With a New Afterword by Vincent Bugliosi

THE WORLD'S #1 TRUE CRIME BESTSELLER

HELTER SKELTER

THE TRUE STORY OF THE MANSON MURDERS

VINCENT BUGLIOSI
with CURT GENTRY

Including a chilling 64-page photographic record of the victims, the killers, and the evidence

BANTAM BOOKS

ISBN 0-553-57435-3

US $6.99 / $8.99 CAN

9 780553 574357

50699

**THE STORY YOU
ARE ABOUT TO READ
WILL SCARE THE
HELL OUT OF YOU**

9:05 A.M., August 9. Three LAPD officers arrive at the Sharon Tate residence in response to a Code 2. They find the first bloody victim in a white Rambler parked in the driveway. Victims two and three—male, Caucasian, probably in his thirties; female, Caucasian, probably in her twenties—are on the lawn. The officers enter the house. In the living room is a long couch. Draped over the back is an American flag. In front of the fireplace is a scene so savage that it will sicken you—a scene that horrifies even the most case-hardened detectives...

November 18, 1969. Deputy district attorney Vincent Bugliosi is assigned the Tate case and the related homicides of supermarket owner Leno LaBianca and his wife Rosemary. For months, Bugliosi collects and sifts through the grisly evidence, listens to the chilling testimony of murderers and accomplices. Slowly, he puts the puzzle pieces together—and emerges with a complete and horrifying picture of the man who ordered the killings, the girls and young men who carried them out, the motive for the seemingly incomprehensible crimes.

Now Vincent Bugliosi tells the whole story —including the never-before-revealed "retaliation" slayings—of the most baffling mass murder case in the annals of American crime...

HELTER SKELTER

"Many of the most startling developments in the Charles Manson murder case were never mentioned in open court or in daily coverage of the case. They are revealed in depth...[in] *Helter Skelter*."
—*San Francisco Chronicle*

"One of the best crime stories ever written."
—*Showcase/Chicago Sun-Times*

"A valuable book on a lurid subject...A record of savagery and official bungling."—*Time*

"Monumental and disturbing epic."
—*Cleveland Press—Plain Dealer*

HELTER SKELTER

"The fullest story of the Manson case anybody ever is likely to get."
—*Wall Street Journal*

"This book for the first time unravels for the public the lethally aberrant behavior of the Manson 'family'…It is an extraordinary chronicle." —*John Barkham Reviews*

"I'm used to it—but the whole tragic, grisly —and well-told—story scared the hell out of me!" —*Attorney Melvin Belli*

"Continuously fascinating…Bugliosi does not disappoint." —*New York Magazine*

HELTER SKELTER

HELTER SKELTER

THE TRUE STORY OF THE MANSON MURDERS

VINCENT BUGLIOSI
PROSECUTOR OF THE TATE-LA BIANCA TRIALS
WITH CURT GENTRY

I.C.C. LIBRARY

BANTAM BOOKS
NEW YORK · TORONTO · LONDON · SYDNEY · AUCKLAND

HELTER SKELTER
A Bantam Book / published by arrangement with
W. W. Norton & Company, Inc.

PUBLISHING HISTORY
W. W. Norton edition published November 1974
Book-Of-The-Month Club edition published December 1974
Playboy Book Club edition published June 1975
A condensed version appeared in BOOK DIGEST *1975*
Serialized in The New York Times *January 1975*
Bantam edition / October 1975
Bantam reissue / September 1995

ISBN 0-553-57435-3

Published simultaneously in the United States and Canada

PRINTED IN THE UNITED STATES OF AMERICA

RAD   0 9 8 7 6 5 4 3 2 1

To Gail and Blanche

Contents

Cast of Characters   xiii

Part 1 THE MURDERS   1
August 9–October 14, 1969   3

Part 2 THE KILLERS   99
October 15–November 17, 1969   101

Part 3 THE INVESTIGATION—PHASE TWO   155
November 18–December 31, 1969   157

Part 4 THE SEARCH FOR THE MOTIVE:
The Bible, the Beatles, and Helter Skelter   281
January–February 1970   283

Part 5 "DON'T YOU KNOW WHO YOU'RE
CRUCIFYING?"   345
March–June 14, 1970   347

Part 6 THE TRIAL   409
June 15–November 19, 1970   411

Part 7 MURDER IN THE WIND   521
November 19, 1970–January 25, 1971   523

Part 8 FIRES IN YOUR CITIES   561
January 26–April 19, 1971   563

Epilogue: A SHARED MADNESS   623

Afterword   665

Index   702

Contents

Cast of Characters

Cast of Characters

Los Angeles Police Department (LAPD)

TATE CASE DETECTIVES:

Helder, Robert J., Lieutenant, Supervisor of Investigations. Headed Tate investigation.

Buckles, Jess, Sergeant.

Calkins, Robert, Sergeant.

McGann, Michael J., Sergeant.

ASSISTED IN TATE INVESTIGATION:

Boen, Jerrome, Latent Prints Section, SID.

Burbridge, Robert, Officer.

Burdick, A. H., Lieutenant. Polygraph examiner, SID.

Clements, Wendell. Civilian fingerprint expert.

Deemer, Earl, Lieutenant.

DeRosa, Jerry Joe, Officer.

Dorman, D. E., Officer.

Galindo, Danny, Sergeant. Also assisted in LaBianca investigation.

Girt, D. L. Latent Prints Section, SID.

Granado, Joe. Forensic chemist, SID. Also assisted in LaBianca investigation.

Henderson, Ed, Sergeant.

Kamadoi, Gene, Sergeant.

Lee, William, Sergeant. Ballistics expert, SID.

Madlock, Robert C., Lieutenant.

Varney, Dudley, Sergeant.

Whisenhunt, William T., Officer.

Wolfer, DeWayne. Criminalist, SID.

LABIANCA CASE DETECTIVES:

LePage, Paul, Lieutenant. Headed LaBianca investigation.

Broda, Gary, Sergeant.
Gutierrez, Manuel "Chick," Sergeant.
Nielsen, Michael, Sergeant.
Patchett, Frank, Sergeant.
Sartuchi, Philip, Sergeant.
ASSISTED IN LABIANCA INVESTIGATION:
Claborn, J., Sergeant. Latent Prints Section, SID.
Cline, Edward L., Sergeant.
Dolan, Harold, Sergeant. Latent Prints Section, SID.
Rodriquez, W. C., Officer.
Toney, J. C., Officer.

Los Angeles County Sheriff's Office (LASO)

ASSIGNED TO THE HINMAN INVESTIGATION:
Guenther, Charles, Sergeant.
Whiteley, Paul, Sergeant.

Los Angeles County District Attorney's Office

Bugliosi, Vincent T., Deputy District Attorney. Prosecuted
the Tate-LaBianca killers.
Kay, Steven, and Musich, Donald, Deputy District Attorneys.
Brought in to assist Bugliosi after Stovitz was taken off the
case.
Stovitz, Aaron, head of the Trials Division. Co-prosecutor of
Manson and the three female defendants until taken off
the case shortly after the start of the trial.

Inyo County District Attorney's Office

Fowles, Frank, Inyo County District Attorney.
Gardiner, Jack, Investigator.
Gibbens, Buck, Deputy District Attorney.

Defense Attorneys

Ball, Joseph. Interviewed Charles Manson and found him
competent to represent himself.
Barnett, Donald. Leslie Van Houten's first attorney was re-
placed by Marvin Part.
Boyd, Bill. Charles Watson's Texas attorney.
Bubrick, Sam. With Maxwell Keith, defended Charles "Tex"
Watson.
Caballero, Richard. Susan Atkins' attorney from November
1969 to March 1970.

Fitzgerald, Paul. First Charles Manson's lawyer, he later quit the Public Defender's Office to represent Patricia Krenwinkel.

Fleischman, Gary. Linda Kasabian's attorney.

Hollopeter, Charles. Charles Manson's attorney for a very brief period.

Hughes, Ronald. Once Charles Manson's "hippie lawyer," he later defended Leslie Van Houten, up until the time he was murdered by the Family.

Kanarek, Irving. Replaced Ronald Hughes as Charles Manson's lawyer.

Keith, Maxwell. Assigned by the Court to represent Leslie Van Houten after the disappearance of Ronald Hughes; also, with Sam Bubrick, defended Charles "Tex" Watson.

Part, Marvin. Leslie Van Houten's attorney for a brief period; was replaced by Ira Reiner.

Reiner, Ira. Replaced Marvin Part as Leslie Van Houten's attorney; was replaced by Ronald Hughes.

Salter, Leon. Robert "Bobby" Beausoleil's attorney.

Shinn, Daye. Replaced Richard Caballero as Susan Atkins' attorney.

Manson Family Members and Associates

Manson, Charles Milles, aka Jesus Christ, God, Soul, the Devil, Charles Willis Manson. Leader of the Family and mass murderer.

Alonzo, Maria, aka Crystal. Released after the murder of Lauren Willett, she was later arrested in connection with an alleged plot to kidnap a foreign diplomat.

Atkins, Susan Denise, aka Sadie Mae Glutz, Sexy Sadie, Sharon King, Donna Kay Powell. Involved in the Hinman, Tate, and LaBianca murders.

Bailey, Edward Arthur. Associated with the Family. May have seen Manson kill a man in Death Valley.

Bailey, Ella Jo, aka Yellerstone. Left Family after learning of the Hinman murder.

Bailey, Lawrence Edward, aka Larry Jones. Present when Tate killers left Spahn Ranch; involved in the Hawthorne shootout.

Baldwin, Linda. Alias used by Family member Madaline Joan Cottage.

Bartell, Susan Phyllis, aka Country Sue. Present when Zero allegedly "committed suicide while playing Russian roulette."

Beausoleil, Robert Kenneth "Bobby," aka Cupid, Jasper, Cherub, Robert Lee Hardy, Jason Lee Daniels. Involved in the Hinman murder.

Big Patty. Alias used by Family member Patricia Krenwinkel.

Brown, Kenneth Richard, aka Scott Bell Davis. Associated with the Family; friend of Zero.

Brunner, Mary Theresa, aka Marioche, Och, Mother Mary, Mary Manson, Linda Dee Moser, Christine Marie Euchts. First girl to join the Manson Family; had a son by Manson; involved in the Hinman murder and the Hawthorne shootout.

Capistrano. Alias used by Family member Catherine Gillies.

Clem. Alias used by Family member Steve Grogan.

Como, Kenneth, aka Jesse James. Escaped convict; associated with Manson Family; involved in Hawthorne shootout.

Cooper, Priscilla. Pleaded guilty to being an accessory after the fact in the murder of Lauren Willett.

Cooper, Sherry Ann, aka Simi Valley Sherri. Fled Barker Ranch with Barbara Hoyt.

Cottage, Madaline Joan, aka Little Patty, Linda Baldwin. Present when Zero died.

Country Sue. Alias used by Family member Susan Bartell.

Craig, James. State prison escapee; associated with Manson Family; pleaded guilty to being an accessory after the fact in the murders of both James and Lauren Willett.

Cravens, Larry. Family member.

Crystal. Alias used by Family member Maria Alonzo.

Cupid. Alias used by Family member Robert "Bobby" Beausoleil.

Davis, Bruce McGregor, aka Bruce McMillan. Involved in the Hinman and Shea murders; present when Zero died; suspect in three other deaths.

DeCarlo, Daniel Thomas, aka Donkey Dan, Daniel Romeo, Richard Allen Smith. Straight Satan motorcycle gang member; associated with the Family; later became a reluctant, but important, prosecution witness.

Donkey Dan. Name given to Daniel DeCarlo by Manson Family girls.

Flynn, John Leo "Juan." Spahn ranch hand; associated with the Family; testified to an extremely incriminating admission by Manson.

Fromme, Lynette Alice, aka Squeaky, Elizabeth Elaine Williamson. One of the earliest Manson Family members; became the Family's ex-officio leader after Manson was arrested.

Gillies, Catherine Irene, aka Capistrano, Cappy, Catherine Myers, Patricia Anne Burke, Patti Sue Jardin. Family member; granddaughter of the owner of Myers Ranch; wanted to go along the night of the LaBianca murders but wasn't needed; present when Zero died.

Glutz, Sadie Mae. Alias used by Family member Susan Atkins.

Good, Sandra Collins, aka Sandy. Married name Mrs. Joel Pugh. Family member.

Goucher, William. Associated with the Manson Family; involved in the murder of James Willett.

Grogan, Steven Dennis, aka Clem Tufts. Involved in the Hinman and Shea murders; was with the killers the night the LaBiancas were killed; involved in the attempted murder of prosecution witness Barbara Hoyt.

Gypsy. Alias used by Family member Catherine Share.

Haught, John Philip, aka Zero, Christopher Jesus. Officially "committed suicide while playing Russian roulette"; was probably murdered.

Hinman, Gary. Befriended the Manson Family; was murdered by them.

Hoyt, Barbara, aka Barbara Rosenburg. Fled the Family before the Barker Ranch raid; became prosecution witness; Family attempted to murder her with an LSD-laden hamburger.

Jones, Larry. Alias used by Family member Lawrence Bailey.

Kasabian, Linda Drouin. Accompanied the killers on the nights of the Tate and LaBianca murders; star witness for the prosecution.

Katie. Alias used by Family member Patricia Krenwinkel.

Knoll, George, aka 86 George. President Straight Satans motorcycle gang. Gave Manson the club sword which was later used in the Hinman slaying and taken along the night the LaBiancas were killed.

Krenwinkel, Patricia Dianne, aka Katie, Marnie Reeves, Big Patty, Mary Ann Scott. Involved in the Tate and LaBianca murders.

Lake, Dianne Elizabeth, aka Snake, Dianne Bluestein. Joined Manson at age 13; became a witness for the prosecution.

Lane, Robert, aka Soupspoon. Arrested in Barker Ranch raid.

Little Patty. Alias used by Family member Madaline Joan Cottage.

Lovett, Charles Allen. Family member involved in the Hawthorne shootout.

Lutesinger, Kitty. Robert "Bobby" Beausoleil's girl friend; fled the Family, then returned to it.

McCann, Brenda. Alias used by Family member Nancy Laura Pitman.

Marioche. Alias used by Family member Mary Brunner.

Minette, Manon. Alias used by Family member Catherine Share.

Monfort, Michael. State prison escapee; associated with the Manson Family; involved in the murders of both James and Lauren Willett.

Montgomery, Charles. Alias used by Family member Charles "Tex" Watson.

Moorehouse, Dean. Father of Family member Ruth Ann Moorehouse; sometime Manson follower.

Moorehouse, Ruth Ann, aka Ouisch, Rachel Susan Morse. Involved in the attempted murder of prosecution witness Barbara Hoyt.

Ouisch. Alias used by Family member Ruth Ann Moorehouse.

Pitman, Nancy Laura, aka Brenda McCann, Brindle, Cydette Perell. Pleaded guilty to being an accessory after the fact in the murder of Lauren Willett.

Poston, Brooks. Former Family member; supplied the prosecution with important evidence regarding Manson's bizarre motive for the murders.

Pugh, Joel. Husband of Family member Sandra Good. Though officially listed as a suicide, he is among the "possible" Manson Family murder victims.

Rice, Dennis. Involved in the attempted murder of prosecution witness Barbara Hoyt; also involved in the Hawthorne shootout.

Ross, Mark. Associated with the Family; Zero's death occurred in his apartment while he was away.

Sadie. Alias used by Family member Susan Atkins.

Sankston, Leslie. Alias used by Family member Leslie Van Houten.

Schram, Stephanie. Fled Barker Ranch with Kitty Lutesinger; testified for the prosecution that Manson was not with her on the nights of the Tate and LaBianca murders.

Scott, Suzanne, aka Stephanie Rowe. Family member.

Share, Catherine, aka Gypsy, Manon Minette. Participated in the "cleanup" following the Shea murder; involved in the Hawthorne shootout.

Simi Valley Sherri. Alias used by Family member Sherry Ann Cooper.

Sinclair, Collie, aka Beth Tracy. Family member arrested in Barker raid.

Smith, Claudia Leigh, aka Sherry Andrews. Family member arrested in Barker raid.

Snake. Alias used by Family member Dianne Lake.

Springer, Alan LeRoy. Member Straight Satans motorcycle gang. Manson admitted the Tate murders to him but his statement could not be used as evidence.

Squeaky. Alias used by Family member Lynette Fromme.

T. J. the Terrible. Alias used by sometime Family member Thomas Walleman.

Todd, Hugh Rocky, aka Randy Morglea. Family member arrested in Barker raid.

True, Harold. Lived at 3267 Waverly Drive, the house next to the LaBianca residence; Manson and other Family members visited him there four or five times.

Tufts, Clem. Alias used by Family member Steve Grogan.

Vance, William Joseph "Bill." Alias of ex-convict David Lee Hamic; associated with the Manson Family.

Van Houten, Leslie Sue, aka LuLu, Leslie Marie Sankston, Louella Alexandria, Leslie Owens. Involved in the LaBianca murders.

Walleman, Thomas, aka T. J. the Terrible. Sometime Family member; was present when Manson shot Bernard Crowe.

Walts, Mark. Hung out at Spahn Ranch; his brother accused Manson of his murder.

Watkins, Paul Alan. Manson's second in command and his chief procurer of young girls; provided Bugliosi with the missing link in Manson's bizarre motive for the murders.

Watson, Charles Denton, aka Tex, Charles Montgomery, Texas Charlie. Involved in the Tate and LaBianca murders.

Wildebush, Joan, aka Juanita. Was with Manson advance group at Barker Ranch; left Family and eloped with Bob Berry, Paul Crockett's partner.

Willett, Lauren. Associated with the Family; murdered on November 10 or 11, 1972, a few days after the body of her husband was discovered; several Manson Family members were linked to her death.

Willett, James. Murdered sometime prior to November 8, 1972; three associates of the Manson Family were charged with the slaying.

Zero. Alias used by Family member John Philip Haught.

HELTER
SKELTER

Part 1

THE MURDERS

"How does it feel
To be
One of the
Beautiful People?"

The Beatles,
"Baby You're a Rich Man,"
Magical Mystery Tour album

Saturday, August 9, 1969

It was so quiet, one of the killers would later say, you could almost hear the sound of ice rattling in cocktail shakers in the homes way down the canyon.

The canyons above Hollywood and Beverly Hills play tricks with sounds. A noise clearly audible a mile away may be indistinguishable at a few hundred feet.

It was hot that night, but not as hot as the night before, when the temperature hadn't dropped below 92 degrees. The three-day heat wave had begun to break a couple of hours before, about 10 P.M. on Friday—to the psychological as well as the physical relief of those Angelenos who recalled that on such a night, just four years ago, Watts had exploded in violence. Though the coastal fog was now rolling in from the Pacific Ocean, Los Angeles itself remained hot and muggy, sweltering in its own emissions, but here, high above most of the city, and usually even above the smog, it was at least 10 degrees cooler. Still, it remained warm enough so that many residents of the area slept with their windows open, in hopes of catching a vagrant breeze.

All things considered, it's surprising that more people didn't hear something.

But then it was late, just after midnight, and 10050 Cielo Drive was secluded.

Being secluded, it was also vulnerable.

Cielo Drive is a narrow street that abruptly winds upward from Benedict Canyon Road. One of its cul-de-sacs, easily missed though directly opposite Bella Drive, comes to a dead end at the high gate of 10050. Looking through the gate, you could see neither the main residence nor the guest house some distance beyond it, but you could see, toward the end of the paved parking area, a corner of the garage and, a little farther on, a split-rail fence which, though it was only August, was strung with Christmas-tree lights.

The lights, which could be seen most of the way from the Sunset Strip, had been put up by actress Candice Bergen when she was living with the previous tenant of 10050 Cielo Drive, TV and record producer Terry Melcher. When Melcher, the son of Doris Day, moved to his mother's beach house in Malibu, the new tenants left the lights up. They were on this night, as they were every night, adding a year-round holiday touch to Benedict Canyon.

From the front door of the main house to the gate was over a hundred feet. From the gate to the nearest neighbor on Cielo, 10070, was almost a hundred yards.

At 10070 Cielo, Mr. and Mrs. Seymour Kott had already gone to bed, their dinner guests having left about midnight, when Mrs. Kott heard, in close sequence, what sounded like three or four gunshots. They seemed to have come from the direction of the gate of 10050. She did not check the time but later guessed it to be between 12:30 and 1 A.M. Hearing nothing further, Mrs. Kott went to sleep.

About three-quarters of a mile directly south and downhill from 10050 Cielo Drive, Tim Ireland was one of five counselors supervising an overnight camp-out for some thirty-five children at the Westlake School for Girls. The other counselors had gone to sleep, but Ireland had volunteered to stay up through the night. At approximately 12:40 A.M. he heard from what seemed a long distance away, to the north or northeast, a solitary male voice. The man was screaming, *"Oh, God, no, please don't! Oh, God, no, don't, don't, don't . . ."*

The scream lasted ten to fifteen seconds, then stopped, the abrupt silence almost as chilling as the cry itself. Ireland quickly checked the camp, but all the children were asleep. He awoke his supervisor, Rich Sparks, who had bedded down inside the school, and, telling him what he had heard, got his permission to drive around the area to see if anyone needed help. Ireland took a circuitous route from North Faring Road, where the school was located, south on Benedict Canyon Road to Sunset Boulevard, west to Beverly Glen, and northward back to the school. He observed nothing unusual, though he did hear a number of dogs barking.

There were other sounds in the hours before dawn that Saturday.

Emmett Steele, 9951 Beverly Grove Drive, was awakened by the barking of his two hunting dogs. The pair usually ignored ordinary sounds but went wild when they heard gunshots. Steele went out to look around but, finding nothing out of place, returned to bed. He estimated the time as between 2 and 3 A.M.

Robert Bullington, an employee of the Bel Air Patrol, a private security force used by many of the homeowners in the affluent area, was parked in front of 2175 Summit Ridge Drive, with his window down, when he heard what sounded like three shots, spaced a few seconds apart. Bullington called in; Eric Karlson, who was working the desk at patrol headquarters, logged the call at 4:11 A.M. Karlson in turn called the West Los Angeles Division of the Los Angeles Police Department (LAPD), and passed on the report. The officer who took the call remarked, "I hope we don't have a murder; we just had a woman-screaming call in that area."

Los Angeles *Times* delivery boy Steve Shannon heard nothing unusual when he pedaled his bike up Cielo Drive between 4:30 and 4:45 A.M. But as he put the paper in the mailbox of 10050, he did notice what looked like a telephone wire hanging over the gate. He also observed, through the gate and some distance away, that the yellow bug light on the side of the garage was still on.

Seymour Kott also noticed the light and the fallen wire when he went out to get his paper about 7:30 A.M.

About 8 A.M., Winifred Chapman got off the bus at the intersection of Santa Monica and Canyon Drive. A light-skinned black in her mid-fifties, Mrs. Chapman was the housekeeper at 10050 Cielo, and she was upset because, thanks to L.A.'s terrible bus service, she was going to be late to work. Luck seemed with her, however; just as she was about to look for a taxi, she saw a man she had once worked with, and he gave her a ride almost to the gate.

She noticed the wire immediately, and it worried her.

In front and to the left of the gate, not hidden but not conspicuous either, was a metal pole on the top of which was the gate-control mechanism. When the button was pushed, the gate swung open. There was a similar mechanism inside the grounds, both being positioned so a driver could reach the button without having to get out of the car.

Because of the wire, Mrs. Chapman thought the electricity might be off, but when she pushed the button, the gate swung open. Taking the *Times* out of the mailbox, she walked hurriedly onto the property, noticing an unfamiliar automobile in the driveway, a white Rambler, parked at an odd angle. But she passed it, and several other cars nearer the garage, without much thought. Overnight guests weren't that uncommon. Someone had left the outside light on all night, and she went to the switch at the corner of the garage and turned it off.

At the end of the paved parking area was a flagstone walkway that made a half circle to the front door of the main house. She turned right before coming to the walk, however, going to the service porch entrance at the back of the residence. The key was secreted on a rafter above the door. Taking it down, she unlocked the door and went inside, walking directly to the kitchen, where she picked up the extension phone. It was dead.

Thinking that she should alert someone that the line was down, she proceeded through the dining room toward the living room. Then she stopped suddenly, her progress impeded by two large blue steamer trunks, which hadn't been there when she had left the previous afternoon—and by what she saw.

There appeared to be blood on the trunks, on the floor next to them, and on two towels in the entryway. She couldn't see the entire living room—a long couch cut off the area in front of the fireplace—but everywhere she could see she saw the red splashes. The front door was ajar. Looking out, she saw several pools of blood on the flagstone porch. And, farther on, on the lawn, she saw a body.

Screaming, she turned and ran back through the house,

leaving the same way she had come in but, on running down the driveway, changing her course so as to reach the gate-control button. In so doing, she passed on the opposite side of the white Rambler, seeing for the first time that there was a body inside the car too.

Once outside the gate, she ran down the hill to the first house, 10070, ringing the bell and pounding on the door. When the Kotts didn't answer, she ran to the next house, 10090, banging on that door and screaming, *"Murder, death, bodies, blood!"*

Fifteen-year-old Jim Asin was outside, warming up the family car. It was Saturday and, a member of Law Enforcement Unit 800 of the Boy Scouts of America, he was waiting for his father, Ray Asin, to drive him to the West Los Angeles Division of LAPD, where he was scheduled to work on the desk. By the time he got to the porch, his parents had opened the door. While they were trying to calm the hysterical Mrs. Chapman, Jim dialed the police emergency number. Trained by the Scouts to be exact, he noted the time: 8:33.

While waiting for the police, the father and son walked as far as the gate. The white Rambler was some thirty feet inside the property, too far away to make out anything inside it, but they did see that not one but several wires were down. They appeared to have been cut.

Returning home, Jim called the police a second time and, some minutes later, a third.

There is some confusion as to exactly what happened to the calls. The official police report only states, "At 0914 hours, West Los Angeles Units 8L5 and 8L62 were given a radio call, 'Code 2, possible homicide, 10050 Cielo Drive.'"

The units were one-man patrol cars. Officer Jerry Joe DeRosa, driving 8L5, arrived first, light flashing and siren blaring.* DeRosa began interviewing Mrs. Chapman, but

---

*The confusion extends to the arrival times of the units. Officer DeRosa would later testify he arrived about 9:05 A.M., which was before he supposedly received the Code 2. Officer Whisenhunt, who came next, set the time of his arrival at between 9:15 and 9:25, while officer Burbridge, who arrived *after* both men, testified he was there at 8:40.

had a difficult time of it. Not only was she still hysterical, she was vague as to what she had seen—"blood, bodies everyplace"—and it was hard to get the names and relationships straight. Polanski. Altobelli. Frykowski.

Ray Asin, who knew the residents of 10050 Cielo, stepped in. The house was owned by Rudi Altobelli. He was in Europe, but had hired a caretaker, a young man named William Garretson, to look after the place. Garretson lived in the guest house to the back of the property. Altobelli had rented the main residence to Roman Polanski, the movie director, and his wife. The Polanskis had gone to Europe, however, in March, and while they were away, two of their friends, Abigail Folger and Voytek Frykowski, had moved in. Mrs. Polanski had returned less than a month ago, and Frykowski and Folger were staying on with her until her husband returned. Mrs. Polanski was a movie actress. Her name was Sharon Tate.

Questioned by DeRosa, Mrs. Chapman was unable to say which, if any, of these people were the two bodies she had seen. To the names she added still another, that of Jay Sebring, a noted men's hair stylist and a friend of Mrs. Polanski's. She mentioned him because she remembered seeing his black Porsche with the other automobiles parked next to the garage.

Getting a rifle from his squad car, DeRosa had Mrs. Chapman show him how to open the gate. Walking cautiously up the driveway to the Rambler, he looked in the open window. There *was* a body inside, in the driver's seat but slumped toward the passenger side. Male, Caucasian, reddish hair, plaid shirt, blue denim pants, both shirt and pants drenched with blood. He appeared to be young, probably in his teens.

About this time Unit 8L62, driven by Officer William T. Whisenhunt, pulled up outside the gate. DeRosa walked back and told him he had a possible homicide. DeRosa also showed him how to open the gate, and the two officers proceeded up the driveway, DeRosa still carrying his rifle, Whisenhunt a shotgun. As Whisenhunt passed the Rambler, he looked in, noting that the window on the driver's side was down and both lights and ignition were off. The pair then checked out the other automobiles and, finding them empty, searched both the garage and the room above it. Still no one.

A third officer, Robert Burbridge, caught up with them. As the three men reached the end of the parking area, they saw not one but two inert forms on the lawn. From a distance they looked like mannequins that had been dipped in red paint, then tossed haphazardly on the grass.

They seemed grotesquely out of place on the well-cared-for lawn, with its landscaped shrubbery, flowers, and trees. To the right was the residence itself, long, rambling, looking more comfortable than ostentatious, the carriage light outside the main door shining brightly. Farther on, past the south end of the house, they could see a corner of the swimming pool, shimmering blue green in the morning light. Off to the side was a rustic wishing well. To the left was a split-rail fence, intertwined with Christmas-tree lights, still on. And beyond the fence was a sweeping, panoramic view that stretched all the way from downtown Los Angeles to the beach. Out there life was still going on. Here it had stopped.

The first body was eighteen to twenty feet past the front door of the residence. The closer they came, the worse it looked. Male, Caucasian, probably in his thirties, about five feet ten, wearing short boots, multicolored bell bottoms, purple shirt, casual vest. He was lying on his side, his head resting on his right arm, his left hand clutching the grass. His head and face were horribly battered, his torso and limbs punctured by literally dozens of wounds. It seemed inconceivable that so much savagery could be inflicted on one human being.

The second body was about twenty-five feet beyond the first. Female, Caucasian, long dark hair, probably in her late twenties. She was lying supine, her arms thrown out. Barefoot, she was wearing a full-length nightgown, which, before the many stab wounds, had probably been white.

The stillness now got to the officers. Everything was quiet, too quiet. The serenity itself became menacing. Those windows along the front of the house: behind any a killer could be waiting, watching.

Leaving DeRosa on the lawn, Whisenhunt and Burbridge went back toward the north end of the residence, looking for another way to get in. They'd be open targets if they entered the front door. They noticed that a screen had been removed from one of the front windows and was leaning up against the side of the building. Whisenhunt also observed a horizontal slit along the bottom of the screen. Suspecting this might have been where the killer or killers entered, they looked for another means of entry. They found a window open on the side. Looking in, they saw what appeared to be a newly painted room, devoid of furniture. They climbed in.

DeRosa waited until he saw them inside the house, then approached the front door. There was a patch of blood on the walk, between the hedges; several more on the right-hand corner of the porch; with still others just outside and to the left of the door and on the doorjamb itself. He didn't see, or later didn't recall, any footprints, though there were a number. The door being open, inward, DeRosa was on the porch before he noticed that something had been scrawled on its lower half.

Printed in what appeared to be blood were three letters: PIG.

Whisenhunt and Burbridge had finished checking out the kitchen and dining room when DeRosa entered the hallway. Turning left into the living room, he found his way partly blocked by the two blue steamer trunks. It appeared that they had been standing on end, then knocked over, as one was leaning against the other. DeRosa also observed, next to the trunks and on the floor, a pair of horn-rimmed glasses. Burbridge, who followed him into the room, noticed something else: on the carpet, to the left of the entrance, were two small pieces of wood. They looked like pieces of a broken gun grip.

They had arrived expecting two bodies, but had found three. They were now looking not for more death, but some explanation. A suspect. Clues.

The room was light and airy. Desk, chair, piano. Then something odd. In the center of the room, facing the fireplace, was a long couch. Draped over the back was a huge American flag.

Not until they were almost to the couch did they see what was on the other side.

She was young, blond, very pregnant. She lay on her left side, directly in front of the couch, her legs tucked up toward her stomach in a fetal position. She wore a flowered bra and matching bikini panties, but the pattern was almost indistinguishable because of the blood, which looked as if it had been smeared over her entire body. A white nylon rope was looped around her neck twice, one end extending over a rafter in the ceiling, the other leading across the floor to still another body, that of a man, which was about four feet away.

The rope was also looped twice around the man's neck, the loose end going under his body, then extending several feet beyond. A bloody towel covered his face, hiding his features. He was short, about five feet six, and was lying on his right side, his hands bunched up near his head as if still warding off blows. His clothing—blue shirt, white pants with black vertical stripes, wide modish belt, black boots—was blood-drenched.

None of the officers thought about checking either body for pulse. As with the body in the car and the pair on the lawn, it was so obviously unnecessary.

Although DeRosa, Whisenhunt, and Burbridge were patrolmen, not homicide detectives, each, at some time in the course of his duties, had seen death. But nothing like this. 10050 Cielo Drive was a human slaughterhouse.

Shaken, the officers fanned out to search the rest of the house. There was a loft above the living room. DeRosa climbed up the wooden ladder and nervously peeked over the top, but saw no one. A hallway connected the living room with the south end of the residence. There was blood in the hall in two places. To the left, just past one of the spots, was a bedroom, the door of which was open. The blankets and pillows were rumpled and clothing strewn about, as if someone—possibly the nightgown-clad woman on the lawn—had already undressed and gone to bed before the killer or killers appeared. Sitting atop the headboard of the bed, his legs hanging down, was a toy rabbit,

ears cocked as if quizzically surveying the scene. There was
no blood in this room, nor any evidence of a struggle.

Across the hall was the master bedroom. Its door was
also open, as were the louvered doors at the far end of the
room, beyond which could be seen the swimming pool.

This bed was larger and neater, the white spread turned
back to reveal a gaily flowered top sheet and a white bottom sheet with a gold geometric pattern. In the center of
the bed, rather than across the top, were two pillows, dividing the side that had been slept on from the side that
hadn't. Across the room, facing the bed, was a TV set, on
each side of which was a handsome armoire. On top of
one was a white bassinet.

Cautiously, adjoining doors were opened: dressing
room, closet, bath, closet. Again no signs of a struggle. The
telephone on the nightstand next to the bed was on the
hook. Nothing overturned or upset.

However, there was blood on the inside left side of the
louvered French door, suggesting that someone, again possibly the woman on the lawn, had run out this way, attempting to escape.

Stepping outside, the officers were momentarily blinded
by the glare from the pool. Asin had mentioned a guest
house behind the main residence. They spotted it now, or
rather the corner of it, some sixty feet to the southeast,
through the shrubbery.

Approaching it quietly, they heard the first sounds they
had heard since coming onto the premises: the barking of
a dog, and a male voice saying, "Shhh, be quiet."

Whisenhunt went to the right, around the back of the
house. DeRosa turned left, proceeding around the front,
Burbridge following as backup. Stepping onto the
screened-in porch, DeRosa could see, in the living room,
on a couch facing the front door, a youth of about
eighteen. He was wearing pants but no shirt, and though
he did not appear to be armed, this did not mean, DeRosa
would later explain, that he didn't have a weapon nearby.

Yelling *"Freeze!,"* DeRosa kicked in the front door.

Startled, the boy looked up to see one, then, moments later, three guns pointing directly at him. Christopher, Altobelli's large Weimaraner, charged Whisenhunt, chomping the end of his shotgun. Whisenhunt slammed the porch door on his head, then held him trapped there until the youth called him off.

As to what then happened, there are contrary versions.

The youth, who identified himself as William Garretson, the caretaker, would later state that the officers knocked him down, handcuffed him, yanked him to his feet, dragged him outside onto the lawn, then knocked him down again.

DeRosa would later be asked, re Garretson:

Q. "Did he fall or stumble to the floor at any time?"

A. "He may have; I don't recall whether he did or not."

Q. "Did you direct him to lay on the ground outside?"

A. "I directed him, yes, to lay on the ground, yes."

Q. "Did you help him to the ground?"

A. "No, he went down on his own."

Garretson kept asking, "What's the matter? What's the matter?" One of the officers replied, "We'll show you!" and, pulling him to his feet, DeRosa and Burbridge escorted him back along the path toward the main house.

Whisenhunt remained behind, looking for weapons and blood-stained clothing. Though he found neither, he did notice many small details of the scene. One at the time seemed so insignificant that he forgot it until later questioning brought it back to mind. There was a stereo next to the couch. It had been off when they entered the room. Looking at the controls, Whisenhunt noticed that the volume setting was between 4 and 5.

Garretson, meantime, had been led past the two bodies on the lawn. It was indicative of the condition of the first, the young woman, that he mistakenly identified her as Mrs. Chapman, the Negro maid. As for the man, he identified him as "the young Polanski." If, as Chapman and Asin had said, Polanski was in Europe, this made no sense. What the officers couldn't know was that Garretson believed Voytek Frykowski to be Roman Polanski's younger brother. Garretson failed completely when it came to identifying the young man in the Rambler.*

At some point, no one recalls exactly when, Garretson was informed of his rights and told that he was under arrest for murder. Asked about his activities the previous night, he said that although he had remained up all night, writing letters and listening to records, he had neither heard nor seen anything. His highly unlikely alibi, his "vague, unrealistic" replies, and his confused identification of the bodies led the arresting officers to conclude that the suspect was lying.

Five murders—four of them probably occurring less than a hundred feet away—and he had heard nothing?

Escorting Garretson down the driveway, DeRosa located the gate-control mechanism on the pole inside the gate. He noticed that there was blood on the button.

The logical inference was that someone, quite possibly the killer, had pressed the button to get out, in so doing very likely leaving a fingerprint.

Officer DeRosa, who was charged with securing and protecting the scene until investigating officers arrived, now pressed the button himself, successfully opening the gate but also creating a superimposure that obliterated any print that may have been there.

Later DeRosa would be questioned regarding this:

Q. "Was there some reason why you placed your finger on the bloody button that operated the gate?"

A. "So that I could go through the gate."

Q. "And that was intentionally done?"

A. "I had to get out of there."

It was 9:40. DeRosa called in, reporting five deaths and a suspect in custody. While Burbridge remained behind at the residence, awaiting the arrival of the investigating officers, DeRosa and Whisenhunt drove Garretson to the

*Why he failed to identify the youth, whom he did know, is unknown. A good guess would be that Garretson was in shock. Also, adding to his confusion, it was about this time that, in looking toward the gate, he saw Winifred Chapman, whom he presumed dead, alive and talking to a police officer.

West Los Angeles police station for questioning. Another officer took Mrs. Chapman there also, but she was so hysterical she had to be driven to the UCLA Medical Center and given sedation.

In response to DeRosa's call, four West Los Angeles detectives were dispatched to the scene. Lieutenant R. C. Madlock, Lieutenant J. J. Gregoire, Sergeant F. Gravante, and Sergeant T. L. Rogers would all arrive within the next hour. By the time the last pulled up, the first reporters were already outside the gate.

Monitoring the police radio bands, they had picked up the report of five deaths. It was hot and dry in Los Angeles, and fire was a constant concern, especially in the hills, where within minutes lives and property could vanish in an inferno. Someone apparently presumed the five people had been killed in a fire. Jay Sebring's name must have been mentioned in one of the police calls, because a reporter phoned his residence and asked his butler, Amos Russell, if he knew anything about "the deaths by fire." Russell called John Madden, president of Sebring International, and told him about the call. Madden was concerned: neither he nor Sebring's secretary had heard from the hair stylist since late the previous afternoon. Madden placed a call to Sharon Tate's mother in San Francisco. Sharon's father, a colonel in Army Intelligence, was stationed at nearby Fort Baker and Mrs. Tate was visiting him. No, she hadn't heard from Sharon. Or Jay, who was due in San Francisco sometime that same day.

Prior to her marriage to Roman Polanski, Sharon Tate had lived with Jay Sebring. Though thrown over for the Polish film director, Sebring had remained friends with Sharon's parents, as well as Sharon and Roman, and whenever he was in San Francisco he usually called Colonel Tate.

When Madden hung up, Mrs. Tate called Sharon's number. The phone rang and rang, but there was no answer.

It was quiet inside the house. Though anyone who called got a ringing signal, the phones were still out. Officer Joe Granado, a forensic chemist with SID, the Scientific

Investigation Division of LAPD, was already at work, having arrived about 10 A.M. It was Granado's job to take samples from wherever there appeared to be blood. Usually, on a murder case, Granado would be done in an hour or two. Not today. Not at 10050 Cielo Drive.

Mrs. Tate called Sandy Tennant, a close friend of Sharon's and the wife of William Tennant, Roman Polanski's business manager. No, neither she nor Bill had heard from Sharon since late the previous afternoon. At that time Sharon had said that she, Gibby (Abigail Folger), and Voytek (Frykowski) were staying in that night. Jay had said he'd be dropping over later, and she invited Sandy to join them. No party was planned, just a quiet evening at home. Sandy, just over the chicken pox, had declined. Like Mrs. Tate, she had tried to call Sharon that morning but had received no answer.

Sandy assured Mrs. Tate that there was probably no connection between the report of the fire and 10050 Cielo Drive. However, just as soon as Mrs. Tate hung up, Sandy put in a call to her husband's tennis club and had him paged. It was important, she said.

Sometime between 10 and 11 A.M., Raymond Kilgrow, a telephone company representative, climbed the pole outside the gate to 10050 Cielo Drive and found that four phone wires had been cut. The cuts were close to the attachment on the pole, indicating that the person responsible had probably climbed the pole too. Kilgrow repaired two of the wires, leaving the others for the detectives to examine.

Police cars were arriving every few minutes now. And as more officers visited the scene, that scene changed.

The horn-rimmed glasses, first observed by DeRosa, Whisenhunt, and Burbridge near the two trunks, had somehow moved six feet away, to the top of the desk.

Two pieces of gun grip, first seen near the entryway, were now under a chair in the living room. As stated in the official LAPD report: "They were apparently kicked under the chair by one of the original officers on the scene; however, no one is copping out."*

A third piece of gun grip, smaller than the others, was later found on the front porch.

And one or more officers tracked blood from inside the residence onto the front porch and walk, adding several more bloody footprints to those already there. In an attempt to identify and eliminate the later additions, it would be necessary to interview all the personnel who had visited the scene, asking each if he had been wearing boots, shoes with smooth or rippled soles, and so on.

Granado was still taking blood samples. Later, in the police lab, he would give them the Ouchterlony test, to determine if the blood was animal or human. If human, other tests would be applied to determine the blood type—A, B, AB, or O—and the subtype. There are some thirty blood subtypes; however, if the blood is already dry when the sample is taken, it is only possible to determine whether it is one of three—M, N, or MN. It had been a warm night, and it was already turning into another hot day. By the time Granado got to work, most of the blood, except for the pools near the bodies inside, had already dried.

Within the next several days Granado would obtain from the Coroner's Office a blood sample from each of the victims, and would attempt to match these with the samples he'd already collected. In an ordinary murder case the presence of two blood types at the crime scene might indicate that the killer, as well as the victim, had been wounded, information which could be an important clue to the killer's identity.

But this was no ordinary murder. Instead of one body, there were five.

There was so much blood, in fact, that Granado overlooked some spots. On the right side of the front porch, as approached from the walk, there were several large pools of blood. Granado took a sample from only one spot, presuming, he later said, all were the same. Just to the right

---

*Since Granado, who arrived after DeRosa, Whisenhunt, and Burbridge, also saw them near the entryway, it would appear that the original officers weren't responsible.

of the porch, the shrubbery appeared broken, as if someone had fallen into the bushes. Blood splatters there
seemed to bear this out. Granado missed these. Nor did he
take samples from the pools of blood in the immediate
vicinity of the two bodies in the living room, or from the
stains near the two bodies on the lawn, presuming, he'd
later testify, that they belonged to the nearest victims, and
he'd be getting samples from the coroner anyway.

Granado took a total of forty-five blood samples. However, for some reason never explained, he didn't run subtypes on twenty-one of them. If this is not done a week or
two after collection, the components of the blood break
down.

Later, when an attempt was made to re-create the murders, these omissions would cause many problems.

Just before noon William Tennant arrived, still dressed
in tennis clothes, and was escorted through the gate by the
police. It was like being led through a nightmare, as he
was taken first to one body, then another. He didn't recognize the young man in the automobile. But he identified
the man on the lawn as Voytek Frykowski, the woman as
Abigail Folger, and the two bodies in the living room as
Sharon Tate Polanski and, tentatively, Jay Sebring. When
the police lifted the bloody towel, the man's face was so
badly contused Tennant couldn't be sure. Then he went
outside and was sick.

When the police photographer finished his work, another officer got sheets from the linen closet and covered
the bodies.

Beyond the gate the reporters and photographers now
numbered in the dozens, with more arriving every few
minutes. Police and press cars so hopelessly jammed Cielo
Drive that several officers were detailed to try and untan-
gle them. As Tennant pushed through the crowd, clutching
his stomach and sobbing, the reporters hurled questions at
him: "Is Sharon dead?" "Were they murdered?" "Has anyone informed Roman Polanski?" He ignored them, but they
read the answers on his face.

Not everyone who visited the scene was as reluctant to
talk. "It's like a battlefield up there," police sergeant Stan-

ley Klorman told reporters, his features grim with the
shock of what he had seen. Another officer, unidentified,
said, "It looked ritualistic," this single remark providing
the basis for an incredible amount of bizarre speculation.

Like the shock waves from an earthquake, news of the
murders spread.

"FIVE SLAIN IN BEL AIR," read the headline on the first
AP wire story. Though sent out before the identity of the
victims had become known, it correctly reported the location of the bodies; that the telephone lines had been cut;
and the arrest of an unnamed suspect. There were errors:
one, to be much repeated, that "one victim had a hood
over his head . . ."

LAPD notified the Tates, John Madden, who in turn
notified Sebring's parents, and Peter Folger, Abigail's father. Abigail's socially prominent parents were divorced.
Her father, chairman of the board of the A. J. Folger
Coffee Company, lived in Woodside, her mother, Inez Mijia Folger, in San Francisco. However, Mrs. Folger was
not at home but in Connecticut, visiting friends following
a Mediterranean cruise, and Mr. Folger reached her there.
She couldn't believe it; she had talked to Abigail at about
ten the previous night. Both mother and daughter had
planned to fly to San Francisco today, for a reunion,
Abigail having made a reservation on the 10 A.M. United
flight.

On reaching home, William Tennant made what was,
for him, the most difficult call. He was not only Polanski's
business manager but a close friend. Tennant checked his
watch, automatically adding nine hours to get London
time. Though it would be late in the evening, he guessed
that Polanski might still be working, trying to tie up his
various film projects before returning home the following
Tuesday, and he tried the number of his town house. He
guessed right. Polanski and several associates were going
over a scene in the script of *The Day of the Dolphin* when
the telephone rang.

Polanski would remember the conversation as follows:
"Roman, there's been a disaster in a house."
"Which house?"

"Your house." Then, in a rush, "Sharon is dead, and Voytek and Gibby and Jay."

"No, no, no, no!" Surely there was a mistake. Both men now crying, Tennant reiterated that it was true; he had gone to the house himself.

"How?" Polanski asked. He was thinking, he later said, not of fire but a landslide, a not uncommon thing in the Los Angeles hills, especially after heavy rains; sometimes whole houses were buried, which meant that perhaps they could still be alive. Only then did Tennant tell him that they had been murdered.

Voytek Frykowski, LAPD learned, had a son in Poland but no relatives in the United States. The youth in the Rambler remained unidentified, but was no longer nameless; he had been designated John Doe 85.

The news spread quickly—and with it the rumors. Rudi Altobelli, owner of the Cielo property and business manager for a number of show-business personalities, was in Rome. One of his clients, a young actress, called and told him that Sharon and four others had been murdered in his house and that Garretson, the caretaker he had hired, had confessed.

Garretson hadn't, but Altobelli would not learn this until after he returned to the United States.

The specialists had begun arriving about noon.

Officers Jerrome A. Boen and D. L. Girt, Latent Prints Section, Scientific Investigation Division, LAPD, dusted the main residence and the guest house for prints.

After dusting a print with powder ("developing the print"), a clear adhesive tape was placed over it; the tape, with the print showing, would then be "lifted" and placed on a card with a contrasting background. Location, date, time, officer's initials were noted on the back.

One such "lift" card, prepared by Boen, read: "8–9–69/10050 Cielo/1400/JAB/ Inside door frame of left French door/ from master bedroom to pool area/ handle side."

Another lift, taken about the same time, was from the "Outside front door/ handle side/above handle."

It took six hours to cover both residences. Later that

afternoon the pair were joined by officer D. E. Dorman and Wendell Clements, the latter a civilian fingerprint expert, who concentrated on the four vehicles.

Contrary to popular opinion, a readable print is more rare than common. Many surfaces, such as clothing and fabrics, do not lend themselves to impressions. Even when the surface is such that it will take a print, one usually touches it with only a portion of the finger, leaving a fragmentary ridge, which is useless for comparison. If the finger is moved, the result is an unreadable smudge. And, as officer DeRosa demonstrated with the gate button, one print placed atop another creates a superimposure, also useless for identification purposes. Thus, at any crime scene, the number of clear, readable prints, with enough points for comparison, is usually surprisingly small.

Not counting those prints later eliminated as belonging to LAPD personnel at the scene, a total of fifty lifts were taken from the residence, guest house, and vehicles at 10050 Cielo Drive. Of these, seven were eliminated as belonging to William Garretson (all were from the guest house; none of Garretson's prints were found in the main house or on the vehicles); an additional fifteen were eliminated as belonging to the victims; and three were not clear enough for comparison. This left a total of twenty-five unmatched latent prints, any of which might—or might not—belong to the killer or killers.

It was 1:30 P.M. before the first homicide detectives arrived. On verifying that the deaths were not accidental or self-inflicted, Lieutenant Madlock had requested that the investigation be reassigned to the Robbery-Homicide Division. Lieutenant Robert J. Helder, supervisor of investigations, was placed in charge. He in turn assigned Sergeants Michael J. McGann and Jess Buckles to the case. (McGann's regular partner, Sergeant Robert Calkins, was on vacation and would replace Buckles when he returned.) Three additional officers, Sergeants E. Henderson, Dudley Varney, and Danny Galindo, were to assist them.

On being notified of the homicides, Los Angeles County Coroner Thomas Noguchi asked the police not to touch the bodies until a representative of his office had examined them. Deputy Coroner John Finken arrived about 1:45, later to be joined by Noguchi himself. Finken made the official determination of death; took liver and environmental temperatures (by 2 P.M. it was 94 degrees on the lawn, 83 degrees inside the house); and severed the rope connecting Tate and Sebring, portions of which were given to the detectives so that they could try to determine where it had been manufactured and sold. It was white, three-strand nylon, its total length 43 feet 8 inches. Granado took blood samples from the rope, but didn't take subtypes, again presuming. Finken also removed the personal property from the bodies of the victims. Sharon Tate Polanski: yellow metal wedding band, earrings. Jay Sebring: Cartier wristwatch, later determined to be worth in excess of $1,-500. John Doe 85: Lucerne wristwatch, wallet with various papers but no ID. Abigail Folger and Voytek Frykowski: no property on persons. After plastic bags had been placed over the hands of the victims, to preserve any hair or skin that might have become lodged under the nails during a struggle, Finken assisted in covering and placing the bodies on stretcher carts, to be wheeled to ambulances and taken to the Coroner's Office, Hall of Justice, downtown Los Angeles.

Besieged by reporters at the gate, Dr. Noguchi announced he would have no comment until making public the autopsy results at noon the following day.

Both Noguchi and Finken, however, privately had already given the detectives their initial findings.

There was no evidence of sexual molestation or mutilation.

Three of the victims—the John Doe, Sebring, and Frykowski—had been shot. Aside from a defensive slash wound on his left hand, which also severed the band of his wristwatch, John Doe had not been stabbed. But the other four had—many, many times. In addition, Sebring had been hit in the face at least once, and Frykowski had been struck over the head repeatedly with a blunt object.

Though exact findings would have to await the autopsies, the coroners concluded from the size of the bullet holes that the gun used had probably been .22 caliber. The police had already suspected this. In searching the Rambler, Sergeant Varney had found four bullet fragments between the upholstery and the exterior metal of the door on the passenger side. Also found, on the cushion of the rear seat, was part of a slug. Though all were too small for comparison purposes, they appeared to be .22 caliber.

As for the stab wounds, someone suggested that the wound pattern was not dissimilar to that made by a bayonet. In their official report the detectives carried this a step further, concluding, "the knife that inflicted the stab wounds was probably a bayonet." This not only eliminated a number of other possibilities, it also presumed that only one knife had been used.

The depth of the wounds (many in excess of 5 inches), their width (between 1 and 1½ inches), and their thickness (⅛ to ¼ inch) ruled out either a kitchen or a regular pocketknife.

Coincidentally, the only two knives found in the house *were* a kitchen knife and a pocketknife.

A steak knife had been found in the kitchen sink. Granado got a positive benzidine reaction, indicating blood, but a negative Ouchterlony, indicating it was animal, not human. Boen dusted it for prints, but got only fragmentary ridges. Mrs. Chapman later identified the knife as one of a set of steak knifes that belonged to the Polanskis, and she located all the others in a drawer. But even before this, the police had eliminated it because of its dimensions, in particular its thinness. The stabbings were so savage that such a blade would have broken.

Granado found the second knife in the living room, less than three feet from Sharon Tate's body. It was wedged behind the cushion in one of the chairs, with the blade sticking up. A Buck brand clasp-type pocketknife, its blade was 3/4 inch in diameter, 3 13/16 inches in length, making it too small to have caused most of the wounds. Noticing a spot on the side of the blade, Granado tested it for blood: negative. Girt dusted it for prints: an unreadable smudge.

Mrs. Chapman could not recall ever having seen this particular knife. This, plus the odd place where it was found, indicated that it might have been left by the killer(s).

In literature a murder scene is often likened to a picture puzzle. If one is patient and keeps trying, eventually all the pieces will fit into place.

Veteran policemen know otherwise. A much better analogy would be two picture puzzles, or three, or more, no one of which is in itself complete. Even after a solution emerges—if one does—there will be leftover pieces, evidence that just doesn't fit. And some pieces will always be missing.

There was the American flag, its presence adding still another bizarre touch to a scene already horribly macabre. The possibilities it suggested ranged from one end of the political spectrum to the other—until Winifred Chapman told the police that it had been in the residence several weeks.

Few pieces of evidence were so easily eliminated. There were the bloody letters on the front door. In recent years the word "pig" had taken on a new meaning, one all too familiar to the police. But what did it mean printed here?

There was the rope. Mrs. Chapman flatly stated that she had never seen such a rope anywhere on the premises. Had the killer(s) brought it? If so, why?

What significance was there in the fact that the two victims bound together by the rope, Sharon Tate and Jay Sebring, were former lovers? Or was "former" the right word? What was Sebring doing there, with Polanski away? It was a question that many of the newspapers would also ask.

The horn-rimmed glasses—negative for both prints and blood—did they belong to a victim, a killer, or someone totally unconnected with the crime? Or—with each question the possibilities proliferated—had they been left behind as a false clue?

The two trunks in the entryway. The maid said they hadn't been there when she left at 4:30 the previous afternoon. Who delivered them, and when, and had this person seen anything?

Why would the killer(s) go to the trouble of slitting and

removing a screen when other windows, those in the newly painted room that was to be the nursery for the Polanskis' unborn child, were open and screenless?

John Doe 85, the youth in the Rambler. Chapman, Garretson, and Tennant had failed to identify him. Who was he and what was he doing at 10050 Cielo Drive? Had he witnessed the other murders, or had he been killed before they took place? If before, wouldn't the others have heard the shots? On the seat next to him was a Sony AM-FM Digimatic clock radio. The time at which it had stopped was 12:15 A.M. Coincidence or significant?

As for the time of the murders, the reports of gunshots and other sounds ranged from shortly after midnight to 4:10 A.M.

Not all of the evidence was as inconclusive. Some of the pieces fitted. No shell casings were found anywhere on the property, indicating that the gun was probably a revolver, which does not eject its spent shells, as contrasted to an automatic, which does.

Placed together, the three pieces of black wood formed the right-hand side of a gun grip. The police therefore knew the gun they were looking for was probably a .22 caliber revolver that was minus a right grip. From the pieces it might be possible to determine both make and model. Though there was human blood on all three pieces, only one had enough for analysis. It tested O-MN. Of the five victims, only Sebring had O-MN, indicating that the butt of the revolver could have been the blunt object used to strike him in the face.

The bloody letters on the front door tested O-M. Again, only one of the victims had this type and subtype. The word PIG had been printed in Sharon Tate's blood.

There were four vehicles in the driveway, but one which should have been there wasn't—Sharon Tate's red Ferrari. It was possible that the killer(s) had used the sports car to escape, and a "want" was broadcast for it.

Long after the bodies had been removed, the detectives remained on the scene, looking for meaningful patterns.

They found several which appeared significant.

There were no indications of ransacking or robbery.

McGann found Sebring's wallet in his jacket, which was hanging over the back of a chair in the living room. It contained $80. John Doe had $9 in his wallet, Frykowski $2.44 in his wallet and pants pocket, Folger $9.64 in her purse. On the nightstand next to Sharon Tate's bed, in plain view, were a ten, a five, and three ones. Obviously expensive items—a videotape machine, TV sets, stereo, Sebring's wristwatch, his Porsche—had not been taken. Several days later the police would bring Winifred Chapman back to 10050 Cielo to see if she could determine if anything was missing. The only item she couldn't locate was a camera tripod, which had been kept in the hall closet. These five incredibly savage murders were obviously not committed for a camera tripod. In all probability it had been lent to someone or lost.

While this didn't completely eliminate the possibility that the murders had occurred during a residential burglary—the victims surprising the burglar(s) while at work—it certainly put it way down the list.

Other discoveries provided a much more likely direction.

A gram of cocaine was found in Sebring's Porsche, plus 6.3 grams of marijuana and a two-inch "roach," slang for a partially smoked marijuana cigarette.

There were 6.9 grams of marijuana in a plastic bag in a cabinet in the living room of the main residence. In the nightstand in the bedroom used by Frykowski and Folger were 30 grams of hashish, plus ten capsules which, later analyzed, proved to be a relatively new drug known as MDA. There was also marijuana residue in the ashtray on the stand next to Sharon Tate's bed, a marijuana cigarette on the desk near the front door,* and two more in the guest house.

Had a drug party been in progress, one of the participants "freaking out" and slaying everyone there? The police put this at the top of their list of possible reasons for the murders, though well aware this theory had several weaknesses, chief among them the presumption that there

_____
*Apparently overlooked by LAPD, this was discovered by Roman Polanski when he visited the residence on August 17.

was a single killer, wielding a gun in one hand, a bayonet in the other, at the same time carrying 43 feet of rope, all of which, conveniently, he just happened to bring along. Also, there were the wires. If they had been cut *before* the murders, this indicated premeditation, not a spontaneous flare-up. If cut *after,* why?

Or could the murders have been the result of a drug "burn," the killer(s) arriving to make a delivery or buy, an argument over money or bad drugs erupting into violence? This was the second, and in many ways the most likely, of the five theories the detectives would list in their first investigative report.

The third theory was a variation of the second, the killer(s) deciding to keep both the money and the drugs.

The fourth was the residential burglary theory.

The fifth, that these were "deaths by hire," the killer(s) being sent to the house to eliminate one or more of the victims, then, in order to escape identification, finding it necessary to kill all. But would a hired killer choose as one of his weapons something as large, conspicuous, and unwieldy as a bayonet? And would he keep stabbing and stabbing and stabbing in a mad frenzy, as so obviously had been done in this case?

The drug theories seemed to make the most sense. In the investigation that followed, as the police interviewed acquaintances of the victims, and the victims' habits and life styles emerged into clearer focus, the possibility that drugs were in some way linked to the motive became in some minds such a certainty that when given a clue which could have solved the case, they refused even to consider it.

The police were not the only ones to think of drugs.

On hearing of the deaths, actor Steve McQueen, long-time friend of Jay Sebring, suggested that the hair stylist's home should be rid of narcotics to protect his family and business. Though McQueen did not himself participate in the "housecleaning," by the time LAPD got around to searching Sebring's residence, anything embarrassing had been removed.

Others developed instant paranoia. No one was sure who the police would question, or when. An unidentified film figure told a *Life* reporter: "Toilets are flushing all over Beverly Hills; the entire Los Angeles sewer system is stoned."

FILM STAR, 4 OTHERS
DEAD IN BLOOD ORGY

Sharon Tate Victim
In "Ritual" Murders

The headlines dominated the front pages of the afternoon papers, became the big news on radio and TV. The bizarre nature of the crime, the number of victims, and their prominence—a beautiful movie star, the heiress to a coffee fortune, her jet-set playboy paramour, an internationally known hair stylist—would combine to make this probably the most publicized murder case in history, excepting only the assassination of President John F. Kennedy. Even the staid New York *Times,* which rarely reports crime on its front page, did so the next day, and many days thereafter.

The accounts that day and the next were notable for the unusual amount of detail they contained. So much information had been given out, in fact, that the detectives would have difficulty finding "polygraph keys" for questioning suspects.

In any homicide, it is standard practice to withhold certain information which presumably only the police and the killer(s) know. If a suspect confesses, or agrees to a polygraph examination, these keys can then be used to determine if he is telling the truth.

Owing to the many leaks, the detectives assigned to the "Tate case," as the press was already calling the murders, could only come up with five: (1) That the knife used was probably a bayonet. (2) That the gun was probably a .22 caliber revolver. (3) The exact dimensions of the rope, as well as the way it was looped and tied. And (4) and (5), that a pair of horn-rimmed glasses and a Buck knife had been found.

The amount of information unofficially released so bothered LAPD brass that a tight lid was clamped on further disclosures. This didn't please the reporters; also, lacking hard news, many turned to conjecture and speculation. In the days that followed a monumental amount of false information was published. It was widely reported, for example, that Sharon Tate's unborn child had been ripped from her womb; that one or both of her breasts had been slashed off; that several of the victims had been sexually mutilated. The towel over Sebring's face became a white hood (KKK?) or a black hood (satanists?), depending on which paper or magazine you read.

When it came to the man charged with the murders, however, there was a paucity of information. It was presumed, initially, that the police were maintaining silence to protect Garretson's rights. It was also presumed that LAPD had to have a strong case against him or they wouldn't have arrested him.

A Pasadena paper, picking up bits and pieces of information, sought to fill the gap. It stated that when the officers found Garretson, he asked, "When are the detectives going to see me?" The implication was obvious: Garretson knew what had happened. Garretson did ask this, but it was as he was being taken through the gate, long after his arrest, and the question was in response to an earlier comment by DeRosa. Quoting unidentified policemen, the paper also noted: "They said the slender youth had a rip in one knee of his pants and his living quarters in the guest cottage showed signs of a struggle." Damning evidence, unless one were aware that all this happened *during*, not before, Garretson's arrest.

During the first few days a total of forty-three officers would visit the crime scene, looking for weapons and other evidence. In searching the loft above the living room, Sergeant Mike McGann found a film can containing a roll of videotape. Sergeant Ed Henderson took it to the Police Academy, which had screening facilities. The film showed Sharon and Roman Polanski making love. With a certain delicacy, the tape was not booked into evidence but was returned to the loft where it had been found.*

In addition to searching the premises, detectives interviewed neighbors, asking if they had seen any strange people in the area.

Ray Asin recalled that two or three months before there had been a large party at 10050 Cielo Drive, the guests arriving in "hippie garb." He got the impression, however, that they weren't actually hippies, as most arrived in Rolls-Royces and Cadillacs.

Emmett Steele, who had been awakened by the barking of his hunting dogs the previous night, remembered that in recent weeks someone had been racing a dune buggy up and down the hills late at night, but he never got a close look at the driver and passengers.

Most of those interviewed, however, claimed they had neither seen nor heard anything out of the ordinary.

The detectives were left with far more questions than answers. However, they were hopeful one person could put the puzzle together for them: William Garretson.

The detectives downtown were less optimistic. Following his arrest, the nineteen-year-old had been taken to West Los Angeles jail and interrogated. The officers found his answers "stuporous and non-responsive," and were of the opinion that he was under the residual effect of some drug. It was also possible, as Garretson himself claimed, that he had slept little the previous night, just a few hours in the morning, and that he was exhausted, and very scared.

Shortly after this, Garretson retained the services of at-

*One writer would later claim that the police found a vast collection of pornography in the residence, including numerous films and still shots of famous Hollywood stars engaged in various sexual acts. Aside from the above, and several unexposed rolls of videotape, the only photographs found anywhere on the property were a set of wedding pictures and a large number of publicity shots of Sharon Tate.

The same writer also claimed that a number of black hoods were found in the loft. Apparently he created them out of the same material as his photos, for nothing even resembling a hood was found.

torney Barry Tarlow. A second interview, with Tarlow present, took place at Parker Center, headquarters of the Los Angeles Police Department. As far as the police were concerned, it too was unproductive. Garretson claimed that although he lived on the property, he had little contact with the people in the main house. He said that he'd only had one visitor the previous night, a boy named Steve Parent, who showed up about 11:45 and left about a half hour later. Questioned about Parent, Garretson said he didn't know him well. He'd hitched a ride up the canyon with him one night a couple of weeks ago and, on getting out of the car at the gate, had told Steve if he was ever in the neighborhood to drop in. Garretson, who lived by himself in the back house, except for the dogs, said he'd extended similar invitations to others. When Steve showed up, he was surprised: no one else ever had. But Steve didn't stay long, leaving after learning that Garretson wasn't interested in buying a clock radio Steve had for sale.

The police did not at this time connect Garretson's visitor with the youth in the Rambler, possibly because Garretson had earlier failed to identify him.

After conferring with Tarlow, Garretson agreed to take a polygraph examination, and one was scheduled for the following afternoon.

Twelve hours had passed since the discovery of the bodies. John Doe 85 remained unidentified.

Police lieutenant Robert Madlock, who had been in charge of the investigation during the several hours before it was assigned to homicide, would later state: "At the time we first found the [victim's] car at the scene, we were going fourteen different directions at once. So many things had to be done, I guess we just didn't have time to follow up on the car registration."

All day Wilfred and Juanita Parent had waited, and worried. Their eighteen-year-old son Steven hadn't come home the previous night. "He didn't call, didn't leave word. He'd never done anything like that before," Juanita Parent said.

About 8 P.M., aware that his wife was too distraught to cook dinner, Wilfred Parent took her and their three other children to a restaurant. Maybe when we get back, he told his wife, Steve will be there.

From outside the gate of 10050 Cielo it was possible to make out the license number on the white Rambler: ZLR 694. A reporter wrote it down, then ran his own check through the Department of Motor Vehicles, learning that the registered owner was "Wilfred E. or Juanita D. Parent, 11214 Bryant Drive, El Monte, California."

By the time he arrived in El Monte, a Los Angeles suburb some twenty-five miles from Cielo Drive, he found no one at home. Questioning the neighbors, he learned that the family did have a boy in his late teens; he also learned the name of the family priest, Father Robert Byrne, of the Church of the Nativity, and called on him. Byrne knew the youth and his family well. Though the priest was sure Steve didn't know any movie stars and that all this was some mistake, he agreed to accompany the reporter to the county morgue. On the way he talked about Steve. He was a stereo "bug," Father Byrne said; if you ever wanted to know anything about phonographs or radios, Steve had the answers. Father Byrne held great hopes for his future.

In the interim, LAPD discovered the identity of the youth through a print and license check. Shortly after the Parents returned home, an El Monte policeman appeared at the door and handed Wilfred Parent a card with a number on it and told him to call it. He left without saying anything else.

Parent dialed the number.

"County Coroner's Office," a man answered.

Confused, Parent identified himself and explained about the policeman and the card.

The call was transferred to a deputy coroner, who told him, "Your son has apparently been involved in a shooting."

"Is he dead?" Parent asked, stunned. His wife, hearing the question, became hysterical.

"We have a body down here," the deputy coroner replied, "and we believe it's your son." He then went on to describe physical characteristics. They matched.

Parent hung up the phone and began sobbing. Later, understandably bitter, he'd remark, "All I can say is that it was a hell of a way to tell somebody that their boy was dead."

About this same time, Father Byrne viewed the body and made the identification. John Doe 85 became Steven Earl Parent, an eighteen-year-old hi-fi enthusiast from El Monte.

It was 5 A.M. before the Parents went to bed. "The wife and I finally just put the kids in bed with us and the five of us just held on to each other and cried until we went to sleep."

About nine that same Saturday night, August 9, 1969, Leno and Rosemary LaBianca and Susan Struthers, Rosemary's twenty-one-year-old daughter by a previous marriage, left Lake Isabella for the long drive back to Los Angeles. The lake, a popular resort area, was some 150 miles from L.A.

Susan's brother, Frank Struthers, Jr., fifteen, had been vacationing at the lake with a friend, Jim Saffie, whose family had a cabin there. Rosemary and Leno had driven up the previous Tuesday, to leave their speedboat for the boys to use, then returned Saturday morning to pick up Frank and the boat. However, the boys were having such a good time the LaBiancas agreed to let Frank stay over another day, and they were returning now, without him, driving their 1968 green Thunderbird, towing the speedboat on a trailer behind.

Leno, the president of a chain of Los Angeles supermarkets, was forty-four, Italian, and, at 220 pounds, somewhat overweight. Rosemary, a trim, attractive brunette of thirty-eight, was a former carhop who, after a series of waitress jobs and a bad marriage, had opened her own dress shop, the Boutique Carriage, on North Figueroa in Los Angeles, and made a big success of it. She and Leno had been married since 1959.

Because of the boat, they couldn't drive at the speed Leno preferred, and fell behind most of the Saturday night freeway traffic that was speeding toward Los Angeles and environs. Like many others that night, they had the radio on and heard the news of the Tate murders. According to Susan, it seemed particularly to disturb Rosemary, who, a few weeks earlier, had told a close friend, "Someone is coming in our house while we're away. Things have been gone through and the dogs are outside the house when they should be inside."

Sunday, August 10, 1969

About 1 A.M. the LaBiancas dropped Susan off at her apartment on Greenwood Place, in the Los Feliz district of Los Angeles. Leno and Rosemary lived in the same neighborhood, at 3301 Waverly Drive, not far from Griffith Park.

The LaBiancas did not immediately return home but first drove to the corner of Hillhurst and Franklin.

John Fokianos, who had a newsstand on that corner, recognized the green Thunderbird-plus-boat as it pulled into the Standard station across the street, and while it was making a U-turn that would bring it alongside his stand, he reached for a copy of the Los Angeles *Herald Examiner*, Sunday edition, and a racing form. Leno was a regular customer.

To Fokianos, the LaBiancas seemed tired from their long trip. Business was slow, and they chatted for a few minutes, "about Tate, the event of the day. That was the big news." Fokianos would recall that Mrs. LaBianca seemed very shaken by the deaths. He had some extra news fillers for the Sunday Los Angeles *Times*, which featured the murders, and he gave them one without charge.

He watched as they drove away. He did not notice the exact time, except that it was sometime between 1 and 2 A.M., probably closer to the latter, as not long after they left the bars closed and there was a flurry of business.

As far as is known, John Fokianos was the last person—excluding their killer(s)—to see Rosemary and Leno LaBianca alive.

At noon on Sunday the hall outside the autopsy room on the first floor of the Hall of Justice was packed with reporters and TV cameramen, all awaiting the coroner's announcement.

They would have a long wait. Although the autopsies had begun at 9:50 A.M., and a number of deputy coroners had been pressed into service, it would be 3 P.M. before the last autopsy was completed.

Dr. R. C. Henry conducted the Folger and Sebring autopsies, Dr. Gaston Herrera those of Frykowski and Parent. Dr. Noguchi supervised and directed all four; in addition, he personally conducted the other autopsy, which began at 11:20 A.M.

Sharon Marie Polanski, 10050 Cielo Drive, female Caucasian, 26 years, 5-3, 135 pounds, blond hair, hazel eyes. Victim's occupation, actress . . .

Autopsy reports are abrupt documents. Cold, factual, they can indicate how the victims died, and give clues as to their last hours, but nowhere in them do their subjects emerge, even briefly, as people. Each report is, in its own way, the sum total of a life, yet there are very few glimpses as to how that life was lived. No likes, dislikes, loves, hates, fears, aspirations, or other human emotions; just a final, clinical summing up: "The body is normally developed . . . The pancreas is grossly unremarkable . . . The heart weighs 340 grams and is symmetrical . . ."

Yet the victims had lived, each had a past.

Much of Sharon Tate's story sounded like a studio press release. It seemed she had always wanted to be an actress. At age six months she had been Miss Tiny Tot of Dallas, at sixteen years Miss Richland, Washington, then Miss Autorama. When her father, a career army officer, was assigned to San Pedro, she would hitchhike into nearby Los Angeles, haunting the studios.

In addition to her ambition, she had at least one other thing in her favor: she was a very beautiful girl. She acquired an agent who succeeded in getting her a few commercials, then, in 1963, an audition for the TV series "Petticoat Junction." Producer Martin Ransohoff saw the pretty twenty-year-old on the set and, according to studio flackery, told her, "Sweetie, I'm going to make you a star."

The star was a long time ascending. Singing, dancing, and acting lessons were interspersed with bit parts, usually wearing a black wig, in "The Beverly Hillbillies," "Petticoat Junction," and two Ransohoff films, *The Americanization of Emily* and *The Sandpiper.* While the latter film, co-starring Elizabeth Taylor and Richard Burton, was being filmed in Big Sur, Sharon fell in love with the magnificently scenic coastline. Whenever she wanted to escape the Hollywood hassle, she fled there. Scrubbed of makeup, she would check into rustic Deetjen's Big Sur Inn, often alone, sometimes with girl friends, and walk the trails, sun at the beach, and blend in with the regulars at Nepenthe. Many did not know, until after her death, that she was an actress.

According to close friends, though Sharon Tate looked the part of the starlet, she didn't live up to at least one portion of that image. She was not promiscuous. Her relationships were few, and rarely casual, at least on her part. She seemed attracted to dominant men. While in Hollywood, she had a long affair with a French actor. Given to insane rages, he once beat her so badly she had to be taken to the UCLA Medical Center for treatment.* Shortly after this, in 1963, Jay Sebring spotted Sharon at a studio preview, prevailed upon a friend for an introduction, and, after a brief but much publicized courtship, they became lovers, a relationship which lasted until she met Roman Polanski.

It was 1965 before Ransohoff decided his protégé was

*LAPD learned of him from Sharon's parents. They also learned, from one of Sebring's ex-girl friends, that he had had an argument with the hair stylist a few nights before the murder, in one of the Hollywood discothèques. After checking the man's alibi, they cleared him of any possible involvement in the murders. The argument itself was minor: he had interrupted Sebring while he was trying to pick up a girl.

ready for her first featured role, in *Eye of the Devil*, which starred Deborah Kerr and David Niven. Listed seventh in the credits, Sharon Tate played a country girl with bewitching powers. She had less than a dozen lines; her primary role was to look beautiful, which she did. This was to be true of almost all her movies.

In the film, Niven became the victim of a hooded cult which practiced ritual sacrifice.

Though set in France, the film was made in London, and it was here, in the summer of 1966, that she met Roman Polanski.

Polanski was at this time thirty-three, and already acclaimed as one of Europe's leading directors. He had been born in Paris, his father a Russian Jew, his mother Polish of Russian stock. When Roman was three, the family moved to Cracow. They were still there in 1940 when the Germans arrived and sealed off the ghetto. With his father's help, Roman managed to escape and lived with family friends until the war ended. Both his parents, however, were sent to concentration camps, his mother dying in Auschwitz.

Following the war, he spent five years at the Polish National Film Academy at Lodz. As his senior thesis, he wrote and directed *Two Men and a Wardrobe*, a much acclaimed surrealistic short. He made several other short films, among them *Mammals*, in which a Polish friend, Voytek Frykowski, played a thief. After an extended trip to Paris, Polanski returned to Poland to make *Knife in the Water*, his first feature-length effort. It won the Critics Award at the Venice Film Festival, was nominated for an Academy Award, and established Polanski, then only twenty-seven, as one of Europe's most promising filmmakers.

In 1965, Polanski made his first film in English, *Repulsion*, starring Catherine Deneuve. *Cul de Sac* followed, which won the Best Film Award in the Berlin Film Festival, the Critics Award in Venice, a Diploma of Merit in Edinburgh, and the Giove Capitaliano Award in Rome. In the news stories following the Tate murders, reporters were quick to note that in *Repulsion* Miss Deneuve went mad and murdered two men, while in *Cul de Sac* the inhabitants of an isolated castle each meet a bizarre fate until only one man is left alive. They also noted Polanski's "penchant for violence," without adding that most often in Polanski's films the violence was less explicit than implied.

Roman Polanski's personal life was no less controversial than his films. After his marriage to Polish film star Barbara Lass ended in divorce in 1962, Polanski became known as the playboy director. A friend would later recall him leafing through his address book, saying, "Who shall I gratify tonight?" Another friend observed that Polanski's immense talent was matched only by his ego. Non-friends, who were numerous, had stronger things to say. One, referring to the fact that Polanski was just over five feet tall, called him "the original five-foot Pole you wouldn't want to touch anyone with." Whether one was captivated by his gaminlike charm or repelled by his arrogance, he appeared to touch off strong emotions in nearly everyone whom he met.

It was not so with Sharon Tate, at least not at first. When Ransohoff introduced Roman and Sharon at a large party, neither was particularly impressed. The introduction was not accidental. On learning that Polanski was considering doing a film spoof of horror movies, Ransohoff had offered to produce it. He wanted Sharon for the female lead. Polanski gave her a screen test and decided she would be acceptable for the part. Polanski wrote, directed, and starred in the film, which eventually appeared as *The Fearless Vampire Killers*, but Ransohoff did the cutting, much to the displeasure of the Polish director, who disavowed the final print. Though the film was more camp than art, Polanski revealed another phase of his multi-faceted talent in his comic portrayal of the bumbling young assistant of a scholarly vampire hunter. Sharon, again, looked pretty and had less than a dozen lines. A victim of the vampire early in the picture, in the last scene she bites her lover, Polanski, creating still another monster.

Before the filming was over, and after what was for Polanski a very long courtship, Sharon and Roman became off-screen lovers too. When Sebring flew to London, Sharon told him the news. If he took it hard, he was careful not to show it, very quickly settling into the role of family friend. There were indications, asides made to a few associates, that Sebring hoped that Sharon would eventually tire of Roman, or vice versa, the presumption being that when this happened he intended to be around. Those who claimed that Sebring was still in love with Sharon were guessing—though Sebring knew hundreds of people, he apparently had few really close friends, and kept his inner feelings very much to himself—but it was a safe guess that although the nature of that love had changed, some deep attachment remained. After the breakup, Sebring was involved with many women, but, as revealed in the LAPD interview sheets, for the most part the relationships were more sexual than emotional, the majority "one night stands."

Paramount asked Polanski to do the film version of Ira Levin's novel *Rosemary's Baby*. The film, in which Mia Farrow played a young girl who had a child by Satan, was completed late in 1967. On January 20, 1968, to the surprise of many friends to whom Polanski had vowed never again to marry, he and Sharon were wed in a mod ceremony in London.

Rosemary's Baby premiered that June. That same month the Polanskis rented actress Patty Duke's home at 1600 Summit Ridge Drive in Los Angeles. It was while they were living there that Mrs. Chapman began working for them. In early 1969 they heard that 10050 Cielo Drive might be vacant. Though they never met in person, Sharon talked to Terry Melcher on the phone several times, making arrangements to take over his unexpired lease. The Polanskis signed a rental agreement on February 12, 1969, at $1,200 a month, and moved in three days later.

Though *Rosemary's Baby* was a smash success, Sharon's own career had never quite taken off. She had appeared semi-nude in the March 1967 issue of *Playboy* (Polanski himself took the photos on the set of *The Fearless Vampire Killers*), the accompanying article beginning, "This is the year that Sharon Tate happens . . ." But the prediction wasn't fulfilled, not that year. Though a number of reviewers commented on her striking looks, neither this nor two other films in which she played—*Don't Make Waves,* with Tony Curtis, and *The Wrecking Crew,* with Dean Martin—brought her much closer to stardom. Her biggest role came in the 1967 film *Valley of the Dolls,* in which she played the actress Jennifer who, on learning that she has breast cancer, takes an overdose of sleeping pills. Not long before her death, Jennifer remarks, "I have no talent. All I have is a body."

There were reviewers who felt that adequately summed up Sharon Tate's performance. To be fairer, to date she hadn't been given a single role which gave her a chance to bring out whatever acting ability she may have had.

She was not a star, not yet. Her career seemed to hesitate on the edge of a breakthrough, but it could easily have remained stationary, or gone the other way.

But for the first time in her life, Sharon's ambition had slipped to second place. Her marriage and her pregnancy had become her whole life. According to those closest to her, she seemed oblivious to all else.

There were rumors of trouble in her marriage. Several of her female friends told LAPD that she had waited to tell Roman of her pregnancy until after it was too late to abort. If she was concerned that even after marriage Polanski remained the playboy, she hid it. Sharon herself often told a story then current in the movie colony, of how Roman was driving through Beverly Hills when, spotting a pretty girl walking ahead of him, he yelled, "Miss, you have a bea-u-ti-ful arse." Only when the girl turned did he recognize his wife. Yet it was obvious that she hoped the baby would bring the marriage closer together.

Hollywood is a bitchy town. In interviewing acquaintances of the victims, LAPD would encounter an incredible amount of venom. Interestingly enough, in the dozens of interview sheets, no one who actually knew Sharon Tate said anything bad about her. Very sweet, somewhat naïve—these were the words most often used.

That Sunday a Los Angeles *Times* reporter who had known Sharon described her as "an astonishingly beautiful woman with a statuesque figure and a face of great delicacy."

But then he didn't see her as Coroner Noguchi did.

Cause of death: Multiple stab wounds of the chest and

back, penetrating the heart, lungs, and liver, causing massive hemorrhage. Victim was stabbed sixteen times, five of which wounds were in and of themselves fatal.

Jay Sebring, 9860 Easton Drive, Benedict Canyon, Los Angeles, male Caucasian, 35 years, 5-6, 120 pounds, black hair, brown eyes. Victim was a hair stylist and had a corporation known as Sebring International . . .

Born Thomas John Kummer, in Detroit, Michigan, he had changed his name to Jay Sebring shortly after arriving in Hollywood, following a four-year stint as a Navy barber, borrowing the last name from the famous Florida sports-car race because he liked the image it projected.

In his personal life, as in his work, appearances were all-important. He drove an expensive sports car, frequented the "in" clubs, even had his Levi jackets custom-made. He employed a full-time butler, gave lavish parties, and lived in a "jinxed" mansion, 9860 Easton Drive, Benedict Canyon. Once the love nest of actress Jean Harlow and producer Paul Bern, it was here, in Harlow's bedroom, that Bern had committed suicide, two months after their marriage. According to acquaintances, Sebring had bought the house because of its "far out" reputation.

It was widely reported that a motion-picture studio had flown Sebring to London just to cut George Peppard's hair, at a cost of $25,000. While the report was probably as factual as another also current, that he had a black belt in karate (he had taken a few lessons from Bruce Lee), there was no question that he was the leading men's hair stylist in the United States, and that more than any other single individual, he was responsible for the revolution in male hair care. In addition to Peppard, his customers included Frank Sinatra, Paul Newman, Steve McQueen, Peter Lawford, and numerous other motion-picture stars, many of whom had promised to invest in his new corporation, Sebring International. While keeping his original salon at 725 North Fairfax in Los Angeles, he planned to open a series of franchised shops and to market a line of men's toiletries bearing his name. The first shop had been opened in San Francisco in May 1969, Abigail Folger and Colonel and Mrs. Paul Tate being among those at the grand opening.

On April 9, 1968, Sebring had signed an application for a $500,000 executive protection policy with the Occidental Life Insurance Company of California. A background investigation, conducted by the Retail Credit Company, estimated his net worth at $100,000, of which $80,000 was the appraised worth of his residence. Sebring, Inc., the original business, had assets of $150,000, with liabilities of $115,000.

The investigators also looked into Sebring's personal life. He had married once, in October 1960, he and his wife, Cami, a model, separating in August 1963, their divorce becoming final in March 1965, the couple having had no children. The report also stated that Sebring had never "used drugs as a habit." LAPD knew otherwise.

They also knew something else the credit company investigators had never discovered. There was a darker side to Jay Sebring's nature that surfaced during numerous interviews conducted by the police. As noted in the official report: "He was considered a ladies' man and took numerous women to his residence in the Hollywood hills. He would tie the women up with a small sash cord and, if they agreed, would whip them, after which they would have sexual relations."

Rumors of this had long circulated around Hollywood. Now picked up by the press, they became the basis for numerous theories, chief among them that some sort of sadomasochistic orgy had been in progress on the night of August 9, 1969, at 10050 Cielo Drive.

LAPD never seriously considered Sebring's odd sexual habits a possible cause of the murders. None of the girls interviewed—and the number was large, Sebring frequently dating five or six different girls a week—claimed that Sebring had actually hurt them, though he often asked them to pretend pain. Nor, as far as could be determined, was Sebring involved in group sex: he was too afraid his private quirks would subject him to ridicule. The mundane truth appeared to be that behind the carefully cultivated public image there was a lonely, troubled man so insecure in his role that even in his sex life he had to revert to fantasy.

Cause of death: Exsanguination—victim literally bled to death. Victim had been stabbed seven times and shot once, at least three of the stab wounds, as well as the gunshot wound, being in and of itself fatal.

Abigail Anne Folger, female Caucasian, 25 years, 5–5, 120 pounds, brown hair, hazel eyes, residence since the first of April, 10050 Cielo Drive. Prior to that she lived at 2774 Woodstock Road. Occupation, heiress to the Folger coffee fortune . . .

Abigail "Gibby" Folger's coming-out party had been held at the St. Francis Hotel in San Francisco on December 21, 1961. The Italianate ball was one of the highlights of the social season, the debutante wearing a bright yellow Dior she had purchased in Paris the previous summer.

After that she had attended Radcliffe, graduating with honors; worked for a time as publicity director for the University of California Art Museum in Berkeley; quit that to work in a New York bookstore; then became involved in social work in the ghettos. It was while in New York, in early 1968, that Polish novelist Jerzy Kosinski introduced her to Voytek Frykowski. They left New York together that August, driving to Los Angeles, where they rented a house at 2774 Woodstock Road, off Mulholland in the Hollywood hills. Through Frykowski, she met the Polanskis, Sebring, and others in their circle. She was one of the investors in Sebring International.

Shortly after arriving in Southern California, she registered as a volunteer social worker for the Los Angeles County Welfare Department, and would get up at dawn each day for assignments that took her into Watts, Pacoima, and other ghetto areas. She continued this work until the day before she and Frykowski moved into 10050 Cielo Drive.

Something changed after that. Probably it was a combination of things. She became depressed over how little such work actually accomplished, how big the problems stayed. "A lot of social workers go home at night, take a bath, and wash off their day," she told an old San Francisco friend. "I can't. The suffering gets under your skin." In May, black city councilman Thomas Bradley ran against incumbent Samuel Yorty for mayor of Los Angeles. Bradley's defeat, after a campaign heavy with racial smears, left her disillusioned and bitter. She did not resume her social work. She was also disturbed about the way her affair with Frykowski was going, and with their use of drugs, which had passed the point of experimentation.

She talked about all these things with her psychiatrist, Dr. Marvin Flicker. She saw him five days a week, Monday through Friday, at 4:30 P.M.

She had kept her appointment that Friday.

Flicker told the police that he thought Abigail was almost ready to leave Frykowski, that she was attempting to build up enough nerve to go it alone.

The police were unable to determine exactly when Folger and Frykowski began to use drugs heavily, on a regular basis. It was learned that on their cross-country trip they had stopped in Irving, Texas, staying several days with a big dope dealer well known to local and Dallas police. Dealers were among their regular guests both at the Woodstock house and after they moved to Cielo Drive. William Tennant told police that whenever he visited the latter residence, Abigail "always seemed to be in a stupor from narcotics." When her mother last talked to her, about ten that Friday night, she said Gibby had sounded lucid but "a little high." Mrs. Folger, who was not unaware of her daughter's problems, had contributed large amounts of both money and time to the Haight-Ashbury Free Medical Clinic, to help in their pioneer work in treating drug abuse.

The coroners discovered 2.4 mg. of methylenedioxyamphetamine—MDA—in Abigail Folger's system. That this was a larger amount than was found in Voytek Frykowski's body—0.6 mg.—did not necessarily indicate that she had taken a larger quantity of the drug, but could mean she had taken it at a later time.

Effects of the drug vary, depending on the individual

nd the dosage, but one thing was clear. That night she
vas fully aware of what was happening.

Victim had been stabbed twenty-eight times.

*Wojiciech "Voytek" Frykowski, male Caucasian, 32
years, 5–10, 165 pounds, blond hair, blue eyes.
Frykowski had been living with Abigail Folger in a
common-law relationship . . .*

"Voytek," Roman Polanski would later tell reporters,
"was a man of little talent but immense charm." The two
had been friends in Poland, Frykowski's father reputedly
having helped finance one of Polanski's early films. Even
in Poland, Frykowski had been known as a playboy. According to fellow émigrés, he had once taken on, and rendered inoperative, two members of the secret police,
which may have had something to do with his exit from
Poland in 1967. He had married twice, and had one son,
who had remained behind when he moved to Paris. Both
there and, later, in New York, Polanski had given him
money and encouragement, hopeful—but knowing Voytek
well, not too optimistic—that one of his grand plans
would come through. None ever quite did. He told people
that he was a writer, but no one could recall having read
anything he had written.

Friends of Abigail Folger told the police that Frykowski
had introduced her to drugs so as to keep her under his
control. Friends of Voytek Frykowski said the opposite—
that Folger had provided the drugs so as not to lose him.

According to the police report: "He had no means of
support and lived off Folger's fortune . . . He used cocaine,
mescaline, LSD, marijuana, hashish in large amounts . . .
He was an extrovert and gave invitations to almost everyone he met to come visit him at his residence. Narcotic
parties were the order of the day.'"

He had fought hard for his life. Victim was shot twice,
struck over the head thirteen times with a blunt object, and
stabbed fifty-one times.

*Steven Earl Parent, male Caucasian, 18 years, 6–0,
175 pounds, red hair, brown eyes . . .*

He had graduated from Arroyo High School in June; dated several girls but no one in particular; had a full-time job as delivery boy for a plumbing company, plus a part-time job, evenings, as salesman for a stereo shop, holding down the two jobs so he could save money to attend junior college that September.

Victim had one defensive slash wound, and had been shot four times.

During the flouroscopy examination that preceded the Sebring autopsy, Dr. Noguchi discovered a bullet lodged between Sebring's back and his shirt. Three more bullets were found during the autopsies; one in Frykowski's body, two in Parent's. These—plus the slug and fragments found in Parent's automobile—were turned over to Sergeant William Lee, Firearms and Explosives Unit, SID, for study. Lee concluded that all the bullets had probably been fired from the same gun, and that they were .22 caliber.

While the autopsies were in progress, Sergeants Paul Whiteley and Charles Guenther, two homicide detectives from the Los Angeles Sheriff's Office, approached Sergeant Jess Buckles, one of the Los Angeles Police Department detectives assigned to the Tate homicides, and told him something very curious.

On July 31 they had gone to 964 Old Topanga Road in Malibu, to investigate a report of a possible homicide. They had found the body of Gary Hinman, a thirty-four-year-old music teacher. He had been stabbed to death.

The curious thing: as in the Tate homicides, a message had been left at the scene. On the wall in the living room, not far from Hinman's body, were the words POLITICAL PIGGY, printed in the victim's own blood.

Whiteley also told Buckles that they had arrested a suspect in connection with the murder, one Robert "Bobby" Beausoleil, a young hippie musician. He had been driving a car that belonged to Hinman, there was blood on his shirt and trousers, and a knife had been found hidden in the tire well of the vehicle. The arrest had occurred on August 6; therefore he had been in custody at the time of the

Tate homicides. However, it was possible that he hadn't been the only one involved in the Hinman murder. Beausoleil had been living at Spahn's Ranch, an old movie ranch near the Los Angeles suburb of Chatsworth, with a bunch of other hippies. It was an odd group, their leader, a guy named Charlie, apparently having convinced them that he was Jesus Christ.

Buckles, Whiteley would later recall, lost interest when he mentioned hippies. "Naw," he replied, "we know what's behind these murders. They're part of a big dope transaction."

Whiteley again emphasized the odd similarities. Like mode of death. In both cases a message had been left. Both printed. Both in a victim's blood. And in both the letters PIG appeared. Any one of these things would be highly unusual. But *all*—the odds against its being a coincidence must be astronomical.

Sergeant Buckles, LAPD, told Sergeants Whiteley and Guenther, LASO, "If you don't hear from us in a week or so, that means we're on to something else."

A little more than twenty-four hours after the discovery of the Tate victims, the Los Angeles Police Department was given a lead by the Los Angeles Sheriff's Office, which, if followed, could possibly have broken the case.

Buckles never did call, nor did he think the information important enough to walk across the autopsy room and mention the conversation to his superior, Lieutenant Robert Helder, who was in charge of the Tate investigation.

At Lieutenant Helder's suggestion, Dr. Noguchi withheld specifics when he met with the press. He did not mention the number of wounds, nor did he say anything about two of the victims' having ingested drugs. He did, again, deny the already much repeated reports that there had been sexual molestation and/or mutilation. Neither was true, he stressed.

Asked about Sharon's child, he said that Mrs. Polanski was in the eighth month of her pregnancy; that the child was a perfectly formed boy; and that had he been removed by post-mortem cesarean within the first twenty minutes after the mother's death, his life probably could have been saved. "But by the time the bodies were discovered, it was too late."

Lieutenant Helder also talked to the press that day. Yes, Garretson was still in custody. No, he could not comment on the evidence against him, except to say that the police were now investigating his acquaintances.

Pressed further, Helder admitted, "There's no solid information that will limit us to a single suspect. It could've been one man. It could've been two. It could've been three.

"But," he added, "I don't feel that we have a maniac running around."

Lieutenant A. H. Burdick began the polygraph examination of William Garretson at 4:25 that afternoon, at Parker Center.

Burdick did not immediately hook up Garretson. In accordance with routine, the initial portion of the examination was conversational, the examiner attempting to put the suspect at ease while eliciting as much background information as possible.

Though obviously frightened, Garretson loosened up a little as he talked. He told Burdick that he was nineteen, from Ohio, and had been hired by Rudi Altobelli in March, just before Altobelli left for Europe. His job was simple: to look after the guest house and Altobelli's three dogs. In return, he had been given a place to stay, thirty-five dollars a week, and the promise of an airline ticket back to Ohio when Altobelli returned.

He had little to do with the people who lived in the main house, Garretson claimed. Several of his replies seemed to bear this out. He still referred to Frykowski, for example, as "the younger Polanski," while he appeared unfamiliar with Sebring, either by name or description, though he had seen the black Porsche in the driveway on several occasions.

Asked to relate his activities prior to the murders, Garretson said that on Thursday night an acquaintance had dropped by, accompanied by his girl. They had brought along a six-pack of beer and some pot. Garretson was sure it was Thursday night, as the man was married "and he brought her up there several other times, you know, on Thursday, when his wife lets him go out."

Q. "Did they use your pad?"

A. "Yes, they did, and I drank some beer while they made out . . ."

Garretson recalled that he drank four beers, smoked two joints, took one dexedrine, and was sick all day Friday.

About 8:30 or 9 P.M. Friday, Garretson said, he went down to the Sunset Strip, to buy a pack of cigarettes and a TV dinner. He guessed the time of his return at about ten, but couldn't be sure, not having a watch. As he passed the main house, he noticed the lights were on, but he didn't see anyone. Nor did he observe anything out of the ordinary.

Then "about a quarter of twelve or something like that, Steve [Parent] came up and, you know, he brought his radio with him. He had a radio, clock radio; and I didn't expect him or anything, and he asked me how I'd been and everything . . ." Parent plugged in the radio, to demonstrate how it worked, but Garretson wasn't interested.

Then "I gave him a beer . . . and he drank it and then he called somebody—somebody on Santa Monica and Doheny—and he said that he would be going there, and so then he left, and, you know, that's when—that's the last time I saw him."

When found in Parent's car, the clock radio had stopped at 12:15 A.M., the approximate time of the murder. Although it could have been a remarkable coincidence, the logical presumption was that Parent had set it while demonstrating it to Garretson, then unplugged it just before he left. This would coincide with Garretson's estimate of the time.

According to Garretson, after Parent left, he wrote some letters and played the stereo, not going to sleep until just before dawn. Though he claimed to have heard nothing unusual during the night, he admitted that he had been "scared."

Why? Burdick asked. Well, Garretson replied, not long after Steve left, he noticed that the handle of the door was turned down, as if someone had tried to open it. And when he tried to use the phone, to learn the time, he found it was dead.

Like the other officers, Burdick found it difficult to believe that Garretson, though admittedly awake all night, heard nothing, while neighbors even farther away heard shots or screams. Garretson insisted, however, that he had neither heard nor seen anything. He was less sure on another point—whether he had gone out into the back yard when he let Altobelli's dogs out. To Burdick he appeared evasive about this. From the yard, however, he couldn't see the main house, though he might have heard something.

As far as LAPD was concerned, the moment of truth was now arriving. Burdick began setting up the polygraph, at the same time reading Garretson the list of questions he intended to ask.

This, too, was standard operating procedure, and more than a little psychological. Knowing a certain question was going to be asked, but not when, built tension, accentuating the response. He then began the test.

Q. "Is your true last name Garretson?"

A. "Yes."

No significant response.

Q. "Concerning Steve, did you cause his death?"

A. "No."

Facing forward, Garretson couldn't see Burdick's face. Burdick kept his voice matter-of-fact as he moved on to the next question, in no way indicating that the steel pens had jerked across the graph.

Q. "You understood the questions?"

A. "Yes."

Q. "Do you feel responsible for Steve's death?"

A. "That he even knew me, yes."

Q. "Huh?"

A. "That he even knew me. I mean he wouldn't have come up that night, and nothing would have happened in other words to him."

Burdick relieved the pressure cup on Garretson's arm, told him to relax, talked to him informally for a while.

Then again the pressure, and the questions, only slightly changed this time.

Q. "Is your true last name Garretson?"

A. "Yes."

Q. "Did you shoot Steve?"

A. "No."

No significant response.

More test questions, followed by "Do you know who caused Mrs. Polanski's death?"

A. "No."

Q. "Did you cause Mrs. Polanski's death?"

A. "No."

Still no significant response.

Burdick now accepted Garretson's explanation, that he felt responsibility for Parent's death, but had no part in causing it or the other murders. The examination went on for another half hour or so, during which Burdick closed off several avenues of investigation. Garretson was not gay; he had never had sex with any of the victims; he had never sold drugs.

There was no indication that Garretson was lying, but he remained nervous throughout. Burdick asked him why. Garretson explained that when he was being taken to his cell, a policeman had pointed at him, saying, "There's the guy that killed all those people."

Q. "I would imagine it would shake you up. But that doesn't mean you're lying?"

A. "No, I'm just confused."

Q. "Why are you confused?"

A. "For one thing, how come I wasn't murdered?"

Q. "I don't know."

Although legally inadmissable as evidence, the police believe in the polygraph.* Though uninformed of it at the time, Garretson had passed. "At the conclusion of the examination," Captain Don Martin, commander, SID, wrote in his official report, "it was the examiner's opinion that

---

*In 1972 a Los Angeles Superior Court judge broke with precedent and permitted the results of a polygraph test to be received into evidence in a marijuana case.

Mr. Garretson was truthful and not criminally involved in the Polanski homicides."

Unofficially, though Burdick believed Garretson "clean" on participation, he felt he was a little "muddy" on knowledge. It was possible that he had heard something, then, fearful, hidden until dawn. This was just conjecture, however.

For all intents and purposes, with the polygraph William Eston Garretson ceased to be a "good suspect." Yet that bothersome question remained: Every single human being at 10050 Cielo Drive had been slaughtered save one; why?

Because there was no immediate answer, and certainly in part because, having been the only warm body on the premises, he had seemed such a likely suspect, Garretson was held for another day.

That same Sunday, Jerrold D. Friedman, a UCLA student, contacted the police and informed them that the call Steven Parent made at approximately 11:45 on Friday night had been to him. Parent was going to build a stereo set for Friedman, and he wanted to talk over the details. Friedman had tried to beg off, saying it was late, but finally gave in and told Parent he could drop by for a few minutes. Parent had asked him the time and, when he told him, said he would be there about 12:30.* According to Friedman, "he never got there."

That Sunday, LAPD not only lost their best suspect to date, another promising lead fizzled out. Sharon Tate's red Ferrari, which the police had thought might have been used as a getaway car, was located in a Beverly Hills garage where Sharon had taken it the previous week for repairs.

That evening Roman Polanski returned from London. Reporters who saw him at the airport described him as "terribly crushed" and "beaten by the tragedy." Though he refused to talk with the press, a spokesman for him denied there was any truth to the rumors of a marital rift. Polan-

*It was possible when Parent asked the time he also set the radio clock.

ski had remained in London, he said, because he hadn't finished his work there. Sharon had returned home early, by boat, because of airline restrictions against travel during the last two months of pregnancy.

Polanski was taken to an apartment inside the Paramount lot, where he remained in seclusion under a doctor's care. The police talked to him briefly that night, but he was, at that time, unable to suggest anyone with a motive for the murders.

Frank Struthers also returned to Los Angeles that Sunday night. About 8:30 P.M. the Saffies dropped him off at the end of the long driveway leading to the LaBianca residence. Lugging his suitcase and camping equipment up the driveway, the fifteen-year-old noticed that the speedboat was still on the trailer behind Leno's Thunderbird. That seemed odd; his stepfather didn't like to leave the boat out overnight. Stowing his equipment in the garage, he went to the back door of the residence.

Only then did he notice that all the window shades had been pulled down. He couldn't recall ever seeing them that way before, and it frightened him just a little bit. The light was on in the kitchen, and he knocked on the door. There was no response. He called out. Again no answer.

Really upset now, he walked to the closest pay phone, which was at a hamburger stand at Hyperion and Rowena. He dialed the number of the house, then, getting no response, tried to reach his sister at the restaurant where she worked. Susan wasn't working that night, but the manager offered to try her apartment. Frank gave him the number of the pay phone.

Shortly after nine she called. She hadn't seen or heard from their mother and stepfather since they had dropped her off at her apartment the previous night. Telling Frank to remain where he was, she called her boy friend, Joe Dorgan, and told him Frank thought something was wrong at the house. About 9:30, Joe and Susan picked up Frank at the hamburger stand, the three driving directly to 3301 Waverly Drive.

Rosemary often left a set of house keys in her own car.

They found them and opened the back door.* Dorgan suggested that Susan remain in the kitchen while he and Frank checked out the rest of the house. They proceeded through the dining room. When they got to the living room, they saw Leno.

He was sprawled on his back between the couch and a chair. There was a throw pillow over his head, some kind of cord around his neck, and the tops of his pajamas were torn open so his stomach was bare. Something was protruding from his stomach.

He was so still they knew he was dead.

Afraid Susan would follow and see what they had, they returned to the kitchen. Joe picked up the kitchen phone to call the police, then, worried that he might be disturbing evidence, put it back down, telling Susan, "Everything's O.K.; let's get out of here." But Susan knew everything wasn't O.K. On the refrigerator door someone had written something in what looked like red paint.

Hurrying back down the driveway, they stopped at a duplex across the street, and Dorgan rang the bell of 3308 Waverly Drive. The peephole opened. Dorgan said there had been a stabbing and he wanted to call the police. The person inside refused to open the door, saying, "We'll call the police for you."

LAPD's switchboard logged the call at 10:26 P.M., the caller complaining about some juveniles making a disturbance.

Unsure whether the person had really made the call, Dorgan had already pushed the bell of the other apartment, 3306. Dr. and Mrs. Merry J. Brigham let the three young people in. However, they were so upset Mrs. Brigham had to complete the call. At 10:35, Unit 6A39, a black-and-white manned by officers W. C. Rodriquez and J. C. Toney, was dispatched to the address, arriving very quickly, five to seven minutes later.

While Susan and Frank remained with the doctor and his wife, Dorgan accompanied the two Hollywood Division officers to the LaBianca residence. Toney covered

---

*Since no one tried the door before using the key, it is unknown whether it was locked.

the back door while Rodriquez went around the house. The front door was closed but not locked. After one look inside, he ran back to the car and called for a backup unit, a supervisor, and an ambulance.

Rodriquez had been on the force only fourteen months; he had never discovered a body before.

Within a few minutes, Ambulance Unit G-1 arrived, and Leno LaBianca was pronounced DOA—dead on arrival. In addition to the pillow Frank and Joe had seen, there was a bloody pillowcase over his head. The cord around his neck was attached to a massive lamp, the cord knotted so tightly it appeared he had been throttled with it. His hands were tied behind his back with a leather thong. The object protruding from his stomach was an ivory-handled, bi-tined carving fork. In addition to a number of stab wounds in the abdomen, someone had carved the letters WAR in the naked flesh.

The backup unit, 6L40, manned by Sergeant Edward L. Cline, arrived just after the ambulance. A veteran of sixteen years, Cline took charge, obtaining a pink DOA slip from the two attendants before they left.

The pair were already on their way down the driveway when Rodriquez called them back. Cline had found another body, in the master bedroom.

Rosemary LaBianca was lying face down on the bedroom floor, parallel to the bed and dresser, in a large pool of blood. She was wearing a short pink nightgown and, over it, an expensive dress, blue with white horizontal stripes, which Susan would later identify as one of her mother's favorites. Both nightgown and dress were bunched up over her head, so her back, buttocks, and legs were bare. Cline didn't even try to count the stab wounds, there were so many. Her hands were not tied but, like Leno, she had a pillowcase over her head and a lamp cord was wrapped around her neck. The cord was attached to one of a pair of bedroom lamps, both of which had overturned. The tautness of the cord, plus a second pool of blood about two feet from the body, indicated that perhaps she had tried to crawl, pulling the lamps over while doing so.

A second pink DOA slip was filled out, for Mrs. Rose-mary LaBianca. Joe Dorgan had to tell Susan and Frank.

There was writing, in what appeared to be blood, in three places in the residence. High up on the north wall in the living room, above several paintings, were printed the words DEATH TO PIGS. On the south wall, to the left of the front door, even higher up, was the single word RISE. There were two words on the refrigerator door in the kitchen, the first of which was misspelled. They read HEALTER SKELTER.

Monday, August 11, 1969

At 12:15 A.M. the case was assigned to Robbery-Homi-cide. Sergeant Danny Galindo, who had spent the previous night on guard duty at the Tate residence, was the first de-tective to arrive, at about 1 A.M. He was joined shortly after by Inspector K. J. McCauley and several other de-tectives, while an additional unit, ordered by Cline, sealed off the grounds. As with the Tate homicides, however, the reporters, who had already begun to arrive, apparently had little difficulty obtaining inside information.

Galindo made a detailed search of the one-story res-idence. Except for the overturned lamps, there were no signs of a struggle. Nor was there any evidence that rob-bery had been the motive. Among the items that Galindo would log into the County Public Administrator's Report were: a man's gold ring, the main stone a one-carat dia-mond, the other stones also diamonds, only slightly small-er; two woman's rings, both expensive, both in plain view on a dresser in the bedroom; necklaces; bracelets; camera equipment; hand guns, shotguns, and rifles; a coin collec-tion; a bag of uncirculated nickels, found in the trunk of Leno's Thunderbird, worth considerably more than their $400 face value; Leno LaBianca's wallet, with credit cards and cash, in the glove compartment of his car; several watches, one a high-priced stopwatch of the type used to clock race horses; plus numerous other easily fenced items.

Several days later Frank Struthers returned to the residence with the police. The only missing items, as far as he could determine, were Rosemary's wallet and her wristwatch.

Galindo was unable to find any indications of forced entry. However, testing the back door, he found it could be jimmied very easily. He was able to open it with only a strip of celluloid.

The detectives made a number of other discoveries. The ivory-handled carving fork found protruding from Leno's stomach belonged to a set found in a kitchen drawer. There were some watermelon rinds in the sink. There were also blood splatters, both there and in the rear bathroom. And a piece of blood-soaked paper was found on the floor in the dining room, its frayed end suggesting that possibly it had been the instrument used to print the words.

In many ways the activities at 3301 Waverly Drive the rest of that night were a replay of those that had occurred at 10050 Cielo Drive less than forty-eight hours earlier. Even to, in some cases, the same cast, with Sergeant Joe Granado arriving about 3 A.M. to take blood samples.

The sample from the kitchen sink wasn't sufficient to determine if it was animal or human, but all the other samples tested positive on the Ouchterlony test, indicating they were human blood. The blood in the rear bathroom, as well as all the blood in the vicinity of Rosemary LaBianca's body, was type A—Rosemary LaBianca's type. All the other samples, including that taken from the rumpled paper and the various writings, were type B—Leno LaBianca's type.

This time Granado didn't take *any* subtypes.

The fingerprint men from SID, Sergeants Harold Dolan and J. Claborn, lifted a total of twenty-five latents, all but six of which would later be identified as belonging to Leno, Rosemary, or Frank. It was apparent to Dolan, from examining those areas where fingerprints should have been but weren't, that an effort had been made to eradi-

cate prints. For example, there was not even a smudge on
the ivory handle of the carving fork, on the chrome handle of the refrigerator door, or on the enamel finish of the
door itself—all surfaces that readily lent themselves to receiving latent fingerprints. The refrigerator door on close
examination showed wipe marks.

After the police photographer had finished, a deputy
coroner supervised the removal of the bodies. The pillowcases were left in place over the heads of the victims; the
lamp cords were cut near the bases, so the knots remained
intact for study. A representative of the Animal Regulation Department removed the three dogs, which, when the
first officers arrived, had been found inside the house.

Left behind were the puzzle pieces. But this time at
least a partial pattern was discernible, in the similarities:

Los Angeles, California; consecutive nights; multiple
murders; victims affluent Caucasians; multiple stab
wounds; incredible savagery; absence of a conventional
motive; no evidence of ransacking or robbery; ropes around
the neck of two Tate victims, cords around the necks of
both LaBiancas. And the bloody printing.

Yet within twenty-four hours the police would decide
there was no connection between the two sets of murders.

SECOND RITUAL
KILLINGS HERE

Los Feliz Couple Slain;
Link to 5-Way Murder Seen

The headlines screamed from the front pages that Monday morning; TV programs were interrupted for updates;
to the millions of Angelenos who commuted to work via
the freeways their car radios seemed to broadcast little
else.*

It was then the fear began.

*Some of the details were garbled. It was reported, for example,
that the pillowcases were white hoods; that the phrase DEATH TO
PIGS had been printed in blood on the refrigerator door, when it
actually appeared on the wall in the living room. But enough information had leaked out for the detectives again to have trouble
finding polygraph keys.

When the news of the Tate homicides broke, even those acquainted with the victims were less fearful than shocked, for simultaneously came the announcement that a suspect had been arrested and charged with the murders. Garretson, however, had been in custody when these new murders took place. And with his release that Monday—still looking as puzzled and frightened as when the police "captured" him—the panic began. And spread.

If Garretson wasn't guilty, then it meant that whoever was was still at large. If it could happen in places as widely separated as Los Feliz and Bel Air, to people as disparate as movie colony celebrities and a grocery market owner and his wife, it meant it could happen anywhere, to anyone.

Sometimes fear can be measured. Among the barometers: In two days one Beverly Hills sporting goods store sold 200 firearms; prior to the murders, they averaged three or four a day. Some of the private security forces doubled, then tripled, their personnel. Guard dogs, once priced at $200, now sold for $1,500; those who supplied them soon ran out. Locksmiths quoted two-week delays on orders. Accidental shootings, suspicious persons reports—all suddenly increased.

The news that there had been twenty-eight murders in Los Angeles that weekend (the average being one a day) did nothing to decrease the apprehension.

It was reported that Frank Sinatra was in hiding; that Mia Farrow wouldn't attend her friend Sharon's funeral because, a relative explained, "Mia is afraid she will be next"; that Tony Bennett had moved from his bungalow on the grounds of the Beverly Hills Hotel to an inside suite "for greater security"; that Steve McQueen now kept a weapon under the front seat of his sports car; that Jerry Lewis had installed an alarm system in his home complete with closed circuit TV. Connie Stevens later admitted she had turned her Beverly Hills home into a fortress. "Mainly because of the Sharon Tate murders. That scared the daylights out of everyone."

Friendships ended, romances broke up, people were abruptly dropped from guest lists, parties canceled—for with the fear came suspicion. The killer or killers could be almost anyone.

A cloud of fright hung over southern California more dense than its smog. It would not dissipate for months. As late as the following March, William Kloman would write in *Esquire:* "In the great houses of Bel Air, terror sends people flying to their telephones when a branch falls from a tree outside."

POLITICAL PIGGY—Hinman.
PIG—Tate.
DEATH TO PIGS—LaBianca.

In each case, written in the blood of one of the victims. Sergeant Buckles still didn't think it important enough to check further.

Deputy Medical Examiner David Katsuyama conducted the LaBianca autopsies. Before starting, he removed the pillowcases from the heads of the victims. Only then was it discovered that in addition to the carving fork embedded in his abdomen, a knife had been stuck in Leno LaBianca's throat.

Since none of the personnel at the scene had observed the knife, this became one of the LaBianca polygraph keys. There were two others. For some reason, though the phrase DEATH TO PIGS had leaked to the press, neither RISE nor HEALTER SKELTER had.

Leno A. LaBianca, 3301 Waverly Drive, male Caucasian, 44 years, 6-0, 220 pounds, brown eyes, brown hair . . .

Born in Los Angeles, son of the founder of the State Wholesale Grocery Company, Leno had gone into the family business after attending the University of Southern California, eventually becoming president of Gateway Markets, a Southern California chain.

As far as the police were able to determine, Leno had no enemies. Yet they soon discovered that he too had a secret side. Friends and relatives described him as quiet and conservative; they were amazed to learn, after his death, that he owned nine thoroughbred race horses, the most prominent being Kildare Lady, and that he was a chronic gambler, frequenting the tracks nearly every racing day, often betting $500 at a time. Nor did they know that he was, at the time of his death, some $230,000 in debt.

In the weeks ahead the LaBianca detectives would do a remarkable job of tracking their way through the tangled maze of Leno LaBianca's complex financial affairs. The possibility that Leno might have been the victim of loan sharks, however, fell apart when it was learned that Rosemary LaBianca was quite wealthy herself, having more than sufficient assets to pay off Leno's debts.

One of Leno's former partners, also Italian, who knew of his gambling habits, told the police he thought the murders might have been committed by the Mafia. He admitted he had no evidence to support this; however, the detectives did learn that for a short time Leno had been on the board of directors of a Hollywood bank which LAPD and LASO intelligence units believed was backed by "hoodlum money." They had been unable to prove this, though several other board members were indicted and convicted of a kiting scheme. The possibility of a Mafia link became one of a number of leads that would have to be checked out.

Leno did not have a criminal record; Rosemary had one traffic citation which dated back to 1957.

Leno left $100,000 in insurance, which, since it was to be divided equally among Susan, Frank, and the three children from his previous marriage, appeared to rule that out as a motive.

Leno LaBianca died in the same house in which he had been born, he and Rosemary moving into the family home, which Leno had purchased from his mother, in November 1968.

Cause of death: Multiple stab wounds. Victim had twelve stab wounds, plus fourteen puncture wounds made by a double-tined fork, for a total of twenty-six separate wounds, any one of six of which could in and of itself have been fatal.

Rosemary LaBianca, 3301 Waverly Drive, female
Caucasian, 38 years, 5–5, 125 pounds, brown hair,
brown eyes . . .

It was probable that even Rosemary did not know a
great deal about her early years. It was believed that she
had been born in Mexico, of American parents, then or-
phaned or abandoned in Arizona. She remained in an
orphanage there until the age of twelve, when she was
adopted by a family named Harmon, who took her to
California. She had met her first husband while working as
a carhop at the Brown Derby Drive-In in Los Feliz in the
late 1940s, while still in her teens. They were divorced in
1958, and it was shortly after this, while working as a
waitress at the Los Feliz Inn, that she met and married
Leno LaBianca.

Her former husband was polygraphed, and cleared of
any involvement in the crime. Former employers, ex-boy
friends, current business associates were interviewed; none
could recall anyone who disliked her.

According to Ruth Sivick, her partner in Boutique Carriage, Rosemary had a good head for business; not only
was the shop successful, Rosemary also invested in stocks
and commodities, and did well. How well was not known
until her estate was probated, and it was learned she had
left $2,600,000. Abigail Folger, the heiress in the Cielo
slayings, had left less than one-fifth that.

Mrs. Sivick had last seen Rosemary on Friday, when
they went buying for the store. Rosemary had called on
Saturday morning, telling her they planned to drive to
Lake Isabella, and wondering if she could drop by that afternoon and feed the dogs. The LaBiancas had three dogs.
All had barked loudly when she approached the house at
about 6 P.M. After feeding them—taking the dog food
out of the refrigerator—Mrs. Sivick checked the doors—
all were locked—and left.

Mrs. Sivick's testimony established that whoever wiped
the refrigerator handle of prints had done so sometime after she had been there.

Rosemary LaBianca—carhop to millionairess to murder
victim.

Cause of death: Multiple stab wounds. Victim had been stabbed a total of forty-one times, any one of six of which could in and of itself have been fatal.

All but one of Leno LaBianca's wounds were to the front of his body; thirty-six of the forty-one inflicted on Rosemary LaBianca were to her back and buttocks. Leno had no defensive wounds, indicating that his hands had probably been bound before he was stabbed. Rosemary had a defensive slash wound on her left jaw. This wound, plus the knife in Leno's throat, indicated that the placing of the pillowcases over the heads of the victims was a belated act, possibly even occurring after they had died.

The pillowcases were identified as the LaBiancas' own, having been removed from the two pillows on their bed.

The knife found in Leno's throat was also theirs; though it was from a different set than the fork, it matched others found in a kitchen drawer. The dimensions of its blade were: length, 4 7/8 inches; thickness, just under 1/16 inch; width at widest point, 13/16 inch; width at narrowest point, 3/8 inch.

The LaBianca detectives later noted in their report: "The knife recovered from his throat appeared to be the weapon used in both homicides."

It was a presumption, and nothing more, since for some reason Dr. Katsuyama, unlike his superior Dr. Noguchi, who handled the Tate autopsies, did not measure the dimensions of the wounds. Nor did the detectives assigned to the LaBianca case ask for these statistics.

The ramifications of this one presumption were immense. A single weapon indicated that there was probably a single killer. That the weapon used belonged in the residence meant that the killer had probably arrived unarmed, his decision to kill the pair occurring sometime after he entered the premises. This in turn suggested: (1) that the killer had arrived to commit a burglary or some other crime, then had been surprised when the LaBiancas returned home; or (2) that the victims knew the killer, trusting him enough to let him in at two in the morning or thereafter.

One little presumption, but it would cause many, many problems later.

As would the estimated time of death.

Asked by the detectives to determine the time, Katsuyama came up with 3 P.M. Sunday. When other evidence appeared to contradict this, the detectives went back to Katsuyama and asked him to recalculate. He now decided Leno LaBianca had died sometime between 12:30 A.M. and 8:30 P.M. on Sunday, and that Rosemary had died an hour earlier. However, Katsuyama cautioned, the time could be affected by room temperature and other variables.

All this was so indecisive that the detectives simply ignored it. They knew, from Frank Struthers, that Leno was a creature of habit. Every night he bought the paper, then read it before going to bed, always starting with the sports section. That section had been open on the coffee table, with Leno's reading glasses beside it. From this and other evidence (Leno was wearing pajamas, the bed hadn't yet been slept in, and so forth) they concluded that the murders had probably taken place within an hour or so after the LaBiancas had left Fokianos' newsstand, or sometime between 2 and 3 A.M. on Sunday.

As early as Monday, police were minimizing the similarities between the two crimes. Inspector K. J. McCauley told reporters: "I don't see any connection between this murder and the others. They're too widely removed. I just don't see any connection." Sergeant Bryce Houchin observed: "There is a similarity, but whether it's the same suspect or a copycat we just don't know."

There were several reasons for discounting the similarities. One was the absence of any apparent link between the victims; another the distance between the crimes. Still another, and more important in formulating a motive, drugs were found at 10050 Cielo Drive, while there were none at 3301 Waverly Drive.

There was one more reason, perhaps the most influential. Even before Garretson was released, the Tate detectives had not one but several very promising new suspects.

August 12-15, 1969

From William Tennant, Roman Polanski's business manager, LAPD learned that in mid-March the Polanskis had given a catered party at Cielo with over a hundred guests. As at any large Hollywood gathering, there were crashers, among them +Herb Wilson, +Larry Madigan, and +Jeffery Pickett, nicknamed "Pic."* The trio, all in their late twenties, were reputedly dope dealers. During the party Wilson apparently stepped on Tennant's foot. An argument ensued, Madigan and Pickett taking Wilson's side. Irritated, Roman Polanski had the three men evicted.

It was a minor incident, in and of itself hardly cause for five savage murders, but Tennant had heard something else: "Pic" had once threatened to kill Frykowski. This information had come to him through a friend of Voytek's, Witold Kaczanowski, an artist professionally known as Witold K.

Not unmindful of the similarity between "Pic" and the bloody-lettered PIG on the front door of the Tate residence, detectives interviewed Witold K. From him they learned that after the Polanskis had left for Europe, Wilson, Pickett, Madigan, and a fourth man, +Gerold Jones, were frequent visitors to the Cielo residence, Wilson and Madigan, according to Witold, supplying Voytek and Gibby with most of their drugs, including the MDA they had taken before they died. As for Jeffrey Pickett, when Gibby and Voytek took over Cielo, he moved into their Woodstock residence. Witold was staying there also. Once, during an argument, Pickett tried to strangle the artist.

---

*Everything in this book is based on fact. In a few instances the names of persons only tangentially involved have been changed for legal reasons, the cross symbol (+) indicating the substitution of a pseudonym for the true name. The persons were and are real, however, and the incidents depicted are entirely factual.

When Voytek learned of this, he told Pickett to get out. Enraged, Pic swore, "I'll kill them all and Voytek will be the first."

Numerous others also felt one or more of the men might be involved, and passed on their suspicions to the police. John and Michelle Phillips, formerly of the Mamas and Papas group and friends of four of the five Tate victims, said Wilson once drew a gun on Voytek. Various Strip habitués claimed Wilson often bragged that he was a hired killer; that Jones was an expert with knives, always carrying one for throwing; and that Madigan was Sebring's "candy man," or cocaine source.

More than ever convinced that the Tate homicides were the result of a drug burn or freakout, LAPD began looking for Wilson, Madigan, Pickett, and Jones.

For ten years Sharon Tate had sought stardom. Now she attained it, in just three days. On Tuesday, August 12, her name moved from the headlines onto theater marquees. *Valley of the Dolls* was rereleased nationally, opening in more than a dozen theaters in the Los Angeles area alone. It was quickly followed by *The Fearless Vampire Killers* and other films in which the actress had appeared, the only difference being that now she was given star billing.

That same day the police told reporters that they had officially ruled out any connection between the Tate and LaBianca homicides. According to the Los Angeles *Times*, "Several officers indicated they were inclined to believe the second slayings were the work of a copycat."

From the start, the two investigations had proceeded separately, with different detectives assigned to each. They would continue this way, each team pursuing its own leads.

They had one thing in common, though that similarity widened the distance between them. Both were operating on a basic assumption: in nearly 90 percent of all homicides the victim knows his killer. In both investigations the chief focus was now on acquaintances of the victims.

In checking out the Mafia rumor, the LaBianca detectives interviewed each of Leno's known business associates. All doubted the murders were Mafia originated. One man told the detectives that if the Mafia had been responsible, he "probably would have heard about it." It was a thorough investigation, the detectives even checking to see if the San Diego company where Leno had purchased his speedboat during their 1968 vacation was Mafia financed; it wasn't, though numerous other businesses in the Mission Bay area were allegedly backed by "Jewish Mafia money."

They even questioned Leno's mother, who told them, "He was a good boy. He never did belong to the association."

The elimination of a possible Mafia link, however, did not leave the LaBianca detectives without a suspect. In questioning neighbors of the pair, they learned that the house to the east, 3267 Waverly Drive, was vacant, and had been for several months. Prior to that it had been a hippie hangout. The hippies didn't interest them, but another former tenant, +Fred Gardner, did, very much.

From his rap sheet and from interviews they learned that Gardner, a young attorney, "has had mental problems in the past and claims he blacks out for periods of time and is not responsible for his actions ..." During an argument with his father, he "grabbed a knife from the kitchen table and chased his father, stating that he would kill him ..." In September 1968, after being married only two weeks, "for no apparent reason [he] administered a vicious beating to his wife, then grabbed a knife from the kitchen drawer and attempted to kill her. She warded off the blows and managed to escape and call the police." Booked for attempted murder, he was examined by a court-appointed psychiatrist, who found he had "uncontrolled aggressions of maniacal proportions." Despite this, the charge had been reduced to simple assault. He was released on probation, and returned to the practice of law.

Since then Gardner had been arrested a number of times, on drunk or drug charges. Following his last arrest, for forging a prescription, he was released on $900 bail, and promptly skipped. A warrant for his arrest had been issued on August 1, nine days before the LaBianca murders. He was believed to be in New York.

When the officers questioned Gardner's ex-wife, she told them she could recall seven separate occasions when Gardner visited the LaBiancas, each time returning with either money or whiskey. When she'd asked him about this, he'd allegedly replied, "It's O.K. I know them and they had better give it to me or else."

Had Gardner, with his penchant for kitchen knives, again tried to put the bite on the LaBiancas, this time the couple saying no? The officers contacted an FBI agent in New York to see if he could determine Gardner's present whereabouts.

Beloved Wife of Roman
Sharon Tate Polanski
1943   1969
Paul Richard Polanski
Their Baby

Wednesday was a day of funerals. More than 150 persons attended Sharon Tate's last rites at Holy Cross Cemetery. Among those present were Kirk Douglas, Warren Beatty, Steve McQueen, James Coburn, Lee Marvin, Yul Brynner, Peter Sellers, John and Michelle Phillips. Roman Polanski, wearing dark glasses and accompanied by his doctor, broke down several times during the ceremony, as did Sharon's parents and her two young sisters, Patricia and Deborah.

Many of the same people, including Polanski, later attended the services for Jay Sebring, at Wee Kirk o' the Heather, Forest Lawn. Additional celebrities included Paul Newman, Henry and Peter Fonda, Alex Cord, and George Hamilton, all former Sebring clients.

There were fewer people, and fewer flashbulbs, as, across the city, six of his high-school classmates carried Steven Parent's body from the small El Monte church where his services had taken place.

Abigail Folger was buried near where she had grown up in Northern California on the San Francisco Peninsula, following a requiem mass in Our Lady of the Wayside Church, which had been built by her grandparents.

Voytek Frykowski's body remained in Los Angeles until relatives in Poland could arrange for it to be returned there for burial.

While the Tate victims were being interred, the police were attempting to re-create their lives, in particular their last day.

Friday, August 8.

About 8 A.M. Mrs. Chapman arrived at Cielo. She did what dishes there were, then commenced her regular household chores.

About 8:30 Frank Guerrero arrived, to paint the room at the north end of the residence. This was to be the nursery. Before starting, Guerrero removed the screens from the windows.

At 11 A.M. Roman Polanski called from London. Mrs. Chapman overheard Sharon's side of the conversation. Sharon was worried that Roman wouldn't be home in time for his birthday, August 18. He apparently assured her that he would be back on August 12 as planned, as Sharon later told Mrs. Chapman this. Sharon informed Roman that she had enrolled him in a course for expectant fathers.

Sharon received several other calls, one of them having to do with a neighbor's kitten that had strayed onto the property; Sharon had been feeding it with an eyedropper. When Terry Melcher had moved out, he'd left behind a number of cats, Sharon promising to look after them. They had since multiplied, and Sharon was caring for all twenty-six, plus two dogs, hers and Abigail's.

Most of the day Sharon wore only bikini panties and a bra. This, according to Mrs. Chapman, was her usual at-home attire in hot weather.

Shortly before noon Mrs. Chapman, noticing that there were paw prints and dog splatters on the front door, washed down the whole exterior with vinegar and water. A small detail, which later would become extremely important.

Steven Parent had lunch at his home in El Monte. Before returning to work at the plumbing supply company, he asked his mother if she would lay out clean clothes so he could make a quick change before going to his second job, at the stereo shop, later that afternoon.

About 12:30 two of Sharon's friends, Joanna Pettet (Mrs. Alex Cord)* and Barbara Lewis, arrived at Cielo for lunch. Mrs. Chapman served them. It was all small talk, the women would later recall, mostly about the expected baby.

About 1 P.M. Sandy Tennant called Sharon. As previously noted, Sharon told her she wasn't planning a party that evening, but did invite her to drop by, an invitation Sandy declined.

(If one believed all the subsequent talk, half of Hollywood was invited to 10050 Cielo Drive for a party that night, and, at the last minute, changed their minds. According to Winifred Chapman, Sandy Tennant, Debbie Tate, and others close to Sharon, there was no party that night, nor was one ever planned. But LAPD probably spent a hundred man-hours attempting to locate people who allegedly attended the non-event.)

Having finished the first coat of paint, Guerrero left about 1:30. He didn't replace the screens, since he intended to return Monday to give the room a final coat. The police later concluded the killer(s) either didn't notice they were off or feared entering a freshly painted room.

About 2 P.M. Abigail purchased a bicycle from a shop on Santa Monica Boulevard, arranging for it to be delivered later that afternoon. About the same time David Martinez, one of Altobelli's two gardeners, arrived at 10050 Cielo and began work. Voytek and Abigail arrived not long after this, joining Sharon and her guests for a late lunch.

About 3 P.M. the second gardener, Tom Vargas, arrived. As he came in the gate, Abigail was driving out in her

---

*This would be actress Joanna Pettet's second close brush with violent death. She had also been a friend of Janice Wylie, who, together with her roommate Emily Hoffert, had been murdered in New York City in the summer of 1963, in what became known as the "career girls murder case."

Camaro. Five minutes later Voytek also left, driving the Firebird.

Joanna Pettet and Barbara Lewis departed about 3:30.

At about that same time Sebring's butler, Amos Russell, served Jay and his current female companion coffee in bed.* About 3:45 Jay called Sharon, apparently telling her he would be over earlier than expected. He later called his secretary, to pick up his messages, and John Madden, to discuss his visit to the San Francisco salon the next day. He didn't mention to either his plans for that evening, but he did tell Madden he had spent the day hard at work on a crest for the new franchise shops.

Just after Sebring called Sharon, Mrs. Chapman told her she had finished her work and was leaving for the day. Since it was so hot in the city, Sharon asked her if she would like to stay over. Mrs. Chapman declined. It was undoubtedly the most important decision she ever made.

David Martinez was just leaving, and he gave Mrs. Chapman a ride to the bus stop. Vargas remained behind, completing his work. While gardening near the house, he noticed Sharon asleep on the bed in her room. When a deliveryman from the Air Dispatch Company arrived with the two blue steamer trunks, Vargas, not wishing to disturb Mrs. Polanski, signed for them. The time, 4:30 P.M., was noted on the receipt. The trunks contained Sharon's clothing, which Roman had shipped from London.

Abigail kept her 4:30 appointment with Dr. Flicker.

Before Vargas left, about 4:45, he went back to the guest house and asked Garretson if he would do some watering over the weekend, as the weather was extremely hot and dry.

Across the city, in El Monte, Steven Parent hurried home, changed clothes, waved to his mother, and was off to his second job.

Between 5:30 and 6 P.M. Mrs. Terry Kay was backing out of her driveway at 9845 Easton Drive when she observed Jay Sebring driving down the road in his Porsche, seemingly in a hurry. Perhaps because her car was block-

---

*LAPD eventually located the girl and determined that she had not accompanied Sebring to the Tate residence that night.

ing his progress, he did not wave in his usual genial manner.

Sometime between 6 and 6:30 P.M. Sharon's thirteen-year-old sister Debbie called her, asking if she could drop by that evening with some friends. Sharon, who tired easily because of her advanced pregnancy, suggested they make it another time.

Between 7:30 and 8 P.M. Dennis Hurst arrived at the Cielo address to deliver the bicycle Abigail had purchased in his father's shop earlier that day. Sebring (whom Hurst later identified from photographs) answered the door. Hurst saw no one else and observed nothing suspicious.

Between 9:45 and 10 P.M. John Del Gaudio, manager of the El Coyote Restaurant on Beverly Boulevard, noted Jay Sebring's name on the waiting list for dinner: party of four. Del Gaudio didn't actually see Sebring or the others, and it is probable that he was off on the time, as waitress Kathy Palmer, who served the four, recalled they waited in the bar fifteen to twenty minutes before a table was available, then, after finishing dinner, left about 9:45 or 10. Shown photographs, she was unable to positively identify Sebring, Tate, Frykowski, or Folger.

If Abigail was along, they must have left the restaurant before ten, as it was about this time that Mrs. Folger called the Cielo number and talked to her, confirming that she planned to take the 10 A.M. United flight to San Francisco the next morning. Mrs. Folger told the police that "Abigail did not express any alarm or anxiety as to her personal safety or the situation at the Polanski house."

A number of people reported seeing Sharon and/or Jay at the Candy Store, the Factory, the Daisy, or various other clubs that night. None of the reports checked out. Several persons claimed to have talked by phone with one or another of the victims between 10 P.M. and midnight. When questioned, they suddenly changed their stories, or told them in such a way that the police concluded they were either confused or lying.

About 11 P.M. Steve Parent stopped at Dales Market in El Monte and asked his friend John LeFebure if he wanted to go for a ride. Parent had been dating John's younger sister Jean. John suggested they make it another night.

About forty-five minutes later Steve Parent arrived at the Cielo address, hoping to sell William Garretson a clock radio. Parent left the guest house about 12:15 A.M. He got as far as his Rambler.

The police also interviewed a number of other girls rumored to have been with Sebring on the evening of August 8.

"Ex-girl friend of Sebring, was supposed to have been with him on 8-8-69—not so—last slept with him 7-5-69. Cooperative, knew he used 'C'—she does not . . ."

". . . dated him steady for three months . . . knew nothing of his way-out bedroom activities . . ."

". . . was to go to a party at Cielo that night, but went to a movie instead . . ."

It was no small assignment, considering the number of girls the stylist had dated, yet none of the detectives was heard to complain. It wasn't every day they got the chance to talk to starlets, models, a *Playboy* centerfold, even a dancer in the Lido de Paris show at the Stardust Hotel in Las Vegas.

There was another barometer to the fear: the difficulty the police had in locating people. To have suddenly moved a few days after a crime would, in ordinary circumstances, be considered suspicious. But not in this case. From a not untypical report: "Asked why she had moved right after the murders, she replied that she wasn't sure why, that like everyone else in Hollywood she was just afraid . . ."

Though the police told the press there had been "no new developments," there were some that went unreported. After testing them for blood, Sergeant Joe Granado gave the three pieces of gun grip to Sergeant William Lee of the Firearms and Explosives Unit of SID. Lee didn't even have to consult his manuals; one look and he knew the grip was from a Hi Standard gun. He called Ed Lomax, product manager for the firm that owns Hi Standard, and arranged to meet him at the Police Academy. Lomax also made a quick ID. "Only one gun has a grip like that," he told Lee, "the Hi Standard .22 caliber Longhorn revolver." Popularly known as the "Buntline Special"—patterned after a pair of revolvers Western author Ned Buntline had made for Marshal Wyatt Earp—the gun had the following specifications: capacity 9 shots, barrel 9 1/2 inches, over-all length 15 inches, walnut grips, blue finish, weight 35 ounces, suggested retail price $69.95. It was, Lomax said, "rather a unique revolver"; introduced in April 1967, only 2,700 had been manufactured with this type grip.

Lee obtained from Lomax a list of stores where the gun had been sold, plus a photograph of the model, and LAPD began preparing a flyer which they planned to send to every police department in the United States and Canada.

A few days after the Lee-Lomax meeting, SID criminalist DeWayne Wolfer went to 10050 Cielo to conduct sound tests to see whether he could verify, or disprove, Garretson's claim that he had heard neither screams nor gunshots.

Using a general level sound meter and a .22 caliber revolver, and duplicating as closely as possible the conditions that existed on the night of the murders, Wolfer and an assistant proved (1) that if Garretson was inside the guest house as he claimed, he couldn't possibly have heard the shots that killed Steven Parent; and (2) that with the stereo on, with the volume at either 4 or 5, he couldn't have heard either screams or gunshots coming from in front of or inside the main residence.* The tests supported Garretson's story that he did not hear any shots that night.

Yet despite Wolfer's scientific findings, there were those at LAPD who still felt that Garretson must have heard something. It was almost as if he had been such a good suspect they were reluctant to admit him blameless. In a summary report on the case made up at the end of August, the Tate detectives observed: "In the opinion of the investigating officers and by scientific research by SID, it is highly unlikely that Garretson was not aware of the screams, gunshots and other turmoil that would result from a multiple homicide such as took place in his near proximity. These findings, however, did not absolutely preclude the fact that Garretson did not hear or see any of the events connected with the homicides."

The evening of Saturday, August 16, Roman Polanski was interviewed for several hours by LAPD. The following day he returned to 10050 Cielo Drive for the first time since the murders. He was accompanied by a writer and a photographer for *Life* and Peter Hurkos, the well-known psychic, who had been hired by friends of Jay Sebring to make a "reading" at the scene.

As Polanski identified himself and drove through the gate, the premises still being secured by LAPD, he commented bitterly to Thomas Thompson, the *Life* writer and a long-time acquaintance, "This must be the world-famous orgy house." Thompson asked him how long Gibby and Voytek had been staying there. "Too long, I guess," he answered.

The blue bedsheet that had earlier covered Abigail Folger was still on the lawn. The bloody lettering on the door had faded, but the three letters were still decipherable. The havoc inside seemed to take him aback for a minute,

*When Officer Whisenhunt searched the guest house following Garretson's arrest, he noticed the volume control on the set was between 4 and 5.

as did the dark stains in the entryway, and once inside the living room, the even larger ones in front of the couch. Polanski climbed the ladder to the loft, found the videotape LAPD had returned, and slipped it into his pocket, according to one of the officers who was present. On climbing back down, he walked from room to room, here and there touching things as if he could conjure up the past. The pillows were still bunched up in the center of the bed, as they had been that morning. They were always that way when he was gone, he told Thompson, adding simply, "She hugged them instead of me." He lingered a long time at the armoire where, in anticipation, Sharon had kept the baby things.

The *Life* photographer took a number of Polaroid shots first, to check lighting, placement, angles. Usually these are thrown away after the regular pictures are taken, but Hurkos asked if he might have several of them, to aid in his "impressions," and they were given to him, a gesture the photographer, and *Life*, would very soon regret.

As Polanski looked at the objects once familiar, now turned grotesque, he kept asking, "Why?" He posed outside the front door, looking as lost and confused as if he had stepped onto one of his own sets to discover everything immutably and grossly changed.

Hurkos later told the press: "Three men killed Sharon Tate and the other four—and I know who they are. I have identified the killers to the police and told them that these men must be stopped soon. Otherwise they will kill again." The killers, he added, were friends of Sharon Tate, turned into "frenzied homicidal maniacs" by massive doses of LSD. The killings, he was quoted as saying, erupted during a black magic ritual known as "goona goona," its suddenness catching the victims unawares.

If Hurkos did identify the three men to LAPD, no one bothered to make a report on it. All publicity to the contrary notwithstanding, those in law enforcement have a standard procedure for handling such "information": listen politely, then forget it. Being inadmissible as evidence, it is valueless.

Also skeptical of Hurkos' explanation was Roman Polanski. He would return to the house several times over the next few days, as if looking for the answer no one else had been able to give him.

There was an interesting juxtaposition of stories on the B, or lead local news, page of the Los Angeles *Times* that Sunday.

The big story, Tate, commandeered the top spot, with its headline, "ANATOMY OF A MASS/MURDER IN HOLLY-WOOD."

Below it was a smaller story, its one-column head reading, "LABIANCA COUPLE,/VICTIMS OF SLAYER,/GIVEN FINAL RITES."

To the left of the Tate story, and just above an artist's drawing of the Tate premises, was a much briefer, seemingly unrelated item, chosen, one suspected, because it was small enough to fit the space. Its headline read, "POLICE RAID RANCH,/ARREST 26 SUSPECTS/IN AUTO THEFT RING."

It began: "Twenty-six persons living in an abandoned Western movie set on an isolated Chatsworth ranch were arrested in a daybreak raid by sheriff's deputies Saturday as suspects in a major auto theft ring."

According to deputies, the group had been stealing Volkswagens, then converting them into dune buggies. The story, which did not contain the names of any of those arrested but did mention that a sizable arsenal of weapons had been seized, concluded: "The ranch is owned by George Spahn, a blind, 80-year-old semi-invalid. It is located in the Simi Hills at 12000 Santa Susana Pass Road. Deputies said Spahn, who lives alone in a house on the ranch, apparently knew there were people living on the set but was unaware of their activity. They said he couldn't get around and he was afraid of them."

It was a minor story, and didn't even rate a follow-up when, a few days later, all the suspects were released, it being discovered they had been arrested on a misdated warrant.

Following a report that Wilson, Madigan, Pickett, and Jones were in Canada, LAPD sent the Royal Canadian Mounted Police a "want" on the four men; RCMP broadcast it; alert reporters picked it up; and within hours the news media in the United States were heralding "a break in the Tate case."

Although LAPD denied that the four men were suspects, saying they were only wanted for questioning, the impression remained that arrests were imminent. There were phone calls, among them one from Madigan, another from Jones.

Jones was in Jamaica, and said he would fly back voluntarily if the police wished to talk to him. They admitted they did. Madigan showed up at Parker Center with his attorney. He cooperated fully, agreeing to answer any questions except those which might tend to involve him in the use or sale of narcotics. He admitted having visited Frykowski at the Cielo residence twice during the week before the murders, so it was possible his prints were there. On the night of the murders, Madigan said, he had attended a party given by an airline stewardess who lived in the apartment below his. He had left about 2 or 3 A.M. This was later verified by LAPD, who also checked his prints against the unmatched latents found at the Cielo address, without success.

Madigan was given a polygraph, and passed, as did Jones, when he arrived from Jamaica. Jones said that he and Wilson had been in Jamaica from July 12 to August 17, at which time he had flown to Los Angeles and Wilson had flown to Toronto. Asked why they had gone to Jamaica, he said they were "making a movie about marijuana." Jones' alibi would have to be checked out, but after his polygraph, and a negative print check, he ceased to be a good suspect.

This left Herb Wilson and Jeffrey Pickett, nicknamed Pic. By this time LAPD knew where both men were.

The publicity had been bad. There was no disputing that. As Steven Roberts, Los Angeles bureau chief for the New York *Times*, later put it, "All the stories had a common thread—that somehow the victims had brought the murders on themselves ... The attitude was summed up in the epigram: 'Live freaky, die freaky.' "

Given Roman Polanski's affinity for the macabre; rumors of Sebring's sexual peculiarities; the presence of both Miss Tate and her former lover at the death scene while her husband was away; the "anything goes" image of the Hollywood jet set; drugs; and the sudden clamp on police leaks, almost any kind of plot could be fashioned, and was. Sharon Tate was called everything from "the queen of the Hollywood orgy scene" to "a dabbler in satanic arts." Polanski himself was not spared. In the same newspaper a reader could find one columnist saying the director was so grief-stricken he could not speak, while a second had him nightclubbing with a bevy of airline stewardesses. If he wasn't personally responsible for the murders, more than one paper implied, he must know who committed them.

From a national news weekly:

"Sharon's body was found nude, not clad in bikini pants and a bra as had first been reported ... Sebring was wearing only the torn remnants of a pair of boxer shorts ... Frykowski's trousers were down to his ankles ... Both Sebring and Tate had X's carved on their bodies ... One of Miss Tate's breasts had been cut off, apparently as the result of indiscriminate slashing ... Sebring had been sexually mutilated ..." The rest was equally accurate: "No fingerprints were found anywhere ... no drug traces were found in any of the five bodies ..." And so on.

Though it read like something from the old *Confidential,* the article had appeared in *Time,* its writer apparently having some tall explaining to do when his editors became aware of his imaginative embellishments.

Angered by "a multitude of slanders," Roman Polanski called a press conference on August 19, where he castigated newsmen who "for a selfish reason" wrote "horrible things about my wife." There had been no marital rift, he reiterated; no dope; no orgies. His wife had been "beautiful" and "a good person," and "the last few years I spent with her were the only time of true happiness in my life ..."

Some of the reporters were less than sympathetic to Polanski's complaints about publicity, having just learned that he had permitted *Life* to take exclusive photos of the murder scene.

Not quite "exclusive." Before the magazine reached the

stands, several of the Polaroid prints appeared in the Hollywood *Citizen News*.

Life had been scooped, by its own photographs.

There were some things Polanski did not tell the press, or even his closest friends. One was that he had agreed to be polygraphed by the Los Angeles Police Department.

Polanski's polygraph examination was conducted by Lieutenant Earl Deemer at Parker Center.

Q.   "Mind if I call you Roman? My name is Earl."

A.   "Sure . . . I will lie one or two times during it, and I will tell you after, O.K.?"

Q.   "Well—all right . . ."

Deemer asked Roman how he first met his wife.

Polanski sighed, then slowly began talking. "I first met Sharon four years ago at some kind of party Marty Ransohoff—a terrible Hollywood producer—had. The guy who makes 'Beverly Hillbillies' and all kinds of shit. But he seduced me with his talk about art, and I contracted with him to do this film, a spoof on the vampires, you know.

"And I met Sharon at the party. She was doing another film for him in London at the time. Staying in London alone. Ransohoff said, 'Wait until you see our leading lady, Sharon Tate!'

"I thought she was quite pretty. But I wasn't at that time very impressed. But then I saw her again. I took her out. We talked a lot, you know. At that time I was really swinging. All I was interested in was to fuck a girl and move on. I had a very bad marriage, you know. Years before. Not bad, it was beautiful, but my wife dumped me, so I was really feeling great, because I was a success with women and I just like fucking around. I was a swinger, uh?

"So I met her a couple of more times. I knew she was with Jay. Then [Ransohoff] wanted me to use her in the film. And I made tests with her.

"Once before I wanted to take her out, and she was being difficult, wanting to go out, not wanting to go out, so I said, 'Fuck you,' and I hung up. Probably that was the beginning of everything, you know."

Q. "You sweet-talked her."

A. "Right. She got intrigued by me. And I really played it cool, and it took me long dating before— And then I started seeing that she liked me.

"I remember I spent a night—I lost a key—and I spent a night in her house in the same bed, you know. And I knew there was no question of making love with her. That's the type of girl she was.

"I mean, that rarely happens to me!

"And then we went on location—it was about two or three months later. When we were on location shooting the film, I asked her, 'Would you like to make love with me?' and she said, very sweetly, 'Yes.' And then for the first time I was somewhat touched by her, you know. And we started sleeping regularly together. And she was so sweet and so lovely that I didn't believe it, you know. I'd had bad experiences and I didn't believe that people like that existed, and I was waiting a long time for her to show the color, right?

"But she was *beautiful*, without this phoniness. She was fantastic. She loved me. I was living in a different house. I didn't want her to come to my house. And she would say, 'I don't want to smother you. I only want to be with you,' etc. And I said, 'You know how I am; I screw around.' And she said, 'I don't want to change you.' She was ready to do everything, just to be with me. She was a *fucking angel*. She was a unique character, who I'll never meet again in my life."

Deemer asked about his first meeting with Sebring. It had occurred in a London restaurant, Polanski said, describing how nervous he had been, and how Jay had broken the ice by saying, "I dig you, man. I dig you." More important, "he seemed happy to see Sharon happy." Roman had remained slightly uncomfortable through their next several meetings. "But when I came to Los Angeles, started living here, he came to our parties, etc. And I started liking Jay very very much. He was a very sweet person. Oh, I know of his hangups. He liked to whip-tie girls. Sharon told me about it. He tied her once to the bed. And she told me about it. And was making fun of him ... To her it was funny, but sad ...

"And he was more and more often a guest of ours. He would just hang around, hang around, and sometimes Sharon would resent his staying too long, because he was always the last to leave, you know.

"I'm sure in the beginning of our relationship there was still his love for Sharon, but I think that largely it disappeared. I'm quite sure."

Q. "So there was no indication that Sharon went back to Sebring at any time?"

A. "*Not a chance!* I'm the bad one. I always screw around. That was Sharon's big hangup, you know. But Sharon was absolutely not interested in Jay."

Q. "Was she interested in any other men?"

A. "No! There was not a chance of any other man getting close to Sharon."

Q. "O.K., I know you have to get on your way. We might as well start. I'll tell you how this works, Roman." Deemer explained the mechanics of the polygraph, adding, "It's important for you to remain quiet. I know you talk a lot with your hands. You're emotional. You're an actor type person, so it's going to be a little difficult for you ... But when the pressure is on, I want you to remain quiet. When it's off, you can talk and even wave your arms. Within reason."

After instructing Polanski to confine his answers to "yes" and "no" and to save any explanations for later, Deemer began the interrogation.

Q. "Do you have a valid California driver's license?"

A. "Yes."

Q. "Have you eaten lunch today?"

A. "No."

Q. "Do you know who took the life of Voytek and the others?"

A. "No."

Q. "Do you smoke cigarettes?"

A. "Yes." There was a long pause, then Polanski began laughing.

Q. "You know what you are going to do, with that screwing around? I'm going to have to start over again!"

A. "Sorry."

Q. "Look at the increase in your blood pressure when

you start to lie about your cigarettes. Boom, boom, boom, just like a staircase. O.K., let's start over again . . .

"Are you now in Los Angeles?"

A. "Yes."

Q. "Did you have anything to do with taking the life of Voytek and the others?"

A. "No."

Q. "Have you eaten lunch today?"

A. "No."

Q. "Do you feel any responsibility for the death of Voytek and the others?"

A. "Yes. I feel responsible that I wasn't there, that is all."

Q. "From running this thing through your mind, repeatedly, as I know you must have, who have you come up with as the target? I don't think it ever crossed your mind that Sharon might be the target, that anyone had that kind of mad on for her. Is there anyone else who was up there that you can think of who would be a target for this type of activity?"

A. "I've thought everything. I thought the target could be myself."

Q. "Why?"

A. "I mean, it could be some kind of jealousy or plot or something. It couldn't be Sharon directly. If Sharon were the target, it would mean that I was the target. It could be Jay was the target. It could be Voytek. It could also be sheer folly, someone just decided to commit a crime."

Q. "What would Sebring be doing, for instance, that would make him a target?"

A. "Some money thing, maybe. I've also heard a lot about this drug thing, drug deliveries. It's difficult for me to believe . . ." Polanski had always believed Sebring to be "a rather prosperous man," yet he'd recently heard he had large debts. "The indication to me is that he must have been in serious financial trouble, despite the appearances he gave."

Q. "That's a hell of a way to collect debts. It's no ordinary bill collector that goes up there and kills five people."

A. "No, no. What I'm talking about is for this reason

he might have got into some dangerous areas to make money, you understand? In desperation, he may have got mixed up with illegal people, you know?"

Q. "Eliminating Sharon and the kid, of the three remaining you think that Sebring would be the logical target, huh?"

A. "The whole crime seems so illogical.

"If I'm looking for a motive, I'd look for something which doesn't fit your habitual standard, with which you use to work as police—something much more far out . . ."

Deemer asked Polanski if he had received any hate mail after *Rosemary's Baby*. He admitted he had, surmising, "It could be some type of witchcraft, you know. A maniac or something. This execution, this tragedy, indicates to me it must be some kind of nut, you know.

"I wouldn't be surprised if I were the target. In spite of all this drug thing, the narcotics. I think the police like to jump too hastily on this type of lead, you know. Because it is their usual kind of lead. The only connection I know of Voytek with any kind of narcotic was he smoked pot. So did Jay. Plus cocaine. I knew he was sniffing. In the beginning I thought it was just an occasional kick. When I discussed it with Sharon, she said, 'Are you kidding? He's been doing it for two years, regularly.' "

Q. "Did Sharon mess with narcotics to any extent, other than pot?"

A. "No. She did take LSD before we met. Many times. And when we met we discussed it . . . I took it three times. When it was legal," he added, laughing. Then, serious again, Polanski recalled the only time they had taken it together. It was toward the end of 1965. It was his third trip, and Sharon's fifteenth or sixteenth. It had begun pleasantly enough, with them talking all night. But then "in the morning she started flipping out and screaming and I was scared to death. And after that she said, 'I told you I couldn't take it and this is the end.' And it was the end, for me and for her.

"But I can tell you this, without question. She took no drugs at all, except for pot, and not too much. And during her pregnancy there was no question, she was so in love with her pregnancy she would do nothing. I'd pour a glass of wine and she wouldn't touch it."

Once more Deemer took him through the questioning, then ended the examination, satisfied that Roman Polanski had no involvement in, or any hidden knowledge of, the murder of his wife and the others.

Before leaving, Roman told him, "I'm devoted now to this thing." He intended to question even his friends. "But I'm going to do it slowly, so they don't get suspicious. No one knows I'm here. I don't want them to know that I'm trying in any way to help the police, you know? I'm hoping in this way they'll have more sincerity."

A. "You have to go on living."

Polanski thanked him, lighted a cigarette, and left.

Q. "Hey, I thought you didn't smoke cigarettes!"

But Polanski had already gone.

On August 20, three days after Peter Hurkos accompanied Roman Polanski to the Cielo residence, a picture of Hurkos appeared in the *Citizen News*. It was captioned:

"FAMED PSYCHIC—Peter Hurkos, famed for his consultation in murder cases (including the current Sharon Tate massacre), opens Friday night at the Huntington Hartford, appearing through Aug. 30."

Madigan and Jones had been eliminated as suspects. Wilson and Pickett remained.

Because of his familiarity with the case, it was decided to send Lieutenant Deemer east to interview the two.

Jeffrey "Pic" Pickett had been contacted through a relative, and a meeting was set up in a Washington, D.C., hotel room. The son of a prominent State Department official, Pickett appeared to Deemer to be "under the influence of some narcotic, probably an excitant drug." He also had a bandaged hand. When Deemer expressed curiosity about it, Pickett vaguely replied that he had cut it on a kitchen knife. Though he agreed to a polygraph, Deemer found that Pickett couldn't remain still or follow instructions, so he interviewed him informally. He claimed that on the day of the murders he had been working in an auto

company in Sheffield, Massachusetts. Asked if he owned
any weapons, he admitted he had a Buck knife, purchased,
he said, in Marlboro, Massachusetts, on a friend's credit
card.

Later Pickett gave Deemer the knife. It was similar to
the one found at Cielo. He also turned over a roll of videotape which he claimed showed Abigail Folger and Voytek
Frykowski using drugs at a party at the Tate residence.
Pickett didn't say how he came into possession of the film
or what use he had intended to make of it.

Accompanied by Sergeant McGann, Deemer went to
Massachusetts. A check of the time cards at the auto company in Sheffield revealed that Pickett's last workday was
August 1, eight days before the homicides. Moreover,
though two stores in Marlboro sold Buck knives, neither
had ever stocked this particular model.

Pickett's status as a suspect rose appreciably, until the
detectives interviewed the friend he had mentioned. Going
through his credit card receipts, he produced the one for
the Buck knife. It had been purchased in Sudbury, Massachusetts, on August 21, long after the murders. The friend
and his wife also recalled something Pickett had apparently forgotten. He had gone to the beach with them the
weekend of August 8-10. Pickett was subsequently polygraphed, twice. Both times it was decided he was telling
the truth and was not involved. Eliminate Pickett.

Flying to Toronto, Deemer interviewed Herb Wilson.
Although initially reluctant to submit to a polygraph, Wilson consented when Deemer agreed not to ask any questions that might make him liable to Canadian prosecution
on narcotics charges. He passed. Eliminate Wilson.

The fingerprints of both Pickett and Wilson were
checked against the unmatched Tate latents, with no
match.

Although the first Tate investigative report—covering
the period August 9-31—concluded that Wilson, Madigan, Pickett, and Jones "have been eliminated at the time
of this report," in early September Deemer and McGann
flew to Ocho Rios, Jamaica, to check out the alibis of Wilson and Jones. The pair claimed they had been there from
July 8 until August 17, "making a movie about marijuana."

Interviews with realtors, servants, and airline ticket agencies supported half their story: they had been in Jamaica at the time of the murders. And it was quite possible they did have something to do with marijuana. Their only regular visitor, excluding female friends, was a pilot who, a few weeks before, had without explanation quit his well-paying job with a leading airline to make unscheduled solo runs between Jamaica and the United States.

As for their moviemaking, however, the detectives evinced some skepticism, the maid having told them the only camera she ever saw in the house was a small Kodak.

The videotape Pickett gave Deemer was viewed in the SID lab. It was decidedly different from the one previously found in the loft.

Apparently filmed during the period the Polanskis were away, it showed Abigail Folger, Voytek Frykowski, Witold K, and an unidentified young lady having dinner in front of the fireplace of the Tate residence. The video machine was simply turned on and left to run, those present after a time seeming to forget it.

Abigail wore her hair tied back in a rather severe chignon effect. She looked both older and more tired than in her other photos; Voytek looked dissipated. Though what appeared to be marijuana was smoked, Voytek seemed more drunk than high. At first Abigail treated him with the exasperated affection one would accord a spoiled child.

But then the mood gradually changed. In an obvious attempt to exclude Abigail, Voytek began speaking Polish. Abigail, in turn, was playing the grand dame, responding to his crude jests with witty repartee. Voytek began calling her "Lady Folger," then, as he became drunker, "Lady F." Abigail talked about him in the third person, as if he wasn't present, commenting upon, with some disgust, his habit of coming down off his drug trips by getting drunk.

To those viewing the tape it must have seemed nothing more than an overly long, exceedingly boring chronicle of a domestic argument. Except for two incidents, which, considering what would happen to two of those present, in this very house, gave it an eeriness as chilling as anything in *Rosemary's Baby.*

As she was serving the dinner, Abigail recalled a time when Voytek, stoned on drugs, looked into the fireplace and saw a strange shape. He had rushed for a camera, hoping to capture the image, a blazing pig's head.

The second incident was, in its own way, even more disturbing. The microphone had been left on the table, next to the roast. As the meat was being carved, it picked up, amazingly loud, over and over and over again, the sound of the knife grating on the bone.

Hurkos was not the only "expert" to volunteer a solution to the Tate homicides. On August 27, Truman Capote appeared on Johnny Carson's "Tonight Show" to discuss the crime.

One person, acting alone, had committed the murders, the author of *In Cold Blood* said authoritatively. He then proceeded to tell how, and why.

The killer, a man, had been in the house earlier. Something had happened "to trigger a kind of instant paranoia." The man then left the premises, went home to get a knife and a gun, and returned to systematically assassinate everyone in the place. According to Capote's deductions, Steven Parent was the last to die.

From the knowledge accumulated in over a hundred interviews with convicted murderers, Capote revealed that the killer was "a very young, enraged paranoid." While committing the murders, he probably experienced a sexual release, then, exhausted, went home and slept for two days.

Although Capote had taken up the single-suspect theory, the Tate detectives had by now abandoned it. Their sole reason for adopting it in the first place—Garretson—was no longer a factor. Because of the number of victims, the location of their bodies, and the use of two or more weapons, they were now convinced that "at least two suspects" were involved.

Killers. Plural. But as to their identity, they had not the slightest idea.

At the end of August there was a summing up, for both the Tate and the LaBianca detectives.

The "First Homicide Investigation Progress Report—

Tate" ran to thirty-three pages. Nowhere in it was there any mention of the LaBianca murders.

The "First Homicide Investigation Progress Report—LaBianca" was seventeen pages long. Despite the many similarities between the two crimes, it contained not one reference to the Tate homicides.

They remained two totally separate investigations.

Although Lieutenant Bob Helder had over a dozen detectives working full time on the Tate case, Sergeants Michael McGann, Robert Calkins, and Jess Buckles were the principal investigators. All were long-time veterans on the force, having worked their way up to the status of detective the hard way, from the ranks. They could remember when there was no Police Academy, and seniority was more important than education and merit examinations. They were experienced, and inclined to be set in their ways.

The LaBianca team, under Lieutenant Paul LePage, consisted, at various times, of from six to ten detectives, with Sergeants Frank Patchett, Manuel Gutierrez, Michael Nielsen, Philip Sartuchi, and Gary Broda the principal investigators. The LaBianca detectives were generally younger, better educated, and far less experienced. Graduates of the Police Academy for the most part, they were more inclined to the use of modern investigative techniques. For example, they obtained the fingerprints of almost everyone they interviewed; gave more polygraph examinations; made more *modus operandi* (MO) and fingerprint runs through the California State Bureau of Criminal Investigation and Identification (CII); and dug deeper into the backgrounds of the victims, even checking the outgoing calls Leno LaBianca had made from a motel while on vacation seven years ago.

They were also more inclined to consider "far out" theories. For example, while the Tate report didn't attempt to explain that bloody word on the front door, the LaBianca report speculated as to the meaning of the writings found inside the residence on Waverly Drive. It even suggested a connection so remote it couldn't even be called a wild guess. The report noted: "Investigation revealed that the singing group the Beatles' most recent album, No. SWBO

101, has songs titled 'Helter Skelter' and 'Piggies' and 'Blackbird.' The words in the song 'Blackbird' frequently say 'Arise, arise,' which might be the meaning of 'Rise' near the front door."

The idea was just sort of tossed in, by whom no one would later remember, and just as promptly forgotten.

The two sets of detectives had one thing in common, however. Though to date the LaBianca team had interviewed some 150 persons, the Tate investigators more than twice that, neither was much closer to "solving" the case than when the bodies were first discovered.

The Tate report listed five suspects—Garretson, Wilson, Madigan, Pickett, and Jones—all of whom had by this time been eliminated.

The LaBianca report listed fifteen—but included Frank and Susan Struthers, Joe Dorgan, and numerous others who were never serious suspects. Of the fifteen, only Gardner remained a good possible, and, though lacking a palm print for positive elimination (one had been found on a bank deposit slip on Leno's desk), his fingerprints had already been checked against those found in the residence with no match.

The progress reports were strictly intradepartmental; the press would never see them.

But already a few reporters were beginning to suspect that the real reason for the official silence was that there was nothing to report.

September 1969

About noon on Monday, September 1, 1969, ten-year-old Steven Weiss was fixing the sprinkler on the hill behind his home when he found a gun.

Steven and his parents lived at 3627 Longview Valley

Road in Sherman Oaks. Running parallel to Longview, atop the hill, was Beverly Glen.

The gun was lying next to the sprinkler, under a bush, about seventy-five feet—or halfway—up the steep hill. Steven had watched "Dragnet" on TV; he knew how guns should be handled. Picking it up very carefully by the tip of the barrel, so as not to eradicate prints, Steven took the gun back to his house and showed it to his father, Bernard Weiss. The senior Weiss took one look and called LAPD.

Officer Michael Watson, on patrol in the area, responded to the radio call. More than a year later Steven would be asked to describe the incident from the witness stand:

Q. "Did you show him [Watson] the gun?"
A. "Yes."
Q. "Did he touch the gun?"
A. "Yes."
Q. "How did he touch it?"
A. "With both hands, all over the gun."

So much for "Dragnet."

Officer Watson took the cartridges out of the cylinder; there were nine—seven empty shell casings and two live rounds. The gun itself was a .22 caliber Hi Standard Longhorn revolver. It had dirt on it, and rust. The trigger guard was broken, the barrel loose and slightly bent, as if it had been used to hammer something. The gun was also missing the right-hand grip.

Officer Watson took the revolver and shells back to Valley Services Division of LAPD, located in Van Nuys, and after booking them as "Found Evidence" turned them over to the Property Section, where they were tagged, placed in manila envelopes, and filed away.

Between September 3 and 5, LAPD sent out the first batch of confidential "flyers" on the wanted Tate gun. In addition to a photograph of a Hi Standard .22 caliber Longhorn revolver, and a list of Hi Standard outlets supplied by Lomax, Deputy Chief Robert Houghton sent a covering letter which asked police to interview anyone who had purchased such a gun, and to "visually check the weapon to see if the original grips are intact." To avoid leaks to the media, he suggested the following cover story:

such a gun had been recovered with other stolen property and the police wished to determine its ownership.

LAPD sent out approximately three hundred of the flyers, to various law-enforcement agencies in California, other parts of the United States, and Canada.

Someone neglected to mail one to the Valley Services Division of the Los Angeles Police Department in Van Nuys.

On September 10—one month after the Tate murders—a large advertisement appeared in newspapers in the Los Angeles area:

REWARD

$25,000

Roman Polanski and friends of the Polanski family offer to pay a $25,000 reward to the person or persons who furnish information leading to the arrest and conviction of the murderer or murderers of Sharon Tate, her unborn child, and the other four victims.

Information should be sent to
Post Office Box 60048,
Terminal Annex,
Los Angeles, California 90069.

Persons wishing to remain anonymous should provide sufficient means for later identification, one method of which is to tear this newspaper page in half, transmit one half with the information submitted, and save the remaining half for matching-up later. In the event more than one person is entitled to the reward, the reward will be divided equally between them.

In announcing the reward, Peter Sellers, who had put up a portion of the money, together with Warren Beatty, Yul Brynner, and others, said: "Someone must have knowledge or suspicions they are withholding, or may be afraid to reveal. Someone must have seen the blood-soaked clothing, the knife, the gun, the getaway car. Someone must be able to help."

Although unannounced in the press, others had already begun their own unofficial inquiries. Sharon's father, Colonel Paul Tate, had retired from the Army in August. Growing a beard and letting his hair grow long, the former intelligence officer began frequenting the Sunset Strip, hippie pads, and places where drugs were sold, looking for some lead to the killer(s) of his daughter and the others.

The police were fearful Colonel Tate's private investigation might become a private war, since there were reports he did not go on his forays unarmed.

Nor were the police happy about the reward. Besides the implication that LAPD wasn't capable of solving the case on its own, such an announcement usually yields only crackpot calls, and of these they already had a surplus.

Most had come in following the release of Garretson, the callers blaming the murders on everyone from the Black Power movement to the Polish Secret Police, their sources imagination, hearsay, even Sharon herself—returned during a seance. One wife called the police to accuse her husband: "He was evasive as to his whereabouts that night."

Hustlers, hairdressers, actors, actresses, psychics, psychotics—all got into the act. The calls revealed not so much the underside of Hollywood as the underside of human nature. The victims were accused of sexual aberrations as peculiar as the minds of the persons who called them in. Complicating LAPD's task were the large number of people—often not anonymous, and in some cases very well known—who seemed anxious to implicate their "friends"—if not directly connecting them with the murders, at least involving them with the drug scene.

There were proponents of every possible theory. The Mafia did it. The Mafia couldn't have done it because the killings were so unprofessional. The killings were *intentionally* unprofessional so the Mafia wouldn't be suspected.

One of the most persistent callers was Steve Brandt, a former gossip columnist. Because he had been a friend of four of the five Tate victims—he had been a witness at

Sharon's and Roman's marriage—the police took him seriously, at first, Brandt supplying considerable information on Wilson, Pickett, and their associates. But as the calls became more and more frequent, the names more and more prominent, it became obvious that Brandt was obsessed with the murders. Sure there was a death list and that he was next, Brandt twice attempted suicide. The first time, in Los Angeles, a friend arrived in time. The second time, in New York, he left a Rolling Stones concert to return to his hotel. When actress Ultra Violet called to make sure he was all right, he told her he had taken sleeping pills. She immediately called the desk man at the hotel, but by the time he reached the room Brandt was dead.

For such a well-publicized crime there were surprisingly few "confessions." It was as if the murders were so horrible that even the chronic confessors didn't want to become involved. A recently convicted felon, anxious to "make a deal," did claim another man had bragged of involvement in the killings, but, after investigation, the story proved bogus.

One after another, leads were checked out, then eliminated, leaving the police no closer to a solution than when the murders were discovered.

Though almost forgotten for a time, by mid-September the pair of prescription glasses found near the trunks in the living room of the Tate residence had, simply by the process of attrition, become one of the most important remaining clues.

Early that month the detectives showed the glasses to various optical company representatives. What they learned was in part discouraging. The frames were a popular model, the "Manhattan" style, readily available, while the prescription lenses were also a stock item, meaning they didn't have to be ground to order. But, on the plus side, they also learned several things about the person who had worn them.

Their owner was probably a man. He had a small, almost volley-ball-shaped head. His eyes were far apart. His left ear was approximately 1/4 to 1/2 inch higher than his right ear. And he was extremely myopic—if he didn't have an extra pair, he would probably have to replace the glasses soon.

A partial description of one of the Tate killers? Possibly. It was also possible that the glasses belonged to someone totally unconnected with the crime, or that they had been left behind as a false clue.

It was at least something to go on. Another flyer, with the exact specifications of the prescription, was sent to all members of the American Optometric Association, the California Optometric Association, the Los Angeles County Optometric Association, and the Ophthalmologists of Southern California, in hopes that it would yield more than had the flyer on the gun.

Of the 131 Hi Standard Longhorn revolvers sold in California, law-enforcement agencies had been able to locate and eliminate 105, a surprisingly large percentage, since many of the owners had moved to other jurisdictions. The search continued, but to date it hadn't yielded a single good suspect. A second gun letter was sent to thirteen different gunshops in the United States which, in recent months, had ordered replacement grips for the Longhorn model. Though the replies to this one wouldn't come back until much later, it too drew a blank.

Nor were the LaBianca detectives having any better luck. To date they had given eleven polygraphs; all had been negative. As a result of an MO run through the CII computer, the fingerprints of 140 suspects were checked; a palm print found on a bank deposit slip was checked against 2,150 suspects; and a fingerprint found on the liquor cabinet was checked against a total of 41,034 suspects. All uniformly negative.

At the end of September neither the Tate nor the LaBianca detectives bothered to write up a progress report.

October 1969

October 10. Two months had passed since the Tate homicides. "What is going on behind the scenes in the Los Angeles Police investigation (if there is such a thing) of the bizarre murder of Sharon Tate and four others?" the Hollywood *Citizen News* asked in a front-page editorial.

Officially, LAPD remained silent, as they had since their last news conference on the case, on September 3, when Deputy Chief Houghton, while admitting that they still didn't know who had committed the murders, said the detectives had made "tremendous progress."

"Exactly what progress?" reporters asked. The pressure was building; the fear remained, if possible even increased, owing to the suggestion, less than subtly hinted at by a popular TV commentator, that perhaps the police were covering for a person or persons "prominent in the entertainment industry."

Meanwhile the leaks continued. The media reported that narcotics had been found in several places at the Tate residence; that some of the victims had been on drugs at the time they died. By October it was also widely reported that the gun sought was a .22 (though it was identified as a pistol, rather than a revolver), and there was even one TV report—which the police quickly broke silence to deny—that pieces of the gun's grip had been found at the crime scene. The TV station stuck by its information, despite the official denial.

A .22, with a broken grip. Several times Bernard Weiss got to wondering about that gun his son Steven had found. Could it be the Tate murder weapon?

But that was ridiculous. After all, the police themselves had the gun, and, had it been the weapon, would surely have returned by now to ask more questions and search the hillside. Since turning the weapon over to them on

September 1, Weiss had heard nothing. When there was no follow-up, Steven had taken it on himself to make a search of the area. He'd found nothing. Still, Beverly Glen wasn't all that far from Cielo Drive, just a couple of miles.

But Bernard Weiss had better things to do than play detective. That was LAPD's responsibility.

On October 17, Lieutenant Helder and Deputy Chief Houghton told reporters that they had evidence which, if it could be traced, might lead to "the killers"—plural—of Sharon Tate and the four others. They refused to be more specific.

The press conference had been called in an attempt to relieve some of the pressure on LAPD. No solid information was released, but a number of current rumors were denied.

Less than a week later, on October 23, LAPD very hastily called another press conference, to announce that they had a clue to the identity of "the killer"—singular—of the five Tate victims: a pair of prescription eyeglasses that had been found at the scene.

The announcement was made only because several papers had that same day already printed the "wanted" flyer on the glasses.

Approximately 18,000 eye doctors had received the flyer from their various member associations; in addition, it had been printed verbatim in the *Optometric Weekly* and the *Eye, Ear, Nose, and Throat Monthly,* which had a combined national circulation of over 29,000. What was surprising was not that the story had leaked, but that it had taken so long for it to do so.

Starved for solid news, the press heralded "a major breakthrough in the case," overlooking the obvious fact that the police had had the glasses in their possession since the day the Tate victims were discovered.

Lieutenant Helder refused comment when a reporter, obviously with excellent connections inside the department, asked if it was true that to date the glasses flyer had yielded only seven suspects, all of whom had already been eliminated.

It was indicative of the desperation of the Tate detectives that the second, and last, Tate progress report, prepared the day before the press conference, stated: "At this time Garretson has not been positively eliminated."

The Tate report, covering the period September 1–October 22, 1969, ran to twenty-six pages, most of which were devoted to closing out the cases against Wilson, Pickett, et al.

The LaBianca report, closed out on October 15, was a little shorter, twenty-two pages, but far more interesting.

In one section of the report the detectives mentioned their use of the CII computer: "A MO run on all crimes where the victims were tied is presently being run. Future runs will be made concentrating on the peculiarities of the robberies, used gloves, wore glasses or disabled the phone."

Robberies. Plural. *Wore glasses, disabled the phone.* The phone at the LaBianca residence was not disabled, nor was there evidence that a LaBianca assailant wore glasses. These references were to Tate.

The conclusion is inescapable: The LaBianca detectives had decided—on their own, and without consulting the Tate detectives—to see if they could solve the Tate, as well as the LaBianca, case.

The second LaBianca report was interesting for still another reason.

It listed eleven suspects, the last of whom was one MANSON, CHARLES.

Part 2

THE KILLERS

"You couldn't meet a nicer group of people."
        Leslie Van Houten, describing
        the Manson Family
        to Sergeant Michael McGann

"At twelve o'clock a meeting round the table
For a seance in the dark
With voices out of nowhere
Put on especially by the children for a lark."
        The Beatles,
            "Cry Baby Cry,"
            "White Album"

"You have to have a real love in your heart to
do this for people."
        Susan Atkins, telling
        Virginia Graham why she
        stabbed Sharon Tate

October 15-31, 1969

The physical distance between Parker Center, headquarters of the Los Angeles Police Department, and the Hall of Justice, which houses the Los Angeles County Sheriff's Office, is four blocks. That distance can be traversed in the time it takes to dial a telephone.

But it isn't always that easy. Though LAPD and LASO cooperate on investigations that involve both jurisdictions, there exists between them a certain amount of jealousy.

One of the LaBianca detectives would later admit that he and his fellow officers *should* have checked with LASO homicide detectives in mid-August to see if they had any similar murders. But it wasn't until October 15, after most of their other leads had evaporated, that they did so.

When they did, they learned of the Hinman murder. And, unlike Sergeant Buckles of the Tate team, they found the similarities striking enough to merit further investigation.

There had been some recent developments in the Hinman case, Sergeants Whiteley and Guenther told them. Less than a week before, Inyo County officers had raided isolated Barker Ranch, located in an extremely rugged, almost inaccessible area south of Death Valley National Monument. The raid, based on charges ranging from grand theft to arson, had netted twenty-four members of a hippie cult known as the "Manson Family." Many of these same people—including their leader, Charles Manson, a thirty-four-year-old ex-con with a long and checkered criminal history—had also been arrested in an earlier raid conducted by LASO, which had occurred on August 16, at Spahn's Movie Ranch in Chatsworth.

During the Barker raid, which took place over a three-day period, two young girls had appeared out of the bushes near a road some miles from the ranch, asking the officers for protection. They claimed they had been attempting to flee the "Family" and were afraid for their lives. One was named Stephanie Schram, the other Kitty Lutesinger.

Whiteley and Guenther had been looking for Kitty Lutesinger ever since learning that she was a girl friend of Bobby Beausoleil, the suspect in the Hinman murder. Informed of her arrest, they drove 225 miles to Independence, the Inyo County seat, to question her.

Kitty, a freckled, frightened seventeen-year-old, was five months pregnant with Beausoleil's child. Though she had lived with the Family, she apparently was not trusted by them. When Beausoleil disappeared from Spahn Ranch in early August, no one would tell her where he had gone. Only after several weeks did she learn that he had been arrested, and, much later, that he had been charged with the murder of Gary Hinman.

Questioned about the murder, Kitty said she had heard that Manson had sent Beausoleil and a girl named Susan Atkins to Hinman's home to get money from him. A fight had ensued, and Hinman had been killed. Kitty couldn't recall who told her this, just that it was the talk at the ranch. She did recall, however, another conversation in which Susan Atkins told her and several other girls that she had been in a fight with a man who had pulled her hair, and that she had stabbed him three or four times in the legs.

Susan Atkins had been arrested in the Barker raid and booked under the name "Sadie Mae Glutz." She was still in custody. On October 13, the day after they talked to Kitty, Sergeants Whiteley and Guenther questioned her.

She told them that she and Bobby Beausoleil were sent to Gary Hinman's house to get some money he had supposedly inherited. When he wouldn't give it to them, Beausoleil pulled out a knife and slashed Hinman's face. For two days and two nights the pair had taken turns sleeping, so Hinman wouldn't escape. Then, on their last evening at the residence, while she was in the kitchen, she had heard Gary say, "Don't, Bobby!" Hinman then staggered into the kitchen bleeding from a chest wound.

Even after this, Hinman didn't die. After wiping the

house of prints (not effectively, since both a palm print and a fingerprint belonging to Beausoleil were found), they were going out the front door when they heard Hinman moaning. Beausoleil went back in, and she heard Gary cry out, "Oh, no, Bobby, please don't!" She also heard "a sound like gurgling as when people are dying."

Beausoleil then hot-wired Hinman's 1965 Volkswagen bus and they drove back to Spahn Ranch.

Whiteley and Guenther asked Susan if she would repeat her statement on tape. She declined. She was transported to the San Dimas sheriff's station, where she was booked for suspicion of murder.

Susan Atkins' statement—unlike that of Kitty Lutesinger—did not implicate Manson in the Hinman murder. Nor, contrary to what Kitty had said, did Susan admit to having stabbed anyone. Whiteley and Guenther strongly suspected she was telling only what she thought they already knew.

Nor were the two LaBianca detectives very impressed. Hinman had been close to the Manson family; several of its members—including Beausoleil, Atkins, even Manson himself—had lived with him at various times in the past. In short, there was a link. But there was no evidence that Manson or any of his followers knew the LaBiancas or the people at 10050 Cielo Drive.

Still, it was a lead, and they proceeded to check it out. Kitty had been released into the custody of her parents, who had a local address, and they interviewed her there. From LASO, Inyo County officials, Manson's parole officer, and others, they began assembling names, descriptions, and fingerprints of persons known to belong to or associate with the Family. Kitty had mentioned that while the Family was still living at Spahn, Manson had tried to enlist a motorcycle gang, the Straight Satans, as his personal bodyguard. With the exception of one biker named Danny, the group had laughed at Manson. Danny had stuck around for several months.

On learning that the motorcycle gang hung out in Venice, California, the LaBianca detectives asked Venice PD if they could locate a Straight Satan named Danny.

Something in Kitty Lutesinger's statement puzzled Whiteley and Guenther. At first they thought it was just a discrepancy. But then they got to wondering. According to Kitty, Susan Atkins had admitted stabbing a man three or four times in the legs.

Gary Hinman hadn't been stabbed in the legs.

But Voytek Frykowski had.

Although rebuffed once before, on October 20 the sheriff's deputies again contacted the Tate detectives at LAPD, telling them what they had learned.

It is possible to measure the Tate detectives' interest with some exactness. Not until October 31, eleven days later, did they interview Kitty Lutesinger.

November 1-12, 1969

November was a month for confessions. Which, initially, no one believed.

After being booked for the Hinman murder, Susan Denise Atkins, aka* Sadie Mae Glutz, was moved to Sybil Brand Institute, the women's house of detention in Los Angeles. On November 1, after completing orientation, she was assigned to Dormitory 8000, and given a bunk opposite one Ronnie Howard. Miss Howard, a buxom former call girl who over her thirty-some years had been known by more than a dozen and a half aliases, was at present awaiting trial on a charge of forging a prescription.

On the same day Susan moved into Dormitory 8000, one Virginia Graham did also. Miss Graham, herself an ex-call girl with a sizable number of aka's, had been picked up for violating her parole. Although they hadn't seen each other for five years, Ronnie and Virginia had

*Police shorthand for "also known as"; "t/n" means "true name."

not only been friends and business associates in the past, going out on "calls" together, but Ronnie had married Virginia's ex-husband.

As their work assignments, Susan Atkins and Virginia Graham were given jobs as "runners," carrying messages for the prison authorities. In the slow periods when there wasn't much work, they would sit on stools in "control," the message center, and talk.

At night, after lights-out, Ronnie Howard and Susan talked also.

Susan loved to talk. And Ronnie and Virginia proved rapt listeners.

On November 2, 1969, one Steve Zabriske appeared at the Portland, Oregon, Police Department and told Detective Sergeant Ritchard that a "Charlie" and a "Clem" had committed both the Tate and LaBianca murders.

He had heard this, the nineteen-year-old Zabriske said, from Ed Bailey and Vern Plumlee, two hippie types from California whom he had met in Portland. Zabriske also told Ritchard that Charlie and Clem were at present in custody in Los Angeles on another charge, grand theft auto.

Bailey had told him something else, Zabriske said: that he had personally seen Charlie shoot a man in the head with a .45 caliber automatic. This had occurred in Death Valley.

Sergeant Ritchard asked Zabriske if he could prove any of this. Zabriske admitted he couldn't. However, his brother-in-law, Michael Lloyd Carter, had also been present during the conversations, and would back him up if Sergeant Ritchard wanted to talk to him.

Sergeant Ritchard didn't. Since Zabriske "did not have last names nor did he have anything concrete to establish that he was telling the truth," Sergeant Ritchard, according to the official report, "did not place any credence on this interview and did not notify the Los Angeles Police Department . . ."

The girls in Dormitory 8000 called Sadie Mae Glutz—as Susan Atkins insisted on being known—"Crazy Sadie."

It wasn't just that ridiculous name. She was much too happy, considering where she was. She would laugh and sing at inappropriate times. Without warning, she would stop whatever she happened to be doing and start go-go dancing. She did her exercises sans underpants. She bragged that she had done everything sexual that could be done, and on more than one occasion propositioned other inmates.

Virginia Graham thought she was sort of a "little girl lost," putting on a big act so no one would know how frightened she really was.

One day while they were sitting in the message center, Virginia asked her, "What are you in for?"

"First degree murder," Susan matter-of-factly replied.

Virginia couldn't believe it; Susan looked so young.

In this particular conversation, which apparently took place on November 3, Susan said little about the murder itself, only that she felt a co-defendant, a boy who was being held in the County Jail, had squealed on her. In questioning Susan, Whiteley and Guenther hadn't told her that it was Kitty Lutesinger who had implicated her, and she presumed the snitch was Bobby Beausoleil.

The next day Susan told Virginia that the man she was accused of killing was named Gary Hinman. She said that she, Bobby, and another girl were involved. The other girl hadn't been charged with the murder, she said, though she had been in Sybil Brand not too long ago on another charge; right now she was out on bail and had gone to Wisconsin to get her baby.*

Virginia asked her, "Well, did you do it?"

Susan looked at her and smiled and said, "Sure." Just like that.

Only the police had it wrong, she said. They had her holding the man while the boy stabbed him, which was silly, because she couldn't hold a big man like that. It was the other way round; the boy held him and she had stabbed him, four or five times.

What stunned Virginia, she would later say, was that

*She was referring to Mary Brunner, first member of the Family, who had had a child by Manson. At this time the police were unaware of her involvement in the Hinman homicide.

Susan described it "just like it was a perfectly natural thing to do every day of the week."

Susan's conversations were not limited to murder. Subjects ranged from psychic phenomena to her experiences as a topless dancer in San Francisco. It was while there, she told Virginia, that she met "a man, this Charlie." He was the strongest man alive. He had been in prison but had never been broken. Susan said she followed his orders without question—they all did, all the kids who lived with him. He was their father, their leader, their love.

It was Charlie, she said, who had given her the name Sadie Mae Glutz.

Virginia remarked that she didn't consider that much of a favor.

Charlie was going to lead them to the desert, Susan said. There was a hole in Death Valley, only Charlie knew where it was, but deep down inside, in the center of the earth, there was a whole civilization. And Charlie was going to take the "family," the chosen few, and they were going to go to this bottomless pit and live there.

Charlie, Susan confided to Virginia, was Jesus Christ.

Susan, Virginia decided, was nuts.

On the night of Wednesday, November 5, a young man who might have been able to provide a solution to the Tate-LaBianca homicides ceased to exist.

At 7:35 P.M. officers from Venice PD, responding to a telephone call, arrived at 28 Clubhouse Avenue, a house near the beach rented by a Mark Ross. They found a youth—approximate age twenty-two, nickname "Zero," true name unknown—lying on a mattress on the floor in the bedroom. Deceased was still warm to the touch. There was blood on the pillow and what appeared to be an entrance wound in the right temple. Next to the body was a leather gun case and an eight-shot .22 caliber Iver & Johnson revolver. According to the other persons present—a man and three girls—Zero had killed himself while playing Russian roulette.

The stories of the witnesses—who identified themselves as Bruce Davis, Linda Baldwin, Sue Bartell, and Catherine

Gillies, and who said they had been staying at the house
while Ross was away—tallied perfectly. Linda Baldwin
stated that she had been lying on the right side of the mattress, Zero on the left side, when Zero noticed the leather
case in a stand next to the bed and remarked, "Oh, here's
a gun." He removed the gun from the case, Miss Baldwin
said, commenting, "There's only one bullet in it." Holding
the gun in his right hand, he had then spun the cylinder,
placed the muzzle against his right temple, and pulled the
trigger.

The others, in various parts of the house, had heard
what sounded like a firecracker popping, they said. When
they entered the bedroom, Miss Baldwin told them, "Zero
shot himself, just like in the movies." Bruce Davis admitted he picked up the gun. They had then called the police.

The officers were unaware that all those present were
members of the Manson Family, who had been living at
the Venice residence since their release following the
Barker Ranch raid. Since when questioned separately all
told essentially the same story, the police accepted the
Russian roulette explanation and listed the cause of death
as suicide.

They had several very good reasons to suspect that explanation, although apparently no one did.

When officer Jerrome Boen later dusted the gun for
latents, he found no prints. Nor were there prints on the
leather gun case.

And when they examined the revolver, they found that
Zero had really been bucking the odds. The gun contained
seven live rounds and one spent shell. It had been fully
loaded, with no empty chambers.

A number of Family members, including Manson himself, were still in jail in Independence. On November 6,
LaBianca detectives Patchett and Sartuchi, accompanied
by Lieutenant Burdick of SID, went there to interview
them.

Patchett asked Manson if he knew anything about either
the Tate or LaBianca homicides. Manson replied, "No,"
and that was that.

Patchett was so unimpressed with Manson that he didn't

:ven bother to write up a report on the interview. Of the
nine Family members the detectives talked to, only one
-ated a memorandum. About 1:30 that afternoon Lieu-
enant Burdick interviewed a girl who had been booked
under the name Leslie Sankston. "During this conversa-
ion," Burdick noted, "I inquired of Miss Sankston if she
was aware that Sadie [Susan Atkins] was reportedly involved in the Gary Hinman homicide. She replied that she
was. I inquired if she was aware of the Tate and LaBianca
homicides. She indicated that she was aware of the Tate
homicide but seemed unfamiliar with the LaBianca homicide. I asked her if she had any knowledge of persons in
her group who might possibly be involved in either the Tate
or LaBianca homicides. She indicated that there were some
'things' that caused her to believe someone from her group
might be involved in the Tate homicide. I asked her to
elaborate on the 'things' [but] she declined to indicate
what she meant and stated that she wanted to think about
it overnight, and that she was perplexed and didn't know
what to do. She did indicate she might tell me the following day."

However, when Burdick again questioned her the next
morning, "she stated she had decided she did not want to
say anymore about the subject and the conversation was
terminated."

Though the interviews yielded nothing, the LaBianca
detectives did pick up one possible lead. Before leaving Independence, Patchett asked to see Manson's personal effects. Going through the clothing Manson had been wearing when arrested, Patchett noted that he used leather
thongs both as laces in his moccasins and in the stitching
of his trousers. Patchett took a sample thong from each
back to Los Angeles for comparison with the thong used
to tie Leno LaBianca's hands.

A leather thong is a leather thong, SID in effect told
him; though the thongs were similar, there was no way to
tell whether they had come from the same piece of
leather.

LAPD and LASO have no monopoly on jealousy. To a
certain extent it exists between almost all law-enforcement
agencies, and even within some.

The Homicide Division of the Los Angeles Police Department is a single room, 318, on the third floor of Parker Center. Although it is a large room, rectangular in shape, there are no partitions, only two long tables, all the detectives working at either one or the other. The distance between the Tate and LaBianca detectives was only a few feet.

But there are psychological as well as physical distances and, as noted, while the Tate detectives were largely the "old guard," the LaBianca detectives were for the most part the "young upstarts." Also, there was apparently some residual bitterness stemming from the fact that several of the latter, rather than the former, had been assigned to L.A.'s last big publicity case, Sirhan Sirhan's assassination of Senator Robert F. Kennedy. In short, there was a certain amount of jealousy involved. And a certain lack of communication.

As a result, none of the LaBianca detectives walked those few feet to tell the Tate detectives that they were following a lead which might connect the two homicides. No one informed Lieutenant Helder, who was in charge of the Tate investigation, that they had gone to Independence and interviewed one Charles Manson, who was believed involved in a strikingly similar murder, or that while there one of his followers, a girl who went by the name of Leslie Sankston, had admitted that someone in their group might be involved in the *Tate* homicides.

The LaBianca detectives continued to go it on their own.

Had Leslie Sankston—true name Leslie Van Houten— yielded to that impulse to talk, she could have told the detectives a great deal about the Tate murders, but even more about the LaBianca slayings.

But by this time Susan Atkins was already doing enough talking for both of them.

• On Thursday, November 6, at about 4:45 P.M., Susan had walked over to Virginia Graham's bed and sat down. They had finished work for the day, and Susan/Sadie was in a talkative mood. She began rapping about the LSD trips she had taken, karma, good and bad vibrations, and the Hinman murder. Virginia cautioned her that she shouldn't be talking so much; she knew a man who had been convicted just on what he told a cellmate.

Susan replied, "Oh, I know. I haven't talked about it to anyone else. You know, I can look at you and there's something about you, I know I can tell things to you." Also, she wasn't worried about the police. They weren't all that good. "You know, there's a case right now, they are so far off the track they don't even know what's happening."

Virginia asked, "What are you talking about?"

"That one on Benedict Canyon."

"Benedict Canyon? You don't mean Sharon Tate?"

"Yeah." With this Susan seemed to get very excited. The words came out in a rush. "You know who did it, don't you?"

"No."

"Well, you're looking at her."

Virginia gasped, "You've got to be kidding!"

Susan just smiled and said, "Huh-uh."*

Later Virginia Graham would be unable to remember exactly how long they had talked—she would estimate it as being between thirty-five minutes and an hour, maybe longer. She would also admit confusion as to whether some details were discussed that afternoon or in subsequent conversations, and the order in which some topics came up.

But the content she remembered. That, she would later say, she would never forget as long as she lived.

She asked the big question first: Why, Sadie, why? Because, Susan replied, we "wanted to do a crime that would shock the world, that the world would have to stand up and take notice." But why the Tate house? Susan's answer was chilling in its simplicity: "It is isolated." The place

---

*The Atkins-Graham-Howard conversations have been taken from LAPD's taped interviews with Virginia Graham and Ronnie Howard; my interviews with both; their trial testimony; and my interview with Susan Atkins. There are, of course, minor variations in wording. Major discrepancies will be noted.

had been picked at random. They had known the owner, Terry Melcher,* Doris Day's son, from about a year back, but they didn't know who would be there, and it didn't matter; one person or ten, they had gone there prepared to do everybody in.

"In other words," Virginia asked, "you didn't know Jay Sebring or any of the other people?"

"No," Susan replied.

"Do you mind me asking questions? I mean, I'm curious." Susan didn't mind. She told Virginia that she had kind brown eyes, and if you look through a person's eyes you can see the soul.

Virginia told Susan she wanted to know exactly how it had come down. "I'm dying of curiosity," she added.

Susan obliged. Before leaving the ranch, Charlie had given them instructions. They had worn dark clothing. They also brought along a change of clothes in the car. They drove up to the gate, then drove back down to the bottom of the hill, parked the car, and walked back up.

Virginia interrupted, "Then it wasn't just you?"

"Oh, no," Susan told her. "There were four of us." In addition to herself, there were two other girls and a man.

When they reached the gate, Susan continued, "he" cut the telephone wires. Virginia again interrupted to ask whether he wasn't worried he'd cut the electrical wires, extinguishing the lights and alerting the people that something was wrong. Susan replied, "Oh, no, he knew just what to do." Virginia got the impression, less from her words than from the way she said them, that the man had been there before.

Susan didn't mention how they got past the gate. She said they had killed the boy first. When Virginia asked why, Susan replied that he had seen them. "And he had to shoot him. He was shot four times."

At this point Virginia became somewhat confused.

---

*Virginia Graham had seen the owner of the house, Rudi Altobelli, interviewed on TV, and although she couldn't remember his name, she knew it wasn't Terry Melcher. This was one reason why, initially, she was inclined to disbelieve Susan Atkins' story. Susan, however, insisted Melcher was the owner, apparently believing he was.

Later she would state, "I think she told me—I'm not positive—I think she said that this Charles shot him." Earlier Virginia had got the impression that although Charlie had instructed them what to do, he hadn't come along. But now it appeared he had.

What Virginia didn't know was that there were two men named Charles in the Family: Charles Manson and Charles "Tex" Watson. The complications this simple misunderstanding would later cause would be immense.

On entering the house—Susan didn't say how they got in—they saw a man on the couch in the living room, and a girl, whom Susan identified as "Ann Folger," sitting in a chair reading a book. She didn't look up.

Virginia asked her how she knew their names. "We didn't," Susan replied, "not until the next day."

At some point the group apparently split up, Susan going on to the bedroom, while the others stayed in the living room.

"Sharon was sitting up in bed. Jay was sitting on the edge of the bed talking to Sharon."

"Oh, really?" Virginia asked. "What did she have on?"

"She had on a bikini bra and panties."

"You're kidding. And she was pregnant?"

"Yeah. And they looked up, and were they surprised!"

"Wow! Wasn't there some kind of a big hassle?"

"No, they were too surprised and they knew we meant business."

Susan skipped on. It was as if she was "tripping out," jumping abruptly from one subject to another. Suddenly they were in the living room and Sharon and Jay were strung up with nooses around their necks so if they tried to move they would choke. Virginia asked why they'd put a hood over Sebring's head. "We didn't put any hood over his head," Susan corrected her. "That's what the papers said, Sadie." "Well, there wasn't any hood," Susan reiterated, getting quite insistent about it.

Then the other man [Frykowski] broke and ran for the door. "He was full of blood," Susan said, and she stabbed him three or four times. "He was bleeding and he ran to the front part," out the door and onto the lawn, "and would you believe that he was there hollering 'Help, help, somebody please help me,' and nobody came?"

Bluntly, without elaboration, "Then we finished him off."

Virginia wasn't asking any questions now. What had begun as a little girl's fairy tale had become a horror-filled nightmare.

There was no mention of what had happened to Abigail Folger or Jay Sebring, only that "Sharon was the last to die." On saying this, Susan laughed.

Susan said that she had held Sharon's arms behind her, and that Sharon looked at her and was crying and begging, "Please don't kill me. Please don't kill me. I don't want to die. I want to live. I want to have my baby. I want to have my baby."

Susan said she looked Sharon straight in the eye and said, "Look, bitch, I don't care about you. I don't care if you're going to have a baby. You had better be ready. You're going to die, and I don't feel anything about it."

Then Susan said, "In a few minutes I killed her and she was dead."

After killing Sharon, Susan noticed there was blood on her hand. She tasted it. "Wow, what a trip!" she told Virginia. "I thought 'To taste death, and yet give life.'" Had she ever tasted blood? she asked Virginia. "It's warm and sticky and nice."

Virginia managed to ask a question. Hadn't it bothered her to kill Sharon Tate, with her pregnant?

Susan looked at Virginia quizzically and said, "Well, I thought you understood. I loved her, and in order for me to kill her I was killing part of myself when I killed her."

Virginia replied, "Oh, yeah, I do understand."

She had wanted to cut out the baby, Susan said, but there hadn't been time. They wanted to take out the eyes of the people, and squash them against the walls, and cut off their fingers. "We were going to mutilate them, but we didn't have a chance to."

Virginia asked her how she felt after the murders. Susan replied, "I felt so elated; tired, but at peace with myself. I knew this was just the beginning of helter skelter. Now the world would listen."

Virginia didn't understand what she meant by "helter skelter," and Susan tried to explain it to her. However, she talked so quickly and with such obvious excitement that Virginia had trouble following. As Virginia understood it, there was this group, these chosen people, that Charlie had brought together, and they were elected, this new society, to go out, all over the country and all over the world, to pick out people at random and execute them, to release them from this earth. "You have to have a real love in your heart to do this for people," Susan explained.

Four or five times while Susan was talking, Virginia had to caution her to keep her voice down, that someone might hear. Susan smiled and said she wasn't worried about that. She was very good at playing crazy.

After they'd left the Tate residence, Susan continued, she discovered that she had lost her knife. She thought maybe the dog had got it. "You know how dogs are sometimes." They had thought about going back to look for it but had decided against it. She had also left her hand print on a desk. "It dawned on me afterwards," Susan said, "but my spirit was so strong that obviously it didn't even show up, or they would have had me by now."

As Virginia understood it, after leaving the Tate residence, they had apparently changed clothes in the car. Then they had driven some distance, stopping at a place where there was a fountain or water outside, to wash their hands. Susan said a man came outside and wanted to know what they were doing. He started to holler at them. "And," Susan said, "guess who he was?"

"I don't know," Virginia replied.

"It was the sheriff of Beverly Hills!"

Virginia said she didn't think Beverly Hills had a sheriff.

"Well," Susan said petulantly, "the sheriff or mayor or something."

The man had started to reach into the car to grab the keys, and "Charlie turned on the key. Boy, we made it. We laughed all the way," Susan said, adding, "If he had only known!"

For a moment Susan remained silent. Then, with her

little girl's smile, she asked, "You know the other two the next night?"

Virginia flashed on the grocery store owner and his wife, the LaBiancas. "Yeah," she said, "was that you?"

Susan winked and said, "What do you think?

"But that's part of the plan," she continued. "And there's more—"

But Virginia had heard enough for one day. She excused herself to go take a shower.

Virginia would later recall thinking, She's got to be kidding! She's making all this up. This is just too wild, too fantastic!

But then she remembered what Susan was in for—first degree murder.

Virginia decided not to say anything to anyone. It was just too incredible. She also decided, if possible, to avoid Susan.

The following day, however, Virginia walked over to Ronnie Howard's bed to tell her something. Susan, who was lying on her own bed, interrupted: "Virginia, Virginia, remember that beautiful cat I was telling you about? I want you to dig on his name. Now listen, his name is Manson—*Man's Son!*" She repeated it several times to make sure Virginia understood. She said it in a tone of childlike wonder.

She just couldn't keep it to herself any longer. It was just too much. The first time she and Ronnie Howard were alone together, Virginia Graham told her what Susan Atkins had said. "Hey, what do you do?" she asked Ronnie. "If this is true—My God, this is terrible. I wish she hadn't told me."

Ronnie thought Sadie was "making it all up. She could have gotten it out of the papers."

The only way to know for sure, they decided, would be for Virginia to question her further, to see if she could learn something that only one of the killers would know.

Virginia had an idea how she could do this without arousing Susan's suspicions. Though she hadn't mentioned it to Susan Atkins, Virginia Graham had more than a passing interest in the Tate homicides. She had known Jay Sebring. A girl friend, who was working as a manicurist for Sebring, had introduced them at the Luau some years ago, shortly after Sebring opened his shop on Fairfax. It was a casual thing—he was neither client nor friend, just someone you'd nod and say "Hi" to at a party or in a restaurant. It was an odd coincidence, Susan copping out to her. But there was another coincidence even odder. Virginia had been to 10050 Cielo Drive. Back in 1962 she and her then husband and another girl had been looking for a quiet place, away from things, and had learned 10050 Cielo Drive was up for lease. There had been no one there to show them around, so they had just looked in the windows of the main house. She could remember little about it, only that it looked like a red barn, but the next day at lunch she told Susan about having been there and asked if the interior was still decorated in gold and white. It was just a guess. Susan replied, "Huh-uh," but didn't elaborate. Virginia then told her about knowing Sebring, but Susan didn't appear very interested. This time Susan wasn't as talkative, but Virginia persisted, picking up miscellaneous bits and pieces of information.

They'd met Terry Melcher through Dennis Wilson, one of the Beach Boys rock group. They—Charlie, Susan, and the others—had lived with Dennis for a time. Virginia got the idea they were hostile toward Melcher, that he was too interested in money. Virginia also learned that the Tate murders had taken place between midnight and one in the morning; that "Charlie is love, pure love"; and that when you stab someone "it feels good when the knife goes in."

She also learned that besides the Hinman, Tate, and La-Bianca murders, "there's more—and more before ... There's also three people out in the desert ..."

Bits and pieces. Susan had said nothing that would establish whether she was or wasn't telling the truth.

That afternoon Susan walked over and sat down on Virginia's bed. Virginia had been leafing through a movie magazine. Susan saw it and began talking. The story she related, Virginia would say much later, was even more bizarre than what Susan had already told her. It was so incredible that Virginia didn't even mention it to Ronnie Howard. No one would believe it, she decided. For Susan Atkins, in one spurt of non-stop talking, gave her a "death list" of persons who would be murdered next. All were celebrities. She then, according to Virginia, described in gruesome detail exactly how Elizabeth Taylor, Richard Burton, Tom Jones, Steve McQueen, and Frank Sinatra would die.

On Monday, November 10, Susan Atkins had a visitor at Sybil Brand, Sue Bartell, who told her about the death of Zero. After Sue left, Susan told Ronnie Howard. Whether she embellished it or not is unknown. According to Susan, one of the girls had been holding Zero's hand when he died. When the gun went off, "he climaxed all over himself."

Susan didn't seem disturbed to hear of Zero's death. On the contrary, it excited her. "Imagine how beautiful to be there when it happened!" she told Ronnie.

On Wednesday, November 12, Susan Atkins was taken to court for a preliminary hearing on the Hinman murder. While there, she heard Sergeant Whiteley testify that it was Kitty Lutesinger—not Bobby Beausoleil—who had implicated her. On being returned to jail, Susan told Virginia that the prosecution had a surprise witness; but she wasn't worried about her testimony: "Her life's not worth anything."

That same day Virginia Graham received some bad news. She was being transferred to Corona Women's Prison, to serve out the rest of her sentence. She was to leave that afternoon. While she was packing, Ronnie came up to her and asked, "What do you think?"

"I don't know," Virginia replied. "Ronnie, if you want to take it from here—"

"I've been talking to that girl every night," Ronnie said. "Boy, she's really weird. She could have, you know."

Virginia had forgotten to ask Susan about the word "pig," which the papers had said was printed in blood on the door of the Tate residence. She suggested that Ronnie question her about this, and anything else she could think of that might indicate whether she was telling the truth.

In the meantime, they decided not to mention it to anyone else.

That same day the LaBianca detectives received a call from Venice PD. Were they still interested in talking to one of the Straight Satans? If so, they were questioning one, a guy named Al Springer, on another charge.

The LaBianca detectives had Springer brought over to Parker Center, where they interviewed him on tape. What he told them was so unexpected they had trouble believing it. For Springer said that on August 11 or 12—two or three days after the Tate homicides—Charlie Manson had bragged to him about killing people, adding, "We knocked off five of them just the other night."

November 12-16, 1969

LaBianca detectives Nielsen, Gutierrez, and Patchett interviewed Springer on tape, in one of the interrogation cubicles of LAPD Homicide. Springer was twenty-six, five feet nine, weighed 130 pounds, and, except for his dusty, ragged "colors," as bikers' jackets are known, was surprisingly neat for a member of an "outlaw" motorcycle band.

Springer, it turned out, prided himself on his cleanliness. Which was one of the reasons he personally hadn't wanted to have anything to do with Manson and his girls, he said. But Danny DeCarlo, the club treasurer of the Straight Satans, had got mixed up with them and had missed meetings, so around August 11 or 12, he, Springer, had gone to Spahn Ranch to persuade Danny to come back. " . . . and there were flies all over the place and they were just like animals up there, I couldn't believe it, you know. You see, I'm really clean, really. Some of the guys get pretty nasty, but I myself, I like to keep things clean.

"Well, in comes this Charlie ... He wanted Danny up there because Danny had his colors on his back, and all these drunkards, they come up there and start harrassing the girls and messing with the guys and Danny walks out with his Straight Satan colors on, and nobody messes with Charlie, see.

"So I tried to get Danny to come back, and Charlie is standing there, and Charlie says, he says, 'Now wait a minute, maybe I can give you a better thing than you've got already.' I said, 'What's that?' He says, 'Move up here, you can have all the girls you want, all the girls,' he says, 'are all yours, at your disposal, anything.' And he's a brainwashing type guy. So I said, 'Well, how do you survive, how do you support these twenty, thirty fucking broads, man?' And he says, 'I got them all hoofing for me.' He said, 'I go out at night and I do my thing.' 'Well,' I said, 'what's your thing, man; run your trip down.' He figured me being a motorcycle rider and all, I'd accept anything including murder.

"So he starts getting in my ear and says how he goes up and he lives with the rich people, and he calls the police 'pigs' and what not, he knocks on the door, they'll open the door, and he'll just drive in with his cutlass and start cutting them up, see."

Q. "This is what he told you?"

A. "This is what he told me verbally, right to my face."

Q. "You're kidding, is that what you really heard?"

A. "Yeah. I said, 'When's the last time you did it?' He says, 'Well, we knocked off five of them,' he says, 'just the other night.'"

Q. "So he told you that—Charlie stated that he knocked over five people?"

A. "Right. Charlie and Tex."

Springer couldn't recall the exact word Manson used: it wasn't "people"; it might have been "pigs" or "rich pigs."

The LaBianca detectives were so startled they had Springer run through it a second time, and a third.

A. "I think you've got your man right here, I really do."

Q. "I'm pretty sure we have, but in this day and age of feeding people their rights, if we're going to make a decent case on him, we can't do it with his statement."

Exactly when had Manson told him this? Well, it was the first time he went to Spahn, and that was either August 11 or 12—he couldn't remember which. But he sure remembered the scene. "I've never seen anything like it in my life. I've never been to a nudist colony or I've never seen real idiots on the loose . . ." Everywhere he looked there were naked girls. Maybe a dozen and a half were of age, eighteen or over, but about an equal number weren't. The young ones were hiding in the bushes. Charlie had told him he could have his pick. He'd also offered to buy him a dune buggy and a new motorcycle if he would stay.

It was true turnabout. Charlie Manson, aka Jesus Christ, trying to tempt a Straight Satan.

That Springer resisted the temptation may have been due in part to his knowledge that other members of his gang had been there on previous occasions: "Everybody got sick of catching the clap . . . the ranch was just out of hand . . ."

During Springer's first visit, Manson had demonstrated his prowess with knives, in particular a long sword. Springer had seen Charlie throw it maybe fifty feet, sticking it, say, eight times out of ten. This was the sword, Springer said, that Charlie used when he "put the chop" to people.

"Did you ever get a corpse with his ear cut off?" Springer abruptly asked. Apparently one of the detectives nodded, as Springer said, "Yeah, there's your man." Charlie had told him about cutting some guy's ear off. If Danny would come in, he could tell them about it. The only problem was, "Danny's scared of these creeps, they've tried to kill him already."

Springer had also mentioned a Tex and a Clem. The detectives asked him to describe them.

Clem was a certified idiot, Springer said: he was an escapee from Camarillo, a state mental hospital. Whatever Charlie said, Clem would parrot it. As far as he could tell, "Charlie and Tex are the ones that had the brains out there." Unlike Clem, Tex didn't say much; he "kept his

mouth shut, real tight. He was real clean-cut. His hair was
a little long, but he was—just like a college student." Tex
seemed to spend most of his time working on dune buggies.

Charlie had a thing about dune buggies. He wanted to
fix them with a switch on the dash that would turn the
taillights off. Then, when the CHP (California Highway
Patrol) pulled them over to cite them, there would be two
guys armed with shotguns in the back, and as the CHP's
came up alongside, "Pow, blow them up."

Q. "Why did he say he wanted to do that?"

A. "Ah, he wants to build up a thing where he can be
leader of the world. He's crazy."

Q. "Does he have a name for his group?"

A. "The Family."

Back to that sword, could Springer describe it? Yeah, it
was a cutlass, a real pirate's sword. Up until a few months
ago, Springer said, it had belonged to the ex-president
of the Straight Satans, but then it had disappeared, and he
guessed one of the members had given it to Charlie.

He had heard, from Danny, that the sword had been
used when they had killed a guy "called Henland, I believe
it was." This was the guy who had his ear cut off.

What did he know about the "Henland" killing? they
asked. According to Danny, a guy named "Bausley" and
one or two other guys had killed him, Springer said.
Danny had told him that "almost beyond a reasonable
doubt he could prove that Bousley or Bausley or whatever
killed this guy and evidently Charlie was in on it or something. Well, anyway, somebody cut his ear." Clem had
also told him, Springer, "how they had cut some fucking
idiot's ear off and wrote on the wall and put the Panther's
hand or paw up there to blame the Panthers. Everything
they did, they blamed on the niggers, see. They hate niggers because they had killed a nigger prior to that."

Five. Plus "Henland" (Hinman). Plus "a nigger." Total
thus far: seven. The detectives were keeping track.

Had he seen any other weapons while at Spahn? Yeah,
Charlie had shown him a whole gunrack full, the first time
he went up there. There were shotguns, deer rifles, .45
caliber hand guns, "and I heard talk of and was told by

Danny that they had a .22 Buntline long barrel, a nine-round. This came from Danny, and he knows guns. And this is what was supposed to have killed that, ah, Black Panther."

Charlie had told him about it. As Al remembered it, Tex had burned this black guy in a deal for a whole bunch of grass. When Charlie refused to give back the guy's money, the black had threatened to get all his Panther brothers up to Spahn Ranch and wipe out the place. "So Charlie pulls out a gun, somebody else was going to do it, but Charlie pulls out a gun and he points it at the guy, and he goes click, click, click, click and the gun didn't go off, four or five times, and the guy stood up and he said, 'Ha, you coming here with an empty gun on me,' and Charlie says click, bam, in the heart area somewhere, and he told me this personally right to my face and that was what the Buntline was used on, the long-barrel job."

After the murder, which had occurred somewhere in Hollywood, the Panther's buddies "took the carcass off supposedly to some park, Griffith Park or one of them ... This is all hearsay, but it is hearsay right from Charlie."

A. "Now, did anybody have their refrigerator wrote on?"

There was a sudden silence, then one of the LaBianca detectives asked, "Why does this come up?"

A. " 'Cause he told me something about writing something on the refrigerator."

Q. "Who said he wrote it on the refrigerator?"

A. "Charlie did. Charlie said they wrote something on the fucking refrigerator in blood."

Q. "What did he say he wrote?"

A. "Something about pigs or niggers or something like that."

If Springer was telling the truth, and *if* Manson wasn't just bragging to impress him, then it meant that Manson was probably also involved in the LaBianca murders. Bringing the total thus far to nine.

But the LaBianca detectives had good reason to doubt this statement, for, contrary to the press reports, DEATH TO

PIGS hadn't been printed in blood on the refrigerator door; the phrase had actually been printed on the living-room wall, as had the word RISE. What had been printed on the refrigerator door was HEALTER SKELTER.

While Springer was being questioned, one of the LaBianca detectives left the room. When he returned a few minutes later, another man was with him.

Q. "Here's another partner, Mike McGann, Al. Let me shove this table down here. He just came in, so you might want to bring him up on what we've talked about."

McGann was one of the Tate detectives. The LaBianca detectives had finally decided to walk those few feet, and share what they had learned. By this time the temptation to say "Hey, look what *we* found" must have been irresistible.

They had Springer run through it again. McGann listened, unimpressed. Springer then began talking about still another murder, that of a cowboy named "Shorty," whom he had met when he first visited the ranch. How and what had he heard about Shorty's death? one of the detectives asked. "I heard about that from Danny." Danny heard, from the girls, that Shorty "got to know too much and hear too much and got worried too much" and "so they just cut his arms and his legs and his head off . . ." Danny had felt very badly about this, because he had liked Shorty.

Ten. *If.*

Q. (*to McGann*) "Anything you want to get in on this?"

Q. "Yeah, I want to ask about why they killed this colored—the Panther supposedly. When did this take place, do you know?"

Springer wasn't sure, but he thought it was about a week before he went up to the ranch. Danny could probably tell them about that.

Q. "Did you connect up the five people that Charlie said that he killed in early August with any particular crime?"

A. "Right, the Tate crime."

Q. "You put that together?"

A. "Right."

They began zeroing in. Anybody else present when Charlie supposedly confessed those five murders to you? No. Was Tate ever specifically mentioned? No. Did you see anyone at the ranch who wore glasses? No. Ever see Manson with a gun? No, only a knife: "he's a knife freak." Were the cutlass and the other knives you saw sharpened on both sides? He thought so but wasn't sure; Danny had mentioned Charlie sending them out someplace to be sharpened. Ever see any rope up there? Yeah, they used all kinds of rope. Do you know there's a $25,000 reward on the Tate murders? Yeah, and "I sure could use it."

Springer had been to Spahn Ranch three times, his second visit occurring the day after his first. He'd lost his hat riding out and had gone back to look for it, but then his bike had broken down and he'd had to stay overnight to repair it. Again Charlie, Tex, and Clem had worked on him to join them. His third and last visit had taken place on the night of Friday, August 15. The detectives were able to establish the date because it was the night before the sheriff's raid on Spahn Ranch. Also, the Straight Satans held their club meetings on Friday, and they had discussed getting Danny away from Charlie. "A lot of the guys in the club were going to go up there and beat his ass, teach him a lesson not to brainwash our members . . ." Eight or nine of them did go to Spahn that night, "but it didn't happen that way."

Charlie had conned some of them. The girls had lured others into the bushes. And when they started breaking up things, Charlie told them that he had guns trained on them from the rooftops. Springer had one of his brothers check the gunrack that Charlie had shown him on his first visit. A couple of rifles were missing. After a time they'd left, in a cloud of exhaust fumes and threats, leaving one of their more sober members, Robert Reinhard, to bring Danny back the following day. But the next morning "the police were all over the place," arresting not only Charlie and the others but also DeCarlo and Reinhard.

All had been released a few days later and, according to Danny, Shorty had been killed not long after this.

Fearing he would be next, Danny had taken his truck and split to Venice. Late one night Clem and Bruce Davis, another of Charlie's boys, had snuck up on the truck. They had succeeded in prying open the door when Danny heard them and grabbed his .45. Danny felt sure, Springer said, that they had come "to off him." And he was scared now, not only for himself but because his little boy was living with him. Springer thought Danny was frightened enough to talk to them. Talking to the Venice detectives would be no problem, since "he's known them most of his life," but getting him to come down to Parker Center was something else. Springer, however, promised he'd try to get Danny to come in voluntarily, if possible the next day.

Springer didn't have a phone. The detectives asked if there was somewhere they could call "without putting any heat on you? Is there some gal you see quite a bit of?"

A.   "Just my wife and kids."

The clean, neat, monogamous Springer didn't conform to their stereotype of a biker. As one of the detectives remarked, "You're going to give the motorcycle gang a whole new image in the world."

Although Al Springer appeared to be telling the truth, the detectives were not greatly impressed with his story. He was an outsider, not a member of the Family, yet the very first time he goes to Spahn Ranch, Manson confesses to him that he's committed at least nine murders. It just didn't make sense. It appeared far more likely that Springer was just regurgitating what Danny DeCarlo, who had been close to Manson, had told him. It was also possible that Manson, to impress the cyclists, had bragged about committing murders in which he wasn't even involved.

McGann, of the Tate team, was so unimpressed that later he wouldn't even be able to recall having heard of Springer, much less talking to him.

Although the interview had been taped, the LaBianca detectives had only one portion transcribed, and that not the section on their case, but the part, less than a page in length, with Manson's alleged confession, "We knocked off

Ive of them just the other night." The LaBianca detectives
hen filed the tape and that single page in their "tubs," as
police case files are known. With other developments in
he case, they apparently forgot them.

Yet the Springer interview of November 12, 1969, was
in a sense an important turning point. Three months after
the Tate-LaBianca homicides, LAPD was finally seriously
considering the possibility that the two crimes were not, as
had long been believed, unrelated. And the focus of at
least the LaBianca investigation was now on a single
group of suspects, Charlie Manson and his Family. It appears almost certain that had the LaBianca detectives continued to pursue the Lutesinger-Springer-DeCarlo lead
they would eventually—even if uninformed of Susan Atkins' confessions—have found the killers of Steven Parent,
Abigail Folger, Voytek Frykowski, Jay Sebring, Sharon
Tate, and Rosemary and Leno LaBianca.

In the meantime, two people—one at Sybil Brand, the
other at Corona—were each, independent of the other,
trying to tell someone what they knew about the killings.
And having no luck.

There is some confusion as to exactly when Susan Atkins first discussed the Tate-LaBianca murders with Ronnie
Howard. Whatever the date, there was a similarity in the
way it came about, Susan first admitting her participation
in the murder of Hinman, then, in her little-girl manner,
attempting to surprise Ronnie with other, more startling
revelations.

According to Ronnie, one evening Susan came over, sat
down on her bed, and started rapping about her experiences. Susan said that she had "dropped acid" (taken
LSD) many times, in fact she had done everything there
was to do; there was nothing left; she'd reached a stage
where nothing shocked her any more.

Ronnie replied that there wasn't much that would shock
her, either. Since age seventeen, when she'd been sent to a
federal penitentiary for two years for extortion, Ronnie
had seen quite a lot.

"I bet I could tell you something that would really blow
your mind," Susan said.

"I don't think so," Ronnie responded.

"You remember the Tate deal?"

"Yes."

"I was there. We did it."

"Really, anyone can say that."

"No, I'll tell you." And tell her Susan Atkins did.

Susan would flash from one thought to another with such rapidity that Ronnie was often left confused. Too, Ronnie's recollection of details—especially names, dates, places—was not as good as Virginia's. Later she would be unsure, for example, exactly how many persons were involved: at one time she thought Susan said five—herself, two other girls, Charlie, and a guy who stayed in the car; another time it was four, with no mention of the man in the car. She knew a girl named Katie was involved in a murder, but which murder—Hinman, Tate, or LaBianca—Ronnie wasn't sure. But she also recalled details Susan either hadn't told Virginia or Virginia had forgotten. Charlie had a gun; the girls all had knives. Charlie had cut the telephone wires, shot the boy in the car, then awakened the man on the couch (Frykowski), who looked up to see a gun pointing in his face.

Sharon Tate's plea and Susan's brutal response were nearly identical in both Ronnie's and Virginia's accounts. However, the description of how Sharon died differed somewhat. As Ronnie understood it, two other people held Sharon while, to quote Susan, "I proceeded to stab her."

"It felt so good the first time I stabbed her, and when she screamed at me it did something to me, sent a rush through me, and I stabbed her again."

Ronnie asked where. Susan replied in the chest, not the stomach.

"How many times?"

"I don't remember. I just kept stabbing her until she stopped screaming."

Ronnie knew a little bit about the subject, having once stabbed her ex-husband. "Did it feel sort of like a pillow?"

"Yeah," Susan replied, pleased that Ronnie understood. "It was just like going into nothing, going into air." But the killing itself was something else. "It's like a sexual release," Susan told her. "Especially when you see the blood spurting out. It's better than a climax."

Remembering Virginia's question, Ronnie asked Susan about the word "pig." Susan said that she printed the word on the door, after first dipping a towel in Sharon Tate's blood.

At one point in the conversation Susan asked, "Don't you remember that guy that was found with the fork in his stomach? We wrote 'arise' and 'death to pigs' and 'helter skelter' in blood."

"Was that you and your same friends?" Ronnie asked.

"No, just three this time."

"All girls?"

"No, two girls and Charlie. Linda wasn't in on this one."

Susan rapped on about a variety of subjects: Manson (he was both Jesus Christ and the Devil); helter skelter (Ronnie admittedly didn't understand it but thought it meant "you have to be killed to live"); sex ("the whole world is like one big intercourse—everything is in and out—smoking, eating, stabbing"); how she would play crazy to fool the psychiatrists ("All you have to do is act normal," Ronnie advised her); children (Charlie had helped deliver her baby, whom she had named Zezozose Zadfrack Glutz; within a couple of months after his birth she had begun fellating him); bikers (with the motorcycle gangs on their side, they "would really throw some fear into the world"); and murder. Susan loved to talk about murder. "More you do it, the better you like it." Just the mention of it seemed to excite her. Laughingly, she told Ronnie about some man whose head "we cut off," either out in the desert or in one of the canyons.

She also told Ronnie, "There are eleven murders that they will never solve." And there were going to be more, many more. Although Charlie was in jail "in Indio," most of the Family was still free.

As Susan talked, Ronnie Howard realized that there were still some things that could shock her. One was that this little girl, who was twenty-one but often seemed much younger, probably *had* committed all these murders. Another was Susan's assertion that this was only the beginning, that more murders would follow.

Ronnie Howard would later state: "I'd never informed on anyone in the past, but this one thing I could not go along with. I kept thinking that if I didn't say anything these people would probably be set free. They were going to pick other houses, just at random. I just couldn't see all those innocent people being killed. It could have been my house next time or yours or anyone's."

Ronnie decided she "just had to tell the police."

It would seem that if one were in jail, talking to a policemen would be relatively easy. Ronnie Howard discovered otherwise.

The dates, again, are vague, but, according to Ronnie, she told +Sergeant Broom,* one of the female deputies at Sybil Brand, that she knew who had committed the Tate and LaBianca murders; that the person who told her had been involved and was now in custody; but that the other killers were on the loose and unless they were apprehended soon there would be more murders. Ronnie wanted permission to call LAPD.

Sergeant Broom said she would pass the request to her superior, +Lieutenant Johns.

After waiting three days and hearing nothing, Ronnie asked Sergeant Broom about the request. Lieutenant Johns didn't think there was anything to the story, the sergeant told her. By this time the lieutenant had probably forgotten all about it, Sergeant Broom said, adding, "Why don't you do the same thing, Ronnie?"

By now, according to Ronnie, she was literally begging. People were going to die unless she warned the police in time. Could you call *for* me? Ronnie asked. *Please!*

It was against the rules for a guard to make a call for an inmate, Sergeant Broom informed her.

On Thursday, November 13, biker Danny DeCarlo came down to Parker Center, where he was interviewed

---

*Since neither the deputy nor her lieutenant was available for interviews, therefore making it impossible to present their version of these incidents, pseudonyms have been used for both.

by the LaBianca detectives. It was not a long interview, and it was not taped. Although DeCarlo had a great deal of information about the activities of Manson and his group, having lived with them for more than five months, at no time had Charlie admitted to him that he was involved in either the Tate or the LaBianca murders.

This made the officers even more skeptical about Springer's tale, and it was probably at this point that they decided to write him off as a reliable source. When Springer came back the following week, he was given some photos to identify but was asked few questions.

Arrangements were made to interview DeCarlo on tape, and at length, on Monday, November 17. He was to come in about 8:30 in the morning.

Ronnie Howard kept after Sergeant Broom, who finally mentioned the subject to Lieutenant Johns a second time. The lieutenant suggested that she ask Ronnie for some details.

Sergeant Broom did, and Ronnie—still without identifying the people involved—told her a little of what she had learned. The killers knew Terry Melcher. They had shot the boy, Steven Parent, first, four times, because he saw them. Sharon Tate had been the last to die. The word "pig" had been written in her blood. They were going to cut out Sharon's baby, but didn't. Again she stressed that more killings were planned.

Sergeant Broom apparently misunderstood Ronnie, for she told Lieutenant Johns that they *had* cut out the baby. And Lieutenant Johns knew this wasn't true.

Your informant is lying, Sergeant Broom informed Ronnie, and told her why.

Ronnie, now almost hysterical, told Sergeant Broom that she had misunderstood what she'd said. Could she talk to Lieutenant Johns herself?

But Sergeant Broom decided that she had already bothered the lieutenant enough. As far as she was concerned, she informed Ronnie, the matter was closed.

There was an irony here, although Ronnie Howard was unaware of it, and wouldn't have appreciated it had she known: Sergeant Broom dated one of the Tate detectives.

But apparently they had other, more important things to talk about.

Virginia Graham was having her own troubles with bureaucracy. Although, unlike Ronnie Howard, she was not yet completely convinced that Susan Atkins was telling the truth, the possibility that there might be more murders worried her too. On November 14, two days after her transfer to Corona, she decided she had to tell someone what she had heard. There was one person at the prison she knew and trusted, Dr. Vera Dreiser, a staff psychologist.

In order for an inmate to talk to a staff member at Corona, it is necessary to fill out a "blue slip," or request form. Virginia made one out, writing on it, "Dr. Dreiser, it is very important that I speak with you."

The form was returned with a notation stating that Miss Graham should fill out another blue slip, to see Dr. Owens, administrator of the unit to which she was assigned. But Virginia didn't want to speak to Dr. Owens. Again she requested a personal interview with Dr. Dreiser.

The request was granted. But not until December. And by then the whole world knew what Virginia Graham had wanted to tell Dr. Dreiser.

November 17, 1969

Danny DeCarlo was due at LAPD Homicide at 8:30 that Monday morning. He didn't show. The detectives called his home first, getting no answer, then his mother's number. No, she hadn't seen Danny, and she was a little worried. Danny was supposed to leave his son with her, so she could baby-sit while he went down to LAPD, but he hadn't even called.

It was possible DeCarlo had skipped. He had been very

frightened when the detectives talked to him the previous Thursday.

There was another possibility, one that they didn't want to think about.

That same day Ronnie Howard had a court appearance in Santa Monica, on the forgery charge. When inmates of Sybil Brand are due in court, they are first transported to the men's jail on Bouchet Street, where a bus picks them up and delivers them to the assigned departments. Before the arrival of the bus, there are usually a few minutes during which each girl is permitted to make one call from a pay phone.

Ronnie saw her chance and got in line. However, time began running out and there were still two girls ahead of her. She paid each fifty cents to let her call first.

Ronnie called the Beverly Hills Police Department and asked to speak to a homicide detective. When one came on the line, she gave him her name and booking number, and told him she knew who had committed the Tate and LaBianca murders. The officer said those cases were being handled by the Hollywood Division of LAPD, and suggested she call there.

Ronnie then called Hollywood PD, giving a second homicide officer the same information. He wanted to send someone over immediately, but she told him she would be in court the rest of the day.

She hung up, however, before the officer could ask which court she would be in.

All day in court Ronnie Howard had the feeling that she was being watched. She was sure that two men, sitting in the back of the courtroom, were homicide detectives, and expected at any minute they would arrange to speak to her. But they never did. When court adjourned, she was taken by bus back to Sybil Brand, Dormitory 8000, and Susan Atkins.

Shortly before 5 P.M., Danny DeCarlo arrived at LAPD Homicide. He had been on his way downtown earlier when he noticed he was low on gas and had pulled into a service station. On leaving, he had made an illegal turn, had been spotted by a black-and-white, and, after the officers checked and found he had some outstanding traffic tickets, had been hauled in. It had taken all day to secure his release.

Unlike Al Springer, Danny DeCarlo looked, talked, and acted like a biker. He was short, five feet four, weighed 130 pounds, had a handlebar mustache, tattoos on both arms, and burn scars on one arm and both legs from motorcycle pile-ups. Wary, frequently glancing back over his shoulder as if expecting to find someone there, he spoke in a colorful jargon that the interviewing officers—Nielsen, Gutierrez, and McGann—unconsciously adopted. Now twenty-five, he had been born in Toronto, then given U.S. citizenship after serving four years in the Coast Guard, his job: weapons expert. Currently he was in business with his father, selling firearms. When it came to the guns at Spahn Ranch, the detectives couldn't have found a better source. When he wasn't getting drunk and chasing girls—which he admitted occupied most of his time—he looked after the weapons. He not only cleaned and repaired them, he slept in the gunroom where they were kept. When a weapon was taken out, Danny knew about it.

He also knew a great deal about Spahn's Movie Ranch, which was located in Chatsworth, not more than twenty miles from downtown Beverly Hills, yet, seemingly, a world away. Once William S. Hart, Tom Mix, Johnny Mack Brown, and Wallace Beery had made movies here; it was said that Howard Hughes had come to Spahn, to oversee personally the filming of portions of *The Outlaw;* and the rolling hills behind the main buildings provided settings for *Duel in the Sun.* Now, except for an occasional Marlboro commercial or a "Bonanza" episode, the main business was renting horses to weekend riders. The movie sets—Longhorn Saloon, Rock City Cafe, Undertaking Parlor, Jail—which fronted on Santa Susana Pass Road, were old now, run down, as was George Spahn, the eighty-one-year-old, near blind owner of the ranch. For years Ruby Pearl, a onetime circus bareback rider turned horse wrangler, had run the riding stable part of the business for George: getting hay, hiring and firing cowboys, making sure they looked after the horses and stable and kept their hands off the too young girls who came for riding lessons. Almost sightless, George depended on Ruby, but at the end of the day she went home to a husband and another life.

Over the years George had sired ten children, each of whom he had named after a favorite horse. He could recall in detail the namesakes but was less clear about the kids. All lived elsewhere, and only a few visited him with any regularity. When the Manson Family arrived, in August 1968, George was living alone in a filthy trailer, feeling old, lonely, and neglected.

This was long before Danny DeCarlo became involved with the Family, but he had often heard the tale from those who were there.

Manson, who originally asked Spahn's permission to stay for a few days, but neglected to mention that there were twenty-five to thirty people with him, assigned Squeaky to look after George.

Squeaky—t/n Lynette Fromme—had been with Manson more than a year at that time, having been one of the first girls to join him. She was thin, red-headed, covered with freckles. Though nineteen, she looked much younger. DeCarlo told the detectives, "She had George in the palm of her hand. She cleaned for him, cooked for him, balanced his checkbook, made love with him."

Q. (*unbelievingly*) "She did?! That old son of a gun!"

A. "Yeah ... Charlie's trip was to get George so he had so much faith in Squeaky that come time for George to go off into the happy hunting ground he'd turn the ranch over to Squeaky. That was their thing. Charlie'd always tell her what to tell George ... and she'd report back to Charlie anything anyone else told him."

Squeaky maintained that she was George's eyes. According to DeCarlo, they saw only what Charlie Manson wanted them to see.

Possibly because he suspected, possibly because his own children on their occasional visits strongly resisted the idea, George never did get around to willing the property to Squeaky. Which, the detectives surmised, was probably why he was still alive out at Spahn Ranch.

George Spahn had frustrated one of Charlie's plans. Danny DeCarlo had played along with, then failed to come through on another——Manson's scheme to get the motorcycle gangs to join him in "terrorizing society," as DeCarlo put it. Danny had met Manson in March 1969, just after separating from his wife. He had gone to Spahn to repair some bikes, and had stayed; "I had a ball," he later admitted. Manson's girls had been taught that having babies and caring for men were their sole purpose in life. DeCarlo liked being cared for, and the girls, at least at first, appeared very affectionate toward "Donkey Dan,"* a nickname they had bestowed upon him because of certain physical endowments.

There were problems. Charlie was against drinking; Danny liked nothing better than to swill beer and lie in the sun——later he testified that while at Spahn he was smashed "probably 90 percent of the time." And, with the exception of a couple of "special sweeties," DeCarlo eventually tired of most of the girls: "They would always try preaching to me. It was always the same shit Charlie preached to them."

With the August 15 visit of the Straight Satans, Manson must have realized that he would never succeed in getting the bikers to join him. After that, Danny was ignored, left out of Family conferences, while the girls denied him their favors. Though he went to Barker Ranch with the group, he stayed only three days. He split, DeCarlo said, because he had begun to believe all the "murder talk" he had heard, and because he had strong suspicions that unless he left he might be next. "After that," he said, "I started watching my back."

When the LaBianca detectives had talked to DeCarlo the previous Thursday, he'd promised to try to locate Manson's sword. He turned it over to Sergeant Gutierrez, who booked it as the personal property of "Manson, Charles M.," probable crime "187 PC"——murder.

---

*Manson told DeCarlo that because he, Manson, was less amply endowed, he needed DeCarlo to keep the girls from running away. This sounds like a Manson con, though DeCarlo maintains it was true.

The sword had accumulated a history. A few weeks after Danny moved to Spahn, the president of the Straight Satans, George Knoll, aka "86 George," had visited him. Manson had admired George's sword and had conned him out of it by promising to pay a twenty-dollar traffic ticket George owed. According to Danny, the sword became one of Charlie's favorite weapons; he had a metal scabbard built for it, next to the steering wheel of his personal dune buggy. When the Straight Satans came to get Danny the night of August 15, they spotted the sword and reclaimed it. On learning that it was "dirty," i.e., had been used in a crime, they had broken it in half. It was in two pieces when DeCarlo handed it over to Gutierrez.

Over-all length, 20 inches; blade length, 15 inches. The width of its razor-sharp blade, the tip of which had been honed on both sides, was 1 inch.

This was the sword, according to DeCarlo, that Manson had used to slice Gary Hinman's ear.

From DeCarlo the detectives now learned that, in addition to Bobby Beausoleil and Susan Atkins, three others had been involved in the murder of Hinman: Manson, Mary Brunner, and Bruce Davis. DeCarlo's primary source was Beausoleil, who, on returning to Spahn after the murder, had bragged to DeCarlo about what he had done. Or, as Danny put it, "He came back with a big head the next day, you know, just like he got him a cherry."

The story, as DeCarlo claimed Beausoleil had related it to him, went as follows. Mary Brunner, Susan Atkins, and Bobby Beausoleil had dropped in on Hinman, "bullshitting about old times and everything like that." Bobby then asked Gary for all his money, saying they needed it. When Gary said he didn't have any money, Bobby pulled out a gun—a 9mm. Polish Radom automatic—and started pistol-whipping him. In the scuffle the gun went off, the bullet hitting no one but ricocheting through the kitchen. (LASO found a 9 mm. slug lodged under the kitchen sink.)

Beausoleil then called Manson at Spahn Ranch and told him, "You'd better get up here, Charlie. Gary ain't cooperating."* A short time later Manson and Bruce Davis arrived at the Hinman residence. Puzzled and hurt, Gary pleaded with Charlie, asking him to take the others and leave; he didn't want any trouble; he couldn't understand why they were doing this to him; they had always been friends. According to DeCarlo, "Charlie didn't say anything. He just hit him with the sword. Whack. Cut part of his ear off or all of it. [Hinman's left ear had been split in half.]

"So Gary went down, and was really going through some changes about losing his ear . . ." Manson gave him a choice: sign over everything he had, or die. Manson and Davis then left.

Though Beausoleil did obtain the "pink slips" (California automobile ownership papers) on two of Hinman's vehicles, Gary continued to insist he had no money. When more pistol-whipping failed to convince him, Bobby again called Manson at Spahn, telling him, "We ain't going to get nothing out of him. He ain't going to give up nothing. And we can't just leave. He's got his ear hacked off and he'll go to the police." Manson replied, "Well, you know what to do." And Beausoleil did it.

"Bobby said he went up to Gary again. Took the knife and stuck him with it. He said he had to do it three or four times . . . [Hinman] was really bleeding, and he was gasping for air, and Bobby said he knelt down next to him and said, 'Gary, you know what? You got no reason to be on earth any more. You're a pig and society don't need you, so this is the best way for you to go, and you should thank me for putting you out of your misery.' Then [Hinman] made noises in his throat, his last gasping breath, and wow, away he went."

Q. "So Bobby told him he was a 'pig'?"

A. "Right. You see, the fight against society was the number one element in this—"

Q. (*skeptically*) "Yeah. We'll get into his philosophy and all that bullshit later . . ."

They never did.

*Since the Hinman residence in Malibu and Spahn's Movie Ranch in Chatsworth were in the same dialing area, this was not a toll call; therefore the telephone company kept no record of it.

DeCarlo went on. Before leaving the house, they wrote on the wall " 'white piggy' or 'whitey' or 'kill the piggies,' something along that line." Beausoleil also dipped his hand in Hinman's blood and, using his palm, made a paw print on the wall; the plan was "to push the blame onto the Black Panthers," who used the paw print as their symbol. Then they hot-wired Hinman's Volkswagen microbus and his Fiat station wagon and drove both back to Spahn Ranch, where Beausoleil bragged about his exploits to De-Carlo.

Later, apparently fearful that the palm print might be identifiable, Beausoleil returned to the Hinman residence and attempted, unsuccessfully, to wipe it off the wall. This was several days after Hinman's death, and Beausoleil later told DeCarlo that he "could hear the maggots eating away on Gary."*

As killers, they had been decidedly amateurish. Not only was the palm print identifiable, so was a latent fingerprint Beausoleil had left in the kitchen. They kept Hinman's Volkswagen and his Fiat at the ranch for several days, where a number of people saw them.† Hinman had played bagpipes, a decidedly uncommon musical instrument. Beausoleil and the girls took his set back to Spahn Ranch, where for a time they remained on a shelf in the kitchen; DeCarlo for one had tried to play them. And Beausoleil did not discard the knife but continued to carry

*Beausoleil, Brunner, and Atkins went to Hinman's residence on Friday, July 25, 1969. Manson slashed Hinman's ear sometime late that night. Hinman was not killed, however, until Sunday, July 27, and it was not until the following Thursday, July 31, that his body was discovered by LASO, following a report from a friend who had been trying to reach Hinman for several days.
†Ironically, on July 28, two LASO deputies—Olmstead and Grap—visited Spahn Ranch on another matter. While there they saw the Fiat, ran a spot check on the license, and learned that it belonged to Gary Hinman. Grap knew Hinman; he also knew he was a friend of the people at Spahn Ranch, and therefore didn't feel there was anything suspicious about the station wagon's being there. At this time, although Hinman was dead, his body had not yet been discovered.
After the discovery of the body on July 31, LASO put out a "want" on Hinman's vehicles. Grap didn't learn of it, or Hinman's death, until much later. If he had known, of course, he could have directed the investigation to Spahn Ranch and the Manson Family months before Kitty Lutesinger implicated Atkins and the others.

it with him; it was in the tire well when he was arrested on August 6, driving Hinman's Fiat.

DeCarlo drew a picture of the knife Beausoleil claimed he had used to stab Hinman. It was a pencil-thin, miniature bowie, with an eagle on the handle and a Mexican inscription. It tallied perfectly with the knife recovered from the Fiat. DeCarlo also sketched the 9 mm. Radom, which as yet hadn't been recovered.

The detectives asked him what other hand guns he had seen at Spahn.

A. "Well, there was a .22 Buntline. When they did that Black Panther, I didn't want to touch it. I didn't want to clean it. I didn't want to be nowhere around it."

DeCarlo claimed he didn't know whose gun it was, but he said, "Charlie always used to carry it in a holster on the front of him. It was more or less always with him."

Sometime "around July, maybe June," the gun "just popped up." When was the last time he saw it? "I know I didn't see it for at least a week before the raid."

The Spahn Ranch raid had taken place on August 16. A week earlier would be August 9, the date of the Tate homicides.

Q. "Did you ever ask Charlie, 'Where's your gun?'"

A. "He said, 'I just gave it away.' He liked it, so I figured it was maybe just stashed."

The detectives had DeCarlo draw the Buntline. It was nearly identical with the photo of the Hi Standard Longhorn model sent out in the LAPD flyer. Later DeCarlo was shown the flyer and asked, "Does this look like the gun you mentioned?"

A. "It sure does."

Q. "What's the difference between that gun and the gun that you saw?"

A. "No difference at all. Only the rear sight blade was different. It didn't have any."

The detectives had DeCarlo run down what he knew about the murder of the Black Panther. Springer had first mentioned the killing to them when they interviewed him. In the interim they had done some checking and had come up with a slight problem: no such murder had ever been reported.

According to DeCarlo, after Tex burned the guy for $2,500 on a grass deal, the Panther had called Charlie at Spahn Ranch, threatening that if he didn't make good he and his brothers were going to wipe out the whole ranch. That same night Charlie and a guy named T. J. went to the Panther's place, in North Hollywood. Charlie had a plan.

He put the .22 Buntline in his belt in back. On a signal T. J. was to yank out the gun, step out from behind Charlie, and plug the Panther. Nail him right there. Only T. J. had chickened out, and Manson had to do the shooting himself. Friends of the black, who were present when the shooting occurred, had later dumped the body in Griffith Park, Danny said.

Danny had seen the $2,500 and had been present the next morning when Manson criticized T. J. for backing down. DeCarlo described T. J. as "a really nice guy; his front was trying to be one of Charlie's boys, but he didn't have it inside." T. J. had gone along with Manson on everything up to this, but he told him, "I don't want to have nothing to do with snuffing people." A day or two later he "fled in the wind."

Q. "Who else got murdered up there? What about Shorty? Do you know anything about that?"

There was a long pause, then: "That was my ace in the hole."

Q. "How so?"

A. "I was going to save that for the last."

Q. "Well, might as well clear the thing up now. Has Charlie got something he can smear on you that—"

A. "No, no way at all. Nothing."

One thing did worry DeCarlo, however. In 1966 he had been convicted of a felony, smuggling marijuana across the Mexican border, a federal charge; he was currently appealing the sentence. He was also under indictment on two other charges: along with Al Springer and several other Straight Satans, he had been charged with selling a stolen motorcycle engine, which was a local charge, and giving false information while purchasing a firearm (using an alias and not disclosing that he had a prior felony conviction), which was federal. Manson was still on parole from a federal pen. "So what if they send me to the same

place? I don't want to feel a shank in my back and find
that little son of a bitch behind me."

Q. "Let me explain something to you, Danny, so you
know where you stand. We're dealing with a guy here who
we are pretty sure is responsible for about thirteen murders. Some of which you don't know about."

The figure thirteen was just a guess, but DeCarlo surprised them by saying, "I know about—I'm pretty sure he
did Tate."

Q. "O.K., we've talked about the Panther, we've
talked about Gary Hinman, we're going to talk about
Shorty, and you think he did Tate, that's eight. Now,
we've got five more. All right? Now, our opinion of Charlie is that he's got a little mental problem.

"'But we're in no way going to jeopardize you or anyone
else if, for no other reason, we don't want another murder. We're in business to stop murders. And in this business there's no sense in solving thirteen murders if somebody else is going to get killed. That just makes fourteen."

A. "I'm a nasty motorcycle rider."

Q. "I don't care what you are personally."

A. "The police's general opinion of me is nothing."

Q. "That's not my opinion."

A. "I'm not an outstanding citizen—"

Q. "As I told you the other day, Danny, you level
with us, all the way, right down the line, no bullshitting—
I'm not going to bullshit you, you're not going to bullshit
me—we level with each other and I'll go out for you a
hundred percent. And I mean it. So that you don't have to
go to the joint."

Q. (*another detective*) "We've dealt with motorcycle
riders before, and with all kinds of people. We've gone out
on a limb to help them because they've helped us. We'll do
our very best to make sure that nobody gets killed, whether
he's a motorcycle rider or the best citizen in the world . . .

"Now tell us what you know about Shorty."

Early that same evening, November 17, 1969, two
LAPD homicide officers, Sergeants Mossman and Brown,
appeared at Sybil Brand Institute and asked to see one
Ronnie Howard.

The interview was brief. They heard enough, however, to realize they were on to something big. Enough, too, to decide it wasn't the best idea to leave Ronnie Howard in the same dormitory with Susan Atkins. Before leaving Sybil Brand, they arranged to have Ronnie moved to an isolation unit. Then they drove back to Parker Center, anxious to tell the other detectives that they had "cracked the case."

Nielsen, Gutierrez, and McGann were still questioning DeCarlo about the murder of Shorty. They already knew something about it, even before talking to Springer and DeCarlo, since Sergeants Whiteley and Guenther had begun their own investigation into the "possible homicide" after talking to Kitty Lutesinger.

They knew "Shorty" was Donald Jerome Shea, a thirty-six-year-old male Causcasian who had worked at Spahn Ranch on and off for some fifteen years as a horse wrangler. Like most of the other cowboys who drifted in and out of Spahn's Movie Ranch, Shorty was just awaiting the day when some producer discovered he had all the potentials of a new John Wayne or Clint Eastwood. Whenever the prospect of any acting job materialized, Shorty would quit work and go in search of that ever elusive stardom. Which explained why, when in late August he disappeared from Spahn, no one thought too much about it. At first.

Kitty had also told LASO that Manson, Clem, Bruce, and possibly Tex had been involved in the killing, and that some of the girls in the Family had helped obliterate all traces of the crime. One thing they didn't know, and now asked Danny, was, "Why did they do it?"

A. "Because Shorty was going to old man Spahn and snitching. And Charlie didn't like snitches."

Q. "Just about the petty bullshit at the ranch?"

A. "That's right. Shorty was telling old man Spahn that he should put him in charge and he would clean everybody up." He would, in short order, run off Manson and his Family. Shorty, however, made a fatal mistake: he forgot that little Squeaky was not only George's eyes, she was also Charlie's ears.

There were other reasons, which Danny enumerated. Shorty had married a black topless dancer; Charlie "had a thing" about interracial marriages, and blacks. ("Charlie had two enemies," DeCarlo said, "the police and the niggers, in that order.") Charlie also suspected that Shorty had helped set up the August 16 raid on Spahn— Shorty had been "offed" about ten days later.* And there was the possibility, though this was strictly conjecture on DeCarlo's part, that Shorty had overheard something about some of the other murders.

Bruce Davis had told him about Shorty's murder, DeCarlo said. Several of the girls had also mentioned it, as had both Clem and Manson. Danny was unclear as to some of the details—how they had managed to catch Shorty off guard, and where—but as for the mode of death, he was more than graphic. "Like they were going to do Caesar," they went to the gunroom and picked up a sword and four German bayonets, the latter purchased from an Army surplus store for a buck each and honed to razor sharpness, then, getting Shorty off by himself, they "stuck him like carving up a Christmas turkey . . . Bruce said they cut him up in nine pieces. They cut his head off. Then they cut his arms off too, so there was no way they could possibly identify him. They were laughing about that."

After killing him, they covered the body with leaves (DeCarlo guessed, but was not sure, that this had occurred in one of the canyons behind the ranch buildings); some of the girls had helped dispose of Shorty's bloody clothing, his automobile, and other possessions; then "Clem came back the next day or that night and buried him good."

Q. (unidentified voice) "Can we break this up for about fifteen minutes, maybe send Danny up to get some coffee? There's been an accident and they want to talk to you guys."

Q. "Sure."

---

*The exact date of Shea's death still remains unknown. It is believed to have occurred on either the night of Monday, August 25, or Tuesday, August 26, 1969.

Q. "I'm going to send Danny up to the eighth floor. I want him back down here in fifteen minutes."

A. "I'll wait right here." Danny was not anxious to be seen wandering the halls of LAPD.

Q. "It won't take more than fifteen minutes. We'll close the door so nobody will know you're in here."

There had been no accident. Mossman and Brown had returned from Sybil Brand. As they related what they had heard, the fifteen minutes stretched to nearly forty-five. Although the Atkins-Howard conversations left many unanswered questions, the detectives were now convinced that the Tate and LaBianca cases had been "solved."* Susan Atkins had told Ronnie Howard details—the unpublished words written at the LaBianca residence, the lost knife at Tate—which only one of the killers could know. Lieutenants Helder (Tate) and LePage (LaBianca) were notified.

When the detectives returned to the interrogation room, they were in a lighthearted mood.

Q. "Now, when we left Shorty, he was in nine pieces and his head and arms were off . . ."

DeCarlo was not told what they had learned. But he must have sensed a change in the questioning. The matter of Shorty was quickly wrapped up. Tate was now the topic. Exactly why did Danny think Manson was involved?

Well, there were two incidents. Or maybe it was the same incident, Danny was not sure. Anyway, "they went out on one caper and they came back with seventy-five bucks. Tex was in on that. And he fucked up his foot, fucking somebody out of it. I don't know whether he put his lights out or not, but he got seventy-five bucks."

There were no calendars at Spahn Ranch, DeCarlo had told them earlier; no one paid much attention to what day it was. The one date everyone at the ranch remembered, however, was August 16, the day of the raid. It was before this.

Q. "How much before?"

A. "Oh, two weeks."

*As will become all too apparent, in this instance "solved" was a misstatement if ever there was one.

If DeCarlo's estimate was correct, this would also be before Tate. What was the other incident?

A. "They went out one night, everybody went but Bruce."

Q. "Who went?"

A. "Charlie, Tex, and Clem. Them three. O.K., the next morning—"

One of the detectives interrupted. Had he actually seen them leave? No, only the next morning— Another interruption: Did any of the girls go that night?

A. "No, I think— No, I am almost positive it was just them three that went."

Q. "Well, do you remember, were the rest of the girls there that night?"

A. "See, the girls were scattered all over the place, and there is no possible way that I could have kept track of who was there and who wasn't there . . ."

So it was possible the girls could have gone without De-Carlo's knowing about it. Now, what about the date?

This one Danny remembered, more or less, because he was rebuilding the engine on his bike and had to go into town to get a bearing. It was "around the ninth, tenth, or eleventh" of August. "And they split that night and they came back the next morning."

Clem was standing in front of the kitchen, DeCarlo said. Danny walked up to him and asked, "What'd you do last night?" Clem, according to Danny, smiled "that real stupid smile of his." Danny glanced back over his shoulder and saw that Charlie was standing behind him. He got the impression that Clem had been about to answer but that Charlie had signaled him to be quiet. Clem said something like "Don't worry about it, we did all right." At this point Charlie walked off. Before starting after him, Clem put his hand on Danny's arm and said, "We got five piggies." There was a great big grin on his face.

Clem told DeCarlo, "We got five piggies." Manson told Springer, "We knocked off five of them just the other night." Atkins confessed to Howard that she stabbed Sharon Tate and Voytek Frykowski. Beausoleil confessed to DeCarlo that he had stabbed Hinman. Atkins told

Howard that *she* had done the stabbing. Suddenly the detectives had a surfeit of confessors. So many that they were thoroughly confused as to who was involved in which homicides.

Skipping Hinman, which, after all, was the sheriff's case, and concentrating on Tate, they had two versions:

(1) DeCarlo felt that Charlie, Clem and Tex—without the help of any of the girls—had killed Sharon Tate and the others.

(2) Ronnie Howard understood Susan Atkins to say that she, two other girls (the names "Linda" and "Katie" had been mentioned, but whether they were involved in this particular homicide was unclear), plus "Charles," plus possibly one other man, had gone to 10050 Cielo Drive.

As for the LaBianca murders, all they knew was that there were "two girls and Charlie," that "Linda wasn't in on this one," and that Susan Atkins was somehow involved in that collective "we."

The detectives decided to try another approach—through the other girls at the ranch. But first they wanted to wrap up a few loose ends. What clothing had the three men been wearing? Dark clothing, DeCarlo replied. Charlie had on a black sweater, Levi's, moccasins; Tex was dressed similarly, he thought, though he may have been wearing boots, he wasn't sure; Clem wore Levi's and moccasins, too, plus an olive-drab field jacket. Had he noticed any blood on their clothes when he saw them the next morning? No, but then he hadn't been looking for any. Did he have any idea which vehicle they took? Sure, Johnny Swartz' '59 Ford; it was the only car working at that time. Any idea where it was now? It had been hauled off during the August 16 raid and, so far as Danny knew, was probably still in the impound garage in Canoga Park. Swartz was one of the ranch hands at Spahn, not a Family member, but he let them borrow his car. Any idea what Tex's true name was? "Charles" was his first name, Danny said; he'd seen the last name once, on a pink slip, but couldn't recall it. Was it "Charles Montgomery"? the detectives asked, using a name Kitty Lutesinger had supplied. No, that didn't sound familiar. What about Clem—does the name "Tufts" ring any bell? No, he'd never heard

Clem called that, but, "That boy that was found shot up in Topanga Canyon, the sixteen-year-old kid. Wasn't his name Tufts?" One of the detectives replied, "I don't know. That's the sheriff's case. We got so many murders now."

O.K., now about the girls. "How well did you know the broads out there?"

A. "Pretty well, man." [Laughter]

The detectives began going through the names the girls had used when arrested in the Spahn and Barker raids. And they immediately encountered problems. Not only had they used aliases when booked, they also used them at the ranch. And not a single alias but several, seemingly changing names like clothes, whenever the mood hit them. As a further complication, they even traded aliases.

As if these weren't problems enough, Danny provided another. He was extremely reluctant to admit that any of the girls might be capable of murder.

The guys were something else. Bobby, Tex, Bruce, Clem, any would kill, DeCarlo felt, if Charlie told him to. (All, it later turned out, had.)

Ella Jo Bailey was eliminated; she'd left Spahn Ranch before the murders. Mary Brunner and Sandra Good were out also; they'd been in jail both nights.

What about Ruth Ann Smack, aka Ruth Ann Huebelhurst? (These were booking names. Her true name was Ruth Ann Moorehouse, and she was known in the Family as "Ouisch." Danny knew this, but for personal reasons didn't bother to enlighten the detectives.)

Q. "What do you know about her?"

A. "She used to be one of my favorite sweeties."

Q. "Do you think she would have the guts to get into a cold-blooded murder?"

Danny hesitated a long time before answering. "You know, that little girl there is so sweet. What really made me sick to my stomach is when she came up one night, when I was up there in the desert, and she said, 'I can hardly wait to get my first pig.'

"Little seventeen-year-old! I looked on her like she was my daughter, just the sweetest little thing you would ever want to meet in your life. She was so beautiful and so sweet. And Charlie fucked her thinking around so much it turned your guts."

The date when she told DeCarlo this was determined to be about September 1. If she hadn't killed by then, she couldn't have been in on LaBianca or Tate. Eliminate Ruth Ann.

Ever know a Katie? Yeah, but he didn't know what her real name was. "I never knew anybody by their real name," DeCarlo said. Katie was an older broad, not a runaway. She was from down around Venice. His description of her was vague, except that she had so much hair on her body that none of the guys wanted to make it with her.

What about a Linda? She was a short broad, Danny said. But she didn't stay long, maybe only a month or so, and he didn't know much about her. She'd left by the time they raided Spahn Ranch.

When Sadie went out on "creepy-crawly" missions, did she carry any weapons? one of the detectives asked.

A. "She carried a little knife . . . They had a bunch of little hunting knives, Buck hunting knives."

Q. "Buck knives?"

A. "Buck knives, right . . ."

They now began firing specific questions at DeCarlo. Ever see any credit cards with an Italian name on them? Anybody ever talk about somebody who owned a boat? Ever hear anyone use the name "LaBianca"? Danny gave "No" answers to all.

What about glasses, anybody at Spahn wear them? "None of 'em wore glasses because Charlie wouldn't let 'em wear glasses." Mary Brunner had had several pairs; Charlie had broken them.

DeCarlo was shown some two-strand nylon rope. Ever see any rope like this up at Spahn? No, but he had seen some three-strand. Charlie had bought about 200 feet of it at the Jack Frost surplus store in Santa Monica, in June or July.

Was he sure about that? Sure he was sure; he'd been along when Charlie bought it. Later he'd coiled it so it wouldn't develop snags. It was the same as they used in the Coast Guard, on PT boats; he'd handled it hundreds of times.

Although DeCarlo was unaware of it, the Tate-Sebring rope was also three-strand.

Probably by prearrangement, the detectives began to lean on DeCarlo, adopting a tougher tone.

Q.   "Did you ever caper with any of the guys?"

A.   "Fuck no. No way at all. Ask any of the girls."

Q.   "Did you have anything to do with Shorty's death?"

DeCarlo denied it, vehemently. Shorty had been his friend; besides, "I've got no balls for putting anybody's lights out." But there was just enough hesitation in his reply to indicate he was hiding something. Pressed, DeCarlo told them about Shorty's guns. Shorty had a matched pair of Colt .45s. He was always hocking, then reclaiming the pistols. In late August or early September—after Shorty had disappeared but supposedly before DeCarlo knew what had happened to him—Bruce Davis had given him Shorty's pawn tickets on the guns, in repayment for some money he owed DeCarlo. Danny had reclaimed the pistols. Later, learning that Shorty had been killed, he'd sold the guns to a Culver City shop for seventy-five dollars.

Q.   "That puts you in a pretty shitty spot, you're aware of that?"

Danny was. And he got in even deeper when one of the detectives asked him if he knew anything about lime. When arrested, Mary Brunner was carrying a shopping list made up by Manson. "Lime" was one of the items listed. Any idea why Charlie would want some lime?

Danny recalled that Charlie had once asked him what to use "to decompose a body." He had told him lime worked best, because he had once used it to get rid of a cat that had died under a house.

Q.   "Why did you tell him that?"

A.   "No particular reason, he was just asking me."

Q.   "What did he ask you?"

A.   "Oh, the best way to ah, ah, you know, to get rid of a body real quick."

Q. "Did you ever think to say, 'Now what in the fuck makes you ask a question like that, Charlie?'"

A. "No, because he was nuts."

Q. "When did that conversation take place?"

A. "Right around, ah, right around the time Shorty disappeared."

It looked bad, and the detectives left it at that. Although privately they were inclined to accept DeCarlo's tale, suspecting, however, that although he probably had not taken part in the murder, he still knew more than he was telling, it gave them some additional leverage to try and get what they wanted.

They wanted two things.

Q. "Anybody left up at Spahn Ranch that knows you?"

A. "Not that I know of. I don't know who's up there. And I don't want to go up there to find out. I don't want nothing to do with the place."

Q. "I want to look around there. But I need a guide."

Danny didn't volunteer.

They made the other request straight out.

Q. "Would you be willing to testify?"

A. "*No, sir!*"

There were two charges pending against him, they reminded him. On the stolen motorcycle engine, "Maybe we can get it busted down to a lesser charge. Maybe we can go so far as to get it knocked off. As far as the federal thing is concerned, I don't know how much weight we can push on that. But here again we can try."

A. "If you try for me, that's fine. That's all I can ask of you."

If it came down to being a witness or going to jail—

DeCarlo hesitated. "Then when *he* gets out of jail—"

Q. "He isn't going to get out of jail on no first degree murder beef when you've got over five victims involved. If Manson was the guy that was in on the Tate murder. We don't know that for a fact yet. We've got a great deal of information that way."

A. "There's also a reward involved in that."

Q. "Yes, there is. Quite a bit of a reward. Twenty-five

grand. Not to say that one guy is going to get it, but even split that's a hell of a piece of cash."

A.   "I could send my boy through military school with that."

Q.   "Now, what do you think, would you be willing to testify against this group of people?"

A.   "He's going to be sitting there looking at me, Manson is, isn't he?"

Q.   "If you go to trial and testify, he is. Now, how scared of Manson are you?"

A.   "I'm scared shitless. I'm petrified of him. He wouldn't hesitate for a second. If it takes him ten years, he'd find that little boy of mine and carve him to pieces."

Q.   "You give that motherfucker more credit than he deserves. If you think Manson is some kind of a god that is going to break out of jail and come back and murder everybody that testified against him—"

But it was obvious DeCarlo didn't put that past Manson.

Even if he remained in jail, there were the others.

A.   "What about Clem? Have you got him locked up?"

Q.   "Yeah. Clem is sitting in the cooler up in Independence, with Charlie."

A.   "What about Tex and Bruce?"

Q.   "They're both out. Bruce Davis, the last I heard, sometime earlier this month, was in Venice."

A.   "Bruce is down in Venice, huh? I'll have to watch myself . . . One of my club brothers said he spotted a couple of the girls down in Venice, too."

The detectives didn't tell DeCarlo that when Davis was last seen, on November 5, it was in connection with another death, the "suicide" of Zero. By this time LAPD had learned that Zero—aka Christopher Jesus, t/n John Philip Haught—had been arrested in the Barker raid. Earlier, in going through some photographs, DeCarlo had identified "Scotty" and "Zero" as two young boys from Ohio, who had been with the Family for a short time but "didn't fit in." One of the detectives had remarked, "Zero's no longer with us."

A.   "What do you mean he's 'no longer with us'?"

Q.   "He's among the dead."

A. *"Oh, shit, is he?"*

Q. "Yeah, he got a little too high one day and he was playing Russian roulette. He parked a bullet in his head."

While the detectives had apparently bought the story of Zero's death, as related by Bruce Davis and the others, Danny didn't, not for a minute.

No, Danny didn't want to testify.

The detectives left it at that. There was still time for him to change his mind. And, after all, they now had Ronnie Howard. They let Danny go, after making arrangements for him to call in the next day.

One of the detectives commented, after Danny had left but while the tape was still on, "I kind of feel like we've done a day's work."

The DeCarlo interview had lasted over seven hours. It was now past midnight on Tuesday, November 18, 1969. I was already asleep, unaware that in a few hours, as a result of a meeting between the DA and his staff that morning, I would be handed the job of prosecuting the Tate-LaBianca killers.

Part 3

THE INVESTIGATION- PHASE TWO

"No sense makes sense."
Charles Manson

November 18, 1969

By now the reader knows a great deal more about the Tate-LaBianca murders than I did on the day I was assigned that case. In fact, since large portions of the foregoing story have not been made public before this, the reader is an insider in a sense highly unusual in a murder case. And, in a way, I'm a newcomer, an intruder. The sudden switch from an unseen background narrator to a very personal account is bound to be a surprise. The best way to soften it, I suspect, would be to introduce myself; then, when we've got that out of the way, we'll resume the narrative together. This digression, though unfortunately necessary, will be as brief as possible.

A conventional biographical sketch would probably have read more or less as follows: Vincent T. Bugliosi, age thirty-five, Deputy District Attorney, Los Angeles, California. Born Hibbing, Minnesota. Graduate Hollywood High School. Attended the University of Miami on a tennis scholarship, B.A. and B.B.A. degrees. Deciding on the practice of law, attended UCLA, LL.B. degree, president graduating class 1964. Joined the Los Angeles County District Attorney's Office same year. Has tried a number of highly publicized murder cases—Floyd-Milton, Perveler-Cromwell, etc.—obtaining convictions in all. Has tried 104 felony jury trials, losing only one. In addition to his duties as deputy DA, Bugliosi is a professor of criminal law at Beverly School of Law, Los Angeles. Served as technical consultant and edited the scripts of two pilot films for Jack Webb's TV series "The D.A." Series star Robert Conrad patterned his part after the young prosecutor. Married. Two children.

That's probably about how it would read, yet it tells nothing about how I feel toward my profession, which is even more important.

"The primary duty of a lawyer engaged in public prose-cution is not to convict, but to see that justice is done . . ."

Those words are from the old Canon of Ethics of the American Bar Association. I'd thought of them often during the five years I'd been a deputy DA. In a very real sense they had become my personal credo. If, in a given case, a conviction is justice, so be it. But if it is not, I want no part of it.

For far too many years the stereotyped image of the prosecutor has been either that of a right-wing, law-and-order type intent on winning convictions at any cost, or a stumbling, bumbling Hamilton Burger, forever trying innocent people, who, fortunately, are saved at the last possible minute by the foxy maneuverings of a Perry Mason.

I've never felt the defense attorney has a monopoly on concern for innocence, fairness, and justice. After joining the DA's office, I tried close to a thousand cases. In a great many I sought and obtained convictions, because I believed the evidence warranted them. In a great many others, in which I felt the evidence was insufficient, I stood up in court and asked for a dismissal of the charges, or requested a reduction in either the charges or the sentence.

The latter cases rarely make headlines. Only infrequently does the public learn of them. Thus the stereotype remains. Far more important, however, is the realization that fairness and justice have prevailed.

Just as I never felt the slightest compunction to conform to this stereotype, so did I rebel against another. Traditionally, the role of the prosecutor has been twofold: to handle the legal aspects of the case; and to present in court the evidence gathered by law-enforcement agencies. I never accepted these limitations. In past cases I always joined in the investigation—going out and interviewing witnesses myself, tracking down and developing new leads, often finding evidence otherwise overlooked. In some cases, this led to the release of a suspect. In others, to a conviction that otherwise might not have been obtained.

For a lawyer to do less than his utmost is, I strongly feel, a betrayal of his client. Though in criminal trials one tends to focus on the defense attorney and his client the accused, the prosecutor is also a lawyer, and he too has a client: the People. And the People are equally entitled to their day in court, to a fair and impartial trial, and to justice.

The Tate-LaBianca case was the farthest thing from my mind on the afternoon of November 18, 1969. I'd just completed a long trial and was on my way back to my office in the Hall of Justice when Aaron Stovitz, head of the Trials Division of the District Attorney's Office, one of the top trial lawyers in an office of 450 deputy district attorneys, grabbed me by the arm and, without a word of explanation, hurried me down the hall into the office of J. Miller Leavy, director of Central Operations.

Leavy was talking to two LAPD lieutenants I'd worked with on previous cases, Bob Helder and Paul LePage. Listening for a minute, I heard the word "Tate." Turning to Aaron, I asked, "Are *we* going to handle it?"

He nodded affirmatively.

My only comment was a low whistle.

Helder and LePage gave us a sketchy résumé of what Ronnie Howard had said. As a follow-up to Mossman and Brown's visit the previous night, two other officers had gone to Sybil Brand that morning and talked to Ronnie for a couple of hours. They had obtained considerably more detail, but there were still huge gaps in the story.

To say that the Tate and LaBianca cases had been "solved" at this point would be a gross overstatement. Obviously, in any murder case finding the killer is extremely important. But it's only a first step. Neither the finding, the arresting, nor the indicting of a defendant has evidentiary value and none are proof of guilt. Once the killer is identified, there remains the difficult (and sometimes insurmountable) problem of connecting him with the crime by strong, admissible evidence, then proving his guilt beyond a reasonable doubt, be it before a judge or a jury.

And as yet we hadn't even made the first step, much less the second. In talking to Ronnie Howard, Susan Atkins had implicated herself and "Charles," presumably meaning Charles Manson. But Susan had also said that others were involved, and we lacked their actual identities. This was on Tate. On LaBianca there was virtually no information.

One of the first things I wanted to do, after reviewing the Howard and DeCarlo statements, was to go to Spahn Ranch. Arrangements were made for me to go out the next morning with several of the detectives. I asked Aaron if he wanted to come along, but he couldn't make it.*

When I returned home late that afternoon and told my wife, Gail, that Aaron and I had been assigned the Tate case, she shared my excitement. But with reservations. She had been hoping that we could take a vacation. It had been months since I'd taken a full day off. Even when I was at home in the evenings, I was either reading transcripts, researching law, or preparing arguments. Although every day I made sure I spent some time with our two children, Vince, Jr., three, and Wendy, five, when I was on a big case I totally immersed myself in it. I promised Gail I'd try to take a few days off, but I honestly had to admit that it might be a while before I could do so.

At that time we were, fortunately, unaware that I would be living with the Tate-LaBianca cases for almost two years, averaging one hundred hours per week, rarely, if ever, getting to bed before 2 A.M. seven days per week. And that the few moments Gail, the kids, and I had together would be devoid of privacy, our home transformed into a fortress, a bodyguard not only living with us but accompanying me everywhere I went, following a threat by Charles Manson that he would "kill Bugliosi."

---

* Although Aaron was my superior in the office, we had been assigned the case as co-prosecutors, each of us having an equal say in its handling. Though neither of us could have foreseen that months later Aaron would be yanked off the case, leaving me to go it alone, I did realize from the start that owing to his other duties as head of the Trials Division his participation would be limited.

November 19-21, 1969

We'd picked a hell of a day for a search. The wind was incredible. By the time we reached Chatsworth, it was almost buffeting us off the road.

It wasn't a long drive, well under an hour. From the Hall of Justice in downtown Los Angeles it's about thirty miles to Chatsworth. Going north on Topanga Canyon Boulevard past Devonshire for about two miles, we made a sharp left onto Santa Susana Pass Road. Once heavily traveled but in recent years bypassed for a faster freeway, the two-lane road winds upward a mile or two. Then, suddenly, around a bend and to the left, there it was, Spahn's Movie Ranch.

Its ramshackle Main Street was less than twenty yards from the highway, in plain view. Wrecked automobile and truck bodies littered the area. There wasn't a sign of life.

There was an unreality to the place, accentuated by the roaring wind and the appearance of total desertion, but even more so by the knowledge, if the Atkins-Howard story was true, of what had begun and ended here. A run-down movie set, off in the middle of nowhere, from which dark-clad assassins would venture out at night, to terrorize and kill, then return before dawn to vanish into the surroundings. It might have been the plot of a horror film, except that Sharon Tate and at least eight other real human beings were now dead.

We pulled off onto the dirt road, stopping in front of the Long Branch Saloon. In addition to myself, there were Lieutenant Helder and Sergeant Calkins of the Tate team; Sergeant Lee of SID; Sergeants Guenther, Whiteley, and William Gleason from LASO; and our guide, Danny DeCarlo. Danny had finally agreed to accompany us, but only on one condition: that we handcuff him. That way, if any members of the Family were still around, they wouldn't think he was voluntarily "flapping to the fuzz."

Though the sheriff's deputies had been to the ranch before, we needed DeCarlo for a specific purpose: to point out the areas where Manson and the Family target-practiced. The object of our search: any .22 caliber bullets and/or shell casings.

But first I wanted to obtain George Spahn's permission to search the ranch. Guenther pointed out his shack, which was to the right and apart from the Western set. We knocked and a voice, that of a young girl, said, "Come right on in."

It was as if every fly in the area had taken shelter there during the storm. Eighty-one-year-old George Spahn was sitting in a decaying armchair, wearing a Stetson and dark glasses. In his lap was a Chihuahua, at his feet a cocker spaniel. A hippie girl of about eighteen was fixing his lunch, while a transistor radio, tuned to a cowboy station, blared "Young Love" by Sonny James.

It seemed as staged as the setting itself: according to DeCarlo, Manson called his girls "young loves."

Because of Spahn's near blindness, Calkins handed him his badge to feel. Once we had identified ourselves, Spahn seemed to relax. Asked for permission to search, he magnanimously replied, "It's my ranch and you're welcome to search it any time you want to, day or night, and as often as you like." I explained his legal rights. Under the law, no search warrant was required, only his permission. If he did give permission, however, it might be necessary at some later date for him to testify to this in court. Spahn still agreed.

There was no mention of Manson and his Family. But Spahn must have known that they were in some way the reason for our being there. Although on other occasions I would interview George at length, our conversation at this time was brief and confined to the search.

Once we went back outside, people began appearing from almost every building. There must have been ten to fifteen, most of them young, most in hippie-type clothes, although a few appeared to be ranch hands. How many, if any, were actual members of the Family we didn't know.

While looking around, I heard some odd sounds coming from a doghouse. Leaning down and looking in, I saw two dogs and, crouched in the corner, a toothless, white-haired old woman of about eighty. I later checked with one of the ranch hands to see if she needed help, but he said she was happy where she was.

It was a very strange place.

About a hundred yards behind the main cluster of buildings there was a drop down to a creek, then, beyond it, the hills rose up and became a part of the Santa Susana mountain range. Rocky, brush covered, the area looked far more rugged than it actually was. I wondered how many times as a boy I'd seen this scene in B-grade cowboy films. According to Lutesinger and DeCarlo, it was here, in the canyons and gullies behind the ranch, and across the road, in Devil's Canyon, that the Family hid out from the police. Here, too, somewhere in this area, if the various accounts were correct, were the remains of Donald "Shorty" Shea.

Charlie's favorite firing spot, DeCarlo said, was in the creek bed, well out of sight from the road. As targets he used fence posts and a trash can. Under the direction of Sergeant Lee, we began searching. Though no shell casings had been found at 10050 Cielo Drive—the Buntline being a revolver, which doesn't automatically eject its shell casings—we wanted to collect both in case the gun or additional evidence was found.

While we were searching the creek bed, I kept thinking about George Spahn, alone and almost defenseless in his blindness. I asked, "Anybody bring a tape recorder?" Calkins had; it was in the back of his car. "Let's go back and get Spahn's consent on tape," I said. "Between now and the time we go to trial, I don't want some s.o.b. putting a knife to Spahn's throat, forcing him to say he didn't give us permission." We went back and taped Spahn's consent. It was for his protection as well as our own; knowing the tape existed could be discouragement.

DeCarlo indicated another area, about a quarter of a mile up one of the canyons, where Charlie and the men sometimes target-practiced. We found a number of bullets and shell casings there. Because of the wind and dust, the search was less thorough than I'd hoped for; however, Sergeant Lee promised to return at a later date and see what he could find.

Altogether, that day we found approximately sixty-eight .22 caliber bullets (approximate because some were fragments rather than whole slugs) and twenty-two shell casings of the same caliber. Lee put them in envelopes, noting where and when found, and took them back to the police lab with him.

While looking around the corral area, I spotted some white nylon rope, but it was two-strand, not three.

Guenther and Whiteley had made their own find, in Danny DeCarlo. That afternoon they interviewed him on the Hinman murder and Beausoleil's confession. The only problem was that the Beausoleil trial had been going on for a week now, and both the prosecution and defense had rested.

Against the objections of Beausoleil's attorney, a continuance was obtained until the following Monday, at which time the prosecution hoped to reopen its case to introduce the confession.

It was agreed that if DeCarlo testified in the Beausoleil trial, LASO would drop the motorcycle engine theft charge against him.

On my return to the Hall of Justice there was a meeting in the office of the then Assistant District Attorney, Joseph Busch. Present in addition to Busch, Stovitz, and myself from the DA's Office were Lieutenant Paul LePage (LaBianca) and Sergeant Mike McGann (Tate) representing LAPD.

The police wanted to wrap up the case, Lieutenant Le-Page informed us. The public pressure on LAPD to solve these murders was unbelievable. Every time Chief Edward M. Davis encountered a reporter, he was asked, "What, if anything, is happening on Tate?"

LAPD wanted to offer Susan Atkins immunity, in exchange for telling what she knew about the murders.

I was in total disagreement. "If what she told Ronnie Howard is true, Atkins personally stabbed to death Sharon

Tate, Gary Hinman, and who knows how many others!
We don't give that gal anything!"

Chief Davis wanted to rush the case to the grand jury,
LePage said. But before that he wanted to break the news
that we had caught the killers in a big press conference.

"We don't even *have* a case to take to the grand jury,"
I told LePage. "We're not even sure who the killers are,
or if they're free or in custody. All we have is a good
lead, but we're getting there. Let's see if, on our own, we
can get enough evidence to nail all of them. If we can't,
then, as a last resort—a very, very last resort—we can
turn to Atkins."

I could sympathize with LAPD; the media were blasting
the department almost daily. On the other hand, it would
be nothing compared to the public response if we let
Susan Atkins walk off scot-free. I couldn't forget Susan
describing how it felt to taste Sharon Tate's blood: "Wow,
what a trip!"

LePage was firm; LAPD wanted to make a deal. I conferred with Busch and Stovitz; they were far less adamant
than I. Against my very strong objections, Busch told Le-
Page that the DA's Office would be willing to settle for a
second degree murder plea for Atkins.

Susan Atkins would be offered a deal. The precise
terms, or whether she would even accept them, remained
unknown.

At eight that night, the citizens of Los Angeles still
thinking that the Tate-LaBianca killers were completely
unknown, two cars sped out of Los Angeles, their destination the last home of the Manson Family: Death Valley.

It seemed more than ironic that, following the murders,
Manson had chosen as his refuge a place so aptly named.

Sergeants Nielsen, Sartuchi, and Granado were in one
car, Sergeants McGann, Gene Kamadoi, and I were in the
other. We broke a few speed limits along the way, arriving
in Independence, California, at 1:30 A.M.

Independence, seat of Inyo County, is not a large town.
The county itself, though second largest in the state, has
less than 16,000 residents, just over one per square mile.

If one were looking for a hideaway, he could find few better.

We checked into the Winnedumah Hotel for what amounted to little more than a long nap. When I got up at 5:30, the temperature had dropped below zero. I slipped my clothes on over my pajamas and was still cold.

Before leaving Los Angeles, I had telephoned Frank Fowles, Inyo County DA, and we had arranged to meet at a nearby café at 6 A.M. Fowles, his deputy Buck Gibbens, and their investigator Jack Gardiner were already there. The three men were, I would soon learn, very conscientious; the help they would give us in the months ahead would be considerable. At the moment they were also very excited. Unexpectedly, they were in the middle of one of the most publicized murder cases in modern history, the Tate case. Then, with puzzled looks, they'd glance across the table at the big-city prosecutor, pajamas sticking out of his cuffs.

Fowles told me that although they had seized some of Manson's belongings during the October raid on Barker Ranch, a number of things remained there, including an old school bus, which was littered with clothing and other items. I suggested that before leaving Independence we obtain a search warrant for the ranch that specifically mentioned the bus.

This caught Fowles by surprise. I explained that if we did find evidence, and wished to use it in a trial, we didn't want it suppressed just because someone suddenly appeared with a pink slip saying, "I'm the real owner of the bus. I only loaned it to Charlie, and you didn't get my permission."

Fowles understood that. It was only, he explained cryptically, that they didn't do things quite that way in Inyo County. We returned to his office and, after waiting for the typist to come to work, I dictated the warrant.

It was necessary to state exactly what we were looking for. Among the items I enumerated were: a .22 caliber revolver; knives and other weapons; rope; wire cutters; wallet, driver's license, and credit cards belonging to Rosemary LaBianca; motor plates to any vehicle; any male and/or female clothing, including footwear.

It was also necessary that I cite the crime—187 PC, murder—and the suspected perpetrators—"tentatively believed to be CHARLES MANSON, CLEM TUFTS, CHARLES MONTGOMERY, SADIE GLUTZ, and one or more additional females." The information was based on the testimony of two "untested informants," whom I did not name but who were Ronnie Howard and Danny DeCarlo.

When typed, the warrant ran to sixteen pages. It was an impressive document, the evidence cited therein more than sufficient to obtain a search warrant. Only I was aware how weak our case actually was.

With McGann and me tagging along, Fowles took the warrant to the office of Judge John P. McMurray. The white-haired jurist was, I guessed, in his seventies; he told us he was near retirement.

A search warrant! Judge McMurray looked at it with amusement. This was the first one he had seen in eighteen years, he told us. In Inyo, he explained, men are men. If you knock on a door and the people inside don't want to let you in, you assume they are hiding something, and bust the door in. A search warrant indeed! But he read and signed it.*

The trip to Barker Ranch would take three hours, leaving us little more than an hour to search before the sun set. En route Fowles told me some of the things he had learned about the Manson Family.† The first few members—in effect, a scouting party—had appeared in the area in the fall of 1968. Since you have to be somewhat different to want to live on the edge of Death Valley, residents of the area had developed a tolerance for people who elsewhere would have been considered odd types. The hippies were no

---

*In 1971, California Governor Ronald Reagan arranged to have Judge McMurray taken out of retirement to try the Angela Davis case. The defense challenged him for cause.

†Exact dates, details, quotes from the investigating officers, etc. I would obtain the following day when going over reports of the various law-enforcement agencies.

When booked, almost all the Family members used aliases. In a number of cases their true names were not known until much later. To avoid confusing the reader as much as I was confused at the time, true names and most-used aliases have been inserted in brackets.

stranger than others who passed through—prospectors, desert rats, chasers after legendary lost mines. There were only a few minor brushes with the authorities—the girls were advised to desist from panhandling in Shoshone, and one made the mistake of giving a marijuana cigarette to a fifteen-year-old girl, who just happened to be the sheriff's niece—until September 9, 1969, when National Park Rangers discovered that someone had attempted to burn a Michigan loader, a piece of earth-moving equipment that was parked in the race-track area of Death Valley National Monument. It appeared a senseless act of vandalism. Automobile tracks leading away from the area were determined to belong to a Toyota. Several persons recalled seeing the hippies driving a red Toyota and a dune buggy. On September 21, Park Ranger Dick Powell spotted a 1969 red Toyota in the Hail and Hall area. The four females and one male who were riding in it were questioned but not detained. Powell later ran a license check, learning that the plates on the Toyota belonged to another vehicle. On September 24, Powell returned to look for the group, but they had gone. On September 29, Powell, accompanied by California Highway Patrolman James Pursell, decided to check out Barker Ranch. They found two young girls there, but no vehicles. As they had found standard in their contacts with this group, the girls gave vague, uncommunicative answers to their questions. As the officers were leaving the area, they encountered a truck driven by Paul Crockett, forty-six, a local miner. With him was Brooks Poston, eighteen, who had previously been a member of the hippie band but was now working for Crockett. On hearing that there were two girls at the ranch, Crockett and Poston appeared apprehensive and, when questioned, finally admitted that they feared for their lives.

Powell and Pursell decided to accompany them back to Barker. The two girls had vanished, but the officers presumed they were still nearby, probably watching them. They began questioning Crockett and Poston.

The officers had come looking for arson suspects, and a possible stolen vehicle. They found something totally unexpected. From Pursell's report: "The interview resulted in some of the most unbelievable and fantastic information we had ever heard: tales of drug use, sex orgies, the actual attempt to re-create the days of Rommel and the Desert Corps by tearing over the countryside by night in numerous dune buggies, the stringing of field phones around the area for rapid communication, the opinion of the leader that he is Jesus Christ and seemed to be trying to form a cult of some sort ..."

The surprises weren't over. Before leaving Barker, Powell and Pursell decided to check out some draws back of the ranch. To quote Powell: "In doing so we stumbled into a group of seven females, all nude or partially so, hiding behind various clumps of sagebrush." They saw one male, but he ran away when they approached. They questioned the girls but received no useful information. In searching the area, the officers found the red Toyota and a dune buggy, carefully camouflaged with tarps.

The officers had a problem. Because of the Panamint mountain range, they couldn't use their police radio. They decided to leave and return later with more men. Before departing, they removed several parts from the engine of the Toyota, rendering it inoperative; the dune buggy had no engine, so they weren't concerned with it.

They would later learn that "as soon as we left, the suspects pulled a complete Volkswagen engine from under a pile of brush, put it in the disabled dune buggy, and drove off within two hours."

A check on the two vehicles revealed "wants" on both. The Toyota had been rented from a Hertz agency in Encino, a town near Los Angeles, on a credit card stolen in a residential burglary. The dune buggy had been stolen off a used-car lot only three days before Powell and Pursell saw it.

On the night of October 9, officers from the California Highway Patrol, the Inyo County Sheriff's Office, and National Park rangers assembled near Barker for a massive raid on the ranch, to commence the following morning.

At about 4 A.M., as several of the officers were proceeding down one of the draws some distance from the ranch, they spotted two males asleep on the ground. Between them was a sawed-off shotgun. The two, Clem Tufts [t/n Steve Grogan] and Randy Morglea [t/n Hugh Rocky

Todd], were placed under arrest. Though the officers were unaware of it, the pair had been stalking human game: Stephanie Schram and Kitty Lutesinger, two seventeen-year-old girls who had fled the ranch the previous day.

Another male, Robert Ivan Lane [aka Soupspoon], was apprehended on a hill overlooking the ranch. Lane had been acting as lookout but had fallen asleep. There was still another lookout post, this one a very well disguised dugout, its tin roof hidden by brush and dirt, on a hill south of the ranch. The officers had almost passed it when they saw a female emerge from the brush, squat, and urinate, then disappear back into the bushes. While two officers covered the entrance with their rifles, one climbed above the dugout and dropped a large rock on the tin roof. The occupants rushed out. Apprehended were: Louella Maxwell Alexandria [t/n Leslie Van Houten, aka Leslie Sankston]; Marnie Kay Reeves [t/n Patricia Krenwinkel]; and Manon Minette [t/n Catherine Share, aka Gypsy].

Those inside the ranch house were caught unawares, and offered no resistance. They were: Donna Kay Powell [t/n Susan Denise Atkins, aka Sadie Mae Glutz]; Elizabeth Elaine Williamson [t/n Lynette Fromme, aka Squeaky]; and Linda Baldwin [t/n Madaline Cottage, aka Little Patty.]

Other members of the raiding party surrounded nearby Myers Ranch, where the group had also been staying, arresting: Sandra Collins Pugh [this was her married name; her maiden name was Sandra Good, aka Sandy]; Rachel Susan Morse [t/n Ruth Ann Moorehouse, aka Ouisch]; Mary Ann Schwarm [t/n Diane Von Ahn]; and Cydette Perell [t/n Nancy Pitman, aka Brenda McCann.]

A total of ten females and three males were arrested during this first sweep of the Barker Ranch area. They ranged in age from sixteen to twenty-six, with the average nineteen or twenty. Two babies were also found: Zezozose Zadfrack Glutz, age one year, whose mother was Susan Atkins; and Sunstone Hawk, age one month, whose mother was Sandra Good. Both were badly sunburned. Mrs. Powell, wife of ranger Dick Powell, who had been brought along as matron, took care of them.

A search of the area revealed a number of hidden vehicles, mostly dune buggies, mostly stolen; a mailbag with a .22 Ruger single-shot pistol inside, also stolen; a number of knives; and caches of food, gasoline, and other supplies. Also found were more sleeping bags than people, indicating that there might be others still in the area.

The officers decided to take the prisoners into Independence and book them, then make a surprise raid at a later date, in case the others returned.

The strategy paid off. The second raid occurred on October 12, two days after the first. CHP officer Pursell and two Park rangers arrived in the area before their support and were hiding in the brush, waiting for the others, when they saw four males walk from one of the washes to the ranch house and enter. Pursell spotted sheriff's deputy Don Ward of the backup unit approaching in the distance. It was already after 6 P.M., the dusk rapidly becoming dark. Not wanting to risk a gunfight at night, Pursell decided to act. While Powell covered the front of the building, Pursell drew his gun and, to quote from his report, "I quickly moved to the back door, flung it open, and making as much use of the wall on the left of the doorway as possible, I ordered all occupants to remain still and place their hands on their heads."

The group, most of whom had been sitting around the kitchen table, were ordered outside, lined up, and searched. There were three females: Dianne Bluestein [t/n Dianne Lake, aka Snake]; Beth Tracy [t/n Collie Sinclair]; and Sherry Andrews [t/n Claudia Leigh Smith]. Plus four males: Bruce McGregor Davis [aka Bruce McMillan]; Christopher Jesus [t/n John Philip Haught, aka Zero, who in less than a month would be shot to death while allegedly playing Russian roulette]; Kenneth Richard Brown [aka Scott Bell Davis, Zero's partner from Ohio]; and one Lawrence Bailey [aka Larry Jones.]

There was no sign of the group's leader, Charles Manson. Pursell decided to recheck the house. It was completely dark now. However, a homemade candle was burning in a glass mug on the table, and, taking that, he began searching the rooms. On entering the bathroom, "I was forced to move the candle around quite a bit, as it made a

very poor light. I lowered the candle toward the hand ba-
sin, and small cupboard below, and saw long hair hanging
out of the top of the cupboard, which was partially open."
It seemed impossible that a person could get into such a
small space, but, without Pursell's having to say anything,
"a figure began to emerge from the tiny cupboard. After I
recovered from the initial shock, I advised the subject to
continue out and not make any false moves. As he
emerged, he made a comment, more or less in a humorous
vein, about being glad to get out of that cramped space.

"The subject was dressed entirely in buckskins, much
differently than all the others we had found ... I asked
the subject who he was. He immediately replied, 'Charlie
Manson.' He was taken to the back door and turned over
to the officers outside."

On re-entering the house, Pursell found still another
male, who was just emerging from the bedroom. He was
David Lee Hamic [aka Bill Vance, an ex-con with more
aliases than Manson.] Pursell noted the time: 6:40 P.M.

None of the suspects were armed, although several
sheath knives were found on the kitchen table.

The prisoners were handcuffed and, hands on heads,
walked single file toward Sourdough Springs, where the officers had left two pickups. En route they encountered two
more females driving a car loaded with groceries. Also
placed under arrest were: Patti Sue Jardin [t/n Catherine
Gillies], and Sue Bartell [aka Country Sue] All the suspects were loaded in the back of one pickup, the second
following immediately behind to provide illumination. As
they neared the Lotus Mine area, about three miles from
Barker, Manson told the officers that he had left his pack
there, near the side of the road. Pursell: "He asked us to
stop and pick it up, which we agreed to do; however, we
could not locate it by his directions, and we refused to let
him loose to search himself as he requested."

On the way to Independence, Manson told Pursell and
Ward that the blacks were going to take over the country
and that he and his group only wanted to find a quiet,
peaceful place away from the conflict. But the establishment, as represented by the police, wouldn't let them
alone. He also told them that they, being both cops and

white, were in deep trouble and should escape to the desert or somewhere while they still had the chance.

Also during the ride, again according to Pursell, "two things happened which indicated to me the leadership exerted over the group by subject Manson. At least twice Charlie made statements that would cause the others to say 'amen' two or three times in unison. Also, a few times when the others would become involved in whispered, giggly conversations, Charlie would simply look at them and immediately they would fall silent.

"The amazing part of the stare," Pursell noted, "was how obvious the results were without a word being spoken."

On arriving in Independence, the suspects were charged with grand theft auto, arson, and various other offenses. The leader of the Family was fingerprinted, photographed, and booked as "MANSON, CHARLES M., aka JESUS CHRIST, GOD."

According to Frank Fowles, although all but three of the eleven vehicles recovered were stolen, there was insufficient evidence to link most of the group with the thefts, and after a few days more than half of those arrested were released. Though most had left the area, two of the girls, Squeaky and Sandy, had rented a motel room and were staying in Independence, so they could run errands for Manson and the others still in custody.

I asked Fowles if he knew why the group had come to the area in the first place. He told me that one of the girls, Cathy Gillies, was the granddaughter of the woman who owned Myers Ranch. The Family had apparently camped there first, then moved to nearby Barker. After the raid a sheriff's deputy interviewed Mrs. Arlene Barker, who was living at Indian Ranch in the Panamint Valley. She told him that about a year ago Manson had visited her, asking permission to camp at Barker Ranch. Like George Spahn, Mrs. Barker presumed there were only a few people and that they intended to stay only a few days. On this visit Manson gave her a gold record which had been presented to the Beach Boys, commemorating one million dollars in sales of their LP "The Beach Boys Today." Manson told her that he was the composer or arranger for the group. Manson had contacted her again, two or three weeks before the October raid, wanting to buy Barker Ranch. She told him she wanted cash; Manson said he'd see her again when he had it.

Apparently Manson felt that if he actually owned the property he would have fewer problems with local law-enforcement agencies.

I was unaware until much later that Manson supposedly had an alternate plan, to get control of Myers Ranch, which called for murdering Cathy's grandmother, and that the plan had been frustrated by something very simple and commonplace: while en route to her home, the three killers he'd chosen had a flat tire.

I asked Fowles about the evidence recovered in the raids and subsequent searches. Were any of the knives Buck brand? Yes, several. Any rope? No. What about wire cutters? Yes, there was a big red pair; they'd found them in the back of what they later learned was Manson's personal, or command, dune buggy. Aside from the Ruger .22 and Clem's shotgun, any other firearms? Not one, Fowles said. In none of the searches did the officers turn up the machine guns, shotguns, rifles, pistols, and large stores of ammunition Crockett, Poston, and others said the Family had.

Throughout the trials that followed, we would remain very aware that those members of the Family still at large probably had access to a sizable cache of arms and ammunition.

Barker Ranch was located in Golar Wash, one of seven dry washes in the Panamint range, approximately twenty-two miles southeast of Ballarat. He had been all over the country, Fowles told me; those dry washes comprised the roughest terrain he had ever seen; we'd have to walk much of it, he said, otherwise our heads would bounce through the roof of the four-wheel-drive jeep Fowles had chosen for the trip.

"Ah, come on, Frank," I said, "it can't be that rough."

It was. The washes were extremely narrow and rock-strewn. Going up them, we'd frequently gain one foot, then with an angry screech of rubber, slide back two. You could smell the tires burning. Finally, Fowles and I got out of the vehicle and walked in front of it, removing boulders as McGann drove forward, foot after foot. It took us two hours to travel five miles.

I asked Fowles to have photographs taken of the washes. I wanted to show the jury how isolated and remote an area the killers had chosen for their hiding place. Circumstantial evidence, a tiny speck, but of such specks, one after another, are strong cases made.

No one would have chosen to live at either Barker or Myers Ranch, which were about a quarter of a mile apart, except for one thing: there was water. There was even a swimming pool at Barker, though, like the stone ranch house and outlying shacks, it was in disrepair. The house was small—living room, bedroom, kitchen, bathroom. I also wanted photos of the cabinet under the sink where Manson hid. It measured 3 by 1½ by 1½ feet. I could see why Pursell was so surprised.

When I saw the large school bus, I couldn't believe Manson had brought it up one of the washes. He hadn't, Fowles told me; he'd driven it in over the road on the Las Vegas side. Even that had been an ordeal, and the condition of the bus showed it. It was a battered green and white. On the side was an American flag decal with the slogan AMERICA—LOVE IT OR LEAVE IT. While Sartuchi and the others searched the house, I went to work on the abandoned bus.

The placement of the warrant took some thought. It had to be left in sight. However, if it was, anyone could come along and remove it. I didn't want a defense attorney contending we hadn't fulfilled the requirements of the search. I put it on one of the racks just under the roof of the bus. You *could* see it, if you looked up.

At least a foot of clothing was piled on the floor. I later learned that wherever the Family stayed, they kept a community clothing pile. When an item was needed, they'd root through the pile until they found it. I got down on my hands and knees and began rooting too. I was looking for two things in particular: clothing with bloodstains, and boots. A bloody boot-heel print had been found on the front porch of the Tate residence. There was a small mark, a little indentation, in the heel that I was hoping we could match up. Although I found several boots, none had such a mark. And when Joe Granado applied the benzidine test to the clothing, the results were uniformly negative. I had all the clothing taken back to L.A. anyway, hoping SID might come up with something in the lab.

There were eight to ten magazines in the bus, half of which were *National Geographics*. Looking through them, I noticed something curious: all dated from 1939 to 1945 and all had articles on Hitler. One also had photographs of Rommel and his Desert Corps.

But that was about all we found. Our search appeared to have yielded little, if anything, of evidentiary value. However, I was anxious to go through the items picked up in the raids.

On the way back to Independence we stopped in Lone Pine. While I was nursing a beer with the officers, Sartuchi remarked that he and Patchett had interviewed Manson in Independence some weeks earlier, questioning him about the Tate as well as the LaBianca murders. The following day when I called Lieutenant Helder, I mentioned this, thinking he probably had a report on the interview. Helder was amazed; he had no idea anyone from LAPD had ever talked to Manson. This was my first indication that the Tate and LaBianca detectives hadn't exactly been working hand in glove.

Helder did have some news. It wasn't good. Sergeant Lee had run a ballistics comparison on the .22 caliber bullets we'd found at Spahn: all were negative to those recovered at 10050 Cielo Drive.

I wasn't about to give up that easily. I still wanted a much more thorough search of Spahn Ranch.

We stayed at the Winnedumah again that night. Up early the next morning, I walked to the courthouse. I'd forgotten what fresh air smelled like. That trees, grass, have scents. In L.A. there are no smells, just smog. A couple of blocks from the courthouse I saw two young girls, one carrying a baby. It was a wild guess but I asked, "Are you Sandy and Squeaky?" They admitted they were. I identified myself and said that I would like to talk to them in the District Attorney's office at 1 P.M. They said they would come if I would buy them some candy. I said I would.

In the DA's office, Fowles opened his files and gave me everything he had on the Manson Family. Sartuchi set to work photocopying.

In going through the documents, I spotted a reference to Crockett and Poston: "Inyo County Deputy Sheriff Don Ward talked to the two miners in Shoshone and has their entire conversation recorded." I wanted to interview the pair, but it would save time if I heard the tape first, so I asked McGann to contact Ward and get it for me.

There was also an October 2, 1969, California Highway Patrol report in which it was stated: "Deputy Dennis Cox has F.I.R. card on suspect Charles Montgomery, 23 years of age (dob 12-2-45)." Field Interrogation Reports are three-by-five cards that are made whenever a person is stopped and questioned. I wanted to see that card. We still knew very little about Tex, who hadn't been arrested in either the Spahn or Barker raids.

After going through the large stack of documents, I started on the evidence seized in the October 10-12 raid. I had Granado test the knives for blood: negative. The wire cutters were large and heavy. It would have been difficult to shinny up a telephone pole with them; still, maybe they were the only pair available. I gave them to the officers so SID could make comparison cuts on the Tate telephone wires. Boots, but no discernible heel mark; I put them aside for SID. I checked the labels on all the clothing, noting that a number of the women's garments, though now filthy, came from expensive shops. I had them taken to L.A. for analysis. I also wanted Winifred Chapman and Susan Struthers to look at them, to see if any of the items might have been the property of Sharon Tate, Abigail Folger, or Rosemary LaBianca.

Squeaky and Sandy kept the appointment. I'd done a little checking before talking to them. Though the information was sketchy, I knew that both had been born in Southern California, and had come from fairly well-to-do families. Squeaky's parents lived in Santa Monica; her father was an aeronautical engineer. Sandy's parents had divorced and remarried; her father was a San Diego stockbroker. According to DeCarlo, when Sandy joined the Family, sometime early in 1968, she had some $6,000 in stocks, which she sold, giving the money to Manson. She and her baby were now on welfare. Both girls had started college, then dropped out, Squeaky attending El Camino Junior College in Torrance, Sandy the University of Oregon and San Francisco State. Squeaky had been one of the earliest members of the Family, I later learned, casting her lot with Manson just months after he got out of prison in 1967.

They were the first Family members I had talked to, other than DeCarlo, who was a fringe member at best, and I was immediately struck by their expressions. They seemed to radiate inner contentment. I'd seen others like this—true believers, religious fanatics—yet I was both shocked and impressed. Nothing seemed to faze them. They smiled almost continuously, no matter what was said. For them all the questions had been answered. There was no need to search any more, because they had found the truth. And their truth was "Charlie is love."

Tell me about this love, I asked them. Do you mean this in the male-female sense? Yes, that too, they answered, but that was only a part. More all-encompassing? Yes, but "Love is love; you can't define it."

Did Charlie teach you this? I asked, genuinely curious. Charlie did not need to teach them, they said. Charlie only turned them around so they could look at themselves and see the love within. Did they believe that Charlie was Jesus Christ? They only smiled enigmatically, as if sharing a secret no one else could possibly understand.

Although Squeaky was twenty-one and Sandy twenty-five, there was a little-girl quality to them, as if they hadn't aged but had been retarded at a certain stage in their childhood. Little girls, playing little-girl games. Including murder? I wondered.

Is your love for Charlie, say, different from your love for George Spahn? I asked Squeaky. No, love is love, Squeaky said; it's all the same. But she'd hesitated just a moment before answering, giving the impression that though these were the words she was supposed to say, there was heresy in them, in denying that Charlie was special. Perhaps to overcome this, she told me about her relationship with George Spahn. She was in love with George, Squeaky said; if he asked her to marry him, she would. George was, she went on, a beautiful person inside. He was also, she added, in an obvious attempt to shock me, very good in bed. She was quite graphic.

"I'm not that interested in your sex life, Squeaky," I told her. "But I am very, very interested in what you know about the Tate, LaBianca, Hinman, and other murders."

Neither expression changed in the slightest. The smiles remained. They knew nothing about any crimes. All they knew about was love.

I talked to them for a long time, asking specific questions now, but still getting pat answers. On asking where they were on a certain date, for example, they'd reply, "There is no such thing as time." The answers were both non-responsive and a guard. I wanted to get past that guard, to learn what they really felt. I couldn't.

I sensed something else. Each was, in her own way, a pretty girl. But there was a sameness about them that was much stronger than their individuality. I'd notice it again later that afternoon, in talking to other female members of the Family. Same expressions, same patterned responses, same tone of voice, same lack of distinct personality. The realization came with a shock; they reminded me less of human beings than Barbie dolls.

Looking at Sandy's almost beatific smile, I remembered something that Frank Fowles had told me, and a chill ran up and down my spine.

While she was still in jail in Independence, Sandy had been overheard talking to one of the other girls in the Family. Sandy had told her, "I've finally reached the point where I can kill my parents."

Leslie, Ouisch, Snake, Brenda, Gypsy—Frank Fowles arranged to have them brought over from the jail, where they were still being held on charges stemming from the

Barker raid. Like Squeaky and Sandy, they accepted my "bribe," candy and gum, and told me nothing of importance. Their answers were as if rehearsed; often they gave identical responses.

If we were to get any of them to talk, I knew, we would have to separate them. There was a cohesion, a kind of cement, that held them together. A part of it was undoubtedly their strange—and to me still puzzling—relationship with Charles Manson. Part was their shared experiences, the world known as the Family. But I couldn't help wondering if another of the ingredients wasn't fear: fear of what the others would say if they talked, fear of what the others would do.

The only way we could find out would be to keep them apart, and owing to the smallness of the jail, it couldn't be done in Independence.

Besides Manson, there was only one male Family member still in custody: Clem Tufts, t/n Steve Grogan. Jack Gardiner, Fowles' investigator, gave me the eighteen-year-old Grogan's rap sheet:

3-23-66, Possession dangerous drugs, 6 mos. probation; 4-27-66, Shoplifting, Cont'd on probation; 6-23-66, Disturbing the peace, Con't on probation; 9-27-66, Probation dismissed; 6-5-67, Possession marijuana, Counseled & released; 8-12-67, Shoplifting, Bail forfeiture; 1-22-68, Loitering, Closed after investigation; 4-5-69, Grand theft money & Prowling, Released insuff. evidence; 5-20-69, Grand theft auto, Released insuff. evidence; 6-11-69, Child molesting & Indecent exposure . . .

Grogan had been observed exposing himself to several children, ages four to five years. "The kids wanted me to," he explained to arresting officers, who had caught him in the act. "I violated the law, the thing fell out of my pants and the parents got excited," he later told a court-appointed psychiatrist. After interviewing Grogan, the psychiatrist ruled *against* committing him to Camarillo State Hospital, because "the minor is much too aggressive to remain in a setting which does not provide containment facilities."

The court decided otherwise, sending him to Camarillo

for a ninety-day observation period. He remained a grand total of two days, then walked away, aided, I would later learn, by one of the girls from the Family.

His escape had occurred on July 19, 1969. He was back at Spahn in time for the Hinman, Tate, and LaBianca murders. He was arrested in the August 16 Spahn raid, but was released two days later, in time to behead Shorty Shea.

Currently, as a result of the Barker raid, he was charged with grand theft auto and possession of an illegal weapon, i.e., the sawed-off shotgun. I asked Fowles the present status of the case.

He said that, at the instigation of Grogan's attorney, he had been examined by two psychiatrists, who had decided that he was "presently insane."

I told Fowles I hoped he would request a jury trial and fight the insanity plea. If I brought Clem to trial in Los Angeles, charged with participating in the Tate murders, I didn't want the defense introducing evidence that a court in Inyo County had already found him insane. Frank agreed to go along with this.

At the moment our case against Grogan was so thin as to be nonexistent. There was no proof that Donald "Shorty" Shea was even dead; to date, no body had been found. As for the Tate murders, all we had was DeCarlo's statement that Clem had told him, "We got five piggies."

There was no way we could use that statement in court if there was a joint trial. In 1965 the California Supreme Court ruled, in the case of *People* vs. *Aranda*, that the prosecution cannot introduce into evidence a statement made by one defendant which implicates a co-defendant.

Since *Aranda* would have a bearing on all the trials involving the Manson Family members, a simplified explanation is in order. For example, if there were a joint trial, with more than one defendant, we couldn't use Susan Atkins' statement to Ronnie Howard, "We did it," the plural being inadmissible because it implicated co-defendants. We could, however, use her statement, "I stabbed Sharon Tate." It is possible to "sanitize" some statements so they don't violate *Aranda*. Susan Atkin's admission to Whiteley and Guenther, "I went to Gary's house with Bobby

Beausoleil" could be edited to "I went to Gary's house," although a good defense attorney can fight, and—depending on the prosecutor and judge—sometimes win the exclusion of even that. But when it came to the pronoun "we," there was no way we could get around it.

Therefore, Manson's statement to Springer, "We knocked off five of them just the other night," was useless. As was Clem's remark to DeCarlo, "We got five piggies."

Manson and Grogan could have made such confessions on nationwide TV and, if there was a joint trial, we could never use their remarks against them.

So we had virtually nothing on Clem.

In going through Grogan's file, I noticed that one of his brothers had made application for the California Highway Patrol; I made note of this, thinking maybe his brother could influence Clem to cooperate with us. DeCarlo had described Grogan in two words: "He's nuts." In his police photograph—big, wide grin, chipped front tooth, moronic stare—he did look idiotic. I asked Fowles for copies of the recent psychiatric reports.

Asked, "Why do you hate your father?" Grogan replied, "I'm my father and I don't hate myself." He denied the use of drugs. "I have my own bennies, adrenalin. It's called fear." He claimed that "love is everything," but, according to one psychiatrist, "he also revealed that he could not accept the philosophy of interracial brotherhood. Quotes supposedly from the Bible with sexual correlation were given in defense of his attitude."

Other quotes from Clem: "I'm dying a little every day. My ego is dying and knows he's dying and struggles hard. When you're free of ego you're free of everything ... Whatever you say is right for yourself ... Whoever you think I am, that's who I am."

The philosophy of Clem? Or Charles Manson? I'd heard the same thoughts, in several instances even identical words, from the girls.

If the psychiatrists had examined one of Manson's followers and, on the basis of such responses, found him insane, what of his leader?

I saw Charles Manson for the first time that day. He was walking from the jail to the courtroom for arraignment on the Michigan loader arson charge, and was accompanied by five sheriff's deputies.

I hadn't realized how small he was. He was just five feet two. He was thin, of slight build, a shade hunchbacked, wore his brown hair very long, almost to his shoulders, and had a good start on a beard, grown—I'd noticed in comparing the LASO and Inyo mug shots—after his arrest in the Spahn Ranch raid. He wore fringed buckskins, which were not inexpensive. Though handcuffed, his walk was casual, not stiff, as though he was completely at ease.

I could not believe that this little guy had done all the things it was said he had. He looked anything but a heavyweight. Yet I knew that to underrate him would be the biggest mistake I could make. For if the Atkins and DeCarlo stories were true, he was not only capable of committing murder himself, he also possessed the incredible power to command others to kill for him.

Manson's girls had talked a great deal about the Indian concept of karma. It was like a boomerang, they said. Whatever you threw out would, eventually, come back to you. I wondered if Manson himself really believed this and if he sensed that, nearly three and a half months after these hideous murders, his own karma was finally returning. He must. You don't assign five sheriff's deputies to an arson suspect. If he didn't know now, he would soon enough, when the jail grapevine repeated some of the questions we'd been asking.

Before leaving Independence, I gave Frank Fowles both my home and office numbers. If there were any developments, I wanted to be notified, whatever the hour. Manson had pleaded not guilty to the arson charge, and his bail had been set at $25,000. If anyone attempted to meet it, I wanted to know immediately, so we could move fast on the murder charges. It might mean revealing our case before we were ready to do so, but the alternative was worse. Aware that he was suspected of murder, once free Manson would probably split. And with Manson at large it would be extremely difficult to get anyone to talk.

That weekend I went through LAPD's files on the Tate-LaBianca murders; the Inyo County files; LASO's reports on the Spahn Ranch raid and other contacts with the Family; and numerous rap sheets. LAPD had conducted over 450 interviews on Tate alone; although they had netted less than had a ten-cent phone call from an ex-hooker, I had to familiarize myself with what had and hadn't been done. I was especially interested in seeing if I could find any link between the Tate-LaBianca victims and the Manson clan. Also, I was looking for some clue as to the motive behind the slayings.

Occasionally writers refer to "motiveless crimes." I've never encountered such an animal, and I'm convinced that none such exists. It may be unconventional; it may be apparent only to the killer or killers; it may even be largely unconscious—but every crime is committed for a reason. The problem, especially in this case, was finding it.

After listening to the seven-hour taped interview with Daniel DeCarlo, I began studying the criminal record of one Manson, Charles M.

I wanted to get to know the man I would be up against.

Charles Manson was born "no name Maddox" on November 12, 1934, in Cincinnati, Ohio, the illegitimate son of a sixteen-year-old girl named Kathleen Maddox.*

Though Manson himself would later state that his mother was a teen-age prostitute, other relatives say she was simply "loose." One remarked, "She ran around a lot,

---

*As with almost everything else written about Manson's early years, even his date of birth is usually given erroneously, although for an understandable reason. Unable to remember her child's birthday, the mother changed it to November 11, which was Armistice Day and an easier date to remember.

drank, got in trouble." Whatever the case, she lived with a succession of men. One, a much older man named William Manson, whom she married, was around just long enough to provide a surname for the youth.

The identity of Charles Manson's father was something of a mystery. In 1936 Kathleen filed a bastardy suit in Boyd County, Kentucky, against one "Colonel Scott,"* a resident of Ashland, Kentucky. On April 19, 1937, the court awarded her a judgment of $25, plus $5 a month for the support of "Charles Milles Manson." Though it was an "agreed judgment," Colonel Scott apparently didn't honor it, for as late as 1940 Kathleen was attempting to file an attachment on his wages. Most accounts state that Colonel Scott died in 1954; though this has never been officially verified, Manson himself apparently believed it. He also stated on numerous occasions that he never met his father.

According to her own relatives, Kathleen would leave the child with obliging neighbors for an hour, then disappear for days or weeks. Usually his grandmother or maternal aunt would have to claim him. Most of his early years were spent with one or the other, in West Virginia, Kentucky, or Ohio.

In 1939 Kathleen and her brother Luther robbed a Charleston, West Virginia, service station, knocking out the attendant with Coke bottles. They were sentenced to five years in the state penitentiary for armed robbery. While his mother was in prison, Manson lived with his aunt and uncle in McMechen, West Virginia. Manson would later tell his counselor at the National Training School for Boys that his uncle and aunt had "some marital difficulty until they became interested in religion and became very extreme."

A very strict aunt, who thought all pleasures sinful but who gave him love. A promiscuous mother, who let him do anything he wanted, just so long as he didn't bother her. The youth was caught in a tug-of-war between the two.

Paroled in 1942, Kathleen reclaimed Charles, then

*His first name remains unknown. Even in official records he is referred to as "Colonel Scott."

eight. The next several years were a blur of run-down hotel rooms and newly introduced "uncles," most of whom, like his mother, drank heavily. In 1947 she tried to have him put in a foster home, but, none being available, the court sent him to the Gibault School for Boys, a caretaking institution in Terre Haute, Indiana. He was twelve years old.

According to school records, he made a "poor institutional adjustment" and "his attitude toward schooling was at best only fair." Though "during the short lapses when Charles was pleasant and feeling happy he presented a likable boy," he had "a tendency toward moodiness and a persecution complex ..." He remained at Gibault ten months, then ran away, returning to his mother.

She didn't want him, and he ran away again. Burglarizing a grocery store, he stole enough money to rent a room. He then broke into several other stores, stealing, among other things, a bicycle. Caught during a burglary, he was placed in the juvenile center in Indianapolis. He escaped the next day. When he was apprehended, the court—erroneously informed that he was Catholic—made arrangements through a local priest to have him accepted at Father Flanagan's Boys Town.

He didn't make its distinguished alumni list. Four days after his arrival, he and another boy, Blackie Nielson, stole a car and fled to the home of Blackie's uncle in Peoria, Illinois. En route they committed two armed robberies—one a grocery store, the other a gambling casino. Among criminals, as in the law itself, a distinction is made between non-violent and violent crimes. Manson had "graduated," committing his first armed robbery at age thirteen.

The uncle was glad to see them. Both boys were small enough to slip through skylights. A week after their arrival in Peoria, the pair broke into a grocery store and stole $1,500. For their efforts, the uncle gave them $150. Two weeks later they tried a repeat, but this time they were caught. Both talked, implicating the uncle. Still only thirteen, Charles Manson was sent to the Indiana School for Boys at Plainfield.

He remained there three years, running away a total of

eighteen times. According to his teachers, "He professed no trust in anyone" and "did good work only for those from whom he figured he could obtain something."

In February 1951, Charles Manson and two other six-teen-year-olds escaped and headed for California. For transportation they stole cars. For support they burglar-zed gas stations—Manson would later estimate they hit fifteen or twenty—before, just outside Beaver, Utah, a roadblock set up for a robbery suspect netted them in-stead.

In taking a stolen vehicle across a state line, the youths had broken a federal law, the Dyer Act. This was the be-ginning of a pattern for Charles Manson of committing federal crimes, which carry far stiffer sentences than local or state offenses.

On March 9, 1951, Manson was ordered confined to the National Training School for Boys, in Washington, D.C., until reaching his majority.

Detailed records were kept on Charles Manson during the time he was there.* On arrival, he was given a battery of aptitude and intelligence tests. Manson's IQ was 109. Though he had completed four years of school, he re-mained illiterate. Intelligence, mechanical aptitude, manual dexterity: all average. Subject liked best: music. Observed his first case worker, with considerable understatement, "Charles is a sixteen-year-old boy who has had an unfa-vorable family life, if it can be called family life at all." He was, the case worker concluded, aggressively antiso-cial.

One month after his arrival: "This boy tries to give the impression that he is trying hard to adjust although he ac-tually is not putting forth any effort in this respect ... I feel in time he will try to be a wheel in the cottage."

After three months: "Manson has become somewhat of an 'institution politician.' He does just enough work to get by on ... Restless and moody most of the time, the boy would rather spend his class time entertaining his friends." The report concluded: "It appears that this boy is a very

*I would not obtain the results of these until much later; how-ever, portions are quoted here.

emotionally upset youth who is definitely in need of some
psychiatric orientation."

Manson was anxious to be transferred to Natural
Bridge Honor Camp, a minimum security institution. Because of his run-away record, school officials felt the opposite—i.e., transfer to a reformatory-type institution—
was in order, but they decided to withhold decision until
after the boy had been examined by a psychiatrist.

On June 29, 1951, Charles Manson was examined by a
Dr. Block. The psychiatrist noted "the marked degree of
rejection, instability, and psychic trauma" in Manson's
background. His sense of inferiority in relation to his
mother was so pronounced, Block said, that he constantly
felt it necessary "to suppress any thoughts about her." Because of his diminutive stature, his illegitimacy, and the
lack of parental love, "he is constantly striving for status
with the other boys." To attain this, Manson had "developed certain facile techniques for dealing with people.
These for the most part consist of a good sense of humor"
and an "ability to ingratiate himself . . . This could add up
to a fairly 'slick' institutionalized youth, but one is left
with the feeling that behind all this lies an extremely sensitive boy who has not yet given up in terms of securing
some kind of love and affection from the world."

Though the doctor observed that Manson was "quite
unable to accept any kind of authoritative direction," he
found that he "accepted with alacrity the offer of psychiatric interviews."

If he found this suspicious, the doctor did not indicate it
in his report. For the next three months he gave Manson
individual psychotherapy. It may be presumed that Charles
Manson also worked on the doctor, for in his October 1
report Dr. Block was convinced that what Manson most
required were experiences which would build up his self-
confidence. In short, he needed to be trusted. The doctor
recommended the transfer.

It would appear that Charles Manson had conned his
first psychiatrist. Though the school authorities considered
him at best a "calculated risk," they accepted the doctor's
recommendation, and on October 24, 1951, he was transferred to Natural Bridge Camp.

That November he turned seventeen. Shortly after his birthday he was visited by his aunt, who told the authorities that she would supply a home and employment for him if he was released. He was due for a parole hearing in February 1952, and, with her offer, his chances looked good. Instead, less than a month before the hearing, he took a razor blade and held it against another boy's throat while he sodomized him.

As a result of the offense, he lost ninety-seven days good-time and, on January 18, 1952, he was transferred to the Federal Reformatory at Petersburg, Virginia. He was considered "dangerous," one official observing, "He shouldn't be trusted across the street." By August he had committed eight serious disciplinary offenses, three involving homosexual acts. His progress report, if it could be called that, stated, "Manson definitely has homosexual and assaultive tendencies." He was classified "safe only under supervision." For the protection of himself as well as others, the authorities decided to transfer him to a more secure institution, the Federal Reformatory at Chillicothe, Ohio. He was sent there on September 22, 1952.

From the Chillicothe files: "Associates with trouble makers ... seems to be the unpredictable type of inmate who will require supervision both at work and in quarters ... In spite of his age, he is criminally sophisticated ... regarded as grossly unsuited for retention in an open reformatory type institution such as Chillicothe ..." This from a report written less than a month after his transfer there.

Then, suddenly, Manson changed. For the rest of the year there were no serious disciplinary offenses. Except for minor infractions of the rules, and a consistently "poor attitude toward authority," his good conduct continued into 1953. A progress report that October noted: "Manson has shown a marked improvement in his general attitude and cooperation with officers and is also showing an active interest in the educational program ... He is especially proud of the fact that he raised his [educational level from lower fourth to upper seventh grade] and that he can now read most material and use simple arithmetic."

Because of his educational advancement and his good

work habits in the transportation unit, where he repaired and maintained vehicles belonging to the institution, on January 1, 1954, he was given a Meritorious Service Award. Far more important to Charles Manson, on May 8, 1954, he was granted parole. He was nineteen.

One of the conditions of his parole was that he live with his aunt and uncle in McMechen. He did, for a time, then, when his mother moved to nearby Wheeling, he joined her. They seemed drawn together, yet unable to stand each other for any length of time.

Since fourteen, Charles Manson's only sexual contacts had been homosexual. Shortly after his release he met a seventeen-year-old McMechen girl, Rosalie Jean Willis, a waitress in the local hospital. They were married in January 1955. For support Manson worked as a busboy, service-station helper, parking-lot attendant. He also boosted cars. He would later admit to stealing six. He appeared to have learned nothing; he took at least two across state lines. One, stolen in Wheeling, West Virginia, he abandoned in Fort Lauderdale, Florida. The second, a 1951 Mercury, he drove from Bridgeport, Ohio, to Los Angeles in July 1955, accompanied by his now pregnant wife. Manson had finally made it to the Golden State. He was arrested less than three months later, and admitted both Dyer Act violations. Taken to federal court, he pleaded guilty to the theft of the Mercury, and asked for psychiatric help, stating, "I was released from Chillicothe in 1954 and, having been confined for nine years, I was badly in need of psychiatric treatment. I was mentally confused and stole a car as a means of mental release from the confused state of mind that I was in."

The judge requested a psychiatric report. Manson was examined on October 26, 1955, by Dr. Edwin McNiel. He gave the psychiatrist a much abbreviated version of his past, stating that he was first sent to an institution "for being mean to my mother." Of his wife, Manson said, "She is the best wife a guy could want. I didn't realize how good she was until I got in here. I beat her at times. She writes to me all the time. She is going to have a baby."

He also told McNiel that "he spent so much time in institutions that he never really learned much of what 'real life on the outside was all about.' He said that now he has a wife and is about to become a father it has become important to him to try to be on the outside and be with his wife. He said she is the only one he has ever cared about in his life."

Dr. McNiel observed: "It is evident that he has an unstable personality and that his environmental influences throughout most of his life have not been good . . . In my opinion this boy is a poor risk for probation; on the other hand, he has spent nine years in institutions with apparently little benefit except to take him out of circulation. With the incentive of a wife and probable fatherhood, it is possible that he might be able to straighten himself out. I would, therefore, respectfully recommend to the court that probation be considered in this case under careful supervision." Accepting the suggestion, on November 7, 1955, the court gave Manson five years probation.

There remained the Florida charge. Though his chances of getting probation on it were excellent, before the hearing he skipped. A warrant was issued for his arrest. He was picked up in Indianapolis on March 14, 1956, and returned to Los Angeles. His probation was revoked, and he was sentenced to three years imprisonment at Terminal Island, San Pedro, California. By the time Charles Manson, Jr., was born, his father was back in jail.

"This inmate will no doubt be in serious difficulty soon," wrote the orientation officer. "He is young, small, baby-faced, and unable to control himself . . ."

Given another battery of tests, Manson received average marks in all the categories except "word meaning," where he had a high score. His IQ was now 121. With some perception, when it came to his work assignment Manson requested "a small detail where he is not with too many men. He states he has a tendency to cut up and misbehave if he is around a gang . . ."

Rosalie moved in with his mother, now living in Los Angeles, and during his first year at Terminal Island she visited him every week, his mother somewhat less frequently. "Manson's work habits and attitudes range from good to poor," noted his March 1957 progress report. "However, as the time of his parole hearing approaches, his work performance report has jumped from good to excellent, showing that he is capable of a good adjustment if he wants to."

His parole hearing was set for April 22. In March his wife's visits ceased. Manson's mother told him Rosalie was living with another man. In early April he was transferred to the Coast Guard unit, under minimal custody. On April 10 he was found in the Coast Guard parking lot, dressed in civilian clothes, wiring the ignition of a car. Subsequently indicted for attempted escape, he pleaded guilty, and an extra five years probation was tacked onto the end of his current sentence. On April 22 the parole request was denied.

Rosalie filed for divorce not long after this, the divorce becoming final in 1958. She retained custody of Charles, Jr., remarried, and had no further contact with Manson or his mother.

April 1958, annual review: His work performance was "sporadic," his behavior continued to be "erratic and moody." Almost without exception, he would let down anyone who went to bat for him, the report noted. "For example, he was selected to attend the current Dale Carnegie Course, being passed over a number of other applicants because it was felt that this course might be beneficial in his case and he urgently desired enrollment. After attending a few sessions and apparently making excellent progress, he quit in a mood of petulance and has since engaged in no educational activity."

Manson was called "an almost classic text book case of the correctional institutional inmate ... His is a very difficult case and it is impossible to predict his future adjustment with any degree of accuracy."

He was released September 30, 1958, on five years parole.

By November, Manson had found a new occupation: pimping. His teacher was +Frank Peters, a Malibu bartender and known procurer, with whom he was living.

Unknown to Manson, he was under surveillance by the FBI, and had been since his release from prison. The federal agents, who were looking for a fugitive who had once lived with Peters, told Manson's parole officer that his "first string" consisted of a sixteen-year-old girl named Judy, whom he had personally "turned out"; as additional support, he was getting money from "Fat Flo," an unattractive Pasadena girl who had wealthy parents.

His parole officer called him in for a talk. Manson denied he was pimping; said he was no longer living with Peters; promised never to see Judy again; but stated that he wished to continue his relationship with Flo, "for money and sex." After all, he said, he had "been in a long time." After the interview the parole officer wrote: "This certainly is a very shaky probationer and it seems just a matter of time before he gets in further trouble."

On May 1, 1959, Manson was arrested attempting to cash a forged U.S. Treasury check for $37.50 in Ralph's, a Los Angeles supermarket. According to the arresting officers, Manson told them he had stolen the check from a mailbox. Two more federal offenses.

LAPD turned Manson over to Secret Service agents for questioning. What then happened was somewhat embarrassing. "Unfortunately for them," read a report of the incident, "the check itself has disappeared; they feel certain subject took it off table and swallowed it when they momentarily turned their backs." The charges remained, however.

In mid-June an attractive nineteen-year-old girl named Leona called on Manson's parole officer and told him she was pregnant by Charlie. The parole officer was skeptical and wanted to see a medical report. He also began checking her background.

With the aid of an attorney, Manson obtained a deal: if he would plead guilty to forging the check, the mail theft charge would be dropped. The judge ordered a psychiatric examination, and Dr. McNiel examined Manson a second time.

When Manson appeared in court on September 28, 1959, Dr. McNiel, the U.S. Attorney's Office, and the probation department *all* recommended against probation. Leona also appeared and made a tearful plea in Manson's behalf. They were deeply in love, she told the judge, and would marry if Charlie were freed. Though it was proved that Leona had lied about being pregnant, and that she had an arrest record as a prostitute under the name Candy Stevens, the judge, evidently moved by Leona's plea and Manson's promise to make good, gave the defendant a ten-year sentence, then suspended it and placed him on probation.

Manson returned to pimping and breaking federal laws.

By December he had been arrested by LAPD twice: for grand theft auto and the use of stolen credit cards. Both charges were dismissed for lack of evidence. That month he also took Leona-aka-Candy and a girl named Elizabeth from Needles, California, to Lordsburg, New Mexico, for purposes of prostitution, violating the Mann Act, still another federal beef.

Held briefly, questioned, then released, he was given the impression that he had "beat the rap." He must have suspected that the investigation was continuing, however. Possibly to prevent Leona from testifying against him, he did marry her, though he didn't inform his probation officer of this. He remained free throughout January 1960, while the FBI prepared its case.

Late in February, Manson's probation officer was visited by an irate parent, +Ralph Samuels, from Detroit. Samuels' daughter +Jo Anne, nineteen, had come to California in response to an ad for an airline stewardess school, only to learn, after paying her tuition, that the school was a fraud. She had $700 in savings, however, and together with another disillusioned student, +Beth Beldon, had rented an apartment in Hollywood. About November 1959, Jo Anne had the misfortune to meet Charles Manson, who introduced himself, complete with printed card, as "President, 3-Star-Enterprises, Nite Club, Radio and TV Productions." Manson conned her into investing her savings in his nonexistent company; drugged and raped her roommate; and got Jo Anne pregnant. It was an ectopic pregnancy, the fetus growing in one of the Fallopian tubes, and she nearly died.

The probation officer could offer little more than a sympathetic ear, however, for Charles Manson had disappeared. A bench warrant was issued, and on April 28 a federal grand jury indicted him on the Mann Act violation. He was arrested June 1 in Laredo, Texas, after police picked up one of his girls on a prostitution charge, and brought back to Los Angeles, where, on June 23, 1960, the court ruled he had violated his probation and ordered him returned to prison to serve out his ten-year sentence. The judge observed: "If there ever was a man who demonstrated himself completely unfit for probation, he is it." This was the same judge who had granted him probation the previous September.

The Mann Act charge was later dropped. For a full year Manson remained in the Los Angeles County Jail, while appealing the revocation. The appeal was denied, and in July 1961 he was sent to the United States Penitentiary at McNeil Island, Washington. He was twenty-six.

According to staff evaluation, Manson had become something of an actor: "He hides his loneliness, resentment, and hostility behind a façade of superficial ingratiation ... An energetic, young-appearing person whose verbalization flows quite easily, he gestures profusely and can dramatize situations to hold the listener's attention." Then a statement which, in one form or another, was to reappear often in his prison records, and, much later, in post-prison interviews: "He has commented that institutions have become his way of life and that he receives security in institutions which is not available to him in the outside world."

Manson gave as his claimed religion "Scientologist," stating that he "has never settled upon a religious formula for his beliefs and is presently seeking an answer to his question in the new mental health cult known as Scientology."

Scientology, an outgrowth of science-fiction writer L. Ron Hubbard's Dianetics, was just coming into vogue at this time. Manson's teacher, i.e., "auditor," was another convict, Lanier Rayner. Manson would later claim that while in prison he achieved Scientology's highest level "theta clear."*

Although Manson remained interested in Scientology much longer than he did in any other subject except music, it appears that, like the Dale Carnegie course, he stuck with it only as long as his enthusiasm lasted, then dropped it, extracting and retaining a number of terms and phrases ("auditing," "cease to exist," "coming to Now") and some concepts (karma, reincarnation, etc.) which, perhaps fittingly, Scientology had borrowed in the first place.

He was still interested in Scientology when his annual progress report was written that September. Furthermore, according to the report, that interest "has led him to make a semi-professional evaluation of his personality which strangely enough is quite consistent with the evaluations made by previous social studies. He appears to have developed a certain amount of insight into his problems through his study of this discipline. Manson is making progress for the first time in his life."

The report also noted that Manson "is active in softball, basketball and croquet" and "is a member of the Drama Club and the Self Improvement Group." He had become "somewhat of a fanatic at practicing the guitar."†

He held one fairly responsible job eleven months, the longest he held any prison assignment, before being caught with contraband in his cell and reassigned to janitorial work.

The annual report that September took a close, hard look at the twenty-eight-year-old convict:

"Charles Manson has a tremendous drive to call attention to himself. Generally he is unable to succeed in positive acts, therefore he often resorts to negative behavior to satisfy this drive. In his effort to 'find' himself, Manson peruses different religious philosophies, e.g., Scientology and Buddhism; however, he never remains long enough

---

*In one of his pamphlets, Hubbard defined a "clear" as "one who has straightened up this lifetime." It is rather hard to see how this might apply to Charles Manson.

†He in fact requested a transfer to Leavenworth, considered a much tougher institution, because "he claimed he would be allowed to practice his guitar more often." The request was denied.

with any given teachings to reap meaningful benefits. Even these attempts and his cries for help represent a desire for attention, with only superficial meaning. Manson has had more than the usual amount of staff attention, yet there is little indication of change in his demeanor. In view of his deep-seated personality problems ... continuation of institutional treatment is recommended."

On October 1, 1963, prison officials were informed, "according to court papers received in this institution, that Manson was married to a Leona Manson in 1959 in the State of California, and that the marriage was terminated by divorce on April 10, 1963, in Denver, Colorado, on grounds of mental cruelty and conviction of a felony. One child, Charles Luther Manson, is alleged to have been of this union."

This is the only reference, in any of Manson's records, to his second marriage and second child.

Manson's annual review of September 1964 revealed a clear conduct record, but little else encouraging. "His past pattern of employment instability continues ... seems to have an intense need to call attention to himself ... remains emotionally insecure and tends to involve himself in various fanatical interests."

Those "fanatical interests" weren't identified in the prison reports, but at least several are known. In addition to Scientology and his guitar, there was now a third. In January 1964 "I Want to Hold Your Hand" became the No. 1 song on U.S. record charts. With the New York arrival of the "four Liverpool lads" the following month, the United States experienced, later than Great Britain but with no less intensity, the phenomenon known as Beatlemania. According to former inmates at McNeil, Manson's interest in the Beatles was almost an obsession. It didn't necessarily follow that he was a fan. There was more than a little jealousy in his reaction. He told numerous people that, given the chance, he could be much bigger than the Beatles. One person he told this to was Alvin Karpis, lone survivor of the Ma Barker gang. Manson had struck up a friendship with the aging gangster after learning he could play the steel guitar. Karpis taught Manson how. Again an observable pattern. Manson managed to get something from almost everyone with whom he associated.

May 1966: "Manson continues to maintain a clear conduct record ... Recently he has been spending most of his free time writing songs, accumulating about 80 or 90 of them during the past year, which he ultimately hopes to sell following release ... He also plays the guitar and drums, and is hopeful that he can secure employment as a guitar player or as a drummer or singer ...

"He shall need a great deal of help in the transition from institution to the free world."

In June 1966, Charles Manson was returned to Terminal Island for release purposes.

August 1966: "Manson is about to complete his ten-year term. He has a pattern of criminal behavior and confinement that dates to his teen years. This pattern is one of instability whether in free society or a structured institutional community. Little can be expected in the way of change in his attitude, behavior, or mode of conduct ..." This last report noted that Manson had no further interest in academic or vocational training; that he was no longer an advocate of Scientology; that "he has come to worship his guitar and music"; and, finally, "He has no plans for release as he says he has nowhere to go."

The morning Charles Manson was to be freed, he begged the authorities to let him remain in prison. Prison had become his home, he told them. He didn't think he could adjust to the world outside.

His request was denied. He was released at 8:15 A.M. on March 21, 1967, and given transportation to Los Angeles. That same day he requested and received permission to go to San Francisco. It was there, in the Haight-Ashbury section, that spring, that the Family was born.

Charles Manson was thirty-two years old. Over seventeen of those years—more than half his life—had been spent in institutions. In those seventeen years, Manson had only been examined by a psychiatrist three times, and then very superficially.

I was surprised, in studying Manson's record, to find no sustained history of violence—armed robbery age thirteen, homosexual rape age seventeen, wife beating age twenty, that was it. I was more than surprised, I was amazed at the number of federal offenses. Probably ninety-nine out of one hundred criminals never see the inside of a federal court. Yet here was Manson, described as "criminally sophisticated," violating the Dyer Act, the Mann Act, stealing from the mails, forging a government check, and so on. Had Manson been convicted of comparable offenses in state courts, he probably would have served *less than five years* instead of over seventeen.

Why? I could only guess. Perhaps, as he said before his reluctant release from Terminal Island, prison was the only home he had. It was also possible that, consciously or unconsciously, he sought out those offenses that carried the most severe punishments. A third speculation—and I wasn't overlooking the possibility that it could be a combination of all three—was a need, amounting almost to a compulsion, to challenge the strongest authority.

I was a long way from understanding Charles Manson. Though I could see patterns in his conduct, which might be clues to his future actions, a great deal was missing.

Burglar, car thief, forger, pimp—was this the portrait of a mass murderer?

I had far more questions than answers. And, as yet, not even a clue as to the motive.

November 24-26, 1969

Although Lieutenants Helder and LePage remained in charge of the Tate and LaBianca cases, the assignments were more jurisdictional than operational, since each was in charge of numerous other homicide investigations. Nineteen detectives had originally been assigned to the two cases. That number had now been cut to six. Moreover, for some odd reason, though there were only two victims in the LaBianca slayings, four detectives remained assigned to that case: Sergeants Philip Sartuchi, Mike Nielsen, Manuel "Chick" Gutierrez, and Frank Patchett. But on Tate, where there were five victims, there were only two detectives: Sergeants Robert Calkins and Mike McGann.

I called Calkins and McGann in for a conference and gave them a list of things I needed done. A few samples:

Interview Terry Melcher.

Check the fingerprints of every known Family member against the twenty-five unmatched latents found at 10050 Cielo Drive.

Put out a "want" on Charles "Tex" Montgomery, using the description on Inyo Deputy Sheriff Cox's August 21, 1969, F.I.R. card (M/C/6 feet/145 pounds/slim build/ruddy complexion/born December 2, 1945). If the case breaks before we arrest him, I told them, we may never find him.

Show photos of every Family member to Chapman; Garretson; the Tate gardeners; and the families, friends, and business associates of the victims. If there's a link, I want to know about it.

Check everyone in the Family to see who wears glasses, and determine if the pair found at the Tate murder scene belongs to a Family member.

"How do we do that?" Calkins asked. "They're not about to admit it."

"I presume you talk to their acquaintances, parents, relatives, to any of the Family members like Kitty Lutesinger and Stephanie Schram who are willing to cooperate," I told him. "If you can check out the glasses with eye doctors all over the United States and Canada, you can certainly check out some thirty-five people."

This was our initial estimate of the size of the Family. We'd later learn that at various times it numbered a hundred or more. The hard-core members—i.e., those who remained for any length of time and who were privy to what was going on—numbered between twenty-five and thirty.

Something occurred to me. "You *did* check out Garretson, didn't you, to see if those glasses were his?"

They weren't sure. They'd have to get back to me on that.

I later learned that although Garretson had been the first—and, for a time, the *only*—suspect in the murders, no one had thought to ascertain if those glasses, the single most important clue found at the murder scene, belonged to him. They hadn't even asked him if he wore glasses. It turned out he sometimes did. I learned this in talking to his attorney, Barry Tarlow. Eventually I was able to get LAPD to contact the police in Lancaster, Ohio, Garretson's home town, where he had returned after his release, and they obtained the specifics of Garretson's prescription from his local optometrist. Not even close.

From the evidence I'd seen, I didn't believe Garretson was involved in the murders, but I didn't want a defense attorney popping up in court pointing a finger, or rather a pair of eyeglasses, at an alternate suspect.

I was also curious about whom those glasses belonged to.

After Calkins and McGann left, I got in touch with the LaBianca detectives and gave them similar instructions regarding the photos and the Waverly Drive latents.

Five of the Manson girls were still in jail in Independence. LAPD decided to bring them to Los Angeles for individual interrogation. They would be confined at Sybil Brand but a "keep away" would be placed on each. This meant they could have no contact with each other or with anyone else LAPD designated—for example, Susan Atkins.

It was a good move on LAPD's part. There was a chance that, questioned separately, one or more might decide to talk.

That evening TV commentator George Putnam startled his listeners with the announcement that on Wednesday he would reveal who had committed the Tate murders. Our office called LAPD, who had their public relations spokesman, Lieutenant Hagen, contact Putnam and other representatives of the media asking them to hold off, because publicity now would hurt our investigation. All the newspapers, wire services, and radio and TV stations agreed to sit on the story, but only for one week, until Monday, December 1. The news was too big, and each was afraid someone else would try for a scoop.

There had been a leak. It wouldn't be the last.

On Tuesday, the twenty-fifth, Frank Fowles, the Inyo County DA, called, and we traded some information.

Fowles told me that Sandra Good had been overheard talking again. She had told another Family member that Charlie was going to "go alibi." If he was brought to trial for the Tate-LaBianca murders, they would produce evidence showing he wasn't even in Los Angeles at the time the murders occurred.

I told Fowles of a rumor I'd heard. According to McGann, a police informant in Las Vegas had told him that Charles "Tex" Montgomery and Bruce Davis had been seen there the previous day, driving a green panel Volkswagen. They had allegedly told someone that they were attempting to raise enough money to bail out Manson; failing in that, they intended to kill someone.

Fowles had heard similar rumblings among the Manson girls. He took them seriously enough to send his own family out of Inyo County over the Thanksgiving weekend. He remained behind, however, ready to forestall any bail attempt.

After hanging up, I called Patchett and Gutierrez of the LaBianca team and told them I wanted a detailed report on Manson's activities the week of the murders. Unlike the Tate detectives, they didn't ask how to do it. They went out and did it, eventually giving me evidence which, together with other information we obtained, would blow any alibi defense to smithereens.

That afternoon McGann and Patchett re-interviewed Ronnie Howard, this time on tape. She provided several details she'd recalled since LAPD last talked to her, but nothing that was of help in the current investigation. We still didn't know who all the killers were.

Wednesday, November 26. "Hung jury on Beausoleil," one of the deputy DAs yelled in the door of my office. "Eight to four for conviction."

The case had been so weak our office hadn't sought the death penalty. Also, the jury hadn't believed Danny De-Carlo. Brought in at the last minute, without adequate preparation, he had not been a convincing witness.

Later that day LASO asked my office if I would take over the prosecution of Beausoleil in his new trial, and I was assigned this case in addition to the two cases I was already handling.

That same morning Virginia Graham decided she had to tell someone what she knew. A few days earlier her husband had visited her at Corona. Whispering through the wire screen in the visitor's room, she told him she had heard something about the Benedict Canyon murders, and didn't know what to do.

He advised her: "Mind your own business."

But, she would later state: "I can see a lot of things I don't say anything about, but this is sick. This is so bad that I don't know who could mind their own business with this."*

Having failed to get an appointment with Dr. Dreiser, Virginia instead went to her counselor. The authorities at Corona called LAPD. At 3:15 that afternoon Sergeant Nielsen arrived at the prison and began taping her story.

Unlike Ronnie, who was unsure whether four or five people were involved in the Tate homicides, Virginia re-called Sadie's saying there were three girls and one man. Like Ronnie, however, she presumed the man, "Charles," was Manson.

The individual questioning of the five girls took place that afternoon and evening at Sybil Brand.

Sergeant Manuel "Chick" Gutierrez interviewed Dianne Bluestein, aka Snake, t/n Dianne Lake, given age twenty-one, true age sixteen. The interview was taped. Listening to the tapes later, I couldn't believe what I was hearing.

Q. "My name is Sergeant Gutierrez and I'm with the

---

*Virginia Graham would later state that she was unaware that Ronnie Howard had already talked to the police. However, a group of girls were transferred from Sybil Brand to Corona shortly before this, and it's possible they carried along some jail scuttlebutt.

Los Angeles Police Department and I work homicide. . . .
I've talked to several of the girls. The girls have been real
nice and we've had some long, long chats. We know a lot
of things that went on over at Spahn. We know a lot that
happened other places. We know who is involved, and
who is not involved. We also know things that maybe you
don't know, that we're not going to tell you until the right
time comes up, but we've got to talk to everybody who
was involved, and I think you know what I'm talking
about. I'm talking about Charlie and the Family and everybody. I don't know how tight you are with the Family.
You're probably real tight with them, but somebody's
going to go down the tubes, and somebody's going to get
the pill in the gas chamber for a whole bunch of murders
which you are a part of, or so some other people have indicated."

There was no evidence whatsoever that Dianne was involved in any of the murders, but "Chick" wasn't deterred
by this.

"Now, I'm here for one specific reason, and that's to listen to you, see what you've got to say, so I can go to the
District Attorney and tell him, 'Look, this is what Dianne
told me, and she's willing to turn state's evidence in return
for her full release.' We're not interested in nailing you.
We're interested in the big guy, and you know who we're
talking about, right, honey?"

A.   [No audible answer]

Q.   "Now, somebody's going to go to that gas chamber, you know that. This is just too big. This is the biggest
murder of the century. You know that and I know it. So, in
order to protect yourself from getting even indicted or
spending the rest of your life in jail, then you're going to
have to come up with some answers . . . We know of
about fourteen murders right now, and you know which
ones I'm talking about."

A.   [Unintelligible]

Gutierrez accused her of involvement in all fourteen.
He then said: "I'm prepared to give you complete immunity, which means that if you are straight with me, right
down the line, I'll be straight with you, and I'll guarantee
you that you will walk out of that jail a free woman ready

to start over again and never go back up there to Independence to do any time. I wouldn't say that unless I meant it, right?"

Actually, Sergeant Gutierrez did not have the authority to guarantee this. The granting of immunity is a complicated procedure, involving the approval not only of the Police Department but also of the District Attorney's Office, with the final decision being made by the Court. Gutierrez offered it to he' as casually as if it were a stick of gum.

Commenting on her silence, Sergeant Gutierrez said, "Now, what's that going to prove, huh? Right now the only thing you're proving to me, honey, is that, heck, you're out there sticking your nose out for a guy by the name of Charlie. Now, what's Charlie? He got you guys in all this problem. You could have been out right now doing your thing, but here you're holding silent for what? For Charlie? Charlie ain't never going to get out of that jail. You know that, right? Didn't we start out on good terms? Huh?"

A. "Yes."

Q. "O.K. And I'm not about to beat you over the head with a hammer or hose and all that. All I want to do is talk to you friendly . . ."

Gutierrez interviewed Dianne for nearly two hours, obtaining from the sixteen-year-old little more than the admission that she liked candy bars.

Later Dianne Lake would become one of the prosecution's most important witnesses. But credit for this goes to the Inyo County authorities, in particular Gibbens and Gardiner, who, instead of threats, tried patient, sympathetic understanding. It made all the difference.

Having got nothing from Dianne, Gutierrez next interviewed Rachel Morse, aka Ouisch, t/n Ruth Ann Moorehouse, age eighteen, Ruth Ann was the girl Danny DeCarlo identified as his "favorite sweetie," the same girl who at Barker Ranch had told him she couldn't wait to get her first pig.

Unlike Dianne, Ruth Ann answered Gutierrez' questions, though most of her replies were lies. She claimed

she'd never heard of Shorty, Gary Hinman, or anyone
named Katie. The reason she knew so little, she explained,
was that she had been with the Family only a short time, a
month or so before the Spahn Ranch raid (all five girls said
this, obviously by prearrangement).

Q. "I want to know everything you know, because
you're going to testify before that grand jury."

A. "I don't know anything."

Q. "Then you're going to hang with the rest of them.
You're going to go to the joint. If you don't start cooperating, you're going to go to the joint, and let me tell you
what it is down there. They may drop that pill on you.
They may drop that cyanide pill on you."

A. (*nearly screaming*) "I haven't done anything! I don't
know anything about it!"

Then, later:

Q. "How old are you?"

A. "Eighteen."

Q. "That's old enough to go to the gas chamber."

There was also no evidence linking her to any of the
homicides, but Gutierrez told her, "Fourteen murders, and
you're involved in each one!" He also promised her complete immunity ("You're either going to go up for murder
or you are going to go free"), and added, "Also, there is a
$25,000 reward."

Manon Minette, aka Gypsy, t/n Catherine Share, who
at twenty-seven was the oldest female member of the
Family, gave the detectives nothing of value. Nor did
Brenda McCann, t/n Nancy Pitman, age eighteen.

It was otherwise, however, with twenty-year-old Leslie
Sankston.

Leslie, whose true name, Van Houten, was not known
to us at this time, was interviewed by Mike McGann.
McGann tried using her parents, conscience, the hideousness of the murders, the implication that others had talked
and involved her—none worked. What did work was
Leslie's little-girl cuteness, her I-know-something-you-don't
game playing. Repeatedly she trapped herself.

Q. "What did you hear about the Tate murders up
there?"

A. "I'm deaf. I didn't hear nothing." [Laughs]

Q. "Five people were killed up there, on the hill. And I know three for sure that went up there. I think I know the fourth. And I don't know the fifth. But I suspect you do. Why are you holding back? You know what happened."

A. "I have a pretty good idea."

Q. "I want to know who was involved. How it went down. The little details."

A. "I told Mr. Patchett [in Independence] I'll tell him if I changed my mind. I haven't changed my mind yet."

Q. "You're going to have to talk about it someday."

A. "Not today ... How did you ever trace it back to Spahn?"

Q. "Who did you see leave the night of the eighth of August?"

A. [Laughs] "Oh, I went to bed early that night. Really, I don't want to talk about it."

Q. "Who went?"

A. "That's what I don't want to talk about."

All these were little admissions, if not of participation, at least of knowledge.

Though she didn't want to talk about the murders, she didn't mind talking about the Family. "You couldn't meet a nicer group of people," she told McGann. "Of all the guys at the ranch, I liked Clem the best; he's fun to be with." Clem, with the idiot grin, who liked to expose himself to little children. Sadie was "really kind of a nice person. But she tends to be on the rough side ..." As Sharon Tate, Gary Hinman, and others had discovered. Bruce Davis was all talk, Leslie continued, always going on about how he was going to dynamite someone, but she was sure it was "only talk." She commented on some of the others, but not Charlie. In common with the four other girls who had been brought down from Independence, she avoided the subject of Manson.

Q. "The Family is no more, Leslie." Charlie was in jail; Clem was in jail; Zero had killed himself playing Russian roulette—

A. *"Zero!"*

Obviously shocked, she dropped her little-girl role and

pressed McGann for details. He told her that Bruce Davis had been present.

A. "Was Bruce playing it too?"

Q. "No."

A. (*sarcastically*) "Zero was playing Russian roulette all by himself!"

Q. "Kind of odd, isn't it?"

A. "Yeah, it's odd!"

Sensing an advantage, McGann moved in. He told her that he knew five people had gone to the Tate residence, three girls and two men, and that one of the men was Charles Manson.

A. "I don't think Charlie was in on any of them."

Leslie said she had heard only four people went to Tate. "I would say that three of them were girls. I would say that there were probably more girls involved than men." Then, later, "I heard one girl who didn't murder someone while they was, they were up there."

Q. "Who is that?"

A. "A girl by the name of Linda."

Susan Atkins had told Ronnie Howard, in regard to the killings the second night, "Linda wasn't in on this one," presumably meaning she had been along the first night, but until now we had been unsure of this.

Questioned, Leslie said she didn't know Linda's last name; that she was at Spahn only a short time and hadn't been arrested with them; and that she was a small girl, maybe five feet two, thin, with light-brown hair.

McGann asked her *who* had told her that Linda had been along on Tate. Leslie replied, petulantly, "I don't remember. I don't remember who told me little details!" Why was she so upset? McGann asked. "Because so many of my friends are getting knocked off, for reasons I don't even know about."

McGann showed her the mug shots taken after the Barker raid. Though she had been present, she claimed she couldn't recognize most of the people. When handed one of a girl booked as "Marnie Reeves," Leslie said, "That's Katie."

Q. "Katie is Marnie Reeves?"

Leslie equivocated. She wasn't sure. She really didn't

know any of these people all that well. Though she had lived with the Family at both Spahn and Barker, she associated mostly with the motorcycle riders. She thought they were neat.

McGann brought the questioning back to the murders. Leslie began playing games again, and in the process making admissions. She implied that she knew of eleven murders—Hinman 1, Tate 5, LaBianca 2, Shea 1, for a total of 9—but she declined to identify the other two. It was as if she were keeping score in a baseball game.

There was a break in the questioning. It's standard police procedure to leave a suspect alone for a while, to think about his or her answers, to provide a transition between "soft" and "hard" interrogation. It also gives the officers an opportunity to visit the can.

When McGann returned, he decided to shock Leslie some more.

Q. "Sadie has already told fifteen people in the jail-house that she was there, that she took part in it."

A. "That's incredible." Then, after a thoughtful pause, "Didn't she mention anyone else?"

Q. "No. Except for Charlie. And Katie."

A. "She mentioned Charlie and Katie?"

Q. "That's right."

A. "That's pretty nauseating."

Q. "She said Katie was there, and I know it was Marnie Reeves, and you know it was Marnie Reeves."

At this point, McGann later told me, Leslie nodded her head affirmatively.

Q. "Sadie also said, 'I went out the next night and killed two more people, out in the hills.' "

A. *"Sadie said that!"*

Leslie was astonished. With good reason. Though we were as yet unaware of it, Leslie knew Susan Atkins had never entered the LaBianca residence. She knew that because she was one of the persons who had.

After this, Leslie refused to answer any further questions. McGann asked her why.

A. "Because if Zero was suddenly found playing Russian roulette I could be found playing Russian roulette."

Q. "We'll give you twenty-four-hour protection from now on."

A. (*laughing sarcastically*) "Oh, that would really be nice! I'd rather stay in jail."

From Leslie we learned that three girls had gone to the Tate residence: Sadie, Katie, and Linda. We also learned that Linda was "one girl who didn't murder someone," the clear implication being that the two other girls had. Beyond Leslie's limited description of Linda, however, we knew nothing about her.

We also knew that Katie was "Marnie Reeves." According to her Inyo arrest sheet, she was five feet six, weighed 120 pounds, had brown hair and blue eyes. Her photograph revealed a not very attractive girl, with very long hair and a somewhat mannish face. She looked older than twenty-two, the age she gave. In comparing the Barker and Spahn photos, it was discovered that she had been arrested in the earlier raid also, at that time giving the name "Mary Ann Scott." It was possible that "Katie," "Marnie Reeves," and "Mary Ann Scott" were all three aliases. She had been released a few days after her arrest at Barker, and her current whereabouts were unknown.

In return, Leslie had learned a few things from McGann: that Tex, Katie, and Linda were still free; and, more important, that Susan Atkins, aka Sadie Mae Glutz, was the snitch.

Even with a "keep away" on the girls, it wouldn't be long before this information got back to Manson.

November 27–30, 1969

We could have used a private line between Independence and L.A.; Fowles and I were averaging easily a dozen calls a day. Thus far, no attempt to meet Manson's bail, or any sign of Tex or Bruce. However, there were reporters all over Independence, and KNXT was sending in a camera crew tomorrow to film Golar Wash. I had Lieutenant Hagen call the TV station. They told him they didn't plan to use the film until Monday, the first, the agreed date, but wouldn't promise an extension to Wednesday, which I wanted.

Although nothing had seen print, the leaks continued. Chief Davis was enraged; he wanted to break the news himself. Someone was talking, and he wanted to know who. Determined to catch the culprit, he suggested that everyone working on the case, at LAPD and in the DA's Office, take a polygraph.

Even his own office ignored the suggestion, and I resisted the impulse to suggest that we concentrate on catching the killers instead.

On Saturday, Sergeant Patchett interviewed Gregg Jakobson. A talent scout, who was married to the daughter of old-time comedian Lou Costello, Jakobson had first met Charles Manson about May 1968, at the Sunset Boulevard home of Dennis Wilson, one of the Beach Boys rock group.

It was Jakobson who had introduced Manson to Terry Melcher, Doris Day's son, while Melcher was still living at 10050 Cielo Drive. In addition to producing his mother's TV show, Melcher was involved in a number of other enterprises, including a record company, and Jakobson had attempted to persuade him to record Manson. After listening to him play and sing, Melcher had said no.

Though Melcher had been unimpressed by Manson, Jakobson had been fascinated with the "whole Charlie Manson package," songs, philosophy, life style. Over a period of about a year and a half, he'd had many talks with Manson. Charlie loved to rap about his views on life, Gregg said, but Patchett wasn't particularly interested in this, and moved on to other subjects.

Did he know a Charles "Tex" Montgomery? Patchett asked. Yes, very well, Jakobson replied; only his real name wasn't Montgomery—it was Watson.

Sunday, November 30. At LAPD from 8:30 A.M. to midnight.

Charles Denton Watson had been arrested in Van Nuys, California, on April 23, 1969, for being on drugs. Though he had been released the next day, he had been fingerprinted at the time of his arrest.

10:30 A.M. Latent Prints Section called Lieutenant Helder. The print of Watson's right ring finger matched a latent found on the front door of the Tate residence.

Helder and I jumped up and down like little kids. This was the first physical evidence connecting the suspects to the crime scene.

Helder sent out fifteen detectives to see if they could locate Watson at any of his old addresses, but they had no luck. They did learn, however, that Watson was from a small town in Texas, McKinney.

Checking an atlas, we found that McKinney was in Collin County. Patchett called the sheriff of Collin, informing him that a former local resident, Charles Denton Watson, was wanted for 187 PC, murder, in California.

The sheriff's name was Tom Montgomery. A coincidence, Watson's using as alias the last name of the local sheriff? It was more than that: Sheriff Montgomery was Watson's second cousin.

"Charles is living here now," Sheriff Montgomery said. "He has an apartment in Denton. I'll bring him in."

The sheriff, we later learned, called Watson's uncle, Maurice Montgomery, saying, "Can you bring Charles over to the jail? We've got some trouble."

Maurice picked up his nephew and drove him to McKinney in his pickup truck. "He didn't say much on the way," the uncle later said. "I didn't know what it was all about, but I guess he knew all the time."

Watson supposedly refused comment and was lodged in the local jail.

Texans are straight shooters, LAPD told me. They'll hold him until we get around to sending an arrest warrant.

Not wanting to take any chances, I suggested we send someone to McKinney with the warrant, and it was decided that Sartuchi and Nielsen would leave at eleven the next morning.

Manson, Atkins, and Watson were now in custody, but two other suspects were still at large. From one of the ranch hands at Spahn, LAPD heard that Linda's last name was Kasabian, and that she was supposedly in a convent in New Mexico.* Marnie Reeves was rumored to be on a farm outside Mobile, Alabama.

That same day Patchett interviewed Terry Melcher regarding his contacts with Manson. He confirmed what Jakobson had already said: he had gone to Spahn Ranch twice, to hear Manson and the girls perform, and was "not enthused"; he had also seen Manson twice before this, while visiting Dennis Wilson. Melcher, however, added one important detail Jakobson hadn't mentioned.

On one of the latter occasions, late at night, Wilson had given him a ride back to his house on Cielo Drive. Manson had come along, sitting in the back seat of the car, singing and playing his guitar. They'd driven up to the gate and let him out, Melcher said, Wilson and Manson then driving off.

We now knew that Charles Manson had been to 10050 Cielo Drive on at least one occasion prior to the murders, although there was no evidence that he had ever been inside the gate.

At 5:30 that Sunday afternoon, while still at LAPD, I talked to Richard Caballero. A former deputy DA now in private practice, Caballero was representing Susan Atkins on the Hinman charge. Earlier Caballero had contacted Aaron Stovitz, wanting to know what the DA's Office had on his client. Aaron laid it out for him: while at Sybil Brand, Susan Atkins had confessed to two other inmates that she was involved not only in the Hinman but also the Tate and LaBianca murders. Aaron gave Caballero copies of the taped statements Ronnie Howard and Virginia Graham had given LAPD.

Under the law of discovery, the prosecution must make available to a defense attorney any and all evidence

*This was probably garbled, "convent" having been mistaken for "commune."

against his client. This is a one-way street. While the defense therefore knows in advance exactly what evidence the prosecution has, the defense isn't required to tell the prosecution anything. Although discovery usually occurs after a formal request to the Court, Aaron wanted to impress Caballero with the strength of our case, hoping his client would decide to cooperate.

Caballero came to Parker Center to see me and the detectives, wanting to know what kind of deal we could offer. In accordance with the earlier discussion between our office and LAPD, we said that if Susan would cooperate with us, we would probably let her plead guilty to second degree murder—i.e., we would not seek the death sentence, but we would ask for life imprisonment.

Caballero went to Sybil Brand and talked to his client. He would later testify: "I told her what the problems were, what the evidence was against her as it was related to me. That included the Hinman case (to which she had already confessed to LASO) and the Tate-LaBianca case. As a result of all this, I indicated to her that there is no question in my mind but they were going to seek the death penalty and that they would probably get it. I told her, 'They have enough evidence to convict you. You will be convicted.' "

About 9:30, Caballero returned to LAPD. Susan was undecided. She might be willing to testify before the grand jury, but he was sure she would never testify against the others at the trial. She was still under Manson's domination. Any minute she could bolt back to him. He said he'd let me know what she finally decided.

It was left hanging there. Though we had the Howard-Graham statements implicating Atkins, and physical evidence linking Watson to the Tate murder scene, our whole case against Manson and the others rested on the decision of Sadie Mae Glutz.

December 1, 1969

7 A.M. Aaron reached me at home. Sheriff Montgomery had just called. If he didn't have a warrant in two hours, he was going to release Watson.

I rushed down to the office and made out a complaint. McGann and I took it to Judge Antonio Chavez, who signed the warrant, LAPD teletyping it to Sheriff Montgomery with just minutes to spare.

I also made out two other complaints: one against Linda Kasabian, the other against Patricia Krenwinkel. The latter, LAPD had learned from LASO, was the real name of Marnie Reeves, aka Katie. Following the Spahn raid, her father, Joseph Krenwinkel, an Inglewood, California, insurance agent, had arranged for her release. On learning this, Sergeant Nielsen had called Krenwinkel, asking where he could reach his daughter. He had told him she was staying with relatives in Mobile, Alabama, and had given him the address. LAPD had then contacted Mobile Police Chief James Robinson, and he had men out looking for her now. Judge Chavez signed these warrants also.

Buck Compton, the Chief Deputy District Attorney, called to inform me that Chief Davis had scheduled a press conference for two that afternoon. Aaron and I were to be in his office at 1:30. "Buck, this is way too premature!" I told him. "We don't even have enough on Manson for an indictment, much less a conviction. As for Krenwinkel and Kasabian, if the story breaks before they're picked up, we may never catch them. Can't we persuade Davis to hold off?" Buck promised to try.

At least part of my worry was unnecessary. Patricia Krenwinkel was arrested in Mobile a few minutes before we arrived in Compton's office. Mobile police had gone to the home of her aunt, Mrs. Garnett Reeves, but Patricia wasn't there. However, Sergeant William McKellar and his partner were driving down the road that runs in front of the residence when they saw a sports car with a boy and a girl inside. As the two cars passed, McKellar "noticed the female passenger pulled her hat down lower over her face." Convinced this was "an effort to avoid identification," the officers pulled a quick U and sirened the car to a halt. Though the girl fitted the teletype description, she said her name was Montgomery (the same alias Watson had used). On being taken to the aunt's home, however, she admitted her true identity. The young man, a local acquaintance, was questioned and released. Patricia Krenwinkel was read her rights and placed under arrest at 3:20 P.M., Mobile time.

1:30 P.M. Buck, Aaron, and I met with Chief Davis. I told Davis that I'd scraped together barely enough evidence against Krenwinkel and Kasabian to get warrants, but it was all inadmissible hearsay: Leslie Sankston's statement to McGann; Susan Atkins' statements to Virginia Graham and Ronnie Howard. We can't get a grand jury indictment on this, I told him, adding, "If Susan Atkins doesn't cooperate, we've had it."

There were over two hundred reporters and cameramen waiting in the police auditorium, Davis said, representing not only all the networks and wire services but newspapers from all over the world. There was no way he could call it off now.

Shortly before the press conference Lieutenant Helder called both Roman Polanski and Colonel Paul Tate, telling them the news. For Colonel Tate, the news meant the end of his months-long private investigation; despite his diligence, he had not come up with anything that was of use to us. But at least now the wondering and suspicion were over.

2 P.M. Facing fifteen microphones and dozens of bright lights, Chief Edward M. Davis announced that after 8,750 hours of police work LAPD had "solved" the Tate case. Warrants had been issued for the arrests of three persons:

Charles D. Watson, twenty-four, who was now in custody in McKinney, Texas; Patricia Krenwinkel, twenty-one, who was in custody in Mobile, Alabama; and Linda Kasabian, age and present whereabouts unknown. It was anticipated that an additional four or five persons would be named in indictments which would be sought from the Los Angeles County grand jury. (Neither Charles Manson nor Susan Atkins was mentioned by name in the press conference.)

These persons, Davis continued, were also involved in the murder deaths of Rosemary and Leno LaBianca.

This came as a big surprise to most of the newsmen, since LAPD had maintained almost from the start that there was no connection between the two homicides. Though a few reporters had suspected the crimes were linked, they had been unable to sell their theories to LAPD.

Davis went on to say: "The Los Angeles Police Department wishes to express their appreciation for the magnificent cooperation rendered by other law enforcement agencies during the development of information regarding both of the above cases, in particular, the Los Angeles Sheriff's office."

Davis did not mention that it had taken LAPD over two months to follow up the lead LASO had supplied them the day after the Tate murders.

Questioned by reporters, Davis credited "tenacious investigation carried on by robbery-homicide detectives" with forcing the break in the case. He stated that the investigators "developed a suspicion which caused them to do a vigorous amount of work in this Spahn Ranch area and the people connected with Spahn Ranch which led us to where we are today."

There was also no mention of that ten-cent telephone call.

The reporters ran for the phones.

Caballero called Aaron. He wanted to interview Susan Atkins on tape, but he didn't want to do it at Sybil Brand, where there was a chance one of the other Manson girls would hear of it. Also, he felt Susan would be inclined to talk more freely in other surroundings. He suggested having her brought to his own office.

Though unusual, the request wasn't unprecedented. Aaron made up a removal order, which was signed by Judge William Keene, and that evening Susan Atkins, escorted by two sheriff's deputies, was taken to Caballero's office, where Caballero and his associate, Paul Caruso, interviewed her on tape.

The tape was for two purposes, Caballero told Aaron. He wanted it for the psychiatrists in case he decided on an insanity plea. And if we went ahead on the deal, he would let us listen to it before we took the case to the grand jury.

December 2, 1969

LAPD called a few minutes after I arrived at the office. All five suspects were now in custody, Linda Kasabian just having voluntarily surrendered to Concord, New Hampshire, police. According to her mother, Linda had admitted to being present at the Tate residence but claimed she had not participated in the murders. It looked as if she wasn't going to fight extradition.

A somewhat different decision had been reached in Texas.

McKinney was less than thirty miles north of Dallas, and only a few miles from Farmersville, where Charles Watson had grown up and gone to school. Audie Murphy had been a Farmersville boy. Now they had another local celebrity.

The news had already broken by the time Sartuchi and Nielsen reached McKinney. Stories in the Texas papers described Watson as having been an A student in high school, a football, basketball, and track star, who still held the state record for the low hurdles. Most local residents

expressed shocked disbelief. "Charles was the boy next
door," one said. "It was drugs that did it," an uncle told
reporters. "He started taking them at college and that was
where the trouble started." The principal of Farmersville
High was quoted as saying, "It almost makes you afraid to
send your kids off to college any more."

On the instruction of Watson's attorney, Bill Boyd, the
Los Angeles detectives were not allowed to speak to his
client. Sheriff Montgomery wouldn't even permit them to
fingerprint him. Sartuchi and Nielsen did see Watson,
however—accidentally. While they were talking to the
sheriff, Watson passed them on the stairs, on his way to the
visitor's room. According to their report, he was well
dressed, clean-shaven, with short, not long, hair. He appeared in good health and looked like "a clean-cut college
boy."

While in McKinney, the detectives established that Watson had gone to California in 1967 and that he hadn't
moved back until November 1969—long after the murders.

Sartuchi and Nielsen returned to Los Angeles convinced
we'd have little cooperation from the local authorities. It
wasn't only a matter of relatives; somehow the whole affair had become involved in state politics!

"Little cooperation" would be a gross exaggeration.

Reporters were busy tracing the wanderings of the nomadic Family and interviewing those members not in custody. I asked Gail to save the papers, knowing the interviews might be useful at a later date. Though still un-
charged with the murders, Charles Manson had now taken
center stage. Sandy: "The first time I heard him sing it was
like an angel . . ." Squeaky: "He gave off a lot of magic.
But he was sort of a changeling. He seemed to change every time I saw him. He seemed ageless . . ."

There were also interviews with acquaintances and relatives of the suspects. Joseph Krenwinkel recalled how in
September 1967 his daughter Patricia left her Manhattan
Beach apartment, her job, and her car, not even picking
up a paycheck due her, to join Manson. "I am convinced
he was some kind of hypnotist."

Krenwinkel was not the only one to make that suggestion. Attorney Caballero talked to reporters outside the Santa Monica courtroom where his client had just entered a not guilty plea to the Hinman murder. Susan Atkins was under the "hypnotic spell" of Manson, Caballero said, and had "nothing to do with the murders" despite her presence at the Hinman and Tate residences.

Caballero also told the press his client was going to go before the grand jury and tell the complete story. This was the first confirmation we had that Susan Atkins had agreed to cooperate.

That same day LAPD interviewed Barbara Hoyt, whose parents had persuaded her to contact the police. Barbara had lived with the Family off and on since April 1969, and had been with them at Spahn, Myers, and Barker ranches.

The pretty seventeen-year-old's story came out in bits and pieces, over several interviews. Among her disclosures:

One evening while at Spahn, about a week after the August 16 raid, she had heard screams that seemed to come from down the creek. They lasted a long time, five to ten minutes, and she was sure they were Shorty's. After that night she never saw Shorty again.

The next day she heard Manson tell Danny DeCarlo that Shorty had committed suicide, "with a little help from us." Manson had also asked DeCarlo if lime would dispose of a body.

While at Myers Ranch, in early September 1969, Barbara had overheard Manson tell someone—she wasn't sure whom—that it had been real hard killing Shorty, once he had been "brought to Now." They'd hit him over the head with a pipe, Manson said, then everyone stabbed him, and finally Clem had chopped his head off. After that they'd cut him up in nine pieces.

While still at Myers, Barbara had also overheard Sadie tell Ouisch about the murders of Abigail Folger and Sharon Tate. Sometime later Ouisch told Barbara that she knew of ten other people the group had murdered.

Not long after this, Barbara and another girl—Sherry Ann Cooper, aka Simi Valley Sherri—fled the Family's Death Valley hideout. Manson caught up with them in

Ballarat, but, because other people were present, had let them go, even giving them twenty dollars for their bus fare to Los Angeles.*

Although very frightened, Barbara agreed to cooperate with us.

That cooperation would nearly cost her life.

About this same time another of Manson's girls agreed to help the police. She was the last person from whom I expected cooperation—Mary Brunner, the first member of the Manson Family.

Following his release from prison in March 1967, Charles Manson had gone to San Francisco. A prison acquaintance found him a room across the bay in Berkeley. In no hurry to find a job, subsisting mostly by panhandling, Manson would wander Telegraph Avenue or sit on the steps of the Sather Gate entrance to the University of California, playing his guitar. Then one day along came this librarian. As Charlie related the story to Danny DeCarlo, "She was out walking her dog. High-button blouse. Nose stuck up in the air, walking her little poodle. And Charlie's fresh out of the joint and along he comes talking his bullshit."

Mary Brunner, then twenty-three, had a B.A. degree in history from the University of Wisconsin and was working as an assistant librarian at the University of California. She was singularly unattractive, and Manson apparently was one of the first persons who thought her worth cultivating. It was possible he recalled the days when he lived off Fat Flo.

"So one thing led to another," DeCarlo resumed. "He moved in with her. Then he comes across this other girl. 'No, there will be no other girls moving in with me!' Mary says. She flatly refused to consider the idea. After the girl had moved in, two more came along. And Mary says, 'I'll accept one other girl but never three!' Four, five, all the

---

*We later received information indicating that Manson may have sent three of his followers to Los Angeles with instructions to either bring back the girls or kill them, but we were never able to prove this. This was the same trip when a flat tire prevented the murder of Cathy Gillies' grandmother, the owner of Myers Ranch.

way up to eighteen. This was in Frisco. Mary was the first."

The Family had been born.

By this time Manson had discovered the Haight. According to a tale Manson himself often told his followers, one day a young boy handed him a flower. "It blew my mind," he'd recall. Questioning the youth, he learned that in San Francisco there was free food, music, dope, and love, just for the taking. The boy took him to Haight-Ashbury, Manson later told Steve Alexander, a writer for the underground paper *Tuesday's Child:* "And we slept in the park and we lived on the streets and my hair got a little longer and I started playing music and people liked my music and people smiled at me and put their arms around me and hugged me—I didn't know how to act. It just took me away. It grabbed me up, man, that there were people that are real."

They were also young, naïve, eager to believe, and, perhaps even more important, belong. There were followers aplenty for any self-styled guru. It didn't take Manson long to sense this. In the underground milieu into which he'd stumbled, even the fact that he was an ex-convict conferred a certain status. Rapping a line of metaphysical con that borrowed as much from pimping as joint jargon and Scientology, Manson began attracting followers, almost all girls at first, then a few young boys.

"There are a lot of Charlies running around, believe me," observed Roger Smith, Manson's parole officer during his San Francisco period.

But with one big difference: somewhere along the line—I wasn't yet sure *how* or *where* or *when*—Manson developed a control over his followers so all-encompassing that he could ask them to violate the ultimate taboo—say "Kill" and they would do it.

Many automatically assumed the answer was drugs. But Dr. David Smith, who got to know the group through his work in the Haight-Ashbury Free Medical Clinic, felt "sex, not drugs, was the common denominator" in the Manson Family. "A new girl in Charlie's Family would bring with her a certain middle-class morality. The first thing Charlie did was to see that all this was worn down.

That way he was able to eliminate the controls that normally govern our lives."

Sex, drugs—they were certainly part of the answer, and I'd soon learn a great deal more about how Manson used both—but they were only part. There was something more, a lot more.

Manson himself de-emphasized the importance of drugs, at least as far as he was concerned. During this period he took his first LSD trip. He later said that it "enlightened my awareness" but added "being in jail for so long had already left my awareness pretty well open." Aware Charlie was.

Manson claimed he foresaw the decline of the Haight even before it came into full flower. Saw police harassment, bad trips, heavy vibes, people ripping off one another and OD'ing in the streets. During the famous Summer of Love, with free rock concerts and Owsley's acid and a hundred more young people arriving every day, he got an old school bus, loaded up his followers, and split, "looking for a place to get away from the Man."

Mary Brunner eventually left her job and joined Manson's wandering caravan. She had a child by him, Michael Manson, the whole Family participating in the delivery, Manson himself biting through the umbilical cord.

Interviewed in Eau Claire, Wisconsin, where she had gone following her release from jail, Mary Brunner agreed to cooperate with the police in return for immunity in the Hinman murder. She supplied numerous details regarding that crime. She also said that in the latter part of September 1969, Tex Watson had told her about the murder of Shorty. They had buried his body near the railroad tracks at Spahn, Tex said, and Gypsy abandoned his car in Canoga Park near a residence the Family had previously occupied on Gresham Street. On the basis of this information, LASO began a search for both the body and the vehicle.

Obviously, Mary Brunner would be an important witness in both the Hinman and Shea cases. Though she had been in jail when the Tate and LaBianca murders occurred, for a time I even considered using her as a witness in that case, since she could testify to the beginnings of the

Family. But I remained very leery of her. According to others I interviewed, her devotion to Manson was fanatical. I just couldn't visualize her testifying against the father of her child.

The Tate case had been big news abroad since the murders occurred, eclipsing even the incident at Chappaquiddick. The arrests commanded just as much attention.

Because of the time difference, it was nearly midnight of December 1 before reports of the "hippie kill cult" reached London. As in the United States, the sensational dispatches dominated the headlines of the papers the next day, led off radio and TV broadcasts.

At eleven that morning a maid in the Talgarth Hotel on Talgarth Road in London, tried to open the door of a room occupied by an American youth named Joel Pugh. It was locked from the inside. Shortly after 6 P.M. the hotel manager unlocked the door with a passkey. "It only opened about one foot," he stated. "There seemed to be a weight behind it." Kneeling down and reaching in, "I felt what seemed like an arm." He hastily called the police. A constable from Hammersmith station arrived minutes later and pushed the door open. Behind it was the body of Joel Pugh. He was lying on his back, unclothed except for a sheet over the lower half of his body. His throat had been slit, twice. There was a bruise on his forehead, slash marks on both wrists, and two bloody razor blades, one less than two feet from the body. There were no notes, although there were some "writings" in reverse on the mirror, along with some "comic-book type drawings."

According to the manager, Pugh had checked into the room on October 27 with a young lady who had left after three weeks. A "hippie in appearance," Pugh was quiet, went out rarely, seemed to have no friends.

There being "no wound not incapable of being self-inflicted," the coroner's inquest concluded that Pugh "took his own life while the balance of his mind was disturbed."

Although the circumstances of the death, including the wounds themselves, were equally if not more consistent with murder, it was considered a routine suicide. No one thought the drawings or writings important enough to take down (the manager later recalled only the words "Jack and Jill"). No attempt was made to determine the time of death. Nor, though Pugh's room was on the ground floor and could be entered and left through the window, did anyone feel it necessary to check for latent prints.

At the time no one connected the death with the big American news that day. If it hadn't been for a brief reference in a letter over a month later, we probably would have remained unaware that Joel Dean Pugh, age twenty-nine, former Manson Family member and husband of Family member Sandra Good, had joined the lengthening list of mysterious deaths connected with the case.

When she and Squeaky moved out of their motel room in Independence, Sandy left some papers behind. Among them was a letter from an unidentified former Family member which contained the line: "I would not want what happened to Joel to happen to me."

December 3, 1969

About eight that night Richard Caballero brought the Susan Atkins tape to LAPD. He requested that no copy be made; however, I was allowed to take notes. In addition to myself, both Lieutenants Helder and LePage and four or five detectives were present while the tape was being played. We said little as, with all the casualness of a child reciting what she did that day in school, Susan Atkins matter-of-factly described the slaughter of seven people.

The voice was that of a young girl. But except for occasional giggles—"And Sharon went through quite a few changes [laughs], quite a few changes"—it was flat, emotionless, dead. It was as if all the human feelings had been erased. *What kind of creature is this?* I wondered.

I'd soon know. Caballero had agreed that before we took the case to the grand jury, I could personally interview Susan Atkins.

The tape lasted about two hours. Although the monumental job of proving their guilt remained, when the tape had ended—Caballero saying to Susan, "O.K., now we're going to get you something to eat, including some ice cream"—we at least knew, for the first time, exactly who had been involved in the Tate and LaBianca murders.

Though Manson had sent the killers to 10050 Cielo Drive, he had not gone along himself. Those who did go were Charles "Tex" Watson, Susan Atkins, Patricia Krenwinkel, and Linda Kasabian. One man, three girls, who would mercilessly shoot and stab five people to death.

Manson, however, did enter the Waverly Drive residence the next night, to tie up Rosemary and Leno LaBianca. He then sent in Watson, Krenwinkel, and Leslie Van Houten, aka Sankston, with instructions to "kill them."

Susan Atkins herself hadn't been inside the LaBianca residence. She had remained in the car with Clem and Linda. But she had heard—from Manson, Krenwinkel, and Van Houten—what had occurred inside.

Though the tape cleared up some mysteries, many remained. And there were discrepancies. For example, although Susan admitted stabbing the big man (Frykowski) five or six times, "in self-defense," she said nothing about stabbing Sharon Tate. In contrast to what she had told Virginia Graham and Ronnie Howard, Susan now claimed that she had held Sharon while Tex stabbed her.

Returning to my office, I did what I do after every interview—converted my notes into a tentative interrogation. I had a lot of questions I wanted to ask Sadie Mae Glutz.

Linda Kasabian waived extradition proceedings and was flown back to Los Angeles that same day. She was booked into Sybil Brand at 11:15 P.M. Aaron was there, as was Linda's attorney, Gary Fleischman. Though Fleischman permitted her to ID some photographs of various Family members which Aaron had, he would not let Aaron question her. Aaron did ask her how she felt, and she replied, "Tired, but relieved." Aaron got the impression that Linda herself was anxious to tell what she knew but that Fleischman was holding out for a deal.

December 4, 1969

CONFIDENTIAL MEMORANDUM

TO: EVELLE J. YOUNGER
         District Attorney

FROM: AARON H. STOVITZ
         Head, Trials Division

SUBJECT: SUSAN ATKINS

A meeting was held today in Mr. Younger's office, commencing at 10:20 A.M. and concluding at 11 A.M. Present at the meeting were Mr. Younger, Paul Caruso, Richard Caballero, Aaron Stovitz and Vincent Bugliosi.

Discussion was had as to whether or not immunity should be given to Susan Atkins in exchange for her testimony at the Grand Jury hearing and subsequent trial. It was decided that she would *not* be given immunity.

Mr. Caballero made it known that at this moment his client may not testify at the trial due to her fear of the physical presence of Charles Manson and the other participants in the Sharon Tate murders.

Discussion was held concerning the value of Susan Atkins' testimony. Agreement was reached upon the following points:

1. That Susan Atkins' information has been vital to law enforcement.

2. In view of her past cooperation and in the event that she testifies truthfully at the Grand Jury, the prosecution will not seek the death penalty against her in any of the three cases that are now known to

the police; namely, the Hinman murder, the Sharon Tate murders, and the LaBianca murders.

3. The extent to which the District Attorney's Office will assist Defense Counsel in an attempt to seek less than a first degree murder, life sentence, will depend upon the extent to which Susan Atkins continues to cooperate.

4. That in the event that Susan Atkins does not testify at the trial or that the prosecution does not use her as a witness at the trial, the prosecution will not use her testimony, given at the Grand Jury, against her.

Caballero had made an excellent deal, as far as his client was concerned. If she testified truthfully before the grand jury, we could not seek the death penalty against her in the Hinman, Tate, and LaBianca cases; nor could we use her grand jury testimony against her or any of her co-defendants when they were brought to trial. As Caballero later put it, "She gave up nothing and got everything in return."

For our part, I felt we got very much the short end. Susan Atkins would tell her story at the grand jury. We'd get an indictment. And that would be all we would have, a scrap of paper. For Caballero was convinced she would never testify at the trial. He was worried that even now she might suddenly change her mind.

We had no choice but to rush the case to the grand jury, which was meeting the following day.

Our case was getting a little stronger. The previous day Sergeant Sam McLarty of the Mobile Police Department had taken Patricia Krenwinkel's prints. On receiving the exemplar from Mobile, Sergeant Frank Marz of LAPD "made" one print. The print of the little finger on Krenwinkel's left hand matched a latent print officer Boen had lifted from the frame on the left French door *inside* Sharon Tate's bedroom. This was the blood-splattered door that led outside to the pool.

We now had a second piece of physical evidence linking still another of the suspects to the crime scene.

But we didn't have either suspect. Like Watson, Kren-winkel intended to fight extradition. She would be held fourteen days without bond. If extradition papers were not there before the fifteenth day, she would be released.

Caballero drove me to his office in Beverly Hills. By the time we arrived, about 5:30 P.M., Susan Atkins was al-ready there, having been taken out of Sybil Brand on the basis of another court order, requested by Aaron. Cabal-lero had suggested that Susan would be much more apt to speak freely with me in the relaxed atmosphere of his of-fice than at Sybil Brand, and Miller Leavy, Aaron, and I had agreed.

Although she had opened up to both Virginia Graham and Ronnie Howard, my interview with Susan Atkins on the Tate-LaBianca murders was the first she had had with any law-enforcement officer. It would also be the last.

Twenty-one years old, five feet five, 120 pounds, long brown hair, brown eyes, a not unattractive face, but with a distant, far-off look, similar to the expressions of Sandy and Squeaky but even more pronounced.

Although this was the first time I had seen Susan At-kins, I already knew quite a bit about her. Born in San Ga-briel, California, she had grown up in San Jose. Her mother had died of cancer while Susan was still in her teens, and, after numerous quarrels with her father, she'd dropped out of high school and drifted to San Francisco. Hustler, topless dancer, kept woman, gun moll—she'd been all these things even before meeting Charles Manson. I had a certain amount of pity for her. I tried my best to understand her. But I couldn't summon up very much compassion, not after having seen the photographs of what had been done to the Tate victims.

After Caballero introduced us, I informed her of her constitutional rights and obtained permission to interview her.

A male and female deputy sheriff sat just outside the open door of Caballero's office, watching Susan's every move. Caballero remained for most of the interview, leav-ing only to take a few phone calls. I had Susan tell me the whole story, from the time she first met Manson in

Haight-Ashbury in 1967 to the present. Periodically I'd halt her narrative to ask questions.

"Were you, Tex, or any of the others under the influence of LSD or any other drug on the night of the Tate murders?"

"No."

"What about the next night, the night the LaBiancas were killed?"

"No. Neither night."

There was something mysterious about her. She would talk rapidly for a few minutes, then pause, head slightly cocked to the side, as if sensing voices no one else could.

"You know," she confided, "Charlie is looking at us right now and he can hear everything we are saying."

"Charlie is up in Independence, Sadie."

She smiled, secure in the knowledge that she was right and I, an outsider, an unbeliever, was wrong.

Looking at her, I thought to myself, This is the star witness for the prosecution? I'm going to build my case upon the testimony of this very, very strange girl?

She was crazy. I had no doubt about it. Probably not legally insane, but crazy nonetheless.

As on the tape, she admitted stabbing Frykowski but denied stabbing Sharon Tate. I'd conducted hundreds of interviews; you get a sort of visceral reaction when someone is lying. I felt that she *had* stabbed Sharon but didn't want to admit it to me.

I had to interview over a dozen witnesses that same night: Winifred Chapman, the first police officers to arrive at Cielo and Waverly, Granado and the fingerprint men, Lomax from Hi Standard, Coroner Noguchi and Deputy Medical Examiner Katsuyama, DeCarlo, Melcher, Jakobson. Each presented special problems. Winifred Chapman was petulent, querulous: she wouldn't testify to seeing any bodies, or any blood, or . . . Coroner Noguchi was a rambler: he had to be carefully prepared so he would stick to the subject. Danny DeCarlo hadn't been believable in the Beausoleil trial: I had to make sure the grand jury believed him. It was necessary not only to extract from very disparate witnesses, many of them experts in their individual fields, exactly what was relevant, but to bring these pieces together into a solid, convincing case.

Seven murder victims, multiple defendants: a case like this was not only probably unprecedented, it required weeks of preparation. Because of Chief Davis' rush to break the news, we'd had only days.

It was 2 A.M. before I finished. I still had to convert my notes to interrogation. It was 3:30 before I finished. I was up at 6 A.M. In three hours we had to take the Tate and LaBianca cases before the Los Angeles County grand jury.

December 5, 1969

"Sorry. No comment." Although grand jury proceedings are by law secret—neither the DA's Office, the witnesses, nor the jurors being allowed to discuss the evidence—this didn't keep the reporters from trying. There must have been a hundred newsmen in the narrow hallway outside the grand jury chambers; some were atop tables, so it looked as if they were stacked to the ceiling.

In Los Angeles the grand jury consists of twenty-three persons, picked by lot from a list of names submitted by each Superior Court judge. Of that number twenty-one were present, two-thirds of whom would have to concur to return an indictment. The proceedings themselves are usually brief. The prosecution presents just enough of its case to get an indictment and no more. Though in this instance the testimony would extend over two days, the "star witness for the prosecution" would tell her story in less than one.

Attorney Richard Caballero was the first witness, testifying that he had informed his client of her rights. Caballero then left the chambers. Not only are witnesses not allowed to have their attorneys present, each witness testifies outside the hearing of the other witnesses.

THE SERGEANT AT ARMS   "Susan Atkins."

The jurors, seven men and fourteen women, looked at her with obvious curiosity.

Aaron informed Susan of her rights, among which was her right not to incriminate herself. She waived them. I then took over the questioning, establishing that she knew Charles Manson and taking her back to the day they first met. It was over two years ago. She was living in a house on Lyon Street in the Haight-Ashbury district of San Francisco, with a number of other young people, most of whom were into drugs.

A.   ". . . and I was sitting in the living room and a man walked in and he had a guitar with him and all of a sudden he was surrounded by a group of girls." The man sat down and began to play, "and the song that caught my attention most was 'The Shadow of Your Smile,' and he sounded like an angel."

Q.   "You are referring to Charles Manson?"

A.   "Yes. And when he was through singing, I wanted to get some attention from him, and I asked him if I could play his guitar . . . and he handed me the guitar and I thought, 'I can't play this,' and then he looked at me and said, 'You can play that if you want to.'

"Now he had never heard me say 'I can't play this,' I only thought it. So when he told me I could play it, it blew my mind, because he was inside my head, and I knew at that time that he was something that I had been looking for . . . and I went down and kissed his feet."

A day or two later Manson returned to the house and asked her to go for a walk. "And we walked a couple blocks to another house and he told me he wanted to make love with me.

"Well, I acknowledged the fact that I wanted to make love with him, and he told me to take off my clothes, so I uninhibitedly took off my clothes, and there happened to be a full-length mirror in the room, and he told me to go over and look at myself in the mirror.

"I didn't want to do it, so he took me by my hand and stood me in front of the mirror, and I turned away and he said, 'Go ahead and look at yourself. There is nothing wrong with you. You are perfect. You have always been perfect.' "

Q. "What happened next?"

A. "He asked me if I had ever made love with my father. I looked at him and kind of giggled and I said, 'No.' And he said, 'Have you ever thought about making love with your father?' I said, 'Yes.' And he told me, 'All right, when you are making love . . . picture in your mind that I am your father.' And I did, I did so, and it was a very beautiful experience."

Susan said that before she met Manson she felt she was "lacking something." But then "I gave myself to him, and in return for that he gave me back to myself. He gave me the faith in myself to be able to know that I am a woman."

A week or so later, she, Manson, Mary Brunner, Ella Jo Bailey, Lynette Fromme, and Patricia Krenwinkel, together with three or four boys whose names she couldn't remember, left San Francisco in an old school bus from which they had removed most of the seats, furnishing it with brightly colored rugs and pillows. For the next year and a half they roamed—north to Mendocino, Oregon, Washington; south to Big Sur, Los Angeles, Mexico, Nevada, Arizona, New Mexico; and, eventually, back to L.A., living first in various residences in Topanga Canyon, Malibu, Venice, and then, finally, Spahn Ranch. En route others joined them, a few staying permanently, most only temporarily. According to Susan, they went through changes, and learned to love. The girls made love with each of the boys, and with each other. But Charlie was complete love. Although he did not have sex with her often—only six times in the more than two years they were together—"he would give himself completely."

Q. "Were you very much in love with him, Susan?"

A. "I was in love with the reflection and the reflection I speak of is Charlie Manson's."

Q. "Was there any limit to what you would do for him?"

A. "No."

I was laying the foundation for the very heart of my case against Manson, that Susan and the others would do anything for him, up to and including murder at his command.

Q. "What was it about Charlie that caused you girls to be in love with him and to do what he wanted you to do?"

A. "Charlie is the only man I have ever met . . . on the face of this earth . . . that is a complete man. He will not take back-talk from a woman. He will not let a woman talk him into doing anything. He is a man."

Charlie had given her the name Sadie Mae Glutz because "in order for me to be completely free in my mind I had to be able to completely forget the past. The easiest way to do this, to change identity, is by doing so with a name."

According to Susan, Charlie himself went under a variety of names, calling himself the Devil, Satan, Soul.

Q. "Did Mr. Manson ever call himself Jesus?"

A. "He personally never called himself Jesus."

Q. "Did you ever call him Jesus?" From my questioning the night before, I anticipated that Susan would be evasive about this, and she was.

A. "He represented a Jesus Christ-like person to me."

Q. "Do you think Charlie is an evil person?"

A. "In your standards of evil, looking at him through your eyes, I would say yes. Looking at him through my eyes, he is as good as he is evil, he is as evil as he is good. You could not judge the man."

Although Susan didn't state that she believed Manson was Christ, the implication was there. Though I was at this time far from understanding it myself, it was important that I give the jury some explanation, however partial, for Manson's control over his followers. Incredible as all this was to the predominantly upper-middle-class, upper-middle-aged grand jurors, it was nothing compared to what they would hear when she described those two nights of murder.

I worked up to them gradually, having her describe Spahn Ranch and the life there, and asking her how they survived. People gave them things, Susan said. Also, they panhandled. And "the supermarkets all over Los Angeles throw away perfectly good food every day, fresh vegetables and sometimes cartons of eggs, packages of cheese that are stamped to a certain date, but the food is still good, and us girls used to go out and do 'garbage runs.'"

DeCarlo had told me of one such garbage run, when, to the astonishment of supermarket employees, the girls had driven up in Dennis Wilson's Rolls-Royce.

They also stole—credit cards, other things.

Q. "Did Charlie ask you to steal?"

A. "No, I took it upon myself. I was—we'd get programmed to do things."

Q. "Programmed by Charlie?"

A. "By Charlie, but it's hard for me to explain it so that you can see the way—the way I see. The words that would come from Charlie's mouth would not come from inside him, [they] would come from what I call the Infinite."

And sometimes, at night, they "creepy-crawled."

Q. "Explain to these members of the jury what you mean by that."

A. "Moving in silence so that nobody sees us or hears us . . . Wearing very dark clothing . . ."

Q. "Entering residences at night?"

A. "Yes."

They would pick a house at random, anywhere in Los Angeles, slip in while the occupants were asleep, creep and crawl around the rooms silently, maybe move things so when the people awakened they wouldn't be in the same places they had been when they went to bed. Everyone carried a knife. Susan said she did it "because everybody else in the Family was doing it" and she wanted that experience.

These creepy-crawling expeditions were, I felt sure the jury would surmise, dress rehearsals for murder.

Q. "Did you call your group by any name, Susan?"

A. "Among ourselves we called ourselves the Family." It was, Susan said, "a family like no other family."

I thought I heard a juror mutter, "Thank God!"

Q. "Susan, were you living at Spahn Ranch on the date of August the eighth, 1969?"

A. "Yes."

Q. "Susan, on that date did Charlie Manson instruct you and some other members of the Family to do anything?"

A. "I never recall getting any actual instructions from

Charlie other than getting a change of clothing and a knife and was told to do exactly what Tex told me to do."

Q. "Did Charlie indicate to you the type of clothing you should take?"

A. "He told me . . . wear dark clothes."

Susan ID'd photos of Watson, Krenwinkel, and Kasabian, as well as a photo of the old Ford in which the four of them left the ranch. Charlie waved to them as they drove off. Susan didn't notice the time, but it was night. There was a pair of wire cutters in the back seat, also a rope. She, Katie, and Linda each had a knife; Tex had a gun and, she believed, a knife too. Not until they were en route did Tex tell them, to quote Susan, that they "were going to a house up on the hill that used to belong to Terry Melcher, and the only reason why we were going to that house was because Tex knew the outline of the house."

Q. "Did Tex tell you why you four were going to Terry Melcher's former residence?"

Matter-of-factly, with no emotion whatsoever, Susan replied, "To get all of their money and to kill whoever was there."

Q. "It didn't make any difference who was there, you were told to kill them; is that correct?"

A. "Yes."

They got lost on the way. However, Tex finally recognized the turnoff and they drove to the top of the hill. Tex got out, climbed the telephone pole, and, using the wire cutters, severed the wires. (LAPD still hadn't got back to me regarding the test cuts made by the pair found at Barker.) When Tex returned to the car, they drove back down the hill, parked at the bottom, then, bringing along their extra clothing, walked back up. They didn't enter the grounds through the gate "because we thought there might be an alarm system or electricity." To the right of the gate was a steep, brushy incline. The fence wasn't as high here. Susan threw over her clothing bundle, then went over herself, her knife in her teeth. The others followed.

They were stowing their clothing in the bushes when Susan saw the headlights of a car. It was coming up the driveway in the direction of the gate. "Tex told us girls to lie down and be still and not make a sound. He went out of sight ... I heard him say 'Halt.'" Susan also heard another voice, male, say "Please don't hurt me, I won't say anything." "And I heard a gunshot and I heard another gunshot and another one and another one." Four shots, then Tex returned and told them to come on. When they got to the car, Tex reached inside and turned off the lights; then they pushed the car away from the gate, back up the driveway.

I showed Susan a photo of the Rambler. "It looked similar to it, yes." I then showed her the police photograph of Steven Parent inside the vehicle.

A. "That is the thing I saw in the car."

There were audible gasps from the jurors.

Q. "When you say 'thing,' you are referring to a human being?"

A. "Yes, human being."

The jurors had looked at the heart of Susan Atkins and seen ice.

They went on down the driveway, past the garage, to the house. Using a scale diagram I'd had prepared, Susan indicated their approach to the dining-room window. "Tex opened the window, crawled inside, and the next thing I knew he was at the front door."

Q. "Did all of you girls enter at that time?"

A. "Only two of us entered, one stayed outside."

Q. "Who stayed outside?"

A. "Linda Kasabian."

Susan and Katie joined Tex. There was a man lying on the couch (Susan ID'd a photo of Voytek Frykowski). "The man stretched his arms and woke up. I guess he thought some of his friends were coming from somewhere. He said, 'What time is it?' ... Tex jumped in front of him and held a gun in his face and said, 'Be quiet. Don't move or you're dead.' Frykowski said something like 'Who are you and what are you doing here?'"

Q. "What did Tex say to that, if anything?"

A. "He said, 'I am the Devil and I'm here to do the Devil's business ...'"

Tex then told Susan to check for other people. In the

first bedroom she saw a woman reading a book. (Susan ID'd a photo of Abigail Folger.) "She looked at me and smiled and I looked at her and smiled." She went on. A man and a woman were in the next bedroom. The man, who was sitting on the edge of the bed, had his back to Susan. The woman, who was pregnant, was lying on the bed. (Susan ID'd photos of Jay Sebring and Sharon Tate.) The pair were talking and neither saw her. Returning to the living room, she reported to Tex that there were three more people.

Tex gave her the rope and told her to tie up the man on the couch. After she'd done this, Tex ordered her to get the others. Susan walked into Abigail Folger's bedroom, "put a knife in front of her, and said, 'Get up and go into the living room. Don't ask any questions. Just do what I say.' " Katie, also armed with a knife, took charge of Folger while Susan got the other two.

None offered any resistance. All had the same expression on their faces, "Shock."

On entering the living room, Sebring asked Tex, "What are you doing here?" Tex told him to shut up, then ordered the three to lie on their stomachs on the floor in front of the fireplace. "Can't you see she's pregnant?" Sebring said. "Let her sit down."

When Sebring "didn't follow Tex's orders ... Tex shot him."

Q.   "Did you see Tex shoot Jay Sebring?"
A.   "Yes."
Q.   "With the gun that he had taken from Spahn Ranch?"
A.   "Yes."
Q.   "What happened next?"
A.   "Jay Sebring fell over in front of the fireplace and Sharon and Abigail screamed."

Tex ordered them to be quiet. When he asked if they had any money, Abigail said she had some in her purse in the bedroom. Susan went with her to get it. Abigail handed her seventy-two dollars and asked if she wanted her credit cards. Susan said she didn't. On their return to the living room, Tex told Susan to get a towel and retie Frykowski's hands; she did, she said, but couldn't get the knot very tight. Tex then took the rope and tied it first around Sebring's neck, then the necks of Abigail and Sharon. He threw the end of the rope over the beam in the ceiling and pulled on it, "which made Sharon and Abigail stand up so they wouldn't be choked to death . . ." Then, "I forget who said it, but one of the victims said, 'What are you going to do with us?' and Tex said, 'You are all going to die.' And at that time they began to plead for their lives."

Q. "What is the next thing that happened?"

A. "Then Tex ordered me to go over and kill Frykowski."

As she raised her knife, Frykowski, who had managed to free his hands, jumped up and "knocked me down, and I grabbed him as best I could, and then it was a fight for my life as well as him fighting for his life.

"Somehow he got ahold of my hair and pulled it very hard and I was screaming for Tex to help me, or somebody to help me, and Frykowski, he was also screaming.

"Somehow he got behind me, and I had the knife in my right hand and I was—I was—I don't know where I was at but I was just swinging with the knife, and I remember hitting something four, five times repeatedly behind me. I didn't see what it was I was stabbing."

Q. "But did it appear to be a human being?"

A. "I never stabbed a human being before, but I just know it was going into something."

Q. "Could it have been Frykowski?"

A. "It could have been Frykowski, it could have been a chair, I don't know what it was."

Susan had changed her story. In my interview with her, and on the tape, she had admitted to stabbing Frykowski "three or four times in the leg." Also, if the story she told Virginia Graham was true, she knew exactly how it felt to stab someone, i.e., Gary Hinman.

Frykowski ran for the front door, "yelling for his life, for somebody to come help him." Tex got to him and hit him over the head several times with "I believe a gun butt." Tex later told her that he had broken the gun hitting Frykowski and that it wouldn't work any more.* Apparently Tex had a knife ready, as he began stabbing Frykowski "as best he could because Frykowski was still fighting." Meanwhile, "Abigail Folger had gotten loose from the rope and was in a fight with Katie, Patricia Krenwinkel . . ."

THE FOREMAN "We have a grand juror who would like to be excused for just a couple of minutes."

A recess was taken. There was more than one pale face in the jury box.

We resumed where Susan had left off. Someone was moaning, she said. Tex ran over to Sebring, "and bent down and viciously stabbed him in the back many times . . .

"Sharon Tate, I remember seeing her struggling with the rope." Tex ordered Susan to take care of her. Susan locked her arm around Sharon's neck, forcing her back onto the couch. She was begging for her life. "I looked at her and said, 'Woman, I have no mercy for you.' And I knew that I was talking to myself, not to her . . ."

Q. "Did Sharon say anything about the baby at that point?"

A. "She said, 'Please let me go. All I want to do is have my baby.'"

"There was a lot of confusion going on . . . Tex went over to help Katie . . . I saw Tex stab Abigail Folger and just before he stabbed—maybe an instant before he stabbed her—she looked at him and let her arms go and looked at all of us and said, 'I give up. Take me.'"

I asked Susan how many times Tex had stabbed Abigail. "Only once," Susan replied. "She grabbed her middle section of her body and fell to the floor."

Tex then ran outside. Susan released her grip on Sharon but continued to guard her. When Tex returned, he told Susan, "Kill her." But, according to the story Susan was now telling, "I couldn't." Instead, "in order to make a diversion so that Tex couldn't see that I couldn't kill her, I grabbed her hand and held her arms, and then I saw Tex

*Although Frykowski had been shot twice, Susan couldn't recall the shooting, leaving in doubt exactly when this occurred.

stab her in the heart area around the chest." Sharon then fell from the couch to the floor. (Susan only mentioned Tex stabbing Sharon Tate once. According to the autopsy report, she had been stabbed sixteen times. According to Ronnie Howard, Susan told her, "I just kept stabbing her until she stopped screaming.")

The next thing she remembered, Susan now testified, was that she, Tex, and Katie were outside, and "I saw Abigail Folger on the front lawn, bent over falling onto the grass . . . I didn't see her go outside . . . and I saw Tex go over and stab her three or four—I don't know how many times . . ." (Abigail Folger had twenty-eight stab wounds.) "While he was doing that, Katie and I were looking for Linda, because she wasn't around . . . and then Tex walked over to Frykowski and kicked him in the head." Frykowski was on the front lawn, away from the door. When Tex kicked him, "the body didn't move very much. I believe it was dead at that time." (Which was not surprising, since Voytek Frykowski had been shot twice, struck over the head thirteen times with a blunt object, and stabbed fifty-one times.)

Then "Tex told me to go back into the house and write something on the door in one of the victims' blood . . . He said, 'Write something that will shock the world.' . . . I had previously been involved in something similar to this [Hinman], where I saw 'political piggy' written on the wall, so that stuck very heavily in my mind . . ." Re-entering the house, she picked up the same towel she had used to tie Frykowski's hands, and walked over to Sharon Tate. Then she heard sounds.

Q. "What kind of sounds were they?"

A. "Gurgling sounds like blood flowing into the body out of the heart."

Q. "What did you do then?"

A. "I picked up the towel and turned my head and touched her chest, and at the same time I saw she was pregnant and I knew that there was a living being inside of that body and I wanted to but I didn't have the courage to go ahead and take it . . . And I got the towel with Sharon Tate's blood, walked over to the door, and with the towel I wrote PIG on the door."

Susan then threw the towel back into the living room; she didn't look to see where it landed. (It fell on Sebring's face, hence the "hood" referred to in the press.)

Sadie, Tex, and Katie then picked up the bundles of spare clothing they'd hidden in the bushes. They left by the gate, Tex pushing the button, and hurried down the hill. "When we got to the car, Linda Kasabian started the car, and Tex ran up to her and said, 'What do you think you're doing? Get over on the passenger side. Don't do anything until I tell you to do it.' Then we drove off."

They changed clothing in the car, all except Linda, who, not having been in the house, had no blood on her. As they were driving away, Susan realized she had lost her knife, but Tex was against going back.

They drove somewhere along "Benedict Canyon, Mulholland Drive, I don't know [which street] ... until we came to what looked like an embankment going down like a cliff with a mountain on one side and a cliff on the other." They pulled off and stopped, and "Linda threw all the bloody clothes over the side of the hill ..." The weapons, the knives and gun, were tossed out at "three or four different places, I don't remember how many."

Susan then described, as she had to Virginia Graham and Ronnie Howard, how after they'd pulled off onto a side street and used a garden hose to wash off the blood, a man and a woman rushed out of the house and threatened to report them to the police. "And Tex looked at him and said, "Gee, I'm sorry. I didn't think you were home. We were just walking around and wanted a drink of water. We didn't mean to wake you up or disturb you.' And the man looked down the street and said, 'Is that your car?' And Tex said, 'No, I told you we were just walking.' The man said, 'I know that is your car. You better get in and get going.'"

They got in the car, and the man, apparently having decided to detain them, reached in to get the keys. Tex quickly started the car, however, and drove off fast.

After stopping at a service station on Sunset Boulevard, where they took turns going to the bathroom to check for "any other blood spots," they drove back to Spahn Ranch, arriving there, Susan guessed, about 2 A.M.

When they pulled up in front of the boardwalk of the old movie set, Charles Manson was waiting for them. He walked over to the car, leaned inside, and asked, "What are you doing home so early?"

According to Susan, Tex told Manson "basically just what we had done. That it all happened perfectly. There was a lot of—it happened very fast—a lot of panic, and he described it, 'Boy, it sure was helter skelter.' "

While at the service station, Susan had noticed blood on the door handles and steering wheel. She now went into the ranch kitchen and got a rag and a sponge and wiped it off.

Q. "How was Charles Manson acting when you arrived back at Spahn Ranch?"

A. "Charles Manson changes from second to second. He can be anybody he wants to be. He can put on any face he wants to put on at any given moment."

Patricia "was very silent." Tex was "nervous like he had just been through a traumatic experience."

Q. "How did you feel about what you had just done?"

A. "I almost passed out. I felt as though I had killed myself. I felt dead. I feel dead now."

After she'd finished cleaning the car, Susan and the others had gone to bed. She thought she had made love to someone, maybe Clem, but then again maybe she had imagined it.

The noon recess was called.

Throughout her testimony Susan had referred to the victims by name. After the recess I established that she hadn't known their names that night, nor had she ever seen any of them before. ". . . when I first saw them, my reaction was, 'Wow, they sure are beautiful people.' "

Susan first learned their identities the day after the murders, while watching the news on TV in the trailer next to George Spahn's house. Tex, Katie, and Clem were also here, and maybe Linda, though Susan wasn't sure.

Q. "As you were watching the television news coverage, did anyone say anything?"

Someone—Susan thought the words came from her

own mouth, but she wasn't positive—said either, "The Soul sure did pick a lulu," or "The Soul sure did a good job." She did remember saying that what had happened had "served its purpose." Which was? I asked.

A. "To instill fear into the establishment."

I asked Susan if any other members of the Family knew they had committed the Tate murders.

A. "The Family was so much together that nothing ever had to be said. We all just knew what each other would do or had done."

We came now to the second night, the evening of August 9 and the early-morning hours of August 10.

That evening Manson again told Susan to get an extra set of clothing. "I looked at him and I knew what he wanted me to do, and I gave a sort of sigh and went and did what he asked me to do."

Q. "Did he say what you were going to go out and do that night?" I asked.

A. "He said we were going to go out and do the same thing we did the last night . . . only two different houses . . ."

It was the same car and the same cast—Susan, Katie, Linda, and Tex—with three additions: Charlie, Clem, and Leslie. Susan didn't notice any knives, only a gun, which Charlie had.

They stopped in front of a house, "somewhere in Pasadena, I believe," Charlie got out, and the others drove around the block, then came back and picked him up. "He said he saw pictures of children through the window and he didn't want to do that house." In the future, however, Manson explained, they might have to kill the children also.

They stopped in front of another house, but saw some people nearby so remained in the car and after a few minutes drove off. At some point Susan fell asleep, she said. When she awakened, they were in a familiar neighborhood, near a house where, about a year before, she, Charlie, and about fifteen others had gone to an LSD party. The house had been occupied by a "Harold." She couldn't recall his last name.

Charlie got out, only he didn't walk up the driveway o

is particular house but the one next door. Susan went
ack to sleep. She woke up when Charlie returned. "He
aid, 'Tex, Katie, Leslie, go into the house. I have the peo-
le tied up. They are very calm.'

"He said something to the effect that last night Tex let
e people know they were going to be killed, which
aused panic, and Charlie said that he reassured the peo-
le with smiles in a very quiet manner that they were not
be harmed . . . And so Tex, Leslie, and Katie got out of
e car."

Susan ID'd photographs of Tex, Leslie, and Katie. Also
f the LaBianca residence, the long driveway, and the
ouse next door.

I asked Susan what else Charlie told the trio. She re-
lied that she "thought," but it may be "my imagination
at tells me this," that "Charlie instructed them to go in
nd kill them." She did recall him saying that they were
to paint a picture more gruesome than anybody had ever
een." He'd also told them that after they were done they
vere to hitchhike back to the ranch.

When Charlie returned to the car, he had a woman's
vallet with him. Then they drove around "in a predomi-
antly colored area."

Q. "What happened next?"

Susan said they stopped at a gas station. Then "Charlie
ave Linda Kasabian the woman's wallet and told her to
ut it in the bathroom in the gas station and leave it there,
oping that somebody would find it and use the credit
ards and thus be identified with the murder . . ."

I wondered about that wallet. To date, none of Rose-
ary LaBianca's credit cards had been used.

After leaving the station, Susan said, she went back to
sleep. "It was like I was drugged" though "I was not on
drugs at the time." When she woke up, they were back at
he ranch.

(At this time we were unaware that Susan Atkins had
nade some significant omissions in her grand jury tes-
imony—including three other attempts at murder that
night. Had we known of them, we probably would have
asked for an indictment of Clem. As it was, however, all
we had against him was Susan's statement that he had

been in the car. And we still had a slim hope that his brother, whom we'd contacted at the Highway Patrol Academy, might persuade him to cooperate with us.)

Susan had not entered the LaBianca residence. However, the next morning Katie told her what had happened inside.

. A. "She told me that when they got in the house they took the woman in the bedroom and put her on the bed and left Tex in the living room with the man ... And then Katie said the woman heard her husband being killed and started to scream, 'What are you doing to my husband?' And Katie said that she then proceeded to stab the woman ..."

Q. "Did she say what Leslie was doing while—"

A. "Leslie was helping Katie hold the woman down because the woman was fighting all the way up until she died ..." Later Katie told Susan that the last words the woman spoke—"What are you doing to my husband?"— would be the thought she would carry with her into infinity.

Afterwards, Katie told Susan, they wrote " 'Death to all pigs' on the refrigerator door or on the front door, and I think she said they wrote 'helter skelter' and 'arise.' "

Then Katie walked into the living room from the kitchen with a fork in her hand, and "she looked at the man's stomach and she had the fork in her hand and she put the fork in the man's stomach and watched it wobble back and forth. She said she was fascinated by it."

Susan also said that it was "Katie, I believe," who carved the word "war" on the man's stomach.

The three then took a shower and, since they were hungry, they went to the kitchen and fixed themselves something to eat.

According to Susan, Katie also told her that they presumed the couple had children and that they would probably find the bodies when they came over for Sunday dinner later that day.

After leaving the residence, "they dumped the old clothing in a garbage can a few blocks, maybe a mile away from the house." Then they hitchhiked back to Spahn Ranch, arriving about dawn.

I had only a few more questions for Susan Atkins.

Q. "Susan, did Charlie oftentimes use the word 'pig' or 'pigs'?"

A. "Yes."

Q. "How about 'helter skelter'?"

A. "Yes."

Q. "Did he use the word 'pigs' and 'helter skelter' very, very frequently?"

A. "Well, Charlie talks a lot ... In some of the songs he wrote, 'helter skelter' was in them and he'd talk about helter skelter. We all talked about helter skelter."

Q. "You say 'we'; are you speaking of the Family?"

A. "Yes."

Q. "What did the word 'pig' or 'pigs' mean to you and your Family?"

A. " 'Pig' was a word used to describe the establishment. But you must understand that all words had no meanings to us and that 'helter skelter' was explained to me."

Q. "By whom?"

A. "Charlie. I don't even like to say Charlie—I'd like to say the words came from his mouth—that helter skelter was to be the last war on the face of the earth. It would be all the wars that have ever been fought built one on top of the other, something that no man could conceive of in his imagination. You can't conceive of what it would be like to see every man judge himself and then take it out on every other man all over the face of the earth."

After a few more questions, I brought Susan Atkins' testimony to an end. As she nonchalantly stepped down from the witness stand, the jurors stared at her in disbelief. Not once had she shown a trace of remorse, sorrow, or guilt.

There were only four more witnesses that day. After Susan Atkins was taken from the room, Wilfred Parent was brought in to identify his son in a high-school prom picture. After identifying photos of the other Tate victims, Winifred Chapman testified that she had washed the front door of the Tate residence shortly before noon on Friday, August 8. This was important, since it meant that in order to leave a print Charles "Tex" Watson had to have been on the premises sometime after Mrs. Chapman left at four that afternoon.

Aaron questioned Terry Melcher. He described meeting Manson; told of how Manson had been along when Dennis Wilson drove him home to 10050 Cielo Drive one night; and described, very briefly, his two visits to Spahn Ranch, the first to audition Manson, the second to introduce him to Michael Deasy, who had a mobile recording unit and who he felt might be more interested in recording Manson than he was.*

According to various Family members, Melcher had made numerous promises to Manson, and hadn't come through on them. Melcher denied this: the first time he went to Spahn, he had given Manson fifty dollars, all the money he had in his pocket, because "I felt sorry for these people"; but it was for food, not an advance on a recording contract; and he'd made no promises. As for Manson's talent, he "wasn't impressed enough to allot the time necessary" to prepare and record him.

I wanted to interview Melcher in depth—I had a feeling that he was withholding something—but, like most of the other grand jury witnesses, he was here for a very limited purpose, and any real digging would have to wait.

Los Angeles Coroner Thomas Noguchi testified to the autopsy findings on the five Tate victims. When he had concluded, the session was adjourned until Monday.

That the proceedings were secret encouraged speculation, which, in some cases, appeared not as conjecture but fact. The headline on the Los Angeles *Herald Examiner* that afternoon read:

TATE KILLERS WILD ON
LSD, GRAND JURORS TOLD

It wasn't true; Susan Atkins had stated the very opposite, that the killers were not on drugs either night. But

---

*Manson gave Deasy some LSD. He had such a frightening "trip" that he wanted nothing more to do with Manson or his Family.

the myth was born, and it persisted, perhaps because it was the easiest explanation for what had happened.

Though, as I'd soon learn, drugs were one of several methods Manson used to obtain control over his followers, they had no part in these crimes, for a very simple reason: on these two nights of savage slaughter, Charles Manson wanted his assassins in complete control of their faculties.

The reality, and its implications, were far more frightening than the myth.

December 6-8, 1969

On Saturday, Joe Granado went to the impound garage in Canoga Park to examine John Swartz' 1959 Ford, which had been held there since the August 16 Spahn raid. This was the car Susan Atkins said the killers had used on both nights.

Granado got a positive benzidine reaction on a spot in the upper right-hand corner of the glove compartment, indicating blood, but there wasn't enough to determine whether it was animal or human.

When I finally got Joe's written report, I noticed the blood wasn't mentioned. Asked about this, Joe said the amount was so small he hadn't bothered to note it. I had Joe prepare a new report, this time including reference to the blood. Our case thus far was basically circumstantial, and in such a case each speck of evidence counts.

"I just had a talk with Gary Fleischman, Vince," Aaron said. "He wants a deal for his client Linda Kasabian. Complete immunity in exchange for her testimony at the trial. I told him maybe we could go along with her pleading to voluntary manslaughter, but we couldn't give her—"

"Christ, Aaron," I interrupted. "It's bad enough that we had to give Susan Atkins something! Look at it this

way—Krenwinkel's in Alabama, Watson's in Texas; for all
we know, we may not be able to extradite them before
the others go on trial; and Van Houten wasn't along on
the night of the Tate murders. If we give deals to Atkins
and Kasabian, who are we going to prosecute for the five
Tate killings? Just Charlie? The people of this city won't
tolerate that. They're shocked and outraged by these
crimes. Drive through Bel Air sometime; the fear is still so
real you can feel it."

According to Fleischman, Linda was anxious to testify.
He had urged her to fight extradition; she'd gone against
his advice and come back to California because she
wanted to tell the whole story.

"O.K., what can she testify to? According to Susan,
Linda never entered either the Tate or LaBianca residences. As far as we know, she wasn't an eyewitness to
any of the murders, with the possible exception of Steven
Parent. More important, as long as we have Susan, Linda's
testimony would be valueless to us, since Susan and Linda
are both accomplices. As you well know, the law is clear
on this: the testimony of one accomplice can't be used to
corroborate the testimony of another accomplice. What
we really need, more than anything else, is corroboration."

This was one of our biggest problems. In a sense it
didn't matter who ended up as our star witness; without
corroboration our case would be lost as a matter of law.
We not only had to find corroboration against *each* of the
defendants, that corroborating evidence had to be completely independent of the accomplice's testimony.

Aaron had seen Linda briefly, when she was booked
into Sybil Brand. I'd never seen her. For all I knew, she
was probably just as freaky as Sadie Mae Glutz.

"Now if Susan bolts back to Charlie," I told Aaron,
"and we're left without a major witness for the trial—as
well we might be—then we can talk about a deal for
Linda. In fact, if that happens, Linda may be our only
hope."

When the grand jury reconvened on Monday, we moved
quickly through the remaining testimony. Sergeant
Michael McGann described what he had found at 10050

Cielo Drive on the morning of August 9, 1969. Sergeant Frank Escalante testified to having rolled Charles Watson's prints on April 23, 1969, when he was arrested on a drug charge; Jerromme Boen of SID described how he lifted the latent from the front door of the Tate residence; and Harold Dolan, also of SID, testified to having compared it to the Watson exemplar, finding eighteen points of identity, eight more than LAPD requires for a positive identification. Sergeant William Lee testified regarding the pieces of gun grip and the .22 caliber bullets. Edward Lomax of Hi Standard matched the grips with his firm's .22 caliber Longhorn revolver, and gave statistics indicating that the gun itself, because of its low production figures, was "rather unique." Gregg Jakobson told of touting Manson to Melcher. Granado testified regarding the rope, the blood on the gun grips, and his discovery of the Buck knife.

It was for the most part highly technical testimony, and the appearance of Daniel DeCarlo provided a respite, as well as more than a little local color.

Aaron asked Danny: "Did you have any particular reason for staying at the ranch?"

A. "Lots of pretty girls up there."

How did he get along with particular girls—for example, Katie?

A. "We talked, that is about it, but I never did nothing. You know, I never snatched her up or anything."

Q. "And is your motorcycle club the kind that goes into a town and scares everybody?"

A. "No, that only happens in the movies."

DeCarlo's appearance, however, was intended for more than comic relief. He testified that Manson, Watson, and others, including himself, target-practiced with a .22 caliber Buntline revolver at Spahn. He said that he had last seen the gun "maybe a week, week and a half" before the sixteenth of August, and never after that. The drawing of the revolver which he had made for LAPD before he knew it was the Tate murder weapon was introduced into evidence. DeCarlo also recalled how he and Charlie had bought the three-strand nylon rope (which, being an ex-Coast Guardsman, he called "line") at the Jack Frost store in Santa Monica in June 1969, and, shown the rope found at Cielo, said it was "identical."

After Susan Atkins, the outlaw motorcyclist looked almost like a model citizen.

Deputy Medical Examiner David Katsuyama followed DeCarlo. Katsuyama had conducted the LaBianca autopsies. I'd have many, many problems with this witness. The grand jury provided only a sample. Aaron was to show Katsuyama a photo of Leno LaBianca's hands, which were bound with a leather thong. DeCarlo was then to retake the stand and describe how Charlie always wore leather thongs around his neck. Sergeant Patchett was to follow and introduce the thongs he had found in Independence among Manson's personal effects. He was also prepared to testify that they were "similar."

Aaron showed Katsuyama the photo, asking what material had been used to tie Leno LaBianca's hands. "Electrical cord," he replied. I managed to suppress a groan: the electrical cord had been around the necks of the LaBianca victims. Would he look at the photo a little more closely? It still looked like electrical cord to him. I finally had to show Katsuyama his own autopsy notes, where he'd written: "The hands are tied together with a rather thin leather thong."

Roxie Lucarelli, an officer with LAPD and a lifelong friend of Leno's, identified photos of the LaBiancas, both Susan and Frank Struthers being still too shaken by the deaths to testify. Sergeant Danny Galindo told what he had found at 3301 Waverly Drive the night of August 10-11, 1969, and stated that a search of the residence revealed no trace of Rosemary LaBianca's wallet.

Of the five girls brought down from Independence, Catherine Share, aka Gypsy, refused to testify, and we had not called Leslie Van Houten, since we were not aware that she was one of the LaBianca killers. The three remaining—Dianne Lake, aka Snake; Nancy Pitman, aka Brenda; and Ruth Ann Moorehouse, aka Ouisch—all denied any knowledge of the murders.

I'd anticipated this. However, I had another reason for calling them. If they appeared as defense witnesses when

we went to trial, any discrepancy between what they told
the grand jury and the trial jury would give me a prior inconsistent statement with which to impeach their testimony.

At 4:17 P.M. the Los Angeles County grand jury began
their deliberations. Exactly twenty minutes later they returned the following indictments: Leslie Van Houten, two
counts of murder and one count of conspiracy to commit
murder; Charles Manson, Charles Watson, Patricia Krenwinkel, Susan Atkins, and Linda Kasabian, seven counts of
murder and one count of conspiracy to commit murder.

We'd got the indictments. And that was about all we
had.

December 9-12, 1969

Neither Aaron nor I logged the calls we received, but it
would be a safe guess that we were getting upward of a
hundred a day, to most of which our only response was
"no comment." The press was frantic. Although the indictments had been made public, the grand jury transcript itself had been "sealed"; it would remain secret until a week
to ten days after the last defendant was arraigned. It was
rumored that one magazine offered $10,000 just to look at
a copy.

An officer, Thomas Drynan, called from Oregon. He had
arrested Susan Atkins in 1966, as part of a holdup gang.
At the time she had been carrying a .25 caliber pistol and
had told Drynan that if he hadn't drawn first she would
have shot and killed him. At this stage of the investigation
such information had no relevance. There was always a
chance, however, that it might be useful later, and I made
a note of his name and telephone number.

My cubicle in the Hall of Justice measured 20 feet by 10
feet, the furnishings consisting of a battered desk, a rick-
ety cot brought in for cat naps at lunch hour, a filing

cabinet, a couple of chairs, and a large table, usually piled high with transcripts and exhibits. A reporter once described the decor as 1930 Chicago. At that I was lucky, since the other deputy DAs had to share their offices. When I had a witness to interview, I'd have to drive everyone else out—not always diplomatically. That left the phone, which, since none of us had secretaries, we had to answer ourselves.

Each day brought new developments. Thus far, although sheriff's deputies had dug up a sizable portion of Spahn Ranch, no trace of the remains of Donald "Shorty" Shea had been found. However, acting on the information supplied by Mary Brunner, LASO searched the neighborhood adjacent to 20910 Gresham Street, Canoga Park, and found, just around the corner from the former Family residence, Shea's 1962 Mercury. It was dirt-covered and rain-streaked, apparently having been abandoned some months before. Inside the vehicle was a footlocker containing Shea's personal effects; dusting it, LASO found a set of palm prints, which were later matched to Family member Bruce Davis. Shea's cowboy boots were also in the car. They were caked with dried blood.

Independence, California, 4 P.M., December 9. Charles Milles Manson, aka Jesus Christ, age thirty-five, address transient, occupation musician, was charged with the Tate-LaBianca murders. Sartuchi and Gutierrez were bringing him to Los Angeles.

We scheduled Manson's arraignment on a different date than that of the other defendants, fearing that if Atkins and Manson met in the courtroom he'd persuade her to repudiate her testimony.

A reporter located Susan Atkins' father in San Jose. He said he didn't believe this claim that Susan was under the "hypnotic spell" of Manson. "I think she is just trying to talk her way out of it. She's sick and she needs help." According to the reporter, Mr. Atkins blamed Susan's involvement on her use of drugs and the leniency of the courts. He said he'd tried for three years to get the courts to keep his rebellious daughter off the streets; had they done so, he implied, this might not have happened.

For Susan, I realized, the Family was her only family. I understood now why Caballero felt it was only a matter of time before she returned to the fold.

On December 10, Susan Atkins, Linda Kasabian, and Leslie Van Houten were brought before Judge William Keene. All three requested and were granted continuances before entering pleas.

This was the first time I had seen Kasabian. She was short, about five feet one, with long, dark-blond hair and green eyes, and was quite obviously pregnant. She looked older than twenty. In contrast to Susan and Leslie, who smiled and giggled through most of the proceedings, Linda seemed on the edge of tears.

Following the grand jury hearing, Judge Keene had called Aaron and me into chambers. At that time he'd told us that since the DA's Office was not discussing the case with the press, he saw no need to issue a "publicity order" (or, as it is most often called, a "gag order") covering the case. However, owing to the incredible amount of pre-trial publicity—a New York *Times* reporter told me that already it far exceeded that given the first Sam Sheppard trial—Judge Keene, without consulting our office, now went ahead and issued a detailed publicity order. Later amended several times, it would run to a dozen pages. In essence, it forbade anyone connected with the case—prosecutors, defense attorneys, police officers, witnesses, and so forth—to discuss the evidence with any representative of the media.

Though unknown to me at the time, the order was already too late to prevent an inside account of the murders from making headlines around the world. The previous evening, attorney Richard Caballero, acting on the basis of an agreement with Susan Atkins, had arranged the sale of the publication rights to her story.

Call from LAPD. Charles Koenig, an attendant at the Standard service station at 12881 Ensenada Boulevard in Sylmar, was cleaning the women's rest room when he noticed the toilet was running. Lifting the lid off the tank, he found, on top of the mechanism, damp but above the waterline, a woman's wallet. He'd checked the driver's license and credit cards, saw the name "Rosemary LaBianca," and immediately called LAPD.

SID was checking the wallet for prints but, because of both the material and the dampness, they doubted they'd find any.

Just the discovery of the wallet was enough for me, for it provided another piece of independent evidence supporting Susan Atkins' story. Apparently the wallet had been there, undiscovered, since Linda Kasabian placed it there the night of the LaBianca murders, exactly four months ago.

At 11 A.M. on December 11 buckskin-clad Charles Manson was brought before Judge William Keene. The courtroom was so packed with reporters and spectators you couldn't have squeezed another person in with a shoehorn. Since Manson lacked funds to hire an attorney, Keene appointed Paul Fitzgerald of the Public Defender's Office to represent him. I'd come up against Paul before on several jury trials and knew he had a good reputation in his office. Manson was arraigned, and a postponement granted until December 22 for the entering of his plea.

In Independence, Sandra Good had told me that once, in the desert, Charlie had picked up a dead bird, breathed on it, and the bird had flown away. Sure, Sandy, sure, I replied. Since then I'd heard a great deal about Manson's alleged "powers"; Susan Atkins, for example, felt he could see and hear everything she did or said.

Midway through the arraignment I looked at my watch. It had stopped. Odd. It was the first time I could remember that happening. Then I noticed that Manson was staring at me, a slight grin on his face.

It was, I told myself, simply a coincidence.

Following the arraignment, Paul Fitzgerald told Ron Einstoss, veteran crime reporter for the Los Angeles *Times:* "There's no case against Manson and these defendants. All the prosecution has are two fingerprints and Vince Bugliosi."

Fitzgerald was right about our case being weak. But I

didn't intend that it should remain that way. Nearly three weeks ago I'd given the Tate detectives, Calkins and McGann, an initial list of things to do, among which were to interview Terry Melcher; check the prints of every known Family member against the unmatched Tate latents; show photographs of Family members to friends and relatives of the victims; determine if the glasses belonged to anyone in the Family.

I called in Calkins and McGann and asked for a progress report. I learned that only one of the things on the list had been done. Melcher had been interviewed. By the LaBianca detectives.

To date LAPD hadn't even begun looking for the Tate weapons and clothing, though Susan Atkins' statements gave us some good clues as to the general area where they should be. Arrangements were made through our office for Susan to be taken from Sybil Brand the following Sunday, to see if she could point out the spots where Linda Kasabian had thrown the various items.

Fitzgerald was not the only one who felt we had no case. The consensus in the DA's Office and the Los Angeles legal community—which I picked up from many sources, usually with some such remark as "Too bad you had to get involved in such a bummer"—was that the case against Manson and most of the other defendants would be thrown out on an 1118 motion.

Under section 1118.1 of the California Penal Code, if at the end of the People's case the court feels the prosecution has failed to put on enough evidence to sustain a conviction on appeal, the judge is empowered to acquit the defendants. They aren't even required to put on a defense to the charges.

Some felt it wouldn't even get that far. *Newsweek* quoted an unnamed Los Angeles County deputy district attorney as saying that our case against Manson was so anemic that it would be thrown out even before we went to trial.

Such talk, in addition to the national exposure that would be accorded any defense attorney connected with the case, was, I suspected, the reason Manson was having so many visitors at the Los Angeles County Jail.

As one deputy sheriff put it, "It's like a bar association convention over here." (Between December 11, 1969, and January 21, 1970, Manson had 237 separate visits, 139 of which were by one or more attorneys.) Among the first lawyers to call on him were Ira Reiner, Daye Shinn, and Ronald Hughes, none of whom I knew at that time, though I'd know all three much better before the trial ended.

Rumors multiplied like bacteria. One was that, prior to the imposition of the gag order, Caballero had sold Atkins' story to a European press syndicate, with the stipulation that the story was not to be released in the United States until after the grand jury transcript was made public. If true, I seriously doubted if American papers would respect such an agreement. There were bound to be leaks.

December 14, 1969

I didn't have to look for a newsstand that sold foreign papers. When I got up that Sunday morning, I needed only to walk out the front door, reach down, and pick up the Los Angeles *Times.*

SUSAN ATKINS' STORY OF
2 NIGHTS OF MURDER

The story covered nearly three pages. Though obviously edited and rewritten, with some additional material on her childhood, it was essentially the same story Susan Atkins had related on the tape made in Caballero's office.

Not until the trial itself would the story-behind-the-story come out. The following is reconstructed from the courtroom testimony. I can make no claim as to its accuracy,

nly that this is what the various participants testified un-
er oath.

Before the imposition of the gag order, Lawrence
chiller, a self-described Hollywood "journalist and
ommunicator," approached Richard Caballero and his law
ssociate, Paul Caruso, asking if they would be interested
a selling Susan Atkins' first-person account of the murders.
fter consulting with Susan, an agreement was reached
nd a "ghost"—Los Angeles *Times* reporter Jerry Cohen,
n leave of absence from the paper—was hired to write
e account.* Using as his main source the December 1
pe, Cohen completed the story in just two days, while
ocked in a room in Schiller's home. To make sure he
aintained "exclusivity," Schiller saw that Cohen had nei-
her carbon paper nor access to a phone, and he destroyed
ll but the finished draft.

According to their subsequent courtroom testimony, Cab-
llero and Caruso understood that initially the story was
o appear in Europe only, with a publication date of Sun-
ay, December 14.

According to Schiller, on December 12 he made three
Xerox copies of the manuscript: one was given to Cabal-
ero; one to a German editor who had bought the rights
or his magazine and who translated it as he flew back to
Germany; and the third flown by special courier to the
London *News of the World*, which had paid $40,000 for
xclusive English rights. Schiller put the original in his
wn safe.

The following day, Saturday, December 13, Schiller
earned (I) that the Los Angeles *Times* also had a Xerox
opy of the manuscript, and (2) that the *Times* intended
o run it in full the following day. Screaming copyright in-
ringement, Schiller tried, unsuccessfully, to stop publica-
ion.

Exactly how the Los Angeles *Times* obtained the story
emains unknown. During the trial Caballero more than

---

*Schiller, though listed as co-author, not only didn't write the
tory, he never even met Susan Atkins.

According to evidence introduced during the trial, the terms of
he agreement were: 25 percent to Schiller; of the remaining 75 per-
ent, 60 percent to Susan Atkins, 40 percent to her attorneys.

hinted that he suspected Schiller, while Schiller attempted to put the blame on Caballero.

Whatever the ethics of the whole matter, the Atkins story created immense problems which would plague both the defense and the prosecution throughout the trial. The story was not only reprinted in newspapers all over the world; even before the trial started it appeared as a paperback book, titled *The Killing of Sharon Tate*.* It was felt by some that the Atkins revelations would make it impossible for the defendants to obtain a fair trial. Although neither Aaron nor I nor, eventually, the trial judge, shared this view, we were all too aware, from the moment the story broke, that finding twelve jurors who hadn't read or heard of the account, and then keeping any mention of it out of the courtroom itself, would be a difficult task.

Few of the Angelenos who read Susan Atkins' story in the *Times* that Sunday were aware that she was at the same time riding around Los Angeles and its environs in a nondescript, though heavily guarded, automobile. We were hoping she would point out the places where the clothing and weapons had been discarded following the Tate murders.

On returning to Sybil Brand that night, Susan wrote a letter to a former cellmate, Kitt Fletcher, in which she told of her excursion: "My attorney is great. He has had me out to his office twice and today he got me out for 7 hours. We went riding in a car up to the Tate mansion and through the canyons. The LAPD wanted me to see if I could recall where certain things happened. It was such a beautiful day my memory vanished."

As in most jails, the mail at Sybil Brand was censored, both letters received and letters sent being read by the authorities. Those which contained what appeared to be incriminating statements were photocopied and given to our office. Under existing case law, this could be done without violating a prisoner's constitutional rights.

Susan/Sadie was in a letter-writing mood. Several of her letters contained damaging admissions which, unlik-

*Published by New American Library, which is owned by the Times Mirror Company, which also owns the Los Angeles *Time*.

er grand jury testimony, could be used against her in the
rial, if we chose to do so. To Jo Stevenson, a friend in
Michigan, she'd written on the thirteenth: "You rember
he Sharon Tate murder and LaBianca murder? Well
ecause of my big mouth to a cell-mate they just indicted
ne and 5 other people ..."*

Even more incriminating, and revealing, was a "kite"
usan sent Ronnie Howard. In jail parlance, a kite is any
legal communication. The letter, which Susan smuggled
o Ronnie via the underground at Sybil Brand, read as fol-
ows:

"I can see your side of this clearly. Nor am I mad at
ou. I am hurt in a way only I understand. I blame no
ne but myself for even saying anything to anybody about
t ... Yes, I wanted the world to know M. It sure looks
ike they do now. There was a so called motive behind all
his. It was to instill fear into the pigs and to bring on
udgment day which is here now for all.

"In the word kill, the only thing that dies is the ego. All
go must die anyway, it is written. Yes, it could have been
our house, it could have been my fathers house also. In
illing someone phisally you are only releasing the soul.
.ife has no boundris and death is only an illusion. If you
an believe in the second coming of Crist, M is he who
as come to save ... Maybe this will help you to under-
tand ... I did not admit to being in the 2nd house because
was not in the 2nd house.

"I went before the grand jury because my attorney said
our testimony was enough to convict me and all the oth-
rs. He also said it was my only chance to save myself.
Then I was out to save myself. I have gone through some
changes since then ... I know now it has all been perfect.
Those people died not out of hate or anything ugly. I am
ot going to defend our beliefs. I am just telling you the
vay it is ... As I write to you I feel more at ease inside.
When I first heard you were the informer I wanted to slit
our throat. Then I snapped that I was the real informer
nd it was my throat I wanted to cut. Well that's all over
with now as I let the past die away from my mind. You

*Spelling and punctuation errors in the Atkins letters are as in
he originals.

know it will all turn out ok in the end anyway, M or no M
Sadie or no Sadie, love will still run forever. I am giving u
me to become that love a little more every day . . ."

Quoting a lyric from one of Manson's songs, Susan end
ed the letter: "Cease to exist, just come and say you lov
me. As I say I love you or I should say I love Me (my
love) in you.

"I hope now you understand a little more. If not, ask."

Ronnie, who was now living in deathly fear of Susan
turned the letter over to her attorney, Wesley Russell, who
passed it on to our office. It would prove far more dam
aging to Susan Atkins than the confession which appeared
in the Los Angeles *Times*.

December 15-25, 1969

When on a case, I made it a habit periodically to scou
LAPD's "tubs," or files, often finding something useful to
my case whose evidentiary value wasn't apparent to the
police.

In going through the LaBianca tubs, I made two discov
eries. The first was the Al Springer interview. Only on
page had been transcribed, the one on which Springe
related how Manson had told him, "We knocked off fiv
of them just the other night."

As desperate as we were for evidence, none of the de
tectives had mentioned the Springer statement to me, no
when I questioned Lieutenants Helder and LePage, wer
they aware they had a confession by Manson in their file
I took the tape and had it transcribed, adding "Intervie
Al Springer" to my own already lengthy list of Things t
Do. Though, because of *Aranda*, Manson's confessio
couldn't be used against him at the trial, it was quite pos
sible he had made other admissions that could.

The second find was a photocopy of a letter mailed t
Manson while he was in jail in Independence. The conter

was innocuous; however, it was signed "Harold." Susan
Atkins had told the grand jury that a guy named "Harold"
had been living at the house next door to the LaBianca
residence when she, Charlie, and a number of others had
gone there for an LSD party a year or so earlier. I had a
feeling this might be the same person, and made another
note for the LaBianca detectives: "Find Harold." This
shouldn't be too difficult, as he had given an address in
Sherman Oaks and two telephone numbers.

Why? The biggest and most puzzling question of all remained: what was Manson's motive? On learning that
Manson often told his followers that he was a Scorpio,
and thinking that possibly his belief in astrology might be
a factor, I obtained back copies of the Los Angeles *Times*
and checked Carroll Righter's "Astrological Forecast" for
his sign.

> August 8: Do whatever you think will help you to
> extend your sphere of influence. Take care of that
> private task wisely and well. Get the information at
> the right source. Then use it cleverly.
>
> August 9: If you go about it tactfully, you can get
> a reluctant associate to understand what you have in
> mind. Cooperate with this individual when some
> problem arises.
>
> August 10: There are fine opportunities all around
> you. Don't hesitate to seize the best one. Extend your
> sphere of influence . . .

You could, I realized, read just about any meaning you
wanted into such forecasts. Including plans for murder?

It was indicative of our desperation that I went to such
unlikely lengths in trying to ascertain why Manson had ordered these murders.

I didn't even know whether Manson read newspapers.

Since the story first broke, LAPD had been receiving inquiries from various police departments regarding unsolved murders in their jurisdictions which they believed
could have been committed by one or more members of

the Manson Family. I went through these reports, eliminating a great many, setting others aside as "possibles."* Though my principal concern was the Tate-LaBianca homicides, I wanted to see if there was a discernible pattern which might help explain the killings at Cielo and Waverly Drives. Thus far, if there was one, I couldn't find it.

In her printed "confession" Susan Atkins had described how, after changing clothes in the car, the Tate killers drove "along a steep embankment," with a mountain on one side, a ravine on the other. "We stopped and Linda got out of the car and threw all the clothes, all drippy with blood . . . over the side."

With the *Times* story on the seat beside them, a TV camera crew from Channel 7, KACB-TV, attempted to re-create the scene. Driving from the gate at 10050 Cielo Drive, they proceeded down Benedict Canyon, all but the driver changing clothes on the way. It took them six minutes and twenty seconds—during which they later admitted they felt more than a little foolish—to complete their change of apparel. At the first spot where they could pull off the road—a wide shoulder opposite 2901 Benedict Canyon Road—they stopped and got out.

Mountain on one side, ravine on the other. Newscaster Al Wiman looked down the steep embankment and, pointing to some dark objects about fifty feet down, said, laughing, "Looks like clothing down there." King Baggot, the cameraman, and Eddie Baker, the sound man, looked too and had to agree.

It was just too easy—if the clothing was in plain view from the road, surely LAPD would have found it by now. Still, they decided to check it out. They were about to descend the slope when the car radio buzzed: they were needed on another story.

While on the other assignment they couldn't get those dark objects out of mind. About 3 P.M. they returned to the spot. Baker went down first, followed by Baggot. They found three sets of clothing: one pair of black trousers, two pairs of blue denim pants, two black T-shirts,

---

*These will be discussed in a later chapter.

one dark velour turtleneck, and one white T-shirt which was spotted with some substance that looked like dried blood. Some of the clothing was partly covered by dirt slides; all of it, however, was in an area about twelve feet square, as if thrown there in one bundle.

They yelled the news up to Wiman, who called LAPD. By the time McGann and three other detectives arrived, shortly before five, it was beginning to get dark, so the TV crew set up artificial lighting. While the detectives placed the clothing in plastic bags, Baggot filmed the incident.

On learning of the find, I asked the Tate detectives to conduct a thorough search of the area, to see if they could locate any of the weapons. I had to make the request not once but many, many times. In the interim, a week after the initial discovery, Baggot and Baker returned to the scene and conducted their own search, finding a knife. It was an old, badly rusted kitchen knife, which, because of its dimensions and dull edge, was eliminated as one of the murder weapons, but it was in plain view less than a hundred feet from where the clothing had been found.

That a TV crew had found the clothing was an embarrassment to LAPD. Faces at Parker Center, however, would be far redder before the end of the following day.

On Tuesday, December 16, Susan Atkins appeared before Judge Keene and pleaded not guilty to all eight counts of the indictment. Keene set a trial date of February 9, 1970. Since this was the same date set for the retrial of Bobby Beausoleil, I was taken off the Beausoleil-Hinman case, and it was assigned to Deputy DA Burton Katz. I wasn't unhappy about this; I had more than enough to do on Tate-LaBianca.

That Tuesday was, for Bernard Weiss, a most trying day.

Weiss hadn't read Susan Atkins' story when it appeared in the Los Angeles *Times,* but a colleague at work had, and he mentioned to Weiss that a .22 caliber revolver had definitely been used in the Tate murders. Odd coincidence, wasn't it, his boy finding a similar type gun?

Weiss thought it might be something more than that.

After all, his son had found the revolver on September 1, a little over two weeks after the Tate murders; they lived not far from the Tate residence; and the road right above the hill where Steven had found the gun was Beverly Glen. That morning Weiss called the Valley Services Division of LAPD in Van Nuys and told them he thought they might have the missing Tate gun. Van Nuys referred him to LAPD Homicide at Parker Center.

Weiss called there about noon, and repeated his story. He observed that the gun his son had found had a broken trigger guard and part of the wooden grip was missing. "Well, it sounds enough like the gun," the detective told him. "We'll check it out."

Weiss anticipated that the detective would call him back; he didn't. That evening on arriving home, Weiss read the Atkins story. It convinced him. About 6 P.M. he again called LAPD Homicide. The officer he'd talked to at noon was out, so he had to repeat the story a third time. This officer told him, "We don't keep guns that long. We throw them in the ocean after a while." Weiss said, "I can't believe you'd throw away what could be the single most important piece of evidence in the Tate case." "Listen, mister," the officer replied, "we can't check out every citizen report on every gun we find. Thousands of guns are found every year." The discussion became an argument, and they hung up on each other.

Weiss then called one of his neighbors, Clete Roberts, a newscaster for Channel 2, and told Roberts the story. Roberts in turn called someone at LAPD.

Although it remains unclear which of the five calls triggered a response, at least one did. At 10 P.M.—three and a half months after Weiss gave the gun to officer Watson—Sergeants Calkins and McGann drove over to Van Nuys and picked up the .22 caliber Hi Standard Longhorn revolver.

POLICE FIND GUN BELIEVED USED IN SLAYING OF 3 TATE VICTIMS

News of the find "leaked" to the Los Angeles *Times* four days later. It was a somewhat selective leak. There were no details as to when or where the gun was found, or by whom, the implication being that it had been discovered by LAPD sometime after the clothing, and in the same general area.

The cylinder contained two live rounds and seven empty shell casings. This tallied perfectly with the original autopsy reports, which stated that Sebring and Frykowski had each been shot once, and Parent five times. There was only one problem: I'd already discovered the autopsy reports were in error.

After Susan Atkins testified that Tex Watson shot Parent four (not five) times, I'd asked Coroner Noguchi to re-examine the Parent autopsy photos. When he did, he found that two of the wounds had been made by the same bullet. This reduced the number of times Parent was shot four; it also left one bullet unaccounted for.

This time I had Noguchi re-examine *all* the autopsy photos. In doing so, he found that Frykowski had been shot not once but twice, the coroners performing the autopsy having overlooked a gunshot wound in the left leg. So the count was again consistent, even if the reports were not.

Bill Lee of SID compared the three pieces of gun grip with the butt of the revolver: a perfect fit. Joe Granado tested some brown spots on the barrel: blood, human, same type and subtype as Jay Sebring's. After test-firing the gun, Lee placed the test bullets and the Tate bullets under a comparison microscope. Three of the four bullets recovered after the Tate murders were either too fragmented or battered for the stria to be matched up. With the fourth, the Sebring bullet, he made a positive ID. There was no doubt whatsoever, he told me, that it had been fired from the .22 Longhorn.

One very important step remained: linking the gun to Charles Manson. I asked the Tate detectives to show it to DeCarlo, to determine if it was the same gun with which Manson and the other men used to target-practice at Spahn. I also requested as complete a history of the gun as they could manage, from the day it was manufactured by Hi Standard to the day it was found by Steven Weiss.

It was decided that there was insufficient evidence to convict either Gypsy or Brenda, and the two hard-core Manson Family members were released from custody. Although Brenda returned to her parents for a short time, both soon rejoined Squeaky, Sandy, and the other Family members at Spahn, lonely George having weakened and let them move back to the ranch.

Manson's frequent court appearances gave me opportunities to study him. Though he'd had little formal schooling, he was fairly articulate, and definitely bright. He picked up little nuances, seemed to consider all the hidden sides of a question before answering. His moods were mercurial, his facial expressions chameleonlike. Underneath, however, there was a strange intensity. You felt it even when he was joking, which, despite the seriousness of the charges, was often. He frequently played to the always packed courtroom, not only to the Family faithful but to the press and spectators as well. Spotting a pretty girl, he'd often smile or wink. Usually they appeared more flattered than offended.

Though their responses surprised me, they shouldn't have. I'd already heard that Manson was receiving a large volume of mail, including many "love letters," the majority of which were from young girls who wanted to join the Family.

On December 17, Manson appeared before Judge Keene and asked to have the Public Defender dismissed. He wanted to represent himself, he said.

Judge Keene told Manson that he was not convinced that he was competent to represent himself, or, in legal jargon, to proceed "in pro per" (in propria persona).

MANSON "Your Honor, there is no way I can give up my voice in this matter. If I can't speak, then our whole thing is done. If I can't speak in my own defense and converse freely in this courtroom, then it ties my hands behind my back, and if I have no voice, then there is no sense in having a defense."

Keene agreed to reconsider Manson's motion on the twenty-second.

Manson's insistence that only he could speak for himself, as well as his obvious enjoyment at being in the spotlight, led me to one conclusion: when the time came, he probably wouldn't be able to resist taking the stand.

I began keeping a notebook of questions I intended to ask him on cross-examination. Before long there was a second notebook, and a third.

On the nineteenth Leslie Van Houten also asked to have her present attorney, Donald Barnett, dismissed. Keene granted the motion and appointed Marvin Part to be Miss Van Houten's attorney of record.

Only later would we learn what was happening behind the scenes. Manson had set up his own communications network. Whenever he heard that an attorney for one of the girls had initiated a move on behalf of his client which could conceivably run counter to Manson's own defense, within days that attorney would be removed from the case. Barnett had wanted a psychiatrist to examine Leslie. Learning of this, Manson vetoed the idea, and when the psychiatrist appeared at Sybil Brand, Leslie refused to see him. Her request for Barnett's dismissal came immediately after.

Manson's goal: to run the entire defense himself. In court as well as out, Charlie intended to retain complete control of the Family.

Manson wanted to represent himself, he told the court, because "lawyers play with people, and I am a person and don't want to be played with in this matter." Most lawyers were only interested in one thing, publicity, Manson said. He'd seen quite a few of them lately and felt he knew what he was talking about. Any attorney previously associated with the DA's Office was not acceptable to him, he added. He had learned that two other defendants had court-appointed attorneys who were once deputy DAs (Caballero and Part).

Judge Keene explained that many lawyers engaged in the practice of criminal law first gained experience in the office of the District Attorney, the City Attorney, or the

U.S. Attorney. Knowing how the prosecution worked was often a benefit to their clients.

MANSON   "It sounds good from there, but not from here."

"Your Honor," Manson continued, "I am in a difficult position. The news media has already executed and buried me . . . If anyone is hypnotized, the people are hypnotized by the lies being told to them . . . There is no attorney in the world who can represent me as a person. I have to do it myself."

Judge Keene had a suggestion. He would arrange for an experienced attorney to confer with him. Unlike other attorneys to whom Manson had talked, this attorney would have no interest in representing him. His function would be solely to discuss with him the legal issues, and the possible dangers, of defending himself. Manson accepted the offer and, after court, Keene arranged for Joseph Ball, a former president of the State Bar Association and former senior counsel to the Warren Commission, to meet with Manson.

Manson talked to Ball and found him "a very nice gentleman," he told Judge Keene on the twenty-fourth. "Mr. Ball probably understands maybe everything there is to know about law, but he doesn't understand the generation gap; he doesn't understand free love society; he doesn't understand people who are trying to get out from underneath all of this . . ."

Ball, in turn, found Manson "an able, intelligent young man, quiet-spoken and mild-mannered . . ." Although he had attempted to persuade him, without success, that he could benefit from the services of a skilled lawyer, Ball was obviously impressed with Manson. "We went over different problems of law, and I found he had a ready understanding . . . Remarkable understanding. As a matter of fact, he has a very fine brain. I complimented him on the fact. I think I told you that he had a high IQ. Must have, to be able to converse as he did." Manson "is not resentful against society," Ball said. "And he feels that if he goes to trial and he is able to permit jurors and the Court to hear him and see him, they will realize he is not the kind of man who would perpetrate horrible crimes."

After Ball had finished, Judge Keene questioned Manson for more than an hour about his knowledge of courtroom procedure, and the possible penalties for the crimes with which he was charged, throughout almost begging him to reconsider his decision to defend himself.

MANSON   "For all my life, as long as I can remember, I've taken your advice. Your faces have changed, but it's the same court, the same structure ... All my life I've been put in little slots, Your Honor. And I went along with it ... I have no alternative but to fight you back any way I know because you and the District Attorney and all the attorneys I have ever met are all on the same side. The police are on the same side and the newspapers are on the same side and it's all pointed against me, personally ... No. I haven't changed my mind."

THE COURT   "Mr. Manson, I am imploring you not to take this step; I am imploring you to either name your own attorney, or, if you are unable to do so, to permit the Court to name one for you."

Manson's mind was made up, however, and Judge Keene finally concluded: "It is, in this Court's opinion, a sad and tragic mistake that you are making by taking this course of action, but I can't talk you out of it. ... Mr. Manson, you are your own lawyer."

It was Christmas Eve. I worked until 2 A.M., then took the next day off.

December 26-31, 1969

A call from LAPD. A cook at the Brentwood Country Club says that the chief steward there, Rudolf Weber, was the man in front of whose house the Tate killers stopped to hose off about 1 A.M. on August 9.

Bringing along a police photographer to take photos of the area, Calkins and I went to see Weber at his home at 9870 Portola Drive, a side street just off Benedict Canyon Drive, less than two miles from the Tate residence. As I listened to Weber's story, I knew he was going to be a good witness. He had an excellent memory, told exactly what he remembered, didn't try to fill in what he did not. He was unable to make a positive identification from the large batch of photos I showed him, but his general description fitted: all four were young (Watson, Atkins, Krenwinkel, and Kasabian were all in their early twenties), the man was tall (Watson was six feet one), and one of the girls was short (Kasabian was five feet one). His description of the car—which had never appeared in the press—was accurate down to the faded paint around the license plates. How was it he could recall such a detail about the car but not their faces? Very simple: when he followed the four down to the car, he turned the flashlight on the license plate; when he saw them on the street, near the hose, they were in the dark.

Weber had a surprise—a big one. Following the incident, thinking perhaps the four people had committed a burglary in the area, he had written down the license number of the vehicle. He had since thrown the piece of paper away—my heart sank—but he still remembered the number. It was GYY 435.

How in the world could he remember that? I asked him. In his job as steward he had to remember numbers, he replied.

Anticipating that this point might be brought up by the defense, I asked Weber if he had read the Atkins story. He said he hadn't.

On returning to my office, I checked the impound report on John Swartz' car: "1959 Ford 4 Dr., Lic. # GYY 435."

When I interviewed Swartz, the former Spahn ranch hand told me that Manson and his girls often borrowed the car; in fact, he had taken the back seat out so they could fit the big boxes in when they went on their "gar-

»age runs." With the exception of one particular night,
hey always asked his permission before taking the car.

What night was that? Well, he wasn't exactly sure of
the date, but it was a week, two weeks before the raid.
What happened that particular night? Well, he'd already
gone to bed in his trailer when he heard his car start up.
He got up and looked out the window just in time to see
the taillights pulling away. Any idea what time that was?
Well, he usually went to bed around ten or thereabouts, so
it was after that. When he woke up the next morning,
Swartz said, the car was back. He'd asked Charlie why
they'd taken the car without asking, and Charlie had told
him that he hadn't wanted to wake him up.

Any other nights during this same period when Manson
borrowed the car? I inquired. Yeah, one other night Charlie, the girls, and some other guys—he was unable to
remember which girls and guys—said they were going
downtown to play some music.

Swartz was unable to date this particular night except
that it was around the same time they took the car without permission. Before or after? He couldn't remember.
Consecutive nights? Couldn't remember that either.

I asked Swartz if he had ever belonged to the Family.
"Never," he very emphatically replied. One time, after the
raid, and after Shorty had dropped from sight, he and
Manson had an argument, Swartz said. Charlie had told
him, "I could kill you any time. I could come into your
sleeping quarters any time." After that Swartz quit his job
at Spahn, where he had been working off and on since
1963, and got a job at another ranch.

What did he know about Shorty's disappearance? Well,
a week or two after the raid Shorty just wasn't around
any more. He'd asked Charlie if he knew where he was,
and Charlie had told him, "He's gone to San Francisco
about a job. I told him about a job there." He didn't exactly feel confident with that explanation, he said, not after having noticed that Bill Vance and Danny DeCarlo
each had one of Shorty's .45 caliber pistols.

Shorty would never willingly part with those matched
pistols, Swartz said, no matter how hard up he was.

Under the Constitution of the United States, extradition is mandatory, not discretionary.* When a state has a valid and duly executed indictment—as we did in the case of Charles "Tex" Watson—there is no legitimate reason why the accused shouldn't be extradited forthwith.

Certain powers in Collin County, Texas, felt otherwise. Bill Boyd, Watson's attorney, told the press he'd fight to keep his client in Texas if it meant going all the way to the United States Supreme Court.

Bill Boyd's father, Roland Boyd, was a powerful southern politician of the Sam Rayburn school. He was also the campaign manager of a candidate who was running for attorney general of Texas. It was his candidate, Judge David Brown, who heard the Watson extradition request, and granted delay after delay after delay to young Boyd's client.

Bill Boyd was himself an aspiring politician. Tom Ryan, the local DA, told a Los Angeles *Times* reporter: "I've heard it said that Bill wants to be President of the United States. And after that he wants to be God."

Time magazine reported: "As swarms of reporters begged for jailhouse interviews with his client, Boyd began dropping ten-gallon hints that Watson's family might go along 'if the offer is substantial.' One photographer offered $1,800. 'We need lots and lots of money,' retorted Boyd. How much? 'About $50,000,' said the lawyer. Though the press balked, Boyd still has not lowered his client's price—and he is quite sure that eventually he will get it."

Meanwhile, Tex apparently wasn't suffering unduly. We heard, from various sources, that his one-man cell was comfortably furnished, that he had his own record player and records. His vegetarian meals were cooked by his mother. He also wore his own clothing, which she laundered. And he was not completely lacking company, his cell adjoining that occupied by the female prisoners.

---

*Subdivision 2 of Article IV reads: "A person charged in any state with treason, felony, or any other crime, who shall flee from justice, and be found in another state, shall on demand of the executive authority of the state from which he fled, be delivered up, to be removed by the state having jurisdiction of the crime."

Though the extradition of Watson was proving difficult, there were indications that Katie Krenwinkel might decide to return voluntarily, on Manson's orders. Squeaky, acting as Charlie's liaison, had sent Krenwinkel a barrage of letters and telegrams, photocopies of which we received from the Mobile, Alabama, authorities: "Together we stand . . . If you go extra is good . . ."

I also presumed that the togetherness referred to in each of the messages meant that Manson intended to conduct a joint, or umbrella, defense.

Since the Family had contacted Krenwinkel but, as far as we could determine, not Watson, I carried my conjecture a step further, guessing that when the case went to trial Manson and the girls would try to put the hat on Watson.

Presuming they would try to prove that Tex, not Charlie, was the mastermind behind the Tate-LaBianca murders, I began collecting every bit of evidence I could find on the Manson-Watson relationship, and the role each played in the Family.

When interrogated in Los Angeles, sixteen-year-old Dianne Lake had been threatened with the gas chamber. And had said nothing. Inyo County Deputy DA Buck Gibbens and investigator Jack Gardiner tried kindness, something Dianne had known little of during her life.

Dianne's parents had "turned hippy" while she was still a child. By age thirteen she was a member of the Hog Farm commune, and had been introduced to group sex and LSD. When she joined Manson, just before her fourteenth birthday, it was with her parents' approval.

Apparently not finding Dianne submissive enough, Manson had, on various occasions: punched her in the mouth; kicked her across a room; hit her over the head with a chair leg; and whipped her with an electrical cord. Despite such treatment, she stayed. Which implies something tragic about the alternatives available to her.

After her return to Independence, Gibbens and Gardiner had a number of lengthy conversations with Dianne. They convinced her that other people did care about her. Gardiner's wife and children visited her regularly.

Hesitantly at first, Dianne began telling the officers what she knew. And, contrary to what she had told the grand jury, she knew a great deal. Tex, for example, had admitted to her that he'd stabbed Sharon Tate. He did it, he told her, because Charlie had ordered the killings.

On December 30, Sartuchi and Nielsen interviewed Dianne in Independence. She told them that one morning, maybe a week or two weeks before the August 16 raid, Leslie had come into the back house at Spahn with a purse, a rope, and a bag of coins. She hid them under a blanket. When, a short time later, a man arrived and knocked on the door, Leslie hid herself. She told Dianne the man had given her a ride from Griffith Park and she didn't want him to see her.

The two LaBianca detectives exchanged looks. Griffith Park was not far from Waverly Drive.

After the man left, Leslie came out from under the blanket and Dianne helped her count the money. There was about eight dollars in change, in a plastic sack.

Because of Leno LaBianca's coin collection, the detectives were very interested in that bag of change.

Q. "O.K., you say you helped Leslie count the money or coins. Did you see any coins in there from another country?"

A. "Canada."

Leslie then built a fire and burned the purse (Dianne recalled it as being brown leather), some credit cards (one was an oil company card), and the rope (it was about 4 feet long and 1 to 1½ inches in diameter). Then she took off her own clothing and burned it too. Had Dianne noticed any blood spots on the clothing? No.

Later, in late August or early September, while they were at Willow Springs, about ten miles from Barker Ranch, Leslie told Dianne that she had stabbed someone who was already dead. Was it a woman or a man? Leslie hadn't said.

Leslie also told Dianne that the murder had occurred someplace near Griffith Park, near Los Feliz; that someone had written something in blood on the refrigerator door; and that she, Leslie, then wiped everything so there would be no prints, even wiping things they hadn't touched. When they left, they took some food with them. What kind of food? A carton of chocolate milk.

Had Leslie said anything about the Tate murders? Leslie had told her she wasn't in on that.

Sartuchi attempted to get more details. The only other thing Dianne could recall was that there had been a big boat outside the house. But she couldn't remember whether Leslie had told her about the boat or whether she had read it in the paper. She did, however, remember Leslie describing it.

Prior to this, the only evidence we had linking Leslie Van Houten with the LaBianca murders was the testimony of Susan Atkins. Since Susan was an accomplice, this would not stand up in court without independent corroboration.

Dianne Lake supplied it.

There was a question, however, as to whether Dianne would be able to testify at the trial. She was obviously emotionally disturbed. She had occasional LSD flashbacks. She feared Manson, and she loved him. At times she thought he was inside her head. Shortly after the first of the year the Inyo County court arranged for her to be sent to Patton State Hospital, in part for treatment for her emotional problems, in part because the court didn't know what else to do with her.

Additions to my list of Things to Do: Check to see if any LaBianca credit cards are still missing. When doctors permit, interview Dianne; find out if anyone else present during back-house incident or Willow Springs conversation. Check with Katsuyama to see if any of the LaBianca stab wounds were post-mortem, i.e., inflicted after death. Ask Susan Struthers if her mother had a brown leather purse and if it is missing. Ask Susan and/or Frank Struthers if either Rosemary or Leno liked chocolate milk.

Tiny details, but they could be important.

The "Harold" whose letter I'd found in the Tate tubs *was* the same "Harold" Susan Atkins had mentioned in her grand jury testimony. His full name was Harold True, and he was a student. When LAPD found him, I was busy with another interview, so Aaron volunteered to talk to him.

From True, who remained friendly to Manson, visiting him several times at the County Jail, Aaron learned that he had met Charlie in March of 1968, while the Family was living in Topanga Canyon. The next day Charlie and about ten others (including Sadie, Katie, Squeaky, and Brenda, but not Tex or Leslie) had shown up at 3267 Waverly Drive, the house True shared with three other youths, and stayed overnight. Manson had visited him maybe four or five times there, before True and the others moved out in September 1968. While they were still living at Waverly, True said, neighbors had frequently complained about their noisy parties.

Aaron hadn't asked True if the LaBiancas had been among the neighbors who complained, and I made a note to check this. When I did, I learned that True couldn't recall having ever seen the LaBiancas; as best he could remember, 3301 Waverly Drive was vacant all the time they were living there.

Going back to the LaBianca investigative reports, I saw that Leno and Rosemary hadn't moved into 3301 Waverly Drive until November 1968, which was after True and the others moved out.

I'd been looking for a possible incident involving the LaBiancas and the Family. I didn't find it. We were left with two facts, however: Manson had been to the house next door to the LaBianca residence on five or six occasions, and he had been as far as the gate to the Tate residence at least once.

Coincidence? Anticipating that this was probably what the Manson defense would argue, I jotted down some ideas for my rebuttal.

Charles Manson was not without a sense of humor. While in the County Jail he had somehow managed to obtain an application for a Union Oil Company credit card. He filled it in, giving his correct name and the jail address. He listed "Spahn's Movie Ranch" as his previous residence, and gave George Spahn as a reference. As for his occupation, he put "Evangelist"; type of business, "Religious"; length of employment, "20 years." He also wrote, in the blank for wife's first name, "None," and gave as his number of dependents "16."

The card was smuggled out of jail and mailed from Pasadena. Someone at Union Oil—obviously not a computer—recognized the name, and Charles Manson didn't get the two credit cards he'd requested.

Another characteristic I'd noticed while observing Manson in court was his cockiness. One possible reason for this was his new notoriety. At the beginning of December 1969 few had ever heard of Charles Manson. By the end of that month the killer had already upstaged his famous victims. An enthusiastic Family member was heard to brag, "Charlie made the cover of *Life!*"

But it was something more. You got the feeling that, despite his verbal utterances, Manson was convinced that he was going to beat the rap.

He wasn't the only one to feel this. Leslie Van Houten wrote her parents that even if convicted she'd be out in seven years (in California a person given life imprisonment is eligible for parole in seven years), while Bobby Beausoleil wrote several of his girl friends that he expected to be acquitted in his new trial, after which he was going to start his own Family.

The problem, at year's end, was that there was a very good chance that at least Manson would be right.

"What if Manson demands an immediate trial?"

Aaron and I discussed this at length. A defendant has a constitutional right to a speedy trial and a statutory right to go to trial within sixty days after the return of the indictment. If Manson insisted on this, we were in deep trouble.

We needed more time, for two reasons. We still desperately lacked evidence to corroborate the testimony of Susan Atkins, presuming—and it was a very big presumption—that she agreed to testify. And two of the defendants, Watson and Krenwinkel, were still out of state. They just happened to be the only two defendants against whom there was scientific evidence of guilt, i.e., the fingerprints at the Tate residence. If there was to be a joint trial, which we wanted, we needed at least one of the two sitting behind that defense table.

I suggested we bluff. Every time we were in court, we should indicate that we wanted to go to trial as quickly as possible. Our hope was that Manson would think this was bad, and start stalling himself.

It was a gamble. There was a very real possibility that Charlie might call our bluff, saying, with his strange little grin, "O.K., let's go to trial right now."

Part 4

THE SEARCH FOR THE MOTIVE

The Bible, the Beatles, and Helter Skelter

"If I'm looking for a motive, I'd look for something which doesn't fit your habitual standard, with which you use to work as police—something much more far out."

**Roman Polanski to
Lieutenant Earl Deemer**

January 1970

Confidential Memo. From: Deputy DA Vincent Bugliosi. To: District Attorney Evelle Younger. Subject: Status of Tate & LaBianca cases.

The memo ran to thirteen pages, but the heart of it consisted of a single paragraph:

"Without Susan Atkins' testimony on the Tate case, the evidence against two out of the five defendants [Manson and Kasabian] is rather anemic. Without her testimony on the LaBianca case, the evidence against five out of the six defendants [everyone except Van Houten] is non-existent."

That was it. Without Sadie, we still didn't have a case.

On January 2, I called a meeting of the Tate and LaBianca detectives, giving them a list of forty-two things that had to be done.

Many were repeat requests: Go to the areas where the clothing and the gun were found and search for knives. Has Granado been able to "make" the boots we picked up in November with the bloody boot-heel print on the Tate walkway? SID must have something by now on the wire cutters, also the clothing the TV crew found. Where is the tape Inyo County Deputy Sheriff Ward made with the two miners, Crockett and Poston? Where are the reports on the Tate, LaBianca, and Spahn Ranch toll calls? Telephone company destroys its records after six months; hurry on this.

Many of the requests were elementary follow-up steps that I felt the detectives should have already done on their own, without our prompting: Get Atkins printing exemplar and compare it with PIG on the front door at Tate. Get same on defendants Van Houten, Krenwinkel, and Watson and compare with printing at the LaBianca residence. Submit a complete report on the stolen credit cards involved in this case (we were hoping to find a sales slip on the rope or the Buck knives). DeCarlo said he was along when Manson purchased the three-strand nylon rope at the Jack Frost store in Santa Monica in June 1969: ask Frost employees if they sold such a rope; also show them the "Family album" to see if they can recall Manson and/or DeCarlo. Also show photos of Manson, Atkins, Kasabian, and the others to employees of the Standard station in Sylmar where Rosemary LaBianca's wallet was found.

After giving the detectives the list, I asked, "I presume that, above and beyond what I've given you, you guys are also conducting your own independent investigations?" The long silence that followed was in itself the answer. Then Calkins complained, "How are we supposed to know to do these things? We're policemen, not lawyers."

"Wait a minute," I said. "These forty-two things have nothing to do with the law. Each and every one pertains to securing evidence and strengthening our case against these people."

"But that isn't our job," Calkins continued to protest.

His remark was so astonishing I came close to losing my temper. *"Investigating a case, gathering evidence, connecting defendants with the corpus delicti of the crime—that isn't a police job?* Come on, Bob. You're the detectives. Aaron and I are the lawyers. Each of us has his own job to do. And if either of us falls down on the job, Manson is going to walk. Think about that."

I could understand if the detectives had other duties, but they were assigned full time to the case.

Unlike Calkins, Mike McGann rarely complained, but he rarely came through either. To a man, the LaBianca detectives were far more conscientious. In the weeks ahead I began giving them assignments that related specifically to the Tate, as well as the LaBianca, murders, knowing they'd do their best. I did this only after checking with Lieutenant Helder, who candidly agreed that Calkins and McGann simply weren't getting the job done.

If it was any consolation to the police—and I'm sure it wasn't—my own list was much longer than theirs. It

anged from such simple items as a reminder to get the
Beatles' album that contained the song "Helter Skelter" to
more than fifty names of potential witnesses I needed to
interview. It also included such detailed specifics as: Obtain exact measurements of all LaBianca wounds—original
officers failed to ask Deputy Medical Examiner Katsuyama for this—in order to determine dimensions of
knives used.

The measurements of the LaBianca wounds were extremely important. If the wound patterns were consistent
with those made by the LaBianca kitchen knives, then the
logical inference was that the defendants had entered the
residence unarmed, then killed the LaBiancas with their
own knives. If Manson had intended to kill these people,
the defense would surely ask, would he have sent in unarmed people to do the job?

Of even greater importance was another item which appeared on all the assignment lists: Get incidents—and witnesses who can testify to same—where Manson ordered or
instructed *anyone* to do *anything*.

Put yourself in the jury box. Would you believe the
prosecutor if he told you that a little runt out at Spahn
Ranch sent some half dozen people, the majority of them
young girls, out to murder for him, their victims not persons they knew and had a grudge against but complete
strangers, including a pregnant woman, and that without
argument they did it?

To convince a jury of this, I would have first to convince them of Manson's domination over the Family, and
particularly over his co-defendants. A domination so total,
so complete, that they would do anything he told them to
do. Including murder.

Each time I interviewed anyone connected with the
Family, I would ask for an example of Manson's control.
Often the witness would be unable to recall specific examples, and I'd have to dig to bring them out: Why did
Manson beat Dianne Lake; was it because she failed to do
something he told her to do? Who assigned the chores at
the ranch? Who put out the guards and lookouts? Can you
recall a single instance where Tex ever talked back to
Charlie?

Getting this evidence was especially difficult because Manson rarely gave direct orders. Usually he'd suggest, rather than command, though his suggestions had the force of commands.

Domination. Unless we could prove this, beyond all reasonable doubt, we'd never obtain a conviction against Manson.

As the defense attorneys requested discovery, I'd take them to my office and let them go through our files on the case. Since Manson was now acting as his own attorney, the files were also made available to him, the only difference being that they were carted over to the County Jail and he examined them there. Eventually, by a court order, secretaries in our office photostated everything in our files, with a copy for each defense counsel.

Only two things were held back. I argued to the court, "We would vehemently resist furnishing Mr. Manson with addresses, and particularly telephone numbers, of prospective witnesses, Your Honor." I also strongly opposed providing the defense with copies of the death photos. We had heard that a German magazine had a standing offer of $100,000 for them. I did not want the families of the victims to open a magazine and see the terrible butchery inflicted on their loved ones.

With only these two exceptions—the court ruling in our favor on both—the prosecution, by law, gave the defense anything they wanted and, discovery being a one-way street, they in turn gave us *nothing.* We couldn't even get a list of the witnesses they intended to call. I was still reading newspaper and magazine articles to pick up leads.

Even this wasn't as simple as it sounds. Many former associates of the Family were in fear of their lives. Several, including Dennis Wilson of the Beach Boys, had received death threats. Since few sources wished to be quoted by name, pseudonyms were often used in the articles. In several instances, I tracked down someone only to find a person I'd already interviewed. And, in more than a few cases, I found fiction posing as fact.

One article claimed that Manson and various other Family members had been present at a party Roman and

Sharon gave at 10050 Cielo in early 1969. Once located, the writer told me his source was Alan Warnecke, a close friend of Terry Melcher's. When I talked to Warnecke, he denied saying any such thing. Eventually I assembled a list of persons who had attended the party, and as many as could be located were interviewed. None had seen Manson or the others at 10050 Cielo Drive, either on the night in question or any other time.

Peter Maas, author of *The Valachi Papers*, wrote an article entitled "The Sharon Tate Murders," which appeared in the *Ladies' Home Journal*. In it was the following paragraph:

" 'How are you going to get the establishment? You can't sing to them. I tried that. I tried to save them, but they wouldn't listen. Now we got to destroy them.' —Charlie Manson to a friend in the summer of 1969."

This was powerful evidence, if true, and I was anxious to learn the source of Maas' quotation.

After easily a dozen calls, I located Maas in New York City. Asked the source of several other statements, he quickly supplied them. But when it came to the key quote mentioned above, which the *Journal* had seen fit to highlight with italics on the first page of the article, Maas said he couldn't remember who had told him that.

Cross off another seemingly promising lead.

On August 9, 1968—exactly a year before the Tate murders—Gregg Jakobson had arranged a recording session for Manson at a studio in Van Nuys. I went there to listen to the tapes, which were now in the possession of Herb Weiser, a Hollywood attorney representing the studio.

My own admittedly unprofessional appraisal was that Manson was no worse than many performers in current vogue.* However, Charlie's musical ability was not my

---

*A folk-song expert later listened to the tapes and found the songs "extremely derivative." From his notes: "Somewhere along the line Manson has picked up a pretty good guitar beat. Nothing original about the music. But the lyrics are something else. They contain an amazing amount of hostility ('You'll get yours yet,' etc.). This is rare in folk songs, except in the old murder ballads, but even there it is always past tense. In Manson's lyrics these are things that are *going to happen.* Very spooky. Overall judgment: a moderately talented amateur."

major concern. Both Atkins and DeCarlo had said that the words "helter skelter" appeared in at least one of Manson's own songs. I'd asked both, "Are you sure he wasn't just playing the Beatles' song "Helter Skelter"? No, each had replied; this was Charlie's own composition. If anywhere in his lyrics I could find "helter skelter," "pig," "death to pigs," or "rise," it would be strong circumstantial evidence.

No luck.

It looked, for a time, as if we'd have better luck with the Watson extradition. On January 5, following a hearing in Austin, Texas Secretary of State Martin Dies, Jr., ordered Watson returned to California. Boyd returned to McKinney and filed a writ of habeas corpus, asking that Dies' order be vacated. The writ was filed with Judge Brown. On January 16, Brown granted a thirty-day continuance on Boyd's request. Tex remained in Texas.

In Los Angeles, Linda Kasabian was arraigned on the sixth and pleaded "not guilty." That same day attorney Marvin Part requested that a court-appointed psychiatrist examine his client, Leslie Van Houten. Judge Keene appointed Dr. Blake Skrdla, who was to make a confidential report to Part. Earlier Part had requested and received permission to interview Leslie on tape. Though the prosecution would neither hear the tape nor see the report, it was a fairly safe assumption that Part, like his predecessor Barnett, was considering an insanity plea.

We didn't have to wait very long for Manson's reaction.

On the nineteenth Leslie requested that Part be relieved as her attorney and Ira Reiner appointed instead.

Owing to the possibly sensitive nature of the testimony, Judge George M. Dell decided to hear the matter in chambers, outside the presence of the public and press.*

Part opposed the substitution, arguing that Leslie Van Houten was mentally incapable of making a rational decision. "This girl will do anything that Charles Manson or any member of this so-called Manson Family says ... This

_____
*The transcripts of in-chambers proceedings were sealed until after the conclusion of the trial. Though there were occasional leaks, in most instances those proceedings are reported here for the first time.

girl has no will of her own left ... Because of this hold
that Charles Manson and the Family has over her, she
doesn't care whether she is tried together and gets the gas
chamber, she just wants to be with the Family."

The appointment of Reiner, Part claimed, would constitute a conflict of interest, one that would definitely hurt
Miss Van Houten.

Part told the court how the switch had come about. A
week or so ago Squeaky had visited Leslie. Although Part
was also present, Squeaky had told her, *"We* think you
ought to have another lawyer," and had shown her
Reiner's card. Leslie had replied, "I'll do anything that
Charlie wants me to do." A few days later Leslie (1) refused to be examined by the psychiatrist, and (2) informed
Part that he was no longer her attorney and that Reiner
was.

Part wanted Judge Dell to listen to the tape he had
made with Leslie. He was sure that, having heard it, the
Court would realize that Leslie Van Houten was incapable
of acting in her own best interests.

It was now obvious that Part felt a joint trial and an
"umbrella" defense would hurt his client. The other defendants were charged with seven murders, Leslie with only
two. And the evidence against her was slight. "To the best
of my knowledge," Part said, referring to the Dianne
Lake statement which he had received through discovery,
"all she did was perhaps stab somebody who was already
dead."

Judge Dell then questioned Ira Reiner, who admitted
that he had talked to Manson "roughly a dozen times." He
also admitted that Manson was one of several people who
had suggested he represent Leslie. He had never actually
represented Manson, however, and he had only gone to
see Miss Van Houten after receiving a written request
from her.

Judge Dell questioned Leslie outside the presence of the
two attorneys. She remained firm in her resolve: she
wanted Reiner.

Part, literally, begged Judge Dell to listen to the tape he
had made with Leslie. Part said, "That girl is insane in a
way that is almost science fiction."

Judge Dell said he would rather not hear the tape. He was concerned with one issue only: whether Miss Van Houten's mental state was such that she could intelligently make a substitution of counsel. To determine this, he appointed three psychiatrists to listen to the tape and examine Leslie, their confidential report, on that single issue, to be made directly to him.

Manson himself appeared before Judge Dell on the seventeenth.

MANSON "I have a motion here—it's a strange motion—probably never been a motion like this ever before—"

THE COURT "Try me."

After examining it, the judge had to agree: "It certainly is an interesting document."

"Charles Manson, also known as Jesus Christ, Prisoner," assisted by six other pro pers, who called themselves "The Family of Infinite Soul, Inc.," had filed a habeas corpus motion on behalf of Manson-Christ, charging that the sheriff was depriving him of his spiritual, mental, and physical liberty, in an unconstitutional manner not in harmony with man's or God's law, and asking that he be released forthwith.

Judge Dell denied the motion.

MANSON "Your Honor, behind the big words and all the confusion and the robes you hide the truth."

THE COURT "Not intentionally."

MANSON "Like sometimes I wonder if you know what is going on."

THE COURT "Sometimes I do too, Mr. Manson. I admit there is some self-doubt ... Yet we in the black robes do our thing, too."

Manson requested a number of items—a tape recorder, unlimited telephone privileges, and so on—which he claimed both the Sheriff's Office and the DA's Office were denying him. Dell corrected him.

THE COURT "The prosecutor is willing to go further than the sheriff has, as a matter of fact."

MANSON "Well, I was going to ask him if he would call the whole thing off. It would save a lot of trouble."

THE COURT   "Disappoint all these people? Never, Mr. Manson."

When Manson again appeared before Judge Dell, on the twenty-eighth, he was still complaining about the limitations of his pro per privileges. For example, he wanted to interview Robert Beausoleil, Linda Kasabian, and Sadie Mae Glutz, but their attorneys had denied permission. Judge Dell informed him they had that right.

MANSON   "I got a message from Sadie. She told me that the District Attorney had made her say what she had said."

Manson was playing to the press, certain that they would pick up the charge, and they did. It was the next best thing to calling Susan on the phone and telling her how to recant.

Aaron played out our bluff, stating that the People were prepared to go to trial.

Manson, to our relief, wanted more time.

Judge Dell assigned the case to Judge William Keene, and granted a continuance to February 9, at which time the trial date would be set.

Our relief was real. Not only was our case still weak, Aaron and I couldn't even agree on the motive.

The prosecution does not have the legal burden of proving motive. But motive is extremely important evidence. A jury wants to know why. Just as showing that a defendant has a motive for committing a crime is circumstantial evidence of guilt, so is the absence of motive circumstantial evidence of innocence.

In this case, even more than in most others, proving motive was important, since these murders appeared completely senseless. It was doubly important in Manson's case, since he was not present when the murders took place. If we could prove to the jury that Manson, and Manson alone, had a motive for these murders, then this would be very powerful circumstantial evidence that he also ordered them.

Aaron and I had been friends for a long time. We had developed a mutual respect that allowed us to say exactly what we felt, and quite often our discussions were heated. This one was no exception. Aaron thought that we should argue that the motive was robbery. I told him quite frankly that I felt his theory was ridiculous. What had they stolen? Seventy-some dollars from Abigail Folger, Rosemary LaBianca's wallet (which they ditched, money intact), possibly a sack of coins, and a carton of chocolate milk. That was it. As far as we knew, nothing else had been taken from either residence. There was, the police reports reiterated, no evidence of ransacking or theft. Items worth thousands of dollars, though in plain view, were left behind.

As an alternative motive, Aaron suggested that maybe Manson was trying to get enough money to bail out Mary Brunner, the mother of his child, who had been arrested on the afternoon of August 8 for using a stolen credit card. Again I played the Devil's advocate. Seven murders, five one night, two the next; 169 separate stab wounds; words written in the victims' own blood; a knife stuck in the throat of one victim, a fork in his stomach, the word WAR carved on his stomach—all this to raise $625 bail?

It wasn't that we lacked a motive. Though Aaron and LAPD disagreed with me, I felt we had one. It was just that it was almost unbelievably bizarre.

When I interviewed Susan Atkins on December 4, she told me, "The whole thing was done to instill fear in the establishment and cause paranoia. Also to show the black man how to take over the white man." This, she said, would be the start of "Helter Skelter," which, when I questioned her before the grand jury the next day, she defined as "the last war on the face of the earth. It would be all the wars that have ever been fought built one on top of the other . . ."

"There was a so called motive behind all this," Susan wrote Ronnie Howard. "It was to instill fear into the pigs and to bring on judgment day which is here now for all."

Judgment Day, Armageddon, Helter Skelter—to Manson they were one and the same, a racial holocaust which would see the black man emerge triumphant. "The karma is turning, it's blackie's turn to be on top." Danny DeCarlo said Manson preached this incessantly. Even a near stranger such as biker Al Springer, who visited Spahn Ranch only a few times, told me he thought "helter skelter" must be Charlie's "pet words," he used them so often.

That Manson foresaw a war between the blacks and the whites was not fantastic. Many people believe that such a war may someday occur. What *was* fantastic was that he was convinced he could personally start that war himself—that by making it look as if blacks had murdered the seven Caucasian victims he could turn the white community against the black community.

We knew there was at least one secondary motive for the Tate murders. As Susan Atkins put it in the Caballero tape, "The reason Charlie picked that house was to instill fear into Terry Melcher because Terry had given us his word on a few things and never came through with them." But this was obviously not the primary motive, since, according to Gregg Jakobson, Manson knew that Melcher was no longer living at 10050 Cielo Drive.

All the evidence we'd assembled thus far, I felt, pointed to one primary motive: Helter Skelter. It was far out, but then so were the murders themselves. It was admittedly bizarre, but from the first moment I was assigned to the case, I'd felt that for murders as bizarre as these the motive itself would have to be almost equally strange, not something you'd find within the pages of a textbook on police science.

The jury would never buy Helter Skelter, Aaron said, suggesting that we offer something they would understand. I told him it wouldn't take me two seconds to dump the whole Helter Skelter theory if he could find another motive in the evidence.

Aaron, however, was right. The jury would never accept Helter Skelter, as is. We were missing far too many bits and pieces, and one all-important link.

Presuming that Manson actually believed that he could start a race war with these acts, what would he, Charlie Manson, personally gain by it?

To this I had no answer. And without it the motive made no sense.

"Always think of the Now ... No time to look back ... No time to say how." This rhyme was repeated in almost every letter Sandy, Squeaky, Gypsy, or Brenda sent to the defendants. Its meaning was obvious: Don't tell them anything.

Through a barrage of letters, telegrams, and attempted visits, the Manson girls tried to get Beausoleil, Atkins, and Kasabian to dump their present attorneys, repudiate any incriminating statements they may have made, and engage in a united defense.

Though Beausoleil agreed that "the whole thing balances on whether the Family stays together in their heads & doesn't break up & start testifying against itself," he decided, "I'm going to keep my present lawyer."

Bobby Beausoleil had always been somewhat independent. Less handsome than "pretty" (the girls had nicknamed him "Cupid"), Beausoleil had had bit parts in several movies, written music, formed a rock group, and had his own harem, all before meeting Manson. Leslie, Gypsy, and Kitty had all lived with Bobby before joining Charlie.

Beausoleil requested that Squeaky and the others not visit him so often. They were taking up all his visiting time, when the person he really wanted to see was Kitty, who was expecting his child in less than a month.

Beausoleil wasn't the only one being pressured. Without Susan Atkins, the prosecution had no case against Manson, and Manson knew it. Family members called Richard Caballero at all hours of the day and night. When cajoling didn't work, they tried threats. Less because of their pressure than that of his own client, Caballero finally gave in and let some of the Manson girls—though not Manson himself—visit Susan.

It was, at best, a holding action. At any moment Susan could insist on seeing Charlie, and Caballero would be unable to prevent it. After Susan's story had appeared in the Los Angeles *Times*, little signs had appeared on the walls at Sybil Brand reading, "SADIE GLUTZ IS A SNITCH." This greatly upset Susan. And each time something like this happened, the scales seemed to tip a little more in Manson's favor.

Manson was also aware that if Susan Atkins refused to testify at the trial, our only hope lay with Linda Kasabian. After a time Linda's attorney, Gary Fleischman, refused to see Gypsy, so persistent had her visits become. If Linda didn't testify, Gypsy told him on numerous occasions, everyone would get off. Fleischman did take her along one time when he went to see his client. Gypsy told Linda—in the presence of several persons—that she should lie and say that on the nights of the Tate-LaBianca murders she had never left Spahn Ranch but remained with her at the waterfall. Gypsy promised to back up her story.

Given a choice between Susan and Linda as the star witness for the prosecution, I much preferred Linda: she hadn't killed anyone. But in the rush to get the case to the grand jury, we'd made the deal with Susan and, like it or not, we were stuck with it. Unless Susan bolted.

Yet this posed its own problems. If Susan didn't testify, we'd need Linda, but without Susan's testimony we had no evidence against Linda, so what could we offer her? Fleischman wanted immunity for his client, yet from Linda's standpoint it would be better to be tried and acquitted than get immunity, testify against Manson and the others, and risk retribution by the Family.

We were very worried at this point. Exactly how worried is evidenced by a telephone call I made. After Manson had been indicted for the Tate-LaBianca murders, the Inyo County authorities had dropped the arson charges against him, though they had a strong case. I called Frank Fowles and asked him to refile the charges, which he did, on February 6. We were that afraid that Manson would be set free.

February 1970

That an accused mass murderer could emerge a counter-culture hero seemed unconceivable. But to some Charles Manson had become a cause.

Just before she went underground, Bernardine Dohrn told a Students for a Democratic Society convention: "Offing those rich pigs with their own forks and knives, and then eating a meal in the same room, far out! The Weathermen dig Charles Manson."

The underground paper *Tuesday's Child,* which called itself the Voice of the Yippies, blasted its competitor the Los Angeles *Free Press* for giving too much publicity to Manson—then spread his picture across the entire front page with a banner naming him MAN OF THE YEAR.

The cover of the next issue had Manson on a cross.

Manson posters and sweat shirts appeared in psychedelic shops, along with FREE MANSON buttons.

Gypsy and other spokesmen for the Family took to the late-night radio talk shows to play Charlie's songs and denounce the prosecution for "framing an innocent man."

Stretching his pro per privileges to their utmost limits, Manson himself granted a number of interviews to the underground press. He was also interviewed, by phone from the County Jail, by several radio stations. And his visitor's list now included, among the "material witnesses," some familiar names.

"I fell in love with Charlie Manson the first time I saw his cherub face and sparkling eyes on TV," exclaimed Jerry Rubin. On a speaking tour during a recess in the Chicago Seven trial, Rubin visited Manson in jail, giving rise to the possibility that Manson might be considering the use of disruptive tactics during his own trial. According to Rubin, Charlie rapped for three hours, telling him, among other things, "Rubin, I am not of your world.

I've spent all my life in prison. When I was a child I was an orphan and too ugly to be adopted. Now I am too beautiful to be set free."

"His words and courage inspired us," Rubin later wrote. "Manson's soul is easy to touch because it lays quite bare on the surface."*

Yet Charles Manson—revolutionary martyr—was a difficult image to maintain. Rubin admitted being angered by Manson's "incredible male chauvinism." A reporter for the *Free Press* was startled to find Manson both anti-Jewish and anti-black. And when one interviewer tried to suggest that Manson was as much a political prisoner as Huey Newton, Charlie, obviously perplexed, asked, "Who's he?"

As yet the pro-Mansonites appeared to be a small, though vocal minority. If the press and TV reports were correct, a majority of young people whom the media had lumped together under the label "hippies" disavowed Manson. Many stated that the things he espoused—such as violence—were directly contrary to their beliefs. And more than a few were bitter about the guilt by association. It was almost impossible to hitchhike any more, one youth told a New York *Times* reporter. "If you're young, have a beard, or even long hair, motorists look at you as if you're a 'kill crazy cultist,' and jam the gas."

The irony was that Manson never considered himself a hippie, equating their pacifism with weakness. If the Family members had to have a label, he told his followers, he much preferred calling them "slippies," a term which, in the context of their creepy-crawly missions, was not inappropriate.

What was most frightening was that the Family itself was growing. The group at Spahn had increased significantly. Each time Manson made a courtroom appearance, I spotted new faces among the known Family members.

It could be presumed that many of the new "converts" were sensation seekers, drawn like moths to the glare of publicity.

*We Are Everywhere, by Jerry Rubin (New York: Harper & Row, 1971).

What we didn't know, however, was how far they would go to gain attention or acceptance.

Leslie Van Houten was legally sane, Judge Dell ruled on February 6, basing his decision on the confidential reports of the three psychiatrists, and granting her motion for a substitution of attorneys.

In court the same day, Manson unexpectedly called our bluff: "Let's have an early trial setting. Let's go tomorrow or Monday. That's a good day for a trial." Keene set a trial date of March 30, the date already assigned Susan Atkins. That gave us a little more time, but not nearly enough.

On February 16, Keene heard Manson's motion for a change of venue. "You know, there has been more publicity on this, even more than the guy who killed the President of the United States," Manson said. "You know, it is getting so far out of proportion that to me it is a joke, but actually the joke might cost me my life."

Though the other defense attorneys would later submit similar motions, arguing that it would be impossible for their clients to obtain fair trials in Los Angeles because of the extensive pre-trial publicity, Manson didn't argue this too strongly. The motion was really "trivial," he said, because "it doesn't seem it could be done anywheres."

Though Keene disagreed with Manson's contention that he couldn't obtain a fair trial, he did observe, in denying the motion, that "a change of venue, even if warranted, would be ineffectual."

This was also the view of the prosecution. It was doubtful if there was any place in California, or the rest of the United States, where the publicity had not reached.

Each time the defense made a motion—and there would be hundreds before the end of the trial—the prosecution had to be prepared to answer. Though Aaron and I shared the verbal arguments, I prepared the written briefs, many of which required considerable legal research. All this was in addition to the heavy investigative responsibilities I had taken on.

Yet the latter job had its special satisfactions. At the start of February there were still huge holes in our case, big areas where we had almost no information whatsoever. For example, I still had very little insight into what made Charles Manson tick.

By the end of the month I had that, and a great deal more. For by then I understood, for the first time, Manson's motive—the reason why he'd ordered these murders.

I rarely interview a witness just once. Often the fourth or fifth interview will bring out something previously forgotten or deemed insignificant, which, in proper context, may prove vital to my case.

When I had questioned Gregg Jakobson before the grand jury, my primary concern had been to establish the link between Manson and Melcher.

Reinterviewing the talent scout, I was surprised to discover that since meeting Manson at Dennis Wilson's home in the early summer of 1968, Jakobson had had over a hundred long talks with Charlie, mostly about Manson's philosophy. An intelligent young man, who flirted off and on with the hippie life style, Gregg had never joined the Family, though he'd often visited Manson at Spahn Ranch. Besides seeing in Manson certain commercial possibilities, Jakobson had found him "intellectually stimulating." He was so impressed that he often touted him to others, such as Rudi Altobelli, the owner of 10050 Cielo Drive, who had been both Terry Melcher's and Sharon Tate's landlord.

I was surprised at the wide variety of people Manson knew. Charlie was a chameleon, Gregg said; he often professed that "he had a thousand faces and that he used them all—he told me that he had a mask for everyone."

Including the jury? I wondered, realizing that if Manson put on the mask of the peace-loving hippie at the trial, I'd be able to use Gregg's remark to unmask him.

I asked Gregg why Manson felt it necessary to don masks.

A. "So he could deal with everyone on their own level, from the ranch hand at Spahn, to the girls on the Sunset Strip, to me."

I was curious as to whether Manson had a "real" face. Gregg thought he had. Underneath it all he had very firm beliefs. "It was rare to find a man who believed in his convictions as strongly as Charlie did—who couldn't be swayed."

What were the sources of Manson's beliefs? I asked.

Charlie rarely, if ever, gave anyone else credit for his philosophy, Gregg replied. But it was obvious that Charlie was not above borrowing.

Had Manson ever mentioned Scientology or The Process?

The Process, also known as the Church of the Final Judgment, was a very strange cult. Led by one Robert De-Grimston, t/n Robert Moore—who, like Manson, was an ex-Scientologist—its members worshiped both Satan and Christ. I'd only begun to look into the group, acting on the basis of a newspaper story which indicated Manson might have been influenced by them.

However, Jakobson said Manson had never mentioned either Scientology or The Process. Gregg himself had never heard of the latter group.

Did Charlie ever quote anyone? I asked Gregg.

Yes, he replied, "The Beatles and the Bible." Manson would quote, verbatim, whole lyrics from the Beatles' songs, finding in them a multitude of hidden meanings. As for the Bible, he most often quoted Revelation 9. But in both cases he usually used the quotations as support for his own views.

Though I was very interested in this odd coupling, and would later question Gregg in depth about it, I wanted to know more about Manson's personal beliefs and attitudes.

Q: "What did Manson say, if anything, about right and wrong?"

A: "He believed you could do no wrong, no bad. Everything was good. Whatever you do is what you are supposed to do; you are following your own karma."

The philosophical mosaic began taking shape. The man I was seeking to convict had no moral boundaries. It was not that he was immoral, but totally amoral. And such a person is always dangerous.

Q: "Did he say it was wrong to kill a human being?"

A: "He said it was not."

Q: "What was Manson's philosophy re death?"

A: "There was no death, to Charlie's way of thinking. Death was only a change. The soul or spirit can't die ... That's what we used to argue all the time, the objective and the subjective and the marriage of the two. He believed it was all in the head, all subjective. He said that death was a fear that was born in man's head and can be taken out of man's head, and then it would no longer exist ...

"Death to Charlie," Gregg added, "was no more important than eating an ice cream cone."

Yet once, in the desert, Jakobson had run over a tarantula, and Manson had angrily berated him for it. He had denounced others for killing rattlesnakes, picking flowers, even stepping on a blade of grass. To Manson it was not wrong to kill a human being, but it was wrong to kill an animal or plant. Yet he also said that nothing was wrong, everything that happened was right.

That Manson's philosophy was riddled with such contradictions apparently bothered his followers little if at all. Manson said that each person should be independent, but the whole Family was dependent on him. He said that he couldn't tell anyone else what to do, that they should "do what your love tells you," but he also told them, "I am your love," and his wants became theirs.

I asked Gregg about Manson's attitude toward women. I was especially interested in this because of the female defendants.

Women had only two purposes in life, Charlie would say: to serve men and to give birth to children. But he didn't permit the girls in the Family to raise their own children. If they did, Charlie claimed, they would give them their own hangups. Charlie believed that if he could eliminate the bonds created by parents, schools, churches, society, he could develop "a strong white race." Like Nietzsche, whom Manson claimed to have read, Charlie "believed in a master race."

"According to Charlie," Gregg continued, "women were only as good as their men. They were only a reflection of their men, all the way back to daddy. A woman was an accumulation of all the men she had been close to."

Then why were there so many women in the Family? I asked; there were at least five girls to every man.

It was only through the women, Gregg said, that Charlie could attract the men. Men represented power, strength. But he needed the women to lure the men into the Family.

As with others I interviewed, I asked Gregg for examples of Manson's domination. Gregg gave me one of the best I'd yet found: he said he had had dinner with the Family on three occasions; each time Manson sat alone on the top of a large rock, the other members of the Family sitting on the ground in a circle around him.

Q.   "Did Tex Watson ever get up on the rock?"

A.   "No, of course not."

Q.   "Did anyone else in the Family get up there?"

A.   "Only Charlie."

I needed many, many more examples like this, so that when I offered all of them at the trial, the jury would be led to the irresistible conclusion that Manson had such a hold over his followers, and specifically his co-defendants, that never in a million years would they have committed these murders without his guidance, directions, and orders.

I asked Gregg about Charlie's ambitions. "Charlie wanted to be a successful recording artist," Gregg said. "Not so much as a means to making money as to get his word out to the public. He needed people to live with him, to make love, to liberate the white race."

What was Manson's attitude toward blacks?

Gregg replied that Charlie "believed there were different levels when it came to race, and the white man occupied a higher level than the black." This was why Charlie was so strongly opposed to black-white sex; "you would be interfering with the path of evolution, you would be mixing up nervous systems, less evolved with more evolved."

According to Jakobson, "Charlie believed that the black man's sole purpose on earth was to serve the white man. He was to serve the white man's needs." But blackie had been on the bottom too long, Charlie said. It was now his turn to take over the reins of power. This was what Helter Skelter, the black-white revolution, was all about.

Gregg and I would talk about this on more than a half

dozen separate occasions. What before had been only fragments, bits and pieces, now began slipping into place.

The picture that eventually emerged, however, was so incredibly bizarre as to be almost beyond belief.

There is a special feeling you develop over years of interviewing people. When someone is lying or not telling everything he knows, you can often sense it.

On reinterviewing Terry Melcher, I became convinced that he was withholding something. There wasn't time for pussyfooting. I told Terry I wanted to talk to him again, only this time he should have his attorney, Chet Lappen, present. When we met in Lappen's office on the seventeenth, I put it to him bluntly: "You're not leveling with me, Terry. You're keeping something back. Whatever it is, eventually it will come out. It would be far better if you told me about it now rather than have the defense surprise us with it on cross-examination."

Terry wavered for a few minutes, then decided to tell me.

The day after news of Manson's involvement in the Tate murders broke, Terry had received a telephone call from London. The caller was Rudi Altobelli, the owner of 10050 Cielo Drive. Rudi had told him, in confidence, that one day in March 1969, while he was taking a shower in the guest house, Manson had knocked on the door. Manson claimed to be looking for Terry, who had moved out some months before, but Altobelli, who was a successful business manager for a number of theatrical stars, suspected that Manson had actually come looking for him, as Manson had worked the conversation around to his own music and songs. In a rather subtle fashion, Altobelli had made it clear that he wasn't interested, and Manson had left.

The guest house! "Terry," I said, "why didn't you tell me this before?"

"I wasn't sure it was relevant."

"Christ, Terry, this places Manson inside the gate of the Tate residence. As you well know, to reach the guest house he'd have to first pass the main house. This means Manson was familiar with the layout of the house and grounds. I don't know what could be any *more* relevant. Where's Altobelli now?"

"Cape Town, South Africa," Melcher reluctantly replied. Checking his address book, he gave me the number of the hotel where he was staying.

I called Cape Town. Mr. Altobelli had just checked out of the hotel, leaving no forwarding address. However, Terry told me that Rudi was planning to return to Los Angeles for a few days sometime soon.

"The minute he hits L.A. I want to know it," I told him. As a safeguard I put out a few feelers of my own, asking others who knew Altobelli to contact me if they saw or heard from him.

The same day I talked to Melcher, half our extradition problems were solved: Patricia "Katie" Krenwinkel waived further proceedings and asked to be returned to California immediately. When she made her first courtroom appearance on the twenty-fourth, she requested Paul Fitzgerald of the Public Defender's Office as her attorney. Fitzgerald told the judge that, barring a possible conflict of interest, his office would be willing to represent her.

Actually there were two possible conflicts of interest: the Public Defender's Office was already representing Beausoleil on the Hinman murder, and Fitzgerald had earlier represented Manson, albeit briefly, before he went in pro per.

A month later Paul Fitzgerald resigned from the Public Defender's Office, after that office decided there was indeed a conflict of interest involved. Whether Fitzgerald's motive was purely idealistic, or he hoped to make a name for himself in private practice by winning an acquittal for his client, or both, the fact remained that he gave up a $25,000 a year salary and a promising career as a public defender to represent Patricia Krenwinkel with virtually no pay.

Terry Melcher didn't call. But another of my contacts did, reporting that Rudi Altobelli had returned to Los Angeles the previous day. I called Altobelli's attorney, Barry

Hirsch, and arranged a meeting. Before leaving the office, I prepared a subpoena and stuck it in my pocket.

Rather than ask Altobelli whether the guest house incident really occurred, and risk a possible denial, I simply laid it out: "Rudi, the reason I'm here is because I want to ask you about the time Manson came to the guest house. Terry told me about it." *Fait accompli.*

Yes, Manson had been there, Rudi said. But did this mean he would have to testify?

Rudi Altobelli was a bright, urbane, and, as I'd later discover, at times quite witty man. The roster of entertainment figures he'd represented included such stars as Katharine Hepburn, Henry Fonda (who for a time had rented the guest house at 10050 Cielo Drive), Samantha Eggar, Buffy Sainte-Marie, Christopher Jones, and Sally Kellerman, to name only a few. However, in common with almost all the other witnesses in this case, he was scared.

On his return from Europe following the murders, he'd found that 10050 Cielo Drive had been sealed by the police. Needing a place to stay, and unsure whether he might have been one of the intended victims—and still might be—he picked the safest place he could think of. He moved in with Terry Melcher and Candice Bergen, who were occupying a beach house in Malibu owned by Terry's mother, Doris Day. Though Terry and Rudi had spent many hours discussing the murders, and possible suspects, Manson's name was never mentioned, Rudi said. When the news broke that Manson had been accused of the murders, a possible motive being his grudge against Melcher, Altobelli decided that he had probably chosen the least safe place in Southern California. He still shivered when recalling it.

He had another reason for fear. In a sense, he too had rejected Manson.

"Tell me about it, Rudi," I suggested. "Then we'll discuss whether you have to testify or not. But first, how do you know it was Manson?"

Because he'd met Manson once before, Altobelli said, during the summer of 1968, at Dennis Wilson's house. Manson was living there at the time, and Rudi had dropped in while Dennis was playing a tape of Manson's music. He'd listened politely, commented that it was "nice," the minimal courtesy possible, then left.

At various times Dennis and Gregg had tried to interest him in Manson and his philosophy. Having worked hard for what money he had, Altobelli said, he was not sympathetic to Manson's sponging, and had told them exactly that.

The incident had occurred about eight or nine on the evening of Sunday, March 23, 1969—Rudi remembered the date because he and Sharon had flown to Rome together the next day, Rudi on business, Sharon to rejoin her husband and to make a movie there. Rudi was alone in the guest house, taking a shower, when Christopher started barking. Grabbing a robe, he went to the door and saw Manson on the porch. While it was possible that Manson had knocked and the shower had muffled the sound, Rudi was irritated that he had opened the outside door and walked onto the porch uninvited.

Manson started to introduce himself but Rudi, somewhat brusquely, without opening the screen door that separated the porch from the living room, said, "I know who you are, Charlie, what do you want?"

Manson said he was looking for Terry Melcher. Altobelli said Terry had moved to Malibu. When Manson asked for his address, Altobelli said he didn't know it. Which was not true.

Prolonging the conversation, Manson asked him what business he was in. Though Altobelli felt sure Manson already knew the answer, he replied, "The entertainment business." He added, "I'd like to talk to you longer, Charlie, but I'm leaving the country tomorrow and have to pack."

Manson said he would like to talk to him when he returned. Rudi told him that he wouldn't be back for over a year. Another untruth, but he had no desire to talk further with Manson.

Before Manson left, Rudi asked him why he had come back to the guest house. Manson replied that the people at the main house had sent him back. Altobelli said that he didn't like to have his tenants disturbed, and he would appreciate it if he wouldn't do so in the future. With that Manson left.

Though one question was uppermost in my mind, before asking it I had Altobelli describe Manson, the lighting on the porch, exactly where each was standing. Since he had met Manson on a prior occasion, there was no question that this was a positive identification, but I wanted to be absolutely sure.

Then I asked it, and held my breath until he answered. "Rudi, who was up front that night?"

"Sharon, Gibby, Voytek, and Jay."

Four of the five Tate victims! This meant that Manson could have seen any or all of them. Prior to my talking to Rudi, we had assumed that Manson had never seen the people he had ordered killed.

"Rudi, all those people are dead. Was there anyone else up front who could testify to this?"

Rudi thought a moment. He had been up at the main house earlier in the evening, actually returning to the guest house only a few minutes before Manson arrived. "I'm not sure," he said, "but I'm almost positive Hatami was there."

Shahrokh Hatami, a native of Iran, was Sharon's personal photographer, and a good friend of both Polanskis. Hatami had been at the house that afternoon, Rudi knew, photographing Sharon while she was packing for her trip.

"I don't want to testify, Mr. Bugliosi," Rudi suddenly said.

"I can understand that. If there is any way I can avoid it, I won't call you to the stand. But realistically, considering the importance of what you've told me, the odds are that I will have to call you." We discussed the subject at some length before I gave him the subpoena.

I then asked him, "Tell me about Sharon."

In the short time he had known her, Rudi said, he had grown very fond of her. She was a beautiful person. Of course she was physically beautiful, but by this he meant something else. She had a kind of warmth, a niceness, which you sensed immediately on meeting her, but which, thus far in her career, no director had ever managed to bring out on the screen. They'd had many long talks. She'd called 10050 Cielo Drive her "love house."

Rudi then told me something he said he had never told anyone else. I knew there was no way I could use it in the trial: it was hearsay, and though there are many exceptions to the hearsay rule, this couldn't come in under any of them.

On the flight to Rome, Sharon had asked him: "Did that creepy-looking guy come back there yesterday?"

So Sharon had seen Manson, the creepy-looking little guy who four and a half months later would mastermind her murder!

Something must have happened to have caused such a strong reaction. A confrontation of some sort. Could it be that Voytek, who had an unpredictable temper, had got into an argument with Manson? Or that Manson had said something offensive to Sharon, and Jay had come to her defense?

I called LAPD and told them to find Shahrokh Hatami.

Lieutenant Helder contacted a friend of Colonel Tate's, who in turn located Hatami. I interviewed him in my office. Very emotionally, the Iranian photographer told me how much he had loved Sharon. "Not romantic, but"—he apologized for his broken English—"one human being loving qualities other human being has."

I told him I doubted if it could be better expressed.

Yes, he'd once sent someone to the back house. One time. He didn't know the date, but it was the day before Sharon left for Europe. It was in the afternoon. He'd looked out the window and noticed a man walking into the yard, hesitant, as if he didn't know where he was going, yet cocky, as if he thought he owned the place. His manner irritated Hatami, and he went out on the porch and asked him what he wanted.

I asked Hatami to describe the man. He said he was short, like Roman Polanski (Polanski was five feet five, Manson five feet two), late twenties, thin, with long hair. What color hair? Dark brown. He didn't have a beard but looked as if he needed a shave. How could he tell that?

He'd walked off the porch onto the stone walk to confront him; they were at most three or four feet apart.

With the exception of the age—Manson was thirty-four, but could easily have been mistaken for younger—the description fitted.

The man said he was looking for someone, mentioning a name Hatami did not recognize.

Could it have been Melcher? I asked. Possible, Hatami said, but he really couldn't remember. It had meant nothing to him at the time.

"This is the Polanski residence," Hatami told him. "This is not the place. Maybe the people you want is back there," pointing. "Take the back alley."

By "back alley" Hatami meant the dirt pathway in front of the residence which led to the guest house. But, as I'd later argue to the jury, to an American "back alley" meant a place where there were garbage cans, refuse. Manson must have felt he was being treated like an alley cat.

I asked Hatami, "What tone of voice did you use?" He illustrated, speaking loudly and angrily. Roman was away, Hatami said, and he felt protective of Sharon. "I wasn't happy that he was coming on the property, and looking at people he doesn't know."

How did the man react? He appeared upset, Hatami said; he turned and walked away without saying "excuse me" or anything.

Just before this, however, Sharon came to the door and said, "Who is it, Hatami?" Hatami told her that a man was looking for someone.

Showing Hatami a diagram of the house and grounds, I had him point to the spots where each was standing. Sharon was on the porch, the man on the walk not more than six to eight feet away, with no obstruction between them. There could be no question that Charles Manson saw Sharon Tate, and she him. Sharon had undoubtedly looked right into the eyes of the man who would order her death. We now had, for the first time, evidence that prior to the murders Manson had seen one of his victims.

Hatami had remained on the walk, Sharon on the porch, while the man went down the path toward the guest house. According to Hatami, he came back up the path in "a minute or two, no more," and left the premises without saying anything.

It was not as abrasive an incident as I was looking for, but, together with Melcher's rejection and Altobelli's subtle putdown, Hatami's "take the back alley" was more than sufficient cause for Manson to have strong feelings against 10050 Cielo Drive. Too, not only were these people obviously establishment, they were establishment in the very fields—entertainment, recording, motion pictures—in which Manson had tried to make it and failed.

There was one discrepancy: the time. Hatami was positive the incident had occurred during the afternoon. Altobelli, however, was equally insistent that it was between eight and nine in the evening when Manson appeared on the guest house porch. While it was possible one or the other was confused, the most logical explanation was that Manson had gone to the guest house that afternoon, found no one there (Altobelli was out most of the afternoon, making arrangements for his trip), then returned that evening. This was supported by Hatami's statement that Manson had come back up the path after "a minute or two, no more," which hardly left time for his conversation with Altobelli.

I had Hatami look at photographs of a dozen or so men. He picked out one, saying it looked like the man, though he couldn't be absolutely sure. It was a photograph of Charles Manson.

In interviewing Hatami, I hadn't mentioned Manson's name. Not until the interview was almost over did Hatami realize that the man he had spoken to that day might have been the man accused of plotting Sharon's murder.

Melcher to Altobelli to Hatami. If I hadn't suspected that Melcher was withholding something, it was possible that we might never have placed Manson inside the gate of 10050 Cielo Drive.

A similar chain, which had begun with my discovery of a short notation in the Inyo County files, led me to the missing piece in the motive for both the Tate and LaBianca murders.

Finally, nearly three months after first requesting it, I obtained the tape Inyo County Deputy Sheriff Don Ward had made with the two miners, Paul Crockett and Brooks Poston.

Ward had interviewed the pair on October 3, 1969, at Independence. This was a week before the Barker raid, and nearly a month and a half before LAPD learned of the Manson Family's possible involvement in the Tate-LaBianca murders. Ward's interview had nothing to do with those murders, only the activities of the "hippie types" who were now living in Golar Wash.

Crockett, a weather-worn miner in his mid-forties, had been prospecting in the Death Valley area in the spring of 1969 when he came across Manson's advance party at Barker Ranch. At this time it consisted of only two persons, a young runaway named Juanita Wildebush and Brooks Poston, a slender, rather docile eighteen-year-old who had been with the Family since June 1968. Nights, Crockett would visit the pair, and the talk would invariably turn to one subject, Charlie. "And I couldn't believe what they were saying," Crockett observed. "I mean, it was so utterly ridiculous." It became obvious to Crockett that these people believed this Charlie to be the second coming of Christ. It was just as obvious that they feared him. And so Crockett, who was no stranger to mysticism, did something perhaps a little odd but at least psychologically effective. He told them that, just like Charlie, he too had powers. And "I planted them with the idea that I had the power to keep Charlie from coming back up there."

Other Family members—including Paul Watkins, Tex Watson, Brenda McCann, and Bruce Davis—would occasionally show up at Barker with messages and supplies, and it didn't take long for the word to get back to Manson.

Initially he scoffed at the idea. But each time he tried to go to Barker something happened: the truck broke down, Spahn Ranch was raided, and so on. Meanwhile Juanita eloped with Bob Berry, Crockett's partner, and Crockett succeeded in "unconverting" several of Manson's most important male followers: Poston; Paul Watkins, who often acted as Manson's second in command; and, somewhat

later, Juan Flynn, a tall, strapping Panamanian cowbo
who had worked at Spahn.

When Crockett first met young Poston, he was "a zom
bie." The phrase was Poston's own. He said that he hae
wanted to leave the Family many times, but "Manson hac
a vise grip on my mind, and I couldn't break the grip. I
didn't know how to leave . . ."

Crockett discovered that Manson had "programmed al
his people to the extent that they're just like him. He ha
put all kinds of things in their heads. I didn't believe it
could be done, but he has done it and I seen it working."
Crockett began "deprogramming" Poston. He put him to
work in his various mining ventures, built up his body, got
him to thinking of other things than Manson.

When Manson finally reached Barker, in September
1969, Crockett, meeting him for the first time, found him
"a very clever man—he borders on genius." Then Manson
told him "some of the weirdest stories. I thought it was all
make-believe, to start with." Before long, Crockett was
not only convinced that Manson was insane, he was sure
"he would think no more of killing one of us than he
would of stepping on a flower; in fact, he'd rather do that
than step on a flower."

Deciding that his own life expectancy was directly proportionate to his usefulness to Manson, Crockett made
himself very useful, volunteering his truck to haul in supplies, and so forth. He and the former Mansonites now
living with him in a small cabin near Barker also began
taking precautions.

Among the weird tales Manson had told Crockett: That
the black man "was getting ready to blow the whole thing
open . . . Charlie has set up the whole thing, it's kind of
like a storybook . . . He says Helter Skelter is coming
down."

"Helter Skelter is what he calls the Negro revolt," Poston explained. "He says the Negroes are going to revolt
and kill all the white men except the ones that are hiding
in the desert . . ." Long before this Manson had told Poston, "When Helter Skelter comes down, the cities are
going to be mass hysteria and the cops—the piggies, he
calls them—won't know what to do, and the beast will fall

nd the black man will take over ... that the battle of Ar-
nageddon will be at hand."

Poston told Deputy Ward, "One of Charlie's basic
creeds is that all that girls are for is to fuck. And that's all
hey're for. And there is no crime, there is no sin, every-
hing is all right, that it's all just a game, like the game of a
ittle kid, only it's a grown-up game, and that God's getting
eady to pull down the curtain on this game and start it
ver again with his chosen people ..."

His chosen people were the Family, Charlie said. He
vould lead them to the desert, where they would multiply
ntil they numbered 144,000. He got this, Poston said,
from reading things into the Bible, from Revelations."*

Also in Revelation, as well as in Hopi Indian legends,
here was mention of a "bottomless pit," Poston said. The
ntrance to this pit, according to Charlie, was "a cave that
e says is underneath Death Valley that leads down to a
ea of gold that the Indians know about." Charlie claimed
hat "every tuned-in tribe of people that's ever lived have
escaped the destruction of their race by going underground,
iterally, and they're all living in a golden city where
here's a river that runs through it of milk and honey, and
a tree that bears twelve kinds of fruit, a different fruit
each month, or something like that, and you don't need to
bring candles nor any flashlights down there. He says it
vill be all lit up because ... the walls will glow and it
won't be cold and it won't be too hot. There will be
warm springs and fresh water, and people are already
down there waiting for him."

Both Atkins and Jakobson had already told me about
Charlie's "bottomless pit." The Family loved to hear Charlie sermonize about this hidden "land of milk and honey."
They not only believed, they were so convinced that such
a place existed that they spent days searching for the hole
in the ground which would lead them to the underground
paradise.

There was also a kind of desperation in the search, because it was here, underground in the bottomless pit, that
they intended to hide and wait out Helter Skelter.

---

*Manson apparently got the 144,000 figure from Revelation 7,
which mentions the twelve tribes of Israel, each numbering 12,000.

It was obvious to both Crockett and Poston that Manson believed Helter Skelter was imminent. And there were the preparations. Manson had arrived at Barker Ranch in September 1969 with about eight others, all heavily armed. More Family members arrived the following week, driving stolen dune buggies and other vehicles. They began setting up lookout posts and fortifications, hiding caches of guns, gasoline, and supplies.

(It did not occur to Crockett and Poston—since neither was aware of the Family's involvement in the Tate-LaBianca murders—that Manson might be fearful of something other than blacks.)

Manson hadn't given up on Poston, but Crockett's "deprogramming" had been very effective. Manson was even more upset about Paul Watkins' leaving him, since Watkins, a good-looking youth with a way with women, had been Manson's chief procurer of young girls.

Crockett, Poston, and Watkins had begun sleeping with their shotguns within reach. On at least three occasions Charlie, Clem, and/or the girls tried to creepy-crawl the cabin. Each time the trio had been lucky and had heard something, aborting the plan. Then one night Juan Flynn arrived "to shoot some bull," and admitted Manson had suggested he kill Crockett. Crockett persuaded Juan—who was far too independent to ever join the Family—that he should leave the area.

Crockett, accustomed to living as free and unencumbered as a mountain goat, was a mite stubborn. He felt he had as much right to be in Death Valley as Manson did. But he was also a realist. With Flynn gone and Watkins in town getting supplies, he and Poston were vastly outnumbered. Figuring "my usefulness to Charlie had already vanished and that he would, if he considered it necessary, liquidate me immediately, if not sooner," Crockett had Poston fill the canteens and pack some grub. Under cover of night they fled the area on foot, walking over twenty rugged miles to Warmsprings, then catching a ride to Independence, where they told Deputy Sheriff Ward about Charles Manson and his Family.

After hearing the tape, I arranged through Frank Fowles for Crockett and Poston to come to Los Angeles.

Though it was Crockett who had broken Manson's hold over Poston, the latter was by far the most articulate. Incidents, dates, places—snap, snap, snap. Crockett, by contrast, was evasive. "I can feel their vibrations. I can't talk freely to you because they might know what I am saying."

Crockett doubted if we could ever convict Manson, because "he does nothing himself. His people do it all for him. He doesn't do anything anybody could pin on him." He added that "all the women have been programmed to do exactly as he says, and they all have knives. He's got those girls so programmed that they don't even exist. They are a copy of him."

Though I was interested in Crockett's contacts with Manson and the Family, I was hopeful that he could give me something more important.

Crockett had helped Poston, Watkins, and Flynn break away from Manson. To do this he must have gained some insight into how Manson had gained control over them in the first place. Others had also said that Manson "programmed" his followers. Did he understand how he accomplished this?

Crockett said he did, but when he tried to articulate it, he became bogged down in a morass of words and definitions, finally saying, "I can't explain it. It's all part of the occult."

I decided I wouldn't be able to use Crockett as a witness.

It was otherwise with Brooks Poston. The tall, gangly youth, with the air of the hayseed about him, was a fund of information about Manson and the Family.

A highly impressionable seventeen-year-old, Brooks Poston had met Manson at Dennis Wilson's house, and from that moment until he finally broke with Manson more than a year later to follow Crockett, "I believed Charlie was JC."

Q. "JC?"

A. "Yeah, that's how Charlie always used to refer to Jesus Christ."

Q. "Did Manson ever tell you that he was JC, or Jesu Christ?"

It wasn't so much stated as implied, Brooks said. Char lie claimed that he had lived before, nearly two thousan years ago, and that he had once died on the cross. (Man son had also told Gregg Jakobson that he had already die once, and that "death is beautiful.")

Charlie had a favorite story which he was fond of tell ing the Family, complete with dramatic gestures an moans of pain. Brooks had heard it often. According to Charlie, while he was living in Haight-Ashbury, he ha taken a "magic mushroom" (psilocybin) trip. He wa lying on a bed, but it became a cross, and he could fee the nails in his feet and hands and the sword in his side and when he looked down at the foot of the cross he sav Mary Magdalene (Mary Brunner), and she was crying and he said, "I'm all right, Mary." He had been fighting it but now he gave up, surrendered himself to death, an when he did, he could suddenly see through the eyes o everyone at the same time, and at that moment he be came the whole world.

With such clues, his followers had little trouble guessin his true identity.

I was curious about something. Up until his arrest i Mendocino County on July 28, 1967,* Charlie had alway used his real name, Charles Milles Manson. On that occa sion, however, and thereafter, he called himself Charle *Willis* Manson. Had Manson ever said anything about hi name? I asked. Crockett and Poston both told me tha they had heard Manson say, very slowly, that his nam was "Charles' Will Is Man's Son," meaning that his wil was that of the Son of Man.

Although Susan Atkins had emphasized Charlie's sur name in talking to Virginia Graham, I hadn't reall thought, until now, how powerful that name was. Ma Son. It was tailor-made for the Infinite Being role he wa now seeking to portray.

*Manson was charged with interfering with the questioning of suspected runaway juvenile, Ruth Ann Moorehouse. He was giver thirty days, suspended, and placed on three years probation. Aske his occupation when booked, he said he was a minister.

But Charlie carried all this yet a step further, Poston said. Manson claimed that the members of the Family were the original Christians, reincarnated, and that the Romans had returned as the establishment.

It was now time, Manson told his closest followers, for the Romans to have their turn on the cross.

Exactly how did Manson "program" someone? I asked Brooks.

He had various techniques, Poston said. With a girl, it would usually start with sex. Charlie might convince a plain girl that she was beautiful. Or, if she had a father fixation, have her imagine that he was her father. (He'd used both techniques with Susan Atkins.) Or, if he felt she was looking for a leader, he might imply that he was Christ. Manson had a talent for sensing, and capitalizing on, a person's hangups and/or desires. When a man first joined the group, Charlie would usually take him on an LSD trip, ostensibly "to open his mind." Then, while he was in a highly suggestible state, he would talk about love, how you had to surrender yourself to it, how only by ceasing to exist as an individual ego could you become one with all things.

As with Jakobson, I queried Poston as to the sources of Manson's philosophy. Scientology, the Bible, and the Beatles. These three were the only ones he knew.

A peculiar triumvirate. Yet by now I was beginning to suspect the existence of at least a fourth influence. The old magazines I'd found at Barker, Gregg's mention that Charlie claimed to have read Nietzsche and that he believed in a master race, plus the emergence of a startling number of disturbing parallels between Manson and the leader of the Third Reich, led me to ask Poston: "Did Manson ever say anything about Hitler?"

Poston's reply was short and incredibly chilling.

A. "He said that Hitler was a tuned-in guy who had leveled the karma of the Jews."

I spent most of two days interviewing Crockett and Poston, obtaining much new information, some of it very incriminating. For example, Manson had once suggested

Poston take a knife, go into Shoshone, and kill the sheriff. In the first real test of his newly found independence, Poston had refused to even consider the idea.

Before Crockett and Poston returned to Shoshone, I told them I wanted to talk to Juan Flynn and Paul Watkins. They weren't sure if Juan would talk to me—that big Panamanian cowboy was an independent cuss—but they thought Paul might. Since he was no longer procuring girls for Charlie, he had some free time on his hands.

Watkins agreed to the interview, and I arranged for Watkins, Poston, and Crockett to stay in a motel in downtown L.A.

"Paul, I need a new love."

Paul Watkins was describing for me how Manson would send him out to recruit young girls. Watkins admitted that he liked his special role in the Family. The only problem was, after he'd located a likely candidate, Charlie would insist on sleeping with her first.

Why didn't Manson pick up the girls himself? I asked.

"He was too old for most of the girls," the nineteen-year-old Watkins replied. "He frightened them. Also, I had a good line." It was also obvious that Watkins was better-looking than Charlie.

I asked Paul where he found the girls. He might go down to the Sunset Strip, where the teenyboppers hung out. Or drive the highways watching for girls who were hitchhiking. Once Charlie, through the connivance of an older woman who posed as Watkins' mother, even had him arrange a phony registration at a Los Angeles high school so he could be closer to the action.

Watkins also described the orgies that took place at the Gresham Street house and at Spahn. For a while there was one about every week. They would always start with drugs—grass, Peyote, LSD, whatever was available—Manson rationing them out, deciding how much each person needed. "Everything was done at Charlie's direction," Paul said. Charlie might dance around, everyone else following, like a train. As he'd take off his clothes, all the rest would take off their clothes. Then, when everyone was naked, they'd lie on the floor, "and they'd play the game of taking twelve deep breaths and releasing them and close eyes and then rub against each other" until "eventually all were touching." Charlie would direct the orgy, arranging bodies, combinations, positions. "He'd set it all up in a beautiful way like he was creating a masterpiece in sculpture," Watkins said, "but instead of clay he was using warm bodies." Paul said that the usual objective during the orgies was for all the Family members to achieve a simultaneous orgasm, but they were never successful.

Manson often staged these events to impress outsiders. If there were guests who he felt could be of some use to him, he'd say to the Family, "Let's get together and show these people how to make love." Whatever the reaction, the impression was a lasting one. "It was like the Devil buying your soul," Watkins said.

Manson also used these occasions to "eradicate hangups." If a person indicated reluctance to engage in a certain act, Manson would force that person to commit it. Male-female, female-female, male-male, intercourse, cunnilingus, fellatio, sodomy—there could be no inhibitions of any kind. One thirteen-year-old girl's initiation into the Family consisted of her being sodomized by Manson while the others watched. Manson also "went down on" a young boy to show the others he had rid himself of all inhibitions.

Charlie used sex, Paul said. For example, when it became obvious that DeCarlo was making no effort to persuade his motorcycle gang to join the Family, Manson told the girls to withhold their favors from Danny.

The fact that Manson directed even the sex lives of his followers was powerful evidence of his domination. I asked Watkins for other examples specifically involving co-defendants. He recalled that once at Spahn Ranch, Charlie told Sadie: "I'd like half a coconut, even if you have to go to Rio de Janeiro to get it." Sadie got right up and was on her way out the door when Charlie said, "Never mind."

It was a test. It was also, by inference, evidence that Susan Atkins would do anything Charles Manson asked her to do.

As with the others, I questioned Watkins about Manson's programming techniques. He told me something very interesting, which apparently the other Family members didn't know. He said that when Manson passed out the LSD, he always took a smaller dose than the others. Though Manson never told him why he did so, Paul presumed that during the "trip" Manson wanted to retain control over his own mental faculties. It is said that LSD is a mind-altering drug which tends to make the person ingesting it a little more vulnerable and susceptible to the influence of third parties. Manson used LSD "trips," Paul said, to instill his philosophies, exploit weaknesses and fears, and extract promises and agreements from his followers.

As Manson's second in command, Watkins had enjoyed Charlie's confidence more than most of the others. I asked him if Manson had ever mentioned Scientology or The Process. Watkins had never heard of The Process, but Manson had told him that while he was in prison he had studied Scientology, becoming a "theta," which Manson defined as being "clear." Watkins said that in the summer of 1968 he and Charlie had dropped into a Church of Scientology in downtown Los Angeles, and Manson asked the receptionist, "What do you do after 'clear'?" When she was unable to tell him anything he hadn't already done, Manson walked out.

One aspect of Manson's philosophy especially puzzled me: his strange attitude toward fear. He not only preached that fear was beautiful, he often told the Family that they should live in a constant state of fear. What did he mean by that? I asked Paul.

To Charlie fear was the same thing as awareness, Watkins said. The more fear you have, the more awareness, hence the more love. When you're really afraid, you come to "Now." And when you are at Now, you are totally conscious.

Manson claimed that children were more aware than adults, because they were naturally afraid. But animals were even more aware than people, he said, because they always lived at Now. The coyote was the most aware creature there was, Manson maintained, because he was completely paranoid. Being frightened of everything, he missed nothing.

Charlie was always "selling fear," Watkins continued. He *wanted* people to be afraid, and the more afraid the better. Using this same logic, "Charlie said that death was beautiful, because people feared death."

I would learn, from talking to other Family members, that Manson would seek out each individual's greatest fear—not so the person could confront and eliminate it, but so he could re-emphasize it. It was like a magic button, which he could push at will to control that person.

"Whatever you do," Watkins advised me, as had both Crockett and Poston, "don't ever let Charlie know you are afraid of him." One day at Spahn, without warning or provocation, Manson had jumped on Watkins and started strangling him. At first Paul resisted, but then, gasping for breath, he suddenly gave up, stopped resisting. "It was really weird," Watkins said. "The instant I stopped fearing him, his hands flew off my throat and he jumped back as if he'd been attacked by an unseen force."

"Then it's like the barking dog," I commented. "If you show fear, it will attack; if you don't it won't?"

"Exactly. *Fear turns Charlie on.*"

Paul Watkins was inherently more independent than Brooks Poston, much less the follower type. Yet he too had remained with the Family for a long period. Other than the girls, was there some reason why he stayed?

"I thought Charlie was Christ," he told me, not blinking an eye.

Both Watkins and Poston had severed the umbilical linking them to Manson. But both admitted to me that they still weren't completely free of him, that even now they would sometimes lapse back into a state where they could feel Manson's vibrations.

It was Paul Watkins who finally supplied the missing link in Manson's motive for the murders. Yet, if I hadn't talked to Jakobson and Poston, I might have missed its importance, for it was from all three, Gregg, Brooks, and Paul, that I obtained the keys to understanding (1) Charles Manson's unique interpretation of the Book of Revelation, and (2) his decidedly curious and complex attitude toward the English musical group the Beatles.

Several persons had told me Manson was fond of quoting from the Bible, particularly the ninth chapter of Revelation. Once Charlie had handed Jakobson a Bible, already open to the chapter, and, while he read it, supplied his own interpretation of the verses. With only one exception, which will be noted, what Gregg told me tallied with what I later heard from Poston and Watkins.

The "four angels" were the Beatles, whom Manson considered "leaders, spokesmen, prophets," according to Gregg. The line "And he opened the bottomless pit . . . And there came out of the smoke locusts upon the earth; and unto them was given power . . ." was still another reference to the English group, Gregg said. Locusts—Beatles—one and the same. "Their faces were as the faces of men," yet "they had hair as the hair of women." An obvious reference to the long-haired musicians. Out of the mouths of the four angels "issued fire and brimstone." Gregg: "This referred to the spoken words, the lyrics of the Beatles' songs, the power that came out of their mouths."

Their "breastplates of fire," Poston added, were their electric guitars. Their shapes "like unto horses prepared unto battle" were the dune buggies. The "horsemen who numbered two hundred thousand thousand," and who would roam the earth spreading destruction, were the motorcyclists.

"And it was commanded them that they should not hurt the grass of the earth, neither any green thing, neither any tree; but only those men which have not the seal of God in their foreheads." I wondered about that seal on the forehead. How did Manson interpret that? I asked Jakobson.

"It was all subjective," Gregg replied. "He said there would be a mark on people." Charlie had never told him exactly what the mark would be, only that he, Charlie, "would be able to tell, he would know," and that "the mark would designate whether they were with him or against him." With Charlie, it was either one or the other, Gregg said; "there was no middle road."

One verse spoke of worshipping demons and idols of gold and silver and bronze. Manson said that referred to the material worship of the establishment: of automobiles, houses, money.

Q. "Directing your attention to Verse 15, which reads: 'And the four angels were loosed, which were prepared for an hour, and a day, and a month, and a year, for to slay the third part of men.' Did he say what that meant?"

A. "He said that those were the people who would die in Helter Skelter . . . one third of mankind . . . the white race."

I now knew I was on the right track.

Only on one point did Jakobson's recollection of Manson's interpretation differ from that of the others. The first verse of Revelation 9 refers to a fifth angel; the chapter ends, however, referring to only four. Originally there were five Beatles, Gregg explained, one of whom, Stuart Sutcliffe, had died in Germany in 1962.

Poston and Watkins—who, unlike Jakobson, were members of the Family—interpreted this much differently. Verse I reads: "And the fifth angel sounded, and I saw a star fall from heaven unto the earth: and to him was given the key of the bottomless pit."

To members of the Family the identity of that fifth angel, the ruler of the bottomless pit, was never in doubt. It was Charlie.

Verse II reads: "And they had a king over them, which is the angel of the bottomless pit, whose name in the Hebrew tongue is Abaddon, but in the Greek tongue hath his name Apollyon."

The king also had a Latin name, which, though it appears in the Catholic Douay Version, was inadvertently omitted by the translators of the King James version. It was Exterminans.

Exterminans, t/n Charles Manson.

As far as Jakobson, Watkins, and Poston knew, Manson placed no special meaning on the last verse of Revelation 9. But I found myself thinking of it often in the months ahead:

"Neither repented they of their murders, nor of their sorceries, nor of their fornication, nor of their thefts."

"The important thing to remember about Revelation 9," Gregg told me, "is that Charlie believed this was happening *now*, not in the future. It's going to begin now and it's time to choose sides ... either that or flee with him to the desert."

According to Jakobson, Manson believed "the Beatles were spokesmen. They were speaking to Charlie, through their songs, letting him know from across the ocean that this is what was going to go down. He believed this firmly ... He considered their songs prophecy, especially the songs in the so-called White Album ... He told me that many, many times."

Watkins and Poston also said that Manson and the Family were convinced that the Beatles were speaking to Charlie through their music. For example, in the song "I Will" are the lines: "And when at last I find you/ Your song will fill the air/ Sing it loud so I can hear you/ Make it easy to be near you ..." Charlie interpreted this to mean the Beatles wanted him to make an album, Poston and Watkins said. Charlie told them that the Beatles were looking for JC and he was the JC they were looking for. He also told them that the Beatles knew that Christ had returned to earth again and that he was living somewhere in Los Angeles.

"How in the world did he come up with that?" I asked them.

In the White Album is a song called "Honey Pie," a lyric of which reads: "Oh honey pie my position is tragic/ Come and show me the magic/ Of your Hollywood song." A later lyric goes: "Oh Honey pie you are driving me frantic/ Sail across the Atlantic/ To be where you belong."

Charlie, of course, wanted *them* to sail across the Atlantic, to join him in Death Valley. While residing in the Gresham Street house (in January and February of 1969, just after the White Album was released), Manson and the girls sent several telegrams, wrote a number of letters, and made at least three telephone calls to England, attempting to reach the Beatles. No luck.

The line "I'm in love but I'm lazy" from "Honey Pie" meant to Charlie that the Beatles loved JC but were too lazy to go looking for him; too, they'd just gone all the way to India, following a man who they'd finally decided was a false prophet, the Maharishi. They were also calling for JC/Charlie in the first eight lines of the song "Don't Pass Me By," in "Yer Blues," and, in the earlier Magical Mystery Tour album, in "Blue Jay Way."

Much of this I would never use at the trial; it was simply too absurd.

The Beatles' White Album, Manson told Watkins, Poston, and others, "set up things for the revolution." *His* album, which was to follow, would, in Charlie's words, "blow the cork off the bottle. That would start it."

Much of the time at the Gresham Street house, according to Poston, Watkins, and others, was spent composing songs for Charlie's album. Each was to be a message song, directed to a particular group of people, such as the bikers, outlining the part they'd play in Helter Skelter. Charlie worked hard on these songs; they had to be very subtle, he said, like the Beatles' own songs, their true meaning hidden beneath the awareness of all but the tuned-in people.

Manson was counting on Terry Melcher to produce this album. According to numerous Family members (both Melcher and Jakobson denied this), Terry had promised to come and listen to the songs one evening. The girls cleaned the house, baked cookies, rolled joints. Melcher didn't show. Manson, according to Poston and Watkins, never forgave Terry for this. Melcher's word was no good, he said angrily on a number of occasions.

Though the Beatles had made many records, it was the double-disk White Album, which Capitol issued in December 1968, that Manson considered most important. Even the fact that the cover was white—with no other design except the embossed name of the group—held significance for him.

It was, and remains, a startling album, containing some of the Beatles' finest music, and some of their strangest. Its thirty songs range from tender love ballads to pop parodies to cacophonies of noise made by taking loops of very diverse tapes and splicing them together. To Charles

Manson, however, it was prophecy. At least this is what he convinced his followers.

That Charlie had renamed Susan Atkins "Sadie Mae Glutz" long before the White Album appeared containing the song "Sexy Sadie" was additional proof to the Family that Manson and the Beatles were mentally attuned.

Almost every song in the album had a hidden meaning which Manson interpreted for his followers. To Charlie "Rocky Raccoon" meant "coon" or the black man. While to everyone except Manson and the Family it was obvious that the lyrics of "Happiness Is a Warm Gun" had sexual connotations, Charlie interpreted the song to mean that the Beatles were telling blackie to get guns and fight whitey.

According to Poston and Watkins, the Family played five songs in the White Album more than all the others. They were: "Blackbird," "Piggies," "Revolution I," "Revolution 9," and "Helter Skelter."

"Blackbird singing in the dead of night/ Take these broken wings and learn to fly/ All your life/ You were only waiting for this moment to arise," went the lyrics of "Blackbird." According to Jakobson, "Charlie believed that the moment was now and that the black man was going to arise, overthrow the white man, and take his turn." According to Watkins, in this song Charlie "figured the Beatles were programming the black people to get it up, get it on, start doing it."

On first hearing the song, I'd thought that the LaBianca killers had made a mistake, writing "rise" instead of "arise." However, Jakobson told me that Charlie said the black man was going to "rise" up against the white man. " 'Rise' was one of Charlie's big words," Gregg said, providing me with the origin of still another of the key words.

Both the Tate and LaBianca murders had occurred in "the dead of night." However, if the parallel had special significance to Manson, he never admitted it to anyone I interviewed, nor, if he knew it, did he admit the dictionary meaning of the phrase "helter skelter." The song "Helter Skelter" begins: "When I get to the bottom I go back to the top of the slide/ Where I stop and I turn and I go for a ride ..." According to Poston, Manson said this was a reference to the Family emerging from the bottomless pit.

There was a simpler explanation. In England, home of the Beatles, "helter skelter" is another name for a slide in an amusement park.

If you listen closely, you can hear grunts and oinks in the background of the song "Piggies."* By "piggies," Gregg and the others told me, Manson meant anyone who belonged to the establishment.

Like Manson himself, the song was openly critical of the piggies, noting that what they really needed was a damned good whacking.

"By that he meant the black man was going to give the piggies, the establishment, a damned good whacking," Jakobson explained. Charlie really loved that line, both Watkins and Poston said; he was always quoting it.

I couldn't listen to the final stanza without visualizing what had happened at 3301 Waverly Drive. It describes piggy couples dining out, in all their starched finery, eating bacon with their forks and knives.

Rosemary LaBianca: forty-one knife wounds. Leno La-Bianca: twelve knife wounds, punctured with a fork seven times, a *knife* in his throat, a *fork* in his stomach, and, on the wall, in his own blood, DEATH TO PIGS.

. "There's a chord at the end of the song 'Piggies,' " Watkins said. "It goes down and it's a really weird chord. After the sound of piggies snorting. And in the 'Revolution 9' song, there's that same chord, and after it they have a little pause and snort, snort, snort. But in the pause, there is machine-gun fire.

"And it's the same thing with the 'Helter Skelter' song," Paul continued. "They had this really weird chord. And in the 'Revolution 9' song there's the same chord again, with machine guns firing and people dying and screaming and stuff."

*Unlike ex-Beatles John Lennon and Paul McCartney, George Harrison refused the authors permission to quote from the lyrics of any of his songs, including "Piggies."

The White Album contains two songs with the word "revolution" in their titles.

The printed lyrics of "Revolution 1," as given on the jacket insert, read: "You say you want a revolution/ Well you know/ We all want to change the world . . ./ But when you talk about destruction/ Don't you know that you can count me out."

When you listen to the record itself, however, immediately after "out" you hear the word "in."

Manson took this to mean the Beatles, once undecided, now favored the revolution.

Manson made much of these "hidden lyrics," which can be found in a number of the Beatles' songs but are especially prevalent in the White Album. They were, he told his followers, direct communications to him, Charlie/JC.

Later on the lyrics go: "You say you got a real solution/ Well you know/ We'd all love to see the plan."

The meaning of this was obvious to Manson: Sing out, Charlie, and tell us how we can escape the holocaust.

Of all the Beatles' songs, "Revolution 9" is easily the weirdest. Reviewers couldn't decide whether it was an exciting new direction for rock or an elaborate put-on. One critic said it reminded him of "a bad acid trip."

There are no lyrics as such, nor is it music in any conventional sense; rather, it is a montage of noises—whispers, shouts, snatches of dialogue from the BBC, bits of classical music, mortars exploding, babies crying, church hymns, car horns, and football yells—which, together with the oft reiterated refrain "Number 9, Number 9, Number 9," build to a climax of machine-gun fire and screams, to be followed by the soft and obviously symbolic lullaby "Good Night."

Of all the songs in the White Album, Jakobson said, Charlie "spoke mostly of 'Revolution 9.'" He said "it was the Beatles' way of telling people what was going to happen; it was their way of making prophecy; it directly paralleled the Bible's Revelation 9."

It was also the battle of Armageddon, the coming black-white revolution portrayed in sound, Manson claimed, and after having listened to it myself, I could easily believe that if ever there were such a conflict, this was probably very much what it would sound like.

According to Poston: "When Charlie was listening to it, he heard in the background noise, in and around the machine-gun fire and the oinking of pigs, a man's voice saying 'Rise.' " Listening to the recording again, I also heard it, twice repeated: the first time almost a whisper, the second a long-drawn-out scream.* This was potent evidence. Through both Jakobson and Poston, I'd now linked Manson, irrevocably, with the word "rise" printed in blood at the LaBianca residence.

In "Revolution I" the Beatles had finally decided to commit themselves to the revolution. In "Revolution 9" they were telling the black man that *now* was the time to rise and start it all. According to Charlie.

Manson found many other messages in this song (including the words "Block that Nixon"), but as far as his philosophy of Helter Skelter was concerned, these were the most important.

Charles Manson was already talking about an imminent black-white war when Gregg Jakobson first met him, in the spring of 1968. There was an underground expression current at the time, "the shit is coming down," variously interpreted as meaning the day of judgment was at hand or all hell was breaking loose, and Charlie often used it in reference to the coming racial conflict. But he wasn't rabid about it, Gregg said; it was just one of many subjects they discussed.

"When I first met Charlie [in June 1968], he really didn't have any of this Helter Skelter stuff going," Paul Watkins told me. "He talked a little bit about the 'shit coming down,' but just barely ... He said when the shit comes down the black man will be on one side and the white will be on the other, and that's all he said about it."

Then, that December, Capitol issued the Beatles' White Album, one of the songs of which was "Helter Skelter."

---

*"It is first heard two minutes and thirty-four seconds into the song, just after the crowd sounds that follow "lots of stab wounds as it were" and "informed him on the third night" and just before "Number 9, Number 9."

The final stanza went: "Look out helter skelter helter skel ter helter skelter/ Look out [background scream] helte skelter/ She's coming down fast/ Yes she is/ Yes she is."

Manson apparently first heard the White Album in Lo Angeles, while on a trip there from Barker Ranch, where most of the Family remained. When Manson returned te Death Valley on December 31, 1968, he told the group according to Poston, "Are you hep to what the Beatles ar saying? Helter Skelter is coming down. The Beatles are telling it like it is."

It was the same expression, except that in place of the word for defecation Manson now substituted "Helter Skel ter."

Another link had been made, this time to the bloody words on the refrigerator door at the LaBianca residence.

Though this was the first time Manson used the phrase it was not to be the last.

Watkins: "And he started rapping about this Beatle al bum and Helter Skelter and all these meanings that didn't get out of it . . . and he builds this picture up and he called it Helter Skelter, and what it meant was the Ne groes were going to come down and rip the cities al apart."

After this, Watkins said, "We started listening to the Beatles' album constantly . . ."

Death Valley is very cold in the winter, so Manson found a two-story house at 20910 Gresham Street in Ca noga Park, in the San Fernando Valley, not too far from Spahn Ranch. In January 1969, Watkins said, "we al moved into the Gresham Street house to get ready fo Helter Skelter. So we could watch it coming down and see all of the things going on in the city. He [Charlie] called the Gresham Street house 'The Yellow Submarine' from the Beatles' movie. It was like a submarine in that when you were in it you weren't allowed to go out. You could only peek out of the windows. We started designing dune buggies and motorcycles and we were going to buy twenty-five Harley sportsters . . . and we mapped escape routes to the desert . . . supply caches . . . we had all these different things going.

"I watched him building this big picture up," Paul not

ed. "He would do it very slowly, very carefully. I swallowed it hook, line, and sinker.

"Before Helter Skelter came along," Watkins said with a sigh of wistful nostalgia, "all Charlie cared about was orgies."

Before Jakobson and I had ever discussed the Beatles, I asked him: "Did Charlie ever talk to you about a black-white revolution?"

A. "Yeah, that was Helter Skelter, and he believed it was going to happen in the near future, almost immediately."

Q. "What did he say about this black-white revolution? How would it come about and what would it accomplish?"

A. "It would begin with the black man going into white people's homes and ripping off the white people, physically destroying them, until there was open revolution in the streets, until they finally won and took over. Then black man would assume white man's karma. He would then be the establishment."

Watkins: "He used to explain how it would be so simple to start out. A couple of black people—some of the spades from Watts—would come up into the Bel Air and Beverly Hills district ... up in the rich piggy district ... and just really wipe some people out, just cutting bodies up and smearing blood and writing things on the wall in blood ... all kinds of super-atrocious crimes that would really make the white man mad ..."

Poston said very much the same thing before I ever talked to Watkins, but with the addition of one very important detail: "He [Manson] said a group of real blacks would come out of the ghettos and do an atrocious crime in the richer sections of Los Angeles and other cities. They would do an atrocious murder with stabbing, killing, cutting bodies to pieces, smearing blood on the walls, writing 'pigs' on the walls ... in the victims' own blood."

This was tremendously powerful evidence—linking Manson not only with the Tate murders, where PIG had been printed in Sharon Tate's blood on the front door of the residence, but also with the LaBianca murders, where

DEATH TO PIGS had been printed in Leno LaBianca's blood on the living-room wall—and I questioned Poston in depth as to Manson's exact words, where the conversation had occurred, when, and who else was present. I then questioned everyone Poston mentioned who was willing to cooperate.

Ordinarily, I try to avoid repetitious testimony in a trial, knowing it can antagonize the jury. However, Manson's Helter Skelter motive was so bizarre that I knew if it was expounded by only one witness no juror would ever believe it.

The conversation had occurred in February 1969, at the Gresham Street house, Poston said.

We now had evidence that six months before the Tate-LaBianca murders Charles Manson was telling the Family exactly how the murders would occur, complete even to writing "pigs" in the victims' own blood.

We now had also linked Manson with every one of the bloody words found at both the Tate and LaBianca residences.

But this would only be the beginning, Manson told Watkins. These murders would cause mass paranoia among the whites: "Out of their fear they would go into the ghetto and just start shooting black people like crazy." But all they would kill would be "the ones that were with whitey in the first place."

The "true black race"—whom Manson identified at various times as the Black Muslims and the Black Panthers—"wouldn't even be affected by it." They would be in hiding, waiting, he said.

After the slaughter, the Black Muslims would "come out and appeal to the whites, saying, 'Look what you have done to my people.' And this would split whitey down the middle," Watkins said, "between the hippie-liberals and all the uptight conservatives ..." And it would be like the War between the States, brother against brother, white killing white. Then, after the whites had mostly killed off each other, "the Black Muslims would come out of hiding and wipe them *all* out."

All except Charlie and the Family, who would have taken refuge in the bottomless pit in Death Valley.

The karma would then have turned. "Blackie would be on top." And he would begin to "clean up the mess, just like he always has done ... He will clean up the mess that the white man made, and build the world back up a little bit, build the cities back up. But then he wouldn't know what to do with it. He couldn't handle it."

According to Manson, Watkins said, the black man had a problem. He could only do what the white man had taught him to do. He wouldn't be able to run the world without whitey showing him how.

Watkins: "Blackie then would come to Charlie and say, you know, 'I did my thing. I killed them all and, you know, I am tired of killing now. It is all over.'

"And then Charlie would scratch blackie's fuzzy head and kick him in the butt and tell him to go pick cotton and go be a good nigger, and we would live happily ever after ..." The Family, now grown to 144,000, as predicted in the Bible—a pure, white master race—would emerge from the bottomless pit. And "It would be our world then. There would be no one else, except for us and the black servants."

And, according to the gospel of Charlie—as he related it to his disciple Paul Watkins—he, Charles Willis Manson, the fifth angel, JC, would then rule that world.

Paul Watkins, Brooks Poston, and Gregg Jakobson had not only defined Manson's motive, Helter Skelter, Watkins had supplied that missing link. In his sick, twisted, disordered mind, Charles Manson believed that *he* would be the ultimate beneficiary of the black-white war and the murders which triggered it.

One day at the Gresham Street house, while they were on an acid trip, Manson had reiterated to Watkins and the others that blackie had no smarts, "that the only thing blackie knows is what whitey has told him or shown him" and "so someone is going to have to show him how to do it."

I asked Watkins: "How to do what?"

A. "How to bring down Helter Skelter. How to do all these things."

Watkins: "Charlie said the only reason it hadn't come down already was because whitey was feeding his young daughters to the black man in Haight-Ashbury, and he said that if his music came out, and all of the beautiful people—'love' he called it—left Haight-Ashbury, blackie would turn to Bel Air to get his rocks off."

Blackie had been temporarily "pacified" by the young white girls, Manson claimed. But when he took away the pacifier—when his album came out and all the young loves followed Pied Piper Charlie to the desert—blackie would need another means of getting his frustrations out and he would then turn to the establishment.

But Terry Melcher didn't come through. The album wasn't made. Sometime in late February of 1969 Manson sent Brooks and Juanita to Barker Ranch. The rest of the Family moved back to Spahn and began preparing for Helter Skelter. "Now there was an actual physical effort to get things together, so they could move to the desert," Gregg said. Jakobson, who visited the ranch during this period, was startled at the change in Manson. Previously he had preached oneness of the Family, complete in itself, self-sufficient; now he was cultivating outsiders, the motorcycle gangs. Before this he had been anti-materialistic; now he was accumulating vehicles, guns, money. "It struck me that all this contradicted what Charlie had done and talked to me about before," Gregg said, explaining that this was the beginning of his disenchantment and eventual break with Manson.

The newly materialistic Manson came up with some wild moneymaking schemes. For example, someone suggested that the girls in the Family could earn $300 to $500 a week apiece working as topless dancers. Manson liked the idea—with ten broads pulling in $3,000 a week and upward he could buy jeeps, dune buggies, even machine guns—and he sent Bobby Beausoleil and Bill Vance to the Girard Agency on the Sunset Strip to negotiate the deal.

There was only one problem. With all his powers, Manson was unable to transform molehills into mountains.

With the exception of Sadie and a few others, Charlie's girls simply did not have impressive busts. For some reason Manson seemed to attract mostly flat-chested girls.

While at the Gresham Street house, Manson had told Watkins that the atrocious murders would occur that summer. It was almost summer now and the blacks were showing no signs of rising up to fulfill their karma. One day in late May or early June of 1969, Manson took Watkins aside, down near the old trailer at Spahn, and confided: "The only thing blackie knows is what whitey has told him." He then added, "*I'm* going to have to show him how to do it."

According to Watkins: "I got some weird pictures from that." A few days later Watkins took off for Barker, fearful that if he stuck around he would see those weird pictures materialize into nihilistic reality.

It was September of 1969 before Manson himself returned to Barker Ranch, to find that Watkins and Poston had defected. Though Manson told Watkins about "cutting Shorty into nine pieces," he made no mention whatsoever of the Tate-LaBianca murders. In discussing Helter Skelter with Watkins, however, Manson said, without explanation, "I had to show blackie how to do it."

LAPD had interviewed Gregg Jakobson in late November of 1969. When he attempted to tell them about Manson's far-out philosophy, one of the detectives replied, "Ah, Charlie's a madman; we're not interested in all that." The following month two detectives went to Shoshone and talked to Crockett and Poston; LAPD also contacted Watkins. All three were asked what they knew about the Tate-LaBianca murders. And all three said they didn't know anything, which, in their minds, was true, none having previously made the connection between Manson and these murders. After the interview with Poston and Crockett, one of the detectives remarked, "Looks like we made a trip for nothing."

Initially, I found it difficult to believe that none of the four even suspected that Manson might be behind the Tate-LaBianca murders. There were, I discovered, several probable reasons for this. When Manson had told Jako son how Helter Skelter would start, he had said nothir about writing words in blood. He had told this to bot Watkins and Poston, even telling Poston about the wor "pigs," but there were no newspapers at Barker Ranc and its location was such that there was no radio recep tion. Though they had heard about the murders on the infrequent supply trips into Independence and Shoshon both stated they hadn't picked up many details.

The main reason, however, was simply a fluke. Thoug the press did report that there was bloody writing at th LaBianca residence, LAPD had succeeded in keeping on fact secret: that two of the words were HEALTER SKELTE

Had this been publicized, undoubtedly Jakobson, Wa kins, Poston, and numerous others would have connecte the LaBianca murders—and probably the Tate murder also, because of their proximity in time—with Manson's ir sane plan. And it seems a safe assumption that at least on would have communicated his suspicions to the police.

It was one of those odd happenstances, for which n one was at fault, the repercussions of which no one coul foresee, but it appears possible that had this happened, th killers might have been apprehended days, rather tha months, after the murders, and Donald "Shorty" Shea and possibly others, might still be alive.

Though I was now convinced we had the motive, othe leads failed to pan out.

None of the employees of the Standard station i Sylmar or the Jack Frost store in Santa Monica coul identify anyone in our "Family album." As for the LaBi anca credit cards, all appeared to be accounted for, whil Susan Struthers was unable to determine if a brown purs was missing from her mother's personal effects. The prob lem was that Rosemary had several brown purses.

By the time LAPD requested the Spahn Ranch phon records, most of the billings for May and July 1969 ha been "lost or destroyed." All the numbers for the othe months—April to October 1969—were identified and though we obtained some minor background informatio on the activities of the Family, we were unable to find an ink between the killers and the victims. Nor did any appear in the phone records of the Tate and LaBianca residences.

Exposure to rain and sunlight over a prolonged period of time breaks down human blood components. Many of the spots on the clothing the TV crew had found gave a positive benzidine reaction, indicating blood, but Granado was unable to determine whether it was animal or human. However, Granado did find human blood, type B, on the white T-shirt (Parent, Folger, and Frykowski were type B), and human blood, "possible type O," on the dark velour turtleneck (Tate and Sebring were type O). He did not test for subtypes.

He also removed some human hair from the clothing, which he determined had belonged to a woman, and which did not match that of the two female victims.

I called Captain Carpenter at Sybil Brand and requested a sample of Susan Atkins' hair. On February 17, Deputy Sheriff Helen Tabbe took Susan to the jail beauty shop for a wash and set. Afterwards she removed the hair from Susan's brush and comb. Later a sample of Patricia Krenwinkel's hair was similarly obtained. Granado eliminated the Krenwinkel sample but, although he wasn't able to state positively that they were the same, he found the Atkins sample "very, very similar" to that taken from the clothing, concluding it was "very likely" the hair belonged to Susan Atkins.*

Some white animal hairs were also found on the clothing. Winifred Chapman said they looked like the hair from Sharon's dog. Since the dog had died shortly after Sharon's death, no comparison could be made. I intended to introduce the hair into evidence anyway, and let Mrs. Chapman state what she had told me.

On February 11, Kitty Lutesinger had given birth to Bobby Beausoleil's child. Even before this, she was an unwilling witness, and the little information I got from her came hard. Later she would return to the Family, leave it, go back. Unsure of what she might say on the stand, I eventually decided against calling her as a witness.

*The points of similarity included color, diameter, length, as well as the medullary characteristics.

I made the same decision in relation to biker
Springer, though for different reasons. Most of his te
timony would be repetitive of DeCarlo's. Also, his mo
damning testimony—Manson's statement, "We got five
them the other night"—was inadmissible because
Aranda. I did interview Springer, several times, and o
remark Manson made to him, re the murders, gave me
glimpse into Manson's possible defense strategy. In di
cussing the many criminal activities of the Family, Mans
had told Springer: "No matter what happens, the girls w
take the rap for it."

I interviewed Danny numerous times, one session lasti
nine hours, obtaining considerable information that hadn
come out in previous interviews. Each time I picked up
few more examples of Manson's domination: Manso
would tell the Family when it was time to eat; he wouldn
permit anyone to be served until he was seated; durir
dinner he would lecture on his philosophy.

I asked Danny if anyone ever interrupted Manson whi
he was talking. He recalled that one time "a couple
broads" started talking.

Q.   "What happened?"

A.   "He threw a bowl of rice at them."

Although DeCarlo was extremely reluctant to testif
Sergeant Gutierrez and I eventually persuaded him that
was in his own best interests to do so.

I had less success with Dennis Wilson, singer and drun
mer for the Beach Boys. Though Wilson initially claime
to know nothing of importance, he finally agreed
"level" with me, but he refused to testify.

It was obvious that Wilson was scared, and not withou
good reason. On December 4, 1969, three days afte
LAPD announced they had broken the case, Wilson ha
received an anonymous death threat. It was, I learned, n
the only such threat, and the others were not anonymous.

Though denying any knowledge of the Family's crimina
activities, Wilson did supply some interesting backgroun
information. In the late spring of 1968, Wilson had twic
picked up the same pair of female hitchhikers while driv
ing through Malibu. The second time he took the gir

home with him. For Dennis, home was 14400 Sunset Boulevard, a palatial residence formerly owned by humorist Will Rogers. The girls—Ella Jo Bailey and Patricia Krenwinkel—stayed a couple of hours, Dennis said, mostly talking about this guy named Charlie.

Wilson had a recording session that night and didn't get home until 3 A.M. When he pulled into the driveway, a strange man stepped out of his back door. Wilson, frightened, asked, "Are you going to hurt me?" The man said, "Do I look like I'm going to hurt you, brother?" He then dropped to his knees and kissed Wilson's feet—obviously one of Charlie's favorite routines. When Manson ushered Wilson into his own home, he discovered he had about a dozen uninvited house guests, nearly all of them girls.

They stayed for several months, during which time the group more than doubled in number. (It was during Manson's "Sunset Boulevard period" that Charles "Tex" Watson, Brooks Poston, and Paul Watkins became associated with the Family.) The experience, Dennis later estimated, cost him about $100,000. Besides Manson's constantly hitting him for money, Clem demolished Wilson's uninsured $21,000 Mercedes-Benz by plowing it into a mountain on the approach to Spahn Ranch; the Family appropriated Wilson's wardrobe, and just about everything else in sight; and several times Wilson found it necessary to take the whole Family to his Beverly Hills doctor for penicillin shots. "It was probably the largest gonorrhea bill in history," Dennis admitted. Wilson even gave Manson nine or ten of the Beach Boys' gold records and paid to have Sadie's teeth fixed.

The newly divorced Wilson obviously found something attractive about Manson's life style. "Except for the expense," Dennis told me, "I got along very well with Charlie and the girls." He and Charlie would sing and talk, Dennis said, while the girls cleaned house, cooked, and catered to their needs. Wilson said he liked the "spontaneity" of Charlie's music, but added that "Charlie never had a musical bone in his body." Despite this, Dennis tried hard to "sell" Manson to others. He rented a recording studio in Santa Monica and had Manson recorded. (Though I was very interested in hearing the tapes, Wilson claimed that he had destroyed them, because "the vibra tions connected with them don't belong on this earth." Wilson also introduced Manson to a number of people i or on the fringes of the entertainment industry, includin Melcher, Jakobson, and Altobelli. At one party, Charli gave Dean Martin's daughter, Deana, a ring and asked he to join the Family. Deana told me she kept the ring which she later gave to her husband, but declined Man son's invitation. As did the other Beach Boys, none c whom shared Dennis' fondness for the "scruffy little guru, as one described him.

Wilson denied having any conflicts with Manson durin this period. However, in August 1968, three weeks befor his lease was to expire, Dennis moved in with Gregg, leav ing to his manager the task of evicting Charlie and th girls.

From Sunset Boulevard the Family moved to Spah Ranch. Although Wilson apparently avoided the group fo a time, he did see Manson occasionally. Dennis told m that he didn't have any trouble with Charlie until Augus 1969—Dennis could not recall the exact date, but he di know it was after the Tate murders—when Manson vis ited him, demanding $1,500 so he could go to the desert When Wilson refused, Charlie told him, "Don't be sur prised if you never see your kid again." Dennis had seven-year-old son, and obviously this was one reason fo his reluctance to testify.

Manson also threatened Wilson himself, but Dennis di not learn of this until an interview I conducted with bot! Wilson and Jakobson. According to Jakobson, not long af ter Dennis refused Manson's request, Charlie hande Gregg a .44 caliber bullet and told him, "Tell Dennis ther are more where this came from." Knowing how the othe threat had upset Dennis, Gregg hadn't mentioned it to him

This incident had occurred in late August or early Sep tember of 1969. Jakobson was startled by the change i Manson. "The electricity was almost pouring out of him His hair was on end. His eyes were wild. The only thing can compare it to . . . is that he was just like an animal i a cage."

It was possible there was still another threat, but this i

strictly conjecture. In going through the Spahn Ranch phone bills, I found that on September 22, 1969, someone called Dennis Wilson's private number from the pay phone at Spahn and that the following day Wilson had the phone disconnected.

Looking back on his involvement with the Family, Dennis told me: "I'm the luckiest guy in the world, because I got off only losing my money."

From rock star to motorcycle rider to ex-call girl, the witnesses in this case all had one thing in common: they were afraid for their lives. They needed only to pick up a newspaper or turn on TV to see that many of the Family members were still roaming the streets; that Steve Grogan, aka Clem, was out on bail, while the Inyo County grand theft charges against Bruce Davis had been dismissed for lack of evidence. Neither Grogan, Davis, nor any of the others suspected of beheading Shorty Shea had been charged with that murder, there being as yet no physical proof that Shea was dead.

Perhaps in her cell at Sybil Brand, Susan Atkins recalled the lyrics of the Beatles' song "Sexy Sadie":

> "Sexy Sadie what have you done
> You made a fool of everyone . . .
> Sexy Sadie you broke the rules
> You laid it out for all to see . . .
> Sexy Sadie you'll get yours yet
> However big you think you are . . ."

Or perhaps it was simply that the numerous messages Manson was sending, by other Family members, were getting to her.

Susan called in Caballero and told him that under no circumstances would she testify at the trial. And she demanded to see Charlie.

Caballero told Aaron and me that it looked as if we'd lost our star witness.

We contacted Gary Fleischman, Linda Kasabian's attorney, and told him we were ready to talk.

From the start Fleischman, dedicated to the welfare c his client, had wanted nothing less than complete immu nity for Linda Kasabian. Not until after I had talked t Linda myself did I learn that she had been willing to tal to us immunity or not, and that only Fleischman had kep her from doing so. I also learned that she had decided t return to California voluntarily, against the advice c Fleischman, who had wanted her to fight extradition.

After a number of discussions, our office agreed to pe tition the Superior Court for immunity, *after* she had tes tified. In return it was agreed: (1) that Linda Kasabia would give us a full and complete statement of her in volvement in the Tate-LaBianca Murders; (2) that Lind Kasabian would testify truthfully at all trial proceeding against all defendants; and (3) that in the event Lind Kasabian did not testify truthfully, or that she refused t testify, for whatever reason, she would be prosecute fully, but that any statement that she gave the prosecutio would not be used against her.

The agreement was signed by Younger, Leavy, Busch Stovitz, and myself on February 26, 1970.

Two days later I interviewed Linda Kasabian. It wa the first time she had discussed the Tate-LaBianca mu ders with anyone connected with law enforcement.

As noted, given a choice between Susan and Linda, I' preferred Linda, sight unseen: she hadn't killed anyon and therefore would be far more acceptable to a jury tha the bloodthirsty Susan. Now, talking to her in Captai Carpenter's office at Sybil Brand, I was especially please that things had turned out as they had.

Small, with long light-brown hair, Linda bore a distinc resemblance to the actress Mia Farrow. As I got to knov her, I found Linda a quiet girl, docile, easily led, yet sh communicated an inner sureness, almost a fatalism, tha made her seem much older than her twenty years. Th product of a broken home, she herself had had two unsuc cessful marriages, the last of which, to a young hippie Robert Kasabian, had broken up just before she went t Spahn Ranch. She had one child, a girl named Tanya, ag two, and was now eight months pregnant with anothe conceived, she thought, the last time she and her husban were together. She had remained with the Family less than a month and a half—"I was like a little blind girl in the forest, and I took the first path that came to me." Only now, talking about what had happened, did she feel she was emerging from the darkness, she said.

On her own since sixteen, Linda had wandered from the east coast to the west, "looking for God." In her quest she had lived in communes and crash pads, taken drugs, had sex with almost anyone who showed an interest. She described all this with a candor that at times shocked me, yet which, I knew, would be a plus on the witness stand.

From the first interview I believed her story, and I felt that a jury would also. There were no pauses in her answers, no evasions, no attempts to make herself appear something she was not. She was brutally frank. When a witness takes the stand and tells the truth, even though it is injurious to his own image, you know he can't be impeached. I knew that if Linda testified truthfully about those two nights of murder, it would be immaterial whether she had been promiscuous, taken dope, stolen. The question was, could the defense attack her credibility regarding the events of those two nights? And I knew the answer from our very first interview: they wouldn't be able to do so, because she was so obviously telling the truth.

I talked to her from 1 to 4:30 P.M. on the twenty-eighth. It was the first of many long interviews, a half dozen of them lasting six to nine hours, all of which took place at Sybil Brand, her attorney usually the only other person present. At the end of each interview I'd tell her that if, back in her cell, anything occurred to her which we hadn't discussed, to "jot it down." A number of these notes became letters to me, running to a dozen or more pages. All of which, together with my interview notes, became available to the defense under discovery.

The more times a witness tells his story, the more opportunities there are for discrepancies and contradictions, which the opposing side can then use for impeachment purposes. While some attorneys try to hold interviews and pre-trial statements to a minimum so as to avoid such problems, my attitude is the exact opposite. If a witness is

lying, I want to know it before he ever takes the stand. I
the more than fifty hours I spent interviewing Linda Ka
sabian, I found her, like any witness, unsure in some de
tails, confused about others, but never once did I catc
her even attempting to lie. Moreover, when she was un
sure, she admitted it.

Though she added many details, Linda Kasabian's stor
of those two nights was basically the same as Susan At
kins'. There were only a few surprises. But they were bi
ones.

Prior to my talking to Linda, we had assumed that sh
had probably witnessed only one murder, the shooting o
Steve Parent. We now learned that she had also seen Ka
tie chasing Abigail Folger across the lawn with ar
upraised knife and Tex stabbing Voytek Frykowski te
death.

She also told me that on the night the LaBiancas were
killed, Manson had attempted to commit three other mur
ders.

Part 5

"DON'T YOU KNOW WHO YOU'RE CRUCIFYING?"

"For there shall arise false Christs,
and false prophets, and shall shew
great signs and wonders; insomuch that,
if it were possible, they shall deceive
the very elect . . . Wherefore, if they
shall say unto you, Behold, he is in
the desert; go not forth . . ."
Matthew 24:24,26

"Just before we got busted in the desert,
there was twelve of us apostles and Charlie."
Family member
Ruth Ann Moorehouse

"I may have implied on several occasions
to several different people that I
may have been Jesus Christ, but I haven't
decided yet what I am or who I am."
Charles Manson

HELTER SKELTER

A CHILLING 64-PAGE PHOTOGRAPHIC RECORD OF THE VICTIMS, THE KILLERS, THE EVIDENCE.

LOS ANGELES AND VICI...

Freeways
Other streets an...

0   5
Miles

SANTA SUSANA MTS.

SAN FERNANDO

Spahn Ranch

CHATSWORTH

CANOGA PARK

BURBANK

GL...

Gun found

Clothing found

Griffith Park

La B...
resid...

SANTA MONICA MTS.

HOLLYWOOD

Tate residence ✕

Benedict Canyon

SANTA...
Topanga Canyon

Hinman ✕ residence

BEVERLY HILLS

MALIBU

SANTA MONICA

LOS ANGE...

VENICE

INGLEWOOD

P A C I F I C

EL SEGUNDO

LYN...

O C E A N

C A L I F O R N I A

REDONDO BEACH

TORRANCE

Area of main map

SAN PEDRO

LO...

DEATH VALLEY AND VICINITY

Main roads
Other roads

0   10   20
Miles

H. Faye

The Murders

10050 Cielo Drive, a secluded cul-de-sac
high above the City of the Angels. Until that night,
Sharon Tate called it her "love house."

First the telephone
wires were cut.

Fearing the gate was electrified,
the killers avoided it.

Instead, they scaled
the embankment to the right
of the gate.

Later, on fleeing the premises,
one of the killers left a
bloody fingerprint on the button
of the gate-control
mechanism. Still later, an LAPD
officer pushed the button,
creating a superimposure which
eradicated the print.

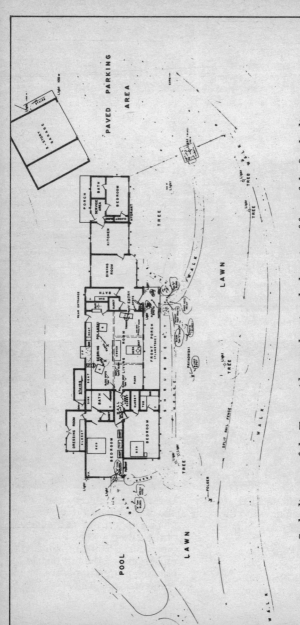

Scale diagram of the Tate residence, showing the location of four of the five bodies. Parent's Rambler was to the right, farther up the paved parking area that led to the gate. The guest house was located to the left, a considerable distance beyond the pool.

Steven Earl Parent, 18, at his high-school prom. A hi-fi enthusiast, he was working at two jobs to save enough money for college that fall.

Steven Earl Parent—murder victim. In the wrong place at the wrong time, Parent was driving toward the gate when the killers arrived. He was the first to die.

After discovering Parent's body, the first officers proceeded up the driveway to the residence. They found the house and grounds frighteningly quiet.

Coffee heiress Abigail Folger, 25, and her Polish lover Voytek Frykowski, 32. They had begun moving out of the Cielo Drive residence, but Sharon asked them to stay until her husband, movie director Roman Polanski returned the following week.

Abigail Folger—murder victim. Her body was also on the lawn, a short distance beyond Frykowski's. She had been stabbed so often her white gown appeared red.

Voytek Frykowsk murder victim Found sprawled on the law near the front do Frykowski had fought hard f his life. He had been sh twice, hit over the head thirte times with a blunt obje and stabbed fifty-one tim

The walkway leading to the front door of the Tate residence. The pools of blood were mute evidence of the furious struggle that occurred here. Only on getting closer did the officers see the bizarre message the killers had left. Printed on the door, in Sharon Tate's own blood, were the letters PIG.

Internationally known men's hair stylist
Jay Sebring, 35, had once been engaged to Sharon Tate.
According to some, he was still in love with her.

American flag was draped over the back of the couch
e living room. On the other side, in front of the fireplace,
a scene so incredible it horrified even the most
hardened detectives.

Beautiful honey-blond actress
Sharon Tate, 26. Though featured in *Valley of the Dolls*
only in death would she receive star billing.

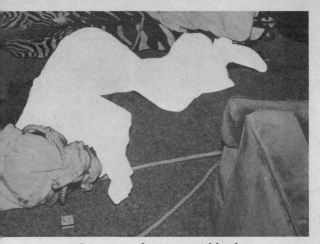

Jay Sebring—murder victim. A bloody
towel covered his face. A rope, looped around his
neck, led to still another body.

Sharon Tate Polanski—
murder victim. Eight months pregnant,
she pleaded for the life of her child.
"Look, bitch, I have no mercy for you,"
one of her killers replied.

The loft over the living room. Before she was stabbed to death, Sharon Tate was hanged from one of the rafters. The rope, left behind by the killers, became an important clue.

Other clues included: a pair of eyeglasses; thre pieces of broken gun grip; and this Buck knife found sticking up from the cushion of a chair in living room.

The Folger-Frykowski bedroom. Abigail Folger was reading when the killers came down the hall. Apparently thinking they were friends of the Polanskis, she looked up and smiled.

Sharon Tate's bedroom, as it appeared the mornin the murders. The bassine atop the armoire, would never be used.

Chased by one of the killers, Abigail Folger had attempted to escape via the door leading from Sharon's bedroom to the pool outside, but they caught her on the lawn.

The guest house at the far end of the estate. Hearing the barking of a dog and a voice saying, "Shhh, be quiet," the police surrounded it, arresting the only person still alive on the premises, nineteen-year-old caretaker William Garretson. Though charged with the five murders, he was released after passing a polygraph test.

Aerial view of the LaBianca residence—
3301 Waverly Drive, in the Los Feliz section of Los Angeles. The house formerly occupied by Harold True, 3267, is to right. The killers parked where the vehicle appears, walked up the curved driveway toward 3267, then cut across to the LaBianca home.

Above and right. Again, as with the five
murders the previous night,
the police found a number of bizarre clues: DEATH TO PIGS
and RISE on the living-room walls, and the misspelled
HEALTER SKELTER on the refrigerator door, all printed in the
blood of one of the victims.

Leno LaBianca was sitting on
the couch, reading the
Sunday paper, when the deadly
nightmare began.

The bedroom. Hearing the
screams of her husband,
Rosemary LaBianca began to
struggle. Her assailants
kept stabbing her even after
she was dead.

Owner of a chain of grocery stores, Leno LaBianca, 44, —med to have nothing in common with the Tate victims, and, —espite the many similarities, the police quickly concluded the two crimes were unrelated.

Rosemary LaBianca, 38. A few days before her death she confided to a friend that someone had been insi◄ their home while she and Leno were away.

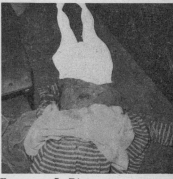

Leno LaBianca—murder victim. In addition to the multiple stab wounds, a knife and fork were found protruding from his body, and the word WAR had been carved on his stomach.

Rosemary LaBianca— murder victim. Wielding knives very similar to those used the previous night, the killers stabbed her forty-one times.

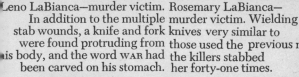

Less than twenty-four hours after the discovery of the word PIG printed on the front door of the Tate residence, one of the homicide detectives assigned to the case was told of a strikingly similar murder which had occurred in Malibu only three weeks earlier, in which the words POLITICAL PIGGY had been printed in the blood of the victim, musician Gary Hinman. Even after the bloody words DEATH TO PIGS were found at the LaBianca residence, he didn't feel the lead worth investigating.

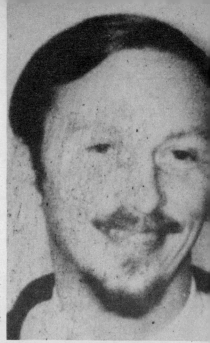

Music teacher Gary Hinman—murder victim. He made the mistake of befriending his killers.

John Philip Haught, aka Christopher Jesus, aka Zero. Murder victim or suicide? The others present claimed he had been playing Russian roulette. Only the gun was fully loaded and clean of prints.

Aspiring actor and
Spahn Ranch cowboy
Donald "Shorty"
Shea—murder victim.
Like Sharon Tate, he
was hoping for
stardom and found
death instead.
His body has never
been found.

Attorney
Ronald Hughes—
murder victim.
His attempt to
defend one of
the Tate-LaBianca
killers cost him
his life. As revealed
here for the first
time, the slaying of
Hughes was "the
first of the
retaliation murders."

Charles Milles Manson, also known as Jesus Christ, God.
Although it was never brought out in court,
Manson bragged of committing thirty-five murders.

The Manso

Burglar, car thief, forger, pimp.
By the age of thirty-two, Manson had spent seventeen years—
more than half his life—in prison.
What happened to transform a small-time hood into one of
the most notorious mass murderers of our time?

Family Album

Charles Manson at the time of the Spahn Ranch raid, August 16, 1969. A week after the Tate murders, all but one of the killers were under arrest, on suspicion of car theft. All were released within forty-eight hours, when it was discovered the warrant was misdated.

Following the October 10-12, 1969, raid on isolated Barker Ranch in Death Valley, Manson was booked for grand theft auto and arson. Standing only five feet two, he hardly looked like a man who could, and did, command others to kill for him.

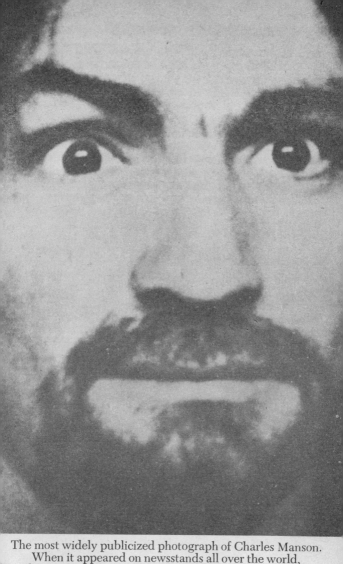

The most widely publicized photograph of Charles Manson. When it appeared on newsstands all over the world, Family members were heard to exclaim proudly, "Charlie made the cover of *Life!*"

Charles Watson,
aka Tex, age 23—murderer.

Susan Denise Atkins,
aka Sadie Mae Glutz, 21—murderer.

Leslie Van Houton, aka LuLu,
age 20—murderer.
LARGE PHOTO COURTESY OF ROBERT HENDRICKSON
AND LAURENCE MERRICK

Patricia Krenwinkel,
aka Katie, age 21—murderer.

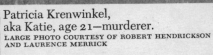

Robert "Bobby" Beausoleil,
aka Cupid, age 22—murderer.
LARGE PHOTO COURTESY OF ROBERT HENDRICKSON
AND LAURENCE MERRICK

Mary Theresa Brunner,
age 25—murderer.

Steve Grogan,
aka Clem, age 17—murderer.

 Bruce McGregor Davis,
age 26—murderer.

Lynette Fromme, aka Squeaky, age 20. Acting head of the Family in Manson's absence, she was arrested in connection with the attempted murder of prosecution witness Barbara Hoyt and given a ninety-day sentence.

PHOTO COURTESY OF
ROBERT HENDRICKSON AND
LAURENCE MERRICK

Sandra Good, aka Sandy, age 25. The daughter of a Diego stockbroker and a former student at San Fra State College, she bragge that the Manson Family h killed defense attorney Ronald Hughes.

Ruth Ann Moorehouse, aka Ouisch, age 17. Arrested in connection with the attempted murder of a prosecution witness, she was released on her own recognizance, then failed to appear for sentencing.

Catherine Gillies, aka Capistrano, age 18. F grandmother owned Myers Ranch. Manson's p to hasten her inheritance was frustrated by a flat ti

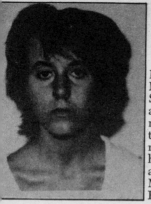

Nancy Pitman, aka Brenda McCann, age 18. She pleaded guilty to being an accessory in the 1972 murder of Lauren Willett, who, together with her murdered husband, James, may have known too much about the slaying of Hughes. Manson once designated Pitman his chief assassin.

Catherine Share, aka Gypsy, age 27. Convicted with five others of armed robbery in a bizarre plot to hijack a 747 and obtain the release of Manson and the other Family members.

A few of the Manson Family children. Manson placed g
emphasis on children because, he said, they had no egos
had not yet been contaminated by their parents and soc

present, some of the children have been adopted. Most, ever, are wards of the courts and live in foster homes. The t records on the children have been sealed.

Right: Aerial photo of Spahn's Movie Ranch. Above shows the main buildings. From this ramshackle movie set, a world of make-believe, the killers went out on their all-too-real nightly missions of murder.

Eighty-one and near blind, ranch owner George Spahn deper on the Manson girls to be his eyes, unaware they were also serving as ears for Charlie. Spahn is shown here with Family member Gypsy.

PHOTO COURTESY OF ROBERT HENDRICKSON AND LAURENCE MERRICK

During the August 16, 1969, raid on Spahn Ranch,
f's deputies arrested twenty-six persons. Only Manson hid,
under one of the buildings. *From far left to right:*
raight Satan motorcycle gang member Danny DeCarlo;
Charles Manson; Straight Satan Robert Reinhard;
and ranch hand Juan Flynn.

Manson Family members and ranch hands alike were p[...]
during the massive raid, which netted a huge
cache of arms, including a submachine gun. However, a[...]
Buck knives, purchased shortly before
the Tate murders, had mysteriously disappeared.

To reach isolated Barker
Ranch, where the
Family hid following the
Shea murder, it was
necessary to go up this
incredibly rugged
dry wash. Only a four-
wheel-drive vehicle
could make it, and then
only if someone
walked ahead and moved
the boulders
out of the way.

PHOTO COURTESY OF TOM ROSS

The submachine gun in its violin case and
Manson's command dune buggy.
In a special scabbard next to the steering wheel is the
sword which Manson used to slice musician
Gary Hinman. It was also taken along on the night
of the LaBianca murders.

Barker Ranch. Manson gave its absentee owner one of
each Boys' gold records in return for letting the Family stay
there. Though in disrepair, the ranch was an oasis
red to most of Death Valley, even having a swimming pool.
    The Family's school bus, in the background,
was brought in from the less rugged Las Vegas side.

Lookouts were posted in dugouts surrounding Barker Ran
but the pre-dawn raid caught the Family off guard.
Among those arrested and taken to Independence to be bo
were Gypsy *(far left)* and Katie, Brenda, Squeaky,
and Sadie *(far right)*. Standing alongside the jeep is Little F
The police were still unaware the nomadic band
was guilty of anything more serious than auto theft.

Entering the bathroom,
officer James Pursell noticed
hair sticking out of a cabinet
under the sink. Inside
he found Charles Manson. The
cabinet measured
only 3 by 1 1/2 by 1 1/2 feet.
PHOTO COURTESY OF TOM ROSS

> ②
> The pass where the Devil you
> Flying along in sight for all to s
> On the edge of infinity
> Santa Suzana is the pass where y
>   look
> Santa Suzana is the pass where y
>   look for
>   love or ligh
> 12 in the night with the ligh
>   brigh
> Shining
> Anyway is right IF you come
> Its so out of sight in Devils C

Among the
seized in the Barker raid
knapsack containing d
of movie magazines an
lyrics of a numb
Manson's songs. A frust
musician who fai
make the big time, M
numbered amor
targets those who had. D
Canyon is located a
from Spahn Ranch, near
Susana Pass. Pe
coincidentally, perhap
the Tate mu
occurred just
"12 in the n

The Physical Evidence

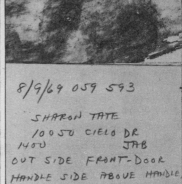

8/9/69 059 593

SHARON TATE
10050 CIELO DR
1400   JAB
OUT SIDE FRONT-DOOR
HANDLE SIDE ABOVE HANDLE

LAPD fingerprint expert Jerrome Boen pointing to the latent print recovered from the front door of the Tate residence. To the right is the lift card he prepared.

Although only twelve points are marked here, comparison between the latent *(left)* and the print of the right ring finger on a fingerprint exemplar belonging to Charles "Tex" Watson *(right)* revealed eighteen points of similarity. LAPD requires only ten points for a positive identification.

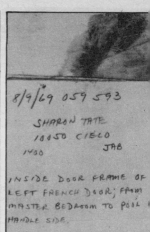

8/9/69 059 593

SHARON TATE
10050 CIELO
1400   JAB

INSIDE DOOR FRAME OF
LEFT FRENCH DOOR; FROM
MASTER BEDROOM TO POOL
HANDLE SIDE.

The location and lift card of the latent fingerprint
found on the inside of the French doors
that led from Sharon Tate's bedroom outside.

The latent *(left)* and the print of the left little finger on a
fingerprint exemplar belonging to
Patricia Krenwinkel revealed seventeen points of similarity
seven more than required for a positive identification.

Following the clues in Susan Atkins' published confession, on December 15, 1969, a TV crew discovered the bloody clothing the killers had worn and discarded on the night of the Tate murders—over four months earlier. Officers from LAPD are shown placing the evidence in plastic bags for inspection in the SID lab.

The nine-shot, .22 caliber Hi Standard Longhorn revolver used by Charles "Tex" Watson to shoot Parent, Sebring, and Frykowski. It was found by ten-year-old Steven Weiss on a hillside behind his home on September 1, 1969. Though the Valley Services Division of LAPD, located in Van Nuys, picked up the gun that same day, it was filed away under "Found Evidence."

OFFICE OF THE
CHIEF OF POLICE
THOMAS REDDIN

SAM YORTY
MAYOR

DEPARTMENT OF
POLICE
150 N. LOS ANGELES ST
LOS ANGELES CALIF 90012
PHONE 624 5211

IN REPLY NO PLEASE GIVE
OUR REF NO 1.6

The following information and request for assistance is
confidential. It is imperative for a successful conclusion
of this case that the contents of this letter not be released
to the news media or the general public.

During the early morning hours of August 9, 1969, a series
of murders occurred in the City of Los Angeles. Pieces of a
broken revolver grip were found at the scene. These have
been identified as those originally used on the right side of
a Hi Standard 22 long rifle "Long Horn" revolver, catalog
number 9399. Revolver further described as follows: 9½"
barrel, 9 shot capacity, 15" overall length, walnut grips,
blue finish, weight 35 oz., price $75. Photo enclosed.

This particular revolver has only been manufactured since
February, 1967. Through the cooperation of the Hi Standard
Manufacturing Company of Hamden, Connecticut, we were furnished
the serial numbers of all revolvers sold to California Hi
Standard distributors. These serial numbers were checked
through the CII and the enclosed listed weapon(s) were sold
in your jurisdiction.

It is requested that you ascertain if this purchaser still
has the revolver in his possession and visually check the
weapon to see if the original grips are intact.

As a cover story, we suggest the following. "Your Department
has some recovered property that is obviously stolen. One
of the articles recovered was a revolver of the above description with the serial numbers partially obliterated. Your
Department checked with the CII and ascertained that the
purchaser in your jurisdiction has such a weapon. You are
checking with him to obtain a lead on the obviously stolen
property you have recovered."

In the event the purchaser has moved, please attempt to
determine his present address.

In the event the purchaser has sold his revolver, please
determine to whom he sold the weapon, their physical description and present address.

In the event the purchaser has loaned his revolver to someone,
please determine to whom he loaned the weapon, their physical
description and present address and the date of loan.

It is requested that you phone collect Robbery-Homicide
Division, Area Code 213, MAdison 4-5211, Extension 2531, the
results of your investigation. Direct your information to Lt.
R. Helder and Sgts. J. Bucklen and M. McGann.

ROBERT A. HOUGHTON, Deputy Chief
Commander, Detective Bureau

Enclosures (2)

Between September 3 and 5, 1969, LAPD sent this letter, together
with a photograph of the Hi Standard model, to police
departments all over the United States and Canada. They
neglected to send one to their own division in Van Nuys,
and it was not until December 16, after persistent calls from
Steven Weiss' father, that the police
discovered they already had the Tate murder gun.

The "HELTER SKELTER" door found at Spahn Ranch.
Although the words HEALTER SKELTER had been found printed
at the LaBianca residence, its importance was missed.

THE PEOPLE VS. CHARLES MANSON

Prosecutor Vincent Bugliosi, chosen from a staff
of 450 lawyers and assigned to the Tate-LaBianca case in
November 1969, he personally gathered much of the
evidence which led to the convictions and death penalty verdi
against Charles Manson, Susan Atkins, Patricia Krenwinkel,
and Leslie Van Houten, after one of the
longest and most sensational trials in American history.

Ronnie Howard. Also known by some twenty other aliases, the former call girl listened in disbelief as her cellmate Susan Atkins bragged of her participation in the Tate, LaBianca, and Hinman murders. Although Atkins first confessed to another inmate, Virginia Graham, it was Howard who first contacted the police.

PHOTO COURTESY OF ROBERT HENDRICKSON AND LAURENCE MERRICK

Linda Kasabian, star witness for the prosecution. Ordered by Manson to slit the throat of an actor, the little hippie girl told him, "I'm not you, Charlie. I can't kill anybody."

PHOTO COURTESY OF ROBERT HENDRICKSON AND LAURENCE MERRICK

Witness Juan Flynn, being interviewed by
prosecutor Vincent Bugliosi during
a recess in the Tate-LaBianca murder trial.
Though marked for death by the Family,
the colorful Panamanian cowboy lived to
testify that Manson told him,
"Don't you know I'm the one who's doing
all of these killings?"

Left: Kitty Lutesinger. Girl friend of killer Bobby Beaus[ole]il
she told sheriff's investigators about Susan Atkins' involve[ment]
in the Hinman murder and inadvertently linked her to the [Tate-LaBianca]
homicides. *Center:* Biker Al Springer. When he said Ma[nson]
was responsible for the Tate-LaBianca murders, the detec[tives]
were skeptical. He vanished before he could share in [the]
$25,000 reward. *Right:* Straight Satan Danny DeCarlo[, who]
liked booze and broads but not murder. The motorcycle[gang]
linked the rope, the sword, and the knives to Manson—but [sud-]
denly hedged when it came to the gun.

Left: Dianne Lake, aka Snake. With the Family since the [age]
of thirteen, she began a new life after the trial. *Center:* Bar[bara]
Hoyt. Her cooperation almost cost her her life. The Fam[ily's]
attempt to eliminate her, by giving her an LSD-laden [ham-]
burger, backfired, changing her to a helpful witness. *R[ight:]*
Stephanie Schram. Manson found her in Big Sur and pla[nned]
to use her as his alibi for the two nights of murder.

The Faces of
Charles Manson.
According
to his disciple
Squeaky: "He
was a changeling.
He seemed to
change every time
I saw him."

The Story on Page One

Calley May Learn Fate Today

TUESDAY

Los Angeles Times

RACING
ENTRIES

FINA

VOL. XC   SIX PARTS—PART ONE   TUESDAY MORNING, MARCH 30, 1971   92 PAGES

Jurors Tell Feelings

MANSON, 3 GIRLS
SENTENCED TO DI

TUESDAY
PREVIEW
EDITION

EXTRA

Los Angeles Times

LATE
SPORT

VOL. XC   FIVE PARTS—PART ONE   ★★★   TUESDAY MORNING, JANUARY 26, 1971   72 PAGES

MANSON VERDICT
ALL GUILTY!

NEWS
SUMMARY

First-Deg
Convictio

Dodgers Get Richie Allen

— Story in Sports —

LOS ANGELES EVENING AND SUNDAY

HERALD EXAMINER

United Press International • Associated Press • Dow Jones

8 STAR
LATEST SPORTS

TODAY'S
COMPLETE NEW YORK
AND AMERICAN STOCKS

VOL C   NO. 193   MONDAY, OCTOBER 5, 1970   8   PRICE TEN CENTS

MANSON LEAPS AT
UDGE, HURLS THREAT

'I'm Going

Polanski On Recovery Road   (Story in Col. 1)

Valley Times

San Fernando Valley's Own Daily Newspaper

FINAL
★ ★ ★

SIX INDICTED
N TATE CASE

TUESDAY   **PREVIEW**   EDITION

MPLETE
OCKS

Los Angeles Times

LATE
SPORTS

IX FIVE PARTS—PART ONE   ★★★   TUESDAY MORNING, AUGUST 4, 1970   74 PAGES   DAILY 10¢

MANSON GUILTY,
NIXON DECLARES

Defense Says

House OKs 18 Vote in All Election
— Story in Cols. 7 —

Nixon Appeals
To Senate for SST
— Story in Cols. 1-3 —

HERALD ╫╫ EXAMINER

SUNS

United Press International • Associated Press • Dow Jones

VOL C NO 300 TUESDAY MARCH

PRICE TEN CENTS

MANSON DEATH THREA

Warns of Terror If Doomed to Di

Cult Head:
'Not Going
To Take It'

Doub
Scho

Blue Chips Skid, Stocks Off

— Story in Cols. 7-8 —

WAR ON POVERTY:
LBJ LOOKS BACK
— Story Page A-6 —

HERALD ╫╫ EXAMINER

8 ST
LATEST S

United Press International • Associated Press • Dow Jones

VOL C NO 296 WEDNESDAY OCTOBER

TODA
AND AMERICA

CATCH MANSON PAL I
SPECTACULAR ESCAPI

Prisoner
Flees 19th
Willy Bran

Tate Slaying Trial Begins
— Story in Cols. 1-3 —

For 'Conscientious
Objectors' A Victory
— Story in Cols. 6-7 —

HERALD ╫╫ EXAMINER

8 ST
TODAY'S
TODA

United Press International • Associated Press • Dow Jones

VOL C NO 81 MONDAY, JUNE 15, 1970 PRICE 10 CENTS

WORLD SPACE RECOR

Russ Cosmonau
Near Third We

LOS ANGELES

FREE
PRESS

KRLA's Pop Chronicles
Free Party to say good-by to Temple
How to start an anti-war military paper

141 Places to go this week—see page 32

Volume 7, #5 (Issue 285) | $6.00 PER YEAR | In two parts: Part One / Copyright 1970 / The Los Angeles Free Press, Inc. | Phone: YES-1970 | January 30 – February 4

25¢

EXCLUSIVE !   EXCLUSIVE !
MANSON INTERVIEW !
First interview with Charles Manson in jail

Los Angeles Herald-Examiner, Sunday, Dec. 7, 1969

Main Characters in Tate Murder Drama

Susan Atkins . . . she gave valuable testimony to the County Grand Jury.

Miss Sharon Tate . . . TV and movie actress was one of five slain last August.

Charles Manson . . . is alleged leader of hippie group

TUESDAY'S CHILD

DO IT - 3
Oily Orgy
Beanery Eat-I

1616 N. Argyle Avenue, Hollywood, California 90028 — 461-4971 — 25 cents — Volume 2 - Number 5 (13) — February 0, 1

MAN OF THE YEAR: CHARLES MANSON

Monster or Revolutionary Martyr
The underground press was divided as to whethe

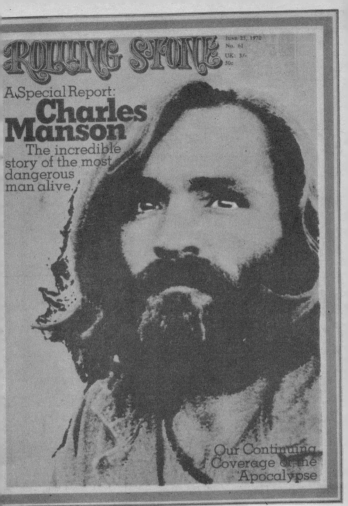

Manson was a sick symbol
of our times or Christ returned. His cult still survives.

		PS	For Credit Department use

union
Union Oil Company of California
Please print

Cards 1 2 3 ___	Code	T	P
Approved by			

Name - (full first name - second initial - last name)	Age	No. of dependents	Wife's first name
Charles M. Manson ✓	35	16	none

Street address		How long at address
441 N. Bauchet		10 Mos. ___ Years

City, state and zip code	Social Security no.
Los Angeles Calif	560-84-846

Previous address (street - city - state)	How long at address
Spahn's Movie Ranch Chatsworth Calif.	1 Years ___ Mo

Employer's name (if self-employed - name of business)	Type of business	Length of employment
Evangalist	Religious	20 Years ___ Mo

Business address (street - city - state)	Position	Monthly salary ☐300 399 ☐400 499 ☐500 699 ☐700 over

Previous employer (if above employment is less than 2 years)	Position	Length of employment ___ Years ___ Mo

Wife's employer	Position	Monthly salary ☐200 299 ☐300 399 ☐400 & over	Length of employ ___ Yrs. ___ Mo

Credit is established with: (include name of oil company credit cards and account number)		Bank used
Name/address George Spahn, Chatsworth	☐ 30 Day ☐ Budget	Republic National
Name/address A Joint Venture 13150 Chandler Van Nuys, Calif.	☐ 30 Day ☐ Budget	Branch No Hollywood
Name/address	☐ 30 Day ☐ Budget	Account no. ☒ Checking
Name/address	☐ 30 Day ☐ Budget	☐ Savings

Number of cards desired 2	Mail statements to ☒ Residence ☐ Business	Applicant agrees to terms and conditions of use printed on credit card.
Date 1 / 1	Residence phone no. 680-7600	Signature Charles M Manson

PLEASE ALLOW APPROXIMATELY 3 WEEKS FOR CREDIT INVESTIGATION AND ISSUANCE

A rare example of Manson's sense of humor.
He applied for a credit card while on trial for mass murder.

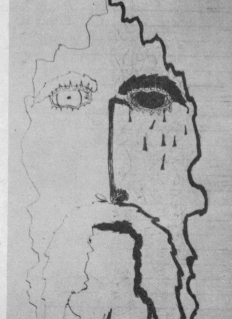

Another side of
Manson is
revealed in one of
his doodlings,
made during the
trial.

THE BUG

"The Bug." Prosecutor Bugliosi, as depicted by Susan Atkins and Leslie Van Houten during the trial. The three female defendants sketched, giggled, or looked bored as witness after witness testified to their savage slaughter.

Prosecutor Bugliosi talks to reporters congratulating him outside the courtroom moments after the jury returned verdicts of guilty against all the defendants on every count of the indictment with which they were charged.
ASSOCIATED PRESS

Manson's attorney Irving Kanarek. The press focused on his bombast and missed his effectiveness. He fought as if he personally were on trial.
PHOTO COURTESY OF ROBERT HENDRICKSON AND LAURENCE MERRICK

...arles "Tex" Watson fought extradition for months,
...en was tried separately. Though the judge referred to him
..."poor Tex," Bugliosi obtained a
...nviction and death penalty verdict against Watson also.

"We're waiting for our father
to be set free." During the trials,
Manson Family members
conducted a vigil outside the Hall of
Justice, at the corner of Temple
and Broadway. *Left to right:* Sandy,
Ouisch, Cathy, and Mary.

"I have X'd myself from your world."
When Manson carved an X
on his forehead, his followers did
likewise. Later, again
following Manson's lead, they changed
the X's into swastikas.
Left to right: Squeaky, Sandy,
Ouisch, Cathy.

PHOTO COURTESY OF ROBERT HENDRICKSON
AND LAURENCE MERRICK

Following the guilty verdicts,
Manson, Atkins, Krenwinkel, and
Van Houten shaved their heads,
as did the girls on the corner, who told
reporters: "You'd better
watch your children because Judgment
Day is coming!"
Left to right, facing camera: Crystal,
Mary, Kitty.
With backs to camera, left to right:
Sandy and Squeaky.

PHOTO COURTESY OF ROBERT HENDRICKSON
AND LAURENCE MERRICK

Charles Manson on his way to Death Row,
San Quentin Prison. With the abolition of the death sentenc[e]
Manson's own sentence was commuted to life
imprisonment. Under present California law, he—and the ot[her]
Tate-LaBianca killers—will
be eligible to apply for parole in 1978.
PHOTO COURTESY OF ROBERT HENDRICKSON AND LAURENCE MERRICK

March 1970

n March 3, accompanied by attorney Gary Fleischman
d some dozen LAPD and LASO officers, I took Linda
asabian out of Sybil Brand. For Linda it was a trip back
    time, to an almost unbelievable night nearly seven
onths ago.

Our first stop was 10050 Cielo Drive.

In late June of 1969, Bob Kasabian had called Linda at
r mother's home in New Hampshire, suggesting a recon-
liation. Kasabian was living in a trailer in Topanga Can-
n with a friend, Charles Melton. Melton, who had re-
ntly inherited $20,000, and had already given away
ore than half, planned to drive to the tip of South
merica, buy a boat, and sail around the world. He'd in-
ted Linda and Bob, as well as another couple, to come
ong.

Linda, together with her daughter, Tanya, flew to Los
ngeles, but the reconciliation was unsuccessful.

On July 4, 1969, Catherine Share, aka Gypsy, visited
elton, whom she had met through Paul Watkins. Gypsy
ld Linda about "this beautiful man named Charlie," the
amily, and how life at Spahn was all love, beauty, and
eace. To Linda it was "as if the answer to an unspoken
rayer."* That same day Linda and Tanya moved to
pahn. Though she didn't meet Manson that day, she did
eet most of the other members of the Family, and they
lked of little else. It was obvious to her that "they wor-
iped him."

That night Tex took her into a small room and told her
far-out things—nothing was wrong, all was right—things

*My interviews with Linda Kasabian were not taped. Exact quota-
ons are from either my interview notes, her trial testimony, or her
arrative letters to me.

347

I couldn't comprehend." Then "He made love to me, an a strange experience took place—it was like being po sessed." When it was over, Linda's fingers were clenche so tightly they hurt. Gypsy later told her that what sh had experienced was the death of the ego.

After making love, Linda and Tex talked, Linda me tioning Melton's inheritance. Tex told her that she shou steal the money. According to Linda, she told him sh couldn't do that—Melton was a friend, a brother. Tex to her that she could do no wrong and that everything shou be shared. The next day Linda went back to the trail and stole $5,000, which she gave to either Leslie or Te She had already turned over all her possessions to th Family, the girls having told her, "What's yours is ou and what's ours is yours."

Linda met Charles Manson for the first time that nigh After all she had heard about him, she felt as if she we on trial. He asked why she had come to the ranch. She r plied that her husband had rejected her. Manson reache out and felt her legs. "He seemed pleased with them Linda recalled. Then he told her she could stay. Befo making love to her, he told her that she had a father han up. Linda was startled by his perception, because sh disliked her stepfather. She felt that Manson could see i side her.

Linda Kasabian became a part of the Family—went garbage runs, had sex with the men, creepy-crawled house, and listened as Manson lectured about the Beatle Helter Skelter, and the bottomless pit. Charlie told he that the black man was together but the white man w not. However, he knew a way to unite the white man, said. It was the only way. But he didn't tell her what was.

Nor did she ask. From the first time they met, Manso had stressed, "Never ask why." When something he said did puzzled her, she was reminded of this. Also of anoth of his favorite axioms, "No sense makes sense."

The whole Family, Linda said, was "paranoid blackie." On weekends George Spahn did a brisk busine renting horses. Occasionally among the riders there woul be blacks. Manson maintained they were Panthers, spyin

the Family. He always hid the young girls when they
re around. At night everyone was required to wear
k clothing, so as to be less conspicuous, and eventually
nson posted armed guards, who roamed the ranch until
vn.

Gradually Linda became convinced that Charles Man-
was Jesus Christ. He never told her this directly, but
day he asked her, "Don't you know who I am?"

She replied, "No, am I supposed to know something?"

He didn't answer, just smiled, and playfully twirled her
und.

Yet she had doubts. The mothers were not allowed to
e for their own children. They separated her and
nya, Linda explained, because they wanted "to kill the
that I put in her" and "at first I agreed to it, I thought
at it was a good idea that she should become her own
rson." Also, several times she saw Manson strike Dianne
ke. Linda had been in many communes—from the
nerican Psychedelic Circus in Boston to Sons of the
rth Mother near Taos—but she'd never seen anything
e this, and, forgetting Charlie's commandment, she did
k Gypsy why. Gypsy told her that Dianne really wanted
be beaten, and Charlie was only obliging her.

Overriding all doubts was one fact: she had fallen in
ve with Charles Manson.

Linda had been at Spahn Ranch a little over a month
en, on the afternoon of Friday, August 8, 1969, Man-
n told the Family: *"Now is the time for Helter Skelter."*

Had Linda stopped there, supplying that single piece of
stimony and nothing else, she would have been a valu-
le witness. But Linda had a great deal more to tell.

That Friday evening, about an hour after dinner, seven
eight members of the Family were standing on the
ardwalk in front of the saloon when Manson came out
d, calling Tex, Sadie, Katie, and Linda aside, told each
get a change of clothing and a knife. He also told
nda to get her driver's license. Linda, I later learned,
as the only Family member with a valid license, except-
g Mary Brunner, who had been arrested that afternoon.
his was, I concluded, probably one of the reasons why

Manson had picked Linda to accompany the others, eac
of whom, unlike her, had been with him a year or more.

Linda couldn't find her own knife (Sadie had it), b
she obtained one from Larry Jones. The handle was br
ken and had been replaced with tape. Brenda foun
Linda's license and gave it to her just about the time Ma
son told Linda, "Go with Tex and do whatever Tex te
you to do."

According to Linda, in addition to Tex, Katie, and he
self, Brenda McCann and Larry Jones were present whe
Manson gave this order.

Brenda remained hard core and refused to coopera
with law enforcement. Larry Jones, t/n Lawrence Baile
was a scrawny little ranch hand who was always trying
ingratiate himself with the Family. However, Jones ha
what Manson considered negroid features and, accordin
to Linda, Charlie was always putting him down, referrin
to him as "the drippings from a white man's dick." Sinc
Jones had been present when Manson instructed the Tat
killers, he could be a very important witness—providing i
dependent corroboration of Linda Kasabian's testimony—
and I asked LAPD to bring him in. They were unable t
find him. I then gave the assignment to the DA's Burea
of Investigation, who located Jones, but he wouldn't gi
us the time of day.

Linda said that after Manson instructed her to go wit
Tex, the group piled into ranch hand Johnny Swartz' o
Ford.

I asked Linda what each was wearing. She wasn't abso
lutely sure, but she thought Sadie had on a dark-blue 7
shirt and dungarees, that Katie's attire was similar, an
that Tex was wearing a black velour turtleneck and dar
dungarees.

When shown the clothing the TV crew had foun
Linda identified six of the seven items, failing to reca
only the white T-shirt. The logical assumption was tha
she hadn't seen it because it had been worn under one
the other shirts.

What about footwear? I asked. The girls, she believe

re all barefoot. She thought, but couldn't be sure, that
x had on cowboy boots.

A number of bloody footprints had been found at the
te murder scene. After eliminating those belonging to
PD personnel, two remained unidentified: a boot-heel
nt and the print of a bare foot—thus supporting Linda's
ollections. Again, as with Susan Atkins, I badly needed
ependent corroboration of Linda's testimony.

I then asked Linda the same question I'd asked
san—had any of them been on drugs that night?—and
eived the same reply: no.

As Tex started to drive off, Manson said, "Hold it," or
ait." He then leaned in the window on the passenger
e and said, "Leave a sign. You girls know what to
ite. Something witchy."

Tex handed Linda three knives and a gun, telling her to
ap them in a rag and put them on the floor. If stopped
the police, Tex said, she was to throw them out.

Linda positively identified the .22 caliber Longhorn
olver. Only at this time, she said, the grip had been in-
t and the barrel unbent.

According to Linda, Tex did not tell them their destina-
n, or what they were going to do; however, she pre-
ned they were going on another creepy-crawly mission.
x did say that he had been to the house and knew the
out.

As we drove up Cielo Drive in the sheriff's van, Linda
owed me where Tex had turned, in front of the gate at
050, then parked, next to the telephone pole. He had
en taken a pair of large, red-handled wire cutters from
e back seat and shinnied up the pole. From where she
s sitting, Linda couldn't see Tex cutting the wires, but
e saw and heard the wires fall.

When shown the wire cutters found at Barker Ranch,
nda said they "looked like" the pair used that night.
ce the wire cutters had been found in Manson's per-
nal dune buggy, her identification linked them not just to
e Family but to Manson himself. I was especially
eased at this evidence, unaware that link would soon be
ered, literally.

When Tex returned to the car, they drove to a sp
near the bottom of the hill and parked. The four th
took the weapons and extra clothing and stealthily walke
back up to the gate. Tex also had some white rope, whi
was draped over his shoulder.

As Linda and I got out of the sheriff's van and a
proached the gate at 10050 Cielo Drive, two large do
belonging to Rudi Altobelli began barking furiously at
Linda suddenly began sobbing. "What are you cryi
about, Linda?" I asked.

Pointing to the dogs, she said, "Why couldn't they ha
been here that night?"

Linda pointed to the spot, to the right of the gat
where they had climbed the embankment and scaled t
fence. As they were descending the other side, a pair
headlights suddenly appeared in the driveway. "Lay dov
and be quiet," Tex ordered. He then jumped up and ran
the automobile, which had stopped near the gate-contr
mechanism. Linda heard a man's voice saying, "Plea
don't hurt me! I won't say anything!" She then saw T
put the gun in the open window on the driver's side a
heard four shots. She also saw the man slump over in t
seat.

(Something here puzzled me, and still does. In additio
to the gunshot wounds, Steven Parent had a defensive st
wound that ran from the palm across the wrist of his le
hand. It severed the tendons as well as the band of h
wristwatch. Obviously, Parent had raised his left hand, t
hand closest to the open window, in an effort to prote
himself, the force of the blow being sufficient to hurl h
watch into the back seat. It therefore appeared that T
must have approached the car with a knife in one hand,
gun in the other, and that he first slashed at Parent, the
shot him. Yet neither Susan nor Linda saw Tex with
knife at this point, nor did either recall the stabbing.)

Linda saw Tex reach in the car and turn off the ligh
and ignition. He then pushed the car some distance up t
driveway, telling the others to follow him.

The shooting put her in a state of shock, Linda sa

"My mind went blank. I was aware of my body, walking toward the house."

As we went up the driveway, I asked Linda which lights had been on that night. She pointed to the bug light on the side of the garage, also the Christmas-tree lights along the fence. Little details, yet important if the defense contended Linda was fabricating her story from what she had read in the papers, since neither these, nor numerous other details I collected, had appeared in the press.

As we approached the residence, I noticed that Linda was shivering and her arms were covered with goose bumps. Though it wasn't cold that day, Linda was now nine months pregnant, and I slipped off my coat and put it over her shoulders. The shivering continued, however, all the time we were on the premises, and often, in pointing out something, she would begin crying. There was no question in my mind that the tears were real and that she was deeply affected by what had happened in this place. I couldn't help contrasting Linda with Susan.

When they reached the house, Linda said, Tex sent her around the back to look for an unlocked window or door. She reported that everything was locked, though she hadn't actually checked. (This explained why they ignored the open nursery window.) Tex then slit a screen on one of the front windows with a knife. Though the actual screen had since been replaced, Linda pointed to the correct window. She also said the slash was horizontal, as it had been. Tex then told her to go back and wait by the car in the driveway.

Linda did as she was told. Perhaps a minute or two later Katie came back and asked Linda for her knife (this was the knife with the taped handle) and told her, "Listen for sounds."

A few minutes later Linda heard "horrifying sounds" coming from the house. A man moaned, "No, no, no," then screamed very loudly. The scream, which seemed continuous, was punctuated with other voices, male and female, begging and pleading for their lives.

Wanting "to stop what was happening," Linda said, "I started running toward the house." As she reached the walk, "there was a man, a tall man, just coming out of the door, staggering, and he had blood all over his face, and he was standing by a post, and we looked into each other's eyes for a minute, I don't know however long, and I said, 'Oh, God, I'm so sorry.' And then he just fell into the bushes.

"And then Sadie came running out of the house, and I said, 'Sadie, *please* make it stop! People are coming!' Which wasn't true, but I wanted to make it stop. And she said, 'It's too late.'"

Complaining that she had lost her knife, Susan ran back into the house. Linda remained outside. (Susan had earlier told me, and the grand jury, that Linda had never entered the residence.) Turning, Linda saw a dark-haired woman in a white gown running across the lawn; Katie was pursuing her, an upraised knife in her hand. Somehow, the tall man managed to stagger from the bushes next to the porch onto the lawn, where he had again fallen. Linda saw Tex hit him over the head with something—it could have been a gun but she wasn't sure—then stab him repeatedly in the back as he lay on the ground.

(Shown a number of photographs, Linda identified the tall man as Voytek Frykowski, the dark-haired woman as Abigail Folger. Examining the autopsy report on Frykowski, I found that five of his fifty-one stab wounds were to the back.)

Linda turned and ran down the driveway. For what seemed like maybe five minutes, she hid in the bushes near the gate, then climbed the fence again and ran down Cielo to where they had parked the Ford.

Q. "Why didn't you run to one of the houses and call the police?" I asked Linda.

A. "My first thought was 'Get help!' Then my little girl entered my mind—she was back [at the ranch] with Charlie. I didn't know where I was or how to get out of there."

She got in the car and had started the engine when "all of a sudden they were there. They were covered with blood. They looked like zombies. Tex yelled at me to turn off the car and get over. He had a terrible look in his eyes." Linda slid over to the passenger side. "Then he started in on Sadie and yelled at her for losing her knife."

Tex had put the .22 revolver on the seat between them. Linda noticed that the grip was broken, and Tex told her it had smashed when he hit the man over the head. Sadie and Katie complained that their heads hurt because the people had pulled their hair while they were fighting with them. Sadie also said the big man had hit her over the head and that "the girl"—it was unclear whether she meant Sharon or Abigail—had cried for her mother. Katie also complained that her hand hurt, explaining that when she stabbed, she kept hitting bones, and since the knife didn't have a regular handle, it bruised her hand.

Q. "How did *you* feel, Linda?"
A. "In a state of shock."
Q. "What about the others, how did they act?"
A. "As if it was all a game."

Tex, Sadie, and Katie changed their clothing while the car was in motion, Linda holding the wheel for Tex. Linda herself didn't change, since there was no blood on her. Tex told them he wanted to find a place to hose the blood off, and he turned off Benedict Canyon onto a short street not too far from the Tate residence.

Linda's account of the hosing incident paralleled Susan Atkins' and Rudolf Weber's. Weber's house was located 1.8 miles from the Tate premises.

From there Tex turned onto Benedict Canyon again and drove along through a dark, hilly country area. He stopped the car on a dirt shoulder off the road, and Tex, Sadie, and Katie gave Linda their bloody clothing, which, on Tex's instructions, she rolled up in one bundle and threw down the slope. Since it was dark, she couldn't see where it landed.

After driving off, Tex told Linda to wipe the knives clean of fingerprints, then throw them out the window. She did, the first knife hitting a bush at the side of the road, the second, which she tossed out a few seconds later, striking the curb and bouncing back into the road. Looking back, she saw it lying there. Linda believed she threw the gun out a few minutes later but she wasn't sure; it was possible that Tex did it.

After driving for a time, they stopped at a gas station—Linda was unable to recall the street—where Katie and Sadie took turns going into the rest room to wash the rest of the blood off their bodies. Then they drove back to Spahn Ranch.

Linda did not have a watch but guessed it must have been about 2 A.M. Charles Manson was standing on the boardwalk in the same spot where he had been when they drove off.

Sadie said she saw some blood on the outside of the car, and Manson had the girls get rags and sponges and wash the car inside and out.

He then told them to go to the bunkhouse. Brenda and Clem were already there. Manson asked Tex how it had gone. Tex told him that there was a lot of panic, that it was real messy, and that there were bodies lying all over the place, but that everyone was dead.

Manson asked the four, "Do you have any remorse?" All shook their heads and said, "No."

Linda did feel remorse, she told me, but she didn't admit it to Charlie because "I was afraid for my life. I could see in his eyes he knew how I felt. And it was against his way."

Manson told them, "Go to bed and say nothing to the others."

Linda slept most of the day. It was almost sundown when Sadie told her to go into the trailer, that the TV news was coming on. Although Linda could not recall seeing Tex, she remembered Sadie, Katie, Barbara Hoyt, and Clem being there.

It was the big news. For the first time Linda heard the names of the victims. She also learned that one, Sharon Tate, had been pregnant. Only a few days earlier Linda had learned that she herself was pregnant.

"As we were watching the news," Linda said, "in my head I kept saying, 'Why would they do such a thing?' "

After Linda and I left the Tate residence, I asked her to show us the route they had taken. She found the dirt shoulder where they had pulled off to dispose of the clothing, but was unable to find the street where Tex had turned off Benedict Canyon, so I had the sheriff's deputy who was driving take us directly to Portola. Once on the street, Linda immediately identified 9870, pointing to the hose in front. Number 9870 was Rudolf Weber's house. She also pointed to the spot where they had parked the car. It was the same spot Weber had indicated. Neither his address, nor even the fact that he had been located, had appeared in the press.

We were back on Benedict looking for the area where Linda had thrown out the knives when one of the deputies said, "We've got company."

Looking out the window, we saw we were being followed by a Channel 2 TV unit. Its presence in the area may have been a coincidence, but I doubted it. More likely, someone at the jail or in the courts had alerted the press that we were taking Linda out. All this time only a few people knew that Linda Kasabian would be a witness for the prosecution. I'd hoped to keep this secret as long as possible. I'd also hoped to take Linda to the LaBianca residence and several other sites, but now that would have to wait. Telling Linda to turn her head away so she wouldn't be recognized, I asked the driver to hightail it back to Sybil Brand.

Once on the freeway, we tried to outrun the TV unit, but without success. They filmed us all the way. It was like a Mack Sennett comedy, only with the press in pursuit of the fuzz.

After Linda was back in jail, I asked Sergeant McGann to get some cadets from the Police Academy, or a troop of Boy Scouts, and conduct a search for the knives. From Linda's testimony, we knew that they had probably been thrown out of the car somewhere between the clothing site and the hill where young Steven Weiss had found the gun, an area of less than two miles. We also knew that since Linda had looked back and seen one of the knives lying in the road, there must have been some illumination nearby, which could be another clue.

The following day, March 4, Gypsy made another visit to Fleischman's office. She told him, in the presence of his law partner Ronald Goldman, "If Linda testifies, thirty people are going to do something about it."

I'd already checked out the security at Sybil Brand. Until her baby was born, Linda was being kept in an isolation cell off the infirmary. She had no contact with the other inmates; deputies brought her meals. After the baby was born, however, she would be reassigned to one of the open dormitories, where she might be threatened, even killed, by Sadie, Katie, or Leslie. I made a note to talk to Captain Carpenter to see if other arrangements could be made.

Attorney Richard Caballero had been able to postpone the inevitable, but he couldn't prevent it. The meeting between Susan Atkins and Charles Manson took place in the Los Angeles County Jail on March 5. Caballero, who was present, would later testify: "One of the first things they wanted to know was whether either one had gotten to see Linda Kasabian yet." Neither having done so, it was decided both should keep trying.

Manson asked Susan, "Are you afraid of the gas chamber?"

Susan grinned and replied that she wasn't.

With that, Caballero must have realized that he had lost her.

Susan and Charlie talked for an hour or so more, but Caballero hadn't the foggiest idea of what they said. "At some point in the conversation they began to talk in sort of a double talk or pig Latin," and "when they reached that point they lost me."

However, the looks they exchanged said it all. It was like a "joyous homecoming." Sadie Mae Glutz had returned to the irresistible Charles Manson.

She fired Caballero the next day.

On March 6, Manson appeared in court and argued a number of novel motions. One asked that the "Deputy District Attorneys in charge of the trial be incarcerated for a period of time under the same circumstances that I have been subject to . . ." Another requested that he "be free to travel to any place I should deem fit in preparing my defense . . ."

There were more, and Judge Keene declared himself

appalled" at Manson's "outlandish" requests. Keene then said he had reviewed the entire file on the case, from his "nonsensical" motions to his numerous violations of the gag order. He had also discussed Manson's conduct with judges Lucas and Dell, before whom Manson had also appeared, concluding that it had become "abundantly clear to me that you are incapable of acting as your own attorney."

Infuriated, Manson shouted, "It's not me that's on trial here as much as this court is on trial!" He also told the judge, "Go wash your hands. They're dirty."

THE COURT "Mr. Manson, your status, at this time, of acting as your own attorney is now vacated."

Against Manson's strong objections, Keene appointed Charles Hollopeter, a former president of the Los Angeles Criminal Courts Bar, as Manson's attorney of record.

"You can kill me," Manson said, "but you can't give me an attorney. I won't take one."

Keene told Manson that if he found an attorney of his own choosing, he would consider a motion to substitute him for Hollopeter. I knew Hollopeter by reputation. Since he'd never be Charlie's bootlicker, I guessed he'd last about a month; I was too generous.

Toward the end of the proceedings, Manson shouted, *There is no God in this courtroom!"* As if on cue, a number of Family members jumped up and yelled at Keene, "You are a mockery of justice! You are a joke!" The judge found three of them—Gypsy, Sandy, and Mark Ross—in contempt, and sentenced each to five days in the County Jail.

When Sandy was searched prior to being booked, among the items found in her purse was a Buck knife.

After this, the sheriff's deputies, who are in charge of maintaining security in the Los Angeles criminal courts, began searching all spectators before they entered the courtroom.

On March 7, Linda Kasabian was taken to the hospital. Two days later she gave birth to a boy, whom she named Angel. On the thirteenth she was returned to the jail, without the child, Linda's mother having taken him back to New Hampshire.

In the interim I had talked to Captain Carpenter, and he had agreed to let Linda remain in her former cell just off the infirmary. I checked it out myself. It was a small room, its furnishings consisting of a bed, toilet bowl, washbasin, and a small desk and chair. It was clean but bleak. Far more important, it was safe.

Every few days I called McGann. No, he hadn't got around to looking for the knives yet.

On March 11, Susan Atkins, after formally requesting that Richard Caballero be relieved as her attorney, asked for Daye Shinn in Caballero's place.

Inasmuch as Shinn, one of the first attorneys to call on Manson after he was brought down from Independence, had represented Manson on several matters and had visited him more than forty times, Judge Keene felt there might be a possible conflict of interest involved.

Shinn denied this. Keene then warned Susan of the possible dangers of being represented by an attorney who had been so closely involved with one of her co-defendants. Susan said she didn't care; she wanted Shinn. Keene granted the substitution.

I hadn't come up against Shinn before. He was about forty, Korean born; according to the press, his main practice, before allying himself with the Manson defense, had been obtaining Mexican domestics for Southern California families.

On leaving the courtroom, Shinn told waiting reporters that Susan Atkins "definitely will deny everything she told the grand jury."

On March 15 we took Linda Kasabian out again. Only this time we used not a conspicuous sheriff's van but unmarked police cars.

I wanted Linda to trace the route the killers had taken the night the LaBiancas were killed.

After dinner that night—Saturday, August 9, 1969—nda and several other Family members were standing tside the kitchen at Spahn. Manson called Linda, Katie, d Leslie aside and told them to get a change of clothing d meet him in the bunkhouse.

This time he mentioned nothing to Linda about knives, t he did tell her again to get her driver's license.

"I just looked at him and, you know, just sort of aded with my eyes, please don't make me go, because," inda said, "I just knew we were going out again, and I new it would be the same thing, but I was afraid to say ything."

"Last night was too messy," Manson told the group hen they assembled in the bunkhouse. "This time I'm ing to show you how to do it."

Tex complained that the weapons they had used the evious night weren't effective enough!

Linda saw two swords in the bunkhouse, one of which as the Straight Satans' sword. She did not see anyone ck them up, but later she noticed the Satans' sword and vo smaller knives under the front seat of the car. In uestioning DeCarlo, I'd learned that one night about this me he'd noticed that the sword had been taken out.

Again the group piled into Swartz' Ford. This time lanson himself slipped into the driver's seat, with Linda ext to him, Clem on the passenger side, Tex, Sadie, Ka-e, and Leslie crowded in back. All wore dark clothing, inda said, except for Clem, who had on an olive-drab eld jacket. As he often did, Manson wore a leather thong round his neck, the two ends extending down to his reastbone, where they were looped together. I asked inda if anyone else was wearing such a thong; she said o.

Before they left, Manson asked Bruce Davis for some noney. Just as DeCarlo took care of the Family guns, Da-is acted as comptroller for the group, taking care of the tolen credit cards, fake ID, and so forth.

As they drove off, Manson told them that tonight they vould divide into two groups: each would take a separate ouse. He said he'd drop off one group, then take the sec-nd group with him.

When they stopped to buy gas (using cash, not a credit card), Manson told Linda to take over the driving. Questioning Linda, I established that Manson—and Manson alone—gave all the instructions as to where they were to go and what they were to do. At no time, she said, did Tex Watson instruct anyone to do anything. Charlie was in complete command.

Following Manson's directions, Linda took the freeway to Pasadena. Once off it, he gave her so many directions she was unsure where they were. Eventually he told her to stop in front of a house, which Linda described as a modern, one-story, middle-class-type home. This was the place where, as described by Susan Atkins, Manson got out, had them drive around the block, then got back in, telling them that, having looked in the window and seen photographs of children, he didn't want to "do" that particular house, though, he added, in the future it might be necessary to kill children also. Linda's account was essentially the same as Susan's.

After riding around Pasadena for some time, Manson again took over the driving. Linda: "I remember we started driving up a hill with lots of houses, nice houses, rich houses, and trees. We got to the top of the hill and turned around and stopped in front of a certain house." Linda couldn't remember if it was one story or two, only that it was big. Manson, however, said the houses were too close together here, so they drove off.

Shortly after this, Manson spotted a church. Pulling into the parking lot next to it, he again got out. Linda believed, but wasn't absolutely sure, that he told them he was going to "get" the minister or priest.

However, he returned a few minutes later, saying the church door was locked.

Susan Atkins had neglected to mention the church in her account. I learned of it for the first time from Linda Kasabian.

Manson again told Linda to drive, but the route he gave her was so confusing that she soon became lost. Later, driving up Sunset from the ocean, there occurred another incident which Susan Atkins had neglected to mention.

Observing a white sports car ahead of them, Manson

ld Linda, "At the next red light, pull up beside it. I'm
ing to kill the driver."

Linda pulled up next to the car, but just as Manson
mped out, the light changed to green and the sports car
omed away.

Another potential victim, unaware to this day how close
death he had come.

Thus far, their wanderings appeared totally at random,
anson seemingly having no particular victims in mind.
s I'd later argue to the jury, up to this time no one in
e vast, sprawling metropolis of seven million people,
hether in a home, a church, or even a car, was safe
om Manson's insatiable lust for death, blood, and mur-
r.

But after the sports-car incident, Manson's directions
came very specific. He directed Linda to the Los Feliz
ction of Los Angeles, not far from Griffith Park, having
r stop on the street in front of a home in a residential
ea.

Linda recognized the house. In June of 1968 she and
r husband had been driving from Seattle to Taos when
ey stopped off in Los Angeles. A friend had taken
em to the house—3267 Waverly Drive—for a peyote
rty. One of the men who were living there, she recalled,
as named Harold. In another of the many coincidences
hich abounded in this case, Linda had also been to the
arold True residence, though at a time none of the
amily members were there.

Linda asked, "Charlie, you're not going to do that
ouse, are you?"

Manson replied, "No, the one next door."

Telling the others to stay in the car, Manson got out.
inda noticed him shove something into his belt, but she
ouldn't see what it was. She watched him walking up the
riveway until it curved and he disappeared from sight.

I presumed, although I couldn't be sure of this, that
Manson had a gun.

For Rosemary and Leno LaBianca, the horror that
ould end in their deaths had begun.

Linda guessed the time was about 2 A.M. Some ten mi
utes later, she said, Manson returned to the car.

I asked Linda if he was still wearing the leather thon
around his neck. She said she hadn't noticed, though sh
did notice, later that night, that he no longer had it.
showed her the leather thong used to bind the wrists
Leno LaBianca, and she said it was "the same kind" Man
son had been wearing.

Manson told Tex, Katie, and Leslie to get out of th
car and bring their clothing bundles with them. Obviousl
they were to be the first team. Linda heard some, thoug
not all, of the conversation. Manson told the trio tha
there were two people inside the house, that he had tie
them up and told them that everything was going to be a
right, and that they shouldn't be afraid. He also instructe
Tex, Katie, and Leslie that they were not to cause fea
and panic in the people as had happened the night before.

The LaBiancas had been creepy-crawled, pacified wit
Charles Manson's unctuous assurances, then set up to b
slaughtered.

Linda heard only bits and pieces of the rest of the con
versation. She did not hear Manson specifically order th
three to kill the two persons. Nor did she see them carry
ing any weapons. She believed she heard Manson say
"Don't let them know you are going to kill them." And
she definitely heard him instruct them that when they wer
done they were to hitchhike back to the ranch.

As the trio started toward the house, Manson got bac
in the car and handed Linda a woman's wallet, telling he
to wipe off the prints and remove the change. In openin
it, she noticed the driver's license, which had a photo of
woman with dark hair. She recalled the woman's firs
name was "Rosemary," while the last name "was eithe
Mexican or Italian." She also remembered seeing a num
ber of credit cards and a wrist watch.

When I asked Linda the color of the wallet, she said
was red. Actually it was brown. She also claimed to hav
removed all the change, but when the wallet was foun
there were still some coins in one of the inner compart
ments. Both were understandable errors, I felt, particu
larly overlooking the extra change compartment.

Manson again took over the driving. Linda was now on the passenger side, Susan and Clem in back. Manson told Linda that when they reached a predominantly colored area he wanted her to toss the wallet out onto a sidewalk, so a black person would find it, use the credit cards, and be arrested. This would make people think the Panthers had committed the murders, he explained.

Manson drove onto the freeway not far from where they had dropped off Tex, Katie, and Leslie. After driving for a long time, he pulled off the freeway and stopped at a nearby service station. Apparently having changed his plans, Manson now told Linda to put the wallet in the women's rest room. Linda did, only she hid it too well, lifting the top of the toilet tank and placing it over the bulb, where it would remain undiscovered for four months.

I asked Linda if she could remember anything distinctive about the station. She remembered there was a restaurant next door and that it seemed "to radiate the color orange."

There was a Denny's Restaurant next to the Standard station in Sylmar, with a large orange sign.

While Linda was in the rest room, Manson went to the restaurant, returning with four milk shakes.

Probably at the same time the LaBiancas were being murdered, the man who had ordered their deaths was sipping a milk shake.

Again Manson had Linda drive. After a long time, perhaps an hour, they reached the beach somewhere south of Venice. Linda recalled seeing some oil storage tanks. All four got out of the car, Sadie and Clem, at Charlie's instructions, dropping behind while he and Linda walked ahead in the sand.

Suddenly Manson was again all love. It was as if the events of the last forty-eight hours had never happened. Linda told Charlie that she was pregnant. Manson took Linda's hand and, as she described it, "it was sort of nice, you know, we were just talking, I gave him some peanuts, and he just sort of made me forget about everything, made me feel good."

Would the jury understand this? I thought so, once they

understood Manson's charismatic personality and Linda's love for him.

Just as they reached a side street, a police car pulled up and two officers got out. They asked the pair what they were doing.

Charlie replied, "We were just going for a walk." Then, as if they should recognize him, he asked, "Don't you know who I am?" or "Don't you remember my name?" They said, "No," then returned to the patrol car and drove off, without asking either for identification. It was, Linda said, "a friendly conversation," lasting only a minute.

Finding the two officers on duty in the area that night should be fairly easy, I thought, unaware how wrong I could be.

Clem and Sadie were already back in the car when they returned. Manson then told Linda to drive to Venice. En route he asked the three if they knew anyone there. None did. Manson then asked Linda, "What about the man you and Sandy met in Venice? Wasn't he a piggy?" Linda replied, "Yes, he's an actor." Manson told her to drive to his apartment.

I asked Linda about the actor.

One afternoon in early August, Linda said, she and Sandy had been hitchhiking near the pier when this man picked them up. He told them he was Israeli or Arab—Linda couldn't recall which—and that he had appeared in a movie about Kahlil Gibran. The two girls were hungry, and he drove them to his apartment and fixed them lunch. Afterward, Sandy napped and Linda and the man made love. Before the girls left, he gave them some food and spare clothing. Linda couldn't remember the man's name, only that it was foreign. However, she felt sure she could find the apartment house, as she had located it when Manson asked her to drive there that night.

When they pulled up in front, Manson asked Linda if the man would let her in. "I think so," she replied. What about Sadie and Clem? Linda said she guessed so. Manson then handed her a pocketknife and demonstrated how he wanted her to slit the actor's throat.

Linda said she couldn't do it. "I'm not you, Charlie," Linda told Manson. "I can't kill anybody."

Manson asked her to take him to the man's apartment. Linda led Charlie up the stairs, but deliberately pointed to the wrong door.

On returning to the car, Manson gave the trio explicit instructions. They were to go to the actor's apartment. Linda was to knock. When the man let her in, Sadie and Clem were to go in also. Once they were inside, Linda was to slit the man's throat and Clem was to shoot him. When finished, they were to hitchhike back to the ranch.

Linda saw Manson hand Clem a gun, but was unable to describe it. Nor did she know if Sadie also had a knife.

"If anything goes wrong," Manson told them, "just hang it up, don't do it." He then slid into the driver's seat and drove off.

Like the church and sports-car incidents, Susan Atkins had not mentioned the Venice incident to me, nor had she said anything about it when testifying before the grand jury. While I felt that she might have forgotten the two earlier incidents, I suspected the third was omitted intentionally, since it directly involved her as a willing partner in still another attempted murder. It was possible, however, that had I had more time to interview Susan, this too might have come out.

The actor's apartment was on the top, or fifth, floor, but Linda did not tell Clem or Sadie this. Instead, on reaching the fourth floor, she knocked on the first door she saw. Eventually a man sleepily asked, "Who is it?" She replied, "Linda." When the man opened the door a crack, Linda said, "Oh, excuse me, I have the wrong apartment."

The door was open only a second or two and Linda caught just a glimpse of the man. She had the impression, though she was unsure of this, that he was middle-aged.

The three then left the building, but not before Sadie, ever the animal, defecated on the landing.

It was obvious that Linda Kasabian had prevented still another Manson-ordered murder. As independent evidence corroborating her story, it was important that we locate not only the actor but the man who answered the door.

Perhaps he'd remember being awakened at 4 or 5 A.M. by a pretty young girl.

From the apartment house Clem, Sadie, and Linda walked to the beach, a short distance away. Clem wanted to ditch the gun. He disappeared from sight behind a sandpile, near a fence. Linda presumed that he had either buried the gun or tossed it over the fence.

Walking back to the Pacific Coast Highway, they hitched a ride to the entrance of Topanga Canyon. There was a hippie crash pad nearby, next door to the Malibu Feedbin, and Sadie said she knew a girl who was staying there. Linda recalled there was also an older man there, and a big dog. The three stayed about an hour, smoking some weed, then left.

They then hitched two rides, the last taking them all the way to the entrance of Santa Susana Pass Road, where Clem and Linda got out. Sadie, Linda learned the next day, remained in the car until it reached the waterfall area.

When Linda and Clem arrived at the ranch, Tex and Leslie were already there, asleep in one of the rooms. She didn't see Katie, though she learned the next day that, like Sadie, she had gone on to the camp by the waterfall. Linda went to bed in the saloon.

Two days later Linda Kasabian fled Spahn Ranch. The manner of her departure, however, would cause the prosecution a great deal of concern.

Rather than taking Linda directly to the LaBianca residence, I had the sheriff's deputy drive to the Los Feliz area, to see if Linda could find the house itself. She did, pointing out both the LaBianca and True houses, the place where they had parked, the driveway up which Manson had walked, and so on.

I also wanted to find the two houses in Pasadena where Manson had stopped earlier that night, but, though we spent hours looking for them, we were, at this time, unsuccessful. Linda did find the apartment house where the actor had lived, 1101 Ocean Front Walk, and pointed out both his apartment, 501, and the door on which she had knocked, 403. I asked Patchett and Gutierrez to locate and interview both the actor and the man who had been living in 403.

Linda also showed us the sandpile near the fence where she believed Clem had disposed of the gun, but though we got out shovels and dug up the area, we were unable to locate the weapon. It was possible that someone had already found it, or that Clem or one of the other Family members had reclaimed it later. We never did learn what type of gun it was.

Having been out since early in the morning, we stopped at a Chinese restaurant for lunch. That afternoon we returned to Pasadena and must have driven past forty churches before Linda found the one where Manson had stopped. I asked LAPD to photograph it and the adjoining parking lot as a trial exhibit.

Linda also identified the Standard station in Sylmar where she'd left the wallet, as well as Denny's Restaurant next door.

Despite all our security precautions, we were spotted. The next day the *Herald Examiner* reported: "In addition to winning immunity, Mrs. Kasabian was given a 'bonus' in the form of a Chinese dinner at Madam Wu's Garden Restaurant in Santa Monica. Restaurant employees confirmed Mrs. Kasabian, defense attorney Fleischman and Prosecutor Bugliosi ate there Sunday."

The paper neglected to mention that our party included a half dozen LAPD officers and two LASO deputies.

We took Linda out twice more, trying to find the two houses in Pasadena. On both occasions we were accompanied by South Pasadena PD officers who directed us to neighborhoods similar to those Linda had described. We finally found the large house atop the hill. Though I had it and the adjoining houses photographed—they were close together, as Manson had said—I decided against talking to the owners, sure they would sleep better not knowing how close to death they had come. We were never able to locate the first house—which both Susan and Linda had described—where Manson looked in the window and saw the photographs of the children.

We did grant Linda one special privilege, which might have been called a "bonus." On the three occasions we took her out of Sybil Brand, we let her call her mother in New Hampshire and talk to her two children. Her attorney paid for the calls. Though Angel was only a month old and much too young to understand, just speaking to them obviously meant a great deal to Linda.

Yet she never asked to do this. She never asked for anything. She told me not once but several times that although she was pleased to be getting immunity, because it meant that eventually she could be with her children, it didn't matter that much if she didn't get it. There was a sort of sad fatalism about her. She said she knew she had to tell the truth about what had happened, and that she had known she would be the one to tell the story ever since the murders occurred. Unlike the other defendants, she seemed burdened with guilt, though, again unlike them, she hadn't physically harmed anyone. She was a strange girl, marked by her time with Manson, yet not molded by him in the same way the others were. Because she was compliant, easily led, Manson apparently had had little trouble controlling her. Up to a point. But she had refused to cross that point. "I'm not you, Charlie. I can't kill anybody."

Once I asked her what she thought about Manson now. She was still in love with him, Linda said. "Some things he said were the truth," she observed thoughtfully. "Only now I realize he could take a truth and make a lie of it."

Shortly after the story broke that Linda Kasabian would testify for the prosecution, Al Wiman, the reporter with the Channel 7 crew which had found the clothing, showed up in my office. If Kasabian was cooperating with us, then she must have indicated where she threw the knives, Wiman surmised. He begged me to pinpoint the area; his station, he promised, would supply a search crew, metal detectors, everything.

"Look, Al," I told him, "you guys have already found the clothing. How is it going to look at the trial if you find the knives too? Tell you what. I'm trying to get someone out. If they won't go, then I'll tell you."

After Wiman left, I called McGann. *Two weeks* had passed since I'd asked him to look for the knives; he still hadn't done it. My patience at an end, I called Lieutenant Helder and told him about Wiman's offer. "Think how LAPD is going to look if it comes out during the trial that a ten-year-old boy found the gun and Channel 7 found both the clothing and the knives."

Bob had a crew out the next day. No luck. But at least during the trial we'd be prepared to prove that they had looked. Otherwise, the defense could contend that LAPD was so skeptical of Linda Kasabian's story that they hadn't even bothered to mount a search.

That they'd failed to find the knives was a disappointment, but not too much of a surprise. Over seven months had passed since the night Linda tossed the knives out of the car. According to her testimony, one had bouncèd back into the road, while the other had landed in the bushes nearby. The street, though in the country, was much traveled. It was quite possible they had been picked up by a motorist or passing cyclist.

I had no idea how often the police had interviewed Winifred Chapman, the Polanskis' maid. I'd talked to her a number of times myself before I realized there was one question so obvious we'd all overlooked it.

Mrs. Chapman had stated that she washed the front door of the Tate residence just after noon on Friday, August 8. This meant Charles Watson had to have left his print there sometime after this.

However, there was a *second* print found at the Tate residence, Patricia Krenwinkel's, located inside the door that led from Sharon Tate's bedroom to the pool.

I asked Mrs. Chapman: "Did you ever wash that door?" Yes. How often? A couple of times a week. She had to, she explained, because the guests usually used that door to get to the pool.

The big question: "Did you wash it the week of the murders, and, if so, when?"

A. "Tuesday was the last time. I washed it down, inside and out, with vinegar and water."

Under discovery, I was only required to make a note of the conversation and put it in our tubs. However, in fairness to both Fitzgerald and his client, I called Paul and told him, "If you're planning on having Krenwinkel testify that she went swimming at the Tate residence a couple of weeks before the murders and left her print at that time, better forget it. Mrs. Chapman is going to testify she washed that door on Tuesday, August 5."

Paul was grateful for the information. Had he based his defense on this premise, Mrs. Chapman's testimony could have been devastating.

There was, in such conversations, something assumed though unstated. Whatever his public posture, I was sure that Fitzgerald knew that his client was guilty, and he knew that I knew it. Though only on rare occasions does a defense attorney slip up and admit this in court, when it comes to in-chambers discussions and private conversations, it's often something else.

There were two items of evidence in our files which I did not point out to the defense. I was sure they had already seen them—both were among the items photocopied for them—but I was hoping they wouldn't realize their importance.

One was a traffic ticket, the other an arrest report. Separately each seemed unimportant. Together they made a bomb that would demolish Manson's alibi defense.

On first learning from Fowles that Manson might claim that he was not in the Los Angeles area at the time of the murders, I had asked LaBianca detectives Patchett and Gutierrez to see if they could obtain evidence proving his actual whereabouts on the subject dates. They did an excellent job. Together with information obtained from credit card transactions and interviews, they were able to piece together a timetable of Manson's activities during the week preceding the start of Helter Skelter.

On about August 1, 1969, Manson told several Family members that he was going to Big Sur to seek out new recruits.

He apparently left on the morning of Sunday, August 3, as sometime between seven and eight he purchased gas at a station in Canoga Park, using a stolen credit card. From Canoga Park, he headed north toward Big Sur. At about four the next morning, he picked up a young girl, Stephanie Schram, outside a service station some distance south of Big Sur, probably at Gorda. An attractive seventeen-year-old, Stephanie was hitchhiking from San Francisco to San Diego, where she was living with her married sister. Manson and Stephanie camped in a nearby canyon that night—probably Salmon or Limekiln Creek, both hippie hangouts—Manson telling her his views on life, love and death. Manson talked a lot about death, Stephanie would recall, and it frightened her. They took LSD and had sex. Manson was apparently unusually smitten with Stephanie. Usually he'd have sex with a new girl a few times, then move on to a new "young love." Not so with Stephanie. He later told Paul Watkins that Stephanie, who was of German extraction, was the result of two thousand years of perfect breeding.

On August 4, Manson, still using the stolen credit card, purchased gas at Lucia. Ripping off the place, which bore a large sign reading "Hippies Not Allowed," must have given him a special satisfaction, as he did it again the next day.

On the night of the fifth Manson and Stephanie drove north to a place whose name Stephanie couldn't recall but which Manson described as a "sensitivity camp." It was, he told her, a place where rich people went on weekends to play at being enlightened. He was obviously describing Esalen Institute.

Esalen was, at this time, just coming into vogue as a "growth center," its seminars including such diverse figures as yogis and psychiatrists, salvationists and satanists. Obviously Manson felt Esalen a prime place to espouse his philosophies. It is unknown whether he had been there on prior occasions, those involved in the Institute refusing to even acknowledge his visits there.*

---

*At 3:07 P.M., July 30, 1969, someone at the Tate residence called the Esalen Institute, Big Sur, California, telephone number 408-667-2335. It was a brief station-to-station call, total charge 95 cents. It is unknown who placed the call, or—since the number is that of the switchboard—who was called.

Since the call occurred just six days before Charles Manson's visit to Esalen, it arouses a certain amount of speculation. A few things are known, however: none of the Tate victims was at Big Sur during the period Manson was there; Abigail Folger had attended semi-

Manson took his guitar and left Stephanie in the van. After a time she fell asleep. When she awakened the next morning, Manson had already returned. He was in less than a good mood, as, later that day, he unexpectedly struck her. Still later, at Barker Ranch, Manson would tell Paul Watkins—to quote Watkins—that while at Big Sur he had gone "to Esalen and played his guitar for a bunch of people who were supposed to be the top people there, and they rejected his music. Some people pretended that they were asleep, and other people were saying, 'This is too heavy for me,' and 'I'm not ready for that,' and others were saying, 'Well, I don't understand it,' and some just got up and walked out."

Still another rejection by what Manson considered the establishment—this occurring just three days before the Tate murders.

With his single recruit, Manson left Big Sur on August 6, making gas purchases that same day at San Luis Obispo and Chatsworth, a few miles from Spahn Ranch. According to Stephanie, they had dinner at the ranch that night and she met the Family for the first time. She felt uncomfortable with them, and, learning that Manson shared his favors with the other girls, told him she would stay only if he would promise to remain with her, and her alone, for two weeks. Surprisingly, Manson agreed. They spent that night in the van, parked not far from the ranch, then drove to San Diego the next day to pick up Stephanie's clothes.

En route, about ten miles south of Oceanside on Interstate 5, they were stopped by California Highway Patrol officer Richard C. Willis. Though pulled over for a mechanical violation, Manson was cited only for having no valid driver's license in his possession. Manson gave his correct name and the ranch address, and signed the ticket

---

nars at Esalen in the past; and several of her San Francisco friends visited there periodically. It is possible that she was simply trying to locate someone, but this is just a guess.

Though both the call and Manson's visit to Esalen remain mysterious, I should perhaps note that, with a single exception—the Hatami-Tate-Manson confrontation on March 23, 1969—I was unable to find a prior link of any kind between any of the Tate-LaBianca victims and their killers.

himself. Officer Willis noted on the ticket that Manson was driving a "1952 cream-colored Ford bakery van, license number K70683." The date was Thursday, August 7, 1969; the time 6:15 P.M.

The ticket, which Patchett and Gutierrez found, proved Manson was in Southern California the day before the Tate murders.

While Stephanie was getting her clothes together, Manson talked to her sister, who was also a Beatles fan. She had the White Album, and Manson told her the Beatles had laid out "the whole scene" in it. He warned her that the blacks were getting ready to overthrow the whites and that only those who fled to the desert and hid in the bottomless pit would be safe. As for those who remained in the cities, Manson said, "People are going to be slaughtered, they'll be lying on their lawns dead."

Just a little over twenty-four hours later, his prediction would be fulfilled, in all its gory detail, at 10050 Cielo Drive. With a little help from his friends.

That night, according to Stephanie, she and Charlie parked somewhere in San Diego and slept next to the van, returning to Spahn Ranch the following day, arriving there about two in the afternoon.

Stephanie was a bit vague when it came to dates. She "thought" the day they returned to Spahn Ranch was Friday, August 8, but she wasn't sure. I anticipated that the defense would make the most of this, but I wasn't concerned, because that second piece of evidence conclusively placed Manson back at the ranch on Friday, August 8, 1969.

According to Linda Kasabian, on the afternoon of August 8 Manson gave Mary Brunner and Sandra Good a credit card and told them to purchase some items for him. At four that afternoon the two girls were apprehended while driving away from a Sears store in San Fernando, after store employees checked and found the credit card was stolen. The San Fernando PD arrest report stated that they were driving a "van 1952 Ford license K70683."

Because of the fine job of digging by the LaBianca detectives, we now had physical proof that Manson was back at Spahn Ranch on Friday, August 8, 1969.

Though both the traffic ticket and arrest report were in the discovery materials, so were hundreds of other documents. I was hoping that the defense would overlook their common denominator: that vehicle description with its telltale license number.

If Manson went with an alibi defense, and I proved that alibi was fabricated, this would be strong circumstantial evidence of his guilt.

There was, of course, other evidence placing Manson at Spahn Ranch that day. In addition to the testimony of Schram, DeCarlo, and others, Linda Kasabian said that when the Family got together that afternoon, Manson discussed his visit to Big Sur, saying that the people there were "really not together, they were just off on their little trips" and that "the people wouldn't go on his trip."

It was just after this that Manson told them: "Now is the time for Helter Skelter."

Bits and pieces, often largely circumstantial. Yet patiently dug out and assembled, they became the People's case. And with almost every interview it became a little stronger.

I spent many hours interviewing Stephanie Schram, who, together with Kitty Lutesinger, had fled Barker Ranch just hours before the October 1969 raid, shotgun-wielding Clem in close pursuit. I often wondered what would have happened to the two girls had the raid been timed just a day later or Clem been a little faster.

Unlike Kitty, Stephanie had severed all contact with the Family. Though we had kept her current address from the defense, Squeaky and Gypsy found her working at a dog-grooming school. "Charlie wants you to come back," they told her. Stephanie replied, "No thanks." Considering what she knew, her forthright refusal was a brave act.

From Stephanie I learned that while at Barker Manson had conducted a "murder school." He had given a Buck knife to each of the girls, and had demonstrated how they should "slit the throats of pigs," by yanking the head back by the hair and drawing the knife from ear to ear (using Stephanie as a very frightened model). He also said they

hould "stab them in either their ears or eyes and then
riggle the knife around to get as many vital organs as
ossible." The details became even gorier: Manson said
hat if the police pigs came to the desert, they should kill
hem, cut them in little pieces, boil the heads, then put the
kulls and uniforms on posts, to frighten off others.*

Stephanie had told LAPD that Manson had spent the
ights of Friday, August 8, and Saturday, August 9, with
er. On questioning her, I learned that about an hour af-
er dinner on August 8, Manson took her to the trailer at
pahn and told her to go to sleep, that he would join her
oon. However, she didn't see him again until shortly be-
ore dawn the next morning, at which time he awakened
er and took her with him to Devil's Canyon, the camp
cross the road from the ranch.

That night—August 9—Stephanie said, "when it got
ark, he left and he came back either sometime during the
ight or early in the morning."

If Manson was planning on using Stephanie Schram as
n alternative alibi, we were now more than ready for
im.

On March 19, Hollopeter, Manson's court-appointed at-
orney, made two motions: that Charles Manson be given
 psychiatric examination, and that his case be severed
rom that of the others.

Enraged, Manson tried to fire Hollopeter.

Asked whom he wished to represent him, Manson re-
lied, "Myself." When Judge Keene denied the change,
Manson picked up a copy of the Constitution and, saying
t meant nothing to the Court, tossed it in a wastebasket.

Manson eventually requested that Ronald Hughes be
ubstituted for Hollopeter. Like Reiner and Shinn, Hughes
ad been one of the first attorneys to call on Manson. He
ad remained on the periphery of the case ever since, his
hief function being to run errands for Manson, as indi-

*Much later I discovered that LASO deputies George Palmer and
William Gleason had obtained much of this same information from
tephanie Schram on December 3, 1969, but LASO had not informed
APD of this.

cated by a document Manson had signed on February 1
designating him one of his legal runners.

Keene granted the substitution. Hollopeter, whom th
press called "one of L.A. county's most successful defens
attorneys," was out, after thirteen days; Hughes, wh
had never before tried a case, was in.

Something of an intellectual, Hughes was a huge, bal
ing man with a long, scraggly beard. His various items (
apparel rarely matched and usually evidenced numerou
food stains. As one reporter remarked, "You could usual
tell what Ron had for breakfast, for the past sever
weeks." Hughes, whom I would get to know well in th
months ahead, and for whom I developed a growing r
spect, once admitted to me that he had bought his sui
for a dollar apiece at MGM; they were from Walt
Slezak's old wardrobe. The press was quick to dub hi
"Manson's hippie lawyer."

Hughes' first two acts were to withdraw the motions fe
the psychiatric examination and the severance. Grante
His third and fourth were requests that Manson be a
lowed to revert to pro per status and to deliver a spee
to the Court. Denied.

Although Manson was displeased with Keene's last tw
rulings, he couldn't have been too unhappy with the d
fense team, which now consisted of four attorneys-
Reiner (Van Houten), Shinn (Atkins), Fitzgerald (Kre
winkel), and Hughes (Manson)—each of whom had bee
associated with him since early in the case.

Unknown to us, there were still changes ahead. Amor
the casualties would be both Ira Reiner and Rona
Hughes, each of whom dared go against Manson's wishe
Reiner would lose considerable time and money for havi
linked himself with the Manson defense. His loss would I
small, however, compared to that of Hughes, who, ju
eight months later, would pay with his life.

On March 21, Aaron and I were walking down the co
ridor in the Hall of Justice when we spotted Irving Ka
arek emerging from the elevator.

Although little known elsewhere, Kanarek was som
thing of a legend in the Los Angeles courts. The attorney

bstructionist tactics had caused a number of judges to
penly censure him from the bench. Kanarek stories were
o common, and usually incredible, as to seem fictional
vhen they were actually fact. Prosecutor Burton Katz, for
xample, recalled that Kanarek once objected to a prose-
ution witness's stating his own name because, having first
eard his name from his mother, it was "hearsay." Such
rivolous objections were minor irritations compared with
Kanarek's dilatory tactics. As samples:

In the case of *People* vs. *Goodman*, Kanarek had
tretched a simple theft case, which should have taken a
ew hours or a day at most, to three months. The amount
tolen: $100. The cost to the taxpayers: $130,212.

In the case of *People* vs. *Smith and Powell*, Kanarek
pent twelve and a half months on pre-trial motions. After
n additional two months trying to pick a jury, Kanarek's
wn client fired him in disgust. *A year and a half* after Ir-
ing Kanarek came onto the case, the jury still hadn't
een selected, nor a single witness called.

In the case of *People* vs. *Bronson*, Superior Court
udge Raymond Roberts told Kanarek: "I am doing my
est to see that Mr. Bronson gets a fair trial in spite of
ou. I have never seen such obviously stupid, ill-advised
uestions of a witness. Are you paid by the word or by
he hour that you can consume the Court's time? You are
he most obstructionist man I have ever met."

Outside the presence of the jury, Judge Roberts defined
Kanarek's modus operandi as follows: "You take intermi-
able lengths of time in cross-examining on the most mi-
ute, unimportant details; you ramble back and forth with
o chronology of events, to just totally confuse everybody
n the courtroom, to the utter frustration of the jury, the
vitnesses, and the judge."

After examining the transcript, the Appellate Court
ound the judge's remarks were not prejudicial but were
ubstantiated by the trial record.

"All we need, Vince," Aaron remarked jocularly to me,
"is to have Irving Kanarek on this case. We'd be in court
en years."

The next day Ronald Hughes told a reporter that "he
nay ask Van Nuys attorney I. A. Kanarek to enter the

case as Manson's lawyer. He mentioned that he and Ma[n]
son conferred with Kanarek at the County Jail Mond[ay]
night."

Though no miracle was involved, the Black Panth[er]
whom Charles Manson had shot and killed in July 19[69]
had resurrected. Only he wasn't a Panther, just a "form[er]
dope dealer," and, contrary to what Manson and t[he]
Family had believed, after Manson shot him he had[n't]
died, though his friends had told Manson that he had. [His]
name was Bernard Crowe, but he was best known by t[he]
descriptive · nickname Lotsapoppa. Our long search f[or]
Crowe ended when an old acquaintance of mine, [Al]
Tolmas, who was Crowe's attorney, called me. He told [me]
he had learned we were looking for his client and arrang[ed]
for me to interview Crowe.

Crowe's story of the incident was essentially the same [as]
that DeCarlo had told LAPD, although even Charl[ie]
didn't know the surprise ending.

After Manson and T. J. had left the Hollywood apa[rt]
ment where the shooting took place, Crowe, who had be[en]
playing dead, told his friends to call an ambulance. Th[ey]
did, then split. When questioned by the police at the hos[pi]
tal, Crowe said he didn't know who had shot him or wh[y.]
He nearly didn't make it; he was on the critical list f[or]
eighteen days. The bullet was still lodged next to his spine.

I was interested in Crowe for two reasons. One, the i[n]
cident proved that Charles Manson was quite capable [of]
killing someone on his own. Though I knew I couldn't g[et]
this into evidence during the guilt phase of the trial, I w[as]
hopeful of introducing it during the penalty phase, wh[ere]
other crimes can be considered. Two, from the descripti[on]
it appeared that the gun Manson had shot Crowe with w[as]
the same .22 caliber Longhorn revolver which, just a litt[le]
over a month later, Tex Watson would use in the Tate hom[
icides. If we could remove the bullet from Crowe's bo[dy]
and match it up with the bullets test-fired from the .[22]
caliber revolver, we'd have placed the Tate murd[er]
weapon in Manson's own hand.

Sergeant Bill Lee of SID wasn't optimistic about th[e]
bullet. He told me that since it had been embedded in th[e]

body for over nine months, it was likely that acids had obliterated the stria to an extent where a positive identification would be difficult. Still, it might be possible. I then talked to several surgeons: they could take out the bullet, they told me, but the operation was risky.

I laid it out for Crowe. We'd like to have the bullet, and would arrange to have it removed at the Los Angeles County Hospital. But there were serious risks involved, and I didn't minimize them.

Crowe declined the operation. He was sort of proud of the bullet, he said. It made quite a conversation piece.

Eventually Manson would have learned, through discovery, of the resurrection of Bernard Crowe. Before this, however, Crowe was jailed on a marijuana charge. As he was being escorted down the hall, he passed Manson and his guard, who were on their way back from the attorney room. Charlie did a quick about-face, then told Crowe, according to the deputies who were present, "Sorry I had to do it, but you know how it is."

Crowe's response, if there was one, went unreported.

Toward the end of March the prosecution nearly lost one of its key witnesses.

Paul Watkins, once Manson's chief lieutenant, was pulled out of a flaming Volkswagen camper and rushed to Los Angeles County General Hospital with second-degree burns on 25 percent of his face, arms, and back. When sufficiently recovered to talk to the police, Watkins told them he had fallen asleep while reading by candlelight, and either that, or a marijuana cigarette he had been smoking, could have caused the fire.

These were only guesses, Watkins told them, as he was "unsure of the origin of the blaze."

Three days *before* the fire, Inyo County authorities had heard a rumor that Watkins was going to be killed by the Family.

As far back as November 1969, I'd asked LAPD to infiltrate the Family. I not only wanted to know what they were planning as far as defense strategy was concerned; I told the officers, "It would be tragic if there was another murder which we could have prevented."

I made this request at least ten times, LAPD finally contending that if they did plant an undercover agent in the Family, he would have to commit crimes, for example, smoke marijuana. For there to be a crime, I noted, there had to be criminal intent; if he was doing it as part of his job, to catch a criminal, it wouldn't be a crime. When they balked at this, I said he didn't even have to be a police officer. If they had paid informers in narcotics, bookmaking, even prostitution cases, surely they could manage to come up with one in one of the biggest murder cases of our time. No dice.

Finally I turned to the DA's Bureau of Investigation and they found a young man willing to accept the assignment. I admired his determination, but he was clean-cut, with short hair, and looked as straight as they come. As desperate as we were for information, I couldn't send him into that den of killers; once they stopped laughing, they'd chop him to pieces. Eventually I had to abandon the idea. We remained in the dark as to what the Family was planning to do next.

April 1970

The words PIG, DEATH TO PIGS, RISE, and HEALTER SKELTER contain only thirteen different letters. Handwriting experts told me it would be extremely difficult—if not impossible—to match the bloody words found at the Tate and LaBianca residences with printing exemplars obtained from the defendants.

It wasn't only the small number of letters involved. The words were printed, not written; the letters were oversize; in both cases unusual writing implements had been used, a towel at the Tate residence, probably a rolled-up piece of paper at the LaBiancas; and all but the two words found on the refrigerator door at the latter residence had been printed high up on the walls, the person responsible having to stretch unnaturally high to make them.

As evidence, they appeared worthless.

However, thinking about the problem, I came up with an idea which, if successful, could convert them into very meaningful evidence. It was a gamble. But if it worked, it would be worth it.

We knew who had printed the words. Susan Atkins had testified before the grand jury that she had printed the word PIG on the front door of the Tate house, while Susan had told me, when I interviewed her, that Patricia Krenwinkel had admitted printing the words at the LaBiancas. Though Susan's grand jury testimony and her statements to me were inadmissible because of the deal we had made with her, she had confessed the printing at Tate to Ronnie Howard, so we had her on that. But we had nothing admissible on Krenwinkel.

The Fifth Amendment to the U.S. Constitution provides that no person "shall be compelled in any criminal case to be a witness against himself." The U.S. Supreme Court has ruled that this is limited to verbal utterances, and that a defendant cannot refuse to give physical evidence of himself, like appearing in a lineup, submitting to a breath-analysis test for drunken driving, giving fingerprint and handwriting exemplars, hair samples, and so on. After researching the law, I drew up very explicit instructions for Captain Carpenter at Sybil Brand, stating exactly how to request the printing exemplars of Susan Atkins, Patricia Krenwinkel, and Leslie Van Houten.

Each was to be informed: "(1) You have no constitutional right to refuse; (2) you have no constitutional right to have your attorney present; (3) your constitutional right to remain silent does not include the right to withhold printing exemplars; and (4) if you submit to this process, this can be used as evidence by the prosecution in your case."

Captain Carpenter assigned Senior Deputy H. L. Mauss to obtain the exemplars. According to my instructions, she informed Susan Atkins of the above, then told her: "The word PIG was printed in blood at the Tate residence. We want you to print the word PIG." Susan, without complaint, printed the exemplar as requested.

Leslie Van Houten and Patricia Krenwinkel were brought in individually and given similar instructions concerning their rights. However, each was told, *orally:* "The words HELTER SKELTER, DEATH TO PIGS, and RISE were printed in blood at the LaBianca residence. We want you to print those words."

In my memo to Captain Carpenter there was one additional instruction for the deputy: "Do not write any of this for them." I wanted to see if Krenwinkel misspelled "helter" as "healter" as she had on the refrigerator door.

Leslie Van Houten printed the exemplar.

Patricia Krenwinkel refused.

We'd won the gamble. We could now use her refusal in the trial as circumstantial evidence of her guilt.

As evidence, this was doubly important, since, before this, I'd had absolutely *no* independent evidence corroborating Linda Kasabian's testimony regarding Patricia Krenwinkel's involvement in the LaBianca murders. And without corroborating evidence, as a matter of law, Krenwinkel would have been entitled to an acquittal on those charges.

Though we'd won that gamble, Krenwinkel herself could just as easily have emerged the winner. Leslie could have refused to make an exemplar also, which would have diluted the force of Katie's refusal. Or Katie could have made the exemplar, the handwriting experts then failing to match her printing with that found at the LaBiancas.

We were less lucky when it came to putting the Tate-Sebring rope and the wire cutters in Manson's possession before the murders, evidence I was counting on to provide the necessary corroboration of Linda Kasabian's testimony as to Manson.

We knew from DeCarlo, who had been present, that Manson had purchased about 200 feet of the white, three-strand nylon rope at the Jack Frost surplus store in Santa Monica in June 1969. However, when Tate detectives finally interviewed Frost—three and a half months after my initial request—he was unable to find a purchase order for the rope. Nor could he definitely state that this was the same rope he had stocked.* An attempt to identify the manufacturer, then trace it back to Frost, also failed. Frost usually picked up his stock in odd lots from jobbers or through auctions, rather than directly from the manufacturer.

Just as these were blind alleys, so was one other—literally. According to DeCarlo, Manson had given part of the rope to George Spahn, for use on the ranch. Spahn's near blindness, however, eliminated him as a witness.

It was then I thought of Ruby Pearl.

For some reason, though the police had visited Spahn Ranch numerous times, none of the officers had interviewed Ruby, George's ranch manager. I found her a fund of valuable information. Examining the Tate-Sebring rope, she not only said it looked like the rope Manson had, she also supplied numerous examples of Manson's domination; recalled seeing the .22 Longhorn at the ranch many times; identified the leather thong found at the LaBiancas' as similar to the ones Manson often wore; and told me that, prior to the arrival of the Family at Spahn, she had never seen any Buck knives there, but that in the summer of 1969 "suddenly it seemed everyone had one."

While disappointed that we couldn't obtain documented proof of the rope sale, I was pleased with Ruby. Being an experienced horse wrangler—as well as a tough, gallant lady who showed not the slightest fear of the Family†—her testimony would carry weight. There was a fine streak of stubborn authority about her.

Another find was Randy Starr, whom I interviewed the same day as Ruby. A sometime movie stunt man who spe-

---

*Frost recalled stocking some three-strand, white nylon rope, but he believed it was ½ inch thick. The Tate-Sebring rope was ⅝ inch thick. While it was possible that Frost had been mistaken, or the rope had been mislabeled, the defense could argue that it simply wasn't the same rope.

†When Manson was brought to Los Angeles from Independence, Ruby Pearl visited him at the jail. "I only came here for one reason, Charlie," she told him. "I want to know where Shorty was buried."

Manson, unwilling to meet her gaze, looked down at the floor and remarked, "Ask the Black Panthers."

"Charlie, you know the Black Panthers have never been up to the ranch," she responded, turning her back on him and walking out.

cialized in fake hangings, Starr said the Tate-Sebring rope was "identical" to a rope he'd once used to help Manson pull a vehicle out of the creek bed. Starr told me, "Manson always kept the rope behind the seat in his dune buggy."

Even more important was Randy Starr's positive identification of the .22 Longhorn revolver, for Starr had once owned the gun and had given it to Manson.*

One question remained unanswered. Why, on the night of the Tate murders, did the killers bring along 43 feet 8 inches of rope? To tie up the victims? Manson accomplished this the next night with a single leather thong. I obtained a glimpse of a possible answer during one of my interviews with DeCarlo. According to Danny, in late July of 1969, Manson had told him that the establishment pigs "ought to have their throats cut and be hung up by their feet." This would really throw the fear into people, Manson said.

The logical inference, I felt, was that the killers brought along the rope intending to hang their victims. It was only a guess, but I suspected it was correct.

The wire cutters presented their own problems. Linda Kasabian said the pair found in Manson's dune buggy looked like the pair that had been in the car that night. Fine. Joe Granado of SID used them to test-cut a section of the Tate telephone wire and concluded that the two cuts were the same. Great. But then officer DeWayne Wolfer, considered LAPD's foremost expert on physical evidence, made some test cuts also, and he concluded that these wire cutters couldn't have been the ones used.

Not about to give up, I asked Wolfer if the tautness of the wire could have been a factor. Possibly, he said. I then asked Wolfer to accompany telephone company representatives to 10050 Cielo Drive and make another cut, only

*The gun, serial number 1902708, had been among a number of weapons taken from the Archery Headquarters in El Monte, California, during a burglary on the night of March 12, 1969. According to Starr, he obtained it in a trade with a man known only as "Ron." Manson was always borrowing the gun for target practice, and Randy finally gave it to him in trade for a truck that had belonged to Danny DeCarlo.

this time I wanted him to sever the wire while it was strung up and tight, the way it was the night of the murders. Wolfer eventually made the test, but his opinion remained unchanged: the actual cut made on the night of the murders and the test cut did not match.

While it was possible that the cutting edge of the wire cutters could have been damaged subseqeunt to the Tate murders, Wolfer's tests literally severed this important link between Manson and the Tate evidence.

When I'd accompanied LAPD to Spahn Ranch on November 19, 1969, we'd found a number of .22 caliber bullets and shell casings. Because of the terrific windstorm, and the necessity of following up other leads, our search had been cursory, however, and I'd asked Sergeant Lee to return and conduct a more thorough search. The much repeated request became even more important when, on December 16, 1969, LAPD obtained the .22 caliber Longhorn revolver. Yet it was not until April 15, 1970, that Lee returned to Spahn. Again concentrating on the gully area some two hundred feet behind George Spahn's residence, Lee found twenty-three more .22 caliber shell casings. Since twenty-two had been found during the first search, this brought the total to forty-five.*

It was not until after the latter search that Lee ran comparison tests on any of the Spahn shell casings. When he finally did, he concluded that fifteen of the forty-five had been fired from the Tate murder gun.†

Belatedly, but fortunately in time for the trial, we now had scientific evidence linking the gun to Spahn Ranch.

Only one thing would have made me happier: if Lee had returned and found the rest of the shell casings before the gun was discovered. As it was, the defense could contend that during the four and a half months between the

---

*None of the .22 caliber bullets recovered during the two searches matched up with the bullets found at the murder scene or those test-fired from the weapon.

†Lee determined this by comparing the rim marks on the Spahn shell casings with (1) the rim marks on the shell casings found in the cylinder of the weapon; (2) the rim marks of shell casings test-fired from the gun; and (3) the firing pin of the gun.

two searches the police and/or prosecution had "planted" this evidence.

For months one item of physical evidence had especially worried me: the pair of eyeglasses found near the trunks in the living room at the Tate murder scene. The natural conclusion was that if they didn't belong to any of the victims, they must belong to one of the killers. Yet neither Watson, Atkins, Krenwinkel, nor Kasabian wore glasses.

I anticipated that the defense would lean heavily on this, arguing that since they didn't belong to any of the defendants, at least one of the killers was still at large. From there it was only a short step to the conclusion that maybe the wrong people were on trial.

This posed an extremely serious problem for the prosecution. That problem, though not the mystery itself, vanished when I talked to Roseanne Walker.

Since Susan Atkins had confessed the murders to both Virginia Graham and Ronnie Howard, it occurred to me that she might have made incriminating statements to others, so I asked LAPD to locate any girls Atkins had been particularly close to at Sybil Brand.

One former inmate who agreed to talk to me, though she wasn't very happy about it, was Roseanne Walker. A pathetic, heavyset black girl who had been sent to Sybil Brand on five drug-related charges, Roseanne had been a sort of walking commissary, selling candy, cigarettes, and makeup to the other inmates. Not until the fifth or sixth time I interviewed her did Roseanne recall a conversation which, though it seemed unimportant to her, I found very significant.

Susan and Roseanne were listening to the radio one day, when the newscaster began talking about a pair of eyeglasses LAPD had found at the Tate murder scene. Amused, Susan remarked, "Wouldn't it be too much if they arrested the person the glasses belonged to, when the only thing he was guilty of was losing his glasses?"

Roseanne replied that maybe the glasses did belong to the killer.

Susan said, "That ain't the way it went down."

Susan's remark clearly indicated that the glasses did *not* belong to the killers.

Other problems remained. One of the biggest concerned Linda Kasabian's escape from Spahn Ranch.

Linda told me that she decided to flee after the night of the LaBianca murders; however, Manson sent her to the waterfall area later that day (August 11) and she was afraid to leave that night because of the armed guards he had posted.

Early the next morning (August 12) Manson sought her out. She was to put on a "straight" dress, then take a message to Mary Brunner and Sandra Good at Sybil Brand, as well as Bobby Beausoleil at the County Jail. The message: "Say nothing; everything's all right." After borrowing a car from Dave Hannum, a new ranch hand at Spahn, Linda went to Sybil Brand, but learned that Brunner and Good were in court; at the County Jail her identification was rejected and she wasn't allowed to see Beausoleil. When she returned to the ranch and told Manson she had been unsuccessful, he told her to try again the next day.

Linda saw her chance. That night she packed a shoulder bag with some clothing and Tanya's diapers and pins, and hid it in the parachute room. Early the next morning (August 13) she again borrowed Hannum's car. On going to get the bag, however, she found Manson and Stephanie Schram sleeping in the room. Deciding to forget the bag, she went to get Tanya, but discovered that the children had been moved to the waterfall area. There was no way she could go there to get Tanya, she said, without having to explain her actions. So she left the ranch without her.

Instead of going to Los Angeles as instructed, Linda began driving to Taos, New Mexico, where her husband was now living. Hannum's car broke down outside Albuquerque. When she tried to have it repaired, using a credit card Bruce Davis had earlier given her for gas, the gas station owner checked and learned the card was no longer valid. Linda then wrote a letter to Hannum, enclosing the keys, telling him where he could find the car, and apologizing. She then hitchhiked the rest of the way.

(Susan Atkins apparently intercepted the letter, as sh
gave Hannum the information and keys, but didn't sho
him the rest of the letter. Understandably unhappy, Ha
num took a bus to Albuquerque to reclaim the vehicle.)

Linda found her husband living with another girl in
commune at Lorien, outside Taos. She told him about th
Tate murders, the events of the second night, and leavin
Tanya at Spahn. Bob Kasabian suggested they return t
Spahn together and get Tanya, but Linda was afraid Mar
son would kill them all. Kasabian said he wanted to thin
about it for a few days. Unwilling to wait, Linda hitcl
hiked into Taos and went to see Joe Sage. Sage, who ha
a reputation for helping people, was a rather colorfu
character. When the fifty-one-year-old Zen monk wasn
busy running his Macrobiotic Church, he was campaigr
ing for president of the United States on an anti-pollutio
ticket. Linda asked Sage for enough money to return t
Los Angeles to get her little girl. Sage, however, bega
questioning Linda, and eventually she told him and
youth named Jeffrey Jacobs about the murders.

Not believing Linda's tale, Sage placed a call to Spab
Ranch, talking first to an unidentified girl, then to Manso
himself. Sage asked Manson—whose reaction can only b
imagined—if Linda's story was true. Manson told hir
Linda had flipped out; that her ego was not ready to die
and so she had run away.

Linda did not talk to Charlie, but she did talk to one o
the other girls—she believed, but was not sure, it wa
Squeaky—who told her about the August 16 raid. The au
thorities had kept Tanya, she learned; she was now in
foster home. Linda also spoke to Patricia Krenwinkel, Ka
tie saying something to the effect, "You just couldn't wai
to open your big mouth, could you?"

Linda subsequently called the Malibu police station an
learned the name of the social worker who was handlin
Tanya's case.* Sage gave Linda enough money for roun

*On calling the social worker, Linda learned that another gir
posing as Tanya's mother, had attempted to reclaim Tanya a sho
time before. Though I couldn't prove it, I suspected that Manso
had sent one of his girls to get Tanya, as insurance that Lind
wouldn't talk.

rip air fare, as well as the name of a Los Angeles attorney, Gary Fleischman, who he felt might be able to help her reclaim Tanya. When Linda saw Fleischman, she did not tell him about the murders, only that she had left the ranch to look for her husband. Eventually, after a court hearing, the mother and daughter were reunited and flew back to Taos. Bob was still involved with the other girl, however, and Linda took Tanya and hitchhiked first to Miami, Florida, where her father was living, then to her mother's home in Concord, New Hampshire. It was here, on December 2, 1969, when the news broke that she was being sought in connection with the Tate murders, that Linda turned herself in to the local police. Waiving extradition, she was returned to Los Angeles the next day.

I asked Linda, "Why, between the time you reclaimed Tanya and the date of your arrest in December, didn't you contact the police and tell them what you knew about the murders?"

She was afraid of Manson, Linda said, afraid that he might find and kill both her and Tanya. Also, she was pregnant, and didn't want to go through this ordeal until after the baby was born.

There were, of course, other reasons, the most important being her distrust of the police. In the drug-oriented world she inhabited, police were considered neither friends nor allies. I felt that this explanation, if properly argued, would satisfy the jury.

An even bigger question remained: "How could you leave your daughter in that den of killers?"

I was concerned not only with the jury's reaction to this, but also with the use to which the defense could put it. That Linda had left Tanya with Manson and the others at Spahn Ranch could be circumstantial evidence that she did not really believe them to be killers, clearly contradicting the main thrust of her testimony. Therefore both the question and her answer became extremely important.

Linda replied that she felt Tanya would be safe there, *just so long as she did not go to the police.* "Something within me told me that Tanya would be all right," Linda said, "that nothing would happen to her, and that now was

the time to leave. I knew I would come back and get he
I was just confident that she would be all right."

Would the jury accept this? I didn't know. This w
among my many concerns as the trial date drew ev
closer.

When contacted by Lieutenant Helder and Sergea
Gutierrez, both Sage and Jacobs verified Linda's story.
was unable to use either as a witness, however, most
their testimony being inadmissible hearsay. Ranch han
David Hannum said he had begun work at Spahn on A
gust 12, and that Linda had borrowed his car that san
day, as well as the next. And a check of the jail recore
verified that Brunner and Good *had* been in court on A
gust 12.

The various interviews yielded unexpected bonuse
Hannum said that once when he killed a rattlesnake, Ma
son had angrily castigated him, yelling, "How would yo
like it if I chopped your head off?" He then added, "I'
rather kill people than animals." At the same time I inte
viewed Linda's husband, Robert Kasabian, I also talked
Charles Melton, the hippie philanthropist from who
Linda had stolen the $5,000. Melton said that in Apr
1969 (before Linda ever met the Family) he had gone t
Spahn Ranch to see Paul Watkins. While there, Melto
had met Tex, who, admiring Melton's beard, commented
"Maybe Charlie will let me grow a beard someday."

It would be difficult to find a better example of Man
son's domination of Watson.

These were pluses. There were minuses. And they wer
big ones.

To prove to the jury that Linda's account of these tw
nights of murder wasn't fabricated out of whole cloth,
desperately needed some third person to corroborate an
part of her story. Rudolf Weber provided that corrobora
tion for the first night. But for the second night I had n
one. I gave LAPD this all-important priority assignment
Find the two officers who spoke to Manson and Linda o
the beach, the man whose door Linda knocked on tha
night, the man and woman at the house next to th

Malibu Feedbin, or any of the drivers who gave them rides. I'd like to have had all these people, but if they could turn up even one, I'd be happy.

Linda had located the spot where the two police officers stopped and questioned them. It was near Manhattan Beach. But, Los Angeles being the megalopolis that it is, it turned out to be an area where there were overlapping jurisdictions, not one but three separate law-enforcement agencies patrolling it. And a check of all three failed to turn up anyone who could recall such an incident.

We had better luck when it came to locating the actor Linda had mentioned. LaBianca detectives Sartuchi and Nielsen found him still living in Apartment 501, 1101 Ocean Front Walk, Venice. Not Israeli but Lebanese, his name was Saladin Nader, age thirty-nine. Unemployed since starring in *Broken Wings*, the movie about the poet Kahlil Gibran, he remembered picking up the two hitchhiking girls in early August 1969. He described both Sandy and Linda accurately, including the fact that Sandy was noticeably pregnant; picked out photos of each; and related essentially the same story Linda had told me, neglecting to mention only that he and Linda had gone to bed.

After questioning Nader, the investigating officers, according to their report, "explained to subject the purpose of the interview, and he displayed amazement that such sweet and sociable young ladies would attempt to inflict any harm upon his body after he assisted them to the best of his ability."

Though their stories jibed, Nader was only partial support for Linda's testimony, as (fortunately for him, and thanks to Linda) he did not encounter the group that night.

One floor down was the apartment of the man on whose door Linda had knocked. Linda had pointed out the door, 403, for us, and I'd asked Gutierrez and Patchett to try to locate the man, hopeful he'd recall the incident. When I got their report, it was on the tenant of 404. Returning, they learned from the landlady that 403 had been vacant during August 1969. It was possible some transient

may have been staying there, she said—it wouldn't ha
been the first time—but beyond that we drew a blank.

According to the rental manager of 3921 Topanga Ca
yon Boulevard—the house next to the Malibu Feedt
where Linda said she, Sadie, and Clem had stopped just b
fore dawn—a group of hippies had moved into the unre
ed building about nine months ago. There had been,
said, as many as fifty different persons living there, but
didn't know any of them. Sartuchi and Nielsen, howeve
did manage to locate two young girls who had lived the
from about February to October 1969. Both were frien
of Susan Atkins, and both recalled meeting Linda Kas
bian. One recalled that once Susan, another girl, and
male had visited them. She remembered the incident-
though not the date, the time, or the other perso
present—because she was "on acid" and the trio "a
peared evil." Both girls admitted that during this peri
they were "stoned" so much of the time their recollectio
were hazy. As witnesses, they would be next to useless.

Nor was LAPD able to locate any of the drivers wh
had picked up the hitchhikers that night.

The LaBianca detectives handled all these investigation
Going over their reports, I was convinced they had dor
everything possible to run down the leads. But we we
left with the fact that of the six to eight persons wh
could have corroborated Linda Kasabian's story of th
events of that second night, we hadn't found even one.
anticipated that the defense would lean heavily on this.

Any defendant may file at least one affidavit of preju
dice against a judge and have him removed from the cas
It isn't even necessary to give a reason for such a cha
lenge. On April 13, Manson filed such an affidavit again
Judge William Keene. Judge Keene accepted Manson
challenge, and the case was reassigned to Judge Charle
H. Older. Though more affidavits were expected—each d
fendant was allowed one—the defense attorneys, after
brief huddle, decided to accept Older.

I'd never tried a case before him. By reputation, th
fifty-two-year-old jurist was a "no nonsense" judge.
World War II fighter pilot who had served with the Flyin

Tigers, he had been appointed to the bench by Governor Ronald Reagan in 1967. This would be his biggest case to date.

The trial date was set for June 15. Because of the delay, we were again hopeful that Watson might be tried with the others, but that hope was quickly dashed when Watson's attorney requested, and received, still another postponement in the extradition proceedings.

The retrial of Beausoleil for the Hinman murder had begun in late March. Chief witness for the prosecution was Mary Brunner, first member of the Manson Family, who testified that she had witnessed Beausoleil stab Hinman to death. Brunner was given complete immunity in exchange for her testimony. Claiming that he had only been a reluctant witness, Beausoleil himself took the stand and fingered Manson as Hinman's murderer. The jury believed Brunner. In Beausoleil's first trial the case against him had been so weak that our office hadn't asked for the death penalty. This time prosecutor Burton Katz did, and got it.

Two things concerned me about the trial. One was that Mary Brunner did everything she could to absolve Manson—making me wonder just how far Sadie, Katie, and Leslie would be willing to go to save Charlie—and the other that Danny DeCarlo hedged on many of his previous statements to LAPD. I was worried that Danny might be getting ready to split, all too aware that he had little reason to stick around. Though the motorcycle engine theft charge had been dropped in return for his testimony in the Hinman case, we had made no deal with him on Tate-LaBianca. Moreover, although he had a good chance of sharing the $25,000 reward, it was not necessary that he testify to obtain it.

DeCarlo and Brunner did testify that same month before the grand jury, which brought additional indictments against Charles Manson, Susan Atkins, and Bruce Davis on the Hinman murder. But testifying before a grand jury in secret and having to face Manson himself in court were two different things.

Nor could I blame Danny for being apprehensive. As

soon as the grand jury indictments were made public, Davis, who had been living with the Family at Spahn, vanished.

May 1970

In early May, Crockett, Poston, and Watkins encountered Clem, Gypsy, and a youth named Kevin, one of the newer Family members, in Shoshone. Clem told Watkins: "Charlie says that when he gets out you all had better not be around the desert."

From a source at Spahn Ranch we learned that Family members there appeared to be "preparing for some activity."

The Manson girls were interviewed so often that they were on a first-name basis with many of the reporters. Inadvertently, several times they implied that Charlie would be out soon. Perhaps significantly, the girls said nothing about his being "acquitted" or "released."

It was obvious that something was being planned.

On May 11, Susan Atkins filed a declaration repudiating her grand jury testimony. Both Manson and Atkins used the declaration as basis for habeas corpus motions, which were subsequently denied.

Aaron and I conferred with District Attorney Younger. Sadie couldn't have it both ways. Either she had told the complete truth before the grand jury and, according to our agreement, we would not seek a first degree murder conviction against her, or, according to her recent declaration, she recanted her testimony, in which case the agreement was breached.

My personal opinion was that Susan Atkins had testified "substantially truthfully" before the grand jury, with these exceptions: her omission of the three other murder attempts the second night; her hedging on whether she had stabbed Voytek Frykowski (which she admitted to me when I interviewed her); and my instinctive, but strong, feeling (corroborated by her confessions to Virginia Graham and Ronnie Howard) that she had lied when she testified that she had not stabbed Sharon Tate. Under Atkins' agreement with our office, "substantially" wasn't good enough—she had to tell the complete truth.

With her declaration, however, the issue was closed. On the basis of her repudiation, Aaron and I asked Younger's permission to seek the death penalty against Susan Atkins as well as the other defendants. He granted it.

Sadie's about-face was not unexpected. Another change, however, caught almost everyone off guard. In court to petition for a new trial, Bobby Beausoleil produced an affidavit, signed by Mary Brunner, stating that her testimony in his trial "was not true," and that she had lied when she said Beausoleil stabbed Hinman to death.

Although obviously stunned, prosecutor Burt Katz argued that the other evidence in the trial was sufficient to convict Beausoleil.

Investigating further, Burt learned that a few days before she was due to testify, Mary Brunner had been visited by Squeaky and Brenda at her parents' home in Wisconsin. She was again visited by Squeaky, this time accompanied by Sandy, two days before she signed the affidavit. Burt charged that the girls, representing Manson, had coerced Mary Brunner into repudiating her testimony.

Called to the stand, Mary Brunner first denied this, then, after conferring with counsel, did another about-face, and repudiated her repudiation. Her testimony in the trial was true, she said. Still later she *again* reversed herself.

Eventually, Beausoleil's motion for a new trial was denied, and he was sent to San Quentin's Death Row to wait out his appeal. The District Attorney's Office was left with a perplexing legal dilemma, however. After her testimony in the Beausoleil trial, the Court had granted Mary Brunner complete immunity for her part in the Hinman murder.

Except for the possibility that she might be tried for

perjury, it looked as if Mary Brunner had managed to beat the rap.

Indicted on the Hinman murder, Manson appeared before Judge Dell to request that he be allowed to represent himself. When Dell denied the motion, Manson requested that Irving Kanarek and Daye Shinn be made his attorneys. Judge Dell ruled there would be "a clear conflict of interest" if Shinn represented both Manson and Susan Atkins. This left Kanarek.

Commenting, "I think we are well aware of Mr. Kanarek and his record," Manson told Judge Dell, "I do not wish to hire this man as my attorney, but you leave me no alternative. I understand what I am doing. Believe me, I understand what I am doing. *This is the worst man in town I could pick,* and you are pushing him on me." If Dell would permit him to represent himself, Manson said, then he would forget about having Kanarek.

"I am not going to be blackmailed," Dell told Manson.

MANSON   "Then I will take it up to the bigger father."

Judge Dell said that Manson could, of course, appeal his decision. However, since Manson was already appealing the revocation of his pro per status in the Tate-LaBianca proceedings, Dell was willing to postpone a final decision until that writ was either accepted or rejected.

Aaron and I discussed the possible Kanarek substitution with District Attorney Younger. In view of his record, with Kanarek on the case the prospect that the trial might last two or more years was very real. Younger asked us if there was any legal basis for removing an attorney from a case. We told him we knew of none; however, I'd research the law. Younger asked me to prepare an argument for the Court, and suggested that it stress Kanarek's incompetency. From what I had learned of Kanarek, I did not feel that he was incompetent. His obstructionism, I felt, was the major issue.

I had no trouble obtaining evidence of this. From judges, deputy DAs, even jurors, I heard examples of his dilatory, obstructionist tactics. One deputy DA, on learning that he had to oppose Kanarek a second time, quit the office; life was too short for that, he said.

Anticipating that Manson would ask to substitute Kanarek on Tate-LaBianca as well as Hinman, I began preparing my argument. At the same time I had another idea which just might make that argument unnecessary.

Maybe, with the right bait, I could persuade Manson to dump Kanarek himself.

On May 25, I was going through LAPD's tubs on the LaBianca case when I noticed, standing against the wall, a wooden door. On it was a multicolored mural; the lines from a nursery rhyme, "1, 2, 3, 4, 5, 6, 7—All Good Children Go to Heaven"; and, in large letters, the words "HELTER SKELTER IS COMING DOWN FAST."

Stunned, I asked Gutierrez, "Where in the hell did you get that?"

"Spahn Ranch."

"When?"

He checked the yellow property envelope affixed to the door.

"November 25, 1969."

"You mean for five months, while I've been desperately trying to link the killers with Helter Skelter, you've had this door, with those very words on it, the same bloody words that were found at the LaBianca residence?"

Gutierrez admitted they had. The door, it turned out, had been found on a cabinet in Juan Flynn's trailer. It had been considered so unimportant that to date no one had even bothered to book it into evidence.

Gutierrez did so the next day.

Again, as I had on numerous other occasions, I told the detectives that I wanted to interview Juan Flynn.

I had no idea how much Flynn actually knew. Along with Brooks Poston and Paul Watkins, the Panamanian cowboy had been interviewed by the authors of a quickie paperback that appeared even before the trial, but he obviously held back a great deal, since many of the incidents I'd learned about from Brooks and Paul were not included.

June 1-14, 1970

Two weeks before the start of the Tate-LaBianca trial, Manson requested, and obtained, the substitution of Irving Kanarek for Ronald Hughes.

I asked for a conference in chambers. Once there, I pointed out that the legal issues in this case were tremendously complex. Even with attorneys known to handle matters expeditiously, the trial could last four or more months. "But," I added, "it is my frank opinion that if Mr. Kanarek is permitted to represent Mr. Manson, the case could last several years." I noted, "It is common knowledge among the legal profession that Mr. Kanarek is a professional obstructionist. I believe the man is conscientious. I believe he is sincere." However, I continued, "there is no way for the Court to stop Mr. Kanarek. Even holding him in contempt will not stop this man, because he will gladly spend the night in jail."

Rather than have the trial become "a burlesque on justice," I had an alternative suggestion, I told the Court. It was one I had considered for a long time and, though I had discussed it with Aaron, I knew it would come as a surprise to everyone else.

"As a possible solution, the prosecution has no objection to permitting Mr. Manson to represent himself, as he has desired throughout, and let him have an attorney of his choice to assist him . . ."

Manson looked at me with a startled expression. This was probably the last thing he had expected to hear from the prosecution.

Although I was hoping that, given this opportunity, Manson would dump Kanarek, I was sincere in making the suggestion. From the start Manson had maintained that only he could speak for himself. He'd strongly implied that, failing in this, he'd make trouble. And there was no question in my mind that this was his reason for choosing Kanarek.

Too, even though lacking formal education, Manson was bright. Having dominated them in the past, he could cross-examine such prosecution witnesses as Linda Kasabian, Brooks Poston, and other ex-Family members with probably more effectiveness than many "straight" attorneys. And, to assist him in legal matters, he would have not only his own lawyer but three other experienced attorneys alongside him at the counsel table. Also, looking far ahead, I was concerned that the denial of Manson's request to defend himself might be an issue on appeal.

Aaron then quoted Manson's own statement, made in Judge Dell's court, that Kanarek was the worst man he could pick.

Kanarek objected so strongly to the proceedings that Judge Older remarked, "Now the things that Mr. Stovitz and Mr. Bugliosi said about you, Mr. Kanarek, while they might appear to be unfair, there certainly is, as a matter of common knowledge among the judges in this court, a good deal of truth in what they say. I am not impugning your personal motives, but you do have a reputation for taking an inordinately long time to do what someone else can do in a much shorter period . . ."

However, Older said, the only reason he was considering the matter was that he wanted to be absolutely sure Manson wanted Kanarek as his attorney. His remarks before Judge Dell had injected some doubt on that point.

In one respect, Manson replied, Kanarek would be the best attorney in town, "in a lot of respects, he would be the worst attorney that I could take." But, Manson continued, "I don't think there is any attorney that can represent me as well as I can myself. I am smart enough to realize that I am not an attorney, and I will sit behind these men and I won't make a scene. I am not here to make trouble . . .

"There is a lot involved here that does not meet the eye. A person is born, he goes to school, he learns what he is told in a book, and he lives his life by what he knows. The only thing he knows is what someone has told him. He is educated; he does what an educated person does.

"But go out of this realm, you go into a generation gap, a free-love society, you get into insane drugs or smoking marijuana." And in this other world the reality differs, Manson noted. Here experience alone is the teacher; here you discover "there is no way that you can know the taste of water unless you drink it or unless it has rained on you or unless you jump in the river."

THE COURT   "All I want to do, Mr. Manson, is find out if you are happy with Mr. Kanarek or if you have second thoughts."

MANSON   "I thought I explained that. I would not be happy with anyone but myself. No man can represent me."

I asked the Court's permission to question Manson. Though Kanarek objected, Charlie was agreeable. I asked him if he had consulted the other defense attorneys as to whether he should be represented by Kanarek. I had heard that two of them, Fitzgerald and Reiner, were very unhappy about Kanarek's entry into the case.

MANSON   "I don't ask other men's opinions. I have my own."

BUGLIOSI   "Do you feel Mr. Kanarek can give you a fair trial?"

MANSON   "I do. I feel *you* can give me a fair trial. You showed me your fairness already."

BUGLIOSI   "I will give you a fair trial, Charlie, but I am out to convict you."

MANSON   "What's a fair trial?"

BUGLIOSI   "That's when the truth comes out."

Declaring, "It would be a miscarriage of justice to permit you to represent yourself in a case having the complications this case has," Older again asked Manson, "Are you affirming Mr. Kanarek as your attorney?"

"I am forced into a situation," Manson replied. "My second alternative is to cause you as much trouble as possible."

A little over a week later we'd get our first sample of what he had in mind.

On being taken to Patton State Hospital in January, sixteen-year-old Dianne Lake had been labeled "schizophrenic" by a staff psychologist. Though I knew the defense would probably try to use this to discredit her testimony, I wasn't too worried, since psychologists are not doctors and are not qualified to make medical diagnoses. The staff psychiatrists, who were doctors, said her problems were emotional, not mental: behavioral disorders of adolescence plus possible drug dependence. They also felt she had made excellent progress and were now sure she would be able to testify at the trial.

With Sergeant Patchett, I visited Patton in early June. The little ragamuffin I'd first seen in the jail in Independence now looked like any teen-ager. She was getting straight A's in school, Dianne told me proudly; not until getting away from the Family, she said, had she realized how good life was. Now, looking back, she felt she had been in a "pit of death."

In interviewing Dianne, I learned a number of things which hadn't come out in her earlier interviews. While they were in the desert together, at Willow Springs, Patricia Krenwinkel had told her that she had dragged Abigail Folger from the bedroom into the living room of the Tate residence. And Leslie Van Houten, after admitting to her that she had stabbed someone, had commented that at first she had been reluctant to do so, but then she'd discovered the more you stabbed, the more fun it was.

Dianne also said that on numerous occasions, in June, July, and August of 1969, Manson had told the Family, "We have to be willing to kill pigs in order to help the black man start Helter Skelter."

And several times—she believed it was in July, about a month before the Tate-LaBianca murders—Manson had also told them, "*I'm* going to have to start the revolution."

The interview lasted several hours. One thing Dianne said struck me as very sad. Squeaky, Sandy, and the other girls in the Family could never love anyone else, not even their parents, she told me. "Why not?" I asked. "Because," she replied, "they've given all their love to Charlie."

I left Patton with the very strong feeling that Dianne Lake had now escaped that fate.

In court on June 9, Manson suddenly turned in his chair so his back was to the judge. "The Court has shown me no respect," Manson said, "so I am going to show the Court the same thing." When Manson refused to face the Court, Judge Older, after several warnings, had the bailiffs remove him from the courtroom. He was taken to the lockup adjoining the court, which was equipped with a speaker system so he could hear, though not participate in, the proceedings.

Although Older gave him several opportunities to return, on the understanding that he would agree to conduct himself properly, Manson rejected them.

We had not given up in our attempt to have Irving Kanarek taken off the case. On June 10, I filed a motion requesting an evidentiary hearing on the Kanarek-Hughes substitution. The thrust of my motion: Manson did not have the constitutional right to have Kanarek as his lawyer.

The right of counsel of one's choice, I argued, was not an unlimited, unqualified, absolute right. This right was given to defendants seeking a favorable verdict for themselves. It was obvious from Manson's statements that he wasn't picking Kanarek for this reason, but rather to subvert, thwart, and paralyze the due and proper administration of justice. "And we submit that he cannot use the right to counsel of his choice in such an ignoble fashion."

Kanarek responded that he would be glad to let the Court read the transcripts of his cases, to see if he used dilatory tactics. I thought I saw Judge Older wince at this, but I wasn't sure. Older's somber expression rarely changed. It was very difficult to guess what he was thinking.

In researching Kanarek's record, I had learned something which was not part of my hour-long argument. For all his filibustering, disconnected ramblings, senseless motions, and wild, irresponsible charges, Irving Kanarek frequently scored points. He noted, for example, that our office hadn't tried to challenge Ronald Hughes, who had never tried a case before, on the grounds that his representation might hurt Manson. And, in conclusion, Kanarek, very much to the point, asked that the prosecution's motion be struck "on the basis there is no basis for it in law."

I'd frankly admitted this in my argument, but had noted that this was "a situation so aggravated that it literally cries out to the Court to take a pioneer stand."

Judge Older disagreed. My motion for an evidentiary hearing was denied.

Although District Attorney Younger had Older's ruling appealed to the California Supreme Court, it was let stand. Though we had tried to save the taxpayers perhaps several million dollars and everyone involved a great deal of time and unnecessary effort, Irving Kanarek would remain on the Tate-LaBianca cases just as long as Charles Manson wanted him.

"If Your Honor does not respect Mr. Manson's rights, you need not respect mine," Susan Atkins said, rising and turning her back to the Court. Leslie Van Houten and Patricia Krenwinkel followed suit. When Older suggested that the defense attorneys confer with their clients, Fitzgerald admitted that would do little good, "because there is a minimum of client control in this case." After several warnings, Older had the girls removed to one of the vacant jury rooms upstairs, and a speaker was placed there also.

I had mixed feelings about all this. If the girls parroted Manson's actions during the trial, it would be additional evidence of his domination. However, their removal from the courtroom might also be considered reversible error on appeal, and the last thing we wanted was to have to try the whole case over again.

Under the current law, *Allen* vs. *Illinois*, defendants can be removed from a courtroom if they engage in disruptive conduct. Another case, however, *People* vs. *Zamora*, raised a subtler point. In that case, in which there were twenty-two defendants, the counsel tables were so situated that it was extremely difficult for the attorneys to communicate with their clients while court was in session. This led to a reversal by the Appellate Court, which ruled that the right of counsel implies the right of consultation between a defendant and his lawyer during the trial.

I mentioned this to Older, suggesting that some type of telephonic communication be set up. Older felt it unnecessary.

After the noon recess the girls professed a willingness to return. Speaking for all three, Patricia Krenwinkel told Older, "We should be able to be present at this play here."

To Krenwinkel it was just that—a play. Remaining standing, she turned her back to the bench. Atkins and Van Houten immediately mimicked her. Older again ordered all three removed.

Bringing all the defendants back into court the next day, Judge Older warned them that if they persisted in their conduct before a jury, they could badly jeopardize their cases. "So I would ask you to seriously reconsider what you are doing, because I think you are hurting yourselves." After again attempting to revert to pro per status, Manson said, "O.K., then you leave me nothing. You can kill me now."

Still standing, Manson bowed his head and stretched out his arms in a crucifixion pose. The girls quickly emulated him. When the deputies attempted to seat them, all resisted, Manson ending up scuffling with a deputy on the floor. Two deputies bodily carried him to the lockup, while the matrons took the girls out.

KANAREK "I would ask medical assistance for Mr. Manson, Your Honor."

THE COURT "I will ask the bailiff to check and see if he needs any. If he does, he will get it."

He didn't. Once in the lockup, out of sight of the press and spectators, Manson became an entirely different person. He donned another mask, that of the complaisant prisoner. Having spent more than half his life in reformatories and prisons, he knew the role all too well. Thoroughly "institutionalized," he played by the rules, rarely causing trouble in the jail itself.

After the noon recess we had several examples of Kanarek in action. Arguing a search-and-seizure motion, he said that Manson's arrest was illegal because "Mr. Caballero and Mr. Bugliosi conspired to have Miss Atkins make certain statements" and that "the District Attorney's Office suborned the perjury."

As ridiculous as this was, subornation of perjury is an extremely serious charge, and since Kanarek was making it in open court, in front of the press, I reacted accordingly.

BUGLIOSI "Your Honor, if Mr. Kanarek is going to have diarrhea of the mouth, I think he should make an offer of proof back in chambers. This man is totally irresponsible. I urgently request the Court we go back in chambers. God knows what this man is going to say next."

THE COURT "Confine yourself to the argument, Mr. Kanarek."

The argument, when Kanarek did eventually get around to making it, left even the other defense attorneys looking stunned. Kanarek stated that since "the warrant of arrest for the defendant Manson was based on illegally obtained and perjured testimony, therefore the seizure of the person of Mr. Manson was illegal. The person of Mr. Manson must, therefore, be suppressed from evidence."

While I was wondering how you could suppress a person, Kanarek provided an answer: he asked that "that piece of physical evidence which is Mr. Manson's physical body" not "be before the Court conceptually to be used in evidence." Presumably, by Kanarek's convoluted logic, witnesses shouldn't even be allowed to identify Manson.

Older denied the motion.

Another aspect of Irving Kanarek was exhibited that day: a suspicious distrust that at times bordered on paranoia. The prosecution had told the Court that we would not introduce Susan Atkins' grand jury testimony in the trial. One would think the introduction of this testimony—in which Susan stated that Charles Manson ordered the Tate-LaBianca murders—would have been the last thing Manson's attorney would want in evidence. But Kanarek, suddenly wary, charged that if we weren't using those statements, "they must be tainted in some way."

Older recessed court for the weekend. The preliminaries were over. The trial would begin the following Monday— June 15, 1970.

Part 6

THE TRIAL

**"If the tale that is unfolding were not
so monstrous, aspects of it would break the heart."**
Jean Stafford

Judge Charles Older's court, Department 104, was located on the eighth floor of the Hall of Justice. As the first panel of sixty prospective jurors was escorted into the crowded courtroom, their expressions changed from boredom to curiosity. Then, as eyes alighted on the defendants, mouths dropped open in abrupt shock.

One man gasped, loud enough for those around him to hear, *"My God, it's the Manson trial!"*

In chambers the chief topic was sequestration. Judge Older had decided that once jury selection was completed, the jurors would be locked up until the end of the trial— "to protect them from harassment and to prevent their being exposed to trial publicity." Arrangements had already been made for them to occupy part of a floor at the Ambassador Hotel. Although spouses could visit on weekends, at their own expense, bailiffs would take all necessary precautions to see that the jury remained isolated from both outsiders and any news about the case. No one was sure how long this would be—estimates of the trial's length ranged from three to six months and up—but obviously it would be severe hardship for those chosen.

STOVITZ "Your Honor has—and I don't say this in comedy—sentenced some felons for less than three months in custody."

THE COURT "No doubt about it."

FITZGERALD "Not at the Ambassador, though."

Although all the attorneys had some reservations about sequestration, only one strongly opposed it: Irving Kanarek. Since Kanarek had screamed the loudest about the taint of publicity adverse to his client, I concluded that Manson, not Kanarek, must have been behind the motion.

411

And I had my own opinion as to why Charlie didn't want the jury locked up.

Rumor had it that Judge Older himself had already received several threats. A secret memo he'd sent the sheriff, outlining courtroom security measures, ended with the following paragraph:

"The sheriff shall provide the trial judge with a driver-bodyguard, and security shall be provided at the trial judge's residence on a 24-hour basis, until such time as all trial and post-trial proceedings have been concluded."

Twelve names were drawn by lot. When the prospective jurors were seated in the jury box, Older explained that the sequestration could last "as much as six months." Asked if any felt this would constitute undue hardship, eight of the twelve raised their hands.*

Envisioning a mass exodus from the courtroom, Older was very strict when it came to excuses for cause. However, anyone who stated that he or she could not vote the death penalty under any circumstances was automatically excused, as was anyone who had read Susan Atkins' confession. This was usually approached obliquely, the prospective juror being asked something like "Have you read where any defendant has made any type of incriminating statement or confession?" to which several answered on the order of "Yes, that thing in the L.A. *Times*." Questioning on this and other issues dealing with pre-trial publicity was done individually and in chambers, to avoid contaminating the whole panel.

After Older finished the initial questioning, the attorneys began their individual voir dire (examination). I was disappointed in Fitzgerald, who led off. His questions were largely conversational, and quite often showed no sign of prior thought. For example: "Have you or any member of your family ever been the unfortunate victim of a homicide?" Fitzgerald asked this not once but twice, before one of his fellow lawyers nudged him and suggested that if the prospective juror was a homicide victim he wouldn't be of much use on a jury.

*Later, after obtaining revised estimates from the various attorneys, Judge Older changed this to "three or more months," after which the hardship excuses abruptly declined.

Reiner was much better. It was obvious that he was doing his best to separate his client, Leslie Van Houten, from the other defendants. It was also obvious that in doing so he was incurring Manson's wrath. Kanarek objected to Reiner's questions almost as often as did the prosecution.

Shinn asked the first prospective juror only eleven questions, seven of which Older ruled improper. His entire voir dire, including objections and arguments, took only thirteen pages of transcript.

Kanarek began by reading a number of questions obviously written by Manson. This apparently didn't satisfy Charlie, as he asked Older if he could ask the jurors "a few simple, tiny, childlike questions that are real to me in my reality." Refused permission, Manson instructed Kanarek: "You will not say another word in court."

Manson contended, Kanarek later told the Court, that he was already presumed guilty; therefore there was no need to question the jurors, since it didn't matter who was selected.

To my amazement, Kanarek, usually a very independent sort, actually followed Manson's instructions and declined to ask further questions.

Lawyers are not supposed to "educate" jurors during voir dire, but every lawyer worth his salt tries to predispose a jury to his side. For example, Reiner asked: "Have you read anything in the press, or heard anything on TV, to the effect that Charles Manson has a kind of 'hypnotic power' over the female defendants?" Obviously Reiner was less interested in the answer than in implanting this suggestion in the minds of the jurors. Similarly, walking the thin line between inquiry and instruction, I asked each juror: "Do you understand that the People only have the burden of proving a defendant guilty beyond a *reasonable* doubt; we do not have the burden of proving his guilt beyond *all* doubt—only a *reasonable* doubt?"

Initially, Older would not permit the attorneys to instruct the prospective jurors in the law. I had a number of heated discussions with him about this before he let us couch such questions in general terms. This was, I felt, an important victory. For example, I didn't want to go through the whole trial only to have some juror decide, "We can't convict Manson of the five Tate murders because he wasn't there. He was back at Spahn Ranch."

The heart of our case against Manson was the "vicarious liability" rule of conspiracy—each conspirator is criminally responsible for all the crimes committed by his co-conspirators if said crimes were committed to further the object of the conspiracy. This rule applies even if the conspirator was not present at the scene of the crime. For example: A, B and C decide to rob a bank. A plans the robbery, B and C carry it out. Under the law, A, though he never entered the bank, is as responsible as B and C, I pointed out to the jury.

From the prosecution's point of view, it was important that each juror understand such gut issues as reasonable doubt, conspiracy, motive, direct and circumstantial evidence, and the accomplice rule.

We hoped Judge Older would not declare Linda Kasabian an accomplice. But we were fairly sure he would,* in which case the defense would make much of the fact that no defendant can be convicted of any crime on the uncorroborated testimony of an accomplice. In researching the law, I found a California Supreme Court case, *People* vs *Wayne*, in which the Court said only "slight" evidence was needed to constitute corroboration. After I brought this to Older's attention, he permitted me to use the word "slight" in my questioning. This, too, I considered a significant victory.

Though Older had ascertained that each prospective juror could, if the evidence warranted it, vote a verdict of death, I went beyond this, asking each if he could conceive of circumstances wherein he would be willing to vote such a verdict against (1) a young person; (2) a female defendant; or (3) a particular defendant even though the evidence showed that he himself did not do any actual killing. Obviously I wanted to eliminate anyone who answered any of these questions negatively.

Manson and the girls caused no disruptions during jury selection. In chambers during the individual voir dire,

*He later did.

however, Manson would often stare at Judge Older for literally hours. I could only surmise that he had developed
his incredible concentration while in prison. Older totally
ignored him.

One day Manson tried it with me. I stared right back,
holding his gaze until his hands started shaking. During
the recess, I slid my chair over next to his and asked,
"What are you trembling about, Charlie? Are you afraid
of me?"

"Bugliosi," he said, "you think I'm bad and I'm not."

"I don't think you're all bad, Charlie. For instance, I
understand you love animals."

"Then you know I wouldn't hurt anyone," he said.

"Hitler loved animals too, Charlie. He had a dog named
Blondie, and from what I've read, Adolf was very kind
to Blondie."

Usually a prosecutor and a defendant won't exchange
two words during an entire trial. But Manson was no ordinary defendant. And he loved to rap. In this, the first of
many strange, often highly revealing conversations we
had, Manson asked me why I thought he was behind these
murders. "Because both Linda and Sadie told me you
were," I replied. "Now, Sadie doesn't like me, Charlie, and
she thinks you're Jesus Christ. So why would she tell me
this if it wasn't true?"

"Sadie's just a stupid little bitch," Manson said. "You
know, I only made love to her two or three times. After
she had her baby and lost her shape, I couldn't have cared
less about her. That's why she told that story, to get attention. I would never personally harm anyone."

"Don't give me that crap, Charlie, because I won't buy
it! What about Lotsapoppa? You put a bullet in his
stomach."

"Well, yeah, I shot that guy," Manson admitted. "He
was going to come up to Spahn Ranch and get all of us.
That was kinda in self-defense."

Manson was enough of a jailhouse lawyer to know that
I couldn't use anything he told me unless I'd first informed
him of his constitutional rights. Yet this, and many subsequent admissions, surprised me. There was a strange sort
of honesty about him. It was devious, it was never direct,

but it was there. Whenever I pinned him down, he might evade, but not once in this, or the numerous other conversations we had, did he flatly deny that he had ordered the murders.

An innocent man protests his innocence. Instead, Manson played word games. If he took the stand and did this, I felt the jury would see through him.

Would Manson take the stand? The general consensus was that Manson's prodigious ego, plus the opportunity to use the witness stand as a forum to expound his philosophy before the world press, would impel him to testify. But—though I had already put in many hours preparing my cross-examination—no one but Manson really knew what he would do.

Toward the end of the recess, I told him, "I've enjoyed talking to you, Charlie, but it would be much more interesting if we did it with you on the stand. I have lots and lots of things I'm curious about."

"For instance?"

"For instance," I replied, "where in the world—Terminal Island, Haight-Ashbury, Spahn Ranch—did you get the crazy idea that other people don't like to live?"

He didn't answer. Then he began to smile. He'd been challenged. And knew it. Whether he'd decide to accept the challenge remained to be seen.

Though silent in court, Manson remained active behind the scenes.

On June 24, Patricia Krenwinkel interrupted Fitzgerald's voir dire to ask that he be relieved as her attorney. "I have talked with him about the way I wish this to be handled right now, and he doesn't do as I ask," she told the Court. "He is to be my voice, which he is not . . ." Older denied her request.

Later the defense attorneys had a meeting with their clients. Fitzgerald, who had given up his Public Defender's job to represent Krenwinkel, emerged with tears in his eyes. I felt very badly about this and, putting my arm around his shoulder, told him, "Paul, don't let it get you down. She'll probably keep you. And if she doesn't, so what? They're just a bunch of murderers."

"They're savages, ingrates," Fitzgerald said bitterly. "Their only allegiance is to Manson."

Fitzgerald didn't tell me what had occurred during the meeting, but it wasn't hard to guess. Directly, or through the girls, Manson had probably told the attorneys: Do it my way or you're off the case. Fitzgerald and Reiner told Los Angeles *Times* reporter John Kendall that all the attorneys had been instructed to "remain silent" and not question prospective jurors.

When, the following day, Reiner disobeyed this order and continued his voir dire, Leslie Van Houten tried to fire him, repeating almost verbatim the words Krenwinkel had used. Older denied her request also.

What Reiner was going through could be gleaned from some of his questions. For example, he asked one prospective juror: "Even if it appears that Leslie Van Houten desired to stand or fall with the other defendants, could you nevertheless acquit her if the evidence against her was insufficient?"

On July 14 both the prosecution and the defense agreed to accept the jury. The twelve were then sworn. The jury consisted of seven men and five women, ranging in age from twenty-five to seventy-three, in occupation from an electronics technician to a mortician.*

It was very much a mixed jury, neither side getting exactly what it wanted.

Almost automatically, the defense will challenge anyone connected with law enforcement. Yet Alva Dawson, the oldest member of the jury, had worked sixteen years as a deputy sheriff with LASO, while Walter Vitzelio had been a plant security guard for twenty years, and had a brother who was a deputy sheriff.

---

*The twelve jurors were: John Baer, an electrical tester; Alva Dawson, a retired deputy sheriff; Mrs. Shirley Evans, a school secretary; Mrs. Evelyn Hines, a dictaphone-teletype operator; William McBride II, a chemical company employee; Mrs. Thelma McKenzie, a clerical supervisor; Miss Marie Mesmer, former drama critic for the now defunct Los Angeles *Daily News;* Mrs. Jean Roseland, an executive secretary; Anlee Sisto, an electronics technician; Herman Tubick, a mortician; Walter Vitzelio, a retired plant guard; and William Zamora, a highway engineer.

On the other hand, Herman Tubick, the mortician, and Mrs. Jean Roseland, a secretary with TWA, each had two daughters in approximately the same age group as the three female defendants.

Studying the jurors' faces as they were sworn, I felt that most appeared pleased to have been selected. After all, they had been chosen to serve on one of the most famous trials of all time.

Older was quick to bring them back to earth. He instructed them that when they came to court the following morning they should bring their suitcases, clothing, and personal items, as from that point on they would be sequestered.

There remained the selection of the alternate jurors. Because of the anticipated length of the trial, Older decided to pick six, an unusually large number. Again we went through the whole voir dire.

Only this time it was without Ira Reiner. On July 17, Leslie Van Houten formally requested that Reiner be relieved as her attorney and Ronald Hughes appointed instead.

After questioning Hughes, Manson, and Van Houten on the possibility of a conflict of interest, Judge Older granted the substitution. Reiner was out, receiving not even so much as a thank-you for the eight months he had devoted to the case. Manson's former attorney, the "hippie lawyer" Ronald Hughes, with his Santa Claus beard and Walter Slezak suits, became Leslie Van Houten's attorney of record.

Ira Reiner had been fired for one reason, and one reason only. He had tried to represent his client to the best of his ability. And he had properly decided that his client was not Charles Manson but Leslie Van Houten.

There was a slight but perceptible smile on Manson's face. With good reason. He had succeeded in forming a united defense team. Although Fitzgerald remained its nominal head, it was obvious who was calling the shots.

On July 21 the six alternates were sworn, and they too were sequestered.* Jury selection had taken five weeks, during which 205 people had been examined and nearly 4,500 pages of transcript accumulated.

It had been a rough five weeks. Older and I had clashed on several occasions, Reiner and Older even oftener. And Older had threatened four of the attorneys with contempt, carrying through on one.

Three were for violations of the gag order: Aaron Stovitz was cited for an interview he had given the magazine *Rolling Stone;* Paul Fitzgerald and Ira Reiner for their quoted remarks in the Los Angeles *Times* story "TATE SUSPECTS TRY TO SILENCE LAWYERS." Though Older eventually dropped the contempt citations against all three, Irving Kanarek was less lucky. On July 8 he was seven minutes late to court. He had a valid reason—it was very difficult to find a parking space at the time court convened—but Older, who had previously threatened Kanarek with contempt when he was just three minutes late, was not sympathetic. He ruled Kanarek in contempt and fined him twenty-five dollars.

While we were busy selecting a jury, two of Manson's killers were set free.

Mary Brunner was reindicted and rearrested for the Hinman murder. Her attorneys filed a writ of habeas corpus. Ruling that she had fufilled the conditions of the immunity agreement, Judge Kathleen Parker granted the writ and Brunner was released.

Meanwhile, Clem, t/n Steve Grogan, pleaded guilty to a grand theft auto charge stemming from the Barker raid. Van Nuys Judge Sterry Fagan heard the case. He was aware of Grogan's lengthy rap sheet. Moreover, the probation department, usually very permissive, in this case recommended that Grogan be sentenced to a year in the County Jail. Aaron also informed the judge that Clem was

*The six alternate jurors were: Miss Frances Chasen, a retired civil service employee; Kenneth Daut, Jr., a state Division of Highways employee; Robert Douglass, an employee of the Army Corps of Engineers; John Ellis, a telephone installer; Mrs. Victoria Kampman, a housewife; and Larry Sheely, a telephone maintenance man.

exceedingly dangerous; and that he had not only been along on the night the LaBiancas were killed, but we also had evidence that he had beheaded Shorty Shea. Yet unbelievably enough, Judge Fagan gave Clem straight probation!

On learning that Clem had returned to the Family at Spahn Ranch, I contacted his probation officer, asking him to revoke Clem's probation. There was more than ample cause. Among the terms of his probation were that he maintain residence at the home of his parents; seek and maintain employment; not use or possess any narcotics; not associate with known narcotics users. Moreover, he had been seen on several occasions, even photographed, with a knife and a gun.

His probation officer refused to act. He later admitted to LAPD that he was afraid of Clem.

Though Bruce Davis had gone underground, most of the other hard-core Family members were very much in evidence. Some dozen of them, including Clem and Mary, haunted the entrances and corridors of the Hall of Justice each day, where they would cast cold, accusing stares at the prosecution witnesses as they arrived to testify.

The problem of their presence in the courtroom—a concern since Sandy had been found carrying a knife—was solved by Aaron. Prospective witnesses are excluded when other witnesses are testifying. Aaron simply subpoenaed all the known Family members as prosecution witnesses, an act which raised a tremendous furor from the defense but made everyone else breathe a little easier.

July 24-26, 1970

TATE MURDER TRIAL STARTS TODAY

HINT PROSECUTION WILL REVEAL "SURPRISE MOTIVE"

SHARON'S FATHER EXPECTED TO BE FIRST WITNESS

Many of the spectators had been waiting since 6 A.M., hoping to get a seat and a glimpse of Manson. When he was escorted into the courtroom, several gasped. On his forehead was a bloody X. Sometime the previous night he had taken a sharp object and carved the mark in his flesh.

An explanation was not long forthcoming. Outside court his followers passed out a typewritten statement bearing his name:

"I have X'd myself from your world . . . You have created the monster. I am not of you, from you, nor do I condone your unjust attitude toward things, animals, and people that you do not try to understand . . . I stand opposed to what you do and have done in the past . . . You make fun of God and have murdered the world in the name of Jesus Christ . . . My faith in me is stronger than all of your armies, governments, gas chambers, or anything you may want to do to me. I know what I have done. Your courtroom is man's game. Love is my judge . . ."

THE COURT "People vs. Charles Manson, Susan Atkins, Patricia Krenwinkel, and Leslie Van Houten.

"All parties and counsel and jurors are present . . .

"Do the People care to make an opening statement?"

BUGLIOSI "Yes, Your Honor."

I began the People's opening statement—which was a preview of the evidence the prosecution intended to intro-

421

duce in the trial—by summarizing the charges, naming the defendants, and, after relating what had occurred at 10050 Cielo Drive in the early-morning hours of August 9, 1969, and at 3301 Waverly Drive the following night, identifying the victims.

"A question you ladies and gentlemen will probably ask yourselves at some point during this trial, and we expect the evidence to answer that question for you, is this:

"What kind of a diabolical mind would contemplate or conceive of these seven murders? What kind of mind would want to have seven human beings brutally murdered?

"We expect the evidence at this trial to answer that question and show that defendant Charles Manson owned that diabolical mind. Charles Manson, who the evidence will show at times had the infinite humility, as it were, to refer to himself as Jesus Christ.

"Evidence at this trial will show defendant Manson to be a vagrant wanderer, a frustrated singer-guitarist, a pseudo-philosopher, but, most of all, the evidence will conclusively prove that Charles Manson is a killer who cleverly masqueraded behind the common image of a hippie, that of being peace loving . . .

"The evidence will show Charles Manson to be a megalomaniac who coupled his insatiable thirst for power with an intense obsession for violent death."

The evidence would show, I continued, that Manson was the unquestioned leader and overlord of a nomadic band of vagabonds who called themselves the "Family." After briefly tracing the history and composition of the group, I observed: "We anticipate that Mr. Manson, in his defense, will claim that neither he nor anyone else was the leader of the Family and that he never ordered anyone in the Family to do anything, much less commit these murders for him."

KANAREK "Your Honor, he is now making an opening statement for us!"

THE COURT "Overruled. You may continue, Mr. Bugliosi."

BUGLIOSI "We therefore intend to offer evidence at this trial showing that Charles Manson was in fact the dictatorial leader of the Family; that everyone in the Family was slavishly obedient to him; that he always had the other members of the Family do his bidding for him; and that eventually they committed the seven Tate-LaBianca murders at his command.

"This evidence of Mr. Manson's total domination over the Family will be offered as circumstantial evidence that on the two nights in question it was he who ordered these seven murders."

The principal witness for the prosecution, I told the jury, would be Linda Kasabian. I then briefly stated what Linda would testify to, interrelating her story with the physical evidence we intended to introduce: the gun, the rope, the clothing the killers wore the night of the Tate murders, and so forth.

We came now to the question that everyone had been asking since these murders occurred: *Why?*

The prosecution does not have the burden of proving motive, I told the jury. We needn't introduce one single, solitary speck of evidence as to motive. However, when we have evidence of motive we introduce it, because if one has a motive for committing a murder, this is circumstantial evidence that it was he who committed the murder. "In this trial, we *will* offer evidence of Charles Manson's motives for ordering these seven murders."

If Manson and the defense were waiting to hear the word "robbery," they'd wait in vain. Instead, Manson's own beliefs came back at them.

"We believe there to be more than one motive," I told the jury. "Besides the motives of Manson's passion for violent death and his extreme anti-establishment state of mind, the evidence in this trial will show that there was a further motive for these murders, which is perhaps as bizarre, or perhaps even more bizarre, than the murders themselves.

"Briefly, the evidence will show Manson's fanatical obsession with Helter Skelter, a term he got from the English musical group the Beatles.

"Manson was an avid follower of the Beatles and believed that they were speaking to him across the ocean through the lyrics of their songs. In fact, Manson told his followers that he found complete support for his philosophy in the words of those songs . . .

"To Charles Manson, Helter Skelter, the title of one of their songs, meant the black man rising up and destroying the entire white race; that is, with the exception of Charles Manson and his chosen followers, who intended to escape from Helter Skelter by going to the desert and living in a bottomless pit, a place that Manson derived from Revelation 9, a chapter in the last book of the New Testament . . .

"Evidence from several witnesses will show that Charles Manson hated black people, but that he also hated the white establishment, whom he called 'pigs.'

"The word 'pig' was found printed in blood on the outside of the front door to the Tate residence.

"The words 'death to pigs,' 'helter skelter,' and 'rise' were found printed in blood inside the LaBianca residence.

"The evidence will show that one of Manson's principal motives for these seven savage murders was to ignite Helter Skelter; in other words, start the black-white revolution by making it look as though the black man had murdered these seven Caucasian victims. In his twisted mind, he thought this would cause the white community to turn against the black community, ultimately leading to a civil war between blacks and whites, a war which Manson told his followers would see bloodbaths in the streets of every American city, a war which Manson predicted and foresaw the black man as winning.

"Manson envisioned that black people, once they destroyed the entire white race, would be unable to handle the reins of power because of inexperience, and would therefore have to turn over the reins to those white people who had escaped from Helter Skelter; i.e., Charles Manson and his Family.

"In Manson's mind, his Family, and particularly he, would be the ultimate beneficiaries of a black-white civil war.

"We intend to offer the testimony of not just one witness but many witnesses on Manson's philosophy, because the evidence will show that it is so strange and so bizarre that if you heard it only from the lips of one person you probably would not believe it."

Thus far all the emphasis had been on Manson. Convicting Manson was the first priority. If we convicted the others and not Manson, it would be like a war crimes trial in which the flunkies were found guilty and Hitler went free. Therefore I stressed that it was Manson who had ordered these murders, though his co-defendants, obedient to his every command, actually committed them.

There was a danger in this, however. I was giving the attorneys for the three girls a ready-made defense. In the penalty phase of the trial, they could argue that since Atkins, Krenwinkel, and Van Houten were totally under Manson's domination, they were not nearly as culpable as he, and therefore should receive life imprisonment rather than the death penalty.

Anticipating long in advance that I'd have to prove the very opposite, I laid the groundwork in my opening statement:

"What about Charles Manson's followers, the other defendants in this case, Susan Atkins, Patricia Krenwinkel, and Leslie Van Houten?

"The evidence will show that they, along with Tex Watson, were the actual killers of the seven Tate-LaBianca victims.

"The evidence will also show that they were *very willing* participants in these mass murders, that by their overkill tactics—for instance, Rosemary LaBianca was stabbed forty-one times, Voytek Frykowski was stabbed fifty-one times, shot twice, and struck violently over the head thirteen times with the butt of a revolver—these defendants displayed that *even apart* from Charles Manson, murder ran through their own blood."

After mentioning Susan Atkins' confessions to Virginia Graham and Ronnie Howard; the fingerprint which placed Patricia Krenwinkel at the Tate murder scene; and the evidence which implicated Leslie Van Houten in the LaBianca murders, I observed: "The evidence will show that Charles Manson started his Family in the Haight-Ashbury district of San Francisco in March of 1967. The Family's

demise, as it were, took place in October of 1969 at
Barker Ranch, a desolate, secluded, rock-strewn hideout
from civilization on the shadowy perimeters of Death Valley. Between these two dates, seven human beings and an
eight-and-a-half-month baby boy fetus in the womb of
Sharon Tate met their death at the hands of these members of the Family.

"The evidence at this trial will show that these seven incredible murders were perhaps the most bizarre, savage,
nightmarish murders in the recorded annals of crime.

"Mr. Stovitz and I intend to prove not just beyond a
reasonable doubt, which is our only burden, but beyond *all*
doubt that these defendants committed these murders, and
are guilty of these murders; and in our final arguments to
you at the conclusion of the evidence, we intend to ask
you to return verdicts of first degree murder against each
of these defendants."

Noting that it would be a long trial, with many witnesses, I recalled the old Chinese proverb, "The palest ink
is better than the best memory," urging the jury to take
detailed notes to aid them in their deliberations.

I closed by telling the jury that we felt confident that
they would give both the defendants and the People of the
State of California the fair and impartial trial to which
each was entitled.

Kanarek had interrupted my opening statement nine
times with objections, all of which the Court had overruled.
When I finished, he moved that the whole statement be
stricken or, failing in that, a mistrial declared. Older denied
both motions. Fitzgerald told the press my remarks were
"scurrilous and slanderous," and called the Helter Skelter
motive "a truly preposterous theory."

I had a strong feeling that by the time of his closing argument to the jury, Paul wouldn't even bother to argue
this.

The defense reserving its opening statements until after
the prosecution had completed its case, the People called
their first witness, Colonel Paul Tate.

With military erectness, Sharon's father took the stand
and was sworn. Though forty-six, he looked younger, and

sported a well-trimmed beard. Before entering the court-room, he had been thoroughly searched, it being rumored that he had vowed to kill Manson. Even though he glanced only briefly at the defendants, and exhibited no discernible reaction, the bailiffs watched him every minute he was in the courtroom.

Our direct examination was brief. Colonel Tate described his last meeting with Sharon, and identified photos of his daughter, Miss Folger, Frykowski, Sebring, and the house at 10050 Cielo Drive.

Wilfred Parent, who followed Colonel Tate to the stand, broke down and cried when shown a photograph of his son, Steven.

Winifred Chapman, the Tate maid, was next. I questioned her in detail about the washing of the two doors; then, wanting to establish a chronology for the jurors, I took her up to her departure from the residence on the afternoon of August 8, 1969, intending to recall her to the stand later so she could testify to her discoveries the next morning.

On cross-examination Fitzgerald brought out that she hadn't mentioned washing the door in Sharon's bedroom until months after the murders, and then she had told this not to LAPD but to me.

This was to be the start of a pattern. Having questioned each of the witnesses not once but a number of times, I had uncovered a great deal of information not previously related to the police. In many instances I had been the only one who had interviewed the witness. Though Fitzgerald initially planted the idea, Kanarek would nurture it until, in his mind at least, it budded into a full-bloomed conspiracy, with Bugliosi framing the whole case.

Kanarek had only one question for Mrs. Chapman, but it was a good one. Had she ever seen the defendant Charles Manson before her appearance in court? She replied that she had not.

Although he had recently married and was not anxious to leave his bride, William Garretson had flown back from his home in Lancaster, Ohio, where he had returned after being released by LAPD. The former caretaker came across as sincere, though rather shy. Although I intended to call both officers Whisenhunt and Wolfer, the former to testify to finding the setting on Garretson's stereo at between 4 and 5, the latter to describe the sound tests he had conducted, I did question Garretson in detail as to the events of that night, and I felt the jury believed him when he claimed he hadn't heard any gunshots or screams.

I asked Garretson: "How loud were you playing your stereo?"

A. "It was about medium . . . It wasn't very loud."

This, I felt, was the best evidence Garretson was telling the truth. Had he been lying about hearing nothing, then surely he would have lied and said the stereo was loud.

Most of Fitzgerald's questions concerned Garretson's arrest and alleged rough handling by the police. At one point later in the trial Fitzgerald would maintain that Garretson was involved in at least some of the Tate homicides. Since there wasn't even a hint of this in his cross-examination, I'd conclude that he was belatedly looking for a convenient scapegoat.

Kanarek again asked the same question. No, he'd never seen Manson before, Garretson replied.

When I'd interviewed Garretson prior to his taking the stand, he'd told me that he still had nightmares about what had happened. That weekend, before his return to Ohio, Rudi Altobelli, who was now living in the main house, arranged for Garretson to revisit 10050 Cielo Drive. He found the premises quiet and peaceful. After that, he told me, the nightmares stopped.

By the end of the day we had finished with three more witnesses: Frank Guerrero, who had been painting the nursery that Friday; Tom Vargas, the gardener, who testified to the arrivals and departures of the various guests that day and to his signing for the two steamer trunks; and Dennis Hurst, who identified Sebring from a photograph as the man who came to the front door when he delivered the bicycle about eight that night.

The stage was now set for the prosecution's main witness, whom I intended to call to the stand first thing Monday morning.

On hearing my opening statement, Manson must have realized that I had his number.

At the conclusion of court that afternoon sheriff's deputy Sergeant William Maupin was escorting Manson from the lockup to the ninth floor of the jail when—to quote from Maupin's report—"inmate Manson stated to undersigned that it would be worth $100,000 to be set free. Inmate Manson also commented on how much he would like to return to the desert and the life he had before his arrest. Inmate Manson commented additionally that money meant nothing to him, that several people had contacted him regarding large sums of money. Inmate Manson also stated that an officer would only receive a six month sentence if caught releasing an inmate without authority."

Maupin reported the bribe offer to his superior, Captain Alley, who in turn informed Judge Older. Though the incident was never made public, Older gave the attorneys Maupin's report the next day. Reading it, I wondered what Manson would try next.

Over the weekend, Susan Atkins, Patricia Krenwinkel, and Leslie Van Houten lit matches, heated bobby pins red-hot, then burned X marks on their foreheads, after which they ripped open the burnt flesh with needles, to create more prominent scars.

When the jurors were brought into court Monday morning, the X's were the first thing they saw—graphic evidence that when Manson led, the girls followed.

A day or so later Sandy, Squeaky, Gypsy, and most of the other Family members did the same thing. As new disciples joined the group, this became one of the Family rituals, complete to tasting the blood as it ran down their faces.

Eight sheriff's deputies escorted Linda Kasabian from Sybil Brand to the Hall of Justice, through an entrance that circumvented those patrolled by the Family. When they reached the ninth floor, however, Sandra Good suddenly appeared in the corridor and screamed, *"You'll kill us all; you'll kill us all!"* Linda, according to those who witnessed the encounter, seemed less shaken than sad.

I saw Linda just after she arrived. Though her attorney, Gary Fleischman, had purchased a new dress for her, it had been misplaced, and she was wearing the same maternity dress she'd worn when pregnant. The baggy tent made her look more hippie-like than the defendants. After I'd explained the problem to Judge Older, he heard other matters in chambers until the dress was located and brought over. Later a similar courtesy would be extended to the defense when Susan Atkins lost her bra.

BUGLIOSI "The People call Linda Kasabian."

The sad, resigned look she gave Manson and the girls contrasted sharply with their obviously hostile glares.

CLERK "Would you raise your right hand, please?"

KANAREK "Object, Your Honor, on the grounds this witness is not competent and she is insane!"

BUGLIOSI "Wait a minute! Your Honor, I move to strike that, and I ask the Court to find him in contempt for gross misconduct. This is unbelievable on his part!"

Unfortunately, it was all too believable—exactly the sort of thing we had feared since Kanarek came on the case. Ordering the jury to disregard Kanarek's remarks, Older called counsel to the bench. "There is no question about it," Older told Kanarek, "your conduct is outrageous ..."

BUGLIOSI "I know the Court cannot prevent him from

speaking up, but God knows what he is going to say in the future. If I were to say something like this in open court, I would probably be thrown off the case by my office and disbarred . . ."

Defending Kanarek, Fitzgerald told the Court that the defense intended to call witnesses who would testify that Linda Kasabian had taken LSD at least three hundred times. The defense would contend, he said, that such drug use had rendered her mentally incapable of testifying.

Whatever their offer of proof, Older said, matters of law were to be discussed either at the bench or in chambers, *not* in front of the jury. As for Kanarek's outburst, Older warned him that if he did that once more, "I am going to take some action against you."

Linda was sworn. I asked her: "Linda, you realize that you are presently charged with seven counts of murder and one count of conspiracy to commit murder?"

A. "Yes."

Kanarek objected, moving for a mistrial. Denied. It was some ten minutes later before I was able to get in the second question.

Q. "Linda, are you aware of the agreement between the District Attorney's Office and your attorneys that if you testify to everything you know about the Tate-LaBianca murders, the District Attorney's Office will petition the Court to grant you immunity from prosecution and dismiss all charges against you?"

A. "Yes, I am aware."

Kanarek objected on four different grounds. Denied. By bringing this in first, we defused one of the defense's biggest cannons.

Q. "Besides the benefits which will accrue to you under the agreement, is there any other reason why you have decided to tell everything you know about these seven murders?"

Another torrent of objections from Kanarek before Linda was able to answer: "I strongly believe in the truth, and I feel the truth should be spoken."

Kanarek even objected to my asking Linda the number of children she had. Often he used a shotgun approach— "Leading and suggestive; no foundation; conclusion and hearsay"—in hope that at least some of the buckshot would hit. Many of his grounds were totally inapplicable. He would object to a "conclusion," for example, when no conclusion was called for, or yell "Hearsay" when I was simply asking her what she did next.

Since I'd anticipated this, it didn't bother me. However, it took over an hour to get Linda up to her first meeting with Manson, her description of life at Spahn Ranch, and, over Kanarek's very heated objections, her definition of what she meant by the term "Family."

A. "Well, we lived together as one family, as a family lives together, as a mother and father and children, but we were all just one, and Charlie was the head."

I was questioning Linda about the various orders Manson had given the girls when, unexpectedly, Judge Older began sustaining Kanarek's hearsay objections. I asked to approach the bench.

Lay people believe hearsay is inadmissible. Actually there are so many exceptions to the hearsay rule that many lawyers feel the law should read, "Hearsay is admissible except in these few instances."* I told Older: "I had anticipated many legal problems in this case, and I have done research on them—because I kind of play the Devil's advocate—but I never anticipated I'd have any trouble showing Manson's directions to members of the Family."

Older said he sustained the objections because he couldn't think of any exception to the hearsay rule that would permit the introduction of such statements.

This was crucial. If Older ruled such conversations inadmissible, there went the domination framework, and our case against Manson.

Shortly after this, court recessed for the day. Aaron, J. Miller Leavy, and I were up late that night, looking for citations of authority. Fortunately, we found two cases—*People* vs. *Fratiano* and *People* vs. *Stevens*—in which the Court ruled you can show the existence of a conspiracy by showing the relationship between the parties, including statements made to each other. Shown the cases the next

*For example, Susan Atkins' confessions to Virginia Graham and Ronnie Howard were hearsay, but admissible under the admission exception to the hearsay rule.

morning, Judge Older reversed himself and overruled Kanarek's objections.

Opposition now came from a totally unexpected direction: Aaron.

Linda had already testified that Manson ordered the girls to make love to male visitors to induce them to join the Family, when I asked her: "Linda, do you know what a sexual orgy is?"

Kanarek immediately objected, as did Hughes, who remarked, in a somewhat revealing choice of words: "We are not trying the sex lives of these people. We are trying the murder lives of these people."

Not only were the defense attorneys shouting objections, many of which Older sustained; Aaron leaned over to me and said, "Can't we skip this stuff? We're just wasting time. Let's get into the two nights of murder."

"Look, Aaron," I told him sotto voce, "I'm fighting the judge, I'm fighting Kanarek, I'm not going to fight you. I've got enough problems. This is important and I'm going to get it in."

As Linda finally testified, in between Kanarek's objections, *Manson* decided when an orgy would take place; *Manson* decided who would, and who would not, participate; and *Manson* then assigned the roles each would play. From start to finish he was the maestro, as it were, orchestrating the whole scene.

That Manson controlled even this most intimate and personal aspect of the lives of his followers was extremely powerful evidence of his domination.

Moreover, among the twenty-some persons involved in the particular orgy Linda testified to were Charles "Tex" Watson, Susan Atkins, Leslie Van Houten, and Patricia Krenwinkel.

The sexual acts were not detailed, nor did I question Linda about other such "group encounters." Once the point was made, I moved on to other testimony—Helter Skelter, the black-white war, Manson's belief that the Beatles were communicating with him through the lyrics of their songs, his announcement, late on the afternoon of August 8, 1969, that "Now is the time for Helter Skelter."

Describing her appearance on the stand, the Los Angeles *Times* noted that even in discussing the group's sex life, Linda Kasabian was surprisingly "serene, soft-spoken, even demure."

Her testimony was also at times very moving. Telling how Manson separated the mothers and their children, and relating her own feelings on being parted from Tanya, Linda said, "Sometimes, you know, when there wasn't anybody around, especially Charlie, I would give her my love and feed her."

Linda was describing Manson's directions to the group just before they left Spahn Ranch that first night when Charlie, seated at the counsel table, put his hand up to his neck and, with one finger extended, made a slitting motion across his throat. Although I was looking the other way and didn't see the gesture, others, including Linda, did.

Yet there was no pause in her reply. She went on to relate how Tex had stopped the car in front of the big gate; the cutting of the telephone wires; driving back down the hill and parking, then walking back up. As she described how they had climbed the fence to the right of the gate, you could feel the tension building in the courtroom. Then the sudden headlights.

A. "And a car pulled up in front of us and Tex leaped forward with a gun in his hand ... And the man said, 'Please don't hurt me, I won't say anything!' And Tex shot him four times."

As she described the murder of Steven Parent, Linda began sobbing, as she had each time she had related the story to me. I could tell the jury was moved, both by the mounting horror and her reaction.

Sadie giggled. Leslie sketched. Katie looked bored.

By the end of the day I had brought Linda to the point where Katie was chasing the woman in the white gown (Folger) with a knife and Tex was stabbing the big man (Frykowski): "He just kept doing it and doing it and doing it."

Q. "When the man was screaming, do you know what he was screaming?"

A. "There were no words, it was beyond words, it was just screams."

Reporters keeping track of Kanarek's objections gave up on the third day, when the count passed two hundred. Older warned Kanarek that if he interrupted either the witness or the prosecution again, he would find him in contempt. Often a dozen transcript pages separated my question and Linda's answer.

BUGLIOSI "We are going to have to go back, Linda. There has been a blizzard of objections."

KANAREK   "I object to that statement."

When Kanarek again interrupted Linda in mid-sentence, Older called us to the bench.

THE COURT   "Mr. Kanarek, you have directly violated my order not to repeatedly interrupt. I find you in contempt of Court and I sentence you to one night in the County Jail starting immediately after this court adjourns this afternoon until 7 A.M. tomorrow morning."

Kanarek protested that "rather than my interrupting the witness, the witness interrupted me"!

By day's end Kanarek would have company. Among the items I wished to submit for identification purposes was a photograph which showed the Straight Satans' sword in a scabbard next to the steering wheel of Manson's own dune buggy. Since the photograph had been introduced in evidence in the Beausoleil trial, I didn't get it until it was brought over from the other court. "The District Attorney is withholding great quantities of evidence from us," Hughes charged.

BUGLIOSI "For the record, I just saw it for the first time a few minutes ago myself."

HUGHES "That is a lot of shit, Mr. Bugliosi."

THE COURT "I hold you in direct contempt of Court for that statement."

Though in complete agreement with Older's earlier citing of Kanarek, I disagreed with his finding against Hughes, feeling if he was in contempt of anyone, it was me, not the Court. Too, it was based on a simple misunderstanding, one which, when explained to him, Hughes quickly accepted. Older was less understanding.

Given a choice between paying a seventy-five-dollar fine or spending the night in jail, Hughes told the Court: "I am a pauper, Your Honor." With no sympathy whatsoever, Older ordered him remanded into custody.

Kanarek learned nothing from his night in jail. The next morning he was right back interrupting both my questions and Linda's replies. Admonishments from the bench accomplished nothing; he'd apologize, then immediately do the same thing again. All this concerned me much less than the fact that he occasionally succeeded in keeping out testimony. Usually when Older sustained an objection, I could work my way around it, introducing the testimony in a different way. For example, when Older foreclosed me from questioning Linda about the defendants watching the news of the Tate murders on TV the day after those murders occurred, because he couldn't see the relevance of this, I asked Linda if, on the night of the murders, she was aware of the identities of the victims.

A.   "No."

Q.   "When was the first time you learned the names of these five people?"

A.   "The following day on the news."

Q.   "On television?"

A.   "Yes."

Q.   "In Mr. Spahn's trailer?"

A.   "Yes."

Q.   "Did you see Tex, Sadie, and Katie during the day following these killings, other than when you were watching television with them?"

A.   "Well, I saw Sadie and Katie in the trailer. I cannot remember seeing Tex on that day."

The relevance of this would become obvious when Barbara Hoyt took the stand and testified (1) that Sadie came in and told her to switch channels to the news; (2) that before this particular day Sadie and the others never watched the news; and (3) that immediately after the newscaster finished with Tate and moved on to the Vietnam war, the group got up and left.

In my questioning of Linda regarding the second night, there was one reiterated theme: Who told you to turn off the freeway? Charlie. Was anyone else in the car giving directions other than Mr. Manson? No. Did anyone question any of Mr. Manson's commands? No.

In her testimony regarding both nights, there were also literally a multitude of details which only someone who had been present on those nights of horrendous slaughter could have known.

Realizing very early how damaging this was, Manson had remarked, loud enough for both Linda and the jury to hear, "You've already told three lies."

Linda, looking directly at him, had replied, "Oh, no, Charlie, I've spoken the truth, and you know it."

By the time I had finished my direct examination of Linda Kasabian on the afternoon of July 30, I had the feeling the jury knew it too.

When I know the defense has something which might prove harmful to the prosecution's case, as a trial tactic I usually put on that evidence myself first. This not only converts a damaging left hook into a mere left jab, it also indicates to the jury that the prosecution isn't trying to hide anything. Therefore, I'd brought out, on direct, Linda's sexual permissiveness and her use of LSD and other drugs.* Prepared to destroy her credibility with these revelations, the defense found itself going over familiar ground. In doing so, they sometimes even strengthened our case.

It was Fitzgerald, Krenwinkel's defense attorney, not the prosecution, who brought out that during the period Linda was at Spahn, "I was not really together in myself . . . I was extremely impressionistic . . . I let others put ideas in me"; and—even more important—that she feared Manson.

Q. "What were you afraid of?" Fitzgerald asked.

A. "I was just afraid. He was a heavy dude."

Asked to explain what she meant by this, Linda replied, "He just had something, you know, that could hold you. He was a heavyweight. He was just heavy, period."

Fitzgerald also elicited from Linda that she loved Manson; that "I felt he was the Messiah come again."

*She had taken LSD about fifty times, she testified, the last time being in May 1969, three months prior to the murders.

Linda then added one statement which went a long way toward explaining not only why she but also many of the others had so readily accepted Manson. When she first saw him, she said, "I thought . . . 'This is what I have been looking for,' and this is what I saw in him."

Manson—a mirror which reflected the desires of others.

Q. "Was it also your impression that other people at the ranch loved Charlie?"

A. "Oh, yes. It seemed that the girls worshiped him, just would die to do anything for him."

Helter Skelter, Manson's attitude toward blacks, his domination of his co-defendants: in each of these areas Fitzgerald's queries brought out additional information which bolstered Linda's previous testimony.

Often his questions backfired, as when he asked Linda: "Do you remember who you slept with on August 8?"

A. "No."

Q. "On the tenth?"

A. "No, but eventually I slept with all the men."

Time and again Linda volunteered information which could have been considered damaging, yet, coming from her, somehow seemed only honest and sincere. She was so open that it caught Fitzgerald off guard.

Avoiding the word "orgy," he asked her, regarding the "love scene that took place in the back house . . . did you enjoy it?"

Linda frankly answered: "Yeah, I guess I did. I will have to say I did."

If possible, at the end of Fitzgerald's cross-examination Linda Kasabian looked even better than she had at the end of the direct.

It was Monday, August 3, 1970. I was on my way back to court from lunch, a few minutes before 2 P.M., when I was abruptly surrounded by newsmen. They were all talking at once, and it was a couple of seconds before I made out the words: "Vince, have you heard the news? *President Nixon just said that Manson's guilty!*"

Fitzgerald had a copy of the AP wire. In Denver for a conference of law-enforcement officials, the President, himself an attorney, was quoted as complaining that the press tended "to glorify and make heroes out of those engaged in criminal activities."

He continued: "I noted, for example, the coverage of the Charles Manson case ... Front page every day in the papers. It usually got a couple of minutes in the evening news. Here is a man who was guilty, directly or indirectly, of eight murders. Yet here is a man who, as far as the coverage is concerned, appeared to be a glamorous figure."

Following Nixon's remarks, presidential press secretary Ron Ziegler said that the President had "failed to use the word 'alleged' in referring to the charges."*

We discussed the situation in chambers. Fortunately, the bailiffs had brought the jury back from lunch before the story broke. They remained sequestered in a room upstairs, and so, as yet, there was no chance of their having been exposed.

Kanarek moved for a mistrial. Denied. Ever suspicious that the sequestration was not effective, he asked that the

---

*On the way back to Washington on *Air Force One*, President Nixon issued a supplementary statement:

"I have been informed that my comment in Denver regarding the Tate murder trial in Los Angeles may continue to be misunderstood despite the unequivocal statement made at the time by my press secretary.

"The last thing I would do is prejudice the legal rights of any person, in any circumstances.

"To set the record straight, I do not now and did not intend to speculate as to whether the Tate defendants are guilty, in fact or not. All the facts in the case have not yet been presented. The defendants should be presumed to be innocent at this stage of the trial."

jurors be voir dired to see if any had heard the news. As Aaron put it, "It would be like waving a red flag. If they didn't know about it before, they certainly will after the voir dire."

Older denied the motion "without prejudice," so it could be renewed at a later time. He also said he would tell the bailiffs to inaugurate unusually stringent security measures. Later that afternoon the windows of the bus used to transport the jury to and from the hotel were coated with Bon Ami to prevent the jurors from seeing the inevitable headlines. There was a TV set in their joint recreation room at the Ambassador; ordinarily they could watch any program they wished, except the news, a bailiff changing the channels. Tonight it would remain dark. Newspapers would also be banned from the courtroom, Older specifically instructing the attorneys to make sure none were on the counsel table, where they might inadvertently be seen by the jury.

When we returned to court, there was a smug grin on Manson's face. It remained there all afternoon. It isn't every criminal who merits the attention of the President of the United States. Charlie had made the big time.

The jury was brought down, and Atkins' defense attorney, Daye Shinn, began his cross-examination of Linda.

Apparently intent on implying that I had coached Linda in her testimony, he asked: "Do you recall what Mr. Bugliosi said to you during your first meeting?"

A. "Well, he has always stressed for me to tell the truth."

Q. "Besides the truth, I'm talking about."

As if anything else were important.

Q. "Did Mr. Bugliosi ever tell you that some of your statements were wrong, or some of your answers were not logical, or did not make sense?"

A. "No, I told him; he never told me."

Q. "The fact that you were pregnant, wasn't that the reason that you stayed outside [the Tate residence] instead of going inside to participate?"

A. "Whether I was pregnant or not, I would never have killed anybody."

Shinn gave up after only an hour and a half. Linda's testimony remained unshaken.

With a heavy, ponderous shuffle, Irving Kanarek approached the witness stand. His demeanor was deceiving. There was no relaxing when Kanarek was cross-examining; at any moment he might blurt out something objectionable. There was also no anticipating him; he'd suddenly skip from one subject to another with no hint of a connecting link. Many of his questions were so complex that even he lost the thought, and had to have the court reporter read them back to him.

It was excruciatingly tiring listening to him. It was also very important that I do so, since, unlike the two attorneys who preceded him, Kanarek scored points. He brought out, for example, that when Linda returned to California to reclaim Tanya, she told the social worker that she'd left the state on August 6 or 7—which, had this been true, would have been *before* the Tate-LaBianca murders occurred. If accurate, this meant that Linda had fabricated all of her testimony regarding those murders. And if she had lied to the social worker to get her daughter back, Kanarek implied, she could very well lie to this Court to get her own freedom.

But mostly he rambled and droned on and on, tiring the spectators as well as the witness. Many of the reporters "wrote off" Kanarek early in the proceedings. Given a choice of defense attorneys, they quoted Fitzgerald, whose questions were better phrased. But it was Kanarek, in the midst of his verbosity, who was scoring.

He was also beginning to get to Linda. At the end of the day—her sixth on the stand—she looked a little fatigued and her answers were less sharp. No one knew how many days of this lay ahead, since Kanarek, unlike the other attorneys, consistently avoided answering Older's questions about the estimated length of his cross-examination.

On my way home that night I was again thankful the jury had been sequestered. You could see the headlines on every newsstand. The car radio had periodic updates.

Hughes: "I am guilty of contempt for uttering a dirty word, but Nixon has the contempt of the world to face." Fitzgerald: "It is very discouraging when the world's single most important person comes out against you." The most reported quote was that of Manson, who had passed a statement to the press via one of the defense attorneys. Mimicking Nixon's remarks, it was unusually short and to the point: "Here's a man who is accused of murdering hundreds of thousands in Vietnam who is accusing me of being guilty of eight murders."

The next day in chambers Kanarek charged the President with conspiracy. "The District Attorney of Los Angeles County is running for attorney general of California. I say it without being able to prove it, that Evelle Younger and the President got together to do this."

If this was so, Kanarek said, "he shouldn't be President of the United States."

THE COURT "That will have to be decided in some other proceeding, Mr. Kanarek. Let's stay with the issues here . . . I am satisfied there has been no exposure of any of these jurors to anything the press may have said . . . I see no reason for taking any further action at this time."

Kanarek resumed his cross-examination. On direct, Linda had stated that she had taken some fifty LSD "trips." Kanarek now asked her to describe what had happened on trip number 23.

BUGLIOSI "I object to that question as being ridiculous, Your Honor."

Though there is no such objection in the rule books, I felt there should be. Apparently Judge Older felt similarly, as he sustained the objection. As well as others when I objected that a question had been repeated "ad nauseam" or was "nonsensical."

Just after the noon recess Manson suddenly stood and, turning toward the jury box, held up a copy of the front page of the Los Angeles *Times*.

A bailiff grabbed it but not before Manson had shown the jury the huge black headline:

MANSON GUILTY,
NIXON DECLARES

Older had the jury taken out. He then demanded to know which attorney, against his express orders, had brought a newspaper into court. There were several denials but no one confessed.

There was no question now that the jury would have to be voir dired. Each member was brought in separately and questioned by the judge under oath. Of the twelve jurors and six alternates, eleven were aware of the full headline; two saw only the words MANSON GUILTY; four only saw the paper or the name MANSON; and one, Mr. Zamora, didn't see anything: "I was looking at the clock at the time."

Each was also questioned as to his or her reaction. Mrs. McKenzie: "Well, my first thought was 'That's ridiculous.'" Mr. McBride: "I think if the President declared that, it was pretty stupid of him." Miss Mesmer: "No one does my thinking for me." Mr. Daut: "I didn't vote for Nixon in the first place."

After an extensive voir dire, all eighteen stated under oath that they had not been influenced by the headline and that they would consider only the evidence presented to them in court.

Knowing something about jurors, I was inclined to believe them, for a very simple reason. Jurors consider themselves privileged insiders. Day after day, they are a part of the courtroom drama. They hear the evidence. They, and they alone, determine its importance. They tend, very strongly, to think of themselves as the experts, those outside the courtroom the amateurs. As juror Dawson put it, he'd listened to every bit of the testimony; Nixon hadn't; "I don't believe Mr. Nixon knows *anything* about it."

My over-all feeling was that the jurors were annoyed with the President for attempting to usurp *their* role. It was quite possible that the statement might even have helped Manson, causing them to be even more determined that they, unlike the President, would give him every benefit of the doubt.

A number of national columnists stated that if Manson was convicted, his conviction would be reversed on appeal because of Nixon's statement. On the contrary, since it was Manson himself who brought the headline to the attention of the jury, this was "invited error," which simply means that a defendant cannot benefit from his own wrongdoing.

One aspect of this did concern me just a little. It was a subtler point. Although the headlines declared that Manson—not the girls—was guilty, it could be argued that as Manson's co-defendants the guilt "slopped over" onto them. Although I assumed this would be an issue they would raise on appeal, I felt fairly certain it would not constitute "reversible error." There are errors in every trial, but most do not warrant a reversal by the appellate courts. This might have, had not Older voir dired the jury and obtained their sworn statements that they would not be influenced by the incident.

Nor did the three female defendants exactly help their case when, the next day, they stood up and said in perfect unison: "Your Honor, the President said we are guilty, so why go on with the trial?"

Older had not given up his search for the culprit. Daye Shinn now admitted that just before court resumed he'd walked over to the file cabinet where the bailiff had placed the confiscated papers and had picked up several and brought them back to the counsel table. He'd intended to read the sports pages, he said, unaware that the front pages were also attached.

Declaring Shinn in direct contempt of Court, Older ordered him to spend three nights in the County Jail, commencing as soon as court adjourned. We were already past the usual adjournment time. Shinn asked for an hour to move his car and get a toothbrush, but Older denied the motion and Shinn was remanded into custody.

The next morning Shinn asked for a continuance. Being in a strange bed, and an even stranger place, he hadn't slept well the night before, and he didn't feel he could effectively defend his client.

These were not all of his troubles, Shinn admitted. "I

am now having marital problems, Your Honor. My wife thinks I am spending the night with some other woman. She doesn't read English. Now my dog won't even talk to me."

Declining comment on his domestic woes, Older suggested that Shinn catch a nap during the noon recess. Motion denied.

Irving Kanarek kept Linda Kasabian on the stand *seven days*. It was *cross*-examination in the most literal sense. For example: "Mrs. Kasabian, did you go to Spahn Ranch because you wanted to seek out fresh men, men that you had not had previous relations with?"

Unlike Fitzgerald and Shinn, Kanarek examined Linda's testimony regarding those two nights as if under a microscope. The problem with this, as far as the defense was concerned, was that some of her most damning statements were repeated two, three, even more times. Nor was Kanarek content to score a point and move on. Frequently he dwelt on a subject so long he negated his own argument. For example, Linda had testified that on the night of the Tate murders her mind was clear. She had also testified that after seeing the shooting of Parent she went into a state of shock. Kanarek did not stop at pointing out the seeming contradiction, but asked exactly when her state of shock ended.

A. "I don't know when it ended. I don't know if it ever ended."

Q. "Your mind was completely clear, is that right?"

A. "Yes."

Q. "You weren't under the influence of any drug, is that right?"

A. "No."

Q. "You weren't under the influence of anything, right?"

A. "I was under the influence of Charlie."

Although Linda remained responsive to the questions, it was obvious that Kanarek was wearing her down.

On August 7 we lost a juror and a witness.

Juror Walter Vitzelio was excused because both he and

his wife were in ill health. The ex-security guard was replaced, by lot, by one of the alternates, Larry Sheely, a
telephone maintenance man.

That same day I learned that Randy Starr had died at
the Veterans Administration Hospital of an "undetermined
illness."

The former Spahn ranch hand and part-time stunt man
had been prepared to identify the Tate-Sebring rope as
identical with the one Manson had. Even more important,
since Randy had given Manson the .22 caliber revolver,
his testimony would have literally placed the gun in Manson's hand.

Though I had other witnesses who could testify to these
key points, I was admittedly suspicious of Starr's sudden
demise. Learning no autopsy had been performed, I ordered one. Starr, it was determined, had died of natural
causes, from an ear infection.

KANAREK "Mrs. Kasabian, I show you this picture."

A.   *"Oh, God!"* Linda turned her face away. It was the
color photo of the very pregnant, and very dead, Sharon
Tate.

This was the first time Linda had seen the photograph,
and she was so shaken Older called a ten-minute recess.

There was no evidence whatsoever that Linda Kasabian
had been inside the Tate residence or that she had seen
Sharon Tate's body. Aaron and I therefore questioned Kanarek's showing her the photograph. Fitzgerald argued
that it was entirely possible that Mrs. Kasabian had been
inside both the Tate and LaBianca residences and had participated in all of the murders. Older ruled that Kanarek
could show her the photo.

Kanarek then showed Linda the death photo of Voytek
Frykowski.

A.   "He is the man that I saw at the door."

KANAREK "Mrs. Kasabian, why are you crying right
now?"

A.   "Because I can't believe it. It is just—"

Q.   "You can't believe what, Mrs. Kasabian?"

A.   "That they could do that."

Q. "I see. Not that *you* could do that, but that *they* could do that?"

A. "I know I didn't do that."

Q. "You were in a state of shock, weren't you?"

A. "That's right."

Q. "Then how do you know?"

A. "Because I know. I do not have that kind of thing in me, to do such an animalistic thing."

Kanarek showed Linda the death photos of all five of the Tate victims as well as those of Rosemary and Leno LaBianca. He even insisted that she handle the leather thong that had bound Leno's wrists.

Perhaps Kanarek hoped that he would so unnerve Linda that she would make some damaging admission. Instead, he only succeeded in emphasizing that, in contrast to the other defendants, Linda Kasabian was a sensitive human being capable of being deeply disturbed by the hideousness of these acts.

Showing Linda the photos was a mistake. And the other defense attorneys soon realized this. Each time Kanarek held up a picture, then asked her to look closely at some minute detail, the jurors winced or squirmed uncomfortably in their chairs. Even Manson protested that Kanarek was acting on his own. And still Kanarek persisted.

Ronald Hughes approached me in the hall during a recess. "I want to apologize, Vince——"

"No apology necessary, Ron. It was a 'heat of the moment' remark. I'm only sorry that Older found you in contempt."

"No, I don't mean that," Hughes said. "What I did was a hell of a lot worse. I was the one who suggested that Irving Kanarek become Manson's attorney."

On Monday, August 10, 1970, the People petitioned the Court for immunity for Linda Kasabian. Though Judge Older signed the petition the same day, it was not until the thirteenth that he formally dropped all charges against her and she was released. She had been in custody since December 3, 1969. Unlike Manson, Atkins, Krenwinkel, and

Van Houten, she had been in solitary confinement the whole time.

My wife, Gail, was worried. "What if she goes back on her testimony, Vince? Susan Atkins did; Mary Brunner did. Now that she has immunity—"

"Honey, I have confidence in Linda," I told her.

I did, yet in the back of my mind was the question: Where would the People's case be if that confidence was misplaced?

The next day Manson passed Linda a long handwritten letter. It seemed, at first, mostly nonsensical. Only on looking closer did one notice that key phrases had been marked with tiny check marks. Extracted, spelling errors intact, they read:

"Love can never stop if it's love . . . The joke is over. Look at the end and begin again . . . Just give yourself to your love & give your love to be free . . . If you were not saying what your saying there would be no tryle . . . Don't lose your love its only there for you . . . Why do you think they killed JC? Answer: Cause he was a Devil & bad. No one liked him . . . Don't let anyone have this or they will find a way to use it against me . . . This trile of Man's Son will only show the world that each man judges himself."

Coming just after she had been granted immunity, the message could only have one meaning: Manson was attempting to woo Linda back into the Family, in hopes that once freed she would repudiate her testimony.

Her answer was to give the letter to me.

Though a number of people had seen Manson pass Linda the letter, Kanarek maintained that she had grabbed it out of his hand!

The most effective cross-examination of Linda Kasabian was surprisingly that of Ronald Hughes. Though this was his first trial, and he frequently made procedural mistakes, Hughes was familiar with the hippie subculture, having been a part of it. He knew about drugs, mysticism, karma, auras, vibrations, and when he questioned Linda about these things, he made her look just a little odd, just a wee bit zingy. He had her admitting that she believed in ESP, that there were times at Spahn when she actually felt she was a witch.

Q. "Do you feel that you are controlled by Mr. Manson's vibrations?"

A. "Possibly."

Q. "Did he put off a lot of vibes?"

A. "Sure, he's doing it right now."

HUGHES "May the record reflect, Your Honor, that Mr. Manson is merely sitting here."

KANAREK "He doesn't seem to be vibrating."

Hughes asked Linda so many questions about drugs that, had an unknowing spectator walked into court, he would have assumed Linda was on trial for possession. Yet Linda's alert replies in themselves disproved the charge that LSD had destroyed her mind.

Q. "Now, Mrs. Kasabian, you testified that you thought Mr. Manson was Jesus Christ. Did you ever feel that anybody else was Jesus Christ?"

A. "The biblical Jesus Christ."

Q. "When did you stop thinking that Mr. Manson was Jesus Christ?"

A. "The night at the Tate residence."

Though I felt confident the jury was impressed with Linda, I was pleased to hear an independent evaluation. Hughes requested that the Court appoint psychiatrists to examine Linda. Older replied: "I find no basis for a psychiatric examination in this case. She appears to be perfectly lucid and articulate. I find no evidence of aberration of any kind insofar as her ability to recall, to relate. In all respects she has been remarkably articulate and responsive. The motion will be denied."

Hughes ended his cross-examination of Linda very effectively:

Q. "You have testified that you have had trips on marijuana, hash, THC, morning-glory seeds, psilocybin, LSD, mescaline, peyote, methedrine, and Romilar, is that right?"

A. "Yes."

Q. "And in the last year you have had the following

major delusions: You have believed that Charles Manson is Jesus Christ, is that right?"

A. "Yes."

Q. "And you believed yourself to be a witch?"

A. "Yes."

HUGHES   "Your Honor, I have no further questions at this time."

The basic purpose of redirect examination is to rehabilitate the witness. Linda needed little rehabilitating, other than being allowed to explain more fully replies which the defense had cut off. For example, I brought out that Linda meant "state of shock" figuratively, not medically, and that she was very much aware of what was going on.

On redirect the prosecution can also explore areas first opened on cross-examination. Since the theft of the $5,000 had come out on cross, I was able to bring in the mitigating circumstances: that after stealing the money, Linda had turned it over to the Family and that she neither saw it again nor benefited from it.

Not until the re-direct was I able to bring out why Linda had fled Spahn Ranch without Tanya.

The delay in getting this in was actually beneficial, I felt, for by this time the jury knew Linda Kasabian well enough to accept her explanation.

Direct. Cross. Redirect. Recross. Re-redirect. Re-recross. Just before noon on Wednesday, August 19, Linda Kasabian finally stepped down from the stand. She had been up there seventeen days—longer than most trials. Though the defense had been given a twenty-page summary of all my interviews with her, as well as copies of all her letters to me, *not once* had she been impeached with a prior inconsistent statement. I was very proud of her; if ever there was a star witness for the prosecution, Linda Kasabian was it.

Following the completion of her testimony, she flew back to New Hampshire for a reunion with her two children. For Linda, however, the ordeal was not yet over. Kanarek asked that she be subject to recall by the defense, and she would also have to testify when Watson was brought to trial.

Randy Starr was not the only witness the People lost during August.

Still afflicted with wanderlust, Robert Kasabian and Charles Melton had gone to Hawaii. I asked Linda's attorney, Gary Fleischman, if he could locate them, but he said they were off on some uncharted island, meditating in a cave, and there was no way to reach them. I'd wanted Melton especially, to testify to Tex's remark, "Maybe Charlie will let me grow a beard someday."

The loss of the other witness was a far greater blow to the prosecution. Saladin Nader, the actor whose life Linda had saved the night the LaBiancas were killed, had moved out of his apartment. He'd told friends he was going to Europe, but left no forwarding address. Although I requested the LaBianca detectives to try to locate him through the Lebanese Consulate and the Immigration Service, they were unsuccessful. I then asked them to interview his former landlady, Mrs. Eleanor Lally, who could at least testify that during August 1969 the actor had occupied Apartment 501, 1101 Ocean Front Walk, Venice. But with Nader's disappearance, we lost the only witness who could even partially corroborate Linda Kasabian's story of that second night.

On August 18, however, we found a witness—one of the most important yet to appear.

Over seven months after I had first tried to get Watkins and Poston to persuade him to come in for an interview, Juan Flynn decided he was ready to talk.

Fearful that he would become a prosecution witness, the Family had launched a campaign of harassment against the tall, lanky Panamanian cowboy that included threatening letters, hang-up phone calls, and cars racing past his trailer in the night, their occupants oinking or shouting "Pig!" All this had made Juan mad—mad enough to contact LASO, who in turn called LAPD.

Since I was in court, Sartuchi interviewed Flynn that afternoon at Parker Center. It was a short interview; transcribed, it ran to only sixteen pages, but it contained one very startling disclosure.

SARTUCHI "When did you first become aware of the

fact that Charles Manson was being charged with the crimes that he is presently on trial for?"

FLYNN "I became aware of the crimes that he is being charged with when he admitted to me of the killings that were taking place . . ."

In his broken English, Flynn was saying that Manson had admitted the murders to him!

Q. "Was there any conversation about the LaBiancas or was that all at the same time, or what?"

A. "Well, I don't know if it was at the same time, but he led me to believe—he told me that he was the main cause for these murders to be committed."

Q. "Did he say anything more than that?"

A. "He admitted—he boasted—of thirty-five lives taken in a period of two days."

When LAPD brought him to my office, I hadn't yet talked to Sartuchi or heard the interview tape, so when in interviewing Flynn I learned of Manson's very incriminating admission, it came as a complete surprise.

In questioning Juan, I established that the conversation had taken place in the kitchen at Spahn Ranch, two to four days after the news of the Tate murders broke on TV. Juan had just sat down to lunch when Manson came in and, with his right hand, brushed his left shoulder—apparently a signal that the others were to get out, since they immediately did. Aware that something was up, but not what, Juan started to eat.

(Ever since the arrival of the Family at Spahn Ranch, Manson had been trying to get the six-foot-five cowboy to join them. Manson had told Flynn: "I will get you a big gold bracelet and put diamonds on it and you can be my head zombie." There were other enticements. When first offered the same bait as the other males, Juan had sampled it eagerly, to his regret. "That damn case of clap just wouldn't go away," Juan told me, "not for three, four months." Though he had remained at Spahn, Juan had refused to be anybody's zombie, let alone little Charlie's. Of late, however, Manson had become more insistent.)

Suddenly Manson grabbed Juan by the hair, yanked his head back, and, putting a knife to his throat, said

"You son of a bitch, don't you know I'm the one who's doing all of these killings?"

Even though Manson had not mentioned the Tate-LaBianca murders by name, his admission was a tremendously powerful piece of evidence.*

The razor-sharp blade still on Juan's throat, Manson asked, "Are you going to come with me or do I have to kill you?"

Juan replied, "I am eating and I am right here, you know."

Manson put the knife on the table. "O.K.," he said. "You kill me."

Resuming eating, Juan said, "I don't want to do that, you know."

Looking very agitated, Manson told him. "Helter Skelter is coming down and we've got to go to the desert." He then gave Juan a choice: he could oppose him or join him. If he wanted to join him, Charlie said, "go down to the waterfall and make love to my girls."

(Manson's "my girls" was in itself a powerful piece of evidence.)

Juan told Charlie that the next time he wanted to contract a nine-month case of syphilis or gonorrhea, he'd let him know.

It was at this point that Manson boasted of killing thirty-five people in two days. Juan considered it just that, a boast, and I was inclined to agree. If there had been more than seven Manson-ordered murders during that two-day period, I was sure that at some point in the investigation we would have found evidence of them. Too, as far as the immediate trial was concerned, the latter statement was useless, as it was obviously inadmissible as evidence.

Eventually Manson picked up the knife and walked out.

*Legally, Manson's statement was an admission rather than a confession.

An admission is a statement by a defendant which is not a complete acknowledgment of guilt, but which tends to prove guilt when considered with the rest of the evidence.

A confession is a statement by a defendant which discloses his intentional participation in the criminal act for which he is on trial and which discloses his guilt for that crime.

And Juan suddenly realized he didn't have much appetit left.

I talked to Juan over four hours that night. Manson' admission was not the only surprise. Manson had tol Juan in June or July 1969, while Juan, Bruce Davis, an Clem were standing on the boardwalk at Spahn, "Well, have come down to it. The only way to get Helter Skelte going is for me to go down there and show the black ma how to do it, by killing a whole bunch of those fuckir pigs."

Among Flynn's other revelations: Manson had threa ened to kill him several times, once shooting at him wit the .22 Longhorn revolver; on several occasions Manso had suggested that Juan kill various people; and Flynn ha not only seen the group leave Spahn on probably the sam night the LaBiancas were killed; Sadie had told him, ju before they left, "We're going to get some fucking pigs."

Suddenly Juan Flynn became one of the prosecution' most important witnesses. The problem now was protect ing him until he took the stand. Throughout our intervie Juan had been extremely nervous; he'd tense at th slightest noise in the hall. He admitted that, because of hi fear, he hadn't had a full night's sleep in months. He aske me if there was any way he could be locked up until came time for him to testify.

I called LAPD and requested that Juan be put in eithe jail or a hospital. I didn't care which, just so long as b was off the streets.

Bemused by this unusual turnabout, Sartuchi, when h picked up Juan, asked him what he wanted to be arreste for. Well, Juan said, thinking a bit, he wanted to confes to drinking a beer in the desert a couple of months ag Since he was in a National Park, that was against the law Flynn was arrested and booked on that charge.

Juan remained in jail just long enough to decide h didn't like it one bit. After three or four days he tried t contact me. Unable to reach me right away, he calle Spahn Ranch and left a message for one of the ranc hands to come down and bail him out. The Family inter cepted the message, and sent Irving Kanarek instead.

Kanarek paid Juan's bail and bought him breakfast. He instructed Juan, "Don't talk to anyone."

When Juan had finished eating, Kanarek told him that he had already called Squeaky and the girls and that they were on their way over to pick him up. Hearing this, Juan split. Though he remained in hiding, he called in periodically, to assure me that he was still all right and that when the time came he would be there to testify.

Although it would never be mentioned in the trial, Juan had a special reason for testifying. Shorty Shea had been his best friend.

August 19-September 6, 1970

After Kasabian left the stand, I called a series of witnesses whose detailed testimony either supported or corroborated her account. These included: Tim Ireland, counselor at the girls' school down the hill from the Tate residence, who heard the cries and screams; Rudolf Weber, who described the hosing incident and dropped one bombshell: the license-plate number; John Swartz, who confirmed that was the number on his car and who told how, on two different nights in the first part of August 1969, Manson had borrowed the vehicle without asking permission; Winifred Chapman, who described her arrival at 10050 Cielo Drive on the morning of August 9, 1969; Jim Asin, who called the police after Mrs. Chapman ran down Cielo screaming, "Murder, death, bodies, blood!"; the first LAPD officers to arrive at the scene—DeRosa, Whisenhunt, and Burbridge—who described their grisly find. Bit by bit, piece by piece, from Chapman's arrival to the examination of the cut phone wires by the telephone company representative, the scene was re-created. The horror seemed to linger in the courtroom even after the witnesses had left the stand.

Since Leslie Van Houten was not charged with the five

Tate murders, Hughes did not question any of these wit
nesses. He did, however, make an interesting motion. He
asked that he and his client be permitted to absen
themselves from the courtroom while those murders wer
discussed. Though the motion was denied, his attempt to
separate his client from these events ran directly counter to
Manson's collective defense, and I wondered how Charli
was reacting to it.

When McGann took the stand, I questioned him a
some length as to what he had found at the Tate res
idence. The relevancy of many of the details—the pieces o
gun grip, the dimensions and type of rope, the absence o
shell casings, and so on—would become apparent to th
jury later. I was especially interested in establishing tha
there was no evidence of ransacking or robbery. I also go
in, ahead of the defense, that drugs had been found. An
a pair of eyeglasses.

Anticipating the next witness, Los Angeles Count
Coroner Thomas Noguchi, Kanarek asked for a confer
ence in chambers. He'd had a change of heart, Kanare
said. Though he'd earlier shown the death photos to Mr
Kasabian, "I have thought about it, and I believe I was i
error, Your Honor." Kanarek asked that the photos, parti
ularly those which were in color, be excluded. Motic
denied. The photos could be used for identification pu
poses. Older ruled; as to their admissibility as evidenc
that motion would be heard at a later time.

Each time Kanarek tried such a tactic, I thought, sure
he can't better this. And each time I found he not on
could but did.

Although I had interviewed Dr. Noguchi several time
I had a last conference with him in my office before v
went to court. The coroner, who had conducted Share
Tate's autopsy as well as supervised those of the oth
four Tate victims, had a habit of holding back little su
prises. There are enough of these in a trial without getti
them from your own witnesses, so I asked him outright
there was anything he hadn't told me.

Well, one thing, he admitted. He hadn't mentioned it
the autopsy reports, but, after studying the abrasions

her left cheek, he had concluded, "Sharon Tate was hung."

This was not the cause of death, he said, and she had probably been suspended less than a minute, but he was convinced the abrasions were rope burns.

I revised my interrogation sheets to get this in.

Although almost all of Dr. Noguchi's testimony was important, several portions were especially so in terms of corroborating Linda Kasabian.

Noguchi testified that many of the stab wounds penetrated bones; Linda had testified that Patricia Krenwinkel had complained that her hand hurt from her knife striking bones.

Linda testified that the two knives she'd thrown out the car window had about the same blade length, estimating, with her hands, an approximate length of between 5½ and 6½ inches. Dr. Noguchi testified that many of the wounds were a full 5 inches in depth. This was not only close to Linda's approximation, it also emphasized the extreme viciousness of the assaults.

Linda estimated the blade width at about 1 inch. Dr. Noguchi said the wounds were caused by a blade with a width of between 1 and 1½ inches.

Linda estimated the thickness as maybe two or three times that of an ordinary kitchen knife. Dr. Noguchi said the thickness varied from ⅛ to ½ inch, which corresponded to Linda's approximation.

Linda—who, on Manson's instructions, had several times honed knives similar to these while at Spahn Ranch—testified that the knives were sharpened on both sides, on one side all the way back to the hilt, on the other at least an inch back from the tip. Dr. Noguchi testified that about two-thirds of the wounds had been made by a blade or blades that had been sharpened on both sides for a distance of about 1½ to 2 inches, one side then flattening out while the other remained keen.*

---

*The other one-third of the wounds, Noguchi said, could have been made by a single-edged blade—but he didn't rule out the possibility that even these might have been made by a double-edged weapon, the unsharpened portion blunting the wound pattern so it appeared, on the surface, that a single-edged blade had been used.

As I'd later argue to the jury, Linda's description o
those two knives—their thickness, width, length, even th
fine point of the double-edged blade—was strong evidenc
that the two knives she was talking about were the sam
knives Dr. Noguchi had described.

In his cross-examination of Noguchi, Kanarek not onl
repeatedly referred to the victims' "passing away," h
spoke of Abigail Folger running to her "place of repose.
It was beginning to sound like a guided tour of Fores
Lawn.

The idiocy of all this was not lost on Manson. He com
plained: "Your Honor, this lawyer is not doing what I ar
asking him to do, not even by a small margin ... He i
not my attorney, he is your attorney. I would like to di
miss this man and get another attorney."

I was not sure whether Manson was serious or no
Even if he wasn't, it was still a good tactical move. Char
lie was in effect telling the jury, "Don't judge me by wha
this man says or does."

Kanarek then questioned Noguchi about each of Mis
Folger's twenty-eight stab wounds. His purpose, as he ad
mitted at the bench, was to establish "the culpability c
Linda Kasabian." Had she run for help, he suggested, pe
haps Miss Folger might still be alive.

There were several problems with this. At least for th
purpose of the questioning, Kanarek was in effect admit
ting Linda's presence at the scene. He was also stressing
over and over and over again, the involvement of Patrici
Krenwinkel. There was nothing unethical about this: Kan
arek's client was Manson. What was surprising was tha
Krenwinkel's own attorney, Paul Fitzgerald, didn't objec
more often.

Aaron spotted the basic fallacy of all this. "You
Honor, had Dr. Christiaan Barnard been present with a
operating room already set up to operate on the victim
the wound to the aorta would still have been fatal."

Later, while the jury was out, Older asked Manson if h
still desired to replace Kanarek. By this time Charlie ha
changed his mind. During the discussion Manson made a
interesting observation as to his own feelings on the pro
ress of the trial thus far: "We did pretty good at the fir

of it. Then we kind of lost control when the testimony started."

Although Channel 7 newscaster Al Wiman had actually been the first to spot the clothing the TV crew found, we called cameraman King Baggot to the stand instead. Had we used Wiman as a witness, he wouldn't have been able to cover any portion of the trial for his station. Before Baggot was sworn, the judge and attorneys conferred with him at the bench, to make sure there was no mention of the fact that Susan Atkins' confession had led them to the clothing. Thus, when Baggot testified, the jury got the impression that the TV crew just made a lucky guess.

After Baggot identified the various items of apparel, we called Joe Granado of SID. Joe was to testify to the blood samples he had taken.

Joe wasn't on the stand very long. He'd forgotten his notes and had to go get them. Fortunately, we had another witness ready, Helen Tabbe, the deputy at Sybil Brand who had obtained the sample of Susan Atkins' hair.

Although I liked Joe as a person, as a witness he left much to be desired. He appeared very disorganized; couldn't pronounce many of the technical terms of his trade; often gave vague, inconclusive answers. Granado's failure to take samples from many of the spots, as well as his failure to run subtypes on many of the samples he had taken, didn't exactly add to his impressiveness. I was particularly concerned about his having taken so few samples from the two pools of blood outside the front door ("I took a random sampling; then I assumed the rest of it was the same") and his failure to test the blood on the bushes next to the porch ("At the time, I guess, I assumed all of the blood was of similar origin"). My concern here was that those samples he had taken matched in type and subtype the blood of Sharon Tate and Jay Sebring, although there was no evidence that either had run out the front door. While I could argue to the jury that the killers, or Frykowski himself, had tracked out the blood, I could foresee the defense using this to cast doubt on Linda's story, so I asked Joe: "You don't know if the random sampling is representative of the blood type of the whole area here?"

A. "That is correct. I would have had to scoop everything up."

Granado also testified to finding the Buck knife in the chair and the clock radio in Parent's car. Unfortunately, someone at LAPD had apparently been playing the radio, as the dial no longer read 12:15 A.M., and I had to bring out that this occurred after Granado observed the time setting.

Shortly after the trial Joe Granado left LAPD to join the FBI.

Denied access to the courtroom, the Family began a vigil outside the Hall of Justice, at the corner of Temple and Broadway. "I'm waiting for my father to get out of jail," Sandy told reporters as she knelt on the sidewalk next to one of the busiest intersections in the city of Los Angeles. "We will remain here," Squeaky told TV interviewers, as traffic slowed and people gawked, "until all our brothers and sisters are set free." In interviews the girls referred to the trial as "the second crucifixion of Christ."

At night they slept in the bushes next to the building. When the police stopped that, they moved their sleeping bags into a white van which they parked nearby. By day they knelt or sat on the sidewalk, granted interviews, tried to convert the curious young. It was easy to tell the hard-core Mansonites from the transient camp followers. Each of the former had an X carved on his or her forehead. Each also wore a sheathed hunting knife. Since the knives were in plain view, they couldn't be arrested for carrying concealed weapons. The police did bust them several times for loitering, but after a warning, or at most a few days in jail, they were back, and after a time the police left them alone.

Nearby city and county office buildings provided restroom facilities. Also public phones, where, at certain prearranged times, one of the girls would await check-in calls from other Family members, including those wanted by the police. Several sob sisters who were covering the trial wrote largely sympathetic stories about their innocent, fresh, wholesome good looks and their devotion. They also often gave them money. Whether it was used for food or other purposes is not known. We did know the Family was adding to its hidden caches of arms and ammunition. The Family was against hunting animals, and it was a safe guess that they were stockpiling for something other than self-protection.

The deaths of her mother and stepfather had caused Susan Struthers to have a nervous breakdown. Though she was slowly recovering, we called Frank Struthers to the stand to identify photographs of Leno and Rosemary La-Bianca and to describe what he'd found on returning home that Sunday night. Shown the wallet found in the Standard station, Frank positively identified it, and the watch in the change compartment, as his mother's. On questioning by Aaron, Frank also testified that he had been unable to find anything else missing from the residence.

Ruth Sivick testified to feeding the LaBianca dogs on Saturday afternoon. No, she saw no bloody words on the refrigerator door. Yes, she had opened and closed the door, to get the food for the dogs.

News vendor John Fokianos, who testified to talking to Rosemary and Leno between 1 and 2 A.M. that Sunday, was followed by Hollywood Division officers Rodriquez and Cline, who described their arrival and discoveries at the crime scene. Cline testified to the bloody writings. Galindo, the first of the homicide officers to arrive, gave a detailed description of the premises, also stating: "I found no signs of ransacking. I found many items of value," which he then enumerated. Detective Broda testified to seeing, just prior to the autopsy of Leno LaBianca, the knife protruding from his throat, which, because of the pillowcase over the victim's head, the other officers had missed.

This brought us to Deputy Medical Examiner David Katsuyama. And a host of problems.

According to the first LaBianca investigative report, "The bread knife recovered from [Leno LaBianca's] throat appeared to be the weapon used in both homicides."

There was absolutely no scientific basis for this, since Katsuyama, who conducted both autopsies, had failed to measure most of the victims' wounds.

However, since the knife belonged to the LaBiancas, if this was let stand the defense could maintain that the killers had gone to the residence unarmed; ergo, they did not intend to commit murder. While a killing committed during the commission of a robbery is still first degree murder, this could affect whether the defendants escaped the death penalty. More important, it negated our whole theory of the case, which was that Manson, and Manson alone, had a motive for these murders, and that that motive was not robbery—a motive thousands of people could have—but to ignite Helter Skelter.

Shortly after I received the LaBianca reports, I ordered scale blowups of the autopsy photos, and asked Katsuyama to measure the length and thickness of the wounds. Initially I presumed there was no way to determine their depth, which would indicate the minimum length of the blade; however, in going over the coroner's original diagrams, I discovered that two of Rosemary LaBianca's wounds had been probed, one to the depth of 5 inches, the other 5½ inches, while two of Leno LaBianca's wounds were 5½ inches deep.

After many, many requests, Katsuyama finally measured the photos. I then compared his measurements with those of the bread knife. They came out as follows:

Length of blade of bread knife: 4⅞ inches.

Depth of deepest measurable wound: 5½ inches.

Thickness of blade of bread knife: just under ⅛₆ inch.

Thickness of thickest wound: ⅜₆ inch.

Width of blade of bread knife: from ⅜ to 1⅜₆ inch.

Width of widest wound: 1¼ inches.

There was no way, I concluded, that the LaBiancas' bread knife could have caused all the wounds. Length, width, thickness—in each the dimensions of the bread knife were smaller than the wounds themselves. Therefore the killers must have brought their own knives.

Recalling, however, how Katsuyama had confused a leather thong for electrical cord before the grand jury, I showed him the two sets of figures and—questioning him in much the same manner as I would in court—asked him: Had he formed an opinion as to whether the bread knife found in Leno LaBianca's throat could have made all of the wounds? Yes, he had, Katsuyama replied. What was his opinion? Yes, it could have.

Suppressing a groan, I asked him to compare the figures again.

This time he concluded there was no way the LaBianca knife could have made all those wounds.

To be doubly safe, the day I was to call him to the stand I interviewed him again in my office. Again he decided the knife could have made the wounds, then again he changed his mind.

"Doctor," I told him, "I'm not trying to coach you. If it's your professional opinion that all the wounds were made by the bread knife, fine. But the figures that you yourself gave me indicate that the bread knife couldn't possibly have caused all the wounds. Now, which is it? Only don't tell me one thing now and something different on the stand. You've got to make up your mind."

Even though he stuck to his last reply, I had more than a few apprehensive moments when it came time to question him in court. However, he testified: "These dimensions [of the bread knife] are much smaller than many of the wounds which I previously described."

Q. "So it's your opinion that this bread knife, which was removed from Mr. LaBianca's throat, could not have caused many of the other wounds, is that correct?"

A. "Yes, it is."

Rosemary LaBianca, Katsuyama also testified, had been stabbed forty-one times, sixteen of which wounds, mostly in her back and buttocks, having been made after she had died. Under questioning, Katsuyama explained that after death the heart stops pumping blood to the rest of the body, therefore postmortem wounds are distinguishable by their lighter color.

This was *very* important testimony, since Leslie Van Houten told Dianne Lake that she had stabbed someone who was already dead.

Though Dr. Katsuyama had come through on direct, I

was worried about the cross-examination. In his initial report the deputy coroner had the LaBiancas dying on the afternoon of Sunday, August 10—a dozen hours after their deaths actually occurred. This not only contradicted Linda's account of the events of that second night, it gave the defense an excellent opportunity to go alibi. Conceivably, they could call numerous people who would testify, truthfully, that while horseback riding at Spahn Ranch that Sunday afternoon they had seen Manson, Watson, Krenwinkel, Van Houten, Atkins, Grogan, and Kasabian.

I not only hadn't asked Katsuyama about the estimated time of death on direct, I hadn't even asked Noguchi this on the Tate murders, because—though I knew his testimony would have supported Linda's—I didn't want the jury to wonder why I asked Noguchi and not Katsuyama.

Since Fitzgerald led off the cross-examination, he always had first chance to explode any bombs in the defense arsenal, and this was certainly a big one. But he only said, "No questions, Your Honor." As, to my amazement, did Shinn, Kanarek, and Hughes.

I could think of only one possible explanation for this: though they had received all these reports through discovery, none of the four had realized their importance.

Susan Atkins had a stomach-ache. Though a fairly minor occurrence, in this instance it led to Aaron Stovitz' being yanked off the Tate-LaBianca case.

Four court days were lost when Susan Atkins complained of stomach pains which the doctors who examined and tested her said "did not exist." After sending the jury out, Judge Older called Susan to the stand, where she dramatically enumerated her ailments. Unimpressed, and convinced, "she is now putting on an act," Older brought the jury back in and resumed the trial. As he was leaving the courtroom, a reporter asked Aaron what he thought of Susan's testimony. He replied, "It was a performance worthy of Sarah Bernhardt."

The next morning Aaron was ordered to appear in District Attorney Younger's office.

After the *Rolling Stone* interview, Younger had told

Aaron: "No more interviews." Being somewhat easygoing by nature, Aaron had trouble complying with the edict. Once, when Younger was in San Francisco, he'd turned on the radio to hear Aaron commenting on some aspect of the day's courtroom proceedings. Though Aaron's comments were not in violation of the gag order, on his return to L.A. Younger warned Aaron, "One more interview and you're off the case."

I accompanied Aaron to Younger's office. There was no way Aaron's comment could be called an interview, I argued. It was simply a passing remark. All of us had made many such during the trial.* But Younger autocratically declared, "No, I've made up my mind. Stovitz, you're off the case."

I felt very badly about this. In my opinion, it was completely unfair. But in this case there was no appeal.

Since I had prepared the case and examined most of the witnesses, Aaron's removal did not affect this portion of the trial. We had agreed, however, that we would share the arguments to the jury, each of which would last several days. Having to handle them all myself added a tremendous burden to the load I was already carrying; in terms of time alone it meant another two hours of preparation each night, when I was already putting in four or five. Although two young deputy DAs, Donald Musich and Steven Kay, had been assigned to replace Aaron, neither was familiar enough with the case to handle either the questioning or the arguments.

Ironically, Steve Kay had once dated Family member Sandra Good, the pair, both of whom had grown up in San Diego, having gone on a date arranged by their mothers.

Sergeants Boen and Dolan of the Latent Prints Section of SID came across as the experts they were. Latents, exemplars, lift cards, smudges, fragmentary ridges, nonconductive surfaces, points of identity—by the time the two

*Although for diplomatic reasons I didn't mention it, Younger, who was currently running for attorney general of California on the Republican ticket, had himself called several press conferences during the trial, much to the displeasure of Judge Older.

officers had finished, the jury had been given a mini-course in fingerprint identification.

Boen described how he had lifted the latent prints found at the Tate residence, particularly focusing on the latent found on the outside of the front door and the latent on the inside of the left French door in Sharon Tate's bedroom.

Using diagrams and greatly magnified photographs I'd ordered prepared, Dolan indicated eighteen points of identity between the print lifted from the front door of the Tate residence and the right ring finger on the Watson exemplar and seventeen points of identity between the print lifted from the door of the master bedroom and the left little finger on the Krenwinkel exemplar. LAPD, he testified, requires only ten points of identity to establish a positive identification.

After Dolan had testified that there has never been a reported case of two separate persons having an identical fingerprint, or of any single person having two matching prints, I brought out, through him, that in 70 percent of the crimes investigated by LAPD's fingerprint men not a single readable print belonging to anyone is obtained. Therefore, I could later argue to the jury, the fact that none of Susan Atkins' prints were found inside the Tate residence did not mean she had not been there, since the absence of a clear, readable print is more common than uncommon.*

No print belonging to Manson, Krenwinkel, or Van Houten had been found at the LaBianca residence. Anticipating that the defense would argue this proved that none of them had been there, I asked Dolan about the handle of the fork found protruding from Leno LaBianca's stomach. It was ivory, he said, a surface which readily lends itself to latent prints. I then asked him: "Did you secure

---

*I could have broken this down further. A print matching that of a defendant is obtained at only 3 percent of the crime scenes visited by LAPD. Therefore 97 percent of the time they don't find a matching print. 97 percent is a powerful statistic when introduced in a case where none of the defendant's prints are found. My reason for not mentioning it in this case was obvious: LAPD had found not one but two matching prints at 10050 Cielo Drive.

anything at all from that fork, a smudge, a trace, a fragmentary fingerprint, anything at all?"

A.   "No, sir, there was not so much as a slight smudge on it; in fact it gave the impression to me"——Kanarek objected, but Older let Dolan finish——"it gave the impression to me that the handle of that particular fork had been wiped." Later, Dolan testified, he'd run a test: he'd grasped the fork with his fingers, then dusted it, "and found fragmentary ridges."

Although Mrs. Sivick had opened and closed the refrigerator door about 6 P.M. on the night of the murders, Dolan had found "not a smudge" on the chrome handle or enamel surface of the door. However, in examining the door, he testified, he did find "wipe-type marks."

Also important were the locations of the Krenwinkel and Watson latents at the Tate residence. That Krenwinkel's print had been found on the inside of the door which led from Sharon Tate's bedroom outside to the pool not only proved that Patricia Krenwinkel had been inside the residence, together with other evidence it indicated that she had probably chased Abigail Folger out this door. Blood spots inside the house, on the door itself, and outside the door were determined to be B-MN, Abigail Folger's type and subtype.* Therefore finding Krenwinkel's print here was completely consistent with Linda Kasabian's testimony that she saw Abigail running from this general direction chased by the knife-wielding Krenwinkel.

Even more conclusive was the position of the Watson print. Although Boen testified that it was on the outside of the front door, he'd also said that it was six to eight inches above the handle, near the edge, the tip of the finger pointing *downward*. As I illustrated to the jury, to leave the print where he did, Watson would have to be *inside* the Tate residence coming out. To make the print had he been outside, he would have had to twist his arm in a very uncomfortable and extremely unnatural direction. (Using the right ring finger and trying it both ways on a door, the reader will see what I mean.)

*Although Parent and Frykowski also had B-MN, there was no evidence Parent ever entered the Tate residence, while there was evidence that Frykowski had run out the front door.

The logical assumption was that Watson left his print while chasing Frykowski, Krenwinkel while in pursuit of Folger.

These were the strong points of the fingerprint testimony. There was one weak spot. Anticipating that the defense would try to make the most of those unidentified latents—twenty-five of the fifty found at the Tate residence, six of the twenty-five found at the LaBianca residence—I brought this out myself. But with several possible explanations. Since, as Dolan testified, no person has two matching fingerprints, it was possible the twenty-five unmatched Tate latents could have been made by as few as three persons, while the six at the LaBiancas' could even have been made by one person. Moreover, I established through Dolan that latent fingerprints can have a long life; under ideal conditions those inside a residence may last for several months. I could afford to point this out, since I'd already established that the two prints I was most concerned about, Krenwinkel's and Watson's, were on surfaces Winifred Chapman had recently washed.

I expected Fitzgerald to hit hardest on that one weak spot. Instead, he attacked Dolan where he was least vulnerable: his expertise. Earlier, I'd brought out that Dolan had been in the Latent Prints Section of SID for seven years, while assigned there conducting over 8,000 fingerprint investigations and comparing in excess of 500,000 latent fingerprints. Fitzgerald now asked Dolan: "Correct me if my mathematics are incorrect, Sergeant, but you testified you went to the scene of 8,000 crimes. If you went to one a day, and worked an average of 200 days a year, you would have been doing this for forty years?"

A. "I would have to figure that out on a piece of paper."

Q. "Assuming that you went to one crime scene per day—is that a fair statement, that you went to one crime scene per day, Sergeant?"

A. "No, sir."

Q. "How many crime scenes did you go to per day?"

A. "Anywhere, for two or three years there, between fifteen and twenty."

Q. "A day?"

A. "Yes, sir."

Fitzgerald had been knocked on his rump. Instead of getting up, dusting himself off, and moving onto safer territory, he set himself up for another pratfall by trying to attack the statistics. Had he done his homework (and, since a fingerprint was the only physical evidence linking his client to the murders, there was no excuse whatsoever for his not doing so) he would have learned, as the jury now did, that since 1940 SID had kept detailed records indicating exactly how many calls each officer made, the number of readable latents he obtained, and the number of times a suspect is thus identified.

Kanarek, in his cross-examination of Dolan, tried to imply that in using benzidine to test for blood, Granado could have destroyed some of the prints at the LaBianca residence. Unfortunately for Kanarek, Dolan noted that he had arrived at the LaBianca residence *before* Granado did.

Though Kanarek did less well with Dolan than some of the other prosecution witnesses, this didn't mean I could relax my guard. At any moment he was apt to do something like the following:

KANAREK "Your Honor, in view of the fact that the Los Angeles Police Department did not even choose to compare Linda Kasabian's fingerprints—"

BUGLIOSI "How do you know that, Mr. Kanarek?"

KANAREK "—I have no further questions of this witness."

THE COURT "Your comment is out of order."

BUGLIOSI "Would Your Honor admonish the jury to disregard that gratuitous remark of Mr. Kanarek's?"

Older did so.

Hughes' cross was brief and to the point. Had the witness compared a fingerprint exemplar of Leslie Van Houten with the latents found at the LaBianca residence? Yes. And none of those prints matched the prints of Leslie Van Houten, is that correct? Yes, sir. No further questions.

Hughes was learning, fast.

Apparently believing Kanarek was really on to something, Fitzgerald reopened his cross examination to ask:

"Now, did you have occasion to compare the latent fingerprints obtained at the Tate residence and the latent fingerprints obtained at the LaBianca residence against an exemplar of one Linda Kasabian?"

A. "Yes, sir, I did."

Q. "What was the result of that comparison?"

A. "Linda Kasabian's prints were not found at either
scene."

FITZGERALD "Thank you."

As much as possible, I tried to avoid embarrassing
LAPD. It wasn't always possible. Earlier, for example, I'd
had to bring in Sergeant DeRosa's pushing the gate-control button, so the jury wouldn't wonder why there was no
testimony regarding that particular print. In my direct examination of eleven-year-old Steven Weiss, I stuck to his
finding the .22 caliber revolver on September 1, 1969, and
did not go into the subsequent events. However, Fitzgerald, on cross, brought out that although an officer had
recovered the gun that same day, it was December 16,
1969, before LAPD Homicide claimed the weapon—after
Steven's father called and told them they already had the
gun they were looking for. Fitzgerald also brought out
how, after Steven had taken care not to eradicate any
prints, the officer who picked up the gun had done so
literally, putting his hands all over it.

I felt sorry for the next witness. The spectators had
barely stopped laughing when officer Watson of the Valley
Services Division of LAPD took the stand to testify that
he was the officer who recovered the gun.

Officer Watson's testimony was essential, however, for
he not only identified the gun—bringing out that it was
missing its right-hand grip and had a bent barrel and broken trigger guard—he also testified that it contained two
live rounds and seven empty shell casings.

Sergeant Calkins then testified that on December 16,
1969, he had driven from Park Center to the Valley Services Division to pick up the .22 caliber revolver.

On cross, Fitzgerald brought out that between September 3 and 5, 1969, LAPD had sent out some three-hundred
gun flyers—containing a photograph and detailed descrip-

tion of the type of revolver they were looking for—to different police agencies in the United States and Canada.

Lest the jury begin wondering why LAPD hadn't recovered the gun from the Valley Services Division immediately after the flyers went out, I was forced to ask Calkins, on redirect: "Did you ever send a flyer to the Valley Services Division of the Los Angeles Police Department in Van Nuys?"

A. "Not to my knowledge, sir."

To avoid further embarrassment to LAPD, I didn't ask how close the Valley Services Division was to the Tate residence.

September 7-10, 1970

Because of the State Bar Convention, court recessed for three days. I spent them working on my arguments, and worrying about a telephone call I'd received.

When court reconvened on the tenth, I made the following statement in chambers:

"One of our witnesses, Barbara Hoyt, has left her parents' home. I don't have all the details, but the mother said Barbara received a threat on her life, that if she testified at this trial she would be killed and so will her family.

"I know two things. I know the threat did not come from the prosecution and it did not come from an aunt I have that lives in Minnesota.

"I think the most reasonable inference is it came from the defense.

"I'm bringing this out because I want the defense attorneys and their clients to know that we are going to prosecute whoever is responsible for subornation of perjury. Not only will we prosecute, when our witnesses take the stand I will do my best to bring out, in front of the jury, that they received threats on their lives. It is relevant.

"I suggest the defendants tell their friends this."

When we returned to the courtroom, I had to leave such concerns behind and focus completely on the evidence we were presenting. It was crucial. Piece by piece we were trying to link the gun to Spahn Ranch and Charles Manson.

On Friday, before our long adjournment, Sergeant Lee of the Firearms and Explosives Unit of SID positively identified the Sebring bullet as having been fired from the gun. Lee also stated that while the other bullets recovered from the Tate scene lacked sufficient stria to make a positive identification, he found no markings or characteristics which would rule out the possibility that they too were fired from the same gun.

When I attempted to question Lee about still another link in this chain, the shell casings we had found at Spahn Ranch, Fitzgerald asked to approach the bench. It was the defense's contention, he said, that the shell casings were the product of an illegal search, and therefore inadmissible.

"Anticipating that just such an objection might be raised," I told the Court, "I obtained George Spahn's permission on tape. Sergeant Calkins should have it," I said. "He was there with me."

Only Calkins didn't have the tape. And now, nearly a week later, he still hadn't found it. Finally, I called Calkins to the stand to testify that we had obtained Spahn's permission. Cross-examined by Kanarek, Calkins denied that the tape had "disappeared" or was "lost"; he just hadn't been able to locate it, he said.

Older finally ruled the search valid, and Lee testified that when examined under a comparison microscope the shell casing he'd test-fired from the gun and fifteen of the shell casings he'd found at Spahn Ranch had identical firing pin compression marks.

Stria, lands, grooves, firing pin marks: after hours of highly technical testimony, and more than a hundred objections, most of them by Irving Kanarek, we had placed the Tate murder gun at Spahn Ranch.

Although he had agreed to testify, Thomas Walleman, aka T. J., was a reluctant witness. He'd never completely broken with the Family. He'd drift away, drift back. He seemed attracted by the easy life style, repelled by the memory of the night he saw Manson shoot Bernard Crowe.

Though I knew I couldn't get the shooting itself in during the guilt trial, I did question T. J. as to the events immediately prior to it. He recalled how, after receiving a telephone call, Manson borrowed Swartz' '59 Ford, got a revolver, then, with T. J. accompanying him, drove to an apartment house on Franklin Avenue in Hollywood. After stopping the car, Manson handed T. J. the revolver and told him to put it in his belt.

Q. "Then you both entered the apartment, is that correct?"

A. "Yes."

This was as far as I could go. I then showed T. J. the .22 caliber Hi Standard revolver and asked: "Have you ever seen that particular revolver before?"

A. "I don't think so. It looks like it, but I don't know for sure, you know."

T. J. was hedging. I wasn't about to let him get away with it. Under further questioning, he admitted that this gun differed from the gun he had seen that night in only one particular: half the grip was missing.

Q. "Now, your first statement, I believe, was to the effect that you didn't think this was the revolver, and then you said it looked like it."

A. "I mean, I don't know *for sure* whether it was the revolver, but *it looks like the revolver*. There are a lot of those made."

I wasn't worried about that little qualification, for Lomax of Hi Standard had already testified that this model was relatively uncommon.

Though qualified, T. J.'s testimony was dramatic, as he was the first witness to connect Manson and the gun.

LAPD contacted me that night. Barbara Hoyt was in a hospital in Honolulu. Someone had given her what was believed to be a lethal dose of LSD. Fortunately, she had been rushed to the hospital in time.

I did not learn many of the details until I talked to Barbara.

After fleeing Barker Ranch, the pretty seventeen-year-old had returned home. Though she had cooperated with us, Barbara was extremely reluctant to testify, and when she was contacted by the Manson girls on the afternoon of September 5 and offered a free vacation in Hawaii in lieu of testifying, she'd accepted.

Among the Family members who'd helped persuade her were Squeaky, Gypsy, Ouisch, and Clem.

Barbara spent that night at Spahn Ranch. The next day Clem drove Barbara and Ouisch to one of the Family hideouts, a house in North Hollywood which was being rented by one of the newer Family members, Dennis Rice.*

Rice took the pair to the airport, bought them tickets, and gave them fifty dollars in cash plus some credit cards, including, not inappropriately, a TWA "Getaway" card. Using assumed names, the two girls flew to Honolulu, where they booked the penthouse suite of the Hilton Hawaiian Village Hotel. Barbara saw little of the islands, however, since Ouisch, sure the police would be looking for Barbara, insisted they remain in the suite.

While there, the pair, who had been close friends, had several long talks. Ouisch told Barbara, "We all have to go through Helter Skelter. If we don't do it in our heads, we'll have to do it physically. If you don't die in your head, you'll die when it comes down." Ouisch also confided that Linda Kasabian was not long for this world; at the most, she had six months to live.

At approximately the same time each morning, Ouisch made a long-distance call. (The number was that of a pay

---

*Rice, thirty-one, had a rap sheet that went back to 1958 and, in common with Clem, had been convicted of offenses ranging from narcotics possession to indecent exposure. He was currently on probation for assaulting a police officer. Though new to the Family, he became one of its most hard-core members.

phone in North Hollywood, three blocks from the Rice residence. At least one of these calls was to Squeaky, the unofficial leader of the Family in Manson's absence.)

Just after the call on the ninth, Ouisch's manner suddenly changed. "She became very serious and looked at me kind of strangely," Barbara said. Ouisch told Barbara that she had to go back to California, but that Barbara was to remain in Hawaii. She called and made a reservation on the 1:15 flight to Los Angeles that afternoon.

They caught a cab to the airport, arriving just before noon. Ouisch said she wasn't hungry, but suggested that Barbara eat something. They went into a restaurant, and Barbara ordered a hamburger. When it arrived, Ouisch took it and went outside, telling Barbara to pay the check.

There was a line at the cash register, and for several minutes Barbara lost sight of Ouisch.

When she came out, Ouisch gave her the hamburger, and Barbara ate it while they were waiting for Ouisch's flight. Just before she was to board, Ouisch remarked, "Imagine what it would be like if that hamburger had ten tabs of acid in it." Barbara's response was, "Wow!" She had never heard of anyone taking more than one tab of LSD, Barbara later said, and the thought was kind of frightening.

After Ouisch left, Barbara began feeling high. She tried to take a bus to the beach but became so sick she had to get off. Panicked, she then started running, and ran and ran and ran until she collapsed.

A social worker, Byron Galloway, saw the young girl sprawled on a curb near the Salvation Army headquarters. Fortuitously, Galloway was employed at the State Hospital, his specialty drug cases. Realizing that the girl was extremely ill, he rushed her to Queen's Medical Center, where her condition was diagnosed as acute psychosis, drug-induced. The doctor who examined her was able to get her name and her Los Angeles address, but the rest made little sense: according to the hospital records, "Patient said, 'Call Mr. Bogliogi and tell him I won't be able to testify today in the Sharon Tate trial.'"

After giving her emergency treatment, the hospital called the police and Barbara's parents. Her father flew to

Hawaii and was able to bring her back to Los Angeles with him the next day.

On receiving the first fragmentary report, I told LAPD I wanted the persons involved charged with attempted murder.

Since Barbara was a witness in the Tate case, the investigation was given to Tate detectives Calkins and McGann.

September 11-17, 1970

Though I knew Danny DeCarlo was afraid of Manson, the motorcyclist did a good job of disguising it while on the stand. When Charlie and the girls smiled at "Donkey Dan," he grinned right back.

I was concerned that DeCarlo might qualify his answers, as he had in the Beausoleil trial. After only a few minutes of testimony, however, my concern suddenly shifted from DeCarlo to Older. When I tried to establish the Manson-Watson relationship through DeCarlo, Older repeatedly sustained the defense objections. He also sustained objections to Manson's dinnertime conversations when he discussed his philosophy about blacks and whites.

Back in chambers Older made two remarks which totally stunned me. He asked, "What is the relevance of whether or not Manson was the leader?" And he wanted an offer of proof as to the relevance of Helter Skelter! It was as if Older hadn't even been present during the trial thus far.

That I was more than a little disturbed at his stance came across in my reply: "The offer of proof is that he used to say that he wanted to turn blacks against whites. Of course, this is only the motive for these murders. That is all it is. Other than that, it is not much else."

I noted: "The prosecution is alleging Mr. Manson *ordered* these murders. It was his philosophy *that led up to* these murders. The motive for these murders was *to ignite Helter Skelter.* I think it is so obviously admissible that I am at a loss for words."

THE COURT   "I would suggest this to you, Mr. Bugliosi. Over the noon hour give some careful thought as to what you contend your proof is going to show. Now, I realize that part of it may have to come in through one witness and part through another. This is not unusual. But so far I can't see any connection between what Mr. Manson believed about blacks and whites in the abstract and any motive."

I sweated through that noon hour. Unless I could establish Manson's domination of the other defendants, I wouldn't be able to convince the jury they had killed on his instructions. And if Older foreclosed me from bringing in Manson's beliefs about the black-white war from De-Carlo, when my heavyweight witnesses on this—Jakobson, Poston, and Watkins—were still to come, then we were in deep trouble.

I returned to chambers armed with citations of authority as to both the admissibility and the relevance of the testimony. Yet even after a long, impassioned plea, it appeared that I had not changed Older's mind. He still couldn't see, for instance, the relevance of Watson's subservience to Manson, or why I was trying to bring out, through DeCarlo, that Tex had an easygoing, rather weak personality. The relevance, of course, was that if I didn't establish both, the jury could very well infer that it was Watson, not Manson, who had ordered these murders.

BUGLIOSI   "I think the Court can tell the relevancy by the fact the defense counsel are on their hind legs trying to keep it out."

KANAREK   "I think the heart of what we have here is this, that Mr. Bugliosi has lost his cool, because he has a monomania about convicting Mr. Manson."

BUGLIOSI   "He is charged with seven murders, and I am going to be tenacious on this ... I intend to go back with these witnesses and find out who Tex Watson was other than a name, Your Honor."

THE COURT   "I am not going to stop you from *trying,* Mr. Bugliosi."

On returning to court, I asked DeCarlo exactly the same question I had asked hours earlier: "What was your impression of Tex Watson's general demeanor?"

KANAREK "Your Honor, I will object to that as calling for a conclusion."

BUGLIOSI *"People* vs. *Zollner,* Your Honor."

I so anticipated Older saying "Sustained" that I almost thought I was imagining it when he said, "Overruled. You may answer."

DECARLO "He was happy-go-lucky. He was a nice guy. I liked Tex. He didn't have no temper or anything that I could see. He never said much."

Glancing back, I saw both Don Musich and Steve Kay staring in openmouthed disbelief. Moments ago in chambers Older had objected to my whole line of inquiry. He'd now completely reversed himself. Going as fast as I could through the questioning, before he again changed his mind, I brought out that whenever Charlie told Tex to do anything, Tex did it.

That Older had gone along with us on the domination issue didn't mean that he saw the relevance of Helter Skelter. My fingers were crossed when I asked: "Do you recall Mr. Manson saying anything about blacks and whites? Black people and white people?"

Stunned and perturbed, Kanarek objected: "It is the same question that he was asking previously!"

THE COURT "Overruled. You may answer."

A. "He didn't like black people."

DeCarlo testified that Manson wanted to see the blacks go to war with the police and the white establishment, both of whom he referred to as "pigs"; that Charlie had told him that the pigs "ought to have their throats cut and be hung up by their feet"; and that he had heard Manson use the term Helter Skelter many, many times. Through all this Kanarek objected repeatedly, often in the midst of DeCarlo's replies. Older told him: "You are interrupting, Mr. Kanarek. I have warned you several times today. I warn you now for the last time."

KANAREK "I don't wish to make unnecessary objections, Your Honor."

THE COURT "Don't you? Then cease from doing it."

Within minutes, however, Kanarek was doing it again, and Older called him to the bench. Very angrily, Older told Kanarek: "You seem to have some sort of physical infirmity or mental disability that causes you to interrupt and disrupt testimony. No matter how many times I warn you, you seem to do it repeatedly, again and again and again . . . You are trying to disrupt the testimony of this witness. It is perfectly clear. Now, I have gone as far as I am going to go with you, Mr. Kanarek."

Kanarek complained, "I am trying to conscientiously follow your orders."

THE COURT "No, no, I am afraid your explanation won't go. I have heard too much from you. I am very familiar with your tactics, and I am not going to put up with it any longer." Older found Kanarek in contempt of Court and, at the conclusion of the day's testimony, sentenced him to spend the weekend in the County Jail.

Danny DeCarlo had never really understood Helter Skelter, or cared to. As he admitted to me, his major interests while at Spahn were "booze and broads." He couldn't see how his testimony about this black-white stuff really hurt Charlie, and he testified to it freely and without qualification. But when it came to the physical evidence—the knives, the rope, the gun—he saw the link and pulled back, not much, but just enough to weaken his identifications.

In interviewing Danny, I'd learned a great many things which were not on the LAPD tapes. For example, he recalled that in early August 1969, Gypsy had purchased ten or twelve Buck knives, which had been passed out to various Family members at Spahn. The knives, according to DeCarlo, were about 6 inches in length, 1 inch in width, ⅛ inch in thickness—very close to the dimensions provided by Kasabian and Noguchi. In going through the sheriff's reports of the August 16 raid, I found that a large number of weapons had been seized (including a submachine gun in a violin case) but not a single Buck knife.

The logical presumption, I'd later argue to the jury, was that after the murders the rest of the Buck knives had been ditched.

I intended to call Sergeant Gleason from LASO to tes-

tify that no knives were found in the raid. First, however, I
wanted Danny to testify to the purchase. He did, but he
qualified it somewhat. When I asked him who bought the
Buck knives, he replied: "I'm not sure. I think Gypsy did,
I'm not sure."

When it came to the Tate-Sebring rope, DeCarlo testified it was "similar" to the rope Manson had purchased
at the Jack Frost store. I persisted: "Does it appear to be
different in any fashion?"

A.   "No."

DeCarlo had told me that Charlie preferred knives and
swords to guns because "in the desert guns could be heard
for a long distance." I asked DeCarlo if, among the guns
at Spahn Ranch, Manson had a special favorite. Yeah,
DeCarlo said, a Hi Standard .22 caliber Buntline revolver.
I showed him the gun and asked him: "Have you ever
seen this revolver before?"

A.   "I saw one similar to it."

Q.   "Does it appear to differ in any fashion?"

A.   "The trigger guard is broken."

Other than that?

A.   "I can't be sure."

Q.   "Why can't you be sure?"

A.   "I don't know. I don't know the serial number of
it. I am not sure that is it."

DeCarlo had cleaned, cared for, and shot the gun. He
had an extensive background in weapons. The model was
unusual. And he had made a drawing of it for LAPD even
before he was told that such a gun had been used in the
Tate homicides. (I'd already introduced the drawing for
identification purposes, over Kanarek's objection that it
was "hearsay.") If anyone should have been able to make
a positive identification of that revolver, it was Danny De-
Carlo. He didn't do so, I suspected, because he was afraid
to.

Though he was a shade weaker on the stand than in our
interviews, I did succeed in getting a tremendous amount of
evidence in through DeCarlo. Though court was interrupted for another three-day recess, DeCarlo's direct took
less than a day and a half of actual court time. I completed it on September 17.

That morning Manson passed word through Fitzgerald and Shinn that he wanted to see me in the lockup during the noon recess. Kanarek was not present, though the other two attorneys were.

I asked Manson what he wanted to talk to me about.

"I just wanted you to know that I didn't have anything to do with the attempted murder of Barbara Hoyt," Manson said.

"I don't know whether you ordered it or they did it on their own," I replied, "but you know, and I know, that in either case they did it because they thought it would please you."

Manson wanted to rap, but I cut him off. "I'm not really in the mood to talk to you, Charlie. Maybe, if you have enough guts to take the stand, we'll talk then."

I asked McGann what was happening on the "Honolulu hamburger case," as the papers had dubbed the Hoyt murder attempt. McGann said he and Calkins hadn't been able to come up with any evidence.

I asked Phil Sartuchi of the LaBianca team to take over. Phil efficiently turned in a detailed report, with information on the airline tickets, credit cards, long-distance calls, and so forth. It was December, however, before the case was taken to the grand jury. In the interim, Ouisch, Squeaky, Clem, Gypsy, and Rice remained at large. I'd often see them with the other Family members at the corner of Temple and Broadway.

On cross-examination Fitzgerald asked DeCarlo: "Is it not true that Mr. Manson indicated to you that he actually loved the black people?"

Danny replied: "Yeah. There was one time he said that."

On redirect I asked DeCarlo about that single conversation. Charlie had told him he loved the blacks, he said, "for having the guts to fight against the police."

Shinn brought out that DeCarlo was aware of, and more than passingly interested in, the $25,000 reward, thereby establishing that he had a reason to fabricate his testimony. Kanarek pursued the subject in detail in his

cross. He also dwelt at length on DeCarlo's fondness for
weapons. Earlier DeCarlo had testified that he loved guns;
would he describe that love? Kanarek asked.

DeCarlo's reply brought down the house. "Well, I love
them more than I do my old lady."

It was easy to see where Kanarek was heading: he was
trying to establish that it was DeCarlo, not Manson, who
was responsible for all the weapons being at Spahn Ranch.

Kanarek switched subjects. Wasn't it true, he asked De-
Carlo, that "during the entire time you were at the ranch
you were smashed?"

A. "I sure was."

Q. "Were you so smashed that on many occasions you
had to be carried to bed?"

A. "I made it a few times myself."

Kanarek hit hard on DeCarlo's drinking, also his
vagueness as to dates and times. How could he remember
one particular Saturday night, for example, and not another night?

"Well, that particular night," DeCarlo responded,
"Gypsy got mad at me because I wouldn't take my boots
off when I made love to her."

Q. "The only thing that is really pinpointed in your
mind, that you really remember, is that you had a lot of
sex, right?"

A "Well, even some of that I can't remember."

Kanarek had scored some points. He brought out that
DeCarlo had testified on an earlier occasion (during the
Beausoleil trial) that while at Spahn he was smashed 99
percent of the time. The defense could now argue that
DeCarlo was so inebriated that he couldn't perceive what
was going on, much less recall specific conversations. Unfortunately for the defense, Fitzgerald unintentionally
undermined this argument by asking DeCarlo to define
the difference between "drunk" and "smashed."

A. "My version of 'drunk' is when I'm out to lunch on
the ground. 'Smashed' is just when I'm walking around
loaded."

September 18, 1970

That afternoon we had a surprise visitor in court—Charles "Tex" Watson.

After a nine-month delay that would necessitate trying him separately, Watson had finally been returned to California on September 11, after U.S. Supreme Court Justice Hugo Black refused to grant him a further stay of extradition. Sergeants Sartuchi and Gutierrez, who accompanied Watson on the flight, said he spoke little, mostly staring vacantly into space. He had lost about thirty pounds during his confinement, most of it during the last two months, when it became obvious his return to Los Angeles was imminent.

Fitzgerald had asked that Watson be brought into court, to see if DeCarlo could identify him.

Realizing that Fitzgerald was making a *very* serious mistake, Kanarek objected, strenuously, but Older granted the removal order.

The jury was still out when Watson entered the courtroom. Though he smiled slightly at the three female defendants, who grinned and blew him kisses, he seemed oblivious to Manson's presence. By the time the jury came in, Watson was already seated and appeared just another spectator.

FITZGERALD "Mr. DeCarlo, you previously testified that a man by the name of Tex Watson was present at Spahn Ranch during the period of time that you were there in 1969, is that correct?"

A. "Yeah."

Q. "Do you recognize Mr. Watson in this courtroom?"

A. "Yeah. Right over there." Danny pointed to where Tex was sitting. Obviously curious, the jury strained to see the man they had heard so much about.

FITZGERALD "Could I have this gentleman identify himself for the Court, Your Honor?"

THE COURT "Will you please stand and state your name."

Watson stood, after being motioned to his feet by one of the bailiffs, but he remained mute.

Fitzgerald's mistake was obvious the moment Watson got up. One look and the jury knew that Charles "Tex" Watson was not the type to order Charles Manson to do anything, much less instigate seven murders on his own. He looked closer to twenty than twenty-five. Short hair, blue blazer, gray slacks, tie. Instead of the wild-eyed monster depicted in the April 1969 mug shot (when Watson had been on drugs), he appeared to be a typical clean-cut college kid.

Offstage, Watson could be made to seem the heavy. Having once seen him, the jury would never think this again.

Since our first meeting in Independence, I had remained on speaking terms with Sandy and Squeaky. Occasionally one or both would drop in at my office to chat. I usually made time for such visits, in part because I was still attempting to understand why they (and the three female defendants) had joined the Family, but also because I was remotely hopeful that if another murder was planned, one or the other might alert me. Neither, I was sure, would go to the police, and I wanted to leave at least one channel of communication open.

I'd had more hopes for Sandy than Squeaky. The latter was on a power trip—acting as Manson's unofficial spokesman, running the Family in his absence—and it seemed unlikely she would do anything to jeopardize her status. Sandy, however, had gone against Manson's wishes on several occasions, I knew; they were minor rebellions (when her baby was due, for example, she had gone to a hospital, rather than have it delivered by the Family), but they indicated that maybe, behind the pat phrases, I'd touch something responsively human.

On her first visit to my office, about two months earlier, we'd talked about the Family credo: Sandy had maintained it was peace; I'd maintained it was murder, and had asked how she could stomach this.

"People are being murdered every day in Vietnam," she'd countered.

"Assuming for the sake of argument that the deaths in Vietnam are murders," I responded, "how does this justify murdering seven more people?"

As she tried to come up with an answer, I told her, "Sandy, if you really believe in peace and love, I want you to prove it. The next time murder is in the wind at Spahn Ranch, I want you to remember that other people like to live just as much as you do. And, as another human being, I want you to do everything possible to prevent it from happening. Do you understand what I mean?"

She quietly replied, "Yes."

I'd hoped she really meant that. That naïve hope vanished when, in talking to Barbara Hoyt, I learned that Sandy had been one of the Family members who had persuaded her to go to Hawaii.

As I left court on the afternoon of the eighteenth, Sandy and two male followers approached me.

"Sandy, I'm very, very disappointed in you," I told her. "You were at Spahn when Barbara's murder was planned. There's no question in my mind that you knew what was going to happen. Yet, though Barbara was your friend, you said nothing, did nothing. Why?"

She didn't reply, but stared at me as if in a trance. For a moment I thought she hadn't heard me, that she was stoned on drugs, but then, very slowly and deliberately, she reached down and began playing with the sheath knife that she wore at her waist. That was her answer.

Disgusted, I turned and walked away. Looking back, however, I saw that Sandy and the two boys were following me. I stopped, they stopped. When I started walking again, they followed, Sandy still fingering the knife.

Gradually they were closing the distance between us. Deciding it was better to face trouble than have my back to it, I turned and walked back to them.

"Listen, you God damn bitch, and listen good," I told her. "I don't know for sure whether you were or weren't involved in the actual attempt to murder Barbara, but if you were, I'm going to do everything in my power to see that you end up in jail!" I then looked at the two males and told them if they followed me one more time, I was going to deck them on the spot.

I then turned and walked off. This time they didn't follow me.

My reaction was, I felt, exceptionally mild, considering the circumstances.

Kanarek felt otherwise. When court reconvened on Monday, the twenty-first, he filed a motion asking that I be held in contempt for interfering with a defense witness. He also asked that I be arrested for violating Section 415 of the Penal Code, charging that I had made obscene remarks in the presence of a female.

September 21-26, 1970

Finding nothing in Sandra Good's declaration "that in my opinion constitutes contemptuous conduct on the part of Mr. Bugliosi," Judge Older dismissed Kanarek's several motions. Again Manson asked to see me in the lockup during the noon recess. He hoped I wasn't taking all this—the attempted murder, the knife incident, the trial—personally.

"No, Charlie," I told him, "I was assigned to this case; I didn't ask for it; this is my job."

By now it should be obvious to me, Manson said, that the girls were acting on their own, that nobody was dominating them. When I raised a skeptical eyebrow, Manson said, "Look, Bugliosi, if I had all the power and control that you say I have, I could simply say, 'Brenda, go get Bugliosi,' and that would be it."

It was interesting, I thought, that Manson should single out Brenda McCann, t/n Nancy Pitman, as his chief assassin.

Later I'd have good reason to recall Manson's remarks.

Nothing personal. But immediately after this, the middle-of-the-night hang-up calls began. They'd continue even after we changed our unlisted number. And several times when I left the Hall of Justice at night, I was followed by various Family members, including Sandy. Only the first time disturbed me. Gail and the kids were circling the block in our car, and I was afraid they would be identified or the license number spotted. When I pretended not to see her, Gail quickly sized up the situation and drove around until I was able to shake my "followers," though, as she later admitted to me, she was far less cool than she appeared.

Though concerned with the safety of my family, I didn't take any of this very seriously until one afternoon when, apparently enraged at the domination testimony that was coming in, Manson told a bailiff, "I'm going to have Bugliosi and the judge killed."

By telling a bailiff this, Manson was making sure we got the message. Older was already under protection. The next day the District Attorney's Office assigned me a bodyguard for the duration of the trial. Additional precautions were taken, which, since they're probably used in protecting others, needn't be enumerated, though one might be noted. In order to prevent a repetition of the events at 10050 Cielo Drive, a walkie-talkie was installed in our home, which provided instant communication with the nearest police station, in case the telephone wires were cut.

Though Older and I were the only trial principals who had bodyguards, it was no secret that several, if not all, of the defense attorneys were frightened of the Family. Daye Shinn, I was told by one of his fellows, kept a loaded gun in each room of his house, in case of an unannounced visitation. What precautions, if any, Kanarek took I never learned, though Manson often assigned him top spot on his kill list. According to another defense attorney, Manson threatened numerous times to kill Kanarek; it was only fair, Manson supposedly said, since Kanarek was killing him in court.

Manson, at one point, had Fitzgerald draw up papers for Kanarek's dismissal. According to Paul, who told the story to me, Kanarek literally got down on his knees and, with tears in his eyes, begged Manson not to fire him. Manson relented and, though they continued to disagree, Kanarek remained on the case.

Each week a member of the Los Angeles Board of Supervisors issued a press release itemizing trial costs to date. Yet even with Kanarek's multitudinous objections, many of which called for lengthy conferences, we were covering a tremendous amount of testimony each day. A veteran court reporter said he'd never seen anything like it in twenty-odd years.

Thus far, Judge Older had done a remarkable job of holding Kanarek in check. Had he granted even half the "evidentiary hearings" Kanarek was always calling for, the ten-year estimate might have become a reality. Instead, each time Kanarek made the request, Older said, "Put your motion in writing with supporting citations." Because of the time involved, Kanarek rarely took the trouble.

For our part, although I'd originally planned to call some hundred witnesses, I'd cut that number down to about eighty. In a case of this magnitude and complexity this was a remarkably low number. Some days saw as many as a half dozen witnesses taking the stand. Whenever possible, I'd use a single witness for several purposes. In addition to his other testimony, for example, I asked DeCarlo the names and approximate ages of each of the Family members, so it would be apparent to the jury that Manson, being older than all of them, was not likely to have played a subservient role.

When I called sheriff's deputy William Gleason to testify that when Spahn Ranch was raided on August 16 not one Buck knife was found, Kanarek, seeing the implication of this, objected, and Older sustained the objection.

I'd almost given up getting this in when Fitzgerald, apparently thinking the absence of such knives was a plus for the defense, asked on cross-examination: "Did you find any Buck knives at the Spahn Ranch on the date of August the sixteenth, 1969?"

A. "No, sir."

The Family's attempt to silence Barbara Hoyt backfired. Once a reluctant witness, she was now very willing to testify.

Barbara not only confirmed Linda's story of the TV incident; she recalled that the previous night, the night of the Tate murders, Sadie called her on the field phone at the back house, asking her to bring three sets of dark clothing to the front of the ranch. When she arrived, Manson told her, "They already left."

Barbara's story was both support for Linda Kasabian's testimony and powerful evidence of Manson's involvement, and, though unsuccessful, Kanarek fought hard to keep it out.

I was not able to bring out the Myers Ranch conversation until after a full half day of argument in chambers, and then, as I'd anticipated, I could only get in part of it.

One afternoon in early September 1969, Barbara had been napping in the bedroom at Myers Ranch when she awoke to hear Sadie and Ouisch talking in the kitchen. Apparently thinking Barbara was still asleep, Sadie told Ouisch that Sharon Tate had been the last to die because, to quote Sadie, "She had to watch the others die."

I got this in, finally. What I couldn't get in, because of *Aranda*, was the rest of the conversation: Barbara had also heard Sadie tell Ouisch that Abigail Folger had escaped and run out of the house; that Katie had caught up with her on the lawn; and that Abigail had struggled so much that Katie had to call for help from Tex, who ran over and stabbed Abigail.

In chambers, Shinn argued that he should be allowed to question Barbara about this. Older, as well as the other defense attorneys, strongly disagreed. By "Arandizing" the conversation—omitting all reference to her co-defendants—this put the onus for all five murders on Susan, Shinn complained, adding, "But other people were there too, Your Honor."

BUGLIOSI "They were, Daye?"

Inadvertently, Shinn had admitted that Susan Atkins was present at the Tate murder scene. Fortunately for both attorney and client, this dialogue took place in chambers and not in open court.

As with the other ex-Family members, I was able to bring in through Barbara numerous examples of Manson's domination, as well as a number of Manson's conversations about Helter Skelter. The one thing I couldn't get in was the Family's attempt to prevent Barbara Hoyt from testifying.

During his cross-examination of Barbara, Kanarek attacked her for everything from her morals to her eyesight.

Aware that Barbara had very poor vision, Kanarek had her take off her glasses, then he moved around the courtroom, asking how many fingers he had up.

Q. "How many can you see now?"

A. "Three."

KANAREK   "May the record reflect she said three and I have two up clearly, Your Honor."

THE COURT   "I thought I saw your thumb."

Kanarek finally proved Barbara had bad eyesight. The issue, however, wasn't her sight but her hearing: she didn't claim to have seen Sadie and Ouisch in the kitchen at Myers Ranch, only to have heard them.

Kanarek also asked Barbara: "Have you been in any mental hospital for the last couple of years?"

Ordinarily I would have objected to such a question, but not this time, for Kanarek had just opened wide the door through which I could, on redirect, bring in the murder attempt.

Redirect is limited to the issues raised on cross-examination. For example, on redirect I had Barbara approximate the distance between the bedroom and the kitchen at Myers Ranch, then conducted a hearing experiment. She passed with no trouble.

Asking to approach the bench, I argued that since Kanarek had implied that Barbara Hoyt was in a mental hospital for an extended period of time, I had the right to bring out that she was in a mental ward only overnight and that it was not because of a mental problem. Older agreed, with one limitation: I couldn't ask who gave her the LSD.

Once I'd brought out the circumstances of her hospitalization, I asked: "Did you take this overdose voluntarily?"

A. "No."

Q. "Was it given to you by someone else?"

A. "Yes."

Q. "Were you near death?"

KANAREK "Calls for a conclusion, Your Honor."

THE COURT "Sustained."

It was good enough. I was sure the jury could put two and two together.

On Saturday, September 26, 1970, an era came to an end. A raging fire swept Southern California. Whipped by eighty-mile-an-hour winds, a wall of flame as high as sixty feet charred over 100,000 acres. Burned in the inferno was all of Spahn's Movie Ranch.

As the ranch hands tried to save the horses, the Manson girls, their faces illuminated by the light of the conflagration, danced and clapped their hands, crying out happily, *"Helter Skelter is coming down! Helter Skelter is coming down!"*

September 27–October 5, 1970

Juan Flynn, who described his job at Spahn Ranch as "manure shoveler," seemed to enjoy himself on the stand. Of all the witnesses, however, the lanky Panamanian cowboy was the only one who openly showed animosity to Manson. When Charlie tried to stare him down, Juan glared back.

After positively identifying the revolver, Juan remarked, "And Mr. Manson on one occasion fired this gun, you know, in my direction, you see, because I was walking with a girl on the other side of the creek."

It was difficult to stop Juan once he got started. The girl had come to Spahn Ranch to ride horses; she'd ignored Manson but went off down the creek with amorous-minded Juan. Charlie was so miffed he'd fired several shots in their direction.

Kanarek succeeded in having all this, except Juan's seeing Manson fire the revolver, struck.

He also tried, but failed, to keep out the two most important pieces of evidence Juan Flynn had to offer.

One night in early August 1969, Juan had been watching TV in the trailer when Sadie came in, dressed in black. "Where are you going?" Juan asked. "We're going to get some fucking pigs," Sadie replied. When she left, Juan looked out the window and saw her get into Johnny Swartz' old yellow Ford. Charlie, Clem, Tex, Linda, and Leslie got in also.

According to Juan, the incident had occurred after dark, about 8 or 9 P.M., and, though he wasn't able to pinpoint the date, he said it was about a week before the August 16 raid. The logical inference was that he was describing the night the LaBiancas were killed.

Juan's story was important both as evidence and as independent corroboration of Linda Kasabian's testimony. Not only did the time, participants, vehicle, and color of Susan Atkins' clothing coincide, Juan also noticed that Manson was driving.

Juan then testified to the kitchen conversation which occurred "a day or so" later, when, putting a knife to his throat, Manson told him, "You son of a bitch, don't you know I'm the one who's doing all of these killings?"

The newsmen rushed for the door.

MANSON ADMITTED MURDERS, SPAHN RANCH COWBOY CLAIMS

Kanarek's objections kept out another piece of extremely damaging evidence.

One night in June or July 1969, Manson, Juan, and three male Family members were driving through Chatsworth when Charlie stopped in front of a "rich house" and instructed Juan to go in and tie up the people. When he'd finished, Manson said, he was to open the door and, to quote Manson, "We'll come in and cut the motherfucking pigs up." Juan had said, "No thanks."

This was in effect a dress rehearsal for the Tate-LaBianca murders. But ruling that "the prejudicial effect far outweighs the probative value," Older wouldn't permit me to question Juan about this.

I was also unable, for the same reason, to get in a comment Manson made to Juan: "Adolf Hitler had the best answer to everything."

That answer, of course, was murder, but, owing to Kanarek's objections, neither of these two incidents was heard by the jury or ever made public.

On cross-examination Fitzgerald brought out an interesting anomaly. Even after Manson had allegedly threatened him, not once but several times, Juan still stuck around. After the raid he'd even accompanied the Family to Death Valley, remaining with them a couple of weeks before splitting to join Crockett, Poston, and Watkins.

That had puzzled me too. One possible explanation was that, as Juan testified, at first he had thought Manson was "bullshitting" about the murders, that "nobody in their right mind is going to kill somebody and then boast about it." Also, Juan was easygoing and slow to anger. Probably more important, Juan was an independent cuss; like Paul Crockett, who didn't leave Death Valley until long after Manson threatened to kill him, he didn't like to be intimidated.

Kanarek picked up on Fitzgerald's discovery. "Now, Mr. Flynn, were you scared to be at the Myers Ranch with Mr. Manson?"

A. "Well, I was aware and precautious."

Q. "Just answer the question, Mr. Flynn. I understand you are an actor, but would you just answer the question please."

A. "Well, I liked it there, you know, because I wanted to think nice things, you know. But every time I walked around the corner, well, that seemed to be the main subject, you know, about how many times they could do me in. Then, finally, I just left."

Q. "Now, Mr. Flynn, will you tell me how you were aware and precautious? How did you protect yourself?"

A.   "Well, I just protected myself by leaving."

Kanarek brought out that when Flynn was interviewed by Sartuchi he'd said nothing about Manson putting a knife to his throat. "You were holding that back, is that it, Mr. Flynn, to spring on us in this courtroom, is that right?"

A.   "No, I told the officers about this before, you see."

Ignoring Flynn's response, Kanarek said: "You mean, Mr. Flynn, that you made it up for the purposes of this courtroom, is that correct, Mr. Flynn?"

Kanarek was charging that Flynn had recently fabricated his testimony. I made a note of this, though as yet unaware how important this bit of dialogue would soon be.

After focusing on all the things I had brought out which were not in the Sartuchi interview, Kanarek asked Juan when he first mentioned the knife incident to anyone.

A.   "Well, there was some officers in Shoshone, you see, and I talked to them." Flynn, however, couldn't recall their names.

Kanarek strongly implied, several times, that Flynn was fictionalizing his story. Juan didn't take kindly to being called a liar. You could see his temper rising.

Intent on proving that Flynn was testifying so he could further his movie career (Juan had had bit parts in several Westerns), Kanarek asked: "You recognize, do you not, that there is lots of publicity in this case against Mr. Manson, right?"

A.   "Well, it is the type of publicity that I wouldn't want, you big catfish."

THE COURT   "On that note, Mr. Kanarek, we will adjourn."

After court I questioned Juan about the Shoshone interview. He thought one of the officers was from the California Highway Patrol, but he wasn't sure. That evening I called the DA's Office in Independence and learned that the man who had interviewed Juan was a CHP officer named Dave Steuber. Late that night I finally located him in Fresno, California. Yes, he'd interviewed Flynn, as well as Crockett, Poston, and Watkins, on December 19, 1969.

He'd taped the whole conversation, which had lasted over nine hours. Yes, he still had the original tapes.

I checked my calendar. I guessed Flynn would be on the stand another day or two. Could Steuber be in L.A. in three days with the tapes and prepared to testify? Sure, Steuber said.

Steuber then told me something I found absolutely incredible. He had already made a copy of the tapes and given it to LAPD. On *December 29, 1969.* Later I learned the identity of the LAPD detective to whom the tapes had been given. The officer (since deceased) recalled receiving the tapes but admitted he hadn't played them. He thought he had given them to someone, but couldn't remember to whom. All he knew was that he no longer had them.

Perhaps it was because the interview was so long, nine hours. Or perhaps, it being the holiday season, in the confusion they were mislaid. Neither explanation, however, erases the unpleasant fact that as early as December 1969 the Los Angeles Police Department had a taped interview containing a statement in which Manson implied that he was responsible for the Tate-LaBianca murders, and as far as can be determined, no one even bothered to book it into evidence, much less play it.

Ordinarily there would have been no way I could introduce the Steuber tape into evidence at the trial, for you cannot use a previously consistent statement to bolster a witness's testimony. However, there is an exception to that rule: such evidence is admissible if the opposing side contends the witness's testimony was recently fabricated and the prior consistent statement was made before the declarant had any reason to fabricate. When Kanarek asked, "You mean, Mr. Flynn, that you made it up for the purposes of this courtroom, is that correct, Mr. Flynn?" he was charging recent fabrication, and opening the door for me to bring the prior consistent statement in.

A lot of doors were opened on cross-examination, but at first the biggest did not look like a door at all. The defense had made much of the fact that Juan did not tell his story to the authorities until long after the events occurred. With this opening, I argued, I should be allowed to bring out the reason why: he was in fear of his life.

Responding to Kanarek's objection, Older said: "You can't go into all of these things on cross and expect the other side to do nothing about them, Mr. Kanarek. You can't paint them in a corner and say they can't work their way out."

Juan was permitted to testify that he didn't go to the police because "I didn't think it was safe for me to do that, you see. I got a couple of threat notes . . ."

Actually, Juan had received three such notes, all handed him by Family members, the last as late as two weeks ago, when Squeaky and Larry Jones had discovered that Juan was living in John Swartz' trailer in Canoga Park. Arguing against their admission, Fitzgerald made an interesting statement: "My life has been threatened three times, and I haven't come forward and talked about it."

BUGLIOSI "Has the prosecution threatened you?"

FITZGERALD "No, I am not saying that." He didn't elaborate.

Older ruled that Juan could testify to the notes, though not the identities of the persons who gave them to him. Juan also testified to the hang-up calls, the cars that raced past in the night, their occupants oinking and screaming, "Motherfucker!" and "Pig!"

I asked him: "And you considered these threats, is that correct?"

A. "Well, they sounded, you know, pretty strong to me."

Q. "Are those among the reasons why you didn't want to come downtown and talk?"

A. "Well, this was one of the reasons, yes."

Q. "Because of fear of your life?"

A. "Yes."

When I asked about the other reasons, Juan described how Manson, Clem, and Tex had creepy-crawled Crockett's cabin at Barker Ranch.

All of this came in because the defense so gratuitously opened the door on cross.

Because Kanarek had questioned Juan about Manson's "programming" of Family members, I was able to bring in a conversation Manson had with Juan in which he explained that he had to "unprogram" his followers to remove the programming placed upon them by their parents, schools, churches, and society. To get rid of the ego, Manson told him, you had to obliterate "all the wants that you had . . . give up your mother and father . . . all the inhibitions . . . just blank yourself out."

Since Manson's techniques differed depending on whether his subject was male or female, I asked what Manson had said about unprogramming the girls. I didn't anticipate that Juan would go into the detail he did.

A. "Well, he says, you know, to get rid of the inhibitions, you know, you could just take a couple of girls and, you know, have them lay down, you know, and have them eat each other, or for me to take a girl up in the hills, you know, and just lie back and let her suck my dick all day long . . ."

KANAREK "Your Honor, Your Honor! May we approach the bench, Your Honor?"

Earlier one of the alternate jurors had written Judge Older a letter complaining about the sexual explicitness of some of the testimony. I didn't look at him, but I suspected he must be having apoplexy. As I passed the counsel table on the way to the bench, I told Manson, "Don't worry, Charlie, I'm keeping all the bad stuff out."

Older struck the entire answer as nonresponsive.

I asked Juan: "Did Mr. Manson discuss with you—*without going into what he said, Juan*—plans that he had to 'unprogram' the people in the Family?" When he replied "Yes," I let it go at that.

What Manson never explained to his Family was that in the process of unprogramming them, he was reprogramming them to be his abject slaves.

Throughout his cross-examination Kanarek had implied, as he had with many of the earlier witnesses, that Juan had been coached by me. I thought Kanarek was going to do this again, for the umpteenth time, when on recross he started: "Mr. Flynn, when a question is asked of you that you think may not help the prosecution in this case—"

BUGLIOSI "Oh, stop arguing."

KANAREK "Your Honor, he's interrupting!"

BUGLIOSI "Be quiet."

THE COURT "Mr. Bugliosi, now, I'm not going to warn you again, sir."

BUGLIOSI "What's he doing, Your Honor? He's accusing me of something and I don't like it."

THE COURT "Approach the bench."

BUGLIOSI "I am not going to take it. I've had it up to here."

My indignation was as much a matter of trial tactics as anything else. If I let Kanarek get away with the same trick time after time, the jury might assume there was some truth to his charges. At the bench I told Older: "I'm not going to be accused of a serious offense by this guy day in and day out."

THE COURT "That's absurd. You interrupted Mr. Kanarek. You made outrageous statements in front of the jury . . . I find you in direct contempt of Court, and I fine you fifty dollars."

To the amusement of the clerk, I had to call my wife to come down and pay the fine. Later the deputy DAs in the office put up a buck each for a "Bugliosi Defense Fund" and reimbursed her.

As with the earlier citation of Hughes, I felt if I was in contempt of anyone, it was Kanarek, not the Court. The following day, for the record, I responded to the contempt, noting among other things that "in the future I would ask the Court to please consider two obvious points: this is a hotly contested trial and tempers become a little frayed; and also take into consideration what Mr. Kanarek is doing which incites a response on my part."

With my citation, we now had a perfect score: every attorney involved in the trial had been either cited for contempt or threatened with it.

The defense tried their best to ridicule Juan's fear of Manson.

Hughes brought out that since Manson was locked up, it was hardly likely he could hurt anyone; did Mr. Flynn actually expect the jury to believe that he was afraid of Mr. Manson?

Juan might have been speaking for all the prosecution

witnesses when he answered: "Well, not of Mr. Manson himself, but the *reach* that he has, you know."

By now I could see the pattern. The more damaging the testimony, the more chance Manson would create a disturbance, thereby assuring that he—and not the evidence itself—would get the day's headlines. Juan Flynn's testimony was hurting him badly. Several times while Flynn was on the stand, Older had to order Manson and the girls removed because of their outbursts. When it happened again, on October 2, Manson turned to the spectators and said: "Look at yourselves. Where are you going? You're going to destruction, that's where you're going." He then smiled a very odd little smile, and added, "*It's your Judgment Day, not mine.*"

Again the girls parroted Manson, and Older ordered all four removed.

Kanarek was livid. I'd just showed the judge the transcript pages where Kanarek accused Flynn of lying. Older ruled: "There is no question: there was an implied, if not express, charge of recent fabrication." Highway patrolman Dave Steuber would be permitted to play that portion of the taped interview dealing with Manson's incriminating admission.*

After establishing the circumstances of the interview, Steuber set up the tape recorder and began playing the tape at the point where the statement had begun. There is something about such physical evidence that deeply impresses a jury. Again, in words very similar to those they had heard him use when he was on the stand, the jurors heard Juan say: "Then he was looking at me real funny . . . And then he grabbed me by the hair like that, and he put a knife by my throat . . . And then he says, 'Don't you know I'm the one who is doing all the killings?' "

---

*Steuber had been investigating a stolen auto report, not murder, when he talked to Flynn, Poston, Crockett, and Watkins in Shoshone. However, realizing the importance of their story, he had spent over nine hours quizzing them on their knowledge of Manson and his Family. After the trial I wrote a letter to the California Highway Patrol, commending Steuber for the excellent job he had done.

Monday, October 5, 1970. Bailiff Bill Murray later said he had a very strong feeling that something was going to happen. You get a kind of sixth sense dealing with prisoners day after day, he said, noting that when he brought Manson into the lockup he was acting very tense and edgy.

Although they had made no assurances that they would conduct themselves properly, Older gave the defendants still another chance, permitting them to return to the courtroom.

The testimony was dull, undramatic. There was, at this point, no clue as to its importance, though I had a feeling Charlie just might suspect what I was up to. Through a series of witnesses, I was laying the groundwork for destroying Manson's anticipated alibi.

LASO detective Paul Whiteley had just finished testifying, and the defense attorneys had declined to cross-examine him, when Manson asked: "May I examine him, Your Honor?"

THE COURT   "No, you may not."

MANSON   "You are going to use this courtroom to kill me?"

Older told the witness he could step down. Manson asked the question a second time, adding, "I am going to fight for my life one way or another. You should let me do it with words."

THE COURT   "If you don't stop, I will have to have you removed."

MANSON   "I will have *you* removed if you don't stop. *I have a little system of my own.*"

Not until Manson made that very startling admission did I realize that this time he wasn't playacting but deadly serious.

THE COURT   "Call your next witness."

BUGLIOSI   "Sergeant Gutierrez."

MANSON   *"Do you think I'm kidding?"*

It happened in less time than it takes to describe it. With a pencil clutched in his right hand, Manson suddenly leaped over the counsel table in the direction of Judge Older. He landed just a few feet from the bench, falling on one knee. As he was struggling to his feet, bailiff Bill

Murray leaped too, landing on Manson's back. Two other deputies quickly joined in and, after a brief struggle, Manson's arms were pinned. As he was being propelled to the lockup, Manson screamed at Older: *"In the name of Christian justice, someone should cut your head off!"*

Adding to the bedlam, Atkins, Krenwinkel, and Van Houten stood and began chanting something in Latin. Older, much less disturbed than I would have expected, gave them not one but several chances to stop, then ordered them removed also.

According to the bailiffs, Manson continued to fight even after he had been taken into the lockup, and it took four men to put cuffs on him.

Fitzgerald asked if counsel might approach the bench. For the record, Judge Older described exactly how he had viewed the incident. Fitzgerald asked if he might inquire as to the judge's state of mind.

THE COURT   "He looked like he was coming for me."

FITZGERALD   "I was afraid of that, and although—"

THE COURT   "If he had taken one more step, I would have done something to defend myself."

Because of the judge's state of mind, Fitzgerald said, he felt it incumbent upon him to move for a mistrial. Hughes, Shinn, and Kanarek joined. Older replied: "It isn't going to be that easy, Mr. Fitzgerald . . . They are not going to profit from their own wrong . . . Denied."

Out of curiosity, after court Murray measured the distance of Manson's leap: ten feet.

Murray wasn't too surprised. Manson had very powerful leg and arm muscles. He was constantly exercising in the lockup. Asked why, he once told a bailiff: "I'm toughening myself up for the desert."

Murray tried to re-create his own leap. Without that sudden shot of adrenaline, he couldn't even jump up on the counsel table.

Though Judge Older instructed the jury to "disregard what you saw and what you have heard here this morning," I knew that as long as they lived they'd never forget it.

All the masks had been dropped. They'd seen the real face of Charles Manson.

From a reliable source, I learned that after the incident Judge Older began wearing a .38 caliber revolver under his robes, both in court and in chambers.

Judgment Day. Echoing Manson, the girls waiting outside on the corner spoke of it in conspiratorial whispers. "Wait till Judgment Day. That's when Helter Skelter will really come down."

Judgment Day. What was it? A plan to break out Manson? An orgy of retribution?

As important was the question of when. The day the jury returned their verdict of "Not guilty" or "Guilty"? Or, if the latter, the day the same jury decided "Life" or "Death"? Or perhaps the day of sentencing itself? Or might it even be tomorrow?

Judgment Day. We began to hear those words more and more often. Without explanation. As yet unaware that the first phase of Judgment Day had already begun, with the theft, from Camp Pendleton Marine Base, of a case of hand grenades.

October 6-31, 1970

Some weeks earlier, on returning to my office after court, I'd found a phone message from attorney Robert Steinberg, who was now representing Virginia Graham.

On the advice of her previous attorney, Virginia Graham had withheld some information. Steinberg had urged her to give this information to me. "Specifically," the phone message read, "Susan Atkins laid out detailed plans to Miss Graham concerning other planned murders, including the murders of Frank Sinatra and Elizabeth Taylor."

Since I was very busy, I arranged to have one of the co-prosecutors, Steve Kay, interview her.

According to Virginia, a few days after Susan Atkins

told her about the Hinman, Tate, and LaBianca murders—probably on November 8 or 9, 1969—Susan had walked over to Virginia's bed at Sybil Brand and begun leafing through a movie magazine. It reminded her, Susan said, about some other murders she had been planning.

She had decided to kill Elizabeth Taylor and Richard Burton, Susan matter-of-factly stated. She was going to heat a knife red-hot and put it against the side of Elizabeth Taylor's face. This was more or less to leave her mark. Then she'd carve the words "helter skelter" on her forehead. After which, she was going to gouge her eyes out—Charlie had shown her how—and—

Virginia interrupted to ask what Richard Burton was supposed to be doing during all this.

Oh, both would be tied up, Susan said. Only this time the rope would be around their necks and their feet, so they couldn't get away "like the others."

Then, Susan continued, she would castrate Burton, placing his penis, as well as Elizabeth Taylor's eyes, in a bottle. "And dig this, would you!" Susan laughed. "And then I'd mail it to Eddie Fisher!"

As for Tom Jones, another of her intended victims, she planned to force him to have sex with her, at knife point, and then, just as he was climaxing, she would slit his throat.

Steve McQueen was also on the list. Before Susan could explain what she had in mind for McQueen, Virginia interrupted, saying, "Sadie, you can't just walk up to these people and kill them!"

That would be no problem, Susan said. It was easy to find out where they lived. Then she'd simply creepy-crawl them, "just like I did to Tate."

She had something choice for Frank Sinatra, Susan continued. She knew that Frank liked girls. She'd just walk up to his door and knock. Her friends, she said, would be waiting outside. Once inside, they'd hang Sinatra upside down, then, while his own music was playing, skin him alive. After which they'd make purses out of the skin and sell them to hippie shops, "so everyone would have a little piece of Frank."

She had come to the conclusion, Susan said, that the

victims had to be people of importance, so the whole world would know.

Shortly after this, Virginia terminated the conversation with Susan. When asked by Steve Kay why she hadn't come forward with the story before this, Virginia explained that it was just so insane that she didn't think anyone would believe her. Even her former attorney had advised her to say nothing about it.

Were these Sadie's own plans, or Charlie's? Knowing as much as I did about Susan Atkins, I doubted if all this came from her. Though I had no proof, it was a reasonable inference that she had probably picked up these ideas from Manson.

In any case, it didn't matter. Reading a transcript of the taped interview, I knew I'd never be able to introduce any of this in evidence: legally, its relevance to the Tate-LaBianca murders was negligible, and whatever limited relevance it did have would be outweighed by its extremely prejudicial effect.

Though Virginia Graham's statement was useless as evidence, a copy of it was made available to each of the defense attorneys under discovery.

It would soon make its own kind of legal history.

Although it was Ronnie Howard who first went to the police, I called Virginia Graham to the stand first, since Susan had initially confessed to her.

Her testimony was unusually dramatic, since this was the first time the jury had heard what had happened inside the Tate residence.

Since their testimony was only against Susan Atkins, only Shinn cross-examined Graham and Howard. His attack was less on their statements than their backgrounds. He brought out, for example, sixteen different aliases Ronnie Howard had used. He also asked her if she made a lot of money as a prostitute.

Asking him to approach the bench, Older said, "You know the rules, Mr. Shinn. Don't give me that wide-eyed innocent stare and pretend you don't know what I am talking about."

SHINN   "Does Your Honor mean I cannot ask a person their occupation?"

The prosecution had made no "deals" with either Virginia Graham or Ronnie Howard. Howard had been acquitted on the forgery charge, while Graham had served out her full sentence at Corona. In both cases, however, Shinn did bring up the reward. When he asked Ronnie if she knew about the $25,000, she bluntly answered: "I think I am entitled to it."

On redirect I asked each: "Are you aware that testifying in court is not a prerequisite to collecting the money?" Objection. Sustained. But the point was made.

The letters Susan Atkins had written to her former cellmates, Ronnie Howard, Jo Stevenson, and Kitt Fletcher, were very incriminating. Although I was prepared to call a handwriting expert to testify to their authenticity, Shinn, in order to save time, stipulated that Susan had written them. However, before they could be introduced in evidence, we had to "Arandize" them, excising any references to Atkins' co-defendants. This was done in chambers, outside the presence of the jury.

Kanarek fought to exclude almost every line. Disgusted at his constant objections, Fitzgerald complained to Older: "I don't have the rest of my life to spend here." Older, equally disgusted, told Kanarek: "I would suggest that you use a little more discretion and not try to clutter up the record with motions, objections, and statements which any ten-year-old child can see are either nonsense or totally irrelevant . . ."

Yet time and again Kanarek pointed out subtleties the other defense attorneys missed. For example, Susan had written Ronnie: "When I first heard you were the informer I wanted to slit your throat. Then I snapped that I was the real informer and it was my throat I wanted to cut."

You don't "inform" on yourself, Kanarek argued; you "confess." This implied that other people were involved.

After nineteen pages of argument, much of it very sophisticated, we finally edited this particular section to read: "When I first heard you were the informer I wanted to slit your throat. Then I snapped that it was my throat I wanted to cut."

Kanarek wanted the line "Love Love Love" excluded from the Stevenson letter because "it refers to Manson."

THE COURT "It sounds more like Gertrude Stein."

Since the "Love" references were among the few favorable things in Susan's letters, Shinn fought to retain them, remarking, "What do you want to do, make a killer out of her?"

LIZ, SINATRA ON SLAY LIST

The Los Angeles *Herald Examiner* broke the story on October 9, in an exclusive article bearing the by-line of reporter William Farr. Learning the night before that the story was going to appear, Judge Older again ordered the windows of the jury bus covered so the jurors couldn't see the headlines on corner newsstands.

Farr's article contained direct quotes from the Virginia Graham statement, which we had turned over to the defense on discovery.

Questioned in chambers, Farr declined to identify his source or sources. After observing that under California law he could not order the reporter to do so, Older excused Farr.

It was obvious that one or more persons had violated the gag order. Older, however, did not press the issue, and there, it appeared, the matter rested. There was no indication at this time that the issue would eventually become a *cause célèbre* and result in the jailing of Farr.

Gregg Jakobson was an impressive and very important witness. I had the tall, modishly dressed talent scout testify in detail to his many conversations with Manson, during which they discussed Helter Skelter, the Beatles, Revelation 9, and Manson's curious attitude toward death.

Shahrokh Hatami followed Jakobson to the stand, to

testify to his confrontation with Manson at 10050 Cielo Drive on the afternoon of March 23, 1969. For the first time the jury, and the public, learned that Sharon Tate had seen the man who later ordered her murder.

In Rudi Altobelli, Kanarek finally met his match. On direct examination the owner of 10050 Cielo Drive testified to his first encounter with Manson at Dennis Wilson's home, and then, in considerable detail, he described Manson's appearance at the guest house the evening before he and Sharon left for Rome.

Extremely antagonistic because Altobelli had refused him permission to visit 10050 Cielo Drive, Kanarek asked: "Now, presently, the premises on Cielo Drive where you live are quite secure, is that correct?"

A. "I hope so."

Q. "Do you remember having a conversation with me when I tried to get into your fortress out there?"

A. "I remember your insinuations or threats."

Q. "What were my insinuations or threats?"

A. "That 'We will take care of you, Mr. Altobelli,' 'We will see about you, Mr. Altobelli,' 'We will get the court up at your house and have the trial at your house, Mr. Altobelli.' "

Altobelli had told Kanarek that if the Court ordered it, he would be glad to comply. "Otherwise, no. It is a home. It is not going to be a tourist attraction or a freak show."

Q. "Do you respect our courts of law, Mr. Altobelli?"

A. "I think more than you, Mr. Kanarek."

Despite defense objections, I had succeeded in getting in perhaps 95 percent of the testimony I'd hoped to elicit through Jakobson, Hatami, and Altobelli.

With the next witness, I suddenly found myself in deep trouble.

Charles Koenig took the stand to testify to finding Rosemary LaBianca's wallet in the women's rest room of the Standard station in Sylmar where he worked. He described how, on lifting the top of the toilet tank, he'd seen the wallet wedged above the mechanism, just above the waterline.

Kanarek cross-examined Koenig at great length about

the toilet, causing more than a few snickers among spectators and press. Then I suddenly realized what he was getting at.

Kanarek asked Koenig if there was a standard procedure in connection with servicing the toilets in the rest room.

Koenig replied that the Standard station operating manual required that the rest room be cleaned every hour. The bluing agent, which is kept in the tank of the toilet, Koenig further testified, had to be replaced "whenever it ran out."

How often was that? Kanarek asked.

As "lead man," or boss of the station, Koenig had not personally cleaned the rest rooms, but rather had delegated the task to others. Therefore I was able to object to this and similar questions as calling for a conclusion on Koenig's part.

Fortunately, court then recessed for the day.

Immediately afterward I called LAPD with an urgent request. I wanted the detectives to locate and interview every person who had worked in this particular station between August 10, 1969 (the date Linda Kasabian testified she left the wallet there) and December 10, 1969 (the date Koenig found it). And I wanted them interviewed before Kanarek could get to them, fearing that he might put words in their mouths. I told the officers: "Tell them, 'Forget what the Standard station operating manual says you should do; forget too what your employer might say if he found you didn't follow the instructions to the letter. Just answer truthfully: Did you personally, at any time during your employment, change the bluing agent in that toilet?'"

To replace the bluing agent, you had to lift the top off the tank. Had anyone done so, he would have immediately seen the wallet. If Kanarek could come up with just one employee who claimed to have replaced the bluing agent during that four-month period, the defense could forcefully contend that the wallet had been "planted," not only destroying Linda Kasabian's credibility as to all of her testimony, but implying that the prosecution was trying to frame Manson.

LAPD located some, but not all, of the former employees. (None had ever changed the bluing agent.) Fortunately, Kanarek apparently had no better luck.

Hughes had only a few questions for Koenig, but they were devastating.

Q. "Now, Sylmar is predominantly a white area, is it not?"

A. "Yeah, I guess so."

Q. "Sylmar is not a black ghetto, is it?"

A. "No."

According to Linda, Manson had wanted a black to find the wallet and use the credit cards, so blacks would be blamed for the murders. My whole theory of the motive was based on this premise. Why, then, had Manson left the wallet in a white area?

In point of fact, the freeway exit Manson had taken was immediately north of Pacoima, the black ghetto of the San Fernando Valley. I tried to get this in through Koenig, but defense objections kept it out, and I later had to call Sergeant Patchett to so testify.

With a single witness, a service-station attendant, the defense—specifically Kanarek and Hughes—had almost knocked two huge holes in the prosecution's case.

By now I had narrowed down my opponents. Fitzgerald made a good appearance but rarely scored. Shinn was likable. For his first trial Hughes was doing damn well. But it was Irving Kanarek, whom most members of the press considered the trial's buffoon, who was scoring nearly all the points. Time and again Kanarek succeeded in keeping out important evidence.

For example, when Stephanie Schram took the stand, Kanarek objected to her testimony regarding the "murder school" Manson had conducted at Barker Ranch, and Older sustained Kanarek's objection. Though I disagreed with Older's ruling, there was no way I could get around it.

On direct Stephanie had testified that she and Manson returned to Spahn Ranch from San Diego in a cream-colored van on the afternoon of Friday, August 8. On cross-examination Fitzgerald asked her: "Could you be mistaken one day?" This indicated to me that Manson might still be planning to go alibi, so on redirect I brought

in the traffic ticket they had been given the previous day.
With the August 8 arrest report on Brunner and Good,
which contained the license number of the same van, I was
now ready to demolish Charlie if the defense claimed he
wasn't even in Southern California at the time of the murders.

Yet I had no way of knowing whether Manson might
have his own surprise bombshell, which he was waiting to
explode.

As it happened, he had.

Sergeant Gutierrez, on the "HELTER SKELTER" door.
DeWayne Wolfer, on the sound tests he'd conducted at the
Tate residence. Jerrold Friedman, on the last telephone
call Steven Parent made. Roseanne Walker, on Atkins' remarks about the eyeglasses. Harold True, on Manson's visits to the house next to the LaBianca residence. Sergeant
McKellar, on Krenwinkel's attempts to avoid recognition just prior to her arrest in Mobile, Alabama. Bits and
pieces, but cumulative. And eventually, I hoped, convincing.

Only a few prosecution witnesses remained. And I still
didn't know what the defense would be. Although the
prosecution had to give the defense a list of all our
witnesses, the defense had no such obligation. Earlier
Fitzgerald had told the press that he intended to call thirty
witnesses, among them such celebrities as Mama Cass, John
Phillips, and Beatle John Lennon, the latter to testify as to
how he interpreted his own song lyrics. But that, and the
rumors that Manson himself planned to testify, were the
only clues to the defense. And even Manson's testifying
was an iffy thing. In my talks with Charlie, he seemed to
vacillate. Maybe I'll testify. Maybe I won't. I continued to
goad him, but was worried that perhaps I'd overplayed my
hand.

The defendants hadn't been in court since Manson's attack on the judge. The day Terry Melcher was to testify,
however, Older permitted their return. Not wanting to
face Manson, Terry asked me, "Can't I go back in the
lockup and testify through the speaker?"

Of all the prosecution witnesses, Melcher was the most

frightened of Manson. His fear was so great, he told me, that he had been under psychiatric treatment and had employed a full-time bodyguard since December 1969.

"Terry, they weren't after you that night," I tried to reassure him. "Manson knew you were no longer living there."

Melcher was so nervous, however, that he had to be given a tranquilizer before taking the stand. Though he came over somewhat weaker than in our interviews, when he finished his testimony, he told me, with evident relief, that Manson had smiled at him, therefore he couldn't be too unhappy with what he'd said.

Kanarek, probably at Manson's request, did not question Melcher. Hughes brought out that when Wilson and Manson drove Terry to the gate of 10050 Cielo Drive that night, they probably saw him push the button. The defense could now argue that if Manson was familiar with the gate-operating device, it would be unlikely he'd have the killers climb over the fence, as Linda claimed they had.

By this time I had proof that *both* Watson and Manson had been to 10050 Cielo Drive on a *number* of occasions before the murders. But the jury would never hear it.

Some months earlier I'd learned that after Terry Melcher had moved out of the residence, but before the Polanskis had moved in, Gregg Jakobson had arranged for a Dean Moorehouse to stay there for a brief period. During this time Tex Watson had visited Moorehouse at least three, and possibly as many as six, times. In a private conversation with Fitzgerald, I told him this and he replied that he already knew it.

Though I intended to introduce this evidence during the Watson trial, I didn't want to bring it in during the current proceedings, and I was hoping that Fitzgerald wouldn't either, since it emphasized the Watson rather than the Manson link.

Though I suspected that Manson had visited there also during the same period, I had no proof of this until the trial was well under way, when I learned from the best possible source that Manson had been to 10050 Cielo Drive "on five or six occasions." My source was Manson himself, who admitted this to me during one of our rap

sessions. Manson denied, however, having been in the
house itself. He and Tex went up there, he said, to race
dune buggies up and down the hills.

But I couldn't use this information against Manson, because, as he well knew, all of my conversations with him
were at his insistence and he was never advised of his constitutional rights.

It was a decidedly curious situation. Although Manson
had vowed to kill me, he still asked to see me periodically—to rap.

Equally curious were our conversations. Manson told
me, for example, that he personally believed in law and
order. There should be "rigid control" by the authorities,
he said. It didn't matter what the law was—right and
wrong being relative—but it should be strictly enforced by
whoever had the power. And public opinion should be
suppressed, because part of the people wanted one thing,
part another.

"In other words, your solution would be a dictatorship,"
I remarked.

"Yes."

He had a simple solution to the crime problem, Manson
told me. Empty the prisons and banish all the criminals to
the desert. But first brand their foreheads with X's, so if
they ever appeared in the cities they could be identified
and shot on sight.

"Do I need two guesses as to who's going to be in
charge of them in the desert, Charlie?"

"No." He grinned.

On another occasion, Manson told me that he had just
written to President Nixon, asking him to turn over the
reins of power to him. If I was interested, I could be his
vice-president. I was a brilliant prosecutor, he said, a master with words, and, "You're right on about a lot of
things."

"What things, Charlie? Helter Skelter, the way the murders came down, your philosophy on life and death?"

Manson smiled and declined to answer.

"We both know you ordered these murders," I told him.

"Bugliosi, it's the Beatles, the music they're putting out.

They're talking about war. These kids listen to this music and pick up the message, it's subliminal."

"You were along on the night of the LaBianca murders."

"I went out a lot of nights."

Never a direct denial. I couldn't wait to get him on the stand.

Manson told me that he liked prison, though he liked the desert, the sun, and women better. I told him he'd never been inside the green room at San Quentin before.

He wasn't afraid of death, Manson responded. Death was only a thought. He'd faced death before, many times, in both this and past lives.

I asked him if, when he shot Crowe, he'd intended to kill him.

"Sure," he replied, adding, "I could kill everyone without blinking an eye." When I asked why, he said, "Because you've been killing me for years." Pressed as to whether all this killing bothered him, Manson replied that he had no conscience, that everything was only a thought. Only he, and he alone, was on top of his thought, in complete control, unprogrammed by anyone or anything.

"When it comes down around your ears, you'd better believe I'll be on top of my thought," Manson said. "I will know what I am doing. I will know *exactly* what I am doing."

Manson frequently interrupted the testimony of Brooks Poston and Paul Watkins with asides. Kanarek's interruptions were so continuous that Older, calling him to the bench, angrily told him: "You are trying to disrupt the testimony with frivolous, lengthy, involved, silly objections. You have done it time and again during this trial . . . I have studied you very carefully, Mr. Kanarek. I know exactly what you are doing. I have had to find you in contempt twice before for doing the same thing. I won't hesitate to do it again."

It was all too obvious, to both Kanarek and Manson, that Poston and Watkins were impressively strong witnesses. Step by step they traced the evolution of Helter Skelter, not intellectually, as Jakobson understood it, but as onetime true believers, members of the Family who had watched a vague concept slowly materialize into terrifying reality.

The cross-examination didn't shake their testimony in the slightest; rather, it elicited more details. When Kanarek questioned Poston, for example, he accidentally brought out a good domination example: "When Charlie would be around, things would be like when a schoolteacher comes back to class."

Hughes asked Poston: "Did you feel you were under Mr. Manson's hypnotic spell?"

A. "No, I did not think that Charlie had a hypnotic spell."

Q. "Did you feel he had some power?"

A. "I felt he was Jesus Christ. That is power enough for me."

Looking back on his time with Manson, Poston said: "I learned a lot from Charlie, but it doesn't seem that he was making all those people free." Watkins observed: "Charlie was always preaching love. Charlie had no idea what love was. Charlie was so far from love it wasn't even funny. *Death is Charlie's trip.* It really is."

Since his extradition to California, Charles "Tex" Watson had been behaving peculiarly. At first he spoke little, then stopped speaking entirely. The prisoners in his cell block signed a petition complaining of the unsanitary condition of his cell. For hours he'd stare off into space, then inexplicably hurl himself against his cell wall. Placed in restraints, he stopped eating and, even though force-fed, his weight dropped to 110 pounds.

Though there was evidence that he was faking at least part of his symptoms, his attorney, Sam Bubrick, asked the Court to appoint three psychiatrists to examine him. Their conclusions differed but they agreed on one point: Watson was rapidly reverting to a fetal state, which, unless immediately treated, could be fatal. Acting on the basis of their examination, on October 29 Judge Dell ruled Watson was at present incompetent to stand trial and ordered him committed to Atascadero State Hospital.

Manson asked to see me during the recess.

"Vince," Manson pleaded through the lockup door, "give me just half an hour with Tex. I'm positive I can cure him."

"I'm sorry, Charlie," I told him. "I can't afford to take that chance. If you cured him, then everyone *would* believe you were Jesus Christ."

November 1-19, 1970

The day before Watson was committed to Atascadero, two court-appointed psychiatrists found seventeen-year-old Dianne Lake competent to testify.

Following her release from Patton, Dianne had received some good news: Inyo County investigator Jack Gardiner and his wife, who had befriended Dianne after her arrest in the Barker raid, had been appointed her foster parents. She would live with them and their children until she finished high school.

Because of *Aranda*, there were some things the jury never heard—for example, that Tex had told Leslie to stab Rosemary LaBianca and, later, to wipe fingerprints off everything they had touched—since Katie had related these things to Dianne, and any reference by Katie to her co-defendants had to be excised.

Dianne could testify to what Leslie had told her she had done; however, the problem here was that Leslie never told Dianne *whom* she had stabbed. She said she had stabbed someone who was already dead; that this occurred near Griffith Park; and that there was a boat outside. From these facts I hoped the jury would conclude that she was talking about the LaBiancas. Dianne also testified that one morning in August Leslie had come into the back house at Spahn and proceeded to burn a purse, a credit card, and her own clothing, keeping only a sack of coins, which the girls divided and spent on food. Dianne, however, was unable to pinpoint the exact date, and though I hoped the jury would surmise this had occurred the morning after the LaBiancas were killed, there was no proof that this was so.

Since this was the only evidence, independent of Linda Kasabian's testimony, which I had linking Leslie Van Houten to the LaBianca homicides, it hurt, and badly, when Hughes on cross brought out that Dianne wasn't sure whether Leslie had told her about the boat or whether she had read about it in the newspapers.

Hughes also focused on a number of minor discrepancies in her previous statements (she'd told Sartuchi the coins were in the purse, while she'd told me they were in a plastic bag), and what could have been one very big bombshell. On direct Dianne had said that she, Little Patty, and Sandra Good, "I believe," had divided the money.

If Sandy was present, this couldn't have been August 10, the morning after the LaBianca murders, since Sandra Good, along with Mary Brunner, was still in custody. However, questioned further, Dianne said Sandy "might not have been there."

In his cross-examination Kanarek brought out that Sergeant Gutierrez had threatened Dianne with the gas chamber. Fitzgerald also came up with a prior inconsistent statement: Dianne had told the grand jury that she was in Inyo County, rather than at Spahn Ranch, on August 8 and 9.

On redirect I asked Dianne: "Why did you lie to the grand jury?"

A. "Because I was afraid that I would be killed by members of the Family if I told the truth. And Charlie asked me not to—he told me not to say anything to anybody who had the power of authority."

On November 4, Sergeant Gutierrez, in search of a cup of coffee, had wandered into the jury room where the female defendants stayed during recesses.

He found a yellow legal pad with the name Patricia Krenwinkel on it. Among the notes and doodlings, Katie had written the words "healter-skelter" three times—misspelling that first word exactly the same way it had been misspelled on the LaBianca refrigerator door.

Older would not permit me to introduce it in evidence, however. I felt he was 100 percent wrong about this: it was unquestionably circumstantial evidence; it had relevance; and it was admissible. But Older ruled otherwise.

Older also gave me a scare when I attempted to introduce Krenwinkel's refusal to make a printing exemplar. Older agreed it was admissible, but he felt Krenwinkel should be given another chance to comply, and ordered her to do so.

The problem here was that this time Krenwinkel just might, on the advice of counsel, make the exemplar, and if she did, I knew there would be real problems.

Katie refused—on the instructions of Paul Fitzgerald!

What Fitzgerald apparently did not realize was that it would be extremely difficult, if not impossible, for LAPD to match the two printing samples. And had LAPD failed to do so, by law Patricia Krenwinkel would have to be acquitted of the LaBianca murders. Her refusal to give an exemplar was the only speck of independent evidence I had supporting Kasabian's testimony regarding Krenwinkel's involvement in these crimes.

Krenwinkel had been given an excellent chance to "beat the rap." To this day I still don't understand why her attorney instructed her as he did and so lost her that chance.

The People's last two witnesses, Drs. Blake Skrdla and Harold Deering, were the psychiatrists who had examined Dianne. On both direct and redirect examination, I elicited testimony from them to the effect that, although a powerful drug, LSD does not impair memory, nor is there any demonstrable medical evidence that it causes brain damage. This was important, since the defense attorneys had contended that the minds of various prosecution witnesses, in particular Linda and Dianne, had been so "blown" by LSD that they could not distinguish fantasy from reality.

Skrdla testified that people on LSD *can* tell the difference between the real and the unreal; in fact, they often have a heightened awareness. Skrdla further stated that LSD causes illusions rather than hallucinations—in other words, that which is seen is actually there, only the perception of it is changed. This surprised a lot of people, since LSD is called a hallucinogenic drug.

When Watkins was on the stand, I personally brought out that although he was only twenty, Paul had taken LSD between 150 and 200 times. Yet, as the jury undoubtedly observed, he was one of the brightest and most articulate of the prosecution witnesses. Skrdla also testified: "I have seen individuals who have taken it several hundred times and show no outward sign of any emotional disturbance while they are not on the drug."

Fitzgerald asked Skrdla: "Would LSD in large doses over a period of time make someone sort of a zombie, or would it destroy rational thought processes?"

If, as I suspected, Fitzgerald was trying to lay the foundation for a defense based on this premise, that foundation collapsed when Skrdla replied: "I have not seen this, counsel."

Dr. Deering was the People's last witness. He finished testifying on Friday, November 13. Most of Monday, the sixteenth, was spent introducing the People's exhibits into evidence. There were 320 of these, and Kanarek objected to every one, from the gun to the scale map of the Tate premises. His strongest objections were to the color death photos. Responding, I argued: "I grant the Court that these photographs are gruesome, there is no question about it, but if in fact the defendants are the ones who committed these murders, which the prosecution of course is alleging, they are the ones who are responsible for the gruesomeness and the ghastliness. It is their handiwork. The jury is entitled to look at that handiwork."

Judge Older agreed, and they were admitted into evidence.

One exhibit never made it into evidence. As mentioned earlier, a number of white dog hairs had been found on the discarded clothing the killers wore the night of the

Tate murders. Shown them, Winifred Chapman told me they looked like the hair of Sharon's dog. When I requested that they be brought over from LAPD, however, I got only excuses. Finally, I learned that while walking across the street to the Hall of Justice, one of the Tate detectives had dropped and broken the vial containing the hairs. He had been able to recover only one. Realizing that the expression "grasping at hairs" would be all too appropriate in this case, I decided against introducing that single hair into evidence.

At 4:27 P.M. that Monday—exactly twenty-two weeks after the start of the trial, and two days short of a year after my assignment to the case—I told the Court: "Your Honor, the People of the State of California rest."

Court was recessed until Thursday, November 19, at which time each of the defense attorneys argued the standard motions to dismiss.

Back in December 1969 a great many attorneys predicted that when we reached this point Manson would have to be acquitted because of insufficiency of evidence.

I doubted if any lawyer in the country felt that way now, including the attorneys for the defense.

Older denied all the motions.

THE COURT "Are you ready to proceed with the defense?"

FITZGERALD "Yes, Your Honor."

THE COURT "You may call your first witness, Mr. Fitzgerald."

FITZGERALD "Thank you, Your Honor. The defendants rest."

Nearly everyone in the courtroom was caught completely off guard. For several minutes even Judge Older seemed too stunned to speak. The ultimate legal issue at a criminal trial is not the defendant's guilt or innocence, as most people believe. The issue is whether or not the prosecution has met its legal burden of proving the guilt of the defendant beyond a reasonable doubt and to a moral certainty.* The defense obviously, but unexpectedly, had decided to avoid cross-examination and to rely on the argument that we hadn't proved the guilt of Manson and his co-defendants beyond a reasonable doubt and, hence, they were entitled to not-guilty verdicts.

The biggest surprise, however, was still to come.

*In American criminal jurisprudence, the term "Not Guilty" is not totally synonymous with innocence. "Not Guilty" is a legal finding by the jury that the prosecution hasn't proven its case. A "Not Guilty" verdict based on the insufficiency of the evidence can result from either of two states of mind on the part of the jury: that they believe the defendant is innocent and did not commit the crime charged, *or*, although they tend to believe he did commit the crime, the prosecution's case was not sufficiently strong to convince them of his guilt beyond a reasonable doubt and to a moral certainty.

Part 7

MURDER IN THE WIND

"You could feel something in the air, you know. You could feel something in the air."

Juan Flynn

"Snitches, and other enemies, will be taken care of."

Sandra Good

"Before his disappearance, Ronald Hughes, the missing defense attorney in the Tate-LaBianca murder trial, confided to close friends that he was in fear of Manson."

Los Angeles *Times*

November 19-December 20, 1970

Fitzgerald said the defense had rested. But the three female defendants now shouted that they wanted to testify.

Calling counsel into chambers, Judge Older demanded to know exactly what was going on.

There had been a split between the defense attorneys and their clients, Fitzgerald said. The girls wanted to testify; their attorneys opposed this, and wanted to rest their case.

Only after an hour of intense discussion did the real reason for the split come out, in an off-the-record admission by Fitzgerald:

Sadie, Katie, and Leslie wanted to take the stand and testify that they had planned and committed the murders—and that Manson was not involved!

Charlie had tried to explode his bombshell, but the attorneys for the girls had managed to defuse it, at least temporarily. Standing up against Manson for the first time, Ronald Hughes observed: "I refuse to take part in any proceeding where I am forced to push a client out the window."

The legal problems thus created were immense, but basically they came down to the question of which took precedence: the right to effective counsel or the right to testify. Worried that whichever course Older took might be reversible error on appeal, I suggested he take the matter to the State Supreme Court for a decision. Older, however, decided that even though the attorneys had rested, and had advised their clients not to take the stand, the right to testify "supersedes any and all other rights." The girls would be permitted to take the stand.

Older asked Manson if he also wished to testify. "No," he replied, then, after a moment's hesitation, added, "That is, not at this time anyway."

On returning to open court, Kanarek made a motion to sever Manson so he could be tried separately.

Charlie was now attempting to abandon ship, while letting the girls sink. After denying the motion, Older had the jury brought in and Susan Atkins took the stand and was sworn. Daye Shinn, however, refused to question her, stating that if he asked the questions she'd prepared, they would incriminate her.*

This created a whole new problem. Returning to chambers, Older remarked: "It is becoming perfectly clear that this entire maneuver by the defense is simply one ... to wreck the trial ... I do not intend to permit this to happen."

Still in chambers, and outside the presence of the jury, Susan Atkins told Judge Older that she wanted to testify to "the way it happened. The way I *saw* it happen."

THE COURT "You are subjecting yourself to the extreme risk of convicting yourself out of your own mouth, do you understand that?"

ATKINS "I understand that." She added that if she was convicted, "let them convict me on the truth. I do not wish to be convicted on a pack of lies taken out of context and just scattered every which way. Because, Mr. Bugliosi, your foundation is just crumbling. I have watched it crumble. You have been a sly, sneaky fox."

BUGLIOSI "Why do you want to put it back together for me, Sadie, if it is crumbling? You should be happy. You can go back to Barker Ranch if it is crumbling. Why do you want to take the stand to help me?"

Shinn said he would ask to be relieved as counsel if Older ordered him to question his client. Fitzgerald replied similarly, adding, "As far as I am concerned, it would be sort of aiding and abetting a suicide."

The matter was unresolved when court recessed for the day.

The following day Manson surprised everyone by saying that he too wanted to testify. In fact, he wanted to go on the stand before the others. Because of possible *Aranda*

---

*Shinn's remarks, in themselves incriminating, were later stricken from the record.

problems, however, it was decided that Manson should first testify outside the presence of the jury.

Manson was sworn. Rather than have Kanarek question him, he requested and received permission to make a statement.

He spoke for over an hour. He began almost apologetically, at first speaking so low that the spectators in the crowded courtroom had to lean forward to hear. But after a few minutes the voice changed, grew stronger, more animated, and, as I'd already discovered in my conversations with him, when this happened his face seemed to change too. Manson the nobody. Manson the martyr. Manson the teacher. Manson the prophet. He became all these, and more, the metamorphosis often occurring in midsentence, his face a light show of shifting emotions until it was not one face but a kaleidoscope of different faces, each real, but only for the moment.

He rambled, he digressed, he repeated himself, but there *was* something hypnotic about the whole performance. In his own strange way he was trying to weave a spell, not unlike the ones he had cast over his impressionable followers.

MANSON   "There has been a lot of charges and a lot of things said about me and brought against the co-defendants in this case, of which a lot could be cleared up and clarified . . .

"I never went to school, so I never growed up to read and write too good, so I have stayed in jail and I have stayed stupid, and I have stayed a child while I have watched your world grow up, and then I look at the things that you do and I don't understand . . .

"You eat meat and you kill things that are better than you are, and then you say how bad, and even killers, your children are. *You* made your children what they are . . .

"These children that come at you with knives, they are your children. You taught them. I didn't teach them. I just tried to help them stand up.

"Most of the people at the ranch that you call the Family were just people that you did not want, people that were alongside the road, that their parents had kicked out, that did not want to go to Juvenile Hall. So I did the best I could and I took them up on my garbage dump and I told them this: that in love there is no wrong . . .

"I told them that anything they do for their brothers and sisters is good if they do it with a good thought . . .

"I was working at cleaning up my house, something that Nixon should have been doing. He should have been on the side of the road, picking up his children, but he wasn't. He was in the White House, sending them off to war . . .

"I don't understand you, but I don't try. I don't try to judge nobody. I know that the only person I can judge is me . . . But I know this: that in your hearts and your own souls, you are as much responsible for the Vietnam war as I am for killing these people . . .

"I can't judge any of you. I have no malice against you and no ribbons for you. But I think that it is high time that you all start looking at yourselves, and judging the lie that you live in.

"I can't dislike you, but I will say this to you: you haven't got long before you are all going to kill yourselves, because you are all crazy. And you can project it back at me . . . but I am only what lives inside each and every one of you.

"My father is the jailhouse. My father is your system . . . I am only what you made me. I am only a reflection of you.

"I have ate out of your garbage cans to stay out of jail. I have wore your second-hand clothes . . . I have done my best to get along in your world and now you want to kill me, and I look at you, and then I say to myself, You want to kill *me*? Ha! I'm already dead, have been all my life. I've spent twenty-three years in tombs that you built.

"Sometimes I think about giving it back to you; sometimes I think about just jumping on you and letting you shoot me . . . If I could, I would jerk this microphone off and beat your brains out with it, because that is what you deserve, that is what you deserve . . .

"If I could get angry at you, I would try to kill every one of you. If that's guilt, I accept it . . .

"These children, everything they done, they done for the love of their brother . . .

"If I showed them that I would do anything for my brother—including giving my life for my brother on the battlefield—and then they pick up their banner, and they go off and do what they do, that is not my responsibility. I don't tell people what to do . . .

"These children [indicating the female defendants] were finding themselves. What they did, if they did whatever they did, is up to them. They will have to explain that to you . . .

"It's all your fear. You look for something to project it on, and you pick out a little old scroungy nobody that eats out of a garbage can, and that nobody wants, that was kicked out of the penitentiary, that has been dragged through every hellhole that you can think of, and you drag him and put him in a courtroom.

"You expect to break me? Impossible! You broke me years ago. You killed me years ago . . ."

Older asked Manson if he had anything further to say.

MANSON   "I have killed no one and I have ordered no one to be killed.

"I may have implied on several different occasions to several different people that I may have been Jesus Christ, but I haven't decided yet what I am or who I am."

Some called him Christ, Manson said. In prison his name was a number. Some now want a sadistic fiend, and so they see him as that. So be it. Guilty. Not guilty. They are only words. "You can do anything you want with me, but you cannot touch me because I am only my love . . . If you put me in the penitentiary, that means nothing because you kicked me out of the last one. I didn't ask to get released. I liked it in there because I like myself."

Telling Manson, "You seem to be getting far afield," Older asked him to stick to the issues.

MANSON   "The issues? . . . Mr. Bugliosi is a hard-driving prosecutor, polished education, a master of words, semantics. He is a genius. He has got everything that every lawyer would want to have except one thing: a case. He doesn't have a case. Were I allowed to defend myself, I could have proven this to you . . .

"The evidence in this case is a gun. There was a gun that laid around the ranch. It belonged to everybody. Anybody could have picked that gun up and done anything they wanted to do with it. I don't deny having that gun. That gun has been in my possession many times.

"Like the rope was there." Sure he'd bought the rope, Manson admitted, 150 feet of it, "because you need rope on a ranch."

The clothes? "It is really convenient that Mr. Baggot found those clothes. I imagine he got a little taste of money for that."

The bloodstains? "Well, they are not exactly bloodstains. They are benzidine reaction."

The leather thong? "How many people have ever worn moccasins with leather thongs?"

The photos of the seven bodies, 169 stab wounds? "They put the hideous bodies on display and they imply: If he gets out, see what will happen to you."

Helter Skelter? "It means confusion, literally. It doesn't mean any war with anyone. It doesn't mean that some people are going to kill other people ... Helter Skelter is confusion. Confusion is coming down around you fast. If you can't see the confusion coming down around you fast, you can call it what you wish."

Conspiracy? "Is it a conspiracy that the music is telling the youth to rise up against the establishment because the establishment is rapidly destroying things? Is that a conspiracy?

"The music speaks to you every day, but you are too deaf, dumb, and blind to even listen to the music ...

"It is not my conspiracy. It is not my music. I hear what it relates. It says 'Rise,' it says 'Kill.'

"Why blame it on me? I didn't write the music."

About the witnesses. "For example, Danny DeCarlo. He said that I hate black men, and he said that we thought alike ... But actually all I ever did with Danny DeCarlo or any other human being was reflect him back at himself. If he said he did not like the black man, I would say 'O.K.' So consequently he would drink another beer and walk off and say 'Charlie thinks like I do.'

"But actually he does not know how Charlie thinks because Charlie has never projected himself.

"I don't think like you people. You people put importance on your lives. Well, my life has never been important to anyone . . ."

Linda Kasabian. She only testified against him because she saw him as her father and she never liked her father. "So she gets on the stand and she says when she looked in that man's eyes that was dying, she knew that it was *my* fault. She knew it was my fault because she couldn't face death. And if she can't face death, that is not my fault. I can face death. I have all the time. In the penitentiary you live with it, with constant fear of death, because it is a violent world in there, and you have to be on your toes constantly."

Dianne Lake. She wanted attention. She would make trouble, cause accidents to get it. She wanted a father to punish her. "So as any father would do, I conditioned her mind with pain to keep her from burning the ranch down."

Yes, he was a father to the young girls and boys in the Family. But a father only in the sense that he taught them "not to be weak and not to lean on me." Paul Watkins wanted a father. "I told him: 'To be a man, boy, you have to stand up and be your own father.' So he goes off to the desert and finds a father image in Paul Crockett."

Yes, he put a knife to Juan Flynn's throat. Yes, he told him he felt responsible for all of these killings. "I do feel some responsibility. I feel a responsibility for the pollution. I feel a responsibility for the whole thing."

He didn't deny that he had told Brooks Poston to get a knife and go kill the sheriff of Shoshone. "I don't know the sheriff of Shoshone. I am not saying that I didn't say it, but if I said it, at the time I may have thought it was a good idea.

"To be honest with you, I don't recall ever saying 'Get a knife and a change of clothes and go do what Tex says.' Or I don't recall saying 'Get a knife and go kill the sheriff.'

"In fact, it makes me mad when someone kills snakes or dogs or cats or horses. I don't even like to eat meat— that is how much I am against killing . . .

"I haven't got any guilt about anything because I have never been able to see any wrong . . . I have always said:

Do what your love tells you, and I do what my love tells me ... Is it *my* fault that your children do what *you* do?

"*What about your children?*" Manson asked angrily, rising slightly in the witness chair as if he were about to spring forward and attack everyone in the courtroom. "*You say there are just a few?*

"*There are many, many more, coming in the same direction.*

"*They are running in the streets—and they are coming right at you!*"

I had only a few questions for Manson, none of which came from the notebooks I'd kept.

Q.   "You say you are already dead, is that right, Charlie?"

A.   "Dead in your mind or dead in my mind?"

Q.   "Define it any way you want to."

A.   "As any child will tell you, dead is when you are no more. It is just when you are not there. If you weren't there, you would be dead."

Q.   "How long have you been dead?"

Manson evaded a direct reply.

Q.   "To be precise about it, you think you have been dead for close to 2,000 years, don't you?"

A.   "Mr. Bugliosi, 2,000 years is relative to the second we live in."

Q.   "Suffice it to say, Department 104 is a long way from Calvary, isn't that true?"

Manson had testified that all he wanted was to take his children and return to the desert. After I reminded him that "the only people who can set you free so that you can go back to the desert are the twelve jurors in this case," and noting that, though he had testified for over an hour, "the jury in this case never heard a single, solitary word you said," I posed one final question: "Mr. Manson, are you willing to testify in front of the jury and tell them the same things that you have testified to here in open court today?"

Kanarek objected. Older sustained the objection, and I concluded my cross.

To my surprise, Older later asked me why I hadn't seriously cross-examined Manson. I'd thought the reason was obvious. I had nothing to gain, since the jury wasn't present. I had lots and lots of questions for Charlie, several notebooks full, *if* he took the stand in the presence of the jury, but in the meantime I had no intention of giving him a dry run.

However, when Older asked Manson if he now wished to testify before the jury, Charlie replied, "I have already relieved all the pressure I had."

As Manson left the stand and passed the counsel table, I overheard him tell the three girls: "You don't have to testify now."

The big question: what did he mean by "now"? I strongly suspected that Manson hadn't given up but was only biding his time.

After the defense had introduced their exhibits, Judge Older recessed court for ten days to give the attorneys time to prepare their jury instructions and arguments.

This being his first trial, Ron Hughes had never argued before a jury before, or participated in drawing up the instructions which the judge would give the jury just before they began their deliberations. He was obviously looking forward to it, however. He confided to TV newscaster Stan Atkinson that he was convinced he could win an acquittal for Leslie Van Houten.

He wouldn't even get the chance to try.

When court resumed on Monday, November 30, Ronald Hughes was absent.

Quizzed by Older, none of the other defense attorneys knew where he was. Fitzgerald said that he had last talked to Ron on Thursday or Friday, and that he sounded O.K. at that time. Hughes often spent his weekends camping at Sespe Hot Springs, a rugged terrain some 130 miles northwest of Los Angeles. There had been floods in the area the past weekend. It was possible that Hughes had been stranded there.

The next day we learned that Hughes had gone to Sespe on Friday with two teen-agers, James Forsher and Lauren Elder, in Miss Elder's Volkswagen. The pair—who were questioned but not held—said that when it began raining, they had decided to return to L.A., but Hughes had decided to stay over until Sunday. When the two tried to leave, however, their auto became mired down, and they were forced to abandon it and hike out.

Three other youths had seen Hughes on the morning of the following day, Saturday the twenty-eighth. He was alone at the time and on high ground, well away from the flood area. Chatting with them briefly, he appeared neither ill nor in any danger. Polygraphed, the three were found to have no additional knowledge and they were not held. Since Forsher and Elder had last seen Hughes a day earlier, they apparently were not polygraphed and their story was taken at face value.

Owing to the continued bad weather, it was two days before the Ventura Sheriff's Office could get up a helicopter to search the area. In the meantime, rumors abounded. One was to the effect that Hughes had deliberately skipped, either to avoid argument or to sabotage the trial. Knowing Ron, I seriously doubted if this was true. I became convinced it wasn't when reporters visited the place where Hughes lived.

He slept on a mattress in a garage behind the home of a friend. According to reporters, the place was a mess— one remarked that he wouldn't even let his dog sleep there. But on the wall of the garage, neatly framed and carefully hung, was Ronald Hughes' bar certificate.

Although there were numerous reports that a man fitting Hughes' description had been seen in various places—boarding a bus in Reno, driving on the San Bernardino freeway, drinking at a bar in Baja—none checked out. On December 2, Judge Older told Leslie Van Houten that he felt a co-counsel should be brought in to represent her during Hughes' absence. Leslie said she would refuse any other attorney.

On December 3, after consulting with Paul Fitzgerald, Older appointed Maxwell Keith co-counsel for Leslie.

A quiet, somewhat shy man in his mid-forties, whose conservative clothing and courtroom manner were in sharp contrast to those of Hughes, Keith had an excellent reputation in the legal community. Those who knew him well described him as conscientious, totally ethical, and completely professional, and it was clear from the start that he would be representing his client and not Manson.

Sensing this, Manson asked to have all the defense attorneys dismissed ("They aren't our lawyers; they won't listen to us") so he and the girls could represent themselves. He also demanded that the case be reopened so they could put on a defense. They had twenty-one witnesses waiting to testify, he said. Both requests were denied.

Keith had his work laid out for him. Before he could prepare his argument, he had to familiarize himself with 152 volumes of transcript, over 18,000 pages.

Though Older granted a delay until he could do so, he told all counsel: "We will continue to meet every day at 9 A.M. until further notice."

Older obviously wanted to count heads.

Several days earlier Steve Kay had overheard Manson tell the girls, "Watch Paul; I think he's up to something." I made sure Fitzgerald learned of the conversation. One missing attorney was one more than enough.

Neither the air search nor a subsequent ground search of the Sespe area yielded any trace of Hughes. The abandoned Volkswagen was found, with a batch of court transcripts inside, but other papers Hughes was known to have had, including a secret psychiatric report on Leslie Van Houten, were missing.

On December 6, Paul Fitzgerald told reporters, "I think Ron is dead." On December 7, an all-points bulletin was issued for Hughes, LASO admitting, "This is something you do when you have no other leads." On December 8, Judge Older went to the Ambassador Hotel to inform the jury of the reason for the delay. He also told them: "It appears fairly certain that you will be sequestered over the Christmas holidays." They took it much better than expected. On December 12, the search for Ronald Hughes was suspended.

The most persistent rumor was that Hughes had been murdered by the Family. There was, at this time, no evidence of this. But there was more than ample cause for speculation.

Though once little more than an errand boy for Manson, during the course of the trial Hughes had grown increasingly independent, until the two had finally split over whether there should be a defense—Hughes strongly opposing his client's taking the stand to absolve Charlie. I also heard from several sources, including Paul Fitzgerald, that Hughes was afraid of Manson. It was possible that he showed this fear, which, in Manson's case, was like waving a red flag before a bull. Fear turned Charlie on.

There could have been several reasons for his murder, if it was that. It may have been done to intimidate the other defense attorneys into letting Manson put on a defense during the penalty trial (one was so shaken by Hughes' disappearance that he went on a bender which ended in his arrest for drunken driving). Equally likely, it could have been a tactic to delay the trial—with the hope that it would result in a mistrial, or set the stage for a reversal on appeal.

Speculation, nothing more. Except for one odd, perhaps unrelated, incident. On December 2, four days after Hughes was last seen alive, fugitives Bruce Davis and Nancy Pitman, aka Brenda McCann, voluntarily surrendered to the police. Two of the Family's most hard-core members, Pitman had been missing for several weeks after failing to appear for sentencing on a forgery charge, while Davis—who had been involved in both the Hinman and Shea murders, who had picked up the gun with which Zero had "committed suicide" but had somehow left no prints, and who was the chief suspect in the slaying of two young Scientology students*—had evaded capture for over seven months.

Maybe it was just the proximity in time that linked the two events in my mind: Hughes' disappearance; Davis and Pitman's surprise surrender. But I couldn't shake the feeling that in some way the two incidents might be related.

*These murders will be discussed in a later chapter.

On December 18—three days before the Tate-LaBianca trial reconvened—the Los Angeles County grand jury indicted Steve Grogan, aka Clem; Lynette Fromme, aka Squeaky; Ruth Ann Moorehouse, aka Ouisch; Catherine Share, aka Gypsy; and Dennis Rice on charges of conspiracy to prevent and dissuade a witness (Barbara Hoyt) from attending a trial. Three other charges, including conspiracy to commit murder, were dismissed by Judge Choate on a 995 motion by the defense.

Although we had presumed—as I suspected the involved Family members had also—that an overdose of LSD could be fatal, we learned from medical experts that there was no known case of anyone's dying from this cause. There were many cases, however, where LSD had resulted in death from misperception of surroundings: for example, a person, convinced he could fly, stepping out the window of a tall building. I thought of Barbara, running through the traffic in downtown Honolulu. That she hadn't been killed was no fault of the Family. The result, however, was that, despite the best efforts of the LaBianca detectives, the DA's Office had a very weak case.

Pending trial, four of the five were released on bail. They immediately returned to the corner outside the Hall of Justice, where they would remain, on and off, during most of the remainder of the trial. Since Ouisch, who had given Barbara the LSD-laden hamburger, was nearly nine months pregnant, Judge Choate released her on her own recognizance. She promptly fled the state.

Nancy Pitman, who had been arrested with Davis, was freed on the forgery charge. She was rearrested a few weeks later while trying to pass Manson a tab of LSD in the visitors' room at the County Jail. After serving thirty days, she was again freed, to rejoin the group on the corner and, subsequently, to become involved in still another murder.

When court reconvened, the four defendants created a disturbance—Manson throwing a paper clip at the judge, the girls accusing him of "doing away with Hughes"—all obviously planned actions to garner the day's headlines.

Older ordered the four removed. As Sadie was being escorted out, she passed behind me. Though I didn't see what happened, I felt it: she knocked over an exhibit board, hitting me on the back of the head. Those who witnessed the incident said it appeared she was lunging for the Buck knife, which was on a nearby table. Thereafter the knife was kept well out of the reach of the defendants.

Maxwell Keith then told the Court that though he now felt himself familiar with the evidence, from having read the transcripts and other documents, he was not at all sure he could effectively represent his client, since he had not been present when the witnesses testified and therefore could not judge their demeanor or credibility. On this basis, he requested a mistrial.

Though Keith argued persuasively, Judge Older denied the motion, observing that every day attorneys argue cases in appellate courts without having been present during the actual trials.

Once this and several other motions were out of the way, it was time for the People's opening argument.*

During the guilt phase of a trial in California, the prosecution delivers an opening argument, which is followed by the opening argument of the defense, and, last, a closing argument (or final summation) by the prosecution. Thus the People have the last word during the guilt trial.

---

*This is entirely separate from the opening statement, which is delivered at the start of the trial.

During the penalty trial, if there is one, each side gives two arguments, with the defense being allowed to argue last.

I had spent several hundred hours preparing my opening argument for the guilt trial, starting even before the beginning of the trial itself. The result was contained in some 400 handwritten pages. But by this time I knew their contents so well I didn't even need to read them, but only glanced at them periodically.

I began by discussing in depth, with charts and other aids, the points of law the jury would have to consider: murder, conspiracy, and so on. The instructions which the judge would give the jury are printed, formal statements of law that use nebulous, abstract terms that often even lawyers don't understand. Moreover, the judge does not tell the jury how these rules of law apply to the facts of the case. Thus, in the jury's mind, the rules are floating lazily in the air with no thread connecting them to anything tangible. In each case I try, I make it a point to supply that link, by the liberal use of common-sense examples, by translating legalese into words and thoughts the jury will understand, and by literally tying those rules to the evidence.

After I had done this, I got into the principal part of my opening argument, summarizing the testimony of each witness, often quoting verbatim the words he had used on the stand, interrelating this testimony with the other evidence, and drawing inferences from it. Though the presentation took three days, it was a tight, cohesive package, and by the time I had finished I felt confident that I had established, beyond all doubt, Manson's control, his motives, his involvement, and the involvement of Watson, Atkins, Krenwinkel, and Van Houten.

Apparently it got to Charlie. At the end of my opening statement, he had tried to bribe deputy Maupin to free him. The night after I completed the first day of my opening argument, he tried to break out of jail.

Though the incident was officially denied by LASO, one of the deputies told me the details. Despite daily searches of both his person and his cell, Manson had managed to

obtain an incredibly long piece of string, at the end of
which he had attached a small weight. By some unknown
means or manner—for the area was supposedly under
constant surveillance—he had got the string across the
walkway in front of his cell and out a window, where it
reached a full ten stories to the ground. One or more con-
federates then attached the contraband. However, something must have happened which prevented Manson from
pulling it up, for when a deputy came around the corner
of the Hall of Justice the next morning he spotted the
string and its cargo: a lid of marijuana and a hacksaw
blade.

Accepting a promise that they would behave, Judge
Older permitted the three female defendants to return to
court the next afternoon. Manson, who said he had no desire to return, remained in the lockup, listening to the proceedings from there.

I had just resumed my argument when Leslie created a
disturbance. Sadie and Katie followed suit, and each of
the three was again ordered removed. This time Sadie was
led in front of the lectern where I was standing. Suddenly,
without warning, she kicked one of the female deputies in
the leg, then grabbed some of my notes, tearing them in
half. Grabbing them back, I involuntarily muttered, beneath my breath, "You little bitch!"

Though provoked, I regretted losing my cool.

The next day the Long Beach *Independent* bore the following front-page headline:

MANSON PROSECUTOR
TAKES SWING AT SUSAN

According to reporter Mary Neiswender: "The chaos
was capped by the chief prosecutor swearing at and attempting to slug one of the defendants ... Bugliosi
slapped the girl's hand, grabbed his notes and then swung at
her shouting, 'You little bitch!' "

In common with everyone else in the courtroom, Judge
Older saw the incident somewhat differently. Describing it
for the record, he branded the charge that I was

struggling with Susan "absolutely false. There was no struggle between Mr. Bugliosi and anybody. What happened was [she] walked by the rostrum and grabbed the notes off the rostrum."

While I'd like to say this was the only inaccurate press coverage during the trial, unfortunately the accounts of several reporters—including a representative of one of the wire services, whose reports appeared in papers all over the country—were often so error-filled that reading them gave one the feeling that the reporters had been attending another trial. On the other hand, such reporters as John Kendall of the Los Angeles *Times* and Bill Farr of the Los Angeles *Herald Examiner* did an excellent job, often catching little nuances even the attorneys missed.

After Krenwinkel had been removed, Judge Older called counsel to the bench and said that he had had it. "It is perfectly obvious to the Court that after lo, these many months, the defendants are operating in concert with each other . . . I don't think any American court is required to subject itself to this kind of nonsense day after day when it is perfectly obvious that the defendants are using it as a stage for some kind of performance . . ." Older then stated that the defendants would not be permitted to return to court during the remainder of the guilt trial.

I had hoped to finish my argument before court recessed for the Christmas holiday, but Kanarek's multitudinous objections prevented my doing so.

The feelings of the jurors at being sequestered over Christmas were exemplified by one who hung up the hotel menu and wrote "BAH, HUMBUG" across it. Though they were permitted family visits, and special parties had been arranged at the Ambassador, it was for most a miserable time. None had anticipated being away from home this long. Many were worried whether they would still have their jobs when the trial ended. And no one, including the judge, would even venture a guess when that might be.

On weekends both jurors and alternates—always accompanied by two male and two female deputies—had taken trips to such places as Disneyland, the movie studios, the San Diego Zoo, many probably seeing more of

Southern California than they had in the whole of their lives. They had dinner at restaurants all over Los Angeles. They went bowling, swimming, even nightclubbing. But this was only partial compensation for their long ordeal.

To keep up morale, the bailiffs exhibited considerable ingenuity. For example, though the trial was perhaps the most widely publicized in history, there were days when most of the action took place in chambers and newsmen could find little to report. At such times bailiff Bill Murray often cut huge sections out of the newspapers, just to make the jurors think they were still in the headlines.

But the strain was getting to them. Older people for the most part, they were set in their ways. Inevitably, arguments broke out, factions developed. One temperamental male juror slapped bailiff Ann Orr one night when, against his wishes, she changed channels on the communal TV. Often Murray and Orr sat up to 4 or 5 A.M., listening to a juror's complaints. As we neared the end of the guilt trial, I began worrying not about the evidence but about the personal disagreements the jurors might be carrying into the jury room with them when they began their deliberations.

It only takes one person to hang up a jury.

I concluded my opening argument on Monday, December 28, by telling the jury what I thought the defense's case would be, thereby lessening the psychological impact of the defense attorneys' arguments.

"The defense will probably argue that there is no conspiracy ... They will tell you that the Helter Skelter motive is absurd, ridiculous, unbelievable ... They will tell you that the interpretation of the Beatles' songs by Manson was normal ... They will tell you that Linda is insane with LSD; that she made up her story to be granted immunity; that Linda's testimony as an accomplice has not been corroborated ... Probably they will tell you the reason why they never put on a defense is because the prosecution never proved their case ... They will tell you that Charles Manson is not a killer; he wouldn't harm a flea.

"They will tell you that Charlie was not the leader of the Family; he never ordered these murders ... They will tell you that this has been a case of circumstantial evidence—as if there is something wrong with circumstantial evidence—completely disregarding the direct evidence by the way of Linda's testimony.

"Out of 18,000 pages of transcript, they will come up here and there with a slight discrepancy between the testimony of one witness and another witness, which of course has to be expected, but they will tell you this means that the People's witnesses are liars."

I then asked the jury as intelligent men and women to conscientiously evaluate the evidence in this case, applying common sense and reason, and thereby reach a just and fair verdict.

"Under the law of this state and nation these defendants are entitled to have their day in court. They got that.

"They are also entitled to have a fair trial by an impartial jury. They also got that.

"That is all that they are entitled to!

"Since they committed these seven senseless murders, the People of the State of California are entitled to a guilty verdict."

Toward the opening of his argument for Patricia Krenwinkel, Paul Fitzgerald said, "If we set out to rebut every witness the prosecution put on that stand we would be here until 1974," unthinkingly emphasizing the strength of the People's case, as well as the defense's inability to answer it.

Fitzgerald's argument was very disappointing. Not only were there many things he could have argued but didn't, he repeatedly misstated the evidence. He said that Sebring was hanged; that all the victims had been stabbed to death; that Tim Ireland heard Parent scream. He referred to Sharon as "Mary Polanski"; he had the killers entering the Tate residence through a bedroom window; he confused how many times Frykowski had been stabbed and struck. He said Linda testified to five knives rather than three; he had Linda driving on the second night when Manson was, and vice versa; he had a deputy who wasn't even present arresting Manson during the Spahn raid; and so on.

The prosecution stressed "murder, murder, murder," Fitzgerald said. "Actually, you have to decide whether it is a murder." The first thing the jury should decide, he continued, is "what crimes, if any, were committed."

"Now, a .22 caliber pistol, it strikes me, is a classically inefficient way to kill somebody . . ."

"It obviously does not make sense to hang anybody . . ."

"If you were a mastermind criminal, if you had absolute power over the minds and bodies of bootlicking slaves, as they were referred to, would you send women out to do a man's job? . . . Women, ladies and gentlemen, are life-givers. They make love, they get pregnant, they deliver babies. They are life-givers, not takers away. Women are adverse to violence . . ."

Only a small portion of Fitzgerald's argument was devoted to the evidence against his client. And rebuttal it was not.

He said that "there is doubt as to whether or not that fingerprint [found at the Tate residence] belongs to Patricia Krenwinkel." Even presuming it did, he said, "It is entirely conceivable, possible, and reasonable that Patricia Krenwinkel was at that house as an invited guest or a friend."

Some friend!

As for Krenwinkel's so-called confession to Dianne Lake, that she dragged Abigail Folger from the bedroom to the living room, that wasn't a confession at all, Fitzgerald said. She didn't say when this occurred or where. Maybe it took place in San Francisco in 1967.

Fitzgerald did spend a great deal of time trying to destroy the credibility of Linda Kasabian. In my argument I had remarked: "Linda Kasabian was on that witness stand, ladies and gentlemen, for eighteen days—an extraordinarily long period of time for any witness to testify in any case. I think you will agree with me that during those eighteen days Linda Kasabian and the truth were companions." Fitzgerald challenged this. But he was unable to cite a single discrepancy in her account.

However, the greater portion of his argument dealt with the case against Charles Manson. All the testimony regarding Manson's philosophy proved, Fitzgerald said, was "that he is some sort of right-wing hippie." Manson, Manson, Manson.

Fitzgerald ended his argument with a long, impassioned plea—not for his client, Patricia Krenwinkel, but for Charles Manson. There was, he concluded, insufficient evidence against Manson.

Not once did he say that there was insufficient evidence against Patricia Krenwinkel.

Nor did he even ask the jury to come back with a not guilty verdict for his client!

Daye Shinn had prepared a chart listing all the witnesses who testified against his client, Susan Atkins. He said he would rebut each.

"The first one on the list is Linda Kasabian, and I believe Mr. Fitzgerald has adequately covered Miss Kasabian's testimony."

He then skimmed over the criminal records of DeCarlo, Howard, Graham, and Walker.

On Danny DeCarlo: "How would you like to have him for your son-in-law? How would you like to have him meet your daughters?"

On Virginia Graham: "How would you like to invite her to your house for Christmas? You would have to hide the silverware.

"Mr. Bugliosi is laughing. At least I did not put him to sleep."

Shinn's entire argument took only 38 pages of transcript.

Irving Kanarek, who followed Shinn, consumed 1,182.

For the most part, Kanarek ignored my argument against Manson. Remaining on the offense rather than taking the defense, he pounded home two names—Tex, Linda. Who was it Linda Kasabian first slept with at Spahn Ranch? Stole the $5,000 for? Accompanied to the Tate residence? Charles "Tex" Watson. The most logical explanation for these murders was the simplest, Kanarek said. "Love of a girl for a boy."

As for his client, Kanarek portrayed him as a peaceful man whose only sin, if he had one, was that he preached and practiced love. "Now the people who brought these charges, they want to get Charles Manson, for some ungodly reason, which I think is related to Manson's life style."

Though many of his statements seemed to me to be too ridiculous for comment, I took many notes during Kanarek's argument. For he also planted little doubts, which, unless rebutted, could grow into bigger ones when the jury began its deliberations.

If the purpose was to start a black-white war, why did it stop the second night? Why wasn't there a third night, and a fourth? ... Why didn't the prosecution bring in Nader, and the policemen on the beach, and the man whose life Linda *claimed* to have saved? ... Are we to believe that by means of a wallet found in a toilet tank Mr. Manson intended to start a race war? ... If Tex pushed Parent's car up the driveway, why weren't his prints found on it?

Several times Kanarek referred to the trial as a "circus," a remark to which Judge Older reacted very strongly. He also reacted, this time without my prompting, to Kanarek's charge that the prosecution had suppressed evidence. "There is no evidence in this case that anyone has suppressed anything," Older said.

At the end of Kanarek's second day of argument, Judge Older told him that he was putting the jury to sleep. "Now, I am not going to tell you how to make an argument," Older said at the bench, "but I would suggest to you that you may not be doing your client the utmost amount of good by prolonging it unduly ..."

He went on for a third day, and a fourth.

On the fifth day the jury sent a note to the bailiff, requesting NoDoz for themselves and sleeping pills for Mr. Kanarek.

On the sixth day Older warned Kanarek, "You are abusing your right to argue just as you have abused practically every other right you have in this case ... There is a point, Mr. Kanarek, at which argument is no longer argument but a filibuster ... Yours is reaching that point."

Kanarek went on another full day before bringing his

argument to an end with the statement: "Charles Manson is not guilty of *any* crime."

Several times during Kanarek's argument Manson had interrupted with remarks from the lockup. Once he shouted, loud enough for the jury to hear, "Why don't you sit down? You're just making things worse."

During one of the noon recesses Manson asked to see me. I'd turned down several earlier requests, with the comment that I'd talk to him when he took the stand, but this time I decided to see what he wanted.

I was glad I did, as it was one of the most informative conversations we had—Manson telling me exactly how he felt about his three female co-defendants.

Manson wanted to clear up a couple of wrong impressions. One was Fitzgerald's reference to him as a "right-wing hippie." Though I personally thought the description had some validity, Manson felt otherwise. He'd never thought of himself as a hippie, he said. "Hippies don't like the establishment so they back off and form their own establishment. They're no better than the others."

He also didn't want me to think that Sadie, Katie, and Leslie were the best he could do. "I've screwed girls that would make these three look like boys," he said.

For some reason it was important to Manson that I believe this, and he re-emphasized it, adding, "I'm a very selfish guy. I don't give a fuck for these girls. I'm only out for myself."

"Have you ever told them that, Charlie?" I asked.

"Sure. Ask them."

"Then why would they do what they're doing for you? Why would they be willing to follow you anywhere—even to the gas chamber at San Quentin?"

"Because I tell them the truth," Manson replied. "Other guys bullshit them and say 'I love you and only you' and all that baloney. I'm honest with them. I tell them I'm the most selfish guy in the world. And I am."

Yet he was always saying that he would die for his brother, I reminded him. Wasn't that a contradiction?

"No, because that's selfish too," he responded. "He's not going to die for me unless I'm willing to die for him."

I had the strong feeling that Manson was leveling with me. Sadie, Katie, and Leslie were willing to murder, even give their own lives, for Charlie. And Charlie personally couldn't have cared less about them.

Though he wasn't even present when the witnesses testified, Maxwell Keith, arguing for Leslie Van Houten, delivered the best of the four defense arguments. He also did what no other defense attorney had dared do during the entire trial. He put the hat on Charles Manson—albeit with a ten-foot pole.

"The record discloses over and over again that all of these girls at the ranch believed Manson was God, really believed it.

"The record discloses that the girls obeyed his commands without any conscious questioning at all.

"If you believe the prosecution theory that these female defendants and Mr. Watson were extensions of Mr. Manson—his additional arms and legs as it were—if you believe that they were mindless robots, they cannot be guilty of premeditated murder." To commit first degree murder, Keith argued, you must have malice aforethought and you must think and plan. "And these people did not have minds to make up . . . Each of the minds of these girls and Mr. Watson were totally controlled by someone else."

As for Leslie herself, Keith argued that even if she did all the things the prosecution contended, she still had committed no crime.

"At best, if you want to believe Dianne Lake, the evidence shows that she was there.

"At best, it shows that she did something after the commission of these homicides that wasn't very nice.

"And at best, it showed that she wiped some fingerprints off after the commission of these homicides, which does not make her an aider and abetter.

"As repugnant as you may feel this is, nobody in the world can be guilty of murder or conspiracy to commit murder who stabs somebody after they are already dead. I'm sure that desecrating somebody that is dead is a crime in this state, but she is not charged with that."

This case, Keith concluded, must be decided on the basis of the evidence, and "on the basis of the evidence, ladies and gentlemen, I say to you: You must acquit Leslie Van Houten."

I began my final summation (closing argument) on January 13.

In my opinion, final summation is very often the most important part of the trial, since it's the last, final word to the jury. Again, several hundred hours had gone into the preparation. I began by meeting head on each of the defense contentions. In this way I hoped to dispose of any questions or lingering doubts that otherwise might distract the jury during the last phase of my argument, during which I summarize, as affirmatively as I can, the highlights and strengths of my case.

Taking on each of the defense attorneys in turn, I cited twenty-four misstatements of either the law or the testimony in Fitzgerald's presentation. As for his suggestion that if Manson ordered these murders he would have sent men rather than women, I asked, "Is Mr. Fitzgerald suggesting that Katie, Sadie, and Leslie were inadequate to do the job? Isn't Mr. Fitzgerald satisfied with their handiwork?" Fitzgerald had also contended that perhaps Linda planted the bloody clothing a few days before it was found. I reminded the jury that Linda was returned to California on December 2, in custody, and that the clothing was found on December 15. "Apparently Mr. Fitzgerald wants you to believe that one night between these dates Linda snuck out of her room at Sybil Brand, rounded up some clothing, put some blood on them, hitchhiked out to Benedict Canyon Road, threw the clothing over the side of the hill, then hitchhiked back to the jail and snuck back into her room."

Fitzgerald had likened the circumstantial evidence in this case to a chain, saying that if one link were missing the chain was broken. I, instead, likened it to a rope, each strand of which is a fact, and "as we add strands we add strength to that rope, until it is strong enough to bind these defendants to justice."

Shinn had raised very few points that needed rebutting. Kanarek had raised a great many, and I took them on one by one. A few samples:

Kanarek had asked why the prosecution didn't have the defendants try on the seven articles of clothing to see if they fitted. I reversed this, asking why, if they didn't fit, the defense didn't illustrate this to the jury.

As for the absence of Watson's prints on Parent's vehicle, I reminded them of Dolan's testimony that 70 percent of the times LAPD goes to a crime scene no readable prints are found. I also noted that in moving his hand, it was very likely Watson had created an unreadable smudge.

When I lacked the answer to a question, I frankly admitted it. But usually I offered at least one and often several possibilities. Whom did the glasses belong to? Frankly, we didn't know. But we did know, from Sadie's statement to Roseanne Walker, that they did not belong to the killers. Why was there no blood on the Buck knife found in the chair? Kanarek had raised this point. It was a good one. We had no answer. We could speculate, however, that Sadie had lost the knife before she stabbed Voytek and Sharon, possibly while she was in the process of tying up Voytek, and that at some later point she borrowed another knife from Katie or Tex. "Much more important than what knife she used was the fact that she confessed stabbing both of the victims to Virginia Graham and Ronnie Howard."

The whole thrust of Irving Kanarek's seven-day argument, I told the jury, was that the prosecution had framed its case against his client, Charles Manson.

"In other words, ladies and gentlemen," I observed, "there are seven brutal murders, so the police and the District Attorney got together and said, 'Let's prosecute some hippie for these murders, someone whose life style we don't like. Just about any hippie will do,' and we just arbitrarily picked on poor Charles Manson.

"Charles Manson is not a defendant in this trial because he is some long-haired vagabond who made love to young girls and was a virulent dissenter.

"He is on trial because he is a vicious, diabolical murderer who gave the order that caused seven human beings to end up in the cold earth. That is why he is on trial."

I also hit, and hard, Kanarek's claim that the prosecution was responsible for the excessive length of the trial. The jury had missed both Christmas and New Year's at home, and I didn't want them entering the jury chambers resenting the prosecution for this.

"Irving Kanarek, the Toscanini of tedium, is accusing the prosecution of tying up this court for over six months. You folks are the best witnesses. Every single, solitary witness that the prosecution called to the stand was asked brief questions, directly to the point. The witnesses were on that stand day after day after day on cross-examination, not on direct examination."

As for Maxwell Keith, he did "everything possible for his client, Leslie Van Houten," I observed. "He gave his best. Unfortunately for Mr. Keith, he had no facts and no law to support him. Mr. Keith, if you look at his argument very closely, never really disputed that Linda Kasabian and Dianne Lake told the truth. Basically, his position was that even if Leslie did the things Linda and Dianne said she did, she is still not guilty of anything.

"I wonder if Max would concede that she is at least guilty of trespassing?"

KEITH "I will."

Max's response surprised me. He was in effect admitting that Leslie had been in the LaBianca residence.

Even if Rosemary LaBianca was dead when Leslie stabbed her, I told the jury, she was guilty of first degree murder as both a co-conspirator and an aider and abetter. If a person is present at the scene of a crime, offering moral support, that constitutes aiding and abetting. But Leslie went far beyond this, stabbing, wiping prints, and so forth.

Also, we had only Leslie's word for it that Rosemary was dead when she stabbed her. "Only thirteen of Rosemary's forty-one stab wounds were post-mortem. What about the other twenty-eight?"

Yes, Tex, Sadie, Katie, and Leslie were robots, zombies, automatons. No question about it. But only in the sense that they were totally subservient and obsequious and servile to Charles Manson. Only in that sense. "This does not mean that they did not want to do what Charles Manson told them to do and weren't very willing participants in these murders. To the contrary, all the evidence goes the

other way. There is no evidence that any of these defen
dants objected to Charles Manson about these two horren
dous nights of murder.

"Only Linda Kasabian, down in Venice, said: 'Charlie,
am not you. I can't kill.'"

The others not only didn't complain, I noted, they
laughed when the Tate murders were described on TV
Leslie told Dianne that stabbing was fun, that the more
she stabbed the more she enjoyed it; while Sadie told Vir
ginia and Ronnie that it was better than a sexual climax.

"The fact that these three female defendants obeyed
Charles Manson and did whatever he told them to do does
not immunize them from a conviction of first degree mur
der. It offers no insulation, no protection whatsoever. If i
did, then hired killers or trigger men for the Mafia would
have a built-in defense for murder. All they would have t
say is: 'Well, I did what my boss told me to do.'"

Mr. Keith also "suggested that Watson and the three
girls had some type of mental disability which prevented
them from deliberating and premeditating, even prevented
them from having malice aforethought." The problem
with this, I told the jury, was that the defense never intro
duced any evidence of insanity or diminished capacity; on
the contrary, I reminded the jury, Fitzgerald described the
girls as "bright, intuitive, perceptive, well educated," while
the evidence itself showed "these defendants were thinking
very, very clearly on these two nights of murder."

Cutting telephone wires, instructing Linda to listen for
sounds, hosing blood off their bodies, disposing of their
clothing and weapons, wiping prints—"their conduct
clearly and unequivocally shows that on both nights they
knew exactly what they were doing, that they intended to
kill, they did kill, and they did everything possible to avoid
detection.

"They were not suffering, ladies and gentlemen, from
any diminished mental capacity. They were suffering from
a diminished heart, a diminished soul."

Still up to his old tricks, Kanarek had constantly interrupted my argument with frivolous objections. Even after
another contempt citation and a $100 fine, Kanarek per-

sisted. Calling counsel to the bench, Judge Older stated: "I have come to the regretful conclusion during the course of the trial that Mr. Kanarek appears to be totally without scruples, ethics, and professional responsibility so far as the trial of this lawsuit is concerned, and I want the record to clearly reflect that."

KANAREK   "May I be sworn?"

THE COURT   "Mr. Kanarek, I wouldn't believe you if you were."

With the defense arguments out of the way, I spent an entire afternoon reviewing the eyewitness testimony of Linda Kasabian. Among the instructions Judge Older was going to give the jury was one regarding the testimony of an accomplice. Both Fitzgerald and Kanarek had read the start of it: "The testimony of an accomplice ought to be viewed with distrust." They stopped there, however. I read the jury the rest: "This does not mean that you may arbitrarily disregard such testimony, but you should give it the weight to which you find it to be entitled after examining it with care and caution in the light of all the evidence in this case."

I then took the evidence of other witnesses, totally independent of Linda Kasabian, and showed how it confirmed or supported her testimony. Linda testified that Watson shot Parent four times. Dr. Noguchi testified that Parent was shot four times. Linda testified that Parent slumped over toward the passenger side. The police photographs show Parent slumped over toward the passenger side. Linda testified that Watson slit the screen horizontally. Officer Whisenhunt testified that the screen was slit horizontally. For the night of the Tate murders alone, I noted forty-five instances where other evidence confirmed Linda's account.

I concluded: "Ladies and gentlemen, the fingerprint evidence, the firearms evidence, the confessions, and all of the other evidence would convince the world's leading skeptic that Linda Kasabian was telling the truth."

I then cited every single piece of evidence against each of the defendants, starting with the girls and ending with Manson himself. I also noted that there were 238 refer-

ences in the transcript to Manson's domination over th
daily lives of his Family and his co-defendants. The infer
ence that he must have also been dominating and directin
them on the two nights of murder was unmistakable,
pointed out.

Thinking back over those many months, I remembere
how difficult it had been to come up with even a few.

Helter Skelter. During the trial the evidence of this ha
come in piece by piece, from the mouths of many wit
nesses. I assembled those pieces now, in one devastatin
package. Very forcefully, and I felt convincingly, I prove
that Helter Skelter was the motive for these murders, an
that that motive belonged to Charles Manson and Charle
Manson alone. I argued that when the words "Helte
Skelter" were found printed in blood, it was like findin
Manson's fingerprints at the scene.

We were nearly finished now. Within a few hours th
jury would begin its deliberations. I ended my summatio
on a very powerful note.

"Charles Manson, ladies and gentlemen, said that he ha
the power to give life. On the nights of the Tate-LaBianc
murders, he thought he had the concomitant right to tak
human life.

"He never had the right, but he did it anyway.

"On the hot summer night of August the eighth, 196
Charles Manson, the Mephistophelean guru who rape
and bastardized the minds of all those who gave them
selves so totally to him, sent out from the fires of hell
Spahn Ranch three heartless, bloodthirsty robots and—u
fortunately for him—one human being, the little hippi
girl Linda Kasabian.

"The photographs of the victims show how very we
Watson, Atkins, and Krenwinkel carried out their maste
Charles Manson's mission of murder . . .

"What resulted was perhaps the most inhuman, nigh
marish, horror-filled hour of savage murder and huma
slaughter in the recorded annals of crime. As the helples
defenseless victims begged and screamed out into the nig
for their lives, their lifeblood gushed out of their bodie
forming rivers of gore.

"If they could have, I am sure that Watson, Atkins, an

Krenwinkel would gladly have swum in that river of blood, and with orgasmic ecstasy on their faces. Susan Atkins, the vampira, actually tasted Sharon Tate's blood ...

"The very next night, Leslie Van Houten joined the group of murderers, and it was poor Leno and Rosemary LaBianca who were brutally butchered to death to satisfy Charles Manson's homicidal madness ...

"The prosecution put on a monumental amount of evidence against these defendants, much of it scientific, all of it conclusively proving that these defendants committed these murders.

"Based on the evidence that came from that witness stand, not only isn't there any reasonable doubt of their guilt, which is our only burden, there is absolutely no doubt whatsoever of their guilt ...

"Ladies and gentlemen, the prosecution did its job in gathering and presenting the evidence. The witnesses did their job by taking that witness stand and testifying under oath. Now you are the last link in the chain of justice.

"I respectfully ask that after your deliberations you come back into this courtroom with the following verdict." I then read in full the verdict the People wished.

I came now to the end of my argument, what the newspapers would call the "roll call of the dead." After each name I paused, so the jurors could recall the person.

"Ladies and gentlemen of the jury," I quietly began, "Sharon Tate ... Abigail Folger ... Voytek Frykowski ... Jay Sebring ... Steven Parent ... Leno LaBianca ... Rosemary LaBianca ... are not here with us now in this courtroom, *but from their graves they cry out for justice.* Justice can only be served by coming back to this courtroom with a verdict of guilty."

Gathering up my notes, I thanked the jury for the patience and attention they had shown throughout the proceedings. It had been a very, very long trial, I noted, and an immense imposition on their personal and private lives. "You have been an exemplary jury. The plaintiff at this trial is the People of the State of California. I have all the confidence in the world that you will not let them down."

After the noon recess, Judge Older instructed the jury. At 3:20 P.M., on Friday, January 15, 1971—exactly seven months after the start of the trial—the jury filed out to begin their deliberations.

The jury deliberated all day Saturday, then took Sunday off. On Monday they sent out two requests: that they be given a phonograph so they could play the Beatles' White Album, which, though introduced in evidence and much discussed, had never been played in court; and that they be permitted to visit the Tate and LaBianca residences.

After lengthy conferences with counsel, Older granted the first request but denied the second. Though admitting that, not having been to either of the death scenes, he too was naturally curious, the judge decided such visits would be tantamount to reopening the case, complete to the recalling of witnesses, cross-examination, and so on.

On Tuesday the jury asked to have Susan Atkins' letters to her former cellmates reread to them. This was done. Probably unprecedented in a case of this magnitude and complexity, at no time did the jury request that any of the actual testimony be reread. I could only surmise they were relying on the extensive notes each had taken throughout the trial.

Wednesday, Thursday, Friday—no further messages were received from the jury. Long before the end of the week the New York *Times* was reporting that the jury had been out too long, that it appeared they were deadlocked.

I wasn't bothered by this. I'd already told the press that I didn't expect them to come back for four or five days at the very minimum, and I wouldn't have been surprised had they stayed out a week and a half.

Nor did I worry about our having proven our case.

What did worry me was human nature.

Twelve individuals, from completely different backgrounds, had been locked up together longer than any jury in history. I thought a great deal about those twelve persons. One juror had let it be known that he intended to write a book about his experiences, and some of the other jurors were apprehensive about how they might be portrayed. The same juror also wanted to be elected foreman, and when he wasn't even in the running, was so piqued that for a day or two he wouldn't eat with the others.* Would he—or any of the other eleven—hang up the jury because of some personal animosity or slight? I didn't know.

Both Tubick and Roseland had daughters about the same age as Sadie, Katie, and Leslie. Would this affect their decision, and if so, how? Again I didn't know.

It was rumored, largely on the basis of glances they had exchanged in court, that the youngest member of the jury, William McBride II, had become slightly enamored of defendant Leslie Van Houten. It was unsubstantiated gossip, yet in the long hours the press waited for some word from the jury room, reporters made bets on whether McBride would vote second degree for Leslie, or perhaps even acquittal.

Immediately after my assignment to the case, I'd requested as much information as was available on the background of Charles Manson. Like much of the evidence, it came in piecemeal. Not until after the People had rested their case did I finally receive the records covering the seven months Manson spent at the National Training School for Boys in Washington, D.C. I found most of the information already familiar, with one startling exception.

If true, it could very well be the seed which—nurtured with hate, fear, and love—flowered into Manson's monstrous, grotesque obsession with the black-white revolution.

Manson had been sent to the institution in March 1951, when he was sixteen years old. In his admission summary, which was drawn up after he had been interviewed, there was a section on family background. The first two sentences read: "Father: unknown. He is alleged to have been a colored cook by the name of Scott, with whom the boy's mother had been promiscuous at the time of pregnancy."

Was Manson's father *black?* Reading through the rest

---

*Alva Dawson, the ex-deputy sheriff, and Herman Tubick, the mortician, had tied. A coin was tossed, and Tubick was made foreman. A deeply religious man, who began and ended each day of deliberations with silent prayer, Tubick had been a stabilizing influence during the long sequestration.

of the records, I found two similar statements, though no additional details.

There were several possible explanations for the inclusion of this statement in Manson's records. The first was that it was totally erroneous: some bureaucratic snafu of which Manson himself may even have been unaware. Another possibility was that Manson had lied about this in his interviews, though I couldn't imagine any conceivable benefit he would derive, particularly in a reform school located in the South. It was also possible that it was true.

There was one further possibility, and in a sense it was even more important than whether the information was true or false. Did young Charles Manson *believe* it to be true? If so, this would go a long way toward explaining the genesis of his bizarre philosophy, in which the blacks finally triumph over the whites but eventually have to hand over the reins of power to Manson himself.

I knew only one thing for sure. Even had I received this information earlier, I wouldn't have used it. It was much too inflammatory. I did decide, however, to ask Manson himself about it, if I got the chance.

I was in bed with the flu when, at 10:15 A.M. on Monday, January 25, court clerk Gene Darrow telephoned and said, "Just got the word. The jury has reached a verdict. Judge Older wants to see all the attorneys in his chambers as soon as they can get here."

The Hall of Justice resembled a fortress, as it had since the jury went out. A secret court order had been issued that same day, which began: "Due to intelligence reports indicating a possible attempt to disrupt proceedings on what has been described as 'Judgment Day,' additional security measures will be implemented . . ." There followed twenty-seven pages of detailed instructions. The entire Hall of Justice had been sealed, anyone entering the building for whatever reason being given a personal effects and body search. I now had three bodyguards, the judge a like number.

The reason for this intensive security was never made public. From a source close to the Family, LASO had heard what they initially believed to be an incredible tale.

While working at Camp Pendleton Marine Base, one of Manson's followers had stolen a case of hand grenades. These were to be smuggled into court on "Judgment Day" and used to free Manson.

Again, we didn't know precisely what the Family meant by Judgment Day. But by this time we did know that at least a part of the story was true. A Family member *had* been working in the arms depot at Pendleton, and after he quit, a case of hand grenades *was* missing.

By 11:15 all counsel were in chambers. Before bringing the jury in, Judge Older said he wanted to discuss the penalty trial.

California has a bifurcated trial system. The first phase, which we had just completed, was the guilt trial. If any of the defendants were convicted, a penalty trial would follow, in which the same jury would determine the penalty for the offense. In this case we had requested first degree murder verdicts against all the defendants. If the jury returned such verdicts, there were only two possible penalties: life imprisonment or death.

The penalty trial is, in most cases, very short.

After conferring with counsel, Judge Older decided that if there was a penalty phase, it would commence in three days. Older also said he had decided to seal the courtroom until after the verdicts were read and all the jurors polled. Once the jurors and the defendants had been removed, the press would be allowed out, and then the spectators.

The girls were brought in first. Though they had usually worn fairly colorful clothing during the trial, apparently there hadn't been time for them to change, as all were wearing drab jail dresses. They seemed in good spirits, however, and were giggling and whispering. On being brought in, Manson winked at them and they winked back. Charlie was wearing a white shirt and blue scarf, and sporting a new, neatly trimmed goatee. Another face, for judgment day.

Single file, the jurors entered the jury box, taking their assigned seats, just as they had hundreds of times before. Only this time was different, and the spectators searched the twelve faces for clues. Perhaps the most common of all courtroom myths is that a jury won't look at the ac-

cused if they have reached a guilty verdict. This is rarely
true. None held Manson's gaze when he stared at them,
but then neither did they quickly look away. All you could
really read in their faces was a tired tenseness.

THE COURT   "All jurors and alternates are present. All
counsel but Mr. Hughes are present. The defendants are
present. Mr. Tubick, has the jury reached a verdict?"

TUBICK   "Yes, Your Honor, we have."

THE COURT   "Will you hand the verdict forms to the
bailiff."

Foreman Tubick handed them to Bill Murray, who in
turn gave them to Judge Older. As he scanned them,
saying nothing, Sadie, Leslie, and Katie fell silent and
Manson nervously fingered his goatee.

THE COURT   "The clerk will read the verdicts."

CLERK   "In the Superior Court of the State of California, in and for the County of Los Angeles, the People of
the State of California vs. Charles Manson, Patricia Krenwinkel, Susan Atkins, and Leslie Van Houten, Case No.
A–253,156. Department 104."

Darrow paused before reading the first of the twenty-
seven separate verdicts. It seemed minutes but was probably only seconds. Everyone sat as if frozen, waiting.

"We, the jury in the above-entitled action, find the defendant, Charles Manson, *guilty* of the crime of murder
of Abigail Folger in violation of section 187, Penal Code
of California, a felony, as charged in Count I of the Indictment, and we further find it to be murder of the first
degree."

Glancing at Manson, I noticed that, though his face was
impassive, his hands were shaking. The girls displayed no
emotion whatsoever.

The jury had deliberated for forty-two hours and forty
minutes, over a nine-day period, a remarkably short time
for such a long and complicated trial. The reading of the
verdicts took thirty-eight minutes.

The People had obtained the verdicts they had requested against Charles Manson, Patricia Krenwinkel, and
Susan Atkins: each had been found guilty of one count of
conspiracy to commit murder and seven counts of murder
in the first degree.

The People had also obtained the verdicts requested against Leslie Van Houten: she had been found guilty of one count of conspiracy to commit murder and two counts of murder in the first degree.

I later learned that although McBride had suggested the possibility of a lesser finding against Leslie Van Houten, when it came time to vote there was only one ballot and it was unanimous.

While the individual jurors were being polled, Leslie turned to Katie and said, "Look at the jury; don't they look sad?" She was right, they did. Obviously it had been a very rough ordeal.

As the jury was being taken out, Manson suddenly yelled at Older: "We are still not allowed to put on a defense? You won't outlive that, old man!"

Kanarek seemed strangely unmoved by the verdict. Though Fitzgerald told the press, "We expected the worst from the start," he appeared thoroughly shaken. Outside court, he told reporters, "We felt we lost the case when we lost our change of venue motion. We had a hostile and antagonistic jury. The defendants had the same chance Sam Sheppard had in Cleveland—none." Fitzgerald further stated that had the trial been held anywhere but in Los Angeles, he was sure they would have won acquittals for all the defendants.

"I don't believe that for one minute," I told the press. "It is just weeping on the part of the defense. The jury was not only fair, they based their verdict solely and exclusively on the evidence that came from that witness stand."

"Yes," I responded to the most frequently asked question, "we will seek the death penalty against all four defendants."

The Manson girls on the corner outside the Hall of Justice first heard the news over the radio. They too were strangely calm. Though Brenda told newsmen, "There's a revolution coming, very soon," and Sandy said, "You are next, all of you," these were Manson's words, delivered in court months before, which they had been mouthing ever since. There were no tears, no outward display of emotion. It was as if they really didn't care. Yet I knew this wasn't true.

Watching the interview later on TV, I surmised that perhaps they had conditioned themselves to expect the worst.

In retrospect, another possibility emerges. Once the lowest of the low in the Manson hierarchy, good only for sex, procreation, and serving men, the girls had now become his chief apostles, the keepers of the faith. Now Charlie was dependent on them. It appears quite likely that they were undisturbed by the verdict because they were already formulating a plan which, if all went well, could set not only Manson but all the other Family members free.

Part 8

FIRES IN
YOUR CITIES

"Mr. and Mrs. America—you are wrong.
I am not the King of the Jews nor am
I a hippie cult leader. I am what you
have made of me and the mad dog devil
killer fiend leper is a reflection of
your society . . . Whatever the outcome of
this madness that you call a fair trial
or Christian justice, you can know
this: In my mind's eye my thoughts
light fires in your cities."

Statement issued by
Charles Manson after
his conviction for the
Tate-LaBianca murders

During the penalty trial the sole issue for the jury to decide was whether the defendants should receive life imprisonment or the death penalty. Considerations like mitigating circumstances, background, remorse, and the possibility of rehabilitation were therefore now relevant.

To avoid prolonging the trial and risk alienating the jury, I called only two witnesses: officer Thomas Drynan and Bernard "Lotsapoppa" Crowe.

Drynan testified that when he arrested Susan Atkins outside Stayton, Oregon, in 1966, she was carrying a .25 caliber pistol. "I asked Miss Atkins what she intended to do with the gun," Drynan recalled, "and she told me that if she had the opportunity she would have shot and killed me."

Drynan's testimony proved that even before Susan Atkins met Charles Manson she had murder in her heart.

On cross-examination Shinn asked Drynan about the .25 caliber pistol.

Q. "The size is very small—it looks like a toy gun—is that correct?"

A. "Well, not to me."

Crowe described how, on the night of July 1, 1969, Manson had shot him in the stomach and left him for dead. The importance of Crowe's testimony was that it proved that Manson was quite capable of committing murder on his own.

On February 1, I rested the People's case. That afternoon the defense called their first witnesses: Katie's parents, Joseph and Dorothy Krenwinkel.

Joseph Krenwinkel described his daughter as an "exceedingly normal child, very obedient." She was a Bluebird, Camp Fire Girl, and Job's daughter, and belonged to the Audubon Society.

FITZGERALD "Was she gentle with animals?"

MR. KRENWINKEL "Very much so."

Patricia had sung in the church choir, Mr. Krenwinkel testified. Though she was not an exceptional student, she received good grades in the classes she liked. She had attended one semester of college, at Spring Hill College, a Jesuit school in Mobile, Alabama, before returning to Los Angeles, where she shared an apartment with her half sister.

The Krenwinkels had divorced when Patricia was seventeen. According to Joseph Krenwinkel, there was no bitterness; he and his wife had parted, and remained, friends.

Yet just a year later, when Patricia was eighteen, she had abandoned her family and job to join Manson.

Dorothy Krenwinkel said of her daughter, "She would rather hurt herself than harm any living thing."

FITZGERALD "Did you love your daughter?"

A. "I did love my daughter; I will always love my daughter; and no one will ever convince me she did anything terrible or horrible."

FITZGERALD "Thank you."

BUGLIOSI "No questions, Your Honor."

Fitzgerald wanted to introduce into evidence a number of letters Patricia Krenwinkel had written to various persons, including her father and a favorite priest at Spring Hill.

All were hearsay and clearly inadmissible. All I would have needed to do was object. But I didn't. Though aware that they would appeal to the sympathies of the jury, I felt that justice should prevail over technicalities. The issue now was whether this girl should be sentenced to death. And this was an issue for the jury to decide, not me. I felt that in reaching that extremely serious decision, they should have any information even remotely relevant.

Fitzgerald was both relieved and very grateful when I let them come in.

Keith handled the direct examination of Jane Van Houten, Leslie's mother. Keith later told me that although Leslie's father didn't want to testify, he was behind Leslie 100 percent. Although, like the Krenwinkels, the Van

Houtens were divorced, they too had stuck by their daughter.

According to Mrs. Van Houten, "Leslie was what you would call a feisty little child, fun to be with. She had a wonderful sense of humor." Born in the Los Angeles suburb of Altadena, she had an older brother and a younger brother and sister, the latter Korean orphans whom the Van Houtens had adopted.

When Leslie was fourteen, her parents separated and divorced. "I think it hurt her very much," Mrs. Van Houten testified. That same year Leslie fell in love with an older youth, Bobby Mackey; became pregnant; had an abortion; and took LSD for the first time. After that she dropped acid at least once and often two or three times a week.*

During her freshman and sophomore years at Monrovia High School, Leslie was one of the homecoming princesses. She tried out again her junior year, but this time she didn't make it. Bitter over the rejection, she ran away with Mackey to Haight-Ashbury. The scene there frightened her, however, and she returned home to finish high school and to complete a year of secretarial training. Mackey, in the meantime, had begun studying with a yoga group. In an attempt to continue their relationship, Leslie joined also, giving up both drugs and sex. Her good intentions were short-lived; within a few months she broke with both Mackey and the group.

Mrs. Van Houten did not testify to the period which followed; possibly she knew little if anything about it. From interviews I'd learned that Leslie went full spectrum. The one-time yoga renunciate was now anxious to "try anything," be it drugs or answering sex-partner ads in the Los Angeles *Free Press*. A long-time friend stopped dating her because she had become "too kinky."

For a few months Leslie lived in a commune in Northern California. During this period she met Bobby Beausoleil, who had his own wandering "family," consisting of Gypsy and a girl named Gail. Leslie became a part

---

*Patricia Krenwinkel had also taken LSD before meeting Manson. Very obese in her early teens, she began using diet pills at fourteen or fifteen, then tried reds, mescaline, and LSD, provided by her half sister Charlene, now deceased, who was a heroin addict.

of the *ménage à quatre*. Gail, however, was jealous, and the arguments became near constant. First Gypsy split, moving to Spahn Ranch. Then, shortly after, Leslie followed, also joining Manson. She was nineteen.

About this time Leslie called her mother and told her that she had decided to drop out and that she wouldn't be hearing from her again. She didn't, until Leslie's arrest.

Keith asked Mrs. Van Houten: "How do you feel about your daughter now?"

A. "I love Leslie very much."

Q. "As much as you always have?"

A. "More."

As the parents testified, one realized that they too were victims, just as were the relatives of the deceased.

Calling the defendants' parents first was a bad tactical error on the part of the defense. Their testimony and plight evoked sympathy from everyone in the courtroom. They should have been called at the very end of the defense's case, just before the jury went out to deliberate. As it was, by the time the other witnesses had testified, they were almost forgotten.

Shinn called no witnesses on behalf of Susan Atkins. Her father, Shinn told me, had refused to have anything more to do with her. All he wanted, he said, was to get his hands on Manson.

A reporter from the Los Angeles *Times* had located Charles Manson's mother in a city in the Pacific Northwest. Remarried and living under another name, she claimed Charles' tales of childhood deprivation were fictions, adding, "He was a spoiled, pampered child."

Kanarek did not use her as a witness. Instead, he called Samuel Barrett, Manson's parole officer.

Barrett was a most unimpressive witness. He thought he first met Manson "about 1956, around that"; he couldn't remember whether Manson was on probation or parole; he stated that since he was responsible for 150 persons, he couldn't be expected to recall everything about each one.

Repeatedly, Barrett minimized the seriousness of the various charges against Manson prior to the murders. The reason he did this was obvious: otherwise, one might wonder why he hadn't revoked Manson's parole. One still did wonder. Manson associated with ex-cons, known narcotics users, and minor girls. He failed to report his whereabouts, made few attempts to obtain employment, repeatedly lied regarding his activities. During the first six months of 1969 alone, he had been charged, among other things, with grand theft auto, narcotics possession, rape, contributing to the delinquency of a minor. There was more than ample reason for parole revocation.

During a recess one of the reporters approached me in the hall. "God, Vince," he exclaimed, "did it ever occur to you that if Barrett had revoked Manson's parole in, say, April of 1969, Sharon and the others would probably still be alive today?"

I declined comment, citing the gag order as an excuse. But it had occurred to me. I had thought about it a great deal.

On direct, Barrett had testified that there was nothing in Manson's prison records to indicate that he was a behavioral risk. Over Kanarek's objections, on cross-examination I had him examine the folder on Manson's attempted escape from federal custody in 1957.

The parade of perjurers began with little Squeaky.

Lynette Alice Fromme, twenty-two, testified that she was from an upper-middle-class background, her father an aeronautical engineer. When she was seventeen, she said, her father kicked her out of the house. "And I was in Venice, sitting down on a curb crying, when a man walked up and said, 'Your father kicked you out of the house, did he?'

"And that was Charlie."

Squeaky placed great importance on the fact that she had met Manson before any of the other girls, excepting only Mary Brunner.

In questioning her about the Family, Fitzgerald asked: "Did you have a leader?"

A.   "No, we were riding on the wind."

No leader, but—

"Charlie is our father in that he would—he would point out things to us."

Charlie was just like everyone else, but—

"I would crawl off in a corner and be reading a book, and he would pass me and tell me what it said in the book ... And also he knew our thoughts ... He was always happy, always ... He would go into the bathroom sometimes to comb his hair, and there would be a whole crowd of people in there watching him because he had so much fun."

Squeaky had trouble denying the teachings of her lord and master. When Fitzgerald tried to minimize the importance of the Beatles' White Album, she replied, "There is a lot in that album, there is a lot." Although she claimed, "I never heard Charlie utter the words 'helter skelter,'" she went on to say that "it is a matter of evolution and balance" and "the black people are coming to the top, as it should be."

Obviously these were not the answers Fitzgerald wanted, and apparently he betrayed his reaction.

FROMME   "How come you're making those faces?"

FITZGERALD   "I'm sorry, continue."

Calling counsel to the bench, Judge Older said, "She can only harm the defendants doing what she is doing."

I explained to Older, "If the Court is wondering why I am not objecting, it is because I feel that her testimony is helpful to the prosecution."

So helpful, in fact, that there was little need for cross-examination. Among the questions I had intended to ask her, for example, was one Kanarek now asked: "Did you think that Charles Manson was Jesus Christ?"

Squeaky hesitated a moment before answering. Would she be the apostle who denied Jesus? Apparently she decided she would not, for she replied: "I think that the Christians in the caves and in the woods were a lot of kids just living and being without guilt, without shame, being able to take off their clothes and lay in the sun ... And I see Jesus Christ as a man who came from a woman who did not know who the father of her baby was."

Squeaky was the least untruthful of the Family members who testified. Yet she was so damaging to the defense that thereafter Fitzgerald let the other defense attorneys call the witnesses.

Keith called Brenda McCann, t/n Nancy Laura Pitman, nineteen. Though not unattractive, Brenda came across as a tough, vicious little girl, filled with hostility that was just waiting to erupt.

Her father "designed the guidance controls of missiles over in the Pentagon," she said. He also kicked her out of the house when she was sixteen, she claimed. The dropout from Hollywood High School asserted there was no such thing as a Family, and Charlie "was not a leader at all. It was more like Charlie followed us around and took care of us."

But, as with Squeaky and the girls who would follow her, it was obvious that Brenda's world revolved around a single axis. He was nobody special but "Charlie would sit down and all the animals would gather round him, donkeys and coyotes and things ... And one time he reached down and petted a rattlesnake."

Questioned by Kanarek, Brenda testified that Linda "would take LSD every day ... took speed ... Linda loved Tex very much . . . Linda followed Tex everywhere . . ."

On cross-examination I asked Brenda: "Would you give up your life for Charles Manson if he asked you to?"

A.   "Many times he has given you his life."

Q.   "Just answer the question, Brenda."

A.   "Yes, I would."

Q.   "Would you lie on the stand for Charles Manson?"

A.   "No, I would tell the truth on the stand."

Q.   "So you would die for him, but not lie for him?"

A.   "That's right."

Q.   "Do you feel that lying under oath is a more serious matter than dying, Brenda?"

A.   "I don't take dying all that seriously myself."

All these witnesses were extremely antagonistic toward their real families. Sandra Good, for example, claimed that her father, a San Diego stockbroker, had disowned her, neglecting to mention that this was only after he had sent her thousands of dollars and was threatened by Manson if he didn't give her more.

Manson had severed their umbilical cords while fastening one of his own. And throughout their testimony it showed. Even more than Squeaky and Brenda, Sandy rhapsodized on Manson's "magical powers." She told the story of how Charlie had breathed on a dead bird and brought it back to life. "I believe his voice could shatter this building if he so desired . . . Once he yelled and a window broke."

It was not until the penalty trial that the jury learned of the vigil of the Family members on the corner of Temple and Broadway. Rather movingly, Sandy testified to life there. "You can hardly see the sky most of the time for the smog. They are always digging; every day there is a new project going; something is always under construction. They are always ripping out something and putting something in, usually of a concrete nature. It is insane out there. It's madness, and the more I am out there the more I feel this X. I am X'd out of it."

After I'd declined to cross-examine Sandy, she very angrily asked, "Why didn't you ask me any questions?"

"Because you said nothing which hurt the People's case, Sandy," I replied. "In fact, you helped it."

I had anticipated that Sandy would testify that Manson wasn't even at Spahn Ranch at the time the murders had occurred. When she didn't, I knew the defense had decided to abandon the idea of using an alibi defense. Which meant they had something else in mind. But what?

Manson and the three female defendants had been allowed to return to court during the penalty phase. They were much quieter now, far more subdued, as if it had finally got through to them that this "play," as Krenwinkel had characterized it, might cost them their lives. While Squeaky and the other Manson girls testified, their mentor looked thoughtful and pulled on his goatee, as if to say: They're telling it like it is.

The female witnesses wore their best clothes for the occasion. It was obvious that they were both proud and happy to be up there helping Charlie.

The jurors shared a common expression—incredulity. Few even bothered to take notes. I suspected that all of them were mulling over the astonishing contrast. On the stand the girls talked of love, music, and babies. Yet while the love and the music and the babies were going on, this same group was going out and butchering human beings. And to them, amazingly enough, there was no inconsistency, no conflict between love and murder!

By February 4, I was fairly sure, from the questions Kanarek had been asking the witnesses, that Manson was not going to take the stand. This was my biggest disappointment during the entire trial, that I wouldn't have the chance to break Charlie on cross-examination.

That same day our office learned that Charles "Tex" Watson had been returned to Los Angeles and ruled competent to stand trial.

Only three days after his transfer to Atascadero, Watson had begun eating regular meals. Within a month, one of the psychiatrists who examined him wrote: "There is no evidence of abnormal behavior at the present time except his silence, which is purposeful and with reason." Another later noted: "Psychological testing gave a scatter pattern of responses inconsistent with any recognized form of mental illness . . ." In short, Tex was faking it. All this information would be useful, I knew, if Tex tried to plead insanity during his trial, which was now scheduled to follow the current proceedings.

Catherine Share, aka Gypsy, was the defense's most effective liar. She was also, at twenty-eight, the oldest female member of the Family. And, of all its members, she had the most unusual background.

She was born in Paris in 1942, her father a Hungarian violinist, her mother a German-Jewish refugee. Both parents, members of the French underground, committed suicide during the war. At eight, she was adopted and brought to the United States by an American family. Her adoptive mother, who was suffering from cancer, committed suicide when Catherine was sixteen. Her adoptive father, a psychologist, was blind. She cared for him until he remarried, at which time she left home.

A graduate of Hollywood High School, she had attended college for three years; married; divorced a year later. A violin virtuoso since childhood, with an unusually beautiful singing voice, she had obtained work in a number of movies. It was on the set of one, in Topanga Canyon, that she became involved with Bobby Beausoleil, who had a minor role. About two months later Beausoleil introduced her to Charles Manson. Though it was, on her part, love at first sight, she continued traveling with the Beausoleil menage for another six months, before splitting for Spahn Ranch. Although she was an avowed Communist when she joined the Family, Manson soon convinced her that his dogma was ordained. "Of all the girls," Paul Watkins had told me, "Gypsy was most in love with Charlie."

She was also the most eloquent in his defense. But, though brighter and more articulate than most of the others, she too occasionally slipped up.

"We are all facing the same sentence," she told the jury. "We are all in a gas chamber right here in L.A., a slow-acting one. The air is going away from us in every city. There is going to be no more air, and no more water, and the food is dying. They are poisoning you. The food you are eating is poisoning you. There is going to be no more earth, no more trees. Man, especially white man, is killing this earth.

"But those aren't Charles Manson's thoughts, those are my thoughts," she quickly added.

During her first day on the stand Gypsy dropped no bombshells. She did try to rebut various parts of the trial testimony. She said that Leslie often went out and stole things, to explain away the back-house incident. She claimed that it was Linda who suggested stealing the $5,000. She also said that Linda didn't want Tanya, and had dumped her on the Family.

It was not until her second day on the stand, on *redirect* by Kanarek, and immediately after Kanarek had asked to approach the witness and speak to her privately, that Gypsy suddenly came up with an alternative motive—one that was designed to clear Manson of any involvement in the murders.

Gypsy claimed that it was Linda Kasabian, not Charles Manson, who had masterminded the Tate-LaBianca murders! Linda was in love with Bobby Beausoleil, Gypsy said. When Bobby was arrested for the Hinman murder,

Linda proposed that the girls commit other murders which were similar to the Hinman slaying, in the belief that the police would connect the crimes and, realizing that Beausoleil was in custody when these other murders occurred, set him free.

The "copycat" motive was in itself not a surprise. In fact, Aaron Stovitz had suggested it as one of several possible motives in his interview with the reporters from *Rolling Stone*. There was only one thing wrong with it. It wasn't true. But in an attempt to clear Manson and to cast doubt on the Helter Skelter motive, the defense witnesses, starting with Gypsy, now began manufacturing their own bogus evidence.

The scenario they had so belatedly fashioned was as transparent as it was self-serving.

Gypsy claimed that on the afternoon of August 8, 1969, Linda explained the plan to her and asked her if she wanted to go along. Horrified, Gypsy instead fled to the mountains. When she returned, the murders had already occurred and Linda was gone.

Gypsy further testified that Bobby Beausoleil was innocent of the Hinman murder; all he had done was drive a car belonging to Hinman. And Manson wasn't involved either. The Hinman murder had been committed by Linda, Sadie, and *Leslie!*

Maxwell Keith quickly objected. At the bench he told Judge Older: "It sounds to me like this girl is leading up to testimony of an admission by my client to her participation in the Hinman, Tate, and LaBianca murders. This is outrageous!"

THE COURT "I don't know if Mr. Kanarek has the faintest idea of what he wants to do."

FITZGERALD "I am afraid so."

KANAREK "I know exactly."

Keith observed: "I talked to this witness yesterday at the County Jail about her testimony. It was sort of innocuous testimony regarding Leslie. And all of a sudden, boom, we are being bombed out of the courtroom."

On cross-examination I asked: "Isn't it true, Gypsy, that what you are trying to do is clear Charles Manson at the expense of Leslie and Sadie?"

A.   "I wouldn't say that. No, it isn't true."

To destroy her credibility, I then impeached Gypsy with a number of inconsistent statements she had previously made. Only then did I return to the bogus motive.

Gypsy had testified that immediately after hearing of the Tate-LaBianca murders, she was sure that Linda, Leslie, and Sadie were involved.

I asked her: "If in your mind Linda, Sadie, and Leslie were somehow involved in the Tate-LaBianca murders, and Mr. Manson was innocent and had nothing to do with it, why haven't you come forward before today to tell the authorities about this conversation you had with Linda?"

A.   "I didn't want anything to do with it. I don't believe in coming to you at all."

Earlier on cross-examination Gypsy had admitted that she loved Manson, that she would willingly die for him. After reminding her of these statements, I said: "All right, and you believe he had nothing to do with these murders, right?"

A.   "Right."

Q.   "And yet you let him stay in jail all these months without coming forward with this valuable information?"

Gypsy evaded a straight reply.

Q.   "When was the first time that you told anyone about this infamous conversation that you had with Linda when she asked you to go out and murder someone?"

A.   "Right here."

Q.   "Today?"

A.   "Uh-huh."

Q.   "So today on the witness stand was the first time that you decided to release all this valuable information, is that right?"

A.   "That's right."

I had her. I could now argue to the jury that here's Manson, being tried for seven counts of murder, and there's Gypsy, out on the corner of Temple and Broadway twenty-four hours a day since the start of the trial, a girl who loves Manson and would give her life for him, but who waits until well into the penalty trial, and on redirect at that, before she decides to tell anyone what she knows.

At 6:01 A.M. on February 9, 1971, a monster earthquake shook most of Southern California. Measuring 6.5 on the Richter scale, it claimed sixty-five lives and caused millions of dollars' worth of damage.

I awoke thinking the Family was trying to break into our house.

The jurors awoke to find water cascading on them from broken pipes above their rooms.

The girls on the corner told reporters Charlie had caused the quake.

Despite the disaster, court resumed at the usual time that morning, with Susan Atkins taking the stand to trigger an earthquake of her own.

Daye Shinn's first question of his client was: "Susan, were you personally involved in the Tate and LaBianca homicides?"

Susan, who was wearing a dark jumper and a white blouse, and looking very little-girlish, calmly replied, "Yes."

Although by this time all counsel knew that the three girls intended to take the stand and "confess," Fitzgerald having mentioned it in chambers nearly a week before, the jury and spectators were stunned. They looked at each other as if disbelieving what they had heard.

Shinn then took Susan through her background: her early religious years ("I sang in the church choir"); the death of her mother from cancer ("I couldn't understand why she died, and it hurt me"); her loss of faith; her problems with her father ("My father kept telling me, 'You're going downhill,' so I just went downhill"); her experiences as a topless dancer in San Francisco; her explanation for why she was carrying a gun when arrested in Oregon ("I was afraid of snakes"); and her introduction to drugs, Haight-Ashbury, and her first fateful meeting with Charles Manson.

Returning to the crimes, she testified: "This whole thing started when I killed Gary Hinman, because he was going to hurt my love ..."

Judge Older called the noon recess. Before leaving the stand, Susan turned toward me and said, "Look at it, Mr. Bugliosi. Your whole thing, man, is just gone, your whole motive. It is so silly. So dumb."

That afternoon, Sadie recited the newly revised version of how the Hinman murder went down. According to Susan, when Manson arrived at the Hinman residence, to persuade Gary to sign over the pink slip on a car they had already purchased, Gary drew a gun on him. As Manson fled, Gary tried to shoot him in the back. "I had no choice. He was going to hurt my love. I had my knife on me and I ran at him and I killed him ... Bobby was taken to jail for something that I did."

The holes in her story were a mile wide. I noted them for my cross-examination.

After the arrest of Beausoleil, Susan testified, Linda proposed committing copycat murders. ". . . and she told me to get a knife and a change of clothes ... she said these people in Beverly Hills had burned her for $1,000 for some new drug, MDA ..."

Before leaving Spahn Ranch, Susan said, "Linda gave me some LSD, and she gave Tex some STP ... Linda issued all the directions that night ... No one told Charlie where we were going or what we were going to do ... Linda had been there before, so she knew where to go ... Tex went crazy, shot Parent ... Linda went inside the house ... Linda gave me her knife." At this point in her narrative, Daye Shinn opened the blade of the Buck knife and started to hand the knife to Susan.

THE COURT "Put that knife back the way it was!"

SHINN "I only wanted to get the dimensions, Your Honor."

Susan skipped ahead in her narrative. She was holding Sharon Tate and "Tex came back and he looked at her and he said, 'Kill her.' And I killed her ... And I just stabbed her and she fell, and I stabbed her again. I don't know how many times I stabbed her ..." Sharon begged for the life of her baby, and "I told her, 'Shut up. I don't want to hear it.' "

Though Susan's words were horrifyingly chilling, her expression for the most part remained simple, even childlike.

There was only one way to describe the contrast: it was incredibly obscene.

In discussing the Hinman murder, Susan had placed Leslie Van Houten at the murder scene. There had never been any evidence whatsoever that Leslie was involved in the Hinman murder.

In discussing the night the LaBiancas were killed, Susan made some additional changes in the cast of characters. Manson didn't go along, she said. Linda drove; Tex creepy-crawled the LaBianca residence; Linda instructed Tex, Katie, and Leslie what to do; Linda suggested killing the actor in Venice. And when they returned to Spahn Ranch, "Charlie was there sleeping."

Just as improbable was another of her fictional embellishments. She had implicated Manson in her conversation with me and in her testimony before the grand jury, she claimed, because I had promised her that if she did so I would personally see that none of the defendants, including Manson, would receive the death penalty.

The best refutation of this was that she had implicated Manson on the tape she made with Caballero, days before our first meeting.

Describing that meeting, Sadie said, "Bugliosi walked in. I think he was dressed similar to the way he is dressed now, gray suit, vest."

Q. "This was way back in 1969, right?"

A. "Right. He looked a lot younger then."

We'd all gone through a lot in the last fourteen months. Shinn then began questioning Susan about Shorty! I asked to approach the bench.

BUGLIOSI "Your Honor, I can't believe what is going on here. He is talking about Shorty Shea now!" Turning to Daye, I said, "You are hurting yourself if you bring in other murders, and you are hurting the co-defendants." Older agreed and cautioned Shinn to be extremely careful.

I was worried that if Shinn continued, the case might be reversed on appeal. What conceivable rationale could there be for having your client take the stand and confess to a murder with which she isn't even charged?

Fitzgerald took over the direct. He asked Susan why the Tate victims were killed.

A. "Because I believed it was right to get my brother out of jail. And I still believe it was right."

Q. "Miss Atkins, were any of these people killed as a result of any personal hate or animosity that you had toward them?"

A. "No."

Q. "Did you have any feeling toward them at all, any emotional feeling toward any of these people—Sharon Tate, Voytek Frykowski, Abigail Folger, Jay Sebring, Steven Parent?"

A. "I didn't know any of them. How could I have felt any emotion without knowing them?"

Fitzgerald asked Susan if she considered these mercy killings.

A. "No. As a matter of fact, I believe I told Sharon Tate I didn't have any mercy for her."

Susan went on to explain that she knew what she was doing "was right when I was doing it." She knew this because, when you do the right thing, "it feels good."

Q. "How could it be right to kill somebody?"

A. "How could it not be right when it is done with love?"

Q. "Did you ever feel any remorse?"

A. "Remorse? For doing what was right to me?"

Q. "Did you ever feel sorry?"

A. "Sorry for doing what was right to me? I have no guilt in me."

Fitzgerald looked beaten. By bringing out her total lack of remorse, he had made it impossible for the defense to persuasively argue that she was capable of rehabilitation.

We had reached a strange situation. Suddenly, in the penalty phase, long after the jury had found the four defendants guilty, I was in a sense having to prove Manson's guilt all over again.

If I cross-examined too strenuously, it would appear that I did not feel that we had proven our case. If I eschewed cross-examination, there was the possibility of leaving a lingering doubt as to guilt, which, when it came time for their deliberations, could influence the jury's vote on penalty. Therefore I had to proceed very carefully, as if trying to walk between raindrops.

The defense, and specifically Irving Kanarek, had tried

to plant such a doubt by providing an alternative to Helter Skelter—the copycat motive. Though I felt the testimony on this was thoroughly unconvincing, this didn't mean I could sit back and presume the jury would feel as I did.

As an explanation for why she was lying to save him, it was important that I conclusively prove to the jury Susan Atkins' total commitment to Manson. At the start of my cross-examination I asked her: "Sadie, do you believe Charles Manson is the second coming of Christ?"

A.   "Vince, I have seen Christ in so many people in the last four or five years, it is hard for me to say which one exactly is the second coming of Christ."

I repeated the question.

A.   "I have thought about it. I have thought about it quite a bit ... I have entertained the thought that he was Christ, yes ... I don't know. Could be. If he is, wow, my goodness!"

After confronting her with her letter to Ronnie Howard, in which she stated, "If you can believe in the second coming of Christ, M is he who has come to save," I asked her: "Even now on the witness stand, Sadie, you think that maybe Charles Manson, the man over there who is playing with his hair, might be Jesus Christ?"

A.   "Maybe. I will leave it at that. Maybe yes. Maybe no."

I persisted until Susan admitted: "He represented a God to me that was so beautiful that I'd do anything for him."

Q.   "Even commit murder?" I asked instantly.

A.   "I'd do anything for God."

Q.   "Including murder?" I pressed.

A.   "That's right. If I believed it was right."

Q.   "And you murdered the five people at the Tate residence for your God, Manson, didn't you?"

Susan paused, then said: "I murdered them for my God Bobby Beausoleil."

Q.   "Oh, so you have two Gods?"

Evasively she replied: "There is only one God and God is in all."

Since Susan had now testified to these matters, the prosecution was able to use her prior inconsistent state-

ments—including her grand jury testimony—for impeachment purposes.

On cross-examination I had Susan repeat the alleged
reasons why they went to the Tate residence. Once she'd
restated the copycat nonsense, I hit her with her statements regarding Helter Skelter's being the motive—made
to me, to the grand jury, and in the Howard letter.

I also brought out that she had told me, and the grand
jury, that Manson had ordered the seven Tate-LaBianca
murders; that Charlie had directed all their activities the
second night; and that none of them had been on drugs either night.

I then led her back through her scenario of the Hinman, Tate, and LaBianca murders, step by step, knowing
she would slip up, which she did, repeatedly.

For example, I asked: "Where was Charles Manson
when you stabbed Gary Hinman to death?"

A. "He left. He left right after he cut Gary's ear."
Having inadvertently admitted this, she quickly added that
she had tried to sew up Hinman's ear.

I then took her back again: Hinman drew a gun on
Manson; Manson ran; Hinman started to shoot Manson;
to protect her love, she stabbed Hinman to death. Just
when, I asked, did she have time to play Florence Night-
ingale?

Susan further claimed that she didn't tell Manson that
she had killed Hinman until after their arrest in the
Barker raid. In other words, though she had lived with
Manson from July to October 1969, she hadn't got around
to mentioning this? "That's right." Why? "Because he
never asked."

She hadn't even told him she committed the Tate and
LaBianca murders, she claimed. Nor, until two days ago,
had she told anyone that Linda Kasabian masterminded
the murders.

Q. "Between August 9, 1969, and February 9, 1971,
how come you never told anyone that Linda was behind
these murders?"

A. "Because I didn't. It's that simple."

Q. "Did you tell *anyone* in the Family that you committed all these murders?"

A.   "No."

Q.   "If you told outsiders like Ronnie Howard and Virginia Graham, how come you didn't tell members of your own Family, Sadie?"

A.   "Nothing needed to be said. What I did was what I did with those people, and that is what I did."

Q.   "Just one of those things, seven dead bodies?"

A.   "No big thing."

I paused to let this incredible statement sink in before asking: "So killing seven people is just business as usual, no big deal, is that right, Sadie?"

A.   "It wasn't at the time. It was just there to do."

I asked her how she felt about the victims. She responded, "They didn't even look like people . . . I didn't relate to Sharon Tate as being anything but a store mannequin."

Q.   "You have never heard a store mannequin talk, have you, Sadie?"

A.   "No, sir. But she just sounded like an IBM machine . . . She kept begging and pleading and pleading and begging, and I got sick of listening to her, so I stabbed her."

Q.   "And the more she screamed, the more you stabbed, Sadie?"

A.   "Yes. So?"

Q.   "And you looked at her and you said, 'Look, bitch, I have no mercy for you.' Is that right, Sadie?"

A.   "That's right. That's what I said then."

BUGLIOSI   "No further questions."

On Tuesday, February 16, after lengthy discussions in chambers, Judge Older told the jury that he had decided to end the sequestration.

Their surprise and elation were obvious. They had been locked up for over eight months, the longest sequestration of any jury in American history.

Though I remained worried about possible harassment from the Family, most of the other reasons for the sequestration—such as mention of the Hinman murder, Susan Atkins' confession in the Los Angeles *Times,* her grand jury testimony, and so on—no longer existed, since the jury heard this evidence when Sadie and the others took the stand.

It was almost as if we had a new jury. When the twelve entered the box the next day, there were smiles on all their faces. I couldn't remember when I'd last seen them smiling.

The smiles would not remain there long. Patricia Krenwinkel now took the stand, to confess her part in the Tate and LaBianca homicides.

An even more improbable witness than Susan Atkins, her testimony regarding the copycat motive was vague, nebulous, and almost devoid of supporting detail. The point in her taking the stand was to take the focus off Manson. Instead, like the other Family members who had preceded her, she repeatedly highlighted his importance. For example, describing life at Spahn Ranch, she said: "We were just like wood nymphs and wood creatures. We would run through the woods with flowers in our hair, and Charlie would have a small flute . . ."

On the murder of Abigail Folger: "And I had a knife in my hands, and she took off running, and she ran—she ran out through the back door, one I never even touched, I mean, nobody got fingerprints because I never touched that door . . . and I stabbed her and kept stabbing her."

Q. "What did you feel after you stabbed her?"

A. "Nothing—I mean, like what is there to describe? It was just there, and it's like it was right."

On the murder of Rosemary LaBianca: According to Katie, she and Leslie took Rosemary LaBianca into the bedroom and were looking through the dresses in her closet when, hearing Leno scream, Rosemary grabbed a lamp and swung at them.

On the mutilation of Leno LaBianca: After murdering Rosemary, Katie remembered seeing Leno lying on the floor in the living room. She flashed, "You won't be sending your son off to war," and "I guess I put WAR on the man's chest. And then I guess I had a fork in my hands, and I put it in his stomach . . . and I went and wrote on the walls . . ."

On cross-examination I asked her: "When you were on

top of Abigail Folger, plunging your knife into her body, was she screaming?"

A. "Yes."

Q. "And the more she screamed, the more you stabbed?"

A. "I guess."

Q. "Did it bother you when she screamed for her life?"

A. "No."

Katie testified that when she stabbed Abigail she was really stabbing herself. My next question was rhetorical. "But you didn't bleed at all, did you, Katie; just Abigail did, isn't that right?"

The defense was contending, through these witnesses, that the words POLITICAL PIGGY (Hinman), PIG (Tate), and DEATH TO PIGS (LaBianca) were the clues which the killers felt would cause the police to link the three crimes. But when I'd asked Sadie why she'd written POLITICAL PIGGY on the wall of the Hinman residence in the first place, she had no satisfactory answer. Nor could she tell me why, if these were to be copycat murders, she'd only written PIG and not POLITICAL PIGGY at Tate. Nor was Katie now able to give a convincing explanation as to why she'd written HEALTER SKELTER on the LaBiancas' refrigerator door.

It was obvious that Maxwell Keith wasn't buying the copycat motive either. On redirect he asked Katie: "The homicides at the Tate residence and the LaBianca residence had nothing to do, did they, with trying to get Bobby Beausoleil out of jail?"

A. "Well, it's hard to explain. It was just a thought, and the thought came to be."

Judge Older was becoming increasingly irritated with Kanarek. Repeatedly, he warned him that if he persisted in asking inadmissible questions, he would find him in contempt for the fifth time. Nor was he very happy with Daye Shinn. Shinn had been observed passing a note from a spectator to Susan Atkins. The week before, the girls on the corner had been seen reading court transcripts which had Shinn's name on them. Confronted with this by Older, Shinn explained: "They borrowed them to look at them."

THE COURT "I beg your pardon? Are you familiar with the publicity order in this case?"

Shinn admitted that he was.

THE COURT "It appears to me, Mr. Shinn, that you are not paying the slightest attention to the publicity order, and you haven't been for some time. I have felt, in my own mind, for a long, long time, that the leak—and there is a leak—is you."

Maxwell Keith very reluctantly called his client, Leslie Van Houten, to the stand. After taking her through her background, Keith asked to approach the bench. He told Older that his client was going to involve herself in the Hinman murder. He had discussed this with her for "hours and hours" but to no avail.

Once she began reciting her tale, the transparency of her fictions became obvious. According to Leslie, Mary Brunner was never at the Hinman residence, while both Charles Manson and Bobby Beausoleil left before the actual killing took place. It was Sadie, she said, who killed Gary.

Though implicating herself in the Hinman murder, at least by her presence, Leslie did try to provide some mitigating circumstances for her involvement in the LaBianca murders. She claimed she knew nothing about the Tate murders and that when she went along the next night she had no idea where they were going or what they were going to do. The murder of Rosemary LaBianca was made to seem almost like self-defense. Only after Rosemary swung at her with the lamp did she "take one of the knives and Patricia had a knife, and we started stabbing and cutting up the lady."

Q. "Up to that time, did you have any intention of hurting anybody?"

A. "No."

Q. "Did you stab her after she appeared to be dead, Les?"

A. "I don't know if it was before or after she was dead, but I stabbed her ... I don't know if she was dead. She was lying there on the floor."

Q. "Had you stabbed her at all before you saw her lying on the floor?"

A. "I don't remember."

Leslie's forgetting such things was almost as improbable as her claim that she hadn't mentioned the murders to Manson until they were in the desert.

Very carefully, Keith tried to establish that Leslie had remorse for her acts.

Q. "Leslie, do you feel sorrow or shame or a sense of guilt for having participated in the death of Mrs. LaBianca?"

A. [Pause]

Q. "Let me go one by one. Do you feel sorrowful about it; sorry; unhappy?"

You could almost feel the chill in the courtroom when Leslie answered: "Sorry is only a five-letter word. It can't bring back anything."

Q. "I am trying, Leslie, to discover how you feel about it."

A. "What can I feel? It has happened. She is gone."

Q. "Do you wish that it hadn't happened?"

A. "I never wish anything to be done over another way. That is a foolish thought. It never will happen that way. You can't undo something that is done."

Q. "Do you feel as if you wanted to cry for what happened?"

A. "Cry? For her death? If I cry for death, it is for death itself. She is not the only person who has died."

Q. "Do you think about it from time to time?"

A. "Only when I am in the courtroom."

Through most of the trial Leslie Van Houten had maintained her innocent-little-girl act. She'd dropped it now, the jury seeing for the first time how cold and unfeeling she really was.

Another aspect of her real nature surfaced when Kanarek examined her. Angry and impatient at some of his questions, she snapped back hostile, sarcastic replies. With each spurt of venom, you could see the jurors drawing back, looking at her as if anew. Whatever sympathy she may have generated earlier was gone now. Even McBride no longer met her eyes.

Leslie Van Houten had been found guilty of two homicides. I felt she deserved the death penalty for her very willing participation in those acts. But I didn't want the jury to vote death on the basis of a crime she didn't even commit. I told her attorney, Maxwell Keith, that I was willing to stipulate that Leslie was not at the Hinman residence. "I mean, the jury is apt to think she was, and hold it against your client, and I don't think that is right."

Also, during cross-examination I asked: "Did you tell anyone—prior to your testimony on the witness stand— that it was you who was along with Sadie and Bobby Beausoleil at Gary Hinman's house?"

A. "I told Patricia about it."

Q. "Actually it was Mary Brunner who was inside the residence, not you, isn't that correct?"

A. "That is what you say."

Although I was attempting to exonerate Leslie of any complicity in the Gary Hinman murder, I did the opposite when it came to the murder of Rosemary LaBianca. By the time I'd finished my cross-examination on this, Leslie had admitted that Rosemary might still have been alive when she stabbed her; and that she not only stabbed her in the buttocks and possibly the neck, but "I could have done a couple on the back." (As I'd later remind the jury, many of the back wounds were not post-mortem, while one, which severed Rosemary LaBianca's spine, would have been in and of itself fatal.)

As with Sadie and Katie, I emphasized the improbabilities in her copycat tale. For example, though she had testified that she was "hopelessly in love" with Bobby Beausoleil, and became aware that these murders had been committed in an attempt to free him, I brought out that she hadn't even offered to testify in either of his trials, when her story, had it been true, could have resulted in his release.

At this point I decided to go on a fishing expedition. Though I had no definite knowledge that this was so, I strongly suspected that Leslie had told her first attorney, Marvin Part, the true story of these murders. I did know that Part had recorded her story and, though I never heard the tape, I recalled Part almost begging the judge to listen to it.

BUGLIOSI "Isn't it true, Leslie, that before the trial started you told someone that Charles Manson ordered these murders?"

A. "I had a court-appointed attorney, Marvin Part, who was insistent on the fact that I was—"

Keith interrupted her, objecting that we were getting into the area of privileged communications. I noted to Judge Older that Leslie herself had mentioned Part by name and that she had the right to waive the privilege. Kanarek also objected, well aware of what I was hoping to bring out.

VAN HOUTEN "Mr. Kanarek, will you shut up so I can answer his question? ... I had a court-appointed attorney by the name of Marvin Part. He had a lot of different thoughts, which were all his own, on how to get me off. He said he was going to make some tape recordings, and he told me the gist of what he wanted me to say. And I said it."

Q. "What did you tell Mr. Part?"

A. "I don't remember. It was a long time ago."

I asked her if she told Part that Manson had ordered these murders.

A. "Sure I told him that."

Did she tell Part that Manson was along the second night, and that when they stopped on Waverly Drive, Manson got out and entered the LaBianca house?

After a number of evasive replies, Leslie angrily answered: "Sure I told him that!"

THE COURT "We will take our recess at this time—"

VAN HOUTEN "Mr. Bugliosi, you are an evil man!"

Each of the Family witnesses denied that Manson hated blacks. But in the light of what I'd recently learned, several put it in a very curious way. When Fitzgerald asked Squeaky: "Did he love the black man or did he hate him?" she had replied: "He loved them. He is his father—the black man is Charlie's father." Gypsy had testified: "First of all, Charlie spent nearly all of his life in jail. So he got to know the black people very, very well.

In fact, I mean, they were like his father, you know."
Leslie had said something very similar, adding: "If Charlie
hated black people he would hate himself."

During a recess I asked Manson, "Charlie, was your father black?"

"What?" He seemed startled by the question, yet
whether because it was such a crazy idea or because I'd
found out something he didn't want known I couldn't tell.
There was nothing evasive about his eventual response,
however; he emphatically denied it.

He seemed to be telling the truth. Yet I wondered. I
still do.

The next witness was no stranger to the stand. Brought
back from New Hampshire at the request of Irving Kanarek, Linda Kasabian was again sworn. Fitzgerald, Keith,
and Shinn had opposed calling her; Kanarek should have
listened to their advice, as Linda again came over so well
that I didn't even cross-examine her. None of her previous
testimony was shaken in the slightest.

Linda, her husband, and their two children were living
together on a small farm in New Hampshire. The foot-
loose Bob Kasabian had turned out to be a pillar of
strength, and I was pleased to hear that their marriage
now seemed to be working.

Ruth Ann Moorehouse, aka Ouisch, age twenty, who'd
once told Danny DeCarlo she couldn't wait to get her first
pig, repeated the now familiar refrain: "Charlie was no
leader." But "the rattlesnakes liked him, he could play
with them" and "he could change old men into young
men."

Adding a few more fictional touches to the copycat motive, Ouisch claimed that Bobby Beausoleil was the father
of Linda Kasabian's second child.

I asked her: "You would do anything to help Charles
Manson and these three female defendants, wouldn't you,
Ouisch?"

When she evaded a direct reply, I asked: "You would
even murder for them, wouldn't you?"

A.   "I could not take a life."

Q. "All right, let's talk about that, Ouisch. Do you know a girl by the name of Barbara Hoyt?"

On the advice of her attorney, Ouisch refused to answer any questions about the Hoyt murder attempt. By law, when a witness refuses to be cross-examined, that witness's entire testimony can be stricken. This was done in Ouisch's case.

Easily the weirdest of all the witnesses was Steve Grogan, aka Clem, age nineteen. He spoke of the "engrams" on his brain; answered questions about his father by talking about his mother; and claimed that the real leader of the Family was not Manson but Pooh Bear, Mary Brunner's child by Manson.

Kanarek complained, at the bench, that Older was smiling at Grogan's replies. Older responded: "I find nothing whatsoever funny about this witness, I can assure you ... Why you would want to call him is beyond my comprehension, but that is up to you ... No jury will ever believe this witness, I promise you that."

The youth who beheaded Shorty Shea appeared to be a complete idiot. He grinned incessantly, made funny faces, and played with his beard even more than Manson. Yet it was more than partly role playing, as several of his very careful replies indicated.

Clem recalled accompanying Linda, Leslie, Sadie, Tex, and Katie one night in a car; he claimed that Linda had given them all LSD first; and he insisted that Manson was not along. But he was very careful not to say that this was the night of the LaBianca murders, to avoid implicating himself.

Many of his responses were almost exact quotations from Manson. For example, when I asked him, "When did you join the Family, Clem?" he replied, "When I was born of white skin."

I also asked him, since it had been brought out on the direct examination, about his arrest in the Barker raid. What had he been charged with? I inquired.

A. "I was arrested on a breach of promise."

Q. "Breach of promise? Some girl you made a promise to, Clem, or what?"

A. "It was a promise to return a truck on a certain date."

Q. "Oh, I get it. Sometimes that is called 'grand theft auto,' too, isn't it, Clem?"

The defense called their next witness: Vincent T. Bugliosi. At the bench Fitzgerald admitted that this was an unusual situation: "On the other hand, in this case Mr. Bugliosi has been an investigator as well as a prosecutor."

Daye Shinn questioned me about my interview with Susan Atkins and her testimony before the grand jury. Why did I feel Susan hadn't told the grand jury the whole truth? he asked. I enumerated the reasons, noting, among other things, my belief that she had stabbed Sharon Tate.

Q. "How did you come to that conclusion?"

A. "She admitted it on the witness stand, Mr. Shinn, for one thing. Also, she told Ronnie Howard and Virginia Graham that she stabbed Sharon Tate."

Shinn was trying to reinstate the "deal" in which the DA's Office agreed not to seek the death penalty against Susan if she testified truthfully. As Older told him at the bench: "Susan Atkins took the stand in this case under oath and testified that she was lying at the grand jury. If there'd been any agreement, that in itself would have been enough to negate it."

Keith asked me if I had either heard the tape Leslie made with Part or discussed its contents with him. I replied that I had not. Kanarek's cross-examination went so far afield that Judge Older finally terminated it.

Others who took the stand in succeeding days included Aaron Stovitz; Evelle Younger, former Los Angeles District Attorney and now California State Attorney General; attorneys Paul Caruso and Richard Caballero; and promoter Lawrence Schiller. Every aspect of the December 4, 1969, agreement; the taping of Atkins' account; the selling of her story; her grand jury testimony; and her firing of Caballero the day after her meeting with Manson was discussed. Shinn's most strenuous cross-examination of the entire trial took place when he had Schiller on the stand: Shinn wanted to know exactly how much Susan's story had earned and in which bank accounts every penny was. Shinn was to receive Susan's share for representing her.

During my cross-examination of these witnesses, I scored a number of significant points. I brought out through Caruso, for example, that during the December 4, 1969, meeting he had stated that Susan Atkins probably wouldn't testify at the trial "because of her fear of Manson."

Kanarek, however, scored one of the biggest points—for the prosecution. In questioning Caballero, Atkins' former attorney, he asked: "What did [Susan Atkins] tell you about the language written in blood at these three homes?"

CABALLERO "I told you not to ask me that question, Irving."

Apparently convinced that Caballero was hiding something favorable to his client, Kanarek repeated the question.

Caballero sighed and said: "She told me that Charles Manson had wanted to bring on Helter Skelter and it wasn't happening fast enough, and the use of the word 'pig' was for the purpose of making them think that Negroes were committing these crimes, because the Panthers and people like that are the ones that used the name 'pig' to mean the establishment, and that was the whole purpose of it, that Helter Skelter wasn't happening fast enough, and Charlie was going to bring on the ruination of the world, and this is why all the murders were committed.

"I asked you not to ask me these questions, Mr. Kanarek."

Having failed abysmally in their attempt to sell the copycat motive, the defense now switched to a new tactic. They called a number of psychiatrists to the stand, hoping to establish that LSD had affected the minds of the three female defendants to the extent that they were not responsible for their acts.

It was not a real defense, but it could be made to seem a mitigating circumstance which, unless thoroughly rebutted, might tip the scales in favor of life imprisonment.

Their first witness, Dr. Andre Tweed, professed to be an expert on LSD, but almost all of his testimony was contrary to that of acknowledged experts in the field.

Tweed claimed he knew of one case where a youth while under LSD heard voices which told him to kill his mother and his grandmother, and he did just that. On the basis of this single, unidentified case, Tweed concluded that "people may perform homicidal acts while under the influence of LSD." It was also his opinion, he said, that LSD probably caused brain damage.

On cross-examination I brought out that Dr. Tweed had only talked to Patricia Krenwinkel for two hours. He had not read the trial transcripts or interviewed any of her friends or relatives. He had never done any controlled research in the field of LSD, had only lectured once on the subject, and had written no papers on it. When I asked him why he considered himself an expert, he rather loftily replied: "What is an expert but what the beholder thinks he is from his experience? Many people consider me an expert, so I have accustomed myself to assuming that I am."

Q. "Do you consider Dr. Thomas Ungerleider of UCLA an expert in LSD?"

A. "Yes, I do."

Q. "More than yourself?"

A. "I am not in a position to judge that. I will leave that to others."

Q. "Do you consider Dr. Duke Fisher of UCLA an expert in the field of LSD?"

A. "Yes."

I then brought out that the two men had written a paper entitled "The Problems of LSD in Emotional Disorders," in which they concluded that "there is no scientific demonstrable evidence of organic brain damage caused by LSD."

Tweed now had to admit that was correct, as far as present evidence went.

On December 24, 1969, Patricia Krenwinkel had been examined by a Mobile, Alabama, psychiatrist, a Dr. Claude Brown. Since Tweed had based his conclusions in part on Brown's report, I was given a copy of it just prior to my cross-examination.

It was a bombshell, as my next question to Dr. Tweed indicated:

Q. "In forming your opinions with respect to Patricia Krenwinkel, did you take into consideration that she told Dr. Brown that on the night of the Tate murders Charles Manson told her to go along with Tex Watson?"

After numerous objections and lengthy conferences at the bench, Dr. Tweed admitted that he had considered this. Still later, Patricia Krenwinkel was recalled to the stand, where, though she denied the truth of the statement, she admitted that she had told Dr. Brown that this was so.

We now had a perfect score. Manson had called Sadie, Katie, and Leslie to the stand in an attempt to exonerate him. Instead, I had now proven that each of the three had previously told others that Manson was behind these murders.

There were other surprises in the Brown report. Krenwinkel also told the doctor that she had fled to Mobile "because she was afraid of Manson finding her and killing her";* that on the day of the Tate murders she was coming *off* an acid trip and wasn't on any drugs that night; and that following the murders "she was always fearful that they would be arrested for what they had done, but 'Charlie said nobody could touch us.' "

This latter statement proved that Katie was well aware of the consequences of her acts.

This was important, since it was obvious from their questions that the defense attorneys were trying to imply that the three female defendants were insane at the time they committed these murders.

Under California law an insanity plea must be entered *before* the start of the trial. A separate sanity phase is then held, after the guilt trial. The defense, however, had

---

*Although harmful to Manson, this could only be helpful to Fitzgerald's client, Patricia Krenwinkel. However, it was not Fitzgerald who brought this out but Keith, after Fitzgerald had concluded his examination.

not entered such a plea at the proper time. Therefore, in one sense, the question of whether the defendants were sane or insane was irrelevant, since this was not an issue which the jury would have to decide. In another sense, however, it was crucial. If the defense could cause the jury to doubt the sanity of the defendants, this could strongly influence their vote on the penalty they were to pay.

Suddenly I was not only having to prove Manson's guilt all over again, I was also having to prove that the girls were legally sane.

In most states, including California, the legal test of insanity is the M'Naghten Rule. Among other things, M'Naghten provides that if a defendant, as a result of mental disease or defect, does not realize that what he did was wrong, then he is legally insane. It is not enough, however, that he personally believe his acts were not wrong. Were this so, every man would be a law unto himself. For instance, a man could rape a dozen women, say, "I don't think it's wrong to rape," and therefore evade criminal punishment. The clincher is whether he knows that society thinks his actions are wrong. If he does, then he cannot be legally insane. And deliberate acts to avoid detection—such as cutting telephone wires, eradicating prints, changing identities, disposing of incriminating evidence—constitute circumstantial evidence that the defendant knows society views his acts as wrong.

Earlier Dr. Tweed had testified that Patricia Krenwinkel didn't believe these murders were wrong. I now asked him on cross: "In your opinion, when Patricia Krenwinkel was committing these murders, did she believe that society thought it was wrong to do what she was doing?"

A. "I believe so."

BUGLIOSI "No further questions."

On March 4, Manson trimmed his beard to a neat fork and completely shaved his head, because, he told newsmen, "I am the Devil and the Devil always has a bald head."

Interestingly enough, this time the three female defendants did not follow Manson's example. Nor, when he occasionally acted up in court, did they parrot him, as they had in the guilt trial. Obviously it had got across to them, albeit belatedly, that such antics only proved Manson's domination.

While denying that LSD can cause brain damage, the next witness, psychiatrist Keith Ditman, testified that the drug can have a detrimental effect on a person's personality. He also stated that a person using LSD is more susceptible to the influence of a second party, and that Leslie's use of the drug, *plus* Manson's influence over her, could have been significant factors in causing her to participate in a homicide.

VAN HOUTEN   "This is all such a big lie. I was influenced by the war in Vietnam and TV."

On cross-examination I got Ditman to concede that not all people react the same to LSD, that it depends upon the personality structure of the person ingesting the drug. I then brought out that Ditman had never examined Leslie; therefore, not knowing what her personality structure was, he couldn't say what effect, if any, LSD had on her mental state.

Nor, turning this around, not having examined her, could he say for certain whether she did or did not have inherent homicidal tendencies.

Keith, on redirect, asked Ditman: "What is meant by inherent homicidal tendencies?"

A.   "That a person has, let's say, more than the average human being, a killer instinct . . ."

Q.   "Psychiatrically speaking, do some people have greater killer instincts than others, in your opinion?"

A.   "Well, some people have a more covert and overt hostility and aggression. In that sense, they are *more capable* of committing crimes of violence, such as murder."

Dr. Ditman had just articulated one of the chief points of the final argument I was preparing to give at the close of the penalty phase.

Dr. Joel Fort, the almost legendary "hippie doctor of the Haight," didn't look the part. The founder of the National Center for Solving Social and Health Problems was fortyish, dressed conservatively, talked quietly, didn't have long hair (in fact he was bald). Angered by his testimony, Manson shouted, "If he ever seen a hippie, it was in the street while he was driving by in his car."

Manson's anger had good cause. Even on direct, Dr. Fort was more helpful to the prosecution than the defense. The author of one book on drugs and co-author of eleven others, Dr. Fort stated that "a drug by itself does not perform a magical transformation—there are many other factors."

On cross-examination I brought out one. Fort said: "It was my feeling [after examining Leslie Van Houten] that Mr. Manson's influence played a very significant role in the commission of the murders."

Another very crucial point came out on cross. To negate the defense's new argument that the girls were on LSD during the murders, and therefore less responsible for their acts, I asked Fort: "Isn't it true, Doctor, that people under the influence of LSD do not tend to be violent?"

A. "That is true."

Still attacking the prosecution's theory of Manson's domination, Kanarek asked Fort: "Now, do you know of any cases where someone has—I mean, other than in the Frankenstein type of picture—do you know where someone has sat down and programmed people to go out, let's say, and commit armed robberies, burglaries, assaults? Do you know of any such instances?"

A. "Yes. In one sense, that is what we do when we program soldiers in a war ... The Army uses a peer group technique and the patriotic ideals that are instilled in citizens of a particular country to bring about this pattern of behavior."

Dr. Fort was typical of many persons who, though opposed to capital punishment in principle, felt that these murders were so savage and senseless, so totally lacking in mitigating circumstances, that justice demanded that these persons be sentenced to death. I learned this in a conversation with him in the hall outside court, in which he stated that he was extremely unhappy that he had been called to testify for the defense in this case. Greatly concerned about the stain the Manson Family had cast on all young people, Dr. Fort offered to testify for the prosecution when I brought Charles "Tex" Watson to trial, an offer which I later accepted.

It was in just such a hallway interview that I discovered how potentially damaging to the defense their next witness could be. Learning that Keith intended to call Dr. Joel Simon Hochman during the afternoon session, I cut my lunch hour short so I could spend a half hour interviewing the psychiatrist.

To my amazement, I learned that Maxwell Keith hadn't even interviewed his own witness. He was calling him to the stand "cold." Had he talked to him for just five minutes, Keith would never have called Hochman. For the doctor, who *had* interviewed Leslie, felt that the use of LSD wasn't an important influence on her; rather, he felt there was something very seriously wrong with Leslie Van Houten.

In his testimony and the psychiatric report he wrote following the examination, Dr. Hochman called Leslie Van Houten "a spoiled little princess" who was unable "to suffer frustration and delay of gratification." From childhood on, she'd had extreme difficulties with impulse control. When she didn't get her way, she went into rages; for example, beating her adopted sister with a shoe.

"From a position of over-all perspective," Hochman noted, "it is quite clear that Leslie Van Houten was a psychologically loaded gun which went off as a consequence of the complex intermeshing of highly unlikely and bizarre circumstances."

Hochman confirmed something I had long suspected. Of the three female defendants, Leslie Van Houten was the least committed to Charles Manson. "She listened to [Manson's] talk of philosophy, but it wasn't her trip." Nor could she "get that into Charlie sexually, and that bothered her a lot. 'I couldn't get it on with Charlie like I could with Bobby,' she said . . ." According to Hochman, Leslie was obsessed with beauty. "Bobby was beautiful, Charles was not, physically. Charles was short. That is something that always turned me off."

Yet she killed at his command.

Keith asked Hochman: "Doctor, did you ask her

whether or not Mr. Manson, during her association with him, had any influence over her in her thought process and in her conduct and activity?"

A. "She denies it. But I don't buy that."

Q. "Why don't you buy that?"

A. "Well, I don't understand why she would stay on the scene that long if there was nothing there for her, on some unconscious basis."

As I'd observe in my final argument, many came to Spahn Ranch but only a few stayed; those who did, did so because they found the blackhearted medicine Manson was peddling very palatable.

According to Hochman, in talking to him Leslie professed "a kind of primitive Christianity, love for the world, acceptance of all things. And I asked her, 'Well, professing that, how can it be you would murder someone?' She said, 'Well that was something inside of me too.' "

Maxwell Keith should have stopped right there. Instead, he asked Hochman: "How do you interpret that?"

A. "I think it's rather realistic. I think that in reality it *was* something inside of her, despite her chronic denial of the emotional aspects of herself, that a rage was there."

Nor did Keith leave it at that. He now asked: "When you say a rage was there, what do you mean by that?"

A. "In my opinion it would take a rage, an emotional reaction to kill someone. I think it is unquestionable that that feeling was inside of her."

Q. "Bearing in mind that she had never seen or heard of Mrs. LaBianca, in your opinion there was some hate in her when this occurred?"

A. "Well, I think it would make it easier for her not to know Mrs. LaBianca ... It is hard to kill someone that you have good feelings towards. I don't think there was anything specific about Mrs. LaBianca.

"Let me make myself clear: Mrs. LaBianca was an object, a blank screen upon which Leslie projected her feelings, much as a patient projects his feelings on an analyst whom he doesn't know ... feelings towards her mother, her father, toward the establishment ...

"I think she was a very angry girl for a long time, a

very alienated girl for a long time, and the anger and rage was associated with that."

Hochman was articulating one of the main points of my final summation: namely, that Leslie, Sadie, Katie, and Tex had a hostility and rage within them that pre-existed Charles Manson. They were different from Linda Kasabian, Paul Watkins, Brooks Poston, Juan Flynn, and T. J. When Manson asked them to kill for him, each said no.

Tex Watson, Susan Atkins, Patricia Krenwinkel, and Leslie Van Houten said yes.

So there had to be something special about these people that caused them to kill. Some kind of inner flaw. Apart from Charlie.

Though he had badly damaged his own case, Keith had tried to put the hat on Manson. Fitzgerald, in his examination of Hochman, did just the opposite. He sought to minimize the importance of Manson's influence over Leslie. Asking Hochman what Manson's influence actually was, he received this reply: "His ideas, his presence, the role he played in his relationship to her, served to reinforce a lot of her feelings and attitudes. It served to reinforce and give her a way of continuing her general social alienation, her alienation from the establishment."

Q. "So, really, all you are saying is that (A) Manson could possibly have had some influence, and (B), if he did have some influence, it would only contribute to the lowering of her restraints on her impulsiveness, is that correct?"

A. "Yes."

Q. "So any influence Manson had on Leslie Van Houten, in terms of your professional opinion, is tenuous at best, is that correct?"*

A. "Let me give you another example that may make it clearer ... Suppose someone comes in and says, 'Let's

---

*There was no meaningful dichotomy between Leslie Van Houten and Fitzgerald's client, Patricia Krenwinkel. Both young girls had joined the Family, submitted to Manson's domination, and ultimately murdered for him. In trying to establish that Manson was not responsible for causing Leslie to kill, Fitzgerald was at the same time establishing that Manson wasn't responsible for Katie's killing either. Hochman's reply badly hurt not only Leslie but Katie and Sadie as well.

eat the whole apple pie.' Obviously your temptation is stimulated by the suggestion, but your final decision on whether or not to eat the whole pie or just one piece comes out of you. So the other person is influential, but is not a final arbiter or decider of that situation . . .

"Someone can tell you to shoot someone, but your decision to do that comes from inside you."

Kanarek, when his turn came, picked up the scent. "And so you are telling us then, in layman's language, that when someone takes a knife and stabs, the decision to do that is a personal decision?"

A. "In the ultimate analysis it is."

Q. "It is a personal decision of the person who does the stabbing?"

A. "Yes."

Ironically, Kanarek and I were now on the same side. Both of us were seeking to prove that, even independent of Manson, these girls had murder within them.

Manson was very impressed by Hochman and at first wanted to be interviewed by him. I was relieved, however, when he later abandoned the idea. I wasn't greatly worried about Manson conning Hochman. But even if Hochman didn't buy Manson's story, Kanarek would make sure he repeated it on the stand. Thus, using Hochman as a conduit, Manson could get almost everything he wanted before the jury, without being subject to my cross-examination.

Hochman found in all three girls "much evidence in their history of early alienation, of early antisocial or deviant behavior." Even before joining the Family, Leslie had more emotional problems than the average person. Sadie actively sought to be everything her father warned her not to be. "She thinks now, in retrospect," Hochman noted, "that even without Charles Manson she would have ended up in jail for manslaughter or assault with a deadly weapon." Katie first had sex at fifteen. She never saw the boy again, and she suffered tremendous guilt because of the experience. Manson eradicated that guilt. He also, in letting her join the Family, gave her the acceptance she desperately craved.

Of the three, Hochman felt Sadie had a little more remorse than the other two—she often talked of wishing her life were over. Yet he also noted, "One is struck by the absence of a conventional sense of morality or conscience in this girl." And he testified, "She does not seem to manifest any evidence of discomfort or anxiety about her present circumstances, or her conviction and possible death sentence. On the contrary, she seemed to manifest a remarkable peacefulness and self-acceptance in her present state."

According to Hochman, all three girls denied "any sense of guilt whatever about anything." And he felt that intellectually they actually believed there is no right or wrong, that morality is a relative thing. "However, I, as a psychiatrist, know that you cannot rationally do away with the feelings that exist on the irrational, unconscious level. You cannot tell yourself that killing is O.K. intellectually when you have grown up all your life feeling that killing is wrong."

In short, Hochman believed that as human beings the girls felt some guilt deep down inside, even though they consciously suppressed it.

Keith asked Hochman: "In your opinion, Doctor, would Leslie be susceptible or respond to intensive therapy?"

A. "Possibly."

Q. "In other words, you don't feel that she is such a lost soul that she could never be rehabilitated?"

A. "No, I don't think she is *that* lost a soul, no."

To a psychiatrist, no one is beyond redemption. This is essential, standard testimony. Yet only one of the defense attorneys, Maxwell Keith, asked the question, and then only on redirect.

Earlier I'd brought out that Hochman had only the word of the girls that they were on LSD either night. I now asked him: "Have you ever read a reported case in the literature of LSD of any individual who committed murder while under the influence of LSD?"

A. "No. Suicide, but not murder."

As I'd later ask the jury, could Watson, Atkins, Krenwinkel, and Van Houten, *all four*, be exceptions?

A large portion of Hochman's testimony had dealt with the mental states of the three girls. Susan Atkins was suffering from a diagnosable condition, he said: an early childhood deprivation syndrome which had resulted in a hysterical personality type.

This was not legal insanity as defined by M'Naghten.

Leslie Van Houten was an immature, unusually impulsive person, who tended to act spontaneously without reflection.

Nor was this legal insanity as defined by M'Naghten.

In his report on Krenwinkel, Dr. Claude Brown, the Mobile psychiatrist, had stated that "at the time I saw Miss Krenwinkel, she showed a schizophrenic reaction." He added, however, that "I do not state with any certainty that this psychosis existed at the time of the alleged murders."

Schizophrenia *may* be legal insanity as defined by M'Naghten. But Dr. Brown's opinion was qualified, and when Fitzgerald asked Dr. Hochman if, on the basis of his examination of Krenwinkel, he agreed that she was, or had been, schizophrenic, Hochman replied, "I would say no."

It remained to bring these points across to the jury, in terms they could easily understand.

On recross-examination I had Hochman define the word "psychotic." He replied that it meant "a loss of contact with reality."

I then asked him: "At the present time, Doctor, do you feel any of these three female defendants are psychotic?"

A.   "No."

Q.   "In your opinion, do you feel that any of these three female defendants have ever been psychotic?"

A.   "No."

BUGLIOSI   "May I approach the witness, Your Honor? I want to ask the witness a question privately."

THE COURT   "Yes, you may."

I had already questioned Dr. Hochman once about this. But I wanted to be absolutely certain of his reply. Once I had received it, I returned to the counsel table and asked him a number of unrelated questions, so the jury wouldn't know what we had been talking about. I then gradually worked up to the big one.

Q. "The term 'insanity,' Doctor, you are familiar with that term, of course?"

A. "Yes."

Q. "Basically, you define the word 'insanity' to be the layman's synonym for 'psychotic'?"

A. "I would say that the word 'insanity' is used generally to mean 'psychotic.' "

Q. "Then, from a psychiatric standpoint, I take it that in your opinion none of these three female defendants are presently insane nor have they ever been insane, is that correct?"

A. "That is correct."

As far as the psychiatric testimony was concerned, with Hochman's reply the ball game was over.

The defense called only three more witnesses during the penalty trial, all hard-core Family members. Each was on the stand only a short time, but their testimony, particularly that of the first witness, was as shocking as anything that had gone before.

Catherine Gillies, whose grandmother owned Myers Ranch, parroted the Family line: Charlie never led anyone; there was never any talk of a race war; these murders were committed to free Bobby Beausoleil.

Coldly, matter-of-factly, the twenty-one-year-old girl testified that on the night of the LaBianca murders, "I followed Katie to the car, and I asked if I could go with her. Linda, Leslie, and Sadie were all in the car. And they said that they had plenty of people to do what they were going to do, and that I didn't need to go."

On direct examination by Kanarek, Cathy stated: "You know, I am willing to kill for a brother, we all are."

Q. "What do you mean by that?"

A. "In other words, to get a brother out of jail, I would kill. I would have killed that night except I did not go . . ."

Q. "What prevented you from going with them, if anything?"

A. "Just the fact that they didn't need me."

Apparently Fitzgerald hoped to soften the harshness of her reply when he asked her: "Have you killed anybody to get someone out of jail?"

With a strange little smile, Cathy turned her head and, looking directly at the jury, replied: "Not yet."

Cathy had testified on direct examination that Katie had told her about the Tate-LaBianca murders. On cross-examination I asked her: "When Katie told you that they had murdered these people, did this disturb you at all?"

A. "Actually it had very little effect on me because I knew why they had done it."

Q. "So it didn't upset you?"

A. "No, it definitely didn't upset me."

Q. "You didn't decide that you would rather not continue living with murderers?"

A. "Obviously not."

Q. "Were you upset that you didn't get to go along with them?"

A. "I wanted to go."

Mary Brunner, first member of the Manson Family, claimed that the police had told her that she would be charged with murder if she did not implicate Manson in the Hinman slaying. She now repudiated this testimony and further denied even being at the Hinman residence.

Keith brought out that Mary Brunner had testified both in the second trial of Bobby Beausoleil and before the Hinman grand jury, and neither time did she say anything about Leslie Van Houten being present when Hinman was killed.

I had no questions for her. The point was made.

Brenda McCann was recalled to the stand, to testify that on the nights of the Tate and LaBianca murders she had seen Manson sleeping with Stephanie Schram in Devil's Canyon.

The groundwork for my cross-examination of Brenda had been laid fifteen months before. I impeached her with her testimony before the grand jury, when she stated that she couldn't remember where she, or Manson, was on either night.

Brenda was the last witness. She completed her testimony on Tuesday, March 16, 1971. That afternoon, after a number of delays—Kanarek, for example, refused to stipulate that Gary Hinman was dead—the defense rested. Wednesday we worked on the jury instructions, and on Thursday the trial entered its final stage. All that now remained were the arguments, the deliberations, and the verdict.

March 18-29, 1971

My opening argument in the penalty trial was brief, lasting less than ten minutes. As with all my arguments during the trial, Manson decided to sit this one out, in the lockup. The psychology behind this was obvious: he didn't want the jury focusing on him when I discussed him.

I began by saying: "I am not going to address myself to the frantic effort by the three female defendants and the defense witnesses to make it look like Charles Manson wasn't involved in these murders. I am sure all of you clearly saw that they were lying on that witness stand to do what they could for their God, Charles Manson.

"Well, Charles Manson has already been convicted. He has already been convicted of seven counts of first degree murder and one count of conspiracy to commit murder.

"The difficulty in your decision, as I see it, is not whether these defendants deserve the death penalty, ladies and gentlemen. In view of the incredibly savage, barbaric, and inhuman murders they committed, the death penalty is the only proper verdict." I then stated the very heart of my argument: *If this case were not a proper case for the imposition of the death penalty, no case ever would be.* In view of what they did, life imprisonment would be the greatest gift, the greatest charity, the greatest handout, as it were, ever given.

"The difficulty in your decision, as I see it, is whether you will have the fortitude to return verdicts of death against all four defendants."

The defense attorneys, I anticipated, would beg for their clients' lives. This was not only commendable, I told the jury, it was also understandable, just as it was understandable that they "argued during the guilt phase that their clients were not involved in these murders, even though during the penalty phase the three female defendants took the stand and said: 'Yes, we were involved.'"

There was absolutely no reason for these defendants to viciously and inhumanly snuff out the lives of these seven human beings, I noted. There were *no* mitigating circumstances.

"These defendants are not human beings, ladies and gentlemen. Human beings have a heart and a soul. No one with a heart and a soul could have done what these defendants did to these seven victims.

"These defendants are human monsters, human mutations.

"There is only one proper ending to the Tate-LaBianca murder trial," I concluded, "verdicts of death for all four defendants."

Kanarek stipulated, at the start of his argument, that "Mr. Manson is not all good." However, he continued, "Mr. Manson is innocent of these matters that are before us."

Why was he on trial then? Kanarek returned to his two favorite themes: "Mr. Manson has had quite a share of troubles because of the fact that he likes girls." And he was only brought to trial "so someone in the District Attorney's Office can have a gold star and say, 'I got Charles Manson.'"

Kanarek's argument stretched over three days. It was occasionally ridiculous, as when he said, "We can perform a public service for the United States of America by giving these people life, because if there is a revolution, this is the kind of thing that could spark it." It was sometimes unintentionally funny, as when he stated that, unlike Patricia Krenwinkel and Leslie Van Houten, "Charles Manson has no family to come here to testify." But mostly he tried to plant little seeds of doubt.

Why, if Susan Atkins lied on the stand to absolve Manson, would she have implicated him in the Hinman murder? Wasn't the fact that Manson himself shot Crowe, to protect the people at Spahn Ranch, evidence that he didn't need to order others to act for him? If these girls were lying about Manson's non-involvement in the murders, wouldn't they have also lied and said they had sorrow and remorse?

Kanarek only briefly mentioned the copycat motive; he didn't even try to argue it. Instead, he suggested still another alternative motive. "But for the fact that at least some of these people [supposedly referring to the Tate victims] were engaged in a narcotic episode of some type, these events would not have taken place."

Daye Shinn, who argued next, fastened on Dr. Hochman's statement that he believed these girls had subconscious if not conscious remorse.

As for Susan, "She is still young," Shinn argued. "She is only twenty-two years old. I believe there is still a hope of rehabilitating her . . . Maybe someday she may be rehabilitated to the extent that she may finally realize what she has done was not right. I believe that she deserves the chance, an opportunity, so that maybe someday she may be released and live the rest of her life out of prison."

This was very bad strategy on Shinn's part, implying that if Susan Atkins was given life imprisonment she might someday be released on parole. By law, the prosecution can't argue this, it is so prejudicial to the defendant.

Of the four defense attorneys, Maxwell Keith gave the best opening argument. He was also the only one who really attempted to rebut my contentions.

"Mr. Bugliosi tells you that if the death penalty is not appropriate in this case, it would never be appropriate. Well, I wonder if it ever is appropriate?

"Mr. Bugliosi read to you at the close of his argument on the guilt phase the roll call of the dead. Let me read to you now, ladies and gentlemen, the roll call of the living dead: Leslie, Sadie, Katie, Squeaky, Brenda, Ouisch, Sandy, Cathy, Gypsy, Tex, Clem, Mary, Snake, and no doubt many more. These lives, and the lives of these three young girls in particular, have been so damaged that it is possible, in some cases, their destruction is beyond repair. I hope not, but it is possible."

Leslie Van Houten, he strongly argued, was capable of rehabilitation. She should be studied, not killed. "I am not asking you to forgive her, although to forgive is divine. I am asking you to give her the chance to redeem herself. She deserves to live. What she did was not done by the real Leslie. Let the Leslie of today die—she will, slowly and maybe painfully. And let the Leslie as she once was live again."

Nowhere in Paul Fitzgerald's argument, which followed, did he state, or even imply, that Manson was responsible for what had happened to Patricia Krenwinkel.

"Patricia Krenwinkel is twenty-three years old," Fitzgerald observed. "With 365 days in the year, there are approximately 8,400 days in 23 years, and approximately 200,000 hours in her lifetime.

"The perpetration of these offenses took at best approximately three hours.

"Is she to be judged solely on what occurred during three of 200,000 hours?"

Just before court commenced on March 23, I walked over to the water cooler. Manson, in the nearby lockup, called out to me, rather loudly, "If I get the death penalty, there is going to be a lot of bloodletting. Because I am not going to take it."

Both the court clerk and Steve Kay overheard the remark. Kay intemperately rushed out of the courtroom and repeated it to the press. Learning of this, I asked the reporters not to print it. The *Herald Examiner* wouldn't agree, and it broke the story with a banner headline:

MANSON DEATH THREAT

Warns of Terror
If Doomed to Die

Before this, however, Judge Older, made aware of what had happened, decided that rather than wait to the close of arguments, he would sequester the jury immediately.

In my final argument I rebutted point by point the earlier defense contentions. For example, the defense had claimed that Linda got her story from listening to the Susan Atkins tapes. Why would Linda need to listen to the tapes, I asked, when she was present both nights?

Kanarek had told the jury that if they returned death penalty verdicts, they would be killers. This was a very heavy argument. As support, he cited the Fifth Commandment: "Thou shalt not kill."

In answer, I told the jury that most biblical scholars and theologians interpret the original language to mean: "Thou shalt not commit murder," which is exactly how it appears in the New English Bible, dated 1970.

The Ten Commandments appear in Exodus, chapter 20, I noted. What Kanarek did not mention, I observed, is that the very next chapter authorizes the death penalty. Exodus 21, verse 12, reads: "Whoever strikes a man a mortal blow must be put to death," while verse 14 of the same chapter reads: "When a man kills another, after maliciously scheming to do so, you must take him even from my altar and put him to death."

Kanarek argued that there was no domination. In addition to all the evidence during the guilt trial, I observed, during the penalty trial, "When Atkins, Krenwinkel, and Van Houten played the part of the sacrificial lamb and admitted their participation in these murders, and then lied on that witness stand and said that Manson wasn't involved, the fact that they were willing to lie on that witness stand just proves, all the more, Manson's domination over them ..." As for the other Family witnesses, Squeaky, Sandy, and the others, "All of them sounded like a broken record on that witness stand. They all have the same thought; they use the same language; each one was a carbon copy of the other. They are all still totally subservient and subject to Charles Manson. They are his X'd-out slaves."

I came now to the copycat motive. My objective was to completely demolish it, yet not dwell on it so long that it would seem that I was giving it credence.

"It is really laughable, ladies and gentlemen," I began, "the way the three female defendants and the defense witnesses sought to take the hat off Charles Manson.

"They had to come up with a motive for these murders other than Helter Skelter. Why? Because no less than ten witnesses during the guilt trial had irrevocably connected Manson with Helter Skelter, so they certainly could not say from that witness stand that the motive for these murders was Helter Skelter. If they said that, they would be saying, 'Yes, Charles Manson masterminded these murders.' So they came up with the copycat motive.

"I could give you between twenty and thirty reasons why it's obvious that this nonsensical story of the defense was fabricated out of whole cloth, but I won't take up your time with it, and I am not going to insult your intelligence." I did point out a few:

Linda Kasabian testified during the penalty trial that she had never heard anyone discuss committing these murders to free Bobby Beausoleil.

Gary Hinman was stabbed not more than four times. Voytek Frykowski was stabbed fifty-one times, Rosemary LaBianca forty-one times, Leno LaBianca twenty-six times. Rather a great difference, if these were copycat slayings.

And, if these murders were to be carbon copies, why weren't the words "political piggy" used at the Tate and LaBianca residences? And why no bloody paw print at the latter two houses?

The most powerful evidence demolishing this ridiculous motive, I noted, was that as early as February 1969, "long before there was any Hinman murder to copy, long before there were any words 'political piggy' to copy, Manson told Brooks Poston and other Family members—including all of his co-defendants—that, quoting Poston: 'He said a group of real blacks would come out of the ghettos and do an atrocious crime in the richer sections of Los Angeles and other cities. They would do an atrocious murder with stabbing, killing, cutting bodies to pieces, smearing blood on the walls, writing 'pigs' on the walls.'

"Writing 'pigs' on the walls," I repeated.

"So writing 'pig' at the Tate and LaBianca residences was simply a part of Manson's blueprint for starting Helter Skelter, not an effort to copy the Hinman murder.

"Incidentally," I observed, "Mr. Kanarek never did try to explain to you why the words 'helter skelter' were printed in blood on the refrigerator door at the LaBianca residence. What does Helter Skelter have to do with freeing Bobby Beausoleil or an alleged $1,000 MDA burn at the Tate residence? Absolutely nothing, that's what. The words 'helter skelter' were found printed in blood on the LaBianca refrigerator door because all of the evidence at this trial shows beyond all doubt that Helter Skelter was the principal reason for these savage murders.

"Yes," I admitted, "there is a connection between the Hinman murder and the Tate-LaBianca murders. But it was not this silly Bobby Beausoleil nonsense. Here is the connection. Mr. Manson not only ordered the Tate-LaBianca murders, he also ordered the Hinman murder. That is the connection."

As for Susan Atkins' claim that Linda Kasabian masterminded these murders, I noted that not until the penalty phase did she say anything about this, and then "all of a sudden Linda Kasabian is Charles Manson."

I noted some of the reasons why this was preposterous, among them the ridiculousness of the docile, subservient Linda taking over the leadership of the Family in just one month. "Only one person ordered these murders, ladies and gentlemen, and his initials are CM. He also has an aka: JC. And he is in that lockup right now listening to me . . ."

The most preposterous thing about all this was that supposedly for one and a half years both Sadie and Gypsy kept this secret in their perjurous bosoms. They not only didn't tell the other members of the Family, they didn't even tell Manson's attorney, though both testified they loved and would willingly die for Charlie.

"And why didn't they tell him about this motive? Because it didn't exist. It was recently fabricated."

As for Manson's alibi, that he was with Stephanie Schram in Devil's Canyon on both of these nights, "Isn't it strange that all of Mr. Manson's X'd-out slaves have testified to this during the penalty trial, and the very person, Stephanie Schram, whom they claim Manson was with, testified that Manson was not with her?"

I then addressed myself to the issue of whether the four defendants should receive the death penalty.

The strongest argument that can be made in support of capital punishment is, I feel, deterrence—that it may save additional lives. Unfortunately, under California law the prosecution could not argue deterrence, only retribution.

"These weren't typical murders, ladies and gentlemen. This was a one-sided war where unspeakable atrocities were committed. If all of these defendants don't receive the death penalty, the typical first-degree murderer only deserves ten days in the County Jail."

As for Fitzgerald's contention that killing these defendants would not bring the seven victims back to life, "If we were to accept that line of reasoning, no one would ever be punished for any crime, since punishing a person does not remove the fact that the crime was committed." For example, "Don't punish a man for arson because the punishment is not going to rebuild the building."

In California, if a defendant is seventeen years of age or younger, he or she cannot be sentenced to death. Though Fitzgerald repeatedly called the three female defendants "children," I reminded the jury that Leslie was twenty-one, Susan twenty-two, Katie twenty-three. "They are adults by any standard, and completely responsible for their acts."

In regard to the defense contention that the three female defendants were insane, I reminded the jury that Dr. Hochman, the only psychiatrist to examine all three, said they are not and have never been insane.

Dr. Hochman testified that we are all capable of killing, I noted. "He did not say that we are all capable of murder. There is a vast difference between killing—as in justifiable homicide, self-defense, or defense of others—and murder. And no one can convince me, ladies and gentlemen, that all of us are capable of murdering strangers for no reason whatsoever like these three female defendants did.

"It takes a special type of person to do what they did. It takes a person who places no value on the life of a fellow human being.

"True, Watson, Atkins, Krenwinkel, and Van Houten committed these murders because Charles Manson told them to, but they would never have committed these murders in a million years if they did not already have murder in their guts, in their system. Manson merely told them to do what they were already capable of doing."

Moreover, there was no evidence that Manson *forced* Watson and the girls to murder for him. "In fact, the inference is that they wanted to go along. That seemed to be the general feeling in the Family. Witness the statement of Cathy Gillies. Witness Susan Atkins' telling Juan Flynn, 'We're going to get some fucking pigs.' Does that sound like someone who is being forced to go out?"

Manson ordered the murders, but Watson and the three girls personally committed them "because they wanted to. Make no mistake about that. If they did not want to murder these victims, *all they had to do was not do it.*"

I examined now the backgrounds of the three girls. Like the other female members of the Family, they had "one common denominator among them. It was obvious that each of them had a revulsion, an antipathy, a seething feeling of disgust for society, for their own parents." Each of the three girls had dropped out of society before even meeting Charles Manson; each had taken LSD and other drugs before meeting Manson; and each had rejected her real family before meeting Manson.

Looking right at juror Jean Roseland, who had two teen-age daughters, I said, "Don't confuse them with the girl-next-door type. These three female defendants had repudiated and renounced their very families and society before they ever met Charles Manson.

"In fact, it was precisely because they had contemptuously disavowed and rejected their families and society that they ended up with Charles Manson. That is the very reason.

"Manson was simply the catalyst, the moving force that

translated their preexisting disgust and hatred for society and human beings into violence."

I anticipated an argument that I felt Maxwell Keith might give. "The thought certainly may enter your mind that as wicked and as vicious as these three female defendants are, by comparison to Charles Manson they are nowhere as wicked and vicious as he is; therefore, let's give Manson the death penalty and these three female defendants life imprisonment.

"The only problem with that type of approach is that these female defendants are given credit, as it were, because of Manson's extreme wickedness and viciousness. Under that type of reasoning, if Adolf Hitler were Charles Manson's co-defendant, Manson should receive life imprisonment because of the indescribably evil Adolf Hitler." Rather than compare the three female defendants with Manson, I told the jury, they should evaluate the conduct of *each* of the defendants and determine whether it warranted the imposition of the death penalty. I then went into the acts of each, starting with Manson, enumerating one by one the reasons they deserved death rather than life.

One question the jury would surely ask, I noted, was: Why no remorse? The answer was simple: "Manson and his co-defendants like to kill human beings. That is why they have no remorse. As Paul Watkins testified, 'Death is Charlie's trip.' "

I came to the end of my argument.

"Now the defense attorneys want you to give these defendants a break. Did these defendants give the seven victims in this case a break?

"Now the defense attorneys want you to give their clients another chance. Did these defendants give the seven victims in this case any chance at all?

"Now the defense attorneys want you to have mercy on their clients. Did these defendants have any mercy at all on the seven victims in this case when they begged and pleaded for their lives?"

I then reminded the jurors that nine months earlier, during voir dire, each had told me he would be willing to vote death if he felt this was a proper case. I reiterated:

"If the death penalty is to mean anything in the State of California, other than two empty words, this is a proper case."

I concluded: "On behalf of the People of the State of California, I can't thank you enough for the enormous public service you have rendered as jurors in this very long, historic trial."

That night after dinner I said to Gail, "There must be *something* I have to do tonight." But there wasn't. For a year and a half, seven days a week, I had been totally immersed in the case. Now all I could do was listen to the closing arguments of the defense attorneys and wait until the jury reached its verdict.

Kanarek began by implying that perhaps I had poisoned the glass of water on the lectern and ended, more than a day later, by reading chapter after chapter from the New Testament.

"Now, this being the Easter season, there is an analogy here between Mr. Manson—this may sound at first blush to be ridiculous, and we are not suggesting that Mr. Manson is the deity or Christlike or anything like that—*but how can we know?*"

Judge Older, who had several times warned Kanarek that he had exhausted all relevant rebuttal, finally brought his sermon to an end at the point of resurrection.

Shinn spent his time attacking the DA's Office and in particular me: "Miss Atkins was drowning without friends ... and she saw Mr. Bugliosi with an oar. She said: Oh, here comes help now. Miss Atkins reached out for that oar. And what do you think Mr. Bugliosi did? He hit her over the head with the oar."

Keith delivered a strong argument against the death penalty itself. Before this, however, he said: "Now strangely, or perhaps not so strangely, I accepted wholeheartedly certain areas of Mr. Bugliosi's argument.

"I accept his exposition to you that Mr. Manson dominated these girls and ordered the homicides.

"I accept that the 'free Bobby Beausoleil' motive is non-sense.

"I accept his telling you that you shouldn't hold the Hinman murder against Leslie.

"I accept his argument that Leslie's testimony and the testimony of the other girls in this case shows Mr. Manson's domination and influence still persists and is all-pervasive."

To deny these things, Keith said, would be to deny the evidence. Thus Keith became the first, and only, defense attorney to accuse Manson of these murders.

Keith, however, said that he did not agree that any of the defendants should receive the death penalty, not even Charles Manson. For in his opinion, Keith said, "Mr. Manson is insane," and in instilling his thoughts into the minds of the three female defendants he had also infected them with his madness.

Keith concluded: "Give Leslie the chance for redemption, to which she is entitled. Remember, Linda Kasabian cut the umbilical cord, in Mr. Bugliosi's words, that tied her to Manson and his Family. Give Leslie the chance to do the same. Give her life. I thank you."

Fitzgerald read a short argument, at the end of which he began describing in detail how the three female defendants would be executed in the gas chamber at San Quentin Prison if the jury returned verdicts of death. This was improper argument, and I objected. When we approached the bench, Paul literally begged Judge Older to let him proceed. "This is extremely important! I can't impress on the Court how important it is!" Because he was so desperate, I decided to back off, agreeing not to object if he would describe this as a hypothetical situation—"Imagine that this is happening"—and not as fact. He did so, after which Judge Older instructed the jury. They left the courtroom at 5:25 P.M. on Friday, March 26, 1971.

While I felt confident that the jury would return a death penalty verdict against Charles Manson, I was less sure when it came to the girls. Only four females had been executed in California history, none of them as young as the defendants.

I had anticipated that the jury would be out at least four days. When I received the call Monday afternoon, after only two days, I knew there could be only one verdict. It was too fast for anything else. Their actual deliberations, I later learned, had taken only ten hours.

Again under extraordinary security precautions, the jury was brought back into the courtroom, at 4:24 P.M. on Monday, March 29, with their verdicts.

Manson and the girls had been brought into the courtroom earlier—the three female defendants now, when it was too late to influence the jury, having shaved their heads also—but before the clerk could read the first verdict, Manson yelled, "I don't see how you can get by with this without letting me put on some kind of defense . . . You people have no authority over me . . . Half of you in here ain't as good as I am . . ." and Older ordered him removed.

Manson's no-defense claim was nonsense. It was obvious that the defense he intended to put on during the guilt phase had been delivered in toto during the penalty phase. The jury's reaction to it was now being delivered, in a courtroom jammed with spectators and press.

The clerk read the first verdict: "We, the jury in the above-entitled action, having found the defendant Charles Manson guilty of murder in the first degree as charged in Count I of the Indictment, do now fix the penalty as death."

KRENWINKEL "You have just judged yourselves."

ATKINS "Better lock your doors and watch your own kids."

VAN HOUTEN "Your whole system is a game. You blind, stupid people. Your children will turn against you."

Judge Older had the three girls removed. They too listened over the loudspeaker as the clerk fixed the penalty for all four defendants as death on all counts.

Judge Older left the bench to shake hands with each juror. "If it were within the power of a trial judge to award a medal of honor to jurors," he told them, "believe me, I would bestow an award on each of you."

For the first time the jurors could speak to the press about their ordeal.

Jury foreman Herman Tubick told reporters that the jury was convinced "the motive was Helter Skelter." Mrs. Thelma McKenzie said the jury had "certainly tried" to find point upon which they could sentence the female defendants to a verdict less severe, "but we couldn't." William McBride remarked: "I felt sympathy for the women but sympathy can't interfere with justice. What they did deserves the death penalty." Marie Mesmer said she felt more pity for Susan Atkins than for the other two girls, because of her background, but that she was shocked when all three showed no signs of remorse. As for Manson, she said: "I wanted to protect society. I think Manson is a very dangerous influence." Jean Roseland, mother of three teenagers, two of them girls, said the most terrible part of the whole trial was Leslie Van Houten "looking at me with those big brown eyes." Mrs. Roseland was convinced Manson's power to manipulate others came not from within himself but "from the voids within the minds and souls of his followers."

Later *Life* ran an article entitled "The Manson Jury: End of a Long Ordeal."

Ironically, there appeared in the same issue an article entitled "Paul McCartney on the Beatles Breakup."

That there had been irreconcilable troubles within the group became apparent, McCartney said, while they were making the White Album.

Colonel Paul Tate was reported to have said, regarding the death sentence verdicts: "That's what we wanted. That's what we expected. But there's no jubilation in something like this, no sense of satisfaction. It's more a feeling that justice has been done. Naturally I wanted the death penalty. They took my daughter and my grandchild."

Mrs. Tate told reporters that she didn't believe any human being should have the power to take a life, that that was up to God.

Roman Polanski declined comment, as did the other relatives of the victims whom the media contacted.

Sandy, Cathy, and the other girls on the corner had threatened to burn themselves to death with gasoline if any of the four were given death sentences. They didn't carry out their threat, though all did later shave their heads.

On learning of the decision, Sandy looked into the TV cameras and screamed: *"Death? That's what you're all going to get!"*

With the exception of the sentencing, the trial was over. It had been the longest murder trial in American history, lasting nine and a half months; the most expensive, costing approximately $1 million; and the most highly publicized; while the jury had been sequestered 225 days, longer than any jury before it. The trial transcript alone ran to 209 volumes, 31,716 pages, approximately eight million words, a mini-library.

For almost everyone, the ordeal was not only long but expensive. A number of the jurors, anticipating that they would be paid by their employers, now found themselves either unpaid or without jobs. Mrs. Roseland, for example, claimed that TWA did not honor a verbal agreement to keep her on salary until the end of the trial, and estimated she lost about $2,700 in back pay. TWA denied there was any such agreement. There were several such denials.

The financial sacrifice on the part of the defense attorneys was enormous. Fitzgerald said: "It's just really wiped me out." He told a reporter that he had lost about $30,000 in income and incurred $10,000 in trial expenses. He had been forced to sell his stereo and other possessions, and had spent $5,000 which he didn't have. Six-times-married Daye Shinn said: "I'm behind in my house payments and child support and my alimonies." Shinn had received $19,000 in royalties from the Atkins book, he said, but he claimed that about $16,000 of it went back to the Manson Family. Kanarek refused to discuss his financial situation. Another of the defense attorneys did tell me, however, that at one point during the trial Manson had ordered Shinn to give Kanarek $5,000 from the Atkins account, to help defray his expenses, but how much more he received, if any, is unknown. Keith, who received a fee from the county, since he was court-appointed, admitted his private practice had gone downhill and that he didn't expect to gain any new clients as a result of the publicity.

The trial cost another attorney his life.

In the avalanche of stories on the Manson verdict, one small item which appeared that same day went almost unnoticed.

The Ventura County Sheriff's Office reported that they had found a body believed to be that of the missing defense attorney, Ronald Hughes. The badly decomposed corpse had been found face down, wedged between two boulders, in Sespe Creek, miles from where Hughes had last been seen alive.

Two fishermen had discovered the body early Saturday but didn't report it until Sunday night, because "we didn't want to spoil our fishing trip."

The cause of death was at this time unknown. Through our office, I ordered an immediate autopsy.

April 19, 1971

Judge Older had set Monday, April 19, 1971 as the date of sentencing.

There was speculation that Older might decide on his own to reduce at least some of the verdicts from death to life. In a previous case Older had done this for a defendant who had poured gasoline on two beds where four children were sleeping, killing one of them. However, I personally felt that since Older had complimented the jurors, he wouldn't turn right around and set aside their verdict.

On the nineteenth the Court heard, and rejected, a number of defense motions, including those for a new trial. Judge Older then asked the defendants if they had anything to say. Only Manson did.

Charlie's left hand was trembling and he seemed near tears. Very meekly, with a quivering voice, he said: "I accept this court as my father. I have always done my best in my life to uphold the laws of my father, and I accept my father's judgment."

THE COURT "After nine and a half months of trial, all of the superlatives had been used, all of the hyperbole has been indulged in, and all that remains are the bare, stark facts of seven senseless murders, seven people whose lives were snuffed out by total strangers . . .

"I have carefully looked, in considering this action, for mitigating circumstances, and I have been unable to find any . . .

"It is my considered judgment that not only is the death penalty appropriate, but it is almost compelled by the circumstances. I must agree with the prosecutor that if this is not a proper case for the death penalty, what would be?"

Speaking to Manson, Judge Older said: "The Department of Corrections is ordered to deliver you to the custody of the Warden of the State Prison of the State of California at San Quentin to be by him put to death in the manner prescribed by law of the State of California."

There was at this time no Death Row for women. A special isolation wing was being constructed at the California Institute for Women at Frontera, and Atkins, Krenwinkel, and Van Houten were sent there to await execution.

It was anticipated that the appeals would take at least two and possibly as long as five years.

In actuality, their fate would be decided in less than one.

After the sentencing, I didn't anticipate ever seeing Charles Manson again. But I'd see him twice more, the last time under very peculiar circumstances.

Epilogue

A SHARED MADNESS

"A more comprehensive description of her
condition will necessitate further study.
But at this time we might suggest the
possibility that she may be suffering from
a condition of *folie à famille*, a kind of
shared madness within a group situation."
Dr. Joel Hochman,
in his psychiatric
report on Susan Atkins

"I lived with Charlie for one year straight
and on and off for two years. I know Charlie.
I know him inside and out. I became Charlie.
Everything I once was, was Charlie. There was
nothing left of me anymore. And all of the
people in the Family, there's nothing left of
them anymore, they're all Charlie too."*
Paul Watkins

"We are what you have made us. We were brought
up on your TV. We were brought up watching
'Gunsmoke,' 'Have Gun Will Travel,' 'FBI,' 'Combat.'
'Combat' was my favorite show. I never missed
'Combat.' "*
Brenda

*From the Robert Hendrickson documentary film, *Manson.*

"Whatever is necessary, you do it. When somebody needs to be killed, there's no wrong. You do it, and then you move on. And you pick up a child and you move him to the desert. You pick up as many children as you can and you kill whoever gets in your way. That is us."*

Sandy

"If you find an apple that has a little spot on it, you cut out that spot."

Squeaky

"You just better hope I never get out."
Bobby Beausoleil

*From the Robert Hendrickson documentary film, *Manson*.

A Shared Madness

Although Manson and the girls had been convicted, the trials, and the murders, were not yet over.

For their part in the attempted murder of prosecution witness Barbara Hoyt, four of the five defendants served only ninety days in the County Jail, while the fifth escaped punishment entirely.

Although I was not assigned to the case, I questioned the way it was handled. Because it was felt that the evidence against the defendants was weak, and because of the expense of flying in witnesses from Hawaii, the DA's Office, LAPD, and the defense attorneys agreed to a "deal." In return for the defendants pleading "no contest" to one count of conspiracy to dissuade a witness from testifying, the prosecutor made a motion to reduce the charge from a felony to a misdemeanor. Judge Stephen Stothers granted the motion, and on April 16, 1971, he sentenced four of the five defendants—Lynette Fromme, aka Squeaky; Steve Grogan, aka Clem; Catherine Share, aka Gypsy; and Dennis Rice—to ninety days in the County Jail. Since they had already served fifteen days, they were back on the streets in seventy-five days.

The fifth defendant, Ruth Ann Moorehouse, aka Ouisch, the girl who actually gave Barbara Hoyt the LSD-laden hamburger, got off scot-free. When it came time for sentencing, she failed to appear. Although a bench warrant was issued for her arrest and she was known to be living in Carson City, Nevada, the DA's Office decided it wasn't worth the trouble to extradite her.

Of the five, three would later be involved in other murders, some attempted, some successful.

Charles "Tex" Watson went on trial in August 1971. A good portion of my preparation took place not in a law li-

brary but in a medical library, since I was relatively sure
that Watson was going to plead not guilty by reason of insanity and put on a psychiatric defense.

The trial had three possible phases——guilt, sanity, and
penalty—each of which presented its own special problems.

Even though defense attorney Sam Bubrick told me
that Watson intended to take the stand and confess, I
knew I still had to present a strong case during the guilt
phase, since it was a safe bet that Watson's testimony
would be self-serving. Too, I had to prove (by evidence
such as Watson's instructing Linda to steal the $5,000) that
although Watson was dominated by Manson, he still had
enough independence to make him legally responsible for
his acts. One of the key issues during the guilt trial, then,
was whether Watson was suffering from diminished mental
capacity at the time of the murders. If he was, and it was
of such a nature that it prevented him from deliberating
and premeditating, the jury would have to find the chief
Tate-LaBianca killer guilty of second rather than first degree murder.

If convicted of any degree of criminal homicide, then
there would be a sanity trial, in which the sole issue would
be whether Watson was sane or insane at the time of the
murders. I anticipated, and quite rightly, that the defense
would call a number of prominent psychiatrists (eight
were called), many of whom would testify that in their
opinion Watson was insane. Therefore I'd not only have to
subject their testimony to withering cross-examination, I'd
also have to present an abundance of evidence showing
that Watson was in full command of his mental faculties
at the time of the murders and that he was well aware
that in the eyes of society what he was doing was wrong.
In short, I had to prove that he wasn't legally insane. Such
evidence as his cutting of the telephone wires, his telling
Linda to wipe the knives of fingerprints, his manner when
talking to Rudolf Weber, and his using an alias when questioned by the authorities in Death Valley a few weeks
after the murders thus became extremely important to
proving my case, in that all were circumstantial evidence

of a consciousness of wrongdoing and guilt on Watson's part.

If Watson was convicted of first degree murder and also found sane, then the jury would have to decide the ultimate question: whether he was to be given life or death. And this meant I would again face many of the same problems I had with the girls in the penalty phase of the earlier trial.

Still another problem was Watson's demeanor. In an obvious attempt to project a college-boy image, Watson dressed very conservatively in court—short hair, shirt and tie, blue blazer, slacks. But he still looked strange. His eyes were glassy, and never seemed to focus. He reacted not at all to the damning testimony of such witnesses as Linda Kasabian, Paul Watkins, Brooks Poston, and Dianne Lake. And his mouth was always slightly gaping, giving him the appearance of being mentally retarded.

Taking the stand on direct examination by the defense, Tex played the part of Manson's abject slave. He admitted shooting or stabbing six of the Tate-LaBianca victims, but denied stabbing Sharon Tate. And everything which showed either premeditation or deliberation he put on Manson or the girls.

My cross-examination so shook Tex that he often forgot he was supposed to be playing the idiot. By the time I'd finished, it was obvious to the jury that he was in complete command of his mental faculties and probably always had been. I also got him to admit that he had stabbed Sharon Tate too; that he didn't think of the victims as people but as "just blobs"; that he had told Dr. Joel Fort that the people at the Tate residence "were running around like chickens with their heads cut off," and that when he said this he had smiled; and I tore to shreds his story that he was simply an unthinking zombie programmed by Charles Manson, as well as cast considerable doubt on his claim that he now felt remorse for what he had done.

Watson's testimony cleared up some mysteries:

Contrary to the findings of LAPD evidence-expert De-Wayne Wolfer, Watson identified the pair of red wire cutters found in Manson's dune buggy as the pair he had used to cut the Tate telephone wires that night.

Also revealed for the first time were Manson's exact instructions to Watson on the night of the murders at 10050 Cielo Drive. Watson testified: "Charlie called me over behind a car ... and handed me a gun and a knife. He said for me to take the gun and knife and go up to where Terry Melcher used to live. He said to kill everybody in the house as gruesome as I could. I believe he said something about movie stars living there."

And Watson admitted that when he entered the LaBianca residence, he was already armed with a knife.

My greatest difficulty during the entire Watson trial came not from the evidence, the defense attorneys, or the defense witnesses, but from the judge, Adolph Alexander, who was a personal friend of defense attorney Sam Bubrick.

Alexander not only repeatedly favored the defense in his rulings, he went far beyond that. During voir dire he remarked: "Many of *us* are opposed to the death penalty." When prosecution witnesses were testifying, he gave them incredulous, unbelieving looks; when defense witnesses took the stand, he industriously took notes. All this was done right in front of the jury. He also frequently cross-examined the prosecution witnesses. Finally, I'd had it. Asking to approach the bench, I reminded Alexander that this was a jury trial, not a court trial, and that I was immensely concerned that by cross-examining the prosecution witnesses he was giving the jury the impression that he didn't believe the witnesses, and since a judge has substantial stature in the eyes of a jury, this could be extremely harmful to the People. I suggested that if he wanted to have certain questions asked, he write them out and give them to the defense attorneys to ask.

Thereafter Alexander cut down on his cross-examination of the prosecution witnesses. However, he still continued to amaze me. When the jury went out to deliberate, he didn't even have the exhibits sent back to the jury room—a virtually automatic act——until after I had demanded that he do so. And once, in chambers and off the record, he referred to the defendant as "poor Tex."

Also off the record was a remark I made to him toward the end of the trial: "You're the biggest single obstacle to my obtaining a conviction of first degree murder in this case."

Despite the problems presented by Judge Alexander, on October 12, 1971, the jury found Watson guilty of seven counts of first degree murder and one count of conspiracy to commit murder. That I had effectively destroyed the testimony of the defense psychiatrists on cross-examination was borne out by the fact that on October 19 it took the jury only two and a half hours to decide that Watson was sane. And on October 21, after remaining out only six hours, they returned with a verdict of death.

The trial had lasted two and a half months and cost a quarter of a million dollars. It also added another forty volumes, 5,916 pages, to the mini-library on the Tate-La-Bianca murders.

Although Judge Alexander thanked the jury for the conscientious job they had done, he remarked, on the day he sentenced Watson, "If I had tried this case without a jury, I possibly would have arrived at a different verdict."

In still other proceedings, Susan Atkins pleaded guilty to the murder of Gary Hinman and was given life imprisonment. In sentencing her, Judge Raymond Choate called her "a danger to any community," who should spend "her entire life in custody."

The defense obtained separate trials for Charles Manson, Bruce Davis, and Steve Grogan on the combined Hinman-Shea murder charges. Despite the fact that the body of Donald "Shorty" Shea hadn't been found (and hasn't to this day), prosecutors Burt Katz, Anthony Manzella, and Steven Kay succeeded in the difficult task of obtaining guilty verdicts against each of the defendants on all of the counts. Verdicts of life imprisonment were returned for Manson and Davis. The Grogan jury voted death, but when it came time for sentencing—two days before Christmas 1971—Judge James Kolts, commenting that "Grogan was too stupid and too hopped up on drugs to decide anything on his own," and declaring that it was really Manson "who decided who lived or died," reduced the sentence to life imprisonment.

During voir dire in his trial, Manson, angered by the judge's refusal to let him represent himself, told the Court: "I enter a plea of guilty. I chopped off Shorty's head." The judge refused to accept the plea, and the next day Manson withdrew it. During another angry outburst, Manson turned to the press and said, "I've told my people to start killing you."

Again Manson was represented by Irving Kanarek. With Irving, he knew it would be a long trial, postponing his trip to San Quentin's Death Row.

Through all the trials, the Manson girls continued their vigil on the corner of Temple and Broadway. Literally in the shadow of the Hall of Justice, in view of the thousands of people who passed that corner every day, they fashioned a bizarre plot to free all the imprisoned Manson Family members.

In late July of 1971 my co-author learned from a Family member in the San Francisco Bay Area that the Family was planning to break out Manson sometime within the next month. Though he was not told how they intended to accomplish this, he was given some additional details: the Family was stockpiling arms and ammunition; they had secretly rented a house in South Los Angeles and were hiding an escaped convict there; and with Manson's escape "Helter Skelter will really start; the revolution will be on."

Wishful thinking? I wasn't sure, and passed the information along to LAPD. When I did, I learned that among the witnesses Manson had called in the Hinman-Shea trial was a Folsom convict named Kenneth Como, also known by the colorful aka Jesse James. Though it hadn't been publicized, when brought to Los Angeles less than a week before, Como had managed to escape from the Hall of Records. LAPD doubted, however, that he was still in the area. As for the Manson escape, they had heard rumors also, but nothing definite. They were inclined to doubt the tale.

On schedule, less than a month later, the Manson Family made their attempt.

Shortly after closing time on the night of Saturday, August 21, 1971, six armed robbers entered the Western Surplus Store in the Los Angeles suburb of Hawthorne. While one kept a shotgun on the female clerk and two customers, the others began carrying rifles, shotguns, and pistols to a van parked in the alley outside. They had collected about 140 guns when they spotted the first police car. LAPD, alerted by a silent alarm, had already sealed off the alley.

The robbers came out shooting. In the ten-minute gun battle that followed, the van was riddled with over fifty bullets, and some twenty bullets crashed into the black-and-whites. Surprisingly, no one was killed, though three of the suspects received slight wounds.

All six robbers were Manson Family members. Apprehended were Mary Brunner, twenty-seven, first member of the Family; Catherine Share, aka Gypsy, twenty-nine, and Dennis Rice, thirty-two, both recently freed after serving ninety-day sentences for their part in the attempted silencing of Barbara Hoyt; Lawrence Bailey, aka Larry Jones, twenty-three, who was present the night the Tate killers left Spahn; and escaped convict Kenneth Como, thirty-three. Another Family member, Charles Lovett, nineteen, got away during the gun fight but was subsequently apprehended.

After their arrest it was learned that the same group was also responsible for the robbery of a Covina beer distributorship on August 13, which netted them $2,600.

The police surmised that through the robberies the group intended to get enough guns and ammunition to stage a San Rafael-type commando raid on the courthouse. Steve Grogan had called Manson as a witness in his trial. It was believed that the day Manson appeared in court the Family intended to storm the Hall of Justice, breaking out both.

Actually, the real plan was far more spectacular. And, given the right circumstances and enough public pressure, it just *might* have worked.

Although never made public before this, according to a Family member who was privy to the planning of the Hawthorne robbery, the real plan was as follows:

Using the stolen weapons, the Family was going to hijack a 747 and kill one passenger every hour until Manson and all the other imprisoned Family members were released.

Extraordinary security measures were taken during the trial of the Hawthorne robbery defendants, in part because the defense had called as witnesses what Judge Arthur Alarcon labeled "the biggest collection of murderers in Los Angeles County at one time." Twelve convicted killers, including Manson, Beausoleil, Atkins, Krenwinkel, Van Houten, Grogan, and Davis, took the stand. Their presence in one place made everyone a little nervous. Especially since by this time the Family had discovered that the Hall of Justice was not escapeproof.

In the early-morning hours of October 20, 1971, Kenneth Como hacksawed his way through the bars of his thirteenth-floor cell, climbed down to the eighth floor on a rope made of bed sheets, kicked in a window in the courtroom of Department 104 (where just a few months earlier I'd prosecuted Manson and his three female co-defendants), then left the building by way of the stairs. Sandra Good picked up Como in the Family van. Though Sandy later smashed up the van and was arrested, Como managed to elude capture for seven hours. Also arrested—but subsequently released, there being no positive proof that they had aided and abetted the escape—were Squeaky, Brenda, Kitty, and two other Family members.

No attempt was made to break out Manson during the Hawthorne trial. However, two of the jurors had to be replaced by alternates after receiving telephone threats that they would be killed if they voted for conviction. The calls were linked to an unidentified female Family member.

Although Gypsy and Rice had previously been given only ninety days for their part in the attempted murder of a prosecution witness, they and their co-defendants found that the courts take shooting at police officers a little more seriously. All were charged with two counts of armed robbery. Rice pleaded guilty and was sent to state prison. The others were convicted on both counts and given the following sentences: Lovett, two consecutive five-year-to-life terms; Share, ten years to life; Como, fifteen years to life; Brunner and Bailey, twenty years to life.

Sandra Good was subsequently tried for aiding and abetting an escape. Her attorney, the one and only Irving Kanarek, claimed she had been kidnapped by Como. The jury didn't buy it, and Sandy was given six months in jail.

The day Como escaped, Kanarek, appearing in Judge Raymond Choate's court, claimed in his patented way: "I allege with no proof at this particular time that this escape was deliberately allowed to take place."

Judge Choate asked Kanarek if he could explain why Como was forced to climb down a rope from the thirteenth to the eighth floor.

"That makes it look good, Your Honor," Kanarek explained.

While Manson was still on trial for the Hinman-Shea murders, I dropped into the courtroom one day. It was a welcome relief to be a spectator for a change.

Manson, who had recently taken to wearing a black storm trooper's uniform in court, spotted me and sent a message by the bailiff that he wanted to speak to me. There were a few things I wanted to ask him about also, so I stayed over after court recessed. Sitting in the prisoner's dock in the courtroom, we talked from 4:30 P.M. to nearly 6 P.M. None of the talk concerned the current charges against him. Mostly we discussed his philosophy. I was especially interested in learning the evolution of some of his ideas, and questioned him at length about his relationship with Scientology and with the satanic cult known as The Process, or the Church of the Final Judgement.

Manson had wanted to speak to me, he said, because he wanted me to know "I don't have no hard feelings." He told me that I had done "a fantastic, remarkable job" in convicting him, and he said, "You gave me a fair trial, like you promised." He was not bitter about the result, however, because to him "prison has always been my home; I didn't want to leave it the last time and you're only sending me back there." There were regular meals, not great, but better than the garbage at Spahn Ranch.

And since you don't have to work if you don't want to, he'd have plenty of time to play his guitar.

"That may be, Charlie, but you don't have any women there," I said.

"I don't need broads," he replied. "Every woman I ever had, *she* asked *me* to make love to her. I never asked them. I can do without them." There was plenty of sex in prison, he said.

Although Manson again claimed that the Beatles' music and LSD were responsible for the Tate-LaBianca murders, he admitted that he had known they were going to happen, "because I even knew what the mice were doing at Spahn Ranch." He then added, "So I said to them: 'Here, do you want this rope? Do you want this gun?' And later I told them not to tell anyone about what happened."

Though careful never to do so in open court, in our private conversations Manson often referred to blacks as "niggers." He claimed he didn't dislike them. "I don't hate anyone," he said, "but I know they hate me."

Returning to the familiar theme of Helter Skelter, I asked him when he thought the black man was going to take over.

"I may have put a clog in them," he replied.

"You mean the trial alerted whitey?"

His reply was a simple, and sad, "Yeah."

Our conversation took place on June 14, 1971. The following day one of the attorneys complained, and Judge Choate conducted an evidentiary hearing in open court. I testified to the gist of our conversation, noting that Manson had asked to speak to me, and not vice versa, and that the current charges were not discussed. There was nothing unethical about this, I observed. Moreover, I'd told Kanarek that Manson wanted to talk to me, but Kanarek had merely walked away.

The bailiff, Rusty Burrell, who had sat in on the conversation, staying overtime because he found it interesting, supported my account. As did Manson himself.

MANSON   "The version the man [indicating me] gave was right on. I am almost sure Mr. Kanarek knew that I had asked to see him. I had wanted to speak to this man for the last year, and it was my request that motivated it."

As for the hearing itself, Manson said: "Your Honor, I don't think this is fair at all. You know, this was my mistake."

Agreeing, and ruling that there had been no impropriety involved, Judge Choate brought the hearing to an end.

The irony of all this was not lost on the press, which reported, with some incredulity, that Manson had taken the stand to defend the man who had convicted him of seven murders!

My interest in the sources of Manson's beliefs stretched back to my assignment to the case. Some of those sources have been mentioned earlier. Others, though inadmissible as evidence in the trial, have more than a passing interest, if only as clues to the genesis of such a sick obsession.

I knew, from Gregg Jakobson and others, that Manson was an eclectic, a borrower of ideas. I knew too, both from his prison records and from my conversations with him, that Manson's involvement with Scientology had been more than a passing fad. Manson told me, as he had Paul Watkins, that he had reached the highest stage, "theta clear," and no longer had any connection with or need for Scientology. I was inclined to accept at least the latter portion of his claim. In my rather extensive investigation, I found no evidence of any kind that Manson was involved with Scientology after his release from prison in 1967.* By this time, he had gone on to do his own thing.

What effect, if any, Scientology had on Manson's mental state cannot be measured. Undoubtedly he picked up from his "auditing" sessions in prison some knowledge of mind control, as well as some techniques which he later put to use in programming his followers.

Manson's link with The Process, or the Church of the

___

*One of Manson's chief disciples, Bruce Davis, was very closely involved with Scientology for a time, working in its London headquarters from about November or December of 1968 to April of 1969. According to a Scientology spokesman, Davis was kicked out of the organization for his drug use. He returned to the Manson Family and Spahn Ranch in time to participate in the Hinman and Shea slayings.

Final Judgement, is more tenuous, yet considerably more fascinating. The leader of the satanic cult is one Robert Moore, whose cult name is Robert DeGrimston. Himself a former disciple of Scientology founder L. Ron Hubbard, Moore broke with Scientology about 1963 to form his own group, after apparently attaining a high position in the London headquarters. He and his followers later traveled to various parts of the world, including Mexico and the United States, and for at least several months, and possibly longer, he lived in San Francisco. He also reportedly participated in a seminar at the Esalen Institute in Big Sur, though whether this coincided with any of Manson's visits there is unknown.

One of DeGrimston's most fervent disciples is one Victor Wild, a young leather goods manufacturer whose Process name is Brother Ely.

Up until December of 1967, Victor Wild's residence, and the San Francisco headquarters for The Process, was 407 Cole Street, in Haight-Ashbury.

From about April through July 1967, Charles Manson and his still fledgling Family lived just two blocks away, at 636 Cole. In view of Manson's curiosity, it appears very likely that he at least investigated the satanists, and there is fairly persuasive evidence that he "borrowed" some of their teachings.

In one of our conversations during the Tate-LaBianca trial, I asked Manson if he knew Robert Moore, or Robert DeGrimston. He denied knowing DeGrimston, but said he had met Moore. "You're looking at him," Manson told me. "Moore and I are one and the same." I took this to mean that he felt they thought alike.

Not long after this I was visited by two representatives of The Process, a Father John and a Brother Matthew. Having heard that I was asking questions about the group, they had been sent from their Cambridge, Massachusetts, headquarters to assure me that Manson and Moore had never met and that Moore was opposed to violence. They also left me a stack of Process literature. The following day the names "Father John" and "Brother Matthew" appeared on Manson's visitor's list. What they discussed is unknown. All I know is that in my last conversation with Manson, Charlie became evasive when I questioned him about The Process.

In 1968 and 1969, The Process launched a major recruiting drive in the United States. They were in Los Angeles in May and June of 1968 and for at least several months in the fall of 1969, returning to England in about October, after claiming to have converted some two hundred American hippies to their sect. Manson was in Los Angeles during both periods. It is possible that there may have been some contact with Manson and/or his group, but I found no evidence of this. I'm inclined to think that Manson's contact with the group probably occurred in San Francisco in 1967, as indicated, at a time when his philosophy was still being formulated. I believe there was at least some contact, in view of the many parallels between Manson's teachings and those of The Process, as revealed in their literature.

Both preached an imminent, violent Armageddon, in which all but the chosen few would be destroyed. Both found the basis for this in the Book of Revelation. Both conceived that the motorcycle gangs, such as Hell's Angels, would be the troops of the last days. And both actively sought to solicit them to their side.

The three great gods of the universe, according to The Process, were Jehovah, Lucifer, and Satan, with Christ the ultimate unifier who reconciles all three. Manson had a simpler duality; he was known to his followers as both Satan and Christ.

Both preached the Second Coming of Christ, a not unusual belief, except in their interpretation of it. According to a Process pamphlet: "Through Love, Christ and Satan have destroyed their enmity and come together for the End: Christ to Judge, Satan to execute the Judgement." When Christ returned this time, Manson said, it would be the Romans, i.e., the establishment, who went up on the cross.

Manson's attiude toward fear was so curious I felt it to be almost unique. At least I felt that until reading in a special issue of *The Process* magazine devoted to fear:

"Fear is beneficial . . . Fear is the catalyst of action. It is the energiser, the weapon built into the game in the beginning, enabling a being to create an effect upon himself, to spur himself on to new heights and to brush aside the bitterness of failure." Though the wording differs, this is almost exactly what Manson preached.

Manson spoke frequently of the bottomless pit, The Process of the bottomless void.

Within the organization, The Process was called (at least until 1969) "the family," while its members were known as brothers, sisters, mothers, fathers.

The symbol of The Process is similar, though not identical, to the swastika Manson carved on his forehead.

Among the precepts of The Process which parallel Manson's own: "The Time of the End is now . . . The Ultimate Sin is to kill an animal . . . Christ said love your enemy. Christ's enemy was Satan. Love Christ and Satan . . . The Lamb and the Goat must come together. Pure Love descended from the Pinnacle of Heaven, united with Pure Hatred raised from the depths of Hell."

One former Process member, being interrogated by LAPD in connection with two motorcycle gang slayings (neither of which was connected with The Process), said of the cult, "They don't like anybody that they can't indoctrinate or anybody that is not with them. They are just totally against what they call the 'gray forces,' the rich establishment or the Negroes—"

Q. "Why don't they like Negroes?"

A. "I don't know. They just don't."

Q. "They have a natural hate for the Negro?"

A. "They have a natural hate but they would also like to use the Negro as a whole to begin some kind of militant thing . . . They are really good at picking out angry people."

This was merely the opinion of one disaffiliated member, and may well not be the official position of The Process itself, but the similarities to Manson's own philosophy are still chilling.

These are only some of the parallels I found. They are enough to convince me, at least, that even if Manson himself may never have been a member of The Process, he borrowed heavily from the satanic cult.*

Nor are these the only connections between the Manson Family and satanists.

Bobby Beausoleil was for a time closely associated with filmmaker Kenneth Anger, who was himself deeply involved in both the motorcycle gang mystique and the occult. Beausoleil starred in Anger's film *Lucifer Rising*, playing the part of Lucifer. This was before he ever met Manson.

In his psychiatric report on Susan Atkins, Dr. Joel Hochman wrote of a portion of her San Francisco period, apparently sometime in 1967 or 1968, before she too met Manson: "At this time she entered into what she now calls her Satanic period. She became involved with Anton LaVey, the Satanist.† She took a part in a commercial production of a witch's sabbath, and recalls the opening night when she took LSD. She was supposed to lie down in a coffin during the act, and lay down in it while hallucinating. She stated that she didn't want to come out, and consequently the curtain was 15 minutes late. She stated that she felt alive and everything else in the ugly world was dead. Subsequently, she stayed on her 'Satanic trip' [for] approximately eight months ..."

During the Tate-LaBianca trial, Patricia Krenwinkel doodled. Her two favorite subjects, according to bailiff Bill Murray, were Devil's heads and the Mendes Goat, both satanist symbols.

Before he killed him, Charles "Tex" Watson told Voytek Frykowski: "I am the Devil and I'm here to do the Devil's business."

An apparently important influence on Manson, in both precept and example, was a dead man: Adolf Hitler. Manson looked up to Hitler and spoke of him often. He told his followers that "Hitler had the best answer to ev-

---

*There is at least one precept Manson did not borrow from the group: unmarried adherents are expected to remain chaste.

†LaVey, founder of the San Francisco–based First Church of Satan, is known, by those knowledgeable in such matters, more as a spectacular showman than as a demonic satanist. He has stated numerous-times that he condemns violence and ritual sacrifice.

erything" and that he was "a tuned-in guy who leveled the karma of the Jews." Manson saw himself as no less a historical figure, a leader who would not only reverse the karma of the blacks but level all but his own Aryan race—his all-white, all-American Family.

There were both surface and substantive parallels between Hitler and Manson.

Both were vegetarians; both were little men; both suffered deep wounds in their youth, the psychological scars at least contributing to, if not causing, their deep hatred for society; both suffered the stigma of illegitimacy, in Manson's case because he himself was a bastard, in Hitler's because his father was.

Both were vagrant wanderers; both were frustrated, and rejected, artists; both liked animals more than people; both were deeply engrossed in the occult; both had others commit their murders for them.

Both were racists; yet there is some evidence that both also believed they carried the blood of the very people they despised. Many historians believe that Hitler was secretly obsessed with the fear that he had a Jewish ancestor. If Manson's prison records are correct, he may have believed his father was black.

Both surrounded themselves with bootlicking slaves; both sought out the weaknesses of others, and used them; both programmed their followers through repetition, repeating the same phrases over and over; both realized and exploited the psychological impact of fear.

Both had a favorite epithet for those they hated: Hitler's was "*Schweinehund*," Manson's was "pigs."

Both had eyes which their followers described as "hypnotic"; beyond that, however, both had a presence, a charisma, and a tremendous amount of personal persuasive power. Generals went to Hitler intent on convincing him that his military plans were insane; they left true believers. Dean Moorehouse went to Spahn Ranch to kill Manson for stealing his daughter, Ruth Ann; he ended up on his knees worshiping him.

Both had an incredible ability to influence others.

Both Manson's and Hitler's followers were able to explain away the monstrous acts their leaders committed by retreating into philosophical abstractions.

Probably the single most important influence on Hitler was Nietzsche. Manson told Jakobson that he had read Nietzsche. Whether true or not—Manson read with difficulty and Nietzsche is not easy reading—both Manson and Hitler believed in the three basic tenets of Nietzsche's philosophy: women are inferior to men; the white race is superior to all other races; it is not wrong to kill if the end is right.

And kill they both did. Both believed that mass murder was all right, even desirable, if it furthered the attainment of some grand plan. Each had such a plan; each had his own grandiose obsession: Hitler's was the Third Reich, Manson's was Helter Skelter.

At some point parallels become more than coincidence. How much of this was conscious borrowing on Manson's part, how much unconscious emulation, is unknown. I do believe that if Manson had had the opportunity, he would have become another Hitler. I can't conceive of his stopping short of murdering huge masses of people.

Some mysteries remain. One is the exact number of murders committed by members of the Manson Family.

Manson bragged to Juan Flynn that he had committed thirty-five murders. When Juan first told me this, I was inclined to doubt that it was anything more than sick boasting on Charlie's part. There is now evidence, however, that even if this wasn't true *then*, the total to date may be very close to, and may even exceed, Manson's estimate.

In November 1969, Susan Atkins told Ronnie Howard, "There are eleven murders that they will never solve." Leslie Van Houten used the same number in her interrogation by Mike McGann, while Ouisch told Barbara Hoyt that she knew of ten people the Family had killed "besides Sharon."

Susan told Virginia Graham that, in addition to the eight Hinman-Tate-LaBianca slayings, "there's more—and more before." One was undoubtedly Shea. Another was probably the "Black Panther" (Bernard Crowe), whom Susan, like Manson himself, erroneously believed dead.

Susan may have been referring to Crowe when, in the tape she made with Caballero, she said that the .22 caliber Longhorn revolver used in the Tate homicides had been used in "other killings," though on the tape this was clearly plural, not singular.

Susan also told Virginia, "There's also three people out in the desert that they done in." According to Virginia, Susan "just said it very nonchalant like, mentioning no names." When Steve Zabriske tried unsuccessfully to convince Portland police that a Charlie and a Clem were involved in both the Tate and the LaBianca murders, he also said that Ed Bailey had told him that he had seen this Charlie shoot a man in the head. The murder had occurred in Death Valley, according to Bailey, and the gun was a .45 caliber automatic. When interrogated by LAPD in May 1970, Bailey, t/n Edward Arthur Bailey, denied this. However, another source, who was for a time close to the Family, claims he heard "there are supposed to be two boys and a girl buried about eight feet deep behind Barker Ranch."

No bodies have ever been found. But then the body of Donald "Shorty" Shea has never been found either.

On October 13, 1968, two women, Clida Delaney and Nancy Warren, were beaten, then strangled to death with leather thongs a few miles south of Ukiah, California. Several members of the Manson Family were in the area at the time. Two days later Manson suddenly moved the whole Family from Spahn to Barker ranch. The Mendocino County Sheriff's Office believed there might be a link. But a belief is not evidence.

At about 3:30 A.M. on December 30, 1968, seventeen-year-old Marina Habe, daughter of writer Hans Habe, was abducted outside the West Hollywood home of her mother as she was returning home from a date. Her body was found on New Year's Day, off Mulholland near Bowmont Drive. Cause of death: multiple stab wounds in the neck and chest.

It has been rumored, but never confirmed, that the victim was acquainted with one or more members of the Family. Though most of his followers were at Barker Ranch, Manson was apparently in Los Angeles on December 30, returning to Barker the following day. Though several persons, including KNXT newscaster Carl George, believed there was a connection, nothing definite has been established, and the murder remains unsolved.

On the night of May 27, 1969, Darwin Orell Scott was hacked to death in his Ashland, Kentucky, apartment. The killing was so savage that the victim, who was stabbed nineteen times, was pinned to the floor with a butcher knife.

Sixty-four-year-old Darwin Scott was the brother of Colonel Scott, the man alleged to be Charles Manson's father.

In the spring of 1969 a motorcycle-riding guru from California who called himself "Preacher" appeared in the Ashland area with several female followers. Dispensing free LSD to local teen-agers, he attempted to set up a commune in an abandoned farmhouse near Huntington. He remained in the area until April, at which time vigilantes burned down the house and drove off the group, because, quoting the Ashland paper, "they didn't like hippies and didn't want any more around." At least four local residents later told reporters that Manson and Preacher were one and the same person. Despite their positive IDs, Manson's presence in California during at least part of this period is fairly well documented, and it would appear that he was in California on the day of Scott's murder.

On May 22, 1969, Manson telephoned his parole officer, Samuel Barrett, requesting permission to travel to Texas with the Beach Boys. Permission was withheld pending verification of Manson's employment with the group. In a letter dated May 27, the same day as Scott's murder, Manson said that the group had left without him and that he had moved from Death Valley back to Spahn Ranch. To categorize Barrett's control over Manson as minimal would be an exaggeration. Barrett did not again talk to Manson until June 18.

Barrett did not note the postmark on the letter. He did note that he didn't receive it until June 3, seven days after it was supposedly written. It is possible that Manson was using the letter as an alibi; it is also possible that he sent one of his killers to murder Scott. But both possibilities are strictly conjecture. The murder of Darwin Scott also remains unsolved.

Early on the morning of July 17, 1969, sixteen-year-old Mark Walts left his parents' home in Chatsworth and hitchhiked to the Santa Monica Pier to go fishing. His pole was later found on the pier. His body was found about 4 A.M. on July 18, off Topanga Canyon Boulevard a short distance from Mulholland. Young Walts' face and head were badly bruised and he had been shot three times in the chest by a .22 caliber weapon.

Though neither a ranch hand nor a Family member, Walts occasionally hung around Spahn Ranch. Although LASO sent investigators to Spahn, they were unable to uncover any evidence linking the killing to anyone there.

Walts' brother, however, called the ranch and told Manson, "I know you done my brother in, and I'm going to kill you." Though he didn't carry through, he obviously felt Manson was responsible.

When Danny DeCarlo had his marathon session with LAPD, he was asked: "What do you know about a sixteen-year-old boy that was shot?"

DeCarlo replied: "That had nothing to do with anybody up there. I'll tell you why, because they were just as shocked about it [as I was]. If they had done it they would have told me."

DeCarlo informed the officers about the brother's call. One asked: "Why do you think he suspected Charlie?" DeCarlo replied: "Because there aren't too many maniacs on the street that would just pull a gun on someone and blow their head off for no reason at all."

LAPD didn't pursue it further, since this was LASO's case. The murder remains unsolved.

In a period of one month—between July 27 and August 26, 1969—Charles Manson and his murderous Family slaughtered nine people: Gary Hinman, Steven Parent, Jay Sebring, Abigail Folger, Voytek Frykowski, Sharon Tate, Leno LaBianca, Rosemary LaBianca, and Donald Shea.

Though it is known that a number of female Family members were involved in the "cleanup" operation that followed Shea's murder, none has ever been tried as an accessory after the fact. Some are still on the streets today.

Manson's arrest on October 12, 1969, did not stop the murders.

As already mentioned, on November 5, 1969, John Philip Haught, aka Christopher Jesus, aka Zero, was shot to death in a beach house in Venice. The four Family members still present when the police arrived claimed he had killed himself while playing Russian roulette. Linda Baldwin, aka Little Patty, t/n Madaline Joan Cottage, said she had been lying on the bed next to him when it happened. The others—Bruce Davis; Susan Bartell, aka Country Sue; and Cathy Gillies—all told the officers they hadn't witnessed the act but had heard the shot.

At least one, and possibly all, lied.

During the penalty phase of the Tate-LaBianca trial, I asked Cathy: "You said that Zero shot himself. Who told you that? Certainly not Zero."

A. "Nobody had to tell me. I saw it happen."

Q. "Oh, you were present?"

A. "Yes."

Q. "Can you explain how it happened?"

A. "I was talking to him and he walked into the next room. Little Patty was lying on the bed. He sat down on the bed next to her. He reached over, grabbed the gun, and shot himself."

Q. "Just like that?"

A. "Yes."

Q. "Out of a clear blue sky?"

A. "Right out of a clear blue sky."

Three big questions remain: why was Zero playing Russian roulette with a fully loaded gun; why, if he took the gun out of the leather case, was the case clean of prints; and why, though Bruce Davis admitted picking up the gun, were neither his prints nor those of Zero on it?

About a week after the story of Manson's involvement in the Tate-LaBianca murders broke in the press, Los Angeles *Times* reporter Jerry Cohen was contacted by a man who claimed he had been present when Zero was shot.

Only Zero hadn't been playing Russian roulette; he had been murdered.

The man was about twenty-five, five feet eight, blond, of slight build. He refused to give Cohen his name. He was, he admitted, "scared to death."

Six or eight persons had been in the Venice pad that night, smoking hash. "It was one of the chicks that killed Zero," he told Cohen. But he wouldn't say which one, only that recently, at another Manson Family gathering, she had sat staring at him for three hours, all the while fingering her knife.

In questioning him, Cohen established that he had become involved with the Family after the Tate-LaBianca murders. He had never met Manson, he said, but he had heard from other Family members that there had been "many more murders than the police know of" and that "the Family is a whole lot larger than you think."

The youth wanted money to get to Marin County, in Northern California. Cohen gave him twenty-five dollars, implying there would be more if he returned to identify Zero's murderer. He never saw him again.

On November 16, 1969, the body of a young girl was found dumped over an embankment at Mulholland and Bowmont Drive near Laurel Canyon, in almost the same spot where Marina Habe's body was found. A brunette in her late teens, five feet nine, 115 pounds, she had been stabbed 157 times in the chest and throat. Ruby Pearl remembered seeing the girl with the Family at Spahn, and thought her name was "Sherry." Though the Manson girls traded aliases often, LASO was able to identify only one Sherry, Sherry Ann Cooper, aka Simi Valley Sherri. She had fled Barker Ranch at the same time as Barbara Hoyt and was, fortunately, still alive. The victim, who had been dead less than a day, became Jane Doe 59 in police files. Her identity is still unknown.

The proximity in time of her death to that of Zero suggests the possibility that she may have been present at the murder, then killed so she wouldn't talk. But this is strictly conjecture, and there is no evidence to support it. Her murder remains unsolved.

On November 21, 1969, the bodies of James Sharp, fifteen, and Doreen Gaul, nineteen, were found in an alley in downtown Los Angeles. The two teen-agers had been killed elsewhere, with a long-bladed knife or bayonet, then dumped there. Each had been stabbed over fifty times.

Ramparts Division Lieutenant Earl Deemer investigated the Sharp-Gaul murders, as did Los Angeles *Times* reporter Cohen. Although the two men felt there was a good possibility that a Family member was involved in the slayings, the murders remain unsolved.

Both James Sharp and Doreen Gaul were Scientologists, the latter a Scientology "clear" who had been residing in a Church of Scientology house. According to unconfirmed reports, Doreen Gaul was a former girl friend of Manson Family member Bruce Davis, himself an ex-Scientologist.

Davis' whereabouts at the times of the murders of Sharp, Gaul, and Jane Doe 59 are not known. He disappeared shortly after being questioned in connection with the death of Zero.

On December 1, 1969, Joel Dean Pugh, husband of Family member Sandy Good, was found with his throat slit in a London hotel room. As noted, local police ruled the death a suicide. On learning of Pugh's demise, Inyo County DA Frank Fowles made official inquiries, specifically asking Interpol to check visas to determine if one Bruce Davis was in England at the time.

Scotland Yard replied as follows: "It has been established that Davis is recorded as embarking at London airport for the United States of America on 25th April 1969 while holding United States passport 612 2568. At this time he gave his address as Dormer Cottage, Felbridge, Surrey. This address is owned by the Scientology Movement and houses followers of this organization.

"The local police are unable to give any information concerning Davis but they understand that he has visited our country more recently than April 1969. However, this is not borne out by our official records."

Davis did not reappear until February 1970, when he was picked up at Spahn Ranch, questioned briefly on the Inyo County grand theft auto charges, then released. After the grand jury indicted him for the Hinman murder, he vanished again, this time not surfacing until December 2, 1970, four days after the mysterious disappearance of Ronald Hughes. As mentioned, when he gave himself up he was accompanied by Family member Brenda McCann.

With three exceptions, these are all the known murders which have been proven, or are suspected to be, linked to the Manson Family. Are there more? I've discussed this with officers from LAPD and LASO, and we tend to think that there probably are, because these people liked to kill. But there is no hard evidence.

As for those three other murders, two of them occurred as late as 1972.

On November 8, 1972, a hiker near the Russian River resort community of Guerneville, in Northern California, saw a hand protruding from the ground. When police exhumed the body, it was found to be that of a young man wearing the dark-blue tunic of a Marine dress uniform. He had been shotgunned and decapitated.

The victim was subsequently identified as James T. Willett, twenty-six, a former Marine from Los Angeles County. This information appeared on radio and TV newscasts on Friday, November 10.

On Saturday, November 11, Stockton, California, police spotted Willett's station wagon parked in front of a house at 720 West Flora Street. When refused entry to the house, they broke in, arresting two men and two women and confiscating a number of pistols and shotguns.

Both women had Manson Family X's on their foreheads. They were Priscilla Cooper, twenty-one, and Nancy Pitman, aka Brenda McCann, twenty. A few minutes after police entered the residence, a third female called, asking to be picked up and given a ride to the house. The police obliged, and also arrested Lynette Fromme, aka Squeaky, twenty-four, ex-officio leader of the Family in Manson's absence.

The two men were Michael Monfort, twenty-four, and James Craig, thirty-three, both state prison escapees wanted for a number of armed robberies in various parts of California. Both had the letters "AB" tattooed on their left breasts. According to a spokesman for the state Department of Corrections, the initials stood for the Aryan Brotherhood, described as "a cult of white prison inmates, dedicated largely to racism but also involved in hoodlum activities, including murder contracts . . ."

While in the house, the police noticed freshly turned earth in the basement. After obtaining a search warrant, they began digging, and early the following morning exhumed the body of Lauren Willett, nineteen. She had been shot once in the head, her death occurring either late Friday night or early Saturday morning, not long after the identity of her slain husband was revealed on news broadcasts.

Questioned by the police, Priscilla Cooper claimed that Lauren Willett had killed herself "playing Russian roulette."

Although, like Zero, Mrs. Willett was not able to contradict this story, the Stockton police were far more skeptical than had been LASO. The three women and two men were charged with her murder.

They were scheduled to go on trial in May 1973. On April 2, however, four of the five surprised the Court by entering guilty pleas. Michael Monfort, who pleaded guilty to the murder of Lauren Willett, was sentenced to seven years to life in state prison. Superior Court Judge James Darrah also ordered consecutive terms of up to five years and two years for James Craig, who had pleaded guilty to being an accessory after the fact to murder and to possessing an illegal weapon, i.e., a sawed-off shotgun. Both girls also pleaded guilty to being an accessory after the fact, and both Priscilla Cooper and Nancy Pitman, aka Brenda, who Manson once indicated to me was his chief candidate for Family assassin, were sent to state prison for up to five years.

Still another Family member, Maria Alonzo, aka Crystal, twenty-one, arrested while trying to smuggle a switchblade knife into the Stockton jail, was subsequently released.

As was Squeaky. There being insufficient evidence to link Lynette Fromme to Lauren Willett's murder, the charges against her were dropped and she was freed, to again assume leadership of the Manson Family.

Monfort, and an accomplice, William Goucher, twenty-three, subsequently pleaded guilty to second degree murder in the death of James Willett, and were sent to state prison for five years to life. Craig, who pleaded guilty to being an accessory after the fact to the murder, was given another prison term of up to five years.

The motive for the two murders is not known. It is known that the Willetts had been associated with the Manson Family for at least a year, and possibly longer. Police surmised that Lauren Willett was killed after learning of the murder of her husband, to keep her from going to the police. As for the murder of James Willett, the official police theory is that Willett himself may have been about to inform about the robberies the group had committed.

There is another possibility. It may be that both James and Lauren Willett were killed because they knew too much about still another murder.

James and Lauren. Something about those first names seemed familiar. Then it connected. On November 27, 1970, a James Forsher and a Lauren Elder drove defense attorney Ronald Hughes to Sespe Hot Springs. After Hughes disappeared, the couple were questioned but not polygraphed, the police being satisfied that when they left the flooded area Hughes was still alive.

At first I thought "Elder" might be Lauren Willett's maiden name, but it wasn't. Nor, in checking the police reports and newspaper articles, was I able to find any description of Forsher and Elder. All I did find were their ages, both given as seventeen, and an address, from which I subsequently learned they had long since moved. All other efforts to track them down were unsuccessful.

It appears unlikely that James Forsher and James Willett were the same person: Willett would have been twenty-four in 1970, not seventeen. But Lauren is a decidedly uncommon name. And, nineteen in 1972, she would have been seventeen in 1970.

Coincidence? There had been far stranger ones in this case.

One thing is now known, however. If an admission by one of Manson's most hard-core followers is correct, Ronald Hughes *was* murdered by the Manson Family.

It was some weeks after the conclusion of the Tate-LaBianca trial before I received the autopsy report I'd requested from Ventura County. The identification, made through dental X-rays, was positive. The body was that of Ronald Hughes. Yet the rest of the autopsy report added little to the newspaper accounts. It noted: "The decedent was observed face down in a pool of water with the head and shoulder wedged under a large rock." One arm was almost completely severed at the shoulder, and there were large open areas in the chest and back. Other than this, "no outward evidence of violence was noted" while "no evidence of foul play [was] indicated by the X-rays." All this was qualified more than a little by the fact that the body was badly decomposed. As for the report's primary findings, there were none: "Nature of death: Undetermined. Cause of death: Undetermined."

The report did note that the stomach contained some evidence of "medication residue." But its exact composition—drugs, poison, whatever—was, like the nature and cause of death, left undetermined.

Completely dissatisfied with the report, I requested that our office conduct an investigation into the death of Hughes. The request was denied, it being decided that since there was no evidence of foul play, such an investigation was unnecessary.

There the matter remained, until very recently. While the Tate-LaBianca trial was still in progress, motion-picture director Laurence Merrick began work on a documentary on the Manson Family. The film, simply titled *Manson*, dealt only briefly with the murders and focused primarily on life at Spahn and Barker ranches. I narrated a few segments, and there were interviews with a number of Manson's followers. The movie was shown at the Venice Film Festival in 1972 and nominated for an Academy Award the following year. During its filming Merrick gained the confidence of the Manson girls. Sandra Good admitted, for example, on film, that when she and

Mary Brunner learned of the Tate murders, while still in the Los Angeles County Jail, "Mary said, 'Right on!' and I said, 'Wow, looks like we did it!' "

Off camera, and unrecorded, Sandy made a number of other admissions to Merrick. She told him, in the presence of one other witness, that to date the Family had killed "thirty-five to forty people." And that "Hughes was the first of the retaliation murders."

The trials did not write finis to the Manson saga. As Los Angeles *Times* reporter Dave Smith observed in *West* magazine: "To pull the curtain over the Manson case is to deny ourselves any possible hint of where the beast may come from next, and so remain afraid of things that go bump in the night, the way we were in August of 1969."

Mass murders have occurred throughout history. Since the Tate-LaBianca slayings, in California alone: labor contractor Juan Corona has been convicted of killing twenty-five migrant farm workers; John Linley Frazier slaughtered Dr. Victor Ohta, his wife, two of his sons, and his secretary, then dumped their bodies in the Ohta swimming pool; in a rampage that lasted several months, Herbert Mullin killed thirteen persons, ranging in age from three to seventy-three; Edmund Kemper III, ruled insane after slaying his grandmother and grandfather, was ruled sane and released, to later kill his mother, one of her friends, and six college coeds; and a possible total of seventeen murders has been attributed to two young ex-convict drifters.

With the exception of the latter pair, however, these were the work of loners, obviously deranged, if not legally insane, individuals, who *committed the murders by themselves.*

The Manson case was, and remains, unique. If, as Sandra Good claimed, the Family has to date committed thirty-five to forty murders, this may be near the U.S. record. Yet it is not the number of victims which makes the case intriguing and gives it its continuing fascination, but a number of other elements for which there is probably no collective parallel in the annals of American crime: the prominence of the victims; the months of speculation, conjecture, and pure fright before the killers were identified; the incredibly strange motive for the murders, to ignite a black-white Armageddon; the motivating nexus between the lyrics of the most famous rock group ever, the Beatles, and the crimes; and, behind it all, pulling the strings, a Mephistophelean guru who had the unique power to persuade *others to murder for him*, most of them young girls who went out and savagely murdered total strangers at his command, with relish and gusto, and with no evident signs of guilt or remorse—all these things combine to make Manson perhaps the most frightening mass murderer and these murders perhaps the most bizarre in American history.

How Manson gained control remains the most puzzling question of all.

During the Tate-LaBianca trials, the issue was not so much how he did this but proving that he did it. Yet in understanding the whole Manson phenomenon, the *how* is extremely important.

We have some of the answers.

During the course of his wanderings Manson probably encountered thousands of persons. Most chose not to follow him, either because they sensed that he was a very dangerous man or because they did not respond to the sick philosophy he preached.

Those who did join him were not, as noted, the typical girl or boy next door. Charles Manson was not a Pied Piper who suddenly appeared on the basketball court at Texas State, handed Charles Watson a tab of LSD, then led him into a life of crime. Watson had quit college with only a year to go, gone to California, immersed himself in the selling as well as the using of drugs, before he ever met Charles Manson. Not just Watson but nearly every other member of the Family had dropped out before meeting Manson. Nearly all had within them a deep-seated hostility toward society and everything it stood for which pre-existed their meeting Manson.

Those who chose to go with him did so, Dr. Joel Hochman testified, for reasons "which lie within the individuals themselves." In short, there was a need, and Manson seemed to fulfill it. But it was a double process of selection. For Manson decided who stayed. Obviously he did not want anyone who he felt would challenge his authority, cause dissension in the group, or question his dogma. They chose, and Manson chose, and the result was the Family. Those who gravitated to Spahn Ranch and stayed did so because basically they thought and felt alike. This was his raw material.

In shaping that material into a band of cold-blooded assassins who were willing to vent, for him, his enormous hostility toward society, Manson employed a variety of techniques.

He sensed, and capitalized on, their needs. As Gregg Jakobson observed, "Charlie was a man of a thousand faces" who "related to all human beings on their level of need." His ability to "psych out" people was so great that many of his disciples felt he could read their minds.

I doubt seriously if there was any "magic" in this. Having had many, many years to study human nature in prison, and being the sophisticated con man that he is, Manson probably realized that there are certain problems that nearly every human being is beset with. I strongly suspect that his "magical powers" were nothing more, and nothing less, than the ability to utter basic truisms to the right person at the right time. For example, any girl, if she is a runaway, has probably had problems with her father, while anyone who came to Spahn Ranch was searching for something. Manson made it a point to find out what that something was, and supply at least a semblance of it, whether it was a father surrogate, a Christ figure, a need for acceptance and belonging, or a leader in leaderless times.

Drugs were another of his tools. As brought out in the psychiatric testimony during the trials, LSD was not a causal agent but a catalyst. Manson used it very effectively, to make his followers more suggestible, to implant ideas, to extract "agreements." As Paul Watkins told me, Charlie always took a smaller dose of LSD than the others, so he would remain in command.

He used repetition. By constantly preaching and lecturing to his subjects on an almost daily basis, he gradually and systematically erased many of their inhibitions. As

Manson himself once remarked in court: "You can convince anybody of anything if you just push it at them all of the time. They may not believe it 100 percent, but they will still draw opinions from it, especially if they have no other information to draw their opinions from."

Therein lies still another of the keys he used: in addition to repetition, he used isolation. There were no newspapers at Spahn Ranch, no clocks. Cut off from the rest of society, he created in this timeless land a tight little society of his own, with its own value system. It was holistic, complete, and totally at odds with the world outside.

He used sex. Realizing that most people have sexual hangups, he taught, by both precept and example, that in sex there is no wrong, thereby eradicating both their inhibitions and their guilt.

But there was more than sex. There was also love, a great deal of love. To overlook this would be to miss one of the strongest bonds that existed among them. The love grew out of their sharing, their communal problems and pleasures, their relationship with Charlie. They were a real family in almost every sense of that word, a sociological unit complete to brothers, sisters, substitute mothers, linked by the domination of an all-knowing, all-powerful patriarch. Cooking, washing dishes, cleaning, sewing—all the chores they had hated at home they now did willingly, because they pleased Charlie.

He used fear, very, very effectively. Whether he picked up this technique in prison or later is not known, but it was one of his most effective tools for controlling others. It may also have been something more. As Stanford University professor Philip Zimbardo, a long-time student of crime and its effects, noted in a *Newsweek* article: "By raising the level of fear around you, your own fear seems more normal and socially acceptable." Manson's own fear bordered on paranoia.

He taught them that life was a game, a "magical mystery tour." One day they would be pirates with cutlasses, slashing at anyone who dared board their imaginary ship; the next they'd change costumes and identities and become Indians stalking cowboys; or devils and witches casting spells. A game. But there was always a pattern behind it:

them versus us. Dr. Hochman testified: "I think that histo-
rically the easiest way to program someone into murdering
is to convince them that they are alien, that they are them
and we are us, and that they are different from us."

Krauts. Japs. Gooks. Pigs.

With the frequent name changing and role playing,
Manson created his own band of schizophrenics. Little
Susan Atkins, who sang in the church choir and nursed
her mother while she was dying of cancer, couldn't be
held responsible for what Sadie Mae Glutz had done.

He brought to the surface their latent hatred, their inherent penchant for sadistic violence, focusing it on a
common enemy, the establishment. He depersonalized the
victims by making them symbols. It is easier to stab a
symbol than a person.

He taught his followers a completely amoral philosophy,
which provided complete justification for their acts. If everything is right, then nothing can be wrong. If nothing is
real, and all of life is a game, then there need be no regret.

If they needed something that couldn't be found in the
garbage bins or communal clothing pile, they stole it.
Step by step. Panhandling, petty theft, prostitution, burglaries, armed robberies, and, last of all, for no motive of
gain but because it was Charlie's will, and Charlie's will is
Man's Son, the final step, the ultimate act of defiance of
the establishment, the most positive proof of their total
commitment—murder.

Comedians punned that "the family that slays together
stays together." But behind the grim jest there was truth.
Knowing they had violated the strictest of all commandments created a bond not less but more binding in that it
was *their* secret.

He used religion. Not only did he find support for much
of his philosophy in the Bible, he often implied that he
was the Second Coming of Christ. He had his twelve apostles, several times over; not one but two Judases, Sadie
and Linda; his retreat to the desert, Barker Ranch; and his
trial, in the Hall of Justice.

He also used music, in part because he was a frustrated

musician but also because he must have known it was the one thing that could get through to more young people than any other.

He used his own superior intelligence. He was not only older than his followers, he was brighter, more articulate and savvy, far more clever and insidious. With his prison background, his ever adaptable line of con, plus a pimp's knowledge of how to manipulate others, he had little trouble convincing his naïve, impressionable followers that it was not they but society which was sick. This too was exactly what they wanted to hear.

All of these factors contributed to Manson's control over others. But when you add them all up, do they equal murder without remorse? Maybe, but I tend to think that there is something more, some missing link that enabled him to so rape and bastardize the minds of his followers that they would go against the most ingrained of all commandments, Thou shalt not kill, and willingly, even eagerly, murder at his command.

It may be something in his charismatic, enigmatic personality, some intangible quality or power that no one has yet been able to isolate and identify. It may be something he learned from others. Whatever it is, I believe Manson has full knowledge of the formula he used. And it worries me that we do not. For the frightening legacy of the Manson case is that it could happen again.

I believe Charles Manson is unique. He is certainly one of the most fascinating criminals in American history, and it appears unlikely that there will ever be another mass murderer quite like him. But it does not take a prophet to see at least some of the potentials of his madness in the world today. Whenever people unquestioningly turn over their minds to authoritarian figures to do with as they please—whether it be in a satanic cult or some of the more fanatic offshoots of the Jesus Movement, in the right wing or the far left, or in the mind-bending cults of the new sensitivity—those potentials exist. One hopes that none of these groups will spawn other Charles Mansons. But it would be naïve to suggest that the chilling possibility does not exist.

There are some happy endings to the Manson story. And some not so happy.

Both Barbara Hoyt and Dianne Lake returned to and graduated from high school, with apparently few if any permanent scars from their time with Manson. Barbara is now studying to be a nurse.

Stephanie Schram has her own dog-grooming shop. Paul Watkins and Brooks Poston formed their own combo and appear at various clubs in the Inyo County area. Their songs were good enough to be used as background music in the Robert Hendrickson documentary film on Manson.

After the fire George Spahn sold his ranch to an investment firm, which planned to turn it into a dude ranch for German visitors to the United States. He's since purchased another ranch, near Klamath Falls, Oregon, and Ruby Pearl is running it for him.

I haven't heard from Juan Flynn recently, but I'm not worried about him. Juan was always able to take care of himself. Though I last saw him in my office, for some reason I visualize him on a big white horse, his pretty girl friend behind him holding on for dear life as they gallop off into the sunset. Which, I suspect, is Juan's own image of himself.

Since the murder of his wife, Roman Polanski has produced several motion pictures, including a new version of *Macbeth*. Critics noticed in his interpretation disturbing parallels to the Tate murders. Polanski himself posed for an *Esquire* interview, holding aloft a shiny knife, and, according to the press, he has recently moved back to Los Angeles, into a home not far from 10050 Cielo Drive.

Polanski's attorney, working in conjunction with LAPD, divided the $25,000 reward as follows: Ronnie Howard and Virginia Graham each received $12,000, while Steven Weiss, the young boy who found the .22 caliber murder weapon, received $1,000.

Neither Danny DeCarlo nor Alan Springer was around to share in the reward. Shortly before the Watson trial, Danny skipped bail on the federal gun charge and fled to Canada; his exact whereabouts are unknown. According to LAPD, biker Al Springer simply "vanished." It is not known whether he is alive or dead.

Ronnie Howard tried working as a cocktail waitress but found it difficult to hold a job. Everywhere she went, she said, she was identified as the "Manson case snitch." Several times she was beaten up on her way home from work, and one night someone fired a bullet through the living-room window of her apartment, missing her head by inches. The would-be assailant was never identified. The next day she told reporters: "I should have kept my mouth shut in the first place."

Virginia Graham had a job as a receptionist in a legal office and seemed well on the way to rehabilitation, when she jumped parole. As this is written, she is still a fugitive.

Seven months after reporter Bill Farr declined to tell Judge Older who gave him the Virginia Graham statement regarding the "celebrity murders" the Manson Family had planned, Judge Older called Farr back into court and ordered him to either do so or be found in contempt.

Under California law the confidentiality of a reporter's news source is protected. However, since the Tate-LaBianca trial, Farr had left the Los Angeles *Herald Examiner* and was now working in a press secretary job. Older said that since he was no longer a reporter he was no longer protected by the law.

Farr argued—and I feel quite persuasively—that if Older's order was permitted to stand, both the news media and the public would suffer, since, if not guaranteed anonymity, many persons would decide not to provide essential information to the press. On both constitutional grounds and his own personal convictions, Farr declined to identify his sources. He did state, on the advice of his attorneys, that he had obtained copies of the Graham statement from two lawyers and another person subject to the gag order. But he declined to name them.

Under orders from Judge Older, defense attorneys Daye Shinn, Irving Kanarek, and Paul Fitzgerald, and prosecutors Steven Kay, Donald Musich, and I all took the stand. All six denied under oath giving the statement to Farr. All I know is that I didn't give Farr the statement.

Judge Older held Farr in civil contempt and sentenced

him to an indefinite jail term. He later served forty-eight days in the Los Angeles County Jail before being freed by an order by U.S. Supreme Court Justice William O. Douglas pending the outcome of a new appeal.

Had Farr been cited for criminal contempt and given consecutive sentences, the maximum penalty would have been sixty-five days in jail and a fine of $6,500. But Older cited him for civil contempt, and gave him an indefinite sentence, which could mean that if Older remains adamant, and the higher courts rule against Farr, he could remain in jail for as long as fifteen years, until fifty-five-year-old Charles Older reaches seventy, the mandatory age of retirement!

Many, though not all, of the hard-core Manson Family members are now serving time in various penal institutions. Other Family members split to follow new leaders. Cathy Gillies, according to the last information I received, was a "mom" with one of the motorcycle gangs. Still others continue to make headlines. Maria Alonzo, aka Crystal, who was released shortly after the Stockton murder, was arrested in March 1974 and charged with allegedly plotting to kidnap a foreign consul general in an attempt to secure the release of two prisoners in the Los Angeles County Jail. As this is written, she has yet to be brought to trial.

For a time there was a spate of books, plays, and motion pictures which, if not glorifying Manson, depicted him in a not wholly unfavorable light. And, for a time, it looked as if a Manson cult was emerging. Not only were there buttons reading "FREE THE MANSON FOUR," that cancerous growth known as the Family again began growing. When interviewed, the new converts—who had never had any personal contact with Manson—looked and talked exactly like Squeaky, Sandy, and the others, giving rise to the very disturbing possibility that Manson's madness might be communicable. But the strange phase quickly passed, and there is little left of the Manson Family now, though little Squeaky, chief cheerleader of the Manson cause, is still keeping the faith.

Although undisputed leader of the Family while Charlie

is in absentia, and presumably involved in the planning of their activities, and though arrested more than a dozen times on charges ranging from robbery to murder, she has only been convicted a few times, and always on minor charges. Moreover, not long ago she found a champion in, of all places, the District Attorney's Office in Los Angeles.

One of the young deputy DAs, William Melcher, first became acquainted with Squeaky while the group was holding its vigil on the corner of Temple and Broadway. For Christmas 1970, Melcher's wife baked cookies for the Manson girls, and a friendship developed. Not long after Squeaky was released on the Stockton murder charge, she was rearrested as a suspect in a Granada Hills armed robbery. Convinced they had the wrong person, Melcher successfully proved this to the police and she was freed. Clearing her was, Melcher told the Los Angeles *Times*, "my greatest satisfaction in three years as a prosecutor." Noting that the group had "a lot of ill-feeling about the police and courts, I wanted them to know that justice also works on their side of the street." Someday he would like to write a book on the girls, Melcher added. "I'd like to write not an exposé of the tragedy and violence, which I do not condone, but a book about the beauty I've seen in that group—their opposition to war, their truthfulness and their generosity."

The fate of Charles Manson, Charles Watson, Susan Atkins, Patricia Krenwinkel, Leslie Van Houten, and Robert Beausoleil was decided on February 18, 1972. That day the California State Supreme Court announced that it had voted 6-1 to abolish the death penalty in the state of California. The opinion was based on Article I, Section 6, of the State Constitution, which forbids "cruel or unusual punishment."*

*In June 1972 the United States Supreme Court ruled, in a 5-4 decision, that the death penalty, if imposed in an arbitrary fashion with the jury being given absolute discretion and no guidelines, constituted "cruel and unusual punishment" in violation of the Eighth Amendment to the U.S. Constitution.
Although a number of states, including California, have since passed laws restoring the death penalty and making it mandatory for certain crimes, including mass murders, at the time this is writ-

The sentences of the 107 persons awaiting execution in California were automatically reduced to life imprisonment.

Manson, in Los Angeles as a defense witness in the Bruce Davis trial, grinned broadly on hearing the news.

In California a person sentenced to life imprisonment is eligible to apply for parole in seven years.

By August 1972 the last prisoners had left California's Death Rows, most to be transferred to the "yards," or general inmate population, of various state penal institutions. Although at this writing Atkins, Krenwinkel, and Van Houten remain in the special security unit constructed for them at the California Institute for Women at Frontera, it is likely that in time they will join the general population also.

In his psychiatric report on Patricia Krenwinkel, Dr. Joel Hochman said that of the three girls Katie had the most tenuous hold on reality. It was his opinion that if she were ever separated from the others and the Manson mystique, it was quite possible she would lose even that, and lapse into complete psychosis.

With regard to Leslie Van Houten, who of the three girls was least committed to Manson, yet still murdered for him, I fear that she may grow harder and tougher; I have very little hope for her eventual rehabilitation.

Writing of Susan Atkins, Los Angeles *Times* reporter Dave Smith expressed something which I had long felt. "Watching her behavior—bold and actressy in court, cute and mincing when making eye-play with someone, a little haunted when no one pays attention—I get the feeling that one day she might start screaming, and simply never stop."

As for the other convicted Manson Family killers— Charles Watson; Robert Beausoleil; Steve Grogan, aka Clem; and Bruce Davis—all are now in the general inmate

---

ten the United States Supreme Court has yet to rule on their constitutionality.

Even if the California law is let stand, it would not affect the Manson Family killers, since the new statute is not retroactive.

population. Tex is no longer playing insane and has a girl friend who visits him regularly. Bobby received a certain amount of national attention when he was interviewed by Truman Capote during a TV documentary on American prisons. Not long afterward his jaw was broken and his hand dislocated in a brawl in the yard of San Quentin. The fight was the result of a power struggle over the leadership of the Aryan Brotherhood, with which Beausoleil had become affiliated. The AB, which is believed responsible for more than a dozen fatal stabbings in various California prisons in the last few years, is the successor to several earlier groups, including a neo-Nazi organization. Its total membership is not known, but it is believed to have about two hundred hard-core inmate followers, and it espouses many of the same racial principles that Charles Manson did. The legacy lives on.

Of all the Manson Family killers, only their leader merits special handling. In October 1972, Charles Manson was transferred to the maximum security adjustment center at Folsom Prison in Northern California. Described as "a prison within a prison," it provides special housing for "problem inmates" who cannot be safely controlled in the general prison population. With the transfer Manson lost not only all of the special privileges afforded those awaiting execution, he also lost his regular inmate privileges, because of his "hostile and belligerent attitude."

"Prison is my home, the only home I ever had," Manson often said. In 1967 he begged the authorities not to release him. Had anyone heeded his warning, this book need never have been written, and perhaps thirty-five to forty people now dead might still be alive.

In convicting him, Manson said, I was only sending him home. Only this time it won't be the same. Observed San Quentin warden Louis Nelson, before Manson was transferred to Folsom: "It would be dangerous to put a guy like Manson into the main population, because in the eyes of other inmates he didn't commit first-class crimes. He was convicted of killing a pregnant woman, and that sort of thing doesn't allow him to rank very high in the prison social structure. It's like being a child molester. Guys like that are going to do hard time wherever they are."

Too, like Sirhan Sirhan, convicted slayer of Senator Robert Kennedy, his notoriety is his own worst enemy. For as long as he remains in prison, Manson will be looking over his shoulder, aware that any con hoping to make a reputation need only put a shiv in his back.

That Manson, Watson, Beausoleil, Davis, Grogan, Atkins, Van Houten, and Krenwinkel will be eligible for parole in 1978 does not mean that they will get it, only that this is the earliest date they will be eligible to apply. The average incarceration in California for first degree murder is ten and a half to eleven years. Because of the hideous nature of their crimes and the total absence of mitigating circumstances, my guess is that all will serve longer periods: the girls fifteen to twenty years, the men—with the exception of Manson himself—a like number.

As for the leader of the Family, my guess is that he will remain in prison for at least twenty-five years, and quite possibly the rest of his life.

In mid-October of 1973 some thirty prisoners in California's toughest lockup, Folsom Prison's 4-A adjustment center, staged what was described by the San Francisco *Chronicle* as a "peaceful protest" against prison conditions.

The man who used and championed fear did not participate. According to the *Chronicle* story: "Mass murderer Charles Manson is among the inmates in 4-A, although prison spokesmen say he is not involved in this demonstration. Manson has been threatened by other inmates in the past, and authorities say he seldom ventures out of his cell for fear of being attacked."

Afterword

Twenty-five years after, as I said in my summation to the jury, Charles Manson "sent out from the fires of hell at Spahn Ranch three heartless, bloodthirsty robots" to commit the savage and nightmarish Tate-LaBianca murders, the nation continues to be fascinated with the Manson murder case. And the question I am always asked, particularly by the news media, is why?

Why has this mass murder case—as opposed to every other, and there have been many—continued to intrigue and captivate millions of people the world over? To the point where five-year anniversaries of the murders, as with no other murder case in America except the assassination of President John F. Kennedy, are marked by articles, news reports, and television specials, not just in the United States, but internationally.* To the point where, as reported in the Los Angeles *Times,* Manson receives more mail than any other inmate in the history of the U.S. prison system, an alarming amount of it from young people who tell him they want to join his Family; where Manson T-shirts are selling well today around the country; where there have been several plays about him, even an opera, *The Manson Family,* that premiered at New York City's Lincoln Center in July of 1990—as well as a CD soundtrack of the opera released in 1992; where the multi-platinum rock band Guns N' Roses sing a Manson composition, "Look at Your Game, Girl," in their latest album; where, believe it or not, avant-garde typographers in California produced a new typeface called Manson in which for $95 art directors, per *Time* magazine, "can set their serial-killer Zeitgeist essays in Manson Regular, Manson Alternate or Manson Bold" (all renamed Mason after criticism); where "Free Manson"

*This year, the British Broadcasting Company and ARD, German National Television, are airing twenty-fifth anniversary specials on the case.

graffiti soils the landscape of Britain's largest cities, and according to the BBC's William Scanlan Murphy, Manson interest in Britain is approaching mini-mania proportions;† where the television adaptation of this book was about the case, when it aired in 1976, the most watched television movie in the history of the medium and, like no other film of a murder case ever, has continuted to be shown, year after year without fail, in the United States and many other countries of the world; where a March 1994 ABC television special on the case produced the highest-ever ratings for a network magazine show debut. Again, why is this so?

After the Tate-LaBianca murders, there was a killer in Los Angeles called "The Trashbag Killer," so named because he picked up drifters and hitchhikers, murdered and dismembered them, then put them in trash bags. He pled guilty to twenty-one murders. Yet, I don't remember this murderer's name. And I would wager that if you were to ask one hundred people in Los Angeles you'd be hard-pressed to find one person who did. This is not that uncommon. At the time of a mass murder, and when the suspected killer is apprehended and tried, there's always considerable publicity. As a general rule, however, within a short time thereafter the murders and the identity of the perpetrator tend to fade from the public's consciousness. But not so with the Manson case. In fact, next to Jack the Ripper, whose identity still hasn't been conclusively established, Manson is probably the most famous and notorious mass murderer ever. So what is it?

---

†In a March 4, 1994, letter to me, Murphy writes:

There are 32 British rock bands that I know about playing both Manson's own songs and songs in support of him, and a further 40 or so in Europe, particularly Germany. Only last week, one of the worst I've heard, 'Charlie's 69 Was A Good Year', came out, recorded by a band called Indigo Prime; I'm sorry to say that it appears to be selling well. For some reason, the neo-Manson cult seems to centre in Manchester, where there are five stores selling 'Free Charles Manson' T-shirts (which are fantastically popular on Rave dance floors) and bootlegged records of his music; however, it's far from exclusive to Manchester—there was an all-Manson concert in London in January, attended by 2,000 people. There is a full-fledged Manson Appreciation Society, 'Helter Skelter UK', based in Warrington, Cheshire. Posters supporting Manson are a common sight in the major cities, especially in the run-up to concerts by the Masonite bands. The majority of the supporters of these bands are under 25. The truly frightening part is the fact that many of them, when asked, turn out to be Manson 'buffs' who have read all they can find about Manson, and strongly approve of Helter Skelter. They are very strong links to ultra-far-right political parties, particularly the British National Party.

A view that's enjoyed some currency is that the murders represent a watershed moment in the evolving social structure of our society. This view holds that the Manson case was the "end of innocence" (the '60s mantra of love, peace, and sharing) in our country, and sounded the death knell for hippies and all they symbolically represented. In Joan Didion's memoir of the era, *The White Album,* she writes: "Many people I know in Los Angeles believe that the Sixties ended abruptly on August 9, 1969 . . . and in a sense this is true." Even now, in 1994, ABC's Diane Sawyer endorses this notion when she says the Manson murders "brought an end to the decade of love," and "something changed in the heart of America" with the murders.

Others feel, less extravagantly, that the murders were emblematic of the counterculture flower gone to seed. As *Time* magazine said in 1989 on the twentieth anniversary of the murders, the three female killers were "any family's daughters, caught up in the wave of drugs, sex and revolutionary blather that had swept up a generation of young people."

Or, some thought for a time after the murders, perhaps Manson and his disciples represented a ten- or twenty-year extrapolation of the direction in which the counterculture movement was going. And so forth.

All of these hypotheses seem to be devoid of supporting empirical evidence. For instance, although the Manson murders may have hastened its descent, the Age of Aquarius, of which Woodstock (one week after the Manson carnage) was at once its finest hour and last gasp, was already in decline. As the decade of dissent and raw excess approached its denouement, the movement's mecca, Haight-Ashbury, was in ruins, and America had begun its retreat from the war in Vietnam—the political *raison d'être* fueling the movement. Moreover, Manson and the madness he wrought did not reflect the soul of the late '60s, when admittedly the anti-establishment movement had reached a feverish crescendo. That movement indeed wanted a new social order, but largely one brought about by peaceful means. Manson advocated violence, murder, to change the status quo. As pointed out in the body of this book, though Manson was a hero to some, according to surveys at the time a majority of young people whom the media labeled "hippies" disavowed Manson, stating that what he espoused, i.e., violence, was antithetical to their beliefs.*

And we certainly know, from the unerring rearview mirror of twenty-five years later, that Manson and these murders did not represent a foreboding extension of the direction in which the anti-establishment movement was going.

The sociological implications and legacy, then, of the murders may be no more than that they constituted a reaffirmation of the verity that whenever people surrender their minds and souls to a dictatorial cult figure, there comes a point for the followers when it is too late to turn back, and (as with the masses following the despots of history) whatever direction he goes in, he takes them with him. With the Reverend Moon, for example, it is a life of sleeping on floors and eating mush while he buys more yachts and mansions. With the Reverend Jim Jones and David Koresh, it was suicide. With Manson, murder.

In searching for a more prosaic explanation for the seemingly timeless resonance of the case, observers have pointed to the fact that Manson and his minions may have murdered as many as thirty-five people, and already had plans to murder celebrities like Frank Sinatra, Liz Taylor, Richard Burton, Steve McQueen, and Tom Jones. But apart from the planned celebrity killings, murders by other mass murderers numbering in the twenties and one in the thirties (John Wayne Gacy, thirty-three) have been confirmed. Others have spoken of the brutality of the murders. But though few, there have been murders even more brutal. Still others have pointed to the prominence of the victims—but they weren't *that* prominent.

Although all of these elements have undoubtedly contributed to the durability of the case, I believe the main reason

---

*Although I view Manson as an aberration who could have occurred at any time, the late '60s obviously provided a much more fertile soil for someone like Manson to emerge. It was a period when the sex and drug revolution, campus unrest and civil rights demonstrations, race riots, and all the seething discontent over Vietnam seemed to collide with each other in a stormy turbulence. And Manson, in his rhetoric, borrowed heavily from these fermentations.

for the continuing fascination with it at such a late date is
that the Manson murder case is almost assuredly the most
bizarre mass murder case in the recorded annals of crime.
And for whatever reason, people are magnetically fascinated by things that are strange and bizarre. If these murders had never happened, and someone wrote a novel with
the same set of facts and circumstances, most people would
put it down after a few pages; because as I understand it, to
be good fiction it has to be somewhat believable, and this
story is just too far out.

There is another compelling reason for the continuing
fascination with the case. The very name "Manson" has
become a metaphor for evil, catapulting him to near mytho-
logical proportions. Charles Manson has come to represent
the dark and malignant side of humanity; and again, there
is a side to human nature that is fascinated by pure, unal-
loyed evil. On a lesser scale, why are there so many
popular books and crime shows on television dealing with
murder—evil's ultimate act? (Across the water, one recalls
George Orwell's 1946 essay, "Decline of the English Murder," in which he speaks of the pleasure he and his country-
men receive from reading about a sensational murder in the
comfort of their drawing rooms.) Since we place so much
value on human life, why do we glorify, in a perverse sort
of way, the extinguishment of life? The answer to that
question, whatever it is, is at least a partial answer to
why people continue to be fascinated by Hitler, Jack the
Ripper—Manson.

As with evil, fright also has its allure. The quality of a
horror movie, we know, is generally considered to be
directly proportionate to the extent to which it terrifies.
Manson, of course, delivers on the fright meter like perhaps
no one else; his Hitlerian stare fixed upon us from places as
diverse as the television screen and the covers of magazines, to the underground albums of his music and his wax
frame at Madame Tussaud's in London. "People worry
about this man the way they worry about cancer and
earthquakes," a reporter wrote in 1979. "Just recently"—he quotes a California state prison official—"a
New York woman phoned to say she had a dream that
Manson made a break and started going after Jews. She

wanted to make sure there's no chance he can escape." Los Angeles *Times* columnist Howard Rosenberg calls Manson "America's preeminent bogeyman." Not only were the murders he ordered the type one doesn't even see in horror movies, but Manson, like no other mass murderer of this century, has added a shivering new dimension to the fright quotient—his diabolical and singular talent for getting others, without asking any questions, to kill complete strangers for him at his command. Dr. David Abrahamsen, a noted psychiatrist who has studied the history of violence in America, says he has never heard of any parallel for such a phenomenon. With other prominent mass murderers—from Charles Starkweather, David Berkowitz, Henry Lee Lucas, Charles Whitman, and Richard Speck to Ted Bundy; from Juan Corona, Dean Corll, Adolfo de Jesus Constanzo, John Wayne Gacy, and Richard Ramirez to Jeffrey Dahmer— without exception they committed the murders by themselves or participated with others in the act. The fright generated by these heavyweights of homicide's rogue gallery, then, was always finite. Because of Manson's ability to control others and get them to vent his spleen on society for him, the probability of death has always been exponential, and therefore much more frightening.

Some have compared Manson with the Reverend Jim Jones and David Koresh. Although to their followers, Jones, Koresh, and Manson were all messianic, and each possessed the uncommon ability to totally control and dominate the lives of those who believed in them, the comparison ends there. During the final moments of Jones and Koresh, in a state of dementia they ordered the suicide of their followers, then proceeded to take their own lives also. Turning their power over others inward by ordering and participating in mass suicide is a far cry from Manson driving down dark streets with his followers randomly looking for homes into which he could send them to commit human slaughter. Prior to the last days of Jones and Koresh, there is no evidence that either had ordered others to murder anyone for them. With Manson, murder was his religion, his credo, his way of life. As Paul Watkins said, "Death is Charlie's trip."

Derivatively, Manson's slavishly obedient followers had

come to share this hellish passion. Telling cellmates Ronnie Howard and Virginia Graham about the act of murder and the Family's plan to start traveling throughout the country, killing people and whole families at random, Susan Atkins had said animatedly, "The more you do it, the better you like it."

If Manson has continued to fascinate mainstream America, he has also done so with its fanatical elements. Today, almost every disaffected and morally twisted group in America, from Satanists to neo-Nazi skinheads, has embraced Manson and the poisons of his virulent philosophy. He has become their spiritual icon, the high priest of anti-establishment hatred. As columnist William Buckley put it, Manson has become "the nation's leading anti-citizen." Wayne McGuire, in *Acquarian Journal,* predicts that "sometime in the future Charles Manson will metamorphose into a major American folk hero." Though Frenchmen will likely stop drinking wine before that happens,* Manson is indeed a hero to many on the jagged margins of our culture. In a 1994 interview, seventeen-year-old +Natalie,† a Satanist, says: "Charles Manson is an idol and role model." The murders happened, she says, because "Manson wanted a new government and anarchy to clear out the garbage, the useless people." Her twenty-year-old boyfriend, +Robert, a fellow Satanist with whom she lives in San Francisco, adds about the Tate-LaBianca victims: "I feel that might is right, and whoever isn't prepared to defend their own life shouldn't cry when their life is taken." +Willie, a twenty-one-year-old white supremacist, says he "got into Manson on the twentieth anniversary of the Tate killings when I went to this heavy metal tribute to him. I had already met all the peace and love cult people and when I ran into the Satan types I liked all the negative aspects they stood for. So ever since, I've been hanging out with

*However, the Manson T-shirts and Guns N' Roses' album show that the attempted apotheosis and romanticizing of Manson is under way. Two screen projects in the works (the British television documentary *Manson: The Man, the Media, the Music,* and the American full-length feature *Manson in the Desert*), whose themes divert the viewer's attention from the murders, unfortunately coalesce with this effort.

†The cross symbol (+) indicates a pseudonym.

people that support Manson.'' Willie feels that as a white man he is the victim of racism in our society, that blacks are "like Neanderthals and overpopulating our culture." If Manson got out, "he would improve the quality of life." +Alex, a forty-two-year-old neo-Nazi who has corresponded with Manson for years, says his "discovery" of Manson can only be compared to his earlier discovery of Adolf Hitler and the National Socialist Party. He calls Manson "the foremost revolutionary leader in the world today," and is special "by virture of a one in a hundred million shot of gene combinations that gives him his ideas, personality, and physical presence."

To the extremists, mass murderers like John Wayne Gacy and Jeffrey Dahmer are no more intriguing than they are to the average citizen. They are merely very sick psychopaths who kill for no reason other than to satisfy their unchecked homicidal urges. Though these killers attract inevitable media attention and interest for a while, they have no followers nor anything to say, and if and when they do talk, not even the extremists listen. The only message these homicidal monsters have to give by their violence is horror. Manson and his murders, on the other hand, are downright hip to the extremists. As misdirected as it was, his violence was political, revolutionary, and therein lies his main appeal to those on the fringes. Also, aware of the flat intellect of most mass killers, the extremists admire and are impressed with Manson's unquestioned intelligence, the offbeat and sometimes searing nature of his insights, his enigmatic answers and allusions, and a mental deftness that allows him to speak in riddles, always with an underlying message. In short, they are drawn to the mystery of Manson.

While a Mansonesque culture and mystique grow outside his prison walls, Charles Manson, inmate I.D.# B-33920, and now fifty-nine, is incarcerated at Corcoran State Prison in Corcoran, California, a town of approximately nine thousand people located in the San Joaquin Valley of Central California, sixty miles south of Fresno. Corcoran is built on what was once Tulare Lake, home of the Tachi Indians. Transferred from San Quentin's Death Row to Folsom State Prison near Sacramento on October 6, 1972, Manson was sent to the California Medical Facility at Vacaville on March 20, 1974; back to Folsom on October 22, 1974; back to San Quentin on June 7, 1975; and back to Vacaville on May 11, 1976, where he remained until July 17, 1985, his longest stay at one prison. He returned to San Quentin on July 18, 1985, and was sent to his present location, Corcoran, on March 15, 1989.

Tip Kindel, public information officer for the California Department of Corrections, says the reason for all the transfers of Manson is that Manson has been "both a disciplinary and a security problem for the Department." It would appear that the fame and outlaw reputation Manson acquired far and wide for the Tate-LaBianca murders has had a measurable effect upon how he perceives himself, causing him to act much more belligerently behind bars. Though he was never a model prisoner, I could find no reference in his prison records during his many years of incarceration before the murders of any assaultive behavior by him against prison personnel. But Kindel reports that since Manson's conviction for the murders, he has physically assaulted prison staff (striking them with his hands, throwing hot coffee or expectorating on them, etc.) six times, the last time in February of 1992, and threatened them on numerous other occasions. Altogether, Manson has been found guilty of fifty-nine "C.D.C. 115s," California Department of Corrections disciplinary write-ups. For the past year, however, according to an official at Corcoran, Manson "has not been disruptive" and "hasn't gotten into any trouble." Prison counselor Ernest Caldren observes that Manson "has a pattern of cycling in his behavior. There are brief periods of cooperation, and then he turns and threatens staff, particularly the inexperienced, with violent behavior."

In 1972 and 1973, while at Folsom, Manson himself was assaulted on two separate occasions by fellow inmates. And a California state prison official says that throughout the years reports have reached prison personnel that one prison gang or another "had a contract on Charlie." However, the only known attempt on his life was while Manson was at the California Medical Facility at Vacaville. The primary reason for sending Manson there was not because of the psychiatric facilities, as many imagined, but because it is considered to be the best place in the California correctional system to take care of a special prisoner like Manson. Vacaville, for the most part, houses the weaker segment of the prison population: those who, because of their physical or mental disability, are more apt to be victims than predators behind bars. On September 25, 1984, it was Manson's misfortune to be working in the hobby shop at Vacaville with one Jan Holmstrom, a member of the Hare Krishna religious group serving a life sentence for the 1974 shotgun murder of his father, a Pasadena gynecologist. (In an ironic scene reminiscent of the Manson murders, Holmstrom wrote "baby killer" in blood on a wall of the family home.) Holmstrom doused Manson with paint thinner and then set him on fire, causing second- and third-degree burns to nearly 20 percent of his body, mostly his face, scalp, and hands. Holmstrom, described by prison officials as a "psychiatric case in remission," said he set Manson ablaze because Manson had objected to his Hare Krishna chants and had threatened him for his religious beliefs. He also claimed, "God told me to kill Manson."

True "solitary confinement" does not exist in the California prison system today. Inmates still use the popular term, however, to refer to the situation where no other inmate shares their cell with them and they are segregated from the general prison population, mingling only with selected prisoners. Manson has spent the majority of his twenty-three years of incarceration for the Tate, LaBianca, Shea, and Hinman murders in this type of housing.

At Vacaville in August of 1980 Manson was given his first prison job—gardener and maintenance man for the Protestant chapel. "It's taken me ten years to get a breath of fresh air," he said. "I'm not about to screw up." Maintaining a clean disciplinary record for close to two years, in June of 1982 he was placed, per his request, on the "main line," the general prison population. Manson's resolve not to screw up lasted (or the lack of it remained undiscovered) until October 29, 1982, when a hacksaw blade, along with marijuana, was found in his cell.* A

---

*Also, upon his arrival back at San Quentin from Vacaville in 1985, a four-inch piece of a hacksaw blade was found in his shoe.

subsequent search of the chapel uncovered four bags of marijuana, one hundred feet of nylon rope, and a mail-order catalog for hot-air balloons. If Manson couldn't hack his way out of prison, he apparently was thinking of "flying the coop." In what must be considered a vapid display, prison officials actually asked the state attorney general's office to file possession of marijuana charges against the man serving nine concurrent life sentences for nine murders, but saner counsel prevailed and no charges were filed.

While at Vacaville, Manson refused to take part in group psychiatric therapy and largely just played word games with psychiatrists during the individual sessions he consented to. One psychiatric evaluation of Manson made by prison doctors stated: "He has above-average intelligence, and the [Rorschach test] drawings seem to point to schizophrenia. This doesn't mean his entire performance was schizophrenic . . . Manson is a passive-aggressive personality with paranoid tendencies."

Manson's response? "Sure I'm paranoid. I've had reason to be ever since I can remember. And now I have to be, just to stay alive. As for schizophrenia, take anybody off the streets and put them in the middle of a prison and you'll see all kinds of split personalities. I've got a thousand faces, so that makes me five hundred schizophrenics. And in my life I've played every one of those faces, sometimes because people push me into a role, and sometimes because it's better being someone else than me." After spending a short time in the psychiatric ward at Vacaville, Manson was transferred out on the recommendation of a psychiatric

---

How does one reconcile Manson's apparent interest in escaping with his desire at Terminal Island in 1967 to stay behind bars? Prison had become his home, he told the authorities back then, and he didn't think he could adjust to the world outside. Even today, I suspect that Manson isn't miserable or even unhappy behind bars. Having spent forty-two of his fifty-nine years in jails, reformatories, and prisons, he obviously has become totally institutionalized, and therefore most likely isn't uncomfortable in an incarcerated setting per se. However, after he got out in 1967 he undoubtedly learned to like having a harem of girls ("Up in the Haight, I'm called the gardener. I tend to all the flower children," he had told Squeaky when they first met.) and riding dune buggies up and down the desert more. Further, like never before, Manson now has to look over his shoulder. He knows that any con who wants to make a name for himself can kill him and then *he* becomes famous.

report which said he was nothing but "a psychiatric curiosity or oddity."

Knowing he may well spend the rest of his life in prison, Manson has either boycotted his parole hearings since his first one in 1978 or used them merely as a forum to sermonize or simply have some fun. In 1978 he regaled the parole board with his comments for three hours. "I'm totally unsuitable for that world out there. I don't fit in at all," a bearded and shaggy-haired Manson allowed in saying he should not be released from prison. But then Manson, never a model of consistency, added: "I'm mad. I'm indignant. I'm mad to every bone in my body that I have to come back to the penitentiary when I didn't break no law." Waving his arms in exclamation and half singing his presentation, Manson said, "I'm not your executioner. I'm not your devil and I'm not your God. I'm Charles Manson." Reminding the board he had spent most of his life behind bars, he said, "I was born and raised all my life in prison." He told the board he had been "asked to come to Scotland, Germany, Australia," but that he wasn't interested. When asked where he would go if released, he responded, "I'd go to the desert, talk to the animals and live off the land." The parole board, in denying parole, said that Manson's crime "eclipses the imagination." The following year Manson sent word from his cell that he had nothing to tell the board, and gave his unit sergeant several $100 bills from a Monopoly set and a Chance card that said "Advance to Go. Collect $200" to deliver to the board members.

Delighting in talking to reporters covering his parole hearings, he told one, "You're in prison more than I am. You've got more rules to live by than I do. I can sit down and relax. Can you?" Grabbing another reporter's arm and pressing his mouth close to her ear, he whispered, "Do you know a way out of here? If you get me out, we can go to the desert and I'll show you things that'll blow your mind."

At his parole hearing in 1981, Manson, in a T-shirt with a small skull and crossed bones, repeatedly stood, sat down, paced, and interrupted the hearing, frequently shouting at the board members. He told the board: "I've been in solitary for ten years. I ain't got no mind. It's gone, man. I don't understand half the things you're saying." Then, "I never really grew up. I went to prison at nine. I don't read or write too good and I've stayed like a little kid. I stopped thinking in 1954.''

In 1986, Manson did not appear at his parole hearing, sending the board, instead, a lengthy written statement. "All of the judgments and the blame that is pushed off on me will be reflected back in the fires of the Holy War that you call crime," he wrote. "I did invoke a balance for life on Earth. From behind the time locks of courtrooms and from the worlds of darkness, I did let loose devils and demons with the power of scorpions to torment. I did unseal seven seals and seven jars in accord with the judgments placed upon me . . . You've drugged me for years, dragging me up and down prison hallways, laying my head on every chopping block you've got, chained me, burnt me, but you cannot defeat me . . . In the all that was said about me, it was not me saying it, and if you see a false prophet, it is only a reflection of your own judgments.''

That same year he wrote President Ronald Reagan at the White House with this advice: "Keep projecting [to kids] what not to do and you make the thought in their brains of what can and will be done." Before signing off with "Easy, Charles Manson," he told Reagan: "I'm the last guy in line but I've got all the thoughts for the balance of order and peace with a one-world government if we all are to survive.''

At his last parole hearing on April 21, 1992, Manson, the defiant swastika still very visible on his forehead, responded to the accusation he had ordered the murders by telling the three-man parole board (now called the Board of Prison Terms): "Everyone says that I was the leader of those people, but I was actually the follower of the children . . . I didn't break God's law and I didn't break man's law.''

As with each of his prior appearances before the board, he did virtually all the talking. The most routine questions launched him into unstoppable, stream of consciousness lectures that contained references to God, the economy, Rambo, the Queen of England, World Wars I and II, the Pope, J. Edgar Hoover, winos, Vietnam, chess, Christian ethics, General MacArthur, President Truman, Ninja warriors, the San Diego Zoo, J. R. Ewing, gangster Frank

Costello, and a myriad of other people and subjects, including the relationship between does and bucks, and dogs and
chickens. And, as always, that which he always returns
to—the need to stop the destruction of the environment.
He told the board they live in a matriarchal world, he in a
patriarchal one. "You back up to your women. I don't back
up to my women." Although the details did not emerge,
Manson acknowledged at the hearing that he has been
getting $500 for his autograph from people on the outside.*

The board, in finding Manson unsuitable for parole, set
1997 for his next hearing, the maximum time (five years)
between parole hearings allowed under the California Penal
Code.

Until her death from cancer in July of 1992, Sharon Tate's
mother, Doris, attended most of the parole hearings for
Manson and his killers, and was successful in mobilizing
national support in the form of 352,000 letters to the parole
board to keep Manson and the others behind bars for life.
"I live with her [Sharon's] screams and her begging for the
life of her baby," she often said. In the late '70s, Mrs. Tate
co-founded the Los Angeles chapter of Parents of Murdered
Children, a group providing mental, emotional, and other
support to its members. Just before her death, Mrs. Tate,
who was the United States' representative at an International Victims' Rights Conference in Stockholm in June
of 1990, formed the Sacramento-based Doris Tate Crime
Victims Bureau. The bureau promotes, among other things,
the enactment of legislation for the rights of crime victims.

Since her mother's passing, Patti Tate, who was eleven
years old when her twenty-six-year-old sister was slain, and

---

*Manson also receives ten cents for every Manson T-shirt sold. In Califor-
nia, the profits of convicted criminals can only be seized if the moneymaking venture is *directly* related to the crime. The T-shirts and Manson's
song in the Guns N' Roses album do not qualify for seizure. (Senate Bill
1330, which is presently before the California legislature, would expand the
scope of seizure to include the sale of anything "the value of which is
enhanced by the notoriety gained from the commission of the crime.")
However, in 1971, the son of Wojiciech (Voytek) Frykowski, one of the five
Tate victims, got a $500,000 judgment against Manson and his four co-
defendants. As a result of a writ of execution on the judgment (with interest
worth $1,200,000 in 1994), in late February of 1994 the son, who lives in
Germany, received his first royalty check for $72,000 from the Manson song
in the Guns N' Roses album.

who bears a striking resemblance to Sharon, has been faithfully and effectively carrying on all of her mother's important work. Speaking of her sister, a misty-eyed Patti says: "She was so sweet and such a gentle soul. I idolized her and there wasn't anything I wouldn't have done for her."

Corcoran is a medium-maximum security institution. Manson is housed in the Security Housing Unit (SHU) in a 6½' × 12½' cell he shares with another inmate. Called a "prison within a prison," SHU is the maximum security section at Corcoran. Manson is issued three meals a day by correctional officers. The food is served on trays through a food port located in each cell door. Breakfast is at 6:30 A.M., lunch at noon, and dinner at 5 P.M. No less than ten hours a week he exercises in a nearby walled yard with ten co-inmates of his. Manson has a radio and television set in his cell, but does not have his beloved guitar, the latter not permitted in SHU. Like all inmates in this unit, he does not have a work assignment. Per the California Department of Corrections, the current annual cost to the taxpayers for housing Manson is $20,525.

Manson carries on running correspondence with as many of the people who write to him as he can. He also apparently writes to some who have no desire to be his pen pal, sending four letters to me in the preceding years. In 1986, the book *Manson in His Own Words* ("as told to Nuel Emmons") was published in hardcover. The thoughts may be Manson's, but the diction clearly is not. Dedicated "to destroying a myth," Manson, instead, tries to perpetuate the myth he and his most ardent followers invented, that the Tate-LaBianca murders were "the girls' " idea. Manson admits, in a roundabout fashion, that he thereafter ordered the two LaBianca killings, but continues to deny ordering the five Tate murders on the first night.

Near the conclusion of his book, Manson writes: "There are days when I get caught up in being the most notorious convict of all time. In that frame of mind I get off on all the publicity, and I'm pleased when some fool writes and offers to 'off some pigs' for me. I've had girls come to visit me with their babies in their arms and say, 'Charlie, I'd do anything in the world for you. I'm raising my baby in your image.' Those letters and visits used to delight me, but that's my individual sickness. What sickness is it that keeps sending me kids and followers? It's your world out there that does it. I don't solicit my mail or ask anyone to come and visit me. Yet the mail continues to arrive and your pretty little flowers of innocence keep showing up at the gate.''

From these relatively benign words, Manson abruptly changes, and after saying he doesn't think he'll ever be released, closes his book in vintage fashion with these ominously ambiguous words: "My eyes are cameras. My mind is tuned to more television channels than exist in your world. And it suffers no censorship. Through it, I have a world and the universe as my own. So . . . know that only a body is in prison. At my will, I walk your streets and am right out there among you.''

Life behind bars hasn't dashed Manson's desire to be a recording star. From his cell in Vacaville in 1982, Manson recorded his second album, titled *Charlie Manson's Good Time Gospel Hour*. Manson sings ballads he composed about his life and that of his pals on San Quentin's Death Row. The sounds of nearby television and flushing toilets can be heard in the background. Manson's first album, called *LIE* (the photo on the jacket is the one of him on the December 19, 1969, cover of *Life* magazine), was taped, portentously, on August 9, 1968, exactly one year before the Tate murders. With several of the Manson Family girls providing choral backup, Manson sings his own compositions. Both albums have gone through several bootleg editions and are considered such rare collectibles that one alternative music store owner told me if he ever got his hands on either one, "I wouldn't sell them. They're too valuable.''

Remarkably, there are some who heap scalding criticism on those in the music industry who never gave Manson a chance when he got out of prison in 1967. If he had been given a real opportunity, they add, most likely the murders would never have taken place. While this is possibly true, that type of "but for" causation could be used to argue that if someone had bought Hitler's paintings in Vienna in 1912 perhaps we wouldn't have had the Second World War.

Being behind bars also hasn't inhibited Manson from reaching America's vast television audience. The media (NBC's *Today Show,* CNN, BBC, Charlie Rose, Tom Snyder, the ABC Special in March of 1994, etc.) have sought him out, enabling him to verbally spew his venom. In a 1988 interview with Geraldo Rivera, he said: "I'm going to chop up some more of you mother-fuckers. I'm going to kill as many of you as I can. I'm going to pile you up to the sky. I figure about fifty million of you. I might be able to save my trees and my air and my water and my wildlife." When Rivera later said, "There's nine dead people out there" (referring to Manson's nine murder convictions), Manson answered, "There's a lot more than nine, son, a whole lot, and there's going to be a whole lot more." When Rivera asked if he told the women in his Family to kill, he responded, "I don't deal with women I got to tell what to do. They *know* what to do." He told Rivera: "I make laws. I'm the lawmaker. I'm the one that lays down the track."

In the twenty-five years since the murders, no event thrust the Manson Family back into the news once again as much as Lynette "Squeaky" Fromme's attempted assassination of President Gerald Ford in 1975. After Manson was transferred from San Quentin back to Folsom in October of 1974, Squeaky and Sandra Good moved to Sacramento (fifteen miles to the west) to be as close to him as possible.* Squeaky, Sandra, and a part-time nurse they had recruited into the Family named Susan Murphy, rented a run-down attic apartment in an old, downtown boardinghouse just a few blocks from the state capitol. On the sunny and crisp morning of September 5, 1975, President Ford was walking through a park in front of the capitol to meet Governor Jerry Brown.

Not only wasn't Squeaky on the Secret Service's list of

---

*Though Squeaky and Sandra were not allowed to visit or even correspond with Manson, a prison spokesman at the time said that the two of them would come to the prison about once a month "to inquire about how Manson was doing." A friend of Squeaky and Sandra told *Time* magazine that the girls believed Manson's imprisonment was part of a grand design, "that he would rise again some day, like Christ. They spend all their time preparing themselves for the day he rises."

dangerous people in town to watch—particularly remarkable when weeks earlier she and Sandra had issued a communiqué to the media in Sacramento that "if Nixon's reality wearing a new face [i.e., Ford] continues to run this country against the law, your homes will be bloodier than the Tate-LaBianca homes and My Lai put together"*—but the President's men inexplicably paid no attention to an elfish woman nearby attired in a bright red robe and matching turban. As Ford stopped at a magnolia tree to shake hands with a cluster of smiling supporters, Squeaky materialized out of the group, grabbed a gun from under her robe and pointed it at Ford, just two feet away. Instantly, Secret Service agent Larry Buendorf seized Squeaky's gun arm and threw her to the ground. In apparent anger, Squeaky cried out, "It didn't go off. Can you believe it? It didn't go off." The reason it didn't go off will probably never be known beyond *all* doubt. To be sure, Squeaky's .45 caliber Army Colt pistol, though loaded with four bullets, had no bullet in the chamber ready to be fired. To fire the gun, Squeaky would have first had to pull the slide back on top of the gun to raise a cartridge from the magazine into the firing chamber, which she hadn't done. Had Squeaky mistakenly thought that squeezing the trigger (Buendorf and another witness reported hearing a metallic clicking sound, which could have been the hammer striking the rear of the firing pin) would be enough to fire the weapon? Because of the belief that Squeaky knew how to operate guns (on the documentary *Manson* she is seen operating the bolt of a rifle), many people, including some in law enforcement, are convinced she had no intention of hurting Ford. Nevertheless, prosecutor Dwayne Keyes, now a Superior Court judge in Fresno, told me he is "absolutely positive she had every intent to kill the President," a state of mind the prosecution had to prove to secure a conviction.

In any event, Squeaky was now competing for the limelight, at least for a while, with her God, Charlie, making

---

*The Manson Family's hatred of former President Nixon stems, of course, from Nixon's headline-capturing declaration during the trial that he believed Manson to be guilty. In author Ed Sander's best-selling book, *The Family*, he quotes a Manson therapist at Vacaville as saying Manson believed his own personal hex on Nixon had caused him to fall.

the September 15, 1975, covers of *Newsweek* and *Time* magazines. At her federal trial she was so obstreperous the judge had her removed from the courtroom for most of the proceedings, but not before she told him that one of the issues at the trial "was as clear as the piano in the front window of your home," an accurate reference. During jury deliberations after a three-week trial in which Squeaky did not testify, "a lot of people," juror Robert Convoy recalled, "believed that with no cartridge in the chamber, the gun wasn't a weapon." Ultimately, however, the jury found Squeaky guilty of attempting to assassinate Ford (prior to 1965, presidential assassination was only a state, not a federal, crime), the first female in American history so charged and convicted. Squeaky was sentenced to life imprisonment.

Was Manson behind the attempt? My instincts from the beginning were that he was not. Though Manson always spoke as if he had no fear of death, telling his followers that death wasn't the end of life, "just another high," even beautiful ("Living is what scares me. Dying is easy," he'd also say, as well as implying he had been resurrected), I saw first-hand how hard he in fact fought for his life during his nine and one-half month trial. Having his death sentence removed just three years earlier, it made no sense to me that he would risk a new sentence of death against someone as remote to him and his interests as Ford. Prosecutor Keyes also believes that Manson was not involved, and his office found no evidence implicating him. Squeaky, the Little Orphan Annie-looking matriarch of the Family during Manson's forced exile, was probably trying to impress Manson by her act. She had to know that successful or not in killing Ford, such a spectacular, grandly anti-societal act would be sure to please him.

Searching Squeaky's apartment pursuant to a warrant after the attempt on Ford, police found a stack of letters, ready to go, from "The International People's Court of Retribution," an impressive-sounding organization whose membership, however, was rather limited—Squeaky, Sandra Good, and Susan Murphy. The letters threatened named corporate executives and U.S. government officials with death if they did not forthwith stop polluting the air and water and destroying the environment. A long list of other addressees was nearby. While on bail after her and Murphy's arrest for conspiring to send threatening communications through the United States mail, Good proceeded to utter, on radio and TV, the same threats, constituting four new federal violations of transmitting death threats by way of interstate commerce.

Good represented herself at her trial, was convicted on all five counts (Murphy on only the conspiracy count), and asked that she be sentenced to the maximum of twenty-five years. The judge gave her fifteen. William Shubb, her appointed "advisory counsel" during the trial and now a U.S. Federal District Court judge in Sacramento, says that if she had been agreeable he is certain a plea could have been negotiated wherein her sentence would have been much less severe.

All of Manson's co-defendants in the Tate-LaBianca murders are, like Manson, still behind bars serving their life sentences.

Charles "Tex" Watson, Manson's chief lieutenant at the murder scenes and the principal killer of the Tate-LaBianca victims, has renounced Manson and is presently at Mule Creek State Prison in Ione, California. He was transferred there in April of 1993 from the California Men's Colony (CMC) in San Luis Obispo, where he had been incarcerated since September 1972. At CMC in 1975, Watson, through the ministry of Raymond Hoekstra (a legendary prison evangelist known as "Chaplain Ray"), became a born-again Christian. As a student chaplain and associate administrator of the Protestant chapel at CMC, Watson baptized, led Bible-study groups, and preached to the inmate congregation. In 1980, Watson founded Abounding Love Ministries (ALMS), a California nonprofit corporation which he and his Norwegian wife, Kristin, run. The two married in 1979 and have three children. Ordained as a minister in 1983, Watson receives donations to his ministry of approximately $1,500 per month from people on a national mailing list to whom he sends religious cassette tapes and a Christian newsletter.

Watson's 1978 book, *Will You Die for Me?*, which he

wrote with Chaplain Ray, chronicles his life with Manson, the murders, and his ultimate conversion to Christianity. Speaking of Manson, to whom he writes, "I had given myself totally," he says he served the power of death and destruction "through one diabolical man who wanted to be God." Believing that Manson "was—perhaps still is—possessed" by the devil, he says Manson's only interest "had been death, but Jesus promised life."

A rather startling admission by Watson to his prison psychiatrist was revealed at his last parole hearing in May of 1990. (Watson elected to waive his January 1993 parole hearing, stipulating to his unsuitability for parole.) The psychiatrist wrote that it had only been "during the last three years of one-on-one therapy that [Watson had] begun to truly experience a sense of deep remorse, both for the crime victims and for the families of the crime victims." When a troubled parole board member asked Watson what, then, had he been feeling the previous eighteen years, Watson responded: "Well, it's not that I haven't experienced that before, but there's been things happening in my life over the last few years that have really brought it home more so." Watson explained that ever since he became a Christian in 1975 it's been "great to know that I have been forgiven by God for what I've done. But I think sometimes we can hide behind that, and the last three years I've had the opportunity to really see myself in a new light in the sense that I've opened myself up to really look at the crime through other people's eyes other than just my own."

Watson's belated epiphany was brought about in large part, he informed the board, by a somewhat incongruous relationship with Suzanne LaBerge (formerly Suzanne Struthers), Rosemary LaBianca's daughter from a relationship before she met Leno. The thrice married and divorced Suzanne, who was twenty-one years old at the time of the murders, began visiting Watson at CMC in 1987. She appeared at the 1990 parole hearing and actually made an impassioned plea for the release of her mother's killer, telling the board Watson had atoned for his terrible crimes, had overcome his past by turning to Christ, and no longer was a threat to society.

In a June 5, 1994, letter to me, Watson wrote: "With my

deepest remorse, I apologize to the people of the world for my part in making Manson what he has become. To the many victims, my heart is full of sorrow for my actions. . . . If anyone should have received the death penalty for their crimes, it was me. I believe that God and his grace gave me a second chance, having a different plan for my life. . . . I have no great ambitions, other than allowing the Lord to use me as a testimony, urging others to Christ.''

While at CMC, Watson completed courses in vocational data processing and office machine repair. His current work assignment at Mule Creek is "tier tender," i.e., keeping clean one of the two tiers in the building where he is housed. A prison spokesperson at Mule Creek advises that since Watson's incarceration for the Tate-LaBianca murders he has received "one disciplinary infraction, of a minor nature, in 1973. He continues to program without incident.''

Susan Atkins, Patricia Krenwinkel, and Leslie Van Houten, like Watson, have each renounced Manson and expressed remorse for the killings. All are still at the California Institution for Women at Frontera. One of only three prisons for women in the state, Frontera has been described by one wag as "a college campus with barbed wire around it.'' Each of the three Manson girls lives in a cottage-like housing unit (two inmates to a unit) at the attractive, well-manicured institution. All three girls have been reviewed for parole consideration, and denied, ten times thus far. It is the common consensus that if any of them are ever released, Van Houten will be the first one, primarily because unlike Atkins and Krenwinkel, she was only involved in the LaBianca, not the Tate murders. Additionally, a well-organized group, "Friends of Leslie," consisting of hundreds of supporters, regularly urge her release to the parole board.

According to a prison spokesperson, "the institutional behavior [of the girls] is viewed as good.'' (Krenwinkel, in fact, has not received one disciplinary write-up in twenty-three years, called "unusual" by a member of the parole board.) Their current custody level is medium security, they are each in the general prison population, and reportedly Krenwinkel and Van Houten are closer to each other socially than either one is to Atkins.

The most well-known of the girls, Susan "Sexy Sadie" Atkins, converted to Christianity even before Watson. Through the intercession in early 1974 of former Family member Bruce Davis, in prison at Folsom for the Hinman-Shea murders, Susan began to contemplate a Christian life. Davis, who had become a born-again Christian, wrote many letters to her, offering guidance and recommending Christian literature, including the New Testament, for her to read. In her 1977 book, *Child of Satan, Child of God* (written with Bob Slosser), she recounts an evening in late September 1974 when, alone in her cell, she softly but solemnly uttered the words that she wanted to be forgiven for her ghastly crimes. "Suddenly," she writes, "there in my thoughts was a door. It had a handle. I took hold of it, and pulled." When the door opened, she says, a flood of brilliant light poured over her. In the center was an even brighter light, which she knew was Jesus. "He spoke to me—literally, plainly, in my nine-by-eleven prison cell. 'Susan, I am really here. I'm coming in your heart to stay. Right now you are being born again . . . You are now a child of God. You are washed clean and your sins have all been forgiven.' " Atkins goes on to say that that night, for the first time in many years, she "slept soundly, free of nightmares—unafraid and warm." On the last page of her book, she writes that she believes "the Lord will one day release me from this place [Frontera] and give me a ministry to people of all kinds, but especially those who are as twisted and lost as I was from my earliest teen years."

She now denies stabbing Sharon Tate, adding, however, that her moral culpability is still the same because she was there and "did nothing to stop it." When she was asked by a reporter in the mid-'80s if she would be willing to say she was sorry to Sharon Tate's mother for her involvement in Sharon's murder, she replied: "There are no words to describe what I feel. 'I'm sorry, please forgive me,' those words are so overused and inadequate for what I feel."

Atkins married one Donald Lee Laisure, a fifty-two-year-old Texan, in September of 1981. Laisure spells his last name with a dollar sign for the *s*. At the time of the marriage he claimed to be worth "999 million dollars plus, and seven times that in foreign countries," and he said he planned to build a $12 million solar home near the Frontera prison so he could be close to his bride. Per news reports, Laisure appeared for the wedding in the prison chapel "resplendent and bespangled in diamond rings, diamond clips, a huge gold belt-buckle, sunglasses, cigar, Western-style hat and an orange leisure suit." Atop his rust-colored Cadillac in the prison parking lot outside was an unfurled Lone Star flag of the state of Texas.

Although Susan had corresponded with Laisure for several years, there were two small details she regrettably had not learned about him. His wealth was nonexistent. Perhaps more importantly, Laisure had the troubling habit of getting married about as often as Paris changes skirt lengths. Susan was his thirty-sixth bride. Three months later she told Laisure, who had had conjugal visits with her in the Prison Family Living Unit Apartments, to "go back to Texas," concluding the marriage was "a drastic mistake." Laisure filed for divorce the following year. In 1987, Susan remarried. Her husband, fifteen years her junior, attends law school in Southern California. She describes this marriage as "the first healthy and successful relationship I've ever had in my life."

In a long, typewritten letter to me on May 11, 1994, Atkins wrote: "Twenty-five years ago you tried three girls between the ages of twenty and twenty-two years old, and one thirty-five-year-old ex-con. Now, twenty-five years later, there are three women about the age of forty-five, all of whom have exemplary prison records, have taken advantage of the educational programs to earn college degrees, have contributed to every charity organization and program available, and have expressed remorse, shame, and regret for their parts in this hideous crime . . . and you have one sixty-year-old ex-con who shows up at his parole board hearings with a swastika carved on his forehead. I think that says it all."

Though Atkins is very critical of Manson, she has said she still prays for him, "that Charlie will turn to Christ." Atkins has obtained, through correspondence, an Associate of Arts degree (two years), graduating with a 3.5 grade point average. She also has completed a course in vocational data processing, and is presently taking paralegal classes. Her current work assignment at Frontera is that of a sewing operator in the Prison Industries program.

In 1976, Leslie Van Houten's conviction for the two LaBianca murders was reversed and sent back for a new trial by the California Court of Appeal, Second Appellate District, on the ground that Judge Charles Older had erred in not granting her motion for a mistrial when her attorney, Ronald Hughes, vanished near the end of the trial. After a hung jury in the first retrial, she was finally reconvicted of the two murders in 1978. As opposed to the guilt phase of her original trial back in 1970–71, in her two retrials Van Houten readily admitted to the jury her full participation in the LaBianca homicides. Her defense was diminished mental capacity based on mental illness induced, in part, by the chronic, prolonged use of hallucinogenic drugs. For a few months before her last trial she was released on a $200,000 bail bond paid for by friends and relatives, and lived for a while with a former writer from the *Christian Science Monitor* who was writing a book about Van Houten. The book reached the first draft level, but was never published.

Van Houten had a short-lived marriage to a man named Bill Cywin in the early '80s. Though not connected to any misbehavior or complicity on her part, during the brief marriage Cywin was found to be in possession of a female prison guard's uniform.

Through correspondence courses, Van Houten acquired a Bachelor of Arts degree in English Literature. She also writes short stories, one of which was included in an anthology of prison literature, and at one time edited the prison newspaper. She is part of a small inmate group that sews quilts for the homeless. Van Houten says she "takes offense to the fact that Manson doesn't own up" to his responsibility for the murders. "I take responsibility for my part, and part of my responsibility was helping to create him. Being a follower does not excuse." Van Houten is presently doing secretarial work at the prison.

Patricia Krenwinkel received a Bachelor of Science degree through correspondence while at Frontera and has also completed a course in vocational data processing. Krenwinkel has never married. The most athletic of the three Manson girls, she plays on the prison softball team and presently is a "camp trainer" in the inmate firefighter's program, training those under her to meet a physical fitness standard they must have in order to fight fires. Both she and Van Houten serve as counselors in a program in which young people with drug abuse problems are brought to the prison.

In 1988, while stating her deep remorse for the murders, Krenwinkel nonetheless told her prison psychiatrist that Abigail Folger, the person she murdered on the night of the Tate murders "could have been something more than she was, a drug abuser." At her 1993 parole hearing, Krenwinkel, crying and her voice cracking, told the board: "No matter what I do, I cannot change one minute of my life. There's nothing I can do outside of being dead to pay for this. And I know that's what you wish, but I cannot take my own life." In the 1994 ABC special, she said that every day "I wake up and know that I'm a destroyer of the most precious thing, which is life, and living with that is the most difficult thing of all." But, she adds, "that's what I deserve—to wake up every morning and know that." Responding to Manson's claim he did not order the murders, she said, "Charlie is absolutely lying. There wasn't one thing done—that was even allowed to be done—without his express permission." She is very concerned about young people who write her and "seem to think that what we did was all right. There is nothing, nothing that we did that is all right. Nothing. If there is anything I can say to these children, it's that he [Manson] is not the man to follow."

All other family members convicted of Manson-related murders, with the exception of one, are also still behind bars. Bruce Davis, convicted of the murders of Donald "Shorty" Shea and Gary Hinman, is presently at the California Men's Colony at San Luis Obispo, California, and Robert Beausoleil, also convicted of the Hinman murder, is at the California Correctional Center at Susanville, California. Only Steven Grogan ("Clem Tufts" in the Family), convicted of Shea's murder, has been released.

Grogan was by all accounts the most unhinged and spaced out (on psychedelic drugs) of all Manson Family members. Even in the Family he was considered crazy. Yet the transformation behind bars for Grogan, eighteen years old at the time he participated in Shea's murder, was remarkable. Burt Katz, who prosecuted Grogan, and is now a retired Los Angeles County Superior Court judge, says he was "favorably impressed" by the change in the openly remorseful Grogan, and felt he had matured into "a thoughtful, sensitive young man." Sergeant William Gleason of the Los Angeles County Sheriff's Department, a lead investigator in the Shea murder, was similarly impressed, calling the change in Grogan "amazing." Grogan became very adept behind bars at painting watercolors and playing his guitar, and obtained an airplane engine mechanic's license.

One of the enduring Manson Family mysteries was cleared up by Grogan. It had become part of Manson Family lore, possibly to frighten all members who had a mutinous thought, that Shea was decapitated by Grogan and had been cut up and buried in nine separate places at Spahn Ranch. However, extensive digging at the ranch by law enforcement had failed to uncover Shea or any part of him. In 1977, Grogan, while at the Deuel Vocational Institution at Tracy, California, asked to see Katz. Determined to prove he had not beheaded Shea, and that Shea had not been cut up into nine pieces, he drew a map for Katz, pinpointing the location of Shea's body. Subsequently, Sergeant Gleason and his partner found Shea's remains in one piece at the spot designated by Grogan—the bottom of a steep embankment about a quarter mile down the road from the ranch. On November 18, 1985, Grogan was released from prison, and was discharged from parole on April 13, 1988.

Although Manson, today, has far more supporters and sympathizers than ever were members of his Family, I know of no group at the present time, in or out of prison, calling themselves the Manson Family and trying to keep the flame alive. The nomadic band of minstrels, waifs, and latent killers he assembled around him in the late '60s is no more, and no new group has emerged to take their place. With two exceptions, all of his former followers have severed their umbilical cord to him, starting new lives. Only

Squeaky and Sandra ("Red" and "Blue," Manson calls them), their faces still suffused with a missionary glow, have remained irrevocably wedded to him, and still fervently preach his gospel.

Squeaky has served most of her life sentence at the Federal Correctional Institution at Alderson, West Virginia. She is presently at the Federal Correctional Institution at Marianna, Florida, transferred there from Alderson on March 3, 1989. Some time back the Associated Press reported her saying that "the curtain is about to come down on all of us, and if we don't turn everything over to Charlie immediately, it's going to be too late." In a 1977 unpublished manuscript about her life with Manson, Squeaky wrote: "People said that I was Manson's main woman . . . [but Manson's] main woman is the truth. She comes before anyone or anything, and he's with her always in life or death." When Squeaky learned, on December 23, 1987, that Manson had written to some friends in Ava, Missouri, that he had testicular cancer,* she escaped within hours from Alderson to come to him, but was apprehended a few days later only two miles away. In a letter to a friend earlier that month, she wrote: "I only live and feel alive when I think of him."

Sandra Good served ten years (five of which, from 1980 to 1985, she spent with Squeaky at Alderson) of her fifteen-year sentence. She now lives in Hanford, California, a town near Manson's prison at Corcoran. Though she does not have visiting privileges, she is content to be geographically close to Manson, and has become the main, spokesperson and cheerleader for him on the outside, telling whoever will listen, including national television audiences, that Manson is innocent of the Tate-LaBianca murders, and would be a "fantastic" person for the country to follow, one who would "give the children back to themselves." Good's boyfriend, George Simpson, does have visiting privileges, and reportedly is an intermediary for Manson.

Good is believed to be the proud guardian of the vest

---

*Manson's personal medical records being confidential, the California Department of Corrections said they cannot confirm whether Manson in fact had, or presently has, the cancer.

Manson frequently wore during the Family's heyday, embroidered by "Charlie's girls" through the years with the images of devils, witches, goblins, and other symbols of black magic and demonology. Also sewn into the vest is the hair of those girls who shaved their heads while conducting their round-the-clock vigil for Manson outside the Hall of Justice during his trial.

As to those who were once members of Manson's flock, or associated with the Family, they have scattered to the four winds and are very protective of their privacy from the media. Because the Manson Family has become synonymous with terror, like those in the Bible's Revelation 9 whose identifying seal on their foreheads their leader often spoke about, all of its former members (even those who, as far as we know, did not participate in any of the execrable crimes committed by the Family) are marked for life. Since they know that few who are aware of their background can ever feel serene in their presence, nearly all of them keep their history a secret in their new lives.

My latest information is that Linda Kasabian moved from New Hampshire and is now living under an assumed name in the Pacific Northwest with her husband and three children. A friend of Linda's when she lived in Milford, New Hampshire, told a reporter that Linda "led a normal life. She drove her kids to school, participated in the PTA, that sort of thing." Barbara Hoyt, whom I was happy to help get into nursing school, is now a registered nurse in the Northwest. Barbara is divorced and living with her daughter in a townhouse she just purchased. She leads a very active life "camping, fishing, painting, and playing volleyball."

Contrary to other reports, Dianne Lake never became a corporate executive or vice-president of a bank. She worked as a bank teller for years, and describes herself today as a "happily married, well adjusted and committed Christian living with my husband and three children in the western part of the United States." Kitty Lutesinger is divorced and raising her two children in California. Steven Grogan is not, as has been reported, working as a house painter in the San Fernando Valley of Los Angeles. Someone very close to him informed me that his occupation (undisclosed) takes him to various states and "he is doing exceptionally well, better than anyone could have anticipated.''

Mary Brunner, the first female member of the Family, who was an assistant librarian at the University of California at Berkeley when she joined Manson, served six and one-half years for her participation in the Western Surplus Store robbery in Hawthorne, California. She is presently living in the Midwest under an assumed name, is single, and is doing clerical work.

Catherine Share served five years for her conviction in the Hawthorne robbery. She now lives in a Southwest state with her second husband and a twenty-three-year-old son who is a senior in college. After divorcing Manson Family associate Kenneth Como in 1981, she says she completely separated herself from the Family. Like Dianne Lake, she says she is ''happily married, and a Christian very active in church affairs.'' Share, who was born in Paris to a Hungarian violinist father and German-Jewish refugee mother, both of whom were members of the anti-Nazi underground French resistance during the Second World War, describes her life today as so clean she hasn't ''gotten a traffic ticket in ten years.'' And like Patricia Krenwinkel and other former Family members, she is deeply concerned about the many young people today who look up to Manson and want to follow him. Because of this, she is in the process of working on a book (*She Was a Gypsy Woman*) with a Texas-based writer which will ''tell the truth'' to these youths about ''who Charles Manson really is.''

During the penalty phase of the Tate-LaBianca trial, Share had testified that the motive for the murders was not Helter Skelter—which I had tied firmly to Manson—but the so-called copycat motive, which had nothing to do with Manson. In a conversation with her in early April of 1994, she acknowledged to me what I had already known (see pages 573–74 and 610–11 of the text): that her testimony was untruthful. She said the copycat motive story (as well, of course, as her testimony that Linda Kasabian, not Manson, had been behind the murders) was a fabrication to save Manson from the gas chamber, and that she had testified to it under his explicit direction.

Catherine Gillies is divorced and living on welfare with

her four children near Death Valley. She is very proud of
the fact that her twin teenage daughters are both honor
students. No one seems to know what became of Stephanie
Schram. Nancy Pitman married Michael Monfort, a former
member of the Aryan Brotherhood, a group Manson allegedly had a loose, arms-length relationship with in the mid-
'70s. She served one year for her accessory-after-the-fact
conviction in the murder of Lauren Willett, a homicide
Monfort pled guilty to. Pitman divorced Monfort in 1990.
She is now single, employed, and living with her four
children in the Pacific Northwest. Her main concern these
days, she says, "is to protect my children" from any
harm brought about by her having once belonged to the
Manson Family.

Little Paul Watkins, the intelligent and articulate youth
who provided me with the missing link for Manson's motive
of Helter Skelter, died in 1990 from leukemia. Paul and his
second wife, Martha, had two girls and lived in Tecopa, a
small desert town at the southernmost edge of Death Valley.
Paul was the founder and first president of the Death Valley
Chamber of Commerce and the unofficial mayor of Tecopa.
He and his wife mined rocks in the area and sold them in
their Tecopa jewelry store. Paul also lectured extensively
on the psychology of cults and the pernicious effects of
substance abuse. His book, *My Life with Charles Manson,*
was published in 1979.

For years, Paul (who composed, sang, and played the
saxophone and flute) and his close friend Brooks Poston
(composition, guitar) had a rock band called the "Desert
Sun" that played at night spots in the Death Valley area.
Brooks, the self-described hayseed from Texas, is now
reportedly a member of a nonviolent cult in New Orleans,
but I have been unable to confirm this.

Dennis Rice served five years for the Hawthorne robbery
and an additional two for violating a condition of his parole
that he stop associating with members of the Manson Family. Today, he is an ordained minister and president of
"Free Indeed" Ministries, Inc. He lives with his second
wife in a Southwest state and speaks, he says, "in high
schools, jails, and prisons all over America on the power of
Jesus Christ to change lives." He has six children, all of
whom, he notes proudly, are "Christians serving God."

Ruth Moorehouse is living with her husband and three children in a midwestern state. The Panamanian cowboy, Juan Flynn, returned to Panama, where he works on a ranch. In early 1994, Juan returned to the Death Valley area to visit old friends. In the late '70s I received a call from Canadian law enforcement looking for Danny DeCarlo, who was born in Canada. I have been unable to find out from the Royal Canadian Mounted Police in Ottawa what became of this matter because the Privacy Act in Canada prohibits the release of this information. I have no idea where DeCarlo is today.

I am frequently asked what happened to the "Manson children." There were eight of them, four belonging to Dennis Rice by his first wife—three boys and a girl. Two of Rice's boys are now pastors in churches located in a Southwest state. The other boy and the girl also live in the Southwest and are very involved in the activities of their local Christian church.

Little is known of Sandra Good's son, Sunstone Hawk, except that he went to college on a football scholarship and was a lineman on the team.

Linda Kasabian's daugher, Tanya, grew up with Linda in New Hampshire. She now lives in the Pacific Northwest, is married, and recently made Linda a grandmother with her first child.

All I was able to learn about Susan Atkins' son, Zezozose Zadfrack, was that he was adopted, reportedly by a physician. The court records have been sealed and Atkins herself does not know where her son is.

Valentine Michael ("Pooh Bear"), the son of Manson and Mary Brunner, was raised by Mary's parents in Eau Claire, Wisconsin. Until the third grade he did not know who his father was and believed his mother to be his older sister. In 1993, Michael told a reporter who tracked him down that he had never visited Manson "nor do I have any desire to see him. He's just some evil person I have nothing to do with." According to Manson Family researcher Bill Nelson, Michael, now twenty-six, lives with his girlfriend and their three-year-old son in a Rocky Mountain state where he is a salesman for a plumbing supply firm. He recently got his real estate license. Michael is deeply appreciative of the fact that his grandparents raised him, and to this day remains closer to them than to his mother.

As to some of those whose lives brought them into contact with Manson and his Family in a significant way, Doris Day's son, record producer Terry Melcher, at whose former home the Tate murders took place and whom Manson unsuccessfully sought to have record him and his music, is now primarily in the hotel and real estate business on the West Coast. He continues, however, to be involved in the music world. Since 1985, he has been the producer of the Beach Boys' recordings. Terry and his wife have become quite active in the civic affairs of the community in which they live.

Gregg Jakobson, who met Manson at Dennis Wilson's home and was the one who introduced Melcher to Manson, whose philosophy on life he found intellectually stimulating, is, to quote him, "half retired and leading the good life" in the charming oceanside community of Laguna Beach, California. Gregg and his wife, comic Lou Costello's daughter, divorced and he has not remarried. He is the part-owner of a Chinese restaurant in nearby Newport Beach, buys and sells antiques, and does a little music composition working with local musicians.

Dennis Wilson, the drummer for the Beach Boys at whose home on Sunset Boulevard Manson, without invitation, moved into with his Family in the late spring of 1968, and who told me, when I sought musical tapes he had made of Manson, that he had destroyed them because "the vibrations connected with them don't belong to this earth," drowned on December 27, 1983, at Marina del Rey, California, while diving off a dock near a friend's boat. The coroner's report provided a possible explanation for the drowning. The alcohol level in Wilson's blood was .26 percent, nearly three times the legal limit for operating a motor vehicle in the state of California. Traces of cocaine and Valium were also found in his system.*

---

*Guns N' Roses wasn't the first rock group to record a Manson song. With minor changes in the lyrics (e.g., "exist" was changed to "resist," "brother" to "lover"), Manson's composition "Cease to Exist" was recorded by the Beach Boys and released on the B side of *Bluebirds over the Mountain* on December 8, 1968, under the new title "Never Learn Not to

George Spahn didn't much care for the rainy Oregon weather nor the ranch he bought there in 1971, and after a year returned to Los Angeles and moved back with his wife, from whom he had been legally separated. Spahn died in late 1974 at the age of eighty-five. One of Spahn's daughters told me that Ruby Pearl, the one-time circus bareback rider and horse wrangler who helped Spahn run the ranch, had accompanied Spahn to Oregon. She bought a smaller ranch in Oregon after Spahn reunited with his wife, and is still living there.

In 1979, Ronnie Howard died in a Los Angeles hospital from injuries sustained in a beating by two unknown male assilants. Laurence Merrick, who produced the 1970 Academy Award-nominated documentary *Manson*, was shot to death in 1977 at his Hollywood studio. The police concluded that both murders were unrelated to Manson or his Family.

After she resolved her parole problems, Virginia Graham opened up a health spa at the Hilton Hawaiian Village Hotel in Honolulu with the $12,000 she received as her share from the Polanski reward money. A survivor, Virginia today is the manager of a fine art gallery in Kailua-Kona, Hawaii,

---

Love.'' The single never got past number 61 on the charts, but both sides of the 45 rpm were included in *20/20*, the Beach boys' last album with Capitol Records the following year. Although the Beach Boys never credited Manson as being the composer, Paul Watkins, Brooks Poston, and Gregg Jakobson each confirmed to me it was Manson's song, and in the 1986 biography of the Beach boys, *Heroes and Villains: The True Story of the Beach Boys*, author Steven Gaines acknowledges this.

Mike Rubin, a New York City writer who has been tracking the rock music scene in America for years, says that in addition to Guns N' Roses, he knows of at least five other rock groups who have either recorded a song of Manson's or a Manson tribute song within the past decade.

In early January of 1994, the industrial hard rock group Nine Inch Nails recorded their most recent album, *Downward Spiral*, at the former Tate residence. Trent Reznor, lead singer and songwriter for the band, says that although he called the jerry-built studio constructed for the recording of the album "Le Pig," and although there are songs in the album like "Piggy" and "March of the Pigs" with confrontational lyrics (the word "pig" was printed in blood by the killers on the front door of the Tate residence and the words "death to pigs" on the living room wall of the LaBianca residence), this was all a coincidence—that the realtor through whom he leased the home failed to tell him it had been the scene of the Tate murders. The "Le Pig" studio was also used by a hard rock group called Marilyn Manson in which lead singer Mr. Manson recorded the vocals for its soon-to-be-released album *Portrait of an American Family*.

and just completed a much expanded version of her 1974 book, *The Joy of Hooking,* titled *Look Who Is Sleeping in My Bed: Madames, Mansions, Murder and Manson.* I appreciated what she said about me in her 1974 book, especially in view of Manson's familiar refrain that I railroaded him. She wrote: "I can't remember how many times we went down to the District Attorney's Office to go over my statement with Vincent Bugliosi. I have to say this about Bugliosi. Although I've never had much love for authority of any kind, he was absolutely fair, straight and honest. He never once even hinted that I might alter my testimony a little bit to help the state's case. He was careful to the other extreme, in fact."

Spahn Ranch was never rebuilt after it was burned to the ground by brush fires that swept the area from Newhall to the sea in September of 1970. The German company that bought the land from George Spahn never developed it into the dude ranch resort for German tourists they had planned. Today, there are no signs that the murderous Manson Family was ever there. All of the ramshackle structures on the ranch are gone and the property, which was eventually sold to the state of California, is deserted, weed-choked land.

The Tate residence went through several owners after Rudi Altobelli, the landlord of the time of the murders. The current owner tore the house down in January of 1994 because he didn't like "the history of the place," and is in the process of constructing an enormous $10 million home that will tower over all other homes in the area. The LaBianca home was owned for years by a Filipino couple, the wife reportedly being a friend of Imelda Marcos. They sold it recently to their daughter and son-in-law.

As for the Manson trial participants today, Irving Kanarek, Manson's lawyer, was ordered to be inactive by the California State Bar on January 29, 1990. He resigned from the bar on October 26, 1990, "with charges pending." I do not know the basis for the charges (being a privileged matter) nor Kanarek's present whereabouts.

Paul Fitzgerald, Patricia Krenwinkel's lawyer, practices law in Beverly Hills and is a prominent member of the criminal defense bar in the Los Angeles area. Fitzgerald, a fine trial lawyer who continues to win more than his share of cases, manages to do so without sacrificing grace and civility in the courtroom, a place inherently inhospitable to both qualities.

Daye Shinn, Susan Atkins' lawyer, was disbarred by the California State Bar on October 16, 1992, for misappropriating a client's money.

Maxwell Keith, the urbane lawyer who replaced Ronald Hughes as Leslie Van Houten's lawyer, is still in the private practice of law in Los Angeles, and this year was honored with a Lifetime Achievement Award from the Los Angeles Criminal Courts Bar Association.

The cause of Ronald Hughes' death in the Sespe Hot Springs area of Ventura County remains a mystery to this day. In 1976, a former member of Manson's Family, understandably wanting to remain anonymous, called me. Without furnishing any additional or supporting information, he stated categorically that Hughes had been murdered by the Manson Family. Lieutenant Greg Husband of the Ventura County Sheriff's office reports that since it was never determined whether Hughes' death was the result of an accident, homicide, or suicide, the Hughes case file is still open, though no investigators are presently assigned to the case. It should be remembered that there is no statute of limitations for the crime of murder.

I write almost full-time, trying cases on a very selective basis. My two most recent nonfiction books, both published in 1991, are *And the Sea Will Tell* and *Drugs in America: The Case for Victory*. I'm presently writing a book on the assassination of President John F. Kennedy. My read on the case? Lee Harvey Oswald killed Kennedy and acted alone.

Curt Gentry, the co-author of this book, went on to write *J. Edgar Hoover: The Man and the Secrets*. Published in 1991, it is the definitive biography of Hoover, and in my opinion and that of many others, a literary *tour de force*.

My co-prosecutor, Aaron Stovitz, has always wanted (and, I feel, is still eminently qualified) to be a judge. In October of 1991, Aaron, who was retired from the DA's office, became a part-time Los Angeles Municipal Court commissioner in San Fernando, a city in the northeast section of Los Angeles County. His sense of humor intact,

Aaron says he is "the Judge Wapner of the San Fernando Valley," and orders anyone who comes to his Small Claims court unprepared "to watch two reruns of *People's Court*."

Judge Charles Older is in retirement, having left the bench in 1987.

In a three-volume work by Jay Robert Nash called *Bloodletters and Badmen,* a who's who of virtually every well-known criminal in American history, Jesse James is on the cover of Volume I, Al Capone on Volume II, and Manson on Volume III. In the elite pantheon of heinous criminals, Manson has made his mark, and he appears to relish this fame, as steeped in infamy as it is.

In the twenty-five years that have elapsed since the atrocities which Charles Manson ordered and masterminded occurred, mass murder, as never before, has almost become a staple in our society. Disgruntled or demented killers flip out, go into a former place of employment, fast-food establishment, law firm, etc., and murder five to ten people or more. Such carnage no longer shocks a desensitized public when reported on the evening news. But fortunately, as of this date, the singularity of Manson's evil and the particular brand of demonic murders he authored have not again been inflicted upon our nation. We can only hope that the ensuing years will be the same.

V.B.
June 1994

Index

Alarcon, Arthur, Judge, 632
Alexander, Adolph, Judge, 628–29
Alexander, Steve, 222
Alexandria, Louella; see Van Houten, Leslie Sue
Alonzo, Maria, 649, 660
Altobelli, Rudi, 8, 13, 20, 48, 50, 70, 299, 303–10, 340, 352, 428, 507
Andrews, Sherry; see Smith, Claudia Leigh
Anger, Kenneth, 639
Asin, Jim, 7, 455
Asin, Ray, 7, 8, 13, 30
Atascadero State Hospital, 514–15, 571
Atkins, Susan Denise, 99, 102–4, 105–7, 110–19, 127–30, 133, 137, 143, 145, 147, 149, 159–60, 164–65, 167, 170, 201, 208–10, 213–14, 217–18, 220, 225–67, 272, 277, 278, 283–84, 288, 291–95, 313, 316, 317, 319, 325–26, 337, 341–69, 378, 383, 390, 394–98, 405–7, 421, 425, 429, 433, 436, 447–48, 464, 489–92, 501, 502–6, 523–24, 536–38, 545, 547–55, 557–58, 566, 573–83, 589–93, 599–603, 607–13, 616–17, 619–21, 629, 632, 639–42, 656, 661–62, 664

Baer, John, 417n
Baggott, King, 264–65, 459
Bailey, Edward Arthur, 105, 642
Bailey, Ella Jo, 148, 233, 339
Bailey, Lawrence Edward, 171, 350, 631
Baker, Eddie, 254–65
Baldwin, Linda, see Cottage, Madaline Joan
Ball, Joseph, 270–71
Barker, Mrs. Arlene, 173–74
Barker Ranch, 101–2, 108, 136, 148, 152, 166–70, 172–77, 205, 209–10, 220, 236, 311–14, 334–36, 374, 376, 426, 474, 509, 515, 580, 589, 642–43, 646, 656
Barnett, Donald, 269
Barrett, Samuel, 566–67, 643
Bartell, Susan, 107, 118, 172
Beach Boys, The, 173, 211, 286, 340, 643
Beatles, The, 1, 99, 288, 300, 317, 321–31, 341, 348, 375, 423, 433, 506, 512–13, 540, 554, 568, 618, 634
Beatty, Warren, 68, 92
Beausoleil, Robert Kenneth (Bobby), 46–47, 102–3, 106, 118, 122, 137–40, 146–48, 164, 181–82, 202–3, 265, 279, 291, 294, 337, 389, 395, 397, 435, 476, 482, 565, 572–73, 576, 584, 586, 588, 603–4, 610–11, 616, 624, 632, 639, 661–64

Benedict Canyon, 4, 41, 111, 264
Benedict Canyon Road, 3, 4, 111, 242, 264, 272, 355
Bennett, Tony, 59
Bergen, Candice, 4, 305
Bern, Paul, 41
Berry, Bob, 311
Benedict Canyon Road, 3
Beverly Glen, 5, 91, 266
Beverly Grove Drive, 5
Big Patty; see Krenwinkel, Patricia
Big Sur, Calif., 36, 372–74, 636
Black Muslims, 332
Black Panthers, 122–23, 139–42, 332, 380, 641
Block, Dr., 188
Bluestein, Dianne; see Lake, Dianne Elizabeth
Boen, Jerrome, 20, 108, 465–66
Boyd, Bill, 219, 274, 288
Boyd, Roland, 274
Bradley, Thomas, 44
Brandt, Steve, 93–94
Brigham, Dr. and Mrs. Merry, 54
Broda, Gary, Sgt., 89, 461
Broom, Sgt. (pseud.), 130–32
Brother Matthew, 636
Brown, Sgt. 142, 159
Brown, Claude, Dr., 592–93, 602–3
Brown, David, Judge, 274, 288
Brown, Kenneth Richard, 171
Brunner, Mary Theresa, 106n, 137, 148–50, 221–22, 233, 254, 292, 375, 389, 392, 395, 397,–98, 419, 420, 448, 510, 567, 584–86, 589, 604, 608, 631–33, 652
Bryant Drive, 32
Brynner, Yul, 68, 92
Bubrick, Sam, 514, 628
Buckles, Jess, Sgt., 21, 46–47, 60, 89, 101
Bugliosi, Gail, 160, 219, 487
Bugliosi, Vincent, Jr., 160, 487
Bugliosi, Vincent T., Deputy District Attorney, birth, schools and degrees, joins L.A. County DA's Office, teaches Beverly Law School, technical consultant TV series, marriage and children, 157; assignment as prosecuting attorney Tate-LaBianca case, 153, 159; immersion in case and intrusion into home life, 160; search of Spahn Ranch, 161–64; opposes Atkins immunity, 164–65; search of Barker Ranch, 165–76; search of Inyo County DA files and raid evidence, 177; interview with Squeaky, Sandy, and other Manson Family girls, 176–80; perusal of Grogan rap sheet, 180–82; sees Manson for first time, 183; study

of DeCarlo tape and Manson criminal record, 184–99; conference with Tate detectives, 199–201; trades information with Inyo DA Fowles, 202; asks LaBianca detectives for report on Manson's activities week of the murders, 201–2; interviews with Manson girls at Sybil Brand, 203–10; apprehension of Watson and suggestion for warrant and pickup, 212–13; conversation with Caballero re deal for Atkins, 213–14; prosecution issues complaint against Krenwinkel and Kasabian, scarcity of evidence against, also Atkins, 215–17; meeting with LAPD Chief Davis, cites weakness of case, 216; LAPD press conference re "solving" of case, 216–17; Watson extradition difficulties, 218–19; requests Gail save papers on Manson Family, 219; Hoyt agrees to cooperate, 220–21; Caballero delivery of Atkins tape to LAPD, revelations and personal reaction, 225–26; confidential memo re Atkins, 227–28; interviews Atkins, 229–30; preparation for taking case to grand jury, 230–31; grand jury, 231–49; re offering of deals, 249–50; grand jury indictments, 250–52; call from Oregon re Atkins' prior arrest, profusion of calls, new developments, 253; discovery of LaBianca wallet and importance as corroboration, plans to have Atkins point out spots where weapons and clothing thrown, 255–57; feeling in L.A. legal community re hopelessness of prosecution's case against Manson, 256–58; scouring LAPD "tubs" for evidence, discovery of Springer interview and "Harold" letter, 262–63; perplexity re Manson's motive, 263–64; TV crew discovers clothing Tate killers wore, Weiss tells LAPD they already have the murder gun, 264–67; need to link gun to Manson, 267; Manson plea for self-representation, judge's reluctant agreement, 268–71; Weber interview and license number revelation, 271–72; Swartz interview, 272–73; Texas politics and Watson extradition, collecting evidence of Manson's domination of Watson, 274–75; Lake interviews and importance of information obtained, 275–77; True interview, 277–78; believes Manson's cockiness due to feeling he will beat rap, fear Manson will request immediate trial, 279–80; memo to Younger re weakness of case, meeting with Tate and LaBianca detectives, after Tate detectives repeatedly fail to deliver gives assignments to La-

Bianca team, 283–86; importance of proving Manson's domination, 285–86; what held back under discovery, 286; search for evidence, 286–87; hears tapes of Manson recording session, Watson extradition blocked, 287–88; discussion with Stovitz re Manson's motive, missing link in Helter Skelter motive, 291–93; pressures and threats against attorneys for Atkins and Kasabian, aware that without Atkins there is no case against Manson, prefers Kasabian over Atkins as star witness, 294–95; has Inyo County refile arson charges against Manson, 295; reinterviews Jakobson, 299–303; interviews Melcher, 303–4; Krenwinkel extradited, 304; interviews Altobelli, 304–8; receives tape of Crockett-Poston interview, 311–15; interviews both, 315–18; interviews Watkins, 318–22; piecing together Manson's motive, Manson's bizarre interpretation of the Bible and Beatles lyrics, Manson's belief in imminent race war, links Manson to bloody words at Tate and LaBianca residences, 322–36; success and failure of various leads, 336–38; interviews Wilson of Beach Boys, 338–41; interviews Kasabian for first time, takes her to Tate residence and other sites, recounting of Family activities from July through night of August 8–9, 1969, 347–57; requests McGann search for knives, 357; fears regarding Kasabian's safety, precautions taken, 357–58, 360; Kasabian taken out of Sybil Brand to trace route killers took on night of August 9–10, 1969, recounting of events of that night, 360–70; press reveals immunity deal for Kasabian, further searches for key sites, assessment of Kasabian as person, 369–70; forces LAPD to search for knives, 370–71; Chapman interview places Krenwinkel at Tate residence week of murders, 371–72; excellent work by LaBianca detectives demolishes Manson's anticipated alibi defense, Manson's trip to Big Sur, Manson's involvement with Esalen Institute, 372–76; Schram interviews, 376–77; assessment of Hughes, 378; thoughts on Kanarek, 378–80; resurrection of Crowe and interview, 380–81; tries to get LAPD to infiltrate Manson Family, 381–82; requests printing exemplars, importance of Krenwinkel's refusal, 383–84; problems of linking Manson to rope and wire cutters, 384–87; shell casings prove murder gun was at Spahn Ranch, 387; Walker interview proves eyeglasses did not belong to killers, 388–89; problems concerning Kasabian's flight from Spahn Ranch, 389–92; Sage, Jacobs, Hannum, Melton, and Robert Kasabian interviews, 392; need for corroboration critical, 392–95; fears DeCarlo will split before trial, 395; personal assessment of Atkins declaration repudiating testimony, 396–97; discovery of Helter Skelter door at LAPD, 399; conference in chambers following substitution of Kanarek for Hughes, 400–2; effort to have Kanarek removed from case, 404–5; reactions to female defendants parroting Manson in court and Kanarek's subornation of perjury charges, 405–7; jury selection, acceptance and swearing in, 411–19; private conversation with Manson, 415–16; fails in attempt to have Grogan's parole revoked, 419–20; delivers People's opening statement, Manson reacts with bribe attempt, 421–29; Kasabian testimony, 430–38; in-chambers discussion of Nixon statement, 439–40; personal opinion of its effect on jurors, 443–44; Kanarek cross-examination of Kasabian, Hughes apology re Kanarek, 440–47; petitions Court for immunity for Kasabian, granted, 447; Hughes cross-examination of Kasabian, 448–50; Sartuchi and Bugliosi interview Flynn, 451–55; other witnesses corroborate Kasabian testimony, Family members' vigil outside Hall of Justice, 455–71; statement in chambers re Hoyt disappearance, 471–72; efforts to link gun to Spahn Ranch and Manson, Hoyt murder attempt, 472–76; problems with Judge Older re establishing Manson-Watson relationship and relevance of Manson's attitude toward blacks, 476–82; conversation with Manson re attempted murder of Hoyt, asks LaBianca detectives to take over Hoyt investigation, 481; Watson's return to California, why courtroom appearance bad tactical move, 483–84; attempts to prevent other murders, confrontation with armed Manson followers and repercussions, 484–87; Manson conversation designating Brenda his chief assassin, 486; hang-up calls, followed by Family, fears for wife and children, death threat by Manson, assigned bodyguard, 487; defense attorneys also afraid of Manson, 487; Hoyt testimony, 489–91; Flynn testimony, 491–99; cited for contempt of court, 498; Graham testimony, 502–6; Jakobson testimony, 506; Koenig testimony and unforeseen problems, 507–9; list of future prosecution witnesses, 510; Melcher testimony, Manson privately admits visits to 10050 Cielo Drive, 511–12; Manson's conversation re his belief in law and order, 512–13; Manson says he can cure Watson, reply, 515; Lake testimony, 515–16; Skrdla and Deering testimony on LSD, 517–18; prosecution rests, 519; Manson and female defendants demand to testify, Older permits, 523; Manson testimony outside presence jury, 524–31; court recess, Hughes disappearance, unsuccessful search, rumored murdered by Family, 531–34; prosecution opening argument, 536–41; defense arguments, response, 541–47; final summation, 547–53; jury deliberation, 554–56; records indicate Manson's father may have been black, 555–56; Judgment Day threat, theft hand grenades confirmed, 556–57; guilt trial verdict, 557–59; start penalty trial, prosecution calls only two witnesses and rests, 563; penalty trial defense, 563–64; bad strategy calling parents first, 566; Barrett testimony, 567; Fromme testimony, 567–69; Good testimony, 569–70; return of Manson and three female defendants to court, doubts as to Manson's taking stand, 570–71; Share testimony re "copycat" motive, 571–74; Atkins testimony, 575–81; jury sequestration ended, 581; Krenwinkel testimony, 582–83; Older berates Kanarek and accuses Shinn of violating publicity order, 583–84; Van Houten testimony, 584–87; Kasabian recalled, 588; Grogan testimony, 589–90; called as defense witness, 590; Caballero-Kanarek clash, 591; challenges Tweed's testimony re effects LSD, 592–94; learns Brown report on Krenwinkel implicates Manson, 592–93; Fort's testimony, 595–97; interview with and testimony of Hochman, 597–603; prosecution's opening argument penalty trial, 605–6; defense arguments, 606–8; Kay reports Manson death threat to press, tries to stop publication but unsuccessful, Older again sequesters jury, 608–9; prosecution's final argument, rebuttal of defense contentions, demolishes "copycat" motive and Kasabian's alleged leadership of Family, 609–15; defense's final arguments, 615–16; jury verdict and reactions, 616–19; sentencing of Manson, Atkins, Krenwinkel, and Van Houten, 620–21; Watson trial, 625–29; rumor of plan to break out Manson, 630; Hawthorne shootout, trial, and bizarre plan to free all Manson Family members, 631–32; Manson defends Bugliosi after long conversation during Hinman-Shea trial, 633–35; Manson's beliefs and sources considered, 635–41; remaining mysteries and discussion of other possible Manson murders, 641–52; analysis of Manson's control over followers, 653–57; fate of Manson Family members, 658–64

Bugliosi, Wendy, 160, 487
Bullington, Robert, 5
Buntline, Ned, 74
Burbridge, Robert, Officer, 7n, 9–12, 14, 455
Burdick, A. H., Lt., 48–51, 108–9
Burke, Patricia Anne; see Gillies, Catherine Irene
Burrell, Rusty, 634
Burton, Richard, 36, 503
Busch, Joseph, 164–65, 342
Byrne, Robert, Rev., 32

Caballero, Richard, 213–14, 217–18, 220, 225–26, 227–29, 231, 255, 258–60, 269, 293–94, 341, 358–60, 577, 590–91
Calkins, Robert, Sgt., 21, 89, 161–62, 200–1, 257, 266, 284, 470–71, 472, 481
Capistrano; see Gillies, Catherine Irene
Capote, Truman, 88, 663
Cappy; see Gillies, Catherine Irene
Carpenter, Capt., 337, 358, 360, 383–84
Carson, Johnny, 88
Caruso, Paul, 218, 259, 590–91
Chapman, Winifred, 5–8, 13–15, 23–25, 69–71, 177, 200, 230, 247–48, 337, 371–72, 427, 455, 468, 519
Chasen, Frances, 419n
Chatsworth, Calif., 47, 101, 134, 138n, 161, 492, 644
Chavez, Antonio, Judge, 215
Choate, Raymond, Judge, 535, 629, 633
Cielo Drive (10050), 3–8, 11, 16, 18–21, 25–26, 30–32, 35, 39, 42–43, 52, 57, 64, 69, 70, 72, 73, 74–75, 78, 103, 117, 147, 163, 176, 200, 213, 226, 230, 248, 250–52, 264, 287, 299, 303, 305, 308, 310, 347, 351–52, 355, 375, 386, 422, 427–28, 455, 466, 487, 507, 628, 658
Cielo Drive (10070), 4, 7
Cielo Drive (10090), 7
Claborn, J., Sgt., 57
Clem; see Grogan, Steven
Clements, Wendell, 21
Cline, Edward L., Sgt., 55, 461
Coburn, James, 68
Cohen, Jerry, 259, 645–47
Como, Kenneth, 631–33
Compton, Buck, 215
Conrad, Robert, 157

Cooper, Priscilla, 648–49
Cooper, Sherry Ann, 220–21, 646
Cord, Alex, 68
Corona Women's Prison, 118, 127, 132, 203
Cottage, Madaline Joan, 107–8, 170, 645
Country Sue; see Bartell, Susan
Cox, Dennis, Deputy Sheriff, 177
Craig, James, 648, 650
Crockett, Paul, 168, 177, 283, 311–18, 335, 396, 493–94, 499n, 529
Crowe, Bernard, 380–81, 473, 513, 563, 641–42
Crystal; see Alonzo, Maria
Cupid; see Beausoleil, Robert Kenneth
Curtis, Tony, 40

Darrah, James, Judge, 649
Darrow, Gene, 556–58
Daut, Kenneth, Jr., 419n, 443
Davis, Angela, 167n
Davis, Bruce McGregor, 107–8, 126, 137–38, 143–46, 148, 150, 152, 153, 171, 202, 207–8, 254, 311, 341, 361, 389, 395–96, 420, 534–35, 629, 632, 635n, 645–48, 664
Davis, Edward, Chief LAPD, 164–65, 216–17, 231
Davis, Scott Bell; see Brown, Kenneth Richard
Dawson, Alva, 417, 443, 555n
Day, Doris, 4, 112, 211, 305
Deasy, Michael, 248
Death Valley, Calif., 165, 311, 324, 330, 426, 493, 626, 642
Death Valley National Monument, 101
DeCarlo, Daniel (Danny), 103, 119–20, 124–26, 130–50, 160–64, 167, 178, 181–82, 205, 220–21, 230, 235, 251–52, 267, 284, 288, 292, 319, 338, 361, 376, 384–86, 395, 476–83, 528, 543, 588, 644, 658
Deemer, Earl, Lt., 80–87, 281, 647
Deering, Harold, Dr., 517–18
DeGrimston, Robert; see Moore, Robert
Delaney, Clida, 642
Del Gaudio, John, 72
Dell, George, Judge, 288–91, 298, 359, 398, 401
Deneuve, Catherine, 37
DeRosa, Jerry Joe, Officer, 7–12, 14–15, 29, 455, 470
Dies, Martin, Jr., 288
Ditman, Keith, Dr., 595
Doe, Jane, #59, 647
Doe, John #85; see Parent, Steven Earl
Dohrn, Bernadine, 296
Dolan, Harold, 57, 251, 465–69, 548
Donkey Dan; see DeCarlo, Daniel
Dorgan, Joe, 53–54, 90
Dorman, D. E., Officer, 21
Douglas, Kirk, 68
Douglass, Robert, 419n
Dreiser, Vera, Dr., 132, 203
Drynan, Thomas, Officer, 253, 563
Duke, Patty, 39

Easton Drive (9845), 71
Easton Drive (9860), 41
Eggar, Samantha, 305
86 George; see Knoll, George
Einstoss, Ron, 256
Elder, Lauren, 531–32, 650
Ellis, John, 419n
Ensenada Blvd. (12881), 255
Esalen Institute, 373–74, 636
Escalante, Frank, Sgt., 251
Euchts, Christine Marie; see Brunner, Mary Theresa
Evans, Mrs. Shirley, 417n

Fagan, Sterry, Judge, 419–20
Farr, William, 506, 539, 659–60
Farrow, Mia, 39, 59, 342
Father Flanagan's Boys Town, 186
Father John, 636
Finken, John, Deputy Coroner, 22
Fisher, Duke, Dr., 592
Fisher, Eddie, 503
Fitzgerald, Paul, 256–57, 304, 378, 405, 411–12, 416–17, 419, 426–28, 431, 437–42, 458, 464, 468–72, 482, 488, 493, 501, 505, 509–11, 516–19, 523, 531–34, 541–45, 547, 550–51, 559, 564, 567–68, 573, 575–78, 587–88, 590, 593n, 599, 602–4, 608, 612, 616
Fleischman, Gary, 226, 249–50, 341–42, 347, 357, 369, 391, 451
Fletcher, Kitt, 260, 505
Flicker, Marvin, Dr., 44, 71
Flynn, John Leo (Juan), 314, 318, 399, 451–55, 491–99, 521, 529, 599, 613, 641, 658
Fokianos, John, 34–35, 64, 461
Folger, Abigail (Gibby), 8, 18–19, 22, 26, 35, 42–45, 68, 70–72, 86–88, 127, 177, 220, 238–40, 305, 307, 337, 344, 354–55, 373n, 403, 458, 467–68, 542, 553, 558, 578, 582–83, 644
Folger, Inez Mijia, 19, 72
Folger, Peter, 19
Fonda, Henry, 68, 305
Fonda, Peter, 68
Forsher, James, 531–32, 650
Fort, Joel, Dr., 595–97, 627
Fowles, Frank, DA, 166–67, 173–77, 179–83, 202, 210, 295, 315, 372
Friedman, Jerrold, 52, 510
Fromme, Lynette Alice, 135, 176–80, 219, 225, 229, 233, 275, 278, 294, 376, 390, 429, 455, 460, 474–75, 481, 484–85, 535, 567–70, 608, 624–25, 632, 648, 660–61
Frykowski, Wojiciech (Voytek), 8, 13, 18–22, 26, 43–48, 65–66, 69, 72, 83, 86–88, 104, 113–14, 127, 146, 226, 238–41, 267, 307, 337, 344, 354–55, 397, 425, 434, 446, 459, 468, 548, 553, 578, 610, 644

Galindo, Danny, Sgt., 21, 56–57, 252, 461
Galloway, Byron, 475
Gardiner, Jack, 166, 180, 275–76, 515
Gardner, Fred (pseud.), 67–68, 90

Garretson, William Eston, 8, 13–14, 20–21, 25, 29–31, 48–52, 59, 71, 73, 74–75, 90, 93, 98, 200–1, 427–28
Gaul, Doreen, 647
George, Carl, 643
Gibbens, Buck, 166, 275–76
Gibran, Kahlil, 366, 393
Gillies, Catherine Irene, 107–8, 173, 603–4, 613, 660
Girt, D. L., 20
Gleason, William, Sgt., 161, 377n, 479, 488
Glutz, Sadie Mae; see Atkins, Susan Denise
Glutz, Zezozose Zadfrack, 129, 170
Golar Wash, 174, 211
Goldman, Ronald, 357
Good, Sandra Collins (Sandy), 148, 170, 176–79, 202, 219, 225, 229, 256, 294, 359, 366, 375, 389, 392, 420, 429, 460, 465, 484–87, 510, 516, 521, 559, 569–70, 608, 618–19, 624, 632–33, 651–52, 660
Goucher, William, 650
Graham, Virginia, 104–7, 110–19, 129, 132, 203, 213–14, 216, 226, 239, 242, 316, 397, 425, 432n, 502–6, 543, 548, 590, 641–42, 659
Granado, Joe, 15–18, 22–23, 57, 74, 165, 176–77, 230, 249, 251, 283, 337, 386, 459–60, 469
Gravante, F., Sgt., 15
Gregoire, J. J., Lt., 15
Gresham Street (20910), 254, 324, 330, 332, 333
Griffith Park, 34, 123, 141, 276
Grogan, Steven, 121, 125–26, 143, 146–48, 167, 169, 174, 180, 207, 220, 226, 243–44, 314, 339, 341, 361, 365–68, 394, 396, 419–20, 464, 474, 481, 535, 589–90, 608, 625, 629, 631–32, 642, 662–64
Guenther, Charles, Sgt., 46–47, 101–3, 143, 161–64, 181
Guerrero, Frank, 69–70, 428
Gutierrez, Manuel ("Chick"), Sgt., 89, 119, 134, 136, 143, 200, 202–6, 254, 368, 372, 392–93, 399, 500, 510, 516
Gypsy; see Share, Catherine

Habe, Marina, 642, 646
Hagen, Peter, Lt., 201, 211
Haight-Ashbury, 222–23, 229, 232, 416, 425, 636
Hamic, David Lee, 172
Hamilton, George, 68
Hannum, David, 389–90, 392
Harlow, Jean, 41
Hatami, Shahrokh, 307–10, 374n, 506–7
Haught, John Philip, 107–8, 118, 152–53, 171, 207–8, 534, 645–47, 649
Helder, Robert J., Lt., 21, 47–48, 89, 97, 110, 159, 161, 176, 199, 212, 216, 262, 308, 392
Henderson, Ed, Sgt., 21, 29
Henry, R. C., Deputy Coroner, 35
Hepburn, Katharine, 305

Herrera, Gaston, Deputy Coroner, 35

Hines, Mrs. Evelyn, 417n

Hinman, Gary, 46, 101–4, 109, 118, 122, 137–40, 146–47, 165, 179, 181–82, 206–7, 209, 213–14, 220, 228, 239, 265, 395, 397–99, 503, 534, 572–73, 575–77, 580–86, 604–5, 607, 610–11, 629, 641, 644

Hitler, Adolf, 317, 415, 493, 614, 639–41

Hochman, Joel Simon, Dr., 597–603, 612, 623, 639, 662

Hollopeter, Charles, 359, 377–78

Houchin, Bryce, Sgt., 64

Houghton, Robert, Asst. Chief LA-PD, 91, 96–97

Howard, Ronnie, 104–5, 111n, 116, 118, 127–33, 142–43, 145–47, 153, 159–60, 164, 167, 181, 203, 208, 214, 216, 226, 241–42, 261–62, 397, 425, 432n, 504–5, 543, 548, 579, 581, 590, 641, 659

Hoyt, Barbara, 220–21, 436, 471–76, 481, 485, 489–90, 535, 589, 625, 631, 641, 646, 658

Hubbard, L. Ron, 636; see also Scientology

Huebelhurst, Ruth Ann; see Moorehouse, Ruth Ann

Hughes, Howard, 134

Hughes, Ronald, 258, 377–80, 400, 404, 447–50, 456, 464, 469, 509, 511, 514, 516, 531–34, 536, 620, 648, 650–51

Hurkos, Peter, 75–76, 85, 88

Hurst, Dennis, 72, 428

Independence, Calif., 102, 108–9, 152, 165–66, 172–73, 176, 183, 201, 207, 210–11, 225, 230, 252, 254, 256, 275–76, 311, 360, 386n, 403, 484

Ireland, Tim, 4, 455, 541

Jack Frost store, 251–52, 336, 384–85, 480

Jacobs, Jeffrey, 390, 392

Jakobson, Gregg, 211, 213, 230, 251, 287, 293, 299–303, 313, 317, 321–36, 340, 477, 506–7, 635, 654

Jardin, Patti Sue; see Gillies, Catherine Irene

Jesus, Christopher; see Haught, John Philip

Johns, Lt. (pseud.), 130–31

Jones, Christopher, 305

Jones, Gerold (pseud.), 65–66, 77–78, 85–86, 90

Jones, Larry; see Bailey, Lawrence Edward

Jones, Tom, 118, 503

Kaczanowski, Witold (Witold K), 65

Kamadoi, Gene, Sgt., 165

Kampman, Mrs. Victoria, 419n

Kanarek, Irving, 378–80, 398–407, 411, 413, 419, 422, 426–27, 430–36, 439–42, 445–48, 454–56, 464, 467–69, 472–73, 481–82, 486, 487–

99, 505–14, 516, 525, 530, 539, 543–45, 547–51, 559, 566, 568–69, 571–73, 578–79, 583, 585–91, 600, 603–5, 606–11, 615, 619, 630, 633–34

Karlson, Eric, 5

Karpis, Alvin, 197

Kasabian, Angel (Nathan), 359–60, 370

Kasabian, Linda Drouin, 129, 147, 149, 208, 210, 213, 215, 217, 218, 226, 236–37, 242, 244, 249–53, 255–57, 283–84, 288, 291, 295, 341–44, 347–71, 375–76, 386–94, 401, 414–15, 430–38, 440–42, 445–51, 455–58, 464, 467, 470, 474, 479, 489, 492, 508–9, 517, 529, 541–44, 547–52, 572–80, 588–89, 599, 609–11, 616, 626–27

Kasabian, Robert, 342, 347, 389–92, 451, 588

Kasabian, Tanya, 342, 347, 370, 389–92, 434, 450

Katie; see Krenwinkel, Patricia

Katsuyama, David, Deputy Medical Examiner, 60, 63–64, 230, 252, 461–64

Katz, Burton, 265, 379, 397, 629

Kay, Steven, 465, 478, 502, 504, 608, 629

Kay, Mrs. Terry, 71

Keene, William, Judge, 255–56, 265, 268–71, 288, 291, 298, 358–59, 377–78, 394

Keith, Maxwell, 532–33, 536, 546, 549–50, 564, 569, 573, 583–88, 590, 593n, 595, 597–98, 601, 604, 607, 614–16, 619–20

Kellerman, Sally, 305

Kendall, John, 417, 539

Kennedy, Robert F., 110, 664

Kerr, Deborah, 37

Kilgrow, Raymond, 16

Kloman, William, 60

Klorman, Stanley, Sgt., 18–19

Knoll, George, 137

Koenig, Charles, 255, 507–9

Koits, James, Judge, 629

Kosinski, Jerzy, 43

Kott, Seymour, 4, 5

Kott, Mrs. Seymour, 4

Krenwinkel, Mrs. Dorothy, 563–64

Krenwinkel, Joseph, 215, 219, 563–64

Krenwinkel, Patricia, 149, 170, 206, 208–10, 215–17, 219, 226, 233, 240–46, 250–53, 275, 278, 283, 304, 337, 339, 344, 361–65, 371, 378, 383–84, 390, 395, 403–6, 416–17, 421, 425, 429, 433, 436–37, 457, 464, 467–68, 501, 510, 516–17, 537, 541–45, 547–49, 552–53, 557–59, 563–64, 582–83, 589, 592–94, 599–604, 607–9, 612–13, 617, 621, 632, 639, 661–64

Kummer, Thomas John; see Sebring, Jay

LaBianca, Leno, 33–35, 53–58, 60–64, 66–68, 90, 108–9, 131, 133, 147, 209, 217, 226, 245–46, 252,

261–64, 277–78, 284–85, 335–37, 344, 363–65, 374, 382–83, 399, 446–47, 461–64, 466, 468, 515, 553, 577, 583, 610, 644
LaBianca, Rosemary, 33–35, 53–58, 60–64, 66–68, 108–9, 131, 133, 147, 177, 209, 217, 226, 245–46, 252, 256, 261–64, 277–78, 284–85, 292, 335–37, 344, 363–65, 374, 382–83, 399, 446–47, 461–64, 466, 468, 507, 515–16, 549, 553, 577, 582–86, 598, 610, 644
Lake, Dianne Elizabeth, 171, 179, 203–5, 252, 275–77, 349, 402–3, 463, 515–17, 529, 542, 546, 549–50, 608, 627, 658
Lally, Eleanor, 451
Lane, Robert Ivan, 170
Lappen, Chet, 303
LaVey, Anton, 639
Lawford, Peter, 41
Leavy, J. Miller, 159, 342
Lee, William, Sgt., 46, 74, 161–63, 176, 251, 267, 380, 387, 472
LeFebure, John, 72–73
Lennon, John, 510
LePage, Paul, Lt., 89, 159, 164–65, 199, 225, 262
Levin, Ira, 39
Lewis, Barbara, 70–71
Lewis, Jerry, 59
Little Patty; see Cottage, Madaline Joan
Lomax, Ed, 230, 251
Longview Valley Road (3627), 90–91
Los Angeles Police Department (LAPD), 5, 7, 19–21, 26n, 27–31, 36n, 39–40, 42, 47, 50, 52, 54, 61, 65–66, 70, 71n, 74–78, 91–93, 96–97, 101, 104, 111n, 119, 127, 130, 132–33, 140, 142, 145, 159, 164–65, 176, 184, 193–94, 201–3, 211–17, 218, 220, 225, 251–52, 255–57, 260, 262–67, 271, 277, 308, 311, 335–36, 350–51, 369, 371, 377, 380, 392, 427, 451–52, 454, 470–71, 474, 479, 495, 508, 517, 519, 548, 625, 627, 642, 644, 658
Los Angeles Sheriff's Office (LASO), 46–47, 61, 161, 183–84, 203, 214–15, 217, 254, 347, 377n, 417, 451, 479, 500, 533, 556, 644, 648
Lovett, Charles Allen, 631
LSD, 45, 76, 84, 110, 127, 223, 230, 248n, 263, 275, 277, 317–18, 333, 373, 431, 437, 442, 475, 490, 517–18, 535, 540, 565, 576, 589, 591–97, 601, 625, 639, 643, 653–54
Lucarelli, Roxie, 252
Lucas, Malcolm, Judge, 359
LuLu; see Van Houten, Leslie Sue
Lutesinger, Kathryn (Kitty), 102–4, 118, 143, 147, 163, 170, 200, 337, 376, 632
Lyon Street, 232

Maas, Peter, 287
McBride, William, II, 417n, 443, 555, 618

McCann, Brenda; see Pitman, Nancy Laura
McCauley, K. J., Inspector, 56, 64
McGann, Michael J., Sgt., 21, 26, 29, 86–89, 124, 126, 134, 143, 164, 167, 177, 200–1, 206–10, 250, 257, 266, 284, 357, 360, 370, 456, 481, 641
McKellar, William, Sgt., 216, 510
McKenzie, Mrs. Thelma, 417n, 443, 618
Mackey, Bobby, 565
McKinney, Texas, 212, 218–19
McLarty, Sam, Sgt., 228
McMillan, Bruce; see Davis, Bruce McGregor
McMurray, John P., Judge, 167
McNeil, Edwin, Dr., 190–91, 193
McQueen, Steve, 27, 41, 59, 68, 118, 503
Madden, John, 15, 19
Maddox, Kathleen, 184–86
Maddox, Luther, 185
Madigan, Larry (pseud.), 65–66, 77–78, 85–86, 90
Madlock, Robert C., Lt., 15, 21, 31
Manson, Charles Luther, 193, 197
Manson, Charles Milles, mentioned at Tate autopsy, tip ignored, 47; cited as suspect on LaBianca investigative report, 98; leader of cult, arrested in Barker and Spahn Ranch raids, 101; linked to Tate and LaBianca murders and a slaying in Death Valley, tip ignored, 105; names Atkins "Sadie Mae Glutz," 107; in jail in Independence, interviewed by LAPD officers, no report made, Sgt. Patchett takes sample leather thongs to L.A. for comparison, 108–9; Springer interview re recruitment and Manson's startling admission re murders, 119–27; Atkins tells Howard Manson is both Christ and Devil, 129; De-Carlo interview concerning Manson and his Family, 130, 133–53; arrival at Spahn Ranch, early days at Spahn, efforts to recruit Straight Satans, 134–37; DeCarlo tells police of involvement in Hinman murder, fondness for guns, murders of Black Panther and Shea, power to make others kill for him, 137–53; quotation from, 155; favorite firing spot Spahn Ranch, 163; seizure of belongings in Barker raid, 166; Bugliosi cites in Barker Ranch search warrant, 167; Family's arrival in Death Valley and apprehension and arrest in Barker raid recounted, 167–73; lessons taught Squeaky and Sandy, 177–79; arraignment on Michigan loader arson charge, Bugliosi sees for first time, describes, 183; background 1934–67, 184–99; birth, illegitimate, mystery father's identity, problems with mother, early years with

aunt, 184–85; turbulent life after mother's release from prison, sent to Gibault School for Boys, runs away, commits first crimes, sent to Boys Town, escape, commits first armed robbery at, 186; sentenced to Indiana School for Boys, runs away 18 times, convicted Dyer Act, confined to National Training School for Boys, 186–87; psychiatric examination, transferred to honor camp, 188; sodomy offense, transfer to federal reformatory at Petersburg, Va., further offenses, transfer to federal reformatory at Chillicothe, Ohio, car thefts, arrival in California, arrest, request for psychiatric help, 189–90; psychiatric examination, probation granted, skips court hearing, arrested, sentenced to Terminal Island, son born, 190–91; escape attempt, divorce, release on parole, 191–92; pimping, under surveillance by FBI, arrested for cashing forged and stolen U.S. Treasury check, deal, 192–93; court-ordered psychiatric examination, Stevens' plea, suspended sentence and probation, 193–94; violates Mann Act, marries Leona Stevens, arrest in Texas, sentenced to McNeil Island, 194–95; staff evaluation, study of Scientology, divorce, reference to second child, obsession with Beatles, returned to Terminal Island, 195–98; request to remain in prison denied, release March, 1967, birth of the Family in San Francisco's Haight-Ashbury, 198; Bugliosi's analysis of criminal record, 198–99; rumor will go alibi, Bugliosi asks LaBianca detectives for detailed report on activities week of the murders, 202; Manson Family girls interviewed concerning, 203–10; Jakobson fascination with "Manson package," 211; Melcher interview, recalls time Manson outside gate 10050 Cielo, 213; not mentioned by name in LAPD press conference, 217; Hoyt disclosures, 220–21; birth of Family recounted, speculation regarding how developed incredible control over others, birth of son, 221–24; revelations on Atkins tape, 226; Atkins-Bugliosi interview, 229–30; Atkins' grand jury testimony re how she met Manson, his direction of Family, his ordering of Tate and LaBianca murders, 231–49; DeCarlo's grand jury testimony concerning, 251–52; charged with Tate-LaBianca murders, brought to L.A., 254; arraignment, Court appoints Fitzgerald to represent, watch-stopping incident, 256; Atkins "kite" to Howard re Manson second coming of Christ, 261–62; Bugliosi discovers Springer statement with Manson confession, 262; Bugliosi perplexity re motive, 263–64; need to link murder gun to, 267; request to dismiss attorney and defend self, Judge Keene reluctantly grants, 268–71; Swartz interviews re borrowing car, Shea disappearance, 272–73; efforts to have Krenwinkel return, plans for umbrella defense, 275; Harold True places Manson in house next to LaBianca residence, prosecution's apprehension that might demand immediate trial, 277–78; rope purchase, 284; importance of establishing domination, 285–86; granted discovery, 286; manipulation of the defense, 288–90; unique motion by "Charles Manson, also known as Jesus Christ; Prisoner," denied, 290–91; claim of DA pressure on Atkins, 291; problems establishing motive, 291–93; pressures on other defendants and their attorneys, 294–95; arson charges refiled, 295; unlikely emergence as counterculture hero, 296–98; request for early trial, change of venue motion denied, 298; Jakobson's talks with Manson, revelations concerning his philosophy, domination, race ideas, Helter Skelter, 299–303; Melcher reluctantly reveals Manson visited Altobelli at guest house, Altobelli and Hatami confirm, Sharon Tate saw man who would order her murder, 303–10; Crockett and Poston taped recollections, 311–15; importance of name change, 316; Poston on programming techniques, 317; Watkins provides missing link in Helter Skelter motive, 318–23; unique interpretation of Bible and Beatles lyrics, 323–36; hint of possible defense strategy, 338; additional examples of domination, 338; messages to Atkins, 341; quotation from, 345; Kasabian interviews, revelations concerning, 344, 347–56; meeting with Atkins, persuades her to change attorneys and recant, 358; Judge Keene revokes pro per status, Hollopeter appointed attorney, 358–59; Kasabian re Manson's activities the night of the LaBianca murders, 361–69; LaBianca detectives report on activities week of murders, proof of presence at Spahn Ranch on August 8, 1969, 372–76; link with Esalen Institute, 373–74; Schram testimony re conducting murder school at Barker, 376–77; substitution of Hughes for Hollopeter, 377–78; resurrection of Crowe and reaction, 380–81; linked to rope, gun, and wire cutters, 386–87; conversation with Sage re Kasabian murder claims, 390; Kasabian's fear of, 391; files affidavit of prejudice against Judge Keene, trial assigned to Judge Older, 394; indictment on Hinman murder, Kanarek substituted for Hughes, conversation with Bugliosi re fair trial, 398–402; turns back on judge, removed to lockup, refusals to return, 404; Kanarek asserts arrest illegal, Bugliosi retort, 406–7; first reaction of prospective jurors, 411; attitude toward jury selection, conversation with Bugliosi, challenged to take stand, 413–16; carving of X on forehead and press statement, 421; prosecution opening statement regarding, 421–26; bribe offer to Maupin, 429; Kasabian testimony regarding, 431–38; declared guilty by President Nixon, own statement, holds up Nixon headline for jury to see, 438–44; passes letter to Kasabian, extract of contents, 448; Hughes cross-examination of Kasabian re Manson's divinity, 449–50; Flynn interview reveals incriminating admission, 451–53; instructions re honing of knives, 457; threatens to dismiss Kanarek, observation on progress of trial thus far, 458–59; how Katsuyama error could provide alibi, 463–64; prints not found at LaBianca residence, 466–67; prosecution efforts to link gun to, 472; Walleman testimony re shooting of Crowe, 473; Hoyt murder attempt, 474–76; DeCarlo testimony regarding race ideas, 479; conversation with Bugliosi, denies ordering Hoyt murder, 480–81; prosecution's efforts to establish racial attitudes, 476–82; Squeaky ex officio leader of Family in his absence, 484; conversation with Bugliosi designating Brenda his chief assassin, threatens to kill Bugliosi and judge, 486–87; threats against Kanarek, feared by other attorneys, 487–88; Flynn animosity toward and testimony against, 491–99; attacks Judge Older, 500–2; Jakobson testimony regarding, 506–7; Melcher testimony regarding, privately admits to Bugliosi visits to 10050 Cielo Drive, 510–11; tells Bugliosi he advocates law and order, 512–13; Poston on Manson's power, 514; request to see Watson, claims can cure, 514–15; instructions to Lake, 516; female defendants attempt to clear of involvement, attorneys' resistance, 523; lengthy testimony outside presence jury, 523–31; possible threat to Fitzgerald overheard,

533; Hughes disappearance after conflict with Manson, 533–34; creates disturbance, again removed from court, 536; Bugliosi's references to in opening argument, 540–41; Kanarek's portrayal as peaceful, non-violent man, remarks from lockup, 543–45; Keith puts hat on Manson during opening argument, 546; Bugliosi references to in final summation, 547–53; possibility father may have been black, 555–56; guilt trial verdict and reaction, 557–59; loyalty of girls to and plans to set free, 559–60; written statement after conviction, 561; Barrett minimizes earlier charges against, 566–67; Fromme testimony concerning, 567–69; Good testimony concerning, 569–70; return to court, 570; indications won't take stand, 571; Share's attempt to absolve, Bugliosi demolishes her story, 571–74; Atkins testimony, Bugliosi's dilemma having to re-prove guilt, 575–82; Van Houten testimony concerning, 584–87; Caruso's remark re Atkins' fear of, 591; Atkins' remarks to Caballero re Helter Skelter motive, 591; mention in Brown report, 593; trims beard and proclaims self the Devil, 594; anger at Fort's testimony, 596; Hochman's testimony and request for interview, 597–600; Gillies testimony in support of, 603–4; Pitman alibi testimony and rebuttal, 604–5; references to in Bugliosi's opening argument penalty trial, 607–8; threatens retribution if given death penalty, 608; references to in Bugliosi's final argument, 609–15; Kanarek implies Manson may be Christ, 615; Keith concedes Manson's domination, 615–16; jury vedict, reactions and comment, 616–20; sentenced, 620–21; references to in Watson trial, 626–28; Hinman-Shea trial and verdict, 629–30; rumor of Family plans to free, 630; Hawthorne shootout and trial, 631–33; defends Bugliosi after conversation during Hinman-Shea trial, 633–35; sources of beliefs considered, 635–41; other possible Manson Family murders, 641–52; Bugliosi's analysis of how obtained power over others, 653–57; sentence reduced to life imprisonment, eligible to apply for parole in 1978, 661–64.

Manson, Charles Jr., 190–91
Manson, Leona Rae, 193–94, 197
Manson, Michael, 223
Manson, Rosalie Jean, 190–92
Manzella, Anthony, 629
Marioche; *see* Brunner, Mary Theresa

Martin, Dean, 40, 340
Martin, Deana, 340
Martin, Don, Capt., 51–52
Martinez, David, 70–71
Marvin, Lee, 68
Marz, Frank, Sgt., 228
Maupin, William, Deputy Sheriff, 429
Mauss, H. L., Deputy, 383
Melcher, Terry, 14, 39, 69, 112, 117, 200, 211–13, 230, 236, 248, 251, 257, 287, 293, 299, 303–6, 310, 334, 340, 510–11, 628
Melcher, William, 661
Melton, Charles, 347–48, 392, 451
Merrick, Laurence, 651–52
Mesmer, Marie, 417n, 443, 618
Minette, Manon; see Share, Catherine
Monfort, Michael, 648–50
Montgomery, Charles; see Watson, Charles Denton
Montgomery, Maurice, 212
Montgomery, Tom, Sheriff, 212, 215
Moore, Robert, 300, 636
Moorehouse, Dean, 511
Moorehouse, Ruth Ann, 148, 170, 179, 205–6, 220, 252, 316n, 345, 474–75, 481, 490, 535, 588–89, 608, 625, 641
Morglea, Randy; see Todd, Hugh Rocky
Morse, Rachel Susan; see Moorehouse, Ruth Ann
Moser, Linda Dee; see Brunner, Mary Theresa
Mossman, Sgt., 142–45, 159
Mulholland Drive, 242
Murphy, Audie, 218
Murray, William, Bailiff, 500–1, 540, 639
Musich, Donald, 465, 478
Myers, Catherine; see Gillies, Catherine Irene
Myers Ranch, 173–74, 220, 221n, 489–90, 493, 603

Nader, Saladin, 393, 451, 544
Neiswender, Mary, 538
Nelson, Louis, Warden, 663
Newman, Paul, 41, 68
Newton, Huey, 297
Nielsen, Michael, Sgt., 89, 119, 134, 143, 165, 200, 203, 215, 218–19, 276, 393
Nielson, Blackie, 186
Nietzsche, Friedrich Wilhelm, 301, 317, 641
Niven, David, 37
Nixon, Richard Milhous, 438–39, 442–44, 512
Noguchi, Thomas, Coroner, 21–22, 35, 40, 46–47, 63, 230, 248, 267, 456–58, 479, 551

Ocean Front Walk (1101), 368, 451
Older, Charles H., Judge, 394, 401–6, 411–15, 418–19, 426–36, 440–47, 456–58, 464–67, 469, 476–79, 486–88, 496–502, 504–6, 509–13,

517–19, 523–24, 527, 530–33, 536–40, 544, 551, 553–54, 556–57, 575–77, 581–84, 587–90, 609, 615–17, 620–21, 659–60
Old Topanga Road (964), 46; see also Hinman, Gary
Orr, Ann, Bailiff, 540
Ouisch, see Moorehouse, Ruth Ann
Owens, Dr., 132
Owens, Leslie; see Van Houten, Leslie Sue

Palmer, George, Deputy Sheriff, 377n
Palmer, Kathy, 72
Parent, Juanita, 31–33
Parent, Steven Earl, 20, 22, 25–26, 31–33, 35, 45–46, 49–52, 68–73, 127, 237, 250, 267, 337, 344, 352, 427, 434, 460, 510, 541, 544, 548, 551–53, 576, 578, 644
Parent, Wilfred, 31–33, 247, 427
Parker, Kathleen, Judge, 419
Parker Center, 31, 48, 80, 101, 126, 130, 143, 265
Part, Marvin, 269, 288–89, 586–87
Patchett, Frank, Sgt., 89, 108–9, 119, 176, 200, 202, 207, 211–13, 252, 368–69, 372, 393, 403, 509
Patton State Hospital, 277, 402–3, 515
Pearl, Ruby, 134–35, 385, 646
Pendleton Marine Base, 502, 557
Peppard, George, 41
Perell, Cydette; see Pitman, Nancy Laura
Peters, Frank (pseud.), 192–93
Pettet, Joanna, 70–71
Phillips, John, 66, 510
Phillips, Michelle, 66
Pickett, Jeffrey (pseud.), 65, 77–78, 85–87, 90, 98
Pitman, Nancy Laura, 170, 179–80, 206, 252, 268, 278, 294, 311, 350, 486, 534–35, 559, 569–70, 604–5, 608, 623, 632, 648
Plumlee, Vernon Ray, 105
Polanski, Barbara Lass, 38
Polanski, Roman, 8, 13, 16, 18–20, 26n, 29, 36–40, 45–48, 52–53, 65, 69, 75–85, 92, 216, 281, 286–87, 307–9, 618, 658
Polanski, Sharon Tate; see Tate, Sharon Marie
Portola Drive (9870), 272, 356–57
Poston Brooks, 168, 177, 283, 311–18, 322–29, 333–36, 339, 396, 399, 401, 451, 477, 494, 499n, 513–14, 529, 599, 610, 627, 658
Powell, Dick, Ranger, 168–71
Process, The, 300, 320, 635–39
Pugh, Joel, 224–25, 647
Pugh, Mrs. Joel; see Good, Sandra Collins
Pursell, James, Patrolman, 168–73
Putnam, George, 201

Ransohoff, Martin, 36–38, 80
Rayner, Lanier, 195
Reagan, Ronald, 167n, 395
Reeves, Mrs. Garnett, 215

Reeves, Marnie; see Krenwinkel, Patricia

Reiner, Ira, 258, 288–89, 377–78, 413, 417–19

Reinhard, Robert, 125

Rice, Dennis, 474, 481, 535, 625, 631

Ritchard, Sgt., 105

Roberts, Clete, 266

Roberts, Raymond, Judge, 379

Roberts, Steven, 78

Robinson, James, Chief, 215

Rodriquez, W. C., Officer, 54–55, 461

Rogers, T. L., Sgt., 15

Rogers, Will, 339

Romeo, Daniel; see DeCarlo, Daniel

Rommel, Erwin, Field Marshal, 169, 176

Roseland, Mrs. Jean, 418, 555, 613, 618–19

Rosenburg, Barbara; see Hoyt, Barbara

Ross, Mark, 107, 359

Rubin, Jerry, 296–97

Russell, Amos, 15, 71

Russell, Wesley, 262

Ryan, Tom, DA, 274

Sadie; see Atkins, Susan Denise

Saffie, Jim, 33

Sage, Joe, 390–92

Sainte-Marie, Buffy, 305

Samuels, Jo Anne (pseud.), 194

Samuels, Ralph (pseud.), 194

Sandy; see Good, Sandra Collins

Sankston, Leslie; see Van Houten, Leslie Sue

Santa Susana Pass Road (1200); see Spahn Movie Ranch

Sartuchi, Philip, Sgt., 89, 108, 165, 175–77, 200, 218–19, 254, 277, 393, 451–52, 481, 494

Schiller, Lawrence, 259–60, 590

Schram, Stephanie, 102, 170, 200, 372–73, 389, 509, 604, 612, 658

Schwarm, Mary Ann; see Von Ahn, Diane

Scientology, 195–98, 222, 300, 317, 320, 635–36, 647

Scott, Colonel, 185, 555, 643

Scott, Darwin Orell, 643–44

Scott, Mary Ann; see Krenwinkel, Patricia

Sebring, Jay, 8, 15, 18–22, 24–28, 35, 41–43, 48, 66, 68, 71–73, 75, 81–84, 117–27, 238–39, 267, 307, 337, 384, 428, 459, 472, 553, 578, 644

Sellers, Peter, 68, 92

Sexy Sadie; see Atkins, Susan Denise

Shannon, Steve, 5

Share, Catherine, 170, 179, 206, 252, 268, 294–95, 296, 347–49, 357–59, 376, 396, 429, 474, 480–81, 535, 571–74, 608, 611, 618–19, 625, 631

Sharp, James, 647

Shea, Donald Jerome (Shorty), 124–25, 141–45, 150–51, 163, 181, 206, 209, 220, 254, 273, 455, 534, 577, 589, 629–30, 641, 644

Sheely, Larry, 419n, 446

Sheppard, Sam, 255, 559

Shinn, Daye, 258, 360, 377–78, 398, 440, 444–45, 487–89, 504–5, 524, 543, 566, 575–77, 583–84, 588, 590–91, 607, 615, 619

Simi Valley Sherri; see Cooper, Sherry Ann

Sinatra, Frank, 41, 59, 118, 502–3, 506

Sinclair, Collie, 171

Sirhan, Sirhan, 110, 664

Sisto, Anlee, 417n

Sivick, Ruth, 62, 461, 467

Skrdla, Blake, Dr., 288, 517–18

Slezak, Walter, 378

Smack, Ruth Ann; see Moorehouse, Ruth Ann

Smith, Claudia Leigh, 171

Smith, Dave, 652, 662

Smith, David, Dr., 222–23

Smith, Richard Allen; see DeCarlo, Daniel

Smith, Roger, 222

Snake; see Lake, Dianne Elizabeth

Soupspoon; see Lane, Robert Ivan

Spahn, George, 77, 134–35, 143, 162–63, 173, 178–79, 268, 348, 385, 387, 436, 472, 658

Spahn Movie Ranch, 47, 101, 103, 119, 123, 125–26, 134, 137–45, 148–51, 160–61, 176–77, 181, 184, 206–9, 213, 215–17, 220, 233–35, 242–43, 247–48, 254, 267–68, 272–73, 276, 278, 283, 285, 293, 295, 299, 319, 330, 334–35, 336, 339, 342, 347–48, 361, 368, 374–76, 385–92, 396, 399, 414–16, 420, 432, 434, 452, 457, 464, 472, 479–80, 482–85, 488, 491–92, 509, 541, 543, 570, 572, 576–77, 582, 598, 607, 631, 633–34, 635n, 642, 643–44, 646, 654–55

Sparks, Rich, 4

Springer, Al, 119–27, 134, 141, 146, 182, 262, 293, 338, 658

Squeaky; see Fromme, Lynette Alice

Stafford, Jean, 409

Starr, Randy, 385–86, 446, 451

Steele, Emmett, 5, 30

Steinberg, Robert, 502, 506

Steuber, David, Officer, 494–95

Stevens, Connie, 59

Stevens, Leona (Candy); see Manson, Leona Rae

Stevenson, Jo, 261

Stothers, Stephen, Judge, 625

Stovitz, Aaron, 159–60, 164–65, 213–14, 216–18, 226–27, 232, 249–50, 253, 278–79, 291–92, 342, 378–79, 396–98, 401, 411, 419–20, 426, 440, 458, 464–65, 573, 590

Straight Satans motorcycle gang, 103, 119–22, 136–37, 141, 361, 435

Struthers, Frank Jr., 33, 53–57, 61, 64, 90, 252, 277, 461

Struthers, Susan, 33–34, 53–56, 61, 90, 177, 252, 277, 336, 461

Summit Ridge Drive (1600), 39

Summit Ridge Drive (2175), 5
Sunset Boulevard, 4, 49, 211, 242, 299, 318, 339–40, 362
Sutcliffe, Stuart, 323
Swartz, John, 147, 249, 272–73, 350, 361, 473, 492
Sybil Brand Institute, 104, 118, 133, 143, 145, 159, 201, 203, 213–14, 217, 226, 229, 257, 260–61, 269, 337, 341–43, 347, 357–58, 370, 383, 388, 459, 503, 547

T. J. the Terrible; see Walleman, Thomas
Tabbe, Helen, Deputy, 337, 459
Tarlow, Barry, 30–31, 201
Tate, Deborah, 68, 70, 72
Tate, Patricia, 68
Tate, Paul, Colonel, 15, 19, 42, 93, 216, 308, 426–27, 618
Tate, Mrs. Paul, 15–16, 19, 42, 618
Tate, Sharon Marie, 8, 15–18, 22–29, 35–41, 47–48, 51, 59, 65–71, 76–85, 92, 111–18, 127, 145–46, 159–60, 165, 206, 220, 226–29, 238–41, 287, 299, 306–9, 337, 355, 371, 382–87, 421–27, 439n, 446–47, 456, 459, 466, 475, 489, 507, 511, 518–19, 541, 548, 551–53, 567, 576–78, 590, 626–27, 641, 644
Taylor, Elizabeth, 36, 118, 502–3, 506
Tennant, William, 16–20, 25, 65
Tennant, Mrs. William (Sandy), 16, 70
Terminal Island Prison, 191, 199, 416
Texas Charlie; see Watson, Charles Denton
Thompson, Thomas, 75–76
Todd, Hugh Rocky, 169
Tolmas, Ed, 380
Toney, J. C., Officer, 54
Topanga Canyon, 148, 233, 278, 347, 368, 394, 572
Tracy, Beth; see Sinclair, Collie
True, Harold, 263, 277–78, 363, 510
Tubick, Herman, 418, 555, 558, 618
Tufts, Clem; see Grogan, Steven
Tweed, Andre, Dr., 592–94

Ungerleider, Thomas, Dr., 592

Vance, William Joseph; see Hamic, David Lee
Van Houten, Jane, 564–66
Van Houten, Leslie Sue, 99, 109–10, 170, 179–80, 206–10, 216, 226, 244–46, 253, 255, 269, 276–79, 283, 288–90, 294, 298, 361–65, 378, 383–84, 395, 403–6, 413, 417, 421, 425, 429, 433, 455–56, 463–66, 469, 501, 516, 531–33, 537, 545–47, 549–50, 553, 558–59, 564–66, 577, 584–90, 593–604, 608–9, 612–13, 616–17, 621, 632, 641, 661–62
Vargas, Tom, 70–71, 428

Varney, Dudley, Sgt., 21–23
Vitzelio, Walter, 417, 445–46
Von Ahn, Diane, 170

Walker, Roseanne, 510, 543, 548
Walleman, Thomas, 141, 473, 599
Walts, Mark, 644
Ward, Don, Deputy Sheriff, 171–72, 177, 283, 311, 314
Warnecke, Alan, 287
Warren, Nancy, 642
Watkins, Paul, 311–14, 318–36, 339, 347, 373, 381, 392, 396, 399, 451, 477, 494, 499n, 513–14, 518, 529, 572, 614, 623, 627, 635, 654
Watson, Charles Denton (Tex), 113, 120–23, 143, 146–48, 167, 177, 202, 210–14, 218–19, 226, 236–43, 251, 253, 267, 274–75, 283, 288, 302, 311, 339, 344, 347–57, 361–71, 392, 433–36, 464, 467–68, 476–78, 483–84, 492, 511, 514–15, 537, 544–45, 549–53, 571, 576–77, 589, 593, 597, 599, 602, 608, 613, 625–29, 653, 658, 661–64
Watson, Michael, Officer, 91, 470
Waverly Drive (3267), 67, 363
Waverly Drive (3301), 34, 53, 57, 60, 64, 89, 201, 226, 230, 252, 264, 278, 422
Waverly Drive (3306), 54
Waverly Drive (3308), 54
Webb, Jack, 157
Weber, Rudolf, 271–72, 355, 392, 455, 626
Weiss, Bernard, 91, 96–97, 265–66
Weiss, Steven, 91, 96–97, 470, 658
Whisenhunt, William T., Officer, 7n, 8–16, 428, 455
White Album (The Beatles), 324–30, 375, 554, 568, 618
Whiteley, Paul, Sgt., 46–47, 101–3, 143, 161, 164, 181, 500
Wild, Victor Floyd, 636
Wildebush, Juanita, 311, 334
Willett, James T., 648
Willett, Lauren, 649–50
Williamson, Elizabeth Elaine; see Fromme, Lynette Alice
Willis, Richard C., Officer, 374
Wilson, Dennis, 117, 211–13, 235, 248, 286, 299, 338–41, 511
Wilson, Herb (pseud.), 65, 77–78, 85–86, 90, 98
Wiman, Al, 264–65, 370–71, 459
Wolfer, DeWayne, ·74–75, 386–87, 428, 510, 627
Woodstock Road (2774), 43

Yorty, Samuel, Mayor, 44
Younger, Evelle, DA, Attorney General, 227, 283, 342, 396–98, 405, 442, 464–65, 590

Zabriske, Steve, 105, 642
Zamora, William, 417n, 443
Zero; see Haught, John Philip
Ziegler, Ron, 439
Zimbardo, Philip, 655

ABOUT THE AUTHOR

VINCENT T. BUGLIOSI received his law degree in 1964 from UCLA law school, where he was president of his graduating class. In his eight-year career as a prosecutor for the Los Angeles District Attorney's Office, he tried close to 1,000 felony and misdemeanor court and jury trials. Of 106 felony jury trials, he lost but one case. His most famous trial was, of course, the Manson case, which became the basis of his best-selling book *Helter Skelter*. But even before the Manson case, in the television series "The D.A.," actor Robert Conrad patterned his starring role after Bugliosi. His most recent nonfiction book, *Till Death Us Do Part*, was also a bestseller and he has recently had his first novel (co-written with Ken Hurwitz) *Shadow of Cain*, published in hardcover. He lives with his wife, Gail, and children, Wendy and Vince, Jr., in Los Angeles, where he is in private practice.

THE CASE THAT SHOCKED A NATION.
THE INCREDIBLE BOOK THAT TELLS WHAT REALLY HAPPENED.

It began August 9 and 10, 1969, when seven people were shot, stabbed, and bludgeoned to death in Los Angeles. It ended when a nation watched in fascinated horror as the killers were tried and convicted. But the real questions went unanswered. How did Manson make his "family" kill for him? How could these young men and women kill again and again without human feelings of any kind? Did the murders go on even after Manson was in jail? And where are the killers today?

HERE ARE THE ANSWERS.

HELTER SKELTER

ADMINISTRATION OF HEALTH AND PHYSICAL EDUCATION PROGRAMS, INCLUDING ATHLETICS

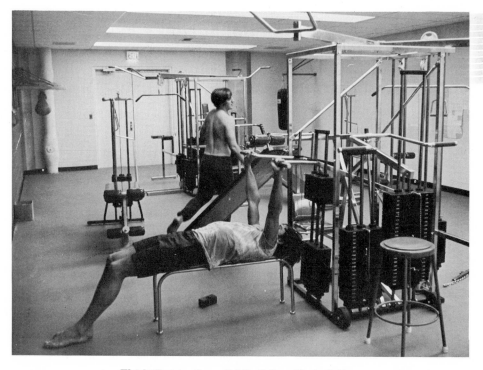

Weight Training Room, Trinity College, Hartford, Conn.

Nebraska Western College, Scottsbluff, Neb. (Shaver & Company, Salina, Kan.)

ADMINISTRATION OF

Health and physical education programs

INCLUDING ATHLETICS

CHARLES A. BUCHER, A.B., M.A., Ed.D.

Professor of Education, New York University,
New York, N. Y.

FIFTH EDITION

With 362 illustrations

Sherwood Elementary School, Greeley, Colo. (Shaver & Company, Salina, Kan.)

THE C. V. MOSBY COMPANY

Saint Louis   1971

To my wife JACKIE

and

my children DIANA, RICHARD, NANCY, *and* JERRY

Preface

The role of administration is becoming increasingly significant in determining the success of health and physical education programs. The manner in which these specialized programs are organized, structured, and supervised determines the results and objectives achieved.

Administration is rapidly becoming a science with a subject matter of its own. If health and physical education specialists are to have outstanding programs in their fields, they must be familiar with administrative theory regarding the structure of organizations, the role of the leader, and the ingredients of outstanding programs. They must also be knowledgeable regarding such administrative functions as community relations, facility management, fiscal accounting, curriculum development, and pupil, teacher, and program evaluation. This fifth edition examines the administration of health, physical education, and athletic programs as a science and brings significant subject matter in administration to the attention of the reader.

This text has been completely revised. All chapters have been brought up to date, with the latest developments and trends in health and physical education included in each subject discussed. For example, new information on administrative theory, personnel administration, adapted physical education, crowd control, health education, facility management, supplies and equipment, audiovisual aids, and pupil, teacher, and program evaluation has been added. Two new chapters — Chapter 1, The Changing Nature of Administration, and Chapter 6, Student Leadership in Physical Education — have been added. Finally, the book has been completely reorganized so that the material is presented in a more meaningful and logical sequence.

The fifth edition is divided into five parts: Part One, The Changing Nature of Administration; Part Two, Administration of Physical Education Programs; Part Three, Health Programs for Students; Part Four, Administrative Functions; and Part Five, Administration of Recreation, Club, and Outdoor Education and Camping Programs. Appendices have also been developed that include such valuable information as sources of equipment and supplies; procedures for care, repair, and storage of equipment; school laws and regulations relating to health and physical education programs; and athletic field and court diagrams.

I would like to thank all the individuals, schools, colleges, and other organizations who contributed photographs, charts, and other materials for this revision.

Dr. Jean Tallman, Chairman, Physical Education Department, Davis and Elkins College, Elkins, West Virginia, is responsible for preparing the excellent Instructor's Manual that the publisher gives to each instructor who adopts this text. The author wishes to thank Dr. Tallman for preparing a manual that will help each instructor to offer a more meaningful course to his or her students.

Charles A. Bucher

Contents

Part one   **THE CHANGING NATURE OF ADMINISTRATION**

     1   The changing nature of administration, 3

     2   Administrative relationships and objectives, 30

     3   The administrative setting, 48

     4   The business administrator, 79

     5   Personnel administration for health and physical education programs, 90

     6   Student leadership in physical education, 116

Part two   **ADMINISTRATION OF PHYSICAL EDUCATION PROGRAMS**

     7   The basic instructional physical education program, 127

     8   The adapted program, 179

     9   The intramural and extramural programs, 206

    10   The interscholastic and intercollegiate varsity athletic programs, 234

    11   Administering physical fitness programs, 279

Part three   **HEALTH PROGRAMS FOR STUDENTS**

    12   The health science instruction program — with implications for physical education, 305

    13   Health service programs for students, including athletes, 344

    14   Providing a healthful environment for students, 386

Part four   ADMINISTRATIVE FUNCTIONS

15   The physical plant, 407

16   Budget making and financial accounting, 464

17   The purchase and care of supplies and equipment including audiovisual materials, 484

18   Legal liability and insurance management, 513

19   Curriculum development, 543

20   Professional and public relations, 572

21   Office management, 588

22   Measurement of pupil achievement, 605

23   Teacher and program evaluation, 629

Part five   ADMINISTRATION OF RECREATION, CLUB, OUTDOOR EDUCATION, AND CAMPING PROGRAMS

24   Community and school recreation, club, and activity programs, 653

25   Outdoor education and camping, 670

APPENDICES

A   Sources of equipment and supplies for athletic, physical education, recreation, outdoor education, and school health programs, 683

B   Care, repair, and storage of uniforms and equipment, 698

C   School laws and regulations on the teaching of health, safety, driver, outdoor, and physical education, 715

D   Field and court diagrams, 730

one

THE CHANGING NATURE OF ADMINISTRATION

Physical Education Bldg., Seattle University, Seattle, Wash.

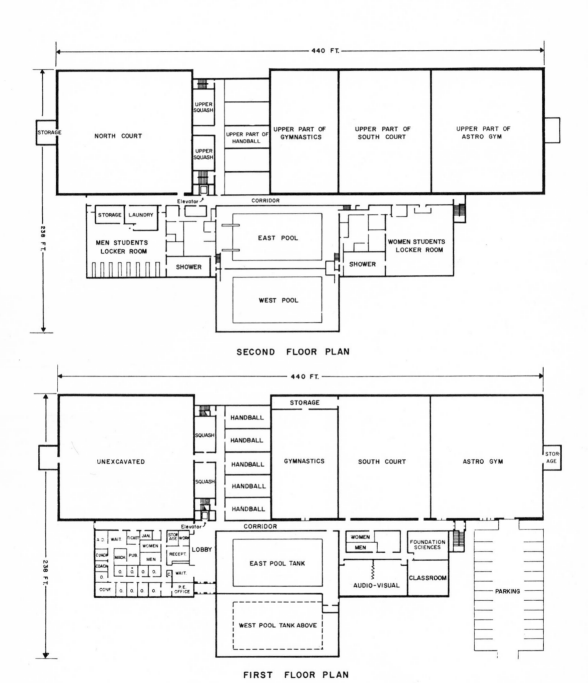

SECOND FLOOR PLAN

FIRST FLOOR PLAN

Physical Education Bldg., Seattle University, Seattle, Wash.

By analyzing several definitions of administration a reader may be better able to understand what a text in administration is designed to cover. Some of the definitions proposed by experts in this field represent analyses of the administrative process based on research; others have been formulated as a result of experience as an administrator or observation of administrators at work.

Based upon Hemphill, Griffiths, and Frederickson's* research, Jenson and Clark† propose the following as a definition of administration: "The administrative process is the way an organization, through working with people, makes decisions and initiates action to achieve its purposes and goals." Halpin,‡ after analyzing administration in education, industry, and government, states that administration refers to a human activity involving a minimum of four components: (1) the *functions or tasks* to be performed, (2) the *formal organization* within which administration must operate, (3) the *work group* or groups with which administration must be concerned,

*Hemphill, J., Griffiths, D., and Frederickson, N.: Administrative performance and personality, New York, 1962, Bureau of Publications, Teachers' College, Columbia University. (This study is sometimes referred to as the "Development of Criteria of Success in School Administration" project.)
†Jenson, T. J., and Clark, D. L.: Educational administration, New York, 1964, The Center for Applied Research in Education, Inc. (The Library of Education).
‡Halpin, A. W.: A paradigm for research on administrative behavior. In Campbell, R. F., and Gregg, R. T., editors: Administrative behavior in education, New York, 1957, Harper & Row, Publishers, p. 161.

and (4) the *leader* or leaders within the organization. Administration has also been defined as a means of bringing about effective cooperative activity to achieve the purposes of an enterprise.

After considerable research and the formulation of a philosophy of administration that is stated later in this chapter, I propose the following definition: *Administration is concerned with the functions and responsibilities essential to the achievement of established goals through associated effort. It is also concerned with that group of individuals who are responsible for directing, guiding, coordinating, and inspiring the associated efforts of individual members, so that the purposes for which an organization has been established may be accomplished in the most effective and efficient manner possible.*

THE SCOPE OF ADMINISTRATION

It has been estimated that there are more than 5 million individuals in the United States today performing administrative work as their main function. This number is large, but as the technology and the specialized functions of this country advance, there will be an increasing number of individuals needed to perform the myriad administrative duties characteristic of the thousands of organizations in society. There are at least as many administrative positions in physical education and health as there are schools and colleges. This, of course, runs into several thousands of positions. In addition, there are many large educational institutions with several persons who assist in the administrative process

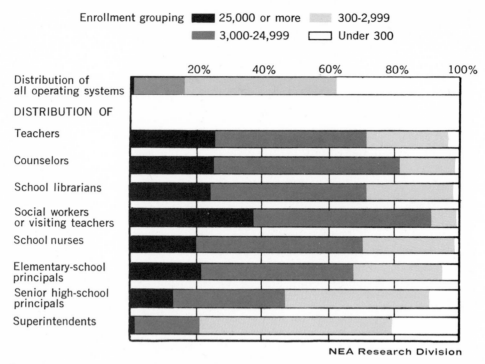

Distribution of personnel by school enrollment, 1968-69. (From Research Division, National Education Association, NEA Research Bulletin **47**:82, 1969.)

concerned with health and physical education programs. Also, there are many agencies such as the YMCAs and Boys' Club, who also have administrative positions. Administration offers many career opportunities for both women and men.

It is essential that individuals who perform administrative work know the many aspects of this particular field. If they are not aware of certain basic facts and are not acquainted with acceptable administrative procedures, many errors may be made. This could result in loss of efficiency, production, and staff morale and in poor human relations, to mention only a few of the possible outcomes. Administration is rapidly becoming a science with a body of specialized knowledge that should be known by all who would administer in a wise and effective manner. Plato in his book, *Laws*, summed it up in a few words that still hold true today: ". . . that God governs all

things, and that chance and opportunity cooperate with Him in the government of human affairs. There is, however, a third and less extreme view, that art should be there also; for I should say that in a storm there must surely be a great advantage in having the aid of the pilot's art. You would agree?"

A PHILOSOPHY OF ADMINISTRATION

People represent the most important consideration in the world. The real worth of a field of endeavor, organization, or idea is found in what it does for human beings. The most important and worthwhile thing that can be said about a particular vocation, organization, or movement is that it contributes to human betterment.

People have goals that represent a variety of human objectives. They include the need for security for oneself and one's family, the desire to be employed in a worth-

Graphic representation of a philosophy of administration.

while and gainful occupation, the wish to worship one's God, the enjoyment of recreation, and the need to obtain an education.

People do not miraculously work together. They do not, as a natural phenomenon, band together and strive to accomplish common objectives. Since many groups of people have common goals, however, they do work together and through associated effort help each other to achieve goals that would be impossible for them to accomplish alone. No one person can establish a school for his children's education, for example, but through the cooperative effort and support of many people a school is made possible. Thus individuals have similar goals that they will work together to attain.

People form organizations to help them fulfill their desires and wishes; they join together and establish a church, a business enterprise, a health association, a governmental agency, a country club, a hospital, or some other type of organization that will help them achieve the goals that they desire. Thus there are thousands of different types of organizations that have been created by human beings who have banded together to achieve objectives that they consider worthwhile.

Organizations, in order to function most

effectively, must have some type of machinery to help them run efficiently, to organize and execute their affairs, and to keep them running smoothly, so that the goals for which they have been created will be achieved. This machinery is administration. It is the framework of organizations. It is the part that helps organizations implement the purposes for which they have been established.

Administration, therefore, exists to help people achieve the goals they desire in order to live happy, productive, healthful, and meaningful lives. It is not an end in itself; rather, it is a means to an end—the welfare of the people for whom the organization exists. Administration exists for people, not people for administration. Administration can justify itself only as it serves the people who make up the organization, helping them to achieve the goals they have as human beings.

It can be seen, then, that in an organization, where the associated efforts of many individuals are necessary, there is no spontaneous and automatic working together of the individuals involved. There are no miraculous thought and planning that result in the achievement of goals and purposes. It is not a natural trait of human beings to cooperate and work side by side in a happy and purposeful manner. This is accomplished through direction, and administration gives this direction.

To a considerable degree, the actions of human beings in society are determined through their association with formal organizations. Formal organizations have leaders and purposes. They depend upon the cooperative efforts of individuals to achieve the objectives that have been set. Many times organizations have failed when their leaders have been of low caliber, when there has been a lack of cooperative effort among 'members, or when the objectives have not been in conformance with what is essential and good for society.

Administration determines in great measure whether an organization is going to progress, operate efficiently, achieve its objectives, and have a group of individuals within its framework who are happy, cooperative, and productive. Administration has to do with directing, guiding, and integrating the efforts of human beings so that specific aims may be accomplished. It refers particularly to a group of individuals, many times called executives, who have as their major responsibility this direction, guidance, integration, and achievement.

Administration is especially concerned with achievement—proof that the organization is producing those things for which it has been established. To be able to achieve these results in a satisfactory manner presupposes an understanding of human relationships and the ability to foresee the future and plan for any eventuality. It demands the capacity to coordinate many different and conflicting types of human personalities. Good administration should ensure that the associated efforts of individuals are productive. To accomplish this, administrators should possess those attributes that are conducive to bringing out the most creative and best efforts on the part of the members of the organization.

Administration also requires close supervision of the facilities, materials, supplies, and equipment essential to the life of the organization. It implies a logical formulation of policies and the effective operation of the organization.

THE IMPORTANCE OF ADMINISTRATION

A study of administration is important for all teachers of health and physical education. A few of the more significant reasons why teachers should understand administration are discussed in the following paragraphs.

1. *The way in which schools and colleges are administered determines the course of human lives.* The lives of both students and teachers are affected by administration. It affects the type of education offered, the climate in which the education takes place, and the goals that are sought. It vitally affects the happiness and achievement of every teacher.

2. *Administration provides an understanding and appreciation of the underlying principles of the science of this field.* Methods, techniques, devices, and procedures used by the administration can be evaluated more accurately and objectively by faculty and staff if they possess administrative understanding. Also, sound administration will be better appreciated and unsound practices more easily recognized. Human resources will have less chance of being exploited, and efficient management and organization will be furthered through such understanding.

3. *A study of administration will assist in deciding whether a person wishes to select this area on a career basis.* Personal qualifications may be better evaluated and possibilities of success better predicted with increased understanding and appreciation of the administrative process.

4. *Most physical education and health educators perform some types of administrative work and therefore an understanding of administration will contribute to better performance in this area.* Adminis-

tration is not restricted to one group of individuals. Most teachers and staff members have reports to complete, equipment to order, evaluations to make, and other duties to perform that are administrative in nature. An understanding of the science of administration will assist in carrying out these assignments.

5. *Administration is fundamental to associated effort.* Goals are reached, ideas are implemented, and an esprit de corps is developed with planning and cooperative action. A knowledge of administration facilitates the achievement of such aims.

6. *An understanding of administration helps to assure continuity.* A fundamental purpose of administration is to carry on that which has proved successful rather than to destroy the old and attempt a new and untried path. An appreciation of this concept by all members of an organization will help to ensure the preservation of the best traditional practices that exist in the organization.

7. *A knowledge of administration helps to further good human relations.* An understanding of sound administrative principles will better assure the cooperation of the various members who make up the organization in order that the greatest efficiency and productivity will be assured.

Outstanding individuals in various walks of life have recognized the importance of administration. *Charles A. Beard,* a famous historian, referred to administration as the key science of the present day. *Henri Fayol,* French engineer and industrialist, stressed the great need for studying administration scientifically, since it is one of the most important elements in all vocations and professions. *Paul Pigors,* American sociologist, felt that the main contribution of administration was to preserve the status quo in society. *Brooks Adams,* American

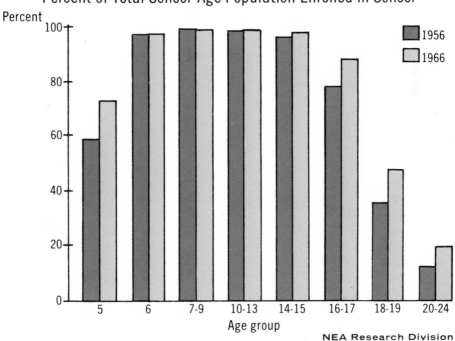

A higher percentage of young people are in school.

lawyer and historian, took an almost opposite view from Pigors' when he advocated administration as being most important because it can help in social change. *James Burnham,* American political philosopher, went further and pointed to the fact that the chief administrators in present-day society had assumed so much power that the social revolution was already in evidence. *Charles E. Merriam,* American political scientist, contended that administration was another outcome of human technology that made it possible for man to better adapt to his complex environment.

The evidence is ample that administration is rapidly becoming a science and that the study of this science is essential to everyone. A study of administration can result in a better-ordered society through more efficiently run organizations. Every individual belongs to formal organizations. Through a democratic approach to administration the individual can aid in carrying on what has proved to be good in the past and steer a course that will ensure progress in the future.

THE DEVELOPMENT OF A THEORY OF ADMINISTRATION

It is increasingly being recognized that administration is not something that is hit or miss, trial and error, or a matter of expediency. Instead, there is evidence to show that a theory of administration is emerging. It is recognized that from a study of this administrative theory one will gain the ability to act wisely in specific situations, and since theory is practical, it provides an accurate picture of how human beings work. Administrative theory will also help in the identification of problems that need to be solved if an effective working organization is to exist.

Textbooks and the professional literature on administration indicate a search for a substance of administration and for a framework of theory that would make the substance a meaningful whole. The tradi-

tional emphasis has been upon the form rather than upon the substance. Organizations such as the National Conference of Professors of Educational Administration, the Cooperative Program in Educational Administration, and the University Council for Educational Administration are helping to give impetus to this new movement and thereby helping to make administration much more of a science than has existed in the past. Although there are some educators who oppose such a trend, it seems assured that administration is in the process of becoming more scientific and thereby characterized by more objectivity, reliability, and a systematic structure of substance. Such theory is explaining what administration is and providing guides to administrative action.

The traditional and modern views of administration

The traditional view of administration revolved around the idea that administration existed in order to carry out the policies that had been developed by the duly constituted policy-forming group, such as a board of education. Modern administration not only carries out policy but also plays an important role in the development of policy, utilizing the knowledge and expertise that come from training and experience.

A study of the history of administration shows that policy-forming groups, such as boards of education, were once held accountable for how the schools were administered, whereas the modern approach delegates administrative responsibilities to the trained school administrator. The old concept of leadership in administration was a sort of passive type of leadership that remained in the background while the policy-forming group provided the strength and skill that were needed to run the schools. Under the modern view of administration, however, strong administrative leadership is a requirement so that technical and ex-

Table 1-1. Instructional organization and practices, 154 middle schools in systems enrolling over 12,000 pupils, 1968-69*

Instructional organization and practices	Number and percent of schools by grade level†							
	Grade 5 (20 schools)		Grade 6 (146 schools)		Grade 7 (154 schools)		Grade 8 (148 schools)	
	Number	Percent	Number	Percent	Number	Percent	Number	Percent
Organization								
Self-contained classrooms	10	50.0%	31	21.2%	3	1.9%	3	2.0%
Partial departmentalization	7	35.0	74	50.7	55	35.7	36	24.4
Total departmentalization	3	15.0	35	24.0	91	59.1	105	70.9
No reply	—	—	6	4.1	5	3.3	4	2.7
Practices								
Subject area teams	4	20.0	45	30.8	51	33.1	52	35.1
Interdisciplinary teams	2	10.0	19	13.0	29	18.8	25	16.9
Small group instruction	7	35.0	55	37.7	63	40.9	66	44.6
Large group instruction	4	20.0	35	24.0	45	29.2	47	31.8
Flexible scheduling	5	25.0	39	26.7	44	28.6	43	29.1
Closed-circuit TV	1	5.0	22	15.1	25	15.6	25	16.9
Independent study	3	15.0	30	20.5	39	25.3	40	27.0
Individualized instruction	4	20.0	39	26.7	47	30.5	48	32.4
Tutorial programs	3	15.0	32	21.9	33	21.4	31	20.9

*From NEA Research Bulletin **47**:51, 1969.
†Percentages are based on the total number of middle schools in the survey, which includes each of the grades. The number of schools with each grade is shown in the column headings.

pert judgments can be made to help the schools to achieve their objectives more effectively. The traditional view of administration claimed the best way to prepare to administer was to practice administering: experience was seen to be the best teacher. The modern view of administration, however, recognizes the value of experience but at the same time maintains that there exists a body of knowledge or theory that, when mastered, can help the administration play a more effective role in the organization with which it is associated.

According to Jenson and Clark,* new perspectives of educational administration are the result of six phenomena:

1. Administration is a science and the administrator is a professional person.
2. An intensive study of administration includes such phenomena as behaviors, social interactions, and human relationships.

*Jenson and Clark, op. cit., p. 37.

3. Application of theory and model constructs are included in the study of administration.
4. Administration is differentiated into two dimensions: content and process.
5. New forces shape new perspectives in administration: new technologies, population trends, value systems, knowledge explosion, ideological conflicts, and so on.
6. Interest of scholars and researchers in the scientific study of the field of administration is increasing.

The preparation of administrators

The modern view of administration is that a professional preparation program for the person who desires to enter the field of administration should include such essentials as: taking foundation work in cognate fields, knowing himself as an individual and as a potential administrator, having competency in administrative skills to be performed, understanding the community, recognizing the importance of instruction, studying and practicing decision making, and realizing the importance of human relations. Finally, there should be on-the-job learning experience that is closely supervised by an experienced professor.

Several types of content, all of which are pertinent to physical education and health administrators, are suggested by Culbertson* as being needed in the preparation of administrators in order to fulfill the following responsibilities.

Making decisions. Content should include a study of concepts and theories that relate to individual, group, and organization decision making. The relationship of such items as basic research, computer technology, and value systems to decision making would also be considered.

Communication. A study of communication—one-way, two-way, and group, as well as organizational communications—should be included. Mass communications and opinion change should also be considered.

Coping with change. A study of the dynamics of change in relation to individuals, groups, and organizations should be made. A study should also be made of barriers to change, how change can be effected, the leadership needed, conflicts, and related topics. For example, Table 1-1 indicates a number of types of instructional organization and practices. The administration plays a key role in bringing about such changes and practices.

Building morale. Content should include how morale is achieved in a modern organization. Special attention should be given to motivation, interpersonal relations, values, organizational loyalty, perception, and so on.

Such content material and preparation, if offered, would produce well-educated administrations, according to the American Association of School Administrators.* The AASA, for example, feels that an administrator (in this case a superintendent of schools, but the points are equally applicable to administrators of physical education and health programs) as a result of his professional training should:

1. Have a deep devotion to the human values that are at the heart of America's purpose and upon which her destiny rests and an understanding of the galaxy of relationships and ethical beliefs upon which those values and ethical principles are based.
2. Be able to make wise and sound decisions toward the improvement of teaching and toward more efficient learning.
3. Know laboratory and classroom environments, tools for teaching, and the structural organization for deployment of staff and pupils.
4. Be well schooled in what science and research show about the expectations, drives, fears, interests, and personal diversities that exist in groups of teachers, children, and young people.
5. Understand the American public—what it is, what it wants, how it is organized, how it can make itself felt, and who leads it.
6. Be efficient in using public funds.
7. Have a combination of personal power, insight, and skill that enables him to get a team of associates to work closely and effectively with him. Some of the most energetic and intellectually astute superintendents (administrators) find themselves carrying more and more burdens because they unknowingly tie in knots the energies and abilities of the men and women closest to them.
8. Have wisdom and good judgment, as well as skill, in oral and written communication.
9. Possess creative, imaginative, and realistic competence in sensing society's evolutionary and emerging aspirations and needs.
10. Have the vision, courage, and patience needed to plan wisely for the future.
11. Be professionally competent in many areas of evaluation.
12. Comprehend the educational needs of adults, children, and youth.

---

*Culbertson, J.: The preparation of administrators. In Behavioral science and educational administration, the Sixty-Third Yearbook of the National Society for the Study of Education, Chicago, 1964, University of Chicago Press.

---

*The education of a school superintendent, Washington, D. C., 1963, American Association of School Administrators, pp. 11-12.

13. Have an education that feeds upon education, that generates an unquenchable thirst for more understanding, and that keeps him far out in front of the doggedly pursuing menace of obsolescence.

The anatomy of administrative leadership

Being the head of a department, division, or school of physical education and health and being the leader of these organizations are two different things. The head can be a person who takes care of the clerical details and occupies the main office in a department or division, but he may not necessarily be the leader of the organization. The administrative leader of an organization is one who helps and influences others in a certain direction as problems are solved and goals achieved. In a school, college, or agency situation the persons influenced are teachers, pupils, clerks, parents, custodians, and any person involved with the organization.

The question as to what makes a leader is a provocative one. Much research has been done in recent years as to what constitutes the administrative leader. Years ago it was felt that combinations of personality characteristics or traits were the ingredients that determined who was a leader. However, research such as that of Gouldner,* indicates that: "At this time there is no reliable evidence concerning the existence of universal leadership traits."

Other studies have provided further information in regard to leadership. Stogdill† states as a result of his research that "the qualities, characteristics, and skills required in a leader are determined to a large extent by the demands of the situation in which he is to function as a leader." In other words, a health or physical education administrative leader in one situation may

not necessarily be a leader in another situation. Different styles of leadership are needed to meet the needs of different settings and situations. Administration therefore is a social process.

Certain traits and attributes that influence leader behavior have been identified. For example, Pierce and Merrill,* in examining research on leadership, found that such qualities as popularity, originality, adaptability, judgment, ambition, persistence, emotional stability, social and economic status, and communicative skills were very important for a person to possess if he hoped to lead. The traits that were found to be most significant were popularity, originality, and judgment.

Goldman† examined the research on leadership and suggests that certain factors are significant. When these factors are related to physical education and health administrative leaders, the following guidelines are worth considering:

1. The administrators of physical education and health programs who possess such traits as ambition, ability to relate well to others, emotional stability, communicative skill, and judgment have greater potential for success in leadership than persons who do not possess these traits.
2. The administrators of physical education and health programs who desire to be leaders of their organization must have a clear understanding of the goals of the organization. The direction in which they desire to lead the organization must be within the broad framework of the goals and objectives of the school district and consonant with the needs of the community they serve.
3. The administrators of physical education and health programs who desire to be leaders of

---

*Gouldner, A. W., editor: Studies in leadership, New York, 1950, Harper & Row, Publishers, p. 34.

†Stogdill, R. M.: Personal factors associated with leadership: a survey of the literature, Journal of Psychology 25:63, 1948.

*Pierce, T. M., and Merrill, E. C., Jr.: The individual and administrative behavior. In Campbell, R. F., and Gregg, R. T., editors: Administrative behavior in education, New York, 1957, Harper & Row, Publishers, p. 331.

†Goldman, S.: The school principal, New York, 1966, The Center for Applied Research in Education, Inc. (The Library of Education), pp. 88-89.

their organizations must understand each of the persons who work with them, including their personal and professional needs.

4. The administrators of physical education and health programs who desire to be leaders of their organizations need to establish a climate within which the organization goals, personal needs of each staff member, and their own personality traits can operate harmoniously.

Administrative tasks

Administration is a process involving pertinent tasks that must be performed if an organization is to progress and achieve its goals. These tasks represent the mission of the organization as delineated into subtasks. For example, the task of the school is to educate, and in order to accomplish this mission certain subtasks are essential. Campbell and his associates* analyzed administrative tasks and came to the conclusion that there were seven operational task areas. These are: (1) school-community relationships, (2) curriculum development, (3) pupil personnel, (4) staff personnel, (5) physical facilities, (6) finance and business management, and (7) organization and structure. In Part Four of this text the following administrative tasks and functions in regard to school health and physical education programs are discussed in detail: the physical education plant, budget making and financial accounting, purchase and care of supplies and equipment, legal liability and insurance management, curriculum planning, professional, school and community relations, office management, measurement of pupil achievement, and teacher and program evaluation. The task of organization and structure is covered in Chapter 3.

Administrative skills

Some administrators are successful and some fail because of the administrative skills they lack. Jenson and Clark,* as a result of their research, have identified three types of administrative skills that are essential: conceptual, technical, and human relations. These skills are necessary for the successful administration of physical education and health programs.

Conceptual skills include the abilities to see the organization as a whole, to originate ideas, to sense problems, and to work out solutions to these problems that will benefit the organization and establish the right priorities and organizational direction. It reduces the risk factor to a minimum.

Technical skills are the administrative skills that relate to the various tasks that must be performed. For example, such tasks as budgeting, curriculum planning, communication, preparing reports, group dynamics, policy development, and public relations, to name only a few, require certain specialized skills if they are to be performed efficiently and accurately.

The third type of skills, *human relations skills*, refers to the administration's ability to have good working relationships among the staff, to get along with people, and to provide a working climate where individuals will not only produce but also grow on the job.

Stages of the administrative process involving decision making

Decision making in the administrative process requires that certain steps be followed. The ordinary problem-solving approach that has been traditionally used includes the recognition of the problem, identifying the alternatives, gathering and organizing facts, weighing alternatives, and finally arriving at a decision. Jenson and Clark,† however, feel that the administration should not stop at the point of arriving at a decision but, instead, feel that it is es-

---

*Campbell, R. F., and others: Introduction to educational administration, ed. 2, Boston, 1962, Allyn and Bacon, Inc.

*Jenson and Clark, op. cit., pp. 56-57.
†Jenson and Clark, op. cit., pp. 53-55.

sential to go on to the stages that involve implementation and assessment. The sequential stages of this process, they feel, are well stated by Burr and his associates*:

1. *Deliberating*   The problem is discussed, facts on the problem are gathered, and the problem is carefully analyzed.

2. *Decision making*   As a result of the deliberation a decision is made. Alternatives are carefully weighed and a choice is made based on the facts.

3. *Programming*   After the decision is made the program is developed so that it is ready for implementation. Questions are asked and actions taken in regard to the resources that are available, the planning that needs to be done, the budget, equipment, and material requirements that exist, and the needs in regard to staff and so on. In other words, information is researched that will provide a successful program and the right direction, in light of the decision that was made.

4. *Stimulating*   After the programming has been developed, it is set into operation. This requires the involvement of people, arousing interest, obtaining commitments, and initiating action. Motivation needs to be encouraged and attitudes developed in this process.

5. *Coordinating*   To effectively implement a program requires the coordination of staff efforts, material resources, proper communication, and other essentials that will assure that the program will be successfully launched.

6. *Appraising*   The last stage in the continuum is evaluating and appraising all stages of the process and the results obtained. It attempts to analyze where the process was successful or where it failed and the reasons for the success or failure. The information gath-

ered will be used in future endeavors.

Rules of administrative organization

Bartholomew* suggests certain rules of organization that he gathered from a study of the field of public and business administration. These have implications for organizing and administering physical education and health programs.

1. *Administrative work may be most efficiently organized by function.* This rule of organization refers to the "doctrine of unity" that holds that all officers engaged in a particular type of work should function under a single authority.

2. *Unified direction should be embodied in the organization.* This refers to the "unity of command," which in essence means that no staff member should be subject to the orders of more than one superior.

3. *Organization may be according to purpose.* Staff, auxiliary, and line activities may be separated.

4. *Organization should be done on a hierarchical basis.* A vertical type of structure that begins at the bottom with production personnel and then goes upward through section heads, division heads, to the organization head should exist. Such units are differentiated on the basis of level of authority and responsibility.

5. *Organization and social purpose cannot be disassociated.* The organization (structure) is a means and not an end in itself.

6. *There is no single correct form of organization.* Such things as size, geography, personnel, and funds available will determine at any given time what is the best organization for a particular situation.

7. *Span of control should be definitely considered in organizational structure.* This

*Burr, J. B., and others: Elementary school administration, Boston, 1963, Allyn and Bacon, Inc., pp. 398-402.

*Bartholomew, P. C.: Public administration, Paterson, N. J., 1959, Littlefield, Adams & Co., pp 4-8.

rule of organization refers to the number of subordinates who can be adequately supervised by one individual. In other words, the number of communication contacts that can be effectively carried on by any administrative office and subordinates will determine the span of control.

ADMINISTRATION AND POLICY FORMATION

Policy serves as a guideline for successful administration. In the areas of health education and physical education, specifically, policy would represent a series of statements that guide the director or administrator and his staff when making decisions so that their program shows organization with a directed purpose.

Policy, whether it represents the philosophy of the total school or college program or merely the department of health and physical education, has the purpose of guiding those persons associated with the program. Wherever there is a successful organization there will be a sophisticated administration supported by well-designed policies. These policies outline the manner in which the organization will operate and are accepted principles of administration set to guide courses of action. Examples of policies are as follows:

> The Department of Health and Physical Education will periodically test its students to determine their physical fitness levels.
>
> The Department of Health and Physical Education will hold monthly departmental meetings.

Policy should not be confused with rules and regulations that are more specific in nature and designed to implement or carry out policy. For example, the policy above, in reference to physical fitness testing, could also have regulations regarding the test to be used, when the test will be conducted, and what will be done with the results.

The need for written policies

Policy, as previously outlined, is a series of statements used to guide the administration and the staff in achieving a successful program. Some schools and colleges operate with a minimum of policy guiding their program. Consequently, this can create a series of small crises when the instructional staff has a number of problems for which they have no predetermined course of action. Policy is the best answer for administrative success since it eliminates chaos and confusion.

Each department in the school or college program needs to develop policies unique to its own area of specialization. School and college health and physical education programs are no exception, and administrators as well as staff in these areas should have the knowledge and ability to formulate policy that best fits their programs.

It should be recognized, however, that too many written policies may be just as ineffective as having no written policies at all. Consequently, there is an urgent need to continuously review and appraise existing policies and practices.

How policy is developed

Policy formation in the public school or college is guided by certain national philosophic concepts. Many of the goals that a school or college hopes to achieve, for example, are dictated by forces greater than the separate schools or colleges. These guided principles were developed many years ago and embodied in the Constitution and the Declaration of Independence and affect and control the major goals of educational institutions. Therefore, regardless of what policies an administrator would like to issue, he has certain boundaries within which he must operate. He is also subordinate to state edicts, whether it be written law or by statements issued through the office of the State Commissioner of Education.

Policy development in public schools and

colleges is basically determined by federal and state constitutions, state educational officials, and the local college board of trustees or school board of education. For example, the federal courts have recently interpreted policy on prayers in the public schools relative to the national constitution. The state constitution has policies governing such procedures as when students may enter or leave school. State education officials set policy on such items as minimum salary schedules and centralization or decentralization of school districts. However, all courses of action that have not been predetermined by the state or federal government concerning the local school are left to the local school board of education, the superintendent, the principal, and the school instructional staff.

When developing policy within the Department of Health and Physical Education, there are many steps to be taken that will culminate in an intelligent, purposeful departmental policy. Whenever policy is under consideration, it is of primary importance that those persons who might be affected by the policy should share in the determination of its nature. Group formulation of policies utilizes the intelligence of more persons and thereby should result in better policy. Also, to be most effective, policy making should be continuous, involving widespread participation of administrators, teachers, and other persons where desired. Old policies often fail to serve as guides in a changing organization, department, school, college, and world.

Why is it important for teachers to share in the policy-making process? Teamwork in the teacher-administrator relationship is a must for an efficient organization and, as such, in the sharing by all the staff in the school or college policy-making procedure. Some of the values of teacher participation in policy making are that as teachers share they will care more about effectively executing the policy they helped to develop. It will bring out many different points of view, which will result in better pretesting of policy and thus eventually make for a sounder policy. It will improve teacher-administrator relationships. It will give the teacher a better feeling of belonging and thereby give the school or college a more enthusiastic supporter.

Although teachers should be involved in policy development, it should be remembered that there is a basic difference between staff participation in decision making and the duties and responsibilities concerned with policy execution.

How to write policy

The actual formation of policy involves a logical organization and administration of philosophic concepts to a meaningful conclusion. This may be the most important task the administrator will have to consider when organizing his or her program; that is, how to construct policy.

Objective policy formation may be determined by values and mandates of our culture, human relations, knowledge of teaching and learning, staff suggestions by such means as a suggestion box, staff meetings, advisory council, and curriculum or other committees.

Regardless of who is selected to help write policy, the basic technique is the same. Those persons who are responsible must research the area for which the policy is to be written. This may be done by such means as reviewing previous policies, surveying the personnel of the department for suggestions, finding out what other outstanding school or college systems are doing, or studying recommendations of professional committees and commissions. After the research has been done and the subject thoroughly studied, the formulation of the policy takes place using wording that is clear, concise, and unambiguous. When a possible policy statement is ready, it can be reviewed by the staff and changes made where necessary. If there is a difference of opinion that cannot be resolved, it may be necessary for the head of the department to make a decision. Furthermore, the upper echelons of administrative authority are consulted and, of course, they should review and approve the final draft of policy.

Where policy needs to be established

Policy needs to be written in the broad areas of administration. The following paragraphs cite a few examples.

Personnel. In a well-designed educational institution, those persons who are associated with the proper functioning of the program must be selected and guided by intelligent policy. There should be policy statements in regard to personnel management. Such policies might include how personnel are appointed to the system. Also, for those individuals whom the organization expects to employ as teachers, there should be written policy available for them to study relative to such matters as what they will encounter in the system in respect to tenure provisions, promotion, transfer, leaves of absence, and sabbatical leaves.

Curriculum. When an educational institution has an intelligent and well-directed staff, it still needs a well-designed curriculum to be a meaningful program. Curriculum organization and development are an important function of any department. Therefore, it is recommended that a set of policies related to curriculum development be designed and written for use as practical guidelines.

Student evaluation. Once a significant curriculum has been adopted, an evaluation process must follow. This involves evaluating student progress toward the stated objectives of the program. Again, there must be policy to serve as a guideline for such evaluation. In addition to such matters as grading, there should be a well-developed policy on promotion, graduation, and successful completion of assigned work.

There are many other areas where policies need to be developed. In the health area, for example, there should be policy on such matters as exclusion from school for health reasons, on matters affecting the psychologic as well as the physical environment, and on how the health science instruction program should be conducted. In physical education there is need for policy in regard to such things as athletics and extra pay for coaching. In addition, a problem such as excuses needs to be governed by written policy.

The department of health and physical education should have a series of policy statements governing its organization and administration. With intelligent and coordinated development a successful and more meaningful program can be offered. One further point should be mentioned. The administration should recognize that in addition to the development of policy there must also be proper dissemination of the information about approved policy. All statements should be in writing and recognized as official acts. In some cases it might be helpful to prepare a handbook on policies concerned with departmental activities.

DEMOCRATIC ADMINISTRATION

The administration should recognize certain steps in the democratic process of a staff and organization working together in order to accomplish group goals. Some of the steps that should be considered are as follows:

1. Goals should be developed through the group process. The goals that are set should be attainable, challenging, and adapted to the capacities of the members.

2. Good morale should be developed among the entire staff. This is essential to constructive group action. A permissive climate must be established in group deliberations. All must feel a sense of belonging and recognize their important contribution in the undertaking. A feeling of "oneness" should pervade the entire group.

3. Group planning must be done in a clearly defined manner. A stated procedure

should be followed. It should be a cooperative undertaking, based upon known needs and flexible enough to allow for unforeseen developments. The fulfillment of plans should bring satisfaction and a feeling of success to all who participated in their formulation and accomplishment. All should share in recognition for a completed job.

4. In staff meetings and other group discussions the administration must encourage the utilization of democratic principles. Each member's contribution must be encouraged and respected. Differences of opinion must be on a "principle" basis rather than on a "personal" basis. The organization's objectives and purposes must be continually kept in mind. All members must be encouraged to facilitate the group process by accepting responsibility, alleviating conflict, making contributions, respecting the opinions of others, abiding by the will of the majority, and promoting good group morale.

5. There must be periodic evaluation of progress. The group should evaluate itself from time to time as to its accomplishments in terms of the organization's goals and the effectiveness of the group process. Each individual must evaluate his own role as a member of the organization in respect to contributions made to the group process and the accomplishments of the group.

Many problems arise when the democratic process is used. Application of the democratic process to the functioning of an organization does not solve all problems. Instead, many situations and difficulties arise because of elements that are inherent in the application of democratic principles. It is important to recognize these problems and cope with them as they arise. Despite such dilemmas, the advantages of the democratic process far outweigh the disadvantages.

The problem of divided opinion

In a democratic organization, it is assumed that the wishes of the majority pre-

vail. There is a question that often arises in this connection: Is the majority always right? Very often an important issue will be determined by one vote. Students of history remember that during post-Civil War days one vote kept Andrew Johnson from being removed from office. Every individual can recall similar situations within organizations where like results have occurred. Is this a weakness of democracy? Should important problems, plans, and issues be decided by such a small difference of opinion?

It seems that the reasoning behind such a dilemma is clear. All who believe in democracy recognize the importance of having as much unanimity of thinking as possible. However, they also recognize that it is much better to have a majority make a decision than to have it made by one person who is an autocrat.

The problem of subjective personal opinion as opposed to scientific fact

In many democratic discussions it appears to some individuals that scientific evidence should dictate policies and that personal opinions must not become involved. On complicated issues situations develop where certain individuals are acquainted with scientific data that in themselves define the issue. Therefore, the conclusion is reached that discussion, voting, or other devices are useless since the course of action is very clear as indicated by known fact.

The answer to such a problem seems to be that there will be acceptance if individuals know and recognize the facts. Generally, acceptance fails to materialize when evidence is not conclusive or when it has not been properly publicized. The democratic process can contribute immeasurably to such enlightenment. Through discussion, facts can be presented and understanding reached. Individuals with reasonable intelligence will accept scientific fact as against personal opinion, if the presentation is clear and the evidence is convincing. William Gerard Hamilton during the late eighteenth century made a statement which has a bearing on this point: "Two things are always to be observed; whether what is said is true in itself, or being so, is applicable. In general, things are partly true, and partly not; in part applicable, and in part not. You are careful therefore to distinguish; and to show how far this is true and applies, and how far not." The democratic process is the most effective method yet devised to show what is true and applies.

The problem of standards

A question that is often raised in connection with the utilization of the democratic process is: What does it do to standards of performance? There is a belief in some quarters that by allowing majority opinion and decisions to prevail, standards of performance are lowered to a "middle level." The individuals who have a low set of standards tend to pull down those with high standards. In effect, this results in a compromise on middle ground. The standards take on mediocrity rather than remain at a high level.

The answer to this problem is difficult. A democracy rests upon the worth of the individual. It has faith in the individual, the goals that he will set, and the standards he wants to follow. The challenge presents itself to those whose standards are high to bring the rest up to their level, rather than to allow themselves to be relegated to a lower one. Such a process may take time. Results are not always immediate in a democracy. Nevertheless, the principles upon which it is based are sound. By utilizing such principles as freedom of discussion and assemblage, it is possible to educate and to elevate standards.

The problem of time

Democratic discussions with their need for deliberation and agreement take time.

Such delay often creates problems, sometimes with serious consequences. There is often too much delay between the need for action, decision, and execution. Democracy is based upon the necessity for individuals to see the need for a course of action and then, after seeing this need, deliberate on it, and finally see that the decision that they have made is put into effect.

It is true that this dilemma often works to the disadvantage of many individuals. However, it does not necessarily have to be this way. It has been seen how rapidly the federal government will act in case of emergency. For example, it did not take long for Congress to declare war after the attack on Pearl Harbor or to vote the necessary supplies and help once our country was at war. The delay occurs when there is misunderstanding, when a situation is not meaningful, and when the course of action is confusing. Perhaps it is wise in many cases to have this lag of time. Hasty action also results in many mistakes.

The element of time is usually important in cases of emergency. Democratic organizations make provisions for action under such conditions. Members of an organization can vest such powers in qualified individuals when necessary. John Locke in his *Treatise on Civil Government* pointed out that sometimes it is inevitable that decisions be made quickly by the executive in charge. It would seem logical that the wise administrator and organization would provide for such emergency action.

The problem of discussion with uninterested and noninformed individuals

Another problem that frequently arises in democratic deliberations is that some individuals who participate in group discussions are many times not interested or competent to discuss intelligently and constructively the subject at hand. Such a situation may be very helpful as an educational device. As individuals become better informed on various topics they contribute more. Many minds are better than one or two. Any group should welcome as much help as possible in solving problems.

The problem of authority

Criticism has often been directed against the democratic process from the standpoint that it results in confusion and poor direction. The authority for certain acts is not clearly established. Furthermore, it is conducive to a conflict of ideas, which results in indecisiveness.

It seems important to recognize the part that democratic principles play in such a problem. A democratic organization vests in its members the right to help determine policies, purpose, and methods. They want a "say" in these important factors that vitally affect their lives. At the same time, however, they vest authority for execution of policy and purpose in administrators who are responsible to the group for their actions. Any democratically run organization has to recognize clearly the definite lines that exist between policy formation and execution. If an individual has been placed in an administrative position, the wherewithal to perform his duties effectively must also be granted. In a sense, all individuals have authority in their respective positions. Authority goes with the job and not with the individual. This is true from the top to the bottom of the organization. There is no "final authority" except as it exists in the entire membership. All organizations that are to be efficient and effective must clearly recognize these principles upon which the functioning of an organization rests.

The future of democracy

The problems that have been listed should not be used to deter the application of democratic principles to any organization. If one takes any other method of government, it would readily be found that problems of much greater magnitude and seriousness exist. Furthermore, the administrator as a leader can do much toward solving and alleviating the difficulties that are associated with democratic dilemmas. Outstanding leadership is essential to any democratic organization. High-quality leadership will stress the importance of group participation, freedom of action, good human relations, and the importance of each individual member. This is important and far outweighs any advantages associated with systems that are not democratic.

ADMINISTRATION AND THE CHALLENGE OF MODERN EDUCATION

Education is America's largest industry. This country has nearly 60 million people in classrooms from coast to coast. There are approximately 2 million teachers in the elementary and secondary schools of the nation. More than $50 billion are spent each year on educational programs. The United States government is investing billions of dollars to ensure a quality education for each of its citizens. Educational construction costs more than $5 billion a year. Expenditures on classroom equipment, such as books, audiovisual devices, and desks, amount to $1 billion a year. Certain leading corporations in the United States have linked themselves to the educational business in such areas as copying machines, microfilms, texts and reading material, programmed instruction, electronics, language laboratories, and learning systems. More than 60% of the antipoverty program in the Economic Opportunity Act is estimated as being allocated directly to education. Job Corps centers rely heavily on educators for help and guidance.

The growth of education during the last few years has been phenomenal. For example, expenditures in 1950 were about $9.3 billion, or 3.5% of our gross national product (the sum of all goods and services). A rise to 6.1% of the gross national product has been projected by the middle 1970's. Ten years ago school and college enrollments were under 40 million. The United States Office of Education foresees enrollments of 62 million by the middle 1970's. Textbook sales have risen from about $200 million to $600 million annually in the past decade, or an annual growth of about 12%. Two-year college enrollments have jumped from less than 300,000 students in 1954 to nearly 1 million today. The following statistics are outlined by the United States Office of Education in a publication that projects the education of the present into the education of the future (1974-1975):

A 71 percent increase in students getting bachelor's degrees, up from 525,000 to 899,000.

Almost twice as many persons getting master's degrees, from 111,000 to 210,000.

Twice as many persons getting doctoral degrees from 15,300 to 31,900.

An 89 percent increase in total spending by colleges and universities, from $11.9 billion to $22.5 billion.

A 74 percent increase in students seeking degrees at colleges and universities, up from 5 million in the fall of 1964 to 8.7 million in the fall of 1974.

A 13.5 percent increase in enrollment at public and private elementary and secondary schools, from 48.1 million in 1964 to 54.6 million in 1974.

A 25.9 percent increase in public and private high school graduates, from 2.7 million to 3.4 million.

An increase of 507,000 public and private elemen-

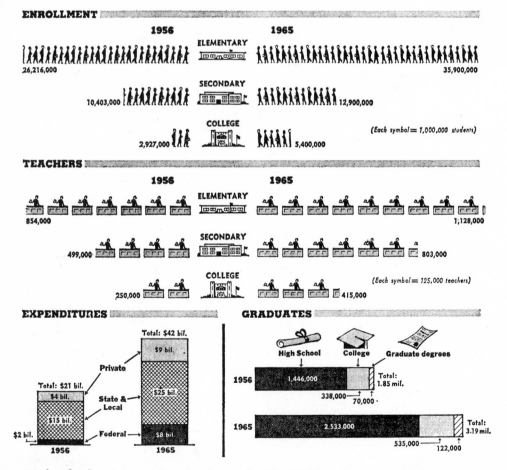

The nation's school system — a decade of growth. (© 1965 by The New York Times Company. Reprinted by permission.)

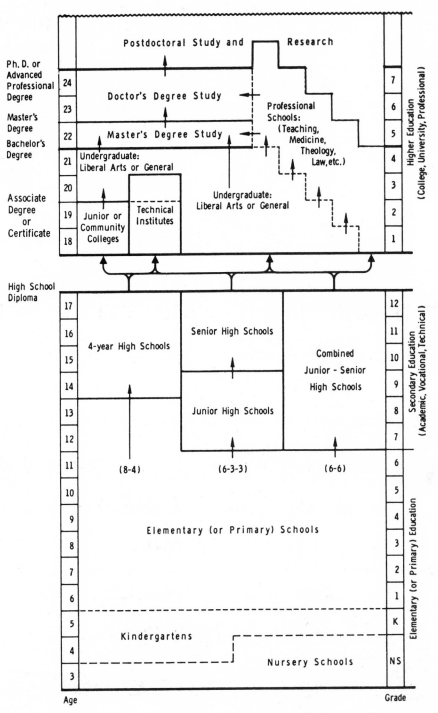

The structure of education in the United States. (From Digest of educational statistics, Washington, D. C., 1965 edition, U. S. Department of Health, Education and Welfare, Office of Education.)

tary and secondary school teachers, from 1.9 million to 2.4 million.

A 47 percent increase in expenditures for elementary and secondary schools, from $26.1 billion to $38.4 billion in the 1974-1975 school year.

The projections indicate that in 1974, the number of high school students will have more than doubled, and the number of degree-seeking college students will have more than tripled the 1954 totals. A decade from now, an estimated 16.4 million students will be in high school.*

The growth in education during recent years and the future expansion predicted place a heavy responsibility upon those persons who provide leadership in this area to offer a program that will preserve the democratic foundations upon which this nation was built, to help develop the potentials of each young person, and to devise educational programs that keep abreast of the times. This Herculean task falls not only upon those individuals who are la-

beled administrators but also upon all educators, whatever role they play in the schools. As such, a study of the facts that comprise the components of educational administration is essential to all, teachers and administrators alike.

THE CHANGING NATURE OF EDUCATION

In addition to the phenomenal growth in enrollments and the cost of running our schools, there have been many significant changes in the manner in which schools and colleges educate our young people. The schools and colleges of America are undergoing a major overhaul. A sampling of some new innovations follows*:

1. The ungraded system in elementary schools that eliminates grade lines in respect to subject matter and student progress

---

*Projections of educational statistics of 1974-75, Washington, D. C., 1965 edition, U. S. Department of Health, Education and Welfare.

*For further discussion of new innovations, see Chapter 3.

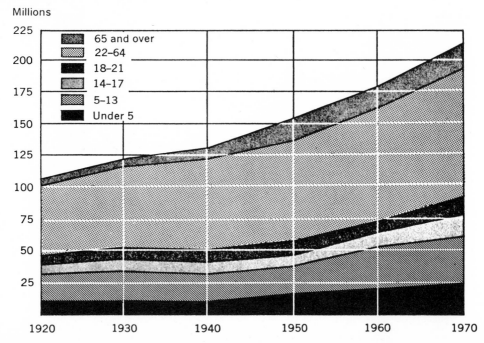

Fifty years of population growth – 1920 to 1970 – has many implications for education. (From NEA Research Bulletin 39:91, 1961.)

2. "Shared time" projects in which both public and parochial school students participate

3. Cooperative buying of school supplies and equipment by several school districts

4. Area schools for rural students desiring modern industrial training

5. Foreign languages offered in the elementary grades

6. Project Head Start—a federally aided program to help slum youngsters enter school better prepared for their new experience

7. Children taught to read with the assistance of a computerized typewriter

8. The new alphabet (Pitman or Initial Teaching Alphabet) with forty-four symbols that represent various sounds being used to provide children with their first experience in reading

9. The new mathematics

10. The new physics

11. The new grammar

12. Team teaching—employing two, three, or more teachers

13. Educational television

14. Teaching machines—giving a student knowledge bit by bit and at his own pace

15. Extension of the school day from 9 A.M. to 5 P.M.

16. Extension of the school year

17. Flexible scheduling with class time ranging from 20 minutes to 1½ or 2 hours

18. Independent study to enable students to carry out advanced work

19. Facilities built underground to cut expense costs

20. The use of educational parks to bring elementary and secondary schools together on campuses

21. Special programs for the gifted students

22. Aid for slum children

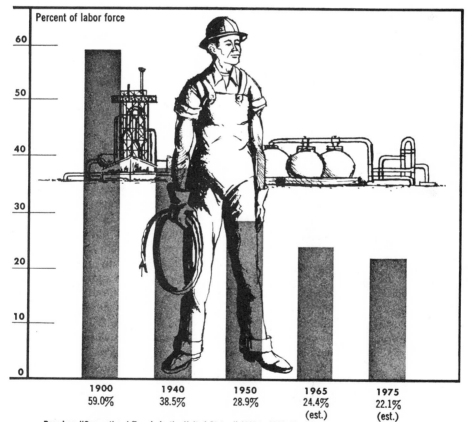

Percent of labor force

1900	1940	1950	1965	1975
59.0%	38.5%	28.9%	24.4%	22.1%
			(est.)	(est.)

Based on "Occupational Trends in the United States," 1900 to 1950, Working Paper No. 5 of the U. S. Department of Commerce, Bureau of the Census; and unpublished data of the U. S. Department of Labor, Bureau of Labor Statistics.

The falling demand for unskilled labor. (From NEA Research Bulletin **38**:12, 1960.)

Education is on the move. New ways of doing things, new facilities, new programs, and the emphasis upon research have become bywords in school systems across the country. Education is not static but instead is a dynamic, constantly changing entity. Educators need to be aware of the changes taking place in the schools and to adapt their own efforts and special fields accordingly. Administration should help in the evaluation of these new innovations, checking the advantages against the disadvantages and weighing their implications for each teacher's field of specialization.

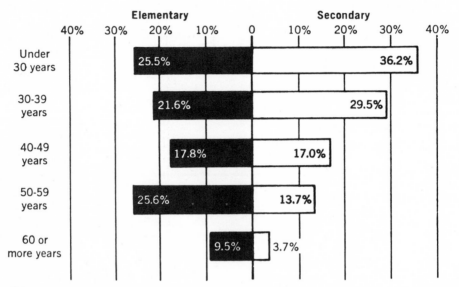

Age distribution of teachers by school level, February, 1965. (From NEA Research Bulletin **43:**68, 1965.)

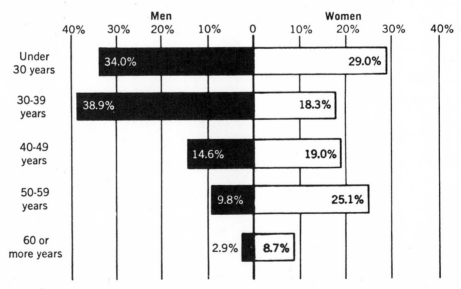

Age distribution of teachers by sex, February, 1965. (From NEA Research Bulletin **43:**68, 1965.)

Education exists in and out of the schools

There is an educational revolution going on in education outside the schools. Business organizations have their education departments. Communications media such as television and radio are in the business of education. Youth groups such as the Campfire Girls and Boy Scouts provide educational experiences, and a multitude of other agencies are also involved. It is therefore important to be realistic about education in America and to be concerned with it in its broadest sense—in and out of the schools. This means teachers, administrators, and educators, in general, must prepare them-selves to give leadership to out-of-school programs as well as those with which they are directly involved in the schools.

Equality of education for everyone

The civil rights movement, Project Head Start, the Job Corps, and other national developments indicate that this country is striving to provide each person, regardless of race, color, creed, or economic means, with a quality education. The implications of such a worthy goal mean federal funds, broadened programs, and educational consumers with different needs and interests.

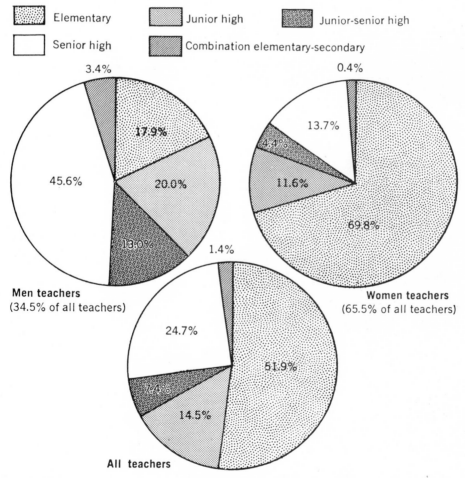

Distribution of classroom teachers by teaching assignment, February, 1965. (From NEA Research Bulletin 43:68, 1965.)

The curriculum reform movement

Knowledge and truth change with history and with the application of the scientific method to social and educational problems. Young people today need to be acquainted with truths that are truths today. The new mathematics and new physics are only a few of the changes in the curriculum reform movement that are taking place in our schools in an attempt to get at the truth. The trivia must be abolished, the overlap and duplication eliminated, and a new look provided where deficiencies and weaknesses exist. There is a need to debate ways of doing this, a need to test results, a need to experiment, a need for new programs, and a need for alternatives.

Education and the arts and sciences are both in the business of education. (Yeshiva University, New York, N. Y.)

The scientific study of teaching and learning

There is a realization that the teaching and learning processes can be improved. New techniques can be utilized, new assignments given, and new projects developed. In the preparation of teachers, all parts of a university must work together. Schools of education and the arts and the sciences are both in the business of education whether they like it or not. Learning can be done more efficiently, and the answers will be learned only as constant experimentation takes place and research and testing are done.

The trend toward more public control

The increase of state and federal outlays for education means that control is also shifting from local to federal sources. Federal and state grants mean that the conditions under which such monies are expended for educational purposes must meet the approval of the upper echelons of governmental authority.

Closer working relationship among the home, school, and community

The community is voicing increased concern about the education of its children. Parent-teacher organizations, advisory councils, and other lay groups want to have a say about how their educational systems are run. Educators can no longer live a cloistered existence and be oblivious to the public voice. Avenues of communication must be established and educational problems aired if they are to be solved effectively.

The belief that all problems can be solved through education

The fact that many Americans are killed each year on the nation's highways has resulted in Americans turning to schools for a solution to this problem. The fact that tests have shown that American children are not physically fit has resulted in the public asking the schools to help remedy the problem. Education is increasingly being looked upon as a panacea for many of the problems with which our society is vexed. Consequently, there are pressures for time in the school schedule, personnel to do the job, and budget allocations to support the suggested reforms.

The internationalization of education

The exchange programs involving faculty and students, the increased speed of transportation, the junior-year abroad, the great amount of travel by Americans to other countries, and the creation of international centers and other evidences of cross-cultural intermingling have resulted in educational concern for people and problems outside the continental United States. Americans no longer live by themselves. What they do and how they think affects not only Americans but also other people around the globe. Education is not limited to the United States but involves the entire globe.

THE CHALLENGE OF THE FUTURE AND THE ADMINISTRATION OF HEALTH AND PHYSICAL EDUCATION PROGRAMS

The changes taking place in education and the goals being sought have vital implications for school health and physical education programs.

1. *Health educators and physical educators must be aware of new developments in general education.* There are so many changes taking place in education today that unless a person continually makes a determined effort to keep abreast of these changes, he is likely to find that he is out of pace with the times. Each health educator and physical educator should read current literature that concerns itself with new trends and practices in education. There are many excellent publications that cover the latest thinking in education. Keeping abreast of new innovations does

not simply mean possessing a superficial knowledge of each development, but, instead, it means being informed as to the nature and scope of the innovation, where and why it is being used, its advantages and disadvantages, and its implications for health and physical education programs.

In addition to being knowledgeable about what is happening in education, some of the new trends may have special implications for school health and physical education programs. For example, in regard to the nongraded elementary school, one might ask the following questions: Should a student be permitted to proceed at his own rate of speed in areas that have a unique relationship to his physical growth and development in the same way that he would proceed in a course in mathematics where the learning involves primarily the mental mechanisms? What is the ideal type of schedule for physical education and health education? Should all class periods be the same length or be of varying lengths? If so, what are they? In what way can programmed instruction be used most effectively in health education and physical education? The answers to such questions will require much thought and investigation, but the end results are very important to the most effective administration of these special fields.

2. *Health educators and physical educators should be continually studying their present programs and practices to determine if they are keeping up with the times.* Just as programs are changing in mathematics, English, and science, so also should programs of school health education and physical education be studied for possible needed changes. Changing for the sake of change itself should not be the case, but sometimes traditional ways of doing things become outmoded and consequently new innovations are needed to keep up with the times. For example, such ideas as the following have been suggested and may possibly warrant further study:

a. Physical education classes meeting in the classroom as well as in the gymnasium
b. Health science classes being taught only by teachers trained and interested in this area
c. A textbook in classes of physical education
d. A conceptualized approach to the teaching of health
e. A program of educational athletics
f. A national curriculum in physical education
g. A movement education emphasis in physical education
h. Perceptual motor skills as a means of improving reading in the early grades
i. New approaches to the teaching of critical health areas such as alcohol, tobacco, narcotics, and sex education
j. Team teaching

3. *Health educators and physical educators should recognize that new challenges to education have administrative implications for their programs.* The tremendous growth and emphasis upon education have special implications for the field of administration. Such factors as policies developed, budgets approved, personnel appointed, facilities and equipment purchased, curricula planned, and special subject matter and activity programs encouraged will determine the direction of school health and physical education programs in the future. The challenge of the increased role for education in American life, with increased funds, personnel, and facilities to accomplish the objectives that have been established, will be met only as sound administrative practices are followed. The challenge means that all health educators and physical educators should understand what does and does not constitute sound administrative practice.

4. *Health educators and physical educators should place more emphasis on research.* There is an urgent need for more emphasis upon research in the fields of health education and physical education. Research is needed to advance the frontiers of knowledge in regard to these special fields, their contributions to mankind, their role in academic achievement, the function they have in personality develop-

ment, and the tangible impacts they have on the health, productivity, and leadership of Americans. These are only a few areas that need to be investigated. In addition to more research being conducted, there needs to be greater emphasis on the training of research workers in professional preparation programs. Also, there should be more outlets for publicizing the research findings. At present, the *Research Quarterly* of the American Association of Health, Physical Education and Recreation (about sixty studies a year), *The Journal of School Health,* and *The School Health Review* are the main outlets, although certain psychologic and physiologic publications do provide other means of communication. However, there should be more outlets with greater implementation of findings at the grass roots level.

5. *Health educators and physical educators must become more scholarly.* Excellence in educational undertakings means that the educators involved—the persons who are doing the teaching and administering—must themselves be scholarly individuals. There is so much cross fertilization in educational endeavors that each teacher and administrator can contribute to the education of our young people in many areas other than his own specialty. This can only be possible as each educator becomes a scholarly individual in his own right. Furthermore, it is important for health education and physical education to be able to stand on an equal footing with academic subjects and not be found wanting when more scholarly discussions are held.

Questions and exercises

1. Define the term *administration* in your own words. Give illustrations to point out the various facets of your definition.
2. Prepare an organization chart for some department, school, or agency with which you are familiar. Discuss significant aspects of the administrative setup of this organization.
3. Prepare a rating sheet that could be utilized

by students to determine the extent of their qualifications for the field of administration.

4. Write an essay discussing the role of the administrator in achieving cooperation from members of an organization.

5. What are some basic principles that should be observed in respect to channels of communication?

6. Why is a study of administration important to you as a physical educator or health educator?

7. Compare the traditional and the modern views of education. What do we mean by a theory of administration, and how does theory help in the practice of administration?

8. What type of preparation should potential administrators receive according to the administrative theorists?

9. What are the qualities that make for administrative leadership? Will the administrative leader be a success in whatever job he assumes?

10. In respect to policy formation discuss the following: (a) what is policy? (b) why is policy needed? (c) how should policy be developed and written? Prepare a sample policy in physical education.

11. Describe a democratic administrator. Compare his characteristics with those of an autocratic administrator.

12. Why is education playing an increasing role in American life?

13. Project health education or physical education 20 years into the future and describe the type of program you would like to see.

Reading assignment in *Administrative Dimensions of Health and Physical Education Programs, Including Athletics:* Chapter 1, Selections 1 to 4.

Selected references

American Association for Health, Physical Education, and Recreation: Developing democratic human relations through health education, physical education and recreation, Washington, D. C., 1951, The Association.

Bender, J. F.: The technique of executive leadership, New York, 1950, McGraw-Hill Book Co.

Bucher, C. A.: Foundations of physical education, ed. 5, St. Louis, 1968, The C. V. Mosby Co.

Bucher, C. A., Koenig, C., and Barnhard, M.: Methods and materials for secondary school physical education, ed. 3, St. Louis, 1970, The C. V. Mosby Co.

Center for the Advanced Study of Educational Administration: Perspectives of educational administration and the behavioral sciences, Eugene, 1965, The University of Oregon.

Educational Personnel Administration Number, Education, December, 1954. (A compilation of fourteen articles on educational personnel administration.)

Goldman, S.: The school principal, New York, 1966, The Center for Applied Research in Education, Inc. (The Library of Education).

Griffiths, D. E.: The school superintendent, New York, 1966, The Center for Applied Research in Education, Inc. (The Library of Education).

Gulick, L., and Urwick, L., editors: Papers on the science of administration, New York, 1937, Institute of Public Administration.

Halpin, A. W., editor: Administrative theory in education, New York, 1958, The Macmillan Co.

Jenson, T. H., and Clark, D. L.: Educational administration, New York, 1964, The Center for Applied Research in Education, Inc. (The Library of Education).

Knezevich, S. J.: Administration of public education, New York, 1962, Harper & Row, Publishers, pp. 223-226.

Kozman, H. C., editor: Group process in physical education, New York, 1951, Harper & Row, Publishers.

Morphet, E. L., and others: Educational organization and administration, Englewood Cliffs, N. J., 1967, Prentice-Hall, Inc.

Simon, H. A.: Administrative behavior, New York, 1957, The Free Press.

Tead, O.: The art of leadership, New York, 1935, Whittlesey House.

Tead, O.: The art of administration, New York, 1951, McGraw-Hill Book Co.

Thompson, J. D., editor: Approaches to organizational design, Pittsburgh, 1966, University of Pittsburgh Press.

Urwick, L.: The elements of administration, New York, 1943, Harper & Row, Publishers.

Willower, D. J., and Culbertson J., editors: The professorship in educational administration, Columbus, Ohio, 1964, The University Council for Educational Administration.

CHAPTER 2 ADMINISTRATIVE RELATIONSHIPS AND OBJECTIVES

Each person associated with the schools and colleges of this country should view himself first as an educator and second as a health educator, physical educator, recreation supervisor, history teacher, or other type of specialist. Each person should see himself working to achieve goals that are common to general education and toward which the schools and colleges are directing their efforts. Each person should view his own special field with a perspective that gives balance to the total enterprise. Each person should strive to appreciate fully what all areas of specialization are attempting to accomplish and the contribution each makes toward helping our young people develop into mature, well-educated adults.

A field of endeavor is characterized by the objectives for which it exists. Objectives help the members of a group to know where they are going, what they are striving for, and what they hope to accomplish. Physical educators and health educators have clearly stated objectives toward which they are working. The student preparing for a career in these fields or administrators and leaders working in these fields should understand the objectives and be guided by them. Objectives, therefore, represent the aims, purposes, and outcomes that are derived from participating in physical education and health education programs.

HEALTH EDUCATION AND PHYSICAL EDUCATION DEFINED

The term *health* as defined by the World Health Organization refers to the total health of the person, including mental, emotional, physical, and social health, and not merely the absence of disease and infirmity. The school health program is designed to achieve this objective through a plan of health instruction, health services, and healthful school living. A definition of school health education as included in the report of the Joint Committee on Health Education Terminology,* is: "The process of providing or utilizing experiences for favorably influencing understandings, attitudes, and practices related to safe living."

The term *physical education* as used in this text is defined as follows: *Physical education, an integral part of the total education process, is a program aimed at the development of physically, mentally, emotionally, and socially fit citizens through the medium of physical activities that have been selected with a view to realizing these outcomes.*

GENERAL EDUCATION

Since school and college health and physical education should first be viewed within the concept of general education, it is appropriate to first define what is meant by general education and second to delineate the role of health and physical education within general education.

The purposes for which education exists have been set forth by many individuals and many organizations. One group of pur-

---

*Report of the Joint Committee on Health Education Terminology, Journal of Health, Physical Education, and Recreation 33:27, 1962.

poses reflects the socioeconomic goals for education as presented in ten characteristics that are desired for the individual American. These characteristics were stated in 1937 by a committee that included a philosopher, a lawyer, a sociologist, a superintendent of schools, and two secretaries of state education associations.

1. Hereditary strength
2. Physical security
3. Participation in an evolving culture
   a. Skills, techniques, and knowledges
   b. Values, standards, and outlooks
4. An active, flexible personality
5. Suitable occupation
6. Economic security
7. Mental security
8. Equality of opportunity
9. Freedom
10. Fair play

Also included in the report of this committee, which included John Dewey and Willard E. Givens, were statements that "education must be universal in its extent and application, universal in its materials and methods, and universal in its aims and spirit." When analyzing and studying this list, one cannot but realize the great implications each of the items has for the fields of school health and physical education.

In 1938 the Educational Policies Commission also set forth certain purposes of education that they felt included a summarization and enlargement of statements that had been published previously by various committees and individuals representing the National Education Association. These purposes were (1) the objectives of self-realization, which are concerned with developing the individual to his fullest capacity in respect to health, recreation, and philosophy of life, (2) the objectives of human relationship, which refer to relationships among people on the family, group, and society levels, (3) the objectives of economic efficiency, which are

concerned with the individual as a producer and a consumer, and (4) the objectives of civic responsibility, which stress the individual's relationship to his local, state, national, and international forms of government.

Today, general education is looked upon as preparing the individual for a meaningful, self-directed existence. For a student to be prepared to accomplish this goal means that he must have an understanding of (1) his cultural heritage and the ability to evaluate it, (2) the world of nature and the ability to adapt to it, (3) the contemporary social scene and the values and skills necessary for effective participation, (4) the role of communication and skill in communicating, (5) the nature of self and others and growth in capacity for continuing self-development and for relating to others, and (6) the role of esthetic forms in human living and the capacity for self-expression through them. Thus the role of general education is a multifaceted undertaking requiring many different experiences and specialties.

HEALTH AND PHYSICAL EDUCATION PROGRAMS CONTRIBUTE TO GENERAL EDUCATION

Health education and physical education are integral parts of general education. Science indicates that these fields of endeavor contribute in many ways.

1. *The mind and body are inseparable.* Physical, mental, social, and emotional development are closely interwoven into the fabric of the human being. A person can think himself into being sick just as sickness can affect his thinking; *psychosomatic* has become an important word in our vocabulary. Intellectual, physical, and emotional developments are closely associated. Endocrinology has shown that mentality changes as body chemistry changes. Biology has linked the cell to the learning experience. Psychology points to the fact

Davenport, Iowa, Public Schools.

that the child's earliest learnings are tactual and kinesthetic.

2. *Motor skills contribute to learning.* Intelligence is not the only answer to achievement in school. Motor learning is involved in readiness skills that are basic to perception, symbolic manipulation, and concept formation. If motor learning during the early years of childhood is deficient, more complex and advanced learning will be impeded. Psychologists Radler and Kephart * point out that motor activity of some type forms the foundation for all behavior, including the higher thought processes. They further stress that human behavior will function no better than the motor skills that are a part of the individual's makeup.

3. *Health and physical education contribute to academic achievement by developing physical fitness.* Research indicates that students who are achieving academically are also physically above average. It appears that physical fitness, at least up to a certain minimum level, is essential for good health and necessary for academic achievement.

4. *Health education and physical education contribute to academic achievement*

through their contribution to social development. Research shows a relationship between scholastic success and the degree to which a student is accepted by his peer group. Similarly, the boy or girl who learns and applies sound principles of personality development or who is well grounded in motor skills, for example, usually possesses social status among his or her peers.

5. *Health education and physical education contribute to the emotional development of educationally subnormal students.* The value of health and physical education programs for educationally subnormal students may be greater than for average boys and girls. Dr. James N. Oliver, lecturer in education at the University of Birmingham, England, has done much research on educationally subnormal boys and has found that systematic and progressive physical conditioning yields marked mental and physical improvement. He believes much of the improvement results from a boy's feelings of achievement that has the side effect of influencing his academic work for the better.

6. *Health education and physical education are integral parts of general education since they possess a subject matter essential to human beings.* Just as it is important to teach English so that people can communicate articulately, history so that they will appreciate their cultural heritage, and fine arts so that they can appreciate and enjoy Picasso and Beethoven, so it is also important to educate people regarding their physical selves so that they may function most efficiently as human beings. A very intelligent group of young people in our schools and colleges today are not going to be physically active, develop skill, stop their sexual promiscuity, drinking, smoking, and use of narcotics unless given some good reasons. They are going to have to understand and know that the time spent in the pursuit of these goals has its rewards. Thus facts and subject matter become a necessity.

*Radler, D. H., and Kephart, N. C.: Success through play, New York, 1960, Harper & Row, Publishers.

Physical education is a part of general education. (Emma Woerner Junior High School, Louisville, Ky.)

RELATIONSHIP OF HEALTH EDUCATION AND PHYSICAL EDUCATION

Health education and physical education as professional fields of endeavor are closely allied, especially in respect to their administrative aspects. In many schools and colleges, both come under one administrative head. They are concerned with the accomplishment of similar objectives. In many small communities both health education and physical education, although not always desirable, are taught by the same person. Professional preparation institutions usually incorporate both areas in the same schools or departments. In the American Association for Health, Physical Education, and Recreation, they are linked together professionally. Individuals working in these specialized areas share facilities, personnel, funds, and other items essential to their programs. General school administrators feel they are closely related.

These are only a few of the reasons why a close administrative relationship should and must exist between these specialized

fields. Although professional persons realize the place of each and the need for specialists in each area, at the same time they also recognize the importance of maintaining a close and effective working relationship. The administrator is a key person in seeing that such a relationship is maintained. In some quarters there has been disunity and strained relations between these areas because the administrator did not assume his role of appeaser and unifier.

In recent years educational thinking has been more and more cognizant of the place of health education and physical education in school and college programs. Each is closely related to the other, but at the same time each is distinct. Each area has its own specialized subject matter content, its specialists, and media through which it is striving to better the living standards of human beings. In the larger professional preparation institutions each has its own separate training program. There is continual agitation for separate certification of its leaders in the various states. Some sections of the country have recognized this

need and have established state certification standards for employment of these
specialized workers.

Although many educators and others feel
that physical education has traditionally
reflected the thinking and work of both
areas, this is an erroneous belief. There is
a definite need for the specialist in each of
the areas of health and physical education.
Each can render a service to humanity.
Each can make a contribution that is distinct and separate from the other's. Each
has its own destiny.

A close relationship among teachers in
these areas, however, is evidenced by the
fact that, to a great degree, they work on
committees together and have professional
books and magazines that cover the literature of both fields. Both are concerned
with the total health of the individual. Both
recognize the importance of activity in developing and maintaining good personal
health. Both are concerned with the physical as well as the social, mental, emotional,
and spiritual aspects. Both recognize the
importance of developing good human relations as a basis for effective living in a
democracy. Both are interested in promoting the total health of the public at large
as a means to enriched living, accomplishment of worthy goals, and increased happiness.

OBJECTIVES OF HEALTH AND PHYSICAL EDUCATION PROGRAMS

The ultimate objectives of school and
college health and physical education programs are similar. The essential difference
lies in the fact that each area attempts to
achieve its goals by utilizing different skills,
media, and approaches. The objectives of
each of the two areas are discussed in the
pages to follow.

Objectives of health education programs

The long-term, overall objective of a
health program is to maintain and improve
the health of human beings. This refers to
all aspects of health, including physical,
mental, emotional, and social. It applies to
all individuals, regardless of race, color,
economic status, creed, or national origin.
Schools and colleges have the responsibility to see that all students achieve and
maintain optimum health, not only from a
legal point of view but also from the standpoint that the educational experience will
be much more meaningful if optimum
health exists. A person learns easier and
better when in a state of good health.

A synthesis of some of the objectives of
the school and college health programs that
have been listed by leaders in the field include the following:

1. To teach scientific health knowledge so that
the individual can make intelligent health
decisions
2. To develop desirable health attitudes in
order that the individual will have an interest in applying health knowledge to his
own daily regimen of living
3. To convey to the consumer that health is a
three-dimensional entity, embodying social,
mental, and physical aspects
4. To contribute to the physical, social, and
emotional development of each boy and
girl
5. To further good personality development
among students
6. To encourage the student to be a wise
consumer and producer with respect to
health goods and services
7. To encourage the correction of remediable
defects among those persons where they
exist
8. To help students and teachers to live
healthfully at school and college
9. To reduce the incidence of communicable
disease in the school, college, and community
10. To appreciate the many health services
available in the school, college, and community
11. To further home-school cooperation in
health matters

The commonly mentioned objectives
concerned with the development of health
knowledge, desirable health attitudes, and
desirable health practices deserve further
discussion.

Development of health knowledge. In order to accomplish the health knowledge objective, health education must present and interpret scientific health data for purposes of personal guidance. Such information will help individuals to recognize health problems and to solve them by utilizing information that is valid and helpful. It also will serve as a basis for the formulation of desirable health attitudes. In the complex society that exists today there are so many choices confronting an individual in regard to factors that affect his health that a reliable store of knowledge is essential.

Individuals should know how their bodies function, causes and methods of preventing disease, factors that contribute to and maintain health, and the role of the community in the health program. Such knowledge will aid the individual to live correctly, help protect his body against harm and infection, and impress upon him the responsibility for his own health and the health of others.

Knowledge of health will vary with different ages. For younger children there should be an attempt to provide experiences that will show the importance of living healthfully. Such settings as the cafeteria, lavatory, and medical examination room offer these opportunities. As the individual grows older, the scientific knowledge for following certain health practices and ways of living can be presented. Some of the areas of health knowledge that should be understood by students and adults include nutrition, the need for rest,

Burnett and Logan, Chicago.

One objective of health education is the cultivation of those habits of living which will promote present and future health. (Washington Irving Elementary School, Waverly, Iowa.)

sleep, and exercise, protection of the body against changing temperature conditions, contagious disease control, drugs, environmental pollution, family living, human sexuality, the dangers of self-medication, and community resources for health.* If such topics are brought to the attention of persons everywhere and if the proper health attitudes and practices are developed, better health will result.

There should also be an adequate knowledge of what constitutes healthful living and adequate health services.

Both the physical and nonphysical environment should be considered in healthful living. School and college buildings, homes, and other places where people congregate should be clean, sanitary, well lighted, and ventilated, provide ample space, and be adjusted to the various health needs of individuals. In addition, the importance of the nonphysical environment should be recognized. This environment reflects how teachers and pupils get along with each other, incentives, organization and administrative structure and procedures, and other items that greatly affect mental and emotional health.

Knowledge of what constitutes adequate health services should also be understood. Such health services as health appraisal, health counseling, communicable disease control, education of the handicapped, and emergency care of injuries should be appreciated by all. Only as this knowledge is imparted will the various services be utilized in a manner most conducive to the health of students.

Development of desirable health attitudes. The term *health attitudes* refers to the health interests of the individual or the motives that impel him to act in a certain way. All the health knowledge that can be accumulated will have little worth unless the individual is interested and motivated to the point that he wants to apply this

knowledge to everyday living. Attitudes, motives, drives, or impulses, if properly established, will result in the individual's seeking out scientific knowledge and utilizing it as a guide to living. This interest, drive, or motivation must be dynamic to the point where it results in behavior changes.

School and college health programs must be directed at developing those attitudes that will result in optimum health. Students should have an interest in, and be motivated toward, possessing a state of buoyant health, being well rested and well fed, having wholesome thoughts free from anger, jealousy, hate, and worry, and feeling strong and possessing physical power to perform life's routine tasks. They should have the right attitudes toward health knowledge, healthful school living, and health services. If such interests as these exist within the individual, proper health practices will be followed. Health should not be an end in itself except in cases of severe illness. Health is a means to an end, a medium that aids in achieving noble purposes and contributes to enriched living.

Another factor that motivates individuals to good health is the desire to avoid the pain and disturbances that accompany ill health. They do not like toothaches, headaches, or indigestion because of the pain or distraction involved. However, developing health attitudes in a negative manner, through fear of pain or other disagreeable conditions, is a questionable approach.

A strong argument for developing proper attitudes or interests should center around the goals one is trying to achieve in life and the manner in which optimum health is an aid in achieving such goals. This is the strongest incentive or interest that can be developed in the individual. If one wishes to become a great artist, an outstanding businessman, or a famed dancer, it is greatly beneficial if he or she has good health. This is important so that the study,

---

*See also Chapter 12.

training, hard work, trials, and obstacles that one encounters can be met successfully. Optimum health will aid in the accomplishment of such goals. As Jennings, the biologist, has pointed out, the body can attend to only one thing at a time. If its attention is focused on a toothache, a headache, or an ulcer, it cannot be focused satisfactorily on some essential work that has to be done. Centering health attitudes or interests on life goals is a dynamic thing because these represent an aid to accomplishment, achievement, and enjoyable living.

Development of desirable health practices. Desirable health practices represent the application of those habits that are best, according to the most qualified thinking in the field, to one's routine of living. The health practices that an individual adopts will determine in great measure the health of that person. If practices or habits harmful to optimum health are engaged in, such as failure to obtain proper rest or exercise, overeating, overdrinking, oversmoking, and the use of harmful drugs and failure to observe certain precautions against contracting diseases, then poor health is likely to follow.

Knowledge does not necessarily ensure good health practices. An individual may have at his command all the statistics as to the results of speeding at 70 miles per hour and of using seat belts, but unless this information is applied it is useless. The health of an individual can be affected only by applying that which is known. At the same time, knowledge will not usually be applied unless an incentive, interest, or attitude exists that impels its application. It can be seen, therefore, that in order to have a good school health program, it is important to recognize the close relationship that exists among health knowledge, health attitudes, and health practices. One contributes to the other.

Another health objective that is sometimes listed is that of skill development. This refers to the development of such skills as those involved in first aid and safety. A mastery of such skills enhances good health.

Recent significant health studies. A significant study in the field of health education was the School Health Education Study,* which was initiated in September, 1961, under a grant from the Samuel Bronfman Foundation of New York City. This study included a synthesis of research in selected areas of health instruction, a national study of health instruction in the public schools, and the development of a concept approach to the teaching of health that identified the key concepts in the teaching of health, statements of concepts for organizing the curriculum, and substantive elements that delineated the subject matter content. All of these concepts are directed at certain behavioral outcomes that are deemed desirable for the student. The School Health Education Study is discussed at greater length in Chapter 12.

Another significant step forward at the state level has developed in New York State. As a result of the increased awareness of health problems, including the widespread use of drugs and narcotics, tobacco, and alcohol, Governor Nelson Rockefeller signed the Speno-Brydges Bill in May, 1967. This law required the teaching of health in all grades throughout the state of New York. A new health curriculum was developed and the program introduced in 1970. As a result of this legislation and the increased interest in health on the part of the citizens of this state, schoolchildren are receiving instruction in the critical

---

*The following reports were published by the School Health Education Study, 1201 16th St. N.W., Washington, D. C.: Synthesis of research in selected areas of health instruction, July, 1963; School Health Education Study: A summary report, June, 1964; School Health Education Study: A call for action, February, 1965; and School Health Education Study: A conceptual approach, February, 1965.

The physical development objective. (Department of Physical Education, University of California at Berkeley.)

health areas of tobacco, drugs, alcohol, and family living and also in such areas as nutrition, mental and emotional health, disease prevention and control, and accident prevention.

What is developing in New York State is increasingly being felt throughout the nation. More and more state departments of education and health, larger and larger groups of citizens, and more governmental officials are beginning to recognize that education is vital to the nation's health and well-being.

Objectives of the school and college physical education programs*

A study of the individual reveals four general directions or phases in which

*Bucher, C. A.: Foundations of physical education, ed. 5, St. Louis, 1968, The C. V. Mosby Co.

growth and development take place—physical development, motor development, mental development, and human relations development. Physical education plays an important part in contributing to each of these phases of human growth and development.

The physical development objective. The physical development objective deals with the program of activities that builds physical power in an individual through the development of the various organic systems of the body. It results in the ability to sustain adaptive effort, the ability to recover, and the ability to resist fatigue. The value of this objective is based on the fact that an individual will be more active, have better performance, and be healthier if the organic systems of the body are adequately developed and functioning properly.

Muscular activity plays a major role in the development of the organic systems of the body. The term *organic* refers to the digestive, circulatory, excretory, heat regulatory, respiratory, and other systems of the human body. These systems are stimulated and trained through such activities as hanging, climbing, running, throwing, leaping, carrying, and jumping. Health is also related to muscular activity; therefore, activities that bring into play all of the fundamental "big muscle" groups in the body should be engaged in regularly. Furthermore, the activity should be of a vigorous nature so that the various organic systems are sufficiently stimulated.

Through vigorous muscular activity several beneficial results take place. The trained heart provides better nourishment to the entire body. The trained heart beats slower than the untrained heart. It pumps more blood per stroke, with the result that more food is delivered to the cells and there is better removal of waste products. During exercise the trained heart's speed increases less and has a longer rest period between beats. After exercise it returns to normal much more rapidly. The end result of this state is that the trained individual is able to perform work for a longer period of time, with less expenditure of energy and much more efficiency, than the untrained individual. This trained condition is necessary for a vigorous and abundant life. From the time an individual rises in the morning until he goes to bed at night, he is continually in need of vitality, strength, endurance, and stamina to perform routine tasks, be prepared for emergencies, and lead a vigorous life. Therefore, physical education aids in the development of the trained individual so that he will be better able to perform his routine tasks and live a healthy, interesting, and happy existence.

The motor development objective. The motor development objective is concerned with performing physical movement with as little expenditure of energy as possible and in a proficient, graceful, and esthetic manner. This has implications for one's work, play, and anything else that requires physical movement. The name *motor* is derived from relationship to a nerve or nerve fiber that connects the central nervous system, or a ganglion, with a muscle. Movement results, as a consequence of the impulse it transmits. The impulse it delivers is known as the motor impulse.

Effective motor movement is dependent upon a harmonious working together of the muscular and nervous systems. It results in greater distance between fatigue and peak performance; it is found in activities involving running, hanging, jumping, dodging, leaping, kicking, bending, twisting, carrying, and throwing; and it will enable one to perform his daily work much more efficiently and without reaching the point of being "worn out" so quickly.

In physical education activities, the function of efficient body movement, or neuromuscular skill as it is often called, is to provide the individual with the ability to perform with a degree of proficiency. This will result in greater enjoyment of participation. Most individuals enjoy doing those particular activities in which they have acquired a degree of mastery or skill. For example, if a child has mastered the ability to throw a ball consistently to a designated spot and has developed batting and fielding power, he will like to play baseball or softball. If he can swim 25 or 50 yards without tiring and can perform several dives, he will enjoy being in the water. If an adult can consistently serve tennis "aces," he will like tennis; if he can drive a ball 250 yards straight down the fairway, he will like golf; and if he can throw ringers, he will like horseshoes. A person enjoys doing those things in which he or she excels. Few individuals enjoy participating in activites in which they have little skill. Therefore, it is the objective of physical education to develop in each individual as many physical skills as possible so that interests will be wide and varied. This will

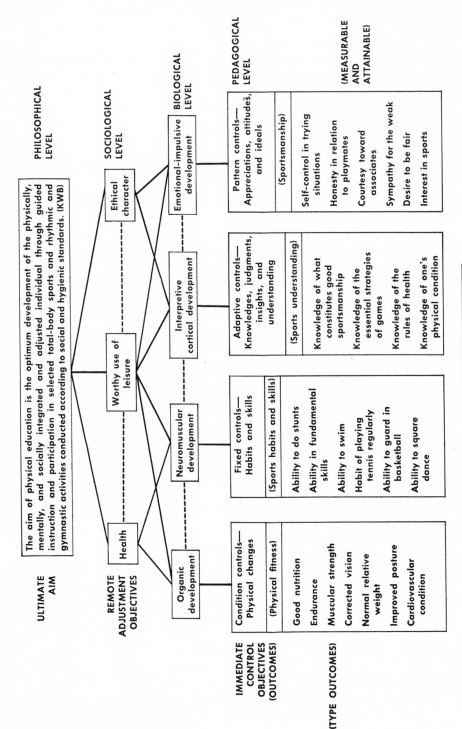

THE PURPOSES OF PHYSICAL EDUCATION

Objectives of physical education. (From Bookwalter, K. W.: Physical education in the secondary schools, Washington, D. C., 1964, The Center for Applied Research in Education, Inc.)

not only result in more enjoyment for the participant, but at the same time will allow for better adjustment to group situations.

Physical skills are not developed in one lesson. It takes years to acquire coordinations, and the most important period for development is during the formative years of a child's growth. The building of coordinations starts in childhood, when an individual attempts to synchronize his muscular and nervous systems for such movements as creeping, walking, running, and jumping. A study of kinesiology shows that many muscles of the body are used in even the most simple of coordinated movements. Therefore, in order to obtain efficient motor movement or skill in many activities, it is necessary to start training early in life and to continue into adulthood. Furthermore, a child does not object to the continual trial-and-error process of achieving

success in the performance of physical acts. He does not object to being observed as an awkward, uncoordinated beginner during the learning period. Most adults, however, are self-conscious when going through the period of learning a physical skill. They do not like to perform if they cannot perform in a creditable manner. The skills they do not acquire in their youth are many times never acquired. Therefore, the physical education profession should try to see that this skill learning takes place at a time when a person is young and willing and is laying the foundation for adult years.

The motor development objective also has important implications for the health and recreational phases of the program. The skills that children acquire will determine to a great extent how their leisure time will be spent. One enjoys participat-

Developing skill in worthwhile physical activities is an objective of physical education. (Department of Physical Education, University of California at Berkeley.)

ing in those activities in which one excels. Therefore, if a child excels in swimming, a great deal of his leisure time is going to be spent at a pool, lake, or beach. If he excels in tennis, he will be found on the courts on Saturdays, Sundays, and after dinner at night. There is believed to be a correlation between juvenile delinquency and lack of constructive leisure-time activity. If we want children to spend their leisure moments in a physically wholesome way, we should see that skills are gained in physical education activities.

The mental development objective. The mental development objective deals with the accumulation of a body of knowledge and the ability to think and interpret this knowledge.

Physical activities must be learned; hence, there is a need for thinking on the part of the intellectual mechanism, with a resulting acquisition of knowledge. The co-ordinations involved in various movements must be mastered and adapted to the environment in which the individual lives, whether it be in walking, running, or wielding a tennis racquet. In all these movements the child must think and coordinate his muscular and nervous systems. Furthermore, this type of knowledge is acquired through trial and error. Then, as a result of experience, there is a changed meaning in the situation. Coordinations are learned, with the result that an act once difficult and awkward to perform becomes easy to execute.

The individual should not only learn coordinations but should also acquire a knowledge of rules, techniques, and strategies involved in physical activities. Basketball can be used as an example. In this sport a person should know the rules, the strategy in offense and defense, the various types of passes, the difference between screening and blocking, and finally the values that are derived from playing in this sport. Techniques that are learned through experience result in knowledge that is also acquired. For example, a ball travels faster and more accurately if one steps with a pass, and time is saved when the pass is made from the same position in which it is received. Furthermore, a knowledge of followership, leadership, courage, self-reliance, assistance to others, safety, and adaptation to group patterns is very important.

Knowledge concerning health should play an important part in the program. All individuals should know about their bodies, the importance of sanitation, factors in disease prevention, the importance of exercise, the need for a well-balanced diet, values of good health attitudes and habits, and the community and school agencies that provide health services. This knowledge will contribute greatly to physical prowess as well as to general health. Through the accumulation of a knowledge of these facts, activities will take on a new meaning and health practices will be associated with definite purposes. This will help each individual to live a healthier and more purposeful life.

A store of knowledge will give each individual the proper background for interpreting new situations that confront him from day to day. Unless there is knowledge to draw from, he will become helpless when called upon to make important decisions. As a result of participation in physical education activities, an individual will be better able to make discriminatory judgments, by which knowledge of values is mentally derived. This means that he has greater power for arriving at a wise decision and that he can better discern right from wrong and the logical from the illogical. Through his experience in various games and sports, he has developed a sense of values, an alertness, the ability to diagnose a tense situation, the ability to make a decision quickly under highly emotionalized conditions, and the ability to interpret human actions.

In physical education activities one also gains insight into human nature. The various forms of activity in physical education are social experiences that enable a participant to learn about human nature. For all children and youth this is one of the main sources of such knowledge. Here they discover the individual's responsibility to the group, the need for followership and leadership, the need to experience success, and the feeling of "belonging." Here they learn how human beings react to satisfactions and annoyances. Such knowledge contributes to social efficiency and good human relations.

The human relations objective. The human relations objective is concerned with helping an individual make personal adjustments, group adjustments, and adjustments as a member of society. Activities in the physical education program offer one of the best opportunities for making these adjustments, if there is proper leadership.

Social action is a result of certain hereditary and derivative tendencies. There are interests, hungers, desires, ideals, attitudes, and emotional drives that are responsible for everything we do. A child wants to play because of his drive for physical activity. A man will steal food because of the hunger drive. America is opposed to totalitarian governments because of its desire for personal freedom. The responses to all these desires, drives, hungers, and the like may be either social or antisocial in nature. The value of physical education reveals itself when we realize that play activities are one of the oldest and most fundamental drives in human nature. Therefore, by providing the child with a satisfying experience in activities in which he has a natural desire to engage, the opportunity is presented to develop desirable social traits. The key is qualified leadership.

All human beings should experience success. This factor can be realized through play. Through successful experience in play activities, a child develops self-confidence and finds happiness in his achievements. Physical education can provide for this successful experience by offering a variety of activities and developing the necessary skills for success in these activities.

If children are happy, they will usually make the necessary adjustments. An individual who is happy is much more likely to make the right adjustment than the individual who is morbid, sullen, and unhappy. Happiness reflects friendliness, cheerfulness, and a spirit of cooperation, all of which help a person to be content and to conform to the necessary standards that have been established. Therefore, physical education should instill happiness by guiding children into these activities where this quality will be realized.

In a democratic society all individuals should develop a sense of group consciousness and cooperative living. This should be one of the most important objectives of the physical education program. Whether or not a child will grow up to be a good citizen and contribute to the welfare of society will depend to a great extent upon the training he receives during his youth. Therefore, in various play activities, the following factors should be stressed: aid for the less-skilled and weaker players, respect for the rights of others, subordination of one's desires to the will of the group, and realization that cooperative living is essential to the success of society. In other words, the golden rule should be practiced. The individual should be made to feel that he belongs to the group and that he has the responsibility of directing his actions in its behalf. The rules of sportsmanship should be developed and practiced in all activities that are offered in the program. Courtesy, sympathy, truthfulness, fairness, honesty, respect for authority, and abiding by the rules will help a great deal in the promotion of social efficiency. The necessity for good leadership and followership should also be stressed as important to the interests of society.

The needs and desires that form the basis for people's actions can be controlled

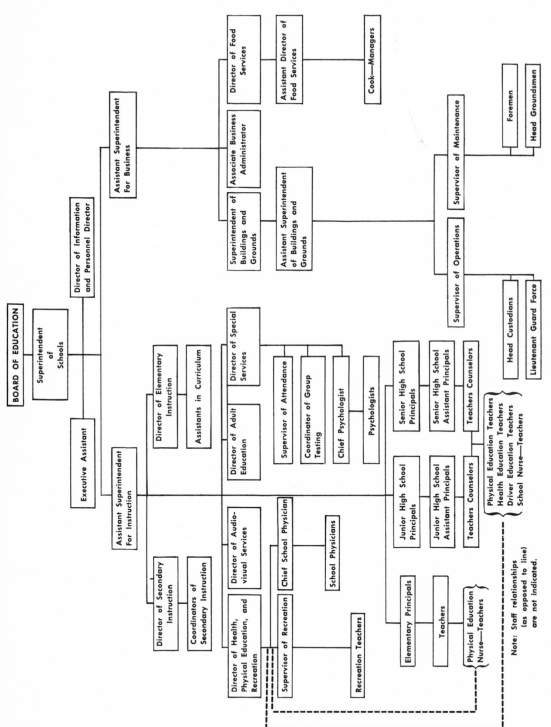

An organization chart for a public school system.

through proper training. This training can result in effective citizenship, which is the basis of sound, democratic living. Effective citizenship is not something that can be developed by artificial stimuli. It is something that is achieved only through activities in which individuals engage in their normal day-to-day routine. Since play activities have such a great attraction for youth, and since it is possible to develop desirable social traits under proper guidance, physical education should realize its responsibility. It should do its part in contributing to good citizenship, the basis of our democratic society. In this chaotic world with its cold wars, hot wars, hydrogen bombs, racial strife, student unrest, imperialistic aims, human ambitions, and class struggles, human relations are more and more important to personal, group, and world peace. Only through a better understanding of one's fellowman will it be possible to build a peaceful and democratic world.

THE ROLE OF ADMINISTRATION IN ACHIEVING OBJECTIVES

Good administration is an essential in the fields of school and college health education and physical education if the goals that have been set for these professions are to be realized. Harmony must be encouraged among the various members of the staff, adequate facilities provided, the program planned and continually reevaluated, a public relations plan established, leadership provided, and many other essentials and details attended to with dispatch if the objectives are to be achieved.

The administrator is a key person; he sets the pace and provides the leadership. If this individual does not assume the responsibilities that go with such a position, there will be apathy and indifference all along the line and consequently the aims for which the professions exist will not be realized. Administrators must continually keep in mind the goals toward which they are working. With these in mind they

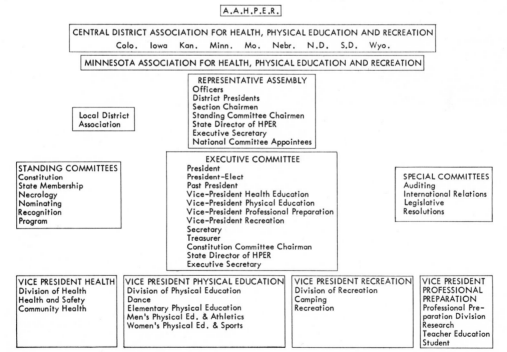

Structure of a state association. (From Minnesota Association for Health, Physical Education, and Recreation News Letter 2:3, 1965.)

should gear their staff relationships, programs, and other factors in a way that will be most efficient and productive from the standpoint of realizing such goals.

Administrators frequently have the areas of both health and physical education within their administrative division. This affords the opportunity to promote the kind of cooperation that is needed to achieve the aims of each. One cannot be promoted at the expense of the other. One cannot be recognized as being more important than the other. If such is the practice progress will be obstructed. Administrators must recognize the important place that each area has in the total picture. All administrative policies must preserve this balance.

If the administrators have only one of these specialized areas within their division, this should not limit their relationship with the other. Both areas are closely allied and it is very important that they work closely together. Administrators will determine in large measure whether or not this becomes a reality.

PROFESSIONAL ORGANIZATIONS

The administrator should be familiar with the role of professional organizations in his work. He should realize that these associations help in the achievement of objectives, promote professional ethics, scholarship, leadership, and high educational standards.

Some of the organizations with which the health educator and physical educator should be familiar are listed below.*

National Education Association
American Association for Health, Physical Education, and Recreation
National Recreation and Park Association
American Academy of Physical Education

American School Health Association
National College Physical Education Association
National Association of Physical Education for College Women
National Junior College Athletic Association
American Physical Therapy Association
Society of State Directors of Health, Physical Education, and Recreation
American Youth Hostels, Inc.
Young Women's Christian Association
Physical Education Society of the Young Men's Christian Associations of North America
Boys' Clubs of America
National Collegiate Athletic Association
National Association of Intercollegiate Athletics
Canadian Physical Education Association
Delta Psi Kappa
Phi Delta Pi
Phi Epsilon Kappa
American College of Sports Medicine

Questions and exercises

1. Survey ten schools or colleges in your area to determine the administrative relationship of health and physical education.
2. Why is it important for health and physical educators to work closely together?
3. Prepare a research paper on the reasons why health and physical education were incorporated in the national association.
4. Why are both health education and physical education specialists needed in the schools?
5. Define health and physical education.
6. List and discuss the objectives of both school and college health and physical education.
7. Interview or correspond with five health educators and five physical educators on the main problems confronting their professions.
8. To what extent are the objectives of school and college health and physical education being achieved today?
9. Define the term *school health program*. Discuss the various aspects of the program.
10. Why are health attitudes so important?
11. What are the goals of physical education in addition to developing an individual physically?

---

*For a detailed discussion of these organizations, refer to Chapter 22 in Bucher, C. A.: Foundations of physical education, ed. 5, St. Louis, 1968, The C. V. Mosby Co.

12. What are some of the benefits to an individual that come from physical activity?
13. How can physical education contribute to the development of good citizenship?
14. Why must there be cooperation to achieve the objectives in health and physical education? What part does the administrator play?

Reading assignment in *Administrative Dimensions of Health and Physical Education Programs, Including Athletics:* Chapter 2, Selections 5 to 10.

Selected references

American Association for Health, Physical Education, and Recreation: Health concepts—guides for health instruction, Washington, D. C., 1966, The Association.

American Association for Health, Physical Education, and Recreation: Knowledge and understanding in physical education, Washington, D. C., 1969, The Association.

American Association for Health, Physical Education, and Recreation: Physical education for college men and women, Washington, D. C., 1965, The Association.

Bauer, W. W.: Teach health, not disease, Journal of Health and Physical Education 12:296, 1941.

Bookwalter, K. W.: Physical education in the secondary schools, New York, 1964, The Center for Applied Research in Education, Inc. (The Library of Education).

Bucher, C. A.: Foundations of physical education, ed. 5, St. Louis, 1968, The C. V. Mosby Co.

Bucher, C. A.: Physical education for life, St. Louis, 1969, McGraw-Hill Book Co. (A textbook for high school courses in physical education.)

Bucher, C. A., and Dupee, R. K., Jr.: Athletics in schools and colleges, New York, 1965, The Center for Applied Research in Education, Inc. (The Library of Education).

Bucher, C. A., Koenig, C., and Barnhard, M.: Methods of materials for secondary school physical education, ed. 3, St. Louis, 1970, The C. V. Mosby Co.

Bucher, C. A., Olsen, E. A., and Willgoose, C. E.: The foundations of health, New York, 1967, Appleton-Century-Crofts.

Bucher, C. A., and Reade, E. M.: Physical education and health in the elementary school, ed. 2, New York, 1971, The Macmillan Co.

Joint Committee of National Education Association and American Medical Association: The physical educator asks about health, Washington, D. C., 1951, American Association for Health, Physical Education, and Recreation.

Joint Committee on Health Problems in Education of National Education Association and American Medical Association: School health services, Washington, D. C., 1964, National Education Association.

Byrd, O. E.: School health administration, Philadelphia, 1964, W. B. Saunders Co.

Grout, R. E.: Health teaching in schools, ed. 4, Philadelphia, 1963, W. B. Saunders Co.

Hillson, M.: Change and innovation in elementary school organization, New York, 1965, Holt, Rinehart & Winston, Inc.

Irwin, L. W., and Mayshark, C.: Health education in secondary schools, St. Louis, 1968, The C. V. Mosby Co.

Joint Committee on Health Problems in Education of National Education Association and American Medical Association: Healthful school living, Washington, D. C., 1969, National Education Association.

Joint Committee on Health Problems in Education of National Education Association and American Medical Association: Health education, Washington, D. C., 1961, National Education Association.

National Committee on School Health Policies of the National Conference for Cooperation in Health Education: Suggested school health policies, ed. 3, Washington, D. C., 1966, National Education Association.

Neff, F. C.: Philosophy and American education, New York, 1966, The Center for Applied Research in Education, Inc. (The Library of Education).

Oberteuffer, D., and Beyrer, M. K.: School health education, ed. 4, New York, 1966, Harper & Row, Publishers.

Smolensky, J., and Bonvechio, L. R.: Principles of school health, Boston, 1966, D. C. Heath & Co.

Van Dalen, D. B.: Health and safety education, New York, 1963, The Center for Applied Research in Education, Inc. (The Library of Education).

Willgoose, C. E.: Health education in the elementary school, ed. 2, Philadelphia, 1964, W. B. Saunders Co.

CHAPTER 3 THE ADMINISTRATIVE SETTING

The administrator, teacher, and leader of physical education and of health education must be cognizant of the roles played by those who administer our educational institutions and the administrative structure of the school, college, and community. Many changes are taking place in the area of educational administration. Since health and physical education programs constitute integral parts of this administrative setting, it is important to understand the changes taking place.

Educational administrators increasingly must have special qualifications and preparation for their duties. School and college administrators need to be well-educated persons who are knowledgeable about the major aspects of managing an educational system or institution. They need to be "idea" men—thinkers with a vision of the future. They should possess a multitude of qualities that enable them to wear the hat of a teacher, architect, speaker, human relations expert, philosopher, and business executive. The administrator should train for his position through an intensive study of the science and theory of administration, and he should also have practical experience as an intern on the job.

ADMINISTRATIVE CHANGES IN SCHOOL ORGANIZATION
School districts

The school administration carries out its duties in a larger school district than was formerly the case, as a result of reorganization, centralization, and consolidation. The number of districts employing only a few teachers is declining rapidly. Enlarge-

ment of school districts has been necessary because of (1) the teacher shortage, (2) small district financial problems, and (3) inadequate curricula.

The school district is the basic administrative unit for the operation of local elementary and secondary schools and is a quasimunicipal corporation established by the state. This basic educational unit ranges through the United States from a one-teacher rural system to a large metropolitan system serving thousands of pupils. A system may be an independent governmental unit or part of a state government, county, or other local administrative unit. The governing body of the system is the school board. The chief administrative officer is the superintendent of schools. The number of basic administrative units reported in 1931 and 1932 was 127,531. Today, there are approximately 30,000 administrative units.

State and federal control

Traditionally, local communities have exercised almost complete control over local education, and the state has not interfered with local operations of school programs. Today, however, local communities have transferred some of their influence over education to state and federal governmental units. The control has advanced proportionately as the amount of state and federal financial aid to schools has increased. If school systems do not have quality educational programs as outlined by the state, fail to follow state and federal laws in such matters as civil rights, or fail to meet certain stipulations as attached to the use of

Shaver & Company, Salina, Kan.

The administrative setting for health and physical education programs. (Valley Winds Elementary School, St. Louis, Mo.)

governmental funds, such financial help can be withheld. This threat of withholding monies is proving to be a strong means of bringing local school districts into line with what is desired by state and federal authorities.

Patterns of school organization

The pattern of school organization at the elementary and secondary levels is in a period of transition. Some of the present patterns of school organization are as follows:

1. The traditional high school or 8-4 system—Under this type of organization the 4-year high school is preceded by the 8-year elementary school.
2. The combined junior and senior high school or 6-6 or 7-5 plan—Under this type of organization the junior and senior high schools are combined under one principal.
3. The emphasis upon junior high school or 6-3-3 system—Under this plan the junior high schools are grouped separately under one principal. Although the junior high school usually includes grades seven through nine, there are exceptions to this type of organization.
4. The 4-year high school or 6-2-4 system—Under this plan the 4-year high school is

similar to the traditional high school in organization, and the junior high school consists of two grades.
5. The middle school or 4-4-4 plan—This type of organization is a new development that retains the old high school idea but usually groups the early elementary grades together and the fifth to eighth (or other) grades in one unit.

There are many arguments that can be set forth for each plan of school organization or such other plans as the 6-3-3-2 or the 8-4-2, which includes 2 years of community college. The physical, psychologic, and sociologic aspects of the school setting and of child growth and development, the need for effective communication between schools, the range of subjects, the facilities provided, and the preparation of teachers are all pertinent to the type of administrative organization selected.

SCHOOL AND COLLEGE STRUCTURE

In this section the roles of the board of trustees, board of education, president of a college, superintendent of schools, principal and other administrative personnel, and lay groups will be discussed, as well as

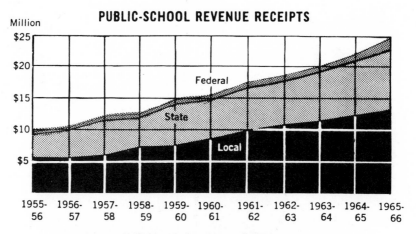

PUBLIC-SCHOOL REVENUE RECEIPTS

Million

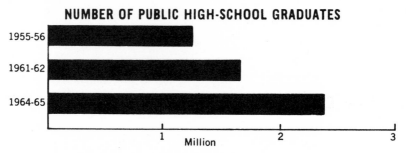

NUMBER OF SCHOOL DISTRICTS
Basic Administrative Units

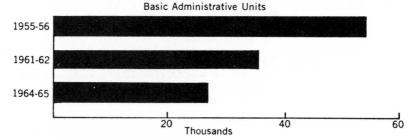

NUMBER OF PUBLIC HIGH-SCHOOL GRADUATES

Changes taking place in public school systems in the United States. (From NEA Research Bulletin 44:23, 1966.)

the place of physical education and health education within the educational framework. Much of this information applies directly to the school structure where most health education and physical education personnel are employed.

The college and university structure is analogous in some ways to the structure of the school system. For example, many of the administrative functions of a board of trustees of a college are similar in scope to those of a board of education, and the pres-

ident of a college has duties similar in some respects to a superintendent of schools. The director of physical education or the director of health education needs to perform many of the same duties in a college as the director does in a school system. A brief discussion of the college and university structure is included here to show the aspects of the structure that are especially unique to higher education.

A college or university is characterized by a governing board, usually known as a

School board meeting. (Mamaroneck, N. Y.)

board of trustees, which is granted extensive powers of control by legislative enactment or by its charter. The governing board of a college usually delegates many of its powers to the administration and faculty of the institution. The administrative officers, usually headed by a president, are commonly organized into such principal areas of administration as academic, student personnel services, business, and public relations. The members of the faculty are usually organized into colleges, schools, divisions, and departments of instruction and research. In large institutions one frequently finds a university senate that is the voice of the faculty and that serves as a liaison between faculty and administration. Health and physical education can have school, division, or department status. The duties of a dean, director, or chairman correspond in many ways to those of a director of health education and/or physical education in a school system.

Board of education, school committee, or board of directors*

The board of education is the legal administrative authority created by the state legislature for each school district. The responsibility of the board is to act on behalf of the residents of the district it represents. It has the duty of appraising and planning the educational program on a local basis. It selects executive personnel and performs duties essential to the successful operation of the schools within the district. The board develops policies that are legal and in the interest of the people it serves. It devises financial means within the legal framework to support the cost of the educational plan. It keeps its constituents informed of the effectiveness and needs of the total program.

Some of the more specific powers of boards of education include purchasing

---

*The term *board of education* is used in this discussion although *school committee* and *board of directors* are used in some sections of the country.

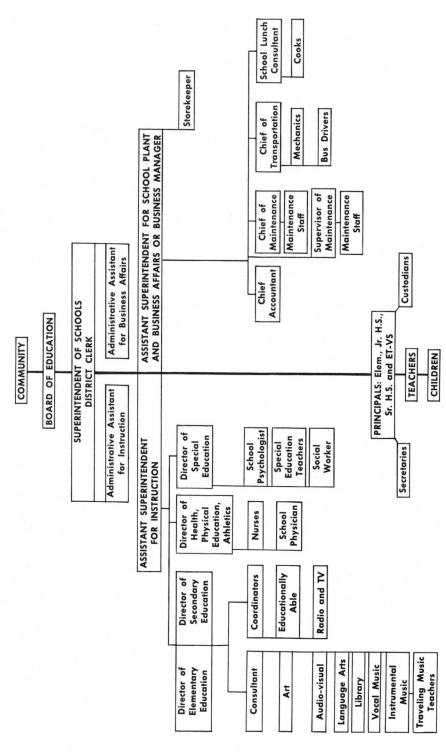

The operational organization chart clarifies channels of communication for the employees of the school district. The superintendent administers school district policies through the assistant superintendents, and they in turn utilize intermediate staff members in the process.

property, planning school buildings, determining the educational program, securing personnel, levying taxes for school purposes, approving courses of study, determining the school calendar, and providing for the school census. The powers of boards of education are fixed by state statutory enactment.

The qualifications for board members are very few. There are usually general requirements that specify citizenship, age, residence, and sometimes ownership of property. In many communities women as well as men are playing very prominent roles. According to surveys that have been conducted, boards of education usually include individuals who are past middle age, have been successful in their community, and are conservative in nature. There has been an improvement in recent years in the organization and composition of boards of education. The addition of women and individuals who are nonpartisan in their outlook, the organization of smaller and less cumbersome boards, and provisions for longer terms of office are resulting in a more stable educational policy.

Boards of education vary in size. There is the usual three-member board in the common-school district that represents the independent one- or two-room school set-up. Township boards of education range from five to nine members, county boards from three to fifteen, and city boards from three to sixteen. The trend is toward small boards of education.

Board of education members are appointed in some cases, and in others they are elected.

The National School Boards Association has indicated the following characteristics of school boards in forty-two cities throughout the nation having more than 300,000 population.

Most school boards have seven, five, or nine members, in that order. Three cities have boards with fifteen members. The composition of school board members (3%

women and 13% Negroes) is broken down as follows: businessmen, 103; lawyers, 66; housewives, 51; physicians, 22; ministers, 11; and college professors, 8.

Most of the 137,000 members of the nation's 25,000 school boards are elected. Among the large cities, only Philadelphia, Pittsburgh, and Washington, D.C., choose boards through a committee of court judges. In Boston, Detroit, Los Angeles, and St. Louis, school boards are elected.

There is a growing feeling among professional and lay leaders alike for the need of reform in respect to school board operations. Reforms have been advocated by such an important group as the New York Committee on Educational Leadership and are receiving support in some of the more progressive sections of the country. These reforms include (1) the transfer of all administrative functions that encumber school board operations to the superintendent of schools, (2) better procedures for screening school board members so that the "office seeks the man rather than the man seeks the office," (3) elimination of the annual public vote on the school budget where required and substituting budget hearings in its place, and (4) improved procedures for selecting superintendents of schools.

General administrative personnel

The administrative personnel that will be discussed include the superintendent of schools, assistant superintendent, clerk of the board, principal, supervisor, director, and lay groups.

Superintendent of schools. Within a large school system where many schools are involved there is a superintendent who has overall charge of the school program. Associate or assistant superintendents are in charge of technical detail, management, or various phases of the program, such as secondary education. There is also a superintendent's position associated with smaller schools. These officers are known as district superintendents. They are responsible for many schools extending over a wide geographic area.

The superintendent's job is to carry out the educational policies of the state and the board of education. He acts as the leader in educational matters in the community. He also provides the board of education with the professional advice it needs as a lay organization. From an executive standpoint, he appraises the entire educational program over which he has control, working closely with the board of education to eliminate weaknesses and to establish a strong system of education. Any large organization needs leadership; so too does the educational system of any community.

The qualifications for the position of superintendent vary in different communities. In some villages and cities the individual must be a resident and in others this is not necessary. The educational requirement varies a great deal. Some communities require a doctorate and others require a minimum of professional training. There is a trend, however, in the direction of increased training. Most superintendents of schools have their bachelor and master's degrees and an increasing number have taken work beyond the master's. Many have their doctorates. Both teaching and administrative experience are frequently listed as requirements.

Assistant superintendent for business services or school business administrator. The business administrator serves as director of business affairs and of buildings and grounds. In a college or university there is also one administrative officer who carries out similar duties. The business administrator usually has direct supervision of the business office staff, the building service and maintenance staff, and general supervision of the custodial staff. He has responsibility for supervising the operation and maintenance of all buildings and grounds. He may perform the duties of the superintendent as directed in the superintendent's absence. (Chapter 4 is devoted to a de-

tailed discussion of the school business administrator.)

Assistant superintendent or director of instructional services. The director of instruction has under his direct supervision the divisions of elementary education, secondary education, adult education, health and physical education, music education, vocational and practical arts, summer school education, and inservice training of teachers. He gives major consideration to the development of curriculum materials, to organization, and to the supervision of instruction and teaching. He may perform the duties of the superintendent of schools as directed in the superintendent's absence. In a college or university the administrative officer in charge of the academic program could be a vice-president, dean, provost, or other officer.

Assistant superintendent or director of personnel services. The director of personnel supervises both professional and nonprofessional employees. He recruits and interviews candidates for positions. He is usually responsible for all pupil personnel services, guidance and psychologic services, handicapped children and special services, as well as attendance and adjustment, including pupil accounting. He may supervise and coordinate the medical services, including medical, dental, and nurse-teacher services. He may coordinate and direct the publications and information services and carry on testing and research activities. He may perform the duties of the superintendent as directed in the superintendent's absence. In a college or university many of these responsibilities are carried out by a dean of men or a dean of women.

Clerk of the board. The clerk of the board of education is usually under the direction of the superintendent of schools. He has custody of the seal of the board, notifies members of the board of regular and special meetings, and has charge of files and records of the board. He sees that all files and records are properly maintained, presents a periodic financial statement, and supervises accounting for tuition pupils. He preaudits and certifies all bills, examines and certifies all payrolls, and keeps an active insurance register. He usually conducts the annual school election and keeps the bond and coupon register of the board and public library, together with necessary reports of bonds and interest due.

Principal. The position of principal is very similar to that of the superintendent. It differs mainly in respect to the extent or scope of responsibility. Whereas the superintendent is usually in charge of all the schools within a particular community, the principal is in charge of one particular school. The duties of the principal include responsibility for executing educational policy as outlined by the superintendent, appraising the educational offering, making periodic reports on various aspects of the program, directing the instructional program, promoting good relationships between the community and the school, and supervising the maintenance of the physical plant.

In many school situations, principals teach in addition to their administrative responsibilities. Some conduct extracurricular activities such as leading the band or coaching a varsity athletic team. Some principals have responsibilities on only one school level, but where various levels are combined in one structural unit, this responsibility may extend from the high school level down through the junior high school and even to the elementary school.

The qualifications for the position of principal vary. There is in evidence a trend toward increased training for such positions. Some communities feel that the principal should have more training than the teachers.

Boards of education must select school administrators from the individuals available. The prestige, money, security, and other factors that the position offers play an important part in determining the quality of individual that can be secured.

Supervisor. This position usually implies a responsibility associated with the improvement of instruction. In some cases the assignment might be much broader in scope and in corporate responsibility for the entire elementary or secondary instructional program. In most cases, however, it usually applies to specific subject matter areas.

Director. The role of the director involves responsibility for functions of specific subject matter area or a particular educational level. The responsibilities have administrative as well as supervisory implications.

Director of health, physical education, and recreation. A common position to be found in educational systems is that of director of health, physical education, and recreation. One state, for example, grants a special certificate for a director of health, physical education, and recreation after a stated program of studies has been accomplished, a stated amount of experience has been had, and other requirements met. Other communities and states have directors of health and physical education. Some have directors of physical education, directors of health, and directors of recreation where the fields of specialization are completely separated.

In a college or university there may be a director who heads up the entire physical education program and a director in charge of the health program, or the two fields may be combined into the same administrative unit, whether it be a college, school, division, or department.

A director's position exists to provide leadership, program, facilities, and other essentials in these special areas. Specific areas of responsibility for a director of health, physical education, and recreation in general include the following:

General duties
1. Implement standards established by the state Department of Education and the

local board of education. (In a college it would be the university administration.)

2. Interview possible candidates for positions in the special areas and make recommendations for these positions.

3. Work closely with the assistant superintendent in charge of business affairs, assistant superintendent in charge of instruction, and subject matter and classroom teachers.

4. Coordinate areas of health, physical education, and recreation.

5. Supervise all inside and outside facilities, equipment, and supplies concerned with special areas—this responsibility includes maintenance, safety, and replacement operations.

6. Maintain liaison with community groups— this responsibility includes such duties as holding educational meetings with doctors and dentists to interpret and improve the school health program, scheduling school facilities for community groups, and serving on various community committees for youth needs.

7. Prepare periodic reports regarding areas of activity.

8. Coordinate school civil defense activities in some school systems.

9. Serve on the school health council.

Health

1. Health services—in some cases includes the supervision of school nurse teachers and dental hygiene teachers and coordination of the work of school physicians. Other responsibilities include preparation of guides and policies for the program of health services, organization of health projects, and obtaining proper equipment and supplies.

2. Health science instruction—includes supervision of health education programs throughout the school system, preparation of curriculum guides and research studies, and upgrading the program in general.

3. Healthful school living—includes general supervision of school plant, psychologic aspects of school program, and formation of recommendations for improvement.

Physical education

1. Supervise total physical education program (class, adapted, intramurals, extramurals, and varsity interscholastic or intercollegiate athletics).

2. Administer schedules, practice and game facilities, insurance, and equipment.

3. Maintain liaison with county, district, and state professional groups.

4. Upgrade program in general.

Recreation

1. Supervise various aspects of the recreation program that, in addition to school program, may include summer and vacation playgrounds, teen centers, and so on.

2. Obtain, where necessary, facilities, equipment, personnel, and supplies.

3. Plan and administer program.

Lay groups

The general public is participating more and more in the work of schools and colleges. Parent-teacher associations, citizens' councils, alumni groups, and study groups are a few of the organizations that express the lay opinion of the community in regard to educational matters. This interest on the part of the public should be encouraged and helped in every way possible. There are more than 10 million members of parent-teacher associations alone throughout the country. The public school program should reflect what the public wants and thinks is best for their children. This can be accomplished only through active "lay" participation. Administrators and other school personnel should make sure that the citizens of the community are adequately informed in respect to educational matters so that the best type of program may be developed.

HEALTH WITHIN THE SCHOOL AND COLLEGE STRUCTURE*

The superintendent and principal or president and dean have the main responsibility for school and college health programs. The attitude they have toward health and the degree to which they recognize the importance of achieving professional objectives will determine the success of the school health program.

Administrators must recognize certain important principles in regard to health so that it may have an important place in the total school and college program. The following are basic concepts: Health should

---

*See also Chapters 12, 13, and 14.

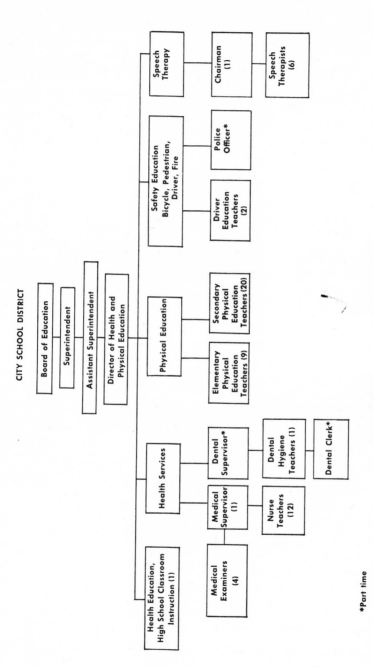

CITY SCHOOL DISTRICT

*Part time

The director of health and physical education in the school structure. (From Bucher, C. A., Koenig, C. R., and Barnhard, M.: Methods and materials for secondary school physical education, ed. 3, St. Louis, 1970, The C. V. Mosby Co.)

Superintendents and principals have important responsibilities for promoting health within the school. (Chandler Street Junior High School, Worcester, Mass.)

be an important and integral part of the overall educational program. All teachers and other personnel should understand and appreciate the importance of promoting health and the contributions they can make through their own work toward realizing such a goal. There should be individuals on the staff who have had special training in this field so that they may take the leadership in developing and promoting an adequate program. There should be coordination of the various instructional aspects of the educational program to ensure adequate coverage of health information and to avoid unnecessary overlapping. There should be provision for concentrated health teaching. Adequate facilities, time, money, and personnel should be provided to carry on this special work properly. A close working arrangement with the community should be recognized as an essential to a well-developed program. There should

be a statement of policies in regard to health that is clear and understood by all.

Terminology for the school and college health program. The following definitions were drawn up by the Committee on Terminology that represented the American Association for Health, Physical Education, and Recreation, the Society of Public Health Educators, and the American Public Health Association. It is presented here for the reader's information.*

Dental examination—The appraisal, performed by a dentist, of the condition of the oral structures to determine the dental health status of the individual.

Dental inspection—The limited appraisal, performed by anyone with or without special dental preparation, of the oral structures to determine the presence or absence of obvious defects.

---

*Report of the Joint Committee on Health Education Terminology, Journal of Health, Physical Education, and Recreation 33:27, 1962.

Health appraisal—The evaluation of the health status of the individual through the utilization of varied organized and systematic procedures such as medical and dental examinations, laboratory test, health history, teacher observation, etc.

Health observation—The estimation of an individual's well-being by noting the nature of his appearance and behavior.

Medical examination—The determination, by a physician, of an individual's health status.

Screening test—A medically and educationally acceptable procedure for identifying individuals who need to be referred for further study or diagnostic examination.

Cumulative school health record—A form used to note pertinent consecutive information about a student's health.

School health program—The composite of procedures used in school health services, healthful school living, and health science instruction to promote health among students and school personnel.

Healthful school living—The utilization of a safe and wholesome environment, consideration of individual health, organizing the school day, and planning classroom procedures to favorably influence emotional, social, and physical health.

Health school environment—The physical, social, and emotional factors of the school setting which affect the health, comfort, and performance of an individual or a group.*

Health science instruction—The organized teaching procedures directed toward developing understandings, attitudes, and practices relating to health and factors affecting health.

School health services—The procedures used by physicians, dentists, nurses, teachers, etc. designed to appraise, protect, and promote optimum health of students and school personnel. (Activities frequently included in school health services are those used to (1) appraise the health status of students and school personnel; (2) counsel students, teachers, parents, and others for the purpose of helping school-age children get treatment or for arranging education programs in keeping with their abilities; (3) help prevent or control the spread of disease; (4) provide emergency care for injury or sudden sickness.)

School health education—The process of providing or utilizing experiences for favorably influencing understandings, attitudes, and practices relating to individual, family, and community health.

Safety education—The process of providing or utilizing experiences for favorably influencing understandings, attitudes, and practices relating to safe living.

Health counseling—A method of interpreting to students or their parents the findings of health appraisals and encouraging and assisting them to take such action as needed to realize their fullest potential.

School health coordination—A process designed to bring about a harmonious working relationship among the various personnel and groups in the school and community that have interest, concern, and responsibility for development and conduct of the school health program.

Essential aspects of the school and college health program. Health within the educational structure will be discussed under three headings: health science instruction, health services, and healthful school and college living.

*Health science instruction.** In the area of health science instruction, scientific knowledge is imparted and experiences are provided so that students may better understand the importance of developing good attitudes and health practices. Information concerning such subjects as nutrition, communicable disease, rest, exercise, sanitation, drugs, alcohol, tobacco, environmental pollution, human sexuality, first aid, and safety is presented.

On the elementary level the responsibility for such health education rests primarily on the shoulders of the classroom teacher, although in some school systems trained specialists are provided as resource persons. On the secondary and college levels, it is recommended that individuals who have had special training in health education be responsible for concentrated health instruction. This is not always the case. Sometimes, in the absence of a trained specialist, the teacher of physical education, home economics, or science or some other teacher is given the responsibility. This procedure, however, is not always desirable

---

*See also Chapter 14.

*See also Chapter 12.

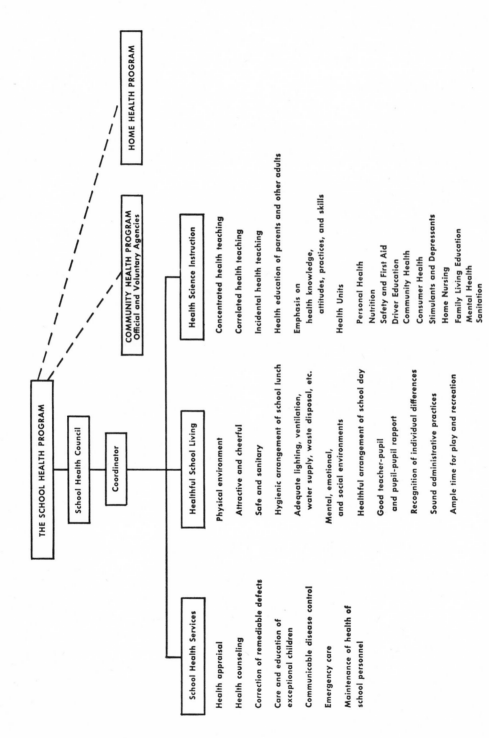

Suggested health education for the schools of the United States. (From Bucher, C. A.: Foundations of physical education, ed. 5. St. Louis, 1968, The C. V. Mosby Co.)

because of the lack of necessary qualifications by persons other than a specialist.

A concentrated course in health education should be required of all students for at least 1 and preferably 2 years at the secondary level. Some states are now requiring health in every grade. At the college level there should be at least a one-semester health course for all students. Health educators should teach such courses, and these subjects should be given the same credit and time allotments as other important ones in the curriculum. Again, this recommendation is not followed in many schools and colleges because of the lack of trained personnel, the fact that other subjects are given a priority listing, and the lack of an appreciation on the part of school and college administrators of the importance of health education. Some schools incorporate health education in the physical education class. When this is the case, it quite often becomes a "rainy day" proposition. Some feel that it is adequately cared for in other subjects, such as science and home economics. Correlating health instruction in various subject matter areas is to be encouraged. However, this in itself is not sufficient.

The emphasis in health education at the primary grade level should be on how to live healthfully, at the intermediate grade level on *why* certain types of health practices are important, and at the secondary level on personal and community health. It should be reiterated that although there is a place for concentrated teaching at the secondary and college levels, at the same time it is important for all subject matter areas to also recognize their possibilities and responsibilities for teaching health.

The possibilities for health education should also be recognized in the various experiences the child has in school. When the school physician gives the medical examination, the dental hygienist examines the child's teeth, an emergency concerned with health exists in the community, or the

curiosity of the child is aroused, "teachable moments" for imparting health information are presented. This type of health education often leaves a greater impression upon young minds than the more formal classroom type.

*Health services.** The health services phase of school and college health programs includes health appraisal, health counseling, correction of defects, provision for the exceptional child, prevention and control of communicable disease, and emergency care of injuries.

In this phase of the health program it is important to recognize concern for mental, emotional, social, and physical health. In providing health services that include all these phases of health, several persons in addition to the health educator play prominent parts.

The classroom teacher has an important responsibility in health services. He or she is probably closer to the child than any other person on the staff and therefore can detect deviations from the normal. The teacher also is in a position to give good advice, provide first aid when necessary, administer certain screening tests, and oversee the general welfare of the child.

The nurse plays a prominent role in the administration of the health program. Through counseling, acting as a resource person for other staff members, developing close relationships with parents, helping physicians, and other responsibilities peculiar to her profession, the nurse is a key person.

The physician has the potential for playing a very important part in school and college programs. Through medical examinations, health guidance, protection of students from communicable diseases, development of health policies, and consultations with parents, it is possible for the physician to exercise a great force for good in the health of the students and parents

---

*See also Chapter 13.

Healthful school living. (Chandler Street Junior High School, Worcester, Mass.)

with whom he comes in contact. It has been the observation of many educators, however, that the physician often does not realize the educational implications of his role in the health program. As a result, he does not take advantage of "teachable moments" that occur whenever a student is being given a medical examination or when conferences are held with parents.

Dentists and dental hygienists play an important role wherever their services are provided. These specialists appraise the dental needs of students. Here again there is an unlimited opportunity to educate the student and the parent on the importance of proper oral hygiene.

Psychologists, psychiatrists, social workers, guidance counselors, speech correctionists, and others are increasingly being brought into school and college health services programs. All have an important part to play and contribution to make to the total health of young people who attend schools and colleges in this country.

*Healthful school and college living.** Healthful living is also an important part of the total health program. In addition to a healthful physical environment, a wholesome emotional environment must also be provided. Both are important to the health of the student.

The physical environment should provide an attractive, safe, and wholesome place for students to congregate. This implies that such important considerations as lighting, ventilation, heating, location, sanitary facilities, play space, equipment, and other essentials are adequately provided for in the buildings and areas that are used for educational purposes. It also means there is proper maintenance by the custodial staff and includes any other factors that influence the physical arrangements of the school or college plant.

The emotional environment is just as important to the student's health as the physical one. To ensure a wholesome emotional environment, proper rapport must exist between the teacher and pupils and among the pupils themselves; educational practices pertinent to such matters as grades, promotions, assignments, schedules, play periods, attendance, class conduct, and discipline must be sound; and the teachers themselves must be well adjusted.

---

*See also Chapter 14.

Other phases of health administration. There are two other aspects of the health program that need special attention—the health council and the health coordinator.

The health council. Every school and every school system should have health councils or committees to help ensure a desirable and adequate health program. This means that there should be a health council for each school and one central health council for all the schools in a particular school system. The number of members comprising such councils may vary from three or four persons in a small school to fifteen or sixteen in a larger school. Potential members of such councils are the school principal, health coordinator, nurse, psychologist, guidance person, custodian, dental hygienist, physician, dentist, physical education teacher, science teacher, home economics teacher, classroom teacher, teacher of handicapped persons, nutritionist, students, parents, public health officer, mayor, clergymen, and any other individual who is particularly related to the health of the school or community and has something to contribute.

Health councils are responsible for coordinating the entire health program of the school. This would include determining subject matter to be taught, resources to be utilized, and experiences to be provided; securing a healthful environment in which to live; arranging inservice training for teaching personnel; encouraging closer school-parent relationships in respect to such important health procedures as medical examinations; promoting sanitary conditions; providing for the safety of children; and distributing health literature.

Representatives from various community and school groups that are interested in health can accomplish much when sitting around a conference table discussing their problems. A spirit of cooperation and "oneness" will aid in developing procedures and taking action that will promote better health for all.

Health coordinator. Health affects many subject matter areas, the school plant, educational practices, and practically every aspect of school life. It is important therefore to have coordination. This means that responsibility must be fixed in one person. By having someone responsible it is possible to integrate health into the total education program and the total community health program.

As a result of the need for coordination of the various phases of health, many schools have appointed health coordinators. In some places this individual is known by another title such as health consultant or health educator. This person, in most cases, is appointed by the administration and has particular qualifications for the job.

The responsibilities of the health coordinator include such duties as integrating and correlating the various phases of health education in the subject matter areas, channeling health information to staff members, keeping records, preparing reports periodically on pertinent health matters, providing leadership for health councils, seeing that established health policies are carried out, appraising and evaluating the total health program, arranging special health examinations when needed, counseling students on health problems, aiding the physician in the performance of his duties, helping in the maintenance of a healthful environment, organizing safety and other programs that promote health, and helping in furthering school-home relationships.

PHYSICAL EDUCATION WITHIN THE SCHOOL AND COLLEGE STRUCTURE

Physical education is increasingly occupying a more important role in the school and college offering. During its early history, physical education was regarded by general school administrators as a fad, an appendage to the educational program, or a necessary evil to be tolerated. In recent years, however, it has been viewed by an increasing number of educators as an integral part of the total educational offering with many potentialities for contributing to enriched living.

Terminology in physical education. Components of the physical education program are characterized by many and varied terms. Since there has been no committee established to work out descriptive terms for the various phases of the program, as in the case of the health program, there is lack of uniformity within the profession. I would like to suggest that the four components of the physical education program, into which it logically divides itself, be called (1) the required class or basic instruction program, (2) the adapted pro-

gram, (3) the intramural and extramural athletics program, and (4) the varsity interschool or intercollegiate athletics program.

The *required class* or *basic instruction program* is the provision of physical education for all students and is characterized by instruction in such matters as the rules, strategies, and skills of the various activities that comprise the program.

The *adapted program* refers to that phase of physical education that meets the needs of the individual who, because of some physical inadequacy, functional defect capable of being improved through exercise, or other deficiency, is temporarily or permanently unable to take part in the regular physical education program.

SCHOOL AND COLLEGE PHYSICAL EDUCATION PROGRAM

Chairman of Department

The Basic Instructional Class Program	Adapted Program	Intramural and Extramural Athletics Program	Varsity Interscholastic or Intercollegiate Athletics Program
Instructional in nature	For special students including those with:	Competitive leagues and tournaments, play and sports days, etc.	For skilled students
Required of all students	Faulty body mechanics	Voluntary in nature	Voluntary in nature
Daily period	Nutritional disturbances (over- and underweight)	For all students	Conducted during out-of-school hours
Credit given	Heart and lung disturbances	Conducted during out-of-class hours	Organized and administered with needs of participant in mind
Variety of activities	Postoperative and convalescent cases	Laboratory period for required class program	Rec.: For high school and college students only
Team games	Hernias, weak and flat feet, menstrual disorders, etc.	Wide variety of activities based on needs and interests of students	Wide variety of activities based on needs and interests of students
Dual and individual games	Nervous instability	Rec.: Intramural athletics—fourth grade through college	
Rhythms and dances	Poor physical fitness	Rec.: Extramural athletics—seventh grade through college	
Games of low organization	Crippling conditions (infantile paralysis, etc.)		
Gymnastics	Provision for physical, mental, emotional, and social welfare of student		
Aquatics	Provision for program during regular class and special classes		
	Restricted and remedial physical activity		
	Utilization of special conditioning exercises, aquatics, and recreational sports		
	Harmonious working relationships with medical and nursing personnel		

The *intramural and extramural athletics program* is voluntary physical education for all students within one or a few schools or colleges. It is characterized by such events as competitive leagues and tournaments and play and sports days and acts as a laboratory period for the required class program. In the intramural program activities are conducted for students of only one school or college, while in the extramural program students from more than one school or college participate.

The *varsity interschool or intercollegiate athletics program* is designed for the skilled individuals in one school or college who compete with skilled individuals from another school or college in selected physical education activities.

Organization. The various departments of physical education throughout the country have many different plans of organization. A few years ago it was quite common to see such titles as Department of Physical Culture or Hygiene. The term *physical training* was also used as a descriptive term for the work performed in this special area.

Today, one also sees a variety of titles associated with physical education work. In some schools and colleges it is the "physical education department," in others the "health and physical education department," and in others it is the "health, physical education, and recreation division." Camping and safety may also be included.

The titles that are given also show to some degree the particular work that is performed within these phases of the total program. In some schools and colleges physical education is organized into a separate unit with the various physical activities, intramural, extramural, and interschool or intercollegiate athletics—comprising this division. In other schools and colleges, health and physical education are combined in one administrative unit. In some cases, although the word *health* is used, there is little evidence of the particular specialized type of health work as it is known

today. This is also true where the word *recreation* is used in the title. In the discussion to follow, the term *physical education* will be used.

There is usually a person designated as head or chairman of the physical education department. The title of director of physical education is also used. In smaller schools, it is quite common to have only one man and one woman on the physical education staff, each acting as the head of his or her separate division.

The duties of the head of a physical education department include coordinating the activities within his particular administrative unit, requisitioning supplies and equipment, preparing schedules, making budgets, holding departmental meetings, teaching classes, coaching, hiring and dismissing personnel, developing community relations, supervising the intramural, extramural, and interscholastic programs, evaluating and appraising the required class program, representing the department at meetings, reporting to the principal, and having overall general responsibility for the activities carried on.

The required class or basic instruction program. * The required class or basic instruction program refers to the instructional program. In some states this phase of the program is required by state law, and in others it is governed by a local regulation. In a few schools and colleges participation is not required but voluntary. Classes are scheduled in much the same way as other subjects. Students, however, are too often assigned on the basis of administrative convenience rather than homogeneously. Physical education people have advocated assigning students to classes in a way that would result in their realizing the greatest physical, social, and other benefits pertinent to this field of work. However, too few schools and colleges have followed these recommenda-

---

*See also Chapter 7.

tions. The emphasis in the class program is instructional and various games and activities are offered at different levels in the school program. On the elementary level, rhythmic activities and simple games are stressed, whereas on the secondary level there is a change to more highly organized games and sports.

A survey of the country will show many inferior programs of physical education if they are compared to the standards that have been set for the profession. In many communities the required class program, although serving the entire student body, is hampered by lack of time, facilities, and leadership. Stress on varsity sports and lack of administrative support have also been influential factors. The leadership that is found in many physical education programs is not resourceful, dynamic, and capable of promoting a sound program.

Where excellent required class or basic instruction programs of physical education exist, they have been developed on the basis of the physical, social, mental, and emotional needs of the students. A broad and varied program of activities, both outdoor and indoor, progressively arranged and adapted to the capacities and abilities of each student, is offered.

The adapted program. * One of the weakest phases of modern physical education programs is the lack of an effective adapted program at all educational levels. Since pupils should be required to take physical education each day they are in school, regardless of their physical condition or how they feel, the program must be adapted to their needs. The boy or girl should not be made to fit the physical education program. Instead, the physical education program should fit the individual. The child with a rheumatic fever history, the boy who has just returned from having an operation to remove his appendix, the girl who suffers menstrual difficul-

ties, mentally retarded and culturally disadvantaged students, and pupils with other health problems can all receive benefits from the physical education program, provided it is geared to their individual differences. To ensure the cooperation of parents, administrators, and others and to work out the best possible program, there should be a close working relationship between the nursing, medical, and other health professions. This procedure will also help to ensure that the prescription recommended properly fits the student's needs. Another consideration that cannot be overlooked is having qualified teachers assigned to the adapted program. The effectiveness of such a program will depend to a great extent upon the type of leadership that is provided.

The intramural and extramural athletics program. * The goal of the intramural and extramural program is to provide competition in games, sports, and other physical activities for the rank and file of the student body. This program is in addition to the required class or basic instruction program. Whereas the required class or basic instruction program is designed to be largely instructional in nature so that basic fundamentals for playing various activities can be learned, the intramural and extramural program is designed to provide an opportunity for students to utilize these learned skills in actual competitive situations.

There is a place in the intramural and extramural program for all students, regardless of degree of skill, strength, age, or field of specialization. It offers an opportunity for friendly competition between groups from the same school or college. Sometimes "sports" and "play" days are also included. These special events involve students from one or many schools who are invited to participate. Teams are composed of students from the same school

---

*See also Chapter 8.

*See also Chapter 9.

and college and from many different schools and colleges.

As many as 90% or 95% of the students participate in the intramural and extramural programs where there is an active interest. Since these programs are conducted on a voluntary basis, this indicates the amount of enthusiasm and interest that can be generated through a well-organized program. High attendance in such a program usually reflects a broad offering of activities, with leagues or some other unit of competition, organized in a manner that appeals to the interest and needs of the students.

In small schools and colleges, intramural and extramural programs are usually conducted by one or two persons who are also in charge of the required class or basic instruction program. This places an additional load on such individuals and consequently some fail to develop the type of program that could be offered if more personnel were available. In larger schools and colleges it is quite common to have a director of intramural athletics. This places the responsibility on one person and usually results in a better-organized and more effective program.

Close coordination should exist between the required class and intramural and extramural programs. Furthermore, department members, student managers, and interested faculty members should be encouraged to help in the conduct of the program. For the best administration of intramural and extramural programs, most schools also give careful consideration to units of competition; a program of fall, winter, and spring activities; eligibility requirements; provisions for medical examination; preliminary training periods; scheduling; variation in types of tournaments; coaching; and awards.

The varsity interschool and intercollegiate athletics program.* The varsity interschool program in athletics is designed for the individuals most highly skilled in sports. It is one of the most interesting and receives more publicity than the other two phases of physical education in the school setup. The reason for this is not that it is more important or renders a greater contribution; instead, it is largely the result of its popular appeal. The fact that sports writers and others discuss it in glowing terms and that it involves competition that pits one school or college against another school or college also increases its public appeal. A spirit of rivalry develops. This seems to be characteristic of the American culture.

The varsity interschool and intercollegiate athletics program has probably had more difficulties attached to it than any of the other phases of the program. The desire to win and to increase gate receipts has resulted in evil practices. Large stadia and sports palaces have been constructed that require large financial outlays for their upkeep.

For many years there has been much controversy over whether or not girls should engage in interscholastic and intercollegiate sports. Some advocate such activities for the girls because they feel they should also be offered the advantages that accrue to boys. On the other hand, others feel that physiologic and social implications indicate that girls should not participate in such activities. As a result of this controversy, some schools and colleges do not have interscholastic and intercollegiate competition for girls and in their place have stressed "sports" and "play" days.

In some schools and colleges the interschool phase of the program comes under a director of athletics. It is his responsibility to arrange the schedules, make the necessary arrangements for athletic events, such as securing officials, and care for the numerous details essential to a well-organized program. For many schools and col-

---

*See also Chapter 10.

leges smaller in size, the individual or individuals who administer the required class and intramural and extramural programs also administer the interschool phase of the total physical education program. Since all are closely related, utilize the same personnel in most cases, share the same facilities, and are interested in achieving the same objectives, it is important that they all come under the jurisdiction of the same department. Such an organization makes it possible for all to accomplish their purposes under the leadership of an individual who recognizes the value and place of each in a well-rounded program.

In connection with financing athletic programs, many schools have what is called a general organization, which is in charge of the finances not only for the athletic program but also for other school activities, such as dramatics and music. This has been used with success in some schools and takes the financial responsibility out of the physical education department and places it in an impartial organization.

Other items of particular importance that should be arranged for in the administration of athletics are provision for medical supervision and an accident plan. Both should be carefully considered by any school desiring to have a sound athletics program.

The organization of physical education in colleges and universities

Physical education is organized as one administrative unit for men and women in a majority of colleges and universities in the United States. The administrative unit

Shaver & Company, Salina, Kan.

A phase of the physical education program. (McPherson High School, McPherson, Kan.)

State College Board of Trustees

President of the College

Vice President

or

Dean of the College

Associate Dean or Head ———— Executive Committee: All Department Chairmen

School of Physical Education, Health, and Recreation

Chairman, Department of Physical Education, Men	Chairman, Department of Physical Education, Women	Chairman, Department of Health Education	Chairman, Department of Recreation	Chairman, Department of Intercollegiate Athletics, Men (Director of Athletics)
Advisory Committee ---	Advisory Committee ---	Advisory Committee ---	Advisory Committee ---	Advisory Committee ---
Basic Instruction for Men ---	Basic Instruction for Women ---	Undergraduate Professional Curriculum ---	Undergraduate Professional Curriculum ---	Administration of Intercollegiate Athletics ---
Undergraduate Professional Curriculum ---	Undergraduate Professional Curriculum ---	Service Courses in First Aid ---	Service Courses, General Elementary Teachers ---	Coordination of Athletic Coaching Courses ---
Graduate Professional Curriculum ---	Graduate Professional Curriculum ---	State Field Service ---	Campus Recreation ---	Coordination of Intercollegiate Athletic Schedules ---
Intramural Sports ---	Intramural Sports ---	Coordination With Community Health Services ---	State Field Service ---	Coordination of Teaching Services of Coaches ---
Supervision of Sports Facilities ---	Extramural Sports ---	Health Education Institutes and Workshops ---	Administration of Outdoor Education Center ---	Coordination of Maintenance and Use of Athletic Facilities ---
Supervision of Aquatics ---	Dance Productions ---	Public and Private School Consultations ---	Recreation Institutes and Workshops ---	Coordination of Conference Affiliation, National Collegiate Athletic Association, American Amateur Athletic Union, etc. ---
Faculty-Staff and Community Instructional Services ---	Faculty-Staff and Community Instructional Services ---		Coordination with Community Recreation Services ---	
Research Laboratory ---	Research Laboratory ---		Public, Private, and Commercial Recreation Consultations ---	

Organization chart for a school of physical education, health, and recreation. (Developed by Don Adee.)

may be either a college, school, division, or department; the administrator in charge of the physical education program may be called a dean, director, supervisor, or chairman. In many institutions of higher learning this administrator is responsible directly to the president or to a dean, but in a few instances, he is responsible to the director of athletics. (In a majority of colleges, athletics are included as part of the same administrative setup with the rest of the physical education program.) In many cases the duties of the athletic director and the administrator of the physical education program are assigned to the same person. Many colleges and universities have intra-

Table 3-1. Total and first-time opening fall degree-credit enrollment in junior colleges, by sex: United States, 1954 to 1974 (adapted)*†

	Total fall enrollment			First-time fall enrollment		
Fall	*Total*	*Men*	*Women*	*Total*	*Men*	*Women*
(1)	*(2)*	*(3)*	*(4)*	*(5)*	*(6)*	*(7)*
1954	282,433	171,752	110,681	129,349	76,517	52,832
1955	308,411	196,671	111,740	139,969	86,176	53,793
1956	347,345	225,635	121,710	162,810	101,610	61,200
1957	369,162	237,679	131,483	167,640	104,037	63,603
1958	385,609	248,040	137,569	174,949	107,744	67,205
1959	409,715	259,754	149,961	181,679	111,257	70,422
1960	451,333	282,155	169,178	213,976	128,570	85,406
1961	517,925	320,156	197,769	243,777	145,665	98,112
1962	589,529	365,624	223,905	260,440	156,163	104,277
1963	624,789	386,660	238,129	271,673	163,062	108,611
1964	710,868	439,509	271,359	322,241	193,407	128,834
1965	791,000	492,000	299,000	384,000	230,000	154,000
1966	866,000	535,000	331,000	383,000	229,000	154,000
1967	944,000	587,000	357,000	388,000	232,000	156,000
1968	1,016,000	631,000	385,000	400,000	239,000	161,000
1969	1,048,000	651,000	397,000	419,000	251,000	168,000
1970	1,086,000	675,000	411,000	448,000	269,000	179,000
			Projected			
1971	1,150,000	714,000	436,000	474,000	284,000	190,000
1972	1,220,000	756,000	464,000	498,000	299,000	199,000
1973	1,291,000	799,000	492,000	519,000	312,000	207,000
1974	1,350,000	832,000	518,000	542,000	325,000	217,000

*Sources and method: Enrollment data from U. S. Department of Health, Education and Welfare, Office of Education circulars: Opening (fall) enrollment in higher education (1954 through 1970). Population data used are consistent with Series B projection in U. S. Department of Commerce, Bureau of the Census, Current population reports: projections of the population of the United States by age and sex to 1985, Series P-25, No. 179.

The projections of total and first-time opening fall degree-credit enrollment in junior colleges are based on the assumptions: (1) Attendance rates of men and of women aged 18 to 21 years in junior colleges will follow the 1954-1970 trends; (2) entrance rates of 18-year-old men and of 18-year-old women into junior colleges will follow the 1954-1970 trends.

Note: Data include 50 states and District of Columbia for all years. Because of rounding, detail may not add to totals.

†From U. S. Department of Health, Education and Welfare, Office of Education: Projections of educational statistics to 1947-75, Washington, D. C., 1965 edition, The Department, p. 12.

mural athletic directors, since in most of these institutions intramural athletics are a part of the physical education program.

Professional programs in physical education are a part of the physical education program at both the undergraduate and the graduate levels. Physical education and health *education* are frequently combined into the same administrative unit, but health *services,* as a general rule, are not organized as part of the physical education unit. Physical education is commonly responsible for the administration of recreation programs for both students and faculty.

THE TWO-YEAR COLLEGE

The junior college, or community college as it is sometimes called, deserves special mention because this type of institution is expanding at such a rapid rate and will continue to do so as the number of college-bound students rise. This means that more and more high school boys and girls upon graduation will find their educational opportunities in this kind of college.

Though there are exceptions, most junior colleges (and by this term the community college is included) have the following three functions:

1. To give 2 years of preprofessional training or general education. A student may graduate with a degree of associate in the arts or sciences after these 2 years or transfer to a 4-year institution for a bachelor's degree. This transfer program is sometimes called the university parallel curricula. Most 4-year colleges and universities will accept transfer students from accredited junior colleges if the academic achievement of the student is high and if the subjects studied mesh with the curricula of the higher institution.
2. To provide a complete program in a semiprofessional field such as secretarial work, home economics, medical laboratory techniques, drafting, and business education.
3. To provide classes for adults who want more education to help them in their jobs or who simply want to study subjects they never had a chance to study before.

The type of curricula offered by junior colleges is usually controlled by the needs and interests of the students they serve. Some junior college curricula are planned almost entirely for students who want a general education and who plan to transfer to a 4-year institution. Other junior colleges enroll the majority of students in semiprofessional courses.

A junior college in an agricultural area may feature agricultural courses, while another junior college in an industrial community may specialize in courses that prepare young people for jobs in nearby factories.

In respect to physical education and health education in the 2-year college, surveys conducted indicate that the pattern of 2 hours weekly for ½ unit credit is the most frequent procedure for physical education. Objectives in most cases stress the students' competence in maintaining good health and balanced personal adjustment. Some colleges are seriously attempting to meet these objectives, but others have not yet developed their programs sufficiently to accomplish this task. Athletics appear to be an especially strong point of physical education at the junior college level because of the great student and public interest. Some colleges provide broad programs of team competition in many sports, whereas others are very limited.

Most 2-year colleges have a health service program for their students, but instruction in personal and community hygiene or health is less usual than instruction in physical education. Where a health course is offered it is usually a one-semester course for 2 credits.

Interviews with deans of instruction, faculty, and students of 2-year colleges indicate that they prefer to have one department chairman in charge of both the health and physical education programs. The department chairman usually is responsible to the dean of students or dean of instruction.

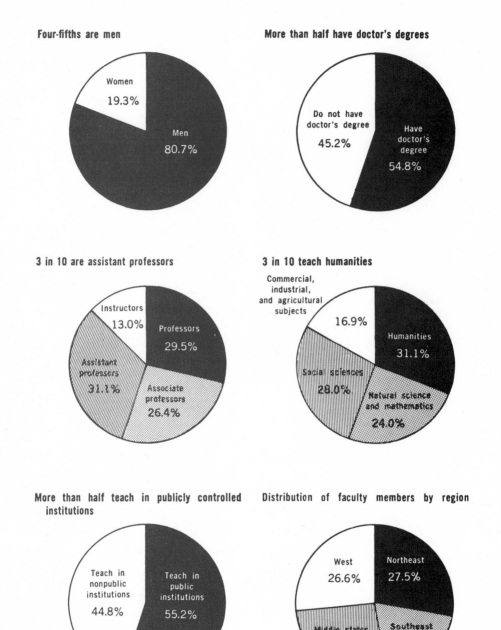

Faculty members in degree-granting institutions. (From NEA Research Bulletin **44**:8, 1966.)

The physical education program in the 2-year college at Flint Community College, Flint, Mich. **A,** Defense is not stressed by all teams in the intramural league. **B,** All swimming classes are coeducational. Classes for beginning swimmers through water safety instructor course are offered in Durham Pool. **C,** Commercial alleys for their bowling classes.

COMMUNITY ORGANIZATION FOR HEALTH

It is important to understand not only the structure of the school and college but also that of the larger community of which it is a part. If programs of health and physical education are to render the most valuable service at the community level, their leaders must clearly understand its structural organization. This important level of government touches human lives to a great degree.

Public health organization at the local level

Health department. There are few, if any, local departments with more impor-

tant functions than the health department. In spite of this, the amount of money set aside and the emphasis placed on this phase of government are usually less than that spent on many other areas, such as for police or fire protection.

The department of health also works more closely with other branches of local government than most other departments. For example, it is closely related to bureaus having control of water supply and purification, garbage collection and disposal, sewerage system and street cleaning, and police department enforcement of the sanitary code. It also works with officers in charge of education, especially in regard to medical and dental inspection of school children. Such essential relationships make it imperative to have a local health department that is efficient and functions properly.

In some cities governed by a commission, health is combined with police and fire administration to form a department of public safety. However, in most cities, especially the larger ones, there is a separate department of health. At the head of the health department in these larger cities there is usually a board of health or a commission, headed by a health commissioner. In a few cities the health activities are guided by a single commissioner, who is appointed by the mayor or city council.

In many cases small or medium-sized cities and villages do not employ full-time health officers, and the public health activities are cared for by a physician who devotes only part time to this work. Under such conditions, a health department in the full sense of the phrase does not exist and the public health activities are bound to be limited.

On some occasions, two or three small communities have felt the need for full-time health personnel and consequently have pooled their efforts and resources and have combined to develop a joint health administration with a full-time health officer. This has resulted in advantages to all communities concerned. It is hoped that this policy will be used to a greater extent by small villages, towns, and cities located within a short enough radius to make such a system practical.

The recognized, successful health departments in larger cities have boards of health presided over by a commissioner of health. These boards enact the sanitary code of the city, issue emergency health orders, and have been given broad powers in all health matters. In some emergency situations such a group has been given the power to imprison persons, destroy property, forbid traffic, and perform similar duties to prevent the spread of disease.

The health department in larger communities is usually divided into certain specialized divisions, each having control over various health aspects of the community. Some of these divisions are as follows:

The *bureau of administration,* which coordinates all the various activities performed and serves as a central communication point with other city functions.

The *division of records,* which collects, preserves, and publishes vital statistics, issues burial permits, registers physicians, assists in enforcing child labor and school attendance laws, and performs statistical work for the department.

The *sanitary division* or *bureau,* which has jurisdiction over sanitary conditions and looks into such matters as reported nuisances and the sanitation of slaughterhouses and stables.

The *bureau of preventable diseases,* which is concerned with preventing and controlling communicable disease, holding tuberculosis and other clinics, disinfecting premises and goods, and supervising a staff of field nurses.

The *division of child hygiene,* which is concerned with child and infant care, eye and dental clinics, supervision of day nurseries, and placement and care of dependent children.

The *food and drug bureau,* which has control over the food and drug supply in the city and inspects premises where foods are stored, handled, sold, or prepared. It also is especially concerned with the persons who prepare or serve food in public eating places.

The *bureau of laboratories,* which carries on research work, maintains supply stations for diphtheria antitoxin and vaccine, and makes scientific studies of various diseases and combats them whenever possible.

The *bureau of hospitals,* which supervises the various hospitals which in large cities are maintained by the department for the care of individuals who have communicable diseases.

Last, but not least, there is the *bureau of public health education.* This bureau is gradually being added to more and more departments of health because it is becoming increasingly evident that individuals are not going to develop good health practices without an educational program. This bureau sends out various types of information concerning health matters, promotes cooperation between department officials and the public, publishes health literature for professional and lay persons, gives health lectures, and organizes exhibitions and other media for publicizing the importance of certain health practices.

The health department, as can be seen from the preceding description, provides many essential and important functions for a community. Unfortunately, many of the activities listed are not carried on by all cities. An analysis of the functions performed indicates a change of emphasis from that of merely eliminating nuisances and fighting epidemics to one of prevention and providing information and services essential for good health.

Health councils. One of the best ways to ensure that all the health resources in a community are being utilized effectively for the benefit of most people is to have a community health council.

A community contains many groups and individuals who are interested in health. With so many interested in such an endeavor, there is need for coordination and a clearinghouse for the solution of health problems. A council or committee that is composed of representatives of various community groups can serve a very useful purpose. Much progress can be made if representatives from such groups as voluntary and professional health agencies, schools, industry, merchants, and others interested in health meet to discuss health problems. Group discussion can take place,

problems can be aired, plans can be made, and work can be done that would never be possible without some type of cooperative effort. The health council is a comparatively new organization but has been found to be most helpful in promoting health in the community. As an agency through which many groups may cooperate to promote health, it has great possibilities for mobilizing public support for necessary health measures.

Voluntary health agencies. Some voluntary health agencies usually exist in communities of any size. These are organizations concerned with health that receive their support from public drives for funds, gifts, membership fees, and donations. Some examples of these are the American Cancer Society, National Tuberculosis Association, National Committee for Mental Hygiene, and the American Red Cross. Voluntary agencies in the field of health take the leadership for solving particular health problems that affect great numbers of American people. Through voluntary contributions and work, these agencies attempt to meet the problems.

Many voluntary health agencies exist now and new ones are being formed periodically. The greatest need at the present time is to coordinate the work that all the various agencies for health—whether they be official, voluntary, or private—are doing. There is considerable confusion in the public's mind because of the numerous agencies that are asking for financial help and support. If the work were better coordinated and organized, the public would have a clearer picture of what is needed and consequently would lend greater support.

Relationship between public health and school health programs

The health of the school child is a major consideration of our educational systems. In 1918 it was placed first on the list of "Cardinal Principles for Education." In 1938 it was reemphasized by the Educational Policies Commission. Conferences have been held, legislation passed, personnel appointed, and programs planned for the express purpose of promoting the health of the youth in our schools. This great emphasis focused on the health of the child and the happiness and fitness of future citizens of the United States means that every effort must be made to accomplish this objective in the most efficient and best way possible. Therefore, all the personnel and resources that are available in the community must be mobilized for this purpose. This is not a one-agency job. Instead, it requires the help and assistance of all organizations affecting the health of the child. Voluntary and official agencies, hospitals, boards of education, and other interested individuals and organizations must pool their resources, facilities, equipment, and knowledge in order that the health of the child may receive utmost consideration.

On the other hand, the solution of community health problems outside the school needs the concerted effort of every agency. Public health programs are to a great degree based upon an enlightened public that understands the health problems of the community and gives its support to the solving of these problems. The school can play a major part in helping to educate the citizens of the community so that health progress may be realized. The school health program should fit into the total community health program in a well-coordinated manner so as to render utmost service to all concerned.

In discussing interrelationships between school and public health programs, it is important to consider the controversy between community health groups and the schools as to who is responsible for administering the various phases of the school health program.

There are primarily three points of view as to where the responsibility lies. One group feels that the board of education should be responsible, another that public health officials should assume the responsibility, and a third group thinks that school health is a joint responsibility of both the board of education and public health officials. It is advisable to consider briefly some of the arguments in favor of each point of view.

Those individuals who advocate board of education control for the school health program set forth many pertinent arguments in their behalf. These arguments can be summed up in the following statements. Board of education supporters point to the fact that the Tenth Amendment to the Constitution of the United States places the authority for education in the hands of the states. The states delegate this authority to the local communities, which in turn vest the authority in the board of education. The board of education, in the absence of legislation to the contrary, is responsible for all education, and health education, therefore, falls logically under their jurisdiction. They point to the fact that teachers, as a result of their training in such areas as psychology and methodology, are much better prepared to instruct children in health matters than are public health officials. They are better prepared to make health services meaningful educational experiences for all pupils. As another argument, they maintain that if public health officials were responsible for the school health program, the teachers would have two bosses, thus making for inefficient administration.

Those individuals who advocate that the school health program should be controlled by public health officials also list many pertinent arguments in their favor. Public health supporters say that health is logically a province of the medical profession and should therefore be under supervision of medical personnel, such as those found in most public health departments. They point to the fact that the school is part of the total community, and therefore such an important matter as health is a responsibility of community health officials. Furthermore, the pupil is in school only 5 days of each week and 180 or so days per year. The rest of the time he is in the larger community outside the school environment. They argue that public health nurses, as a result of their training and experience, are the best qualified to develop and administer a health services program, especially in respect to home-school-community relationships. They maintain that according to law the control of communicable diseases is a prerogative of public health officials and that they can do the job much more efficiently than can the board of education.

Finally, there is a group of persons who maintains that the school health program should be controlled jointly by both the board of education and public health officials. These point out that there will be better utilization of personnel, facilities, and community resources and that, consequently, greater health progress can be made if there is joint control with both working together for the good of all.

There does not seem to be a simple solution to this controversy as to where the responsibility for school health lies. Probably the answer to this problem will vary according to the community. The solution would seem to depend upon how each community can best meet the health needs of the people who inhabit its particular geographic limits. The type of administrative setup that most fully meets the health needs and makes for greatest progress should be the one that is adopted. Vested interests should not be considered, and the health interests of the consumer should be the primary concern. *Health is everybody's business,* and everyone should strive for the best health program possible in his community, state, nation, and world.

COMMUNITY ORGANIZATION FOR PHYSICAL EDUCATION

Physical education within the larger community outside of the school is usually in-

corporated in the programs sponsored by recreation people or by voluntary and private agencies such as the Boys' Club, YMCA, churches, and camps. Since these organizations and programs are considered in detail in the last two chapters of this book, they will not be discussed here.

Questions and exercises

1. Draw a structural organization chart for your school or college showing the various administrative divisions. Discuss the responsibilities of each of the divisions. Give special attention to the health and physical education divisions.
2. In regard to the board of education of the community in which you live, list the composition of the board, powers of the board, and qualifications of board members.
3. Discuss the role of the superintendent of schools, principal, and college administrators in a selected community.
4. Define each of the following: (a) health program, (b) health services, (c) health appraisal, (d) health counseling, (e) health education, (f) healthful school living, (g) health coordination, (h) health council, and (i) health educator.
5. What part does a health coordinator play in the school health program?
6. Describe in detail the three main divisions of the total school physical education program.
7. Discuss the relationship of local government to school health. What administrative provisions have been made for these important considerations?
8. Discuss in detail the organization and administration of a program of physical education in a junior college of your choice.

Reading assignment in *Administrative Dimensions of Health and Physical Education Programs, Including Athletics:* Chapter 3, Selections 12 to 15.

Selected references

Blackwell, T. E.: College and university administration, New York, 1966, The Center for Applied Research in Education, Inc. (The Library of Education).

Bookwalter, K. W.: Physical education in the secondary schools, Washington, D. C., 1964, The Center for Applied Research in Education, Inc. (The Library of Education).

Brickman, W. W.: Educational systems in the United States, New York, 1964, The Center for Applied Research in Education, Inc. (The Library of Education).

Brimm, R. P.: The junior high school. New York, 1963, The Center for Applied Research in Education, Inc. (The Library of Education).

Bucher, C. A.: Foundations of physical education, ed. 5, St. Louis, 1968, The C. V. Mosby Co.

Bucher, C. A.: Physical education for life, St. Louis, 1969, McGraw-Hill Book Co.

Bucher, C. A., and Dupee, R. K., Jr.: Athletics in schools and colleges, Washington, D. C., 1965, The Center for Applied Research in Education, Inc. (The Library of Education).

Bucher, C. A., Koenig, C., and Barnhard, M.: Methods and materials for secondary school physical education, ed. 3, St. Louis, 1970, The C. V. Mosby Co.

Bucher, C. A., Olsen, E., and Willgoose, C. The foundations of health, New York, 1967, Appleton-Century-Crofts.

Bucher, C. A., and Reade, E. M.: Physical education and health in the elementary school, ed. 2, New York, 1971, The Macmillan Co.

Byrd, O. E.: School health administration, Philadelphia, 1964, W. B. Saunders Co.

Educational Policies Commission: School athletics —problems and policies, Washington, D. C., 1954, National Education Association.

Eichhorn, D. H.: The middle school, New York, 1966, The Center for Applied Research in Education, Inc. (The Library of Education).

Ferguson, D. G.: Pupil personnel services, New York, 1963, The Center for Applied Research in Education, Inc. (The Library of Education).

Gauerke, W. E.: School law, New York, 1965, The Center for Applied Research in Education, Inc. (The Library of Education).

Goldhammer, K.: The school board, New York, 1964, The Center for Applied Research in Education, Inc. (The Library of Education).

Hillson, M.: Change and innovation in elementary school organization, New York, 1965, Holt, Rinehart & Winston, Inc.

Jenson, T. H., and Clark, D. L.: Educational administration, New York, 1964, The Center for Applied Research in Education, Inc. (The Library of Education).

Joint Committee on Health Problems in Education of National Education Association and American Medical Association: School health services, Washington, D. C., 1964, National Education Association.

Joint Committee on Health Problems in Education of National Education Association and American Medical Association: Healthful school living, Washington, D. C., 1969, National Education Association.

Joint Committee on Health Problems in Education of National Education Association and American Medical Association: Health education, Washington, D. C., 1961, National Education Association.

Linder, I. H., and Gunn, H. M.: Secondary school administration: problems and practices, Columbus, Ohio, 1963, Charles E. Merrill Books, Inc.

Morphet, E. L., Johns, R. L., and Reller, T. L.: Educational administration, Englewood Cliffs, N. J., 1967, Prentice-Hall, Inc.

Reynolds, J. W.: The junior college, New York, 1965, The Center for Applied Research in Education, Inc. (The Library of Education).

Willgoose, C. E.: Health education in the elementary school, ed. 2, Philadelphia, 1964, W. B. Saunders Co.

Wynn, R. D.: Organization of public schools, New York, 1964, The Center for Applied Research in Education, Inc. (The Library of Education).

CHAPTER 4 THE BUSINESS ADMINISTRATOR*

In recent years the position of school or college business administrator has grown extensively. The exact position, with its inherent responsibilities, is still in a stage of development. The business administrator is a person trained and experienced in the field of education with a background of business—or a person trained in business with a knowledge of educational techniques. The business administrator is part of the administrative team. He is a specialist making a contribution to the united efforts of the group in supporting the procedures of improving the educational opportunity of the pupils and the staff. School business administration has long been accepted to mean "that phase of school administration having responsibility for the efficient and economic management of the business affairs of the schools."†

The American Association of School Administrators and the Association of School Business Officials of the United States and Canada have now jointly agreed that school business administrators may be defined as follows:

The school business administrator shall be that employee member of the school staff who has been designated by the Board of Education and/or the Superintendent to have general responsibility for the administration of the business affairs of a school district. In any type of administrative organization, he shall be responsible for carrying out the general administration of the district and such other duties as may be assigned to him. Unless otherwise provided by local law or customs (as in dual control areas), he shall report to the Board of Education through the Superintendent of Schools.*

The school or college business administrator is an important member of the administrative team who has a significant contribution to make in the decision-making process as well as in executing business functions. He is well versed in education matters as well as in business management, and teaching experience is highly desirable. He is in a position to participate under the superintendent's or president's leadership and in making educational decisions as well as doing an efficient job of serving the district or college by providing educational activities for the staff and pupils.

Since health educators and physical educators must work closely with school business administrators, special consideration is given to this key school or college administrator and the role he plays in the administration of school and college programs in general and in school and college health and physical education programs in particular.

THE COLLEGE BUSINESS MANAGER

The college business manager, or the vice president of business affairs as he is sometimes called, is responsible for budget

*Thanks are due Mr. H. J. Stevens, Assistant Superintendent of Business Affairs, Nanuet, New York Public Schools, for his help in writing this chapter.

†Linn, H. H.: School business administration, New York, 1956, The Ronald Press Co., p. 21.

*Association of School Business Officials: The school business administrator (Bulletin 21), Evanston, Ill., 1960, The Association.

preparation and fiscal accounting, investment of endowment and other monies, planning and construction of buildings, data processing, management of research and other contracts, business aspects of student loans, and intercollegiate activities.

Most key business officers have earned a master's or a doctor's degree, usually in business administration. However, some are certified public accountants and some have taken courses in management institutes. Most college business managers are recruited outside the academic world.

For the purposes of this chapter, the term *business administrator* is used, and the duties of such an educational officer are discussed in terms of schools and the school district. However, the functions that are outlined for the business administrator, the problems discussed, and the working relationship with health and physical ed-

ucation personnel are similar to or have implications for college as well as for school health educators and physical educators.

RESPONSIBILITIES OF THE BUSINESS ADMINISTRATOR

The business administrator's responsibilities are varied. He is as familiar with employee health insurance problems as he is with the butterfat content in milk. In the smaller school district, the business responsibilities are incorporated into the duties of the chief school administrator. As districts enlarge, there is a need to hire a person to oversee all the nonteaching areas of the district so that the chief school administrator is free to devote more time to the educational program of the district. No two districts are alike in the handling of business responsibilities.

Following are some of the administra-

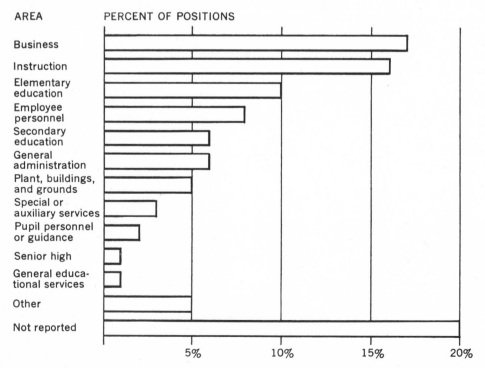

Major areas of assignment of 935 associate and assistant superintendencies. (From NEA Research Bulletin 40:26, 1962.)

tor's duties as listed by Frederick W. Hill,* past president of the Association of School Business Officials:

1. Budget and financial planning—This is an area in which the business official has to be sensitive to the needs of the staff in order to carry out a program. He also has to have a sixth sense to understand how much the community can expend on the program. This can be related to the accompanying isosceles triangle. There has to

Program

be a direct relationship among all the components that make up the three sides of the triangle.

2. Purchasing and supply management —The business official must utilize the best purchasing techniques to obtain maximum value for every dollar spent. After purchases are made and goods received, he is responsible for warehousing, storage, and inventory control. An article offered at the cheapest price is not always the most economical to purchase.

3. Plans—The business official works with administrators, teachers, architects, attorneys, and citizens of the community in developing plans for expansion of building facilities.

4. Personnel—The business official's duties vary in relation to the size of the district. In a small district he may be in charge of the nonteaching personnel, and in a large district he may be in charge of all personnel. In this capacity he has to

*Hill, F. W.: The rightful role of the school business official, School Business Affairs 29:63, 1963.

maintain records, pay schedules, retirement reports, and other personnel records.

5. Staff improvement—The business official is always interested in upgrading the people under his jurisdiction by providing workshops and inservice courses concerning latest developments in the field.

6. Community relations—Without community support the school would not operate. Some administrators tend to forget this when they become too far removed from the community. There is always a need to interpret the business area to the public.

7. Transportation—It has often been said that boards of education find themselves spending too much time on the three B's—buses, buildings, and bonds. When this occurs, it is time to look into the hiring of a business official.

8. Food services—The business official is

The business administrator is responsible for purchasing supplies and equipment. (Courtesy Nissen Corporation, Cedar Rapids, Iowa.)

responsible for the efficient management of the lunchroom.

9. Accounting and reporting—The business official establishes and supervises the financial records and accounting procedures.

10. Debt service—The business official is involved with various capital developments and financial planning through short-term and long-term programs. Part of the financial rating of a school or a college district is judged on the way its debt service is handled.

11. Insurance—The business official must be familiar with a large schedule of insurance provisions ranging from fire and liability to health insurance. He has to maintain records for proof in case of loss.

12. Legal matters—The business official has to be familiar with education law and he has to know when to consult with attorneys.

13. System analysis—The business official must constantly question existing systems to see if they can be changed so that the job can be done more efficiently. New methods are being introduced utilizing data processing that will be a challenge as well as an aid to the business official.

FUNCTIONS OF BUSINESS MANAGEMENT IN THE EDUCATIONAL PROGRAM

The business administrator is in a position to serve the educational program. His function is strictly limited by the size of the educational triangle—program, receipts, expenditures. The greater the perimeter of the triangle, the larger will be his sphere of operations. This applies to all departments in the system. Likewise, in times of inflation, the expenditures and receipts may increase, the program side will also increase, but the actual program could remain the same. Hence, it is obvious that the business administrator must project expenditures and receipts ahead if a constant program is going to be maintained.

The business office represents a means

to an end, and it can be evaluated in terms of how well it contributes to the realization of the objectives of education.

OBJECTIVES OF BUSINESS MANAGEMENT

In serving schools and colleges, the business administrator constantly has a goal to help them obtain the greatest educational service possible from each tax or aid dollar spent. He should take a democratic approach on decisions affecting others. A decision will then be reached that will be for the best, with the assurance that the educational benefits are worth the cost.

The business administrator is part of the team of administrators—along with presidents, principals, superintendents, and board members—who may be expected to look into the years ahead and have some ideas in regard to the future plans of the school or college.

RELATIONSHIP WITH HEALTH AND PHYSICAL EDUCATION DEPARTMENTS

The business administrator has a very close working relationship with physical educators and health educators.

Director of health and physical education

In a large school district the business administrator works directly with the director of the department on budgetary and financial matters. It is important that all matters concerning physical education programs in the various buildings of the school district be approved by the building principal before they go to the central office. This is especially true in the secondary school because the physical education program is one part of the total curriculum. After the programs have been approved by the principal, they should be presented by the principal to the central office. If any program is to be modified, the principal is notified accordingly. Purchasing of materials is done on a bid basis, and when substitutes are offered for specified items, the business administrator should consult with the director of the department. The director then acts as a consultant in determining the quality of the items being purchased. One of the most serious mistakes that can be made when working with the business administrator is to "pad" the budget request for supplies and materials. The old expression "murder will out" comes to the fore at this point. The physical education person may decide that he needs twenty-four basketballs for next year, but he decides to list thirty-six on his budget request—hoping for the twenty-four—and if he receives thirty-six, he will have that many extra in the storage closet. Likewise, the business administrator should not make blind deletions in the requisitions without a consultation. There has to be a feeling of rapport between the two areas—so when the physical educator requests twenty-four basketballs, he will know he will receive twenty-four, unless a mutual budget change has been made.

A teacher in the physical education department should analyze the community and school philosophy to determine how much emphasis is to be placed on the program. This will have a direct bearing on the expenditures. In some school districts the academic program is a runner-up to the athletic program. A new teacher to a school system soon finds out how liberal or conservative the district is when he commences to submit purchase requisitions. An early meeting with the business administrator would be very helpful in determining the financial philosophy of the school district toward the health and physical education program. Such a meeting would also spare some embarrassment in the future.

The health educator

The health educator plays a significant role in the school and college curriculum today. Educational growth is most effective when the students are progressing health-fully as well as intellectually. It has been found that one of the reasons for the lack of educational attainment has been the physical inability to cope with the school or college program. Many items come to the business office that can be passed on to the health educator such as teaching aids for the health program.

The myth of the school nurse-teacher functioning as a school nurse—minus the teaching—is now being overcome. In today's modern school the nurse-teacher is looked upon as a resource person to be brought into the classroom as a specialist to augment teaching units.

The business administrator and the school nurse-teacher must work together at all times. New schools are now being equipped with furnishings in color that have replaced the characteristic standard white equipment. The waiting rooms for health suites are now equipped with comfortable lounge furniture. The medications, equipment, and other supplies are not purchased at the local drug stores but on a bid basis through national supply houses.

The business administrator, as a member of the administrative team, has to be sensitive to change in growing school districts. Perhaps it was acceptable for the school nurse-teacher to combine her duties and become the attendance officer when the school district was small, but can her salary be justified if she has to use several hours a day on the telephone verifying absences or making home visits of truants? A non-teaching clerical person could be utilized for these duties at a considerable saving in salary, and this would also relieve the school nurse-teacher to perform other duties that would be more effective in the curriculum.

The dental hygienist

The dental hygienist is a relatively new addition to the health education team. Until recent years most school districts have utilized the services of the local dentists to make an annual dental inspection. In some districts the dentists were paid for this service. In other districts the dentists did it on a volunteer basis. In the latter school districts it is more difficult to initiate the idea of hiring an individual to make dental inspections. It must be emphasized that a dental hygienist is more than just a tooth inspector. A dental hygienist should be utilized in the classroom as a consultant, similar to the school nurse-teacher. At the time the dental hygienist's schedule is prepared, consideration should be made for classroom visitations to discuss dental hygiene with the students. It is the responsibility of the school business administrator to provide a means for the dental hygienist to obtain materials and equipment to carry out her function in the school district.

OTHER AUXILIARY SERVICES

The business administrator renders many additional services that have a direct bearing on health and physical education programs.

Team transportation

The business administrator is usually responsible for the transportation program. A good business administrator, with an educational background, will be cognizant of the importance of exercise of not only the mind but also of the body. He will, therefore, make a provision in his transportation program for buses to carry athletic teams to sport contests so that they will arrive safely on time at their destinations. The director of athletics must be informed as to the type of facilities that will be available to him so that he can plan accordingly. This involves a direct relationship between the director of athletics and the transportation supervisor. All requests for special athletic trips should be in writing and acknowledged by the secondary school principal or college administrator where he is involved. This is necessary since the principal or college administrator will be aware of any conflicts with other parts of his program. The business administrator finds it very difficult to schedule special athletic trips on a moment's notice, although it is understandable when games are canceled for reason of weather or other unforeseen events. The director of athletics should submit a monthly calendar of athletic events, listing the date, time and place of departure, event, destination, number of participants, time of pickup, and remarks (see accompanying sample).

Month of April

April 8

Depart: 3:00 P.M.
From: Senior High School
Team: Junior Varsity Baseball
To: Jones High School
Students: 35
Pickup: 5:30 P.M.
Remarks:

April 9

Depart: 3:00 P.M.
From: Junior High School
Team: Varsity Tennis
To: Albany High School
Students: 5
Pickup: 5:00 P.M.
Remarks: Station wagon requested;
          Coach Lewis will drive.

April 10

Depart: 3:00 P.M.
From: Senior High School
Team: Varsity Baseball and
       Varsity Tennis
To: Baseball to Jones High School
    Tennis to Albany High School
Students: 40
Pickup: Baseball—5:00 P.M.
        Tennis—5:30 P.M.
Remarks: One bus for both teams—
          drop off baseball first.

The events scheduled on April 8 are very routine and the transportation supervisor can request a bus accordingly. The events on April 9 are a little more complex and the director of athletics can state a preference for a station wagon. It is much more economical for a school district or college to furnish a station wagon to transport five students rather than a sixty-passenger bus. The events on April 10 are more complex, and the remarks indicate that one bus can be utilized for both teams. It is necessary to list the number of participants so that the proper size bus, or buses, can be assigned. This calendar should be submitted in triplicate (carbons) to the business administrator. After the transportation department has scheduled the trips, the business administrator initials all three copies and returns two copies to the athletic director. The director keeps one copy and the other copy is sent to the principal or college administrator. The procedure for submitting transportation requests could vary in different schools. The administrator might receive the schedule for approval before the business office.

Facilities, equipment, and supplies

The business administrator has a responsibility to provide adequate indoor and outdoor facilities and sufficient equipment and supplies for the health and physical education department, and the latter has the responsibility to keep these items in the best condition possible.

There are three phases related to facilities, equipment, and supplies.

The first phase is to secure needed items in order to provide a program. The size of the health suite and gymnasium, the field acreage, and the quantity and quality of the equipment are all related to money. The health educator and physical educator can present to the business administrator alternate programs with price tags for the business administrator to transfer into tax rates for the board of education or board of trustees. This is usually done prior to a building program.

The second phase is in regard to a main-

Bethesda Public Schools, Bethesda, Md.

tenance program. The director of health and physical education is usually the custodian of all the equipment and supplies. He has an obligation to the district to see that health supplies, uniforms, bats, balls, and other equipment are not unnecessarily damaged. He should delegate responsibility to the various teachers and coaches to supervise all participants at all times. Locker room damage can be extensive after a game if the players are not under continual supervision. Damaged uniforms can be repaired if the physical education personnel are aware of deteriorating conditions. Usually it is much more economical to repair them rather than to replace them.

The use of the grounds requires cooperation between the physical educator and the superintendent of buildings and grounds. There must be a direct line of communication between these two positions. The former is primarily interested in a first-rate physical education program, and the latter is primarily interested in first-rate facilities. Neither one can be first rate without cooperation between the two individuals involved and a mutual understanding of each other's problems.

The third phase of the utilization of facilities, equipment, and supplies relates to replacement of existing units. Equipment does wear out, and the life of the equipment does depend somewhat on the second phase. The business administrator, in his capacity as the director of the budget, prefers to replace items over a period of years—not all at once. It is a budget hardship to replace all football uniforms, for example, in 1 year, whereas the budget can absorb the cost if a few uniforms are replaced annually.*

At times there are some large replacement expenses that cannot be avoided, for example, replacing bleachers. The business administrator is in a position to include this in the budget as a capital expense or perhaps add it to a bond issue. But such a large budget item does merit special consideration from the business administrator. Too many special considerations added to the budget from the department will soon give people the impression that the program receives greater emphasis than the other phases of the instructional program. One of the ways to obtain economical and efficient use of the facilities, equipment, and supplies is for the business administrator and health and physical educators to reside as taxpayers in the community where they are employed.

Insurance*

The business administrator has to maintain a constant vigil on developments in the health and physical education insurance programs. Athletics represent one of the most important areas of coverage. Some schools and colleges do not provide an athletic insurance program. If a student is injured in an athletic event, the family would then be responsible for all medical expenditures. There would be be no provision for the school or college to reimburse the family for its expense. Of course, the school or college is always open to a lawsuit by the parents in an effort to reclaim expenses. This is expensive for the school or college, for if the claim is settled in favor of the parents, the school's or college's insurance premiums for the next few years are increased. If the lawsuit is settled in favor of the school or college, the insurance company has already placed a sum of money in reserve until the final decision is reached. This is also costly because the premium is increased during the time the money is in reserve. An intangible effect is the damage to the school's or college's public relations.

An alternative is to provide an opportunity for the students to purchase athletic insurance or, better yet, for the school or

---

*See also Chapter 17.

*Insurance is also discussed in Chapter 18.

college to purchase a policy for students participating in sports. Of course, the latter is the best method because all students are covered, regardless of their wealth, and the students' liability policy is not subject to suit. Most parents are only interested in recovering monies actually spent, and they are satisfied accordingly. Usually a blanket policy purchased by the school or college can be obtained at a lesser unit cost than a policy purchased by individuals. The athletic insurance program can be administered by a local or regional broker, relieving the school or college of going into the insurance business.

It is the responsibility of the director of physical education to supply accurate lists of participating students to the business office prior to the starting time of the sports. It is imperative for the various coaches to become aware of the insurance coverage so that when accidents do happen, they can inform the athletes as to the proper procedure to follow in filing reports and claims. Usually the business office will supply policies for every participant in a covered athletic team. The coach should not only be knowledgeable, but he should also show concern for accident victims. This is not only a form of good public relations, but it may also make the difference in the parents minds concerning a lawsuit. The coaches then must be instructed in the proper attitude to take when such mishaps occur.

Medical examinations

The business administrator has a responsibility to the department to ascertain that there are enough physicians appointed by the board of education or that the health services are adequate to serve the needs of the school district or college. Every student participating in physical education should have a medical examination before he enters into activities. In athletics there should be a medical examination before each sport season. This means that if a

student is participating in football, basketball, and baseball, he would have three medical examinations.

A student was injured in a sectional wrestling meet and later died from the injury. Even though the school's liability carrier was not involved in the case, the adjuster was collecting material. His first request was the boy's medical examination that permitted him to participate in wrestling.

Coaches must be made aware of the significance of allowing a student to participate in a sport without a proper medical examination.

It is obvious that there is a direct relationship between the school or college business administrator and health and physical educators. They are dependent on the business administrator not only for supplies but also for guidelines in carrying out their program within the policies of the board of education or board of trustees. The purchase and care of supplies and equipment are discussed in detail in Chapter 17, but all the procedures usually originate in the office of the school business administrator. The staff of the health and physical education department can work with the business administrator in order to reach their objectives. It is important to realize that the business administrator and health and physical education personnel do have the same objective—to educate each child to the maximum of his ability. With that premise in mind, all the insignificant petty grievances, political overtones, and selfish desires will disappear into oblivion.

All personnel should respect the organizational structure and philosophy of the school or college. Subordinates that bypass their department heads, for instance, do not make good leaders. The first criterion of a good leader is that he must be a good follower. It is one thing to read the various school philosophies, but it is still another to be able to carry out the philosophy. Before joining the staff of a particular school or college, a teacher should become familiar with its philosophy and be prepared to live by it.

PROBLEMS IN WORKING WITH BUSINESS ADMINISTRATORS

Some of the pitfalls and problems encountered by business administrators in working with health and physical educators, as seen through the eyes of business administrators, are as follows:

1. Overestimation of budget requests with the idea of expecting a reduction in the request
2. Not being able to justify budget requests as they relate to the total educational program
3. Deadlines not met in submitting requests for transportation, supplies, and so on
4. Lack of awareness of the school district or college philosophy in regard to the place of the athletic program in the curriculum; hence, budget complications
5. Lack of cooperative planning in regard to the transportation equipment that is available and the scheduling of special athletic events away from school or college necessitating the use of buses
6. Late notification to the business administrator's office when a special athletic event is cancelled that requires the cancellation of a prearranged bus
7. Negligence in filing accident reports on students injured in sports or classes, no matter how insignificant an accident may seem at the time
8. Incomplete records on students participating in sports—especially in regard to the requirement that all students receive a physical examination *before* trying out for the sport
9. Lack of concern for accident victims
10. Lack of knowledge as to an injured student's rights and privileges under the student accident policy
11. Failure to realize that the educational goals represented in the philosophy of the school or college take priority over selfish, petty, and political interests
12. Lack of respect for the "chain of command" —a health and physical education teacher should not bypass the director of the department when communicating with the business office
13. Lack of interest in the facilities at his disposal, causing breakdowns and extra added expense

GUIDELINES FOR HEALTH AND PHYSICAL EDUCATORS

Some of the guidelines for health and physical educators to follow as viewed by business administrators are as follows:

1. All matters concerning health and physical education programs in the buildings of the district should be approved by the building principal before going to the school business administrator.

2. The school business administrator should also keep the central administration informed of any budget changes for the athletic programs since the curriculum will also be affected.

3. Supplies that are to be purchased should be accompanied by a complete specification, including model, catalogue size, and so on. Bids must be accepted on equivalents, but sometimes bids are received on substitutes. Health and physical educators should make themselves available to the business administrator to evaluate bids submitted.

4. Requisitions should be submitted after a careful study of the needs of the health and physical education department.

5. A teacher in the health and physical education department should be aware of the community's sentiment toward health and physical education programs and let that be one guideline for the curriculum.

6. The director of the health and physical education program should meet with the business administrator to determine the financial philosophy of the school or college toward the educational program.

7. The director of the health and physical education programs should keep the business administrator informed on new materials and ideas in his field.

8. All requests for special trips should be in writing on forms provided by the business office.

9. A monthly calendar should be submitted by the director of health and physical education, listing all athletic events and all pertinent transportation details.

10. The director of health and physical education should cooperate with the insurance program by submitting lists of students participating in sports, reporting accidents, and following through with physical examinations.

11. All personnel should be instructed in regard to administrative policies for dealing with accidents.

Questions and exercises

1. Interview a business administrator to obtain the following information: (a) the relations he has with health educators and/or physical educators, (b) how the business aspects of health education and/or physical education programs can be most effectively carried out, and (c) what a new teacher of health education and/or physical education should know about business administrators.

2. Why is a person who is a specialist in business management needed in school or college systems today?

3. Read one book or one article in a school or college administration magazine of your choice that concerns itself with the role of the business administrator in schools or colleges. Give a report to the class.

4. How is business management of health education and/or physical education carried on at the college level?

Reading assignment in *Administrative Dimensions of Health and Physical Education Programs, Including Athletics:* Chapter 3, Selection 11.

Selected references

Casey, L. M.: School business administration, New York, 1964, The Center for Applied Research in Education, Inc. (The Library of Education).

Hill, F. W.: The school business administrator, Evanston, Ill., 1960, American Association of Business Officials of the United States and Canada.

Hill, F. W.: The rightful role of the school business official, School Business Affairs 29:63, 1963.

Hill, F. W., and Colmey, J. W.: School business administration in the smaller community, Minneapolis, Minn., 1964, T. S. Denison & Co., Inc.

Knezevich, S. J., and Fowlkes, J. G.: Business management of local school systems, New York, 1960, Harper & Row, Publishers.

Linn, H. H.: School business administration, New York, 1956, The Ronald Press Co.

Naughton, J. J.: Profile of the chief school business administrator, Connecticut Teacher 34:16, April, 1967.

Roe, W. H.: School business management, New York, 1961, McGraw-Hill Book Co.

Stevens, H. J.: Are you issuing blank checks? School Management 9:80, 1965.

CHAPTER 5   PERSONNEL ADMINISTRATION FOR HEALTH AND PHYSICAL EDUCATION PROGRAMS

Personnel administration requires the recognition of, and adherence to, sound principles. Some important principles essential to effective personnel administration are discussed in the following paragraphs.

PRINCIPLES OF PERSONNEL ADMINISTRATION

Cooperation

To achieve cooperation implies that the specialties and unique abilities of individuals must be noted and utilized in situations where their services will be rendered under optimum conditions. The permanency of cooperation will depend upon the degree to which the purposes of the organization are achieved and individual motives are satisfied. The function of administration is to see that these essentials are accomplished.

The individual as a member of an organization

Administration should seek to imbue the organization with the theme that every individual has a stake in the enterprise. The undertakings can be successful only as all persons contribute to the maximum of their potentials, and with success will then come increased satisfaction to each individual. Above all, it must be recognized that submergence of self is necessary for the achievement of the organization's goals.

The fallacy of final authority

The authority that does exist belongs to the job and not to the person. The admin-istrator should never feel powerful and all-important. Authority does not reside in one human being but in the best thinking, judgment, and imagination that the organization can command. Every individual has the authority that goes with his position and only that much. In turn, this authority is conditioned by other members whose work is closely allied to his achieving the objectives for which the organization exists. Authority comes from those who perform the more technical aspects of the organization's work as well as from those who, because of their positions, are responsible for the ultimate decisions. Department heads, foremen, and staff consultants issue reports interpreting the facts. Their judgments, conclusions, and recommendations contribute to the formulation of the final decisions that are the responsibility of the administrator. If these interpretations, judgments, conclusions, and recommendations are not accepted, the organization may fail. Its best thinking has been ignored. Furthermore, individuals cannot be induced to contribute their efforts in an organization that has little respect for their thinking. Authority is not resident in one person. Instead, it permeates the entire organization from top to bottom.

Staff morale

There are certain conditions that are known to contribute to staff morale. Some of the more important of these will be discussed. The administration should continually strive to create such conditions in their organizations. The degree of good staff morale that exists will be in direct proportion to the degree to which such conditions are satisfied.

Leadership. The quality of the leader will determine staff morale to a great degree. From the top down, there should be careful selection of all individuals who act in leadership capacities. Other things being equal, individuals will contribute better service, produce more, have an overall better morale, and have more respect for individuals who are leaders in the true sense of the word.

Physical and social environment. A healthful physical and social environment is essential to good staff morale. The health of the worker must be provided for. There must be good lighting to protect the eyes, good air to protect the lungs, and adequate safety precautions to protect the body. There must be provisions for mental health that include proper supervision, provision for advancement, provision for any emergency that may arise, and provision for intellectual improvement. Anything that is conducive to physical, mental, and emotional health is important to the morale of the individual and in turn to his efficiency as a member of the organization.

The social environment is also an important consideration. The individuals with whom one works and the activities in which one engages can strengthen or dampen the spirit. An individual is the product of his interactions with others. Therefore, in order to improve oneself it is very important to associate with those who can contribute to this improvement. Since the working day represents, to a great degree, the majority of an individual's social relationships, it is important that these relationships be wholesome and conducive to individual improvement.

Advancement. Human beings like to feel that they are "getting ahead in the world." This is an important consideration in developing and continuing a high degree of staff morale. This consideration necessitates informing each member of an organization as to what is essential for progress. Opportunities should be provided for self-improvement in learning new skills, gaining new knowledge, and having new experiences. In addition, encouragement should be given those who are anxious to improve and are willing to devote extra time and effort for such a purpose.

Recognition of meritorious service. Another requirement, similar to advancement, which is requisite for staff morale, is recognition for outstanding contributions to the organization. As has been previously pointed out, all human beings need to be recognized. Those who make outstanding contributions to the organization should be so honored. This is very important to further greater achievements.

Individual differences. An important principle of personnel management is the recognition of individual differences and different types of work. Individuals differ in many ways—abilities, skills, training, and physical, mental, and social qualities. There are also various types of work that require different skills, abilities, and training.

These differences in individuals and types of work must be recognized by the administrator. One of his or her main duties in respect to personnel should be to make sure that the right person is in the right niche. An individual who is a "round peg in a square hole" does not contribute to his own or the organization's welfare. To be placed in a position that should be held by a person with lesser qualifications or vice versa is unjust and devastating in its results.

It is important for the administrator to recognize in some formal way individual differences that exist in the organization. A system of status must exist for purposes of communication and orderly procedure. Such systems of status must be readily understood, authoritative, and authentic. These systems of status not only make for better communication but also provide the basis for personnel improvement and advancement within the organization. Furthermore, they help to develop a sense of responsibility in the individual. The status that is granted any one person should be in line with capacities and importance of the function he performs. Many disruptive features can develop in status systems if there is not recognition of individual abilities, if the system is allowed to become an end rather than a means to an end, and if proper incentives are not provided at each level.

QUALIFICATIONS OF THE ADMINISTRATOR

Although the qualities of a good administrator need to be considered in relation to the qualities of the persons in the or-

ganization he is attempting to lead, nevertheless it is helpful to recognize certain leadership characteristics that appear to be necessary if an administrator is to be successful on the job. The identification of these qualities is essential to help determine whether or not one should go into this important field if the occasion arises. This identification will also help in evaluating the type of administration one is experiencing in his own organization, whether he be an administrator or hold another position.

The qualifications of an administrator are many. Some (administrative mind, integrity, ability to instill good human relations, ability to make decisions, health and fitness for the job, willingness to accept responsibility, understanding of work, command of administrative technique, and intellectual capacity) are discussed in the following sections. There has been no at-

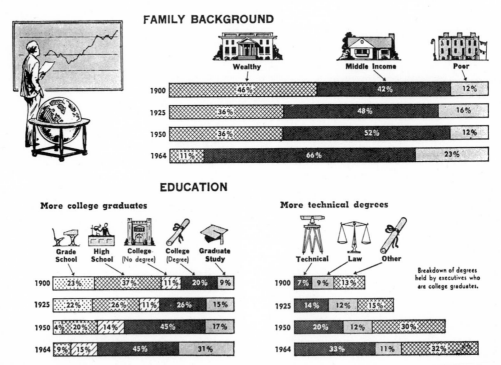

Nation's executives: changes in background and education. (© 1965 by The New York Times Company. Reprinted by permission.)

tempt to list these in order of importance, although in the discussion of each, one may be able to discern the most essential and important qualifications.

Administrative mind

A research project that involved a self-analysis of nearly 1,000 executives, all of whom were presidents of industrial organizations, pointed up the following important considerations for the person who wants to be a good administrator. Using time effectively, ability to get other people to do things, building a team, setting the direction, finding expert advice, making crisis decisions, negotiating, and effective self-improvement were considered important. Personal improvement, especially

directed along lines involving public speaking, planning work, memory skills, conference leadership, writing, producing better ideas, and reading, were also considered necessary.

Some individuals have qualities that, perhaps, have been developed through training and experience and that peculiarly adapts them to administrative work. These individuals are able to analyze situations objectively, have the ability to clarify generalizations, and possess the quality of administering in a constructive manner rather than in an exploitative way. Such persons are sensitive to human relations and the important part they play in the successful functioning of any organization. These individuals think in imagina-

Table 5-1. Mean maximum scheduled salaries,* teacher and administrative personnel, 1952-63 to 1968-69 (reporting systems with enrollments of 25,000 or more)†

Position	School year							Percent increase, 1968-69 over 1962-63
	1962-63	1963-64	1964-65	1965-66	1966-67	1967-68	1968-69	
Classroom teachers	$ 7,819	$ 8,213	$ 8,611	$ 9,025	$ 9,788	$10,530	$11,254	43.9%
Supervisory personnel assigned to individual buildings								
Supervising principals								
Elementary	10,597	11,345	11,732	12,499	13,295	14,378	15,428	45.6
Junior high	11,297	11,981	12,301	13,115	14,058	15,120	16,289	44.2
Senior high	12,064	12,682	13,236	14,062	14,973	16,188	17,408	44.3
Assistant principals								
Elementary	9,882	10,129	10,649	11,316	12,027	12,825	13,596	37.5
Junior high	10,186	10,419	10,820	11,460	12,120	13,207	14,128	38.7
Senior high	10,298	10,770	11,298	11,889	12,656	13,776	14,766	43.4
Counselors	9,094	9,183	9,421	10,314	10,960	11,844	12,525	37.7
Central-office adminstrators								
Supervisors	11,040	12,286	11,756	12,469	13,572	14,492	15,716	42.4
Consultants and/or coordinators	..	..	..	..	13,938	15,094	16,140	..
Directors	13,043	13,520	14,184	14,853	16,011	17,061	18,252	39.9
Assistant superintendents	15,990	16,669	17,675	18,415	19,246	20,466	21,746	36.0

*Highest salaries scheduled, exclusive of long-service increments or special supplements.
†From NEA Research Bulletin, May, 1969, p. 42.

tive terms. They are able to see into the future and plan a course of action with an open mind. They recognize problems in order of importance, are able to analyze a situation, develop various plans of action, and reach logical conclusions. They have the ability to organize.

Integrity

One of the most important qualifications of any administrator is integrity. Whether or not a leader can inspire the staff, have their cooperation, and achieve the purposes of the organization will depend to a great degree upon his or her integrity. Everyone likes to feel that an administrator is honest and sincere, keeps promises, can be trusted with confidential information, and is an individual in whom one has faith. Such confidence cannot emanate from administrators unless they have integrity. Failure to fulfill this one qualification will result in low morale and an inefficient organization.

Ability to instill good human relations

Ray O. Duncan, former president of the American Association for Health, Physical Education, and Recreation (AAHPER), suggested the following as considerations for administrators: be friendly and considerate, be alert to the opinions of others, be careful what you say and how you say it, be honest and fair, be wise enough to weigh and decide, be able to tolerate human failings and inefficiency, be able to acquire humility, and plan well for staff meetings.

The ability to get along with associates in work is an essential qualification for an administrator. Only through cooperative effort is it possible for an organization to achieve its goals. This cooperative effort is greatest when the individuals responsible for the coordination of human efforts have the welfare of the various members of the organization at heart. This means that an administrator must be able to con-

vert the abilities of many individuals into coordinated effort. This is done in many ways. Some of these methods include setting a good example, inspiring confidence, selecting proper incentives, possessing poise, making the right decisions in tense moments, having an impersonal attitude, cooperating and helping others when necessary, and developing and practicing ethical standards. The administrator must be adept at the art of persuasion, which takes into consideration such important items as the points of view, interests, and other factors characterizing those to be persuaded.

There is very little associated effort without leadership. The administrator must be a leader and possess the attributes and qualities that people expect if they are to follow and contribute their best to achieve the purposes for which the organization has been established.

Ability to make decisions

The administrator must be able to make decisions when the situation necessitates such action. This presumes an understanding of what constitutes the important and the unimportant in the particular situation that is in question, the ability to foresee future developments and the results of a decision, and a knowledge of what is reasonable and what is unreasonable. It also assumes knowledge as to what is in the best interests of the organization and what is not, and what has the best chance for success and what has the least chance.

Decision is essential in order to accomplish objectives at the most opportune time. The administrator should have the capacity and be willing to make a decision. Many times if a decision is not forthcoming lethargy, suspense, and poor morale are created. The administrator who procrastinates beyond a reasonable time, is afraid of making the wrong decision, thinks only of his or her own security, and is oblivious to the organization's needs

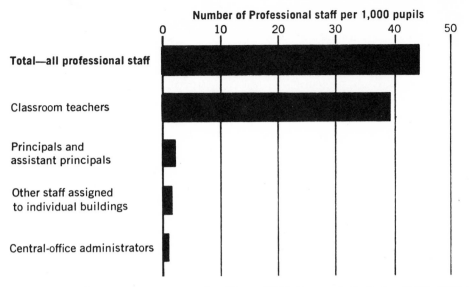

Professional employees per 1,000 pupils. (From NEA Research Bulletin **43**:77, 1965.)

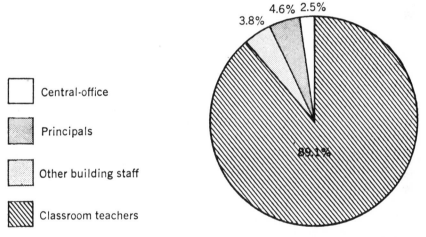

Distribution of the professional staff of all public school systems, 1964-1965. (From NEA Research Bulletin **43**:77, 1965.)

should never hold an administrative position.

Health and fitness for the job

Good health and physical fitness are essentials for the administrator. They often have a bearing on making the right decisions. Socrates once said that people in a state of bad health often made the wrong decisions in regard to affairs of state. Jennings, the famous biologist, pointed out that the body can attend to only one thing at a time. Therefore, if attention is focused on a pain in the chest, a stomach ailment, or a nervous condition, it is difficult to focus it on the functions that an administrator must perform. Poor health may cause poor administration.

Vitality and endurance are essential to the administrator. They affect one's manner, personality, attractiveness, and disposition. Administrative duties often require long hours of tedious work under the most trying conditions. Failure to have the necessary strength and endurance under such conditions could mean the inability to perform tasks that are essential to the welfare of the organization. Members of an organization have confidence in those administrators who watch over their interests at all times. It is possible for an administrator to retain this confidence continuously only if he or she is in good health and physically fit to perform arduous duties.

When considering health and fitness for the job, it is important to recognize the many facets of health. The administrator should possess not only physical but also mental, emotional, and social health. Emotional stability, especially, is a must.

Willingness to accept responsibility

Every administrator must be willing to accept responsibility. There are duties to be performed that greatly influence the welfare of many individuals. Plans have to be fulfilled if the purposes of the organization are to be accomplished. Action is required to ensure production and render services. The person who accepts an administrative job is morally bound to assume the responsibility that is part and parcel of that position. A good administrator will experience a feeling of dissatisfaction whenever he fails to meet responsibilities.

Understanding of work

The administrator will benefit from having a thorough understanding of the specialized work in which the organization is engaged. If it concerns a particular industry, it will be an advantage to know the production process from the ground up. If it is government, knowledge of related legislative, executive, and judicial aspects will help. If it is education, familiarity with that particular field will be an asset. If it is a specialized field within education or other area, it is necessary to have a knowledge of the particular specialty and also the part it plays in the total educational process. It is difficult to guide purposefully unless the individual knows his particular educational specialty and how it relates to other subject-matter areas. One often reads about the Congressman who was once a page in the Senate, the railroad executive who was a yard worker, the bank president who started as a bookkeeper, and the superintendent of schools who many years before started as a teacher. The technical knowledge and understanding of the total functioning of an organization are best gained through firsthand experience. An administrator will find that detailed knowledge of an organization's work is of great help in successfully guiding its operations.

Command of administrative technique

Administrative technique in many ways is similar to the first qualification listed —administrative mind. There is one essential difference. Administrative mind refers more to the "know how" and temperament of the individual, whereas *administrative technique* refers to the application of this knowledge and ability. An individual who possesses this quality can plan and budget his or her time and effort and also the time and work of others, in the most effective way possible. Time is not spent on details when more important work should be done. Tasks are performed in a relaxed, efficient, calm, and logical manner. Work is accomplished in conformance with established standards. Duties are effectively executed, including those that involve strong pressure and great amounts of time. Resources for performing the job are utilized.

It has been said there are three conditions that burn out an administrator in a short length of time: performing his own duties in a tense, highly emotional manner, performing too many details, and being part of an organization that is not considerate of its administrators.

Intellectual capacity

Intellectual capacity in itself will not guarantee a good administrator. In fact, the so-called intellectual often makes a very poor administrator. Such traits as absent-mindedness and tardiness are often not compatible with acceptance of responsibility. The intellectual sometimes cannot make decisions because he visualizes so many sides of an issue. Furthermore, such an individual is often not interested in people but in books, figures, or other data instead. This makes a poor leader since lack of interest in human beings results in poor followership.

However, one should not gain from this discussion that intellectual capacity should be disregarded. To be a good administrator one must be intellectually competent. One should be able to think and reason logically, to apply knowledge effectively, to communicate efficiently, and to possess other factors that are closely allied to the intellectual process. There have been many so-called "brains" who failed miserably as administrators, whereas most good administrators can be classified as at least average in respect to their intellectual capacities.

Space has not permitted a discussion of all the qualifications of the administrator. Others, such as courage and initiative, are also important. There is in addition the ability to be an ambassador for the organization. Liaison work with higher echelon groups in the organization and also with outside groups is important. It is necessary at times to stand up and fight for one's own department or division. To a great degree this will determine whether it is respected and has equal status with other administrative divisions.

THE ADMINISTRATOR AS A LEADER

In the last 25 years research findings have indicated that some beliefs, such as certain qualities per se indicate who the leaders are, that leaders are born and not made, and that some of us will lead and others will follow, are not exactly true. Instead, in recent years research seems to indicate that personal characteristics must be related to the characteristics of the followers, because of the interaction of the two that takes place. The identification of qualities of certain individuals as leaders without relating these qualities to the persons they are going to try to lead has little meaning.

Stogdill* studied the relationship of personality factors to leadership and found that the leader of a group exceeds the average of the group in respect to such characteristics as intelligence, scholarship, acceptance of responsibility, participation, and socioeconomic status.

Berelson and Steiner† surveyed the scientific findings in the behaviorial sciences and formulated some propositions and hypotheses relating to leadership. In essence some of these are as follows:

1. The closer an individual conforms to the accepted norms of the group, the better liked he will be; the better liked he is, the closer he conforms; the less he conforms, the more disliked he will be.
2. The higher the rank of the member within the group, the more central he will be in the group's interaction and the more influential he will be.
3. In general, the "style" of the leader is determined more by the expectations of the membership and the requirements of the situation than by the personal traits of the leader himself.
4. The leadership of the group tends to be vested in the member who most closely conforms to the standards of the group of the matter in question or who has the most information and skill related to the activities of the group.
5. When groups have established norms, it is extremely difficult for a new leader, however capable, to shift the group's activities.

*Stogdill, R. M.: Personal factors associated with leadership, a survey of the literature, Journal of Psychology **25**:63, 1948.
†Berelson, B., and Steiner, G. A.: Human behavior: an inventory of scientific findings, New York, 1964, Harcourt, Brace & World, Inc., pp. 341-344.

6. The longer the life of the leadership, the less open and free the communication within the group and probably the less efficient the group in the solution of new problems.

7. The leader will be followed more faithfully the more he makes it possible for the members to achieve their private goals along with the group goals.

8. Active leadership is characteristic of groups that determine their own activities, passive leadership of groups whose activities are externally imposed.

9. In a small group, authoritarian leadership is less effective than democratic leadership in holding the group together and getting its work done.

Other studies that provide pertinent information on leadership include those of Myers,* Hemphill,† Homans,‡ and Halpin.§

The physical educator or health educator who desires to exercise a leadership role in his or her organization should study the administrative theory reflected in the research studies available on this subject. This will help to better assure success as a leader in any particular situation.

MAJOR ADMINISTRATIVE DUTIES

Gulick and Urwick‖ have utilized the word POSDCORB to outline the functions of an administrator. This is based on Henri Fayol's work, *Industrial and General Ad-*

---

*Myers, R. B.: The development and implications of a conception for leadership education, Unpublished doctoral dissertation, University of Florida, 1954.

†Hemphill, J. K.: Administration as problem solving. In Halpin, A. W., editor: Administrative theory in education, Chicago, 1958, Midwest Administration Center, University of Chicago.

‡Homans, G. C.: The human group, New York, 1950, Harcourt, Brace and World, Inc.

§Halpin, A. W.: A paradigm for the study of administrative research in education. In Campbell, N. R., and Gregg, R. T., editors: Administrative behavior in education, New York, 1957, Harper & Row, Publishers.

‖Gulick, L., and Urwick, L., editors: Papers on the science of administration, New York, 1937, Institute of Public Administration.

ministration. An organization of duties under these major headings is apropos to the section under discussion although the semantics of the subject in some cases is not appropriate to modern administration. POSDCORB refers to the functional elements of (1) planning, (2) organizing, (3) staffing, (4) directing, (5) coordinating, (6) reporting, and (7) budgeting.

Planning

Planning is the process of outlining the work that is to be performed, in a logical and purposeful manner, together with the methods that are to be utilized in the performance of this work. The total plan will result in the accomplishment of the purposes for which the organization is established. Of course this implies a clear conception of the aims of the organization.

In order to accomplish this planning, the administrator must have vision to look into the future and to prepare for what he sees. He must see the influences that will affect the organization and the requirements that will have to be met.

Organizing

Organizing refers to the development of the formal structure of the organization, whereby the various administrative coordinating centers and subdivisions of work are arranged in an integrated manner, with clearly defined lines of authority. The purpose behind this structure is the effective accomplishment of established objectives. Organizational charts aid in clarifying such organization.

This formal structure should be set up in a manner that avoids red tape and provides for the clear assignment of every necessary duty to some responsible individual. Whenever possible, standards should be established for acceptable performance for each duty assignment.

The coordinating centers of authority are developed and organized chiefly on the basis of the work to be done by the organization, services performed, individuals available in the light of incentives offered, and efficiency of operation. A single administrator cannot perform all the functions necessary, except in the smallest organizations. Hence, responsibility must be assigned to others in a logical manner. These individuals occupy positions along the line, each position being broken down in terms of its own area of specialization. The higher up the line one goes, the more general is the responsibility; the lower down the line one goes, the more specific is the responsibility.

Staffing

The administrative duty of staffing refers to the entire personnel function of selection, assignment, training, and providing and maintaining favorable working conditions for all members of the organization. The administrator must have a thorough knowledge of the staff. He or she must select with care and ensure that each subdivision in the organization has a competent leader and that each employee is assigned to the job where he can be of greatest service. Personnel should possess energy, initiative, and loyalty. The duties of each position must be clearly outlined. All members of the organization must be encouraged to utilize their own initiative. They should be rewarded fairly for their services. The mistakes and blunders of employees must be brought to their attention and dealt with accordingly. Vested interests of individual employees must not be allowed to endanger the general interests of all. The conditions of work should be made as pleasant and as nearly ideal as possible. Both physical and social factors should be provided for. Services rendered by the individual increase as the conditions under which he works improve.

Directing

Directing is a responsibility that falls to the administrator as the leader. He or she must direct the operations of the organization. This means distinct and precise decisions must be made and embodied in instructions that will ensure their completion. The administrator must direct the work in an impersonal manner, avoid becoming involved in too many details, and see that the organization's purpose is fulfilled according to established principles. Executives have a duty to see that the quantity and quality of performance of each employee are maintained.

The administrator is a leader. His or her success is determined by his ability to guide others successfully toward established goals. Individuals of weak responsibility and limited capability cannot perform this function successfully. The good administrator must be superior in determination, persistence, endurance, and courage. He must clearly understand his organization's purposes and keep them in mind as he guides and leads the way. Through direction, it is essential that faith be created in the cooperative enterprise, in success, in achievement of personal ambitions, in the integrity of the leadership provided, and in the superiority of associated efforts.

Coordinating

Coordinating means interrelating all the various phases of work within an organization. This means that the organization's structure must clearly provide for close relationships and competent leadership in the coordinating centers of activity. The administrator must meet regularly with chief assistants. Here arrangements can be made for unity of effort, reports can be submitted on progress, and obstacles to coordinated work can be eliminated. Good coordination also means that all factors must be considered in their proper perspective.

This duty requires the development of a faith that runs throughout the organization. Coordination can be effective only if there is faith in the enterprise and in the need for coordinated effort. Faith is the motivating factor that stimulates human beings to continue rendering service so that goals may be accomplished.

There should also be coordination with administrative units outside the organization where such responsibilities are necessary.

Reporting

Reporting is the administrative duty of supplying information to administrators or executives higher up on the line of authority or to other groups to which one is responsible. It also means that subordinates must be kept informed through regular reports, research, and continual observation. In this respect the administrator is a point of intercommunication. In addition to accepting the responsibility for reporting to higher authority, he must continually know what is going on in the area under his jurisdiction. Members of the organization must be informed on many topics of general interest, such as goals to be achieved, progress being made, strong and weak points, and new areas proposed for development. This information will come from various members of the organization.

Budgeting

As the word implies, budgeting refers to financial planning and accounting. It is the duty of the administrator to allocate to various subdivisions the general funds allotted to the organization. This must be done in a manner that is equitable and just. In carrying out this function, he must keep the organization's purposes in mind and apportion the available money to those areas or projects that will help most in achieving these purposes. It also means that controls must be established to ensure that certain limits will be observed, so-called budget padding will be kept to a minimum, and complete integrity in the handling of all the budgetary aspects of the organization will be maintained.

QUALIFICATIONS OF HEALTH AND PHYSICAL EDUCATORS

The most important consideration in administration is personnel. The members of an organization determine whether it will succeed or fail. Administration must take into account the qualifications of health and physical educators, factors that promote cooperation, principles of good human relations, the fallacy of final authority, the importance of decisiveness, the need for good staff morale, and other principles to be observed in personnel management.

Qualifications for health educators

The qualifications of health educators based on the recommendations from five national conferences on professional preparation as presented in adapted form are as follows*:

Health education

Knowledge of (1) what constitutes well-balanced and well-functioned health teaching and (2) implications of different age and developmental levels of human beings for teaching health and also for curricular organization of materials.

Skill in (1) detecting health interests and needs and motivating students to achieve and maintain an optimum level of personal health and (2) selecting and using acceptable methods, materials, and resources for health education as well as skill in health counseling.

School health services

Knowledge of the roles played by various professional health personnel in the referral and follow-up duties of teachers and the opportunities afforded in school health services for health education.

Skill in establishing school health policies for various health services, such as emergency care, observing children for deviations from good health, using screening techniques and health records, encouraging health corrections, and cooperating with home and community in child health problems.

---

*Preparing the health teacher, recommendations from five national conferences on professional preparation, Washington, D. C., 1961, American Association for Health, Physical Education, and Recreation, p. 26.

Healthful school living

Awareness of opportunities that exist in the school environment for the teaching of health, the relationship of facilities and other aspects of the physical environment to health, and the relationship of discipline, promotion, and other such practices to psychologic health.

Skill in the improvement of environmental conditions, the development of potentialities of the school lunch program as a medium of education, and the application of sound mental health principles to the school setting.

The personality of the health educator is of particular concern. The individual must be well adjusted and well integrated emotionally, mentally, and physically if he or she is to do a good job in developing these characteristics in others. Such a person must also be interested in human beings and possess skill and understanding in human relations so that health objectives may be realized.

It is very important that the health educator have a mastery of certain scientific knowledge and specialized skills and have proper attitudes. Such knowledge, skills, and attitudes will help the health educator identify the health needs and interests of individuals with whom he comes in contact, provide a health program that will meet these needs and interests, and promote the profession so that human lives may be enriched. This means that many experiences should be included in the training of persons entering this specialized field. These experiences can be divided into general education, professional education, and specialized education.

General education experiences should provide knowledge and skill in the communicative arts, understanding in sociologic principles, an appreciation of the history of various peoples with their social, racial, and cultural characteristics, and the fine and practical arts that afford a means of expression, a means of releasing the emotions, a medium for richer understanding of life, and a medium for promoting mental health. The behavioral sciences are espe-cially important for the health educator. The science area is also very important to the health educator and should include anatomy and kinesiology, physiology, bacteriology, biology, zoology, chemistry, physics, and also such behavioral sciences as child and adolescent psychology, human growth and development, general psychology, mental hygiene, and sociology.

In professional education it is important for the health educator to have a mastery of the philosophies, techniques, principles, and evaluative procedures that are characteristic of the most advanced and best thinking in education.

The specialized health education area should include personal and community health, nutrition, family and child health, first aid and safety, sex education, drugs and narcotics, tobacco and alcohol, methods and materials, organization and administration of school health programs, public health, including the basic principles of environmental sanitation and ecology, communicable disease control, and health counseling. The qualifications for teachers of health to be certified in New Jersey are listed on p. 102.

Qualifications for physical educators

The following are some special qualifications of the physical educator.

The physical educator should be a graduate of an approved teacher training institution that prepares teachers for physical education. The college or university should be selected with care.

Since physical education is based upon the foundational sciences of anatomy, physiology, biology, kinesiology, sociology, and psychology, the leader in this field should be well versed in these areas.

The general education of physical educators is under continuous scrutiny and criticism. Speech, knowledge of world affairs, mastery of the arts, and other aspects of this area are important in the preparation of the physical educator. Since his

HEALTH EDUCATION

AUTHORIZATION. This certificate is required for teaching health education in the elementary and secondary schools.

REQUIREMENTS

I. A bachelor's degree based upon a four-year curriculum in an accredited college

II. Successful completion of *one* of the following:

    A. A college curriculum approved by the New Jersey State Department of Education as the basis for issuing this certificate

OR

    B. A program of college studies including:

general background

1. A total of thirty semester-hour credits in *general background* courses distributed in at least three of the following fields: English, social studies, science, fine arts, mathematics, and foreign languages. Six semester-hour credits in English and six in social studies will be required.

2. A minimum of eighteen semester-hour credits in *professional education* courses distributed over four or more of the following groups including at least one course in each starred area. A maximum of three semester-hour credits will be accepted in health education. These eighteen credits do not include student teaching.

    ° Methods of teaching health education

professional education

    ° Educational psychology. This group includes such courses as psychology of learning, human growth and development, adolescent psychology, educational measurements, and mental hygiene.

    ° Health education. A maximum of three semester-hour credits will be accepted in this area. This group includes such courses as personal health problems, school health problems, nutrition, health administration, and biology.

    Curriculum. This group includes such courses as principles of curriculum construction, the high school curriculum, a study of the curriculum in the specific field, and extracurricular activities.

    Foundations of education. This group includes such courses as history of education, principles of education, philosophy of education, comparative education, and educational sociology.

    Guidance. This group includes such courses as principles of guidance, counseling, vocational guidance, educational guidance, research in guidance, and student personnel problems.

3. A minimum of forty semester-hour credits in the *field of specialization* distributed among the following four areas, and covering both the elementary and secondary fields, with major emphasis on health education.

    Bacteriology, biology, and chemistry

    Psychology and sociology, including mental hygiene, adolescent psychology, sociology, and educational sociology

specialized field

    Health education, including anatomy, physiology, child growth and development, personal and community health, foods and nutrition, health aspects of home and family life, health counseling, safety and first aid, and organization, administration, and supervision of school health programs

    Methods of teaching, including a study of the public school health education curriculum

student teaching

4. One hundred and fifty clock hours of *approved student teaching*. At least ninety clock hours must be devoted to responsible classroom teaching; sixty clock hours may be employed in observation and participation. This requirement is in addition to the eighteen credits in professional education.

PHYSICAL EDUCATION

AUTHORIZATION. This certificate is required for teaching physical education in elementary and secondary schools. (Health education shall be included in this authorization if the curriculum contains at least eighteen semester-hour credits in this field.)

REQUIREMENTS

I. A bachelor's degree based upon a four-year curriculum in an accredited college

II. Successful completion of *one* of the following:

    A. A college curriculum approved by the New Jersey State Department of Education as the basis for issuing this certificate

OR

    B. A program of college studies including:

general background

      1. A minimum of thirty semester-hour credits in *general background* courses distributed in at least three of the following fields: English, social studies, science, fine arts, mathematics, and foreign languages. Six semester-hour credits in English and six in social studies are required.

professional education

      2. A minimum of eighteeen semester-hour credits in *professional education* courses distributed over four or more of the following groups, including at least one course in each starred area. A maximum of three semester-hour credits will be accepted in health education. These eighteen credits do not include student teaching.

        * Methods of teaching physical education in elementary and secondary schools

        * Educational psychology. This group includes such courses as psychology of learning, human growth and development, adolescent psychology, educational measurements, and mental hygiene.

        * Health education. A maximum of three semester-hour credits will be accepted in this area. This group includes such courses as personal health problems, school health problems, nutrition, health administration, and biology.

        Curriculum. This group includes such courses as principles of curriculum construction, the high school curriculum, a study of the curriculum in the field of specialization, and extracurricular activities.

        Foundations of education. This group includes such courses as history of education, principles of education, philosophy of education, comparative education, and educational sociology.

        Guidance. This group includes such courses as principles of guidance, counseling, vocational guidance, educational guidance, research in guidance, and student personnel problems.

student teaching

      3. One hundred and fifty clock hours of *approved student teaching*. At least ninety clock hours must be devoted to responsible classroom teaching; sixty clock hours may be employed in observation and participation. This requirement is in addition to the eighteen credits in professional education.

      4. A minimum of forty semester-hour credits in the *field of specialization,* distributed among the following areas and covering both the elementary and secondary fields:

        Anatomy, physiology, kinesiology

        Coaching, development of personal skills, nature and function of play

        History, principles, and organization and administration of physical education

specialized field

        Materials and methods in physical education for the elementary grades and materials and methods in physical education for the high school

        Health education including personal and community hygiene, first aid, and safety

position requires frequent appearances in public, adequate knowledge and skill in the art of communication are essential.

Physical education work is strenuous and therefore demands that members of the profession be in a state of buoyant, robust health in order that they may carry out their duties with efficiency and regularity. It should also be remembered that physical educators are supposed to build healthy bodies. Therefore, they should be a good testimonial for their preachments.

Many moral and spiritual values are developed through participation in games and other physical education activities. It is essential, therefore, that the teacher of physical education have a proper background and possess such qualities that he or she will stress fair play, good sportsmanship, and a sound standard of values. The nature of his or her leadership should be such that the highest standards of moral and spiritual values are developed.

The physical educator should have a sincere interest in the teaching of physical education. Unless the individual has a firm belief in the value of his work and a desire to help extend the benefits of such an endeavor to others, he will not be an asset to the profession. A sincere interest in the teaching of physical education means that one enjoys teaching individuals, participating in the gamut of activities incorporated in such programs, helping others to realize the happiness and thrilling experiences of participation that he himself enjoys, and helping to develop citizenship traits conducive to democratic living. One must have a sincere love of the out-of-doors and of all the activities that make up the physical education program either indoors or out in the open. This means that anyone interested in physical education should enjoy sports and other activities. If there is not a liking for these activities, the individual is in the wrong profession.

The physical educator should possess an acceptable standard of motor ability. Physical skills are basic to the profession. To be able to teach various games and activities to others, it is necessary to have skill in many of them. The physical educator must enjoy working with people, with whom there is continuous association in an informal atmosphere when teaching physical education activities. The values of such a program will be greatly increased if the physical educator teaches in a manner conducive to happiness, cooperation, and a spirit of friendship. The qualifica-

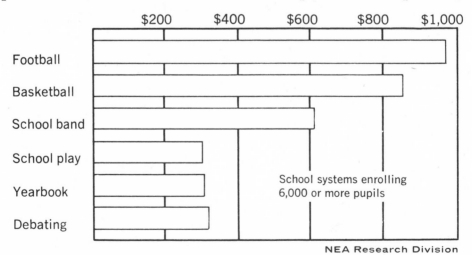

NEA Research Division

Average maximum annual salary supplements 1967-1968 for the physical educator qualified to coach selected pupil-participating activities. (From NEA Research Bulletin **46:**79, 1968.)

Freshman majors in health and physical education at Illinois State University working in flag football under the direction of experienced faculty members.

Leadership is an essential for the professions of health and physical education. An Illinois State University senior gives a demonstration lesson on badminton to a group of high school girls. Observing in the background is the supervising staff member.

HOW DO YOU MEASURE UP AS A MEMBER OF THE UNITED TEACHING PROFESSION?*

As a first step in determining your professional stature, place a check mark beside the questions you can answer *yes*.

As an individual, do you—

_____Join the united teaching profession — local, state, and national associations — and promote unified professional membership among your colleagues?

_____View your dues as an investment in your profession rather than just another expense?

_____Believe that being a member of the united teaching profession involves more than paying dues — that it includes participating actively, familiarizing yourself with the objectives of your associations, sharing in goal setting, and being a change agent?

_____Identify with your positional organizations (classroom teachers, principals, supervisors, or administrators)?

_____Identify with the associations representing your subject matter area?

_____Keep informed on educational issues through professional journals?

_____Abide by the Code of Ethics of the Education Profession?

_____Participate in political action by discussing issues, campaigning for candidates, and running for offices if you are so inclined?

_____Inform yourself about the economic benefits which may be offered by your local and state organizations?

___Credit union___Life insurance___Health and accident insurance___Personal liability insurance___Income protection insurance___Tax-deferred annuity program___Installment financing___Home mortgage loans___Discount buying

As a member of your local association, do you—

_____Attend meetings?

_____Volunteer for assignments?

_____Accept committee appointments?

_____Participate in in-service education programs?

_____Lend your efforts in negotiations with the school board by contributing your ideas, serving on the negotiating team, or working on supportive committees?

_____Have a thorough knowledge of grievance procedures so that you can help in referring aggrieved colleagues to the proper persons?

_____Defend teacher rights?

_____Do your part to see to it that classroom teachers, as the largest segment of your association, have an impact commensurate with their number?

_____Work for minority-group involvement in your association program?

_____Reach out to the new teacher, acquaint him with your association's services, encourage him to participate in its activities, and accept him as a member of the team?

_____Support candidates for professional offices who have a record of service to the association; who are committed to the association's goals rather than to their own personal advancement; who speak for the membership?

_____Encourage your association to work with Student NEA chapters in nearby colleges?

_____Promote the Future Teachers of America by supporting FTA chapters and by serving as a sponsor?

_____Make sure your association is represented at meetings of your state education association as well as at those of the state classroom teachers association?

_____Make sure that your association uses its full quota of delegates to the Representative Assemblies of the NEA and of its Association of Classroom Teachers?

_____Serve as a delegate to state and national conventions if named?

*From Heflin, J.: How do you measure up? Today's Education, NEA Journal **5**:64, 1969.

HOW DO YOU MEASURE UP AS A MEMBER OF THE UNITED TEACHING PROFESSION?—cont'd

As a member of the state association, do you—

_____Participate in state and regional meetings?

_____Accept committee assignments?

_____Prepare yourself for office?

_____Read your state association journal and newsletter?

_____Keep abreast of progress in your state association's legislative program?

_____Vote for candidates for public offices who are favorable to the state legislative program?

_____Join your state positional association?

_____Familiarize yourself with its program and services?

As a member of the National Education Association, do you—

_____Make your influence felt in the NEA Representative Assembly by studying NEA resolutions and reports and discussing them with delegates?

_____Attend regional and national conferences?

_____Identify with the Association of Classroom Teachers or your positional association and take advantage of its services?

_____Read TODAY'S EDUCATION and the *NEA Reporter?*

_____Support the NEA DuShane Emergency Fund?

_____Inform yourself and your colleagues about NEA services?

___Life insurance___Accident insurance___Tax-deferred annuity program___NEA Mutual Fund___Auto leasing___Research___Publications and other materials___Field service___Salary and negotiation consultant services___Instructional activities___Legislative work ___Travel program___Job referral service___Public relations___Promotion of high standards of teacher preparation, certification, and performance___Protection of professional, civil, and human rights

Next, write the names of the following in the blanks provided:

Your local association president_____

Your state education association president_____

The president of your state association of classroom teachers or of your positional association_____

Your NEA state director(s)_____

The NEA president_____

The president of NEA's Association of Classroom Teachers or of your positional association
_____

The NEA executive secretary_____

The NEA headquarters city_____

See how you measure up as a member of the united teaching profession.

tions for teachers of physical education to be certified in New Jersey are listed on p. 103.

QUALITIES THAT MAKE FOR SUCCESSFUL TEACHING

Several persons were interviewed as to the qualities and characteristics they thought existed in the best teachers to whom they were exposed. A list of those qualities that were mentioned most frequently are as follows:

1. Teacher knew his subject matter well.
2. Teacher took a personal interest in each student.
3. Teacher was well respected and respected his students.
4. Teacher stimulated his students to think.
5. Teacher was interesting and made his subject matter come to life.

6. Teacher was an original thinker and creative in his methods.
7. Teacher was a fine speaker, presented a neat experience, and was generally well groomed.
8. Teacher had a good sense of humor.
9. Teacher was fair and honest in his dealings with his students.
10. Teacher was understanding and kind.

PROBLEMS OF BEGINNING TEACHERS

Beginning teachers need considerable encouragement and help. The administration should be aware of this need and work to ensure that it is met. As a guide to some of the problems of beginning teachers, a survey of fifty teachers indicated the following:

1. Difficulties arising as a result of the lack of facilities
2. Large size of classes, making it difficult to teach effectively
3. Teaching assignments in addition to the primary responsibility of teaching health education or physical education
4. Discipline problems with students
5. Conflicting methodology between what the beginning teacher was taught in professional preparing institution and established patterns of experienced teachers
6. Clerical work—difficulty in keeping records up to date
7. Problems encountered in obtaining books and supplies
8. Problems encountered in obtaining cooperative attitude from other teachers
9. Lack of departmental meetings to discuss common problems
10. Failure to find time for personal recreation

WORKING EFFECTIVELY WITH GENERAL SCHOOL AND COLLEGE ADMINISTRATORS

School and college health and physical education programs are part of general education. Consequently, such items as the budgets allocated, facilities provided, and personnel appointed are subject to the thinking and decisions of general educators. Presidents of colleges, deans, superintendents of schools, principals, and administrators of instructional and business services, through their decisions and actions, affect these special programs in elementary and secondary schools and in colleges and universities of the nation. It is therefore important to get the thinking of these general administrators in respect to programs of school health, physical education, and recreation. The information that follows was taken from a review of general administration books and interviews with general administrators for the purpose of determining what constitutes effective working relationships between general school administrators and health and physical educators.

What constitutes effective working relations between general school administrators and health and physical educators?

Effective working relationships between general administrators and health and physical educators may be discussed under the headings of (1) responsibilities of gen-

Table 5-2. Major problems of teachers*

	Urban	Suburban	Rural
Large class size	40.4%	33.4%	30.6%
Classroom management and discipline	23.3	10.8	12.1
Inadequate assistance from specialized teachers	22.5	21.0	30.3
Inadequate salary	34.9	24.5	30.3
Inadequate fringe benefits	27.7	22.3	31.3
Ineffective grouping of students into classes	24.3	18.2	24.2
Lack of public support for schools	27.8	17.4	23.7
Ineffective testing and guidance program	21.1	14.2	20.8

*From NEA Research Bulletin 46:116, 1968.

eral administrators, (2) responsibilities of health and physical educators, (3) common points of conflict, and (4) checklist for effective working relationships.

Some responsibilities of general administrators. There are many responsibilities of general administrators that have an impact upon good working relationships. A few of the more important are listed in the following paragraphs:

1. *Administrators should possess a sound understanding of human nature so as to work effectively with people.* General administrators should not look upon the administrative process in an impersonal manner but, instead, should always keep in mind the human dimensions. As such, human problems should be given high priority.

2. *Administrators should understand their own administrative behavior.* They should see conflicts where they exist and not fabricate them where they do not exist. They should give an accurate account of group expectations although they may not be in agreement with them. They should recognize the differences and rationale between their own views and those of other people.

3. *Administrators should exercise wisely the authority vested in the administrative position.* The authority goes with the office and not with the person. Administrators should recognize that the administrative position exists to further the goals of the school system and the education of children and youth. It should never be used as a personal vendetta.

4. *Administrators should establish effective means of communication among members of the school system.* Opportunities should be readily available for a discussion of personal and/or professional problems, new ideas, and ways of improving the effective functioning of the organization.

5. *Administrators should provide maximum opportunity for personal self-fulfill-*

ment. Each person has a basic psychologic need of being recognized, having self-respect, and possessing a feeling of belonging. Within organization requirements, general administrators should make this possible for each teacher on the job and every member of the school organization, regardless of subject area or job role.

6. *Administrators should provide leadership.* General administrators speak for their schools. They are the acknowledged leaders both in the internal and external functioning of the educational program. Such responsibility implies leadership qualities that will bring out the best individual effort on the part of each member of the staff and a total coordinated endeavor working toward common goals.

7. *Administrators should provide clearcut policies and procedures.* Policies and procedures are essential to efficient functioning of the school organization; therefore, they should be carefully developed, thoroughly discussed with members who are concerned, put in written form in clear concise language, and then followed.

8. *Administrators should plan meaningful faculty meetings.* Meetings of the staff should be carefully planned and efficiently conducted. Meetings should not, as a regular rule, be called on impulse and dominated by the general administrator. Plans and procedures agreed upon should be carried out.

9. *Administrators should make promotions on the basis of merit with an absence of politics and favoritism.* Promotions should be arrived at through a careful evaluation of each faculty member's qualifications and objective criteria.

10. *Administrators should protect and enhance the mental and physical health of the faculty and staff.* In carrying out this responsibility the general administrator should eliminate petty annoyances and worries that can weigh heavily upon staff members, attempt to increase the satisfactions that each person derives from the or-

ganization, promote friendly relationships, develop an esprit de corps, improve respect for and social status of staff members in the community, and establish a climate of understanding that promotes goodwill.

Some responsibilities of health and physical educators. All the responsibilities of health educators and physical educators cannot be discussed in the limited space available for this subject. A few of the more important responsibilities that affect good working relationships with general administrators are listed:

1. *Health and physical educators should lend thought and energy to supporting the total educational program.* Each staff member must see his or her responsibility to the total educational program. This means serving on committees, attending faculty meetings, contributing ideas, and giving support to worthy new developments regardless of the phase of the total program to which it belongs. Also, the staff member should view his or her own field of specialization in proper perspective with the total educational endeavor.

2. *Health and physical educators should take an interest in the administrative process.* Such interest can be tangibly shown by participating in policy making and decision making, doing some role playing as to the problems and pressures faced by the general administrator in his job, and contributing ideas that will help cut down on administrative red tape and thus streamline the educational process.

3. *Health and physical educators should carry out their individual responsibilities with dispatch and efficiency.* Each teacher or staff member has a job to do. If each job is performed effectively, the total school organization will function more efficiently. Only as each person assumes the responsibility for doing his or her own job in a responsible manner can the educational effort be accomplished effectively.

4. *Health and physical educators should get their reports in on time.* Purchase req-

uisitions, attendance, excuse, accident, and the multitude of other forms and reports that have to be completed and then collated in the general administrator's office must be done on time. Punctuality on the part of all staff members makes the general administrator's life much easier.

5. *Health and physical educators should be loyal to the administration.* Each staff member has the responsibility to be loyal to the administrators of his school organization. There can be differences of opinion and disagreement on the administrative process and the way it is conducted, but loyalty to the leaders is essential.

6. *Health and physical educators should observe proper administrative protocol.* Administrators do not appreciate a teacher going over their heads to a higher authority without their knowing about it. There are lines of authority that must be recognized and followed in every organization. Schools are no exception to the rule.

7. *Health and physical educators should be professional.* In relationships with colleagues, general administrators, or the public in general, a staff member should recognize that there is a professional way of behaving. Confidences are not betrayed, professional problems are ironed out with the people concerned, and personality conflicts are discussed with discretion.

Common points of conflict between general administrators and health and physical educators. Although there are many implications for conflict in the listing of responsibilities for general administrators and for health and physical educators, some additional areas where poor working relationships occur are listed as follows:

1. The failure on the part of general administrators to recognize health and physical educators as vital subjects of the academic and educational process
2. A failure on the part of general administrators to see health education and physical education as two distinct and separate fields
3. The existence of an authoritarian and un-

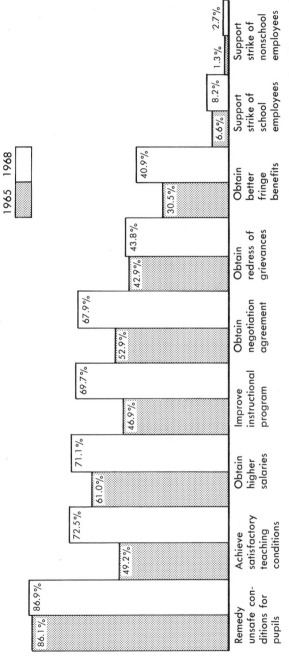

Purposes of teacher strikes: percents of teachers believing strike is justified, 1965 and 1968. Percents are based on total who approve of striking, *not* on total sample. (From NEA Research Division, Today's Education **57**:85, 1968.)

democratic administration with the general administrator ruling with an iron hand

4. The failure to outline clearly goals and responsibilities for the organization and for each member of the organization
5. The existence of some teachers' unions and organizations that obstruct rather than further the democratization of administration
6. The failure of general administrators to provide dynamic leadership
7. The failure of the administrator to provide clearly defined policies
8. The practice of administrators encroaching upon classes and schedules without good reason or adequate previous announcement
9. The assignment of unreasonable teaching loads and extra class assignments
10. The failure of teachers to read bulletins that contain important administrative announcements
11. The failure of teachers to conscientiously assume the duties and responsibilities associated with administrative routine, such as the checking of attendance
12. The failure of teachers to handle disciplinary cases properly
13. The existence of unsatisfactory plant, buildings, and working conditions
14. The lack of adequate teacher materials and equipment
15. Overemphasis upon athletics

What administrative groups worry about

The professional magazine, *Nation's Schools*,* conducted an opinion poll to determine what schoolmen worry most

*Schoolmen worry most about teacher, money shortages, Nation's Schools 81:81, 1968.

about. A 4% sampling was done of 16,000 school administrators in 50 states that brought a 54% response. An 8% sampling was done of 8,000 school board members, which brought a 22% response. Presented here in adapted form are some of the main worries of school officials.

Superintendents of schools
Shortages of teachers
Inadequate funds
Militant teachers
Overcrowded conditions
Relations with school board
Transportation problems
Student problems of dress
Desegregation
New curricula
Community pressures
Use of drugs

School board members
Inadequate funds
Shortages of teachers
Militant teachers
Overcrowded conditions
Transportation problems
Relations with school administrators
Desegregation
Vandalism
Community pressures
New curricula
Student problems of dress
Use of drugs

CHECKLIST FOR EFFECTIVE WORKING RELATIONSHIPS BETWEEN GENERAL ADMINISTRATORS AND HEALTH AND PHYSICAL EDUCATORS

	Yes	No
1. Job descriptions of all school personnel are formulated, written, and disseminated to each individual involved.	___	___
2. Policies are cooperatively formulated.	___	___
3. Teachers are encouraged to participate in the determination of policies. Administration utilizes committees of faculty to develop policies.	___	___
4. Policies cover priorities in the use of physical education facilities.	___	___
5. Policies have been developed and are in writing for the major areas of the educational enterprise as well as specifically for the fields of health education and physical education.	___	___

CHECKLIST FOR EFFECTIVE WORKING RELATIONSHIPS BETWEEN GENERAL ADMINISTRATORS AND HEALTH AND PHYSICAL EDUCATORS —cont'd

	Yes	No
6. Departmental policies and procedures are up to date and complete.		
7. Board of education establishes and approves policies and programs.		
8. Health and physical educators know the policies for their school system and work within this framework.		
9. Open channels of communication are maintained between administrator and teacher.		
10. Inservice education is provided teachers.		
11. Teachers are encouraged to participate in the activities of professional organizations.		
12. Supervisors act in an advisory and not an administrative capacity.		
13. The teaching load of all teachers is equitable in that the following factors are considered: work hours per week, number of students per week, and number of after-school activities scheduled.		
14. Athletics are open to all students and conducted according to sound educational principles.		
15. Policies are in writing and disseminated and cover the organization and administration of varsity interscholastic athletics.		
16. Coaches are certified in physical education.		
17. The group process is effectively used in faculty and committee meetings.		
18. There is a strong belief in and a willingness to have a democratic administration.		
19. Faculty meetings are well organized.		
20. New staff members are oriented in respect to responsibilities, school policies, and other items essential to their effective functioning in the school system.		
21. Departmental budgets and other reports are submitted on time and in proper form.		
22. Staff members attend faculty meetings regularly.		
23. Staff members participate in curriculum studies.		
24. Classroom interruptions are kept to an absolute minimum.		
25. Proper administrative channels are followed.		
26. Relationships with colleagues are based on mutual integrity, understanding, and respect.		
27. The administration is interested in the human problems of the school organization.		
28. Maximum opportunity is provided for personal self-fulfillment consistent with organization requirements.		
29. Department heads are selected on the basis of qualifications rather than seniority.		
30. Staff members are enthusiastic about their work.		
31. All personnel are provided opportunities to contribute to the improved functioning of the school system.		
32. The school board's executive officer executes policy.		
33. Faculty and staff assignments are educationally sound.		
34. The administration works continually to improve the working conditions of school personnel.		
35. Out-of-class responsibilities are equitably distributed.		
36. The administration provides recreational and social outlets for the staff.		
37. The administration recognizes and records quality work.		
38. Health and physical educators seek to improve themselves professionally.		

Continued.

CHECKLIST FOR EFFECTIVE WORKING RELATIONSHIPS BETWEEN GENERAL ADMINISTRATORS AND HEALTH AND PHYSICAL EDUCATORS —cont'd

	Yes	No
39. Health and physical educators view with proper perspective their special fields in the total educational enterprise.	___	___
40. Health and physical educators organize and plan their programs so as to best meet the needs and interests of their students.	___	___
41. Health and physical educators continually evaluate themselves and the professional job they are doing in the school system.	___	___
42. Budgetary allocations are equitably made among departments.	___	___
43. The administration is sensitive to the specific abilities and interests of teachers and staff.	___	___
44. Health and physical educators take an active role in school planning.	___	___
45. Health and physical education objectives are consistent with general education objectives.	___	___
46. The administration recognizes and gives respect and prestige to each area of specialization in the school system.	___	___
47. Health and physical educators are consulted when new facilities are planned in their areas of specialization.	___	___
48. Funds are available for professional libraries, professional travel, and other essentials for a good inservice program.	___	___
49. Health and physical educators carefully consider constructive criticism when given by the administration.	___	___
50. The administration is skilled in the organization and administration of a school system.	___	___

Questions and exercises

1. Draw up a list of competencies that you consider essential for all teachers.
2. Draw up a list of competencies that in your opinion are essential for teachers of health and/or physical education.
3. Define the term *administration* in your own words and give illustrations to point out the various facets of your definition.
4. Discuss the qualifications of a good administrator, giving concrete examples to support the importance of each qualification listed.
5. Prepare an organization chart for some department, school, or agency with which you are associated. Discuss significant aspects of the administrative setup of this organization.
6. Prepare a rating sheet that could be utilized by students to determine the extent of their qualifications for the field of administration.
7. From your own experience, prepare a list of principles that you feel are essential to good personnel relations.
8. Prepare two skits, one dramatizing some aspects of good personnel relations and the other pointing up some poor practices in regard to such relations.
9. What is meant by the term *fallacy of final authority?* Cite two illustrations to support the idea involved.
10. Interview five general administrators and summarize their feelings about health education and physical education.
11. Write an essay of approximately 500 words on the subject: "Ways in which health education and/or physical education can become more important in the eyes of general administrators."
12. Read one general administration book and summarize its comments on health education and/or physical education.
13. What do you feel are the responsibilities of health educators and/or physical educators in the total educational program?
14. If you were a general administrator, what kind of a health educator or physical educator would you hire for your school or college system? Outline the type of person you would want working for you.

Reading assignment in *Administrative Dimensions of Health and Physical Education Programs, Including Athletics:* Chapter 4, Selections 16 to 20.

Selected references

Bucher, C. A.: Foundations of physical education, ed. 5, St. Louis, 1968, The C. V. Mosby Co.

Byrd, O. E.: School health administration, Philadelphia, 1964, W. B. Saunders Co.

Douglass, H. R.: Modern administration of secondary schools, Boston, 1963, Ginn & Co.

Jenson, T. J., and Clark, D. L.: Educational administration, New York, 1964, The Center for Applied Research in Education, Inc. (The Library of Education).

Moore, H. E.: The administration of public school personnel, New York, 1966, The Center for Applied Research in Education, Inc. (The Library of Education).

NEA Report of the Project on Instruction: Schools for the sixties, New York, 1963, McGraw-Hill Book Co.

One of the major responsibilities of all educators is to develop the leadership essential to the democratic society in which we live. All phases of the educational process should be concerned with carrying out and fulfilling this function. A democratic form of government depends upon an enlightened populace capable of assuming responsibility for its own governance and self-direction.

Physical educators have the ability to develop leadership qualities in the students who participate in their programs. Many opportunities exist in curricular and extracurricular physical education programs to enable students to assume leadership responsibilities under the direction and guidance of experienced physical educators. Under qualified supervision students can develop such attributes as cooperation, self-control, and good human relations and become imbued with the desire to serve other people. In addition, students can become involved with such responsibilities as planning and evaluating the programs in which they participate. To achieve the best results, however, the climate in which they participate should be friendly and permissive, be a place where initiative and creativity are encouraged, and provide frequent opportunities to discuss problems with their classmates and teachers and to understand clearly the meaning of good leadership. Finally, certain principles must be recognized if successful student leadership is to be developed. These principles include a clear delineation of student and staff responsibilities and a leadership program where

individual development and self-direction are encouraged.

When a program of student leadership is established with such principles and conditions in mind, it will not only help each student to grow and develop but it will also be of value to the fields of physical education and health. Students frequently become more interested in these specialized fields and often decide to pursue a career in them as a result of seeing firsthand the opportunities they provide. Student leadership also renders a valuable service to the department by making it possible for more students to receive individualized instruction from their better skilled classmates; by providing better safety conditions under which activity participation can take place, since more spotters and other staff members are available; and by providing for the maximum utilization of class time as a result of a larger and more effective instructional staff. Many times student leadership also enables the teacher to spend more of his or her time in teaching rather than having to give attention to small clerical details such as attendance taking and equipment and supply management. Furthermore, it helps to enrich the program by providing expanded leadership for such extras as exhibitions, demonstrations, and intramural and interscholastic athletics.

ADVANTAGES AND DISADVANTAGES FOR THE STUDENT

I have spoken to many students who have engaged in student leadership responsibilities in their respective physical education programs. As seen through their eyes, there are many advantages and disadvantages to serving in a student leadership capacity. An analysis of their evaluations of such a responsibility indicates that many of the disadvantages, however, can be eliminated if the program is conducted in a sound educational manner.

Students who have taken on student leadership responsibilities find that they are recognized by classmates and faculty as leaders who have special skills and personal attributes that qualify them for such a role. They also mention some of the more tangible material rewards that go with such a responsibility, for example, special uniforms, lockers, award dinners, assembly programs, and other forms of recognition. Those students who are interested in physical education or health as a possible career point out that they are provided an opportunity to learn more about the field and to get experience as a leader in this area of specialization. Furthermore,

they point out that leadership qualities are developed with such experience, such as the ability to think, analyze problems, and make judgments concerning how a class should be conducted. The social experiences, such as associating with other leaders within their own school as well as student leaders in other schools, are also rewarding.

Student leaders feel that they gain a sense of duty and responsibility from their experience. They learn to abide by a code of ethics that has been established so that their responsibilities as a leader can be carried out as effectively as possible. They enjoy the responsibilities that are given to them and find that the additional duties help to develop their health and bodies.

Student leaders have also commented on the disadvantages that accrue from taking on such responsibilities. Some students indicate that they are asked to take on duties in order that the teacher may get an additional rest period. Others say they are requested to assume duties for which they are not qualified, for ex-

Student leaders. (Rich Township High School, Park Forest, Ill.)

ample, teaching certain skills in which they are not proficient. Some students have found that the leadership program is poorly organized and administered and as a result they are not motivated to develop leadership qualities. In addition, they point out that some of the jobs assigned are menial in nature and not related to the development of leadership traits. In addition to pointing out disadvantages that evolve from the teacher's actions, they also point the finger at certain students who are autocratic and undemocratic in the execution of their responsibilities, thus preventing the achievement of desirable educational goals.

An interesting observation of some student leaders is that at times they feel that only a few select students are given the opportunity to have leadership experiences and, as a result, many potential leaders are overlooked. Students feel that more persons should be provided with the opportunities to develop leadership traits through such an experience. A last observation of students is that the actual leaders who have gone through the training program are sometimes combined with the leaders-in-training in many of the experiences, social and curricular, that are provided. The students who make this observation indicate that they do not feel this procedure is the best one to follow since there is much duplication in the program provided.

QUALIFICATIONS OF THE STUDENT LEADER

The student leader obviously must have certain qualifications if he is to achieve the goals for which a leadership program is established. Since the student leader will have an impact on all the students with whom he works, it is important that such exposure yield sound educational results. Therefore, it is important to have established standards by which student leaders are selected. There are five quali-

fications that should be used as a guide in the selection of student leaders.

Personality

The personality of the student leader should be conducive to interaction with the other students and faculty in a harmonious and desirable manner. A student leader should be cheerful and friendly, possess a sense of humor, and be able to smile at himself. He should be enthusiastic about and enjoy his work, but at the same time he must command the respect of his classmates and be viewed as the leader who must guide and make decisions for the welfare of the entire class.

Intelligence and scholarship

Above-average intelligence and the application of this intelligence as demonstrated by getting passing grades in all subjects should be a requirement of the student leader. Intelligence and sound judgment are needed as a basis for making wise decisions, solving problems, and gaining the respect of one's classmates.

Interest in other people

Leadership cannot be exercised by a person unless he has a sincere interest in other people. The student leader should have an understanding of the needs of human beings and possess a desire to serve them. In addition, he should have a sympathetic attitude toward classmates with less skill who are awkward and uncoordinated in physical movement. Also, he should demonstrate qualities of good sportsmanship at all times.

Health and a love of physical activity

The student leader in physical education should exemplify the qualities that he is trying to develop in other students. Good health and sport skills and general motor ability are important considerations for the student leader in this field of specialization. In addition to providing a desirable image of the physical education leader, these qualities are prerequisites to the energy and productivity that are needed to carry out the responsibilities associated with the job of student leader.

Leadership qualities

In addition to the qualities that have been discussed as essential to a student's leadership role, other qualities are also necessary. These qualifications include the need to recognize the importance of the democratic process in teaching, the ability to efficiently organize classes and groups for activities, and other attributes such as dependability, desire, resourcefulness, initiative, industriousness, and patience.

METHODS OF SELECTING THE STUDENT LEADER

There are several methods utilized by physical educators to select student leaders. Some physical educators advocate the appointment of temporary leaders during the first few sessions of a class until the students become better known to their classmates and instructor. Some of the methods by which student leaders are selected are discussed in the following paragraphs.

Volunteers

Students are asked to volunteer to become a student leader. It may happen that the least qualified persons are the ones who volunteer. If this method is used, it should probably be used with the understanding that the student leader will serve for only a relatively short period of time. Also, there can be a rotation of student leaders with this method so that all volunteers may have such an experience.

Appointment by the teacher

The physical education instructor may appoint the student leader, utilizing his experience and judgment as a basis for his selection, based upon the qualities that are needed for such a position. One of the limitations of this procedure is that it is not democratic since it does not involve the students who are going to be exposed to the student leader. However, if the teacher has the objective of letting each student in the class have a student leadership experience, he can overcome this limitation.

Election by the class

Another method of selecting student leaders is to have the students in the physical education class vote and elect the person or persons they would like to have serve in this capacity. A limitation of this method is that the person selected is often the most popular student as a result of his participation in sports, student government, or some other school activity. Being the most popular student does not mean that he is qualified to be a leader. This is a democratic procedure, however, and if the guidelines for selection of a leader are established and if the proper climate prevails, it can be an effective method.

Selection based on test results

A battery of tests is sometimes used by physical educators as a means of selecting student leaders. Tests of physical fitness, motor ability, sports skills, and/or other instruments that indicate leadership and personality characteristics yield useful information. They provide tangible evidence that a person has some of the desirable qualifications that are needed by a student leader in a physical education class. In addition, if the physical educator desires to have the entire class participate in the student leadership program, the test results may also be of value to the teacher in helping each student to identify weaknesses that need to be overcome during the training period.

Selection by Leaders' Club

Physical educators sometimes organize Leaders' Clubs as a means of providing a continuing process for the selection of student leaders. The students who are members of the Leaders' Club, under the supervision of a faculty advisor, select new students to participate as leaders-in-training. Then, after a period of training, these students in turn become full-fledged student leaders. This method, with its advantages and disadvantages, is discussed at greater length in the paragraphs to follow.

TRAINING THE STUDENT LEADER

One method of selecting and training student leaders is through a Leaders' Club. These clubs commonly have their own constitution, governing body, faculty advisor, and training sessions.

The written constitution of a Leaders' Club usually states the purpose of the club, requirements for membership, qualifications and duties of officers, financial stipulations, procedures for giving awards and honors, and other rules governing the organization.

The governing body of the Leaders' Club may consist of a president, vice-president, treasurer, and secretary, all of whom are elected by the members of the club.

The faculty advisor is a teacher who works closely with the leaders to ensure that the objectives of the Leaders' Club are accomplished. The faculty advisor exercises close supervision over the affairs of the club and, in addition, provides inspiration and motivation to the leaders, encouraging creativity, and helping the students to achieve their goals.

The Leaders' Club usually has regular meetings on a weekly, biweekly, or monthly basis.

The Leaders' Club involvement in the selection and training of student leaders

In some schools, the students who are interested in becoming student leaders apply for membership in the Leaders' Club. Certain requirements are usually established as a means of judging whether or not a student is eligible for membership in the Club. In one school these requirements are listed as follows:

1. Grade of 80% or above in physical education
2. Scholastic average of at least 70% in major subjects
3. Passing grades in all subjects
4. Satisfactory health record
5. Membership in school's general organization
6. Recommendation of the physical education teacher as to personality, character, and quality of work
7. All-around physical performance
8. Good rating on physical fitness tests

When a student's application to membership in a Leaders' Club is accepted, a period of training for one semester usually follows. During this period students learn the requirements and responsibilities of a student leader, practice demonstrating and leading as an assistant in physical education classes, and become familiar with the rules of games, the techniques of officiating, and other responsibilities that go with the role of student leader.

After the training period has ended, the qualifications of the trainees are again reviewed by the Leaders' Club. Such items as scholastic average, health and medical record, character, recommendations of physical education teachers, performance on skill tests, scores on written tests of rules, ability to officiate, and skill proficiency are examined. The next step may be the personal interview. The big hurdle is frequently a visit before the entire governing body of the Leaders' Club. Here the candidate's record is reviewed, pertinent questions are asked, and action is taken. The faculty advisor, however, usually makes the final judgment.

Some physical educators feel that the Leaders' Club involvement in the selection and training of student leaders is quite formal and not in the best interests of the goals of the leadership program. These critics especially question the personal interview at the end of the training period and action being taken by a student's peers in determining whether or not a student should become a member of the Leaders' Club. Furthermore, some physical educators object to clubs and societies in general as being contrary to the democratic ideals that should guide any leadership program.

Methods of guiding the student leader

There are several methods that have proved effective in guiding student leaders, either during their training period or while they are actually serving as full-fledged student leaders. These methods include movies, guest lecturers, leaders' physical education period, and meetings. *Movies* can be shown on such subjects as strategies involved in sports or how to play a game or sport. *Guest lecturers,* such as visiting physical education teachers, sports personalities, and educational specialists in such areas as motor learning and teaching techniques, can be utilized advantageously. A *leaders' physical education period,* where the student leaders themselves comprise the class and the faculty advisor covers various duties that the student leader must assume, can be helpful. *Meetings* in which the faculty advisor offers advice and instruction, problems are discussed, and other matters involving the student leader are covered are also an excellent medium of guiding student leaders.

HOW THE STUDENT LEADER MAY BE UTILIZED

Student leaders may be used in the physical education program in several capacities.

Class leaders

There are many opportunities in the basic physical education instructional class period where student leaders can be utilized to advantage. These include:

1. Acting as squad leader, where the student takes charge of a small number of students for an activity
2. Being a leader for warm-up exercises at the beginning of the class period
3. Demonstrating how activities—skills, games, strategies—are to be performed
4. Taking attendance
5. Supervising the locker room
6. Providing safety measures for class participation, such as acting as a spotter, checking equipment and play areas, and providing supervision
7. Assuming measurement and evaluation responsibilities, such as helping in the testing program, measuring performance in track and field, and timing with a stop watch

Officials, captains, and other positions

Student leaders can gain valuable experience by serving as officials within the class and intramural program, being captain of an all-star or other team, coaching an intramural or club team, and acting as scorers and timekeepers.

Committee members

Many committee assignments should be filled by student leaders so that they gain valuable experience. These include being a member of a *rules committee,* where rules are established and interpreted for games and sports; serving on an *equipment and grounds committee,* where standards are established for the storage, maintenance, and use of these facilities and equipment; and participating on a *committee for planning special days or events* in the physical education program, such as play, sports, or field days.

Supply and equipment manager

Supplies and special equipment are needed in the physical education program when the various activities are being taught. This includes such equipment as basketballs, archery, golf, and hockey equipment, and audiovisual aids. The equipment must be taken from the storage areas, transferred to the place

STUDENT LEADERSHIP SURVEY OF NINE NEW YORK STATE SCHOOLS

Questions

1. Do you use any kind of student leadership in your physical education classes?

2. If yes, do you use boys or girls or both?

3. What are their duties?
   Squad leaders, demonstrators, etc.

4. Do you use student leaders during athletic events at your school?

5. Do your student leaders in any way help formulate curriculum through suggestions to the teacher?

6. Do you use your athletic captains in a leadership role during practice or game situations? How?

7. Do you find the work of student leaders beneficial to the overall implementation of the program?

8. How do you select your leaders—teacher-appointed, class-elected, squad-elected classes, athletics?

9. How long do they serve?

10. Do you feel that the system of student leadership you have now is adequate, should be enlarged or changed, or done away with? Why?

Utilization of student leaders. Survey conducted by Norman Peck. See answers on facing page.

where the activity will be conducted, and then returned to the storage area. The student leader can help immeasurably in this process and profit from such an experience.

Program planner

Various aspects of the physical education program need to be planned, and students should be involved. Student leaders, because of their special qualifications and interest, are logical choices to participate in such planning. Their knowledge and advice can be utilized to ensure that the program meets the needs and interests of the students who participate in the program. Any curriculum development program should involve such students.

Questions*	Rye	Rye Neck	Mamaroneck	New Rochelle	Valhalla	Hastings	Port Chester	Scarsdale	Bronxville
1	Yes	Yes	Yes	Yes	Yes	Yes	Yes — senior high only	Yes	No
2	Yes	Girls only	Yes	Yes	Yes	Yes	Yes	Yes	—
3	Squad leaders Demonstrators	Squad leaders Demonstrators	Squad leaders Demonstrators Spotters Instructors	Squad leaders	Squad leaders to set up equipment	Squad leaders Demonstrators	Squad leaders	Leaders in various physical education activities	—
4	Yes — varsity club members	Yes — varsity club members	Yes — "M" club members	Yes — varsity club members	Yes — varsity club members	Yes — varsity club members	No	Yes — varsity club members	Yes — leaders club (girls) and varsity club (boys)
5	No	No	Yes — through suggestion to teacher	No	No	Yes — through G.O. council	No	To very limited extent — not important part of program	No
6	Yes	No	Yes	Yes — strategy	Yes — sportsmanship and training	Yes — strategy	Yes	Yes	Yes
7	Yes	Yes — in school service functions	Yes — in all areas and functions	Yes — very much	Yes — in most cases	Yes — in all cases	Doubtful — sometimes good and sometimes poor	Yes	Yes — very much
8	Class — teacher appointed Athletics — appointed by teacher	Class — teacher appointed Athletics — elected by team	Class — high school teacher appointed Athletics — elected by team	Class — teacher appointed Athletics — elected by team	Class — teacher appointed Athletics — elected by team	Class — teacher appointed Athletics — elected by team	Class — teacher appointed Athletics — elected by team	Class varies with age groups and instructors Athletics — elected by lettermen	Leaders club Teachers selected Varsity club elected by team
9	Class — rotating basis Captain — elected for season	Class — rotating — equal chance for all Captain — elected for season	Class — usually for unit of instruction Captain — elected for season	Class — rotating basis, day — week unit Captain — elected for season	Class — one period all must serve Captain — elected for season	Class — unit Captain — elected for season	Class — rotating basis Captain — elected for season	Class varies — depends on ability and athletics — elected for season	Leaders club Varsity club for all year Captain — elected for season
10	Increasing	Expand to include boys' physical education classes	Change in curriculum will allow for more student leadership	Enlarge program and include safety techniques	Adequate	Increasing	Increasing	Adequate	Needs improvement

*See opposite page.

Record keeper and office manager

Attendance records and inventories must be taken, filing and recording done, bulletin boards kept up to date, visitors met, and other responsibilities attended to. These necessary functions provide worthwhile experiences for the student leader and benefit the program.

Special events coordinator

There are always a multitude of details to attend to when play days, sports days, demonstrations, and exhibitions are planned and conducted. Student leaders should be involved in the planning of these events and also in their actual conduct.

EVALUATION OF THE PROGRAM

An evaluation of the student leadership program should take place periodically to determine the degree to which the program is achieving its stated goals. Students should be involved in this evaluation. Such questions as the following might be asked. "Are the experiences that are provided worth while?" "Are the students developing leadership qualities?" "Is the teacher providing the necessary leadership to make the program effective?" "Are any of the assigned tasks incompatible with the objectives sought?" "If a Leaders' Club exists, is it helping to make for a better leaders' program?"

Questions and exercises

1. What are some of the qualities needed by student leaders?
2. Do a job analysis of a student leader in each of three different schools and evaluate the responsibilities assigned in terms of the development of leadership traits.
3. What are the disadvantages and advantages of being a student leader?
4. Develop a constitution for a Leaders' Club, including those requirements that you feel are most necessary for a sound educational leadership program.
5. Interview three experienced physical educators who were student leaders during their high school days and draw up a list of guidelines for a student leadership program based on their experiences and their evaluation of their own experience.

Selected references

Bell, M. M.: Are we exploiting high school girl athletes? Journal of Health, Physical Education, and Recreation 41:53, 1970.

Bookwalter, K.: Physical education in the secondary schools, New York, 1964, The Center for Applied Research in Education, Inc. (The Library of Education).

Jaeger, E., and Bockstruck, E.: Effective student leadership, Journal of Health, Physical Education, and Recreation 30:52, 1959.

Physical education for girls in high school, Curriculum Bulletin No. 6, Board of Education of the City of New York, 1965-1966.

two

ADMINISTRATION OF PHYSICAL
EDUCATION PROGRAMS

Colorado Springs Public Schools, Colorado Springs, Colo.

Washington State College, Pullman, Wash.

CHAPTER 7   THE BASIC INSTRUCTIONAL PHYSICAL EDUCATION PROGRAM*

The basic instructional physical education program should provide students with the opportunity to receive instruction, develop essential physical skills, and have enjoyable educational experiences. It is here that opinions are formed and attitudes developed in respect to the physical education program and profession. The fact that some individuals grow into adulthood with an indifferent or unfavorable attitude toward physical education can often be traced back to the physical education they were exposed to in school and college. To some individuals it was something that was jammed down their throats. To others it was presented in an uninteresting manner and seemed unimportant—something to "skip" as often as possible. To still others it was an experience where they were ignored because they had little skill.

Physical education should be presented in a scientific and interesting manner. Students should receive joy and satisfaction from participating in the various activities. Physical education carries its own drive and the teacher should attempt to preserve this natural drive throughout childhood years and into adulthood. It

has been said that if children are exposed to good physical education programs during their formative years there would be no necessity for required physical education programs in later school and college years. The individual would develop skills and attitudes toward physical education that would result in joy and satisfaction from participation. The individual on his or her own initiative would then want to continue such enjoyable experiences.

ENCOURAGING NEW DEVELOPMENTS IN THE TEACHING OF PHYSICAL EDUCATION

There have been several new developments that have emerged in recent years and that augur well for the teaching of physical education in the future. These are (1) getting at the "why" of physical activity, (2) movement education, (3) perceptual-motor programs, (4) the Broadfront Program, and (5) the Battle Creek Physical Education Project.

Getting at the "why" of physical activity

An encouraging new development in physical education is the progress being made toward incorporating the "why" of physical activity into physical education programs, particularly at the high school level. Traditionally, physical education has consisted entirely of physical activity with very little explanation being given to students as to *why* they should be active. Physical education appears to have operated under the assumption that participa-

*School and college physical education programs will be discussed in the next four chapters. This chapter is concerned with the basic instructional physical educational class or service program. Chapter 8 concerns itself with the adapted physical education program. Chapter 9 deals with the intramural and extramural athletic programs, and Chapter 10 is concerned with interscholastic and intercollegiate varsity athletic programs.

tion in games, sports, and other activities alone will develop an understanding of the potential values of these activities, although it is widely accepted that students will function more positively if they know, understand, and appreciate the reasons for participating in various forms of physical activity. Today, it is being increasingly recognized that students need to understand basic concepts about health and fitness in order to be truly physically educated.

The American Association for Health, Physical Education, and Recreation has had a committee working for several years identifying the knowledge and understanding needed in physical education.* This report has been prepared by an outstanding group of leaders and is divided into an introduction and four parts: Introduction, Why Teach A Body of Knowledge in Physical Education?; Part I, Activity Performance (covers such items as basic sport skills, body mechanics, concepts fundamental to movement, skills in strategies and activity patterns, rules and procedures, and protective requirements); Part II, Effects of Activity, Immediate and Long Term; Part III, Factors Modifying Participation in Activities and the Effects of Participation; and Part IV, Standardized Tests.

In keeping with the trend toward getting at the "why" of physical activity, a few textbooks have been published that outline the material that is essential for boys and girls to know in order to be physically educated. I recently published a text entitled *Physical Education for Life*,† which is specifically designed for this purpose and for the use of high school boys and

girls. The material included in this text is outlined here in order to give the reader some idea as to what material might be included regarding the "why" of physical activity.

Physical Education for Life includes a full coverage of sports and activities appropriate for both sexes, for boys only, and for girls only. Part One concentrates on such topics as the organic systems of the body related to and affected by physical activity, the requirements for good body mechanics, exercises to correct some atypical posture conditions, how physical movement takes place and the laws of physics that apply to such movement, how skills are learned based on the latest scientific principles of motor learning, the requirements for and the ingredients of a personal regimen for achieving and maintaining physical fitness, and isometric and isotonic exercises for high school students. Furthermore, a chapter is devoted to safety guidelines and first aid procedures common to participation in physical education activities. Each chapter concludes with a series of questions and answers covering additional information pertinent to the subject of the chapter.

Part Two consists of twenty chapters. Each chapter presents a different physical education activity, ranging from archery, badminton, and basketball to dancing, gymnastics, and wrestling. Each chapter includes the history of the activity, terminology, rules of the game, and recommendations for attire, equipment, etiquette, and safety precautions. There is a progressive treatment of the basic skills involved in the beginning, intermediate, and advanced ability levels of each activity. Each chapter ends with a discussion of strategy and activities for improving skill.

When a high school student appreciates and understands the "why" of physical education as well as the physical activity in which he participates, there is a better assurance that he will develop the neces-

*American Association for Health, Physical Education, and Recreation: Knowledge and understanding in physical education, Washington, D. C., 1969, The Association.

†Bucher, C. A.: Physical education for life, St. Louis, 1969, Webster Division, McGraw-Hill Book Co.

sary attitudes and habits and remain physically active all of his life.

Movement education

Movement education is a significant new approach to teaching physical education. It frees the individual student to work and progress at his own pace while it offers opportunities for creative expression and exploration. It helps the student to better understand the physical laws that govern human movement. Physical skills are developed through an individualized problem-solving technique.

Movement education is being introduced into many elementary schools throughout the nation, and various aspects of movement education are taking root in secondary schools and colleges as well.

What is movement education? Experts do not agree on a single definition. They do agree, however, that movement education is dependent on physical factors in the environment and on the individual's ability to intellectually and physically react to these factors. Movement education attempts to help the student to become mentally as well as physically aware of his bodily movements. It is based on a conceptual approach to human movement. Through movement education, the individual develops his own techniques for dealing with the environmental factors of force,

Elementary school physical education. (Henderson County Schools, Hendersonville, N. C.)

time, space, and flow as they relate to various movement problems.

Movement education employs the problem-solving approach. Each skill that is to be explored presents a challenge to the student. Learning results as the student accepts and solves increasingly more difficult problems. For this reason, the natural movements of childhood are considered to be the first challenges that should be presented to the student.

Traditional physical education emphasizes the learning of specific skills through demonstration, drill, and practice. Movement education emphasizes the learning of skill patterns through individual exploration of the body's movement potential. Traditional physical education stresses the teacher's standard of performance. Movement education stresses the individual child's standard of performance.

Perceptual-motor foundations

Another development in physical education that should be noted is the increased recognition of perceptual-motor foundations. For some time there has been an increased recognition of the importance of meaningful perceptual-motor programs for underachievers in the elementary schools. Research conducted by psychologists, physical educators, and others has shown that motor activity, when properly presented, can enhance perceptual development.

One of the most significant developments of this interest has been the publication of the report of a task force of the AAHPER, which studied such subjects as the evolution of perceptual-motor behavior with implications for the teaching-learning process. It also explored interdisciplinary implications and identified areas for future study and research.* This study indicates there is a relationship between physical

---

*American Association for Health, Physical Education, and Recreation: Perceptual-motor foundations: a multidisciplinary concern, Washington, D. C., 1969, The Association.

education and the development of perceptual-motor skills and that perceptual-motor skills are essential to learning and scholastic achievement. Therefore the conclusion is drawn that physical education, through the contribution that can be made in this area, has the potential for contributing to and facilitating the educational and academic achievement of certain children in our schools.

The Broadfront Program

Ellensburg, Washington, has developed a comprehensive program in physical education, health, and recreation. The project was started as a result of a Title III grant from the national government. It is designed to help each boy and girl in elementary, junior high, and senior high school develop physical skills, desirable attitudes, and knowledge about physical education, health, and recreation. It not only focuses attention on the normal boy and girl but also the handicapped and the retarded student. Furthermore, it is concerned with linking the school and community together in a program with both student and adult participation. Specifically, the Broadfront Program has five major aspects: (1) the acquisition of skills on the part of the student in individual sports, (2) health education, (3) a community-school program, (4) outdoor education and school camping, and (5) an adapted health and physical education program.

Broadfront is designed to accomplish such goals as ensuring that students develop skill competency in at least two lifetime sports, providing inservice education for classroom teachers both elementary and secondary, utilizing professors and major students from nearby colleges, instructing the adult population of Ellensburg, Washington, in lifetime sports, utilizing all facilities in both the school and community, and providing for the orientation of student teachers who are majors in physical education, as well as elementary school education majors, so that they will understand and appreciate the program.

The Battle Creek Physical Education Curriculum Project

The Battle Creek Curriculum Project represents an effort on the part of a public school system working with a university to develop and implement a model curriculum for physical education at both the elementary and secondary educational levels. The project team consists of specialists in physical education, curriculum development, child growth and development, sociology, physiology, and educational measurement. The major objectives of the project are to first identify a body of knowledge that can form the framework for a curriculum model. This was accomplished by an intensive search of the literature to find out such things as the influence of physical activity on man's biologic, sociologic, and psychologic development and the relationship of man's various activity patterns to culture and environment. The second objective was to take the findings of this intensive search of the literature and organize it in terms of such things as a philosophy that would act as a guide for the curriculum model and also as a guide for general and behavioral objectives and outcomes. Finally, the development of a model program in physical education will be derived from the previous two steps. The Battle Creek Project has national implications for physical education programs.

THE BASIC INSTRUCTIONAL PROGRAM—INSTRUCTIONAL IN NATURE

The basic instructional program of physical education is the place to teach, not a setting for free play and intramurals or an opportunity for the varsity team to practice. The entire period should be used to teach skills, strategies, understandings, and essential knowledge concerning the relation of physical activity to physical, mental, emotional, and social development.

Skills should be taught from a scientific approach so that the various kinesiologic factors that affect movement are understood clearly by the student. Utilization of demonstrations, super-8 films, loop films, models, slide films, posters, and other visual aids and materials can help in clarifying instruction. Team teaching enables the master teacher of specific skills to be utilized more extensively than in the past.

The material presented throughout the school life of the child should be sequential in development and progressive in application. Just as a student advances in mathematics from simple arithmetic to algebra, geometry, and calculus, so in physical education the pupil should progress from basic skills and materials to more complex and involved skills and strategies.

Standards should be established for student achievement. When boys and girls advance from one grade to another they should have achieved certain standards in various physical education activities, just as they master various levels of skills and understandings in subject matter areas of instruction.

The physical education class should involve more than physical activity itself. As the student understands more fully the importance of sports and activities in life, what happens to the body during exercise, the relation of physical activity to man's biologic, psychologic, and sociologic development, the history of various activities, and the role of physical activity in the cultures of the world, the class takes on more intellectual respectability and meaning for the student and the profession in general.

Just as textbooks are used in other courses in the educational system, so should physical education use a textbook, with regular assignments being given. Textbooks should contain not only material on physical skills but should also get at the subject matter with which physical education is concerned.

Records that follow a child from grade to grade should be kept throughout his school life. These records will indicate the degree to which the objectives have been achieved by the student, his physical status, his skill achievement, his knowledge about the field, his social conduct, and other aspects that will help to interpret in a meaningful manner what physical education has done for the student and what still needs to be done.

There should also be homework in physical education. The subject matter needs to be mastered, the skills acquired, and standard of physical fitness achieved. Much of this information, skill, and various standards can be met at least partially through homework assignments.

Guidelines

The basic instructional physical education period cannot be conducted in a "hit-and-miss" fashion. It must be planned in accordance with the needs and interests of the individuals it serves.

Some of the initial considerations in planning and developing a physical education program are suggested*:

1. The basic instructional physical education program, adapted program, and intramural, extramural, and varsity interscholastic and intercollegiate athletic programs all represent important components of the total physical education program. They must remain in proper balance at all school and college levels and be geared to the needs and interests of the student.

2. A sound philosophy is essential as a basis for the construction of any physical education program.

3. The needs of the individual and of society, as reflected in the objectives of

---

*Also see Chapter 11 on Administering School and College Physical Fitness Programs.

A golf class in the required physical education class program for men. (Department of Physical Education and Athletics, University of Michigan.)

The maxim that physical education carries its own drive should be preserved for every individual who comes in contact with the program. A basketball class in the required physical education class program for men. (Department of Physical Education and Athletics, University of Michigan.)

physical education, represent a main consideration in the establishment of a program of physical education.

4. The fact that physical education contributes to the social, mental, emotional, and physical needs of the individual should be kept in mind.

5. The physical education instructional program should get at the why of the activity as well as the physical activity itself. Provisions should be made for studying, discussing, and assimilating knowledge regarding the subject matter of physical education.

6. The health and recreational aspects of the program must be emphasized. This can best be done by close coordination with the school and college health and recreation programs.

7. Physical education should recognize the importance of coeducational activities for social growth and provide for them in the program.

8. Provisions should be made so that *all* individuals may participate in and benefit from the physical education program.

9. The maxim that "physical education carries its own drive" should be preserved in every individual who comes in contact with the program. Joy and satisfaction should be outcomes from physical education that are guarded jealously.

10. Physical education should receive equal consideration with other subjects in the school and college offerings in respect to necessary supplies, facilities, and administrative support.

11. Qualified leadership is an essential in all phases of the physical education program.

12. Physical education should be planned, organized, and conducted in a manner that will exploit the educational possibilities to the fullest.

13. The program should include a wide variety of activities that can be engaged in by all individuals, indoors and outdoors, and that meet safety, hygienic, and social standards.

14. Instruction in activities should be on a progressive basis and organized in a way that is systematic and most meaningful to the student.

15. Physical education should contribute to the democratic way of life.

16. A program of measurement and evaluation should be developed so that progress toward goals may be noted and weaknesses detected.

The next step in considering the basic instructional program is to examine some of the administrative problems surrounding its organization and administration. These include scheduling, time allotment, size of classes, teaching loads, and grouping; administrative policies concerned with the advisability of having physical education on a required or elective basis, substitutions, credit allowances, class attendance, and excuses; separation of boys and girls in grades one to six; physical education specialist or classroom teacher in the elementary school and the question of self-defense courses; items of class management concerned with planning, dressing and showering, costume, roll taking, grading, and records; matters relating to activities, such as criteria for their selection, classification, and coeducational aspects; and program considerations at the elementary, junior high school, senior high school, and college levels.

SCHEDULING

The manner in which physical education classes are scheduled reflects the physical education leadership in the school or college and the attitude of the central administration. The physical education class will be more meaningful for students if it is scheduled in a manner that is linked to their interests, rather than in the interest of administrative convenience.

Scheduling should be done according to a definite plan. Physical education should not be inserted in the overall master scheduling plan wherever there is time left over after all the other subjects have been provided for. This important responsibility cannot be handled on a hit-and-miss basis, since that disregards the interests and needs of the students. Instead, at the secondary educational level, for example, physical education classes should be scheduled first on the master plan, along with such subjects as English and science that are required of all students most of the time they are in school. This allows for progression and for grouping according to the interests and needs of the individual participants. The three important items to take into consideration in scheduling classes are (1) the number of teachers available, (2) the number of teaching stations available, and (3) the number of students who must be scheduled. This is a formula that should be applied to all subjects in the school offering. Physical education will be scheduled correctly, as will other subjects, if this formula is followed.

All students should be scheduled. There should be no exceptions. If the student can go to school or college he should be enrolled in physical education. Special attention should be given, however, to the exceptional individual to ensure that he is placed in a program suited to his needs. Also, special attention should be given to the so-called "dub" who needs extra help in the development of physical skills.

At the elementary and secondary levels, but especially at the elementary, scheduling should be done on 1-year basis. Special attention should be given to the needs and interests of students in respect to such items as the availability of facilities, equipment, and supplies and the weather. Planned units of work will usually become increasingly longer as the student progresses in grades, because of his longer interest span, greater maturity, and the increased complexity of the acitivities.

All students should be scheduled for physical education. (Henderson County Schools, Hendersonville, N. C.)

Every physical educator should make a point of presenting to the central administration his or her plans for scheduling physical education classes. The need for special consideration in this area should be discussed with the principal, scheduling committee, and others involved. Through persistent action along this line, progress will be made. The logic and reasoning behind the formula of scheduling classes according to the number of teachers and teaching stations available and the number of students who must be scheduled cannot be denied. It must be planned in this way if there is to be progression in instruction and if a meaningful program is to result.

The innovation of flexible scheduling into school programs has implications for the administration of school physical education programs. Flexible scheduling assumes that the traditional system of having all subjects meet the same number of times each week for the same amount of time each period is passé. Flexible scheduling provides that class periods be of varying lengths, depending on the type of work being covered by the students, methods of instruction, and other factors pertinent to such a system. Whereas the master plan makes it difficult, if not impossible in many

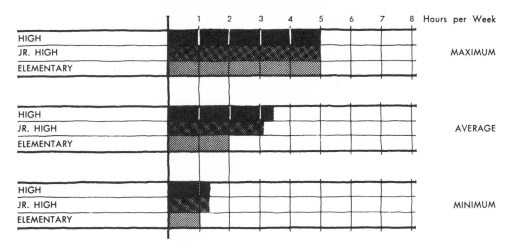

Time spent by students in the physical education program. (From Partial shelter for physical education: a study of the feasibility of the use of limited shelters for physical education, College Station, Texas, 1961, Texas Engineering Experiment Station, Texas A & M University.)

cases, to have flexible scheduling, the advent of the computer has made such an innovation practical and common.

Flexible scheduling also makes it possible to schedule activities for students of differing abilities in a different manner so that all are not required to have a similar schedule based on a standard format of the school day. Under the traditional system all students who were the slowest, for example, took as many courses as the brightest. Under flexible scheduling, some students may take as few as four courses and some as many as eight.

Part of the student's school day will not be scheduled. However, this time is not wasted. Individual study, homework time, skill practice session, conferences with teachers, library study, and many other activities may be scheduled as needed. Such flexible scheduling makes better use of human and physical resources within the school and also offers the student an opportunity to accept responsibility and to make decisions on his own.

Physical educators must give considerable thought as to what type of scheduling should be utilized in physical education classes, what length of periods is best, and

what allocations of time should be fed to the computer. Some schools are experimenting with this problem.

Time allotment

Just as scheduling practices vary from school to school, college to college, and state to state, so does the time allotment. In some states there are laws that are mandatory in nature and require that a certain amount of time each day or week be devoted to physical education, whereas in others permissive legislation exists. For grades one to twelve the requirement varies in different states from none, or very little, to a daily 1-hour program. Some require 20 minutes daily and others 30 minutes daily. Other states specify the time by the week, ranging from 50 minutes to 300 minutes. The college and university level does not usually require as much physical education as grades one to twelve. The usual practice in higher education is to require physical education two times a week for 2 years.

The general consensus among physical education leaders is that in order for physical education to be of value it must be given with regularity. For most individuals this means daily periods. There is also agreement among experts in the field of health that exercise is essential to everyone from the cradle to the grave. Smiley and Gould point out the exercise needs of individuals at various ages:

Ages 1 through 4
Free play during hours not occupied by sleeping

Ages 5 through 8
Four hours a day of free play (running, jumping, dancing, climbing, teetering, etc.) and of loosely organized group games (tag, nine pins, hoops, beanbags, etc.)

Ages 9 through 11
At least three hours a day of outdoor active play (hiking, swimming, gymnastics, group games and relays, soccer, volleyball, broad-and-high jump, 25- and 50-yard dashes, folk dancing, etc.)

Ages 12 through 14
At least two hours a day of outdoor active play (hiking, swimming, gymnastics, group games, relays, soccer, volleyball, indoor baseball, basketball, baseball, tennis, 60-yard dash, the jumps, shot-put, low hurdles, short relays, folk and gymnastic dancing). Still no endurance contests

Ages 15 through 17
At least one and one-half hours a day of outdoor active play (hiking, swimming, apparatus work, group games and relays, soccer, volleyball, indoor baseball, basketball, baseball, tennis, football, golf, ice hockey, 60-yard dash, the jumps, shot-put, low hurdles, short relays, folk and gymnastic dancing). Still no endurance contests

Ages 18 through 30
At least one hour a day of active outdoor exercise (all the types listed in the preceding paragraph and, if examined and found physically fit, in addition, cross-country running, crew, wrestling, boxing, fencing, and polo)

Ages 31 through 50
At least one hour a day of moderate outdoor exercise (golf, tennis, riding, swimming, handball, volleyball, etc.)

Ages 51 through 70
At least one hour a day of light outdoor exercise (golf, walking, bowling, gardening, fishing, croquet, etc.)*

---

*Smiley, D. F., and Gould, A. G.: A college textbook of hygiene, New York, 1940, The Macmillan Co., pp. 346-347.

Daily physical education period at elementary and secondary school levels

The time-allotment recommendation usually considered adequate is a daily physical education period for each student. This should represent the minimum requirement. Some individuals feel that, especially in the elementary schools, a program cannot be adapted to a fixed time schedule. However, as a standard, there seems to be agreement that a daily experience in such a program is needed. Such a recommendation is made and should always be justified on the basis of value and contribution to the student and his needs. There should be provision for regular, instructional class periods and, in addition, laboratory periods where the skills may be put to use.

On the secondary level especially, there is a feeling that a full 60-minute period is needed. Since time for dressing and showering is required, this leaves only approximately 45 minutes on the floor or playground. Some have suggested a double period every other day rather than a single period each day. This might be feasible if the daily class periods are too short. However, the importance of daily periods should be recognized and achieved wher-

Students should have a daily period of physical education. (Henderson County Schools, Hendersonville, N. C.)

ever possible. Administrators should work toward providing adequate staff and facilities to allow for a daily period.

One of the most intensive and enlightening public interpretation programs ever carried on in modern times in support of a daily program of physical education was conducted in California. The California Association for Health, Physical Education, and Recreation rendered an outstanding service to the profession in cataloguing, describing, and interpreting the values inherent in the daily program of physical education in their state. They incorporated their scientific evidence and research findings in a special issue of the *Journal of the California Association for Health, Physical Education, and Recreation.**

This special issue included supporting statements from such people and organizations as the President of the United States, citizens' committees, American Medical Association, California Heart Association,

physiologists and psychologists, educators, and parent-teachers' associations. As a result of this intensive and aggressive campaign, the public became much better informed regarding the need for daily physical education.

The President's Council on Physical Fitness and Sports has made this statement in regard to the daily physical education period:

The unanimous support for recommendations of the President's Council on Physical Fitness by a national jury of eminent medical leaders accompanying similar support by the American Medical Association and its committee on Exercise and Physical Fitness, Medical Aspects of Sports, and the Joint Committee of the AMA and its National Education Association indicate the sound position the President's Council has taken in recommending daily physical education instruction involving vigorous exercise in grades 1 to 12.*

Size of classes

Some school and college administrators feel that physical education classes can accommodate more students than the so-

---

*Values inherent in the daily program of physical education: fitness for California children and youth, Journal of the California Association for Health, Physical Education, and Recreation, special issue, March, 1965.

*President's Council on Physical Fitness, Washington, D. C., distributed in 1965 (mimeographed).

Girls' physical education. (State Teachers College, East Stroudsburg, Pa.)

called academic classes, such as English or social studies. This is a misconception that has developed over the years and is in need of correction. Physical educators themselves are in many cases at fault for such a practice. Some have failed to interpret their field of endeavor adequately to the central administration. Others have followed the practice of throwing a ball to a class and utilizing free play, with little or no organization. This has led some administrators to feel that the same type of teaching job would be done with a small class, and therefore they see no reason to incur the administrative problems and extra expense of more staff and smaller classes.

The problem of class size seems to be more pertinent at the secondary than at other educational levels. At the elementary levels, for example, the classroom situation represents a unit for activity and the size of this teaching unit is usually reasonable. However, there are some schools that combine various classrooms for physical education, resulting in large classes that are not desirable.

Classes in physical education should be approximately the same size as is prevalent for the other subjects in the school or college offering. This is just as essential for effective teaching, individualized instruction, and progression in physical education as it is in other subjects. Physical education contributes to educational objectives on at least an equal basis with other subjects in the curriculum. Therefore, the size of the class should be comparable so that an effective teaching job can be accomplished and the objectives of education attained.

The standard established by LaPorte's committee* after considerable research points up the acceptable size of physical education classes. It recommends not more than thirty-five students as the suitable size for activity classes. Normal classes should never exceed forty-five for one instructor. Of course, if there is a lecture scheduled it may be possible to have a larger number of students in the class. For remedial and corrective classes the suitable class size is from twenty to twenty-five and should never exceed thirty. With flexible scheduling, the size of classes can be varied to meet the needs of the teacher, facilities, and type of activity being offered.

The American Association for Health, Physical Education, and Recreation* points out that class size should not exceed thirty-five.

Teaching loads

The load of the physical education teacher should be of prime concern to the administrator. In order to maintain a top level of enthusiasm, strength, and other essential characteristics, it is important that the teaching load be adjusted so that the physical educator is not overworked.

The New York State Physical Fitness Conference† recommended that one full-time physical education teacher should be provided for every 240 elementary pupils and one for every 190 secondary pupils enrolled. If such a requirement became universal it would aid considerably in providing adequate staff members in this field and avoid an overload for so many of the teachers.

LaPorte's national study‡ made recommendations in respect to teaching load at precollege educational levels that should

*LaPorte, W. R.: The physical education curriculum (a national program), ed. 6, Los Angeles, 1955, University of Southern California Press, pp. 50-51.

*American Association for Health, Physical Education, and Recreation: Administrative problems in health education, physical education, and recreation, Washington, D. C., 1953, The Association, p. 70.
†Report to the Commissioner of Education on the State Fitness Conference, Albany, N. Y., 1952, State Education Department, p. 7.
‡LaPorte, W. R., op. cit., p. 51.

be considered carefully by any teacher or administrator striving to meet acceptable standards. It recommends that class instruction per teacher not exceed 5 clock hours or the equivalent in class periods per day, or 1,500 minutes a week. It never should exceed 6 clock hours per day or 1,800 minutes a week. This maximum should include afterschool responsibilities. A daily load of 200 students per teacher is recommended and never more than 250. Finally, each teacher should have at least one free period daily for consultation and conferences with students.

It is generally agreed that the normal teaching load in colleges and universities should not exceed 15 hours per week.

Grouping

Homogeneous grouping in physical education classes is very desirable. To render the most valuable contribution to students, factors influencing performance must be taken into consideration in organizing groups for physical education instructional work or competition. The lack of scientific knowledge and measuring techniques to obtain such information and the administrative problems of scheduling have handicapped the achievement of this goal in most schools and colleges.

The reasons for grouping are sound. Placing individuals with similar capacities and characteristics in the same class will make it possible to better meet the needs of each individual. Grouping individuals with similar skill, ability, and other factors aids in equalizing competition. This helps the student to realize more satisfaction and benefit from playing. Grouping makes for more effective teaching. Instruction can be better organized and adapted to the level of the student. Grouping facilitates progression and continuity in the program. Furthermore, grouping makes for a better learning situation for the student. Being in a group with persons of similar physical characteristics and skills ensures some success, a chance to excel, recognition, a feeling of belonging, and security. Consequently this helps the social and personality development of the individual. Finally, homogeneous grouping helps protect the child. It ensures his participation with individuals who are similar in physical characteristics. This protects the child physically, emotionally, and socially.

The problem of grouping is not as pertinent in the elementary school, especially in the lower grades, as it is in the junior high school and upper levels. At the lower levels the grade classification appears to serve the needs of children. As children grow older, the complexity of the program increases, social growth becomes more diversified, competition becomes more intense, and consequently, there is a greater need for having similar individuals in the same group.

At the present time students are homogeneously classified on such bases as grade, sex, health, physical fitness, multiples of age-height-weight, ability, physical capacity, motor ability, interests, educability, speed, skill, and previous experience. Such techniques as health examinations; tests of motor ability, physical capacity, achievement, and social efficiency; conferences with students; and determination of physiologic áge are utilized to obtain such information.

The Sacramento, California, public schools have outlined the various aspects of their physical education program from the elementary grades through the junior college level. Their course of study for the senior high school girls lists the following procedure for grouping in physical education.

I. Basis of classification
   A. Physical examination
     1. Personal history
     2. Menstrual history
     3. Posture test
     4. Feet
     5. Other findings

B. Medical examination
  1. Teeth
  2. Nose, throat
  3. Heart
  4. Nutrition
  5. Blood pressure
  6. Review of findings in physical examinations
II. Classification of physical education activities based upon the above findings
  A. Active or unrestricted physical education
    1. Team sports
    2. Individual sports
    3. Dancing
    4. Gymnastics and unorganized games
    5. Drill
  B. Restricted or modified physical education
    1. Modified games
    2. Posture exercises
    3. Relaxation
  C. Remedial physical education
    1. Exercises for general muscle tone
    2. Menstrual exercises
    3. Posture exercises
    4. Feet exercises
    5. Special, individual exercises
    6. Relaxing
  D. Rest
    This activity includes girls who are under a physician's care and have organic or functional handicaps sufficiently serious to recommend a period of complete rest during their physical education period.

The suggestions of the American Association for Health, Physical Education, and Recreation* are appropriate when considering recommendations for grouping:

1. The need for grouping students homogeneously for instruction and competition has long been recognized, but the inability to scientifically measure such important factors as ability, maturity, interest, and capacity has served as a deterrent from accomplishing this goal.

2. The most common procedure for grouping today is by grade or class.

3. The ideal grouping organization

---

*American Association for Health, Physical Education, and Recreation: Administrative problems in health education, physical education, and recreation, Washington, D. C., 1953, The Association, pp. 71-72.

would take into consideration all factors that affect performance—intelligence, capacity, interest, knowledge, age, height, weight, and so on. To utilize all these factors, however, is not administratively feasible at the present time.

4. Some form of grouping is essential to provide the type of program that will promote educational objectives and protect the student.

5. On the secondary and college levels, the most feasible procedure appears to be to organize subgroups within the regular physical education class proper.

6. Classification within the physical education class should be based on such factors as age, height, and weight statistics and other factors, such as interest and skill, that are developed as a result of observation of the activity.

7. For those individuals who desire greater refinement in respect to grouping, utilization of motor capacity, motor ability, attitude, appreciation, and sports-skills tests may be used.

ADMINISTRATIVE POLICIES

The administrator of any physical education program is perennially confronted with such questions as: Should physical education be required or elective? How much credit should be given? Is it possible to substitute some other activity for physical education? What should be the policy on class attendance? How should one deal with excuses? What provision should be made for sex differences? Should there be courses in self-defense? These and other questions are answered in the following paragraphs.

Should physical education be required or elective?

There is general agreement that physical education should be required at the elementary level. However, there are many advocates on both sides of the question as to whether it should be required or elective on the secondary and college levels. Both groups are sincere and feel that their beliefs represent what is best for the student. Probably most specialists feel that the program should be required. Some school administrators feel it should be elective. Following are some of the arguments presented by each.

Required

1. Physical education represents a basic need of every student just as English, social studies, and other experiences do. It became part of the school or college offering as a required subject to satisfy such needs and therefore should be continued on the same basis.

2. The student is compelled to take so many required courses that the use of electives is limited, if not entirely eliminated, in some cases. Therefore, unless physical education is a required course, many students will not have the opportunity to partake of this program because of the pressures placed on them by the required courses.

3. The student looks upon those subjects that are required as being the most important and the most necessary for success. Therefore, unless physical education is on the required list, it becomes a subject of second-rate importance in the eyes of the students.

4. Various subjects in the curriculum would not be provided for unless they were required. This is probably true of physical education. Until state legislatures passed laws requiring physical education, this subject was ignored by many school administrators. If physical education were on an elective basis the course of some administrative action would be obvious. Either the subject would not be offered at all or the administrative philosophy would so dampen its value that it would have to be eliminated because of low enrollment.

5. Even under a required program, physical education is not fulfilling its potentialities for meeting the physical, social, and mental needs of students. If an elective program were instituted, deficiencies and shortages would increase, thus further handicapping the attempt to meet the needs of the student.

Elective

1. Physical education "carries its own drive." If a good basic program is developed in the elementary school, with students acquiring the necessary skills and attitudes, the drive for such activity will carry through in the secondary school and college. There will be no need to require such a course, because students will want to take it voluntarily.

2. Objectives of physical education are focused on developing skills and learning activities that have carryover value, living a healthful life, and recognizing the importance of developing and maintaining one's body in its best possible condition. These are goals that cannot be legislated. They must become a part of each individual's attitudes and desires if they are to be realized. A person is more or less "master of his own fate" in regard to his body. He can do with it what he chooses. This is characteristic of life. The student should be guided in setting up his standard of values. However, he makes the final choice as to how he will achieve those values.

3. Many children and young adults do not like physical education. This is indicated in their manner, attitude, and desire to get excused from the program and to substitute something else for the course. Under such circumstances the values that accrue to these individuals are not great. Therefore, it would be best to place physical education on an elective basis where only those students participate who actually desire to.

The question of whether a program should be required or elective will not be decided within a few months or years. It will require considerable study. There are good points on both sides of the issue. A compromise may be possible. The present setup of our educational systems that places some subjects on a pedestal, making them required and focusing attention on them because they have been offered traditionally, may be the reason for the difficulty. Perhaps if a reevaluation of the entire educational system were to take place with each subject evaluated on its contribution to the enriched living of the individual, its value throughout life, and the contributions it can make to an interesting, vigorous, and active life, it would be found that some of the so-called academic subjects might go the way that Latin, for example, has gone. It might be found that many of them are not practical and functional in present-day living. Sometimes the social pressures of the times and the emphasis on material values and false standards govern individuals' choices to too great an extent. When a true set of standards can be established in the mind of every individual so that wise choices can be made, many subjects can be placed on an elective basis. Until then, it is important to make them a requirement.

Should substitutions be allowed for physical education?

A practice exists in some school and college systems that allows students to substitute some other activity for their physical education requirement. This practice should be scrutinized very carefully and resisted aggressively by every administrator.

Some of the activities that are used as substitutions for physical education are athletic participation, Reserve Officers' Training Corps, war service, and band.

There is no substitute for a good program of physical education. In addition to healthful physical activity it is concerned also with developing an individual socially, emotionally, and mentally. It develops in the individual many skills that can be utilized throughout life for worthy use of leisure time. These essentials are lost if a student is permitted to take some other activity in place of physical education. Professional persons who condone substitutions for their physical education classes are not clear as to the goals of their profession. It is important that physical educators recognize that there is no adequate substitute for a well-planned, well-organized, and well-conducted physical education class.

Should credit be given for physical education?

Whether or not credit should be given for physical education is another controversial problem with which the profession is continually confronted. Here again can be found advocates on both sides. There are those who feel the joy of the activity and the values derived from participation are sufficient in themselves without giving credit. On the other hand, there are those who feel that physical education is the same as any other subject in the curriculum and should also be granted credit.

The general consensus among physical education leaders is that if physical education is required for graduation and if it contributes to educational outcomes, credit should be given, just as in other subjects. The credit given should be justified by the contribution physical education makes to the achievement of outcomes toward which all of education is working.

What policy should be established on class attendance?

It is important for every department of physical education to have a definite policy on class attendance that covers absenteeism and tardiness. Since it is felt that students should attend school and colleges regularly, it follows that they should also attend classes regularly, including physical education.

Regular attendance in physical education is essential in order to derive the values and outcomes that accrue from participation. Since attendance is necessary in order to achieve such outcomes, every physical education department should have a clear-cut policy on attendance regulations. These regulations should be few in number and clearly stated in writing so that they are recognized, understood, and strictly enforced by teachers and students. They should allow for a reasonable number of absences and tardinesses, which can always occur in emergency situations over which the student has no control. Perfect attendance at school or college should not be stressed. Many harmful results can develop if students feel obligated to attend classes when they are ill and should be home in bed. There should probably be some provision for makeup work when important experiences are missed. However, makeup work should be planned and conducted so that the student derives essential values from such participation, rather than enduring it as a disciplinary measure. There should also be provision for the readmission of students who have been ill. A procedure should be established so that the program is adapted to these individuals.

A final point to remember is the importance of keeping accurate, up-to-date attendance records. Unless meaningful records are kept, administrative problems will increase.

What about excuses?

The principal, nurse, or physical educator frequently receives a note from a parent or family physician asking that a student be excused from physical education. Many abuses develop if all such requests are granted. Many times for minor reasons the student does not want to participate and obtains the parent's or family physician's support.

Tom Peiffer, a physical educator in the

PHYSICAL EDUCATION EXCUSE

NAME ....

GRADE .... ADVISOR .... GYM PERIOD ....

DATES—EXCUSED FROM .... TO ....

DOCTOR ....

REASON ....

....

NO PHYS. ED. ....

MODIFIED PROGRAM

    FULL PROGRAM EXCEPT COMPETITIVE SPORTS ....

    PARTICIPATION EXCEPT ....

SCHOOL SCHEDULE ADJUSTMENT, IF ANY ....

....

Physical education excuse form. (From Bucher, C. A., Koenig, C. R., and Barnhard, M.: Methods and materials for secondary school physical education, ed. 3, St. Louis, 1970, The C. V. Mosby Co).

New York State public schools, conducted a survey to determine both the extent of required physical education and practices in regard to physical education excuses in secondary schools, colleges, and universities. The questionnaire used in the survey was sent to schools selected at random from fifteen states situated in various sections of the United States. The questionnaire was sent to the high school in the largest city, to a suburban school of that city, to one city in the state with a population of 20,000 to 25,000, to one city in the state with a population of 10,000 to 15,000, and to one community with a population of 3,000 to 5,000. On the college level, questionnaires were sent to one state university, one private institution, and one teacher training institution. Questionnaires were sent to seventy-five secondary schools and sixty-seven colleges and universities. Replies were received from forty-five secondary schools and forty colleges and universities. Among the secondary schools, 37.9% required 4 years of physical education, 28.8% required 3 years, 20% required 2 years, and 13.3% required 1 year. In higher education, 60% of the colleges required 2 years, 25% required 1 year, 10% required 3 years, and 5% did not have a requirement. The number of days per week devoted to physical education is also shown in diagram on p. 145.

Peiffer's survey showed that high schools permitted a student to be excused on the basis of a parental note, a memorandum from the family physician, or the discretion of the physical education teacher. While some schools would accept the recommendation of any of these three persons, other schools would accept only an excuse from the school physician. At the college level most programs accept the college physician's excuse or permit the instructor of each class to use his own discretion in granting excuses to his students.

The reasons listed as to why excuses in physical education were granted were an interesting part of the preceding survey.

Secondary schools grant most of their excuses for participation in athletics and for being in the school band. Some schools permit their athletes to be excused only on the day of the game, while others grant a blanket excuse for the entire sports season. Other reasons for excuses on the secondary level, in addition to athletics, included makeup tests, driver training, counseling, a too-heavy extracurricular load, and medical reasons. At the college level, excuses were granted to athletes, veterans, students who could pass physical fitness tests, honor students, older students, for medical reasons, in "hardship cases," and so on.

Another part of the questionnaire on excuses attempted to discover what was done with the students who were excused. Students in secondary schools were sent to study halls; required to score, officiate, or help around the physical education department; write reports; remain on the sidelines; or report after school. At the college level most colleges did nothing except follow a pattern of failing a student in some cases if he exceeded the legal number of excused absences per semester. A few either required the student to observe the class, substitute a health class, or study in the gymnasium or left it up to the instructor's discretion.

Some school systems have exercised control over the indiscriminate granting of requests for excuses from physical education. Policies have been established, sometimes through conferences and rulings of the board of education, requiring that all excuses must be reviewed and approved by the school physician before they will be granted. Furthermore, family physicians have been asked to state specific reasons for requesting excuse from physical education. This procedure has worked out very satisfactorily in some communities. In other places physical educators have taken particular pains to work very closely with medical doctors. They have established a physical education program in collabora-

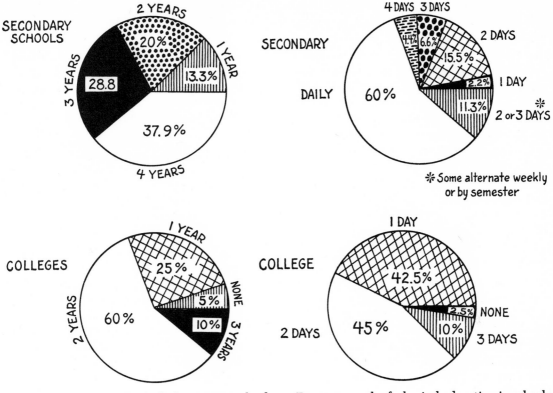

Extent of required physical education in schools surveyed.

Days per week of physical education in schools surveyed.

FORM 860-D   DSP   11-57-500 BKS.   U-857-44603

DENVER PUBLIC SCHOOLS
Department of Health Service

HEALTH EXCUSE FROM SCHOOL

Date..

To the parents or guardian of:..

We consider it best that your child return home today because of the following

health reasons:..

....

....

If the illness continues or becomes worse, please have the child seen by your own

physician; and be sure he / she is well before returning to school.

....
School Physician or Nurse

....
School Principal

tion with the school physician so that the needs of each individual are met, regardless of his or her physical condition. They have met with the local medical society in an attempt to clear up misunderstandings in regard to the purpose and conduct of the program. Family physicians have been brought into the planning. As a result of such planning, problems in regard to excuses from physical education have been considerably reduced.

There probably is a correlation between the respect, prestige, and degree to which physical education is understood in any community and the number of excuses that are requested. Furthermore, respect, prestige, and understanding are reflected in the type of leadership that exists. It has been found that in those communities where parents, family physicians, and the lay public in general understand physical education, the number of requests for excuses is relatively small. In such communities, the values that can be derived from participation in the program are clearly recognized, and since most parents and physicians want children to have worthwhile experiences, they encourage rather than attempt to limit such participation. The leadership of any program can eliminate many of the administrative problems in regard to excuses, provided physical education is properly interpreted to the public at large.

A few years ago, a conference concerned with close cooperation between physical education and medical doctors drew up a list of statements in respect to the problem under discussion. These are as follows:

1. Orient the student, parent, and physician at an early date in regard to the objectives of the physical education program.
2. Route all requests for excuse through the school physician. In the absence of the physician the school nurse should have this responsibility. The sympathetic and informed nurse can be a real asset to the physical education program.
3. Discard permanent and blanket excuses. The

school physician should share in planning certain areas of the individual physical education program. Instead of being categorically excused, boys and girls can be given an activity in keeping with their special needs.
4. Students involved in the excuse request should have a periodic recheck as to need for excuse (this tends to reduce requests up to 50%).
5. Conferences between the school physicians and the head of the physical education department on the local level need to be emphasized.
6. The problem of excuse from physical education should be tied up with the total guidance program of the school. It helps also if the administrator and classroom teachers are familiar with the general physical education aims.

Should boys and girls be separated for physical education in grades one to six?

There is disagreement as to whether or not boys and girls should be separated for physical education classes in the elementary school.

Those persons who advocate keeping the pupils together list such reasons as the following to support their position:

1. Separation hinders the social objective.
2. Separation causes unnecessary curiosity on the part of both boys and girls.
3. Schools cannot provide the resources and teachers needed to conduct separate programs.
4. Interests of both boys and girls prior to the adolescent period are much the same.
5. Playing together can carry over to later years, resulting in a happy, shared recreational life.

Those persons who advocate separating the sexes, at least during some of the elementary school years, list such reasons as the following to support their position:

1. Girls are too emotional.
2. Boys are interested in feats requiring strength, endurance, and skill, whereas girls are primarily interested in grace and moderate amounts of skill.
3. Girls and boys shy away from each other and want to be separated in physical activities.

4. Physical activities that the boys like, placing heavy demands on organic vitality, are not appropriate for girls.
5. A segregated program can do more to accomplish the separate objectives of both boys and girls.
6. A program that brings boys and girls together results in boys taking over key positions. Also, boys are more demanding, resulting in less time for girls to practice skills and have fun.

An analysis of the characteristics of boys and girls at the various grade levels shows that in the first and second grades the boys and girls have no preference as to sex, and, at the third grade, boys and girls are just beginning to become conscious of the distinctions between them. Interests and abilities of boys and girls during the first three grades are not significant. Therefore, it is recommended that through the third grade, boys and girls might well take their physical education classes together.

At the fourth-, fifth-, and sixth-grade levels the physical education classes for boys and girls might well be separated, at least for many of the activities that are offered in the program. The reasons that undergird such a statement are well founded. Starting with the fourth grade, open antagonisms become apparent; boys like to rough it up and are more aggressive, girls are more subdued and do not like loud, boisterous action. Girls are nearing puberty at this level and developing at a very rapid rate. During the fifth and sixth grades interests are entirely different, with girls liking rhythmic movement and boys liking tests of strength and endurance. Each sex teases the other continuously. Boys are farther ahead than girls in skill, rules, knowledge, and strategy in many activities.

There should be opportunities, however, for boys and girls to get together periodically in activities that lend themselves to an integrated situation, such as some form of rhythmic activity.

Should the physical education specialist or the classroom teacher conduct the physical education class in the elementary school?

This question has been discussed on a perennial basis for many years. There are educators who advocate the classroom teacher handling physical education classes and also many supporters who want a specialist to take over this responsibility. The issue is quite involved and limited space does not permit taking up in depth each side of the issue. These facts, however, should be pointed out. The classroom teacher has limited professional education in physical education. Some classroom teachers are not interested in teaching physical education. Furthermore, there is increased interest in physical education today, which implies that qualified and interested persons should handle these classes. There is a trend toward more emphasis on movement education, physical fitness, skills, and other aspects of education with which physical education is concerned. There is a need for more research on physical education programs as they relate to the learning and growth of children. There is an increased emphasis upon looking to the specialist in physical education for help and advice in planning and conducting the elementary school program. These developments have implications for a sound inservice program to help the classroom teacher do a better job in physical education.

In light of the present status of physical education in the elementary schools of this country, such recommendations as the following should be very carefully considered. Each elementary school should be staffed with a man or woman specialist in physical education. The classroom teacher may find her best contribution to physical education programs in kindergarten to grade three, but to do her best job she needs preparation in this special field and the advice and help of a physical education specialist in her school. Although the classroom teacher can contribute much to the physical education program in grades four to six, factors such as the growth changes and interests taking place in boys and girls and the more specialized program that exists at this level make it imperative to seek the help of a specialist. A specialist possesses the ability, experience, and training required to meet the needs of growing boys and girls as well as gain their respect and interest. Another statement should be made in regard to the elementary school physical education program. The specialist and the classroom teacher should pool and share their experiences so that the most desirable learning experience may be provided children in the physical education program. Each teacher has much to contribute and should be encouraged to do so.

What about self-defense courses?

There are many arguments pro and con concerning self-defense courses for both men and women. On the affirmative side, the arguments include the need to be prepared in case of attack from a robber, assailant, rapist, and molester. The advocates further stress that knowing the various tricks of dirty fighting and self-defense will enable one to defend himself in various kinds of emergency situations. The increase in crime on our streets and in our homes, others say, makes it necessary to know how to deal with such situations if they arise.

Those persons who oppose self-defense courses argue that a little knowledge is a bad thing; a gangster or criminal always has the advantage with weapons he may carry, the surprise of his attack, and his greater strength and experience. Those opposed also indicate that the tricks learned in such courses may be used to the detriment of friends and associates in playful situations. They also stress that the number of instances of attack do not warrant devoting time to such a course.

Furthermore, some persons stress that such courses are entirely opposed to the values that physical education stresses, namely, social effectiveness and sportsmanship. Finally, some educators indicate that the majority of the students exposed to such courses would find such instruction ineffective in warding off assailants. One further objection of some physical educators is that such courses for women should be opposed because they are not feminine in nature.

CLASS MANAGEMENT

Good class management requires planning. Forethought is needed in order to have a group of students act in an orderly manner, accomplish the tasks that have been established, and have an enjoyable, satisfying, and worthwhile experience. The leader who is in charge of a class where these optimum conditions exist has spent considerable time in planning the details of the class from start to finish. Good class management does not just happen. It requires considerable thought, good judgment, and the making of many plans before the class begins.

There are many reasons for good organization. These should be recognized by every teacher and administrator. Some of these are listed below:

1. It gives meaning and purpose to instruction and to the activities.

2. It results in efficiency, the right emphasis, and the best use of the time that is available.

3. It more fully ensures that the needs and interests of the students will be satisfied.

4. It more fully ensures progression and continuity in the program.

5. It provides for measurement and progress toward objectives.

6. It ensures provision for child health and safety.

7. It encourages program adaptations to each individual's needs and interests.

8. It reduces errors and omissions to a minimum.

9. It helps to conserve the instructor's time and strength and aids in giving her or him a sense of accomplishment.

Some guides with which the teacher and administrator should concern themselves are as follows:

1. There should be long-term planning —for the semester and the year, as well as daily, weekly, and seasonal.

2. A definite time schedule should be planned for each period, taking into consideration time to be devoted to showering and dressing, taking roll, class activity, and other essentials.

3. The activity should be carefully planned so that it proceeds with precision and dispatch, with a minimum amount of standing around and a maximum amount of activity for each student.

4. The physical education class period should be regarded primarily as an instructional period. It is not one for free play. However, in order to have sustained interest and as much satisfaction and joy result from the class as possible, there should be provision for using the instruction received in actual activity.

5. There should be a definite system established for such essentials as taking roll, keeping essential records, grading, adhering to policy on uniform, and dressing and showering.

6. Attention should be given to the preparation of materials to be used in class. The teacher should know beforehand the materials to be used, and they should be ready when the class begins.

7. The setting for the class should be safe and healthful. The equipment should be safe and line markings, arrangements for activities, and other essential details attended to.

8. Procedures to be followed in locker room should be established, to provide for traffic, valuables, clothes, and dressing and showering.

9. A procedure should be established for falling in, taking attendance, organizing for activity, and dismissal.

10. The instructor should always use good English and explain things in a simple, clear, and informative manner. During explanations the class should be attentive.

11. The instructor should always be prompt and punctual for class meetings.

12. The instructor should be tactful and considerate of every pupil. Pupils should not be condemned for making mistakes. It should be remembered that an educational situation is a normal and natural setting for mistakes.

13. Pupils should be encouraged and motivated to do their best.

14. All pupils should be treated in the same manner. There should be no favorites.

15. A planned program of measurement and evaluation should be provided to determine progress being made by pupils and the effectiveness of teaching.

16. The instructor and the class should dress in suitable costume.

17. There should be as few rules of behavior as possible, making sure that those that are established are adhered to. Pupils should participate in the establishment of such rules.

18. The instructor should circulate among the entire class, giving help to those who are in need of it. Individual differences should be adequately provided for.

19. The instructor should have a good command of his subject. The values of demonstrations, visual aids, and other techniques to promote learning should be recognized.

20. Desirable attitudes and understandings toward physical fitness, skill learning, good sportsmanship, and other concepts inherent in physical education should be stressed at all times.

21. Standards of achievement and specific goals that are attainable should be established. Pupils' progress should be

recorded so that they know how they are advancing toward these goals.

Some of the factors concerned with class management that deserve special attention are dressing and showering, costume, taking roll, grading, and records. Each of these will be discussed in more detail.

Dressing and showering

Such factors as the age of the student, time allowed, grade participating, and type of activity should be considered in a discussion of dressing and showering for physical education classes.

The problem of showering and dressing is not so pertinent at the lower elementary level where the age of the participants and type of activities as a general rule do not require special costumes and showering. Also the time allotted is too short in many cases. In the upper elementary and at the junior and senior high school and college levels, however, it is a problem.

Physical education, by its very nature, embodies activities that result in considerable running, jumping, throwing, and other vigorous movements. Participation also frequently results in perspiration. In the interests of comfort and good hygiene practices, provisions should be made for special clothing and showering. The unpleasant features of a student's returning to class after participating in physical education activity, with clothes dripping from perspiration and with the accompanying odors, are not in conformance with establishing good habits of personal cleanliness and grooming. Therefore, all schools should make special provisions for places to dress in comfortable uniforms and for showering. Such places should be convenient to the physical education areas, be comfortable, and afford privacy. Although girls are increasingly becoming accustomed to using a gang shower, there are still many who prefer the private cubicles. In the interests of these individuals, such facilities should be

provided. There should also be some type of towel service. In many schools there are facilities for laundering towels that have worked out very satisfactorily.

In order to ensure that a maximum number of pupils take advantage of the facilities for showering and dressing, it is important that proper attitudes and understanding be developed. The right attitudes toward cleanliness, personal grooming, and sanitation should be developed in each individual. If this is done, the right health practices will be followed and the question of whether or not to establish a rigid rule requiring showers will not be necessary. It should be a matter of education rather than one of coercion. In addition, there should be a reasonable time allotted for showering and dressing. This should be kept at a minimum in order to allow a maximum of time for activity, but at the same time adequate time should be allowed to dress and shower.

Costume

There are many reasons for the use of special costumes in physical education classes above the elementary level:

1. It makes for better appearance if an individual is dressed in a costume that fits the activity in which he is engaging.
2. It provides for more comfort and allows for freedom of movement.
3. It is more economical, since it saves on street clothes. If purchased in lots by the school there can be a considerable saving to the student. Those students who cannot afford uniforms should have them provided free of charge.
4. If all students have the same uniform, it aids morale and promotes equality.
5. It is safer without dangling sleeves or wide skirts to cause accidents.

The costumes do not have to be elaborate. For girls they can be simple, washable shorts and blouse or one-piece suits. For boys white cotton jerseys and trunks will suffice. Of course, suitable shoes should also be worn. An important con-

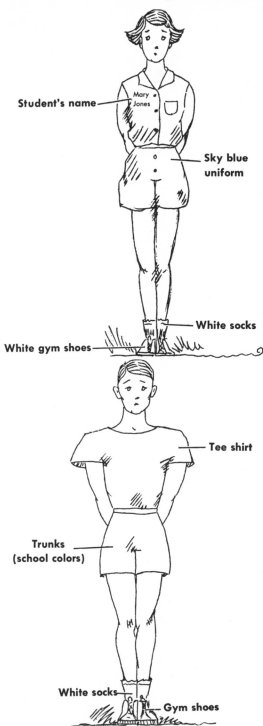

Student's name

Mary Jones

Sky blue uniform

White socks

White gym shoes

Tee shirt

Trunks (school colors)

White socks

Gym shoes

Physical education uniforms for high school girls and boys. (Courtesy Division of Health and Physical Education, Chicago Public Schools, Chicago, Ill.)

sideration is to keep the uniform clean. The instructor should establish a policy on clean uniforms and work diligently toward seeing that hygienic standards are met by all.

Taking roll

There are many methods of taking roll. If a method satisfies the following three criteria, it is usually satisfactory. (1) It is economical of time—roll taking should not consume too much time. It is essential to get into activity as soon as possible, and routine details should be kept to a minimum. (2) It should guarantee accuracy—it is important to know accurately after the class has been held who was present and who was not. This means taking into consideration those who might come to class late or leave early. (3) It should not be complicated. Any system that is used should be very simple and easy to administer.

A number of questions arise in respect to roll taking: Should it be taken on the gymnasium floor or playground or in the swimming pool, shower, or locker room? Or should it be taken on the way to or from the gymnasium or place where the physical education activity is held? When should it be taken? Should it be taken at the beginning of the period; after the class has started, in order to ensure the inclusion of tardy students; or at the end of the period? Who should take it? Should it be taken by the instructor, an assistant instructor, the shower or locker attendant, or squad leader? These questions are pertinent and must be answered by the physical educator in each local situation and in accordance with the influences that play upon the physical education class.

Some of the methods for roll taking that may be used are as follows:

1. *Having numbers on the floor*—each member of the class is assigned a number that he must stand on at the time the signal for "fall in" is given. The person

taking attendance records the numbers that are not covered.

2. *Reciting numbers orally*—each member of the class is assigned a number that he must say out loud at the time the signal for "fall in" is given. The person taking attendance then records the numbers that are not given.

3. *Tag board*—each member of the class has a number that is recorded on a cardboard or metal tag that hangs on a peg on a board in a central place. Each member of the class who is present removes his tag from the board and places it in a box. The person taking attendance records the absentees from the board.

4. *Delaney system*—a special system developed by Delaney involves using a folder with cards that are turned over when a person is absent. It is a cumulative system that records the attendance of pupils over a period of time. There are adaptations of this system that are used elsewhere.

5. *Squad system*—the class is divided into squads and the squad leader takes the roll for his squad and in turn reports to the instructor.

6. *Issuing towels and equipment*—the roll is taken when a towel is issued to each student or when it is turned in, or when a basket with uniform is issued or returned.

7. *Signing a book or register*—students are required to write their names in a book or register at the beginning of the class. Some systems require the writing of a name at the beginning of a period and crossing it out at the end of a period. The

Courtesy Mrs. C. Eaton.

Squad form of attendance taking. (Glastonbury High School, Glastonbury, Conn.)

LEADER																			GRADE		
NAME	AGE	WGT																SQUAD			

Attendance record.

Squad # _____

Dental Note _____

Physical Education Department
Class Data

Class _____

NAME (LAST) FIRST	SEPTEMBER	OCTOBER	NOVEMBER	DECEMBER	JANUARY	MID TERM	FEBRUARY	MARCH	APRIL	MAY	JUNE	FINAL
1												
2												
3												
4												
5												
6												
7												
8												
9												
10												

Cumulative class record.

person taking attendance records the names not entered.

Records

Records are essential in keeping valuable information in regard to pupils' welfare. They also are essential to efficient program planning and administration. They should, however, be kept to a minimum and should be practical and functional. They should not be maintained just as "busy" work and for the sake of filling the files. Instead they should have "use" and a place in the program.

Some of the records should be concerned directly with the welfare of the pupil and others with certain administrative factors.

Those records that concern the welfare of the student are the health records, the cumulative physical education form, anecdotal accounts, attendance reports, grades, and accident reports.

Health records are essential. They contain information on the health examination and other appraisal techniques, health counseling, and any other data pertaining to the student's health.

The cumulative physical education record should start when the student first attends school and contain information about activities engaged in, afterschool play, test, anecdotal accounts, interests, needs, and any other pertinent information that should be known in respect to the student and his participation in the physical education programs.

There should be special records for attendance and grades and any special occurrences that have a bearing on the child and that are not recorded in other records.

If a student is involved in an accident, a full account of the circumstances surrounding the accident should be recorded. Usually special forms are provided for such purposes.*

---

*See Chapters 10 and 14 for more information on accidents.

The records dealing with administrative factors are concerned with general administrative information and equipment records. These would include a list of the year's events: activities; records of teams; play days, sports days, intramurals; events of special interest; techniques utilized that have been helpful; budget information; and any other data that would be helpful in planning for succeeding years. The memory of the human being often fails over a period of time, with the result that many good ideas are lost and many activities and techniques of special value not utilized because they are forgotten.

There should be records in regard to equipment, facilities, and supplies. Such records should show the material needing repair, new materials needed, and also the location of various materials, so that they can easily be found.

There is also a need for records in regard to such items as locker or basket assignments and any other pertinent information that is essential to the efficient running of a physical education program.

PHYSICAL EDUCATION ACTIVITIES

Physical education activities represent the heart of the program. They are the means for accomplishing objectives. They represent the media that attract the attention of the student and through participation aid him in the achievement of life's goals. Because they are so important to the physical education profession, they must be selected with considerable care.

Criteria for selection

1. Activities should be selected in terms of the values they have in achieving the objectives of physical education. This means they would not only possess potentialities for developing physical fitness but also would have implications for developing the intellectual, emotional, and social makeup of the individual.

2. Activities should be interesting and

challenging. They should appeal to the students and present them with situations that challenge their skill and ability. For example, golf always presents the challenge of getting a lower score.

3. They should be adaptable to the growth and developmental needs and interests of children and youth. The needs of individuals vary from age to age. Consequently, activities and the pattern of organization must also change if these needs are to be met. The activity must be suited to the child, not the child to the activity. Wherever possible, students should be allowed some choice in the activities in which they participate.

4. Activities should be modifications of racially old, fundamental movements such as running, jumping, throwing, walking, and climbing.

5. Activities, of course, must be selected in the light of the facilities, supplies, equipment, and other resources available in the school, college, or community. One cannot plan an extensive tennis program if only one court is available.

6. Activities should be selected not only with a view to their present value while the child is in school but also with a view to postschool and adult living. Skills learned during school and college days have potentialities for use throughout life, thus contributing in great measure to enriched living. Patterns for many skills utilized in adult leisure hours are developed while the individual is in the formative years of childhood.

7. Activities must be selected for health and safety values. Such an activity as boxing has been in question as to its effect on the health and the safety of individuals.

8. The local education philosophy, policies, and school or college organization must be taken into consideration.

9. School activities should provide situations that are similar to those children experience in natural play situations outside the school environment.

Washington State College, Pullman, Wash.

10. Activities should provide the student with opportunities for creative self-expression.

11. Activities should be selected which have potentialities to elicit the correct social and moral responses through high-quality leadership.

12. Activities should reflect the democratic way of life.

Classification

One survey* produced a list of physical education activities offered throughout the country, here classified into various categories. These do not necessarily meet criteria that have been listed. They merely indicate current offerings in physical education programs in the United States:

Team games

Baseball	Soccer
Basketball	Softball
Code ball	Speedball
Field hockey (women only)	Touch football
Flag football (men only)	Volleyball
Football (men only)	

Outdoor winter sports

Ice hockey	Snow games
Roller skating	Snowshoeing
Skating	Tobogganing
Skiing	

*Bucher, C. A.: Foundations of physical education, ed. 5, St. Louis, 1968, The C. V. Mosby Co.

Other activities
Camping and outdoor activities
Combatives
Correctives
Fly-tying
Games of low organization
Movement education
Relays
Self-testing activities

Rhythms and dancing

Folk dancing	Square dancing
Gymnastic dancing	Social dancing
Modern dancing	Tap dancing
Rhythms	

Formal activities
Calisthenics
Marching

Water activities

Canoeing	Swimming
Diving	Sailing
Lifesaving	Water games
Rowing	

Gymnastics

Acrobatics	Rope climbing
Apparatus	Stunts
Obstacle course	Trampoline
Pyramid building	Tumbling

Dual and individual sports

Archery	Darts (women only)
Badminton	Deck tennis
Bait and fly casting	Fencing
Bowling	Fishing
Checkers (women only)	Golf

Dual and individual sports—cont'd.

Handball	Skish
Horseback riding	Table tennis
Horseshoes	Tennis
Paddle tennis	Tether ball
Rifle	Track and field
Rope skipping	Wrestling (men only)
Shuffleboard	

LaPorte[*] has compiled a list of physical education activities, together with time allotments, that meet acceptable criteria (Table 7-1).

The state of California lists the following types of activities:

1. Aquatics, where facilities are available
2. Gymnastics and tumbling
3. Individual and dual sports
4. Mechanics of body movement and health aspects of physical activity
5. Rhythms and dance
6. Team sports
7. Combatives for boys[†]

---

[*]LaPorte, op. cit., pp. 28-33.
[†]California State Department of Education, Bureau of Health Education, Physical Education, and Recreation. Letter dated August 14, 1964, from C. Carson Conrad, Chief, Bureau of Health Education, Physical Education, and Recreation, Sacramento, Calif.

Table 7-1. List of physical education activities[*]

A. Primary level (grades 1 to 3)	
1. Rhythmical activities	25%
2. Fundamental rhythms	20%
3. Hunting games	20%
4. Relays	15%
5. Stunts and self-testing activities	10%
6. Athletic games of low organization	10%
	100%
B. Elementary level (grades 4 to 6)	
1. Athletic games of low organization	25%
2. Rhythmical activities	30%
3. Hunting games	15%
4. Individual athletic event (self-testing)	10%
5. Relays	10%
6. Tumbling stunts	10%
	100%

[*]From LaPorte, W. R.: The physical education curriculum (a national program), ed. 6, Los Angeles, 1955, University of Southern California Press, pp. 28-33.

Table 7-1. List of physical education activities—cont'd

C. Junior high school (grades 7 to 9) and senior high school (grades 10 to 12)

	Junior high school (elementary)		Senior high school (advanced)	
	Boys (weeks)	Girls (weeks)	Boys (weeks)	Girls (weeks)
1. **Aquatics**				
Swimming, diving, lifesaving	18	18	18	18
2. **Dancing**				
Folk, square, tap, modern (girls)	12	18	12	18
3. **Team sports**				
A. Court and diamond games Volleyball, softball, basketball, nine-court basketball (junior high school girls)	18	18	18	18
B. Field sports				
Soccer, speedball, touch football (boys), field ball (junior high girls), field hockey (senior high girls)	18	12	18	12
4. **Gymnastics**				
Tumbling, pyramids, apparatus, relays, stunts, body mechanics, and posture exercises	12	12	12	12
5. **Individual and dual sports**				
Tennis, badminton, handball, golf, or archery	18	18	18	18
Additional sports from following: boating and canoeing, bowling, hiking and camping, horseshoes, fencing, fly and bait casting, paddle tennis, riding, skating, snowshoeing, squash, table tennis, trampoline, wrestling	12	12	12	12
	Total of 108 weeks		Total of 108 weeks	

D. College (grades 13 to 16) (Each activity is a one-semester course of an advanced type.)

1. Apparatus
2. Archery
3. Badminton
4. Diving
5. Fencing
6. Folk dancing
7. Golf
8. Handball
9. Lifesaving
10. Modern dance (creative, interpretive)
11. Social dancing
12. Social (recreational) games
13. Squash (or squash racquets)
14. Swimming
15. Tap and clog dancing
16. Tennis
17. Tumbling
18. Wrestling
19. Team games (when needed)
20. Specialties (winter activities, etc., when needed)
21. Restricted and remedial for subnormal cases

Coeducational activities

The need for more coeducational activity is being recognized. Past history shows that activities for boys and girls have been combined at the lower elementary levels but at the upper elementary, secondary, and college levels they have been separated. A common sight on college campuses and even at the secondary level is separate sets of facilities for the men and women or boys and girls. In the light of education objectives, this does not seem to be in the interests of what the profession is striving to attain in the schools.

Men and women are continually together in work, home, social, and other situations throughout life. If they are to adjust properly in such situations, it is essential that attention be given to this matter in their childhood and youth years. Our country is faced with the problems of increased divorce rates and disintegration of family life. Individuals who have not had the opportunity to play, work, and socialize with the opposite sex in childhood and youth often find it difficult to adjust satisfactorily when they become adults. Furthermore, if family life is to be a happy experience, the various members of the families should be attuned to such items as the others' interests, temperaments, likes, dislikes, and habits. Such adjustment is obtained only through constant association in a variety of situations. The physical education program should encourage and provide for such associations, rather than be indifferent or oppose such a natural phenomenon. The contributions this specialized field can make to such an objective are very great and should be utilized to the fullest.

PROGRAMS

Many aspects of the elementary, junior high, senior high, and college physical education basic instructional programs have already been discussed. This information will not be repeated. Instead, certain administrative guides are suggested for each level to aid the administrator, teacher, or

---

Co-Educational P. E.

Last Name	First Name	Period	Section	Standing

INDICATE YOUR CHOICE (1 for first, 2 for second, etc.)

10th Grade	11th Grade	12th Grade
	Badm't'n & P'g P'g - ____	Archery - - - - ____
Dancing - - - - ____	Dancing - - - - ____	Badm't'n & P'g P'g - ____
Sports - - - - ____	Sports - - - - ____	Dancing - - - - ____
____ - - - ____	____ - - - ____	Sports - - - - ____
____ - - - ____	____ - - - ____	Tennis - - - - ____
		____ - - - - ____

Coeducational physical education. (From Bucher, C. A., Koenig, C. R., and Barnhard, M.: Methods and materials for secondary school physical education, ed. 3, St. Louis, 1970, The C. V. Mosby Co.)

other interested person in the conduct of a physical education program.

Program for kindergarten through grade six

The various aspects of the physical education program for elementary school, including characteristics of children at various ages, opportunities they need, and activities that meet these needs and characteristics, were developed by a group of experts at the National Conference on Physical Education for Children of Elementary School Age. The following information has been taken from their report because of its value to all persons interested in elementary school physical education. *Of course, the discussion of movement education recorded earlier in this chapter indicates a vital and important emphasis on elementary school physical education programs.*

PROGRAM*

Growth is a continuous process—an emerging—an unfolding. At no time does a child abruptly

*Report of National Conference of Physical Education for Children of Elementary School Age: Physical education for children of elementary school age, Chicago, 1951, The Athletic Institute, Inc.

complete a particular stage of development and begin the next. Neither is there a time when all children in a group are at exactly the same stage of growth.

Any classification into groups along the route of growth is artificial. The following chart [Tables 7-2 and 7-3 on pp. 160 and 161] is merely a device to help give a picture of activities that seem to suit the changing needs of children. The subdivision and classifications used serve as convenient labels for periods of growth through which children gradually move, each child holding to a path that is his alone.

Program for grades seven and eight

Facilities, time, pupils, and teacher load are some of the factors that will determine the basic physical education instructional program for grades seven and eight. The absence or presence of a swimming pool, for example, would influence the type of program offered.

Boys and girls in grades seven and eight are in a period of rapid physical growth with awkwardness and lack of coordination frequently in evidence. Muscles, bones, heart, and lungs are experiencing the growth spurt. Boys surpass girls in strength and speed, and interests in different types of physical activities are common. There is keen interest in competitive activities, and this motivating factor may create the desire to want to continue par-

Text continued on p. 166.

There is need for coeducational activity. (Wisconsin State College, La Crosse, Wis.)

Table 7-2. Early childhood—5 to 8 years of age—kindergarten through third grade[*]

What they are like	What they need OPPORTUNITIES	What to do
Their large muscles (trunk, legs, and arms) are more developed than the smaller muscles (hands and feet)	To experience many kinds of vigorous activities that involve many parts of the body To engage in many developmental activities for small muscles	Activities such as hanging, running, jumping, climbing, dodging, or throwing at an object. Beanbag Toss, Jacks, Bouncing Balls, Hopscotch, O'Leary
They have a short attention span	To engage in many activities of short duration	Choice of activity where a child can change frequently, and activities that can be started quickly, such as Magic Carpet, Pincho, Hill Dill, and stunts
They are individualistic and possessive	To play alone and with small groups To play as an individual in larger groups	Individual activities, such as throwing, catching, bouncing, kicking, climbing, stunts, running, hopping, skipping, building blocks, jumping. Dance activities which allow for expression of self, such as clowns, aviators, firemen, tops, aeroplanes. Activities that may use small numbers of children, such as Stride Ball, Cat and Rat, Hill Dill, Cowboys and Indians, Tag. Singing games such as Looby Loo, Bluebird, Sing a Song of Sixpence
They are dramatic, imaginative, and imitative	To create and explore To identify themselves with people and things	Invent dance and game activities, such as Cowboys, Circus, Christmas toys; work activities such as pounding, sawing, raking, and hauling. Other play activities: farmers, postmen, grocers, elevators, bicycles, leaves, scarecrows
They are active, energetic, and responsive to rhythmic sounds	To respond to rhythmic sounds such as drums, rattles, voice and nursery rhythms, songs, and music	Running, skipping, walking, jumping, galloping, dodging, swimming. Singing and folk games such as Oats, Peas, Beans, and Barley Grow; Farmer in the Dell; Dixie Polka
They are curious and want to find out things	To explore and handle materials with many types of play	Using materials such as balls, ropes, stilts, beanbags, bars, ladders, trees, blocks. Games and activities such as hiking, Run-Sheep-Run, Huckle-Buckle, Bean-stalk
They want chances to act on their own and are annoyed at conformity	To make choices, to help make rules, to share and evaluate group experiences	Variety of activities with minimum of rules, such as Center Base, Exchange, Midnight, and Red Light. Make-up activities, dances, and games
They are continuing to broaden social contacts or relationships	To cooperate in play and dance, to organize many of their own groups	Group games, such as simple forms of Dodge Ball, Kickball. Dance and rhythmic activities, such as Gustaf's Skoal, Dance of Greeting, Bow Balinda
They seem to be in perpetual motion	To play many types of vigorous activities	Running, jumping, skipping, galloping, rolling

[*]From Report of National Conference on Physical Education for Children of Elementary School Age: Physical education for children of elementary school age, Chicago, 1951, The Athletic Institute, Inc.

Table 7-3. Middle childhood—9 to 11 years of age—fourth through sixth grades*

What they are like	What they need OPPORTUNITIES	What to do
They grow steadily in muscles, bone, heart, and lungs	To engage in strenuous activity that regularly taxes these organs to the limits of healthy fatigue	Running, jumping, climbing, and hard play
They enjoy rough and tumble activities	To participate in activities that use the elements of roughness	Bumping, pushing, contact activities such as King of the Ring, Poison Pen, Indian Wrestle, Hand Wrestle, Beater Goes 'Round
Sex differences begin to appear with girls taller and more mature than boys. Sex antagonisms may appear	To enjoy their roles as boys and girls, to have wholesome boy-girl relationships in activities and to participate separately for some activities	Activities such as folk dances, mixers, squares, modern Brothers and Sisters, Last Couple Out. Group games such as Volleyball type games, Newcomb or Fist Ball, Softball. Others may be enjoyed separately or together
They respond differently in varying situations	To participate in wide range of activities and organizations using many kinds of materials	Individual, dual, or small and large group activities such as swimming, tumbling, stilts, track, catch, handball, relays, Crows and Cranes, Crackers, Bombardment; folk dances, mixers, and simple square dances such as Csebogar, Captain Jinks, Life on the Ocean Wave
They have a strong sense of rivalry and crave recognition	To succeed in activities that stress cooperative play along with activities that give individual satisfaction	Self-testing activities such as track events, stunts, chinning, sit-ups, push-ups, ball-throwing, for distance and accuracy. Group and team play such as Newcomb, Kickball, Circle or Square Soccer, End Ball, Club Snatch, Progressive Dodge Ball
They may show increasing independence and desire to help	To plan, lead, and check progress	Assist with officiating, serve as squad leaders, act as scorers, help with equipment, elect captains, help with younger children and each other
They want to be liked by their own classmates, to belong. They have a strong loyalty to teams, groups, or "gangs"	To belong to groups, to be on many kinds of teams To engage in a wide range of activities	Group games such as Bounce Volleyball, Line Soccer, Keep Away, Hit Pin Kickball, Net Ball. Partner play such as Deck Tennis (Ring Toss), Tennis, Aerial Darts, Horseshoes
They want approval, but not at the expense of their group relationships	To gain respect and approval of others	Participate in activities in which they achieve in the eyes of their group

*From Report of National Conference on Physical Education for Children of Elementary School Age. Physical education for children of elementary school age, Chicago, 1951, The Athletic Institute, Inc.

Table 7-4. Later childhood—early adolescence—12 to 13 years of age—seventh and eighth grades*

What they are like	What they need OPPORTUNITIES	What to do
This is a period of rapid physical growth that is frequently uneven in various parts of the body. Awkwardness and inability to coordinate sometimes occur	To develop skill and coordination and to take part in activities that do not call attention to their awkwardness or put them in embarrassing situations	Skills in various activities such at batting, throwing, catching, kicking, dribbling, and serving, as used in—Softball, Soccer, Volleyball, Basketball. Skills in body controls as—how to walk, to run, to stand, to sit, to relax. Individual activities as—rope jumping, horseshoes, target throw, jumping, skating, hiking, skiing, and swimming
Muscles, heart, lungs, and bones share liberally in the growth spurt	Vigorous activity to stimulate each of these organs to attain its fullest development	Activities conducted as vigorously as possible with respect for individual reaction
Boys and girls are showing differences in interests and in abilities. Boys tend to surpass girls in strength and speed; girls are usually more interested in dance forms than boys are	To participate in some activities in separate groups and some together. For girls to have more dance in program than boys have	Activities recommended in groupings as follows:

	Boys alone	Girls alone	Both together
Group sports			
Soccer	Yes	Yes	No
Touch football	Yes	No	No
Softball	Yes	Yes	Yes
Basketball	Yes	Yes	No
Volleyball	Yes	Yes	Yes
Individual, dual, and group sports			
Track	Yes	Yes	No
Badminton	Yes	Yes	Yes
Tennis	Yes	Yes	Yes
Swimming	Yes	Yes	Yes
Outing activities	Yes	Yes	Yes
Formal dancing			
Square	Yes	Yes	Yes, preferably
Social	Yes	Yes	Yes, preferably
Creative	Yes	Yes	Yes, preferably
Folk	Yes	Yes	Yes, preferably

What they are like	What they need OPPORTUNITIES	What to do
Interest in members of one's own sex broadens to include an interest in members of the opposite sex	To have coeducational activities in small and large groups	Activities such as Square, Social, and Creative Dance, Tennis, Swimming, and Outing Activities, Volleyball, Table Tennis, Badminton
Great loyalty to groups as clubs, gangs, and teams, and there is a keen desire for group acceptance	To belong to various teams and to plan and develop their own groups	Many teams in all team games such as class teams, homeroom, club, counting off for teams and voting for captains who choose teams

*From Report of National Conference on Physical Education for Children of Elementary School Age: Physical education for children of elementary school age, Chicago, 1951, The Athletic Institute, Inc.

Table 7-4. Later childhood—early adolescence—12 to 13 years of age—seventh and eighth grades—cont'd

What they are like	What they need OPPORTUNITIES	What to do
Strong desire for individual recognition and the urge to be free of adult restrictions	To take part in activities of their own choosing, to be leaders and captains of groups, to create and modify games, and to evaluate progress	Squad-leader directed activities as: a. Testing skills—sit up, push-up b. Officiating in games c. Assigning positions on teams
Emotions are easily aroused and swayed	To be frequently in situations requiring practice of fair play, when winning or losing	Wide variety of activities requiring individual decisions and scoring as in: a. High and broad jumps (boys only) b. Ball-throwing events c. Running against time d. Stunts and tumbling, as jump stick, Indian wrestle, pull-up, sit-up Officiating at games as umpiring in Softball, timing in races and relays
The interest span lengthens. They may want to continue in activities beyond fatigue to exhaustion	To participate in activities that are modified to overcome fatiguing factors as time, speed, distance, and pressures to win. To learn when to stop	Games that involve skills of major sports as: Line Soccer (Soccer), Keep Away (Basketball), End Ball (Basketball), Touch Football (Football), Newcomb (Volleyball), Long Base (Softball) Modifications of standard games involve changing fatiguing factors, as: a. Shortening playing periods in vigorous sports: shorter halves in soccer, shorter quarters in basketball b. Frequent time-outs c. Restricting space: Three-Court Soccer, Six-Court Basketball, One-Basket Basketball
There is a keen interest in competitive activities	To compete in a variety of activities that involve a wide range of skills and organization	Self-testing types with competition against self as tumbling, track events. Skill tests as throwing for baskets, pitching at a target. Games not highly organized as Bombardment, End Ball, Ten Trips, Kick Over, Fist Ball
The enjoyment of organized team sports is keen	To give every boy and girl an opportunity to be a participating member on the types of teams that challenge his interest and ability	Wide variety of team sports such as Soccer, Volleyball, Softball, Basketball, Field Ball. Many teams in each sport organized on such bases as skill and ability, age-height-weight, squads

Table 7-5. Suggested time allotment for a physical program, grade seven*†

	Periods per year	
	Boys	Girls
Conditioning and body mechanics		
Calisthenics, fundamental movement, and posture training	3	5
Aquatics		
Swimming, diving, and water safety	35	35
Lifesaving, skin and scuba diving		
Self-testing activities		
Gymnastics		
Tumbling, stunts, and apparatus	10	15
Track and field	10	15
Weight training	10	
Games		
Group games	4	8
Individual and dual sports		
Archery, horseshoes, fly and bait casting	10	10
Badminton, table tennis, shuffleboard, and quoits	10	10
Tennis and golf	10	10
Bowling, deck tennis, and fencing	4	4
Ice skating and skiing	2	2
Wrestling	8	
Team sports		
Soccer	5	5
Speedaway or speedball	5	5
Softball	7	7
Touch football	10	
Basketball	10	10
Volleyball	5	7
Rhythms, marching, and dancing	10	20
Evaluation, skill, and knowledge tests	7	7
Physical fitness tests	5	5
Total	180	180

*From University of the State of New York, The State Education Department, Bureau of Secondary Curriculum Development: Physical education in the secondary schools, Curriculum Guide, Albany, 1964, State Department of Education, pp. 50-51.

†The suggested number of periods assume a daily schedule. If less than a daily period or fewer facilities are available, appropriate adjustments in the schedule will be necessary.

Table 7-6. Suggested time allotment for a physical education program, grade eight*†

	Periods per year	
	Boys	Girls
Conditioning and body mechanics		
Calisthenics, fundamental movement, and posture training	3	5
Aquatics		
Swimming, diving, and water safety	35	35
Lifesaving, skin and scuba diving		
Self-testing activities		
Gymnastics		
Tumbling, stunts, and apparatus	10	20
Track and field	15	10
Weight training	10	
Games		
Group games	2	4
Individual and dual sports		
Archery, horseshoes, fly and bait casting	10	5
Tennis and golf		5
Bowling and deck tennis		5
Ice skating and skiing		5
Wrestling	15	
Team sports		
Soccer	9	10
Speedaway	5	10
Softball	5	10
Touch football	15	
Basketball	15	10
Volleyball	10	15
Rhythms, marching, and dancing	10	20
Evaluation, skill, and knowledge tests	6	6
Physical fitness tests	5	5
Total	180	180

*From University of the State of New York, The State Education Department, Bureau of Secondary Curriculum Development: Physical education in the secondary schools, Curriculum Guide, Albany, 1964, State Department of Education, pp. 50-51.

†The suggested number of periods assume a daily schedule. If less than a daily period or fewer facilities are available, appropriate adjustments in the schedule will be necessary.

ticipating beyond fatigue to exhaustion. The enjoyment of organized sports is common. The students develop loyalty to groups, have a desire for peer-group approval, and a strong desire for recognition. Emotions are easily aroused.

Boys and girls in the seventh and eighth grades need to have opportunities to participate in activities in which they can experience success—activities that do not emphasize their awkwardness, that provide vigorous activity, that provide for group participation, and that challenge their interest and physical capabilities.

A description of children's characteristics and needs at the seventh and eighth grade levels together with physical education activities suited to these needs is taken from the report of the National Conference on Physical Education (Table 7-4).

The State Department of Education for New York State* has suggested programs for grades seven and eight together with suggested time allotments (Tables 7-5 and 7-6).

Program for grades nine through twelve

A discussion of characteristics and the physical education program for youth 14 through 17 years of age, or grades nine through twelve, is included here.

During this period students display marked characteristics in regard to physical growth and development. In respect to skeletal growth, the girls are about 2 years ahead of the boys. Some girls reach adult height at about 14 years, whereas others continue to grow for several years beyond this age. In the case of boys, some attain adult height at about 16 years and others continue their growth to 20 years or later.

Bone growth is completed with sexual maturity.

In regard to muscular development, the "awkward age" is ending and there is a definite improvement in coordination. The muscles of boys are becoming hard and firm whereas those of girls remain softer. Posture is improving and control and grace are in evidence, especially by those who have participated in rhythmic activities such as dancing, swimming, and sports.

In respect to organic development, the heart increases in size, with a question being raised as to strenuous competitive sports, since the heart and arteries may be disproportionate in size. The puberty cycle is completed in the majority of cases. There may be a period of glandular instability with fluctuations in respect to energy level. Some characteristic ailments at this age would include headache, nosebleed, nervousness, palpitation, and acne.

The characteristics of the secondary school students are many. The boy or girl of 14 through 17 may have reached physiologic adulthood but needs many new experiences for fuller development. He is emotional and is seeking a feeling of belonging in the life around him. This attempt to adjust may result in some emotional instability. The desire to conform to the standards of the "gang" or group with whom he is closely associated is often greater than the desire to conform to adult standards. However, there are cases of "hero worship," and in such cases adults have considerable influence on youth. This age group is capable of competing in more highly organized games. Groups and "cliques" evolve in accordance with interests and physical maturation. Boys as a rule like to be regarded as big, strong, and healthy, whereas girls desire to be attractive. In both sexes there is interest and an attempt to be physically attractive. As a result, good grooming increases. Appetite is good at this age. Various sexual manifestations during this age may cause undue

*From University of the State of New York, The State Education Department, Bureau of Secondary Curriculum Development: Physical education in the secondary schools, Curriculum Guide, Albany, 1964, State Department of Education, pp. 50-51.

self-consciousness. Since girls mature before boys, girls are, as a rule, more interested in boys than boys are in girls.

The needs of youth at these ages are many. There is a need for adult guidance, which should allow for considerable freedom and choice on the part of youth. Family life is important and plays a steadying influence on the child at a time when life is becoming more and more complex. There is a need for wholesome activity and experiences where excess emotions and energy can be properly channeled. Certain physical education activities require separate participation on the part of boys and girls. However, there is a need for many experiences where boys and girls play together. Coeducational activities should be adapted to both sexes so that no physiologic or other harm results. Social dancing is very important at this level. Also, at this age students are interested and receive much satisfaction from sports. Although individual differences determine the amount of sleep needed, most can profit from 8 to 10 hours. There is need for a planned after-school program that is adapted to the needs of youth and that includes active recreation as well as the manipulative or contemplative activities.

The types of activities that will best meet the needs of the secondary school student should be wide and varied. Team games of high organization occupy an increasingly important place at the junior high and even more at the senior high school level. The junior high and early senior high school programs should be mainly exploratory in nature, offering a wide variety of activities with the team games modified in nature and presented in the form of lead-up activities. Toward the end of the senior high school period there should be opportunity to select and specialize in certain activities that will have a carryover value after formal education ceases. Furthermore, many of the team games and other activities are offered in a more intensive manner

and in larger blocks of time as one approaches the terminal point of the secondary school. This allows for greater acquisition of skill in selected activities.

As a general rule, boys and girls at the secondary level, including both junior and senior high, can profit greatly from rhythmic activities such as square, folk, and social dancing; team sports such as soccer, field hockey, softball, baseball, touch football, volleyball, and speedball; individual activities such as track and field, tennis, paddle tennis, badminton, hiking, handball, bowling, archery, and fly casting; many forms of gymnastics such as tumbling, stunts, and apparatus activities; and various forms of games and relays. These activities will comprise the major portion of the program at the secondary level. Of course the activities would be adapted to boys and to girls as they are played separately or on a coeducational basis.

A sample physical education program* for ninth-grade girls meeting twice weekly is presented in Table 7-7. The program indicates the types of activities that help to meet the objectives sought.

Program for colleges and universities

A recent survey of 406 colleges and universities indicated the following statistics in regard to the required physical education program in these institutions:

1. Of the 406 colleges and universities, 89.6% have required men's physical education programs.
2. A uniform requirement was maintained in physical education for all departments within the college or university in 90.2% of the institutions surveyed.
3. Most colleges and universities require 2 years of physical education.
4. Credit for physical education, which is applied toward graduation, is given in 81% of the institutions surveyed.

---

*Bucher, C. A., Koenig, C., and Barnhard, M.: Methods and materials for secondary school physical education, ed. 3, St. Louis, 1970, The C. V. Mosby Co.

Table 7-7. Physical education program for girls in grade nine*

Month and number of weeks		Physical fitness	Physical skills	Knowledge and appreciation	Social development
Sept.	3	Posture Strength	Archery Stance	Archery Etiquette	Individual responsibilities in class
Oct.	4	Endurance Speed	Technique Hockey	Safety Hockey	Program planning Group cooperation

Nov.	1	Agility
		Accuracy
		Balance
			Dribble
			Drive
			Dodge
			Lunge
			Tackle
				History
				Rules
				Offensive and
				  defensive
				  strategies
					Teamwork

Total	8		Test	Test	
Nov.	3	Posture Balance	Badminton Serve	Badminton Etiquette	Partnership etiquette

Dec.	3	Agility
		Accuracy
			Forehand
			Backhand
			Volleyball
			Single tap
			Serve
			Smash
			Test
				Doubles rules
				Volleyball
				History
				Etiquette
				Offensive and
				  defensive
				  strategies
				Rules
				Rotation
					Improved group
					relationships and
					teamwork

Total	6			Test	
Jan.	4	Endurance Speed	Basketball Passes	Basketball History	Teamwork New groups

Feb.	2	Accuracy
		Balance
		Agility
			Dribble
			Pivot
			Foul-shooting
			Goal-shooting
			Test
				Offensive and
				  defensive
				  strategies
				Rules
				Notebook
					Leadership

Total	6			Test	
Feb.	2	Strength Endurance	Modern dance Types of movement	Modern dance History	Group planning Creativity
Mar.	3	Balance Agility Posture Poise Grace	Axial Swing Sustained Percussive Locomotor Leaps Skips	Noted performers Values Purposes Test	Cooperation Leadership
Total	5		Turns		

Apr.	4	Strength
		Endurance
		Balance
		Agility
		Posture
			Stunts
			Tumbling
			Apparatus
			Parallel bars
			High bar
			Ladder
			Rings
				Values of
				  training
				Olympic
				  performers
				Safety
				  procedures
				Spotting
					Safety
					  consciousness
					Leadership
					Group planning
					Cooperation

Total	4		Test		

*From Bucher, C. A., Koenig, C., and Barnhard, M.: Methods and materials for secondary school physical education, ed. 3, St. Louis, 1970, The C. V. Mosby Co.

Table 7-7. Physical education program for girls in grade nine—cont'd

Month and number of weeks		Physical fitness	Physical skills	Knowledge and appreciation	Social development
May	4	Strength	Tennis	Tennis	Partnership
		Endurance	Forehand	History	etiquette
June	3	Agility	Backhand	Etiquette	New groups
		Speed	Serve	Doubles rules	Teamwork
		Accuracy	Volley		Leadership
			Softball	Softball	Cooperation
			Base-playing	History	
			Base-running	Rules	
			Batting	Scoring	
			Bunting	Base-playing	
			Catching	Test	
			Throwing		
			Fielding		
Total	7		Test		

5. Most colleges and universities permit the election of physical education courses for credit over and above the institution requirement.
6. The most common formula applied in these colleges and universities is to give one-half credit for each hour of participation in physical education.
7. Physical education grades were averaged together with the student's point-hour grade ration in 71.8% of the institutions surveyed.
8. Students are excused from participation in physical education for such reasons as medical, varsity athletics, ROTC, and marching band.
9. Swimming was the activity most frequently required of all students.
10. Of the 406 colleges and universities, 87.5% administer skill tests or physical performance tests.
11. In the last 5 years the requirement for physical education remained the same in 70.7% of the colleges, increased in 18.2%, and decreased in 10.9%.
12. In the last 5 years the physical education program increased its emphasis on physical fitness activities in 33% of the institutions, on leisure time activities in 15.2% of the institutions, and remained about the same in 51.1% of the institutions.*

Oxendine* conducted a more recent survey on the status of required physical education in 723 colleges and universities in the United States. His survey indicated that 87% of these institutions require physical education for all students, with another 7% having a requirement for students in certain departments or schools. Two-thirds of the institutions that require physical education indicate that the requirement is for a 2-year period. Oxendine's survey also indicated that programs of physical education are on a sounder academic basis in large institutions than in small ones, in public compared to private institutions, and in coeducational as compared to noncoeducational institutions. Finally, Oxendine's survey indicated the trends toward more emphasis on "recreation" and "fitness" activities and on coeducational classes. There is less emphasis on team sports and all-male or all-female classes.

The college and university physical education program is the terminal point for

*Carra, L. D., Kent State University, letter dated Nov. 25, 1964.

*Oxendine, J. B.: Status of required physical education programs in colleges and universities, Journal of Health, Physical Education, and Recreation **40**:32, 1969.

formal physical education in the lives of many students. The age range of individuals in colleges and universities is very wide, incorporating those as young as 16 and as old as 60. However, most college students are in their late teens or early twenties. These individuals have matured in many ways. They are entering the period of greatest physical efficiency. They have developed the various organic systems of the body. They possess a high degree of strength, stamina, and coordination. In this respect the program does not have to be restricted for the average college population. College and university students have many interests. They want to prepare themselves adequately for certain vocations. They desire to be a success in their chosen fields of work. Such an objective offers potentialities for the physical education teacher who can show how the outcomes derived from the physical education program can contribute to success in their work. College students are interested in the opposite sex and are beginning to look for a marital partner. They want to develop socially. This has implications for a broad coeducational program. They are interested in developing skills that they can use throughout life and from which they will obtain a great deal of enjoyment.

The physical education program at the college and university level should ensure that these students leave school with skills in their possession for future participation in many enjoyable and worthwhile sports activities. The emphasis should be on leisure-time or recreational skills. If a student possesses sufficient skill in swimming, badminton, golf, or tennis, for example, when he or she leaves school, the chances are that he will engage in such activities throughout adult years. If the physical education program does not see that such skills are developed, the individual may never have another opportunity to acquire them. This responsibility rests heavily upon the physical educator's shoulders.

In formulating a program at the college and university level one needs to remember that many students enter with limited activity backgrounds. Therefore, the program should be broad and varied at the start, with opportunities to elect activities later. There should be considerable opportunity for instruction and practice in those activities in which a student desires to specialize. As much individual attention as possible should be given to ensure the necessary development of skill.

Most colleges offer physical education twice a week for 2 years. There are others, however, where the requirement is for 1, 3, or 4 years' duration. It would seem that the longer the requirement, the greater would be the assurance that the individual would leave school with the necessary skills. Some colleges and universities require only that the allotted time be put in, while others state that certain standards of achievement must be met. Both requirements are important if the objectives of physical education are to be realized. It would seem that sports skills are as important to the development of the "whole" individual as being able to compute some mathematical problem, operate a typewriter, or use a slide rule.

The program of activities should be based on the interests and needs of students and the facilities and staff available. There is an important place for coeducation at the college level in such activities as tennis, dancing, swimming, badminton, volleyball, and golf. Some of the experiences that might be included in the women's program are as follows: team activities —field hockey, soccer, speedball, basketball, softball, and fieldball; aquatics in all forms; dancing—folk, square, social, and modern; individual activities—bowling, table tennis, skating, badminton, archery, tennis, deck tennis, horseback riding, and hiking; formal activities—tumbling and stunts; and camping activities. Some of the activities that have been popular in men's programs are

Coeducational physical education. (Washington State College, Pullman, Wash.)

team activities—basketball, touch football, softball, volleyball, soccer, and speedball; aquatics in all forms; dancing—folk, square, and social; individual activities—skating, fishing, squash, badminton, tennis, golf, bowling, archery, hiking, horseshoes, handball, fencing, and wrestling; formal activities—tumbling and apparatus work; and camping activities.

A publication of the President's Council on Physical Fitness and Sports entitled *Fitness for Leadership** contains many suggestions for college and university programs in physical education.

Some of the pertinent suggestions for physical education programs in this report include the recommendation that physical achievement tests should be utilized to assess student needs and assure progress. Special help and prescribed programs should be offered to help physically under-

developed students. Another suggestion is to institute a requirement that would make it necessary for all students to demonstrate and develop proficiency in swimming, conditioning exercises, and several other physical activities.

Special considerations for junior college physical education programs

The growth of the 2-year college in recent years has been phenomenal. Approximately one and one-half million students are enrolled in about 900 junior colleges from coast to coast. In many respects the activities for the 2-year college are the same as those for the 4-year institution. However, since approximately 70% of community college students will terminate their education after 2 years of study, there is a need to provide skills and interests to enrich their leisure and stimulate a desire to keep themselves fit throughout their lifetimes.

Most of the 2-year colleges require students to take physical education both

---

*President's Council on Physical Fitness and Sports: Fitness for leadership, Washington, D. C., 1964, U. S. Government Printing Office.

Table 7-8. Coeducational carryover physical activities offered in California junior colleges[*]

Activity	Number of schools in which taught	Rank	Offered	Rank
Aquatics	16	4	109	3
Archery	20	2	87	4
Badminton	15	5-6-7	74	5
Bowling	10	8	38	8
Fencing	4	12	10	12
Folk and square dance	9	9-10	17	10
Golf	21	1	132	2
Ice skating	1	13-14	6	13
Modern dance	8	11	15	11
Sailing	1	13-14	3	14
Social dance	15	5-6-7	44	7
Tennis	18	3	157	1
Tumbling, gymnastics, and trampoline	9	9-10	22	9
Volleyball	15	5-6-7	73	6

[*]Eiland, H. J.: Emphasis in junior college physical education programs should be on carryover physical recreation activities, Journal of Health, Physical Education, and Recreation 36:35, 1965.

years. Most of the programs require 2 hours each week and stress the successful completion of the service program as a requirement for graduation.

The California 2-year colleges take into consideration their responsibility for a wide variety of coeducational carryover physical activities. Table 7-8 shows information accumulated from the spring schedules of twenty-two junior colleges in California.

INTERRELATIONSHIPS OF ELEMENTARY, SECONDARY, AND COLLEGE AND UNIVERSITY PROGRAMS

Provision should be made for close interrelationships of the physical education programs at the elementary, secondary, and college levels. Continuity and progression should mark the program from the time the student enters school until he or she graduates. Overall planning is essential to guarantee that duplication of effort, waste of time, omissions, and shortages do not occur in respect to the goal of ensuring

that each student become physically educated.

Continuity and progress do not exist today in many of the school systems of the United States. To a great degree each institutional level is autonomous, setting up its own program irrespective of the other levels and with little regard as to what has preceded and what will follow. Many are concerned only with their own little niche and not with the overall program. If the focus of attention is on the student—the consumer of the product—then it would seem that program planning would provide the student with a continuous program, developed in the light of his needs and interests, from the time he starts school until the time he finishes. There should also be consideration given to adult years. Directors of physical education for the entire community should shoulder this responsibility and ensure that such a program exists. Some communities like Great Neck, Long Island, and Long Beach, California, have directors over all the school and community physical education and recreation programs. This offers many possibilities for ensuring a continuous program for community residents "from the cradle to the grave."

A system of standardized and meaningful record keeping is essential to ensure continuity and progression. Regardless of which elementary or secondary school the student attends, his records should follow him when he passes on to the next level. These records would show the activities engaged in by the student, progress made, weaknesses, measurement and evaluation results, notations on conferences and counseling, and any other pertinent information that would be helpful in planning a purposeful physical education program.

Good interrelationships among the various institutional levels are a must if physical education is to provide the best type of program possible in the light of the needs and interests of those they serve.

PROVIDING FOR THE HEALTH OF THE STUDENT

Every effort must be put forth by the physical education staff to safeguard the health of all individuals in the program. To accomplish this objective satisfactorily there must be a close working relationship with staff members in the school health program. Every child should have periodic health examinations with the results of these examinations scrutinized very carefully by the physical educator. Frequent conferences should be held with the school physician. A physical education program must be adapted to the needs and interests of each student. The physical educator must assume responsibility for health guidance and health supervision in the activities over which he is responsible. The school physician should be consulted when students return after periods of illness, when accidents occur, when students want excuses from the program, and at any other time that qualified advice is needed.

Special precautions must be taken to make activity safe for the student. The desire to win in sports competition must not be used to exploit a student's health. If a disagreement arises, the physician's decision should be final. These and many other phases of the physical education department's interrelationship with the school health program must be carefully attended to.

CRITERIA FOR EVALUATING PHYSICAL EDUCATION ACTIVITY CLASSES

Piscopo has developed the accompanying checklist for evaluating physical education activity classes. It should help in better understanding the essentials of this phase of the physical education program.

CRITERIA FOR EVALUATING PHYSICAL EDUCATION ACTIVITY CLASSES*

	Poor (1)	Fair (2)	Good (3)	Very good (4)	Excellent (5)
Meeting physical education objectives					
1. Does the class actively contribute to the development of physical fitness?	☐	☐	☐	☐	☐
2. Does the class activity foster the growth of ethical character, desirable emotional and social characteristics?	☐	☐	☐	☐	☐
3. Does the class activity contain recreational value?	☐	☐	☐	☐	☐

*From Piscope, J.: Quality instruction: first priority, The Physical Educator 21:162, 1964.

Continued.

CRITERIA FOR EVALUATING PHYSICAL EDUCATION ACTIVITY CLASSES—cont'd

	Poor (1)	Fair (2)	Good (3)	Very good (4)	Excellent (5)
Meeting physical education objectives–cont'd					
4. Does the class activity contain carryover value for later life?	☐	☐	☐	☐	☐
5. Is the class activity accepted as a regular part of the school curriculum?	☐	☐	☐	☐	☐
6. Does the class activity meet the needs of *all* students in the group?	☐	☐	☐	☐	☐
7. Does the class activity encourage the development of leadership among students?	☐	☐	☐	☐	☐
8. Does the class activity fulfill the safety objective in physical education?	☐	☐	☐	☐	☐
9. Does the class activity and conduct foster a better understanding of democratic living?	☐	☐	☐	☐	☐
10. Does the class activity and conduct cultivate a better understanding and appreciation for exercise and sports?	☐	☐	☐	☐	☐

Perfect score: 50   *Actual score:_____*

	Poor (1)	Fair (2)	Good (3)	Very good (4)	Excellent (5)
Leadership (teacher conduct)					
1. Is the teacher appropriately and neatly dressed for the class activity?	☐	☐	☐	☐	☐
2. Does the teacher know the activity thoroughly?	☐	☐	☐	☐	☐
3. Does the teacher possess an audible and pleasing voice?	☐	☐	☐	☐	☐
4. Does the teacher project an enthusiastic and dynamic attitude in class presentation?	☐	☐	☐	☐	☐
5. Does the teacher maintain discipline?	☐	☐	☐	☐	☐
6. Does the teacher identify, analyze, and correct faulty performance in guiding pupils?	☐	☐	☐	☐	☐
7. Does the teacher present a sound, logical method of teaching motor skills, for example, explanation, demonstration, participation, and testing?	☐	☐	☐	☐	☐
8. Does the teacher avoid the use of destructive criticism, sarcasm, and ridicule with students?	☐	☐	☐	☐	☐
9. Does the teacher maintain emotional stability and poise?	☐	☐	☐	☐	☐
10. Does the teacher possess high standards and ideals of work?	☐	☐	☐	☐	☐

Perfect score: 50   *Actual score:_____*

	Poor (1)	Fair (2)	Good (3)	Very good (4)	Excellent (5)
General class procedures, methods, and techniques					
1. Does class conduct yield evidence of preplanning?	☐	☐	☐	☐	☐
2. Does the organization of the class allow for individual differences?	☐	☐	☐	☐	☐

CRITERIA FOR EVALUATING PHYSICAL EDUCATION ACTIVITY CLASSES—cont'd

	Poor (1)	Fair (2)	Good (3)	Very good (4)	Excellent (5)

General class procedures, methods, and techniques–cont'd

3. Does the class exhibit maximum pupil activity and minimum teacher participation? e.g., overemphasis on explanation and/or demonstration?

☐	☐	☐	☐	☐

4. Are adequate motivational devices such as teaching aids and audiovisual techniques effectively utilized?

☐	☐	☐	☐	☐

5. Are student or squad leaders effectively employed where appropriate?

☐	☐	☐	☐	☐

6. Does the class start promptly at the scheduled time?

☐	☐	☐	☐	☐

7. Are students with medical excuses from the regular class supervised and channelled into appropriate activities?

☐	☐	☐	☐	☐

8. Is the class roll taken quickly and accurately?

☐	☐	☐	☐	☐

9. Are accurate records of pupil progress and achievements maintained?

☐	☐	☐	☐	☐

10. Are supplies and equipment quickly issued and stored?

☐	☐	☐	☐	☐

Perfect score: 50   *Actual score:___*

Pupil conduct

1. Are the objectives of the activity or sport clearly known to the learner?

☐	☐	☐	☐	☐

2. Are the students interested in the class activities?

☐	☐	☐	☐	☐

3. Do the students really enjoy their physical education class?

☐	☐	☐	☐	☐

4. Are the students thoroughly familiar with routine regulations of class roll, excuses, and dismissals?

☐	☐	☐	☐	☐

5. Are the students appropriately uniformed for the class activity?

☐	☐	☐	☐	☐

6. Does the class exhibit a spirit of friendly rivalry in learning new skills?

☐	☐	☐	☐	☐

7. Do students avoid mischief or "horseplay"?

☐	☐	☐	☐	☐

8. Do students take showers where facilities and nature of activity permit?

☐	☐	☐	☐	☐

9. Do slow learners participate as much as fast learners?

☐	☐	☐	☐	☐

10. Do students show respect for the teacher?

☐	☐	☐	☐	☐

Perfect score: 50   *Actual score:___*

Continued.

CRITERIA FOR EVALUATING PHYSICAL EDUCATION ACTIVITY CLASSES—cont'd

	Poor (1)	Fair (2)	Good (3)	Very good (4)	Excellent (5)
Safe and healthful environment					
1. Is the area large enough for the activity and number of students in the class?	☐	☐	☐	☐	☐
2. Does the class possess adequate equipment and/or supplies?	☐	☐	☐	☐	☐
3. Are adequate shower and locker facilities available and readily accessible?	☐	☐	☐	☐	☐
4. Is the equipment and/or apparatus clean and in good working order?	☐	☐	☐	☐	☐
5. Does the activity area contain good lighting and ventilation?	☐	☐	☐	☐	☐
6. Are all safety hazards eliminated or reduced where possible?	☐	☐	☐	☐	☐
7. Is first aid and safety equipment readily accessible?	☐	☐	☐	☐	☐
8. Is the storage area adequate for supplies and equipment?	☐	☐	☐	☐	☐
9. Does the activity area contain a properly equipped rest room for use in injury, illness, or rest periods?	☐	☐	☐	☐	☐
10. Does the activity area contain adequate toilet facilities?	☐	☐	☐	☐	☐

Perfect score: 50   *Actual score:*____

	Perfect score	*Criteria* *Actual score*
Meeting physical education objectives	50	
Leadership (teacher conduct)	50	____
General class procedures, methods, and techniques	50	____
Pupil conduct	50	____
Safe and healthful environment	50	____
Total points	250	____

Questions and exercises

1. Write a 300-word essay on the total physical education program, bringing out the three main components and the contributions that each phase makes to the education of the individual.
2. Outline a physical education program for one of the educational levels. Show how the experiences that you include in your program contribute to the goals of physical education.
3. Select a school or college and evaluate its entire program in the light of the findings disclosed in this chapter.
4. What are some initial considerations that must be brought about before a program can be planned?
5. Develop a set of standards that could be used to evaluate a physical education program.
6. Develop a list of principles that would serve as guides in the scheduling of physical education activities.
7. What part does each of the following play in scheduling: (a) time allotment, (b) size of classes, (c) teaching stations, (d) teaching loads, (e) grouping, and (f) administrative philosophy?

8. Have a class discussion on each of the following:
   (a) Physical education should be elective in school.
   (b) The Reserve Officers' Training Corps is not a substitute for physical education.
   (c) Credit should be given for physical education.
   (d) Attendance should be voluntary in physical education.
   (e) All excuses should be accepted in physical education.
9. What are some essential points to keep in mind in regard to good class management?
10. Outline what you consider to be a desirable grading procedure in physical education.
11. Prepare a list of principles to guide the selection of activities in physical education.
12. What place do coeducational activities have in the physical education program? Justify your stand.
13. Develop a plan to ensure continuity in physical education from the elementary through the college level.
14. How can physical education and health education work together to help promote the health of each individual?
15. Why is an adapted program needed in physical education?

Reading assignment in *Administrative Dimensions of Health and Physical Education Programs, Including Athletics:* Chapter 5, Selections 21 to 27.

Selected references

American Association for Health, Physical Education, and Recreation: Children in focus, 1954 Yearbook, Washington, D. C., 1954, The Association.

American Association for Health, Physical Education, and Recreation: Broadfront, Journal of Health, Physical Education, and Recreation **38:**10, 1967.

American Association for Health, Physical Education, and Recreation: Knowledge and understanding in physical education, Washington, D. C., 1969, The Association.

American Association for Health, Physical Education, and Recreation: Perceptual-motor foundations: a multidisciplinary concern, Washington, D. C., 1969, The Association.

Association for Childhood Education International: Physical education for children's healthful living, Washington, D. C., 1968, The Association.

Baker, G. M.: Survey of the administration of physical education in public schools in the United States, Research Quarterly **33:**632, 1962.

Battle Creek Physical Education Curriculum Proj-

ect Team: Battle Creek Physical Education Curriculum Project, Journal of Health, Physical Education, and Recreation **40:**25, 1969.

Bookwalter, K. W.: Physical education in the secondary schools, New York, 1964, The Center for Applied Research in Education, Inc. (The Library of Education).

Bucher, C. A., editor: Methods and materials in physical education and recreation, St. Louis, 1954, The C. V. Mosby Co.

Bucher, C. A.: Foundations of physical education, ed. 5, St. Louis, 1968, The C. V. Mosby Co.

Bucher, C. A.: Physical education for life, St. Louis, 1969, McGraw-Hill Book Co. (A textbook in physical education for high school boys and girls.)

Bucher, C. A., Koenig, C., and Barnhard, M.: Methods and materials for secondary school physical education, ed. 3, St. Louis, 1970, The C. V. Mosby Co.

Bucher, C. A., and Reade, E. M.: Health and physical education in the modern elementary school, New York, 1971, The Macmillan Co.

Espenschade, A. S.: Physical education in the elementary schools—what research says to the teacher, Washington, D. C., March, 1963, Department of Classroom Teachers, American Educational Research Association of the National Education Association.

Fitness for California Children and Youth: Values inherent in the daily program of physical education, Journal of the California Association for Health, Physical Education and Recreation, March, 1965 (special issue).

LaPorte, W. R.: The physical education curriculum (a national program), ed. 6, Los Angeles, 1955, University of Southern California Press.

Oxendine, J. B.: Status of required physical education programs in colleges and universities, Journal of Health, Physical Education, and Recreation **40:**32, 1969.

Physical education in the junior college, Journal of Health, Physical Education, and Recreation **36:**33, 1965.

President's Council on Physical Fitness: Fitness for leadership, Washington D. C., 1964, Superintendent of Documents.

Reams, D., and Bleier, T. J.: Developing team teaching for ability grouping, Journal of Health, Physical Education, and Recreation **39:**50, 1968.

Report of the National Conference on Physical Education for Children of Elementary School Age: Physical education for children of elementary school age, Chicago, 1951, The Athletic Institute, Inc.

The University of the State of New York, The State Education Department, Bureau of Secondary Curriculum Development: Physical education in the secondary schools, Curriculum Guide, Albany, 1964, State Department of Education.

Von Bergen, E.: Flexible scheduling for physical education, Journal of Health, Physical Education, and Recreation 38:29, 1967.

Wisconsin State Department of Education: Standards for physical education: grades one through twelve, Madison, Wis., May, 1964, State Department of Education.

CHAPTER 8   THE ADAPTED PROGRAM*

The term *adapted* is used here, although in many books and programs other terms, such as *corrective, individual, modified, therapeutic, remedial, special, restricted,* and *atypical* are used. The adapted program refers to that phase of physical education that meets the needs of the individual who, because of some physical inadequacy, functional defect capable of being improved through physical activity, or other deficiency, is temporarily or permanently unable to take part in the regular physical education program. It also refers to a significant segment of a school or college student population that does not fall into the classification "average" or "normal" for their age or grade. These students deviate from their peers on a physical, mental, emotional, or social measure or on a combination of these traits.

Many times health examinations such as medical, physical fitness, or other type indicate that some pupils are not able to participate in regular physical activity programs. For example, those students with organic weakness and functional or growth abnormalities need special attention. Other students who are atypical include the culturally disadvantaged, mentally retarded, emotionally disturbed, poorly coordinated,

and gifted or creative. Special adaptations also need to be made for these students.

The principle of individual differences is being recognized increasingly by educators. Education is for each and every individual in a democracy. The observance of this principle has resulted in special provisions in the schools for backward as well as for superior children, for those with heart disturbances, defective sight, physical disabilities, and other deviations from the normal, and for those who are culturally deprived or emotionally disturbed.

The principle of individual differences that applies to education as a whole should also apply to physical education. Most administrators believe that as long as a student can come to school or college, he should be required to participate in physical education. If this tenet is adhered to, it means that programs must be adapted to individual needs. Many children and young adults who are recuperating from long illnesses or operations or who are suffering from other abnormal conditions require special consideration in their program of activities.

It cannot be assumed that all individuals in physical education classes are normal. Unfortunately, many programs are administered on this basis. One estimate has been made that one out of every eight students in our schools is handicapped to the extent that special provision should be made in the educational program.

Schools and colleges will always have students who, because of many factors such as heredity, environment, disease, accident, or other reason, will have physical or other

---

*A detailed discussion of the care and education of exceptional children is given in Chapter 13 on school health services. Much of this material is pertinent to the adapted program but will not be repeated here. However, the reader may wish to read that important section.

This chapter is designed to outline briefly the adapted program as a component of total school and college physical education programs.

form 86C 3000 3-46

PHYSICAL EXAMINATION RECORD

NEW TRIER TOWNSHIP HIGH SCHOOL
WINNETKA, ILLINOIS

NAME _____ _____ _____
          LAST   FIRST

PARENT OR GUARDIAN _____

ADVISER _____ TELEPHONE _____

ADDRESS _____ PHYSICIAN _____

DENTIST _____

PLEASE CHECK IF YOU HAVE HAD THE FOLLOWING DISEASES

Chickenpox
Whooping Cough
Mumps
Scarlet Fever
Typhoid Fever
Diphtheria
Rheumatism
Tonsillitis
Vaccination (for Smallpox)
Diphtheria Immunization
Measles

What operations have you had? _____

Give type of operation and dates _____

What serious injuries have you had? _____

Specify injury and date _____

Remarks _____

	Date				
	Age				
	Weight	Height	Weight	Height	Weight	Height
	Development				
	Nourishment				
SKIN	Acne				
	Ringworm				
	Plantar Warts				
EYES	Vision R L	R L	R L
	Exophthalmos				
	Conjunctiva				
EARS	Hearing R L	R L	R L
	Discharge R L	R L	R L
	Cerumen R L	R L	R L
NOSE	Obstruction				
SINUSES					
MOUTH					
THROAT	Tonsils				
	Advise Removal				
	Removed				
NECK	Thyroid				
	Pulsation of Vessels				
CHEST					
LUNGS	Palpation				
	Percussion				
	Auscultation				

(Continued Below)

HEART	Murmurs			
PULSE	At Rest			
	After Exercise, 20 hops			
	After 2 Min. Rest			
SPINE AND POSTURE				
ABDOMEN				
HERNIA				
GENITALS	Varicocele			
	Hydrocele			
	Speech Defect			
NERVOUS SYSTEM	Coordination			
	Tremor			
FEET				
	Classification			
	Reason			
	Length of Time			
SUMMARY	Comments and Suggestions			
	Excused from Swimming			
	How Long?			
	Excused from Showers			
	How Long?			
REMARKS				

Class "A"—Unrestricted physical education activity.
Class "B"—Regular physical education but no intramural competition.
Class "C"—Restricted physical education activity (special classes).
Class "D"—Supervised rest.

X—Means defect present.
XX—Means defect needs attention—parents notified.
XXX—Means defect needs immediate attention—parents notified.

Physical examination record. This record is an aid in adapted program. (New Trier Township High School, Winnetka, Ill.)

LOS ANGELES CITY SCHOOL DISTRICTS
Health Education and Health Services Branch—Auxiliary Services Division
Corrective Physical Education Section

CORRECTIVE PHYSICAL EDUCATION ACTIVITY GUIDE
A Guide for the Teacher and Physician
In Planning a Restricted Program of Physical Education

Pupil_____ Date_____

School_____ Corrective Phys. Ed. Teacher_____

I. TYPES OF MOVEMENTS	OMIT	*MILD	**MODERATE	UNLIMITED	REMARKS
Bending					
Climbing					
Hanging					
Jumping					
Kicking					
Lifting					
Pulling					
Pushing					
Running					
Stretching					
Throwing					
Twisting					

II. TYPES OF EXERCISES	OMIT	*MILD	**MODERATE	UNLIMITED	REMARKS
Abdominal					
Arm					
Breathing					
Foot					
Head					
Knee					
Leg					
Trunk					
Relaxation					

III. TYPES OF POSITIONS	LIMITED	UNLIMITED
Lying supine		
Lying prone		
Sitting		
Standing		

Recommended until_____ 196_

Remarks:

Signature of Physician

IV. TYPES OF ACTIVITIES	YES	NO
Competitive sports		
Games——Sitting		
Games requiring standing but no running or jumping		
Officiating		
Swimming		
Coeducational activities		
Social dancing		
Square dancing		
Sports and games		

*Very little activity.
**Half as much as the unlimited program.

impairment. Many of these students have difficulty in adjusting to the demands that society places upon them. It is the responsibility of physical education programs to help each and every individual who comes into class. Even though a person may be atypical, this is not cause for neglect. In fact, it should represent an even greater challenge to see that he enjoys the benefits of participating in physical activities adapted to his needs. Provision for a sound adapted program has been a shortcoming of physical education throughout the nation because of a lack of properly trained teachers, the financial cost of remedial instruction, and the fact that many administrators and teachers are not aware of their responsibility and the contribution they can make in this phase of physical education. These obstacles should be overcome as the public becomes aware of the need of educating *all* individuals in *all* phases of the total education program.

Parker has grasped the importance of

providing for the exceptional person in these words:

The exceptional person needs an opportunity to become a responsible citizen; to become an economically efficient producer and consumer of goods, or services; to develop an understanding of human relationships of home, neighborhood, and wider social groups; and to realize whatever personal potentialities the Creator has bestowed. For an exceptional child it means a well-planned curriculum of many rich experiences of the kinds he is capable of having, which brings to him some measure of ability to make and keep friends, to share with others some if not all of the common social experience, to care for himself personally and for his home, perhaps even to earn his living or a reasonable part of it, and to enjoy life as he must live it.*

Stone and Deyton frame the value of adapted physical education in these terms:

These children receive health and vocational guidance from interested teachers, who have discovered the value of rehabilitation through corrective physical education. Through these cooperative efforts, physically and psychologically atypical children are trained to face and accept their handicaps, to realize their limitations, and to adapt to them. The aims of the corrective programs for these children are to meet the physical and emotional needs of each one, to prove to each individually that there is a place for him which he alone can fill best, to help fit himself for that place, and within his handicap to allow him to "play, too."†

EXTENT OF ATYPICAL CONDITIONS AMONG STUDENTS

Although records are insufficient, there have been several estimates as to the number of children with handicapping conditions in the nation's schools. One estimate indicates that 8% to 10% of school-age children are handicapped, emotionally disturbed, brain injured, or auditorily impaired or have chronic health problems.

It has been conservatively estimated that at least 3 million children in the United States between the ages of 4 and 19 years are physically handicapped. The great majority of these boys and girls, approximately 83%, are in the elementary schools.

Some specific figures in regard to handicapping conditions have been given. One source states that there are approximately 10,000 children who are totally blind and 58,000 children of school age who have partial sight. There are more than 500,000 in each of the following classifications: crippled, deaf, or hard of hearing. There are approximately 700,000 speech-handicapped children, and a similar number of children are considered socially maladjusted. Each year in the United States more than 126,000 babies are born with some degree of mental retardation. At present there are more than 7 million mentally retarded children and adults in the United States. According to the Director of Programs for the Handicapped of the AAHPER, 4 million children of school age in the United States have physical, mental, or emotional handicaps. In addition to the handicapped, there are those students with poor motor ability, low physical fitness, and weight problems who represent 20% to 25% of the total school population. The Ford Foundation indicates at least 50% of the children living in cities are culturally disadvantaged. There are also over 500,000 children with special health problems.

OBJECTIVES OF THE ADAPTED PROGRAM

Physical education can be of great value to the atypical individual in many ways. It can help in identifying deviations from normal and in referring students to proper individuals or agencies, when necessary. It can help the atypical person to have a happy, wholesome play experience. It can help the student to achieve, within his limitations, physical skill and exercise. It

---

*Parker, R.: Physical education for the handicapped, Journal of Health and Physical Education 17:254, 1946.
†Stone, E. B., and Deyton, J. W.: Corrective therapy for the handicapped child, New York, 1951, Prentice-Hall, Inc., pp. 1-2.

can provide many opportunities for the learning of skills that are appropriate for the handicapped person to achieve success. Finally, physical education can help to contribute to a more productive life on the part of the handicapped individual by developing those physical qualities that are needed to meet the demands of day-to-day living.

Some of the objectives that have been set forth for the adapted program are listed here. The first list for the physically handicapped was established by the University of the State of New York:

1. To correct faulty body mechanics for the purpose of giving the vital organs better opportunity to perform their functions.
2. To build up positive physical fitness by improving muscle tone and by developing functional harmony and poise.
3. To correct and develop habits of and attitudes toward health and physical activity.
4. To improve and develop habits of *individually* correct body mechanics in motor activities.*

Daniels and Davies developed a very comprehensive list of objectives for the adapted physical education program, which represents a worthy guide for administrators everywhere. The list follows:

1. Accomplish needed therapy or correction for conditions which can be improved or removed (pertains particularly to temporary disabilities such as reduced dislocations and post appendectomies).
2. Aid in the adjustment and/or resocialization of the individual when the disability is permanent (permanent disabilities like amputation, cerebral palsy can benefit greatly from adapted physical education programs).
3. Protect the condition from aggravation by acquainting the student with his limitations and capacities and arranging a program within his physiological work capacity or exercise tolerance.

4. Provide students with an opportunity for the development of organic power within the limits of the disability.
5. Provide students with an opportunity to develop skills in recreational sports and games within the limits of the disability.
6. Provide students with an opportunity for normal social development through recreational sports and games appropriate to their age group and interests.
7. Contribute to security through improved function and increased ability to meet the physical demands of daily living.*

An analysis of these objectives indicates that through their accomplishment the needs of every individual will be provided for, regardless of whether he has a temporary or a permanent disability, whether he has a need for organic, mental, emotional, or social adjustment, or whether he needs a broad or limited program. These are excellent goals for physical educators.

PLANNING THE ADAPTED PHYSICAL EDUCATION PROGRAM

To have an effective adapted physical education program requires considerable thought and planning. The Bureau of Health Education, Physical Education, and Recreation of the California State Department of Education has prepared a special publication for distribution to their schools and physical educators.† Among many outstanding features of this publication are suggestions for planning an adapted physical education program. These suggestions presented in adapted form include the following:

1. Instruction and practice in basic skills of locomotion and skills for physical

---

*University of the State of New York: Physical education syllabus, book 4. Secondary schools (grades 7 to 12), boys, Albany, 1944, University of State of New York Press.

*Daniels, A. S., and Davies, E. A.: Adapted physical education, ed. 2, New York, 1965, Harper & Row, Publishers, pp. 82-88.
†Dexter, G.: Special physical education classes for physically handicapped minors, Sacramento, Calif., June, 1964, California State Department of Education, pp. 3-4.

recreation should be provided for all age groups.

2. The regular physical education program in the intermediate grades and secondary schools should provide for a minimum of two units in the mechanics of body movement.

3. Where there is a need for special help by students in overcoming poor body alignment, there should be special classes in those schools in which such classes are possible and by individual assignments in regular classes in other schools.

4. From kindergarten through high school, each teaching unit should be planned to teach motor skills for movement patterns that will, in turn, provide for a successful experience in those physical activities included in the program.

5. Where the pupil's ability is limited he should either be permitted to participate in regular courses if the experience can be successful, or provision should be made for other units of instruction that will provide the special help needed.

6. If a student's condition is such that rest and relaxation are needed, such should be possible.

7. Policies concerned with pupils who are absent from class should take into consideration the welfare of the student.

8. When assigning students with severe physically handicapping conditions to special classes or when following other procedures to provide special instruction for pupils, all experiences should be regarded and operated as integral parts of the total, regular physical education program.

9. A special program should be offered to those pupils who score below the twenty-fifth percentile of the California Physical Performance Tests or a similar battery of tests.

10. Both school and family physicians should understand the nature and scope of the adapted physical education program in order to intelligently recommend a student's participation in physical education.

CONTRIBUTION OF PHYSICAL EDUCATION TO VARIOUS TYPES OF ATYPICAL CONDITIONS

There is no one way to group students in the adapted program. As has been indicated, there are many different types of boys and girls in the program. It would be wise for the physical educator and health educator to sit down with the school physician, school psychologist, and/or nurse and include in their planning the various types of atypical students they have in their institution. The discussion in this section includes the following atypical conditions: (1) physically handicapped, (2) mentally retarded, (3) emotionally disturbed, (4) culturally disadvantaged, (5) poorly coordinated, and (6) physically gifted and creative students.

Physically handicapped students

Various methods have been utilized to classify physically handicapped persons. Three types of classification that have been used are given here.

Hilleboe's* classification includes the following five categories:

1. Orthopedic defectives
   a. Children with posture defects
   b. Crippled children
2. Visual defectives
3. Hearing defectives
4. Speech defectives
5. Respiratory-cardio-nutritional defectives

The University of the State of New York† lists the following specific deficiencies or growth abnormalities that require adapted physical education activities:

1. Heart and lung disturbances
2. Postoperative and convalescent patients

---

*Hilleboe, G. L.: Finding and teaching atypical children, New York, 1930, Bureau of Publications, Teachers College, Columbia University, p. 25.

†University of the State of New York: Physical education syllabus, book 4. Secondary schools (grades 7 to 12 inclusive), boys, Albany, 1944, University of State of New York Press.

3. Faulty body mechanics, including posture
4. Underweight
5. Overweight
6. Nervous instability
7. Functional defects
8. General muscular weakness resulting from lack of exercise, or systemic deficiences
9. Conditions, congenital or acquired, affecting bone or muscle mechanism
10. Certain eye conditions

LaPorte* points to the fact that corrective cases may be classified under the following headings:

1. Nutrition (overweight and underweight)
2. Poor posture
3. Weak and flat feet
4. Functional and organic heart conditions
5. Hernias
6. Infantile paralysis and other crippling conditions
7. Neurasthenia or nervous instability
8. Menstrual and endocrine disorders

Whatever the physical disability, a physical education program must be provided. Some handicapped students will be able to participate in a regular program of physical education with certain minor modifications. A separate adapted program must be provided for those students who cannot participate in the basic instructional program of the school. The physically handicapped student cannot be allowed to sit on the sidelines and become only a spectator. The handicapped student needs to have the opportunity to develop and maintain adequate skill abilities and fitness levels.

Physical handicaps, which may stem from congenital or hereditary causes or may develop later in life through environmental factors, such as malnutrition, disease, or accident, sometimes cause negative psychologic and social traits to develop because of the limitations imposed on the individual. A physically handicapped student is occasionally ignored or rebuffed by

---

*LaPorte, W. R.: The physical education curriculum (a national program), ed. 6, Los Angeles, 1955, University of Southern California Press, p. 59.

classmates who do not understand the nature of the disability or who ostracize the student because his disability prevents him from participating fully in the activities of the school. These attitudes toward the handicapped force them to withdraw in order to avoid becoming hurt and result in their becoming further isolated from the remainder of the student body.

Some experts have noted that the limitations of the handicap often seem more severe to the observer than they are in fact to the handicapped individual. When this misconception occurs, the handicapped student must prove his abilities in order to gain acceptance and a chance to participate and compete on an equal basis with his nonhandicapped classmates.

The blind or deaf student or the student with a severe speech impairment has a different set of problems from the orthopedically handicapped student. The partially sighted, the blind, the deaf, and the speech-impaired student cannot communicate with great facility. The orthopedically handicapped student is limited in the physical education class but not necessarily in the academic classroom. The student with vision, hearing, or speech problems may be limited in both physical education and the academic classroom.

There is a lack of physical educators who are specially trained to teach physically handicapped students. School systems find that the cost of providing special classes taught by specially trained physical educators is sometimes prohibitive. Where there are no special classes, the physical educator must provide, within the regular instructional program, those activities that will meet the needs of the handicapped student. Further, placing the physically handicapped student in a regular physical education class will help give him a feeling of belonging. This advantage is not always possible where separate adapted classes are provided.

Some handicapped students will be able

Name of child_____ Date_____
Birthday of child_____ School attended (if any)_____
Address_____ Phone_____
Parent, guardian, or other informant_____
Reason for examination:_____

Date Last Seen

Name of clinics, { Clinic_____ _____
hospitals, or doctors { Private M.D._____ _____
serving child { Specialist_____ _____

PAST AND FAMILY HISTORY: (Parent present ☐ or if not, nurse obtains data from home)
Birth: (type, weight, trauma, etc.)_____ Convulsions_____
Mother's health during this pregnancy_____
Health, age, sex of siblings_____
Child stat up_____ Talked_____ Walked_____ Child's difficulty first noted_____
Diseases_____ Accidents_____
Operations: T&A_____ Others_____

PHYSICAL EXAMINATION: Height_____ Weight_____
Vision test (current) Rt._____ Lt._____ Comments_____
Hearing test (current) Rt._____ Lt._____ Comments_____
Check below (o) if essentially negative or (x) if abnormal and describe on back of sheet.
Mouth_____ Glands_____ Heart_____ Genitalia_____ Skin_____ Coordination_____
Teeth_____ Eyes_____ Abdomen_____ Hernia_____ Gait_____ Skel. deform._____
Tonsils_____ Ears_____ Extremities_____ Nutrition_____ Allergies_____ Toilet habits_____

IMPRESSION OF CHILD AND MEDICAL RECOMMENDATIONS FOR EDUCATIONAL PROGRAM:
1. General physical condition is_____
2. Health practices seem to be_____
3. Family attitudes apparently are_____

4. Specific health problems include: Vision ☐ Hearing ☐ Motor Incoordination ☐ Hyperactivity ☐
Convulsive Disorder ☐ (on medication ☐ no medication ☐) Frequency of Episodes_____
Date of last episode, etc._____
Other:_____

5. Recommendations:
Further attention to_____
Placement in limited P.E. ☐   Regular P.E. ☐   Swimming ☐
Other:_____

_____   _____
Date of Evaluation   Signature of Physician

FORM #08 DSP 8-64-500 B-821-54560

Health evaluation of pupils for placement in special education programs. (Health Services Department, Denver Public Schools, Denver, Colo.)

to participate in almost all of the activities that nonhandicapped students enjoy. Blind students, for example, have successfully engaged in team sports where they can receive aural cues from their sighted teammates. Some athletic equipment manufacturers have placed bells inside game balls; the blind student is then able to rely on this sound as well as the supplementary aural cues. Ropes or covered wires acting as hand guides also enable the blind student to participate in track and field events. Still other activities such as swimming, dance, calisthenics, and tum-

_____   DENVER PUBLIC SCHOOLS
  (Date)   HEALTH SERVICE DEPARTMENT
        REFERRAL OF PUPIL FOR HEALTH REASONS

I am sending_____ _____
                        (Name)   (Rm. or Sect.)

to the office or nurse at _____ for:
                              (Time)

    Cold symptons ... ☐   Nausea............ ☐   Stomach-ache...... ☐
    Headache............ ☐   Skin Rash.......... ☐   Toothache.......... ☐

    Injury_____

    Other reason_____

    _____
                                                  (Teacher)
Office or nurse reply:
    Will remain in clinic ☐   Will return to class ☐
    Home contacted, pupil going home ☐

    Comments_____

    _____

                    Signature_____
STOCK NO. 10704   (Office Personnel or Nurse)
FORM 804   DSP   8-68-3500 PADS   G-123-60827

Referral of pupil for health reasons. (Health Services Department, Denver Public Schools, Denver, Colo.)

bling require little adaptation or none at all, except in regard to heightened safety precautions.

In general, deaf students will not be restricted in any way from participating in a full physical education program. Some deaf students experience difficulty in those activities requiring precise balance, such as balance-beam walking, and may require some remedial work in this area. The physical educator should be prepared to offer any extra help that is needed.

Other physically handicapped students will have a variety of limitations and a variety of skill abilities. Appropriate program adaptations and modifications must be made in order to meet this range of individual needs. The physician is the individual most knowledgeable about the history and limitations of a student's handicap. He is therefore in the best position to recommend a physical activity program for the student. The student's abilities and levels of fitness should be tested in those areas where medical permission for participation has been granted. This will insure not only a proper program for the individual but will also help in placing the student in the proper class or section of a class. Careful records should be kept showing the student's test scores, activity recommendations, activities, and progress through the program.

The adapted and the regular physical education programs should be as similar as possible. Where the programs are totally divergent, the physically handicapped student is isolated from his classmates. When the programs are as similar as possible, the handicapped student can be made to feel a part of the larger group and will gain self-confidence and self-respect. Physically handicapped students need the challenge of a progressive program. They welcome the opportunity to test their abilities, and they should experience the fun of a challenge and the success of meeting it. The handicapped should be given an opportunity to seek extra help and extra practice after school hours. During this time they can benefit from more individualized instruction than is possible during the class period. The fitness level of each student, his ability, recreational needs, sex, age, and interest will help to determine the activities the student will engage in pleasurably. Safe facilities and safe equipment are essential. Intramural and club programs should be provided, but they should be of such a nature that physically handicapped students can enjoy them in a safe and controlled atmosphere that precludes the danger of injury.

Mentally retarded students

In some schools, special physical education classes are offered for mentally retarded students, while in still other schools the mentally retarded participate in the regularly scheduled physical education classes.

Mental retardation can be a result of hereditary abnormalities, a birth injury, or an accident or illness that leads to impairment of brain function. There are degrees of mental retardation ranging from the severely mentally retarded, who require custodial care, to the educable mentally retarded, who function with only a moderate degree of impairment.

Many agencies are conducting research in the field of mental retardation in an attempt to discover the causes of mental retardation, the nature of mental retardation, and the methods through which retardation may be prevented. Some agencies are operating innovative training schools for the mentally retarded. The Joseph P. Kennedy, Jr., Foundation is spearheading much of the research concerned with mental retardation and is also a leader in providing camping and recreational programs for the mentally retarded. The Kennedy Foundation has also sponsored training programs for teachers of the mentally retarded. The United States government is sponsoring experimental physical education programs for mentally retarded persons staffed by special education teachers, specially trained physical edu-

cators, vocational rehabilitation technicians, and architectural engineers. Special programs and special equipment have been designed especially for use by the mentally retarded. Climbing devices, obstacle courses, and unique running areas, as well as a swimming pool, are part of the special facilities. The objectives of this program include social and personal adjustment and development of physical fitness, sports skills, and general motor ability.

Mentally retarded students show a wide range of intellectual and physical ability. Experts seem to agree that a mentally retarded child is usually closer to the norm

Special fitness awards for the mentally retarded, AAHPER–Kennedy Foundation.

for his chronologic age in physical development than he is in mental development. Some mentally retarded students are capable of participating in a regular physical education class, while others have been able to develop only minimal amounts of motor ability. In general, most mentally retarded students are 2 to 4 years behind their normal peers in motor development alone.

Despite a slower development of motor ability, mentally retarded students seem to reach physical maturity faster than do normal boys and girls of the same chronologic age. The mentally retarded tend to be overweight and to lack physical strength and endurance. Their posture is generally poor, and they lack adequate levels of physical fitness and motor coordination. Some of these physical problems develop because the mentally retarded have had little of the play and physical activity experiences of normal children. The problems of some mentally retarded youngsters are further multiplied by attendant physical handicaps and personality disturbances.

The mentally retarded require a physical educator with special training, special skills, and a special brand of patience. The mentally retarded lack confidence and pride and need a physical educator who will help them to change their negative self-image. The physical educator must be able to provide a program designed to give each student a chance for success. The physical educator must be ready to praise and reinforce each minor success. The physical educator must be capable of demonstrating each skill, give simple and concise directions, and be willing to participate in physical education activities with the students. Discipline must be enforced and standards adhered to, but the disciplinary approach must be a kind and gentle one.

The physical educator must be especially mindful of the individual characteristics of each mentally retarded student. Those students who need remedial work should be afforded this opportunity, while those students who can succeed in a regular physical education program should be placed in such a class or section.

Most mentally retarded students need to be taught how to play. They are frequently unfamiliar with even the simplest of childhood games, and they lack facility in the natural movements of childhood, such as skipping, hopping, and leaping. The mentally retarded are often seriously deficient in physical fitness and need work in postural improvement. Further, the mentally retarded find it difficult to understand and remember game strategy such as the importance of staying in the right position, and cannot relate well to the rules of sports and games.

The majority of mentally retarded students need a specially tailored physical education experience. For those who can participate in a regular physical education class, care must be taken so that these students are not placed in a situation where they will meet failure. In a special physical education class, the mentally retarded student can be exposed to a variety of physical education experiences. Physical fitness and posture improvement, along with self-testing activities and games organized and designed according to the ability and interests of the group, will make up a vital part of the special program. In such a class, activities can be easily modified and new experiences introduced before interest wanes. Research has indicated that specially tailored physical education classes can help mentally retarded students to progress very rapidly in their physical skill development. Movement education is especially suited to the mentally retarded. These students have often not engaged in the natural play activities of childhood and need to develop their gross motor skill abilities in order to be able to find success in some of the more sophisticated motor skills.

Emotionally disturbed students

The emotionally disturbed student presents special problems for the physical educator, who must be concerned not only with teaching but also with the safety of the students in the class.

A single emotionally disturbed student can have a disastrous effect on a class and can affect the behavior of the rest of the students in that class. Effective teaching cannot take place when discipline deteriorates.

Emotionally unstable students have difficulty maintaining good relationships with their classmates and teachers. Some of their abnormal behavior patterns stem from a need and craving for attention. Sometimes the disruptive student exhibits gross patterns of aggressiveness and destructiveness. Other emotionally unstable students may be so withdrawn from the group that they refuse to participate in the activities of the class, even to the extent of refusing to report for class. In the case of physical education, the emotionally disturbed student may refuse to dress for the activity when he does report. These measures draw both student and teacher reaction and focus attention on the nonconforming student.

Emotionally unstable students are often restless and unable to pay attention. In a physical education class they may poke and prod other students, refuse to line up with the rest of the class, or insist on bouncing a game ball while a lesson is in progress. These are also ploys to gain attention. The student behaves in the same manner in the academic classroom for the same reason.

Some emotionally disturbed students may have physical or mental handicaps that contribute to their behavior. Others may be concerned about what they consider to be poor personal appearance such as extremes of height or weight or physical maturity not in keeping with their chronologic age. Still other emotionally disturbed students may simply be in the process of growing up and are finding it difficult to handle their adolescence.

If negative student behavior stems from some aspect of a student's personality, then the physical educator must take positive steps to resolve the problem so that teaching can take place. The physical educator must deal with each behavioral problem on an individual basis and seek help from those school personnel who are best equipped to give aid. The school psychologist and the student's guidance counselor will have information that will be of help to the physical educator. A conference with these individuals may reveal methods that have proved effective with the student in the past. Further, the observations made by the physical educator will be of value to the continuing study of the student.

The physical educator will find that not all emotionally disturbed students are continual and serious behavior problems. The physical educator should have a private conference with the student whose behavior suddenly becomes negative and try to understand why the student has reacted in a way unusual for him. Such a conference will lead to mutual understanding and often help to allay future problems with the same student.

Much of the physical educator's task is student guidance. In individual cases of disruptive behavior, the physical educator should exhaust all of his personal resources to alleviate the problem before enlisting aid from other sources. Any case of disruptive behavior demands immediate action on the part of the physical educator to prevent minor problems from becoming major ones.

The majority of school pupils enjoy physical activity and physical education. They look forward to the physical education class as one part of the school day in which they can express themselves and gain a release of tension in an atmosphere that encourages this. For this reason, the student who is disruptive in the classroom is often one of the best citizens in the physical education class.

Physical education is in a unique position to help the emotionally disturbed student. Most students profit from the activities of physical education, and through their actions in this phase of the school curriculum teaching personnel can gain many insights into understanding student behavior. Individual knowledge of each student is of utmost importance in physical education and in understanding individual behavior patterns. Recognizing a student's needs and problems early in the school year will help in offsetting future behavior problems.

While physical education classes are conducted in a less formal manner than are classroom subjects, this does not mean that lower standards of behavior are acceptable. Students should know what the standards are on the first day of class and should be expected to adhere to these standards in all future classes.

Respect for the individual student is a necessity. No student likes to be criticized or embarrassed in front of his peers. When a student is singled out from a group and used as a disciplinary example, the atmosphere in the class will deteriorate. Respect for the student means maintenance of respect for the teacher. If disciplinary matters are handled on a one-to-one basis, rapport is enhanced. If the disruptive student knows that the physical educator expects him to behave in a bizarre manner, he will react in just this way. Good behavior should be expected until the student acts otherwise. Constant failure only abets disruptive behavior. If a student is known to be hostile and disruptive, an attempt should be made to avoid placing him in situations where he feels inadequate and shows this in his behavior. If, for example, a disruptive student does not run well, he may still make a superior goalie in soccer, a position that

would not require him to run. If the emotionally disturbed student has a special skill talent, he might be asked to demonstrate for the class. This will give him the recognition and attention he needs. Praise should be given for a skill that is well performed.

No student is going to participate in extra class activities unless he really wants to. Therefore, behavioral standards should be set for each activity, and it should be available to all students in the school who meet the standards. Acceptance into a club or participation on an intramural team may help the disruptive student gain self-respect and peer recognition and approval.

Culturally disadvantaged students

Recently, culturally disadvantaged students have become a real concern to various communities and to the schools serving these communities. It is a common error for the public to associate only the black child with cultural deprivation. Professional educators especially must realize that cultural deprivation crosses all color lines and ignores none of them. The culture of poverty is especially apparent in the large urban centers. Culturally disadvantaged persons may be found in Appalachia, suburbia, and isolated small towns and rural villages all across the United States.

The culturally disadvantaged student feels isolated from the mainstream of life. His home and neighborhood environments serve as negative influences, destroying his confidence, robbing him of a chance for success, and defeating any aspirations he may have. A culturally disadvantaged student does not achieve success in school because the cultural standards of the school and the home environment are usually inconsistent. Even schools in ghetto or slum areas are staffed by teachers who represent the middle-class segment of society. Continual failure in the classroom negatively affects the school behavior of the culturally disadvantaged student. His short attention span, emotional instability, excitability, and restlessness often contribute to disruptive behavior patterns.

In physical education the culturally disadvantaged student can be given an opportunity to meet success. Physical activity has a strong appeal for these youngsters whether they are students in a school in their neighborhood or community or part of the student body in a school in an affluent area.

The physical educator is the most important single factor in a school physical education program for the disadvantaged. The physical educator should have a sincere interest in these students and must be willing to assume the responsibility for physically educating them. He should have an adequate background and special training in general education and physical education courses concerned with teaching the disadvantaged. These courses will help him come to a fuller understanding of the culturally disadvantaged student and the educational problems he faces. The physical educator should have the ability to develop rapport with the culturally disadvantaged so that he can better respect, understand, and help these students. The physical educator should be able to provide an enriched program that will help to motivate the culturally disadvantaged student to make the best use of his physical, intellectual, and creative abilities.

Through physical education activities many general educational knowledges, skills, and abilities can be enhanced. Through folk dances, for example, it is possible to acquaint the student with the dress and customs of various cultures. This knowledge will help a class in history to become more interesting to the student and will help him to develop pride in his own culture. Through a sport such as baseball, mathematics can be brought to life. The students will be able to see the rela-

tionship between mathematics and its uses in determining baseball batting averages, computing team won-lost percentages, and the importance of understanding angles as applied to laying out a baseball diamond.

The school physical education program frequently is the only supervised physical activity program for the culturally disadvantaged student. These students usually do not have a neighborhood recreational facility available and must conduct their sports and games on unsupervised streets or in dangerously littered lots. The school physical education experience must be designed to afford this student the physical education and recreational activities that are denied him elsewhere. There must be a wide choice of physical education activities offered so that these students can select not only those experiences they find pleasurable but also those in which they can find success.

The program should include activities that will help these students to increase their physical fitness and optimum skill levels. Lack of structured programs outside the school denies culturally disadvantaged students the opportunity to participate in a regular program of physical activity. This often prevents these students from maintaining even minimal fitness levels. Competitive sports and games must be a part of the class program, but time must also be alloted for the individual to compete with himself to raise a physical fitness test score or to improve in a skill performance.

Culturally disadvantaged students need to develop a background in the lifetime sports. Swimming, dancing and tennis, as well as other recreational activities such as bowling, should be included in the program. There should be records, a phonograph, and a variety of rhythm instruments. The culturally disadvantaged enjoy rhythmic activities and find that they are successful in such areas as dance, gymnastics, and tumbling, where they can demonstrate their creativity and express their individuality. Many warm-up activities, as well as many games, can be done to a musical accompaniment.

The culturally disadvantaged are especially conscious of their individuality, and the program must allow ample opportunity for self-expression and creativity. Teacher recognition and praise for the most minor accomplishment is of utmost importance to the continued success of these students. If possible, culturally disadvantaged students should not be in a large class because little teaching takes place and because the individual student becomes lost in the mass.

Poorly coordinated students

The student with low motor ability is often ignored by the physical educator. He may be unpopular with his classmates because he is considered a detriment in a team sport. He may be undesirable as a partner in a dual sport and may wind up paired with an equally uncoordinated and awkward partner. The student with low motor ability needs special attention so that he can improve his physical skill performances, derive pleasure from success in physical activity, and gain a background in lifetime sports.

Poorly coordinated students are frequently placed in regular physical education classes when they have no mental or physical handicaps. The only concession made to their problem is through ability grouping in schools where facilities and personnel are adequate. Even then, ability grouping sometimes is used only to separate the "duds" from the "stars," thus increasing the poorly coordinated student's feelings of inadequacy. The poorly coordinated student may be held up to ridicule by fellow students as well as by physical education teachers, who use him as an example of how not to perform a physical skill.

The poorly coordinated student will resist learning new activities because the challenge this presents offers little chance for success. The challenge of a new skill or activity to be learned may create such tension within the student that he becomes physically ill. In other instances this tension may result in negative behavior.

Poor coordination may be the result of several factors. The student may not be physically fit, or he may have poor reflexes, or he may not have the ability to use mental imagery. For some reason such as a lengthy childhood illness, the poorly coordinated student may not have been normally physically active. Other poorly coordinated students may enter the secondary school physical education program from an elementary school that lacked a trained physical educator, had no facilities for physical education, or had a poor program of physical education.

In working with poorly coordinated students the physical educator must exercise the utmost patience. He must know why the student is poorly coordinated and be able to devise an individual program for each student that will help him to move and perform more effectively. The physical educator must be sure that the student understands the need for special help and try to motivate him to succeed. When a skill is performed with even a modicum of improvement, the effort must be praised and the achievement reinforced.

With a large class and only one instructor, there can be relatively little time spent with each individual. Buddy systems—that is, pairing a poorly coordinated student with a well-coordinated partner—often enables both students to progress faster. The physical educator must be careful not to push the student beyond his limits. A too difficult challenge coupled with the fatigue that results from trying too hard may result in retardation, rather than acceleration, of improvement. Any goal set for the poorly coordinated student must be a reasonable one.

The objectives of the program for poorly coordinated students will not differ from the objectives of any physical education program.

Before a program is devised, the status of the students will need to be known so that their individual abilities and needs can be identified. Physical fitness and motor ability testing should be on-going phases of the program. Through the physical education program the students should come to realize that their special needs are being met because they are as important as the well-skilled students in the eyes of the physical educator.

Separating students into ability groups may cause poorly coordinated students to feel that they are being pushed out of the way. If ability grouping is used, the poorly coordinated must receive adequate instruction, a meaningful program, and have equal access to good equipment and facilities.

If a student has poor eye-hand or eye-foot coordination, he will not succeed in such activities as tennis or soccer. Activities should be chosen that suit the abilities of the students and at the same time help them to develop the needed coordinations. Work on improving fitness and self-testing activities should form only a part of the program. Appropriate games, rhythmics and dance, and such activities as swimming and archery will help to stimulate and maintain interest. Physical fitness clubs, swimming clubs, and other clubs open to all students will also benefit the poorly coordinated.

With carefully arranged teams and schedules in an intramural program, the poorly coordinated can be given a chance to compete with other students on their own level of ability. Preparation for intramural competition should be a part of the class program.

Dancing lends itself to coeducational instruction. When classes can be combined and coeducational instruction offered, the poorly coordinated will have an opportunity to develop social skills. Different groupings for different activities will stimulate interest and provide students with a variety of partners.

The student's progress should be evaluated periodically. When an adequate level of success has been attained in a particular activity, the student should be assigned to a faster moving and more highly skilled group. A selection of activities should be offered that will appeal to the poorly coordinated and guide their selections in relation to their abilities.

Physically gifted and creative students

Gifted and creative students in physical education also need a specially tailored physical education experience.

The physically gifted student has superior motor skill abilities in many activities and maintains a high level of physical fitness. This student may be a star athlete, but in general he is simply a good all-around performer. In a game situation, he always seems to be in the right place at the right time. The physically gifted student learns quickly and requires a minimum of individual instruction. He is usually enthusiastic about physical activity and practices his skills of his own volition. Any individual instruction he does require is in the form of coaching rather than remedial correction. The physically gifted student has a strong sense of kinesthetic awareness and understands the principles of human movement. The student may not be able to articulate these latter two qualities, but observation by the physical educator will reveal that the student has discovered how to exploit his body as a tool for movement.

The creative student also has a well-developed sense of kinesthetic awareness and knows how to use his body properly. This student is the girl who dances with ease and grace or who is highly skilled in free exercise. It is the boy who is the lithe

The creative and gifted student has developed a kinesthetic awareness. (Graceland Fieldhouse, La Moni, Iowa.)

tumbler or gymnast. These students develop their own sophisticated routines in dance, tumbling, gymnastics, apparatus, and synchronized swimming. They may or may not be extraordinarily adept in other physical education activities, but they are as highly teachable as are the physically gifted.

The beginning physical educator may find it especially difficult to teach a student who possesses many more physical abilities than the teacher does. However, there is no student in school who knows all there is to know about an activity. Many experiences will still be new to them.

The physically gifted and creative students may not have attempted a wide range of activities, but they may have experienced all the activities offered in the school physical education program. Both the physically gifted and the creative student as well as the average student will be stimulated and challenged by the introduction of new activities. The creative student in dance may be introduced to a

new kind of music, or the boy skilled on apparatus may enjoy adding new moves to his routines. The athlete may be a good performer, but perhaps he needs to become a better team player. Or he may rely on his superior skills rather than on a complete knowledge of the rules and strategies of sports and games.

A well-planned physical education program will be adaptable to the needs of all the students it serves. But before the program can be definitively developed, the specific needs, limitations, and abilities of the students in the program must be defined. The activities offered must be adapted to the needs of the students, since the students cannot be adapted to the program.

The exceptional student needs a structured program of physical activity, since this is a vital part of his mental, social, emotional, and physical development. Some schools have made it a policy to excuse athletes from the activity program when their varsity sport is in season. This is a disservice to the student, especially when the varsity sport and the unit being taught in class are different. A student benefits from physical activity in a regular program. The physical educator can keep the interest of the exceptional student high by adopting some tested methods.

A leader's program has proved valuable in many schools. Leaders can assist the physical educator in innumerable ways, and they develop a sense of responsibility for the program because they are directly involved. Members of Leaders' Clubs have served as gymnastics and tumbling spotters in classes other than their own and can assist as officials in both the class program and during intramural contests. Members of Leaders' Clubs thus still participate in the activities of their own class, but at the same time receive the benefit of extra exposure to activities. Movies, film strips, loop films, and slides interest and benefit all students. The exceptional student can compare his performance with those of experts and can gain new insights into skills.

Textbooks in physical education are not in wide use in secondary school physical education programs. Students can benefit from the use of a textbook, special outside readings, assignments, and research problems, and these provide an additional challenge for the exceptional student.

Many highly skilled or creative students will be able to assist those students who have low motor skill abilities. By working on a one-to-one basis, the amount of individualized instruction will be increased. The student with low motor ability will receive the special assistance he needs, and the gifted student will be helped to realize that not all students possess high levels of ability.

The exceptional student can assist in the intramural program by acting as a coach on a day when his team is not playing. Coaching a team will help the student to become more cognizant of the importance of team play, sportsmanship, and the need for rules.

A skilled gymnast may not benefit from a beginning unit in tumbling. If his class is on this unit, the exceptional student can be assigned to work on advanced skills or on an advanced routine. A girl who shows great creativity in dance can be assigned to design a new dance or to devise some new steps.

SCHEDULING THE ADAPTED PROGRAM

Before scheduling a student in the adapted program, a thorough understanding should be gained of the boy's or girl's atypical condition and the type of procedure that will best meet his or her total development.

Because of the shortage of funds, space, and staff, many scheduling difficulties arise in respect to the adapted program. Many times equipment has to be improvised, special groups must be scheduled within the regular class period, and staff members have to devote out-of-school time to this important phase of the total physical education program. Unfortunately, some teachers solve the problem by sending the exceptional student to study hall or letting him observe from the bleachers, thus failing to provide for a modified program.

There is a feeling among physical education leaders that scheduling atypical children and youth in separate groups is not always satisfactory. Many educators who have studied this problem feel that the atypical student should take his physical education along with the normal students and, to provide for the handicapped condition, the program be modified and special methods of teaching used. In such cases, the administrator should make sure that the modification of the program for the student is physically and psychologically sound. Sometimes mental and emotional defects can be minimized if the teacher acquaints other students with the general

ANNUAL PHYSICAL ACTIVITY FORM

Junior and Senior High School

Sponsored by Bureau of School Health Service, Division of Pupil Personnel Services, New York State Department of Education and New York State Heart Assembly, Inc.

Date _____

To Dr. _____

From Dr. _____ School Physician
_____ School
_____
Address

Re: _____   _____
Name of pupil   Grade in school

All pupils registered in the schools of New York State are required by the education law to attend courses of instruction in physical education   These courses are required to be adapted to meet individual needs. This means that a pupil who is unable to participate in the entire program should have his activities modified to meet and/or improve his condition. The physical education classes are approximately _____ minutes in length and are held___times a week.

The final responsibility for the determination of a student participation rests with the school physician. Your recommendation will assist him in making a decision. If further clarification is needed, the school physician will arrange a conference with you.

This child may participate in all physical education class activities and in competitive sports, intramural and interscholastic.   Yes_____ No_____

DIAGNOSIS: _____

If activity is limited, please check what he may do, in the following list:

PHYSICAL EDUCATION CLASS ACTIVITIES

( ) Basketball   ( ) Trampoline   ( ) Square dancing
( ) Baseball   ( ) Tumbling   ( ) Social dancing
( ) Football   ( ) Volleyball   ( ) Apparatus
( ) Soccer   ( ) Wrestling   ( ) Archery
( ) Softball   ( ) Track   ( ) Field hockey
                                            ( ) Swimming

INTRAMURAL AND INTERSCHOLASTIC SPORTS

( ) Basketball   ( ) Wrestling   ( ) Golf
( ) Baseball   ( ) Track and field   ( ) Swimming
( ) Football   ( ) Cross country   ( ) Cheerleading
( ) Soccer   ( ) Bowling

1. Does this child require a rest period during school hours?   Yes_____ No_____
2. Duration of restrictions: weeks_____ months_____ school year_____
3. Do you wish the patient to return to you for reevaluation?   Yes_____ No___Date___

_____ _____ M. D. _____
Date   Address
Prepared and pretested by: Nassau TB, Heart and Public Health Association, Inc.

Adapted physical education record. (Bureau of School Health Service, Division of Pupil Personnel Services, New York State Department of Education and New York State Heart Assembly, Inc.)

LAST NAME	FIRST NAME	MIDDLE NAME	SCHOOL	GRADE

CHANGE IN PHYSICAL EDUCATION ASSIGNMENT

The physical education assignment of the above student may be changed as indicated on this form when approved by the committee members appearing below.

ASSIGNMENT TO SPECIAL PHYSICAL EDUCATION CLASS	WITHDRAWAL FROM SPECIAL PHYSICAL EDUCATION CLASS
Person Originating Recommendation Title	Person Originating Recommendation Title
Reason for Recommendation:	Reason for Recommendation:
Recommended for	Recommended for withdrawal from
Rest_____ Modified_____ Orthopedic _____	Rest_____ Modified_____ Orthopedic _____
Recommended by Committee	**Recommended by Committee**
School Physician Date	School Physician Date
School Nurse Date	School Nurse Date
School Counselor Date	School Counselor Date
Special Physical Education Teacher Date	Special Physical Education Teacher Date
Chairman, Physical Education Dept. Date	Chairman, Physical Education Dept. Date
Approved by Date	**Approved by** Date
Date admitted to class_____	Date withdrawn from class_____
	Number weeks in special class_____
Return to P.E. Department Chairman	Return to P.E. Department Chairman

7500 5-56 - 9881

LONG BEACH PUBLIC SCHOOLS
SPECIAL PHYSICAL EDUCATION TRANSFER

INDIVIDUAL REMEDIAL PHYSICAL EDUCATION
PUPIL PASS   DATE.............................

BK. NO.
OR SEC......................   NAME ....
ASSIGNED TO:

DAY	PERIOD	ROOM NO.	SUBJECT	TEACHER'S SIGNATURE
MON.				
TUE.				
WED.				
THU.				
FRI.				

RELEASED FROM:

DAY	PERIOD	ROOM NO.	SUBJECT	TEACHER'S SIGNATURE
MON.				
TUE.				
WED.				
THU.				
FRI.				

TEACHER..

THIS CARD MUST BE RETURNED TO THE TEACHER OF INDIVIDUAL REMEDIAL PHYSICAL EDUCATION WHEN COMPLETELY SIGNED.

FORM PEH   95—REMEDIAL CLASSES, PUPIL PASS—SCHOOL DISTRICT OF PHILADELPHIA (JAN. 1961)

Please Admit _____

| (Name) | (Adviser) | (Period) | (Group or Class) |

New Trier Township High School—Winnetka, Illinois

PHYSICAL EDUCATION CLASS ADJUSTMENT DUE TO SICKNESS OR INJURY

East Gymnasium ___( )   Athletic Field _____( )   Free Throwing _____( )   Badminton _____( )
Main Gymnasium ___( )   Field House _____( )   Horseshoes ____ ____( )   Hand Ball _____( )
North Gymnasium __( )   Natatorium _____( )   Playing Catch _____( )   Running _____( )
South Gymnasium __( )   Nurse's Office _____( )   Special Exercise ____( )   Tennis _____( )
Stage Gymnasium __( )   Training Room _____( )   Table Tennis _____( )   Walking _____( )
Locker Room _____( )

Remarks: _____

Monday	Tuesday	Wednesday	Thursday	Friday

NOTE: Instructor should initial proper date if student reports and does satisfactory work. If assignment is for more than one day, the card should be left in attendance book. If assignment is of long duration, the books will be changed to check attendance.

problems of the handicapped person and encourages their cooperation in helping the student to make the right adjustment and maintain his self-esteem and social acceptance. There also seems to be a trend, at least in secondary schools, to follow an adapted sports program rather than to have a corrective type of program.

In the larger schools it sometimes has been possible to schedule special classes for students with some types of abnormalities. There also have been special schools established for the severely handicapped. These two types of procedures have not always proved satisfactory, however, because of the financial cost and the feeling that boys and girls should be scheduled with normal students for social and psychologic reasons.

In some smaller schools and colleges where there is a staff problem, those students needing an adapted program have been scheduled as a separate section within the regular physical education class period. In some cases group exercises have been devised together, with the practice of encouraging pupils to assist one another in the alleviation of their difficulties. These methods are not always satisfactory but, according to the schools and colleges concerned, are much better than not doing anything about the problem. In other schools and colleges, atypical pupils have been scheduled during special periods, where individual attention can be given to them.

The procedure that any particular school or college follows in scheduling students for the adapted program will depend upon its educational philosophy, finances, facilities and staff available, and the needs of the students.

SELECTION OF ACTIVITIES FOR ADAPTED PHYSICAL EDUCATION

The activities should be selected for the adapted physical education program with the needs of the atypical student in mind. It must usually be done on an individual basis after consultation with proper medical authorities. The activities should be selected in light of the objectives so that worthwhile skills are developed, a proper state of organic fitness is maintained, and the social and emotional needs of the student are considered. In no case should an activity ever aggravate an existing injury or atypical condition. Of course, all activities should be appropriate to the age level of the student and be ones in which he can find success. As far as possible and practical, activities should reflect the regular program of physical education offered at the school or college. The fewer changes made in the original activity, the more the atypical person feels that he is being successful and not different from the other students. Activities should contribute to the development of basic movements and skills. There should be as much group activity as possible since the socializing benefits of participation are important in providing students with a feeling of belonging and being a part of a group.

THE TEACHER IN THE ADAPTED PROGRAM

The physical education teacher who works with children and youth in the adapted program needs special training in order to do the job effectively. It requires more than a knowledge of sports and routine physical education.

In discussing the qualifications of health and physical educators, much has been said about the training needed by physical education teachers. These qualifications are very important and necessary for the teacher in the adapted program. However, in addition to these qualifications, the teacher should understand the student with the atypical condition—the various atypical conditions, their causes, and treatment. The teacher should like to work with students who need special help and be able to establish a good rapport so as to instill confidence and faith in the work that needs to be done. The teacher should appreciate

the various mental and emotional problems that confront an atypical person and the methods and procedures that can be followed to cope with these problems. The teacher must in some ways be a psychologist, creating interest and stimulating motivation toward physical activity for the purpose of hastening improvement. The teacher should be sympathetic to the advice of medical personnel. She or he should be willing to give corrective exercise under the guidance of physicians and to plan the program with their help. In addition, it is necessary to know the implications of medical and other findings for the adapted physical education program, to be familiar with the medical, psychologic, or other examinations of each student, and, with the help of the physician, psychologist, social worker, or other specialist, to work out a program that best meets the needs of the student.

Since some of the most effective work with children in the adapted program can be done at the elementary level, this has implications for the classroom teacher as well as the physical education specialist. In many elementary schools across the country there exists the "self-contained" classroom where the same teacher has the children for all subjects. The classroom teacher should therefore have sufficient knowledge, understanding, and training in the adapted program to provide adequately for her children's needs in this area.

THE ADAPTED PROGRAM IN SCHOOLS AND COLLEGES

The administrator of physical education should understand the components that make up a well-rounded adapted program and should strive toward including these essential phases in his particular school or college system.

One of the best descriptions that has been developed to point out the broad outlines of an adapted program primarily for the physically handicapped was published

Physical Inspection

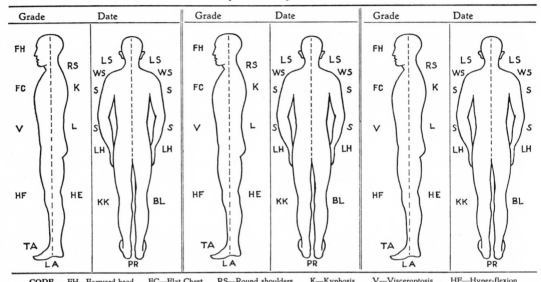

CODE — FH—Forward head   FC—Flat Chest   RS—Round shoulders   K—Kyphosis   V—Visceroptosis   HF—Hyper-flexion
HE—Hyper-extension   TA—Transverse arch   LA—Longitudinal arch   LS—Low shoulder   WS—Winged scaula   S—Scoliosis
LH—Low hip   KK—Knock knee   BL—Bow leg   PR—Pronation   Circle letters and indicate degree with 1, 2, 3 EXAMPLE (FH2)

Physical inspection. (Long Beach, Calif., Public Schools.)

PE 27 3M 7-56 9912

LONG BEACH UNIFIED SCHOOL DISTRICT
PERMANENT INDIVIDUAL EXERCISE CARD — DEPARTMENT OF PHYSICAL EDUCATION

Name_____ Grade_____ Semester_____ Year_____ Period_____

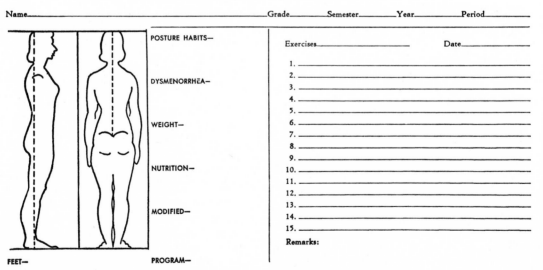

Permanent individual exercise card. (Long Beach, Calif., Public Schools.)

in the Yearbook of the American Association for Health, Physical Education, and Recreation entitled *Children in Focus.** It will be valuable for any administrator to have the main points of this program reproduced here in slightly adapted form:

1. **Health examinations.** A thorough examination should be given to all students by either the school or the family physician.

2. **Classification for physical education based on the examination.** The results of the health examination will determine the type of handicap, if any, and whether the student should be in the regular or adapted program.

3. **Conference with students needing special consideration.** Conference can uncover student's needs, interests, limitations, and capabilities in the area of adapted physical education.

4. **Scheduling accomplished in accordance with school policy or size of school.** A suggested plan is as follows:

(a) Large schools—separate classes.

(b) Medium-sized schools—student spends some time in special class and also in regular class; suggest one day a week in special class and the other days in regular class.

(c) Smaller schools—both handicapped and nonhandicapped in same class but program is modified and adapted to meet the needs of the handicapped within the regular group of normal students.

5. **Phases of the adapted program.** The program may involve three areas:

(a) Special conditioning—includes developmental exercises to meet student needs such as to increase muscle power, help postural deviations, or improve range of motion.

(b) Aquatics—aquatic activities to meet student needs, such as those concerned with remedial, recreational, and adjustment factors.

(c) Recreational sports—sports are considered the best type of physical activity. Students should be transferred from exercise therapy to active sports therapy or placed directly in adapted sports program in preference to exercises. Recreational sports may contribute in such areas of development as adjustment and socialization.

6. **Evaluation of progress.** Evaluation can be accomplished through the utilization of such tech-

niques as tests, conferences, standards of behavior, etc. Objective measures, if available, should receive first consideration.

7. **Records.** A record that contains data on the handicapped condition, physician's recommendations, program objectives for the student, recommended activities, record of special treatments, consultations, progress rating, and other pertinent information should be kept.

8. **Relationships.** An effective adapted program recognizes the importance of harmonious working relationships between medical and nursing personnel, the home, the school administrators, and other teachers.

ADMINISTRATIVE PRINCIPLES

The following statement was prepared for general use in schools and colleges rather than for special schools for handicapped children. It was approved by the Board of Directors, American Association for Health, Physical Education, and Recreation, and endorsed in principle by the Joint Committee on Health Problems in Education, American Medical Association and National Education Association:

It is the responsibility of the school to contribute to the fullest possible development of the potentialities of each individual entrusted to its care. This is a basic tenet of our democratic faith.

1. *There is need for common understanding regarding the nature of "adapted physical education."*

Adapted physical education is a diversified program of developmental activities, games, and sports suited to the interests, capacities, and limitations of students with disabilities who may not safely or successfully engage in unrestricted participation in the vigorous activities of the general program.

2. *There is a need for "adapted physical education" in schools and colleges.*

The number of children of school age in the United States with physical handicaps is alarmingly high. Of the 33,500,000 in the age groups five to nineteen, approximately 4,000,000 children have physical handicaps which need some kind of special educational consideration. (Of these, 65,000 are blind or partially seeing; 335,000, orthopedic disabilities; and 500,000 each, deaf or hard of hearing, organic heart disease, and delicate or undeveloped.) The major disabling conditions each affecting thousands of children are cerebral palsy, poliomyelitis, tuberculosis, traumatic injuries,

---

*Daniels, A.: What provision for the handicapped? In American Association for Health, Physical Education, and Recreation: Children in focus, 1954 Yearbook, Washington, D. C., 1954, The Association.

and heart disease. Further evidence indicates that, on the college level, there is a significant percentage of students who require special consideration for either temporary or permanent disabilities.

3. *"Adapted physical education" has much to offer the individual who faces the combined problem of seeking an education and overcoming a handicap.*

"Adapted physical education" should serve the individual by:

(a) Aiding in discovering deviations from the normal and making appropriate referrals where such conditions are noted.

(b) Guiding students in the avoidance of situations which would aggravate their conditions or subject them to undue risks of injury.

(c) Improving general strength and endurance of individuals who are poorly developed and of those returning to school following illness or injury.

(d) Providing opportunities for needed social and psychological adjustment.

4. *The direct and related services essential for the proper conduct of adapted physical education should be available in our schools.*

These services should include:

(a) Adequate and periodic health examinations.

(b) Classification for physical education based on the health examination and other pertinent tests and observations.

(c) Guidance of individuals needing special consideration with respect to physical activity, general health practices, recreational pursuits, and vocational planning.

(d) Arrangement of appropriate physical education programs.

(e) Evaluation of progress through observations, appropriate measurements, and consultations.

(f) Integrated relationships with other school personnel, medical and its auxiliary services, and the family to assure continuous guidance and supervisory services.

(g) A cumulative record for each individual, which should be transferred from school to school.

5. *It is essential that adequate medical guidance be available for teachers of adapted physical education.*

Programs of adapted physical education should not be attempted without the diagnosis, written recommendation, and supervision of a physician. Problems of correction may be very profound. Where corrective measures are deemed necessary, they must be predicated upon medical findings and accomplished by competent teachers working with medical supervision and guidance. There should be an effective referral service between physicians, physical education, and parents, aimed at proper safeguards and maximum student benefits.

6. *Teachers of adapted physical education have a great responsibility as well as unusual opportunity.*

Physical educators engaged in teaching adapted physical education should have adequate professional education fitting them for this work. They must be motivated by the highest ideals with respect to the importance of total student development and satisfactory human relationships. They must have the ability to establish rapport with students who may exhibit social maladjustment as a disability. It is essential that they be professionally prepared to implement the recommendations provided by medical personnel for the adapted physical education program.

7. *Adapted physical education is necessary at all school levels.*

The student with a disability faces the dual problem of overcoming a handicap and acquiring an education which will enable him to take his place in society as a respected citizen. Failure to assist a student with his problems may sharply curtail the growth and development process. Offering adapted physical education in the elementary grades, and continuing through the secondary school and college, will assist the individual to improve function and make adequate psychological and social adjustments. It will prevent attitudes of defeat and fears of insecurity. It will be a factor in his attaining maximum growth and development within the limits of the disability. It will help him face the future with confidence.*

ADAPTED PHYSICAL EDUCATION— AN ESSENTIAL

Physical education programs should give increasing attention to the educational needs of individual children and youth, including those who are physically handicapped or who otherwise deviate from the normal. Physical education programs can offer remedial work as well as modify the program so that each boy and girl receives maximum benefit from participation. Furthermore, by providing an adapted program, students can be expected to be

*Committee on Adapted Physical Education, American Association for Health, Physical Education, and Recreation.

present for each class period and not excused or allowed to observe from the sidelines because of some atypical condition.

In order to have an effective adapted program, the physical education administrator and his staff must work harmoniously with the school and college medical staff, parents, and community agencies. Through cooperative effort each student can learn to live at his highest level of health.

Questions and exercises

1. What is meant by the term *adapted physical education?*
2. What are the objectives of the adapted physical education program?
3. What is the relationship between the principle of individual differences and the adapted physical education program?
4. How should students be classified for the adapted program?
5. What are the various methods of scheduling students for the adapted program? List the advantages and disadvantages of each.
6. What qualifications does the teacher of physical education need to work in the adapted program?
7. Outline an adapted physical education program for a high school or college.
8. Read three references on adapted physical education and give a report to the class on these readings.
9. How can the physical educator best adapt his program to the needs of the mentally retarded student?
10. What special physical education needs does the creative student have?
11. To what other resources can the physical educator turn when he needs assistance in understanding and working with the atypical student?

Reading assignment in *Administrative Dimensions of Health and Physical Education Programs, Including Athletics:* Chapter 6, Selections 28 to 33.

Selected references

Activity programs for the mentally retarded, Journal of Health, Physical Education, and Recreation 37:24, 1966.

Adapted physical education, Journal of Health, Physical Education, and Recreation 40:45, 1969.

American Association for Health, Physical Education, and Recreation: Project on recreation and fitness for the mentally retarded, Challenge, May, 1968.

Clarke, H. H., and Clarke, D. H.: Developmental and adapted physical education, Englewood Cliffs, N. J., 1963, Prentice-Hall, Inc.

Conant, J. B.: Slums and suburbs, New York, 1964, New American Library.

Cratty, B. J.: Social dimensions of physical activity, Englewood Cliffs, N. J., 1967, Prentice-Hall, Inc.

Daniels, A. S., and Davies, E. A.: Adapted physical education, ed. 2, New York, 1965, Harper & Row, Publishers.

Dexter, G.: Special physical education classes for physically handicapped minors, Sacramento, Calif., June, 1964, State Department of Education.

Duggar, M. P.: Dance for the blind, Journal of Health, Physical Education, and Recreation 39:28, 1968.

Fantani, M. D., and Weinstein, G.: The disadvantaged: challenge to education, New York, 1968, Harper & Row, Publishers.

Frankel, E. C.: Toward a rebirth of creativity, Journal of Health, Physical Education, and Recreation 38:65, 1967.

Hein, F. V.: Health classification vs. medical excuses from physical education, Journal of School Health 32:14, 1962.

Kretchmar, R. T.: The forgotten student in physical education, Journal of Health, Physical Education, and Recreation 31:21, 1960.

Mathews, D. K., Kruse, R., and Shaw, V.: The science of physical education handicapped children, New York, 1962, Harper & Row, Publishers.

National Society for the Study of Exceptional Children: The education of exceptional children, forty-ninth yearbook, National Society for the Study of Education, Chicago, 1950, University of Chicago Press.

Ratchick, I., and Koenig, F. G.: Guidance and the physically handicapped child, Chicago, 1963, Science Research Associates, Inc.

Riessman, F.: The culturally deprived child, New York, 1962, Harper & Row, Publishers.

Schoon, J. R.: Some psychological factors in motivating handicapped students in adapted physical education, The Physical Educator **19:**138, 1962.

Stein, J. U.: A practical guide to adapted physical education for the educable mentally handicapped, Journal of Health, Physical Education, and Recreation 33:30, 1962.

Wienke, P.: Blind children in an integrated physical education program, The New Outlook for the Blind **60:**73, 1966.

CHAPTER 9   THE INTRAMURAL AND EXTRAMURAL PROGRAMS

Intramurals and *extramurals* refer to that phase of the school or college physical education program that is geared to the abilities and skills of the entire student body and consists of voluntary participation in games, sports, and other activities. It offers intramural activities within a single school or college and such extramural activities as "play" and "sports" days that bring together participants from several institutions. It is a laboratory period for sports and other activities, whose fundamentals have been taught in the basic instructional program. It affords competition for all types of individuals, the strong and the weak, the skilled and the unskilled, the big and the small. It also includes both sexes, separately and in corecreational programs. It is not characterized by the highly organized features of varsity sports, including commercialization, many spectators, considerable publicity, and stress on winning. It is a phase of the total physical education program, however, that should receive considerable emphasis.

OBJECTIVES

The objectives of intramural and extramural activities are compatible with the overall objectives of physical education and also with those of education in general. The objectives as listed by the University of Connecticut men's *Intramural Sports Handbook* are presented here in adapted form:

1. To provide the students at the institution with opportunities for fun, enjoyment, and fellowship through participation in sports.
2. To provide the students at the institution

with opportunities that will be conducive to their health and physical fitness.
3. To provide the students at the institution with opportunities for release from tensions and aggressions and to provide for a feeling of achievement through sports participation, all of which are conducive to mental and emotional health.

The objectives of the intramural and extramural programs may be classified under four headings: (1) health, (2) skill, (3) social development, and (4) recreation. Each objective will be discussed briefly.

Health

Intramural and extramural activities contribute to the physical, mental, social, and spiritual health of the individual. They contribute to physical health through participation in activity that affords healthful exercise. Such characteristics as strength, agility, speed, body control, and other factors that prove their worth in day-to-day living are developed. They contribute to mental health by providing opportunities for interpretive thinking, making decisions under highly charged emotional situations, and keeping one's mind occupied in worthwhile pursuits. They contribute to social health through group participation and working toward the achievement of group goals. They contribute to spiritual health through practical applications of the "golden rule," fair play, sportsmanship, and high standards of conduct.

Skill

Intramural and extramural activities offer the opportunity for every individual to display and develop his or her skill in var-

BOYS' INTRAMURAL STAFF APPLICATION
New Trier Township High School – Winnetka, Illinois

The Boys Intramural Sports Staff is dedicated to the task of providing sports competition and recreation for all New Trier boys. Most of the organization and administration of this program is done by students. If you are interested in becoming a member of the I.M. Sports Staff, fill out this application and return it to the I.M. Office.

Important: This application must be completely filled out to be considered.

Name _____ Adviser _____ Phone _____
    first (nickname)   last

Address _____ Class of 19____ Grade average

to date _____

Do you (or will you) have a job that will interfer with your probable assignment in I.M. Sports? _____

In which of the following areas would you like to work?

Supervising games and tournaments	Point Staff	Publicity
____ team sports	____ recorder	____ writing
____ individual sports	____ participation and awards	____ display
		____ radio

In what interscholastic sports have you participated (indicate year)? _____

In what other extracurricular activities do you participate and what offices do you hold? _____

Approximately what is your I.M. point total as of the date below? _____

READ THE FOLLOWING ITEMS CAREFULLY BEFORE YOU SIGN AND RETURN THIS APPLICATION

When I sign this application I understand that:

1. I am offering my service gratis, with no expectation of receiving special privileges or awards of any kind, except that of serving the students of New Trier High School.

2. I am willing to work one afternoon per week (3:40 until about 5:15 P.M.) and occasionally two. (This does not always apply to the point and publicity staffs.)

3. I am to conduct myself with the dignity and leadership necessary for a student leader at New Trier High School.

_____   _____
    date of application   student's signature

(Do not write below this line.)

_____ Date received   _____ Date rating sheet was sent

_____ Date of interview   _____ I.M. point total

_____ Accepted   _____ rejected

Boys' intramural staff application. (From Intramurals for senior high schools, The Athletic Institute, Chicago, Ill.)

ious physical education activities. Through specialization and voluntary participation they offer an opportunity to excel and to experience the thrill of competition. It is generally agreed that an individual enjoys those activities in which he has developed skill. Participation in athletics offers the opportunity to develop proficiency in various activities in group situations where individuals are equated according to their skill, thus providing for equality of competition. This helps to guarantee greater success and more enjoyment of participation. In turn there will be a carryover into adult living of skills that will enable many to spend leisure moments in a profitable and enjoyable manner.

Social development

Opportunities for social development are numerous in intramural and extramural activities. Through many social contacts, coeducational experiences, playing on teams, and other situations desirable qualities are developed. Individuals learn to subordinate their desires to the will of the group, develop sportsmanship, fair play, courage, group loyalty, social poise, and other desirable traits. Voluntary participation exists in such a program, and students who desire to play under such conditions will live by group codes of conduct. These experiences offer good training for citizenship, adult living, and human relations that are so essential in present-day living.

Recreation

Intramural and extramural programs help to establish a permanent interest in many sports and physical education activities. This interest and enthusiasm will carry over into adult living and provide the basis for many happy leisure hours. These programs also provide the basis for recreation during school days, when idle moments can have potentialities for fostering antisocial as well as constructive social behavior.

RELATION TO INTERSCHOLASTIC AND INTERCOLLEGIATE VARSITY ACTIVITIES

Both intramural and extramural activities and interscholastic and intercollegiate varsity athletics are integral phases of the total physical education program. As has been pointed out, the total physical education program is made up of the basic instructional class program, the adapted program, the intramural and extramural program, and the interscholastic and intercollegiate varsity athletic programs. Each has an important contribution to make to the achievement of physical education objectives. The important thing is to maintain a proper balance so that each phase enhances and does not restrict the other phases of the total program.

Whereas intramurals and extramurals are for the entire student body, interscholastic and intercollegiate varsity athletics are for those individuals who are skilled in various physical activities. Intramurals and extramurals are conducted primarily on a school and college basis, while interscholastic and intercollegiate varsity athletics are conducted, as the name implies, on an interschool or intercollege basis.

There is no conflict between these two phases of the program if the facilities, time, personnel, money, and other factors are apportioned according to the degree to which each phase achieves the educational outcomes desired, rather than the degree of public appeal and interest stimulated. One should not be designed as a training ground or farm system for the other. It should be possible for a student to move from one to the other, but this should be incidental in nature, rather than planned.

If conducted properly, each phase of the program can contribute to the other, and through an overall, well-balanced program the entire student body will come to respect sports and the great potentials they have for improving physical, mental, social, and emotional growth. When a physical education program is initially developed, it would seem logical to first provide an intramural program for the majority of the students, with the interscholastic or inter-

collegiate varsity athletic program coming as an outgrowth of the former. The first concern should be for the many or majority, and the second for the few or minority. This is characteristic of the democratic way of life. Although the intramural and extramural athletic programs are designed for every student, in practice they generally attract the poor and moderately skilled individuals. The skilled person finds his niche in the program for those of exceptional skill. This has its benefits in that it is an equalizer for competition.

PLAY, SPORTS, AND INVITATION DAYS

Play, sports, and invitation days are rapidly growing in popularity and deserve a prominent place in the extramural athletic program of any school or college. Although they have been utilized mainly by girls' and women's physical education programs, they are equally important for boys and men at the elementary, junior high school, senior high school, and college levels. They have received the endorsement of the American Association for Health, Physical Education, and Recreation, the Division for Girls' and Women's Sports, and many other prominent associations concerned with physical education. They are an innovation that should receive more and more stress in those places where overemphasis on athletics, highly competitive sports for children of elementary and junior high school ages, and the desire to win at any cost are threatening the accomplishment of the goals of physical education programs.

Sports days refer to that phase of the program where one or several schools or colleges participate in physical education activities. Schools or colleges may enter several teams in various sports. When organized in this manner, each team is identified with the institution it represents. Sports days may also be used to culminate a season of activity for participants within

```
┌──────────────────────────────────────────────────────────────────────┐
│                         PLAYER'S PERMIT                                │
│                                                                        │
│   Name _____ Address _____ School _____ Date ____   │
│                                                                        │
│   is physically fit and has our permission to participate in the play day to be held on │
│                                                                        │
│   _____ at _____.  │
│                                                                        │
│                             Physician _____     │
│                             Parent or Guardian _____     │
│                             High School Principal _____    │
│                                                                        │
└──────────────────────────────────────────────────────────────────────┘
```

the same school or college. When several schools or colleges particpate in a sports day, the number of activities may range anywhere from one to eight, although it is generally agreed that having too many activities sometimes works to a disadvantage rather than an advantage. There are no significant awards for the various events and the publicity is not of a nature that builds up the desire to win.

Play days usually refer to a day or part of a day that is set aside for participation in physical education activities. It may be for students from the same school or college, from several institutions in the same community, or from many schools and colleges in various communities. In the play day each team is composed of individuals from different educational organizations. Here the organization loses it identity, whereas it was maintained in the sports day. The teams usually are labeled by distinctive colored uniforms, arm bands, numbers, or some other device. The activities can be individual as well as team in nature and competitive or noncompetitive. It would be noncompetitive, for example, if several students desired to engage in an activity like riding, not for the purpose of competing against one another but simply for the sociability of the occasion.

An *invitation day* is informal in nature, as are the sports and play days. In this event two schools or colleges usually meet for competition in an activity. This practice has worked out successfully at the end of a seasonal activity, when the winning intramural team or representatives from several teams compete against a similar group from another school or college. The emphasis, however, is not on placing selected, highly skilled players on one team in order to enhance the chances of winning but on the social benefits and fun that can be gained from the occasion.

The advantages of play, sports, and invitation days are very much in evidence. They offer opportunities for the entire student body to participate in wholesome competition, regardless of skill. They offer the student an opportunity to participate in many and varied activities in a spirit of friendly rivalry. They stress both social and physical values. They eliminate the pressures and undesirable practices associated with highly competitive athletics. They are available to the entire student body. They are especially adaptable for immature youngsters who should not be exposed to the practices and pressures of high-level competition. They add interest to student participation and offer innumerable opportunities for leadership.

ACTIVITIES

The activities that comprise the intramural and extramural programs represent the substance that will either attract or divert attention. Therefore, it is important that the right activities be selected. Some ad-

INTRAMURAL EQUIPMENT

The following Intramural supplies are available to you. List items desired.

You are responsible for each item.

Please leave your I.D. card.

_____	Bow
_____	Arrows
_____	Badminton bird
_____	Badminton racket
_____	Basketball
_____	Football
_____	Golf balls
_____	Golf clubs
_____	Handball ball
_____	Handball glove, pr.
_____	Horseshoes
_____	Paddleball ball
_____	Paddleball paddle
_____	Ping Pong ball
_____	Ping Pong paddle
_____	Smashball ball
_____	Smashball paddle
_____	Soccer ball
_____	Softball ball
_____	Softball bat
_____	Softball glove
_____	Softball mask
_____	Squash ball
_____	Squash racquet
_____	Tennis balls
_____	Tennis racket
_____	Volleyball ball
_____	Volleyball net
_____	

O-2879 **You will be fined for equipment kept overnight.**

Intramural equipment. (From Intramurals for senior high schools, The Athletic Institute, Chicago, Ill.)

ministrative guides that may be listed to help in the selection of these activities are as follows:

1. Activities should be selected in accordance with the season of the year and the conditions and influences that prevail locally.
2. Activities should be presented in a progressive manner from the elementary through the college level.
3. Activities should be selected in accordance with the needs and interests of the students.
4. Activities that have implications for adult living should be given a prominent place in the program.

5. Corecreational activities should be provided.
6. The activities that are included in the physical education class program should have a bearing on the activities that are included in the intramural and extramural programs. The latter should act as a laboratory for the former.
7. Many desirable activities require little special equipment and do not require long periods of training in order to get the participant in physical condition.
8. Consideration should be given to such activities as field trips, story-telling, dramatics, hiking, handicraft, and others of a more recreational nature.
9. Activities in the elementary school should be selected with special attention to the ability of the child.

The following lists of activities are identified in a publication of The Athletic Institute[*]:

Individual and dual sports

Achievement tests	Physical fitness
Archery	Rope climbing (boys)
Badminton	Scuba diving
Basketball goal	Shooting
and foul	Shuffleboard
Billiards	Skiing
Bowling	Swimming
Deck tennis	Table tennis
Golf	Tennis
Gymnastics	Track and field
Handball	Tumbling
Horseshoes	Weight training
Paddle tennis	Wrestling (boys)

NOTE: Boxing is not approved as an activity.

Club or group activities

Camping and cookouts	Hosteling
Canoeing	Ice skating
Cycling	Marching tactics
Dance—social, folk,	Outdoor skills
square, and modern	Rifle
Figure skating	Roller skating
Fishing	Rowing
Fly or bait casting	Sailing
Hiking	Tumbling
Horseback riding	

[*]Matthews, D. O., editor: Intramurals for the senior high school, Chicago, 1964, The Athletic Institute.

Team sports

Baseball (boys)	Speedball
Basketball	Soccer
Blooper ball	Softball
Field hockey	Swimming
Gymnastics	Touch (or flag) football
Ice hockey	Track and field
Kick ball	Volleyball
Lacrosse	Water games (water polo,
Speed-a-way	water basketball)

NOTE: Tackle football for boys may be included in team sports only if the proper conditioning and training, instruction, coaching, officiating, and supervision are provided and the recommended protective equipment is used.

Corecreational activities

Badminton	Ice skating
Bowling	Picnics and outings
Canoeing	Roller skating
Curling	Shuffleboard
Cycling	Skiing
Dance—social, folk,	Softball
square, and modern	Swimming
Deck tennis	Table tennis
Golf	Tennis
Horseback riding	Volleyball

UNITS AND TYPES OF COMPETITION FOR INTRAMURAL AND EXTRAMURAL ACTIVITIES

The careful selection of appropriate units and types of competition will help to enhance the values that accrue from intramural and extramural activities.

Units of competition

There are many ways of organizing competition for the intramural and extramural programs. The units of competition should be such as to lend interest, create enthusiasm, and allow for identity with some group where an esprit de corps can be developed and where a healthy flavor is added to the competition.

At the elementary level, the classroom provides a basis for such activity. It may be desirable in some cases to organize on some other basis, but the basic structure of the homeroom lends itself readily to this purpose.

At the junior and senior high school levels, several units of organization are possible. Organization may be by grades or classes, homerooms, age, height, weight, clubs, societies, residential districts, physical education classes, study groups, or the arbitrary establishment of groups by staff members. The type of unit organization will vary from school to school and from community to community. The staff member in charge of the program should try to determine the method of organization best suited to the local situation.

At the college or university level there are also several possible units for organization. It can be on the basis of fraternities or sororities, classes, colleges within a university, departments, clubs, societies, physical education classes, boarding clubs, churches, residential districts, geographic units or zones of the campus, dormitories, marital status, social organizations, assignment by lot, honorary societies, or groups set up in an arbitrary manner. Again, the best type of organization will vary from situation to situation.

Types of competition

There are several different ways of organizing competition. Three of the most common are on the bases of leagues, tournaments, and meets. These methods of organization take many forms, with league play popular in the major sports, elimination tournaments utilized to great extent after league play has terminated, and meets held to culminate a season or year of sports activity.

Individual and group competition may be provided. Individual competition is adaptable to such activities as tennis, wrestling, and skiing, whereas group competition is adaptable to such team activities as basketball, softball, and field hockey.

Various types of tournament competition have been widely written up in books specializing in intramurals and other aspects of sports. For this reason only a brief discussion of these items will be included here.

The round robin tournament is probably one of the most widely used and one of the best types of competition, since it allows for maximum play. It is frequently utilized in leagues, where it works best when there are not more than eight teams. Each team plays every other team at least once during the tournament. Each team continues to play to the completion of the tournament and the winner is the one who has the highest percentage, based on wins and losses, at the end of scheduled play.

The elimination type of tournament does not allow for maximum play; the winners continue to play, while the losers drop out. A team or individual is automatically out when it or he loses. However, this does represent the most economical form of organization from the standpoint of time in determining the winning player or team.

The single or straight elimination type of tournament is set up so that one defeat eliminates a player or team. Usually there is a drawing for positions, with provisions for the seeding of the better players or teams on the basis of past experience. Such seeding provides for more intense competition as the tournament moves toward the finals. Under such an organization, byes are

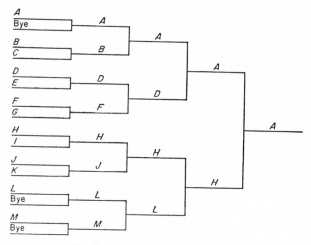

Single-elimination tournament.

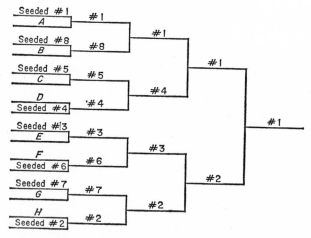

Single-elimination tournament with seedings.

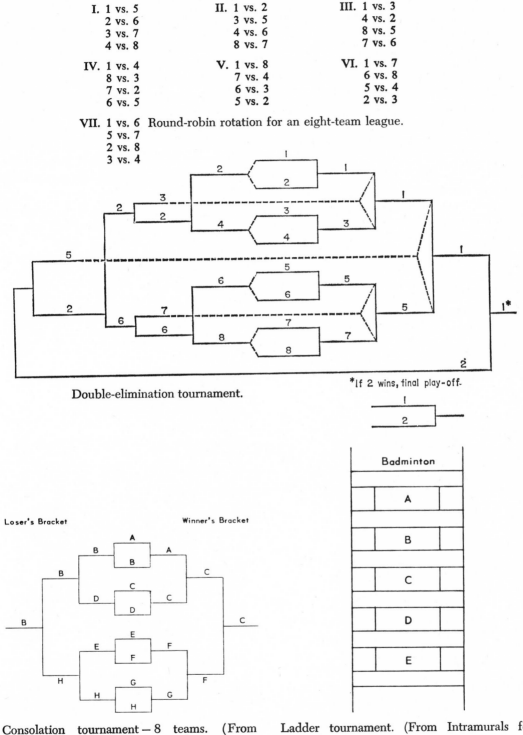

I. 1 vs. 5
2 vs. 6
3 vs. 7
4 vs. 8

II. 1 vs. 2
3 vs. 5
4 vs. 6
8 vs. 7

III. 1 vs. 3
4 vs. 2
8 vs. 5
7 vs. 6

IV. 1 vs. 4
8 vs. 3
7 vs. 2
6 vs. 5

V. 1 vs. 8
7 vs. 4
6 vs. 3
5 vs. 2

VI. 1 vs. 7
6 vs. 8
5 vs. 4
2 vs. 3

VII. 1 vs. 6   Round-robin rotation for an eight-team league.
5 vs. 7
2 vs. 8
3 vs. 4

*If 2 wins, final play-off.

Double-elimination tournament.

Consolation tournament — 8 teams. (From Intramurals for senior high schools, The Athletic Institute, Chicago, Ill.)

Ladder tournament. (From Intramurals for senior high schools, The Athletic Institute, Chicago, Ill.)

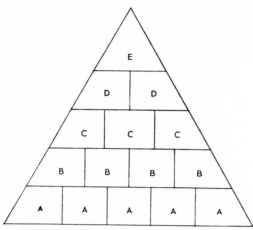

Any A may challenge any B.
Any B may challenge any C.
Any C may challenge any D.
Either D may challenge E.

Pyramid tournament. (From Intramurals for senior high schools, The Athletic Institute, Chicago, Ill.)

awarded in the first round of play whenever the number of entrants does not equal a multiple of two. Although such a tournament is a timesaver and is quick, it is weak in the respect that it does not adequately select the second- and third-place winners. The actual winner may achieve the championship because another player who is better has a bad day. Another weakness is that the majority of participants play only once or twice in the tournament.

The double elimination tournament does not have some of the weaknesses of the single elimination because it is necessary for a team or individual to have two de-

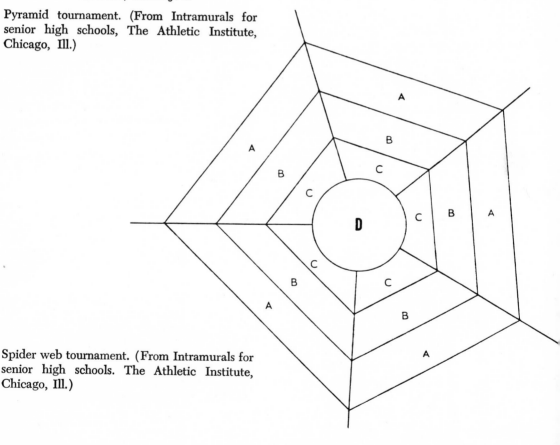

Spider web tournament. (From Intramurals for senior high schools. The Athletic Institute, Chicago, Ill.)

Note: Any A may challenge any B.
Any B may challenge any C.
Any C may challenge D.

feats before being eliminated. This principle is also characteristic of various types of consolation elimination tournaments that permit the player or team to play more than once.

In some consolation tournaments all the players who lose in the first round and those who, because they received a bye, did not lose until the second round get to play again to determine a consolation winner. In other similar tournaments they permit any player or team who loses once, irrespective of the round in which the loss occurs, to play again. There are also other tournaments such as the Bagnall-Wild Elimination Tournament that place emphasis on second and third places.

The ladder type of tournament adapts well to individual competition. Here the contestants are arranged in ladder or vertical formation with rankings established arbitrarily or on the basis of previous performance. Each contestant may challenge the one directly above or in some cases two above, and if he wins the names change places on the ladder. This is a continuous type of tournament that does not eliminate any participants. However, it is weak from the standpoint that it may drag and interest may wane.

The pyramid type of tournament is similar to the ladder variety. Here, instead of having one name on a rung or step, there are several names on the lower steps, gradually pyramiding to the top-ranking individual. A player may challenge anyone in the same horizontal row and then the winner may challenge anyone in the row above him.

The spider web tournament takes its name from the bracket design, which is the shape of a spider's web. The championship position is at the center of the web. The bracket consists of five (or any other selected number) lines drawn radially from the center and the participant's names are placed on concentric lines crossing these radial lines. Challenges may be made by persons on any concentric line to any person on the next line closer to the center. This type of tournament provides more opportunity for activity.

The type of tournament organization adopted should be the one that is best for the group, activity, and local interests. The goal should be to have as much participation as possible for the facilities and time available. Tournaments make for more student interest and enthusiasm and are an important part of intramural and extramural athletic programs.

AWARDS, POINT SYSTEMS, RECORDS, AND ELIGIBILITY

Awards, point systems, records, and eligibility requirements may present problems in the organization and administration of intramural and extramural competition.

Awards

There are arguments pro and con in respect to awards for intramural and extramural competition. Some of the arguments for awards are that they stimulate interest, serve as an incentive for participation, and recognize achievement. Some of the arguments against awards are that they make for a more expensive program, a few individuals win most of the awards, and they are unnecessary, since individuals would participate even if no awards were given. Leaders who oppose awards also stress the ideas that there should be no expectation of awards for voluntary, leisure-time participation; it is difficult to make awards on the basis of all factors that should be considered; the incentive is artificial; and the joy and satisfaction received are enough reward in themselves.

One study indicates that approximately four out of five intramural directors give awards. Letters, numerals and similar awards are used most frequently in the junior high schools. Medals and trophies are given more extensively on the junior college and college levels.

NORFOLK CITY PUBLIC SCHOOLS

INTRAMURAL  CERTIFICATE

This is to certify that ⤸

_____

HAS COMPLETED THE REQUIREMENTS OF THE PHYSICAL EDUCATION

DEPARTMENT AND IS AWARDED THIS CERTIFICATE FOR

PARTICIPATION IN_____FOR THE YEAR_____

ASSISTANT DIRECTOR_____   PRINCIPAL_____

TEACHER_____   TEACHER_____

When awards are given, they should be inexpensive. They can take the form of medals, ribbons, certificates, plaques, cups, or letters.

Point systems

Most intramural programs have some type of point system that is cumulative in nature and many times figured on an all-year basis. The keeping of such points makes for continued interest and enthusiasm over the course of the school year. It also encourages greater participation.

A system of keeping points should be developed that takes into consideration those factors that stimulate wholesome competition over a period of time, maintains continued interest, and is in conformance with the objectives sought in the total program. The system should be readily understood by all and easy to administer. Under such conditions points should be awarded on the basis of such considerations as contests won, championships gained, standing in a league or order of finish, participation, sportsmanship, and contribution to the objectives of the program.

A point system used by one school system is based on the following items:

Each entry: 10 points
Each win: 2 points
Each loss: 1 point
Forfeits: 0 points
Each team championship: 10 points
Second-place team championship: 6 points
Third-place team championship: 3 points
Each individual championship: 6 points
Second-place individual championship: 4 points
Third-place individual championship: 3 points
Each game an official works: 3 points
Being homeroom representative: 10 points
Each meeting attended by homeroom representative: 2 points

Records

Efficient administration of the program will necessitate the keeping of records. These should not be extensive in nature but should contain the information needed to determine the worth of the program and the progress being made.

Such records allow for comparison with other schools of a similar nature. They show the degree to which the program is providing for the needs of the entire student body and the extent to which students are participating. They show the activities that are popular and the ones that are not as popular. They focus attention on the best units of competition, needs of the program, administrative procedures that are effective, and leadership strengths and

Sample intramural basketball score card. (From Intramurals for senior high schools, The Athletic Institute, Chicago, Ill.)

INTRAMURAL ATHLETICS

NAME_____

1ST SEMESTER				2ND SEMESTER			
SPORTS	SOPH. YR:	JR. YR:	SR. YR:	SPORTS	SOPH. YR:	JR. YR:	SR. YR:
FOOTBALL	7	7	7	BASKETBALL	7	7	7
VOLLEYBALL	7	7	7	WRESTLING	2	2	2
TUG-OF-WAR	2	2	2	BOWLING	10	10	10
SHUFFLEBOARD S	3	3	3	GYMNASTICS	2	2	2
HORSESHOES-S	3	3	3	TRACK	2	2	2
BADMINTON-S	3	3	3	SOFTBALL	3	3	3
FUNGO HITTING	1	1	1	HANDBALL-S	3	3	3
FOOTBALL KICK	1	1	1	HORSESHOES-D	2	2	2
HANDBALL-D	2	2	2	BADMINTON-D	2	2	2
SHUFFLEBOARD D	2	2	2	TABLE SHUFFLEBOARD			
TABLE SHUFFLEBOARD				LONG-S	3	3	3
LONG-D	2	2	2	SHORT-S	3	3	3
SHORT-D	2	2	2	PING PONG - S	3	3	3
GOLF	1	1	1	PING PONG - D	2	2	2
TENNIS	1	1	1	FREE THROWS	1	1	1
INDOOR SHOT	1	1	1	ROPE CLIMB	1	1	1
MINATURE GOLF	1	1	1	BONGO	1	1	1

1 2 3 4 5 6 7 8 9 10 11 12 13	
14 15 16 17 18 19 20 21 22 23 24 25 26 27 =	1 CREDIT
28 29 30 31 32 33 34 35 36 37 38 39 40 41 =	2 CREDITS
42 43 44 45 46 47 48 49 50 51 52 53 54 55 =	3 CREDITS
56 57 58 59 60 61 62 63 64 65 66 67 68 69 =	4 CREDITS
70 OR MORE =	5 CREDITS
HOME ROOM	CREDIT

Intramural athletics. (From Intramurals for senior high schools, The Athletic Institute, Chicago, Ill.)

INTRAMURAL SOFTBALL SCORE CARD

DATE _____ TIME _____ DIAMOND _____

UMPIRE _____ SCORE KEEPER _____

TEAM:		INNING									SYMBOLS
NAME: First Last		1	2	3	4	5	6	7	8	9	Walk - W
1.											Single-1B
											Double-2B
											Triple-3B
2.											Home run-HR
											Fly out-F.O.
											Ground out-G.O.
3.											Pop out-P.O.
											Strike out-K
4.											Sacrifice-Sac.
											Fielders Choice-F.C.
5.											For Error-1BE,2BE, etc.
6.											Fill in bottom half of diag. if runner scores.
7.											Write "0" in bottom half of
8.											diag. if runner is picked off, out stealing, etc.
9.											
TOTALS	Runs										Final Score
	Hits										

Sample Intramural softball score sheet. (From Intramurals for senior high schools, The Athletic Institute, Chicago, Ill.)

PROTEST FORM

Protesting Team _____

Quarter and Time Remaining _____

Score At Time Of Protest _____

Ball Possession At Time Of Protest _____

Situation: (Be Specific)

_____
Head Official

Protest form for intramural officials. (From Intramurals for senior high schools, The Athletic Institute, Chicago, Ill.)

weaknesses. Record keeping is an important phase of the program that should not be overlooked.

Eligibility

There is a need for a few simple eligibility rules. These should be kept to a minimum, since the intramural and extramural programs should render a contribution to the vast majority of the student body.

It is generally agreed that there should be no scholarship rules. There should be rules that forbid varsity players from participating in activities when they are on the varsity team or squad. Professionals should be barred from those activities in which they are professional. A student should be allowed to participate on only one team in a given activity during the season. Students, of course, should be regularly enrolled in the school and carrying what the institution rules is a normal load. Unsportsmanlike conduct should be dealt with in a manner that is in the best interests of the individual concerned, the program, and the established goals. Certain activities by their very nature should not be engaged in by individuals with certain health defects. Therefore, such individuals should be cleared by the health department of the school before participation is allowed in such activities.

The eligibility rules established by one college that have implications for high schools as well as colleges are as follows:

1. All men students of the college in good standing shall be eligible to compete in any activity promoted by the Intramural Department, except as provided later in these articles.
2. A varsity man is one who is retained by the coach after the final cut has been made.
3. The varsity and freshman coaches are requested to pass on the list of their respective squads. Participation on these squads will automatically make a man ineligible for intramural athletics in that particular sport.
4. A man may represent but one team in a given sport in a given season.

5. A team shall forfeit any contest in which an ineligible player was used. The director shall eliminate any points made by an ineligible man in meets. These infractions of the rules must be discovered within forty-eight hours after the contest.
6. Members of the freshman or varsity squads who become scholastically ineligible in any particular sport shall be ineligible to participate in any allied intramural activity.
7. The director may declare a man ineligible to participate in intramural athletics for unsportsmanlike conduct toward officials or opponents.
8. A man receiving a varsity award is ineligible to participate in that particular intramural sport until one complete season has passed since earning his letter.*

INTRAMURAL AND EXTRAMURAL PROGRAMS IN THE ELEMENTARY SCHOOL

The intramural and extramural programs in the elementary school should be outgrowths of the instructional program. They should consist of a broad variety of activities including stunts, rhythmic activities, relays, and tumbling. They should be suited to the age and sex differences of children at this level. They should be carefully supervised. The younger children in the primary grades probably will benefit most from free play. In the upper elementary grades, recess periods and afterschool activity can take place on both intragrade and intergrade bases. The programs should be broad, varied, and progressive in nature, with participants similar in maturity and ability.

A committee of the American Association for Health, Physical Education, and Recreation adopted the following policy statement with respect to elementary school boys and girls:

The kind of competitive sports planned for children in the elementary school must be based on what is best for the growth and de-

---

*From the Handbook of intramural athletics, Michigan State College.

```
                                       RES.
Team Name_____League:  HALL, FRAT., IND.   Sport _____
                                      (Circle One)
REGISTER THE DAYS AND HOURS YOUR TEAM PREFERS NOT TO PARTICIPATE.  BE SPECIFIC.  IF POSSIBLE,
THIS TIME WILL BE AVOIDED.   YOU MAY BE SCHEDULED ON THESE DAYS _____

Manager's Name_____Telephone Number _____
Address_____   Room Number _____
```

MANAGER'S COLUMN	PLAYER'S SIGNATURE
This certifies that I understand the Intra-mural Eligibility Rules and have completely checked all the players on my team. If there is any discrepancy, I will assume full re-sponsibility. If there is any question about rules or eligibility, I will contact the Intramural Office.	This certifies that I have read and understand the Intramural Eligibility Rules, and will comply witn them. Also, that I have not, and will not play with any team, other than the one listed above. (Rule 6, Sec. D., I.M. Handbook). Failure to comply with this rule will result in my suspension from I.M. compe-tition.

Manager's Signature

TEAM ROSTER

MANAGER'S COLUMN	PLAYER'S SIGNATURE
1.	
2.	
3.	
4.	
5.	
6.	
7.	
8.	
9.	
10.	
11.	
12.	
13.	
14.	
15.	
16.	
17.	
18.	
19.	
20.	
21.	
22.	
23.	
24.	

Michigan State intramural sports roster. (From Intramurals for senior high schools, The Athletic Institute, Chicago, Ill.)

velopment of boys and girls at this level of maturity.

In the elementary school, children grow at variable rates, and at the same chronological age there are many differences in maturity. In children who are growing rapidly growth demands much of their energy. Emotional pressures may drive the child past the stage of healthful participation. Bone ossification and development are incomplete.

In consideration of these factors, the kinds of competition indicated in the following program outline are recommended as best meeting the physical activity needs of elementary school boys and girls:

1. First, as a foundation, all children should have broad, varied, and graded physical education under competent instruction through all grades. In many of the activities in this program, the competitive element is an important factor. The element of competition provides enjoyment and, under good leadership, leads to desirable social and emotional as well as physical growth.

2. Based upon a sound, comprehensive instructional program in grades five through eight, children should have opportunity to play in supervised intramural games and contests with others who are of corresponding maturity and ability within their own school. In grades below the fifth, the competitive elements found in the usual activities will satisfy the needs of children.

3. As a further opportunity to play with others, beyond the confines of their own school or neighborhood, play or sports day programs may be planned with emphasis on constructive social, emotional, and health outcomes. Teams may be formed of participants coming from more than a single school or agency, thus making playing together important.

Tackle football and boxing should not be included in the program because of common agreement among educational and medical authorities that these activities are undesirable for children of elementary school age.

Schools should plan with parents and community agencies to insure the kind of program outlined above is part of the educational experiences of every child.

It should be kept in mind that the child is important in this setting and not the teacher, parent, school, or agency.*

INTRAMURAL AND ENTRAMURAL PROGRAMS IN THE JUNIOR HIGH SCHOOL

In the junior high school the main concentration in athletics should be on intramurals and extramurals. It is at this particular level that students are taking a

*National Conference on Physical Education for Children of Elementary School Age: Physical education for children of elementary school age, Chicago, 1951, The Athletic Institute, Inc., p. 22.

special interest in sports, but at the same time their immaturity makes it unwise to allow them to engage in a highly organized interscholastic program. The program at this level should provide for both boys and girls, appeal to the entire student body, have good supervision by a trained physical education person, and be adapted to the needs and interests of the pupils.

Many authoritative and professional groups have gone on record in favor of broad intramural and extramural programs and against a varsity interscholastic, competitive program. They feel this is in the best interests of youth at this age level.

The junior high school provides a setting for giving students fundamental skills in many sports and activities. It is a time of limitless energy when physiologic changes and rapid growth are taking place. Youth in junior high schools should have proper outlets to develop themselves in a healthful manner.

INTRAMURAL AND EXTRAMURAL PROGRAMS IN THE SENIOR HIGH SCHOOL, COLLEGE, AND UNIVERSITY

At both the high school and college levels the intramural and extramural programs should receive a major emphasis. At this time the interests and needs of boys and girls require such a program. These students want and need to experience the joy and satisfaction that are a part of playing on a team, excelling in an activity with one's own peers, and developing skill. Every high school, college, and university should see to it that a broad and varied program is part of the total physical education plan.

The intramural and extramural programs for boys and girls should receive more emphasis than they are now getting at the senior high school and college levels. They are basic to sound education. They are settings where the skills learned and developed in the instructional program can be put to use in a practical situation, with all the fun that comes from such competition. They should form a basis for the utilization of skills that will be used during leisure time, both in the present and in the future.

There should be adequate personnel for such programs. Good leadership is needed if the programs are to prosper. Each school should be concerned with developing a plan where proper supervision and leadership are available for afterschool hours. Qualified officials are also a necessity in order to ensure equal and sound competi-

---

NEW TRIER TOWNSHIP HIGH SCHOOL

Winnetka, Illinois

Boys' Intramural Sports

MATCH NOTICE
(for individual or doubles matches)

Adviser _____

Name _____

REMINDER: You are scheduled to play a _____

match tomorrow _____ .

If you wish, you may play any time BEFORE the scheduled date and time by making arrangements with your opponent.

The winner must turn in the score by 8:45 the morning following the scheduled time.

Matches may not be postponed without the consent of the I. M. Office, G211.
        I. M. 65

New Trier Township High School boys' intramural sports match notice. (From Intramurals for senior high schools, The Athletic Institute, Chicago, Ill.)

tion. Facilities, equipment, and supplies should be apportioned on an equitable basis for the entire physical education program. There should be no monopoly on the part of any group or any program.

The college and university level offers an ideal setting for play and sports days for both boys and girls.

Sports clubs should be encouraged in those activities having special appeal to groups of students. Through such clubs greater skill is developed in the activity and the social experiences are well worthwhile.

Corecreational activities should play a prominent part in the programs. Girls and boys need to participate more together. Many of the activities in the high school and college programs adapt themselves well to both sexes. Such activities include volleyball, softball, tennis, badminton, table tennis, folk and square dancing, bowling, swimming, and skating. In some cases the rules of the games will need to be modified. The play and sports days that are conducted also offer a setting where both sexes can participate and enjoy worthwhile competition together.

INTRAMURAL AND EXTRAMURAL PROGRAMS FOR GIRLS AND WOMEN*

Most of what has been discussed thus far is applicable to girls and women as well as to boys and men. The objectives, play and sports days, activities, units of competition, and programs at the various institutional levels have been discussed with both sexes in mind. At the same time, women have progressed so rapidly in the intramural and extramural phases of the physical education program that it seems wise to make special reference to them.

According to many leaders in the field, intramurals and extramurals are preferred and emphasized for women as against var-

---

*See also Chapter 10.

sity interscholastic athletics. They point out that certain biologic, social, and psychologic characteristics of girls and women adapt better to this type of organization and program. The Division for Girls' and Women's Sports of the American Association for Health, Physical Education, and Recreation has pointed out that sports, when conducted in the right manner, contribute to such desirable outcomes as fitness for living and to the development of the most desirable and attractive qualities for womanhood. These include many physical, mental, and social qualities.

The program should be composed of a wide variety of team and individual sports and other activities that may be played among the girls themselves or in mixed groups. Girls have spearheaded the drive for sports and play days and so these deserve special emphasis. There should be qualified women leaders directing all phases of the program, although men should work very closely with them and lend support and help at every opportunity. Women should officiate in their own activities. Every safeguard should be taken to protect girls from harmful practices. There should be no commercial exploitation or harmful publicity attached to the program.

GENERAL ADMINISTRATIVE POLICIES FOR ORGANIZATION AND ADMINISTRATION OF INTRAMURAL AND EXTRAMURAL PROGRAMS

Some general administrative policies for the organization and administration of the intramural and extramural programs follow.

General administration

Intramural and extramural activities should be centered in the physical education program. However, they should be separate divisions of the overall program, receiving equal consideration with the instructional and interscholastic or intercol-

HEALTH AND PHYSICAL EDUCATION DEPARTMENT

GIRLS' INTRAMURAL ATHLETIC REPORT

Season_____

Activity	Number of teams	Number of pupils participating	Pupils participating in at least 80% of games
Apparatus and tumbling			
Archery			
Badminton			
Basketball			
Bowling			
Camping			
Croquet			
Deck tennis			
Fencing			
Field hockey			
Folk dancing			
Golf			
Handball			
Horseshoes			
Ice skating			
Lacrosse			
Modern dance			
Paddle tennis			
Shuffleboard			
Skiing			
Soccer			
Social dancing			
Softball			
Speedball			
Swimming and water safety			
Table tennis			
Tap dancing			
Tennis			
Volleyball			
Other			

Number of different girls in intramural program _____ (Do not count any girl more than once even though she participates in two or more activities)

GIRLS' INTERSCHOOL ACTIVITIES

How many interschool activities were held for girls: sports days_____;
     invitation games_____; other invitation activities_____.
Total number of girls who participated in these activities_____.
How many different girls are represented by these figures?_____

School _____
Date _____   Teacher's name _____

Girls' intramural athletic report.

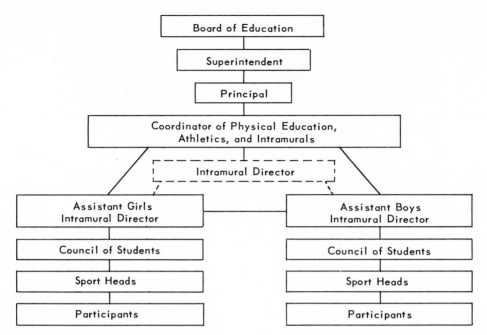

Suggested organization chart for intramurals. (From Intramurals for senior high schools, The Athletic Institute, Chicago, Ill.)

legiate athletics divisions in respect to staff, finances, facilities, equipment, supplies, and other essentials. There should be one staff member who has direct responsibility for this program. Such an individual should be one who is well trained in physical education and whose chief interest is intramural and extramural activities. This may not be possible in some smaller schools or colleges. However, it is necessary that the person in charge have adequate time and a sincere interest to do a commendable job in this area. Along with the director there should be assistant directors, supervisors, student managers, and other staff members as needed, depending upon the size of the school or college. There should also be adequate provision for officials. These should be selected and trained with care because of their importance to the program. Varsity players when carefully selected make good officials. Also, varsity coaches, staff members, and student managers should be considered for this work. A list of policies governing the various

features of the program should be prepared in written form and well publicized. Sometimes these are effectively publicized through a handbook.

An important feature of the overall administration of an intramural or extramural program is the establishment of a council. This usually is an elected council with representatives from the students, central administration, intramural staff, health department, and faculty. This body could be most influential in the establishment of policy and practices for a broad program of athletics for all students.

A significant development on the national scene was the establishment of the National Intramural Sports Council as a joint project of the Division of Men's Athletics and the Division of Girls' and Women's Sports of the American Association for Health, Physical Education, and Recreation. The purpose of creating the organization was to provide national leadership for intramural programs across the country.

Matthews has developed a set of intra-

G. A. A. POINT RECORD

School_____

Name_____   Letter, Yr._____ All City Yr._____

Verifications of earned points in transferred cases will be complete, with instructors signature on this card.

5M 8-57 ⬥8

SCHOOL YEAR	Total brought forward	Archery	Basketball	Badminton	Bicycling	Dancing	Deck Tennis	Demonstration	Executive Board	Field Ball	Golf	Hiking	Horseback Riding	Kittenball	Refereeing	Scholarship	Shuffle Board	Shooting	Ice Skating	Roller Skating	Swimming	Table Tennis	Tennis	Tobogganing	Tumbling	Volley Ball			TOTAL
9th																													
10th																													
11th																													
12th																													

Girls' Athletic Association record.

mural administration principles that will be helpful to schools and colleges alike in establishing and administering sound intramural and extramural programs. These principles in adapted form are as follows:

1. Policies relative to intramurals should have rapport with the total welfare of the educational institution. Example: they should complement and supplement the academic program. Units of competition should not reflect racial or religious groupings.
2. Good human relationships and attitudes should be stressed. Example: rating plans, supervision, officiating, meetings, rules, etc. should stress sportsmanship.
3. Student planning and management should be encouraged. Example: the administrative council represents an opportunity for student involvement. Team manager, captains, scorers, etc. offer such opportunities as well.
4. The health and welfare of all participants should be protected. Example: periodic physical examinations are mandatory, and constant and close inspection of facilities and equipment is a must.
5. Competition should be equalized so that all participants experience success. Example: a constant loser will soon drop from intramurals and for this as well as other reasons

competition should enable all participants to be successful in this phase of the educational program.
6. A variety of activities should be offered. Example: students should be consulted and activities should reflect strenuous and nonstrenuous, team and individual, and also corecreational activities. At least five different sports should be offered.
7. The officiating should be carefully selected and supervised. Example: a program that involves training and orientation for the officials as well as testing and observation is important.
8. Grievances and protests should receive fair and equal treatment. Example: channels for grievances should be established, thus helping to assure some degree of satisfaction and success for all concerned.
9. Rules of eligibility and procedures should be established and publicized. Example: committees and/or the council should carefully establish the rules and see that all concerned are provided with copies of the same.
10. The program should be financed in a manner consistent with school policy. Example: the intramural program is an important part of total educational program and therefore should be subsidized financially through monies allocated by the

SUGGESTED PHYSICAL EXAMINATION FORM

(Cooperatively prepared by the National Federation of State High School Athletic Associations and the Committee on Medical Aspects of Sports of the American Medical Association) Physical examination for athletes cannot be rendered before August 1 preceding school year concerned.

PLEASE LETTER   (Name of Student)   (City and School)
SIGNIFICANT PAST ILLNESS OR INJURY_____HEIGHT_____
_____WEIGHT_____
EYES, EARS, NOSE, AND THROAT 20/   20/   _____ HEARING   /15   /15
LUNGS _____
HEART _____BLOOD PRESSURE_____
ABDOMEN _____
GENITALIA _____ HERNIA _____
MUSCULO-SKELETAL _____
REFLEXES _____
URINALYSIS _____ DATE OF LAST IMMUNIZATIONS
BLOOD COUNT, X-RAY (if indicated)_____ POLIO _____
                                           TETANUS _____
File in high school office   OTHERS _____

I certify that I have on this date examined the above student and recommend him (or her) as being physically able to compete in supervised activities NOT CROSSED OUT BELOW:

BASEBALL   FOOTBALL   ROWING   SOFTBALL   TRACK
BASKETBALL   HOCKEY   SKATING   SPEEDBALL   VOLLEYBALL
CROSS COUNTRY   GOLF   SKIING   SWIMMING   WRESTLING
FIELD HOCKEY   GYMNASTICS   SOCCER   TENNIS   OTHERS_____

DATE OF EXAMINATION:_____SIGNED: _____
                                           Examining Physician

Suggested physical examination form. (From Intramurals for senior high schools, The Athletic Institute, Chicago, Ill.)

MICHIGAN STATE INTRAMURAL INJURY HOSPITAL SLIP

Name _____   Student Number _____   Date of Injury _____ 19___

Age _____
The above named student was injured in { □ Scheduled / Informal □ } _____ activity.

Body location and type of injury

Time injury reported _____

SUPERVISOR _____

Frank Beeman
Intramurals

R-367   Give detailed report of ACTION causing injury

Basic Cause

Michigan State intramural injury hospital slip. (From Intramurals for senior high schools, The Athletic Institute, Chicago, Ill.)

TEAM NOTICE--INTRAMURAL SPORTS

NEW TRIER TOWNSHIP HIGH SCHOOL, Winnetka, Illinois

Adviser Room _____

REMINDER: Your _____ team plays tomorrow.

_____ .

Your opponents are _____ .

Sign up the players below who can play tomorrow.

1. _____   2. _____   3. _____

4. _____   5. _____   6. _____

7. _____   8. _____   9. _____

IMPORTANT: If you have enough players, then keep this sheet for your own use. If you do not have enough players, you MUST RETURN THIS SHEET TO THE I.M. OFFICE IMMEDIATELY.
    I.M. 60

Team notice for intramural sports. (From Intramurals for senior high schools, The Athletic Institute, Chicago, Ill.)

board of education or central administration.*

Health examinations

Health examinations should be required of all participants as a safeguard to their health. Sometimes this is taken care of through the annual health examination and at other times through special examinations given before a seasonal activity starts.

Finances

The finances involved in intramural and extramural programs are raised in various ways. Since these programs have as many contributions to make to educational objectives as other parts of the educational program, or more, they should be financed out of board of education and central administration funds, just as other phases of the program are financed. They should be in-

---

*Matthews, D. O.: Intramural administration principles, The Athletic Journal **46**:82, 1966.

cluded in the regular physical education budget and supported through regularly budgeted school or college income.

There is another method of financing the programs that has proved quite satisfactory in some high schools and colleges. This plan incorporates the cost of running the programs in the regular activity fee that includes such student activities as dramatics, the interscholastic athletic program, musicals, and band concerts. This allows for stable funds that are in proportion to the student enrollment and can be anticipated in advance. Also, this method eliminates any additional charges to the student.

Other methods of financing that are utilized but that are questioned in some quarters are using money taken from athletic gate receipts, charging spectators to see the games, requiring an entry fee, and special fund-raising projects like athletic nights, carnivals, and presentation of talented athletic and other groups. Some of the arguments against such practices are that they create a wrong emphasis on gate receipts and result in many evils, that they discourage spectators from attending and students from participating, and that they require special projects to raise money, which should not be necessary for such a valuable phase of the educational program.

Publicity and promotion

It is essential that the student body, faculty, and public in general understand the intramural and extramural programs, the individuals they serve, the activities offered, and the objectives they attempt to attain. Such information can be disseminated to the right individuals only through a well-planned and organized publicity and promotion program.

The newspapers should be encouraged to give appropriate space to these activities. Brochures, bulletin boards, and the school newspaper can help to focus attention on the program. Notices can be prepared and sent home to parents in the elementary and secondary schools. A handbook can be prepared that explains all the various aspects of the total program and given to all students and others who are interested. Record boards can be constructed and placed in conspicuous settings. Clinics can be held in the various sports. Orientation talks and discussions can be held in school and college assemblies and at other gatherings. Special days can be held with considerable publicity and such catch slogans as "It Pays to Play" can be adopted. Through utilizing several devices and techniques, a good job of publicity and promotion can be done, with consequent greater participation among the student body and better understanding among the public.*

Time of day

The time when intramural and extramural activities should be held will depend upon the school or college level, facilities, season of year, community, and other influences.

One of the most popular and convenient times in many schools is late afternoon. This has proved best for elementary and

*See also Chapter 20 on public relations for more information on publicity and promotion.

```
              INTRAMURAL GAME BLANK

    SPORT _____        DATE _____

    PLAYER _____       H.R. ____ SCORE _____
                              *VS*
    PLAYER _____       H.R. ____ SCORE _____

    _____              _____
          LOSING PLAYER                       POINT FOR GAME
    THIS BLANK MUST BE COMPLETELY FILLED OUT AND RETURNED
    BY WINNER TO INTRAMURAL MANAGER OR ROOM 701 ON DAY OF
    CONTEST OR A FORFEIT WILL RESULT.
```

Intramural game blank. (From Intramurals for senior high schools, The Athletic Institute, Chicago, Ill.)

junior and senior high schools. For some seasons of the year—namely, spring and fall—it has also been popular in college. It is a time that is economical, does not require lights, and has the outdoors available. It also ensures faculty supervision to a greater degree.

Evenings have been used quite extensively at the college level during the winter. This is not recommended at the elementary or junior and senior high school levels.

Some schools utilize hours within the school day. However, it should be remembered that the physical education class is primarily an instructional period, and to use this period for such a program does not seem to be in conformance with the standards set in the profession. However, some schools have satisfactorily utilized free, activity, and club periods for the program where facilities would allow.

Noon hour has been popular in some schools, especially at the elementary and secondary levels, and particularly in rural schools where students do not go home for lunch. Since students will be active anyway, such a period offers possibilities in selected situations, if strenuous activities are not offered.

Recess periods in the elementary school have proved to be a good time for many communities to conduct some of their intramural activities.

Saturdays have also been utilized in some situations. Although the weekend has proved to be a problem in some localities because many individuals have work to do or have planned this time to be with their parents, it has worked successfully in many communities.

The time before school in the morning has also proved satisfactory in a few schools. Getting up early in the morning does not seem to be a handicap to some individuals.

Special days are set aside in some schools for "field days" when classes are abandoned by administrative decree and all the students participate in a day or a half-day devoted entirely to activities that comprise the program.

AN INTRAMURAL PROGRAM EVALUATION CHECKLIST*

A program can be evaluated in terms of the stated principles and objectives or according to prevalent acceptable standards.

How does the intramural program measure up to acceptable minimum standards? By taking a few minutes to check off the items listed below, a quick evaluation can be made of the present status of the excellence of the program.

Yes	No	*Philosophy and objectives*
____	____	1. Is a written philosophy or a set of objectives available to the participants?

Yes	No	*Organization and administration*
____	____	1. Is the director professionally qualified to administer the program?
____	____	2. Does the director devote at least 7.5 hours per week to administering his program?
____	____	3. Are students included in the management of the program?
____	____	4. Is there an advisory committee composed of students and faculty?

Yes	No	*Units of competition*
____	____	1. Are students classified according to ability, age, height, or weight within the competitive unit?
____	____	2. Within the basic unit, are students permitted to choose the members of their teams?

*From Matthews, D. O.: Intramural administration principles, The Athletic Journal 46:82, 1966. Reproduced courtesy The Athletic Journal.

Continued.

AN INTRAMURAL PROGRAM EVALUATION CHECKLIST—cont'd

Yes   No   Program of activities

_____ _____ 1. Does the director consult with the students to make sure that their interests are of prime consideration in the choice of activities in the program?

_____ _____ 2. Are there both strenuous and nonstrenuous sports in the program?

_____ _____ 3. Are there both team and individual sports in the program?

_____ _____ 4. Are there at least five different sports making up the program?

_____ _____ 5. Does at least one corecreation activity make up part of the program?

Yes   No   Time periods

_____ _____ 1. Does the hour immediately after school receive top priority for scheduling?

_____ _____ 2. Is the noon hour utilized as a time period for intramurals?

Yes   No   Methods of organizing competition

_____ _____ 1. Is the round robin tournament used whenever possible in preference to others?

Yes   No   Point system of awards

_____ _____ 1. Is recognition of any kind given to the participants for their achievements?

_____ _____ 2. Is the award primarily for achievement instead of incentive for participants?

Yes   No   Rules and regulations

_____ _____ 1. Are the rules defining such things as eligibility, health, safety, forfeits, postponements, and team membership distributed to all participants?

_____ _____ 2. Is the lack of good sportsmanship regarded as a rule violated?

_____ _____ 3. Is equipment provided for all the activities offered?

Yes   No   Publicity

_____ _____ 1. Is there a special bulletin board for intramural information?

Yes   No   Finances

_____ _____ 1. Does the board of education through the school budget provide funds for the operation of the program?

Rating scale

A "yes" answer must be given in each category if a program is to be considered *good* or *excellent*.

Excellent	15 to 22
Good	13 to 14
Fair	10 to 12
Poor	9 or below

Questions and exercises

1. What is the place of intramural and extramural programs in the total physical education plan of a school or college? How do they complement and supplement the other phases of the total program?

2. To what extent are the objectives of intramurals and extramurals compatible with those of general education? Give specific evidence to support your answer.

3. Survey at least three schools on either the high school or the college level to determine if there is proper balance between the intramural and extramural and the interschool programs. Prepare a statement of findings.

4. Prepare a plan for a sports or play day that could be held in your school.

5. Why have sports, play, and invitation days increased so much in popularity during the last few years?

6. Develop a set of principles that could be used as guides for the selection of activities in intramural and extramural programs.

7. Draw up a seasonal list of activities that could be offered in a school of your choosing. Take into consideration facilities, climate, leadership, and other essential influences.

8. Identify the following: round robin tournament, unit of competition, straight elimination tournament, and ladder tournament.

9. Prepare a debate on the question: Should awards be given in intramural and extramural programs?

10. Develop what you consider to be ideal intramural and extramural programs at the elementary, junior high school, senior high school, or college level.

11. What are some important considerations in administering athletic programs for girls and women? Discuss in detail.

Reading assignment in *Administrative Dimensions of Health and Physical Education Programs, Including Athletics:* Chapter 7, Selections 34 to 38.

Selected references

American Association for Health, Physical Education, and Recreation: Girls sports organization handbook, Washington, D. C., 1961, The Association.

American Association for Health, Physical Education, and Recreation: Intramural sports for college men and women, Washington, D. C., 1961, The Association.

Anton T., and Toschi, L.: A practical approach to intramural sports, Portland, Me., 1964, J. Weston Walsh.

The Athletic Institute: Intramurals for the senior high school, Chicago, 1964, The Athletic Institute, Inc.

Bucher, C. A.: Field days, The Journal of Health and Physical Education 19:22, 1948.

Bucher, C. A., editor: Methods and materials in physical education and recreation, St. Louis, 1954, The C. V. Mosby Co.

Bucher, C. A.: Foundations of physical education, ed. 5, St. Louis, 1968, The C. V. Mosby Co.

Bucher, C. A., and Cohane T.: Little league baseball can hurt your boy, Look, Aug. 11, 1963, p. 74.

Bucher, C. A., and Dupee, R. K., Jr.: Athletics in schools and colleges, New York, 1965, The Center for Applied Research in Education, Inc. (The Library of Education).

Cummings, P.: The dictionary of sports, New York, 1949, A. S. Barnes & Co.

Division for Girls' and Women's Sports: Special events in the girls' sports program, Washington, D. C., 1961, The American Association for Health, Physical Education, and Recreation.

Educational Policies Commission: School athletics ⌐problems and policies, Washington, D. C., 1954, National Education Association.

Forsythe, C. E.: The administration of high school athletics, Englewood Cliffs, N. J., 1962, Prentice-Hall, Inc.

Grieve, A. W.: Directing high school athletics, Englewood Cliffs, N. J., 1963, Prentice-Hall, Inc.

Jacobson, R. O.: Intramurals are recreation for all in the high school, School Activities 35:183, 1964.

Mallory, O.: Co-recreational intramurals, School Activities 35:68, 1963.

Matthews, D. O.: Intramural administration principles, The Athletic Journal 46:82, 1966.

Report of the Joint Committee on Athletic Competition for Children of Elementary and Junior High School Age: Desirable athletic competition for children, Washington, D. C., 1952, American Association for Health, Physical Education, and Recreation.

Rule books for all boys' sports. Available from the National Federation of State High School Athletic Associations, 7 S. Dearborn St., Chicago, Ill.

Rule books for all girls' sports. Available from the Division for Girls' and Women's Sports, American Association for Health, Physical Education, and Recreation, 1201 16th St., N. W., Washington, D. C.

Watkins, J. H.: Intramurals in the junior high school, Journal of the American Association for Health, Physical Education, and Recreation 21:281, 1950.

CHAPTER 10 THE INTERSCHOLASTIC AND INTERCOLLEGIATE VARSITY ATHLETIC PROGRAMS

Each phase of the educational process must have clear-cut objectives if it is to justify its existence. This is essential in order to know where it is heading, what it is striving for, and what it hopes to accomplish. Interscholastic and intercollegiate varsity athletic programs are no exception to this rule.

The aim of all education is the enrichment of life. This is the ultimate goal upon which attention has been focused. The objectives of athletics as part of the physical education program are more definite and specific than this aim, and through them the ultimate goal is brought nearer to realization. Therefore, it is essential that everyone associated with this work help in the achievement of these goals.

The executive secretary of the Missouri State High School Activities Association* indicates that school athletic programs should include the development of the following goals for its youth. They are presented here in adapted form:

1. An appreciation of why the school provides an athletic program
2. A knowledge of the values of athletics to the individual and society
3. An understanding of the rules essential to playing the game
4. The ability to think as an individual and as a team member

5. Faith in and respect for the democratic processes
6. An appreciation of the values of group ideals
7. The development of motor skills
8. Health and physical fitness
9. An understanding and appreciation of what constitutes wholesome recreation and entertainment
10. The desire to be successful and excel
11. Moral and ethical standards
12. Self-discipline, emotional maturity, and self-control
13. Social competence
14. Recognition of the importance of conforming to the rules
15. Respect for the rights of others and those in authority
16. Good human relationships

An era of great expansion in athletics started in the post–World War II period. The physical defects revealed by the draft, the value of sports in building morale, and the emphasis on physical fitness during the war and during the present period of national emergency have combined to encourage athletics to a degree that has never been equaled in the history of this country.

The emphasis on athletics has been the focus of much attention and controversy and consequently the program should be considered carefully by all interested in administration. Interscholastic and intercollegiate athletics have a definite place in senior high school and college programs of physical education. Such competition can help players achieve a higher standard of mental, moral, social, and physical fitness, provided the overall objectives of physical education are kept in mind.

*Keller, I. A.: School athletics—its philosophy and objective, American School Board Journal 153:22-23, 1966. Reprinted, with permission, from the American School Board Journal, August, 1966. Copyright assigned 1967 to The National School Boards Association. All rights reserved.

Varsity crew in rowing tank with mirrors. (Trinity College, Hartford, Conn.)

Angell Field, Stanford University, with an intercollegiate dual meet in progress. Note the television coverage of this meet. The rim of Stanford Stadium is visible in the center background.

RELATIONSHIP TO TOTAL PHYSICAL EDUCATION PROGRAM

Varsity interscholastic and intercollegiate athletics represent an integral part of the total physical education program. They should develop out of the intramural and extramural athletic programs.

Athletics, with the appeal they have to youth, should be the heart of physical education and should aid in achieving goals that will help to enrich living for all who participate.

The challenge of providing sound educational programs in varsity interscholastic and intercollegiate athletics is one that all physical education personnel should recognize. The challenge can be met and resolved if physical educators aggressively bring to the attention of administrators, school and college faculties, and the public in general the true purposes of athletics in a physical education program. It is important to stress that there is a need for having an athletic program that meets the needs of all; that such a program is organized and administered with the welfare of the individual in mind; that it is conducted in the light of educational objectives that are not compromised when exposed to pressures from sports writers, alumni, and townspeople; and that it provides leadership trained in physical education.

In actual practice the organization of athletics takes two forms. At times they are organized as an integral part of the physical education structure and at other times as a separate unit apart from physical education. Some departments of athletics that operate as separate units evolved from the nineteenth century, when they were not considered an integral part of education. If athletics are looked upon as intrinsically related to education, they should be a part of the physical education program.

THE ATHLETIC COUNCIL

Most colleges and many schools have some type of athletic council, board, or committee that establishes athletic policies for the institution. It may involve only faculty members or it may also involve students. Such councils, boards, or committees are responsible for giving the athletic program proper direction in the educational program.

The composition of such committees or councils varies widely from school to school and college to college. In a school, the principal may serve as chairman, or this position may be held by the director of physical education or other faculty member. The committee may include coaches, members of the board of education, faculty members, students, or members of the community at large. In a college or university, the composition of the committee may consist of administrators, faculty members, students, athletic director, coaches, and others.

THE ATHLETIC DIRECTOR

The athletic director implements the athletic policies as established by the council, board, or committee. Responsibilities of the athletic director include preparing the budget for the sports program, purchasing equipment and supplies, scheduling athletic contests, arranging for officials, supervising eligibility requirements, making arrangements for transportation, seeing that medical examinations of athletes and proper insurance coverage are adequate, and supervising the program in general.

A rating card was developed by Kelliher for the evaluation of the effectiveness of the athletic director. It is reproduced here for the benefit of the reader.

RATING CARD FOR ATHLETIC DIRECTORS FOR EVALUATING THE ADMINISTRATION OF AN ATHLETIC PROGRAM

A high school rating card has been adapted from Kelliher's college criteria.* These evaluation items assist the athletic director in checking the effectiveness of his program.

The actual rating card includes a column for evaluating each of these thirty-six items. The column is headed "Performance in this Area Is Given: Great Attention; Moderate Attention; Little Attention."

A. Financial soundness
    1. He operates on a sound financial basis.
    2. There is equitable balance in the budget for all sports.

*Kelliher, M. S.: Successful athletic administration, Journal of Health, Physical Education, and Recreation 30:31, 1959.

RATING CARD FOR ATHLETIC DIRECTORS FOR EVALUATING THE ADMINISTRATION OF AN ATHLETIC PROGRAM—cont'd

B. Organization of the department

   3. He handles the business of the department efficiently and promptly.

   4. All members of the department handle their work assignments efficiently.

   5. He operates effectively without waste of time or materials.

   6. He develops close cooperation between all members of his staff.

   7. Policies and procedures are written out and are made clear to both players and staff members.

   8. He cooperates with other departments of the school and maintains good relations with the administration.

   9. He is fair and firmly in control of his staff and never fails to recognize organizational channels.

  10. He is easily available to anyone with an interest in the athletic program.

C. Professional status of the staff

  11. His operations are in harmony with the philosophy and objectives of the school and of the physical education department.

  12. His operations are in harmony with the spirit and rules and regulations of interscholastic athletics as established by the state high school athletic association.

  13. He is able to justify the athletic program as an important phase of education.

  14. The director is an educator. His status in the school is comparable to other department heads and is considered high.

  15. He cooperates with the administration; he works with the faculty and keeps them well informed.

D. Well-being of the staff

  16. He has developed a high degree of esprit de corps among all members of his department.

  17. He cooperates with the administration in the selection of staff members who believe in high standards of competitive athletics.

  18. He develops a staff of men with high professional standards and education.

  19. He is loyal to the administration and to his staff and gets facts before making a move.

E. Well-being of the students

  20. The health protection of athletes is rated high.

  21. He insists that athletes strive to keep up with their class.

  22. The best possible education for the boy is the most important criterion.

  23. He produces a program that appeals to a large number of participants.

  24. He considers the after-graduation success of former athletes a measure of success of the athletic department.

  25. He prefers that athletes carry on a career program.

  26. He has understanding of and cooperates with general student body interests.

  27. Students assigned to work in the department give reasonable service for experience and credit earned.

F. Public relations

  28. There is an efficient program of public relations.

  29. He maintains friendly relations with press and radio.

  30. He conducts athletics in an efficient, crowd-pleasing manner.

  31. He insists that squad members are school representatives at all times and that they conduct themselves accordingly.

  32. The activities of the department are well received by the administration, faculty, and community.

  33. The record of sportsmanship of all competitive teams under his administration is high.

G. Care of property and equipment

  34. Teams are well equipped, neat, and clean.

  35. The equipment of the department is cared for in an excellent manner and according to sound procedures.

  36. The buildings and grounds under the supervision of the director are kept in excellent condition.

THE COACH

One of the most popular phases of physical education professional work is that of coaching. Many students who show exceptional skill in some interscholastic sport such as basketball, baseball, or football feel that they would like to become members of the profession so that they may coach. They feel that since they have proved themselves outstanding athletes in high school, they will be successful in coaching. This, however, is not necessarily true. It may seem paradoxic to the layman, but there is insufficient evidence to show that exceptional skill in any activity necessarily guarantees success in teaching that activity. Many other factors such as personality, interest in youth, knowledge of human growth and development, psychology, intelligence, integrity, leadership, character, and a sympathetic attitude carry great weight in coaching success.

Coaching should be recognized as teaching. Because of the nature of his position, a coach may be in a more favorable position to teach concepts that make for effective daily living than any other member of a school faculty. Youth, with their inherent drive for activity and action and their quest for the excitement and competition found in sports, look up to the coach and in many cases feel that he is the type of individual to be emulated. Therefore, the coach should recognize his influence and see the value of such attributes as character, personality, and integrity. Although a coach must know thoroughly the game he is coaching, these other characteristics are of equal importance.

The coach of an athletic team has within himself the power to build future citizens who possess traits that are desirable and acceptable to society, or citizens who have a false conception as to what is right and proper. The coach is sometimes tempted to seek outcomes not educational in nature by the insecurity of his position, the emphasis on winning teams, student and alumni pressure, the desire for lucrative gate receipts, and the publicity that goes with winning teams. Unless the coach is an individual of strong character and is willing to follow an unswerving course in the direction of what he knows to be right, many evil practices may enter the picture.

Coaching is characterized in some schools and colleges by insecurity of position. Whether a coach feels secure depends to a great extent upon the school, college, community, and the administration. Coaching offers an interesting and profitable career to many individuals. However, one should recognize the possibility of finding himself in a situation where the pressure to produce winning teams may be so great as to cause unhappiness, insecurity, and even the loss of a job.

Coaching is only one phase of the physical education profession; and coaching is teaching. Because of this close relationship with physical education and the education field in general, a coach should be thoroughly qualified as a physical education person. He needs a background in physical and biologic science, skills, behavioral sciences, education, and the humanities. Only in this way can he best serve youth who are interested in athletics.

There are four qualifications that are found in the outstanding coach. First, he has an ability to teach the fundamentals and strategies of his sport; he *must* be a good teacher. Second, he understands the boy or girl who is a player. The coach needs to understand how a youth functions at his particular level of development—with full appreciation of skeletal growth, muscular development, and physical and emotional limitations. Third, he understands the game he coaches. Thorough knowledge of techniques, rules, and similar information is basic. Fourth, he has a desirable personality and character. Patience, understanding, kindness, honesty, sportsmanship, sense of right and wrong, courage, cheerfulness, affection, humor, energy, and

Varsity basketball. (Trinity College, Hartford, Conn.)

enthusiasm are imperative, since the youngsters will be idolizing and emulating his every move.

Too often coaches are chosen because of one qualification—they have played the game. Most principals, superintendents of schools, and college presidents would be flattered to have an All-American coaching their football teams. In terms of the welfare of youth, however, the other qualifications are even more important, and the administration will be most likely to find a coach with these qualifications in a person who has been trained in physical education.

It is just as important to employ a coach who has been trained in his field as it is to employ a science teacher who has been prepared to teach in his subject matter area. Who has heard of an administrator employing a science instructor whose training was in history but who had dabbled in science on an extracurricular basis and had won the science fair contest in high school? Athletics is one part of the total physical education program, not an end in itself. Basic experiences in sports techniques, first aid, anatomy and physiology, philosophy of physical education, and other courses will make a person a better coach in the educational setting.

School and college administrators, physical educators, coaches, state certificating officers, and others should try to arrive at some common standards for employing a coach rather than having it done on a hit-or-miss basis.

Professional preparation of the coach

About one-fourth of all coaches in the junior and senior high schools in this country have no professional preparation, and the percentage is much higher among college coaches. The only qualification many coaches have is the fact that they have played the game or sport in high school, college, or the professional ranks. It is generally recognized that the best preparation that a coach can have is training in the field of physical education. In light of this fact, several states are attempting to see that coaches, particularly at the precollege level, have at least some training in the field of physical education.

A group of persons has been working as a committee in the American Association for Health, Physical Education, and Recreation to encourage certification of coaches. They feel that a coach should be prepared in each of the following five areas:

Medical aspects of athletic coaching
Principles and problems of coaching
Theory and techniques of coaching
Kinesiologic foundations of coaching
Physiologic foundations of coaching

The Men's Physical Education Department at California State College, Long Beach, has initiated a coaching emphasis minor program that includes the following:

Departmental approval required for admittance to program courses in:
Scientific foundations
Behavioral problems in athletics and
physical education
Athletic injuries

Field work in coaching or student teaching
in coaching
Coaching courses
Electives

The preparation of the coach is receiving more and more attention and, in time, at least a minimum of preparation will be required in many states. This is in keeping with the great growth of sports in our society and the need to safeguard the best interests of American youth.

SOME ADMINISTRATIVE CONSIDERATIONS IN VARSITY ATHLETIC PROGRAMS

There are many administrative considerations pertinent to the conduct of an interscholastic or intercollegiate varsity athletic program. Some of the more important of these are: (1) crowd control, (2) health of the players, (3) contracts, (4) officials, (5) protests and forfeitures, (6) game management, (7) schedules and practice periods, (8) awards, (9) records, and (10) transportation. Each will be discussed in the following paragraphs.

Crowd control

Crowd control at athletic contests is becoming of increasing importance in light of recent dissent, riots, and disturbances on both high school and college campuses

Interscholastic wrestling. (Richwoods Community High School, Peoria Heights, Ill.)

and in public gathering places. The elimination of night athletic activities has been on the increase, particularly in our large cities. School districts and college authorities are taking increased precautions to avoid any disturbances. More police are being brought in to help supervise the crowds at athletic contests, sportsmanship assemblies are being held, townspeople are being informed, administrators are discussing the matter, and careful plans are being developed.

The Sixth National Conference of City and County Directors of the AAHPER, which was held in Washington, D. C., in December, 1968, spent considerable time on the subject of crowd control at athletic contests. A summary of their discussions as reported in their proceedings is reproduced here.

APPROACHES TO CROWD CONTROL*

Summary of reports: small group discussions

The nature and seriousness of the problems in crowd control have recently become more drastic and bizarre as they have occurred in increasing frequency. They take on the collective character of a deliberate attempt either to ignore or confront the system. This social problem may be impossible to eliminate completely, but an attempt must be made to cope with the immediate symptoms. Our only hope is for imaginative and coordinated efforts by the school administration, the majority of students, and community authorities to promote standards of conduct conducive to continuing spectator sports in comparative tranquility. The alternatives are to allow a disruptive element to completely negate the nature of school athletics, to play with no spectators, or to abandon the activity.

The following will present some causes of crowd control problems and some approaches to solutions.

Some causes of problems
Lack of anticipation of, and preventive planning for, possible trouble
Lack of proper facilities
Poor communication resulting in lack of information
Lack of involvement of one or more of the following: school administration, faculty, student body, parents, community, press, and law enforcement agencies
Lack of respect for authority and property
Attendance at games of youth under the influence of narcotics
Increased attitude of permissiveness
School dropouts, recent graduates, and outsiders

Some approaches to solutions
Develop written policy statements, guidelines, and regulations for crowd control.
1. Consult the following before writing policy statements or promulgating regulations: school administration, athletic director, coaches, faculty members involved in the school sports program, school youth organizations, local police departments.
2. Properly and efficiently administer regulations and provide for good communications.
3. Constantly evaluate regulations and guidelines for their relevance and effectiveness.
4. Make guidelines and regulations so effective that the director of athletics who follows them is secure in knowing he has planned with his staff for any eventuality and has sufficient help, appropriately briefed, for any situation that may arise.

Provide adequate facilities.
1. Plan and design stadiums, fieldhouses, and gymnasiums for effective crowd control.
2. Provide for adequate rest room facilities.
3. Establish a smoking area when indoor contests are held.
4. Complete preparation of facilities before game time.

*From Sixth National Conference of City and County Directors, American Association for Health, Physical Education, and Recreation: Crowd control, Washington, D. C., 1968, The Association, pp. 17-22.

Continued.

APPROACHES TO CROWD CONTROL—cont'd

Teach good sportsmanship throughout the school and the community.

1. Begin education in good sportsmanship in the earliest grades and continue it throughout the school life.
2. Make frequent approving references to constructive and commendable behavior.
3. Arrange for program appearances by faculty members and students jointly to discuss the true values of athletic competition including good sportsmanship.
4. Make use of all news media through frequent and effective television, radio, and press presentations and interviews, commentaries, and frequent announcement of good sportsmanship slogans.
5. Distribute a printed Code of Ethics for Good Sportsmanship.
6. Include the good sportsmanship slogan in all printed programs at sports events.
7. Urge the use of athletic events as an example in elementary school citizenship classes, stressing positive values of good conduct at games, during the raising of the flag and singing of the national anthem; courtesy toward visitors.
8. Involve teachers in school athletic associations, provide them with passes to all sports events, and stress the positive values of their setting an example of good sportsmanship.

Intensify communications prior to scheduled games.

1. Arrange for an exchange of speakers at school assembly programs; the principals, coaches, or team captains could visit the opposing school.
2. Discuss with appropriate personnel of the competing school the procedures for the game, including method and location of team entry and departure.
3. Provide superintendent or principal, athletic director, and coach with a copy of written policy statement, guidelines, and regulations.
4. Meet all game officials and request them to stress good sportsmanship on the field.
5. Meet with coaches and instruct them not to question officials during a contest; stress the importance of good sportsmanship and the fact that their conduct sets the tone for spectator reaction to game incidents.
6. Instruct students what to expect and what is expected of them.
7. Schedule preventive planning conferences with local police to be assured of their full cooperation and effectiveness in spectator control.

Inform the community.

1. Request coaches and athletic directors to talk to service groups and other community groups.
2. Stress the need for exemplary conduct of coaches at all times.
3. Invite community leaders (non-school people) to attend athletic events.
4. Post on all available notice boards around town, in factories and other public places, posters showing the Sportsmanship Code of Ethics and Guidelines in brief.
5. Release constructive information and positive statements to news media and request publication of brief guidelines on sports pages.
6. Provide news media with pertinent information as to ways in which the community may directly and indirectly render assistance in the crowd control problem.

Involve law enforcement personnel.

1. Police and other security personnel should be strategically located so as to afford the best possible control.
2. Law enforcement professionals should handle *all* enforcement and disciplining of spectators.
3. Strength in force may be shown by appearance of several policemen, motorcycles, police cruise cars, et cetera, at and near the site of the game.
4. Women police may be stationed in women's rest rooms.
5. Civil Defense organizations could patrol parking areas.
6. A faculty member from the visiting school may be used as a liaison with police and local faculty in identifying visiting students.
7. Attendants, police, county sheriffs, deputies should be in uniform. Uniformed authority figures command greater respect.

Use supervisory personnel other than police.

1. Select carefully teacher supervisors who are attentive and alert to signs of possible trouble.
2. Identify faculty members by arm bands or other means.
3. Provide for communication by means of walkie-talkie systems.

APPROACHES TO CROWD CONTROL—cont'd

4. Assign some faculty members to sit behind the visiting fans; this reduces verbal harassment of visitors.
5. Employ paid ticket takers and paid chaperones to mingle strategically among the crowd and to remain on duty throughout the game, including half-time.
6. Issue passes to junior high physical education teachers to provide more adult supervision.

Plan for ticket sales and concession stands.

1. Arrange for advance sale of student tickets to avoid congestion at the gate.
2. Sell tickets in advance only to students in their own schools, and avoid sale of tickets to outsiders and non-students.
3. Provide for a close check at the gate or entrance.
4. Arrange for concession stands to be open before the game, during half-time, and after the game, but closed during actual play.
5. Channel the flow of traffic to and from concession stands by means of ropes, or other means; keep traffic moving.

Prepare spectators and contestants.

1. Encourage as many students as possible to be in the uniforms of the athletic club, pep club, booster clubs, band, majorettes, cheer leaders.
2. Bus participants to and from the site of the game.
3. Have participants dressed to play before leaving for a game or contest.
4. Adhere to established seating capacity of stadiums and gymnasiums.
5. Request home team fans to remain in their own stands until visiting team fans have left.
6. Try to arrange for a statewide athletic association regulation prohibiting all noise makers including musical instruments except for the school band or orchestra under professional supervision.
7. Request the assistance of visiting clubs.
8. Educate cheerleaders, student leaders, band captains, pep squads, and faculty supervisors by means of a one day conference program.
9. Keep spectators buffered from the playing area as much as practical.
10. Request that elementary school children be accompanied by an adult.

Miscellaneous.

1. Inform and involve school superintendents fully when problems arise in connection with sports events.
2. Impose severe penalties on faculty and student leaders guilty of poor conduct.
3. Publish the identity of offenders at games and notify parents, if possible; any penalties inflicted should also be noted. (Note: If the offense leads to Juvenile Court action, care should be taken not to contravene laws about publishing names of juvenile offenders.)
4. Consistently enforce rules and regulations; this is a necessity.
5. Work toward the assumption of responsibility for strong regulation and enforcement of team behavior on the part of the state athletic associations.
6. Attempt to work with the courts toward greater cooperation.
7. Avoid overstressing the winning of games.
8. Discontinue double headers and triple headers.
9. After-game incidents away from the proximity of the stadium or gymnasium are out of the control of school officials, but cause bad public reaction.

Summary

Sound safety controls and crowd controls at school athletic functions are a must! Greater concentration on treating the causes of the problem is essential. Preliminary groundwork is the key to good crowd control. Coordination and cooperation of school and law enforcement agencies is the key to success.

Youth should be taught to know what to expect and what is expected of them. Consistent enforcement of rules and regulations is a necessity if youth is to respect authority. Adult behavior should be such that it may be advantageously and admirably emulated by youth whose actions hopefully may result in deserving praise instead of negative criticism and disapproval.

The athletic program is a constructive and valuable school activity. It should be permitted to function in a favorable, healthful, and friendly environment.

Health of the players

Interscholastic and intercollegiate athletics should contribute to the health of the players. Through wholesome physical activity the participant should become more physically, mentally, emotionally, and socially fit.

Medical examination. One of the first requirements for every participant in an athletic program should be a medical examination to determine physical fitness and capacity to engage in such a program.

*See also Chapter 13.

HEALTH QUESTIONNAIRE FOR SPORTS CANDIDATES

(To be completed by parents or family physician and returned to team physician or trainer)

Name .... Birth Date ....

Home Address ....

Parent's Name .... Tel. No. ....

Family Physician .... Tel. No. ....

1. Has had injuries requiring medical attention	YES	NO
2. Has had illness lasting more than a week	YES	NO
3. Is under physician's care now	YES	NO
4. Takes medication now	YES	NO
5. Wears glasses	YES	NO
Contact lenses	YES	NO
6. Has had surgical operation	YES	NO
7. Has been in hospital (except for tonsillectomy)	YES	NO
8. Do you know of any reason why this individual should not participate in all sports?	YES	NO

Please explain any "YES" answers to above questions:

....

....

....

9. Has had complete poliomyelitis immunization, by inoculations (Salk) or oral vaccine (Sabin)	YES	NO
10. Has had tetanus toxoid, and booster inoculation within past 3 years	YES	NO

....

PARENT OR PHYSICIAN

Health questionnaire.

The strenuous nature of athletics and the demands placed upon the participant make it imperative that a thorough medical examination be required. This should be a practice in all schools and colleges and for all individuals.

The medical examination may be conducted by the family, school, or college physician. The trend appears to be to have the examination given by the family physician. However, the best method of administering the examination should be determined in light of local conditions. The school or college physician should review the examination results and health histories or otherwise determine if there are any defects or other conditions that would be aggravated by participation. No student should be permitted to participate unless a physician can state that he is fit for such competititon.

Safety. Everything possible should be done to ensure that the safety of the participant is provided for. Only well-trained and qualified coaches should be permitted to be on the staff. Such a coach will always conduct his program with the health of the players in mind. He will have a knowledge of first aid. He will be continually alert to stop players from further participation if they are unduly fatigued; have received head, spine, or neck injuries; or are dazed. He will not allow a player who has been unconscious as a result of injury to resume play until a thorough check and approval have been given by a qualified physician. He will work closely with the team or school physician, trying to make every effort possible to guard the health of his players.

Proper conditioning and training should take place before any player is subjected to competition. Such conditioning and training should be progressive in nature and allow for gradual achievement of a state of acceptable physical fitness. There should always be enough players on the squad to allow for substitutions in the event a person is not physically or otherwise fit for play.

Proper facilities and equipment should be available to guard the safety and health of the players. This means that facilities are constructed according to recommended standards in respect to size, surfacing, and various safety features. Protective equipment should be provided as needed in the various sports. If desirable facilities and equipment are not available, such competition should not be provided.

Games should be scheduled that result in equal and safe competition. The desire of small schools to defeat larger schools, where the competition is not equal, often brings disastrous results to the health and welfare of the players. Under such circumstances, one often hears the remark, "They really took a physical beating." Competition should be as equitable as possible.

Prompt attention should be given to all injuries. Injured players should be examined by a physician and given proper treatment. There should be complete medical supervision of the athletic program. The trainer is not a substitute. A medical doctor should be present at all games and practices, if at all possible. The doctor should be the one to determine the extent of an injury. A player after being ill or hurt should not be permitted to participate again until the coach receives an approved statement from the family, school, or college physician.

Proper sanitary measures should be taken. Individual towels and drinking cups should be provided. The day of the "team" towel and the "team" drinking cup has passed. Equipment and uniforms should be cleaned as often as necessary. Locker, dressing, shower, toilet, and other rooms that are used by players should be kept clean and in a sanitary condition. Playing areas should be kept clean and safe. Gymnasia should be properly heated, and every measure taken to ensure as nearly ideal conditions as possible for students engaging in the athletics program.

Injuries and insurance. * The state athletic association in many states sponsors an athletic insurance plan. Such plans pay various medical, x-ray, dental, hospitalization, and other expenses according to the terms of the plan. There are also some private insurance companies that have such plans. The Wisconsin Interscholastic Athletic Association with its Athletic Accident Plan, recognized as one of the better types of athletic insurance, was a pioneer in the field. This plan covers injuries while practicing for or participating in interscholastic athletics. It has a premium rate for "all sports" coverage and also one for all sports except football. As pointed out by this association, the purpose of the plan is to provide enrolled athletes with benefits that will help to meet the costs of medical, dental, and hospital care in the event of accidental injury resulting from participation in physical education or athletics sponsored by a participating school. The amount of any payment for an injury shall be only in the amount of the actual expenses incurred but not in excess of the amounts listed in the schedule of allowance for such injury. In order to collect benefits, plan requirements must be met.

The insurance covered by various state and independent plans usually includes benefits for accidental death or dismemberment, hospital expenses, x-ray fees, physicians' fees, and surgical and dental expenses. Dental benefits may or may not be included in the schedule of surgical benefits. In some plans, catastrophe benefits are also available for injuries requiring extensive medical care and long-term hospitalization. Coverage is normally provided on a deductible basis, with the insurance company paying 75% to 80% of

the total cost over the deductible amount up to a maximum of $2,500 to $5,000.

After the Wisconsin High School Athletic Association inaugurated its school athletic insurance in 1930, several other state high school athletic associations followed suit. The number of such athletic insurance plans reached twenty-five in the 1940's. However, the commercial insurance industry, seeing the promise and need for athletic insurance, gradually came into the market, some of them providing many attractive premiums. Many school administrators were sympathetic to this type of coverage. Increasingly, the commercial insurance people have gained a strong foothold in the school athletic insurance program and today many schools and colleges utilize their policies.

State high school athletic associations in a few states still operate successful benefit plans, primarily by adopting many of the benefits utilized by the insurance industry, namely, nonallocated benefits, catastrophic coverage, and nonduplication of benefits.

California is the only state in this country that by law requires schools to furnish accident insurance for pupils. However, most school districts voluntarily purchase athletic insurance or make it available to parents.

Every school and college should have a written policy in regard to financial and other responsibilities associated with injuries. The administrator, parents, and players should be thoroughly familiar with the responsibilities of each in regard to injuries.

Contracts

Written contracts are usually essential in the administration of interscholastic and intercollegiate athletics. On the college level, in particular, games are scheduled many months or years in advance. Memories and facts tend to fade and become obscure with time. In order to avoid misunderstanding and confusion, it is best to

---

*See also Chapter 18.

have in writing a contract between the schools or colleges concerned.

Contracts should be properly executed and signed by official representatives of both schools and colleges. Many athletic associations provide specially prepared forms for use of member schools or colleges. Such forms usually contain the names of the schools, dates, and circumstances and conditions under which the contest will be held. Furthermore, they usually provide for penalties if the contract is not fulfilled by either party.

Officials

The officials will greatly influence the interscholastic or intercollegiate athletic program and determine whether it is conducted in a manner that will be of most benefit to the players and the schools or colleges concerned. Officials should be well qualified. They should know the rules and be able to interpret them accurately; recognize their responsibility to the players; be good sportsmen; and be courteous, honest, friendly, cooperative, impartial, and able to control the game at all times.

In order to ensure that only the best officials are utilized, machinery should be established to register and determine those who are qualified. Officials should be required to pass examinations on rules and to demonstrate their competency. Rating scales have been developed that aid in

---

Sec. XI	Officials Rating Card	NYSPHSAA

Sport .... League .... Game Date ....

Varsity ....   Score

Jr. Varsity .... Home Team ....

Jr. High .... Visiting Team ....

NAME OF OFFICIAL	RATING	CODE	
Referee	....	EXCELLENT	5
		GOOD	4
Umpire	....	ACCEPTABLE	3
		POOR	2
Other	....	UNSATISFACTORY	1
Other	....	NO SHOW	0

CRITERIA — GAME CONTROL   JUDGEMENT — RULES — SPEED   ACCURACY   APPEARANCE
GAME DIFFICULTY — PERSONALITY

COMMENTS ....
....
....
....
....

Any rating of 0, 1 or 2 must be accompanied by reasons or a letter.
This card must be mailed within one week following game.

COACH .... ATH. DIR. ....

Officials rating card of the New York State Public High School Athletic Association.

making such estimates. Most athletic associations have some method of registering and certifying those acceptable officials whom they wish to use. The Division for Girls' and Women's Sports of the AAHPER has a rating committee that certifies officials. In some states the officials who are used, in turn, rate the schools or colleges as to facilities, environment, and circumstances surrounding the game.

Subject to contract differences, officials usually are chosen by the home team with approval of opponents. The practice of the home team selecting officials without any consideration of the wishes of other schools or colleges or regard for impartial officiating has resulted in relations that have not been in the best interests of players or of athletics in general. A growing practice of having the conference or association select officials to be used has many points in its favor.

Officials should be duly notified of such details as the date and time of the contests to which they have been assigned. Officials' fees usually vary from school to

school and from college to college, although some associations have set up standard rates. It is usually considered best to pay a flat fee that includes salary and expenses, rather than to list both separately.

Protests and forfeitures

There should be a set procedure for handling protests and forfeitures in connection with athletic contests. Of course, there should be careful preventive action beforehand in order to avoid a situation where such protests and forfeitures will occur. Proper interpretation of the rules, good officiating, elimination of undue pressures, and proper education of schools, colleges, and coaches on the objectives of interscholastic and intercollegiate athletics will act as preventive measures against such action.

However, the essential procedure for filing protests and forfeitures of contests should be established. This procedure should be clearly stated in writing and contain all the details, such as the person

Athletics, with the appeal it has for youth, should be the heart of physical education. Scene from 1950 Michigan–Michigan State game. (Department of Physical Education and Athletics, University of Michigan.)

DEPARTMENT OF PHYSICAL EDUCATION
ATHLETIC REPORT

School _____ Sport _____ Game No. _____

Game with _____ Played at _____

Date _____ Score _____ Opponents _____
(your score)

Referee _____ Umpire _____ H. L. _____
Rating of officials: (Use numerals: 1-excellent, 2-good, 3-fair, 4-poor)

Attendance _____ Receipts _____ Guarantee (paid) _____
Received _____

Weather conditions _____ Principal's lists were (not) exchanged _____

	Player (full name)	No.	Position	List total participation			Remarks
				Quarters	Innings	Events	
1							
2							
3							
4							
5							
6							
7							
8							
9							
10							
11							
12							
13							
14							
15							
16							
17							
18							
19							
20							
21							
22							
23							
24							
25							

Scorer _____ Record compiled by _____
Time _____ Signature of Coach _____

Athletic report.

HEALTH AND PHYSICAL EDUCATION DEPARTMENT

BOYS' INTERSCHOLASTIC ATHLETIC PROGRAM

Season _____

Activity	Duration of season			Total number of games played						Number of boys participating		
	Date of first practice	Date of last game		Won		Lost				Varsity	Jr. Varsity	Total
			Varsity	Jr. Varsity	Varsity	Jr. Varsity	Varsity	Jr. Varsity				
Baseball												
Basketball												
Cross country												
Football												
Golf												
Ice hockey												
Soccer												
Swimming												
Tennis												
Track and field												
Others												

Number of different boys in interscholastic program _____. (Do not count any boy more than once even though he participated in two or more activities.)

List any school honors or outstanding individual achievements, such as team or individual championships W. I. A. A. selections, etc.:

_____

_____

School _____

Date _____

_____ Teacher's name

Boys' interscholastic athletic program.

ATHLETIC PERMIT

ATHLETIC APPLICATION FOR_____
(SPORT)

Name_____
(last)   (first)

I hereby apply for the privilege of trying out for the

_____team in_____
(sport)   (yr.)

I recognize my responsibilities if I try out for the above sport. I will make it a point to so govern myself that my association with the sport will bring honor to it and the school, and expect to be asked to withdraw from the team in case I do not.

If extended the above privilege I will:

A.   Train consistently as advised by the coach.
B.   Abide by all training rules.
C.   Make a serious endeavor to keep up my studies.
D.   Make it a point to abide by the rules and regulations of the student body.
E.   So conduct myself, at all times, that I will bring credit to my team.

I promise on my word of honor to do the above.

SIGNED_____

PARENTS WAIVER

Date_____

This is to certify that

_____

has my permission to train for and compete in

_____
(sport)

I assume for myself full responsibility should any accident occur to him either in training for such competition or in the competition itself, or in traveling to and from various fields where contests are played or practices held.

Signature_____

Athletic permit.

to whom the protest should be sent, time limits involved, person or group responsible for action, and any other information that is necessary. A frequent reason for a protest is the utilization of ineligible players. Most associations require the forfeiture of any game in which ineligible players participate.

Game management

Since there are so many details in connection with game management it is possible to include only a brief statement of the more important items. In order to have an efficiently conducted contest, it is important to have good organization. There must be someone responsible. Attention must be given to details. There must be planning. Many details must be attended to before the game, during the game, and after the game. Forsythe discusses such items. The various ones that he includes are reproduced here as a checklist for the administrator responsible for such management:

Before-game preparation (home contests)
   a. Contracts
   b. Eligibility records
   c. Physical examinations
   d. Parents' permission
   e. Athletic officials
   f. Equipment
   g. Field or court
   h. Publicity
   i. Courtesies to the visiting school
   j. Reserve games
   k. Tickets
   l. Contest programs
   m. Concessions
   n. Ushers
   o. Police protection and parking
   p. Reserved areas
   q. Cheerleaders
   r. Scoreboards
   s. Conditions of stadium, bleacher, or gymnasium
   t. Bands and half-time arrangements
   u. Decorations
   v. Public-address system
   w. Physician at contest
   x. Scorers, timers, judges

Game responsibilities (home contests)
   a. Supplies and equipment
   b. Tickets
   c. Ushers
   d. Contest programs
   e. Officials' quarters
   f. Visiting team quarters and courtesies
   g. Flag raising
   h. Intermission program
   i. Players' benches
   j. Physician
   k. Bands
   l. Contracts
   m. Contract guarantees and payments
   n. Eligibility lists
   o. Scoreboard arrangements
   p. Guards for dressing room
   q. Extra clothing for substitutes
   r. Concessions
   s. Cheerleaders
   t. Police
   u. Public-address system
   v. Rest rooms
   w. Guarding extra equipment

After-game responsibilities (home contests)
   a. Payment of officials
   b. Payment of visiting school
   c. Storage of equipment
   d. Contest receipts
   e. General financial statement
   f. Concessions report
   g. Record of officials
   h. Participation records
   i. Filing of contest data

Preparation for out-of-town games
   a. Transportation
   b. Parents' permits
   c. Finances for trip
   d. Equipment
   e. Game details
   f. Eligibility records
   g. Game contract
   h. Trip personnel
   i. Participation record books*

Schedules and practice periods

The trend in athletics is to limit the length of seasons for various sports. If this is not done, overemphasis often results with a particular sport monopolizing the

*Forsythe, C. E.: The administration of high school athletics, Englewood Cliffs, N. J., 1962, Prentice-Hall, Inc., chap. 7.

time of students and allowing only little time for other activities. Football has often been accused of this with its fall practice before school or college starts, postseason games that run into the new year, spring practice, and summer work in preparation for the fall season. Such a schedule is not in the interests of the students' general welfare.

There should be defined limits in respect to the length of seasons. These should have the approval of school and college authorities. The length of seasons should be so arranged that they interfere

---

STATEMENT OF PHILOSOPHY REGARDING AWARDS

There are arguments pro and con in respect to awards for athletic participation. Some of the arguments for awards are: they stimulate interest, they serve as an incentive for participation, and they recognize achievement. Some of the arguments against awards are: they make for a more expensive program, a few individuals win most of them, they are unnecessary since students would participate even if no awards were given, it is difficult to make awards on the basis of all factors that should be considered, and the incentive is artificial since the joy and satisfaction received are enough reward in themselves.

Although the conferring of awards is overdone in many cases, the practice of giving out valuable awards indiscriminately cannot be justified educationally or financially. The responsibility of the physical education department is to teach boys and girls to play for the "love of playing" without any thought of an award. It is the feeling of this committee that the human desire for recognition is most natural. The receiving of an award for achievement in athletics in the form of a ribbon, emblem, certificate, or simple medal fosters personal pride in accomplishment. Academically, we recognize students with high grades. We select valedictorians and members of local and national honor societies.

Awards are symbols of achievement and should not be recognized as a prize. In Greek times the olive wreath given to a victor was the most coveted award that could be obtained by a Greek athlete. The importance of such an award was not its material value, but what it symbolized. The custom of awarding insignia or letters by school and college authorities to athletic teams in order to foster school spirit and personal pride in accomplishment and set up high ideals of sportsmanship is almost universal. Because of the long tradition of granting awards and because of the fact that this is a common practice in other activities of life, simple awards — mere symbols of achievement with little or no monetary value — seem to be justifiable.

The school should consider such factors as attitude, dependability, school citizenship, scholarship, participation, and improvement, as well as athletic prowess, in establishing a policy for the conferring of awards. Such a practice would make it advisable for many school officials to be involved in the determination of who receives awards. Furthermore, the basis for students receiving awards should be broadened to include as many levels and kinds of achievement as possible while still keeping the award meaningful as a form of recognition.

Principles for administering athletic awards

1. Awards should have little or no monetary value and should serve as a symbol of achievement.
2. Awards should not detract from the primary goal, namely, the enjoyment of the activity for the activity itself.
3. Opportunities should be provided for all students to obtain awards.
4. Good sportsmanship, scholarship, character, attitude, and citizenship should be considered along with participation and achievement in the conferring of awards.
5. Awards should be presented as a culminating activity of the physical education program.
6. Money for awards should come from the budgeted school funds and not be secured through clubs, alumni, and civic organizations.
7. Awards and dinners or other events given in honor of athletes, should be sponsored *only* by school authorities and not by clubs, alumni, or civic organizations.
8. There should be no major and minor distinction in presenting awards.

as little as possible with other school and college work. They should provide for adequate practice before the first game so that the players are in good physical condition. There should be limits as to the total number of games, depending upon the sport, and also upon the number of games played in any 1 week. Postseason games are not considered advisable by many educators. Teams that are as nearly as possible of equal ability and equal skill should be scheduled.

Awards

The basis for awards in interscholastic and intercollegiate athletics is the same as that for intramural and extramural athletics. As pointed out, there are arguments for and against giving awards. Some individuals feel that the values derived from playing a sport—joy and satisfaction, physical, social, and other values—are sufficient in themselves and that no awards should be given. Others point to the fact that awards are symbolic of achievement and are traditional in our culture and should be given.

The policy that will be adopted in respect to awards should be determined locally. A definite policy should be established that cuts across all the affairs of the school or college. At the present time the practice of giving awards in the form of letters, insignia, or some other symbol is almost universal. It is recommended that when awards are given they should be very simple and of very little monetary value. Some state athletic associations, for example, have stated that the award should not cost more than $1.00. Furthermore, it seems wise not to distinguish between so-called major and minor sports when giving awards. They should be treated on an equal basis.

On p. 253 is the statement of the philosophy and principles for administering athletic awards used in one school system.

Records

The good administrator and coach will keep accurate records of all the details concerned with the administration of interscholastic or intercollegiate athletics. There should be records of students' participation, for eligibility purposes and to show the extent of the program; records of the conduct of various sports from year to year so that they can be compared over a period of time and also compared with other schools and colleges; statistical summaries of player and game performance that will help the coach to determine weaknesses in game strategy or identify players' performances and other items essential to well-organized play; records of equipment and supplies; officials' records; financial records, and other items in connection with the conduct of the total program. Good business and good administration demand good record keeping.

Transportation

Transporting athletes to games and contests presents many administrative problems. Such questions arise as; Who should be transported? In what kind of vehicles should athletes be transported? Is athletics part of a regular school or college program? Should private vehicles or school- and college-owned vehicles be used? What are the legal implications involved in transporting athletes in school- and college-sponsored events?

It appears that the present trend is to view athletics as an integral part of the educational program so that public funds may be used for transportation purposes. At the same time, however, statutes vary from state to state, and any person administering athletic programs should examine carefully the statutes in their own state.

The feeling among many administrators in regard to transportation is that athletes and representatives of the school or college concerned, such as band and cheerleaders, should travel only in transportation provided by the educational institution. Where private cars belonging to coaches, students, or other persons are used, the administrator should be sure to determine whether he is in conformity with the state statutes regarding liability. Under no circumstances should students or other representatives be permitted to drive unless they are authorized drivers and recognized as such by the state statutes. Under most circumstances it is recommended that students not be used as drivers.

SOME ADMINISTRATIVE PROBLEMS

There are many problems with which the administration of any interscholastic or intercollegiate athletic program has to contend. Some that are particularly prominent at the present time are those concerned with (1) gate receipts, (2) tournaments and championships, (3) eligibility, (4) scholarships, (5) recruitment, (6) proselyting, and (7) scouting.

Gate receipts

Gate receipts are the source of many evils in athletics. Too often they become the point of emphasis rather than the valuable educational outcomes that can accrue to the participant. When this occurs, athletics cannot justify existence in the educational program. Furthermore, the emphasis on gate receipts results in a vicious cycle—the money increases the desire for winning teams so that there will be greater financial return, which in turn results in greater financial outlays to secure and develop even better teams. This goes on and on, with a false set of standards forming the basis for the program.

Throughout the country interscholastic and intercollegiate athletics are financed through many different sources. These include gate receipts, board of education and central university funds, donations, special projects, students' fees, physical education department funds, magazine subscriptions, and concessions. In high schools a "general organization" quite frequently handles the funds for athletics. Some colleges finance part of the program through endowment funds.

It has long been argued by leaders in the physical education profession that athletics have great educational potentials. They are curricular in nature rather than extracurricular. This means they contribute to the welfare of students like any other subject in the curriculum. Upon this basis, therefore, the finances necessary to support such a program should come from board of education or central university funds. Athletics should not be self-supporting or used as a means to support part or all of the other so-called extracurricular activities of a school or college. They represent an integral part of the educational program and as such deserve to be treated in the same manner as other aspects of the program. This procedure is followed in some schools and colleges with benefits to all concerned and should be an ideal toward which all should strive.

Tournaments and championships

The question frequently arises as to whether postseason tournaments and championship playoffs should be conducted as part of an athletic program. It is generally agreed by physical education leaders that all the educational values that can be derived from athletics can be gained without ever playing a tournament or championship game. The main purposes of such ventures are usually to make money, to entertain the public, and to crown a winner. Furthermore, many evils enter the picture when tournaments and championships are conducted. As a result of such contests the emphasis on winning becomes more pronounced, participation often results in physical and emotional strain on players, spectator pressure increases, gambling often enters the picture, and the emphasis is on a few individuals.

Eligibility

Standards in regard to the eligibility of contestants are essential. These should be in writing, disseminated widely, and clearly understood by all concerned. They should be established well ahead of a season's or year's play so that the student, coaches, and others will not become emotional when they suddenly realize they will lose their chance to win a championship because they cannot use a star player who is ineligible.

Standards of eligibility in interscholastic circles usually include an age limit of not more than 19 or 20 years; a requirement that an athlete be a bona fide student; rules on transfer students that frequently require their being bona fide residents in the community served by the school; satisfactory grades; a limit of three or four on number of seasons of competition allowed (playing in one game usually constitutes a season); regular attendance at school; permission to play on only one team during a season; and a requirement that the participant have a medical examination, anateur status, and parent's consent. These regulations vary from school to school and from state to state.

The National Federation of State High School Athletic Associations considers a student ineligible for amateur standing if (1) he has accepted money or compensation for playing in an athletic contest, (2) he has played under an assumed name, (3) he has competed with a team whose players received pay for their playing, and (4) he has signed a contract to play with a professional team.

Eligibility requirements at the college and university level include rules in respect to such items as residence, undergraduate status, academic average, amateur status, limits of participation, and transfer. In general, most players must have been in residence for at least 1 year (sometimes waived for small colleges); be a bona fide, fully matriculated student carrying on a full program of studies; have a satisfactory grade-point average; and have had only 1 year of freshman competition and 3 years of varsity competition. Also, a student cannot participate after the expiration of four consecutive 12-month periods following the date of his initial enrollment in an institution of higher learning. Amateur status is also a requirement.

Scholarships

Should athletes receive scholarships or special financial assistance in schools and colleges? This subject is argued pro and con and is mainly a problem at the college level. Those in favor of scholarships and financial assistance claim that a student who excels in sports should receive aid just as much as one who excels in music or any other activity. They claim that such inducements are justified in the educational picture. Those opposed point to the fact that scholarships should be awarded on the basis of the need and general academic qualifications of a student, rather than his skill in some sport.

One solution is to have a list of criteria drawn up for the purpose of making such grants and have them handled by an all-school or all-college committee. This plan is based on the premise that scholarships and student aid should not be granted to the athletic or to any other department. Instead, they should be handled on an all-school or all-college basis and given to students who need them most and are best qualified. In this way, those students who are in need of assistance, regardless of the area in which they specialize, will be the ones who will receive aid.

Recruitment

The recruitment of athletes in order to develop star and winning teams is not condoned for any educational institution. The procedure for admittance should be the same for all students, regardless of whether they are athletes, chemistry students, music students, or others. No special consideration should be shown to any particular group. The same standards, academic and otherwise, should prevail. In this respect the statements below apply equally well to high schools and colleges:

> The athletic teams of an institution should be composed of bona fide students who were attracted to the institution by its educational program. Special efforts to recruit students of athletic prowess for the primary purpose of developing winning athletic teams are unworthy of an institution of higher education. . . .
>
> The encouragement or condonation by an institution of outside organizations engaged in the recruitment or subsidization of athletes is symptomatic of an unwholesome athletic situation. Where such an organization exists, the institution affected by the efforts of this organization will be expected to repudiate these efforts and to take effective steps to prevent relationships between its students and the organization.*

Proselyting

Proselyting is a term applied to a high school or college that has so strongly over-emphasized athletics that it has stooped to unethical behavior to secure outstanding talent for winning teams. High schools are not troubled with this problem as much as colleges, but in some quarters they also have difficulties. There have been incidents where a father was provided employment so that he would move his family to a particular section of a city or a particular community so that his boy would be eligible to play with the local team. However, thanks to vigilant state athletic associations, such incidents have

been kept to a minimum. The following represent some of the rules in force in many states to eliminate special inducements to attract athletes. These rules have been established by many state high school athletic associations:

1. A student shall not be allowed to receive for participation in athletic contests any sweater, blanket, or trophy of any sort except the unattached letter, monogram, or other insignia of the school.
2. A student shall not receive any award from an individual or an organization other than an educational institution of this Association.
3. No student shall be given any trip or excursion of any kind by any individual, group, or organization outside of this Association.
4. An association school shall not receive any award from any individual, groups, or organization outside of this Association.
5. Local individuals, local organizations, or local groups may give complimentary dinners to local athletes or members of athletic teams, provided such dinners meet with the approval of the local superintendent of schools.*

Scouting

Scouting has become an accepted practice at high school and college levels. By watching another team perform, the formations and plays used will be known and certain weaknesses will be discovered. One coach said that his scouting consisted of watching players to determine little mannerisms they had that would give away the play that was going to be used.

Many schools and colleges are spending considerable money in this manner. Some schools and colleges scout a rival team every game during the season. Some use three or four persons on the same scouting assignment, and such schools and colleges take moving pictures at length so that the

---

*Commission on Colleges and Universities, North Central Association of Colleges and Secondary Schools: An interpretation of the revised policy on intercollegiate athletics of the North Central Association, Chicago, 1952, The Association, pp. 11-12.

*Joint Committee: Administration problems in health education, physical education, and recreation, Washington, D. C., 1953, American Association for Health, Physical Education, and Recreation, p. 126.

opponent's play can be studied in great detail. Such money, it is felt by some physical educators, could be spent more wisely if used to enhance the value of the game for the participants, rather than to further any all-important effort to win.

Many unethical practices have entered into scouting. Coaches have been known to have scouts observe secret practice sessions and utilize other unethical methods. DeGroot pointed out that the Code of Ethics of the American Football Coaches Association has the following to say on scouting: "It shall be considered unethical under any circumstances to scout any team, by any means whatsoever, except in regularly scheduled games. Any attempt to scout practice sessions shall be considered strictly unethical. The head football coach of each institution shall be held responsible for all scouting. This shall include the use of moving pictures.*

Many coaches feel that the only reason they want to scout is that they themselves are being scouted. Therefore, they feel it will work to their disadvantage unless they follow the same procedure. If something could be done to eliminate or restrict scouting, considerable time and money could be put to much more advantageous use.

INTERSCHOLASTIC ATHLETICS AT THE ELEMENTARY AND JUNIOR HIGH SCHOOL LEVELS

Since athletics was first introduced into the educational picture, there has been a continual pushing downward of these competitive experiences into the lower educational levels. Educational athletics started at the college level with a crew race between Harvard and Yale in 1852. Then other sports were introduced to the

campuses throughout the United States. As higher education athletic programs expanded and gained recognition and popularity, the high schools felt that sports should also be a part of their educational offerings. As a result, most high schools in America today have some form of interscholastic athletics. In recent years, junior high schools have also felt the impact of interscholastic athletic programs. A survey made by the National Association of Secondary-School Principals, and including 2,296 junior high schools, showed that 85.2% had some program of interscholastic athletics while 14.8% did not.

There should not be any interscholastic athletics at the elementary school level. In kindergarten to grade six physical activities should be geared to the developmental level of the child. Starting with grade four it may be possible to initiate an intramural program on an informal basis. However, there should not be undue emphasis on developing skill in a few sports or requiring children to conform to adult standards of competition.

The special nature of grades seven through nine, representing a transition period between the elementary school and the senior high school and between childhood and adolescence, has raised a question in the minds of many educators as to whether an interscholastic athletic program is in the best interests of the students concerned.

Many of the guidelines of the American Academy of Pediatrics listed below apply to the junior high school level, as well as to the elementary school level, and to the type of athletic competition that should be offered:

1. All children should have opportunities to develop skill in a variety of activities.
2. All such activities should take into account the age and developmental level of child.
3. a. Athletic activities of elementary school children should be part of an over-all school program. Competent medical supervision of each child should be ensured.

---

*DeGroot, D. S.: Code of Ethics of the American Football Coaches Association, The Journal of the American Association for Health, Physical Education, and Recreation **24**:51, 1953.

b. Health observation by teachers and others should be encouraged and help given by the physician.

4. Athletic activities outside of the school program should be on an entirely voluntary basis without undue emphasis on any special program or sport, and without undue emphasis upon winning. These programs should also include competent medical supervision.

5. Competitive programs organized on school, neighborhood and community levels will meet the needs of children twelve years of age and under. State, regional and national tournaments; bowl, charity and exhibition games are not recommended for this age group. Commercial exploitation in any form is unequivocally condemned.

6. Body-contact sports, particularly tackle football and boxing, are considered to have no place in programs for children of this age.

7. Competition is an inherent characteristic of growing developing children. Properly guided it is beneficial and not harmful to their development.

8. Schools and communities as a whole must be made aware of the needs for personnel, facilities, equipment and supplies which will assure an adequate program for children in this age group.

9. All competitive athletic programs should be organized with the cooperation of interested medical groups who will ensure adequate medical care before and during such programs. This should include thorough physical examinations at specified intervals, teaching of health observation to teachers and coaches, as well as attention to factors such as: (a) injury; (b) response to fatigue; (c) individual emotional needs; and (d) the risks of undue emotional strains.

10. Muscle testing is not, per se, a valid estimate of physical fitness, or of good health.

11. Participation in group activities is expected of every child. When there is a failure to do so, or lack of interest, underlying physical or emotional causes should be sought.

12. Leadership for young children should be such that highly organized, highly competitive programs would be avoided. The primary consideration should be a diversity of wholesome childhood experiences which will aid in the proper physical and emotional development of the child into a secure and well-integrated adult.

The research in regard to a highly organized athletics at the junior high school level indicates points of substantial agreement, as listed in the following section*:

1. The junior high school educational program should be adapted to the needs of boys and girls in grades seven, eight, and nine. This is a period of transition from elementary school to senior high school and from childhood to adolescence. It is a time when students are trying to understand their bodies, gain independence, achieve adult social status, acquire self-confidence, and establish a system of values. It is a time when a program of education unique to this age group is needed to meet the abilities and broadening interests of the student.

2. The best educational program at the junior high school level is one that provides for program enrichment to meet the needs of students in grades seven through nine, rather than using the senior high school or other educational level as a blueprint to follow.

3. There is need for a distinct and separate educational climate for these grades in order to ensure that the program will not be influenced unduly by either the elementary or the senior high school.

4. There is a need for teachers (including coaches) whose full responsibilities involve working with grades seven, eight, and nine and whose training has included an understanding of the needs of these students and of the educational program required to meet those needs.

5. The junior high school should provide for exploratory experiences with specialization being delayed until senior high school and college.

6. The junior high school should provide for the mental, physical, social, and emotional development of students.

---

*New York State Education Department: Interscholastic athletics at the junior high school level, Albany, 1965, The Department. (Charles Bucher, consultant, New York State Department of Education.)

7. Out-of-class as well as in-class experiences should be provided.

8. There should be concern for the development of a sound standard of values in each student.

9. The principal and other members of the administration have the responsibility for providing sound educational leadership in all school matters. The type of physical education and athletic programs offered will reflect the type of leadership provided.

10. The physical education program at the junior high school level should consist of a class program, an adapted program, and intramural and extramural programs (the interscholastic athletic program is controversial).

11. The interscholastic athletics program, if offered, should be provided only after the prerequisites of excellent physical education class, adapted, and intramural and extramural programs have been developed, and only as special controls in regard to such items as health, facilities, game adaptations, classification of players, leadership, and officials have been provided.

12. The physical education program should be adapted to the needs of the junior high school student. There is a need for a wide variety of activities, based on physical and neuromuscular maturation, that will contribute to the development of body control, enable each student to experience success, provide for recognition of energy output and fatigue, and take into consideration the "growth spurt" of early adolescence.

13. The physical education program should represent a favorable social and emotional climate for the student. There should be freedom from anxiety and fear, absence of tensions and strains, a feeling of belonging for each student, a social awareness that contributes to the development of such important traits as respect for the rights of others, and an atmosphere that is conducive to growing into social and emotional maturity.

14. Personal health instruction should be closely integrated into the physical education program.

15. Coeducational activities should be provided.

16. All physical activities should be carefully supervised medically and conducted under optimum health and safety conditions.

17. Students who are not physiologically mature should not engage in activities where there is danger of body contact, a high degree of skill is required, great amounts of endurance are necessary, and highly competitive conditions are present.

18. The menstrual cycle and reproductive organs of girls require special consideration in the selection and conduct of activities.

19. Physiologic maturity is the best criterion for determining whether a student is physiologically ready for participation in most interscholastic athletic activities.

20. Competition itself is not the factor that makes athletics dangerous to the physiologically mature student. Instead, such items as the manner in which the program is conducted, type of activity, facilities, leadership, and physical condition of the student are the determining factors.

21. Physiologic fitness can be developed without exposure to an interscholastic athletic program.

22. Competitive athletics, if properly conducted, have the potential for satisfying such basic psychologic needs as recognition, belonging, self-respect, and feeling of achievement, as well as providing a wholesome outlet for the physical activity drive. However, if conducted in the light of adult interests, community pressures, and other questionable influences, they can prove psychologically harmful.

23. Interscholastic athletics, when conducted in accordance with desirable standards of leadership, educational philosophy, activities, and other pertinent factors, have the potential for realizing beneficial social

effects for the student, but when not conducted in accordance with desirable standards they can be socially detrimental to the student.

24. Of all competitive activities, tackle football, ice hockey, and boxing are subject to most criticism as being of questionable value for junior high school students.

INTERSCHOLASTIC ATHLETICS AT THE HIGH SCHOOL LEVEL

The responsibility of the school for the interscholastic athletic program is one that cannot be avoided. Therefore, it is essential that all administrators be aware of the best practices recommended for the various phases of the total program. The Joint Committee on Standards for Interscholastic Athletics of the National Association of Secondary School Principals, the National Federation of State High School Associations, and the American Association for Health, Physical Education, and Recreation have established standards.* These make it possible for every school to examine its athletic program in a critical manner and see how well it meets recommended practices. The preface to the list of standards includes the following statements:

Basic to any consideration of acceptable standards in interscholastic athletics for secondary schools in this statement of the GUIDING POLICIES for the organization, administration, and development of a program of athletics for the youth of our schools:

1. Athletics are to be an integral part of the secondary school program and should receive financial support from tax funds on the same basis as other recognized parts of the total educational program. As part of the curriculum, high school sports are to be conducted by secondary school authorities and all instruction provided by competent, qualified, and accredited teachers so that desirable, definite educational aims may be achieved.

---

*Joint Committee Report: Standards in athletics for boys in secondary schools, The Journal of the American Association for Health, Physical Education, and Recreation **22**:16, 1951.

2. Athletics are for the benefit of all youth. The aim is maximum participation, a sport for every boy and every boy in a sport, in a well-balanced intramural interscholastic program with emphasis on safe and healthful standards of competition.

3. Athletics are to be conducted under rules which provide for equitable competition, sportsmanship, fair play, health, and safety. High school sports are for amateurs who are bona fide undergraduate high school students. These youths must be protected from exploitation and the dangers of professionalism. Pre-season, post-schedule, post-season, all-star games, or similar types of promotions are not consistent with this principle. It is necessary to develop a full understanding of the need for observance of local, league, sectional, state, and national standards in athletics.

The Constitution of the California Interscholastic Federation lists the following "Cardinal Athletic Principles" and "Code of Ethics":

CARDINAL ATHLETIC PRINCIPLES

To be of maximum effectiveness, the athletic program will:

1. Be a well-coordinated part of the secondary school curriculum.
2. Justify the use of the tax funds and school facilities because of the educational aims achieved.
3. Be based on the spirit of amateurism.
4. Be conducted by secondary school authorities.
5. Provide opportunities for many students to participate in a wide variety of sports in every sport season.
6. Eliminate professionalism and commercialism.
7. Prevent "All-Star" contests or other promotional events.
8. Foster training in conduct, game ethics, and sportsmanship for participants and spectators.
9. Include a well-balanced program of intramural sports.
10. Engender respect for local, state, and national rules and policies under which the school program is conducted.

CODE OF ETHICS

It is the duty of all concerned with high school athletics:

1. To emphasize the proper ideas of sportsmanship, ethical conduct, and fair play.

2. To eliminate all possibilities which tend to destroy the best values of the game.
3. To stress the values derived from playing the game fairly.
4. To show cordial courtesy to visiting teams and officials.
5. To establish a happy relationship between visitors and hosts.
6. To respect the integrity and judgment of sports officials.
7. To achieve a thorough understanding and acceptance of the rules of the game and the standards of eligibility.
8. To encourage leadership, use of initiative, and good judgment by the players on the team.
9. To recognize that the purpose of athletics is to promote the physical, mental, moral, social, and emotional well-being of the individual players.
10. To remember that an athletic contest is only a game—not a matter of life or death for player, coach, school, officials, fan, community, state, or nation.*

INTERCOLLEGIATE ATHLETICS

It is at the college and university level that overemphasis has taken place to the largest extent in the field of varsity athletics. Commercialization flourishes when 60,000 people gather for a sports spectacle, the cost of tickets ranges from $2.00 to $8.00, and large stadia, long trips, and many scholarships predominate. A few colleges have established "easy courses" in the curriculum so that athletes will not have to meet the usual academic standards. Records have been falsified to enable some to meet entrance requirements. Others have been given tuition, board, spending money, and sometimes even a car to attract them. Players have been recruited from various sections of the country through unethical means. Alumni pressure for winning teams, the firing of coaches, and other undesirable practices have been in evidence in some quarters.

Much of the responsibility for eliminating the abuses from college athletic circles

---

*California Interscholastic Federation: Constitution and by-laws, 1959, The Federation.

has been placed upon the shoulders of the various regional accrediting agencies. One of the largest of these has the following to say in regard to policy:

1. Some of the most serious abuses of athletics really arise from the abuses of instruction. It is not good university and college practice to permit soft spots in the curriculum. Students call these "snap" courses. They are too easy or too frivolous to occupy the time of university or college students. Their presence aids and abets corruption of athletics. The same applies to low standards of entrance and performance in any of the colleges or courses of the university. Sub-college standards of academic work anywhere in the institution afford a hiding place for youths who lack the ability to be university students or young men whose athletic duties prove too exacting to permit them to pass courses of truly university grade.

2. The notion that institutions of higher education have a responsibility for providing public entertainment in the form of athletic spectacles is alien to the true functions of such institutions.

3. The manner in which an institution spends its funds is the best possible evidence of the values it fosters. A college or university will give financial support to programs and activities in proportion to the importance it attaches to them. A first-rate educational institution will in the very nature of things devote as much of its income as possible to functions that bring a high educational return. This applies to all phases of operation, not alone to athletics.

4. The chief administration officer of a college or university is ultimately responsible for the wholesome conduct of the intercollegiate athletics in his institution, and this ultimate responsibility he cannot properly delegate to subordinate officers. It is his duty to be well informed about the athletic policies and practices of his institution and to take the necessary steps to assure that the athletic program is making its full contribution to the attainment of educational objectives.

5. A high quality institution does not resort to athletic renown as a means of securing public support. Rather, it makes its appeal on the basis of its educational merit. If athletic prominence is an indispensable element in the public relations of a college or university, that fact is of itself a reflection on the academic worth of the institution.

6. When the winning of contests per se becomes the major emphasis of an athletic program, this results almost inevitably in practices

that are detrimental to the moral tone and educational seriousness of purpose of the institution. This emphasis can have such far-reaching consequences, sometimes penetrating to the very core of institutional integrity, that the existence of an unsatisfactory athletic situation in an institution will be regarded as a serious enough weakness to justify the denial of accreditation.[*]

Bucher and Dupee have surveyed the standards for high school and collegiate athletics and have summarized the selected recommended standards for these educational levels. They are presented here for the information and reference of the reader.

Summary of selected recommended standards for varsity interscholastic and intercollegiate athletics[†]

1. Organization
    (a) The wholesome conduct of the athletic programs should be the ultimate responsibility of the school administration.
    (b) Athletic policy should be adopted, evaluated, and supervised by a faculty committee.
    (c) Athletic policy should be implemented by the director of physical education and the director of athletics.
    (d) Athletics should be organized as an integral part of the department of physical education.
2. Staff
    (a) All members of the coaching staff should be members of the faculty.
    (b) All coaches should be hired on their qualifications to assume educational responsibilities, and not on their ability to produce winning teams.
    (c) All coaches should enjoy the same privileges of tenure, rank, and salary which are accorded other similarly qualified faculty members.
    (d) All public school coaches should be certified in physical education.

[*]Commission on Colleges and Universities, North Central Association of Colleges and Secondary Schools: An interpretation of the revised policy of intercollegiate athletics of the North Central Association, Chicago, 1952, The Association.

[†]Bucher, C. A., and Dupee, R. K., Jr.: Athletics in schools and colleges, New York, 1965, The Center for Applied Research in Education, Inc. (The Library of Education), pp. 99-101.

3. Finances
    (a) The financing of interscholastic and intercollegiate athletics should be governed by the same policies that control the financing of all other educational activities within an institution.
    (b) Gate receipts should be considered an incidental source of revenue.
4. Health and safety
    (a) An annual physical examination should be required of all participants; a physical examination on a seasonal basis would be preferable.
    (b) Each school should have a written policy for the implementation of an injury-care program.
    (c) Each school should have a written policy concerning the responsibility for athletic injuries and should provide or make available athletic accident insurance.
    (d) All coaches should be well qualified in the care and prevention of athletic injuries.
    (e) A doctor should be present at all contests at which injury is possible.
    (f) Only that equipment offering the best protection should be purchased.
    (g) Proper fitting of all protective equipment should be insured.
    (h) Competition should be scheduled only between teams of comparable ability.
    (i) Games should not be played until players have had a minimum of three weeks of physical conditioning and drill.
    (j) Playing fields should meet standards for size and safety.
5. Eligibility
    (a) All schools should honor and respect the eligibility rules and regulations of respective local, state, and national athletic associations.
    (b) A student who is not making normal progress toward a degree or diploma should not be allowed to participate.
6. Recruiting
    (a) The athletic teams of each school should be composed of bona fide students who live in the school district or who were attracted to the institution by its educational program.
    (b) All candidates for admission to a school should be evaluated according to the same high standards.
    (c) All financial aid should be administered with regard to need and according to the same standards for all students. The recipient of financial aid should be given

a statement of the amount, duration, and conditions of the award.

7. Awards
   (a) The value of athletic awards should be limited.
   (b) There should be no discrimination between awards for different varsity sports.
   (c) The presentation of all-star, most valuable-player, and most-improved-player awards should be discouraged.

GIRLS' AND WOMEN'S ATHLETICS

The question of highly organized athletics for girls is a controversial matter. The questions of how much, how little, and what is a happy medium are frequently raised with enthusiastic supporters on both sides of the issue. There seems to be a general consensus of opinion that athletics can render a valuable service to girls. The question arises as to what type of program can best render this service. Girls can develop a better state of total fitness, skills for worthy use of leisure time, and other desirable qualities and attributes, just as boys and men can. However, it must be recognized that girls and women are not boys and men. There are many biologic, social, and

---

Student's Name_____ School_____

Entered H.S._____19____   Initiated_____19____   School Group (Check) ☐ 1 ☐ 2

AWARD REQUIREMENTS
(Check when completed.)

Year in H. S.	1	2	3	4
Scholarship				
Sportsmanship				
Heart Examination				
Satisfactory P. E. Grade				
Others: (Local)				

POINTS EARNED

Fresh._____
Soph._____
Junior_____
Senior_____
Total (to date)

AWARDS RECEIVED

1st Local_____19____
2nd Local_____19____
1st State_____19____
2nd State_____19____
GAA Pin_____19____

APPROVED BY: (Adviser)
_____
_____
_____
_____
_____

PARTICIPATION POINTS (To be given only for participation in the elective sports program; i.e., intramural, after-school, noon-hour, etc.)

Year in H. S.	1	2	3	4
Archery				
Tests				
Badminton				
Tests				
Basketball				
Tests				
Bowling				
Tests				
Campcraft				
Dance				
Folk Dance Tests				
Rhythm Tests				
Tap Tests				
Hiking				
Hockey				
Tests				
Leaders Class				
Test				
Total				

Year in H. S.	1	2	3	4
Brought Forward				
Rebound Tumbling Stunts				
Soccer				
Tests				
Softball				
Tests				
Speedball				
Swimming				
Red Cross Tests:				
Beginners				
Intermediate				
Swimmers				
Advanced				
Survival Tests				
Jr. Life Saving				
Sr. Life Saving				
Dives				
Total				

Year in H. S.	1	2	3	4
Brought Forward				
Tennis				
Tests				
Tumbling Stunts (Check) 1, 2, 3, 4, 5, 6, 7, 8, 9, 10, 11, 12, 13, 14, 15, 16, 17, 18, 19, 20, 21, 22, 23, 24, 25, 26, 27, 28, 29, 30, 31, 32, 33, 34, 35, 36, 37, 38, 39, 40				
Tumbling				
Volley Ball				
Tests				
Other Activities: (Write in)				
Total Activity Pts.				

Award Granted_____19____   By_____

Sample record of the Illinois League of High School Girls' Athletic Associations. (From Felshin, J.: Girls' sports organization handbook, Washington, D. C., 1961, The Division for Girls' and Women's Sports.)

other differences that must be taken into consideration. It is impossible to take the boys' program and duplicate it for the girls without any changes.

The girls' program should be concerned especially with the individual sports and activities, as well as the team games. The women in charge and those doing the officiating should be qualified. Official girls' rules should be followed. The girls' games should be separated from the boys', except in coeducational activity, which should occupy a prominent place in the program. The social aspects should be stressed, jumping and body contact should be limited or eliminated altogether. Health safeguards should be observed, limited seasons and restrictions on the amount of competition of any one girl should be enforced. Publicity and commercial aspects should be controlled so that the girls are not exploited.

If athletics for girls are conducted in a sound manner, many benefits can accrue. Some of these benefits have been brought out by the American Association for Health, Physical Education, and Recreation:

The values or purposes may be summarized thus: to satisfy the human desire of belonging to a group which represents the school; to stimulate greater interest in the physical education class program, and wider participation in the intramural program; to develop and maintain physical fitness among players; to provide opportunities for girls to become participants as well as spectators; to strengthen individual qualities, such as initiative, resourcefulness, loyalty, cooperation, and other similar qualities, through game experiences of great importance to the individual; to encourage girls to become skilled in activities as a personal and social asset; to offer challenging competition to the accelerated or gifted student in physical education; to offer opportunities for participation in activities that may be continued throughout life.*

---

*Joint Committee: Administration problems in health education, physical education, and recreation, Washington, D. C., 1953, American Association for Health, Physical Education, and Recreation, p. 117.

Procedures and practices in respect to interscholastic and intercollegiate athletic competition for girls vary from state to state. Some schools and colleges have broad programs of interscholastic athletics, others do not have any, and some have modified programs. In those having modified programs, play days, sports days, invitation games, and telegraphic meets are increasingly playing a more prominent part. Most states do not set up specific requirements for girls' athletics but feel that their established regulations apply to both girls and boys. A few states have athletic associations for girls that are similar to those for boys.

The Division for Girls' and Women's Sports of the American Association for Health, Physical Education, and Recreation is the most influential organization affecting athletics for girls and women. This organization is comprised of leaders in the field of physical education and recreation. The purpose of the organization is to develop, promote, and supervise desirable sports programs for girls and women. In order to accomplish this purpose, guiding principles and standards have been developed and publicized. The DGWS also publishes many official guides in various sports, scorebooks, pamphlets on desirable practices, and special publications concerned with such matters as menstruation, teaching materials, audiovisual resource list, and special events for girls' and women's programs.

Guiding principles and standards established by the DGWS are concerned with the sports program, leader, and participant. The organization feels that the program should be developed on the basis of such factors as individual differences among girls and women and the environment in which the activity is conducted. The leaders of these programs should have a full understanding of the needs and interests of girls and women and be exemplary in their conduct. The participant should develop skill and other characteristics in accordance with her potential, and the activities in which she engages should contribute to her health and welfare. Competition should be so designed as to enable each player to participate and at the level of her ability. Officials should understand the role of girls and women and sports, and the rules of the DGWS should be the official rules of all contests.

Recommendations of Division of Girls' and Women's Sports

The recommendations of the Division of Girls' and Women's Sports of the American Association for Health, Physical Education, and Recreation with regard to competitive sports for various age level groupings represent a definitive statement of standards for girls' and women's athletics:

In junior high school, it is desirable that intramural programs of competitive activities be closely

integrated with the basic physical education program. Appropriate competition at this level should be comprised of intramural and informal extramural events consistent with social needs and recreational interests. A well-organized and well-conducted sports program should take into account the various skill levels and thus meet the needs of the more highly skilled.

In senior high school, a program of intramural-extramural participation should be arranged to augment a sound and inclusive instructional program in physical education. It should be recognized that an interscholastic program will require professional leadership, time, and funds in addition to those provided for the intramural programs. Facilities should be such that the intramural and instructional programs need not be eliminated or seriously curtailed if an interscholastic program is offered.

Specifically, the following standards should prevail:

1. The medical status of the player is ascertained by a physician and the health of the players is carefully supervised.
2. Activities for girls and women are planned

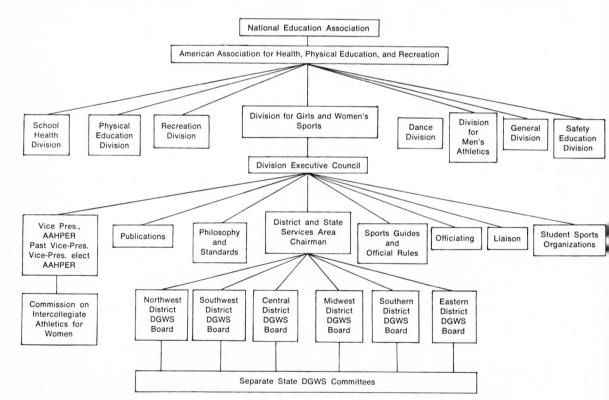

DGWS organizational chart. (From Philosophy & standards for girls' and women's sports, American Association for Health, Physical Education, and Recreation, 1969, p. 50.)

to meet their needs, not for the personal glorification of coaches and/or sponsoring organizations.

3. The salary, retention, and promotion of an instructor are not dependent upon the outcome of the games.

4. Qualified women teach, coach, and officiate wherever and whenever possible, and in all cases the professional background and experience of the leader meet established standards.

5. Rules approved by DGWS are used.

6. Schedules do not exceed the ability and endurance relative to the maturity and

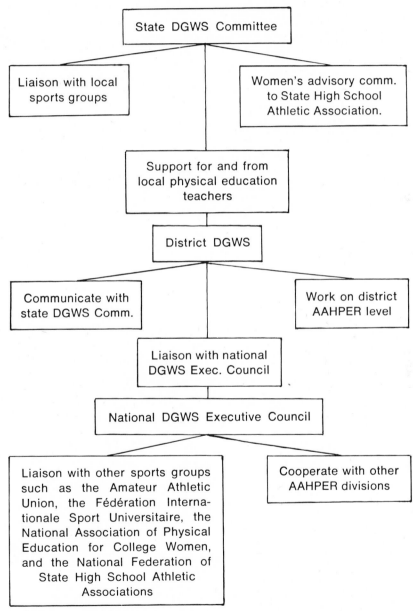

Relations of DGWS to other sports and policy-making groups. (From Philosophy and standards for girls' and women's sports, American Association for Health, Physical Education, and Recreation, 1969, p. 51.)

Junior high school. (Waterloo, Iowa.)

physiological conditioning of the participants. Standards for specific sports are defined by DGWS and appear in sports guides, published by the American Association for Health, Physical Education, and Recreation, 1201 16th St. N. W., Washington, D. C.

7. Sports activities for girls and women are scheduled independently from boys' and men's sports. Exceptions will occur when the activities and/or time and facilities are appropriate for both.

8. Girls and women may participate in appropriate corecreational activities or teams. Girls and women may not participate as members of boys and men's teams.

9. The program, including health insurance for players, is financed by budgeted school or organization funds rather than entirely by admission charges.

10. Provision is made by the school or organization for safe transportation by bonded carriers, with chaperones who are responsible to the sponsoring group.

In colleges and universities it is desirable that opportunities be provided for the highly skilled beyond the intramural program. Regulations for the conduct of collegiate competition have been developed by the National Joint Committee on Extramural Sports for College Women and are available from the committee for any specific sport activity. While the statements of NJCESCW

apply to approval for state-wide or wider geographical tournaments, the principles may also be applicable to or guide the conduct of local and district tournaments.

In addition to the standards previously listed, other standards pertinent to the colleges are:

1. The amount and kind of intercollegiate competition should be determined by the women's physical education department.

2. The financial arrangements relative to all intercollegiate sport events should be administered with the approval of the women's physical education department.

3. The time involved in relation to intercollegiate competition should not interfere with the academic program of the institution sponsoring the event and should not make excessive demands upon the participants' academic schedules.

4. All housing arrangements relative to visiting participants should be approved by the women's physical education department.[*]

The DGWS cooperates with many national sports organizations. This is becoming increasingly common as the desire for more desirable competitive sports experiences for girls and women becomes a part of our culture. A few of the cooperative relationships are Council for National Cooperation in Aquatics, Women's National Aquatics Forum, United States Field Hockey Association, United States Women's Lacrosse Association, United States Volleyball Association, International Joint Softball Rules Committee, National Federation of State High School Athletic Associations, Amateur Athletic Union, United States Track and Field Federation, United States Gymnastics Federation, United States Olympic Development Committee, Athletic and Recreation Federation for College Women, and the National Association for Physical Education of College Women.[†]

---

[*]Division for Girls' and Women's Sports: Philosophy and standards for girls and women's sports. Washington, D. C., 1969, AAHPER, pp. 34-35.

[†]Crawford, E.: DGWS cooperates with national sports organizations, Journal of Health, Physical Education, and Recreation 36:25, 1965.

Girls' and women's athletics are occupying an increasingly prominent role in the nation's schools and colleges. The programs appear to be well supervised and controlled and free of many of the abuses and problems associated with boys' and men's athletics. A large measure of the credit for developing such a sound program is due to the Division for Girls' and Women's Sports of the American Association for Health, Physical Education, and Recreation.

Criteria for the evaluation of programs in girls' and women's sports

The accompanying criteria have been established by the Division for Girls' and Women's Sports to assist administrators and others in determining if their program meets acceptable standards.

ATHLETIC ASSOCIATIONS

An individual school or college, by itself, finds it difficult to develop standards and

---

CRITERIA FOR EVALUATION*

Standards and guidelines established by the Division for Girls and Women's Sports should be used to evaluate program on local, regional, and national levels.

The sports program should be evaluated frequently according to criteria based on sound educational philosophy and scientific research.

Frequent evaluation of the program is necessary to ascertain if the objectives are being realized. The following list of criteria may be of help in this evaluation:

1. The administrator assumes responsibility for the realization of the values and objectives of the sports program.
2. Professionally qualified teachers and leaders are selected and delegated appropriate responsibility and authority to administer the program.
3. The objectives and policies which govern the sports program are determined by competent professional leaders.
4. The objectives of the program are concerned with the total growth and development of the individual.
5. Educational objectives take precedence over matters of expediency.
6. The educational and recreational aims of the school or sponsoring agency are realized through the sports program.
7. In all situations the spirit of fair play predominates.
8. The program is planned using knowledge based on current research.
9. The program is planned and conducted with primary concern for the welfare of the individual player.
10. The program is considered to be both worthwhile and enjoyable by the players and the leaders alike.
11. Sports experiences are so conducted that maximum values are realized by the participant.
12. Participants in sports activities have a voice in the planning and execution of the program.
13. The diversity within the program meets the needs of all age and skill levels.
14. Qualified women direct, coach, and officiate the program.
15. Trained officials are used in the program.
16. The most recent DGWS rules, standards, skills, and tactics of specific sports are used; where these are not specified, the leader employs professional judgment.
17. The participant meets her responsibility in perpetuating the spirit of good sportsmanship.
18. The total sports program includes instruction, intramurals, and extramurals.
19. Established DGWS standards and guidelines are used in frequent evaluations of the program.
20. Financing of the total sports program is included in the school recreational budget.

*From Division for Girls' and Women's Sports: Philosophy and standards of girls' and women's sports, Washington, D. C., 1969, American Association of Health, Physical Education, and Recreation, pp. 26-27.

control athletics in a sound educational manner. However, by uniting with other schools and colleges such a project is possible. This has been done on local, state, and national levels in the interest of better athletics for high schools and colleges. By establishing rules and procedures well in advance of playing seasons, the necessary control for conducting a sound athletic program is provided educators, coaches, and others. It aids them in resisting pressures of alumni, students, spectators, townspeople, and others who do not always have the best interests of the program in mind.

There are various types of athletic associations. The ones that are most prevalent in high schools and colleges are student athletic associations, local conferences or leagues, state high school athletic associations, National Federation of State High School Athletic Associations, National Collegiate Athletic Association, and various college conferences.

The student athletic association is an organization within a school that is designed to promote and participate in the conduct of the athletic program of that school. It is usually open to all students in attendance. Through the payment of fees it often helps to support the athletics program. Such associations are found in many of the high schools throughout the country. They can be very helpful in the development of a sound athletic program.

There are various associations, conferences, or leagues that bind together athletically several high schools within a particular geographic area. These are designed in the main to regulate and promote wholesome competition among the member schools. They usually draw up schedules, approve officials, handle disputes, and have general supervision over the athletic programs of the member schools.

The state high school athletic association that now exists in almost every state is a major influence in high school athletics. It is open to all professionally accredited high schools within the state. It has a constitution, administrative officers to conduct the business, and a board of control. The number of members on the board of control varies usually from six to nine. Fees are usually paid to the association on a flat basis or according to the size of the school. In some states there are no fees, since the necessary revenue is derived from the gate receipts of tournament competition. State associations are interested in a sound program of athletic competition within the confines of the state. They concern themselves with the usual problems that have to do with athletics, such as rules of eligibility, officials, disputes, and similar items. They are interested in promoting good high school athletics, equalizing athletic competition, protecting participants, and guarding the health of players. They are an influence for good and have won the respect of educators in the various states.

The National Council of Secondary School Athletic Directors

The American Association for Health, Physical Education, and Recreation recently established the National Council of Secondary School Athletic Directors. The increased emphasis in sports and the important position of athletic directors in the nation's secondary schools seemed to warrant an association where increased services could be rendered to enhance the services given to the nation's youth. The membership in the National Council is open to members of the AAHPER who have primary responsibility in directing, administering, or coordinating interscholastic athletic programs. The purposes of the Council are as follows:

> To improve the educational aspects of interscholastic athletics and their articulation in the total educational program
> To foster high standards of professional proficiency and ethics
> To improve understanding of athletics throughout the nation

To establish closer working relationships with related professional groups

To promote greater unity, good will, and fellowship among all members

To provide for an exchange of ideas

To assist and cooperate with existing state athletic directors' organizations

To make available to members special resource materials through publications, conferences, and consultant services

The National Federation of State High School Athletic Associations

The National Federation of State High School Athletic Associations was established in 1920 with five states participating. At the present time nearly all the states are members. The National Federation is particularly concerned with the control of interstate athletics. Its constitution states this purpose:

The object of this Federation shall be to protect and supervise the interstate athletic interests of the high schools belonging to the state associations, to assist in those activities of state associations which can best be operated on a nationwide scale, to sponsor meetings, publications and activities which will permit each state association to profit by the experience of all other member associations, and to coordinate the work so that waste effort and unnecessary duplication will be avoided.

The National Federation has been responsible for many improvements in athletics on a national basis, such as doing away with national tournaments and working toward a uniformity of standards.

The National Collegiate Athletic Association

The National Collegiate Athletic Association began in the early 1900's. The alarming number of football injuries and the fact that there was no national control of the game of football led to a conference of representatives of universities and colleges, primarily from the eastern section of the United States, on December 12, 1905. Preliminary plans were made for a national body to assist in the formulation of sound requirements for intercollegiate athletics, particularly football, and

the name Intercollegiate Athletic Association was suggested. At a meeting March 31, 1906, a constitution and bylaws were adopted and issued. On December 29, 1910, the name of the association was changed to National Collegiate Athletic Association. The purposes of the NCAA are to uphold the principle of institutional control of all collegiate sports; to maintain a uniform code of amateurism in conjunction with sound eligibility rules, scholarship requirements, and good sportsmanship; to promote and assist in the expansion of intercollegiate and intramural sports; to formulate, copyright, and publish the official rules of play (in eleven sports); to sponsor and supervise regional and national meets and tournaments for member institutions; to preserve athletic records; and to serve as headquarters for collegiate athletic matters of national import.

National Association of Intercollegiate Athletics

Also on the college and university levels is the National Association of Intercollegiate Athletics, which has a large membership, especially among the smaller schools. This organization has recently become affiliated with the American Association for Health, Physical Education, and Recreation.

The National Junior College Athletic Association

The National Junior College Athletic Association is an organization of junior colleges who sponsor athletic programs. It has nineteen regional offices with an elected regional director for each. Regional business matters are carried on within the framework of the constitution and bylaws of the parent organization. The regional directors hold an annual legislative assembly in Hutchinson, Kansas, are run by an executive committee, and determine the policies, program, and procedures for the organization. The *Juco Review* is the official publication of the organization.

Standing and special committees are appointed each year to cover special items and problems that develop. Membership, which costs $75.00 annually, entitles each member to the services provided by the NJCAA.

National championships are conducted in such sports as basketball, cross country, football, wrestling, baseball, track and field, golf, and tennis. National invitation events are also conducted in such activities as soccer, swimming, and gymnastics.

The NJCAA is affiliated with the National Federation of State High School Athletic Associations and the National Association of Intercollegiate Athletics. It is also a member of the United States Track and Field Federation, Basketball Federation, the United States Collegiate Sports Council, United States Olympic Committee, United States Gymnastics Federation, National Basketball Committee, and American Association for Health, Physical Education, and Recreation.

Some of the services offered by the NJCAA to its members include an insurance plan for athletics, recognition in official records, publications, film library, and participation in events sponsored by the association.

Other organizations

In higher education, there are in addition many leagues, conferences, and associations formed by a limited number of schools for athletic competition. Examples are the "Ivy League" and the "Big Ten Conference." These associations regulate athletic competition among their members and settle problems that may arise in connection with such competition.

EXTRA PAY FOR EXTRA SERVICES*

One of the most popular topics for discussion at school meetings in recent years

---

*National Congress of Parents and Teachers: PTA guide to what's happening in education, New York, 1965, Scholastic Book Services, pp. 203-210.

is: Should teachers receive extra pay for extra services? Parents, taxpayers, and school boards have been trying to decide whether or not athletics, coaches, band leaders, dramatics supervisors, publication consultants, and others who do work in addition to their teaching load should receive additional compensation for such services.

A sensible solution to this problem is essential to the good morale of a school staff. Besides, since school systems are demanding more and more services, some policy must be formulated to cover the extra duties that are being heaped on the shoulders of our teachers.

To help solve the extra-pay dilemma, many surveys, studies, and conferences have been conducted during recent years. The National Education Association, the American Association for Health, Physical Education, and Recreation, several state organizations, local boards of education, and other groups have been busy gathering data on the problem. They have found that many communities give extra pay for extra services. However, this is by no means standard procedure.

My own study has shown that practices in selected school systems across the country generally fall into five groups:

Extra pay is provided for all school activities that require work beyond the normal school day.

Extra pay is given only in the area of athletics.

Release time is provided for extra work.

Supplemental teachers are hired.

All school activities are considered part of the normal teaching load, and no additional pay is given.

Practices across the country

The public schools in one school system in South Dakota pay for all extra activities. The assistant football coach receives $250 a year and the ticket manager, $150. Intramural activities pay $50 per sport. The band director gets $600; the supervisor of school publications, $250; the staff member in charge of the school radio program, $175; and the printing instructor, $250. In a school system in Tennessee extra pay is given at varied rates, ranging all the way from $15 a month for a special teacher of spastic children to $75 a month for a senior high school coach.

In a community on Long Island, New York, extra pay for extra work is based on five criteria: the time required for the activity, the number of students involved, the pressure to which a teacher may be subjected by public performances, the closeness with which the activity is related to the curriculum, and the extent to which the activity is a teaching rather than a supervisory or an advisory function. On the basis of these criteria, each extracurricular activity is placed in one of five categories, each carrying its own rate of pay. The pay ranges from $360 to $880 a year for the various kinds of activity.

The salary policies for coaching selected sports in Class AA schools in the state of Iowa are reported as follows*:

1. All but one of the assigned coaches was given monetary compensation for coaching.
2. Eleven schools reported that they gave an extra free period to some of the head coaches during the season in which they coached.
3. Sixty-nine out of the seventy-one schools have a salary schedule for coaching.
4. Of the schools reporting, 73% indicated they used the lock-step method of payment, 13%, the percentage method of payment, and 11%, the annual increment method of payment.
5. Eight schools permit coaches to come into their system on advance coaching salary steps as a result of past experience.
6. Coaches' salaries vary from school to school and sport to sport.
7. Five schools reported payments to coaches on a merit basis.
8. Most schools pay assistant coaches.

---

*Mauro, D. R.: Salary policies for teaching of selected sports in class AA schools of Iowa, Iowa Journal of Health, Physical Education, and Recreation, May, 1969.

The State College Area School District in Pennsylvania has established a rating method for extra pay for extra duty that involves nine criteria. An illustrated version of this rating method is seen in Table 10-1.

Many schools faced with the extra-pay problem pay for coaching duties only. A city in Utah follows this practice. There the annual pay for senior high school athletic coaches is $474 more than that of other teachers with similar training and experience, except for teachers of special education, who receive the same rate as coaches. In a Kentucky city some athletic coaches receive as much as $800 in extra compensation, but the board of education has not supplemented the salaries of teachers in charge of band, dramatics, and other activities. A few individual schools give some of these teachers part of the proceeds from plays and other activities that they supervise. A city in New York pays its athletic instructors supplementary salaries ranging from $600 for the football coach to $3.00 an hour for athletic league coaches in grade schools.

Some schools throughout the country do not give extra pay. Instead, release time is provided. As Benjamin C. Willis, former superintendent of schools in Chicago, pointed out: "In our salary schedule we do not provide extra pay for extra services. We make an exception for teachers who work beyond the normal school day—that is, those who have additional classes because of the shortage of space. We pay extra compensation for this extra time. In regard to the coaching of athletics, we adjust the teaching schedule to compensate for this work."

In one city in California, junior college supplemental teachers are hired to take on certain activities. The supervisor of personnel research reports that the supplemental teachers are assigned to an afterschool activity that is not part of the full day's program and that requires up to 40 hours a month. The activity may be in drama, music, stagecraft, journalism, yearbook,

Table 10-1. Rating method — extra pay for extra duty*†

I. All athletics and nonclass-related activities										
Criteria	A	B	C	D	E	F	G	H	I	
Possible rating scores	1-10	1-10	1-5	1-5	1-5	1-20	1-20	1-5	1-5	
Weighted value	4	4	3	2	2	3	2	1	2	
Example	5	3	2	2	0	0	2	0	0	Raw rating
Activity xx (rating X value)	20	12	6	4	0	0	4	0	0	Weighted rating 46 — Final rounded 45

CRITERIA

A *Hours*—total out of school
B *Weekend*—vacation hours—Friday 3—Sunday
C *Students*—directly involved
D *Experience*—training necessary
E *Injury risk*—to pupil (other than normal classroom risk)
F *Pressures*—crowd, spectator, community, faculty, administration
G *Responsibility*—equipment, facilities, funds
H *Environmental influence*—outdoor, indoor weather conditions
I *Travel supervision*—bus trips, etc.

A&B: Hours	rating
550-600	10
500-549	9
450-499	8
400-449	7
350-399	6
300-349	5
250-299	4
200-249	3
150-199	2
100-149	1
under 100	.5

C: Students	
150 pupils or more	5
100-149	4
50- 99	3
25- 49	2
under 25	1

II. Rating method—class-related activities									
Criteria	A	B	C	D	E	F	G	H	I
Possible ratings	1-10	1-10	1-5	1-5	1-5	1-20	1-20	1-5	1-5
Weighted value	4	4	1	1	2	1	1	1	2

*From Solley, P. M.: Extra pay for extra duty, Today's Education, **58**:54, 1969.
†State College Area School District guide, "Extra Pay for Extra Duty."

speech, or other areas. Such teachers receive $6.16 an hour.

Finally, there is the great mass of schools where coaching, band, orchestra, and similar activities are considered part of the normal teaching load and no additional pay is provided. The school system of a community in Missouri is typical of this group. These schools "believe in paying all teachers well," writes a member of the school administration. "In turn, they expect teachers to do the work for which they are hired. No . . . teacher has been paid above schedule. . . . A full explanation of the situation is given at the time of employment." In a town in Connecticut, pressure for extra pay has been exerted by coaches and other groups. The board of education has held, however, that their duties are part of their regular job.

Roundup of suggestions

The many-faceted problem of extra pay and extra services concerns a large number of educators, administrators, and laymen. Various ideas of solving it have been advanced, of which the following are perhaps the most pertinent.

The educational program in all school systems should rest on a sound financial base. Teachers' salaries should be sufficient to provide a comfortable living. Faculty members should not have to seek extra work in school or elsewhere to make ends meet.

If possible, there should be enough staff

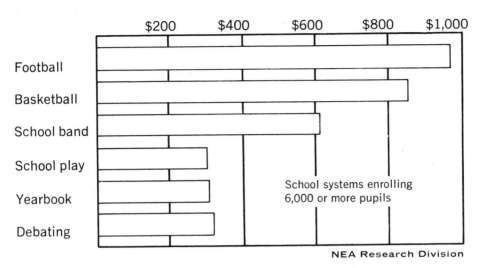

Average maximum annual supplements 1967-1968 for selected pupil-participating activities. (From NEA Research Bulletin **46**:79, 1968.)

members in every school to make it unnecessary for anyone to take on an extra load.

Extra work means loss of efficiency. A teacher can perform at his best for only a certain number of hours a day, then the law of diminishing returns sets in.

All teachers work beyond the school day. They prepare teaching assignments, grade papers, keep records, and take on other professional responsibilities. It is difficult, therefore, to determine what is "extra work."

Extra work in education is not comparable to extra work in business or industry. Professional ethics dictate that positions in public service cannot be categorized in the same way as can those involving only personal gain.

Teaching loads should be equalized as far as possible. If inequalities exist that cannot be corrected through extra staff, extra pay is justified.

Where extra pay is provided, it should be distributed equitably for all who work beyond a normal school day. Teachers should perform extra work only in areas where they are qualified.

The most acceptable form of compensation for additional duties appears to be extra salary. The practice of release time does not seem to meet the wishes of most teachers.

The problem of extra pay for extra service is not an easy one to resolve. Convincing arguments can be given for or against the views that have been presented. Since local needs differ, a nationwide solution cannot be prescribed. However, any community that is wrestling with this problem may well be guided by the foregoing points. They represent the thinking of many teachers and administrators throughout the country.

Educators state their views

Thurston, a consultant on teacher salaries and negotiations of the Office of Professional Development and Welfare of the National Education Association, proposes an index relationship in respect to extra pay for extra services. This reflects the time spent in the activity as a ratio to the basic schedule. The formula, shown on p. 276 shows how this would work.

EXTRA PAY FOR EXTRA SERVICES*

$$\frac{\text{Number of hours spent in activity per day}}{\text{Number of hours in school day}} \times \frac{\text{Length of activity per school year (days, weeks, months)}}{\text{Length of normal school year}} = \text{Basic time index}$$

Example 1. High school basketball coach who spends 2 hours per day with his squad. Season lasts 5 months in 10-month year with an 8-hour day.

$2/8 \times 5/10 = \text{basic index} = .125$

Example 2. High school chemistry teacher spends 1 hour, twice a month with science club. School operates on 8-hour day and 200-day year.

$1/8 \times 20/200 = \text{basic index} = .0125$

These time indices may be applied on a B.A. base, base of degree held, step on B.A. scale, or step on teacher's basic salary scale.

*From Thurston, J. P.: Secondary school athletic administration: a new look, Report of the Second National Conference on Secondary School Athletic Administration, Washington, D. C., January 12-15, 1969, pp. 82-83.

A dean of the School of Education, Syracuse University, believes that ideally the teacher should be released from teaching duties to offset extraschool services, "thus maintaining a balanced load and a uniform salary schedule. In many school situations the administration is not in a position to do this and must load certain teachers . . . with extra duties, including dramatics, band, athletics, supervision of school paper, and so on. Where teachers are assigned such responsibilities over and above the regular teaching load, certainly extra compensation should be provided. This is only fair to those who are called upon to carry added responsibilities."

A professor of elementary education, Graduate School of Education, Indiana University, thinks that "the services would be part of the regular load of the people directing them. If these activities are added to an already full load the teacher ought to be paid extra at a rate comparable to his regular salary. This is an area where people can be easily exploited unless a definite policy exists to protect them."

And from an executive secretary emeritus of the American Association of School Administrators comes this statement: "Under ordinary circumstances the assignment of any teacher should be a full load, but not an extra one. In general, then, there should be no extra pay for extra work. When the situation, manpower-wise, is such that members of the regular staff must temporarily accept an unreasonable load, they should be compensated for this assignment. . . . Regular overtime assignments reflect a condition of understaffing, and the best answer is not that of overloading and extra pay but of additional staff."

The answer to the important question—Should teachers receive extra pay for extra services?—must be resolved in each community. A satisfactory solution, however, requires these essentials:

The educational program must rest on a sound financial foundation.

Salaries should compensate adequately for the work performed.

As far as possible, normal loads should be assigned to all teachers. Whenever teaching loads cannot be held to a desirable level, the teacher should be provided with extra compensation.

CONCLUDING STATEMENT ON ATHLETICS

The standards for athletics at school and college levels have been clearly stated. There should be no doubt in any individual's mind as to the types of interscholastic and intercollegiate programs that are sound educationally and in the best interests of students who will participate in them. It is the responsibility of administrators and others concerned with such programs to implement the various standards that have been established. *In every case, it is not a question of deemphasis but a question of reemphasis along educational lines. Good leadership will make the interscholastic program a force for good in education that has no equal.*

Athletics are a part of the total physical education program. The objectives that have been stated earlier in this book for physical education also apply to inter-school and intercollegiate athletics. The administrator can evaluate his or her program in terms of the extent to which the listed objectives are being achieved. There should be no question as to where a school stands.

The Educational Policies Commission Report on School Athletics* provides guidelines for physical educators, coaches, administrators, and other individuals interested in a sound school athletic program. This report contains 100 questions that can be used to evaluate any school athletic program. *The information in this report represents the ideals toward which all educators should be striving.*

Questions and exercises

1. Develop a set of standards that could be used to appraise an athletic program at the high school or college level.
2. Have a debate on the question: Resolved: that all gate receipts for interscholastic athletic contests should be abolished.
3. Write a profile of what you consider to be the ideal coach.
4. As a Director of Athletics what plans would you have to make for a season of play in basketball? Outline in detail.
5. What are some essential points to keep in mind in respect to each of the following: (a) contracts, (b) officials, (c) protests and forfeitures, (d) game management, (e) schedules, (f) awards, (g) records, and (h) medical examinations?
6. Describe in detail how athletic insurance works.
7. As a Director of Athletics, what administrative policy would you recommend in respect to each of the following: (a) gate receipts, (b) tournaments and championships, (c) eligibility, (d) scholarships, (e) recruiting, (f) proselyting, and (g) scouting?
8. What is the role of the Athletic Association in the conduct of athletics?
9. Develop a set of guiding administrative principles for girls' athletics.
10. Write an essay of 500 words on the topic: Desirable sports competition for children.
11. Debate the following question: Do national playoffs in sports constitute a desirable activity for children under 12 years of age?
12. What practical suggestions can you make for eliminating the "big business" aspects of intercollegiate athletics?
13. Read the Educational Policies Commission report on "School Athletics" and give a report to the class.

Reading assignment in *Administrative Dimensions of Health and Physical Education Programs, Including Athletics:* Chapter 8, Selections 39 to 47.

Selected references

American Association for Health, Physical Education, and Recreation: Administrative problems in health education, physical education, and recreation, Washington, D. C., 1953, The Association, Area V.

American Association for Health, Physical Education, and Recreation: Coaches handbook—a practical guide for high school coaches, Washington, D. C., 1960, The Association.

American Association for Health, Physical Education, and Recreation: Approaches to problems of public school administration in health, physical education and recreation, Proceedings of the Sixth National Conference of City and

*Educational Policies Commission: School athletics — problems and policies, Washington, D. C., 1954, National Education Association.

County Directors, Washington, D. C., 1968, The Association.

American Association for Health, Physical Education, and Recreation: Secondary school athletic administration, Washington, D. C., 1969, The Association.

Bucher, C. A., editor: Methods and materials in physical education and recreation, St. Louis, 1954, The C. V. Mosby Co.

Bucher, C. A.: Foundations of physical education, ed. 5, St. Louis, 1968, The C. V. Mosby Co.

Bucher, C. A., and Cohane, T.: Little league baseball can hurt your boy, Look, Aug. 11, 1953, p. 74.

Bucher, C. A., and Dupee, R. K., Jr.: Athletics schools and colleges, New York, 1965, The Center for Applied Research in Education, Inc. (The Library of Education).

Bucher, C. A., Koenig, C., and Barnhard, M.: Methods and materials for secondary school physical education, ed. 3, St. Louis, 1970, The C. V. Mosby Co.

Division for Girls' and Women's Sports: Philosophy and standards for girls and women's sports, Washington, D. C., 1969, American Association for Health, Physical Education, and Recreation.

Educational Policies Commission: School athletics—problems and policies, Washington, D. C., 1954, National Education Association.

Forsythe, C. E.: The administration of high school athletics, Englewood Cliffs, N. J., 1962, Prentice-Hall, Inc.

George, J. F., and Lehmann, H. A.: School athletic administration, New York, 1966, Harper and Row, Publishers.

Grieve, A. W.: Directing high school athletics, Englewood Cliffs, N. J., 1963, Prentice-Hall, Inc.

Healey, W. A.: The administration of high school athletic events, Danville, Ill., 1961, The Interstate Printers & Publishers, Inc.

Hixson, C. G.: The administration of interscholastic athletics, New York, 1967, J. Lowell Pratt and Co.

Joint Committee on Athletic Competition for Children of Elementary and Junior High School Age: Desirable athletic competition for children, Washington, D. C., 1952, American Association for Health, Physical Education, and Recreation.

Ray, R. F.: Trends in intercollegiate athletics, Journal of Health, Physical Education, and Recreation 36:21, 1965.

Reed, W. R.: Big time athletics' commitment to education, Journal of Health, Physical Education, and Recreation 34:29, 1963.

Rogers, F. R.: The future of interscholastic athletics, New York, 1929, Bureau of Publications, Teachers College, Columbia University.

Rule books for all boys' sports. Available from the National Federation of State High School Athletic Associations, 7 S. Dearborn St., Chicago, Ill.

Rule books for all girls' sports. Available from the Division for Girls' and Women's Sports, American Association for Health, Physical Education, and Recreation, 1201 16th St. N.W., Washington, D. C. 20036.

The administration of physical fitness programs requires an understanding of the nature and scope of fitness and also of some of the historical background responsible for the current physical fitness emphasis. School and college physical educators and health educators will render a greater service to their students when they become more knowledgeable about physical fitness.

Fitness is the ability of the individual to live a full and balanced life. It involves physical, mental, emotional, social, and spiritual factors and the capacity for their wholesome expression. All are closely interwoven into the fabric of the whole person.

The totally fit person has a healthy and happy outlook on life. He satisfies such basic needs as physical well-being, love, affection, security, and self-respect. He likes people and lives happily with them. As he grows older, he develops a maturity that is characterized by submersion of self and an interest in serving humanity. He makes peace with his God and believes in and exemplifies high ethical standards.

A fit person is one who (1) *physically* has a strong organic base, exhibits vigor, is active, is skilled in some physical activities, and enjoys a sense of well-being; (2) *socially* recognizes the principle once stated by Justice Stone that "no man can live unto himself alone" and, therefore, understands and respects the rights of others, likes people, practices service above self, and makes satisfactory group adjustments; (3) *mentally* has a healthy outlook on life, thinks independently and constructively, has good judgment, is resourceful, and wants to be fit; and (4) *emotionally* has stability and self-control, faces reality in an honest manner, and has high ethical standards.

Henderson County Schools, Hendersonville, N. C.

Henderson County Schools, Hendersonville, N. C.

Weight lifting in the required physical education program at Washington State College helps to build physical fitness.

PHYSICAL FITNESS

Physical fitness, as one aspect of total fitness, involves three important concepts. It is related to the tasks the person must perform, his potential for physical effort, and the relationship of his physical fitness to his total self. The same degree of physical fitness is not necessary for everyone. It should be sufficient to meet the requirements of the job, plus a little extra as a reserve for emergencies. A football player or a foot soldier in the Army needs a different type of physical fitness from that required by a train conductor or a stenographer. The question of "fitness for what" must always be asked. Furthermore, discussion of the physical fitness of a person must be within the context of his own human resources and not to those of others. It depends on his potentialities in the light of his own physical makeup. Finally, physical fitness cannot be considered by itself but, instead, as it is affected by mental, emotional, and spiritual factors as well. Human beings function as a whole and not in segmented parts.

COMPONENTS OF PHYSICAL FITNESS

The attempt to define and break down the term *physical fitness* has led to the identification of certain specific components that collectively make up physical fitness. Such factors as resistance to disease, or the ability of the body to keep its disease-fighting equipment in good shape; muscular strength, or the ability to exert force against a resistance; muscular endurance, or the ability to repeat activities involving resistance; and cardiorespiratory endurance, or the ability of the circulatory and respiratory systems to support activities requiring sustained effort, such as distance running or swimming—these make up the components of physical fitness set forth by most authorities.

Larson and Yocom* list ten components of physical fitness—namely, resistance to disease, muscular strength and endurance, cardiovascular-respiratory endurance, muscular power, flexibility, speed, agility, coordination, balance, and accuracy. McCloy and Young† list components such as the speed of muscular contraction, dynamic energy, ability to change direction, agility, dead weight, and flexibility. Cureton‡ appraises physical fitness in terms of physique and organic efficiency, which he says implies anatomic and physiologic soundness, and adds a component that he calls "motor fitness." This motor fitness, according to Cureton, includes endurance, power, strength, agility, flexibility, and balance.

Morehouse and Miller§ include a psychologic component that to them implies possession of necessary emotional stability, drive or motivation, intelligence, and educability.

As can be seen from these statements of leaders in the field of physical education, there is not complete agreement as to what physical fitness is and what its components are. Research is needed to obtain more valid evidence about this important aspect of health and physical education work.

DEVELOPING PHYSICAL FITNESS

The question of how to obtain physical fitness is a controversial point. Since we do not know exactly what it is and what its components may be, the answer as to how one obtains it is also somewhat nebulous. We do know, however, that heredity plays an important role. The form and structure of the body is determined largely by parents. Heredity sets certain direction and limitations to development. Good nutrition is essential. Good health habits—such as having proper rest, relaxation, and sleep and otherwise providing good care for the body—are necessary. The important contributions of mental, emotional, spiritual, and social health must be considered. In addition, there is increasing recognition of the importance of physical activity. The value of exercise in developing many of the components of physical fitness and, in addition, in contributing to mental, social, and emotional well-being is an important factor.

Up to now there has been a reserved caution in regard to the benefits of exercise, with many persons feeling that it is unimportant as a contributor to the fit individual. However, research is proving the value of physical activity in physical fitness. A statement from Steinhaus* is a fitting conclusion to this section:

The muscles are by weight about 43 percent of the average adult male human body. They expend a large portion of all the kinetic energy of the adult body. The cortical centers for the voluntary muscles extend over most of the lateral psychic zones of the brain, so that their culture (the culture of muscles) is brain building. They are in a most intimate and peculiar sense organs of the will. They have built all the roads, cities, and machines in the world, written all of the books, spoken all the words, and, in fact, done everything that man has accomplished with matter. If they are undeveloped or grow flabby, the dreadful chasm between good intentions and their execution is liable to appear and widen. Character might be in a sense defined as a plexus of motor habits.

Methods of developing physical fitness

Some of the methods of utilizing physical activity in the development of physical

*Larson, L. A., and Yocom, R.: Measurement and evaluation in physical, health and recreation education, St. Louis, 1951, The C. V. Mosby Co., p. 162.

†McCloy, C. H., and Young, N. D.: Tests and measurements in health and physical education, ed. 3, New York, 1954, Appleton-Century-Crofts, pp. 4-5.

‡Cureton, T. K.: Physical fitness appraisal and guidance, St. Louis, 1947, The C. V. Mosby Co., p. 21.

§Morehouse, L. E., and Miller, A. T., Jr.: Physiology of exercise, ed. 5, St. Louis, 1967, The C. V. Mosby Co., p. 268.

*Steinhaus, A. H.: Health and physical fitness from the standpoint of the physiologist, Journal of Health and Physical Education 7:225, 1936.

Youth Fitness Achievement Award. (Courtesy American Association for Health, Physical Education, and Recreation.)

fitness include circuit training, interval training, weight training, weight lifting, isometric exercises, and the Exer-Genie.

Circuit training involves a series of exercises, usually around ten, that are performed in a progressive manner. Physical activity is performed at each of the ten stations. The training is done on a time basis and progress is checked against the clock. The length and nature of activities performed can be changed as the performer becomes stronger.

Interval training requires physical activ-ity involving distance to build endurance, an increase of speed, an increase in the number of repetitions, and the rest or recovery period. As the performer becomes stronger the recovery interval is reduced. Its main contribution is in the area of cardiovascular endurance development.

Weight training utilizes resistance exercises, taking into consideration the number of repetitions of resistance exercises and also the duration and intensity of the exercises being performed.

Weight lifting involves the lifting of

Fitness. (Courtesy American Association for Health, Physical Education, and Recreation.)

weights and usually involves only a few repetitions.

Isometric exercises are exercises whereby muscles contract and build up tension and hold without any shortening or lengthening. (*Static* or *isometric* is derived from the words *iso*, meaning same, and *metric*, meaning length.) They are valuable in developing strength.

In *calisthenic exercises* the muscles contract so that they shorten and the ends are brought together (concentric), or the muscles lengthen and the ends go away from the center, as in the beginning of a pull-up when one lowers himself into a hanging position (eccentric) (isotonic).

The *Exer-Genie* can utilize either isometric or isotonic exercises. It is an instrument sold commercially that involves rope and handles. The amount of strength required to pull the ropes in various positions can be adjusted, thus enabling a progressive development of strength and endurance.

HISTORICAL BACKGROUND OF CURRENT PHYSICAL FITNESS EMPHASIS

The subject of fitness is not new to the American educational system. There have been numerous times during the educational history of this country when educators have been called upon to upgrade the fitness of American youth. World Wars I and II both caused the pendulum to swing toward more emphasis in this direction.

During the past few years there has been a renewed stress on the subject of fitness. Results of some physical fitness tests have revealed the softness of American children and youth as compared to children and youth in other countries. Although some of these tests have been criticized by many physical education leaders as not possessing validity, they have stirred up considerable interest in the area of physical fitness. The information forthcoming from these tests caught the ears of the President of

NAME _____

SCHOOL _____ / ____ Entrance Date SCHOOL _____ / ____ Entrance Date SCHOOL _____ / ____ Entrance Date

PRIMARY WASHINGTON MOTOR FITNESS TEST:

KEY: S = Score; P = Points; R = Rating

RATING: S = Superior; G = Good; A = Average; BA = Below Average; NI = Needs Improvement

	AGE	POWER			STRENGTH & ENDURANCE									SPEED			PHYSICAL FITNESS
		Standing Broadjump			Bench Push Ups			Curl Up			Squat Jump			30 Yard Dash			
		S	P	R	S	P	R	S	P	R	S	P	R	S	P	R	P	R
GRADE I																		
Fall																		
Repeat																		
Spring																		
GRADE II																		
Fall																		
Repeat																		
Spring																		
GRADE III																		
Fall																		
Repeat																		
Spring																		

PFI (OREGON SIMPLIFICATION)

AAHPER FITNESS TEST KEY: S = Score; % = Percentile

	Age	Hgt.	Wgt.	Leg Lift	Back Lift	Push Up	Pull Up	PFI	Stdg. BJ.		50 yd. Dash		40 yard Shuttle Run		Softball Throw		Wall Volley	
									S	%	S	%	S	%	S	%	S	%
GRADE IV																		
Fall																		
Repeat																		
Spring																		
GRADE V																		
Fall																		
Repeat																		
Spring																		
GRADE VI																		
Fall																		
Repeat																		
Spring																		

-2-

PFI (OREGON SIMPLIFICATION)

AAHPER FITNESS TEST Key: S = Score; % = Percentile

	Age	Hgt.	Wgt.	Leg Lift	Back Lift	Push Up	Pull Up	PFI	Stdg. B.J. S	%	50 Yard Dash S	%	40 Yard Shuttle Run S	%	600 Yard Run S	%	Pull Ups S	%	Sit Ups S	%
GRADE VII																					
Fall																					
Repeat																					
Spring																					
GRADE VIII																					
Fall																					
Repeat																					
Spring																					
GRADE IX																					
Fall																					
Repeat																					
Spring																					
GRADE X																					
2nd Test																					
3rd Test																					
GRADE XI																					
Follow Up																					
GRADE XII																					
Follow Up																					

LIFETIME SPORTS PROFICIENCY

Sport	Date Listed	Signature of Instructor

DEVELOPMENTAL CLASSES

Grade Level _____ Date _____ PFI _____

Grade Level _____ Date _____ PFI _____

Grade Level _____ Date _____ PFI _____

Grade Level _____ Date _____ PFI _____

Grade Level _____ Date _____ PFI _____

Cumulative physical fitness record, Broadfront Program, used at Ellensburg Public Schools, Ellensburg, Wash.

the United States, with the result that a program of action was established in high government circles.

A President's Conference on Fitness of American Youth, held at the United States Naval Academy, Annapolis, Maryland, June 18-19, 1956, initiated a government-sponsored program in fitness that was destined to influence considerably the fields of health education and physical education. It was attended by 150 leaders in sports, education, medicine, public relations, government, and other areas. Most of the conferees were presidents, directors, or other top officials of organizations interested in the fitness of American youth. At the closing session of the conference the Vice-President announced that a President's Council on Physical Fitness, composed of members of the Cabinet, would be established to help improve the mental and physical health of the nation's young people. The President also announced that a President's Citizens' Advisory Committee on the Fitness of American Youth would be established. These committees have been functioning since their formation. The Advisory Committee, according to the President, "is to examine and explore the facts and, thereafter, to alert America on what can and should be done to reach the much-desired goal of a happier, healthier, and more totally fit youth in America."

A summary of some of the recommendations resulting from group discussions at this conference shows the challenge that fitness has for the schools:

1. There is a need for more research.
2. An agency or commission on fitness for American youth should be created.
3. Much is being done at the present time for the fitness of American youth. However, it is not enough and what is being done is very poorly coordinated.
4. Youth must be involved in much of the planning.
5. Programs must be fitted to the needs of the individual child and they must reach *all* the children.

6. Better school health examinations are needed.
7. The fitness of this nation is based on the fitness of its people. If there is something we need and know we need—this nation should have it!
8. There should be more and better leadership.
9. Leaders should themselves believe in fitness and provide a fitting example for the youth of this country.
10. Community leadership should be drawn from schools, recreation agencies, parents, law enforcement agencies, labor, management, youth groups, and the whole gamut of community life.
11. Higher salaries and other inducements for attracting qualified leadership into this work should be provided.
12. Families should make the best possible use of their own resources. Home space should be provided for children's play.
13. School facilities should receive maximum use. Other facilities, such as camps, fairgrounds, parks, etc., should also be used.
14. Foundations should be urged to contribute to the support of fitness endeavors.
15. Colleges and universities and mass communication media can help gain public support.
16. Parents must be impressed with the importance of taking an active interest in fitness of children—spending time with them, teach sportsmanship, loyalty, spirit, etc.
17. Youth must be sold on importance of being physically fit.
18. Fitness programs should begin in the home, and all members of the family should engage in these activities.
19. The schools do not represent the only facet of community life that should have a role in building fitness—churches, social agencies, veterans groups, government agencies, sports groups, and others can play an important part.
20. Girls should receive as much attention as boys.
21. Greater financial support is needed for better and larger programs.

The present administration has emphasized the role of the schools and colleges in physical fitness. The recommendations of the President's Council on Physical Fitness and Sports are discussed later in this chapter.

PHYSICAL ACHIEVEMENT AND THE SCHOOLS

According to the President's Council on Physical Fitness and Sports much progress has been made during the 1960's in improving the physical achievement standards of American youth—for example: 9.2 million children are participating in school physical activity programs; four out of every five pupils now successfully pass standardized physical fitness tests (only two out of three passed in 1961); 68% of all schools have strengthened their physical activity programs; the number of parochial schools providing physical education instruction has doubled; seventeen states have raised their school physical education requirements; and teaching positions for health and physical education have increased by 27%—school enrollments have increased 11%.

Although much progress has been made in recent years, there is much left to be done—for example: 14% of children in school today do not participate in any physical activity program, and an additional 27% participate only 1 or 2 days per week; only four schools in ten provide physical education programs 5 days per week; and 23% of the schools have administered the American Association of Health, Physical Education, and Recreation seven-item physical achievement test, but on this test only 57% of the boys and 51% of the girls were reported to have scored "satisfactory" on all items.

The charts on pp. 290 and 292 reflect a comparison of American youngsters tested in 1958 and their counterparts tested in 1965. The statistics reflect a general improvement over the years.

WHAT SCHOOLS AND COLLEGES CAN DO

Education in its broadest sense means preparation for life. It should help each in-

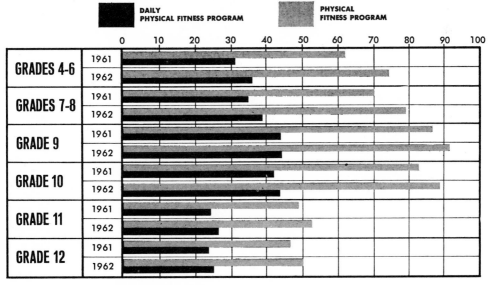

U. S. OFFICE OF EDUCATION SURVEY

The following findings are based on a scientific sampling of the public, private and church-related schools. Every effort was exerted to maintain a proper balance between these various types of schools, between schools of various sizes and between the various instructional levels (elementary, secondary and combined).

Pupil participation on physical fitness programs. (Courtesy The Advertising Council, Inc., New York, N. Y.)

dividual to become all he is capable of being. Therefore, it is inexorably tied in with fitness. Education must be concerned with developing in each individual optimum health, vitality, emotional stability, social consciousness, knowledge, wholesome attitudes, and spiritual and moral qualities. Only as it accomplishes this task will it achieve its destiny in the American way of life.

Schools and colleges have the responsibility for providing many opportunities for understanding and developing fitness. Of all the agencies involved in carrying out the President's fitness program, the schools and colleges are the focal point. The fact that some 60 million children and youth can be reached through them is an important reason for recognizing their worth. The schools and colleges also have the needed facilities and their teachers are trained for carrying out such a program. The school and college can instill children and youth with a desire for fitness. Education can likewise equip youngsters with the necessary tools to attain and maintain fitness throughout life. Their qualified teachers can also provide leadership in community programs that have valuable contributions to make.

The schools and colleges should be fitness conscious. Programs must be so constituted that experiences and services contribute to fitness. This means that health knowledge, attitudes, and practices are stressed; that protective health services are provided; that physical activities are available to and engaged in by *all*—not just the few who are skilled; that necessary facilities are provided; that the environment is conducive to proper growth and development; that experiences in every area stress proper social and ethical behavior.

Leadership in the schools and colleges should exemplify fitness—fitness is the responsibility of all disciplines and all teachers and staff. It should permeate the entire program and all persons connected with it.

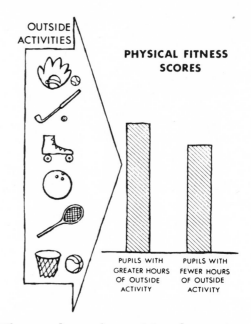

Those students who participated more in activities outside the school had higher fitness scores than those pupils with fewer hours of physical activity outside the school. (Physical fitness achievement in selected physical education programs, Albany, 1965, The University of the State of New York.)

It is not the responsibility of only one area and just a few people.

The schools and colleges represent only one force for developing a fit populace. The home, church, recreational agency, volunteer groups, and other persons and organizations also have major contributions to make. Schools and colleges should work closely with and play a leading role in mobilizing the entire resources of each community to do the job.

Children and youth must want to be fit. Unless the desire to be fit is resident in each child, the way of life that results in fitness will not be achieved. By the time they leave school and college behind and enter into adult life, the importance of fitness in achieving personal ambitions and desires, in feeling well and happy, in living most and serving best, and in contributing to a strong nation must be inculcated

Boys and girls who participated in high quality physical education programs improved more in physical fitness than did those pupils participating in minimum programs. (Physical fitness achievement in selected physical education programs, Albany, 1965, The University of the State of New York.)

in every boy and girl who attends our schools and colleges.

There is a responsible role for the schools and colleges to pursue, but a very necessary one. It is a challenge we must take up if we are not to become a nation of "softies" and unfit individuals.

Health education and physical education can contribute much to the development of total fitness. Many benefits accrue to those persons who have experiences in these specialized fields. They possess an understanding of the human body—its needs and its limitations—the ability to discriminate fad from scientific fact, the interest and desire to be physically fit, the resources to spend leisure hours in a manner that contributes to fitness, and the skill in activities that provide release from strains and tension associated with modern living. They are also provided with experiences that contribute to wholesome personal and group adjustments and opportunities for creative expression. These

are only a few of the many benefits that can be listed. These values, however, do not automatically accrue. Leadership is the key to their fulfillment.

Leaders in health, physical education, and recreation must never lose sight of the fact they are working with the "whole" individual. Programs should make provision for the selected activities that best develop all aspects of self. They should also be concerned with the contributions their respective fields can make, individually and collectively, to this "whole" development.

More specifically, some essential points that school and college health and physical education and recreation programs must consider if they are to adequately promote the health and well-being of boys and girls who attend our schools are listed here:

1. School and college health and physical education programs must be available to *all* children and youth and based on their individual differences.

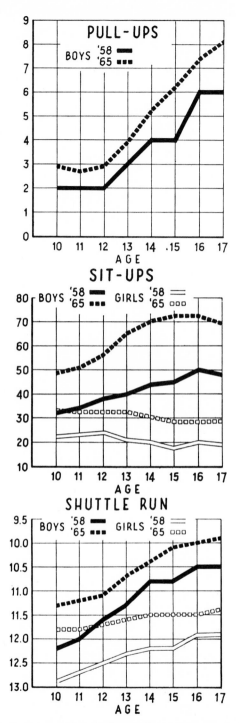

PULL-UPS

BOYS '58 ▬
'65 ■■■

SIT-UPS

BOYS '58 ▬ GIRLS '58 ═
'65 ■■■ '65 □□□

SHUTTLE RUN

BOYS '58 ▬ GIRLS '58 ═
'65 ■■■ '65 □□□

Comparison of youth fitness data between 1958 and 1965. (From Hunsicker, P. N., and Reiff, G.: A survey and comparison of youth fitness, 1958 to 1965, Ann Arbor, 1965, University of Michigan, Cooperative Research Project No. 2418.)

2. Every student should have one period of each school day devoted to the physical education program. College youth should have a required and a voluntary program to meet their needs. Anything less is inadequate.

3. Sports and games should not be limited to only the varsity squads in football, basketball, or baseball. Every student should get into the act, whether he is a dub or skilled, weak or strong, boy or girl.

4. Boys and girls need professionally trained teachers in the fields of health and physical education. Furthermore, the ratio of teachers to students in such classes should be the same as for English, mathematics, or geography.

5. Children and youth should participate in physical education programs that include class periods, intramurals, play, sports, and field days, adapted activities, and scholastic and collegiate sports.

6. Physical activities contribute to physical fitness as they are planned around the following three essentials: *Frequency*—regular daily workouts are needed to develop and maintain a state of optimum health. *Intensity*—big muscles must be vigorously used, with resulting stimulation of the heart and breathing rates. As many muscles should be put into action as possible. *Duration*—1 hour a day, with frequent rest periods, should be devoted to physical activity.

7. In addition to the benefits received from the physical activity program, young people should also understand the importance of being in good health and the factors that build fitness. There should be a comprehensive program of health instruction for all pupils based on their interests and needs.

8. Many health services are essential to promoting physical fitness in the schools and colleges. Most important is a good medical examination in which health defects can be uncovered and steps taken to ensure their correction.

A PHYSICAL FITNESS CHECKLIST*

	Yes	No
Medical aspects		
1. Thorough dental and health examination each year	___	___
(a) Fit heart and circulatory system, digestive system, nervous system, etc.	___	___
(b) Proper body development, according to age and sex (height and weight, etc.)	___	___
2. Correction of remedial health defects, i.e., vision, hearing, overweight etc.	___	___
Physical activity		
1. At least 1½ to 2 hours a day spent in vigorous physical activity, preferably outdoors	___	___
2. Adequate muscular strength and endurance	___	___
3. After running 50 yards, heart and breathing return to normal rates within 10 minutes	___	___
4. Average skill in running, jumping, climbing, and throwing	___	___
5. Control of body in activities involving balance, agility, speed, rhythm, accuracy	___	___
Posture		
1. When standing upright, string dropped from tip of ear passes through shoulder and hip joints and middle of ankle	___	___
2. When sitting in a chair, trunk and head are erect, weight balanced over pelvis, or trunk slightly bent forward	___	___
3. When walking, slumping is avoided, body is in proper balance, and excessively wasteful motions of arms and legs are eliminated	___	___
Health habits		
1. Rest: at least 8 hours of sleep each night	___	___
2. Diet: consists of four servings daily from each of the four basic food groups	___	___
(a) Meat, poultry, fish, and eggs		
(b) Dairy products		
(c) Vegetables and fruits		
(d) Bread and cereals		
3. Cleanliness:		
(a) Daily bath	___	___
(b) Teeth brushed after every meal	___	___
(c) Clean hair, nails, and clothing	___	___
4. Abstain from use of tobacco and alcohol	___	___

*From Bucher, C. A., Koenig, C., and Barnhard, M.: Methods and materials for secondary school education, ed. 3, St. Louis, 1970, The C. V. Mosby Co.

9. There should be coordination between school, college, and community programs to ensure the conduct of sound out-of-school and college programs of recreation, sports, and athletics. Efforts to expand public and private facilities such as YMCA's, Boys' Clubs, and playgrounds must be continued. Present facilities meet only about 15% of our public needs.

10. A healthful environment is essential to fitness. Safe, sanitary, and attractive facilities and equipment, plus an atmosphere that is conducive to optimum mental and emotional health, are necessary.

11. Motivation for fitness must be developed. Students and the public must be oriented as to the importance of fitness for living. People will change only if sufficiently motivated.

12. There should be homework in physi-

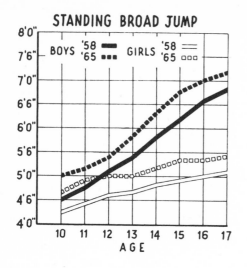

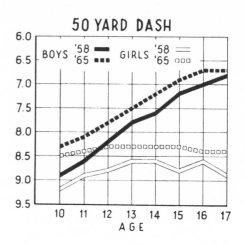

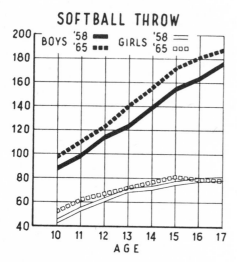

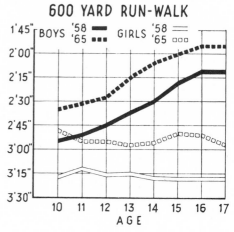

Comparison of youth fitness data between 1958 and 1965. (From Hunsicker, P. N., and Reiff, G.: A survey and comparison of youth fitness, 1958 to 1965, Ann Arbor, 1965, University of Michigan, Cooperative Research Project No. 2418.)

cal activities. It cannot all be done in the gymnasium, swimming pool, or playground. Activities must be taught that may be enjoyed away from the conventional gymnasium and athletic fields. The program should include many kinds of home activities that can be conducted in backyards or basements.

13. If the schools and colleges are going to build strong bodies, they need the necessary equipment and facilities. Taxpayers and administrators must recognize the importance of this work and supply the necessary funds.

14. Health and physical education should receive equal recognition with other subjects in the curriculum. This means credit and other considerations should be

given. Participation in musical organizations, military training, driver education, or other activities should not be permitted to serve as a substitute for physical education.

15. Health and physical education classes should be scheduled early in the program if the needs of students are to be met. In many cases this means they will be scheduled before other subjects. Other things being equal, the school subjects that have the greatest number of pupils enrolled should receive first consideration. The number of staff members and teaching stations are also considerations.

16. Utilization of valid techniques to determine which students are below par in physical fitness is needed, so that special programs may be provided.

17. A progressive program should be provided in health and physical education from kindergarten through college.

THE PRESIDENT'S COUNCIL AND PHYSICAL FITNESS*

The President's Council on Physical Fitness and Sports continues to be active in promoting the cause of physical fitness throughout the United States. In a recent year it attracted more than 10,000 persons to physical fitness clinics that were conducted by Council staff members and outstanding sports and physical education experts. It continues to award the Presidential Physical Fitness Awards to boys and girls who qualify. The number of young people receiving the award exceeds 100,000 in a year. It has established over 130 schools throughout the nation as physical fitness demonstration centers. It has been active in poverty areas in organizing programs of swimming, basketball, and other sports. These are only a few of the projects the Council is undertaking.

*President's Council on Physical Fitness: Youth physical fitness—suggested elements of a school-centered program, parts 1 and 2, Washington, D. C., July, 1961, The Council.

The President's Council on Physical Fitness and Sports, an extension of the President's Council on Youth Fitness established in 1956, came into being by Executive Order on March 4, 1968. Its purpose is to "expand opportunities to engage in exercise, active recreation and sports."

The President of the United States has urged the adoption of the recommendations of his Physical Fitness Council by the schools in order to ensure a basic program of physical developmental activity. A summary of these recommendations and the suggestions for implementing them follow.

Recommendations

1. Identify pupils who have a low level of muscular strength, agility, and flexibility through appropriate testing and require them to participate in a prescribed developmental activity and exercise program.

2. Devote a minimum of 15 minutes a day in the physical education period to vigorous exercises and developmental activities.

3. Use valid tests to determine the physical fitness level of students.

4. Provide a comprehensive program of health education and physical education.

Implementation

1. Utilize three simple tests (pull-ups, sit-ups, and squat-thrusts) to determine pupils who are physically below par.

2. Arrange for all pupils to have a minimum of 15 minutes each day of vigorous physical activity.

3. Test physically underdeveloped boys and girls every 6 weeks until they reach the minimum level.

4. Utilize a validated physical fitness test.

5. Utilize the physical fitness test results for diagnosis and motivation.

6. Provide for testing at least twice yearly.

7. Continually improve and upgrade

total programs of health and physical education.

8. Provide for a qualified person to coordinate the total program.

FURTHER RECOMMENDATIONS OF PRESIDENT'S COUNCIL FOR EMPHASIZING PHYSICAL FITNESS IN HEALTH AND PHYSICAL EDUCATION PROGRAMS

Programs of health education and physical education recommended by the President's Council should include the following items.

Health and safety education

Direct instruction relating to specific health concepts and problems should be provided at every grade level. The topics treated should be in keeping with the interests, needs, and maturational level of the children as they progress grade by grade. Such direct instruction would be augmented by the teaching of healthful and safe behavior through the health appraisal procedures, by capitalizing on interest-arousing events, by correlating health and safety with other subjects, and by other means.

Grades 1 to 3; Ages 6 to 8. At this level, much of the child's health learning relates to developing good practices in daily living at home, in the school, and in the community. Health needs include attention to cleanliness; nutrition; sleep, rest, and relaxation; healthful physical activities; acquaintance with the dentist, nurse, and physician; learning about community health agencies; care of the eyes, ears, and teeth; and elementary concepts of prevention and control of disease.

Grades 4 to 6; Ages 9 to 11. Increasing attention is given to the understanding of *why* health practices should be followed. Elementary treatment of the scientific bases of healthful and safety behavior is carried forward. New units are introduced on the body structure and function, simple first-aid procedures, elementary principles of mental and emotional health, and other topics.

Grades 7 to 9; Ages 12 to 14. Direct instruction in health and safety should amount to at least one semester of five regular periods per week during the 3 years. At this level, heavier emphasis should be given to the physiological and other scientific bases and to the use of scientific methods in solving health and safety problems. The focus should be on problems of adolescence and should include units on: growth and develop-

ment; differences in rate of growth; physical maturation; acne and skin disorders; effects of maintaining an adequate diet; use of tobacco, alcohol, and other drugs; getting along with parents; establishing friendships; desirable relationships with the opposite sex; introduction to vocations, including health careers; importance of exercise and physical forms of recreation; and other related topics.

Grades 10 to 12; Ages 15 to 18. Instruction centers around problems of adult living and of family and community health. Important topics include: emotional health; chronic disease, such as heart disease, cancer, diabetes, and mental illness; instruction concerning consumer health (intelligent utilization of health services and products); national and international health organizations; health careers; health and safety aspects of civil defense; safety in the home, in transportation, recreation; more advanced first aid; the role of exercise in developing and maintaining health and fitness; exercise and weight control; health problems relating to alcohol, tobacco, and narcotics.

Adequate coverage of these topics requires, at a minimum, the equivalent of a full semester of daily periods of regular length. Two full semesters are recommended.

Physical education

The physical education curriculum should include a core of physical fitness activities designed to develop strength, speed, agility, balance, coordination, flexibility, muscular endurance, good posture and body mechanics, and organic efficiency. Activities and exercises should affect all parts and systems. The curriculum should also include a broad scope and balance of physical activities that promote well-rounded physical, social, and intellectual development. Activities should become progressively more complex in organization and skills, and more demanding of physical development and control grade by grade.

The programs should be adapted to the needs, interests, and capacities of each child and youth, including those pupils who, for physical and other reasons, are unable to participate safely and successfully in the general program. All pupils should be motivated to achieve high levels of physical fitness, compatible with their capabilities.

Grades 1 to 3; Ages 6 to 8. Emphasis should be placed upon learning the fundamentals of movement and building a foundation of physical fitness.

Walking, running, hopping, skipping, balancing, jumping, sliding, catching, climbing, hanging, throwing; elementary rhythmical activities, creative movement experience, and simple games which set the stage for later, more complicated activity skills; activities on the jungle gym and other types of playground equipment; simple stunts and tumbling; elementary swimming wherever possible—all of these activities and more should be included. Active participation and vigorous movement should be highlighted.

Grades 4 to 6; Ages 9 to 11. The "fitness core" should have continued emphasis, giving particular attention to development of the back, chest, shoulders, and arms. This age group is ready for elementary calisthenics. Class instruction should include fundamentals of sports skills in several team sports, track and field, and simple forms of individual and dual sports. Opportunity to practice the skills and to gain knowledge in organized games should be provided.

Folk dances and other rhythmical activities are important as are relays, simple games involving running, tumbling, and simple gymnastics. Vigorous outdoor activities such as skating and cycling should be encouraged.

Screening for physical capacity as well as physical achievement testing should begin at this level and continue periodically thereafter. Simple tests of skills and knowledge should also be used.

Grades 7 to 9; Ages 12 to 14. The physical fitness core should include advanced conditioning and developmental activities, e.g., weight-resistance exercises, and the activities should increase in intensity, frequency, and distance. The wide range of individual differences among these youngsters in prepubertal and pubertal stages of development should be noted and programs adjusted accordingly.

The curriculum should include a broad range of offerings in sports and other activities. Emphasis should be given to skillful participation in team sports and increasing attention to individual and dual sports that carry over to recreation hours. Intramural and extramural sports programs should be conducted.

Folk, square, and social dancing are important activities for this age group. Also to be highlighted are stunts, tumbling, gymnastics, and trampolining; aquatics (whenever feasible), with emphasis on survival tactics; combative activities, e.g., wrestling (for boys); and outing activities, e.g., hiking, camping, and hunting.

Grades 10 to 12; Ages 15 to 18. The fitness core continues to be stressed with more opportunities for individual leadership provided.

The broad program is carried forward with particular emphasis on sports, rhythmics, and other activities that carry over into recreation hours throughout life. Specialization in such activities should be encouraged. Ways of maintaining physical fitness at various age levels under varying circumstances should be taught. Additional attention should also be given to outing activities and recreational activities for the family unit, particularly those that promote physical aspects of fitness.*

PHYSICAL FITNESS TESTING

The history of physical fitness testing goes back many years. It probably started as part of the physical education profession at the time when anthropometry was utilized. Anthropometry involved the measuring of the body and its parts, since size seemed to be related to strength. Then there was the emphasis on strength testing, often through use of dynamometers. The work of Dudley A. Sargent and his development of the Intercollegiate Strength Test are characteristic of this early era. It was soon realized, however, that strength testing alone could not measure the functional capacity of individuals. This realization led to cardiorespiratory testing. Schneider expressed this concept when he said:

Physical exertion overtaxes the circulatory mechanism long before it exhausts skeletal musculature; and while it is not easy to overwork the muscles, the heart can quite readily be overworked. The convalescent from infectious disease is limited in his exercise not by what his muscles can do but by the strength of his heart. Hence today the general opinion is that strength tests do not permit us to draw satisfactory conclusions regarding the efficiency of the entire body.†

As a result of this emphasis on functional capacity, many tests were developed, most of which involved changes in frequency of heart rate and blood pressure as a result of exercise. Examples of these are Tuttle's Pulse Ratio Test, McCurdy-Larson's Organic Efficiency Test, Carlson's

---

*President's Council on Physical Fitness: Youth physical fitness—suggested elements of a school-centered program, parts 1 and 2, Washington, D. C., July, 1961, The Council.

†Schneider, E. C.: Physical efficiency and the limitations of efficiency tests, American Physical Education Review 28:405, 1923.

Fatigue Test Curve, and Brouha's Step Test.

In 1925 strength testing was revived by Frederick Rand Rogers with his emphasis on physical capacity tests in the administration of physical education. More recent developments in strength testing have been accomplished by Harrison Clarke, who developed the tensiometer for use with orthopedic disabilities and by Hans Kraus and Ruth P. Hirschland, who devised a six-item test of "minimum muscular fitness" that appraises flexibility as well as strength.

During World War II, when physical fitness was a major objective, several performance type tests were developed. Some of these were the Army Air Force Test, the Army Physical Efficiency Test, the Navy Standard Physical Fitness Test, and the Victory Corps Tests.

Several tests with which to measure physical fitness are available today. Some of these have been scientifically validated, whereas others have been presented without objective evidence of validity. Validity and reliability are important criteria of a test, but administrative efficiency may place one test ahead of another. Validity, however, is the weak point in most physical fitness tests today.

Not all physical fitness tests measure the same kind of physical fitness. The evidence is that tests of physical fitness do not correlate very highly. Therefore, when selecting a fitness test it is necessary to select one that measures the kind of fitness the program is aiming to achieve.

It is difficult to identify the items we want to measure in physical fitness. Many experts feel we are a long way from having an all-purpose test and that it would be better to test component parts of physical fitness (posture, strength, balance, endurance), by means of several tests of each component. Then, through a partial correlation process it would be possible to determine the most valid test of each component. In turn, these most valid tests could be combined into a battery. Most physical fitness tests measure component factors that are not truly comprehensive.

GIRLS' PHYSICAL FITNESS TEST RECORD

Name _____ Grade _____ Period _____

School _____ Age ____ Ht. ____ Wt. ____ Test 1 Classification _____

Age ____ Ht. ____ Wt. ____ Test 2 Classification _____

Test No.	1		2	
Date				
Event	Score	Percentile	Score	Percentile
Modified Pull-Ups				
Sit-Ups (Max 50)				
Broad Jump				
50-yd. Dash				
Shuttle Run				
Modified Push-Ups				
600-yd. Run-Walk				
Softball Throw				
P.F.I.—Average percentile of 5 events				

They stress primarily arm strength, leg strength, and endurance. However, there are other considerations. For example, a husky body requires more strength for one pull-up than does a slight one. In addition to body build, physiologic age (when dealing with children) should also be considered. These and similar factors may account for the difficulty in validating tests.

The possibility of a universal battery of tests is remote because of disagreement among experts as to the nature of physical fitness. How much of it is esthetic and how much is a matter of health or expediency? Many physical education leaders feel it is important that the profession consider the adoption of a single tool of measurement. They feel this is of utmost importance if we are to propose a program that will become widely adopted and provide an answer to the present demand for an emphasis on physical fitness.

Tables 11-1 and 11-2 list the physical fitness components and tests that measure these components, as well as the selected tests of physical fitness.

The American Association for Health, Physical Education, and Recreation* has developed its own physical fitness test for national use. It consists of seven basic items plus a swimming test:

1. Pull-ups (modified for girls to flexed arm hang); to test arm and shoulder girdle strength
2. Sit-ups: to test strength of abdominal muscles and hip flexors
3. Shuttle run: to test speed and change of direction
4. Standing broad jump: to test explosive power of leg extensors
5. 50-yard dash: to test speed
6. Softball throw for distance: to test skill and coordination
7. 600-yard walk or run: to test cardiovascular system
8. Swimming test (jump into water, rest, and swim 15 yards): to test protective powers in the water

Norms have been established for girls and boys in grades five through twelve

*AAHPER youth fitness test manual, American Association for Health, Physical Education, and Recreation, 1201 16th St. N. W., Washington, D. C. 20036.

PHYSICAL FITNESS TEST RECORD						
Name			Grade	Age	Wt.	Ht.
School			Period		Squad	
Test No.	1		2		3	
Date						
Event	Score	Points	Score	Points	Score	Points
Pull Ups						
Sit Ups						
Push Ups						
Burpee 60						
Broad Jump						
	Total Points		Total Points		Total Points	
	Quartile		Quartile		Quartile	
Superior	277-Up		329-Up		400-Up	
Excellent	243-276		289-328		336-399	
Average	208-242		248-288		290-335	
Fair	174-207		208-247		245-289	
Unsatisfactory	Below 174		Below 208		Below 245	

Table 11-1. Physical fitness components and tests*

Component	Selected tests
Arm and shoulder strength	Pull-ups, push-ups, parallel bar, dips, rope climb
Speed	50-yard dash, 100-yard dash
Agility	Shuttle run, agility run
Abdominal and hip strength	Sit-ups, sit-ups with knees flexed, 2-minute sit-ups
Flexibility	Trunk flexion standing, trunk flexion sitting, trunk extension (prone position)
Cardiorespiratory endurance	600-yard run, half-mile run, mile run, 5-minute step test
Explosive power	Standing broad jump, vertical jump
Static strength	Grip strength, back lift, leg lift
Balance	Bass test, Brace test, tests on balance beam
Muscular endurance	Push-ups, chest raisings (prone position, hands behind neck, legs held down), V-sit (against time)

*From Hunsicker, P.: Physical fitness—what research says to the teacher, Washington, D. C., 1963, National Education Association, p. 17.

Improvised equipment for pull-up.

Final position for sit-up.

30 FT.
Starting the shuttle run.

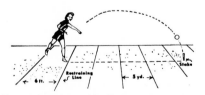
Measuring the softball throw for distance.

Measuring the standing broad jump.

Test items from AAHPER Youth Fitness Test Manual. (From NEA Journal **51:**33, 1962.)

Table 11-2. Selected tests of physical fitness*

Test	Source
AAHPER Youth Fitness Test	American Association for Health, Physical Education, and Recreation, 1201 16th St. N.W. Washington, D. C. 20036.
AAHPER-U. S. Office of Education Committee on Physical Fitness for Girls	Journal of HPER, pp. 308-311, 354-355, June, 1945.
All-round Muscular Endurance	Anderson, John E.: Endurance of young men, Society for Research in Child Development, vol. X, serial No. 40, No. 1, Washington, D. C., 1958, American Association for Health, Physical Education, and Recreation.
Army/Air Forces Physical Fitness Test	AAHPER Research Quarterly 15:12-15, March, 1944.
Army Physical Fitness Test	War Department, FM 21-20, 1945.
California Physical Fitness Test	California State Department of Education, Feb., 1948.
Harvard Step Test	AAHPER Research Quarterly 14:31-36, March, 1943.
Illinois Physical Fitness Test for High School Boys	Illinois State Department of Public Instruction, Bulletin No. 6, 1944.
Indiana High School Physical Condition Test	Indiana State Office of Public Instruction, Bulletin No. 136, Sept., 1944.
The JCR Test	AAHPER Research Quarterly 18:12-29, March, 1947.
Kraus-Weber Test of Minimum Muscular Fitness	AAHPER Research Quarterly 25:178-188, May, 1954.
Larson Muscular Strength Test	AAHPER Research Quarterly 11:82-96, Dec., 1940.
McCloy Strength Test	McCloy, H. C., and Young, N. E.: Tests and measurements in health and physical education, ed. 3, New York, 1954, Appleton-Century-Crofts, pp. 128-152.
Navy Standard Physical Fitness	Bureau of Naval Personnel, Training Division, Physical Fitness Section, 1943.
New York State Physical Fitness Test	New York State Education Department, 1948.
Youth Physical Fitness	President's Council on Youth Fitness: Youth physical fitness, Washington, D. C., 1961, United States Government Printing Office.
Rogers Strength Test	Clarke, H. Harrison: Application of measurement to health and physical education, ed. 3, New York, 1959, Prentice-Hall, Inc. pp. 182-213.

*From Hunsicker, P.: Physical fitness—what research says to the teacher, Washington, D. C., 1963, National Education Association, p. 17.

and for college students and may be obtained from the Association. A manual gives, in addition, complete directions for testing each item.

The State Department of Education of New York State* is an example of many state groups that have developed their own physical fitness tests for local use. The New York test consists of seven components that

---

*New York State physical fitness test, The University of the State of New York, The State Education Department, Albany, New York.

are measured to obtain a total physical fitness score:

1. Posture—evaluated by means of a posture rating chart
2. Accuracy—measured by means of a target throw, utilizing a softball and a circular target
3. Strength—evaluated by pull-ups for boys and modified pull-ups for girls
4. Agility—evaluated by means of the sidestep
5. Speed—evaluated by means of the 50-yard dash

6. Balance—evaluated by means of the squat-stand

7. Endurance—evaluated by means of the treadmill

Norms have been established and are listed in a manual, together with a description of the test.

Resources and materials for physical fitness*

At the present time the quantity of materials for teaching physical fitness continues to increase. Nationwide interest in this problem, fostered by the President's Council on Physical Fitness and Sports, as well as increased emphasis on health status, drugs, and medical care, has all brought this about. Physical educators have found greater interest in the reception for their programs among parents and lay people and have found it an ideal time to expand and extend their programs and facilities.

There is a wealth of material presently available to teachers for use in physical education classes. Following are some of the more well-known physical fitness test batteries and exercise programs which have been developed recently as part of this campaign for fitness:

1. *Youth Physical Fitness*—suggested elements of a school-centered program, President's Council on Youth Fitness, July, 1961, Superintendent of Documents, Washington, D. C., 40¢.

Part One—A discussion of the current concept and foundations of physical fitness programs, including suggested standards for instruction and complementary programs.

Part Two—Suggested tests and activities and developmental exercises for boys and girls, grades 4 to 12. Standards for different age levels are included with suggested test items, all of which have been adapted from the AAHPER test.

2. *Youth Fitness Test Manual*, American Association for Health, Physical Education, and Recreation, Washington, 1965, $1.00.

This booklet contains explanations for the administration of seven suggested test items, together with percentile scores for boys and girls at different age levels.

The association has also developed record forms for this testing program, and special awards and emblems which may be presented to students participating in this program.

3. *Vim*—A complete exercise plan for girls 12 to 18 years of age, and

4. *Vigor*—A complete exercise plan for boys 12 to 18 years of age, President's Council on Physical Fitness, May, 1964, Superintendent of Documents, Washington, D. C., 25¢ each.

These booklets contain helpful hints and facts about fitness for youngsters and include a daily exercise plan suitable for them to follow.

5. *Adult Physical Fitness*—A program for men and women, President's Council on Physical Fitness, Superintendent of Documents, Washington, D. C., 35¢.

This is an adult program for home exercising with which the teacher should be familiar.

6. *Royal Canadian Air Force Exercise Plans for Physical Fitness*—5BX, for men; 10BX, for women, Queen's Printer and Controller of Stationery, Ottawa, Canada, Revised, 1962, $1.00.

This, too, is an adult home exercise plan with which the teacher should be familiar.

7. *Physical Fitness for Girls*, William Hillcourt, and

8. *Physical Fitness for Boys*, William Hillcourt, A Golden Magazine Special, Golden Press, Inc., New York, 1967, $1.00.

There are many other materials available in this area of physical fitness. Many state departments of education have developed their own testing instruments (California, Oregon, Washington, Iowa, Virginia, New York) as have some cities (Tucson, Denver, Omaha, Louisville, Kansas City). A movie entitled *Why Physical Education?** which has been produced for use in junior and senior high schools discusses physical fitness and total fitness as the goal of physical education programs.

Some films and materials related to physical fitness are listed below:

Films

1. Girls are better than ever (13½ min.)   Free
    Modern Talking Picture Service
    1212 Avenue of the Americas
    New York, N.Y. 10036

2. Time of our lives (27 min.)   Free
    Associated Films, Inc.
    600 Madison Avenue
    New York, N.Y. 10022

---

*From Bucher, C. A., Koenig, C., and Barnhard, M.: Methods and materials for secondary school physical education, ed. 2, St. Louis, 1965, The C. V. Mosby Co.

---

*Why Physical Education? 16 mm., sound and color, 14 minutes, $150.00, produced by Wexler Film Productions, available from Henk Newenhouse, Inc., 1017 Longaker Road, Northbrook, Ill.

3. Badhe chalo (11 min.)

Express postage collect

Information Service of India
Film Section
3 East 64th St.
New York, N.Y. 10021

4. Rhythmic ball exercises (1966) (13 min.)

Free

Embassy of Finland
Press Section
1900 Twenty-Fourth St. N. W.
Washington, D. C. 20008

5. Physically fit (Don Schollander) (4½ min.)

Free

Modern Talking Picture Service
1212 Avenue of the Americas
New York, N.Y. 10036

6. Focus of fitness (19 min.)   Free
Eastman Kodak Co.
Audio-Visual Service
343 State St.
Rochester, N.Y. 14650

Materials

	Single price	*Per 100*
Adolescent years		
As others see us	$.15	$.08
How teens set the stage for smoking	.10	.02
Why girls menstruate	.10	.02
Fitness		
Physical fitness	$.05	.02
Exercise and fitness	.05	.02
Safeguarding the health of the athlete	.05	.02
Seven paths to fitness	.10	.02
Tips of athletic training (vols. I-VI)	.05	.02

American Medical Association,
535 N. Dearborn St.
Chicago, Illinois 60610

Booklets, pamphlets, and articles on physical fitness.

AMA and AAHPER Joint Committee on Exercise and Fitness: Health problems revealed during physical activity, Journal of Health, Physical Education, and Recreation 37:7, 1967.

Bender, J. A., Kaplan, H. M., and Pierson, J. K.: Injury control through isometrics and isotonics, Journal of Health, Physical Education, and Recreation 38:2, 1967.

Brooks, B. W.: Views of physical fitness from four educational philosophies, The Physical Educator 24:1, 1967.

Collins, G. J.: Physical achievements and the schools, Bulletin 1965, no. 13, U. S. Department of Health, Education and Welfare, Office of Education, 1965, U. S. Government Printing Office.

Cooper, K. H., M.D.: How to feel fit at any age, Reader's Digest, March, 1968.

Doherty, J. K.: The nature of endurance in running, Journal of Health, Physical Education, and Recreation 35:44, 1964.

Flint, M. M.: Selecting exercises, Journal of Health, Physical Education, and Recreation 35:2, 1964.

Gerenstein, S.: Procedures and equipment for weight training in the high school program, Journal of Health, Physical Education, and Recreation 38:1, 1967.

Hillcourt, W.: Physical fitness for girls, New York, 1967, Golden Press, Inc.

Hillcourt, W.: Physical fitness for boys, New York, 1967, Golden Press, Inc.

Hunsicker, P. A., and Reiff, G. G.: A survey and comparison of youth fitness 1958-1965, Journal of Health, Physical Education, and Recreation 37:1, 1966.

Larson, L. A.: Research turns the spotlight on health and fitness, Journal of Health, Physical Education, and Recreation 36:4, 1965.

Marshall, J. W., and McAdam, R. E.: A buddy plan of active resistance exercise, Journal of Health, Physical Education, and Recreation 35:3, 1964.

McCarthy, J.: Fitness for activity, The Physical Educator 22:4, 1965.

Pennington, G.: Fitness honor roll, The Physical Educator 21:4, 1964.

Ponthieux, N. A., and Barker, D. G.: Relationship between socioeconomic status and physical fitness measures, The Research Quarterly 36:4, 1965.

Ponthieux, N. A., and Barker, B. G.: Relationship between race and physical fitness, The Research Quarterly 36:4, 1965.

Rosenstein, I., and Frost, R. B.: Physical fitness of senior high school boys and girls participating in selected physical education programs in New York State, The Research Quarterly 35:3, 1964.

Steinhaus, A. H.: Fitness beyond muscle, The Physical Educator 23:3, 1966.

Weiss, R. A.: Is physical fitness our most important objective? Journal of Health, Physical Education, and Recreation 35:2, 1964.

Yarnall, C. D.: Relationship of physical fitness to selected measures of popularity, The Research Quarterly 37:2, 1966.

Questions and exercises

1. Outline what you consider to be an effective physical fitness program for a high school.
2. Write an essay on the Kraus-Weber tests and their role in a school physical fitness program.
3. What were some of the high points of President Eisenhower's Conference on Fitness of American Youth?
4. Develop your own definitions of fitness and physical fitness.
5. What are the components of physical fitness?
6. Evaluate the statement of fitness made by the American Association for Health, Physical Education, and Recreation.
7. What are some of the tests for physical fitness? Evaluate each in the light of criteria in the chapter on Measurement and Evaluation.

Reading assignment in *Administrative Dimensions of Health and Physical Education Programs, Including Athletics:* Chapter 5, Selection 27.

Selected references

AMA and AAHPER Joint Committee: Exercise and fitness, Journal of Health, Physical Education, and Recreation **35:**5, 1964.

American Association for Health, Physical Education, and Recreation: Youth fitness test manual, Washington, D. C., 1961, The Association.

Bookwalter, K. W., and Bookwalter, C. W.: Fitness of secondary youth, Washington, D. C., 1956, American Association for Health, Physical Education, and Recreation.

Bucher, C. A.: Highlights of President's Conference on Fitness of American Youth, unpublished paper, 1956.

Bucher, C. A.: Foundations of physical education, ed. 5, St. Louis, 1968, The C. V. Mosby Co.

Clarke, H. H.: Objective strength tests of affected muscle groups involved in orthopedic disabilities, Research Quarterly **19:**11, 1948.

Collins, G. J., and Hunter, J. S.: Physical achievement and the schools, Bureau of Educational Research and Development, Office of Education Bulletin, 1965, No. 13.

Cureton, T. K.: Physical fitness appraisal and guidance, St. Louis, 1947, The C. V. Mosby Co.

Espenschade, A.: Restudy of relationships between physical performances of school children and age, height, and weight, Research Quarterly **34:**144, 1963.

Gallagher, J. R., and Brouha, L.: Physical fitness, Journal of the American Medical Association **125:**834, 1944.

Hunsicker, P.: Physical fitness—what research tells the teacher, Washington, D. C., 1963, National Education Association.

Johnson, W. R., editor: Science and medicine of exercise and sports, New York, 1960, Harper & Row, Publishers.

Journal of the American Association for Health, Physical Education, and Recreation, Sept., 1957, entire issue.

Kraus, H., and Hirschland, R. P.: Minimum muscular fitness tests in school children, Research Quarterly **25:**178, 1954.

President's Conference on Fitness of American Youth: Fitness of American youth, Journal of Health, and Physical Education, and Recreation **28:**3, 1957.

President's Council on Youth Fitness: Youth physical fitness—suggested elements of a school-centered program, parts 1 and 2, Washington, D. C., July, 1961, The Council.

Report of the National Conference on Fitness of Secondary School Youth: Youth and fitness: a program for secondary schools, Washington, D. C., 1958, American Association for Health, Physical Education, and Recreation.

Steinhaus, A. A.: Fitness—a definition and guide to its attainment, Journal of Health, Physical Education, and Recreation **16:**175, 1945.

Weiss, R. A.: Is physical fitness our most important objective? Journal of Health, Physical Education, and Recreation **35:**2, 1964.

three

HEALTH PROGRAMS FOR STUDENTS

THE HEALTH SCIENCE INSTRUCTION PROGRAM — WITH IMPLICATIONS FOR PHYSICAL EDUCATION*

The *health science instruction* phase of the total school and college program refers to the provision of learning experiences for the purpose of influencing knowledge, attitudes, and conduct relating to individual and group health.

Health science instruction is important in the educational program for many reasons, not the least of which are that healthy students learn more rapidly, are better adjusted, and get along better with their classmates. For these and other reasons schools and colleges should attempt to help each student to achieve and maintain a state of optimum health.

Throughout the history of education the schools and colleges have indicated an interest in health. In 1918 the report of a commission on education of the National Education Association listed health as its first objective. The Educational Policies Commission, an important policy-making group in education, pointed out that an educated person understands basic facts concerning health and disease, protects his own health and that of his dependents, and

strives to improve the health of the community. The American Council on Education, another policy-making group, has encouraged schools and colleges to help pupils improve and maintain their health. White House Conferences on Education have stressed physical and mental health as important educational objectives.

There are well-supported reasons for these statements emphasizing the importance of health in education. Research has shown that the healthy person has a better chance to be a success in school and college, to be more effective scholastically and academically, and to be more productive. In addition to these factors, it should be noted that the school acts in loco parentis and, as such, has a legal as well as a moral responsibility to concern itself with the health of the student.

If schools and colleges accept their responsibility for, and do an effective job in, health science instruction, the program should result in the following:

1. Students will become more intelligent citizens on matters concerning health; for example, they will understand the value in fluoridating water supplies.
2. Students will better understand the values of health and the contribution health can make to human productivity, happiness, and effectiveness.
3. Students will be better health consumers—they will not be taken in by quackery, frauds, and gimmicks that advertise shortcuts to health.

Many children and youth are attending

*The school and college attempt to promote health in children and youth through a specialized program that contributes to the understanding, maintenance, and improvement of the health of students and school personnel, including health services, health science instruction, and healthful school living. The healthful school and college living phase of the health program will be considered in Chapters 14 and 15. The health services phase of the total health program will be considered in Chapter 13.

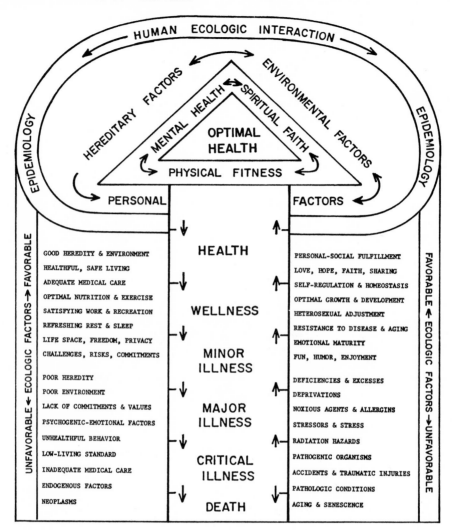

An ecologic model of health and disease. Examples of favorable and unfavorable dynamic, interacting, hereditary, environmental, and personal ecologic factors and conditions that are determinants of the levels of health and disease on a continuum extending from zero health (death) to optimal health. (From Hoyman, H. S.: Journal of School Health **35:**113, 1965.)

schools and colleges with different kinds of health problems and disabilities, and few live at their optimum level of physical and emotional efficiency. Students are involved in accidents caused by carelessness. They suffer from remediable physical defects. They find it difficult to be realistic in respect to the demands of their environment. They contract needless diseases and infections.

A recognition of the need for health science instruction in the schools and colleges has developed through the years, as educators and the lay public have come to realize the importance of providing learning experiences that will result in healthful living for more people. Furthermore, they have come to see more clearly the relationship of knowledge, attitudes, and practices in respect to health.

The importance of health has been taught by educators since early times.

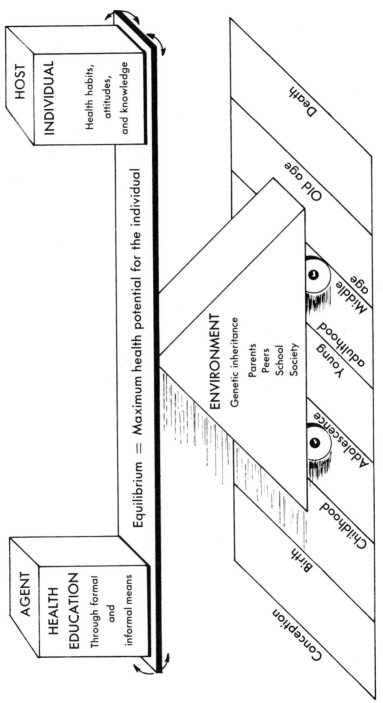

Epidemiology of health. From Mayshark, C.: Epidemiology of health, Journal of Health, Physical Education, and Recreation 39:49, 1968.

Older generations tell about how they received instruction in physiology, learned how to trace the flow of blood through the body, and memorized long definitions of various anatomic and physiologic aspects of the human body. This approach to health education has changed over the years. Toward the end of the nineteenth century some new ideas were introduced into school and college curricula. This resulted from a feeling on the part of certain individuals that the evil effects of alcoholic beverages should be taught. They also felt there should be a greater emphasis on the hygienic aspects of living. As a result, these concepts became an important part of health teaching, especially in colleges.

This emphasis continued until the early twentieth century. Then, the impact of World Wars I and II gave health education the impetus it needed to become firmly embedded as an important part of school and college programs. The public became aroused, for example, by the number of defects discovered in young men through Selective Service examinations. The results of such a disclosure included passing state laws, developing courses of study, publishing textbooks concerned with health education, and providing for the training of special teachers in this area. Today, there is increased recognition that health education can play a very important role in helping to make individuals aware of their responsibility for their own health and also that of others. Health is regarded as "everybody's business."

There is increased emphasis upon health teaching in our schools and colleges today and upon such topics as drugs, ecology, sex education, alcohol, tobacco, personality development, and accident prevention. Professional preparation institutions are placing greater emphasis on instructing teachers about their responsibilities in this area. There is closer cooperation between the school or college and community health officers. Medical doctors, dentists, and other representatives of professional services are taking more interest in health. School and college administrators and their teaching and professional staffs are voicing concern about students and their health. More research is providing new and better directions to help the schools and colleges in changing the health behavior of many boys and girls.

THE NATURE AND SCOPE OF HEALTH SCIENCE INSTRUCTION

One of the revealing studies in the area of health education and the schools is the School Health Education Study. This study has determined the nature and scope of health education in the public schools of the United States, the kind of instruction students receive, how much boys and girls know about health matters, who teaches these pupils, how the subject is organized and scheduled in the school program, the health content areas that are emphasized, and many other factors of importance to all educators and persons interested in health. The project involved such procedures as a survey of 135 public school systems regarding the health practices of approximately 16 million students in more than 1,000 elementary schools and 359 secondary schools. The following represents a sampling of some of the findings in this study:

Most health instruction in the elementary schools is taught by the classroom teacher, without supervisory assistance, and is included in the curriculum in combination with other subjects.

On the average, in those districts with secondary grades, a separate class in health education is offered in grades 7 and 8 by 61.2 percent of the large, 69.1 percent of the medium, and 48.0 percent of the small school districts. The average percentage of districts scheduling a separate class of health education in grades 9 through 12 is 52.2 percent of the large, 43.1 percent of the medium, and 31.8 percent of the small school districts.

On the average, health education is a required subject for all students in grades 7 and 8 in 55.6 percent of the large, 62.2 percent of the medium, and 48.0 percent of the small school districts of the sample group of districts that included secondary grades; in grades 8 through 12, 25.0 percent of the large, 37.5 percent of the medium, and 24.9 percent of the small districts require health education of all students.

In all districts, two-thirds or more of the health classes in grades 7, 8, and 9 and 90 percent or more in grades 10, 11, and 12 in all districts are taught by the teacher with a combined major in health and physical education, or with specialization in physical education only. The percentage reported varied by grades and within districts.

In the majority of secondary schools, boys and girls are separated for health instruction. In those instances where combined classes are scheduled, these tended to be the pattern more frequently in grades 7 and 8 than in the upper grades. Percentages of responses vary throughout the grades and among the districts. The majority of responses indicate that separate classes in health education for boys and girls are held because of staff, space, and scheduling problems. The nature of the subject matter as a reason for a separation was mentioned to a far lesser extent and then mainly by the medium and small districts only.

At the secondary level the large districts rely to a far greater extent than do the medium or small districts on local curriculum guides and local community influence in determining course content. The small districts depend heavily on the state course of study as a resource for deciding what to teach in health education.*

Some instructional problems involved with health science instruction, as cited by school administrators in the School Health Education Study, are ineffectiveness of instructional methods, parental and community resistance to certain health topics, insufficient time allocated for health instruction, lack of coordination, inadequate professional staff, lack of interest among teachers, and neglect of the health education course when combined with the physical education experience.

The School Health Education Study revealed that many health misconceptions exist among students. A brief sampling of these misconceptions includes the following:

1. Commercial medicines are safe to purchase if the label clearly indicates

*School Health Education Study: A summary report, Washington, D. C., 1964, National Education Association.

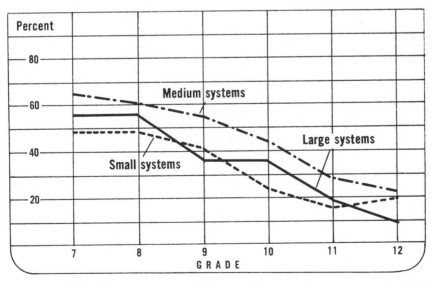

Percent of public school systems in sample group requiring a separate health class of all students. (From School Health Education Study: Summary report of a nationwide study of health instruction in the public schools, 1961 to 1963, Washington, D. C., 1964, School Health Education Study.)

the dose and contents, or if recommended by a pharmacist.

2. The use of "pep" pills and sleeping pills does not require medical supervision.

3. The purpose of fluoridating water supplies is to purify water and make it safe to drink.

4. Unrefrigerated chicken salad is not a potential source of food poisoning.

5. Chronic diseases can be transmitted from person to person.

6. Venereal disease can be inherited.

In respect to the basic health science course in colleges and universities, a survey conducted a few years ago showed that better than 80% of the institutions included in the survey offered a personal health course for their students. In some cases the course was offered on an elective basis, in other cases it was required. Teacher preparatory programs, in particular, provided the setting for most of the required courses.

The college survey also showed that in

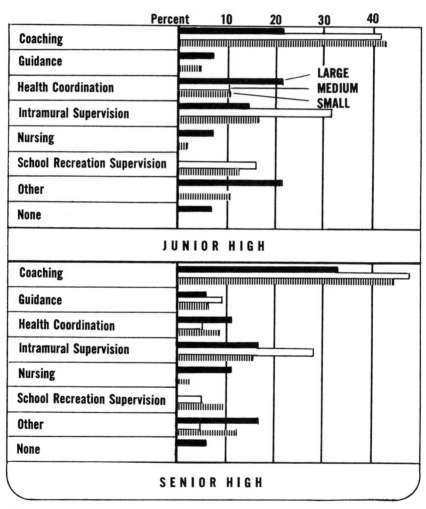

Responsibilities other than teaching for teachers assigned to health instruction on the secondary level in the sample group, 1961-1962. (From School Health Education Study: Summary report of a nationwide study of health instruction in the public schools, 1961 to 1963, Washington, D. C., 1964, School Health Education Study.)

most cases the basic health science course was offered by the Health and Physical Education Department. However, in other cases it was offered by Departments of Biology or Zoology, Science Department, Department of General Education, Home Economics Department, College Health Service, College of Medicine, and College of Nursing.

The college survey further showed that

Table 12-1. Undergraduate majors of teachers of health*

Major	Teachers	Major	Teachers
Physical education	775	Psychology	4
Health education and		Business	4
physical education	289	Nursing	4
Science	173	Education	3
Biology	100	Special education	3
Home economics	99	Recreation	3
Social studies	32	Physiology	2
English	24	Physics	2
History	18	Guidance	2
Social science	16	Music	2
Health education	15	Industrial arts	1
Elementary education	13	French	1
Chemistry	8	Theology	1
Mathematics	6	Speech	1
Art	5	Political science	1
Physical science	4		

*From Michigan Department of Education: Patterns and features of school health education in Michigan public schools, East Lansing, 1969, Michigan State Department of Education, p. 7.

Table 12-2. Undergraduate minors of teachers of health*

Minor	Teachers	Minor	Teachers
Health education	258	Driver education	4
Physical education	128	Art	3
Science	68	Natural science	2
Biology	58	Spanish	2
Social studies	39	Physiology	2
English	34	Psychology	2
History	32	German	1
Social science	32	French	1
Mathematics	16	Journalism	1
Home economics	15	Conservation	1
Physical science	8	Economics	1
Elementary education	7	Political science	1
Business	7	Dance	1
Education	6	Language	1
Speech	6	Guidance	1
Geography	5	Commercial	1
Chemistry	5	Literature	1
Recreation	5	Nursing	1
Industrial arts	5	Zoology	1

*From Michigan Department of Education: Patterns and features of school health education in Michigan public schools, East Lansing, 1969, Michigan State Department of Education, p. 7.

the basic health science course was offered on the average for two or three semester or quarter hour credits and was taught by a variety of persons including health educators, physical educators, biologists, and physicians. Some of the topics covered in the courses included mental health, family health, nutrition, reproduction, tobacco, alcohol, narcotics, preparation for marriage, personal appearance, disease control, health appraisal, and care of the body.

The School Health Education Study and other research findings indicate more and more the need for health science instruction in schools and colleges. The growth and development characteristics of students, the social demands of dating, the preparation for marriage, and the pressures of the peer group are important considerations. Youth must be helped to make informed wise choices in meeting the pressing problems they face each day of their lives. These studies have shown that students are weak in health content concerning fatigue, sleep and rest, mental health, and habit-forming substances; that exposure to alcohol tends to occur first at 13 to 14 years of age; that dietary practices become increasingly worse throughout the teen-age years; that the greatest number of smokers begin smoking between 10 and 15 years of age; and that annually venereal diseases infect more than 250,000 young persons 15 to 19 years of age.

Tables 12-1 and 12-2 indicate the training that teachers of health in one state have had. As the tables show, physical educators play a major role in teaching health in today's schools.

ADMINISTRATION OF THE HEALTH SCIENCE INSTRUCTION PROGRAM

The manner in which health science instruction is administered will vary with the local situation. At the outset, however, it should be recognized that health education should be taught by individuals who are trained in the methodology of teaching. An individual who has studied educational psychology and other subjects that yield knowledges and techniques important to effective teaching is better prepared to do a good job of instruction in health than is the individual who does not have such training. This does not exclude using representatives of the health department and voluntary health agencies as consultants and resource persons. They can be invaluable in drawing up courses of study and in the presentation of various phases of the health education program.

Local administration will again determine where health science instruction should be located within the school or college structure. In some schools and colleges it is placed in such areas as physical education, science, and home economics. In other schools and colleges it is a separate area by itself. In most schools and colleges health is administratively located in the health and physical education department. In the larger schools especially, and in colleges and universities, there may be a separate health education department with full-time personnel who have been trained in the area of health education. Such an administrative arrangement is conducive to good interrelationships between the school and college and public health agencies, to the development of a health council, and to a well-coordinated and well-integrated health program. In smaller and medium-sized schools and colleges, there should also be full-time health educators charged with this important responsibility.

The physical education person many times is assigned such responsibilities as coaching, intramurals, and special events in addition to physical education classes. If the responsibility for health education is given to a teacher of physical education, in addition to these numerous other duties, some responsibility is going to suffer. In many cases, with pressure for winning teams, the class instruction program is neglected. School and college administrators should recognize that health education is a very important part of the school or college offering. It should be assigned only to qualified persons and should receive ample time and facilities to make it effective.

Every school and college, regardless of size, should have someone on its staff assigned to coordinate the various aspects of the health program. In larger schools and colleges this might be a full-time position. In smaller schools and colleges it could be the principal, chairman of the health department, or some qualified staff member who has interest and responsibility in this area.

The administration of the health education program should also include a health council or committee. The *health council* would be composed of representatives from the central administration, subject matter areas, students, parents, professional groups, custodial staff, and others whose duties have particular bearing on the health of the student. Such a group of individuals, regardless of type or size of school, can play an important part in planning and carrying out the health education program. They can be instrumental in providing the necessary funds, materials, staff, and experiences that make for an outstanding program. They would have as a major responsibility the identification and solution of health problems.

THE SCHOOL HEALTH TEAM

The following paragraphs discuss those persons who are participants in the school health team.

Teacher of health

The teacher of health is a key person if the health science program is to be effective. This person should possess an understanding of what constitutes a well-rounded health program and the teacher's part in it. Preparation should include a basic understanding of the various physical, biologic, and behavioral sciences that help to explain the importance of health

to the optimum functioning of the individual, including understanding of such areas as structure and growth of the human body, nutrition, and mental health. The teacher should be interested in the health needs and interests of pupils, possess personal characteristics that exemplify good health, and acquire knowledge and skill for presenting health knowledge in a meaningful and interesting manner to all students. The teacher should be competent to organize health teaching units in terms of the health needs and interests of students, motivate the child to be well and happy, and be aware of the individual differences of the pupils. The teacher should also be able and willing to interpret the school health program to the community and enlist its support in solving health problems.

Health coordinator

The health coordinator is a person on the staff who has special qualifications that enable him to serve as a coordinator, supervisor, teacher, or consultant for health education. He is concerned with developing effective working relationships with school, college, and community health programs and coordinating the total school or college health program with the general educational program. A health coordinator can render valuable service in seeing that a well-rounded health program exists. Health instruction can be more carefully planned. In addition to the direct health teaching, there can also be provision for the correlation and integration of health instruction with many subject matter areas. Resource materials can be provided for the classroom and other teachers involved in health teaching. School, college, and community relationships can be developed. The total health program can be guided to function as an integrated whole. Each administrator should recognize the importance of the position of health coordinator and designate a person qualified for such a responsibility. The Nebraska State

The school health coordinator should*:

Coordinate the health activities of all school personnel.

Provide leadership in the development of a health curriculum based upon the progression of health knowledge, concepts, and activities from kindergarten through high school.

Serve as a liaison person between school, public, and voluntary health agencies to establish desirable working relationships and coordination of school and community health efforts.

Be a resource person for teachers needing help with health education materials, references, teaching aids, and methods.

Establish good relationships with the community's professional medical and dental resources so that the school's program is properly understood.

Promote inservice training for the teaching of health through faculty meetings, small group meetings, workshop sessions with nurses and other school health personnel, and individual interviews with teachers.

With the assistance of the school health council, study needs and present activities of the school health program; from the findings make recommendations that will develop an improved program.

*From Health policies and procedures for Nebraska schools, Lincoln, Nebraska Department of Health and the Nebraska Department of Education, p. 8.

Departments of Health and Education outline the responsibilities for the health coordinator.

School or college administrator

The school or college administrator is a key figure in making important decisions in regard to health programs, such as the personnel appointed to teach health courses, the methods of instruction, the topics to be covered, and the budget essential to having the necessary equipment and supplies. Therefore, a school or college administrator, to be effective in the health science program, should be sympathetic and interested in meeting the health needs and interests of students, in seeing that the health courses include topics that meet these needs and interests, and in assuring that health is taught by competent faculty members in a way that will motivate behavior.

School or college physician

The school or college physician can be an effective member of the health team by discussing results of medical examinations with teachers, drawing implications from the medical examinations for health science instruction, stressing to administrators and the community in general the need for instruction in health, visiting classes, and periodically being a visiting lecturer in the health classes.

Nurse

The nurse works closely with medical personnel on one hand and with students, teachers, and parents on the other. As the person who engages in such duties as administering health tests, assisting in medical examinations, screening for hearing and vision, holding parent conferences, keeping health records, teaching health classes, helping to control communicable disease, and coordinating school, college, and community health efforts, she can play an effective and important role in giving support and direction to the health instruction program. The school nurse can help in the identification of the topics that need to be covered, emphasizing the health needs of the students, and interpreting to administrators the importance of health in the school or college program.

Physical educator

Although the physical educator may not be qualified or interested in teaching health courses, he can contribute much to the health program. His training in such areas as first aid and the foundational sciences and his direction of the physical education program places him in a position to impress upon students the importance of gaining desirable health knowledge, developing desirable health attitudes, and forming desirable health practices. Physical education can be a setting for correlated health teaching with the many opportunities that continually arise that are closely related to the health and fitness of students.

Dentist

The dentist employed to work with school children is frequently involved in such duties as conducting dental examinations of pupils, giving or supervising oral prophylaxis, and advising on curriculum material in dental hygiene. The health teacher can be helped by the dentist in the selection of curriculum material for classroom teaching, by discovering dental problems of students, and by participating himself in the classroom experiences of pupils as a resource person.

Dental hygienist

The dental hygienist usually assists the dentist and does oral prophylaxis. The teacher of health can therefore benefit from a close working relationship with this specialist in much the same way as she or he works with the dentist.

Custodian

All aspects of the school or college health program must be carefully coordinated— the health instruction program, health services, and healthful living. Therefore, the cleanliness of the building and a healthful physical environment are contributions to the health program. The custodian can be invited to help plan pertinent aspects of the health curriculum that specifically relate to his area of responsibility, to have the school or college be a model of cleanliness and of good health practices, and to adhere to proper health standards in respect to such items as lighting, ventilation, and heating.

Nutritionist

The nutritionist can contribute to health science instruction by contributing to the subject matter to be covered concerning nutrition, in speaking to classes about food and nutrition, and in discussing nutritional problems of students.

Guidance counselor

An individual on the school staff that is too frequently overlooked as an effective member of the school health team is the guidance counselor. Since many academic problems are health related and since the guidance counselor is interested in helping each student to have a successful school experience, his or her interest must at times concern itself with areas of health. As such, the guidance counselor can make suggestions for health topics to be discussed in classes, and he can be an effective guest speaker in health classes to discuss the relationship of health to scholastic and vocational success.

CONTENT AREAS FOR THE HEALTH SCIENCE INSTRUCTION PROGRAM

There is considerable knowledge and information that may be taught in health education. With all the literature that is available in such forms as textbooks, resource books, pamphlets, and promotional material, it is important that content be selected with care. At present there is little uniformity in the content of health education courses being taught in the schools and colleges throughout the country.

Some basic principles for selecting curriculum experiences in the health science instruction program are as follows:

1. The content of health science instruction should be based on the needs and interests of the students. Such considerations as developmental characteristics of children and youth and psychologic drives of students, such as security, approval, success in athletics, appearance, and peer-group approval, are considerations in relating teaching to the interests of students.

2. The problems and topics covered must be appropriate to the maturity level of the students.

3. The materials used should be current and scientifically accurate. The course should not be a textbook course. Many materials and experiences should be provided.

4. Pupils should be able to identify with the health problems discussed. As such, the problems should be geared to or related to the daily living experiences of the student body.

5. Health should be recognized as a multidisciplinary subject, and, as such, subject matter, projects, and methods of teaching should take cognizance of the new developments in the related sciences.

6. Health science instruction should be taught in light of a rapidly changing society, new knowledge, and ways of affecting the behavior of human beings.

7. Health teaching should take place in an environment that represents a healthful psychologic and physical environment.

8. The teacher of health science, in order to be most effective in her subject, must exemplify good health, be well informed, and be a happy and successful individual.

9. The basic concepts in health should be identified and taught.

10. The new technologic techniques and aids should be utilized in improving visual presentations of health material to students.

11. Considerations should be given to students' previous health experiences.

12. Planning for health science instruction should be a total school or college endeavor with teachers, specialists, and consultants participating. Furthermore, health instruction should permeate the entire school or college curriculum.

13. Objectives of the school or college health program, including knowledge, attitudes, practices, and skills, need to be reviewed and the program planned intelligently and meaningfully in light of these goals.

14. The community should be involved in health science instruction, including personnel from the health department, voluntary health associations, medical and dental professions, and other health associations and agencies.

15. School health science instruction should be closely integrated with home conditions.

16. New methods of organizing for teaching, including the nongraded school, team teaching, individualized instruction, and programmed instruction, should be considered.

17. Constant research and evaluation of the program should take place to provide the best instructional program for the students concerned.

18. Health instruction in general should share the same prestige and respect in the eyes of school or college administrators, teachers, and students as other respected school or college offerings, with time allotments and other considerations receiving equal attention.

19. Many interesting and meaningful experiences should be provided health classes to help in solving the health problems of students.

Student health needs and interests

It has been pointed out that content areas in health education should be selected on the basis of the needs and interests of the students being served. Therefore, the question arises as to how such interests and needs can be determined. Some ways in which this vital information may be obtained include an analysis of the health records that every school and college should keep in a cumulative manner and that contain such valuable information as the results of health appraisal and health counseling. Teacher observations offer some indication of student interests, desires, and health problems. Tests of knowledge, attitudes, and habits uncover superstitions and other health problems, together with the accuracy of the health knowledge possessed by the student. Conferences with parents, teachers, and students reveal many health interests and needs. A student interest survey will offer valuable information. A study of current literature concerned with scientific information in the field of health is essential. New knowledge and new health problems are revealed each day through experimentation and research on the part of the medical and other professions. Finally, a study of the community will show the health problems that are peculiar to the local setting.

The Joint Committee on Health Problems of the National Education Association and the American Medical Association suggests the following bases for determining needs and problems of students:

> An analysis of biological needs of human beings.
> An analysis of the characteristics of children of different age levels: their growth and developmental needs.
> Health problems are revealed through a study of mortality records by age groups.
> Health status by age groups as revealed on health records, accident and illness records, special studies, and surveys.
> Analysis by age groups of activities related to health in which the majority of boys and girls engage.
> Analysis of environmental health hazards at school and in the home and community.
> Analysis of citizenship responsibilities relating to health.

> Analysis of major social trends relating to health.
> Analysis of vocational opportunities in health education.*

Although the specific health course of study will vary from community to community, it is still necessary to recognize that the basic health needs of students and the general content areas of health education are similar. To a great degree, what takes place is the specific adaptation of these general areas to local situations.

It seems important for the general information of the reader to point out some of the basic health needs of students and also the general health content areas, as listed by leaders in the field. Finally, it seems essential to discuss briefly some of the controversial content areas.

A Denver, Colorado, research project, concerned with a study of health needs, examined textbooks and programs of health in use throughout the United States and discussed health needs of students with teachers and physicians. The study resulted in the following list of eighteen broad areas that represented health needs of students†:

1. Keeping physically fit
2. Group health
3. Cause of disease
4. Protection from disease
5. Structure and function of the body
6. Dental health
7. Good eating habits
8. Selection and composition of food
9. Stimulants and narcotics
10. Rest and relaxation
11. Personal appearance
12. Personality development
13. Social health
14. Heredity and eugenics

*Joint Committee on Health Problems in Education of National Education Association and American Medical Association: Health education, Washington, D. C., 1961, National Education Association, pp. 127-129.

†Corliss, L. M.: A report of the Denver research project on health interests of children, The Journal of School Health 32:355, 1962.

15. First aid
16. Home nursing
17. Safety
18. Vocations in health

Health content areas based on needs and interests of students

The Joint Committee on Health Problems in Education of the National Education Association and the American Medical Association* suggests the following areas of health content at the junior high school educational level:

Physical growth and development
Living practices
Health maintenance and improvement
Food and nutrition
Mental health
Personality development
Family life
Sex adjustment
Safety and first aid
Community health

For the senior high school educational level the Joint Committee on Health Problems in Education of the National Education Association and the American Medical Association suggested the following areas of health content:

1. Structure and function of the human body; scientific concepts relative to normal and abnormal function; contributions of scientific research and medical practice to information relative to maintenance of normal function.
2. The balanced regimen of food, exercise, rest, sleep, relaxation, work, and study; evaluation of individual health needs.
3. Mental health, personal adjustment, development of emotional maturity, establishment of maturing sex roles, boy-girl relations.
4. Preparation for marriage, family life, child care; health implications of heredity and eugenics; good budgeting; health aspects of housing; budgeting for health insurance, medical and dental services; spending the health dollar wisely.

5. Communicable and noncommunicable diseases with emphasis on adolescent and adult disease problems; prevention and control of disease and illness including heart disease, cancer, diabetes, mental illness, alcoholism.
6. Consumer health education: choosing health products and services; scientific health care as contrasted with fads, quackery, and charlatanism; evaluating sources of information; awareness of nature of advertising appeals and "gimmicks" used to sell products.
7. Personal and community programs and practices in accident prevention and emergency care; driver education; recreational and occupational safety; fire prevention; civil defense and disasters.
8. Protection from hazards of poisons, drugs, narcotics; environmental hazards of radiation, air pollution, water contamination; chemical hazards in food production, processing, and distribution.
9. Community health: local, state, national, and international; tax-supported and voluntary health agency programs; contributions of individual citizens to community health.
10. Health careers in medicine, dentistry, nursing, public health, teaching, hospital administration, laboratory services, dietetics, physical therapy, occupational therapy, and allied professions.*

In Table 12-4 Hoyman presents a schematic health science spiral curriculum for kindergarten to grade twelve.

The health education content areas and the number of schools that include this area in their health science course, as reflected in a survey conducted in the fall of 1968 in which 810 schools returned the questionnaire, are shown in Table 12-3.

The content and basic aims of the New York State Health Education Programs are reflected in the diagram on p. 319.†

The health education program in Los Angeles includes the following topics and

---

*Joint Committee on Health Problems in Education of National Education Association and American Medical Association, op. cit., pp. 204-205.

*Joint Committee on Health Problems in Education of National Education Association and American Medical Association, op. cit., pp. 234-235.
†New York State Department of Education, New York State Program in the Health Sciences, Albany.

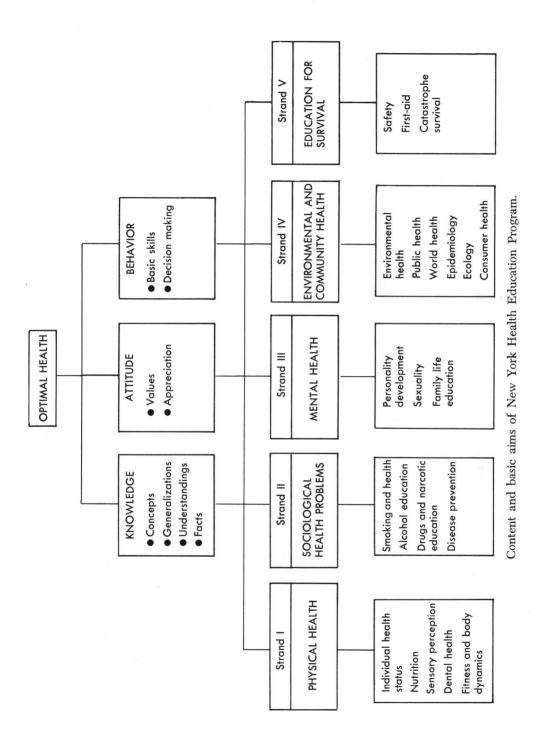

Content and basic aims of New York Health Education Program.

Table 12-3. Health education content areas*

Subject area	Schools	Subject area	Schools
Personal health	263	Hit and miss	5
Smoking, tobacco	155	Child care	4
Drugs	150	Menstruation	4
Sex education	150	Civil defense	3
Alcohol	148	Heart	3
Anatomy and physiology	113	Sanitation	3
First aid	112	Self-help	3
Communicable disease	109	Those required by	
Nutrition	81	state law	3
Mental health	52	Sight and hearing	3
Safety	41	Genetics	2
Growth and development	37	Major health problems	2
Physical fitness	30	School health	2
Marriage and family living	20	Immunization	1
Public and community health	19	Psychology	1
All areas	10	Recreation	1
Dental health	9	Young adult problems	1
Cancer	6	Regular physicial examination	1
Personality	6	Daily shower in physical	
Personal relations	5	education	1

*The Department of Education: Patterns and features of school health education in Michigan public schools, East Lansing, 1969, Michigan State Department of Education, p. 9.

units in their junior high and senior high school programs*:

Junior high school

    Unit 1—Introduction to health science
    Unit 2—Growing and maturing
    Unit 3—Achieving personal health
    Unit 4—Food for growth and health
    Unit 5—Addicting, habit-forming, and other
        dangerous substances
    Unit 6—Progress in community health
    Unit 7—First aid and safety

Senior high school

    Unit 1—Orientation to health needs
    Unit 2—Guidelines for improved nutrition
    Unit 3—Transitions to maturity
    Unit 4—Narcotics, alcohol, tobacco, and other
        harmful substances
    Unit 5—Progress in public health
    Unit 6—Consumer health protection
    Unit 7—Essentials of first aid

HEALTH CONCEPTS

The concept approach to teaching various subject matter fields of specialization has won much acclaim in educational cir-

*Langan, J. J.: Health education in Los Angeles schools, National Association of Secondary Schools Bulletin, March, 1968.

cles in recent years. It is felt that the decisions that people make and their behavior patterns are determined largely by their concepts. Concepts that evolve can have an impact on cognition (knowledge, intellectual abilities, and skills) and values, attitudes, and appreciations.

Recognizing the value of the concept approach, the school health study has developed an outline entitled *A Conceptual Approach to Health Education*.

The concept approach outlined by the school health education study recognizes the three dimensions of health—mental, physical, and social. These are closely interwoven. Furthermore, it stresses the triad of health education—the unity of man in respect to his physical, mental, and social aspects; the knowledges, attitudes, and practices as factors important to influencing health behavior; and the focus of health education upon the individual, family, and community. All these components of the triad are interdependent and constantly interacting.

The study identified three key concepts,

Table 12-4. A schematic health science spiral curriculum for kindergarten to grade twelve*†

Major health instruction areas	Primary grades				Intermediate grades			Junior high grades			Senior high grades		
	K	1	2	3	4	5	6	7	8	9	10	11	12
1. Human ecology and health, disease, longevity	X	X	X	X	X		X			X			X
2. Human growth, development, maturation, aging	X	X	X	X	X		X			X			X
3. Healthful living and physical fitness	X	X	X	X	X		X			X			X
4. Nutrition and personal fitness	X	X	X	X	X		X			X			X
5. Alcohol, tobacco, and narcotics	X	X	X	X	X		X			X			X
6. Prevention and control of disease	X	X	X	X		X			X			X	
7. Community and environmental health	X	X	X	X		X			X			X	
8. Consumer health education	X	X	X	X		X			X			X	
9. Rise of modern scientific medicine	X	X	X	X		X			X			X	
10. Safety education	X	X	X	X	X		X	X		X			X
11. First aid and home nursing	X	X	X	X		X			X		X		X
12. Personality development and mental health	X	X	X	X		X		X			X		X
13. Family-life and sex education	X	X	X	X		X		X			X		X
14. Current health events and problems	X	X	X	X	X	X	X	X	X	X	X	X	X

*From Hoyman, H. S.: An ecologic view of health and health education, The Journal of School Health 25:118, 1965.

†In kindergarten to grade three the X's denote topics, in grades four to twelve, units, or major parts of combined units.

Note: Separate health courses may be scheduled at the junior and senior high school levels as a part of the health science spiral curriculum where this method of scheduling is preferred.

Nutrition instruction as part of the health education program.

ten conceptual statements, and thirty-one substantive elements that represent the conceptual framework for health. The ten concepts into which the key concepts are delineated are:

> Growth and development influences and is influenced by the structure and functioning of the individual.
> Growth and development follows a predictable sequence, yet is unique for each individual.
> Protection and promotion of health is an individual, community, and international responsibility.
> The potential for hazards and accidents exists, whatever the environment.
> There are reciprocal relationships involving man, disease, and environment.
> The family serves to perpetuate man and to fulfill certain health needs.
> Personal health practices are affected by a complexity of forces, often conflicting.
> Utilization of health information, products, and services is guided by values and perceptions.
> Use of substances that modify mood and behavior arises from a variety of motivations.
> Food selection and eating patterns are determined by physical, social, mental, economic, and cultural factors.*

SEX EDUCATION, DRUGS, AND OTHER CRITICAL CONTENT AREAS IN HEALTH SCIENCE INSTRUCTION

The question often arises as to whether such critical subjects as sex, narcotics, or alcohol education should be provided for in the health science instruction program. The fact that some of these problems are more pronounced in certain communities, and possibly restricted to some population groups, together with the fact that such education might tend to stimulate curiosity, are reasons put forth for not including them in courses of study.

On the other hand, instruction in regard to the ill effects of narcotics and alcohol is required by law in many states. Furthermore, it is felt that if children and youth

---

*From Sliepcevich, E. M., and Nolte, A. E.: The school health education study, The National Elementary Principal 47:43, 1968.

are provided with the facts, intelligent instruction in these subjects will act as a preventive measure. In the area of sex education, it is believed that the term *sex education* creates opposition among many parents and church groups and consequently should not be used. If it is introduced in the natural process of instruction without undue emphasis, much good can be done.

Some of the best thinking in the field emphasizes the fact that the nature of the instruction will depend upon the local situation. Where a narcotics or alcohol problem exists, there should be provision in the school curricula for the presentation of sociologic, physiologic, and psychologic facts, as well as the legal aspects of such a problem. Students should understand these facts and be guided intelligently in making the right decisions and establishing a sound standard of values.

Health education is not the only area in which discussions of sex, narcotics, and alcohol should take place. Social studies, biology, general science, physical education, and other classes also have a responsibility. Many phases of these subjects logically fit into certain aspects of these courses. Teachers must appreciate the importance of such instruction and the need for treating these subjects objectively on the basis of the facts. It is not necessary for the teacher to take a definite stand and act in the capacity of a minister preaching on the subject. Instead, if students obtain the necessary facts through research or some other method and then interpret them intelligently, the right answers will be clear. The students make their own decisions, not on the basis of the teacher's position but on the basis of the facts they have collected.

In regard to sex education, the emphasis should be on the psychologic and sociologic aspects rather than only on the biologic aspects. The end result should be to have students recognize what is desirable

RESOLUTIONS

DRUG ABUSE EDUCATION

Whereas, Drugs and medicines make a positive contribution to personal and community health, and
Whereas, A large segment of our population looks to drugs to alleviate a host of physiological, psychological and social discomforts, and
Whereas, The best deterrent to drug abuse is the individual's value system and his assessment of the consequences associated with drug involvement, and
Whereas, Those who develop school policies must be fully informed regarding the nature of drugs, psychosocial motivations, legal considerations, and the content and process of their communities' teacher inservice training and student instructional programs, and
Whereas, The nature of the problem is such that the school program must draw together the students, the total staff, and the community.
Be it Resolved:
1. That schools develop intensive inservice programs with assistance from specialists with experience and background in developing educational programs, including specialists in group process training and communications,
2. That planned programs be developed to involve and inform parents and community leaders regarding their roles in preparing young people to mature successfully in our culture,
3. That school programs for students be developed having these elements:
   a. a sequential plan beginning in the elementary years,
   b. emphasis on the decision-making process and why people use drugs,
   c. increasing understanding of the social conditions that promote drug use and abuse,
   d. a total institutional attitude which encourages acceptance of all children and an understanding that their individual needs, when frustrated, may lead to drug abuse,
4. That drug misuse education should be an important part of the total health education curriculum.

SEX EDUCATION

Whereas, Problems related to family life, sex education, and related interpersonal relationships are of concern to children and youth and have a bearing on their present and future welfare, and
Whereas, Children and youth need reliable information and interpretation from competent adults on issues bearing on their emotional and social well-being, and
Whereas, They learn best when there are cooperative relationships among families, schools, and communities, and
Whereas, There is concern that both critics and proponents have presented sex education issues in a sensational manner which inhibits the further development of a sound program,
Be it Resolved:
1. That a total institutional approach to human sexuality be initiated in the schools,
2. That schools develop sequential K-12 health education programs which encompass family life and sex education,
3. That schools assume leadership in involving parents and other responsible community leaders in the development and interpretation of school programs in family life and sex education,
4. That schools employ competent staff professionally prepared to assume leadership in the development and direction of comprehensive health education programs,
5. That inservice programs for better understanding of the schools responsibility be developed.

Adopted by the Representative Assembly of the American Association for Health, Physical Education, and Recreation, meeting at the 84th Anniversary Convention, Boston, Massachusetts, April 15, 1969.

Table 12-5. Suggested treatment of drugs in state health education curriculum guides (eleven states included)*

State	Grade level	Outline of content
A	7-12	Suggests collecting popular magazine articles on drugs and discussing reasons for A.M.A. acceptance or rejection (sic). Suggests pointing out the dangers to consumer health of over-gullibility to patent medicine advertising, and that the danger of patent medicines is delay in proper diagnosis and treatment. One of twelve content areas deals with stimulants and depressants.
B	1-12	Primary level—dangers in the incorrect use of medicines Junior high level—effects of alcohol, drugs, and tobacco on body and social functions Senior high level—analyzing effects of narcotics, drugs, tobacco and alcohol, and the use of patent medicines
C, D, E	7-12	Grades 7-9—suggests discussion of hazards of self-diagnosis and self-medication, review of medicine chest contents, evaluation of drug advertising Grades 10-12—suggests more comprehensive practice of the above and guest lectures on drugs by physicians and pharmacists
F	7-12	Discusses the importance of following prescription directions under the topic "Home Nursing." Mentions narcotics and stimulants with alcohol.
G	K-12	Defines the responsibility of informing students of dangers of drug abuse
H	K-12	Mentions narcotic drugs only in conjunction with alcohol and tobacco
I, J, K	1-12	Nothing on drugs

*From Smith, M. C., Mikeal, R. L., and Taylor, J. M.: Drugs in the health curriculum: a needed area, The Journal of School Health 39:334, 1969.

behavior and what constitutes a healthy sexuality rather than only to become acquainted with a body of factual knowledge such as that concerned with the reproductive organs. Students should be taught to live the finest type of lives possible. Sex education should not be a separate course but should be included and discussed in every course where its various aspects arise during regular discussions. Parents and representative community groups should be consulted and asked to participate in any discussions relative to the planning for instruction in this area. It is very important to have well-trained and qualified teachers handling such instruction. If the right type of leadership is provided, the result can be very beneficial to all concerned, but if poor leadership exists,

many harmful results can come from such discussion.

A resource unit in family life and sex education has been developed by the Committee on Health Guidance in Sex Education of the American School Health Association. The subunit titles for grades seven to twelve are listed here:

Grade 7
    Unit 1. Understanding ourselves
    Unit 2. The family
    Unit 3. Review of male and female
        reproductive process

Grade 8
    Unit 1. Emotions and behavior
    Unit 2. Dating
    Unit 3. The family
    Unit 4. Review of the female
        reproductive process

Unit 5. Review of the male
reproduction process
Grade 9
Unit 1. Mental and emotional health
Unit 2. Family relationships
Unit 3. Boy-girl relationships
Grades 10 and 11
Unit 1. Psycho-social development
Unit 2. Boy-girl relationships in light of both
immediate and long-range goals
Unit 3. Family planning
Unit 4. Growth and reproduction
Grade 12
Unit 1. Preparation for marriage
Unit 2. Adjustments in marriage
Unit 3. Planning for parenthood
Unit 4. Family living
Unit 5. Attitudes toward sex and sexual behavior*

HEALTH SCIENCE INSTRUCTION AT THE PRESCHOOL AND ELEMENTARY SCHOOL LEVELS†

The committee on Health Education for Pre-School Children of the American School Health Association lists the following as a topical outline of content for preschool children:

Cleanliness and grooming
Dental health
Eyes, ears, nose
Rest and sleep
Nutrition
Growth and development
Family living

---

*As quoted from Mayshark, C., and Irwin, L. W.: Health education in secondary schools, ed. 2, St. Louis, 1968, The C. V. Mosby Co., pp. 136-137.

†The December, 1964, issue of *The Journal of School Health* has a detailed report of the study committee on health education in the elementary school of the American School Health Association. It presents in detail various health topics that may be covered at this grade level, together with basic understandings, and skills, motivational techniques and activities, materials, books, and visual aids pertinent to getting information across to students, together with suggestions for evaluation. There is also a section entitled "Workable ideas for the elementary school." The issue of *The Journal of School Health* should be of interest to those who want to know more about health science instruction at the elementary education level.

Understanding ourselves and getting along
Prevention and control of disease safety*

For each of these topics the committee has identified key concepts, suggested learning experiences, and means of evaluation.

Health education at the elementary level is aimed primarily at having the child develop good health habits and health attitudes, and at helping him live happily, healthfully, and safely. This is achieved in great measure by adapting good health practices to the regular routine of school and home living, rather than by dispensing technical, factual knowledge concerning health. The responsibility for the guidance, planning, and stimulation of good health practices and attitudes falls upon the classroom teacher. She is the guiding influence and her understanding of good health will determine to a great degree how effective such a program actually is.

The type of health program offered should be adapted to the child's level and planned in accordance with his or her interests and needs. It should also be remembered that health education is a continuous process and cannot be compartmentalized within a definite subject area or within a class period. It embraces all the activities and subjects that are a part of the child's life.

It is difficult to prescribe the amount of time that should be devoted to the teaching of health on the elementary level because the needs and interests of pupils vary. However, the amount of time devoted to health education should be equal to the other major areas of the curriculum.

At the primary grade level the emphasis should be more on the child and his daily routine as it is affected by certain health practices and attitudes. His various routines and associations at school and at home form the basis for the health emphasis. The importance of a healthful classroom

---

*Health instruction: suggestions for teachers, The Journal and School Health 39:11, 1969.

environment is stressed. Such items as cleanliness, eating, use of lavatories, safety, and good mental hygiene are brought out as the child plays, eats, and performs those many experiences that are common to all youngsters of his age.

The committee on Health Education for Elementary School Children of the American School Health Associations lists the following as a topical outline of content for this age group:

Grades 1, 2, and 3
  Cleanliness and grooming
  Rest and exercise
  Sleep and rest
  Growth
  Posture
  Role of physician and dentist
  Individual responsibility for one's health
  Responsibility for the health of others
  Dental health
  Vision and hearing
  Babies
  Nutrition
  Making new friends
  Being alone sometimes
  Family time
  Protection from infection
  Food protection
  Safety
Grades 4, 5, and 6
  Health care
  Cleanliness and grooming
  Vision and care of eyes
  Hearing and care of ears
  Heart
  Teeth
  Exercise, rest, and sleep
  Nutrition
  Growth and development
  Family living
  Understanding ourselves
  Getting along with others
  Making decisions
  Environmental health
  Prevention and control of diseases
  Safety and first aid*

For each of these topics the committee has identified key concepts, suggested learning experiences, and means of evaluation.

The Joint Committee on Health Prob-

lems in Education of the National Education Association and the American Medical Association* has suggested areas for health teaching in the kindergarten and primary grades. These areas pertain to school and home experiences relating to:
  Food and nutrition
  Exercise, rest, and sleep
  Eyes, ears, and teeth
  Clothing
  Cleanliness and grooming
  Mental and emotional health
  Communicable disease control
  Safety
  Home, schools, and neighborhoods

In the upper elementary years the values of certain health practices are brought out. A planned progression in instruction is developed. Although there is still stress on the actual practices and attitudes concerned with the daily routines and associations, more factual information is incorporated to form the basis for such habits. Furthermore, more and more responsibility is placed on the child for his own self-direction and self-control.

The utilization of trips and textbooks that point up the value of healthful living, interesting and inspiring stories, visual aids, class discussions, and projects can become a part of the experiences of each child so that the need for certain behavior is dramatically and effectively stamped upon his mind and total being.

Since health experiences should be based on the needs and interests of the child, the wise teacher will utilize various means of obtaining accurate information about these needs and interests. Such techniques as talks with parents and pupils, observations of children under various situations, a perusal of health records, a study of the home environment and community together with scientific measuring devices that have been developed to determine

---

*Health instruction: suggestions for teachers, The Journal of School Health 39:22, 34, 1969.

*Joint Committee on Health Problems in Education of National Education Association and American Medical Association, op. cit., p. 149.

health knowledge and attitudes will be utilized. A health education program that is not based on accurate knowledge of needs and interests will fail to accomplish its objective of helping individuals to live a happier and healthier life.

HEALTH INSTRUCTION ACTIVITIES FOR THE ELEMENTARY SCHOOL

The Joint Committee on Health Problems in Education of the National Education Association and the American Medical Association has listed some of the health instruction activities in which pupils in intermediate and elementary grades can engage:

1. Conducting animal feeding experiments and experiments to test for food nutrients
2. Taking field trips to local dairies, markets, restaurants, bakeries, water supply and sewage treatment plants, and housing projects
3. Visiting museums
4. Preparing charts and graphs for visualizing class statistics, such as absence due to colds or school accidents
5. Making pin maps of sources of mosquitoes, rubbish depositories, and slum areas
6. Making health posters
7. Setting up room and corridor health exhibits
8. Preparing health bulletin boards and displays
9. Making murals and dioramas
10. Maintaining class temperature charts
11. Arranging a library corner of health materials on the subject being studied
12. Using sources of printed material—reference books, texts, bulletins, newspapers, and magazines—for the study of a particular topic
13. Giving reports in various ways—chalkboard talks, dramatizations, role-playing, panels
14. Serving on the safety patrol
15. Joining the bicycle safety club
16. Participating in a home or school cleanup campaign
17. Planning menus
18. Preparing meals for class mothers or other guests
19. Sharing health programs with primary grades
20. Securing a health examination
21. Having all dental corrections made
22. Taking inoculations
23. Keeping records of growth through charts or graphs
24. Keeping diaries of health practices
25. Studying text or references to find answers to problems
26. Thinking through solutions to problems
27. Applying in daily practices health principles learned*

Health suggestions for the classroom teacher

The classroom teacher is the key school person involved in the health of the elementary school child. The organization of the school with the self-contained classroom enables her to continually observe the pupils and to note deviations from normal. Continuous contact with the same children over a long period of time also makes it possible for her to know a great deal about their physical, social, emotional, and mental health. She can help them develop the right knowledge, attitudes, and practices. Some of the responsibilities that fall to the classroom teacher in regard to the health of her pupils require that she do the following:

1. Possess an understanding of what constitutes a well-rounded school health program and the teacher's part in it.

2. Meet with the school physician, nurse, and others in order to determine how she can best contribute to the total health program.

3. Become acquainted with parents and homes of her students and establish parent-school cooperation.

4. Discover the health needs and interests of her pupils.

5. Organize health teaching units that are meaningful and in terms of the health needs and interests of her students.

6. See that children needing special care are referred to proper places for help.

7. Be versed in first-aid procedures.

8. Participate in the work of the school health council. If none exists, interpret the need for one.

9. Provide an environment for children

---

*Joint Committee on Health Problems in Education of National Education Association and American Medical Association, op. cit., pp. 187-188.

while at school that is conducive to health-ful living.

10. Continually be on the alert for children with deviations from normal behavior and signs of communicable diseases.

11. Provide experiences for living healthfully at school.

12. Help pupils assume an increasing responsibility for their own health as well as for the health of others.

13. Set an example for the child of what constitutes healthful living.

14. Motivate the child to be well and happy.

15. Be present at health examinations of pupils and contribute in any way helpful to the physician in charge.

16. Follow through in cooperation with the nurse to see that remediable health defects are corrected.

17. Interpret the school health program to the community and enlist its support in solving health problems.

18. Provide a well-rounded class physical education program.

19. Help supervise various activities that directly affect health—school lunch, rest periods, and so on.

20. Become familiar with teaching aids and school and community resources for enhancing the health program.

21. Be aware of the individual differences of pupils.

HEALTH SCIENCE INSTRUCTION AT THE SECONDARY LEVEL*

Since many aspects of health education at the secondary level are covered in this chapter under the topics of Content Areas

*The December, 1964, issue of *The Journal of School Health* has a detailed report of the study committee on health education in the junior high school and senior high school. It presents in detail various health topics pertinent to these educational levels, together with health problems, suggested learning experiences or activities, and evaluation techniques. Furthermore, there are many workable ideas presented.

for the Health Science Instruction Program, Concentrated, Correlated, Integrated, and Incidental Health Teaching, and Organization of Classes, this discussion will be limited to a brief summary of some of the points of emphasis in health education at the secondary level.

The changes taking place in American society and the research data available emphasize a need to stress certain areas of health instruction. These include alcohol education, community health problems, health careers, international health activities, sex education, venereal disease education, tobacco and narcotics, nutrition and weight control, environmental hazards, and consumer health education.

Health and the structural organization of the secondary school

The structural organization of the secondary level differs from the elementary level. At the elementary level, the classroom teacher frequently takes overall charge of a group of children. She teaches them in various subjects, stays with them throughout the entire day, and supervises their activities. At the secondary level, the student has many different teachers. These teachers specialize in subject matter to a greater degree than they specialize in pupils. There is departmentalization into such subject matter areas as mathematics, social studies, and English. This structural organization affects health education tremendously.

First, this structural organization points up the need for concentrated courses in health education, such as those found in the other subject matter areas. Health education as a subject should receive equal consideration with the other important subjects in the secondary school offering, in all aspects such as scheduling, facilities, and staff. The minimum time that should be allotted has been stated as a daily period for at least two semesters, at the seventh-, eighth-, or ninth-grade level, and a daily period for two semesters, preferably at the eleventh- or twelfth-grade level.

Second, this structural organization emphasizes the need for a specialist in the teaching of health education. Just as specialists are needed in English and the other subjects offered at the secondary level, so are they needed in the field of health education. The body of scientific knowledge, the training needed, and the importance of the subject make such a specialist a necessity.

Third, this structural organization stresses the need for coordination and cooperation. Health cuts across many subject matter areas, as well as the total school life of the child. In order that it may be properly treated in the various subject matter areas such as science, home economics, and social studies, in order that the physical environment and the emotional environment may be properly provided for, in order that health services may be most effectively administered, and in order that close cooperation and coordination between the school and the rest of the community may be obtained, there is an essential need for some type of coordinating machinery. There is a need for a school health council or committee where individuals representing various interests and groups can pool their thinking and bring about cooperative efforts. There is a need for some individual to act in the capacity of a health coordinator, to spearhead the movement for cooperation and coordination, and to develop good relationships among the various departments and interests represented in the total school situation, as well as with those in the broader community.

In order to have an effective, sound health education program at the secondary level, the central administration must provide the type of leadership that leaves no doubt as to the importance of health in the lives of the many children who attend the schools. Such administrative leadership will reflect itself from the very top to the very bottom of the school structure and be felt at the grass roots of all community enterprises.

The junior high school. The junior high school was created to meet the physical, mental, and socioemotional needs of the preadolescent and early adolescent boys and girls who make up grades seven, eight, and nine. These grades represent a period of transition when the characteristics of growth and development, although varying from individual to individual, form a relatively uniform pattern during the age period of 12 to 14 years.

Junior high school students are in need of knowledge and proper attitudes that will result in desirable health practices. The fact that students may not be interested in such information represents a challenge for the junior high school educational program. The consumption of many sweets as a substitute for essential foods, omission of breakfast, and other undesirable practices, an interest in personal grooming, a need to understand one's bodily makeup, the maturing sexual drive, and other factors make it imperative to get across health information at this time. Health education activities contribute feelings of satisfaction and understanding that may never be possible of accomplishment in the regular academic program.

Health content should be adapted to the needs and interests of the students in this age group. Stress should be on the personal health problems of the students themselves, and how hereditary factors affect their health, how good or poor health manifest themselves, and how health practices affect the attainment of life ambitions and goals. Such topics as food, rest, exercise, first aid, safety, alcohol and narcotics, mental health, communicable disease, growth and functions of the human body, personality development, family life, and community health would be covered.

The health teaching that takes place in

the junior high school should take into consideration the developmental tasks that characterize the early adolescent. These include the desire for independence of adults, self-respect, and peer identification, as well as accepting one's physical makeup, adjusting to the opposite sex, and establishing a standard of values.

The committee on Health Education for Junior High School of the American School Health Association lists the following as a topical outline of content for this age group:

Health status
Cleanliness and grooming
Rest, sleep, and relaxation
Exercise
Posture
Recreation and leisure-time activities
Sensory perception
Nutrition
Growth and development
Understanding ourselves
Personality
Getting along with others
Family living
Alcohol
Drugs
Smoking and tobacco
Environment
Air and water pollutions
Consumer health
Disease*

For each of these topics the committee has identified key concepts, suggested learning experiences, and means of evaluation.

The senior high school. During grades ten, eleven, and twelve, the stress continues to be on many subject-matter areas that were stressed for the health content in the junior high school years. However, the material and experiences presented would be more advanced and adapted to the age group found in the later high school years. Such topics as the structure and function of the human body could stress more scientific concepts as found

through research, evaluation of individual health needs in the light of proper balance in one's daily routine, and the means of attaining proper emotional maturity and mental health.

The committee on Health Education for Senior High School of the American School Health Association lists the following as a topical outline of content for this age group:

Health status
Fatigue and sleep
Exercise
Recreational activities
Sensory perception
Nutrition
Growth and development toward maturity
Family living
Alcohol
Drugs
Smoking and tobacco
Health protection
Noise pollution
Health agencies
Health careers
World health
Safety and accidents*

For each of these topics the committee has listed key concepts, suggested learning experiences, and means of evaluation.

Although personal health receives considerable attention during the high school years, a major part of the teaching is concerned with problems of adult and family living and community health. Such health areas as preparation for marriage and family life, communicable and noncommunicable disease control, evaluation of professional health services, environmental health, industrial health, Civil Defense, consumer health education, accident prevention, emergency care, protection from environmental hazards such as radiation, health agencies at the local, state, national, and international levels, and the various health careers open to high school students receive great stress.

*Health instruction: suggestions for teachers, The Journal of School Health 39:48, 1969.

*Health instruction: suggestions for teachers, The Journal of School Health 39:71, 1969.

Some students will not be going to college. This means that the senior high school years offer the last opportunity to impress boys and girls with their health responsibilities—to themselves, their loved ones, and the members of their community.

Health education at the secondary level can represent an experience that will have a lasting effect for the betterment of human lives. The leadership provided, the methods used, and the stress placed upon such an important aspect of living will determine in great measure the extent to which each school will fulfill its responsibility.

HEALTH SCIENCE INSTRUCTION AT THE COLLEGE AND UNIVERSITY LEVEL

The college and the university also have responsibilities for health science instruction. Health is important to everyone regardless of the type of work he may do.

Years ago the college and university health education offerings consisted mainly of lectures on various aspects of the anatomy and physiology of the human body. These were usually given by medical personnel and were often a collection of uninteresting facts unrelated to the student's interests and health problems. In more recent years this type of presentation has changed. The emphasis has shifted from the factual medical knowledge to health problems which students themselves encounter in day-to-day living and also to those subjects in which students are especially interested. Consequently, discussions are now held on subjects concerned with family living, personal and community health, mental health, drugs, environmental health, nutrition, the prevention of disease, and related subjects.

The Third National Conference on Health in Colleges recommended major health instruction courses appropriate to special groups of students. It also suggested "a minimum of 45 class hours or

three to four semester credits" for a basic or general health course in "personal and community health." Other recommended procedures for college health courses that have been set forth include (1) the 3- or 5-hour one-semester required or elective course, (2) the 2-hour per week course for two credits, (3) the 2-hour course shared with a physical education requirement, and (4) the 1-hour per week course for one credit. Such a course should meet frequently enough to maintain the student's interest and to cover the subject adequately. Furthermore, the lecture method of presentation should not be the only one used.

The President's Commission on Higher Education stressed the importance of health instruction for college students. It particularly stressed instruction based directly on the practical problems of personal and community health.

The American College Health Association has recommended that every college and university have a requirement in health education for all students who fall below acceptable standards on a college-level health knowledge test.

The junior college is in a particularly strategic position to offer health instruction. The 2-year college reaches a significant segment of the population that does not go on to the 4-year colleges and universities. Furthermore, research has shown that junior college students have demonstrated as much as 25% more interest in health problems than high school students. Junior college students are more mature and this may be an explanation of their increased interest in health problems. Topics such as sex instruction, marriage, mental health, emotional health, alcohol, tobacco, and narcotics are of particular interest to this segment of the college population.

It is generally felt that a health education department should be established to coordinate the instruction in health, that student needs should represent an important consideration for the determination of subject matter content, that only qualified faculty members be permitted to teach health education classes, and that classes be limited to a maximum of thirty-five students. Testing of new students is also recommended, after which those students who fall below desirable standards are required to take the required health education course.

Presently, health education courses offered in colleges and universities are listed in college catalogues under such names as Personal Hygiene, Health Education, Personal and Community Health, Health Science, Hygiene, Healthful Living, Health and Safety, Health Essentials, and Problems of Healthful Living. Courses are taught in such departments as health, physical education, and recreation; health education; biology; education; health and safety; basic studies; psychology; and biologic sciences. Students required to take such courses vary from only those students in schools of education or in departments of health, physical education, and recreation, or elementary education major students, to liberal arts students. In some institutions courses are required for women but not for men.

There is a need for a uniform requirement for all college students to demonstrate that they know basic facts in the field of health. Those students who fail to meet such standards should be required to take a course in this area. Such a requirement is basic to the general education, productivity, and health of each person.

HEALTH EDUCATON FOR ADULTS

Adults are the guiding force in any community. The prestige they have, the positions they occupy, and their interests determine the extent to which any project or enterprise will be a success. Therefore, if the schools are to have an adequate health education program, if the knowl-edge that is disseminated, attitudes that are developed, and practices that are encouraged are to become a permanent part of the child's being and routine, the adult must be taken into consideration. Unless this is done, the schools' efforts will be of no avail.

There is a great need for parental education and for education in regard to the many health problems that confront any community. Adults are interested not only in children's health problems but also in the causes of sickness and death in the population and ways in which they can live a healthier life. Adult education is rapidly spreading across the length and breadth of this country. It is important that health education become one of the areas considered in any such program.

Schools and colleges should play a key part in adult education programs through the facilities, staff, and other resources at their disposal. They should cooperate fully with the many official and voluntary health agencies and other interested community groups in the furtherance of health objectives. Adult education programs in the area of health should be designed to discover community health problems, understand the health needs of children, and understand school health programs. Such discovery and understanding should lead to active participation in meeting health needs and in solving health problems. Such a program would also lend itself to growth in respect to health knowledge, attitudes, and practices.

METHODS OF TEACHING HEALTH

Methods of teaching health, such as lecture, recitation, and assignments in the textbook, represent a limited array of approved techniques for the modern health class. Although good textbooks are important and the other methods have value under select conditions, there are many other methods that can motivate students and create interest in health topics.

The methods used should be adapted

to the group of students being taught, be in accordance with the objectives sought, be capable of use by the instructor, stimulate interest among the students, and be adaptable to the time, space, and equipment in the school program. Some of the more popular methods for teaching health are discussed in the following paragraphs.

Problem solving is one of the most effective and best methods for teaching health. Health topics can be stated in the form of problems and then a systematic approach can be utilized by the students to obtain an answer. For example, the problem can be stated: "What are the effects of narcotics on health?" A systematic approach to this problem might include (1) stating the nature and scope of the problem, (2) defining the various possible solutions to the problem, (3) collecting scientific information to support each of the various aspects of the problem, (4) analyzing the information gathered as to its source, authoritativeness, date of origin, and other pertinent factors, and (5) drawing conclusions for the solution of the problem.

Textbook assignments may be given, followed by class discussions based on the readings.

Field trips can include planned visits to an agency or place where health matters are of importance, such as a hospital, local health department, water purification plant, health clinic, or fire department.

Class discussions on health topics of interest can be encouraged among the members of the class.

Demonstrations are an excellent method to show how something functions or is constructed, such as good and poor forms of posture or first-aid procedures.

Experiments, such as observing the growth of animals when certain types of diet are administered, are informative.

Independent study in which the students are assigned health topics for investigation is helpful.

Resource people, such as doctors, den-

tists, firemen, or other specialists, can be brought in to speak to health classes.

Audiovisual aids, such as films, television, filmstrips, slides, radio, and recordings, are helpful in presenting certain types of health material to the students in an interesting and clear manner.

Graphic materials such as posters, graphs, charts, bulletin boards, and exhibits are valuable for motivating students in regard to health matters, arousing interest, attracting attention, and visualizing ideas.

Interviews can be arranged in which students may be assigned to interview such persons as officers of the local health department, representatives of safety councils, members of voluntary health agencies, and heads of medical and dental societies for the purpose of getting the views of specialists and their recommendations on health matters.

Panels can be made up of students for an informal exchange of ideas or points of view regarding pertinent health matters.

Buzz sessions in which a class is organized into small groups of students for the purpose of discussing health topics, permitting each student more opportunity for discussion, is an excellent method.

Class committees can be formed by dividing a class and assigning topics for exploration.

Dramatizations, such as a play or a skit, can be put on by a class to bring to the pupils' attention a health matter such as the importance of safety on the playground.

Surveys in regard to health problems in the school, college, or community that need investigation and more information as to their solution can be suggested. Survey forms can be constructed by pupils themselves or else standard forms may be available under certain conditions.

Games and quizzes patterned after popular shows on radio or television can provide interesting methods and challenge the thinking of students.

Health aids can be provided in which

community health agencies may offer opportunities for students to obtain experience by keeping records or engaging in various types of activities where the jobs do not require experience and special training. Working on a Red Cross blood program is an example.

CONCENTRATED, CORRELATED, INTEGRATED, AND INCIDENTAL HEALTH TEACHING

Four ways of including health education in the school offering are through concentrated, correlated, integrated, and incidental teaching. Each of these will be discussed.

Concentrated health teaching

Concentrated health education refers to the provision in the school offering for regularly scheduled courses that are confined solely to a consideration of health, rather than a combination with some other subject matter area. It implies a scheduled time for class meetings and a planned course of study. It is recommended that such courses be given on the secondary school level. Furthermore, such courses should be held for a daily class period at least one semester during the ninth or tenth grade and also during the eleventh or twelfth grade.

It is the general consensus that concentrated health education is a necessity. If the objectives for which the school health program has been established are to be achieved, time must be made available in the curricular offering of the school. Health has been listed as one of the main objectives in the field of education. Therefore, it would seem logical to assume that in order to achieve such an objective proper provisions must be made.

Concentrated health education courses required of all students result in many educational benefits. There is a specialized body of knowledge to impart that can best be given to students in a concentrated

manner, rather than by depending upon some other subject to provide this information. It allows for better planning, teaching progression, and evaluation. It further allows for the giving of credit, such as is given for any other course that is offered separately. It is more likely to result in health instruction by teachers who have specialized in this particular area and who are qualified and interested in participating in such a course. When offered as a separate course it enables boys and girls to be in the same class, as in other subjects. This is not true if it is combined with physical education, where boys and girls are usually in separate groups. It offers greater opportunities for discussion of personal health problems, with guidance and counseling in regard to these problems, and for the utilization of teaching methods appropriate to such a course.

The importance of concentrated health education is clearly recognized in the upper 6 years of school by one superintendent of schools who says:

. . . In the upper six years some of the health instruction may be provided for in other subjects, science and home economics, for example, but there must be at least a one-unit health course taught by a specialist, Only through such a course can justice be done to the extensive content of the complete health education course, since specialists in other subjects have their own objectives to satisfy and can be expected to subordinate satisfaction of health objectives. Moreover, maturing students, particularly those in the senior high school, need the challenge of being exposed to the teaching of a health specialist. Much can be said for diffusing health content through the high school program of studies, so long as diffusion does not result in confusion, if not chaos, and so long as provision is made for an adequate degree of specialization through the one-unit course.*

Correlated health teaching

Correlated health education refers to the practice of including health concepts in the

---

*Miller, J. L.: An administrator looks at the school health program, The Journal of Educational Sociology **22:**27, 1948.

various subject matter areas. For example, in the area of history the relationship of the rise and fall of various groups of people could be related to their health and the prevalence of disease, as could the increased speed of transportation and the transfer of disease from one country to the other. In the area of English, a study of the works of literature could be selected with a view to pointing up the health problems of individuals during various periods of history. The relationship of music and of art to mental health could be brought out. Mathematics could be used as a tool to figure the costs of various health projects. Science could bring out the health aspects in relation to the structure and functions of the human body. Home economics provides an excellent setting for teaching such things as nutrition and personal cleanliness. There is hardly a subject matter area that cannot be correlated with health education.

Correlated health education should be a part of every school health program. This necessitates definite planning to ensure that such an important subject is emphasized at every opportunity. Schools with

health coordinators have found that such a person can perform an outstanding job in this area by meeting with teachers in the various subject matter areas and discussing and planning the contributions they can make to health education. Although correlated health education is very important and should be included in every school, it should not be regarded as a substitute for concentrated health instruction. Even when there is a concentrated health program there should also be a correlated health program that permeates the entire school offering. When both correlated and concentrated health education are provided for, in adequate amounts and in the right manner, the best results are obtained. A survey of Michigan schools shows the various subjects with which health is correlated in that state.

Integrated health teaching

In integrated health teaching, health learnings are integrated into other aspects of the classroom program. Learning experiences are organized around a central objective. Whereas in correlated teaching health

Table 12-6. Health education correlation*

Subject	Schools	Subject	Schools
Science	244	Conservation	1
Physical education	217	Driver education	1
Home economics	183	Educational guidance	1
Biology	165	Elective living	1
General science	34	Home arts	1
Family living	29	Home living	1
Sociology	11	Household mechanics	1
Social studies	10	Life adjustment	1
Psychology	6	Modern problems	1
Orientation	4	Nursing	1
Civics	3	Personal biology	1
Guidance	3	Personal living	1
Reading	3	Physics	1
Art	2	Political science	1
Chemistry	2	Sex education	1
Life science	2	Social living	1
Natural science	2	Teen living	1
Physiology	2		

*From State Department of Education: Patterns and features of school health education in Michigan public schools, East Lansing, 1969, Michigan State Department of Education, p. 4.

is brought into various subject matter areas, such as physical education and mathematics, in integrated health teaching various parts of a unit of study are related to a central theme. Two such themes might be that of living in a city or planning a visit to a foreign country. Health is one consideration involved in the planning, discussion, and assignments concerning this central theme. Health factors, for example, can be a very important consideration in living in a large metropolitan city or in going to a foreign country. There are problems concerned with water supply, sewage supply, fire prevention, disease control, immunizations, and medical examinations. Integrated health teaching finds its best setting in the elementary school.

Incidental health teaching

Incidental health education refers to that education that takes place during normal teaching situations, other than in regular health classes, where attention is focused on problems concerned with health. Such occasions may arise as the result of a question asked by a student; a problem that is raised in class; a personal problem that confronts a member of the class, a family, or the community; or a sudden illness, accident, or special project. It represents an opportunity for the teacher, physician, dentist, or nurse to provide information that is educational in nature. When a child has his eyes examined or his chest x-rayed, for example, many questions arise and opportunities are afforded to give the child information that will have a lasting and beneficial value. In many cases this will benefit the health of the child more than information given in more formalized, planned class situations. Teachers and others should constantly keep in mind the necessity for continually being alert to these "teachable moments." When a child is curious and wants information, this establishes a time for dynamic health education. Incidental health education can be planned for in advance. Situations and incidents should

be anticipated and utilized to their fullest in the interests of good health.

ORGANIZATION OF CLASSES

Many problems arise in connection with the organization of health science classes. Some of the more prevalent of these are concerned with whether boys and girls should meet together or separately, time arrangement, and scheduling.

Class membership

Boys and girls should be scheduled for health classes in a way that is in the best interests of all concerned. This would mean that where health science instruction is a combined program with physical education, and where the boys and girls are in separate classes, it would probably be best to conduct the health classes in a similar manner. On the other hand, if health science and physical education are not combined, it would seem that they should be handled in the same manner as any other subject. This would mean there would be mixed groups. The fact that the subject matter is health science should not mean separation of sexes. It should be pointed out, however, that some leaders in the field maintain this concept is wrong and advocate keeping the sexes separate as a means of getting better organization.

It is generally agreed that if boys and girls meet as a mixed group for health science they should continue as a mixed group throughout the entire course. It does not seem wise to have them meet separately when certain topics are considered. To do so tends to overstress and play up as "hush hush" certain aspects of health science. This creates confusion and encourages undue curiosity. It is best to treat the subjects in a natural and educational manner.

Time arrangement

There are many time arrangement patterns being followed in respect to health science. This is true especially on the secondary level.

The *Suggested School Health Policies—A Charter for School Health* recommends that "specific courses in health should be provided for all pupils in both junior and senior high schools. The minimum time allotment for the junior high school health course should be a daily period for at least two semesters, during the seventh, eighth, or ninth grade. The minimum time allotment for the health course in the senior high school should be a daily period for at least two semesters, preferably during the eleventh or twelfth grade. Health courses should receive credit equal to that given for courses in other areas. Health courses should be given in regular classrooms, adequately equipped. The classes should be comparable in size to those in other subject matter areas."*

The Joint Committee on Health Problems in Education of the National Education Association and the American Medical Association reaffirmed this stand when they pointed out that the trend appears to be toward concentrated health courses, one early in the high school, the other late in the senior high school period.

RESOURCES

The teacher or other individuals interested in obtaining help in planning, organizing, and administering a health education program can consult numerous persons and organizations for guidance and help. There are also many materials available for their use. Within the school itself, resource help exists in the form of staff members who possess specialized knowledge, such as the school physician, nurse, and home economics and physical education teachers. The community also offers numerous resources that can enrich the health education program immensely. In addition to the school and community, the state and nation also have rich resources that in many cases are available merely for the asking.

The organizations at the local, state, and national levels that offer resources for the field of health education can be listed and discussed under the following headings: (1) professional agencies and associations, (2) official agencies, and (3) commercial organizations.

Professional agencies and associations

Under professional agencies and associations can be listed such organizations as voluntary health agencies, medical, dental, and nursing associations, council of social agencies, and other health education associations. Some of the more prominent are listed here:

Voluntary health organizations

American Cancer Society, 219 E. 42nd St., New York, N. Y. 10017

American Heart Association, 44 E. 23rd St., New York, N. Y. 10010

American National Red Cross, National Headquarters, Washington, D. C. 20006

American Social Health Association, 1740 Broadway, New York, N. Y. 10019

American Hearing Society, 919 18th St. N. W., Washington, D. C. 20006

Child Welfare League of America, 44 E. 23rd St., New York, N. Y. 10010

National Committee for Mental Hygiene, 1740 Broadway, New York, N. Y. 10019

National Foundation, 800 2nd Ave., New York, N. Y. 10017

National Safety Council, 425 N. Michigan Ave., Chicago, Ill. 60611

National Society for the Prevention of Blindness, 16 E. 40th St., New York, N. Y. 10016

National Society for Crippled Children and Adults, 2023 W. Ogden Ave., Chicago, Ill. 60612

National Tuberculosis Association, 1740 Broadway, New York, N. Y. 10019

Professional associations

American Academy of Pediatrics, 1801 Hinman Ave., P. O. Box 1034, Evanston, Ill. 60201

American Association for Health, Physical Education, and Recreation, 1201 16th St. N. W., Washington, D. C. 20036

American Dental Association, 211 E. Chicago Ave., Chicago, Ill. 60611

---

*National Committee on School Health Policies: Suggested school health policies, ed. 3, Chicago, 1962, American Medical Association.

American Hospital Association, 840 N. Lakeshore Dr., Chicago, Ill. 60610

American Medical Association, 535 N. Dearborn St., Chicago, Ill. 60610

American Nurses Association, 10 Columbus Circle, New York, N. Y. 10010

American Public Health Association, 1740 Broadway, New York, N. Y. 10019

American School Health Association, 515 E. Main St., Kent, Ohio 44240

Child Study Association of America, 9 E. 89th St., New York, N. Y. 10019

National Education Association, 1201 16th St. N. W., Washington, D. C. 20036

National League of Nursing, 10 Columbus Circle, New York, N. Y. 10019

Official agencies

Official agencies, such as state departments of health, state departments of education, and public health departments, offer a rich source of help. They offer guidance and consultant services, disseminate information and materials in various forms for use in health classes, and make available films and other visual aids.

Government agencies on the national level provide resources in various forms, including consultant services, health reports, and grants-in-aid, and publish various materials of interest and use to all those teaching health education.

State colleges and universities, as well as private institutions, should be kept in mind when seeking resources for health. In many such institutions the staffs, with their various specialists, are available for use in the schools. Many times they will conduct workshops and institutes to provide inservice training to local schoolteachers. Many have libraries of films and other materials that may be rented at a very nominal fee.

Thought and planning are required in order to use these various resources effectively. The right persons to contact should be known, materials that are borrowed should be returned on time, and consultant services should be handled in a considerate manner.

The names of some official agencies follow:

Atomic Energy Commission, Washington, D. C.

Department of Agriculture, Washington, D. C. (Bureau of Animal Industry and Bureau of Home Economics and Human Nutrition)

Department of Commerce, Bureau of the Census, Washington, D. C.

Department of Health, Education, and Welfare, Washington, D. C. (Office of Education, Office of Special Services, Public Health Service, and Social Security Administration)

Department of the Interior, Bureau of Mines, Washington, D. C.

Department of State, Washington, D. C.

Executive Office of the President, National Security Resources Board, Civilian Defense Office (Federal Civil Defense Administration), Washington, D. C.

Government Printing Office, Superintendent of Documents, Washington, D. C.

State boards of health, located in the state capitals

State departments of education, located in the state capitals

State universities and colleges

Tennessee Valley Authority, Health and Safety Division, Knoxville, Tenn.

World Health Organization, Palais des Nations, Geneva, Switzerland

Commercial organizations

There are many commercial companies that dispense health materials. Although this material should be evaluated with care, much of it will prove helpful in the field of health education. Some of the commercial companies are listed:

The American Institute of Baking, 400 E. Ontario, Chicago, Ill. 60611

The Cereal Institute, 135 S. LaSalle St., Chicago, Ill. 60603

General Mills, Inc., 9200 Wayzata Blvd., Minneapolis, Minn. 55426

The Evaporated Milk Association, 228 N. LaSalle St., Chicago, Ill. 60601

The Florida Citrus Fruit Commission, Lakeland, Fla. 33802

The National Livestock and Meat Board, 36 S. Wabash Ave., Chicago, Ill. 60603

Sunkist Growers, Box 2706, Terminal Annex, Los Angeles, Calif. 90054

The United Fresh Fruit and Vegetable Association, 777 14th St. N. W., Washington, D. C. 20005

The Wheat Flour Institute, 309 W. Jackson Blvd., Chicago, Ill. 60606

RATING SCALE TO EVALUATE HEALTH EDUCATION MATERIALS*

Suitable material meets all of these criteria

	Yes	No
1. Is appropriate to the course of study.	___	___
2. Is a reinforcement of other materials.	___	___
3. Is significantly different.	___	___
4. Is impartial, factual, and accurate.	___	___
5. Is up-to-date.	___	___
6. Is nonsectarian, nonpartisan, and unbiased.	___	___
7. Is free from undesirable propaganda.	___	___
8. Is free from excessive or objectionable advertising.	___	___
9. Is free or inexpensive and readily available.	___	___

Pamphlets

	Excellent	Good	Fair	Poor
1. Readability of type.	___	___	___	___
2. Appropriateness of illustrations.	___	___	___	___
3. Organization of content.	___	___	___	___
4. Logical sequence of concepts.	___	___	___	___
5. Important aspects of topic stand out.	___	___	___	___
6. Material directed to one specific group such as teachers, pupils, or parents.	___	___	___	___
7. Reading level appropriate for intended group.	___	___	___	___
8. Based on interest and needs of intended group.	___	___	___	___
9. Positively directed in words, description, and actions.	___	___	___	___
10. Directed toward desirable health practices.	___	___	___	___
11. Minimal resort to fear techniques and morbid concepts.	___	___	___	___
12. In good taste; avoids vulgarity, stereotypes, and ridicule.	___	___	___	___
Total rating	___	___	___	___

Posters

	Excellent	Good	Fair	Poor
1. Realistic and within experience level.	___	___	___	___
2. Appeals to interest.	___	___	___	___
3. Emphasizes positive behavior and attitudes.	___	___	___	___
4. Message clear at a glance.	___	___	___	___
5. Little or no conflicting detail.	___	___	___	___
6. In good taste.	___	___	___	___
7. Attractive and in pleasing colors.	___	___	___	___
Total rating				

Recommended for use

1. For use by:
   a. pupils ___ b. teachers ___ c. parents ___ d. adults ___
2. Appropriate grade level:
   a. primary ___ b. elementary ___ c. junior high school ___ d. secondary ___
   e. college ___ f. adult ___

Not recommended for use and why

Date _____ Evaluated by _____

*From Osborn, B. M., and Sutton, W.: Evaluation of health education materials, The Journal of School Health 34:72, 1964. (Rating scale prepared by members of the school activities subcommittee.)

EVALUATION

Chapters 17 and 18 discuss in detail the evaluation process concerning school and college health programs. These chapters should be reviewed by the reader for the evaluation of the health science instruction program.

Periodic evaluations of school and college health science instruction programs should provide information on the knowledge achieved by the students, the degree to which student needs are being met, the extent to which objectives are achieved, the value of certain methods of teaching, the effectiveness of the teaching, and the strengths and weaknesses of the program.

Instruments that have been found to be effective in evaluating the health science instruction program include the following:

1. Observation of students in respect to their behavior and skills
2. Checklists
3. Questionnaires
4. Rating scales
5. Interviews with students and parents
6. Tests—standardized and teacher-made
7. Examples of students' work
8. Diaries and other records kept by students
9. Case studies of individual students

CHECKLIST FOR EVALUATING THE HEALTH SCIENCE INSTRUCTION PROGRAM*

General

	Yes	No
1. The school has a clear statement of the philosophy and principles upon which an effective school health instruction program is based.	___	___
2. Teachers on the staff appreciate the importance of health instruction and understand the contributions it makes to the total education program.	___	___
3. The school administration has assigned a qualified person from the staff to coordinate the entire school health program and provides him time to carry out his duties and responsibilities.	___	___
4. The school has an active health committee that helps in planning and coordinating the school health program.	___	___
5. The school provides a physical environment and an emotional atmosphere that helps to make possible the achievement of the goals of the health instruction program.	___	___
6. Teachers and other school staff members set a good example, in terms of good physical and mental health habits and attitudes, as part of the health instruction program.	___	___
7. The health instruction program is based upon the health needs, problems, interests, and abilities of the pupils.	___	___
8. The school has developed a teaching guide outlining a progressive plan of health instruction from grades 1 through 12.	___	___
9. The school has established definite goals of achievement in relation to habits, understanding, attitudes, and skills for each.	___	___
10. The school administration promotes the integration of health and safety instruction with all curricular areas and extracurricular activities of the school.	___	___
11. The school includes in its in-service education program opportunities for its staff to become better qualified for conducting the health instruction program.	___	___

*From State of Ohio Department of Education: A guide for improving school health instruction programs, Columbus, Ohio, 1963, State of Ohio Department of Education, Division of Elementary and Secondary Education.

CHECKLIST FOR EVALUATING THE HEALTH SCIENCE INSTRUCTION PROGRAM—cont'd

General—cont'd

12. The school administration provides adequate materials, such as books, charts, filmstrips, and pamphlets needed for the program. ____ ____
13. Textbooks used in health classes are authoritative, up-to-date, written in an interesting manner, and suitable for the grade level in which they are used. ____ ____
14. The school evaluates its health instruction periodically to determine its effectiveness in achieving established goals. ____ ____

Elementary program

Yes   No

15. In grades 1 to 3 sufficient time is provided during the school day for incidental and integrated teaching of health. ____ ____
16. In grades 4 to 6 a minimum of three periods a week is allotted for direct health instruction. ____ ____
17. The planned health instruction is supplemented in the upper grade by incidental teaching, correlation, and integration. ____ ____
18. Classroom teachers meet the state's minimum standards relative to college preparation in health education. ____ ____
19. The health instruction program centers around the daily living of the child instead of rote learning of health facts and rules. ____ ____
20. The program provides many interesting and worthwhile activities that are helpful to the child in solving his health problems related to growth, development, and adjustment. ____ ____
21. If the school attempts to integrate health instruction with large teaching units, the services of a health educator are utilized in planning those phases of unit dealing with health. ____ ____
22. The health instruction program includes the major health areas and problems. ____ ____

Junior and senior high schools

Yes   No

23. The time required for direct health instruction at the junior high school level is equivalent to one full semester of daily classes. ____ ____
24. The time provided for direct health instruction in the senior high school is equivalent to one full semester of daily classes. ____ ____
25. In addition to specific health courses, health instruction is correlated with other subject areas and programs. ____ ____
26. Teachers of health classes in the school have at least a minor in health education or a major in health and physical education. ____ ____
27. The health teacher is keenly interested in the health instruction program and attempts to achieve the potentialities inherent in the program. ____ ____
28. The number of pupils assigned to health classes is no greater than those assigned to other classes in the school. ____ ____
29. The school provides suitable classrooms and adequate facilities for health classes. ____ ____
30. The teacher utilizes the films, materials, and other resources available to him from local and state health agencies. ____ ____
31. The content of the program is interesting and meaningful to the pupils and helps them meet their health problems. ____ ____
32. The school has established definite policies relative to the teaching of controversial areas in health education. ____ ____
33. The health instruction program in the junior high school includes the health areas recommended by leaders in the field. ____ ____
34. The health instruction program in the senior high school includes the health areas recommended by leaders in the field. ____ ____

Questions and exercises

1. What is the relationship of health education to the total school health program?
2. Write an essay of 250 words citing evidence to show the need for health education.
3. What part do the superintendent and principal play in the development of a desirable health education program for the schools?
4. If a physical education person is teaching health education, what should be his or her qualifications in order to do an acceptable job?
5. Identify: (a) health coordinator, (b) school health council, (c) health services, (d) concentrated health teaching, (e) incidental health teaching, (f) Joint Committee on Health Problems, (g) official agencies, and (h) problem-solving activities.
6. How should health education classes be organized?
7. What are eight content areas in health education? Which do you feel are most important in your school? What are the controversial content areas?
8. How does health education vary at the elementary, junior high school, senior high school, and college levels?
9. What are the resources available to individuals in the area of health education?

Reading assignment in *Administrative Dimensions of Health and Physical Education Programs, Including Athletics:* Chapter 9, Selections 48 to 54.

Selected references

A Report of the National Conference on Coordination of the School Health Program: Teamwork in school health, Washington, D. C., 1962, American Association for Health, Physical Education, and Recreation.

A Statement From the Society of State Directors of Health, Physical Education, and Recreation: Guidelines for effective health planning by schools and voluntary health agencies, Journal of Health, Physical Education, and Recreation 34:26, 1963.

American Academy of Pediatrics, Committee on School Health: School health policies, Chicago, 1954, The Academy.

American Association for Health, Physical Education, and Recreation: Children in focus, their health and activity, 1954 Yearbook, Washington, D. C., 1954, The Association.

Anderson, C. L.: Health principles and practices, ed. 6, St. Louis, 1970, The C. V. Mosby Co.

Anderson, C. L.: School health practice, ed. 4, St. Louis, 1968, The C. V. Mosby Co.

Bucher, C. A., Olsen, E., and Willgoose, C.: The foundations of health, New York, 1967, Appleton-Century-Crofts.

Byrd, O. E.: School health administration, Philadelphia, 1964, W. B. Saunders Co.

Cauffman, J. G.: Evaluating a health education curriculum guide, Journal of Health, Physical Education, and Recreation 34:20, 1963.

Grout, R. E.: Health teaching in schools, ed. 5, Philadelphia, 1968, W. B. Saunders Co.

Hanlon, J. J., and McHose, E.: Design for health, Philadelphia, 1963, Lea & Febiger.

Harris, W. H.: Suggested criteria for evaluating health and safety teaching materials, Journal of Health, Physical Education, and Recreation 35:26, 1964.

Hein, F. V.: Critical issues in health and safety education, The Journal of School Health 35:70, 1965.

Hoyman, H. S.: An ecologic view of health and health education, The Journal of School Health 35:110, 1965.

Joint Committee on Health Problems in Education of National Education Association and American Medical Association: Health education, Washington, D. C., 1961, National Education Association.

Joint Committee on Health Problems in Education of National Education Association and American Medical Association: The physical educator asks about health, Washington, D. C., 1951, National Education Association.

Kirkendall, L. A.: Sex education as human relations, New York, 1950, Inor Publishing Co.

Mayshark, C., and Irwin, L.: Health education in secondary schools, ed. 2, St. Louis, 1968, The C. V. Mosby Co.

National Committee on School Health Policies: Suggested school health policies, ed. 2, Washington, D. C., 1962, National Education Association.

National Tuberculosis Association: A health program for colleges, A report of the Third National Conference on Health in Colleges, New York, 1948, The Association.

Oberteuffer, D.: Vital ties between health and education, NEA Journal 53:57, 1964.

Oberteuffer, D., and Beyer, M. K.: School health education, ed. 4, New York, 1966, Harper & Row, Publishers.

Pollock, M. B.: The significance of health education for junior college students, The Journal of School Health 34:333, 1964.

Report of the Study Committee on Health Education in the Elementary and Secondary School of the American School Health Association: Health instruction—suggestions for teachers, The

Journal of School Health, vol. 34, 1964. (Entire issue.)

Richardson, C. E.: Community resources and the school health program, The Journal of School Health 33:314, 1963.

School Health Education Study: A summary report, Washington, D. C., 1964, School Health Education Study, 1201 16th St. N. W.

School Health Education Study: Health education: a conceptual approach, Washington, D. C., 1965, School Health Education Study, 1201 16th St. N. W.

Sheets, N. L.: Health can be interesting, The Journal of School Health 33:132, 1963.

Smith, S. L.: Implication of the report of the NEA project of instruction for health education, The Journal of School Health 34:432, 1964.

Smolensky, J., and Bonevchio, L. R.: Principles of school health, Boston, 1966, D. C. Heath & Co.

Willgoose, C. E.: Health education in the elementary school, ed. 3, Philadelphia, 1969, W. B. Saunders Co.

CHAPTER 13 HEALTH SERVICE PROGRAMS FOR STUDENTS, INCLUDING ATHLETES

The health of school children and college students is a most important consideration for educators, parents, physicians, coaches, and others who desire to develop a fit populace. Effective school and college health service programs are essential in the achievement of this goal. Without satisfactory health services, the health of school children and college students cannot be adequately developed, maintained, and protected.

The history of health services shows that years ago schools and colleges stressed primarily provision for sanitary facilities and a clean environment. This was accomplished through a system of inspections and procedures. As more thinking has been given to this subject, however, there has been increased attention focused on those measures essential to the maintenance and improvement of the student's health. As a result, physicians, dentists, and other specialists have become more closely related to the schools and colleges. In turn, this has meant better detection of health defects, a more complete followthrough to ensure the correction of such defects, closer medical supervision of athletic programs, more adequate means for preventing and controlling communicable disease, an increased realization of the potentialities of the medical examination as an educational tool, and more attention to the eyes, throat, ears, nose, and teeth. As the need for better health services was recognized by the public at large, state laws were passed to provide these services. These laws required such procedures as periodic medical examinations and regular checking of vision and

hearing. They also stressed the need for nurses, who were trained not only in their particular area but also in the field of education. Today, there is a feeling that in order to adequately educate the student, health services must be an essential part of the program.

Health services cover a broad area. They include the procedures established to:
1. Appraise the health status of students and educational personnel
2. Counsel students, parents, and other persons concerning appraisal findings
3. Encourage the correction of remediable defects
4. Help plan for the health care and education of handicapped (exceptional) children
5. Help prevent and control disease
6. Provide emergency care for the sick and injured
7. Promote environmental sanitation
8. Promote the health of school and college personnel

THE HEALTH OF THE ATHLETE

The health of the athlete is of such importance to the students who read this text that this special section is being included. Although the entire chapter has implications for all who participate in physical education classes, this particular section emphasizes some of the essential health services for athletes. The growth of sports and athletic programs at both school and college education levels supports this emphasis.

Health services for athletes involves continuous medical attention, sound policies

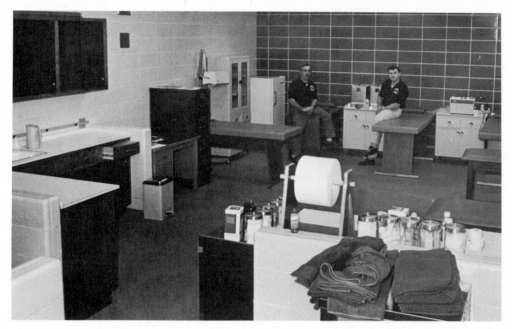

Training room for athletes. (Trinity College, Hartford, Conn.)

and procedures, and the availability of qualified personnel. A close working relationship should exist between coaches, trainers, athletic directors, and school and college administrators and medical society representatives if the athlete is to be adequately protected from injury and harm.

The American Medical Association, through its Committee on the Medical Aspects of Sports, the National Trainers' Association, and such athletic organizations as the National Federation of State High School Athletic Associations, has done an outstanding job in preparing materials, making recommendations to safeguard the health of the athlete, and outlining such procedures as first aid for athletic injuries. A few of the selected materials relating to health services for the athlete are included here. They include a checklist to help evaluate five major factors in the health supervision of athletes, disqualifying conditions for sports participation, and first aid procedures for athletic injuries. Furthermore, a suggested sports candidate's ques-

tionnaire, health examination form, and a student participation and parental approval form are also shown.*

THE PLACE OF HEALTH SERVICES IN SCHOOLS AND COLLEGES

The health services program must be well publicized so that educators, coaches, and the public in general will understand why such services are essential. Only as this need is understood will there be adequate planning and provision for such services.

*A Joint Statement of The Committee on the Medical Aspects of Sports of the American Medical Association and the National Federation of State High School Athletic Associations: Safeguarding the health of the athlete, Chicago, 1965, The American Medical Association.

The Committee on the Medical Aspects of Sports, American Medical Association: A guide for medical evaluation of candidates for school sports, Chicago, 1966, The American Medical Association.

The Committee on the Medical Aspects of Sports, American Medical Association: First aid chart for athletic injuries, Chicago, 1965, The American Medical Association.

SAFEGUARDING THE HEALTH OF THE ATHLETE*

A joint statement of the Committee on the Medical Aspects of Sports of the American Medical Association and the National Federation of State High School Athletic Associations

A checklist to help you evaluate five major factors in health supervision of athletics.

Participation in athletics is a privilege involving both responsibilities and rights. The athlete's responsibilities are to play fair, to keep in training, and to conduct himself with credit to his sport and his school. In turn he has the right to optimal protection against injury as this may be assured through good conditioning and technical instruction, proper regulations and conditions of play, and adequate health supervision.

Periodic evaluation of each of these factors will help to assure a safe and healthful experience for players. The checklist below contains the kinds of questions to be answered in such an appraisal.

PROPER CONDITIONING helps to prevent injuries by hardening the body and increasing resistance to fatigue.

1. Are prospective players given directions and activities for preseason conditioning?
2. Is there a minimum of three weeks of practice before the first game or contest?
3. Are precautions taken to prevent heat exhaustion and heat stroke?
4. Is each player required to warm up thoroughly prior to participation?
5. Are substitutions made without hesitation when players evidence disability?

CAREFUL COACHING leads to skillful performance, which lowers the incidence of injuries.

1. Is emphasis given to safety in teaching techniques and elements of play?
2. Are injuries analyzed to determine causes and to suggest preventive programs?
3. Are tactics discouraged that may increase the hazards and thus the incidence of injuries?
4. Are practice periods carefully planned and of reasonable duration?

GOOD OFFICIATING promotes enjoyment of the game and the protection of players.

1. Are players as well as coaches thoroughly schooled in the rules of the game?
2. Are rules and regulations strictly enforced in practice periods as well as in games?
3. Are officials qualified both emotionally and technically for their responsibilites?
4. Do players and coaches respect the decisions of officials?

RIGHT EQUIPMENT AND FACILITIES serve a unique purpose in protection of players.

1. Is the best protective equipment provided for contact sports?
2. Is careful attention given to proper fitting and adjustment of equipment?
3. Is equipment properly maintained, and are worn and outmoded items discarded?
4. Are proper areas for play provided and carefully maintained?

ADEQUATE MEDICAL CARE is a necessity in the prevention and control of injuries.

1. Is there a thorough preseason health history and medical examination?
2. Is a physician present at contests and readily available during practice sessions?
3. Does the physician make the decision as to whether an athlete should return to play following injury during games?
4. Is authority from a physician required before an athlete can return to practice after being out of play because of disabling injury?
5. Is the care given athletes by coach or trainer limited to first aid and medically prescribed services?

*From Committee on the Medical Aspects of Sports of the American Medical Association and the National Federation of State High School Athletic Associations: Tips on athletic training, XI, Chicago, Illinois, 1969, The American Medical Association.

SUGGESTED
SPORTS CANDIDATES' QUESTIONNAIRE

(To be completed by parents or family physician)

Name_____Birth date_____

Home address_____

Parents' Name_____Tel. No._____

1. Has had injuries requiring medical attention	Yes	No
2. Has had illness lasting more than a week	Yes	No
3. Is under a physician's care now	Yes	No
4. Takes medication now	Yes	No
5. Wears glasses	Yes	No
contact lenses	Yes	No
6. Has had a surgical operation	Yes	No
7. Has been in hospital (except for tonsillectomy)	Yes	No
8. Do you know of any reason why this individual should not participate in all sports?	Yes	No

Please explain any "Yes" answers to above questions:

_____

_____

9. Has had complete poliomyelitis immunization by inoculations (Salk) or oral vaccine (Sabin)	Yes	No
10. Has had tetanus toxoid and booster inoculation within past 3 years	Yes	No
11. Has seen a dentist within the past 6 months	Yes	No

_____

Parent or Physician

Suggested sports candidates' questionnaire. (From Committee on the Medical Aspects of Sports, American Medical Association: A guide for medical evaluation of candidates for school sports, 1966, The Association, p. 2. Reprinted with permission of the American Medical Association.

The Joint Committee of the American Medical Association and the National Education Association* has listed the following as reasons why health services should exist:

1. They contribute to the learning experience and the realization of other educational aims.
2. They facilitate adaptation of school and college programs to individual needs.
3. They help in maintaining a healthful environment.
4. They help children secure the medical or dental care they need.
5. They possess inherent values for increasing students' understanding of health and health problems.

Health services contribute to the realization of educational aims. Educational committees, conferences, and other important groups have continually listed health as one of the objectives of education. Health services are necessary to attain this objective.

Health services minimize the hazards of school and college attendance. They make it possible for the student to attend school and college under safe conditions. Through emergency care, it is possible to greatly re-

*Joint Committee of American Medical Association and National Education Association: School health services, ed. 2, Washington, D. C., 1964, National Education Association, pp. 7-8.

SUGGESTED HEALTH EXAMINATION FORM

(Cooperatively prepared by the National Federation of State High School Athletic Associations and the Committee on Medical Aspects of Sports of the American Medical Association.) Health examination for athletes should be rendered after August 1 preceding school year concerned.

(Please Print)   Name of Student_____   City and School _____

Grade_____Age_____Height_____Weight_____Blood Pressure_____

Significant Past Illness or Injury_____

Eyes_____ R 20/ ; L20 /; Ears_____ Hearing R   /15; L   /15

Respiratory_____

Cardiovascular_____

Liver_____Spleen_____Hernia_____

Musculoskeletal_____Skin_____

Neurological_____Genitalia_____

Laboratory: Urinalysis_____Other:_____

Comments_____

Completed Immunizations: Polio_____ Tetanus_____
                                            Date   Date

| Instructions for use of card | Other_____

I certify that I have on this date examined this pupil and find him (her) physically able to compete in supervised activities NOT CROSSED OUT BELOW.

BASEBALL	FOOTBALL	ROWING	SOFTBALL	TRACK
BASKETBALL	HOCKEY	SKATING	SPEEDBALL	VOLLEYBALL
CROSS COUNTRY	GOLF	SKIING	SWIMMING	*WRESTLING
FIELD HOCKEY	GYMNASTICS	SOCCER	TENNIS	OTHERS_____

*Weight loss permitted to make lower weight class: Yes_____ No_____; if "Yes" may lose _____pounds.

Date of Examination:_____Signed:_____
                                                                  Examining Physician

Physician's Address_____Telephone_____

STUDENT PARTICIPATION AND PARENTAL APPROVAL FORM

Name of student:_____Name of School:_____
                        First   Last   Middle Initial

Date:_____Date of Birth:_____Place of Birth:_____

This application to compete in interscholastic athletics for the above high school is entirely voluntary on my part and is made with the understanding that I have not violated any of the eligibility rules and regulations of the State Association.

| Instructions for use of card | Signature of Student:_____

PARENT'S OR GUARDIAN'S PERMISSION

I hereby give my consent for the above high school student to engage in State Association approved athletic activities as a representative of his high school, except those crossed out on reverse side of this form by the examining physician, and I also give my consent for the above student to accompany the team as a member on its out-of-town trips.

Signature of Parent or Guardian:_____

Date:_____Address:_____
                                      (Street)   (City or Town)

NOTE: This form is to be filled out completely and filed in the office of the high school principal or superintendent of schools before student is allowed to practice and/or compete.

Suggested health examination form. (From Committee on the Medical Aspects of Sports, American Medical Association: A guide for medical evaluation of candidates for school sports, 1966, The Association, p. 3. Reprinted with permission of the American Medical Association.)

duce the harmful effects of injuries in the event of accidents. Adequate precautions are taken against the spread of communicable disease. Medical examinations identify health defects, making for safer participation in athletics and other school activities. These are only a few of the many hazards that can be removed or minimized through effective health services.

Health services help youth to adapt better to school and college programs. Through careful and regular checking of vision and hearing and general physical condition and correction of defects, students will better assume their responsibilities. Deficiencies, defects, and weaknesses that are prevalent will be noted and provided for.

Health services have potentialities for educating the parents as well as the students. They have potentialities for developing proper attitudes toward health, developing proper habits, and imparting scientific information. Through the medical examination, for example, the teacher, nurse, physician, coach, and others have an opportunity to educate students and parents about various aspects of health.

The forty-first annual report of the Health Service Department of the Denver schools* includes a report on the basic functions that this department performs in the education of children and youth in that city. Since this school system has won national recognition for its school health services program, this information is given to provide a better understanding of what all schools should be trying to accomplish in this area:

Health services to assure a safe and wholesome school environment
1. Selection of healthy adult employees
2. Implementation of city health and building regulations
3. Application of control measures to stop the spread of illnesses.
   a. Implementation of official health rules
   b. Prompt attention to ill children and exclusion from school
   c. Immunizations for those who request it
4. Health consultations and periodic evaluations for adult personnel

Health services to detect conditions among pupils that would diminish their most effective participation in educational activities
1. Routine screening tests for vision, hearing, physical growth, and dental health
2. Periodic medical appraisals to evaluate general development and significant physical conditions and defects
3. Screening tests on preschool children for hearing and vision

*Corliss, L. M.: Forty-first annual report, 1965-1966, Health Service Department, Denver Public Schools, Denver, Colo.

Health services to assist in health instruction for all pupils
1. Cooperative efforts with instruction department on materials and inservice training
2. Educational emphasis on all health procedures
3. Work with faculties for classroom health units
4. Tuberculosis testing

Health services to promote followup care and correction of pupils' health problems and deficiencies
1. Nurse counseling with pupils, parents, teachers, social workers, and other school personnel
2. Intercommunications between school health personnel and private physicians and/or clinics
3. Cooperation with other community health agencies

Health services to assist with other needs of some pupils
1. Medical appraisal of those with physical, mental, and emotional problems that seem to interfere with learning
   a. Placement in special educational classes
   b. Assistance from consultant psychiatrists
2. Dental clinic services
3. Help in first-aid care of injuries
4. Medical reports on "battered" children

Additional health service department responsibilities
1. Continual evaluation of department activities
2. Close rapport and administrative planning with medical and dental profession and with official and nonofficial health agencies
3. Continued cooperative programs with other departments within the schools and with community and civic groups
4. Assistance with health, disability, and retirement leaves for adult personnel.

Table 13-1, taken from the Denver Report, indicates the recommended timing and frequency of routine school health services in respect to grades.

THE RESPONSIBILITY FOR SCHOOL HEALTH SERVICES

The question is frequently raised as to whether school health services should fall within the province of school personnel or public health department personnel. Both the school and the public health department are vitally interested in seeing that such services are provided. Both have specialized personnel who can render important contributions to the successful administration of health services. The school is especially interested in the educational aspects of such services and the vast potentialities they have for educating the children and the public. It has personnel who are specially trained in educational methods and techniques. In many communities it also has physicians on the staff who perform medical examinations and other health services. On the other hand, the public health department has specialists in sanitation, epidemiology, and other areas pertinent to the health services program.

Since both the school and the public health department have interests in health services, each local community should decide how such a program can best be carried out. In some communities the public health department is better staffed and qualified to perform many of the health services. In other communities the school has the better staff and other requisites. In many cases, health services should be a cooperative endeavor, where the health department and the school work together, sharing their resources and planning a program in the light of these conditions.

EDUCATION VERSUS TREATMENT

With the school becoming an increasingly important social organization of the community, the question often arises as to whether it should provide treatment as part of its health services program. The philosophy on which the school program is based establishes it mainly as an agency concerned with education. The educational aspects of the health services program represent the major contribution of the schools. By identifying health defects, making referrals to medical, dental, and other experts, counseling, providing for emergency

care, making special provisions for the handicapped, and establishing and encouraging measures to prevent and control communicable diseases, the school is carrying out its responsibilities in health services. However, in some communities, as a result of agreement and consultation among public health, medical and dental professions, educators, and others, provisions have been made to provide dental treatment, occupational therapy, and other services. Such programs are exceptions to the rule, however, and usually are initiated as a result of a need for expediency and because it is felt that such a practice is the best way to handle certain health problems. Treatment is not usually a part of the school health program.

HEALTH SERVICES

The rest of the chapter will be concerned with a discussion of the various health services: (1) health appraisal, (2) health counseling, (3) correction of remediable defects, (4) care and education of exceptional children, (5) communicable disease control, (6) emergency care, (7) environmental sanitation, and (8) health of school and college personnel. Each of these health services will be considered in respect to how it fits into the total health program. Some of the various techniques that are used and administrative problems that arise, together with acceptable procedures to be followed, will be discussed.

Health appraisal

Health appraisal is that phase of health service that is concerned with evaluating the health of the student in as objective a way as possible, through examinations, observations, and records.

The cooperation of many individuals is needed to do an acceptable job in health service. Teachers, administrators, physicians, dentists, psychologists, public health officials, social workers, parents, and lay leaders must all work together. **Through**

Table 13-1. Recommended timing and frequency of routine health services*

Type of service	K	1	2	3	4	5	6	7	8	9	10	11	12
Medical appraisals													
All pupils with possible health problems at any grade level	X	X	X	X	X	X	X	X	X	X	X	X	X
When private physicians have not reported on pupils in grades 1, 6, and 9, or on new pupils at any other grade level		X					X			X			
All pupils who participate in varsity sports											X	X	X
All pupils who participate in school swimming classes								X	X	X	X	X	X
ROTC and NDCC members, if private physician reports are not obtained											X	X	X
All pupils being considered for placement in special education at any grade level	X	X	X	X	X	X	X	X	X	X	X	X	X
Weight and growth measurements													
In first semester (routinely) and on all new pupils and referred pupils; often done cooperatively with physical education teachers as part of fitness program	X	X	X	X	X	X	X	X	X	X			
Hearing screening tests													
At certain grades as shown on all new pupils, on referred pupils, and those with known defects	X	X		X				X					
Vision screening tests													
At certain grades as shown; on new pupils, referred pupils, and those with known defects	X	X		X		X		X			X		
Dental inspections													
At grades shown and at about 5-year intervals—high school pupils inspected and DMF rates ascertained	X	X	X	X		X	X	X	X				
Immunizations													
Once each year in each school for those in need of certain protections and at parents' request	X	X	X	X	X	X	X	X	X	X	X	X	X
Special services													
Tine test for tuberculosis								X					
Scalp ringworm inspections	All grades as needed												
Other nuisance diseases	All grades as needed												
Color vision rechecks								X					

*From Corliss, L. M.: Forty-first annual report, 1965-1966, Health Service Department, Denver Public Schools, Denver, Colo.

DISQUALIFYING CONDITIONS FOR SPORTS PARTICIPATION*

Conditions	Contact†	Noncontact endurance‡	Others§
General			
Acute infections:			
Respiratory, genitourinary, infectious mononucleosis, hepatitis, active rheumatic fever, active tuberculosis, boils, furuncles, impetigo	X	X	X
Obvious physical immaturity in comparison with other competitors	X	X	
Obvious growth retardation	X		
Hemorrhagic disease:			
Hemophilia, purpura, and other bleeding tendencies	X		
Diabetes, inadequately controlled	X	X	X
Jaundice, whatever cause	X	X	X
Eyes			
Absence or loss of function of one eye	X		
Severe myopia, even if correctable	X		
Ears			
Significant impairment	X		
Respiratory			
Tuberculosis (active or under treatment)	X	X	X
Severe pulmonary insufficiency	X	X	X
Cardiovascular			
Mitral stenosis, aortic stenosis, aortic insufficiency, coarctation of aorta, cyanotic heart disease, recent carditis of any etiology	X	X	X
Hypertension on organic basis	X	X	X
Previous heart surgery for congenital or acquired heart disease	X	X	
Liver			
Enlarged liver	X		
Spleen			
Enlarged spleen	X		
Hernia			
Inguinal or femoral hernia	X	X	
Musculoskeletal			
Symptomatic abnormalities or inflammations	X	X	X
Functional inadequacy of the musculoskeletal system, congenital or acquired, incompatible with the contact or skill demands of the sport	X	X	
Neurological			
History or symptoms of previous serious head trauma or repeated concussions	X		
Convulsive disorder not completely controlled by medication	X	X	
Previous surgery on head or spine	X	X	
Renal			
Absence of one kidney	X		
Renal disease	X	X	X
Genitalia			
Absence of one testicle	X		
Undescended testicle	X		

*Committee on the Medical Aspects of Sports, American Medical Association: A guide for medical evaluation of candidates for school sports, Chicago, Illinois, 1966, The Association, pp. 4-5.
†Lacrosse, baseball, soccer, basketball, football, wrestling, hockey, rugby, etc.
‡Cross country, track, tennis, crew, swimming, etc.
§Bowling, golf, archery, field events, etc.

the active cooperation of all, the necessary plans will be made for continuous evaluation and appraisal. If a health council exists, this body can play a major role in coordinating the various aspects of the program.

Planning should provide for desirable facilities and procedures for health appraisal. There should be provision for privacy and quiet so that the best type of examinations and other techniques can be used in an acceptable manner.

The aims of health appraisal include identifying students in need of medical or

---

NOTICE TO PARENTS ABOUT HEALTH APPRAISALS FOR SCHOOL PUPILS

Pupil's Name_____ Grade_____ Room or Section_____

It is important for the school to have some health information about every pupil. Health appraisals are strongly recommended for all pupils whenever they enroll in school and thereafter as your physician recommends.

If possible, please have your family or clinic physician send a report of a recent examination to the schools. Will you ask him to send it on special forms supplied by the schools?

Health clearance is required periodically for participation in swimming classes, ROTC, and certain other school activities. In addition, annual school medical appraisals are required for varsity sports.

In order to have health information of value to the school, we would appreciate your responses on the following:

1. Allergies_____
2. Convulsions or seizures_____
3. Diabetes_____
4. Frequent colds or sore throats_____
5. Frequent stomach-aches_____
6. Headaches_____
7. Heart trouble_____

8. Serious operations or accidents_____
_____
9. Known exposure to tuberculosis Yes____ No____
10. Vision_____ Hearing_____
11. Contagious diseases_____
_____
12. Other health problems, such as kidney trouble, ulcers, etc._____

HEALTH PRACTICES

1. *Eating:* Breakfast Yes____ No____ Between-meal snacks_____
2. *Rest and sleep:* Average hours_____
3. *Exercise and/or recreation outside of school:* Sports, clubs, music lessons, etc._____
_____
4. *Work activities outside of school*_____
5. *Emotional health:* Assuming responsibilities_____
   Getting along with others_____ Liking school_____

IMMUNIZATION RECORD AND TUBERCULIN TESTING (Please state year last given)

Smallpox vaccination_____   Rubeola (*measles*)_____ Mumps_____
Diphtheria-Tetanus_____   Rubella (*3-day measles*)_____
Polio: Type of Sabin (oral) doses I_____ II_____ III_____ Trivalent_____
Tuberculin test: Date_____ Negative_____ Positive_____

If a recent health examination has not been performed by a private or clinic physician, please indicate your choice below.

I will have our family or clinic physician give this
examination and send a report to school. . . _____
                                                                        (Sign here)

I wish the school medical appraisal. . . . . _____
                                                                        (Sign here)

Date_____

(Please Return This Sheet Promptly to the School Nurse)

Notice to parents about health appraisals for school pupils. (Denver Public Schools, Denver, Colo.)

dental treatment, those who have problems relating to nutrition, and those who are in need of treatment by a psychiatrist or guidance clinic. In addition, the objectives of health services are to measure the growth of pupils; identify students with non-remediable defects so that modified programs may be provided, such as for crippled or mentally retarded pupils; identify students who need additional examinations, such as x-ray studies; and identify students who need programs apart from the school setting, such as the blind and deaf.

The techniques used in health appraisal that will be discussed here include medical, psychologic, and dental examinations, screening for vision and hearing, teacher observations, and health records.

Examinations. Examinations are effective means of health appraisal.

Medical examinations. There are many important considerations for the administrator to keep in mind if medical examinations are to fulfill their objective. The following are some administrative guides.

TYPES. Both periodic and referral examinations should be given to students. *Periodic* medical examinations are given at stated intervals. *Referral* examinations are those that are given to students who have health problems needing special attention and who have been referred to the proper professional source. Such students may be referred to the physician as a result of teacher's observations, screening examinations, health records, or other indications that special attention is needed. The *examination of athletes* is also a type of medical examination that needs to be considered.

PLANNING. Medical examinations require planning. Young children should be informed as to their nature and purposes. The teacher can play an important role in explaining some of these purposes and procedures. Desirable attitudes can be developed so that children and parents look forward to such an event with interest and anticipation. The various instruments that are used, such as the stethoscope, can be shown and discussed. Planning should also

---

I hereby give permission and request that

_____

be given the medical examination required for swimmers. I understand there is a small additional cost for this swimming program.

To my knowledge, my child does not have diabetes, epilepsy, chronic sinus or ear infection, or any other physical condition that would make it unsafe for him to swim.

| _____ | _____ |
| (Date) | (Signature of Parent) |

PARENT PERMIT FOR PUPIL TO PARTICIPATE IN SWIMMING CLASS

Department of Health Service
Department of Health Education
DENVER PUBLIC SCHOOLS

STOCK NO. 10753
FORM 853   DSP   4-59-15M   V-238—45140

take into consideration the provision of adequate facilities, having parents present, and making available the necessary health records.

FREQUENCY. At least four periodic medical examinations should be given during the time a child is in the elementary and secondary schools. There should be a minimum of one examination at the time of entrance to school, one at the intermediate grade level, one at the junior or early high school level when the student is entering the adolescent period, and one toward the termination of the high school period. The desirable procedure, however, would be to have a medical examination each year. Referral examinations should be given at any time that health problems are detected. There is also a need for more medical examinations for students who are engaging in the athletic phase of the physical education program and for those whose health conditions are such that the physician recommends examinations at more frequent intervals.

EXAMINER. There is a trend toward having the family physician conduct the medical examination. It is felt that through a more complete knowledge of the family history and a closer personal relationship, a better job can be done. However, since some families do not have their own physicians, since it means an additional outlay of funds, and for other reasons, many schools must rely on a school physician to administer the examination. The procedure that is utilized in each community should be a local prerogative and based upon the type of examination that will produce the best results.

PERSONNEL IN ATTENDANCE. The personnel that should be in attendance at the medical examination for young children would include the physician, nurse, child, teacher, and parents. At the secondary school level, the child should have progressed to the point where he or she assumes the responsibility for his own health, and so the need

for parents at the examination is not as great. Special attention should be given to sending a written invitation to parents, listing the date and time of the examination. The presence of parents at these medical examinations provides an excellent opportunity for educating them in regard to their child's health, as well as their own.

SETTING. The place where the examination is held should be conducive to good results. The physical and the emotional atmosphere should receive attention. There should be privacy for disrobing, so that interruptions will not occur, and quiet so that distractions will be reduced to a minimum. The examination room should also provide ample space for personnel, equipment, and supplies and should be attractive. Tension, hurry, and excitement should be reduced to a minimum. The entire setting should be friendly and informal.

RECORDS AVAILABLE. Essential health records should be brought up to date and be available at the time of the examination. These would include students' health cards, vision and hearing records, height-weight statistics, accident reports, and any other information that will help the physician to better interpret the results of the examination.

SCOPE. The periodic medical examination will include inspection or examination of such items as the following:

Eyes and lids	Nose
Throat and mouth	Teeth and gums
Heart: before and	Lymph node and
after exercise	thyroid gland
Nutrition	Lungs
Posture	Scalp and skin
Feet	Bones and joints
Speech	Nervous system
Behavior attitudes	Inguinal and um-
Ears: canal and	bilical region for
drums	hernia in males

TIME. The examination that is administered by the school physician should be of sufficient length to detect any health defects and also make the experience educational in nature. The minimum average

HEALTH RECORD

Parents or Guardians—Mr. and Mrs.	
Occupation of Father	Session Teacher
Occupation of Mother	Family Doctor	Family Dentist

(Right margin labels: Last Name, First Name, Address, Telephone)

MEDICAL EXAMINATION

MEDICAL EXAMINATION	1	2	3	4
1. Date of Examination				
2. Age				
3. Weight				
4. Height				
5. Hearing Rt.				
Lt.				
6. Eyes Rt.				
Lt.				
7. Test with glasses	Yes No	Yes No	Yes No	Yes No
8. Ring Worm				
9. Plantar Warts				
10. Hair				
11. Personal Hygiene				
12. Pulse before exercise				
13. Pulse after exercise				
14. Heart				
15. Lungs				
16. Tremor				
17. Abdomen				
18. Hernia				
19. Ears				
20. Nose				
21. Tonsils				
22. Adenoids				
23. Teeth				
24. Thyroid				
25. Glands				
26. Nutrition				
27. Skin				
28. P. E. Classification				
Unrestricted (A or B)				
Partially Restricted (C)				
Rest Only (D)				
Permanent Excuse				
Temporary Excuse				
29. Swimming				
Permanent Excuse				
Temporary Excuse				
Doctor's Initials				

HISTORY OF DISEASE

Columns: Chicken Pox | St. Vitus Dance | Diphtheria | Measles | Mumps | Pneumonia | Scarlet Fever | Rheumatic Fever | Whooping Cough | Tonsillitis | Hay Fever | Asthma | Date of Vaccination for Small Pox | T. B. in Family? | Date of Skin Test

Headaches: Never	Menstruation Regular
Occasionally	Irregular
Frequently	Dysmenorrhea
Operations: Tonsils	Injuries
Others:	

Postural Findings Scoliosis	L R	L R	L R	L R
Shoulder High				
Hip High				
Feet: Pronation				
Long. Arch				
Transverse Arch				
Head Forward				
Round Shoulders				
Hollow Back				
Abdomen				
Body Balance				
Posture Grade				
Corrective Gym				

COMMENTS:

Explanation of Terms: "O"—Normal; "X"—Slight Defect; "XX"—Moderate; "XXX"—Marked.

Girl's health record. (Highland Park High School, Highland Park, Ill.)

time per student should be 15 minutes or four per hour.

Examination of athletes. Administrative guides for athletic examinations are as follows:

1. Medical examinations should be administered to all engaged in athletics previous to actual participation and as they are needed during the time the sport is in progress. This refers to all forms of strenuous athletics, whether it be interscholastic, intramural, or part of the class program.

2. There should be adequate provision for medical service at all athletic contests.

3. A physician's recommendation should accompany any athlete returning to competition after a period of illness.

4. Examinations for participation in athletics should preferably be conducted by the family physician. In instances where this is not feasible, the school physician should perform this service.

Psychologic examinations. With the increased emphasis on mental health, various psychologic examinations are being used more extensively. These examinations, however, represent only a very small part of the mental health services that should be available. Mental health programs are concerned with helping students to adjust satisfactorily to the school or college environment, detecting individual behavior problems, aiding the teacher, parent, and others to better understand human behavior, and helping in every way possible to appraise personality and to discover mental handicaps, emotional difficulties, and maladjustments.

Psychologic examinations and tests that appraise such factors as students' abilities, attitudes, personalities, intelligence, and social adjustment offer techniques for obtaining much information. The administration and interpretation of the findings of such techniques should be handled by qualified individuals.

Dental examinations and inspections. Following are administrative guides governing school dental services.

EMPHASIS. The emphasis in school den-

H-6 3M 9-36

LONG BEACH CITY SCHOOLS
HEALTH SERVICE DEPARTMENT
ATHLETIC PHYSICAL EXAMINATION REPORT

Name_____ School_____ Class_____

Age_____

Type of Athletic Activity—F. B., Basket Ball, Track, B. B., Class A. B. C.

Height_____Weight_____Standard_____Chest Circum.

In_____   Ex_____

Standing, Posture_____ Musculature_____ Nutrition_____

Skin_____ Superficial Glands_____

Hands_____ Arms_____ Abdomen_____

Hernia_____ Genitalia_____ Leg_____

Feet_____

Sitting: Hair_____ Teeth_____ Eyes, Reflexes_____

R._____   R._____

Vision—   Corrected—

L._____   L._____

R._____

Hearing—   Nose_____ Gums_____

L._____

Tongue_____ Tonsils_____ Pharynx_____

Ears_____ Chest_____ Heart_____

Pulse, sitting_____ After exercise_____

2 min. later_____ Temp._____ Lungs_____

Blood Pressure Systolic_____ Diastolic_____

Knee Reflexes_____

Urine Analysis: Sp. Grav._____ Alb._____ Sugar_____

Summary

Advice   Date_____

Athletic physical examination report. (Long Beach, Calif., Public Schools.)

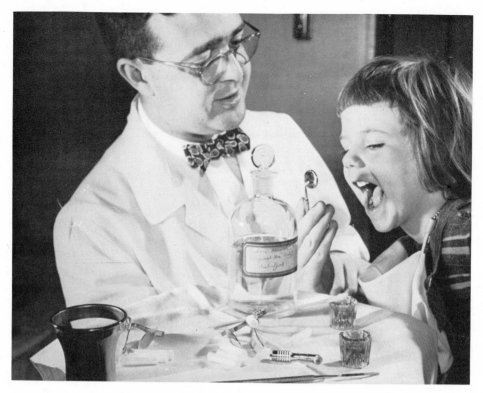

Dental inspection. (Indiana State Department of Health.)

FORM 79 5M 8-48 ◆

New Trier Township
High School

DENTAL CERTIFICATE

Winnetka
Illinois

This is to certify that I have examined the teeth of

STUDENT'S NAME _____ ADVISER _____

(Last)   (First)

RECORD OF EXAMINATIONS

Date	Clean	Under Repair	Under Treatment	Remarks	Dentist's Signature

tal services should be on health education. Children and parents should develop proper attitudes toward dental caries and oral hygiene. Periodically, they should consult their family dentist for the necessary examination, care, and advice.

PERSONNEL. The personnel in the school particularly concerned with dental health include the teacher, nurse, physician, and dental hygienist. The staff will depend upon the community philosophy concerning dental care. If the emphasis is upon education, it will be different than if it is on treatment. When a dental hygienist is a member of the school staff, she often has a variety of duties, including acting as a resource person for classroom teachers regarding dental health, making topical applications of sodium fluoride, cleaning children's teeth, and administering limited dental inspections.

NATURE. A difference of opinion exists as to whether or not schools should provide dental examinations for pupils. Those in favor of such a practice point to its value as a motivating device to encourage parents and children to visit the dentist. Furthermore, they say it helps children in the low-income classes and focuses attention on the dental needs of children. Those not in favor of such a practice argue that as a result of school examinations children and parents visit their dentist less often and in some cases even substitute this examination for regular dental care. They further point out that it is the responsibility of everyone to make provisions for his own dental care and that the school is not the agency responsible for providing such a service. The question of the school's responsibility should be decided in each local community through conferences with dentists, educators, parents, and others interested in the problem. It can then be resolved in a manner that will best meet the needs of the children.

DENVER PUBLIC SCHOOLS

APPOINTMENT FOR CARE AT SCHOOL DENTAL CLINIC

1350 Clarkson

Telephone 222-1055

PLEASE TAKE THIS APPOINTMENT WITH YOU TO THE CLINIC

Pupil's name_____ Room Number_____

Address_____

The above-named pupil has been approved for treatment at the school dental clinic and the "Parent Request" slip is on the Health Record. He/she is to begin such treatment on the date and at the hour stated below.

Date_____, 19_____   Hour_____

_____Nurse

_____School

IF FOR ANY REASON YOUR CHILD CANNOT KEEP HIS APPOINTMENT, NOTIFY THE DENTAL CLINIC IMMEDIATELY BY CALLING 222-1055.

Appointment for care at school dental clinic. (Denver Public Schools, Denver, Colo.)

SCOPE. The scope of the school dental program usually concerns itself with the dental inspections and prophylaxis or cleaning. There are a few schools, however, that treat emergency cases and provide other dental care for children of parents who cannot afford such services. Dental inspection may be used to determine dental needs, to help communities meet the needs, and for purposes of evaluating the dental health program.

DENTAL PROBLEMS. The problems concerned with dental health are dental caries, or decayed teeth; malocclusion, a condition in which the teeth do not uniformly fit together when the jaws are closed; and periodontal diseases in which the tissues surrounding the teeth become infected, such as gingivitis (inflammation of the gums) or Vincent's infection (trench mouth). Although dental caries is the most common problem, the others should receive due consideration.

Dental caries can best be prevented and controlled through good dental hygiene that includes frequent brushing, especially after eating; reducing sugar intake; topical fluoride applications; and fluoridation of water supplies, which experiments have shown reduces dental caries from 40% to 65%.

EDUCATIONAL IMPLICATIONS. The educational implications of dental health services are far reaching. Pupils and parents can be motivated to practice good oral hygiene and to visit their dentist regularly. The proper attitudes can be developed, resulting in good dental habits.

Screening for vision and hearing defects
Vision. Screening for vision requires a consideration of many factors.

VISION HEALTH SERVICES. The vision health services program in the school is concerned with the examinations given by physicians and appraisal of visual acuity. The appraisal of visual acuity is accomplished through continuous observations by the teacher and screening examinations. Both are necessary for the continual and satisfactory appraisal of the vision of school children.

FREQUENCY OF SCREENING TESTS. Tests of visual acuity should be given annually. The optimum time for such screening is immediately after the opening of school in the fall. They can be given to children in the early grades, as soon as they are old enough to cooperate satisfactorily. If possible, there should be a complete eye examination before the child enters school. A screening test for color acuity should be given during the early school years so that guidance can be given in regard to vocational opportunities.

ADMINISTRATION OF SCREENING TESTS. The teacher, after proper instruction and training, is qualified to administer various screening devices for vision. These devices, however, are only for purposes of detecting those individuals who need special care in respect to their vision. Their use is not a diagnostic technique.

SELECTION OF SCREENING DEVICES. The particular device that is utilized for checking visual acuity, together with the plans for appraisal, should be selected and arranged through conferences of school administrators, teachers, nurses, physicians, ophthalmologists, and optometrists.

It has been found that with young children, the Snellen E chart seems effective. For older children, the Snellen and Massachusetts Vision Tests have received wide recommendation. These devices should be administered according to prescribed instructions and pupils should be properly prepared for the examinations.

If needed, there are techniques for determining color acuity, such as the Holmgren test, and for determining muscle balance, such as the "cover test."

REFERRALS. The results of the screening examinations should be recorded and studied. In the light of these results and the teacher's observations, children with difficulties should be referred to the proper

DENVER PUBLIC SCHOOLS
Health Service Department

HOME REPORT ON VISION SCREENING

Date_____ School_____

Recently, _____
was given a vision screening test at school and seemed to have some visual
difficulty. Although glasses may not be needed, we urge you to have an
examination to recheck this condition. Would you please take this report
to an eye specialist to be completed so that it may be returned promptly to
the school nurse.

Thank you,

_____   _____
(Principal)   (School Nurse)

Report From Eye Specialist

I have examined the above pupil on _____ and found the

following eye condition:_____

_____

_____

My recommendations are:_____

_____

_____

_____   _____
(Date)   (Signature of Examiner)

Home report on vision screening. (Denver Public Schools, Denver, Colo.)

place for an eye examination. According to the Joint Committee of the National Education Association and the American Medical Association, "parents should be urged to secure eye examinations for children who are in the following categories: (1) those who consistently exhibit symptoms of visual disturbance, regardless of the results of the Snellen test, (2) older children (eight years and older) who have a visual acuity of 20/30 or less in either eye, with or without symptoms, and (3) younger children (seven years of age or less) who have a visual acuity of 20/40 or less in either eye, with or without symptoms."*

---

*Joint Committee of American Medical Association and National Education Association, op. cit., pp. 81-82.

DENVER PUBLIC SCHOOLS

Department of Health Service

PARENTS' NOTIFICATION OF VISION TEST

The school vision test of...
indicates that some difficulty with the vision exists. A more thorough examination should be made to determine the nature of the trouble and to make any correction, if such is necessary. If your child has not recently had his eyes tested by a doctor it would be advisable to consult your family physician.

School Nurse

Principal

FORM 973 DSP 6-51-50M P-312-36564

TEACHER'S OBSERVATIONS. The teacher as well as the parent should be alert to visual difficulties and problems among children. By being aware of certain actions and manifestations of the child from day to day under varying situations, it is possible to detect many eye difficulties that should be referred for examination. Many of these eye difficulties might go unnoticed unless the alert teacher or parent is aware of certain characteristics that indicate vision problems.

The Joint Committee has listed certain manifestations of visual difficulty in children before they begin to read and after reading activities have begun:

Before the child begins to read:
Attempts to brush away blur
Blinking more than usual
Frequent rubbing of the eyes
Squinting when looking at distant objects
Frequent or continuous frowning
Stumbling over small objects
Undue sensitivity to light
Red, encrusted, or swollen eyelids
Recurring styes
Inflamed or watery eyes

Crossed eyes, "wall" eye, or "wandering" eye (regardless of degree)
After reading activities have begun:
Holding a book too far away from or too close to the face when reading
Inattention during reading periods, chalkboard, chart or map work
Difficulty in reading or in other work requiring close use of the eyes
Inability, or lack of desire, to participate in games requiring distance vision
Poor alignment in written work
Tilting head to one side or thrusting head forward when looking at near or distant objects
Irritability when doing close work
Shutting or covering one eye when reading*

Hearing. Following are administrative guides for conduct of health services in regard to hearing.

SCOPE. The main responsibility of the schools in respect to auditory health services is to detect those pupils with hearing difficulties as early as possible. This can

---

*Joint Committee of American Medical Association and National Education Association, op. cit., p. 76.

be accomplished through such means as teacher observations and screening tests. A counseling and followthrough program that aims at remedying the defect should also be a part of the total plan.

FREQUENCY. Continuous observations should be a part of the school routine. Annual screening tests during the elementary years and one every 2 years at the secondary level are recommended. There should be a minimum of three tests during the first 8 years of school. It is also recommended that a preschool test of auditory acuity should be given wherever possible.

TECHNIQUE. The pure-tone audiometer is recommended as one of the most effective techniques for pupils of all school ages. This is a reliable instrument and allows for checking of either or both ears.

REFERRALS. Students with a hearing loss in one or both ears should be rechecked to determine the accuracy of screening. If results are consistent, parents should be informed and encouraged to follow through with more complete examination.

Teachers who observe mouth breathing, ear discharge, or other abnormalities or characteristics that might arouse suspicion of hearing loss should refer the case to the proper authorities.

TEACHER'S OBSERVATIONS. The teacher can play an important part in continually observing the child for indications of hearing loss. She is also a key person in administering screening techniques. She should be watchful for such mannerisms as speech difficulties, requests for repetition of questions, turning of head to better hear what is said, and inattention, together with such noticeable characteristics as discharging ears, earaches, and other departures from the normal makeup of the child. Through such observations the teacher will detect individuals who need to be referred for more careful study and examination. All teachers should be alert for such manifestations.

PERSONNEL. Teachers, nurses, or technicians may be utilized in administering the various screening devices. All should be well trained in the use and purpose of such instruments. They should recognize that these are screening instruments and not diagnostic devices. There should be a careful check to determine that the instruments are in good working order and yield accurate results.

Teachers' observations. Teachers' observations are of great importance in detecting the health needs of school children. Furthermore, they increase in importance in the absence of nurses and doctors. Although this subject has been discussed previously, it is of such great importance that it is considered again here in more detail. Teachers, through observations of the appearance and behavior of pupils from day to day, become very well acquainted with each individual child. Any deviations from normal in appearance and in action will be detected very quickly by the alert teacher. For many of the health needs this provides the only means of discovering problems. Very often they would not be detected through medical examinations and other health services. Therefore, the teacher's role in health services, through her continual association and observation of children, is a major one.

Such observations, after careful examination by nurses and physicians, may disclose various deficiencies. They may show that some children are maladjusted socially and emotionally, are undernourished, are in the early stages of a communicable or other disease, have some neurologic difficulties or other physical defects, or have developed poor health habits. Along with referral to nurses and physicians, the parents should also be informed of such discoveries. It should be reemphasized that in no case does the teacher diagnose. Instead, she refers the matter to the nurse, physician, and parent for further action.

The oft-quoted report from the health manual of the Massachusetts Department of Education and Department of Public Health* lists the various physical and behavior conditions for which the teacher should be alert in regard to the children with whom she associates each day:

1. *Eyes*
   a. Styes or crusted lids
   b. Inflamed eyes
   c. Crossed eyes
   d. Repeated headaches
   e. Squinting, frowning, or scowling
   f. Protruding eyes
   g. Watery eyes
   h. Rubbing of eyes
   i. Excessive blinking
   j. Twitching of the lids
   k. Holding head to one side

2. *Ears*
   a. Discharge from ears
   b. Earache
   c. Failure to hear questions
   d. Picking at the ears
   e. Turning the head to hear
   f. Talking in a monotone
   g. Inattention
   h. Anxious expression
   i. Excessive noisiness of child

3. *Nose and throat*
   a. Persistent mouth breathing
   b. Frequent sore throat
   c. Recurrent colds
   d. Chronic nasal discharge
   e. Frequent nose bleeding
   f. Nasal speech
   g. Frequent tonsillitis

4. *Skin and scalp*
   a. Nits on the hair
   b. Unusual pallor of face
   c. Eruptions or rashes
   d. Habitual scratching of scalp or skin
   e. State of cleanliness
   f. Excessive redness of skin

5. *Teeth and mouth*
   a. State of cleanliness
   b. Gross visible caries
   c. Irregular teeth
   d. Stained teeth

e. Offensive breath
f. Mouth habits such as thumb-sucking

6. *General condition and appearance*
   a. Underweight—very thin
   b. Overweight—very obese
   c. Does not appear well
   d. Tires easily
   e. Chronic fatigue
   f. Nausea or vomiting
   g. Faintness or dizziness

7. *Growth*
   a. Failure to gain regularly over 3-months' period
   b. Unexplained loss in weight
   c. Unexplained rapid gain in weight

8. *Glands*
   a. Enlarged glands at one side of neck
   b. Enlarged thyroid

9. *Heart*
   a. Excessive breathlessness
   b. Tires easily
   c. Any history of "growing pains"
   d. Bluish lips
   e. Excessive pallor

10. *Posture and musculature*
    a. Asymmetry of shoulders and hips
    b. Peculiarity of gait
    c. Obvious deformities of any type
    d. Anomalies of muscular development

11. *Behavior*
    a. Overstudious, docile, and withdrawing
    b. Bullying, overaggressive, and domineering
    c. Unhappy and depressed
    d. Overexcitable, uncontrollable emotions
    e. Stuttering or other forms of speech difficulty
    f. Lack of confidence, self-denial, and self-censure
    g. Poor accomplishment in comparison with ability
    h. Lying (imaginative or defensive)
    i. Lack of appreciation of property rights (stealing)
    j. Abnormal sex behavior
    k. Antagonistic, negativistic, continually quarreling

---

*Commonwealth of Massachusetts: Health in the schools—a manual of the school health program, Boston, 1951, Massachusetts Department of Education with the collaboration of Massachusetts Department of Public Health, pp. 23-24.

Health records. Following are some administrative guides in connection with health records:

1. As part of the overall school or college record, there should be a health record

that contains a complete appraisal of the student's health. This should include such items as health history, vision and hearing data, teacher's observations, results of various medical, psychologic, dental, and other examinations given, reports of all confer-ences held with student, health defects that have been corrected, and any other information that has a bearing on the health of the student.

2. The health record should follow the student wherever he goes—when he moves

---

HS-29
4-60-20M

COLUMBUS PUBLIC SCHOOLS
Elementary Immunization Record Card (K-6)

Name.. School.................................... Teacher.......................

Room.......................

This section pertains to pupils in **ALL GRADES.**	This section pertains to pupils in **ALL GRADES.**
SMALLPOX VACCINATION	**POLIOMYELITIS — 3 injections**
☐ Requirement met by a written statement of parent or physician, or by a scar	☐ School records show immunization completed
	☐ Completed by written statement of parent or physician
	☐ Received 1st injection................................ Date
	☐ Received 2nd injection (1-month interval)............ Date
	☐ Received 3rd injection (7-month interval)............ Date
This section pertains to all pupils in **GRADES K-2.**	This section pertains only to pupils in **GRADES 3-6** who did not receive injections for diphtheria and tetanus in grades K-2.
DIPHTHERIA, WHOOPING COUGH, TETANUS — 3 injections + 1 Booster	**DIPHTHERIA, TETANUS — 2 injections + 1 Booster**
☐ School records show immunization completed	
☐ Completed by written statement of parent or physician	☐ Completed by written statement of parent or physician
☐ Received 1st injection................................ Date	☐ Received 1st injection................................ Date
☐ Received 2nd injection (1-month interval)............ Date	☐ Received 2nd injection (1-month interval)............ Date
☐ Received 3rd injection (1-month interval)............ Date	☐ Received booster injection (1-year interval)............ Date
☐ Received booster injection (1-year interval)............ Date	

☐ Parental objection (written)

COLUMBUS PUBLIC SCHOOLS
Secondary Immunization Record Card (7-12)

Name.. School.................................... Teacher.......................

Room.......................

All **THREE** sections of this card pertain to **ALL PUPILS.**

(1) SMALLPOX VACCINATION

☐ Requirement met by a written statement of parent or physician, or by a scar

(2) POLIOMYELITIS — 3 injections	**(3) TETANUS — 2 injections plus 1 Booster**
☐ School records show immunization completed	☐ School records show immunization completed
☐ Completed by written statement of parent or physician	☐ Completed by written statement of parent or physician
☐ Received 1st injection................ Date	☐ Received 1st injection................ Date
☐ Received 2nd injection (1-month interval)............ Date	☐ Received 2nd injection (1-month interval)............ Date
☐ Received 3rd injection (7-month interval)............ Date	☐ Received booster injection (1-year interval)............ Date

☐ Parental objection (written)

from one community to another or when he is transferred from one school to another.

3. The records should be cumulative in nature, pointing out the complete health history of the student, together with a continuous appraisal of his health.

4. The health record should be made available to school or college medical and other personnel who are concerned with and who work toward the maintenance and improvement of a student's health. Professional ethics should govern the handling of such information.

5. The health record, if kept up to date and accurate, will prove a very useful and effective device in furthering the health of all students.

Health histories

1. The history of the student's health should be in recorded form as an aid to teachers, nurses, physicians, and others in order to understand better the total picture of the student's health.

2. This record should be kept on a prepared form and should contain a complete history of communicable diseases, operations, accidents, immunizations, dental history, emotional maladjustments, physical abnormalities, nutritional problems, athletic injuries, menstruation, and any other factors that would be of help in better interpreting the total health picture.

3. The health history should be brought up to date before the medical examination is given so that the examining physician may use it as an aid.

Height-weight records. Following are administrative guides in connection with height-weight records:

1. The teacher, or students under supervision, should measure and record the height and weight of pupils at least three times a year. It is recommended that this be done at the beginning, middle, and toward the end of the year.

2. Height-weight records should not be utilized as a device to diagnose such elements as nutritional status. Instead, they should be used as indications that some health problems may exist if, for example, a child's weight does not increase during

Form 750H 4M U—8-50

Name_____Adviser_____

Street_____ | Age_____Date of Birth_____

Village_____Tel. No._____ | School Year_____

New Trier Township High School
Winnetka, Illinois

TUBERCULIN TEST RECORD

Skin test given_____, Read_____, Result_____ _____M. D.
        (date)   (date)   (reading)   (signed)

X-Ray_____Film_____X-Ray by_____M. D.
    (date)   (number)

Report on | X-Ray Diagnosis
X-RAY FILM |

No._____ |
                Signed_____M. D.

To — New Trier Township High School:

    I hereby authorize the tuberculin test (and if advised by physicians) an X-Ray for my (son) (daughter)

_____to be done with the rest of the student body at New Trier High School as
        (child's name)   explained in your letter.

I prefer that the above described test NOT be given } _____ | _____ Signed_____
         (parent's signature)   (date)   (parent)

any 3-month period. They are best utilized not when compared against the height and weight of other children but when used as a comparison and history of a child's own growth from time to time.

3. Height-weight records provide an interesting and worthwhile phase of health education since students are interested in observing their growth and become curious as to some of the reasons that encourage or deter growth.

Accident records.* Accident records, as a means of health appraisal, provide information as to reasons for physical abnormalities and emotional maladjustment that may occur in children. They also provide a medium of promoting safety. They should be carefully kept and contain complete information.

Health counseling

In the light of the findings gathered through appraisal techniques, health matters are discussed with students and parents. Such problems as the need for medical and dental treatment, better health practices, diagnostic examinations, special services, and analysis of behavior problems are discussed. Through such counseling procedures a better understanding of the health of children and youth is achieved.

Health counseling is an important phase of the total health services program. As health needs and problems are revealed through medical examinations and other techniques, it is essential that defects be corrected, advice given, and a planned procedure established to provide for these needs and eliminate the problems. Health counseling by qualified persons can help in achieving these goals.

Purposes. One general objective of health counseling is to provide students and parents with a better understanding of their

health needs and the procedures that should be followed in order to satisfy these needs. Also, health counseling serves as a device for health education. Through conferences and discussion regarding health problems it is possible to develop sound health attitudes. Facts are presented that indicate the need for following acceptable health practices. The parent and student are motivated to alter their behavior in accordance with acceptable health standards. In addition, health counseling can help to develop a feeling of responsibility in pupils and parents for the correction of health defects and for promoting school and community health programs.

The objectives of health counseling have been well stated by the Joint Committee on Health Problems in Education of the National Education Association and the American Medical Association:

1. To give students as much information about their health status, as revealed by appraisal, as they can use to good advantage.
2. To interpret to parents the significance of health conditions and to encourage them to obtain needed care for their children.
3. To motivate students and their parents so that they will want and accept needed treatment and to accept desirable modifications of their school programs.
4. To promote each student's acceptance of responsibility for his own health, in keeping with his stage of maturity.
5. To encourage students and their parents to utilize available resources for medical and dental care to best possible advantage.
6. To encourage, if necessary, the establishment or enlargement of treatment facilities for students from needy families.
7. To contribute to the health education of students and parents.
8. To obtain for exceptional students educational programs adapted to their individual needs and abilities.*

---

*For further discussion of accident records see Chapter 18 on Legal Liability and Insurance Management.

*Reprinted with permission of the Joint Committee on Health Problems in Education of National Education Association and American Medical Association, School health services, Chicago, 1964, National Education Association and American Medical Association, pp. 111-112.

In utilizing counseling as part of the health services program, it should be clearly recognized that it has limitations. Counselors cannot always change individuals. This has been true, for example, of some handicapped individuals who are subject to pity, ridicule, or scorn by their fellow beings. Counselors can only help individuals to understand themselves, realize their potentialities, and live out their natural lives in a happy and productive manner. In some individuals, however, the social and physical environments have left their stamp so indelibly that counseling can do only a limited amount of good.

The counselor. The classroom teacher, school principal, physician, nurse, psychologist, physical education teacher, social worker, recreation leader, guidance person, and others have potentialities as counselors in the field of health. All have relationships with students that place them in a position to offer helpful advice and guidance. Whether or not they carry out such responsibilities effectively will depend on certain basic requirements.

Basic requirements for the counselors are concerned with their interest in people, personality, and competency in counseling skills.

To be effective, a counselor must be interested in people from the standpoint of service. The desire to help others live a happy and successful life and to help eliminate those problems that handicap the achievement of such goals must predominate in the counselor's mind.

A second basic requirement is the counselor's personality. Counseling procedure involves divulging personal problems and other matters that are brought out only when there is good rapport between the counselor and student or parent. Personality is a key to the establishment of a warm and cooperative counselor-client rapport. The counselor's personality must reflect such essentials as friendliness, interest in others' problems, and the desire to help.

He must be a good listener and respecter of the views of others. A good counselor does not talk down to the pupil but confers with the student in an atmosphere of mutual understanding and respect.

A third requirement is competency in counseling skills. As in all specialized services, there are certain competencies that are essential to doing a good job. Studies have shown that the person who has developed competency in counseling gets more effective results and does a better job than the unskilled individual. Skills are necessary in establishing rapport with clients, understanding the implications of behavior patterns, communicating with students, analyzing pupil problems, conducting group discussions, administering conference procedures, and preparing records.

Conference method. The conference method of counseling that brings about a face-to-face relationship between the counselor, the pupil, and the parent is the best method for achieving desirable results. The use of written notices and standard forms is not recommended because of the possibility of misinterpretation and the lack of a clear understanding of the problems involved.

The success of the conference method will depend on the skill and the degree to which the counselor has planned for the conference. It is essential that the counselor have all the necessary records at hand, together with a complete understanding of the community, home, and problems surrounding the pupil in question.

The counselor must establish the proper relationship among the individuals who are present. A friendly and understanding atmosphere is necessary for the achievement of the desired results. The discussion of health matters must be carried on effectively and in a sound manner so that the pupil and parent will recognize the problems that exist and endorse the action that must be taken. No school person engaged in health counseling should attempt to di-

REQUEST FOR HEALTH INFORMATION

DENVER PUBLIC SCHOOLS

CONFIDENTIAL: for Professional Use Only.

IDENTIFICATION OF PUPIL

TO:_____
Physician or Clinic

_____
Address

_____
Clinic Number

We would appreciate your answering the items checked below to help us plan the best school program for this pupil for these reasons:

_____
(Name)

_____
(Address)

_____
(School)   (Birth Date)

_____
(Father's Name)

_____
(Mother's Name)

Thank you,

_____ M.D.

Date of request_____

Director, School Health Services
414 Fourteenth Street, Denver, Colorado

_____ Diagnosis?_____

_____ Is treatment completed?_____

_____ May pupil have full school activities?_____

_____ If pupil should have limited physical activities, how limited and for how long?_____

_____ Any other suggestions for this child's program at school?_____

_____
Date of This Report   Signature of Physician

Request for health information. (Denver Public Schools, Denver, Colo.)

agnose diseases or select a physician or dentist for a pupil.

When the conference comes to an end there should be a common understanding among the counselor, pupil, and parent as to the next steps to be taken in the elimination of the health problems.

Correction of remediable defects

Two phases of school health services have been discussed. The student's health must first be appraised. Second, there must be a counseling procedure whereby the student and his parents are informed of health needs and problems so that the necessary action can be taken. After health appraisal and health counseling have been accomplished, the job is not completed. Next there must be a followthrough to see that remediable defects are corrected.

Students have many health defects that can be corrected. Dental caries is an example. It has been estimated that about 50% of 2-year-old children have one or more teeth that are carious. When they start school the number has risen to three and the number increases as the child progresses in school. In regard to vision defects it has been pointed out that eye problems increase from about 15% at 6 years of age to about 32% at 14 years of age.* Laxity in the correction of remediable defects seems to be especially prevalent in respect to teeth and eyes. There are also many other defects that can be corrected in the areas of malnutrition, hearing, speech, postural defects, diseased tonsils and adenoids, and emotional disorders.

The school has the responsibility for not only detecting such defects, whenever possible, but also putting forth every effort to see that they are corrected. The school's responsibility is to help every child attain optimum health; to encourage the removal of physical handicaps, defects, or anomalies that might constitute an obstacle to growth through correction or other helpful adjustment; and to guide parents, school staff, children, and others involved to a greater understanding of the factors related to better total health.

Community philosophy. The philosophy in respect to the methods that will be used to correct remediable defects will depend upon the community and the public at large. Although it is generally believed that the school should be concerned with educating parents and the public as to the importance of correcting such defects, rather

than with becoming a treatment agency, this belief and practice do not exist in all communities. Basically, the schools should not treat. They are not equipped with the personnel, facilities, and other necessities for such a purpose. However, it is a community prerogative to decide such an issue. As a result, in some communities the school provides for the correction of dental, nutritional, postural, and other defects. In other communities this is considered a parental responsibility, and the school takes over only when indigent parents cannot afford such services. In many communities the school does not treat in any way. The community must decide which method is most effective for the correction of defects.

Getting results. To obtain the best results in the correction of remediable defects, there must be planning, conferences, and accurate record keeping.

The teacher, nurse, health counselor, principal, and school physician should play active roles in planning such a program. A written plan should be developed and distributed so that all will be acquainted with the procedure that is to be followed. The responsibility for record keeping, home visitation, periodic checkups to see if defects have been corrected, and all other essential phases of the plan should be clearly designated. Good results will not be obtained if planning is a "hit-and-miss" affair. It will be effective only if it is done in advance of the detection of defects. If necessary, it should also be reviewed and amended periodically.

A second requisite for getting results is home and school conferences. As has been previously pointed out, written notices are cold and formal and do not achieve the desired results, as do personal conferences. If possible, the parents should come to the school for such purposes, since it helps to give the school prestige. However, where parents are reluctant to come to school, there should be visits to the home, preferably by the nurse. This also affords an op-

---

*Joint Committee of American Medical Association and National Education Association, op. cit., p. 72.

portunity to observe home conditions that affect the health of the child. At these conferences or visitations every attempt should be made to interest the pupil and the parent in the correction of the defects.

Two of the main reasons why health defects are not corrected are lack of money to provide the necessary service and indifference on the part of both pupil and parent. Conferences should aim at eliminating the indifference and attempting to provide the ways and means when the money problem exists. In most communities there are charitable organizations, civic groups, or others who will be happy to defray such expenses.

A third requirement for getting good results is accurate record keeping. As a part of health appraisal the defects should be properly recorded. It is essential to keep a record of all conferences and home visitations. Progress that has been made should be noted. Accurate and complete records will make it possible to know the current status of each pupil.

Community resources. Community resources should be tapped for aid in the correction of remediable defects. Public clinics, welfare agencies, and voluntary organizations should be utilized to give aid to indigent families where financial status prevents such treatment. A list of the hospitals, specialists, and clinics for various types of treatment could be provided when parents want additional information. In most cases it is better to suggest the names of several specialists rather than just one.

The school should work cooperatively with the various community agencies interested in this work. In some cases, time during the school day might be provided for students who must have treatment. Literature and other information prepared by various community agencies might be distributed. Meetings between leaders in the school and community agencies might be held to plan a program. A community health council is an ideal place for discussing and formulating plans for the correction of remediable defects. By mobilizing and utilizing community resources, remediable defects will be corrected.

Care and education of exceptional students*

The term *exceptional* refers to those students who are handicapped mentally, physically, socially, or emotionally and also to those who are gifted intellectually or in other ways.

A democratic society rests on the premise that all individuals should have equal opportunities to develop the various talents that they possess. This means that all children and youth in our schools should be granted the right to have an education adapted to their particular physical, mental, social, and emotional endowments. Therefore, whether an individual is gifted, normal, or handicapped, he should have the right to pursue the educational program that is best adapted to his particular needs and that enables him to achieve his potentialities as a human being. This is an important consideration in a democratic society that recognizes the worth of each individual and his right to "life, liberty, and the pursuit of happiness."

In any discussion of the care and education of the exceptional child, it is important to consider (1) identifying the exceptional student, (2) discovering the exceptional child, (3) adapting the educational program, and (4) discussing the personnel that should be concerned with the care and education of the exceptional student.

Who are the exceptional students? Exceptional children include those students with superior intellectual capacity, the mentally retarded, those with handicaps derived from physical defects or disease, and those who are emotionally disturbed or socially maladjusted.

---

*See also Chapter 8 on The Adapted Program.

According to one source,* out of every 1,000 students about 59 will have some physical handicap that requires special attention. These 59 can be broken down as follows: partially seeing and blind, 2; hard of hearing and deaf, 15; speech defective, 15; crippled, 10; lowered vitality, 15; and epileptic, 2. In the same group of 1,000 students, about 40 will deviate markedly in respect to mental ability.

The prevalence of exceptional school children is evident in every community. These children should be identified and referred for special services, and the educational program should be adapted to their needs and abilities.

Discovering the exceptional student. It is very important that each school develop a planned procedure for determining those pupils who are exceptional. It is very simple to identify some cases, such as those that are crippled, defective in their speech, or socially maladjusted. However, in others, where cardiac defects or tuberculosis causes the handicap, it is not as easy.

The exceptional child may be identified through the various phases of health appraisal that are conducted as part of the health services program. Through a thorough medical examination, the cardiac-handicapped student, for example, will be identified; through a psychologic examination the mentally or emotionally maladjusted pupil will be singled out; and through screening procedures, those with vision and hearing handicaps will be known.

The health history that should be a part of every student's health record is another source for information leading to the identification of exceptional characteristics. A health history that lists all the significant diseases, accidents, and other aspects of the health history of a child should also list any exceptional characteristics that exist.

---

*Joint Committee of American Medical Association and National Education Association, op. cit., p. 129.

Teachers' observations also play a very important part. Through continuous observations on the part of a teacher, deviations from normal behavior will be identified. The individual who is listless might require further examination, a child who displays exceptional talent might be a genius in the class, or a child who finds it difficult to keep up with other boys his age in physical education activities should have further attention. Many of the children who fall into the exceptional group will have to be identified by teachers who work with them every day if they are to be singled out for special help.

Conferences with parents, teacher conferences with the school nurse, certain classroom tests, and reports from family physicians will help to identify exceptional individuals.

All of these methods should be carefully considered as potential media for identifying the many exceptional children who are regularly attending the public schools.

Adapting the educational program to the exceptional student. Some administrative guides for adapting the educational program and caring for the exceptional child are suggested here:

1. The school, as a general rule, should not undertake the treatment of handicapped students. However, it should do everything within its power to see that the necessary medical care is provided those who need such service. Through its referral service the school can carry out this responsibility.

2. Exceptional pupils should be treated as individuals rather than dealt with as groups of children with similar characteristics. Consideration should be given to each student.

3. Whether or not the exceptional individual is part of the regular group in the school situation, a part of a separate group, or in a separate school will depend upon the individual. The decision should be based on the question of which situa-

tion will allow the greatest possibility for improvement of the child's condition and for his total growth and development.

4. Special classes will aid certain individuals such as students who are hard of hearing, have speech and visual defects, and are severely crippled, homebound, or mentally retarded.

5. There is a need for an adequate supervisory program in connection with special classes for exceptional children. Good supervision will ensure periodic examinations to determine the status of the individual in respect to his exception, make

sure that the program is as much like a regular school program as possible, and see that the child is returned to the regular class with normal children as soon as possible.

6. There are many different courses of action for the education and care of exceptional students. A few methods for making provisions for the various classifications are listed. This listing, however, is in no way complete, and special resources should be consulted for a more complete description of the school's responsibility.

The *deaf*, when so classified by a com-

The school should do everything within its power to help obtain the necessary medical care for the handicapped child. (United States Office of Education, Department of Health, Education, and Welfare.)

The orthopedically handicapped child. (United States Office of Education, Department of Health, Education, and Welfare.)

petent specialist, are those that have a hearing loss of 70 decibels or more. Generally, they should be placed in special schools.

The education and care of the *hard of hearing* will vary with hearing loss (slight —loss of 20 to 30 decibels; mild to moderate—loss of 30 to 40 decibels; moderate to severe—loss of 40 to 70 decibels; and severe—loss of more than 70 decibels). Provisions can be made, such as special arrangements for seating and instruction, hearing aids, speech and lipreading, special classes, and special schools.

The *blind* (20/200 in better eye with glasses) may be provided for either by a special school or by special classes where braille is used.

The *partially sighted* (between 20/70 and 20/200 with glasses) can be provided for by proper fitting of correct glasses, sight-saving classes, provision within regular classroom, proper seating, advantageous scheduling of classes, and special materials, such as typewriters.

The *orthopedically handicapped* child should be cared for in regular classes whenever it is possible. Special provisions for children handicapped in this group include: "(1) transportation in school buses with an attendant, (2) physical and occupational therapy, (3) speech therapy, if needed, and (4) general health supervision by the teacher under the general direction of the school medical adviser and nurse, if such are available."*

The *speech defective* student's first need is a complete examination with medical and surgical care, if necessary, to remove the cause of the speech defect. Speech defects such as stuttering, stammering, and phonetic difficulties can be aided through work with a speech correctionist, especially in the case of young children. Special classes are usually not needed; the student can attend regular classes and get the necessary treatment at a speech clinic or other place.

Malnourished and *undervitalized* children will usually be cared for on both an individual and a community basis. Health education aimed at raising the nutritional status of the home, a careful perusal of health histories to identify the causes, adjustment of the school program, and in some cases provision for special rest rooms will contribute to the solution of the defects.

The *mentally retarded* child (50 to 70 intelligence quotient, or I.Q.) should have a program that stresses, according to his individual abilities, proper health, safety, and social habits; information and skills essential to constructive community living, such as care of children, proper maintenance of the home, and the community health resources that are available; and skills for creative and leisure-time activities that will lead to cultural development.†

The *mentally gifted* child (I.Q. of approximately 140 or over) has been helped in at least four ways: (1) an accelerated program adapted according to his ability to achieve higher standards, (2) enrichment of his curriculum so that it is adapted more to his abilities, (3) attendance in special classes, and (4) addition of elective courses.*

Cardiac-handicapped children should be provided for after complete examination by competent medical personnel. A few will require special classes, others will require modified programs, and some will need instruction to help them understand and live within certain restrictions.

The *tubercular-handicapped* child, if he has a case of active tuberculosis, should not be in school. The school programs for children who have had the disease should be adapted to their needs. This should be done in consultation with the appropriate medical person. This may mean only part-time attendance at school, provision for rest periods, limited physical activity, and special transportation.

Emotionally atypical students should be provided for in relation to their maladjustments. Some will need the help of a qualified psychologist or psychiatrist. Others will be helped by the guidance counselor or teacher. In most cases the teacher can play a key role in providing an emotional atmosphere where the child reacts favorably to the group.

The *socially exceptional* should also be provided for in relation to the extent of their maladjustments. Children with the most severe cases will need confinement to institutions; the rest will need rehabilitation, care, or developmental opportunities to restore them to normalcy.

The National Committee on School Health Policies points out other ways that the school can make special provisions for handicapped pupils:

Specially constructed chairs and desks—for the orthopedically disabled children.
Appropriate seating arrangements—"down front" for children with vision or hearing defects.
Provision of hearing aids.
Scheduling of classes all on one floor.

---

*Joint Committee of American Medical Association and National Education Association, op. cit., p. 136.
†Ibid., p. 143.

*Ibid., p. 145.

Rest periods and facilities (cots) for resting—for children with cardiac and other impairments.

Permission to attend school for only part of the day.

Adaptation of physical education requirements.

Transportation to and from school.*

Such provisions enable many handicapped pupils to attend regular classes.

Personnel. The teachers who work with exceptional children should be well trained for their duties. Whether or not the child is able to adjust satisfactorily to the group, improve, and be educated and cared for in a desirable manner will depend to a great degree upon the teacher.

Teachers should be well prepared for the particular grade or subject to which they are assigned. In addition, they should be trained to work with exceptional children with specific disabilities. The nature or type of disability will determine the training needed. The teacher should be emotionally stable and have the type of temperament that is suitable for working with abnormal children. The size of classes for exceptional children should be smaller than for regular classes. If progress is to be achieved, the individual approach must be applied as much as possible.

In addition to the teacher, there are other individuals in the school and community who can render contributions to this phase of the health service program. Where they are part of the school staff, the nurse, guidance director, school physician, psychologist, social worker, and director of special education should work closely with the teacher and school administrator in planning the program. Other individuals, such as ophthalmologists, psychiatrists, orthopedists, speech correctionists, otologists, directors of agencies dealing with the handicapped, and members of state de-

partments of health and education, should be utilized for advice, planning, referrals, inservice education, and other contributions to this phase of the health service program.

Communicable disease control

Whenever students congregate there is the possibility of spreading disease. The school, as a place for children and youth to congregate, is unique in that the law requires attendance. Therefore, if it is compulsory to go to school, there should also be certain protective measures and precautions taken to ensure that everything is done to guard the health of the child. This includes the necessary procedures for controlling communicable disease. Although students are not required to go to college, higher educational institutions also have the responsibility for communicable disease control.

The problem of communicable disease control can be discussed under two main headings, first, responsibility, and second, the various measures that should be applied in the school situation.

Responsibility. The legal responsibility for communicable disease control rests with state and local departments of health. This means that public health officials have control over school and college personnel in this matter. In most cases, however, this is a case of cooperation rather than compulsion. School and college officials should work closely with public health officials so that cases of communicable disease are reported and proper measures taken to prevent other children from contracting the disease.

The responsibility for communicable disease control falls upon many individuals. These include public health personnel, school and college administrative personnel, nurse, school physician, teacher, custodian, and the parent. The teacher, parent, and nurse must be continually vigilant to notice symptoms of various communicable

---

*National Committee on School Health Policies: Suggested school health policies, ed. 3, Chicago, 1962, American Medical Association, p. 31.

diseases, isolate such individuals immediately, and refer these cases to the school, college, or family physician. There must be close cooperation among these three since all three play key roles in the control of communicable diseases. If the parent plays his or her role effectively and the child is isolated immediately, he will lessen considerably the exposure of other individuals to disease. If the child is in school, the alert teacher and nurse will take the necessary precautions.

The superintendent, principal, university physician, and other administrative officers have the responsibility for establishing policy, working cooperatively with public health officials, providing encouragement and inservice training for teachers, and developing among parents and the public in general an understanding that will be most conducive to communicable disease control.

The custodian, through his or her control over the sanitation of the equipment and facilities, can perform his responsibilities so effectively that a healthful environment is always in evidence and thus the spread of disease is decreased.

The school or college physician should

DENVER PUBLIC SCHOOLS
Department of Health Service

HOME CONTROL OF COMMUNICABLE DISEASES

TO PARENTS:

The control of communicable ("catching") diseases during the school year is a difficult problem and a grave responsibility for both parents and school. The first responsibility must fall upon the home. In addition to knowing your children are immunized against those communicable diseases which are preventable, the following information is given to help control acute illnesses. Because parents know the normal appearance of their children they should be the first to detect signs of illness.

1. Observe your child every morning and **do not send him to school if he shows any signs of illness.** Keep an ill child at home for his own safety as well as the safety of other children.

2. **Do not send a sick child to school** for the nurse or teacher to decide whether he should be in school. If in doubt, keep him at home, and when necessary call the family doctor.

3. Keep your child away from sick persons.

4. If your child is sick, keep other children away from him.

Some of the signs and symptoms of acute illness are:

1. Restlessness at night. (This is often the first sign of an acute illness.)
2. Running nose.
3. Sneezing and coughing.
4. Sore throat.
5. Rash.
6. Vomiting.
7. Red, watery eyes.
8. Flushed face.
9. Headache.
10. Unusually tired.

The cooperation of all parents is sincerely requested.

L. M. CORLISS, M.D.
Director of Health Service

STOCK NO. 10871
FORM 971 DSP

Enlisting parental support in communicable disease control.

advise the teacher, nurse, administrative officers, and others who are closely related to the whole problem of communicable disease control as to the necessary measures that should be provided. Through his specialized knowledge, he can contribute much toward the establishment of an effective and workable plan.

Control measures. There are many control measures that every school or college should follow to prevent the spread of disease. Some of the more important of these measures are discussed here.

*Healthful environment.** Some of the provisions for a healthful environment that are necessary for the control of communicable disease include sufficient space to avoid undue crowding, adequate toilet and washroom facilities, proper ventilation and heating, safe running water, properly installed drinking fountains, use of pasteurized milk, a system of exclusions and control of admissions for students who may have communicable disease, and policies toward student and teacher absences that do not require teachers to be in school when they may be ill and capable of spreading communicable disease germs.

Isolation of students. The student who is a "suspect" in regard to some communicable disease should immediately be isolated from the group. Isolating a student does not constitute diagnosis. The details and procedures followed in each school or college regarding isolation should be in writing and clearly understood by all concerned. The adopted plan should have the approval of the health service staff.

The teacher should be continually on the lookout for "suspects." Some indications of communicable disease that should be recognized by the teacher are the following:

Unusual pallor or flushed face
Unusual listlessness or quietness
Red or watery eyes
Eyes sensitive to light

Skin rash
Cough
Need for frequent use of toilet
Nausea or vomiting
Running nose or sniffles
Excessive irritability
Jaundice*

After the teacher isolates the "suspect" from the group, the student should not be left alone. Furthermore, the nurse or school or college physician should be notified. In the event neither of these individuals is available, the teacher and school administrator must decide on exclusion. The best solution is to arrange for the student to return to his home or to be sent to the infirmary, where the services of a physician should be procured as soon as possible. Furthermore, the case should be reported to the local health authorities.

Readmitting students to school or college. After having a communicable disease a student should not be readmitted to school or college until it is certain that his return is in the best interests of the health of both the student concerned and also the other students with whom he will come in contact. There should be strict conformance to the law that governs communicable diseases. In addition, there should be approval for such readmission indicated in writing by a qualified physician or the local health department. In minor cases a note from the parent or the decision of the nurse or other staff member may suffice.

Immunization. Every student should receive immunization against preventable diseases. Most of this should be done in the preschool years when danger from such diseases is prevalent. Every child should be immunized against tetanus, poliomyelitis, diphtheria, smallpox, and whooping cough. The school can play an important part in the health education of parents to see that children are immunized

---

*See also Chapter 14.

*Joint Committee of American Medical Association and National Education Association, op. cit., p. 210.

against these diseases before starting school. The children who come to school and have not received the benefit of such services need special attention. It is a public health and medical problem and should be dealt with through members of these professions. If the community decides that the school is the best place for immunization, the school should cooperate fully and keep complete records on initial immunizations and booster doses. Written permission should be secured from parents concerned.

Attendance. There should not be an overemphasis on perfect attendance for school children. This often results in children coming to school regardless of the condition of their health and the danger to others. Furthermore, state aid should be based on some method other than attendance.

Epidemics. The viewpoint on closing schools and colleges during epidemics has changed somewhat in recent years. Formerly, it was generally believed that schools should be closed. Today, it is felt that under many circumstances they should remain open. The deciding factor is whether or not the school provides regular inspections, observations, adequate staff, and facilities to screen out those who indicate signs of having the disease. If this service can be performed and if the closing of schools will result in many contacts on playgrounds and other places where children congregate, then, according to the latest thinking, the schools should remain open. This is particularly true in urban areas. Many times in rural areas, where children will not come in contact with each other if schools are closed, it may be advisable to have schools closed.

If an epidemic occurs during a vacation period it is often wise to postpone the opening of school, since such opening might result in increased contact with the disease.

Emergency care

Elementary and secondary schools are responsible for providing each student with the necessary protection and care. The school acts in loco parentis (in place of the parent) and it is assumed that the child will receive the same care and protection

---

SAN FRANCISCO DEPARTMENT OF PUBLIC HEALTH
IMMUNIZATION AND TEST CONSENT

Date_____

Name_____ Address_____ Phone No._____

School_____ Grade_____ Room_____ Phy. Ed. Period_____ P.E. Teacher_____ Birthdate_____

In looking over your child's health record, it is recommended that the following immunizations and/or tests be given. Please sign your name opposite the recommended procedure if you wish your child to have the benefit of the test or immunization.

If your child has had a positive Tuberculin Test in the past, it will probably remain positive and should not be repeated. If your child's test was ever positive, please indicate when or approximately when

Negative Tuberculin Tests may be repeated yearly.

F 1515 1-56

Immunizations and Tests	Recommended	Parent's Signature
Smallpox Vaccination		
Diphtheria Pertussis Tetanus } D.P.T.		
Polio Vaccination		
Tuberculin Test		

PLEASE RETURN TO PUBLIC HEALTH NURSE

Table 13-2. First-aid supplies and how to use them*

Suggested supplies	What they are for
Tincture of green soap	Washing injured parts
Hospital cotton, roll	Large soft pads or dressings
Absorbent cotton, sterilized, roll, box or "picking" package	Swabs or pledgets for applying medication or wiping wounds
Dressings, large or small pads, sterilized, in individual transparent envelopes	For protecting injuries
Dressings, finger, in envelopes	For protecting very small injuries
Adhesive tape, roll, one inch	Fastening dressings, or splints
Scissors, bandage or blunt	Cutting dressings
Toothpicks	For making swabs
Alcohol 70% (water 30%) or rubbing alcohol	Disinfecting skin and minor wounds
Mercurochrome, 2% aqueous	Minor injuries especially in young children
Other disinfectant, if ordered by physician	As ordered by physician
Mineral oil, bottle, or petroleum jelly, tube or jar, white or yellow, but not medicated	For removing ointments; in eye to relieve irritation from foreign body; for burns if no other ointment is at hand
Boric acid ointment U.S.P.	For very small minor first-degree burns only
Epsom salts	In hot water, a handful to a basin, for soaking sprains, bruises, or infection when ordered by a physician
Baking soda, powder	Teaspoonful to a pint of warm water for mouthwash, or gargle if ordered
Salt, crystal or tablets	Same as baking soda, or with baking soda as directed
Hot-water bottle with cover	Local relief of pain
Ice bag	Local relief of pain
Two warm blankets	For prevention of chilling
Tourniquet (three feet of soft rubber tubing and a stick or pencil)	USE ABOVE place from where red blood spurts. Call doctor at once. Release every 15 minutes to allow circulation to reach parts, then reapply if necessary
Eye droppers	Dropping liquid medicines. Cleanse after using and boil before using
Ear syringe, soft rubber	For ears only when ordered by physician
Graduated medicine glass†	For measuring liquid medicines
Drugs for internal use	Only when ordered by physician and as directed by him

*From American Association of School Administrators: Health in schools, Twentieth Yearbook, Washington, D. C., 1951, National Education Association, pp. 394-395. (Prepared by American Medical Association.)

†Graduated medicine glass is most accurate and should be used whenever possible. In emergency, this table may be used:

20 drops (water solution)	1 c.c. (metric)
1 teaspoon (measuring spoon, not table silver)	5 c.c.
1 tablespoon (measuring spoon, not table silver)	15 c.c.
1 wineglass	50 c.c.
1 tumbler	250 c.c.

during the hours of school that he normally would receive at home. Children often become sick or injured during school hours. Therefore, the school must provide the necessary attention until this can be undertaken by the parents.

According to the Joint Committee on Health Problems, the school has four responsibilities in respect to emergency care procedures. These are "(1) giving immediate care, (2) notifying the pupil's parents, (3) arranging for the pupil to get home, and, (4) guiding parents, when necessary, to sources of treatment."*

Some administrative guides for emergency care are as follows:

1. Every school and college should have a written plan for emergency care. It should be carefully prepared by the school administration with the help of the school or college physician, parents, medical and dental professions, hospitals, nurse, teachers, and others interested and responsible in this area. The time to plan and decide on procedure is before an accident occurs. This should be one of the first administrative responsibilities that is accomplished.

The written plan should contain such essentials as first-aid instructions; procedures for getting medical help, transportation, and notifying parents; staff responsibilities, supplies, equipment, and facilities available; and any other information that will help clarify exactly what is to be done in time of emergency.

The plan should be reviewed periodically and revised so that it is continually up to date. It should be posted in conspicuous places and discussed periodically with school staff and community groups, whenever necessary.

2. As many staff members as possible should be trained in first-aid procedures. There is a need for special knowledge and training in respect to emergency care that might entail first aid for broken bones, use of artificial respiration, control of hemorrhage, and proper care of patients suffering from shock. The more staff members that are trained in these specific first-aid procedures, the better coverage there is for accidents that may occur at any time when school activities are in progress.

Some schools have the American Red Cross give inservice courses in first-aid procedures. Such inservice training will help to ensure that the staff is competent along this line.

When a nurse is on duty it would usually be expected that her responsibility includes seeing that proper first-aid procedures are carried out.

Professional preparation institutions should give due consideration to instruction in first-aid and emergency care procedures as part of the training of all teachers and school and college personnel.

3. A health room for first aid and emergency care should be available.* It should possess the necessary equipment and supplies; have good lighting; be clean, of adequate size, and always available for emergency cases.

A basic list of first-aid supplies, together with a statement as to what they are for, has been developed by the American Medical Association. See p. 380.

In addition to furniture and routine equipment, the health room should also have available as a minimum the following:

Stethoscope	Tuning fork for
Thermometer, clinical	hearing tests
Sphygmomanometer	Mouth mirror
Electric ophthalmoscope	Probes, dental
Electric otoscope	Forceps
Reflex hammer	Syringes
Tape measure	Needles
Platform scale	Eye droppers
(not a spring model)	Graduated medicine
Illuminated eye	glasses
test charts	

*Joint Committee of American Medical Association and National Education Association, op. cit., pp. 222-223.

*See description in Chapter 15.

first aid chart for athletic injuries

FIRST AID, the immediate and temporary care offered to the stricken athlete until the services of a physician can be obtained, minimizes the aggravation of injury and enhances the earliest possible return of the athlete to peak performance. To this end, it is strongly recommended that:

ALL ATHLETIC PROGRAMS include prearranged procedures for obtaining emergency first aid, transportation, and medical care.

ALL COACHES AND TRAINERS be competent in first aid techniques and procedures.

ALL ATHLETES be properly immunized as medically recommended, especially against tetanus and polio.

Committee on the
Medical Aspects of Sports
AMERICAN MEDICAL ASSOCIATION

to protect the athlete at time of injury, FOLLOW THESE FIRST STEPS FOR FIRST AID

STOP play immediately at first indication of possible injury or illness.

LOOK for obvious deformity or other deviation from the athlete's normal structure or motion.

LISTEN to the athlete's description of his complaint and how the injury occurred.

ACT, but move the athlete *only* after serious injury is ruled out.

BONES AND JOINTS

fracture Never move athlete if fracture of back, neck, or skull is suspected. If athlete *can* be moved, carefully splint any possible fracture. Obtain medical care at once.

dislocation Support joint. Apply ice bag or cold cloths to reduce swelling, and refer to physician at once.

bone bruise Apply ice bag or cold cloths and protect from further injury. If severe, refer to physician.

broken nose Apply cold cloths and refer to physician.

HEAT ILLNESSES

heat stroke Collapse—with dry warm skin—indicates sweating mechanism failure and rising body temperature. THIS IS AN EMERGENCY; DELAY COULD BE FATAL. Immediately cool athlete by the most expedient means (immersion in cool water is best method). Obtain medical care at once.

heat exhaustion Weakness—with profuse sweating—indicates state of shock due to depletion of salt and water. Place in shade with head level or lower than body. Give sips of dilute salt water. Obtain medical care at once.

sunburn If severe, apply sterile gauze dressing and refer to physician.

IMPACT BLOWS

head If any period of dizziness, headache, incoordination or unconsciousness occurs, disallow any further activity and obtain medical care at once. Keep athlete lying down; if unconscious, give nothing by mouth.

teeth Save teeth, if completely removed from socket. If loosened, do not disturb; cover with sterile gauze and refer to dentist at once.

solar plexus Rest athlete on back and moisten face with cool water. Loosen clothing around waist and chest. Do nothing else except obtain medical care if needed.

testicle Rest athlete on back and apply ice bag or cold cloths. Obtain medical care if pain persists.

eye If vision is impaired, refer to physician at once. With soft tissue injury, apply ice bag or cold cloths to reduce swelling.

MUSCLES AND LIGAMENTS

bruise Apply ice bag or cold cloths and rest injured muscle. Protect from further aggravation. If severe, refer to physician.

cramp Have opposite muscles contracted forcefully, using firm hand pressure on cramped muscle. If during hot day, give sips of dilute salt water. If recurring, refer to physician.

strain and sprain Elevate injured part and apply ice bag or cold cloths. Apply pressure bandage to reduce swelling. Avoid weight bearing and obtain medical care.

OPEN WOUNDS

heavy bleeding Apply sterile pressure bandage using hand pressure if necessary. Refer to physician at once.

cut and abrasion Hold briefly under cold water. Then cleanse with mild soap and water. Apply sterile pad firmly until bleeding stops, then protect with more loosely applied sterile bandage. If extensive, refer to physician.

puncture wound Handle same as cuts; refer to physician.

nosebleed Keep athlete sitting or standing; cover nose with cold cloths. If bleeding is heavy, pinch nose and place *small* cotton pack in nostrils. If bleeding continues, refer to physician.

OTHER CONCERNS

blisters Keep clean with mild soap and water and protect from aggravation. If already broken, trim ragged edges with sterilized equipment. If extensive or infected, refer to physician.

foreign body in eye Do not rub. Gently touch particle with point of clean, moist cloth and wash with cold water. If unsuccessful or if pain persists, refer to physician.

lime burns Wash thoroughly with water. Apply sterile gauze dressing and refer to physician.

EMERGENCY PHONE NUMBERS

Physician	Phone:	
Physician	Phone:	
Hospital	Ambulance	
Police	Fire	Other

The staff responsible for the health room should be fixed and such responsibility should include training and competency in first-aid procedures.

4. Proper emergency equipment and supplies, in addition to being located in the health room, should also be available in strategic school or college locations that are accident-prone because of activity courses and in places remote from the health room. Such locations might include gymnasium, laboratories, shops, school buses, annexes, and buildings housing school activities apart from the central unit.

5. School and college records should contain complete information on each student. This might include such information as his address; parent's name, address, and phone number; business address of parent and phone number; family physician, address, and phone number; family dentist, address, and phone number; parent instruction in case of emergency; choice of hospital; and any other pertinent information.

6. There should be a complete record of every accident, including first aid given and emergency care administered in the event of illness. Such information preserves for future reference the procedures followed in each case. This record is very important in the event questions arise in the future. Time results in forgetfulness, misinterpretation, misunderstanding, and inaccurate conclusions being drawn. Records can also be used to disclose hazards that should be eliminated and weak spots in procedures for emergency care that should be improved. Finally, such records aid in impressing upon students, staff, parents, and other individuals who are concerned the importance of good procedures for safe and healthful living.

7. The legal aspects of problems involved in regard to emergency care should be discussed and understood by the entire school or college staff. Such discussion will make for a better understanding of the laws of a particular state or locality and show the importance of avoiding negligence in duty.

8. Insurance plans for staff, athletes, and students should be made clear. They should be in writing and well publicized so that each individual will know the extent to which expenses, claims, and other items will be paid in event of accident, or the extent to which he can or should procure additional coverage.

9. Disasters in the form of fires, floods, tornadoes, and air raids can occur at any time. In order to provide proper emergency care under such circumstances, there must be advance planning. Schools and colleges should recognize their responsibility along this line. Adequate insurance coverage should be maintained. Supplies for emergency care should be on hand. Responsibilities should be fixed in key positions. Plans should be laid for taking children to safest place possible. Drills should be conducted. Close cooperation should exist between the schools and such organizations as Civil Defense or the Red Cross.

Environmental sanitation

Another health service responsibility of schools and colleges is that of ensuring a sanitary environment. Since many aspects of this topic are covered in Chapter 14, as well as earlier in this chapter, it will be discussed only briefly here. Some aspects of environmental sanitation that need particular attention are the school's or college's responsibility for ensuring a safe water supply; sanitary sewage disposal; and cafeterias, kitchens, locker rooms, showers, and swimming pools.

If desirable environmental sanitation standards are adhered to, it will not only help to reduce the incidence of the spread of disease but also will be conducive to a more comfortable, pleasant environment that will contribute to optimum learning.

Health of school and college personnel

Educational organizations need to give attention to the health of school and college personnel in order to ensure the most efficient carrying out of duties by teachers, administrators, and other members of the staff; to provide examples for children and young people that are worth emulating; and to promote the most healthful and pleasant environment possible. Boards of education, boards of trustees, and other persons who are involved in making pertinent decisions, therefore, need to concern themselves with such matters as sick leave, health insurance, sabbatical leaves, retirement provisions, maternity leaves, medical examinations, exclusion from school or college of teachers with health conditions that have implications for students' health and well-being, and other matters that concern the health of all employees of the school district or college. The health of school and college personnel is as important a consideration as health of school and college students.

Questions and exercises

1. What are the component parts of a school or college health service program? What is the importance to the student of each part?
2. What is the relationship between health services and the other phases of the school or college health program?
3. Prepare a speech to be given in class that could be used to point out to the parent-teacher association the importance of the development of a desirable health services program.
4. What should be the relationship between the public health department and the school or college health department in relation to school health services?
5. Discuss the advantages and disadvantages of the theory: "The school is a place for both education and treatment."
6. Outline what you consider to be a sound health appraisal program for an elementary school.
7. Describe the nature and scope of the school medical examination. Relate how it can be an educational experience for boys and girls.
8. Prepare a list of arguments to be presented to the board of education to justify the addition of a psychologist to the school staff.
9. What part do the teacher's observations play in a health services program? What are his or her responsibilities in the matter?
10. Identify pure-tone audiometer, whisper test, Massachusetts Vision Test, caries, Snellen E Chart, followthrough, and exceptional child.
11. What are the essential health records that should be maintained to conduct a desirable health services program?
12. Prepare a mock health counseling conference with a child and his mother after a medical examination that has revealed several defects that need correction.
13. What recommendations could you make in order to ensure the greatest possible correction of remediable health defects?
14. Take one type of exceptional child, do considerable research on the type of educational program that is best suited to this particular individual, and make recommendations to the class.
15. After careful study of all factors involved, outline a program for a particular community as to how the public health department and school health education division can most effectively work together for communicable disease control.
16. Prepare a written plan for emergency care of injuries for your school or college, which will then be submitted to the class for approval and then presented to the school health services division of your institution for comment.

Reading assignment in *Administrative Dimensions of Health and Physical Education Programs, Including Athletics:* Chapter 10, Selections 55 to 58.

Selected references

Committee on the Medical Aspects of Sports of the American Medical Association: The team physician, The Journal of School Health 37:497, 1967.

Corliss, L. M.: Multiple handicapped children—their placement in the school education program, The Journal of School Health 37:113, 1967.

Day, H. P.: University administration views the health service, American College Health Association Journal 15:140, 1966.

DeBoer, L.: Application of screening method for the detection of heart disease in children, Journal of School Health 33:81, 1962.

Eiserer, P. E.: The school psychologist, New York, 1963, The Center for Applied Research in Education, Inc. (The Library of Education).

Ferguson, D. G.: Pupil personnel services, New

York, 1963, The Center for Applied Research in Education, Inc. (The Library of Education).

Forbes, O.: The role and functions of the school nurse as perceived by 115 public school teachers from three selected counties, The Journal of School Health 37:101, 1967.

Gibbons, H.: Recognizing the educational implications of visual problems, Journal of School Health 32:280, 1962.

Goolishian, H. A.: School health services, The Journal of School Health 44:313, 1968.

Hein, F. V.: Health classification vs. medical excuses from physical education, Journal of School Health 32:14, 1962.

Joint Committee on Health Problems in Education of National Education Association and American Medical Association: Health appraisal of school children, ed. 2, Washington, D. C., 1961, National Education Association.

Joint Committee on Health Problems in Education of National Education Association and American Medical Association: Health education, Washington, D. C., 1961, National Education Association.

Joint Committee on Health Problems in Education of National Education Association and American Medical Association: School health services, ed. 2, Washington, D. C., 1964, National Education Association.

Kleinschmidt, E. E.: Current problems in school health service, Journal of School Health 32:222, 1962.

Lampe, J.: For the medical director, Journal of School Health 32:269, 1962.

Lowman, L.: A message to school health services, Journal of School Health 32:17, 1962.

National Committee on School Health Policies: Suggested school health policies, ed. 3, Chicago, 1962, American Medical Association.

Neilson, E. A.: Health education and the school physician, The Journal of School Health 39:377, 1969.

Ryan, A. J.: Providing medical services for athletes, School Activities, November, 1967.

Schneeweiss, S. M., and Locke, A.: New horizons in school health services: the computer, The Journal of School Health 37:349, 1967.

Shaffer, T. E.: What health services do school-age children need? Journal of the American Association for Health, Physical Education, and Recreation 23:16, 1962.

Tower, B., and Fay, P.: Can contracted school health services work? The Journal of School Health 38:339, 1968.

Wetzel, N. C.: New dimensions in the simultaneous screening and assessment of school children, Journal of Health, Physical Education, and Recreation, vol. 37, January, 1966.

Yankauer, A., Jr., and others: Study of case-finding methods in elementary schools; methodology and initial results, American Journal of Public Health 53:656, 1962.

A healthful school or college environment means not only having safe physical facilities, proper equipment, water, and other essentials, but it also means having a healthful psychologic environment where students benefit from practices and conditions conducive to their mental and emotional health. Therefore, this chapter concerns itself with both the physical and psychologic environment.

THE PHYSICAL ENVIRONMENT

The general health features of the physical environment will be discussed here under the following headings: site, building, lighting, heating and ventilation, furniture, plant sanitation, and acoustics.

Site

There are many aspects to consider in the selection of a suitable site. These considerations will differ, depending on the community. Whether it is a rural or an urban community will have a bearing on the location of the site. In an urban community it is desirable to have the school situated near transportation facilities, but at the same time located away from industrial concerns, railroads, noise, heavy traffic, fumes, and smoke. Consideration should be given to the trends in population movements and future development of the area in which the buildings are planned. Adequate space for play and recreation should be provided. Some standards recommend 5 acres of land for elementary schools, 10 to 12 acres for junior high schools, and 20 acres for senior high

schools. The play area should consist of a minimum of 100 square feet for every child. The National Council on Schoolhouse Construction* has suggested that, although larger sites may be used, standards that provide a minimum of 5 acres plus an additional acre for each 100 pupils of projected enrollment for elementary schools and a minimum of 10 acres plus an additional acre for each 100 pupils of projected enrollment for junior and senior high schools should be followed. Thus an elementary school of 200 pupils would have a site of 7 acres, for example, and a high school of 500 pupils a site of 15 acres.

Attention should be given to the esthetic features of a site because of its effect on the physical and emotional well-being of students and staff. The surroundings should be well landscaped, attractive, and free from disturbing noises or odors.

The American Association of School Administrators and the National Council on Schoolhouse Construction can supply detailed information on the selection of a site.

Building

Some trends in modern building construction have already been discussed and consideration of some of the special areas is still to come. Suffice it to say here that the trend is toward one-story construction at the precollege educational level, where that is possible, with stress on planning from a functional rather than an ornamen-

---

*National Council of Schoolhouse Construction, East Lansing, Michigan.

Lighting for gymnasium at University of California at Irvine.

tal point of view. The building should be constructed from the standpoint of use. As much natural lighting as possible should be utilized. The materials used should make the building attractive and safe. According to the National Safety Council a high percentage of children's accidents occur in school buildings. Every precaution should be taken to protect against accidents from fire, slippery floors, and other dangers. The walls should be painted with light colors and treated acoustically. Doors should open outward. Space for clothing should be provided.

These are only a few of the considerations in planning a school building. It is important that an architect plan such facilities with special regard to the educational needs of those who utilize it. Educators should formulate a plan and use it in discussions with the architect.

Lighting*

Proper lighting is important to conserve vision, to prevent fatigue, and to improve morale. There should be proper lighting as to both quality and quantity. In the past it has been recommended that natural light should come into the room from the left and that artificial light should be provided as needed. There is a trend now toward allowing natural light from more than one direction. Artificial light, moreover, should come from many sources rather than one, so as to prevent too much concentration of light in one place. Switches for artificial light should be located in many parts of the room.

Light intensity in most classrooms, according to expert opinion, usually varies from 15 to 100 footcandles.* Most authorities suggest between 30 and 70 footcandles for reading and close work. In gymnasia and swimming pools it is recommended that intensity range from 10 to 50 footcandles. Glare is undesirable and should be eliminated. Fluorescent lights should be properly installed and adjusted for best results. Strong contrasts of color such as light walls and dark floors should be avoided.

Windows, according to most experts,

---

*A good source of information for acceptable standards on lighting is the Illuminating Engineering Society, New York, N. Y.

*A footcandle is the unit by which light is measured in intensity at a given point.

should extend as far up toward the ceiling as possible and should consume space equal to about one-fourth to one-fifth of the floor area.

Window shades aid in controlling light. They should be durable, of light color, and located in the middle of the window so that they may be adjusted either up or down.

Heating and ventilation*

Efficiency in the classroom, gymnasium, special activities rooms, and other places is determined to some extent by thermal comfort. Thermal comfort is determined in the main by heating and ventilation.

The purposes of heating and ventilation are many. Some of the more common are to remove excess heat, unpleasant odors, and, in some cases, gases, vapors, fumes, and dust from the room; to prevent rapid temperature fluctuations; to diffuse the heat within a room; and to supply heat to counteract loss from the human body through radiation and otherwise.

Heating standards vary according to the activities engaged in, the clothing worn by the participants, and section of the country. The following represents an approximate average of various suggested standards for temperatures:

1. Classrooms, offices, and cafeterias— 68° to 76° F. (30 inches above floor)
2. Kitchens, closed corridors, shops, and laboratories—65° to 68° F. (60 inches above floor)
3. Gymnasia and activity rooms—55° to 65° F. (60 inches above floor)
4. Locker and shower rooms—70° to 78° F. (60 inches above floor)
5. Swimming pools—80° to 85° F. (60 inches above the deck)

In respect to ventilation, the range of recommendations is from 8 to 21 cubic feet of fresh air per minute per occupant.

*A good source for ventilating and heating information is the American Society of Heating, Refrigerating, and Air-Conditioning Engineers, New York, N. Y.

Adequate ventilating systems are especially needed in dressing, shower, and locker rooms, toilet rooms, gymnasia, and swimming pools. The recommended humidity ranges from 35% to 60%. The type and amount of ventilation will vary with the specific needs of the particular area to be served.

Furniture

The furniture that students use most is desks and chairs. Seats and desks that are adjustable and movable are recommended by most educators. There are many different kinds of seats and desks that are available in both wood and metal. The desk should be of proper height and fit the pupil comfortably and properly. Desks should be arranged to provide the best light for the students.

Plant sanitation

Various items concerned with plant sanitation should not be overlooked. Sanitation facilities should be well provided and well maintained. The water supply should be safe and adequate. If any question exists, the local or state health department should be consulted. In regard to water supply, one authority suggests that at least 20 gallons per pupil per day is needed, for all purposes.

Drinking fountains of various heights should be recessed in corridor walls and should be of material that is easily cleaned. Approximately one drinking fountain should be provided for every 75 students. A stream of water should flow from the fountain in such a manner that it is not necessary for the mouth of the drinker to get too near the drain bowl.

Water closets, urinals, lavatories, and washroom equipment such as soap dispensers, toilet paper holders, waste containers, mirrors, bookshelves, and hand-drying facilities should be provided as needed.

Waste disposal should be adequately cared for. There should be provision for cleanup and removal of stray paper and other materials that make the grounds and buildings a health and safety hazard as well as unsightly. Proper sewage disposal and prompt garbage disposal should also be provided.

Acoustics

Concentration is necessary in many kinds of school, college, and recreational work. Noise distracts attention, causes nervous strain, and results in the loss of many of the activity's benefits. Therefore, noise should be eliminated as effectively as possible. This can be achieved by acoustical treatment of such important places as corridors, gymnasia, swimming pools, shops, music rooms, and libraries.

Acoustical materials include plasters, fibers, boards, tiles, and various types of fabrics. Some areas should be given special attention. Floor covering that reduces noise can be used in corridors, and acoustical material can be used in walls. In classrooms, special attention should be given to materials that absorb sound in the upper walls and to tight floor coverings. In cafeterias there should be sound-absorption materials on floors, tables, counter tops, ceilings, and walls. Furthermore, the kitchen with its noises should be separated from the dining room. The music room and shop areas should be isolated as much as possible in addition to having acoustically treated walls. Swimming pools and gymnasia need special treatment to control the various noises associated with joyous and enthusiastic play participation. Ceiling and wall acoustical treatment will help control noises in the gymnasium, while the use of mineral acoustical material, which will not be affected by high humidity, will be found helpful in the swimming pool.

Special considerations for a healthful environment for physical education

Physical educators including teachers, coaches, and others should contribute to a healthful environment by providing safe and sanitary conditions for their program and the construction and maintenance of safe facilities.

Outdoor physical education facilities. Playing fields and playgrounds should have good turf and be clear of rocks, holes, and uneven surfaces. A dirty, dusty surface, for example, can aggravate such conditions as emphysema, chronic bronchitis, and allergies. Artificial turf is now coming into use and has been proved to be very satisfactory. Safety precautions should be provided in terms of well-lined areas, regularly inspected equipment, and fenced-in playfields and playgrounds, particularly where there is heavy traffic adjoining these facilities. Rubber asphalt, synthetic materials, and other substances that require little maintenance and help to free an area from cinders, gravel, stones, and dust are being used more and more on outdoor surfaces. In some sections of the country limited shelters are also being used to provide protection from the rain, wind, and sun. All outdoor areas should provide for sanitary drinking fountains and toilet facilities as needed.

Indoor physical education facilities. Just as safe and properly constructed equipment should be a part of outdoor facilities, so should they be a part of indoor physical education facilities. There should be adequate space provided for all the activity phases of the program whether they be in the gymnasium, swimming pool, or auxiliary areas. Mats should be used as a protective measure on walls and other areas where participants may be injured. Drinking fountains should be recessed and doors should open away from the playing floor. Proper flooring should be used—tile-cement floors are sometimes undesirable where activity takes place. Space should be provided for the adapted physical education program where students in wheelchairs and on crutches can be accommodated.

Clothing and equipment. Clothing and equipment used in physical education activities should meet health standards. If not, odors and germs will thrive, causing an unpleasant environment that may help to spread disease. Gymnasium mats, for example, should be kept clean. Regular physical education clothing, not street clothes, should be worn in most classes. Social dancing or similar activities, of course, would be exceptions. Clean clothing, including all types of athletic costumes, should be required. Footwear should be fitted properly. Socks should be clean. Many schools provide facilities for laundering physical education clothing.

Shower and locker facilities. Special attention should be paid to shower facilities. The shower room should be kept clean and plenty of soap and warm water should be available. Proper heating and ventilation should be provided; a nonslip floor surface should be installed; and ceilings should be constructed so as to prevent condensation. The drying area should be washed daily so as to prevent athlete's foot and other contaminations. A towel service should be initiated if it doesn't already exist. Adequate time should be allowed in the program to take a good shower.

Locker rooms should provide dressing as well as storage lockers for all students starting with the upper-grade elementary

Richwoods Community High School, Peoria Heights, Ill.

school. Adequate space should be provided so that dressing is not done in cramped quarters. Occasional locker inspections are considered to be necessary.

Swimming pools. Swimming pools need special attention whether they are of the indoor or outdoor variety. First, the pool should be properly constructed to provide for adequate filtration, circulation, and chlorination. There should be a daily diary kept of such things as temperature of water, hydrogen ion concentration, residual chlorine, and other important matters. Regulations should be established and students acquainted with them in regard to pool use. A list of pool regulations advocated by the National Education Association and the American Medical Association include:

1. Everyone using the pool should have an overall bath, in the nude, with soap and water, washing carefully the armpits, the genital and rectal areas, and the feet.
2. Before taking a shower, the bladder should be emptied. Pupils needing to urinate during the swimming period should be excused to go to the toilet.
3. Anyone leaving the pool to go to the toilet must take another cleansing bath with soap and water before returning.
4. Pupils should expectorate only in the overflow trough.
5. Boys and men should swim in the nude or wear sanitized trunks. Girls and women should wear sanitized tank suits.
6. Girls and boys with long hair should wear rubber bathing caps. Caps keep hair, dandruff, and hair oil from contaminating the water. They also keep hair out of the eyes.
7. Each pupil should be inspected by the instructor or the pool guard before he enters the pool. Pupils with evidence of skin infection, eye infection, respiratory disease, open cuts or sores, or bandages should be excluded.
8. There must be no rough or boisterous play and no running or playing tag in or around the pool area.
9. Pupils should wear ear plugs or nose clips if these have been recommended by their physicians. Some pupils, on medical recommendation, may need to be excused, at least temporarily, from participation in the aquatic program.

10. A qualified person, either the instructor or other person qualified as a lifeguard, should be on duty whenever the pool is in use. No pupil should enter the pool unless a guard is present. All doors leading to the pool should be locked when the pool is not in use and a guard on duty.

11. Since dirt from shoes may be tracked into the pool and contaminate the water, spectators should be prohibited from entering the pool deck.*

Athletics. All the suggestions previously stated for a healthful environment refer to athletics as a phase of the total physical education program. In addition, athletes need some special considerations. All athletes should have medical examinations and medical supervision. The coach should be concerned about the health of the athlete at all times. This responsibility ranges from not putting undue pressure on an athlete to win to providing proper competition with teams of comparable ability. The coach also has great influence on the health habits of the athlete and as such should use it in a way that will reduce the amount of cigarette smoking, use of drugs, undue weight reduction brought about by crash diets, and improper nutrition.

The Joint Committee on Health Problems of the National Education Association and the American Medical Association has set forth a set of guidelines for safeguarding the health of the athlete. These can be found in Chapter 13, p. 346.

THE PSYCHOLOGIC ENVIRONMENT

The World Health Organization defines health as follows: "Health is a state of complete physical, mental, and social well-being, and not merely the absence of disease or infirmity." In order to have a mentally healthful and educational en-

vironment, therefore, one should not be concerned merely with providing the proper physical facilities. It is necessary also to take into consideration the administrative practices that play such an important part in providing for the total health of the child. It has been estimated that one of every ten school children is emotionally disturbed. This fact shows the necessity for coming to grips with this problem in every way possible. Health and physical educators should be especially concerned with mental and emotional health because of their close relationship with physical health and illness. During the last few years the psychosomatic aspects of education have increasingly been given more attention.

Mental health implies a state of mind that allows the individual to adjust in a satisfactory manner to whatever life has to offer. Good mental health cannot be thought of as a subject included in the school curriculum. Instead, it must permeate the total life of the educational institution. It means that programs are flexible and geared to individual needs, a permissive climate prevails, children are allowed considerable freedom, and students become self-reliant and responsible for their own actions. It means that the child is recognized and has a satisfying educational experience. The National Association for Mental Health points out that the well-adjusted person is the one who has the right attitudes and feelings toward himself, other people, and the demands that life places upon him. George Preston* has listed the qualities of mental health and says it consists of being able to live (1) within the limits imposed by bodily equipment, (2) with other human beings, (3) happily, (4) productively, and (5) without being a nuisance.

School and college programs offer an

---

*Joint Committee on Health Problems in Education of the National Education Association and the American Medical Association: Healthful school environment, Washington, D. C., 1969, The Association, pp. 234-235.

*Preston, G. H.: The substance of mental health, New York, 1943, Holt, Rinehart & Winston, Inc., p. 112.

excellent laboratory for developing good human relations, democratic methods, responsibility, self-reliance, and other essentials to happy and purposeful living. The degree to which this laboratory is utilized for such purposes depends upon administrative officers, teachers, custodians, and other staff members. Such important considerations as the administrative policies established, teachers' personalities, program, human relations, and professional help that is given will determine to what extent educational programs justify their existence in human betterment. Some of the important implications for a healthful and educational environment are discussed in more detail.

Administrative practices

A few of the administrative practices that have a bearing upon the mental and emotional health of the students and participants deal with organization of the school day, student achievement, play and recreation, homework, attendance, personnel policies, administrative emphasis, and discipline.

Organization of the school day. The organization of the school day will have a bearing upon whether a healthful environment is provided for the child. The length of the school day must be in conformance with the age of the child. Classes should be scheduled in a manner that does not result in excessive fatigue. Subjects that require considerable concentration should be scheduled when the individual is more mentally efficient. Usually this is during the early part of the day. Boredom and tension will arise from scheduling similar classes close together, without any breaks. The program should be flexible to allow for variety, new developments, and satisfying children's interests. Adequate periods of rest and play should be provided, not only as a change from the more arduous routine of close concentration but also as a necessity for utilizing the big muscles of the body. "Big-muscle" activity is essential during the growing years. The length of classes should be adequate for instructional purposes but not so excessively long that the law of diminishing returns sets in.

Student achievement. Success is an experience essential to the development of self-confidence and an integrated person. One who experiences success will be better stimulated to do good work than one who consistently fails. The child or youth who consistently fails is likely to have behavior disorders. In view of this, it is important that educational programs recognize their responsibility for developing each individual. Experiences should be provided that are adapted to the individual and are planned so that each person will have a series of successful experiences.

Individual differences. It is important to recognize that individuals differ. They differ in respect to intellect, physique, skill, personality, and many other qualities. In a fifth-grade class, for example, although the average chronologic age may be 11 years, the mental age could range from 6 to 16 years. Similar differences abound in other characteristics.

It is very important for administrators, teachers, and leaders to recognize that these differences do exist and that programs must be planned accordingly. The same goals cannot be established for all. If goals are standardized, some individuals will become frustrated because it is impossible for them to achieve the standards, and others will become very bored because there is no challenge. Goals that are within reach for everyone should be established. Administrators and teachers sometimes become so engrossed in the idea of setting high standards that they forget to consider the individual.

Grades. Excessive emphasis should not be placed on marks. Too often the individual is interested more in the mark received than in the knowledge, attitudes, and self-improvement inherent in the activity. It seems that, if marks must be given, as broad a category as possible should be used. These could be stated in terms such as "passed" and "did not pass" or "satisfactory" and "unsatisfactory." Whenever possible, descriptive statements of the student's progress should be given without any marks whatsoever. Parent-teacher conferences are probably the best way to evaluate a student's progress in the most effective manner. These procedures are being followed in some elementary schools with excellent results.

Marks, although supposedly an index of the quality of work done, are poor guides for such purposes. Many tests that are given as a basis for marks do not measure what they are supposed to measure and have been found to be unreliable when rated by various persons. Furthermore, the human element always enters the picture.

Marks stimulate competition that is unhealthy in many of its aspects. Too often the underlying reason for such competition is to prove superiority over someone rather than to prove a mastery in a particular subject matter field or skill. Under such circumstances harm frequently results to the mental health and personalities of students.

Tests and examinations. It is generally agreed that some method is needed to check on the progress that has been made in the acquisition of knowledge, skills, or attitudes. Harmful effects of such tests and examinations result when they are used by teachers and leaders to instill fear in the individual. Frequently, individuals harm themselves physically, mentally, and emotionally when they become worked up over an approaching examination. They stay up all night cramming, cannot sleep, are tense, and generally find it a very trying experience. This is especially true at the college educational level. Students should understand that examinations are a means by which greater help can be given to them. Such help is not possible unless information

is gained as to what the person knows at certain points along the way.

Intelligence ratings. Intelligence ratings can be of some value in the hands of a trained person. It is important to recognize, however, that such measuring devices are not definite, exact, and accurate in indicating the mental capacity of an individual. Furthermore, intelligence is only one factor that makes for success of an individual. In fact, it has been shown through Terman's study of gifted children, where all received high intelligence ratings, that intelligence does not necessarily ensure the achievement of prominent position in life.

Furthermore, intelligence ratings are often in error. One test should never be used as the criterion. Instead, several tests should be given before definite conclusions are drawn. Even then, as the work of Allison Davis and others at the University of Chicago has shown, intelligence tests measure a person's environment and the cultural experiences open to him to a greater extent than they do his native intelligence.

Play and recreation. The impression that achievement in so-called academic subjects is the only criterion necessary to ensure successful living is erroneous. In addition, there should be achievement in the areas of human relations, personality development, physical development, acquisition of skills for leisure hours, and other areas even more vital to the success of the individual than so-called scholastic achievement.

Dr. William Menninger and other experts in the field of psychiatry point to the contributions of play and recreation to mental health. Furthermore, to achieve success in the competitive society of today, a person needs a sound body that possesses stamina and endurance and that will support long hours of work. Also, the skills in physical activities, music, industrial arts, and allied areas that are learned during the early years of an individual's life will determine to a great degree his hobbies or leisure-time pursuits during adult years.

For these and other reasons, it is important that physical education and other subjects falling into this category be recognized for the contribution they can make to the total growth of the individual. There are many persons in mental institutions today who were capable of working out the most difficult problems in calculus and were expert in their knowledge of geography and other subjects. Many of these individuals might have been spared their illness if they had recognized the importance of developing other skills that would have afforded a more balanced life.

Homework. Educators are increasingly recognizing that homework should be assigned in a manner that is in the best interest of the whole child. If it is given for the purpose of busywork, to keep someone occupied during hours after dinner at night, or solely for enabling a person to surpass his classmates, it cannot be justified. Children as well as adults need time for play and recreation. They are entitled to time after school for such purposes. For young children in elementary school, homework assignments should take into consideration that young bodies need great amounts of physical activity. Ample exercise is necessary for body organs and muscles that are developing and gaining strength for future years. In junior high school, the homework assigned should be reasonable in nature. In high school it should not be given in such large amounts that it requires late hours of work. Instead, it should promote achievement and allow the student opportunity for independent work and help to promote the development of the whole individual.

Attendance. In many states financial aid is based upon school attendance. In some cases this has resulted in harmful effects to the health of children. Administrators have been known to stress attendance to the point at which students come to school with colds and other illnesses when they should be home in bed. This not only endangers their own health, but at the same time it exposes many innocent children to harmful germs.

It is important to have regular attendance at school. However, if the student is ill and in need of rest or parental and medical care, it is much better that he stay home. In order not to abuse this privilege, administrators, teachers, and others should try to educate the parents as to what constitutes good reasons for absences from school.

Furthermore, if the student is well enough to attend school, then it would seem that he should attend all classes. Too often a student is dismissed from a physical education class because of some minor disorder. If the program is adapted to the needs of the individual, special consideration can be given to such cases. It is just as important that regular attendance prevail in physical education as in social studies, mathematics, or any other subject.

Personnel policies. The administration's personnel policies in regard to teachers and other staff members will determine in some measure whether or not a healthful environment is created. A teacher who is required to punch a clock when she comes to work in the morning and leaves at night, is never greeted with a smile, never experiences an enjoyable conversation with the principal, is held responsible for many unnecessary details, is required to be at work regardless of how she feels, receives no administrative support when subject to community prejudices, and finds that the administrative policies that are established do not give her happiness, security, and confidence in doing her job cannot help but reflect such policies in her dealings with students and colleagues.

Administrators should try to establish the best possible working conditions for all members of a staff. Only if they feel

Table 14-1. Analysis of 193 student discipline provisions in negotiation agreements[*]

Clause	Agreements with clause	
	Number	Percent
Joint committee established to study disciplinary policy	11	5.7%
Board disciplinary policy or public law tied into agreement by contract language	22	11.4
General statement of teacher board disciplinary philosophy	156	80.8
Reasons for disciplinary action		
Disruptive behavior	52	26.9
Persistent misbehavior	40	20.7
Gross offenses	39	20.2
Physical violence (assault, fighting)	18	9.3
Gambling, drugs, alcohol, tobacco, pornography, weapons	14	7.3
Disrespect or insubordination	10	5.2
Vandalism, arson, theft, extortion	9	4.7
False bomb reports, inciting violence	6	3.1
Abusive language	5	2.6
Threatening or belligerent manner	4	2.1
Truancy/skipping	3	1.6
Health/physical appearance	3	1.6
Procedures for initial identification and handling of disciplinary problems		
Reasonable force for protection and restraint	19	9.8
Child sent to office or principal notified	6	3.1
Teacher reports punishable offenses and points out emotional or disciplinary problem students to principal	47	24.4
Parents called to conference	28	14.5
Punishment for offenses		
Temporary exclusions from class		
By teacher	56	29.0
By principal	1	9.5
Detention	6	3.1
Corporal punishment	14	7.3
Transfer to another class (before suspension)	13	6.7
Suspension	32	16.6
Expulsion	4	2.1
Limitation on punishment	6	3.1
Special consideration given to teachers with one or more children who have emotional or behavior problems		
Reduced class size only	1	0.5
More or longer relief periods and/or reduced class size	2	1.0
Equal distribution of problem children among teachers	1	0.5
General statement	1	0.5
Need for help from specialists recognized		
Psychiatrists, psychologists, physicians, counselors	103	53.4
Law enforcement personnel	80	41.5
Special classes or services for emotional and behavior problem children		
Special classes exist	6	3.1
Expansion of special education	2	1.0
Board to prepare program	1	0.5
Removal from classroom of those who cannot adjust	6	3.1
Record of disciplinary cases kept	4	2.1
Miscellaneous clauses	7	3.6

[*]From NEA Research Bulletin 47:59, 1969.

happy and well adjusted in their jobs will a healthful environment exist.

Administrative emphasis. The administrative emphasis should be on the children and on those experiences that will help them to grow and develop into healthy and educated human beings. It should not be on subject matter material, with rigid and inflexible programs designed to pump as much factual knowledge as possible into the heads of students. Administrative policies should be established that reflect human beings as the center of the program, allow for flexibility, encourage initiative on the part of the teacher, are adapted to the needs and interests of the participants, and provide in every way for a healthful physical and nonphysical environment.

Discipline. The school and college should be a place where individuals receive joy and satisfaction from their experiences. A spirit of cooperation should exist among the administration, staff, and members of the organization. The emphasis in student discipline should be on self-government. As much freedom as possible should be given. The individual who is surrounded on all sides by restrictions and who is not trusted will rebel. As many educators have discovered, abrupt use of authority invites resistance. There should be a permissive attitude toward individual variations from acceptable behavior, coupled with a firm but kind insistence upon higher standards of conduct. Responsibility should go along with freedom. A climate of opinion should be established that allows as much freedom as possible without encroaching on the rights of others. A strong student government can be one of the best educational devices for self-discipline.

Regulations should not be accepted just because they are regulations. Rather, they should be accepted because they are essen-

Burnett and Logan, Chicago.

The school should be a place where individuals receive joy and satisfaction from their experiences. (Washington Irving Elementary School, Waverly, Iowa.)

tial to securing the rights of everyone so that all can enjoy and benefit from the programs that are offered.

If antisocial behavior develops, it is important to look into the reasons for such behavior and work to eliminate the causes, rather than to abruptly and harshly discipline some person. Unless this is done, such antisocial behavior will continue to show itself. Furthermore, in time it may become so obstreperous as to require isolation of the individual from society. If a constructive approach is taken, such measures may be avoided.

The teacher

Good mental health in a school program is tied up very closely with the teacher. The manner in which the teacher and student interact with one another is very important. It is important for the teacher to think of youngsters as living, feeling, and developing human beings who pursue different and varied courses on their ways to maturity. They are not inanimate objects or receptacles into which the instructor pours knowledge.

One of the main responsibilities of any teacher in health or physical education should be student counseling. Quite frequently specialists in these areas are the ones to whom the child goes in search of information. Anyone who is to perform such an important job as counseling should be well adjusted, understand himself, and get along well with others.

The teacher must be in good physical condition in order to do a good job. A teacher may come to a job in excellent physical condition, but if large classes are assigned, the salary is insufficient, and outside work is necessary, physical harm may result. Furthermore, if there is no provision for sick leave and as a result the teacher must be on the job even when sick or ill, her physical condition will suffer. When this happens, the students also suffer.

The teacher's personality has important implications for the mental and emotional health of those with whom he or she comes in contact. The teacher who is happy, wears a smile, is kind, considerate, and likes people in general will impart these qualities to the students. It is bound to "rub off" in the daily interaction that takes place. Conversely, the teacher or leader who is sarcastic, depressed, prejudiced, and intolerant will also impart these qualities to the children with whom he or she associates. The leader's personality is also reflected in the appearance of the classroom and the teaching methods employed.

Administrators should be cognizant of the factors that result in maladjusted personalities for members of their staffs. A few years ago the National Educational Association found that many faculty members were plagued by personal and working conditions that influenced their mental outlooks. Some of these were as follows: financial difficulties, economic problems, serious illness of relatives or friends, unsatisfactory progress of pupils, matters of personal health, being unmarried and without normal family relationships, disciplinary problems, an official rating by a superior, possible loss of position, work on a college course, being unhappily married, and religious problems. Many of these frustrating factors could have been eliminated.

All teachers should have satisfactory working conditions. They should receive an adequate salary to eliminate financial worries, be encouraged to develop out-of-school interests in the community, have hobbies in which they can engage after school hours and during vacation periods, and have adequate provisions for sick and sabbatical leaves and leaves of absence so that proper rest and adequate educational standards may be assured. Furthermore, there should be ample opportunities provided for affiliation with professional groups and the development of cultural and other interests conducive to better leadership qualifications. By providing such essentials teachers and leaders will be made happier and have better mental and emotional health. In turn, this will be reflected in the total health of the children with whom they come in contact.

Human relationships

Human relationships are a most important consideration if one is to grow into a happy, successful, and well-adjusted individual. Of all the traits that should be developed in health and physical education, human relationships rank toward the top of the list. Through counseling, participation in group games and activities under good leadership, and other phases of the programs, the potentialities are great for developing good human relationships.

Each individual should be made to feel that he belongs to the group and has something to contribute in its behalf. There must never be an attempt to make a member of the group feel insignificant and unimportant. More praise should be dispensed than criticism. Every attempt should be made to help each person maintain his self-respect. The atmosphere that pervades the classroom, gymnasium, or recreation center should be relaxed and friendly. The emotional needs of every individual should be taken into consideration in the class or group activities that are held.

The teacher should have good relationships with his or her colleagues. Any faculty or staff that is infested with cliques, jealousies, and strife communicates these attitudes to the students. This is just as true here as in the case of quarreling parents who communicate their feelings to their children. If one is to help others develop good human relationships, one must set an example worthy of emulation.

There must be good human relationships among the children themselves. They are

Each individual should be made to feel that she belongs to the group and has something to contribute in its behalf. (Alabama College, Montevallo, Ala.)

dependent upon the feeling of the group toward them and whether or not they are accepted. It is important to have status among one's associates. The teacher can play an important part in helping to see that everyone gains recognition. This is especially important with such individuals as the dull child in the classroom, the awkward, uncoordinated youngster on the playfield, and the intellectually gifted student in a recreation setting.

The teacher should be careful not to accentuate any characteristic that makes a child markedly different from the rest of the group. This applies to the whole realm of deviations, including scholastic, physical, mental, social, and economic.

Professional services

The factors discussed thus far in respect to the nonphysical environment have been largely preventive in nature. They have attempted to show the importance of providing an environment where the individual has freedom, self-respect, and security and experiences satisfaction in his activities. However, despite emphasis upon preventive measures, there will always be some individuals who become behavior problems and will need professional help.

The teacher can play an important part by identifying those individuals who need help. He can also render guidance and such other aid as is possible in the school or college situation. The teacher can often do a great deal of good by studying the student thoroughly in respect to his school, home, and community environment. Through such study and by working closely with parents, many minor maladjustments can be eliminated. If further help is needed, he should refer the child to the proper professional persons.

In some schools there are counselors who have had preparation that goes beyond that of the ordinary teacher or leader. Their special knowledge of guidance and mental hygiene should be utilized in dealing with problem cases.

With the increasing emphasis being placed upon mental hygiene, many schools and colleges are utilizing the services of social workers, psychologists, and psychiatrists. The more serious cases should be referred to such professional people. They are trained in dealing with such problems and can render a great deal of personal help as well as promote a more healthful environment.

Recently, there has been a marked growth of child guidance clinics across the country. These are sponsored by various organizations interested in securing professional guidance for individuals with behavior problems. These clinics guide parents and community groups in good mental hygiene practices and needs, aid children who have various mental maladjustments, and seek support and understanding within the community to help promote better mental hygiene. They have trained people on their staffs who are competent to assist in preventing and solving problems that involve psychology.

CHECKLIST FOR ADMINISTRATIVE PRACTICES FOR A HEALTHFUL ENVIRONMENT

Organization of the school day

Length of the school day   *Yes   No*

   1. The length of the school day should be adapted to the age of the child, starting with one-half day in kindergarten.   ___ ___

   2. Play and rest periods are provided in accordance with pupil needs.   ___ ___

Continued.

CHECKLIST FOR ADMINISTRATIVE PRACTICES FOR A HEALTHFUL ENVIRONMENT—cont'd

Scheduling   *Yes*   *No*

1. Subjects demanding diligent application are scheduled early in the day.   ___   ___
2. Subjects requiring more mental concentration and academic effort are interspersed with those requiring less mental effort.   ___   ___
3. The amount of time devoted to a specific task is assigned with regard to the age, readiness, and needs of the child.   ___   ___
4. There is ample time between classes to ensure student promptness without excessive haste.   ___   ___
5. A leisurely lunch break is provided for each pupil.   ___   ___
6. The educational program is a flexible one, so that it is possible to schedule special programs or activities without hindering the regular program.   ___   ___

Student achievement

Individual differences

1. There is provision in the school program for individual differences among children in respect to physical handicaps, readiness to learn, academic ability, and environmental background.   ___   ___
2. Consideration is given to the physical and mental growth of each child.   ___   ___
3. The abilities of each child are recognized and instruction is adjusted to individual ability.   ___   ___

Grades

1. Provision is made for clerical and special assistance in helping the teacher to spend more time with teaching responsibilities.   ___   ___
2. The program is planned so that each child experiences a series of educational successes.   ___   ___
3. Goals are adjusted to fit each pupil, and marks are used to indicate progress toward stated goals.   ___   ___
4. Provision is made for a descriptive evaluation along with the grade.   ___   ___

Reporting pupil progress

1. The means used to report pupil progress include personal conferences, checklists, graphs, letters, progress reports, and report cards.   ___   ___
2. Problems, weaknesses, and potential of child are items for teacher-parent conferences.   ___   ___

Tests and examinations

1. Examinations are used as a means of helping pupil and teacher discover the progress that has been made in the acquistion of knowledge.   ___   ___
2. Tests help the learner attain satisfaction and a sense of achievement when he is doing as well as he should.   ___   ___
3. Tests help the teacher judge how effective his teaching methods are.   ___   ___
4. Tests assist in making administrative judgments in respect to grouping and other procedures.   ___   ___
5. Tests provide emphasis on diagnosis rather than on rating of overall merit, upon individual improvement rather than comparison with others, and are used more as guides than as final measures.   ___   ___

Intelligence ratings

1. Intelligence tests are selected and administered by a trained person.   ___   ___
2. Tests are used with a view to how the children can profit with suitable instruction.   ___   ___

CHECKLIST FOR ADMINISTRATIVE PRACTICES FOR A HEALTHFUL ENVIRONMENT—cont'd

Yes *No*

Physical education and recreation

1. Physical education class size ranges from thirty to forty pupils. —— ——
2. Physical education is offered daily and stresses basic skills and movement experiences. —— ——
3. The physical education program is concerned with the social, mental, and emotional aspects of the child, as well as the physical. —— ——
4. Recreational activities are based on pupil interests. —— ——

Homework

1. Homework is assigned in accordance with the age, interest, ability, and needs of the child. —— ——

Pupil attendance

1. The school nurse determines whether the child should attend school and when he should be sent home. —— ——
2. The child does not return to school after sickness until he is able to attend all classes. —— ——
3. The nurse and attendance officer play a major role in communication with the parent regarding proper health practices. —— ——

Discipline

1. Behavior is evaluated with the knowledge that misconduct is a sign of maladjustment and an attempt is made to find the cause. —— ——
2. The staff upholds the same general standards of behavior. —— ——
3. All pupil abilities are recognized and an effort is made to maintain the self-respect of the child through the use of praise. —— ——
4. Fear is not used as a technique of control. —— ——
5. Children are encouraged to assist in developing standards of behavior and to assist in their enforcement. —— ——

Student grouping

1. Grouping is flexible so that administration and organization exist only to expedite the process of learning. —— ——
2. Differences in learners and subject matter are considered in grouping. —— ——
3. Promotion practices are flexible. —— ——
4. Grouping is such that children do not bear labels, for example, "fast group" or "slow learner." —— ——

Teacher-pupil relationships

1. There is cooperative thinking and effort between teachers and pupils rather than emphasis upon the sole direction and authority of the teacher. —— ——
2. The teacher sets a good example for the pupil. —— ——
3. A primary teacher responsibility is that of pupil counseling. —— ——
4. The pupil is made to feel that he is part of the group and contributes to it. —— ——
5. The atmosphere of the classroom is relaxed and friendly. —— ——
6. The teacher shows interest in each pupil. —— ——
7. The teacher recognizes the various environmental factors that compose pupil personality and behavior. —— ——
8. The teacher has good relationships with his colleagues. —— ——
9. The teacher has an enthusiastic and confident attitude. —— ——
10. The teacher enjoys his work and takes pride in it. —— ——
11. The teacher is secure in his job. —— ——

Continued.

CHECKLIST FOR ADMINISTRATIVE PRACTICES FOR A HEALTHFUL ENVIRONMENT—cont'd

Professional services

1. The administration provides for guidance, psychologist, psychiatrist, and social worker services.   ___ ___
2. Specialists in "1" work closely with the home in providing necessary help for the child.   ___ ___

Personnel policies

1. Relationships between administrators and teachers are harmonious.   ___ ___
2. The administration promotes good social and professional relations among members of the staff.   ___ ___
3. Administrators help educate the public to its true responsibilities to the schools and seek the support and assistance of the public in the promotion of educational goals.   ___ ___

The teacher
Qualities

1. The teacher likes children.   ___ ___
2. The teacher is well adjusted and mentally healthy.   ___ ___
3. The teacher understands the growth and development of children.   ___ ___
4. The teacher is able to identify children with serious problems and knows how and when to refer them for help.   ___ ___
5. The teacher helps pupils meet their basic emotional needs.   ___ ___
6. The teacher has a pleasing appearance and manner and is physically healthy, patient, and impartial.   ___ ___
7. The teacher respects the child's personality, understands his limitations, and creates an overall atmosphere of security.   ___ ___

Working conditions

1. The physical conditions of the job are good (salary, sick leave, class load).   ___ ___
2. Administration is aware of factors that might affect the mental health of the teacher and help to eliminate such problems.   ___ ___

Improving instruction

1. Administration utilizes opportunities to commend teacher achievement and effort.   ___ ___
2. The beginning teacher is helped over the rough spots and is also assisted in obtaining a broad professional orientation.   ___ ___

Questions and exercises

1. Define what is meant by the "physical" and "nonphysical" environments. What are the implications of each for total health?
2. Prepare a research report on administrative practices for a healthful and educational environment as they relate to a school with which you are very familiar.
3. Prepare a list of administrative practices in health, physical education, or recreation that are nationally in evidence and should be eliminated in order to provide greater total health.
4. What part does each of the following play in mental health of school children: (a) organization of the school day, (b) achievement, (c) marks, (d) play and recreation, (e) homework, (f) attendance, and (g) discipline?
5. How does the mental and emotional health of a teacher affect the mental and emotional health of school children?
6. Consult case studies in some social agency and report on the teacher's role in these cases.
7. To what degree are the physical features of

a school related to mental and emotional health?

8. Why is it so important to have good human relationships within the school?

9. How can the school and community coordinate their efforts to further better physical, mental, emotional, and. social health for all residents?

10. What is the role of professional services in the school program?

Reading assignment in *Administrative Dimensions of Health and Physical Education Programs, Including Athletics:* Chapter 11, Selections 59 to 62.

Selected references

Ahmann, J. S., and Glock, M. D.: Evaluating pupil growth, Boston, 1958, Allyn & Bacon, Inc., pp. 6, 449, 501-504.

Ahmann, J. S., Glock, M. D., and Wardeberg, H. L.: Evaluating elementary school pupils, Boston, 1960, Allyn & Bacon, Inc., pp. 8-9.

American Association for Health, Physical Education, and Recreation: Administrative problems in health education, physical education, and recreation, Washington, D. C., 1953, The Association, chaps. 2, 4-7.

American Association for Health, Physical Education, and Recreation: School safety policies with emphasis on physical education, athletics, and recreation, Washington, D. C., 1964, The Association.

American Association of School Administrators: Health in schools, Twentieth Yearbook, Washington, D. C., 1951, National Education Association, chap. 6.

American Medical Association, Committee on Medical Aspects of Sports: Proceedings of the National Conference on the Medical Aspects of Sports—I through IX, Chicago, 1960-1967, The Association.

American Medical Association, Committee on Medical Aspects of Sports: Tips on athletic training—I through IX, Chicago, 1960-1967, The Association.

American Public Health Association: Suggested ordinance and regulations covering public swimming pools, New York, 1964, The Association.

Association for Supervision and Curriculum Development: Fostering mental health in our schools, 1950 Yearbook, Washington, D. C., 1950, The Association, a department of the National Education Association.

Carroll, H. A.: Mental hygiene, New York, 1951, Prentice-Hall, Inc.

Daniels, A. S., and Davies, E. A.: Adapted physical education, ed. 2, New York, 1965, Harper & Row, Publishers.

Educational Policies Commission: Educational objectives—education for all-American youths: a further look, Washington, D. C., 1952, The Commission, p. 15.

Florida State Department of Education: A checklist, as evaluation in physical education, Tallahassee, Fla., 1961, The Department.

Grout, R. E.: Health teaching in schools, Philadelphia, 1968, W. B. Saunders Co.

Illinois Office of Public Instruction: Guidelines for evaluating programs in physical education, Springfield, Ill., Office of Public Instruction.

Indiana State Board of Health: Indiana physical education score card, Indianapolis, 1960, The Board.

Jacobs, L.: Mental health in the school health program, The Journal of School Health **22:**288, 1952.

Joint Committee on Health Problems in Education of National Education Association and American Medical Association: Mental hygiene in the classroom, Washington, D. C., 1949, National Education Association.

Joint Committee on Health Problems in Education of National Education Association and American Medical Association: School health services, Washington, D. C., 1964, National Education Association.

Joint Committee on Health Problems in Education of National Education Association and American Medical Association: Healthful school living, Washington, D. C., 1957, National Education Association.

Joint Committee on Health Problems in Education of National Education Association and American Medical Association: Health education, Washington, D. C., 1961, National Education Association.

Michigan Department of Education: A suggested checklist for evaluating the physical education program, Lansing, Mich., 1962, The Department.

Miller, F., chairman: Evaluative criteria, Washington, D. C., 1960, National Study of Secondary School Evaluation.

New York Department of Education: A guide for the review of secondary school physical education, Albany, N. Y., 1964, The Department.

Oberteuffer, D., and Beyrer, M. K.: School health education, ed. 4, New York, 1966, Harper & Row, Publishers.

Ohio Association of Health Physical Education and Recreation: Evaluative criteria for physical education, Columbus, Ohio, 1963, Ohio Department of Education.

Texas Education Agency: Suggestions for planning the secondary school physical education program, Austin, Texas, 1961, The Agency.

four

ADMINISTRATIVE FUNCTIONS

Women's gymnasium. (College of San Mateo, San Mateo, Calif.)

CHAPTER 15 THE PHYSICAL PLANT

Estimates of that portion of the total school or college plant devoted to health and physical education programs range as high as 50% to 75%. This large investment of money, time, and personnel requires considerable thought and planning. Physical education facilities should reflect the program in action. Furthermore, administrators, teachers, and other personnel in these special areas should participate in this planning, and, as such, they need to be knowledgeable about facilities and the various procedures for developing a healthful and efficient school plant. They need to know the needs of the programs involved, the latest trends in facilities, the common errors that are made, how they can work most effectively with the architect, and health features that should be considered.

BASIC CONSIDERATIONS IN PLANNING

At the outset, two principles should be very much in the minds of health and physical educators in relation to facility management: (1) facilities emanate as a result of program needs and (2) cooperative planning is essential to avoid common mistakes. The objectives, activities, teaching methods and materials, administrative policies, and equipment and supplies represent program considerations regarding facilities. The educational and recreational needs of both the school and community, the thinking of both school administrators and health and physical educators, and the advice of both architects and lay persons are other considerations if facilities are to be planned wisely.

Another set of principles basic to facility planning relate particularly to the optimum promotion of a healthful environment for the students. Included in this set of principles is the provision for facilities that take into account physiologic needs of the student, including proper temperature control, lighting, water supply, and noise level. A second principle would be the provision of facilities that take into account protection against accidents. The facilities would be planned so that the danger of fire, the possibility of mechanical accidents, and the hazards involved in student traffic would be eliminated or kept to a minimum. A third principle would concern itself with protection against disease. This would mean attention to such items as proper sewage disposal, sanitation procedures, and water supply. Finally, a fourth principle is the need to provide a healthful psychologic environment. This would have implications for space, location of activities, color schemes, and elimination of distractions through such means as soundproof construction.

A third set of principles has been developed by Bookwalter.* These may be used as guides for the planning, construction, and utilization of facilities for school health and physical education programs:

1. *Validity.* Standards for space, structure, and fixtures must be compatible with

---

*Bookwalter, K. W.: Physical education in the secondary schools, Washington, D. C., 1964, The Center for Applied Research in Education, Inc. (The Library of Education), pp. 84-86.

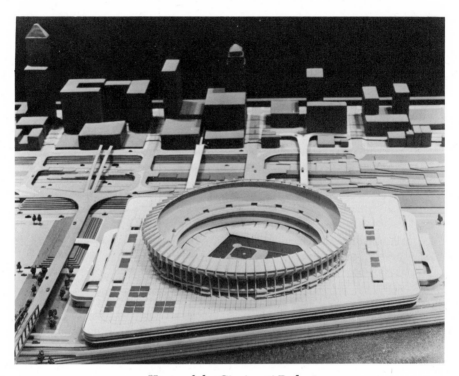

Home of the Cincinnati Reds.

Richards physical education building. (Brigham Young University, Provo, Utah.)

Gymnasium. (Princeton University, Princeton, N. J.)

the rules essential for the effective conduct of the program. According to the New York State Department of Education, the number of teaching stations needed for a school will depend upon school enrollment, physical education class size, periods of physical education scheduled each week for a teaching station, the number of periods of physical education each week for which a pupil is scheduled, activities offered, and pupils in out-of-class programs.

2. *Utility.* Facilities should be adaptable for different activities and programs without affecting such items as safety and effective instruction.

3. *Accessibility.* Facilities should be readily and directly accessible for the individuals who will be using them.

4. *Isolation.* Facilities should be planned so as to reduce to a minimum distractions, offensive odors, noise, and undesirable activities and groups.

5. *Departmentalization.* Functionally related services and activity areas should be continuous or adjacent for greatest economy and efficiency.

6. *Safety, hygiene, and sanitation.* The maintenance of proper health standards should be a major consideration in all facility planning.

7. *Supervision.* Facilities should take into consideration the need for proper teacher supervision of activities under his jurisdiction. Therefore, visibility and accessibility are essential considerations.

8. *Durability and maintenance.* Facilities should be easy and economical to maintain and should be durable.

9. *Beauty.* Facilities should be attractive and esthetically pleasing with the utilization of good color dynamics and design.

10. *Flexibility and expansibility.* Changes in enrollments, program, and other considerations for future expansion should be considered. Modern thinking has stressed the principle of flexibility in regard to physical education facilities. Flexibility should provide for immediate change through folding partitions, such as doors that separate gymnasia, for overnight change with very little effort in cases in which partitions cannot be removed

immediately, and for greater change that can be made within a period of 1 or 2 months, such as during the summer vacation.

11. *Economy.* The best use of money, space, time, energy, and other essential factors should be considered as they relate to facility planning.

A summary of some of the important guidelines and principles for facility planning for school and college health and physical education programs include the following:

1. All planning should be based on goals that recognize that the total physical and nonphysical environments must be safe, attractive, comfortable, clean, practical, and adapted to the needs of the individual.

2. The planning should include a consideration of the total school or college health and physical education facilities and the recreational facilities of the community. The programs and facilities of these areas are essential to any community. Since they are closely allied, they should be planned coordinately and based on the needs of the community. Each should be part of the overall community pattern.

3. Facilities should be geared to health standards. They play an important part in protecting the health of individuals and in determining the educational outcomes.

4. Facilities play a part in disease control. The extent to which schools and colleges provide for play areas, ample space, sanitary considerations, proper ventilation, heating, and cleanliness will to some extent determine how effectively disease is controlled.

5. Administrators must make plans for facilities long before an architect is consulted. Technical information can be procured in the forms of standards and guides from various sources, such as state departments of education, professional literature, building score cards, and various manuals. Information may also be secured from such important groups as the American Association of School Administrators, National Council on Schoolhouse Construction, and American Institute of Architects.

6. Standards should be utilized as guides and as a starting point. They will prove to be very helpful. However, it is important to keep in mind that standards cannot always be used entirely as developed. They usually have to be modified in the light of local needs, conditions, and resources.

7. Building and sanitary codes administered by the local and state departments of public health and the technical advice and consultation services available through these sources should be known and utilized by administrators in the planning and construction of facilities. Information concerned with acceptable building materials, specifications, minimum standards of sanitation, and other details may be procured from these informed sources.

8. Health, physical education, and recreation personnel should play important roles in the planning and operation of facilities. The specialized knowledge that such individuals have is very important. Provisions should be made so that their expert opinion will be utilized in the promotion of a healthful and proper environment.

9. Facilities should be planned with an eye to the future. Too often, facilities are constructed and outgrown within a very short time. Units should be sufficiently large to accommodate peak-load participation in the various activities. The peak-load estimates should be made with future growth in mind.

10. Planning should provide for adequate allotment of space to the activity and program areas. They should receive priority in space allotment. The administrative offices and service units, although important, should not be planned and developed in a spacious and luxurious manner that goes beyond efficiency and necessity.

Text continued on p. 415.

Rifle range and gymnasium of physical education building. See also next two illustrations. (University of Alaska, College, Alaska.)

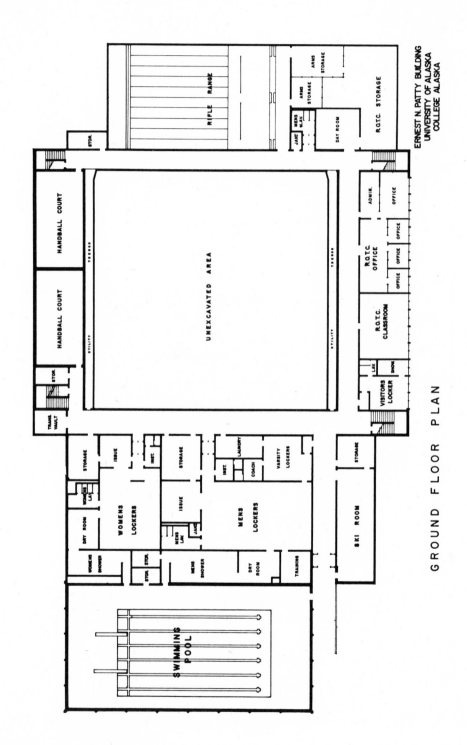

GROUND FLOOR PLAN

ERNEST N. PATTY BUILDING
UNIVERSITY OF ALASKA
COLLEGE ALASKA

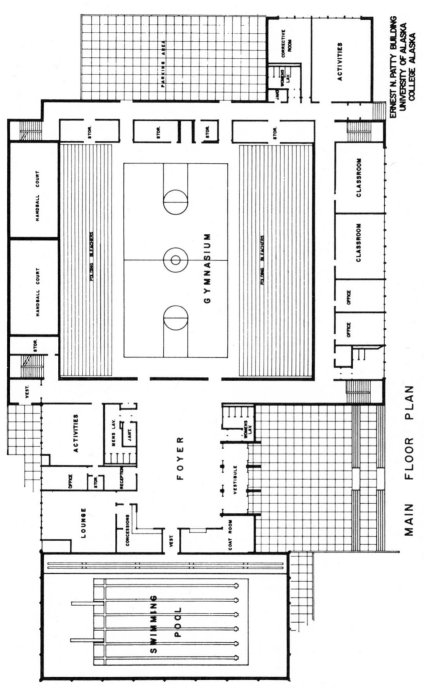

MAIN FLOOR PLAN

Floor plans of physical education building. (University of Alaska, College, Alaska.)

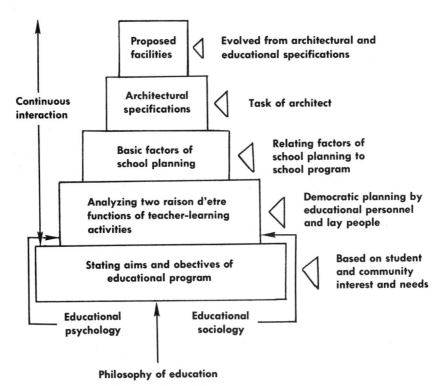

A procedure for planning facilities for schools. (From MacConnell, J. D.: Planning for school buildings, Englewood Cliffs, N. J., 1957, Prentice-Hall, Inc. Reprinted by permission.)

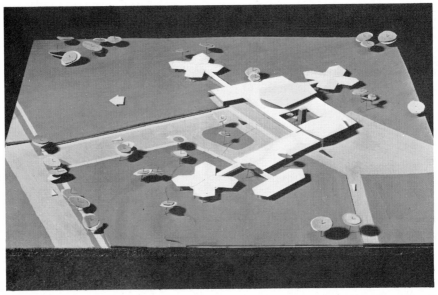

Suter, Hedrich-Blessing, Chicago.

Planning should include consideration of the total school health and physical education facilities as well as the recreational facilities of the community. (Model of Heathcote School, Scarsdale, N. Y.)

11. Geographic and climatic conditions should be taken into consideration in planning facilities. By doing this, the full potentialities for conducting activities outdoors as well as indoors can be realized.

12. Architects do not always pay as much attention as they should to the educational and health features when planning buildings and facilities. Therefore, it is important that they be briefed on certain requirements that educators feel are essential in order that the health and welfare of children, youth, and adults may be provided for. Such a procedure is usually welcomed by the architect and will aid him in rendering a greater service to the community.

13. Facilities should take into consideration all the necessary safety features so essential in programs of health, physical education, and recreation. Health service substations near the gymnasium and other play areas, proper surfacing of activity areas, adequate space, and proper lighting are a few of these considerations.

14. It should be kept in mind that the construction of school or college health, physical education, and recreational facilities often tends to set a pattern that will influence parents, civic leaders, and others. This in turn will promote a healthful and safe environment for the entire community.

COMMON ERRORS OF HEALTH AND PHYSICAL EDUCATION PERSONNEL IN FACILITY MANAGEMENT

Some common mistakes made by health and physical educators in facility management include the following:

1. Failure to adequately project enrollments and program needs into the future (Facilities are difficult to expand or change, so this is a significant error.)
2. Failure to provide for multiple use of facilities
3. Failure to provide for adequate accessibility for students in health and physical education classes and also for community groups for recreation purposes
4. Failure to observe basic health factors in planning facilities in regard to lighting, safety, and ventilation
5. Failure to provide adequate space for the conduct of a comprehensive program of physical education activities
6. Failure to provide appropriate accommodations for spectators
7. Failure to soundproof areas of the building where noise will interfere with educational functions
8. Failure to meet with the architect to present views on program needs
9. Failure to provide adequate staff offices
10. Failure to provide adequate storage space
11. Failure to provide adequate space and privacy for medical examinations
12. Failure to provide large enough entrances to transport equipment
13. Failure to observe desirable current professional standards
14. Failure to provide for adequate study of cost in terms of durability, time, money, and effective instruction
15. Failure to properly locate teaching stations with service facilities

THE PLANNING TEAM

Planning for meaningful facilities is a team effort. It includes such persons as members of the board of education or board of trustees, representatives of the administration, students, custodians, curriculum specialists, educational consultants, members of the community, and selected teachers and department heads.

WORKING WITH THE ARCHITECT

The architect is the specialist in facility planning and the leader in the designing of school and college buildings. As such, he is an important consideration for all persons engaged in health and physical education work. The architect, through his training and experience, is a specialist who is competent to give advisory service in all aspects of facility management.

The qualifications of the architect include:

1. The architect should be legally qualified to practice in the state and should be in good standing in his profession. He must be a man of unquestioned professional character and integrity and must possess high ethical standards.
2. The architect should have had previous successful experience in designing buildings that demonstrate his competence in architectural work. The buildings previously designed by the architect should also reflect a careful study of the peculiar needs of each client.
3. The architect should possess the vision and imagination to translate the educational aims and program specified by the educator into functional buildings. There should be an avoidance of stereotypes. The architect should not possess set, preconceived ideas which are hard to change. He must be able and willing to mold design to fit needs.
4. The architect must have a record of working cooperatively and harmoniously with his clients, educational advisors, and contractors.
5. The architect must have an adequate staff of trained personnel to carry out the building program without undue delay. The architect should either have qualified engineering services available in his own organization or should specify qualified engineering specialists who will work with him.
6. The architect should keep abreast of recent research and study concerning materials and mechanical equipment used in school buildings.
7. The architect should show such economy in the use of space and materials as is consistent with educational needs.
8. The architect should be competent in the field of site planning and the utilization of space for educational and recreational purposes.
9. The architect must give adequate supervision to his buildings. This is a very important part of the architect's services.
10. The architect should be informed concerning state and municipal building regulations and codes and must show care in complying with them.
11. The architect must demonstrate sound business judgment, proper business procedures, and good record keeping on the job.*

Physical educators should carefully think through their own ideas and plans for their special facilities and submit them in writing to the architect during the early stages of school and college planning. There should also be several conferences in which the architect and physical education specialist exchange views in regard to the educational and architectural possibilities to be considered.

Many architects know little about programs of health and physical education and therefore welcome the advice of specialists in these fields. The architect might be furnished with such information as the names of school or college plants where excellent facilities exist, kinds of activities that will constitute the program, space requirements for various activities, storage and equipment areas needed, temperature requirements, relation of dressing, showering, and toilet facilities to program, teaching stations needed, best construction materials for activities, and lighting requirements. The physical educator may not have all this information readily available, including some of the latest trends and standards recommended for his field and endeavor. However, such information can be obtained through professional organizations, other schools where excellent facilities have been developed, and facility books developed by experts in the area.

Mr. William Haroldson, Director of Health and Physical Education for the Seattle, Washington, Public Schools, has developed a procedural outline in cooperation with three architectural firms, in

*From Leu, D. J.: Planning education facilities, New York, 1965, The Center for Applied Research in Education, Inc. (The Library of Education), p. 50.

which are listed some essential considerations for health and physical educators in their relationships and cooperative planning with architects. Some of the main points stressed in this outline are discussed.

Educational specifications

Adequate educational specifications provide the basis for good planning by the architect:

1. General description of the program, such as the number of teaching stations necessary to service the health and physical education programs for a total student body of approximately _____ boys and _____ girls.

2. Basic criteria as pertain to the gymnasium: the number of teaching periods per day, capacities, number and size of courts, lockers, and projected total uses contemplated for the facility.

   a. Availability to the community
   b. Proximity to parks
   c. Parking
   d. Size of groups that will use gymnasium after school hours
   e. Whether locker rooms will or will not be made available to public use

3. Specific description of aspects of the health and physical education programs that are of concern to the architects.

   a. Class size and scheduling, both present and possible future; number of instructors, present and future
   b. Preferred method of handling students, for example, flow of traffic in classrooms, locker rooms, shower rooms, and going to outside play area (This item has a direct bearing on the design of this area.)
   c. Storage requirements and preferred method of handling all permanent equipment and supplies (Here, unless a standard has been established, requirements should be specific—for example, request should state number and size of each item rather than "ample storage.")
   d. Team and other extracurricular use of facilities (It is of assistance to the architect if the educational specifications can describe a typical week's use of the proposed facility, which would include a broad daily program, afterschool use, and potential community use.)

Meeting with the architect

At this point, it is advisable to meet with the architect to discuss specifications in order to ensure complete understanding and to allow the architect to point out certain restrictions or limitations that may be anticipated even before the first preliminary plan is made.

Design

The factors to be considered in the design of the facility and discussed with the architect should include the following:

1. *Budget.* An adequate budget should be allowed. Gymnasia are subject to extremely hard usage, and durability should not be sacrificed for economy.
2. *Acoustics.* Utilize the service of acoustical consultants.
3. *Public address system.* How is it to be used—for instruction, athletic events, general communication?
4. *Color and design.* Harmonize with surrounding neighborhood if it is a new school or match other areas if it is an addition to an old school.
5. *Fenestration* (window treatment). Consider light control, potential window breakage, vision panel; gymnasium areas should have safety glass (preferred) or wire protectors.
6. *Ventilation.* The area should be zoned for flexibility of usage. This means greater ventilation when a larger number of spectators are present, or a reduction for single class groups, or isolated areas, such as locker rooms. Special attention must be given to proper ventilation of uni-

form drying rooms, gymnasium storage areas, locker and shower areas. (Current and off-season uniform storage areas require constant ventilation when plant is shut down.) Ventilation equipment should have a low noise level.

7. *Supplementary equipment in the gymnasium.* Such equipment should be held to a minimum. Supplementary equipment, such as fire boxes, should be recessed.

8. *Compactness and integration.* Keep volume compact—large, barnlike spaces are unpleasant, costly to heat and maintain. Integrate as far as budget permits.

9. *Mechanical or electrical features.* Special attention should be given to location of panel boards, chalk boards, fire alarm, folding doors, and so on.

Further critique with the architect

1. The architect begins the development of his plans from his understanding of the initial requirements that he has considered in relation to the design factors listed.

2. When it becomes evident that the basic plan is set, the architect usually will call in consulting engineers to discuss the structural and mechanical systems prior to approval of the plan by the school district. These systems will have been given previous attention by the architect but cannot be discussed with the consultants other than in generalities before the plan is in approximate final form.

3. A further series of meetings are then held with school personnel regarding approval of preliminary plans and proposed structural and mechanical systems and the use of materials after the incorporation in the preliminary plans.

4. If supplementary financing by governmental agencies other than the school district is involved, the drawing or set of drawings will have been submitted to those agencies with a project outline or specifications as soon as the plan has been sufficiently developed to establish the area. If the other agency approves the application as submitted by the architect, the final preliminary working drawings are started.

Final processing

It is advisable that all matters that can be settled are decided during preliminary planning in order to save time. If this method is used, greater clarity is assured and less changing or misunderstanding results. Preliminary plans are drawn with the intent of illustrating the plan for the school district; working drawings are technical in nature and are often difficult to interpret. However, should school personnel wish to check the working drawings before their completion, they should be welcome to do so.

GENERAL TRENDS IN FACILITY CONSTRUCTION

In respect to educational buildings in general, there has been considerable change. Traditionally rectangular in shape, buildings of all shapes and sizes have appeared in recent years, including round, semicircular, quadrangular, hexangular, oval, and pentangular buildings. New types of rooms have also been introduced, including large rooms for team teaching and large lecture groups; classrooms of various shapes and sizes; special rooms including those for dramatics, science, band, choral groups, business machines, and television broadcasting; and more office and conference rooms for such people as counselors and health program and administrative assistants. Furthermore, with the greater use of overhead lighting, there has been a trend to more windowless rooms. In fact, some buildings have no windows whatsoever.

School sites are getting larger and are being located away from busy industrial centers. More space is also being provided for parking.

The designs of school buildings and other facilities concerned with health and physical education programs and recreation today stress two factors: the educational needs of the children and others who pursue programs in such areas and the need for economy at a time when construction costs are so high.

The trend is to do away with many of the so-called frills in order to achieve economy but at the same time not to compromise educational standards. Educational leaders advocate taking greater advantage of labor-, material-, and space-saving devices. For example, they suggest that the ceilings in regular classrooms be cut down from the traditional 12 feet to 8 feet. They maintain that good lighting can be gained under most conditions with only 8-foot ceilings. Also, multipurpose halls can be constructed to double as exhibit and social areas, and gymnasia can be used for physical education and community purposes rather than merely for spectator entertainment.

It has further been pointed out that several practices are not economical in some of the construction going on today. An example of this is the application of Gothic and Colonial architecture merely to enhance appearance. Buildings should be planned with emphasis on the functional, inside aspects, rather than on the outside ornamentation. Also, it is not economical to have a large auditorium constructed that will be only half filled except on commencement day.

These features have received the support of the American Association of School Administrators. Bright plastic floor covering, improved lighting, and colorful painted walls are important. Classrooms should be large, with movable furniture, work alcoves, and conference rooms. Large, well-planned play areas are important features in the selection of a school site, with 10 to 20 acres of land frequently being used for such sites. Both on the elementary and secondary levels, one-story buildings are becoming increasingly common. Single-story construction is safer more economical and decreases noise. Walls are being constructed with special attention to acoustical treatment to reduce noise. Ceilings

Main entrance to Storey gymnasium. (Cheyenne Public Schools, Cheyenne, Wyo.)

that slope are being increasingly utilized in order to improve light distribution and to reduce the space to be heated. Many rooms and facilities are being located to facilitate community use. Finally, there is evidence of the practicability of single-loaded corridors, which run along the outer walls of the building. In this way classrooms open onto the hall from only one side.

Flexibility of design is an important trend in facility management today, with the inclusion of folding partitions and multiple use of facilities for different types of activities.

Some new materials that are being used are as follows:

1. *Structural steel.* One of the most versatile of building materials, used in various shapes, sizes, and strengths, providing for greater stability, flexibility, and adaptability.
2. *Structural pine.* Used for such purposes as laminated beams to form roof structures and uprights of buildings and other purposes, providing economy of design, beauty, safety, and ease of maintenance.
3. *Concrete block.* Increasingly being used to enclose framework and as interior walls; economical and easily removed from non–load-bearing walls to develop flexibility.
4. *Stone.* Used to a great extent for attractive exteriors on schools and for permanence.
5. *Corrugated steel.* Provides an economical method of long-span roofing.
6. *Carpeting of classrooms.* Helps eliminate noise and is easy to clean and maintain with less man hours required.

NEW FEATURES IN THE CONSTRUCTION OF PHYSICAL EDUCATION FACILITIES

There are many new trends in facilities and materials for physical education programs. New paving materials, new types of equipment, improved landscapes, new construction materials, new shapes for swimming pools, partial shelters, and synthetic grass are just a few of the many new developments. Combination indoor-outdoor pools, physical fitness equipment for outdoor use, all-weather tennis courts, and lines that now come in multicolors for various games and activities are other new developments.

In gymnasium construction some of the new features include the utilization of modern engineering techniques and materials. This has resulted in welded steel and laminated wood modular frames; arched and gabled roofs; domes that provide areas completely free from internal supports; exterior surfaces of aluminum, steel, fiber glass, and plastics; different window patterns and styles; several kinds of floor surfaces of nonslip material; prefabricated wall surfaces; better lighting systems with improved quality and quantity and less glare. Facilities are moving from use of regular glass to either plastic and fiber glass panel or to overhead skydome. Lightweight fiber glass, sandwich panels, or fabricated sheets of translucent fiber glass laminated over an aluminum framework are proving popular. They require no painting, the cost of labor and materials is lower, there is no need for shades or blinds to eliminate glare, and the breakage problem is reduced or eliminated.

Locker rooms and service areas are including built-in locks that involve combination locks with built-in combination changers that permit the staff to change combinations when needed. There is more extensive use of ceramic tile because of its durability and low-cost maintenance. Wall-hung toilet compartment features permit easier maintenance and sanitation with no chance for rust to start from the floor. Odor control is being effectively handled by new dispensers. New thin-profile heating, ventilating, and air-conditioning fan coil units are now being used.

Houston's Astrodome. (Courtesy Houston Sports Association, Inc., Houston, Tex.)

Air-supported tennis court enclosure. (Airshelters, Division of Birdair Structures, Inc., Buffalo, N. Y.)

Shaver & Company, Salina, Kan.

Graceland Fieldhouse, Lamoni, Iowa.

Forman School, Litchfield, Conn. (Courtesy Educational Facilities Laboratories, New York, N. Y.)

Shaver & Company, Salina, Kan.

Graceland Fieldhouse, Lamoni, Iowa.

Shaver & Company, Salina, Kan.

Graceland Fieldhouse, Lamoni, Iowa.

Shaver & Company, Salina, Kan.
Graceland Fieldhouse, Lamoni, Iowa.

The health suite is being modernized by making it more attractive and serviceable. There is also a trend toward better ventilation, heating, and lighting and more easily cleaned materials on walls and floors to guarantee improved sanitation.

New developments in regard to indoor swimming pools include automatic control boards, where one person can have direct control over all filters, chlorinators, chemical pumps, and level controllers; much larger deck space area constructed of nonslip ceramic tile; greater use of diatomaceous earth rather than sand filters to filter out small particles of matter including some bacteria; underwater lighting; water-level deck pools (where the overflow gutters are placed in the deck surrounding the pool instead of in the pool's side walls and provision is made for grating that is designed so that the water that overflows is drained to a trench under the deck without the possibility of debris returning to the pool); air-supported roofs that can serve as re-

movable tops in a combination indoor-outdoor pool; and movable bulkheads.

New developments in regard to outdoor swimming pools involve new shapes—including oval, wedge, kidney, figure eight, cloverleaf, and bean shaped—as well as modern accessories, including gas heaters, automatic water levelers, and retractable roofs and sides. More supplemental recreational facilities, such as shuffleboard courts, volleyball, and horseshoes, and more deck equipment, including guard rails, slides, and pool covers, are being included around larger pools.

A brief listing of some new features that are being used in many school buildings in the area of health and physical education have been developed by the Educational Facilities Laboratories.* This is a nonprofit organization financed by the Ford Foundation. It enters into joint research projects

---

*Educational Facilities Laboratories, 477 Madison Ave., New York, N. Y. 10022.

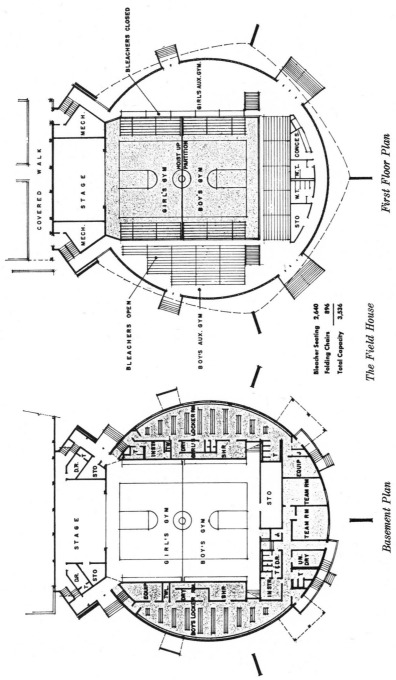

Basement Plan

First Floor Plan

The Field House

Bleacher Seating	2,640
Folding Chairs	896
Total Capacity	3,536

Geodesic field house. (From Conventional gymnasium *vs.* geodesic field house: case studies of educational facilities No. 1, New York, Educational Facilities Laboratories, Inc.)

with schools interested in testing the practicality of some new kind of facility, design, or material.

The geodesic field house has been compared, in cost of construction, with a conventional gymnasium (see accompanying illustration) and found to be slightly less expensive. This type of structure has applicability primarily to programs in which strong emphasis is placed on athletics and spectator appeal or to communities that need a very large auditorium. For these reasons it seems that the geodesic field house has limited value for the general physical education program.

Bubble tops for swimming pools and tennis courts make it possible to use them as outdoor facilities in summer and as indoor facilities in the winter. The roof made of vinyl-coated fabric costs less per square foot in contrast to a wooden dome or a geodesic dome.

Partial shelters for physical education activities have been studied and are in use in many Texas public schools. They are considered practical for elementary school physical education in which change from school clothes many times is not required. These partial shelters protect children from extremes of climate and, at the same time,

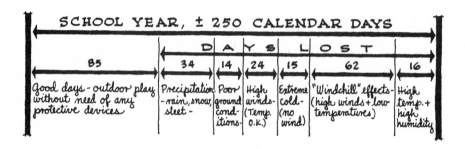

SCHOOL YEAR, ± 250 CALENDAR DAYS						
	D A Y S L O S T					
85	34	14	24	15	62	16
Good days - outdoor play without need of any protective devices	Precipitation - rain, snow, sleet -	Poor ground conditions -	High winds - (Temp. O.K.)	Extreme cold - (no wind)	"Windchill" effects - (high winds + low temperatures)	High temp. + high humidity

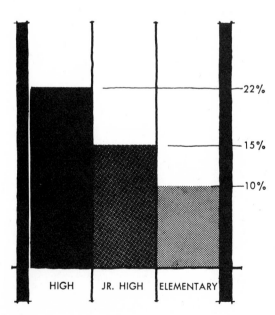

—22%

—15%

—10%

HIGH   JR. HIGH   ELEMENTARY

BUILDING SPACE DEVOTED TO PHYSICAL ACTIVITIES

Charts showing amount of space devoted to physical activities in schools, the implications of weather conditions for the physical education program, and some ideas for partial shelters for physical education programs. (From Shelter for physical education: a study of the feasibility of the use of limited shelters for physical education, College Station, Texas, Texas Engineering Experiment Station, Texas A & M University.)

allow for exercise in the open air. They are of course more economical than traditional facilities.

New artificial turf has been developed and successfully tried. The initial reaction of students and teachers is that the turf provides excellent traction and helps the acoustics. It is easily cleaned with a vacuum.

Rubber-cushioned tennis courts are being used in some places. They consist of tough durable material about 4 inches thick, with the individual advantages of clay, turf, and composition courts being combined into one type of surfacing.

Other new developments in health and physical education facilities that have come into use in schools across the country are

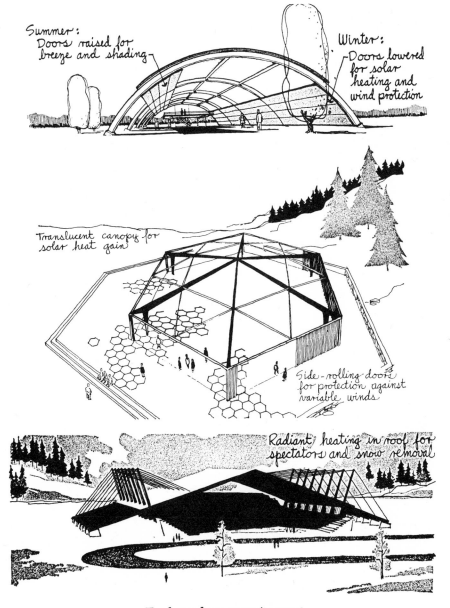

Summer:
Doors raised for breeze and shading

Winter:
Doors lowered for solar heating and wind protection

Translucent canopy for solar heat gain

Side-rolling doors for protection against variable winds

Radiant heating in roof for spectators and snow removal

For legend see opposite page.

numerous. Sculptured play apparatus has been produced by a number of firms. It is designed to be more conducive to imaginative movements and creativity than conventional equipment. Hard-surfaced, rubberized, all-weather running tracks, radiant heating of decks on swimming pools, floating roofs with the elimination of non–load-bearing walls, interior climate control, better indoor and outdoor lighting, rubber padding for use under apparatus, park-school concept with land being used for school and recreational purposes, outdoor skating rinks, translucent plastic materials for swimming pool canopies and other uses, electrically operated machinery to move equipment and partitions and bleachers, and auxiliary gymnasia used for both activity and classroom use are a few more of the new developments in facilities for health and physical education programs.

Park-school facilities

The park-school complex is another innovation that should be mentioned. In this type of setup the school is erected near a park, and the park facilities are used by both the school and the community. This has implications particularly for physical education and recreation programs, since the school usually uses the park facilities during school hours and the recreation department uses them after school hours, on weekends, and during vacation periods.

TEACHING STATIONS

The teaching station concept should be taken into consideration when scheduling physical education classes. A teaching station is the space or setting where one teacher or staff member can carry on physical education activities for one group of students. The number and size of teaching stations available together with the number of teachers on the staff, the size of the group, the number of times the group meets, the number of periods in the school or college day, and the program of activities are important items to consider in planning.

According to the participants in the National Facilities Conference,* the following formulas are listed for determining the number of teaching stations needed.

---

*Participants in National Facilities Conference: Planning areas and facilities for health, physical education, and recreation, Washington, D. C., 1965, American Association for Health, Physical Education, and Recreation, p. 83.

Overpass to athletic facilities. A unique feature of overall campus planning permits access to facilities from parking lots and academic buildings without the necessity of crossing a main thoroughfare. (University of California at Irvine.)

Secondary schools and colleges

The formula for computing the number of teaching stations needed for physical education in colleges and secondary schools would be as follows:

$$\frac{\text{Minimum number of teaching stations} = \dfrac{\text{Number of students}}{\text{Average number of students per instructor}} \times}{}$$

$$\frac{\text{Number of periods class meets each week}}{\text{Total number of class periods in school work}}$$

For example, if a school system projects its enrollment to 700 students and plans six class periods a day with an average class size of thirty students, and physical education is required daily, the formula would read as follows:

$$\text{Minimum number of teaching stations} = \frac{700 \text{ students}}{30 \text{ per class}} \times$$

$$\frac{5 \text{ periods per week}}{30 \text{ periods per week}} = \frac{3{,}500}{900} = \mathbf{3.9}$$

Colleges could substitute pertinent facts into the same formula to determine the number of teaching stations they would need.

Elementary schools

The formula for computing the number of teaching stations needed for physical education in the elementary schools would be as follows:

$$\text{Minimum number of teaching stations} = \frac{\text{Number of class-rooms of students}}{} \times$$

$$\frac{\text{Number of physical education periods per week per class}}{\text{Total periods in school week}}$$

For example, in an elementary school with six grades, with three classes at each level (approximately 450 to 540 students), ten 30-minute physical education periods per day, and physical education conducted on a daily basis, the teaching station needs would be calculated as follows:

$$\text{Minimum number of teaching stations} = 18 \text{ classroom units} \times$$

$$\frac{5 \text{ periods per week}}{50 \text{ periods per week}} = \frac{90}{50} = \mathbf{1.8}$$

Shaver & Company, Salina, Kan.

Gymnasium. (McPherson High School, McPherson, Kan.)

ROOMS	FLOORS									LOWER WALLS							UPPER WALLS					CEILINGS	
	Asphalt, Rubber Linoleum Tile	Cement, Abrasive and Non-absorbent	Maple, hard	Terrazzo Abrasive	Tile, ceramic	Brick	Brick, glazed	Cinder Block	Concrete	Plaster	Tile, ceramic	Wood Panel	Moisture-proof	Brick	Brick, glazed	Cinder Block	Plaster	Acoustic	Moisture-resistant	Concrete or Structure Tile	Structure Tile	Tile, acoustic	Moisture-resistant
Apparatus Storage Room			1					2	1	C													
Classrooms	2	1									2				2	1	*		C	C	1	1	
Clubroom	2	1									2				2	1			C	C	1	1	
Corrective Room		1		2	1		2		1		2		2	2	1	2					1	1	
Custodial Supply Room		1		2					1														
Dance Studio	2	1																					
Drying Room (equip.)	1		2	2	1	2	1	1					1	1						C	1	C	
Gymnasium	1	1			2	1					2		2		2	1	*		C	C	1	C	
Health-Service Unit	1	1			2	1			1		2		2		2	1					1	1	
Laundry Room		2		1	2	1	2		1	C			1				*				*	1	
Locker Rooms		3		2	1	2	2	3		1			1		1	2				C	1	1	
Natatorium				1	2	1	3	2	1			**	2	2	1		*	*	C	C	1	*	
Offices	2	1			2	1		1		1			2		2	1					1	1	
Recreation Room	2	1		2	1		2	1		1		*	2		1	2	*		C	C	1	1	
Shower Rooms		3	2	1	1	2	2	2	1		1		2		2	2		*		C	1	1	
Special-activity Room	2	1	1	2		1	1	1			1	*	1		1	1			C	C	1	C	
Team Room	3		2	1	2	2	3	2	1		2	*	1		1	2				C	1	C	
Toilet Rooms	3		2	1	1	2	2	2	1		2	**	1		1	1				C	1	1	
Toweling-Drying Room (bath)	3		2	1	1	2	2	2	1		2	*	2		2	2		*			1	1	*

Note: The numbers in the Table indicate first, second, and third choices. "C" indicates the material as being contrary to good practice. An * indicates desirable quality.

Suggested indoor surface materials. (From Participants in National Facilities Conference: Planning areas and facilities for health, physical education, and recreation, revised, Chicago, 1965, The Athletic Institute.)

INDOOR FACILITIES

Several special areas and facilities are needed by programs of health, physical education, and recreation. A few of the indoor areas that are important and prominent in the conduct of these specialized programs are briefly discussed in this section.

Administrative and staff offices*

It is important, as far as it is practical and possible, for professional persons working in health, physical education, and recreation to have a section of a building set aside for administrative and staff offices. As a minimum there should be a large central office with a waiting room. The central office will provide a place where the secretarial and clerical work can be performed, space for keeping records and files, and storage closets for office supplies. The waiting room can serve as a reception point where students and visitors can wait until staff members are ready to see them.

Separate offices for the staff members should be provided, if possible. This allows for a place where conferences can be held in private and without interruption. This is a very important consideration for health counseling and for discussing scholastic, family, recreational, and other problems. If separate officers are not practical, a desk should be provided for each staff member. In this event, there should be a private room available to staff members for conferences.

Other facilities that make for a more efficient and enjoyable administrative and staff setup are staff dressing rooms, departmental library, conference room, and toilet and lavatory facilities.

Locker, shower, and drying rooms

Health, physical education, and recreation activities require facilities for storage of clothes, showering, and drying. These

*See also Chapter 21 on Office Management.

are essential to good health and for a well-organized program. The reason such facilities are often not fully utilized is that poor planning makes them inadequate and uncomfortable.

Locker and shower rooms should be readily accessible to activity areas. Locker rooms should not be congested places that students want to get out of as soon as possible. Instead, they should provide ample room, both storage and dressing type lockers, stationary benches to sit upon, mirrors to aid in dressing, recessed lighting fixtures, and drinking fountains.

An average of 14 square feet per individual at peak load, exclusive of the space utilized by the lockers, is required to provide proper space.

Storage lockers should be provided for each individual in the school or recreational program. An additional 10% should be installed for purposes of expanded enrollments or membership. These are lockers for the permanent use of each individual and can be utilized to hold essential clothing and other supplies. They can be smaller than the dressing lockers and some recommended sizes are these: 7½ by 12 by 24

Women's locker room. (University of California at Irvine.)

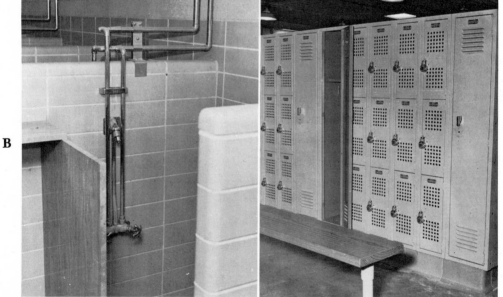

A, Dual-shelf system in the girls' dressing room. Books, purses, and other in-hand objects go on the lower shelf. Bobby pins, combs, compacts, and lipstick, of course, need to be at hand on the smaller upper shelf. **B,** A girl's shower stall. Picture taken from an upper angle. **C,** Locker arrangement utilized in both girls' and boys' locker rooms. The perforated storage lockers are 9 inches wide, 20 inches high, and 15 inches deep. Hook hangers provide a place to hang gymnasium wear. Each student has his own personal lock rented from the school. Shelves in the dressing lockers were lowered from 12 inches to 16 inches to make room for the large folios that many students carry. The dressing lockers are 8 inches high, 12 inches wide, and 15 inches deep. There is room for books, shoes, and clothes. (Courtesy Spring Branch Independent School District, Houston, Tex.)

inches, 6 by 12 by 36 inches, and 7½ by 12 by 18 inches. The basket type lockers are not looked upon with favor by many experts, because of the hygiene factor, the fact that an attendant is required for good administration of this system, and the necessity of carting the baskets from place to place.

Dressing lockers are utilized by participants only when actually engaging in activity. They are large in size, usually 12 by 12 by 54 inches or 12 by 12 by 48 inches in elementary schools and 12 by 12 by 72 inches for secondary schools and colleges and for community recreation programs.

Shower rooms should be provided that have the gang type shower for boys and a combination of the gang and cubicle type showers for girls. Some facility planners recommend that girls have a number of shower heads equal to 40% of the enrollment at peak load and the boys, 30% of the enrollment at peak load. Another recommendation is one shower head for four boys and one for three girls at peak load. These should be 4 feet apart. If showers are installed where a graded change of water temperature is provided and where the individual progresses through such a gradation, the number of shower heads can be reduced. The shower rooms should also be equipped with liquid soap dispensers, good ventilation and heating, floors constructed of nonslip material, and recessed plumbing. The ceiling should be dome-shaped so that it will more readily shed water.

The drying room adjacent to the shower room is an essential. This should be equipped with proper drainage, good ventilation, towel bar, and a ledge that can be used to place a foot upon while drying.

A report of a conference on the planning of facilities for health, physical education, and recreation lists the following common errors in service facilities:

Failure to provide adequate locker and dressing space

Failure to plan dressing and shower area so as to reduce foot traffic to a minimum and establish clean, dry aisles for bare feet

Failure to provide a nonskid surface on dressing, shower, and toweling room floors

Failure to properly relate teaching stations with service facilities

Inadequate provision for drinking fountains

Failure to provide acoustical treatment where needed

Failure to provide and properly locate toilet facilities to serve all participants and spectators

Failure to provide doorways, hallways, or ramps so that equipment may be moved easily

Failure to design equipment rooms for convenient and quick check-in and check-out

Failure to provide mirrors and shelving for boys' and girls' dressing facilities, and lipstick tissues for girls

Failure to plan locker and dressing rooms with correct traffic pattern to swimming pool

Failure to construct shower, toilet, and dressing rooms with sufficient floor slope and properly located drains

Failure to place shower heads low enough and in such a position that the spray is kept within the shower room.

Failure to provide shelves in the toilet room*

Gymnasia

The type and number of gymnasia that should be part of a school or recreational plant will depend upon the number of individuals who will be participating, the variety of activities that will be conducted in this area, and the school level concerned.

General construction features to which most individuals will agree include smooth walls, hardwood floors (maple preferred—laid lengthwise), recessed lights, recessed radiators, adequate and well-screened windows, and storage space for the apparatus and other equipment utilized. It is also generally agreed that in schools it is best to have the gymnasium located in a separate wing of the building to isolate the noise and also as a convenient location for

*Planning facilities for health, physical education, and recreation, revised edition, Chicago, 1956, The Athletic Institute, Inc., p. 70.

Men's gymnasium. (College of San Mateo, San Mateo, Calif.)

community groups that will be anxious to use such facilities.

The American Association for Health, Physical Education, and Recreation has listed several important factors to keep in mind when planning the gymnasium:

1. Hard maple flooring which is resilient and nonslippery.
2. Smooth interior walls to a height of 10 or 12 feet.
3. Upper walls need not be smooth.
4. The ceiling should reflect light and absorb sound, and there should be at least 22 to 24 feet from the floor to exposed beams.
5. Windows should be ten to twelve feet above floor and placed on long side of room.
6. Heating should be thermostatically controlled, radiators recessed with protecting grill or grate if placed at floor level.
7. Sub-flooring should be moisture- and termite-resistant and well ventilated.
8. Prior consideration must be given concerning the suspension of apparatus from the ceiling and the erection of wall-type apparatus.
9. Mechanical ventilation may be necessary.
10. Proper illumination meeting approved standards and selectively controlled for various activities must be designed.
11. Floor plates for standards and apparatus

must be planned, as well as such items as blackboards, electric clocks and scoreboards, public address system, and provisions for press and radio.
12. Floor markings for various games should be placed after prime coat of seal has been applied and prior to application of the finishing coats.*

The number of teaching stations desired will play an important part in deciding the size and number of the gymnasia. A teaching station is a place where a group meets with a teacher or leader for the conduct of certain activities. The degree to which a varied program is offered, the facilities available, and the number of staff members assigned will determine the number of teaching stations utilized in any program.†

In addition to an adequate number of teaching stations, it is also important to give attention to official size courts, ade-

---

*American Association for Health, Physical Education, and Recreation: Administrative problems in health education, physical education, and recreation, Washington, D. C., 1953, The Association, p. 83.

†See also pp. 428-429.

This unit provides:

Two teaching stations

One standard inter-school basketball court

Two court areas for instruction and intra-mural basketball

Two court areas for volleyball, newcomb, etc.

Four court areas for badminton, paddle tennis, etc.

Two circle areas for instruction, dodge ball, and circle games

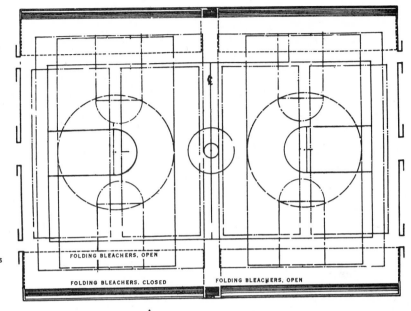

A

This unit provides:

Two teaching stations

One standard inter-school basketball court

Two court areas for in-struction and intra-mural basketball

Three court areas for volleyball, new-comb, etc.

Six court areas for badminton, paddle tennis, etc.

Four circle areas for instruction, dodge ball, and circle games

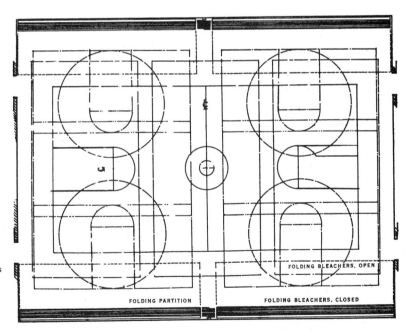

B

A, Illustrative plan of two teaching stations for junior high school gymnasium. **B,** Illustrative plan of two teaching stations for senior high school gymnasium. (From Participants in National Facilities Conference: Planning areas and facilities for health, physical education, and recreation, revised, Chicago, 1965, The Athletic Institute.)

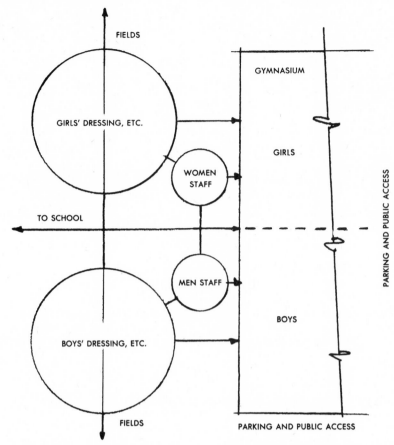

Orientation of gymnasium to related areas. (From Participants in National Facilities Conference: Planning areas and facilities for health, physical education, and recreation, revised, Chicago, 1965, The Athletic Institute.)

quate space for safe and enjoyable participation, and spectator space, if such is desired. When spectator space is provided, bleachers that can be telescoped and recessed in the walls are advisable, as they do not take space away from activity participation.

Many gymnasia have folding doors that divide them into halves, thirds, or fourths and allow for activities to be conducted simultaneously on each side. This has proved satisfactory where separate gymnasia could not be provided.

In elementary schools that desire only one teaching station a minimum floor space of 36 feet by 52 feet is required. Where two

teaching stations are desired, floor space of 52 feet by 72 feet may be divided by a folding partition. In junior and senior high schools where only one teaching station is desired, a minimum floor space of 48 feet by 66 feet is necessary. If two teaching stations are necessary, an area 66 feet by 96 feet of floor space, exclusive of bleachers, will provide these teaching stations of minimum size. The folding partition that provides the two teaching stations should be motor driven. Where seating capacity is desired, additional space will be needed. If more than two teaching stations are desired, the gymnasium area may be extended to provide an additional

Special exercise room. (University of Maine at Portland.)

station or activity rooms may be added. Of course, the addition of a swimming pool will also provide an additional teaching station.

Other considerations for gymnasia should include provisions for basketball backboards, mountings for various apparatus that will be used, recessed drinking fountains, places for hanging mats, outlets for various electric appliances and cleaning devices, proper line markings for activities, bulletin boards, and other essentials to a well-rounded program.

Common errors in construction of gymnasia are as follows:

Provision for spectator space at the sacrifice of instructional space.

Failure to mark floor for possible court games such as badminton, basketball, and volleyball.

Construction of a combination auditorium-gymnasium when separate facilities could be provided.

Installation of permanent bleachers instead of folding bleachers, resulting in loss of maximum use of floor space.

Failure to provide ventilated space below a built-up gymnasium floor.

Natural lighting construction permitting leakage and glare problems.*

---

*Planning facilities for health, physical education, and recreation, revised edition, Chicago, 1956, The Athletic Institute, Inc., p. 63.

Special activity areas

Although gymnasia are large and take up considerable space, there should still be additional areas for activities essential to school programs of health, physical education, and recreation.

Wherever possible additional activity areas should be provided for remedial or adapted activities, apparatus, handball, squash, weight lifting, dancing, rhythms, fencing, and dramatics and for various recreational activities such as arts and crafts, lounging and resting, and bowling. The activities to be provided will depend on interests of participants and type of program. The recommended size of such auxiliary gymnasia is 30 by 50 by 24 feet, or preferably 40 by 60 by 24 feet.

Another special room especially desirable in the elementary school is the all-purpose room that could be used for all types of activities, including games, music, dramatics, and social events.

In reference to special activity areas, it should also be pointed out that regulation classrooms can be converted into these special rooms. This may be feasible where the actual construction of such costly facilities may not be practical.

The remedial or adapted activities room should be equipped with such items as horizontal ladders, mirrors, mats, climbing

Special tennis structure. (Brigham Young University, Provo, Utah.)

ropes, stall bars and benches, pulley weights, dumbbells, Indian clubs, shoulder wheels, and such other equipment as is suited for the particular needs of the individuals participating.

Auxiliary rooms

The main types of auxiliary areas found in connection with school and college health and physical education and recreation facilities are supply, checkout, custodial, and laundry rooms.

Supply rooms should be easily accessible from the gymnasium and other activity areas. In these rooms will be stored balls, nets, standards, and other equipment needed for the programs that are offered. The size of these rooms will vary according to the number of activities offered and the number of participants.

Checkout rooms should be provided on a seasonal basis. They will house the equipment and supplies used in various seasonal activities.

Custodial rooms provide a place for storing equipment and supplies utilized in the maintenance of these specialized facilities.

Laundries should be adequate in size to accommodate the laundering of such essential items as towels, uniforms, and swimming suits.

SWIMMING POOLS

In the year 1900 there were very few indoor swimming pools in the public schools in the United States. Today, however, there are approximately 2,500 swimming pools in public schools.

According to Gabrielsen,* schools should have swimming pools for many reasons. Swimming is the number one recreation activity in America, and it is often listed by elementary and secondary school students as their favorite activity. Teaching all children how to swim could reduce the more than 8,000 deaths by drowning that occur in the United States each year. Knowing how to swim leads to many other excellent aquatic activities such as surfing, sailing, canoeing, fishing, scuba diving, and water skiing.

Gabrielsen in his report cited the major

---

*Professor M. A. Gabrielsen, New York University. From a speech given at the Conference on Planning, Constructing, Utilizing Physical Education, Recreation, and Athletic Facilities, sponsored by the Ohio Department of Education, Columbus, Ohio, December 10, 1969.

Swimming pool complex. (Brigham Young University, Provo, Utah.)

Dartmouth College swimming pool. See also pp. 440 and 441.

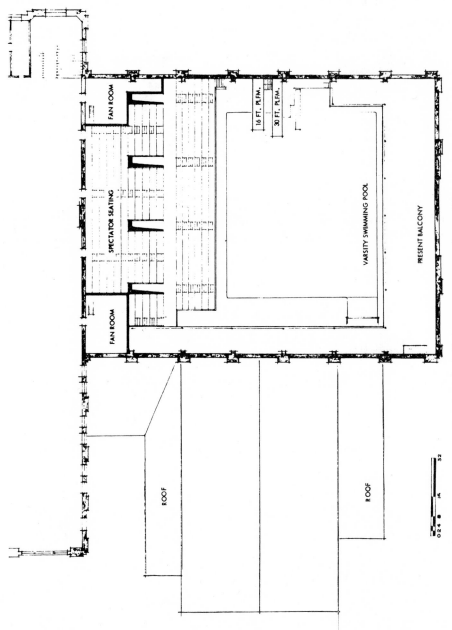

Dartmouth College swimming pool—cont'd.

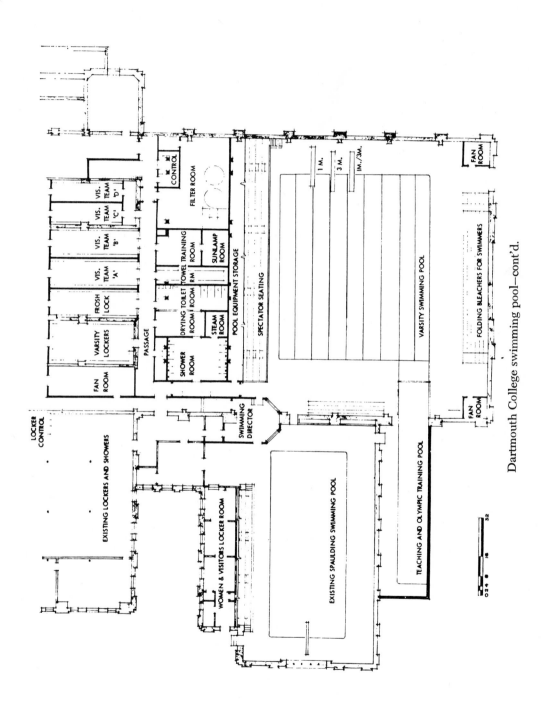

Dartmouth College swimming pool—cont'd.

design decisions that must be made if a school or college decides to construct a pool. These include such items as the nature of the program to be conducted in a pool, type of overflow system to be used, dimensions and shape of pool, depth of the water, type of finish, type of filters and water treatment system, construction material to be used, amount of deck area, climate control, illumination, and number of spectators to be accommodated. The range in cost of pools can vary from $2.65 per square foot to $17.00 per square foot depending upon the material used, the design, and the geographic location. Cost of pool enclosures vary from about $2.50 to $3.50 per square foot for air structures, to $7.00 to $9.00 per square foot for prefabricated, lightweight aluminum dome frames supporting reinforced plastic roof tents of acrylic panels, to $18.00 to $25.00 per square foot for steel frame with masonry or fireproof panel walls, steel roof trusses, beams, or joints, and fire-resistive metal or concrete plank roof deck.

Some mistakes that Gabrielsen says should be avoided in the construction of a pool include entrances to the pool from the locker rooms opening onto the deep rather than the shallow end of the pool, pool base finished with slippery material such as glazed tile, insufficient depth of water for diving, improper placement of ladders, insufficient rate of recirculation of water to accommodate peak bathing loads, inadequate storage space, failure to use acoustical material on ceiling and walls, insufficient illumination, slippery tile on decks, and an inadequate overflow system at the ends of the pool.

Finally, in this report are listed some trends and innovations in pool design and operation. These include: the Rim-Flow Overflow System, inflatable roof structure, the skydome design, pool tent cover, floating swimming pool complex, prefabrication of pool tanks, automation of pool recirculating and filter systems, regenerative cycle filter system, adjustable height diving platform, variable depth bottoms, fluorescent underwater lights, automatic cleaning systems, and wave making machines.

Present types of swimming pools have in the main two objectives, one to provide instructional and competitive programs and the other for recreation.

The swimming pool should be located on or above the ground level, have southern exposure, be isolated from other units in the building, and be easily accessible from the central dressing and locker rooms. Materials that have been found most adaptive to swimming pools are smooth, glazed, light-colored tile or brick.

The standard indoor pool is 75 feet in length. The width should be a multiple of 7 feet, with a minimum of 35 feet. Depths vary from 2 feet 6 inches at the shallow end to 4 feet 6 inches at the outer limits of the shallow area. The shallow or instructional area should comprise about two-thirds of the pool. The deeper areas taper to 9 to 12 feet in depth. An added but important factor is a movable bulkhead that can be used to divide the pool into various instructional areas.

The deck space around the pool should be constructed of a nonslip material and provide ample space for land drills and demonstrations. The area above the water should be unobstructed. The ceiling should be at least 25 feet above the water if a 3-meter diving board will be used. The walls and the ceiling of the pool should be acoustically treated.

The swimming pool should be constructed so as to receive as much natural light as possible, with the windows located on the sides rather than on the ends. Artificial lighting should be recessed in the ceilings. Good lighting is especially important in the areas where the diving boards are located. Underwater lighting is beautiful but not an essential.

There should be an efficient system for adequately heating and circulating the

Swimming pool. (Alabama College, Montevallo, Ala.)

water. The temperature of the water should range from 75° to 80° F.

If spectators are to be provided for, it is recommended that a gallery that is separate from the pool room proper be erected along the length of the pool.

An office adjacent to the pool where records and first-aid supplies can be kept is advisable. Such an office should be equipped with windows that overlook the entire length of the pool. Also, there should be lavatory and toilet facilities available.

The swimming pool is a costly operation. Therefore, it is essential that it be planned with the help of the best advice obtainable. Specialists who are well acquainted with such facilities and who conduct swimming activities should be brought into conferences with the architect, a representative from the public health department, and experts in such essentials as lighting, heating, construction, and acoustics.

The checklist at the end of this chapter should be consulted for further standards regarding swimming pools.

HEALTH SCIENCE INSTRUCTION FACILITES

The health science instruction program should have facilities especially designed to meet the needs of educating students in respect to health matters. The National Facilities Conference stresses the following standards:

1. Space for 35 square feet per pupil, maximum of 30 pupils
2. Flexible teacher location
3. Provision for various teaching methods, including laboratory demonstration
4. Flexibility of seating
5. Hot and cold running water and gas outlet
6. Educational-exhibit space
7. Storage space
8. Provision for using audio-visual devices (electrical outlets, window shades, screens)
9. Access to health service unit
10. Exemplary environmental features

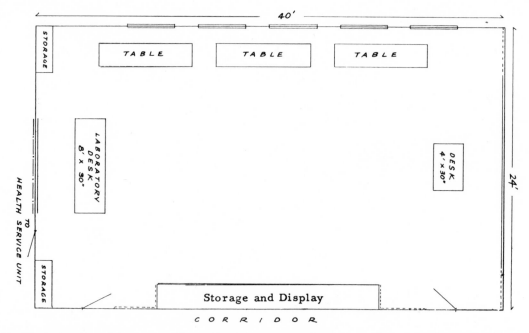

Health instruction laboratory. (From Participants in National Facilities Conference: Planning areas and facilities for health, physical education, and recreation, revised, Chicago, 1965, The Athletic Institute.)

11. Adequate handwashing facilities, drinking fountains, and toilets
12. Air-conditioning
13. Accessible to and usable by the disabled
14. Planned jointly for community use*

The recommended sizes in square feet for a floor plan for a health instruction laboratory are given in Table 15-1.

Classrooms

Classrooms utilized for health instruction should include the requirements discussed in relation to seating, lighting, color of walls and ceilings, heating and ventilation, acoustics, and sanitation. All classrooms should be healthful, comfortable, and adaptable, regardless of whether they are

---

*Participants in National Facilities Conference: Planning areas and facilities for health, physical education, and recreation, Washington, D. C., 1965, American Association for Health, Physical Education, and Recreation, p. 209.

being used for health instruction or some other subject.

There is one feature, however, that should receive consideration if there is not a special room set aside for such a purpose. This is the use of audiovisual equipment. There are ample resources for audiovisual material that can be utilized very effectively in any health instruction program. There should be available projection and sound equipment including an opaque projector, slide projector, filmstrip projector, motion picture projector, and turntables. There should also be outlets for electrical connections. Projection equipment should be installed in the rear of the room and audio equipment outlets in the front. There should be shades or other facilities for darkening the room. Finally, a screen should be available.

Another consideration in any health instruction room is a large display board that

Table 15-1. Recommended sizes in square feet of health service facilities for schools of various sizes*

	Enrollment					
	200 to 300	301 to 500	501 to 700	701 to 900	901 to 1,100	1,101 to 1,300
Waiting room	80	80	100	100	100	120
Examining room†	200	200	200	240	240	240
Rest room (total area for boys and girls)‡	100	180	220	260	300§	340§
Toilets (48 square feet total area—provide one for girls and one for boys)						

Optional areas
Dental clinic   100 square feet for all schools
Office space   80 square feet for each office provided
Eye examination   120 square feet minimum for all schools

*From Participants in National Facilities Conference: Planning areas and facilities for health, physical education, and recreation, Chicago, 1965, The Athletic Institute, p. 211. Based on data from State Department of Education: School planning manual, School Service Section, vol. 37, 1954, Richmond, Va.
†Examining room areas include 6 square feet for clothes closet and 24 square feet for storage closets.
‡For determining the number of cots, allow one cot per 100 pupils up to 400 pupils, and one cot per 200 pupils above 400. Round out fractions to nearest whole number. Allow 50 square feet of floor space for each of the first two cots and 40 square feet for each additional cot.
§In schools enrolling 901 to 1,100, a three-cot rest room is suggested for boys and a four-cot rest room for girls, and in 1,101-pupil to 1,300-pupil schools, a three-cot rest room is suggested for boys and a five-cot rest room for girls.
Note: For larger schools, add multiples of the above areas to obtain total needs.

can be used to illustrate the material that is presented.

Health service facilities

The health services are a very important part of the health program and require adequate facilities to carry out the responsibilities that are assigned to this health area. DeWeese and Moore* made an extensive study of the health service facilities and concluded that at least 720 square feet of floor surface should be provided and include the following:

1. Administrative office

2. Library for health science instruction material
3. Rest rooms
4. Examination room
5. Conference facilities
6. Space for first-aid care and treatment
7. Space for scientific and educational displays
8. Storage and toilet facilities

Health service suite. To have a practical health service setup that can accommodate examination work, a suite is needed rather than just one room. Experts recommend at least four rooms, which include examining, waiting, and rest rooms for boys and for girls. In addition there should be toilet facilities for each sex. Several exits from the examining room are recommended as a means of expediting the conduct of health services and eliminating confusion.

*DeWeese, A. O., and Moore, V. M.: The organization of a school health service comprising from 500 to 1000 pupils from kindergarten through high school, Journal of School Health 34:415, 1964.

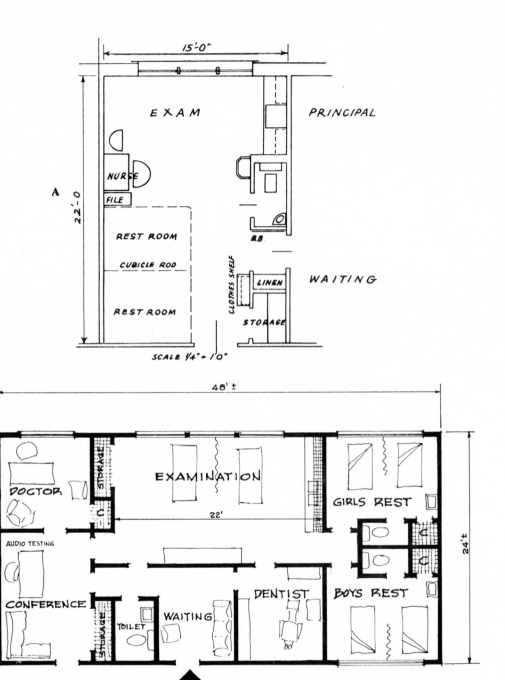

A, Health suite for elementary school—seven classrooms. **B,** Suggested health suite for over 1,100-pupil school. **C,** Suggested health suite for up to 700-pupil school. (From Participants in National Facilities Conference: Planning areas and facilities for health, physical education, and recreation, revised, Chicago, 1965, The Athletic Institute.)

The health service suite may also become the nurse's headquarters. In this case, there should be room for various items that are needed in her work, such as health records, desk, and files.

The color and furnishings of the waiting room should provide an attractive and cheerful atmosphere. A desk for clerical help can also be provided. There should be screens, if necessary, to give privacy to the examining and rest rooms that are part of the health suite and attached to the waiting room.

The examining room should be large enough to accommodate all the necessary equipment, supplies, and measuring devices. Provisions for eye testing, weighing, first aid, examining procedures, parent interviews, and other essentials should be kept in mind.

The rest rooms should be large enough to hold necessary cots, tables, and other items. They should also be equipped with subdued lighting, walls and ceilings that keep noise to a minimum, and other conveniences that contribute to rest.

A Committee on School Health Service Facilities of the American School Health Association conducted an extensive study of health service units throughout the country. This committee, recognizing that there could be no standard health unit that would meet the needs of schools everywhere, did, however, indicate what an average health unit might be, on the basis of statistical information gathered from their survey. According to this committee, the elementary school health service unit consisting of approximately 400 square feet would probably contain the following:

Examination room	Waiting room
Cot room	Dental ex-
Toilet room	amination room,
Storage spaces	in some cases
Testing and dressing room	

Health service units for secondary schools would require approximately 600 to 700 square feet of floor space and consist of the following:

Examination room	Storage spaces
Two cot rooms	Waiting room
Two toilet rooms	Testing room

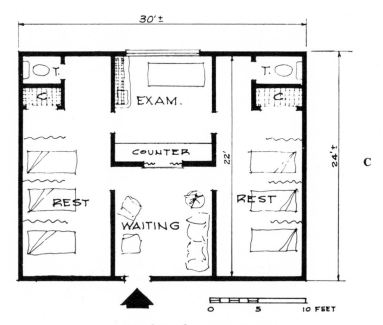

For legend see opposite page.

The following general statements help describe some essential considerations for a health service unit:

1. Future expansion should be considered.
2. The unit should be located near the administrative area, for ease of supervision, and away from noisy areas such as the shops, gymnasia, and music rooms.
3. Finishes should be of a type that can be easily maintained.
4. Attractive colors are important.
5. Service facilities such as sinks, lavatories, counters, and toilets should be of appropriate size for the pupils to be served.
6. Telephones are a necessity.

Cafeteria

The school lunch is a vital factor in the general health of any child and is an important part of his educational experiences. Furthermore, the cafeteria in any school or college recreational or other building is an important consideration and concern of individuals engaged in health, physical education, and recreation work.

The cafeteria should be easily accessible from anywhere within the building, as well as the service driveway. The size depends upon the number of individuals to be served. In general, from 10 to 12 square feet per person is required at peak load for the dining area.

The kitchen area will depend in size upon the number of meals to be prepared. The kitchen should contain all the equipment and supplies essential to the preparation and serving of good meals. Such equipment as ranges, ovens, sinks, dish-washing machines, refrigerators, tables, service trucks, counters, and kitchen machines such as mixers, peelers, and slicers should be provided.

The dining-room part of the cafeteria should be equipped with the necessary tables and chairs, serving counter, re-frigerated counters, silver, napkins, plates, trays, drinking fountain, and other essentials.

The physical appearance of the cafeteria should be attractive, with adequate lighting, light colors, and floors that are easy to clean. The cafeteria should be quiet and conducive to enjoyable and satisfactory eating conditions.

OUTDOOR FACILITIES

The outdoor facilities that will be discussed in this section are (1) play areas, (2) game areas, (3) outdoor swimming pools, and (4) camps.

Play areas

Many things must be taken into consideration when planning outdoor facilities for schools and colleges. The location, topography, soil drainage, water supply, size, shape, and natural features are a few important considerations before a site is selected. The outdoor facilities should be as near the gymnasium and locker rooms as possible and yet far enough from the classrooms so that the noise will not be a disturbing factor.

The play areas should serve the needs and interests of the students for the entire school year and at the same time should provide a setting for activities during vacation periods. The needs and interests of the citizens of the community must also be taken into consideration, since the play areas can be used for part of the community recreation program. This is especially important in some communities where such facilities can be planned as education and recreation centers. Since the community uses the areas after the school day is over, the plan is feasible.

The size of the playground area should be determined on the basis of activities offered in the program and the number of individuals who will be using the facilities at peak load. Possibilities for expansion should also be kept in mind.

Playground and recreation areas will be discussed under the three headings of elementary, junior high, and senior high school.

Elementary school. The activities program in the elementary school suggests what facilities should be available. Children of the primary grades engage in big muscle activity involving adaptations of climbing, jumping, skipping, kicking, throwing, leaping, and catching. The children in the intermediate and upper elementary grades utilize not only these activities but also such other ones as games of low organization, team games, and fundamental skills used in playing these games.

The playground area for an elementary school should be located near the building and should be easily accessible from the elementary classrooms. The kindergarten children should have a section of the playground for their exclusive use. This should be at least 5,000 square feet in size and separated from the rest of the playground. It should consist of a surfaced area, a grass area, and a place for sand and digging. The sand area should be enclosed to prevent the sand from being scattered. It is also wise to have a shaded area where storytelling and similar activities may be conducted. Some essential equipment would include swings, slides, seesaws, climbing structures, tables, and seats.

The children older than kindergarten age in the elementary school should have play space that includes turf, apparatus, shaded, multiple-use paved, and recreation areas.

The turf area provides space for many field and team games. Provisions for speed ball, soccer, field hockey, softball, and field ball could be included.

The apparatus area should provide such equipment as climbing bars in the form of a Jungle Jim, horizontal bars, and Giant Strides. There should be ample space to provide for the safety of the participants.

The shaded area may provide space for

Outdoor gymnasium. (University of Tampa, Tampa, Fla.)

such activities as marbles, hopscotch, or ring toss and also storytelling.

The multiple-use paved area may serve for a variety of purposes and activities on a year-round basis by both school and community. It can house basketball, tennis, and handball courts, games of minimum organization, and other activities. This area should be paved with material that takes into consideration resiliency, safety, and durability. Rapid and efficient drainage is essential. Lines may be painted on the area for the various types of games. Schools should allow additional space adjacent to this area for possible future expansion.

Other recreation areas that have important implications for the community are a landscaped, parklike area, a place for quiet activities such as dramatics and informal gatherings, a wading pool, a place for older adults to congregate, and a place for children to have gardening opportunities.

Junior high school. The junior high school play and recreation area, planned and developed for the children who attend the school and also for the adults in the community, should be located on a larger site than that for the elementary school.

Some suggestions have been made that it consist of from 10 to 25 or more acres. Local conditions will play a part in deciding the amount of area available.

Many of the facilities of the elementary school will be a part of the junior high school. In many cases, however, the various areas should be increased in size. There should be a place for small children, apparatus, quiet games, and a wading pool, as in the elementary schools. The multiple-use paved area of turf area for games should be increased in size.

The program for junior high school girls will stress a broad base in fundamentals for participation in such activities as archery, volleyball, tennis, and hockey.

The boys' program will include soccer, touch football, baseball, speed ball, softball, and golf. A track should also be included. Therefore, the necessary facilities should provide for those activities that will be part of the regular physical education class as well as the intramural program.

A landscaped, parklike area should be provided for the various recreational activities in which people in the community will like to engage, such as walking, picnicking, skating, and fly casting.

Tennis complex of ten courts. (College of San Mateo, San Mateo, Calif.)

Senior high school. The senior high school physical education program is characterized to a more pronounced degree by a team game program in various activities. This emphasis, together with the fact that facilities are needed for the recreational use of the community, requires an even larger area than those for the two previous educational levels. Estimates range from 10 to 40 acres for such a site.

Most of the areas that have been listed in discussing the elementary and junior high schools should again be included at the senior high school. This means there would be facilities for young children, such as apparatus, pool, and a place for quiet activities. Where there was an increase in size of many areas at the junior high over the elementary level, there should again be an increase in size at the high school level over the junior high.

There should be considerably more space for the various field games so that not only can physical education class instruction take place but also at the same time full-sized official fields will be available for such activities as softball, field hockey, soccer, speed ball, lacrosse, football, and baseball. This would be on an intramural as well as an interscholastic basis. Also, the community recreation program could make use of these facilities.

Football and track can be provided for in an area of approximately 4 acres, with the football field being placed within the track oval. A baseball field is questionable in such an area, because track and baseball are both spring sports. Baseball needs an

Table 15-2. Recommended dimensions for game areas*†

	Elementary	Upper grades	High school (adults)	Area size (sq. ft.)
Basketball	40′ × 60′	42′ × 74′	50′ × 84′	5,000
Volleyball	25′ × 50′	25′ × 50′	30′ × 60′	2,800
Badminton			20′ × 44′	1,800
Paddle tennis			20′ × 44′	1,800
Deck tennis			18′ × 40′	1,800
Tennis		36′ × 78′	36′ × 78′	7,200
Ice hockey			85′ × 200′	17,000
Field hockey			180′ × 300′	54,000
Horseshoes		10′ × 40′	10′ × 50′	1,000
Shuffleboard			6′ × 52′	648
Lawn bowling			14′ × 110′	7,800
Tetherball	10′ circle	12′ circle	12′ circle	
Croquet	38′ × 60′	38′ × 60′	38′ × 60′	2,275
Handball	18′ × 26′	18′ × 26′	20′ × 34′	1,280
Baseball			350′ × 350′	122,500
Archery		50′ × 150′	50′ × 300′	20,000
Softball (12″ ball)‡	150′ × 150′	200′ × 200′	250′ × 250′	62,500
Football—with 440-yard track—220-yard straightaway			300′ × 600′	180,000
Touch football		120′ × 300′	160′ × 360′	68,400
6-man football			120′ × 300′	49,500
Soccer			165′ × 300′	57,600

*From Planning facilities for health, physical education, and recreation, revised edition, Chicago, 1956, The Athletic Institute, Inc., p. 26.
†Table covers a single unit; many of above can be combined.
‡Dimensions vary with size of ball used.

area of about 350 feet by 350 feet. This allows for a minimum of 50 feet from home plate to the backstop and also allows for adequate space outside the first and third base lines.

Game areas

The recommended dimensions for game areas for school physical education programs have been outlined by a group of experts as shown in Table 15-2. An area of about 1 acre will accommodate four tennis courts, four handball courts, three badminton courts, and two volleyball courts.

There should be a separate area for high school girls with a minimum area of 320 feet by 280 feet, which is approximately 2 acres in size. Such an area will permit basic physical education instructional classes to be held and also provide fields for softball, field hockey, soccer, speedball, lacrosse, and other activities.

High school boys should also be adequately provided for in addition to the many courts areas that include basketball, softball, and other activities. There should be proper space for track if desired, an oval one-fourth mile in length or at least a straightaway of 380 feet and 15 to 20 feet in width. Of course, there is also the need for the interschool athletic area, which usually includes football, track, baseball, and soccer.

Not to be forgotten should be the winter activities. With such activities gaining increased popularity, provision should be made for skiing, sleds, skating, and other winter activities.

The New York State Department of Education* recommends that the outdoor facilities for the basic needs of a physical education and recreation program, from kindergarten to grade twelve, should consist of a minimum of 12 acres of land. This

*New York State Department of Education: Planning the outdoor physical education facilities, Albany, 1964, The Department.

area should be divided into an elementary area of 3 acres; courts area of 1 acre; high school girls' area of 2 acres, a high school boys' intramural area of 3 acres, and an interschool athletic area of 3 acres. The interschool athletic area would be used for baseball in the spring and summer and football or soccer in the fall. A quarter-mile track could also be added, but in this case the interschool athletic program should have 7 acres of land. The recommendation further points out that if archery, golf, natural theater, picnic area, skiing, and tobogganing area are desired, additional land will be necessary.

Outdoor swimming pools

The outdoor swimming pool is a popular and important facility in many communities. To a great degree climatic conditions will determine the advisability of such a facility.

Outdoor pools are built in various shapes, including oval, circular, T-shaped, and rectangular. Rectangular pools are most popular because of easier construction and because they lend themselves better to competitive swimming events.

The size of pools varies, depending upon the number of persons they are to serve. One recommendation has been made that 12 square feet of water space per swimmer be allotted for swimming purposes or, if the deck is taken into consideration, 20 square feet of space for swimming and walking area per swimmer.

The decks for outdoor pools should be larger than those for indoor pools. This larger space will serve to accommodate more people and also provide space for sunbathing.

Shower facilities should be provided to ensure that every swimmer takes a soapy shower in the nude before entering the water. A basket system for storing clothes has been found practical instead of the locker type of system that is used inside. In cases where the pool is located adjacent to

Swimming pool. (Wallace Rider Farrington High School, Honolulu, Hawaii.)

the school, it sometimes is practical to use the locker and shower facilities of the school. However, it is strongly advised that wherever possible separate shower and basket facilities be provided. Toilets should also be provided for the convenience of the swimmers.

Since swimming is popular at night as well as in the daytime, lights should be provided in order that a great percentage of the population may participate in this healthful and enjoyable activity.

Diving boards generally are of wood or metal, but in recent years glass and plastic ones have proved popular. The standard heights of boards are 1 and 3 meters. The 1-meter board should be over water 9 to 10 feet in depth and the 3-meter board over water 10 to 12 feet in depth. The board or any diving takeoff area should have a nonskid covering. The boards should be securely fastened to the ground or foundation.

The rules and regulations concerning diving equipment should be clearly posted near the diving areas. Roping off and patrolling the area is a good safety precaution.

The checklist at the end of the chapter provides further information on swimming pool standards.*

Camps†

Since camping is becoming an increasingly popular activity in both school and recreational programs, it should receive consideration.

Camps should be located within easy reach of the school and community. They should be in locations that are desirable from the standpoints of scenic beauty, safety, accessibility, water, and natural resources pertinent to the program offered. Activities usually offered include fishing, hiking, swimming, campcraft, boating, nature study, and appropriate winter sports. The natural terrain and other resources can contribute much toward such a program.

There should be adequate housing, eating, sanitary, waterfront, and other facilities essential to camp life. These do not have to be as elaborate as those in the home or school but instead can be very simple. Adequate facilities for protection

---

*For more information on swimming pools, see pp. 438-443.
†See Chapter 25.

against the elements are essential, however. Facilities should also meet acceptable standards of health and sanitation. In general, camp structures should be adapted to the climatic conditions of the particular area in which the camp is located. It is wise to consult public health authorities when selecting a camp site. Sometimes existing facilities can be converted to camp use. The camp site should be purchased outright or a long-term lease acquired.

CHECKLIST FOR FACILITY PLANNERS*

General

	Yes	No
1. A clear-cut statement has been prepared on the nature and scope of the program, and the special requirements for space, equipment, fixtures, and facilities dictated by the activities to be conducted.	___	___
2. The facility has been planned to meet the total requirements of the program as well as the special needs of those who are to be served.	___	___
3. The plans and specifications have been checked by all governmental agencies (city, county, and state) whose approval is required by law.	___	___
4. Plans for areas and facilities conform to state and local regulations and to accepted standards and practices.	___	___
5. The areas and facilities planned make possible the programs which serve the interests and needs of all the people.	___	___
6. Every available source of property or funds has been explored, evaluated, and utilized whenever appropriate.	___	___
7. All interested persons and organizations concerned with the facility have had an opportunity to share in its planning (professional educators, users, consultants, administrators, engineers, architects, program specialists, building managers, and builder—a team approach).	___	___
8. The facility and its appurtenances will fulfill the maximum demands of the program. The program has not been curtailed to fit the facility.	___	___
9. The facility has been functionally planned to meet the present and anticipated needs of specific programs, situations, and publics.	___	___
10. Future additions are included in present plans to permit economy of construction.	___	___
11. Lecture classrooms are isolated from distracting noises.	___	___
12. Storage areas for indoor and outdoor equipment are adequately sized. They are located adjacent to the gymnasia.	___	___
13. Shelves in storage rooms are slanted toward the wall.	___	___
14. All passageways are free of obstructions; fixtures are recessed.	___	___
15. Facilities for health services, health testing, health instruction, and the first-aid and emergency-isolation rooms are suitably interrelated.	___	___
16. Buildings, specific areas, and facilities are clearly identified.	___	___
17. Locker rooms are arranged for ease of supervision.	___	___
18. Offices, teaching stations, and service facilities are properly interrelated.	___	___
19. Special needs of the physically handicapped are met, including a ramp into the building at a major entrance.	___	___
20. All "dead space" is used.	___	___
21. The building is compatible in design and comparable in quality and accommodation to other campus structures.	___	___
22. Storage rooms are accessible to the play area.	___	___

*Adapted from Participants in National Facilities Conference: Planning areas and facilities for health, physical education, and recreation, Washington, D. C., 1965, American Association for Health, Physical Education, and Recreation, pp. 256-260.

CHECKLIST FOR FACILITY PLANNERS–cont'd

General–cont'd   *Yes*   *No*

23. Workrooms, conference rooms, and staff and administrative offices are inter-related.   ____ ____
24. Shower and dressing facilities are provided for professional staff members and are conveniently located.   ____ ____
25. Thought and attention have been given to making facilities and equipment as durable and vandalproof as possible.   ____ ____
26. Low-cost maintenance features have been adequately considered.   ____ ____
27. This facility is a part of a well-integrated master plan.   ____ ____
28. All areas, courts, facilities, equipment, climate control, security, etc. conform rigidly to detailed standards and specifications.   ____ ____
29. Shelves are recessed and mirrors are supplied in appropriate places in rest rooms and dressing rooms. Mirrors are not placed above lavatories.   ____ ____
30. Dressing space between locker rows is adjusted to the size and age level of students.   ____ ____
31. Drinking fountains are conveniently placed in locker-room areas or immediately adjacent thereto.   ____ ____
32. Special attention is given to provision for the locking of service windows and counters, supply bins, carts, shelves, and racks.   ____ ____
33. Provision is made for the repair, maintenance, replacement, and off-season storage of equipment and uniforms.   ____ ____
34. A well-defined program for laundering and cleaning of towels, uniforms, and equipment is included in the plan.   ____ ____
35. Noncorrosive metal is used in dressing, drying, and shower areas except for enameled lockers.   ____ ____
36. Antipanic hardware is used where required by fire regulations.   ____ ____
37. Properly placed hose bibbs and drains are sufficient in size and quantity to permit flushing the entire area with a water hose.   ____ ____
38. A water-resistant, coved base is used under the locker base and floor mat, and where floor and wall join.   ____ ____
39. Chalkboards and/or tackboards with map tracks are located in appropriate places in dressing rooms, hallways, and classrooms.   ____ ____
40. Book shelves are provided in toilet areas.   ____ ____
41. Space and equipment are planned in accordance with the types and number of enrollees.   ____ ____
42. Basement rooms, being undesirable for dressing, drying, and showering, are not planned for those purposes.   ____ ____
43. Spectator seating (permanent) in areas which are basically instructional is kept at a minimum. Roll-away bleachers are used primarily. Balcony seating is considered as a possibility.   ____ ____
44. Well-lighted and effectively displayed trophy cases enhance the interest and beauty of the lobby.   ____ ____
45. The space under the stairs is used for storage.   ____ ____
46. Department heads' offices are located near the central administrative office, which includes a well-planned conference room.   ____ ____
47. Workrooms are located near the central office and serve as a repository for departmental materials and records.   ____ ____
48. The conference area includes a cloak room, lavatory, and toilet.   ____ ____
49. In addition to regular secretarial offices established in the central and department chairmen's offices, a special room to house a secretarial pool for staff members is provided.   ____ ____
50. Staff dressing facilities are provided. These facilities may also serve game officials.   ____ ____

Continued.

CHECKLIST FOR FACILITY PLANNERS–cont'd

General–cont'd

	Yes	No
51. The community and/or neighborhood has a "round table"—planning round table.		
52. All those (persons and agencies) who should be a party to planning and development are invited and actively engaged in the planning process.		
53. Space and area relationships are important. They have been carefully considered.		
54. Both long-range plans and immediate plans have been made.		
55. The body comfort of the child, a major factor in securing maximum learning, has been considered in the plans.		
56. Plans for quiet areas have been made.		
57. In the planning, consideration has been given to the need for adequate recreation areas and facilities, both near and distant from the homes of people.		
58. Plans recognize the primary function of recreation as being enrichment of learning through creative self-expression, self-enhancement, and the achievement of self-potential.		
59. Every effort has been exercised to eliminate hazards.		
60. The installation of low-hanging door closers, light fixtures, signs, and other objects in traffic areas has been avoided.		
61. Warning signals—both visible and audible—are included in the plans.		
62. Ramps have a slope equal to or greater than a 1-foot rise in 12 feet.		
63. Minimum landings for ramps are 5 feet × 5 feet, they extend at least 1 foot beyond the swinging arc of a door, have at least a 6-foot clearance at the bottom, and have level platforms at 30-foot intervals on every turn.		
64. Adequate locker and dressing spaces are provided.		
65. The design of dressing, drying, and shower areas reduces foot traffic to a minimum and establishes clean, dry aisles for bare feet.		
66. Teaching stations are properly related to service facilities.		
67. Toilet facilities are adequate in number. They are located to serve all groups for which provisions are made.		
68. Mail services, outgoing and incoming, are included in the plans.		
69. Hallways, ramps, doorways, and elevators are designed to permit equipment to be moved easily and quickly.		
70. A keying design suited to administrative and instructional needs is planned.		
71. Toilets used by large groups have circulating (in and out) entrances and exits.		

Climate control

	Yes	No
1. Provision is made throughout the building for climate control—heating, ventilating, and refrigerated cooling.		
2. Special ventilation is provided for locker, dressing, shower, drying, and toilet rooms.		
3. Heating plans permit both area and individual room control.		
4. Research areas where small animals are kept and where chemicals are used have been provided with special ventilating equipment.		
5. The heating and ventilating of the wrestling gymnasium have been given special attention.		

Electrical

	Yes	No
1. Shielded, vaporproof lights are used in moisture-prevalent areas.		
2. Lights in strategic areas are key controlled.		
3. Lighting intensity conforms to approved standards.		

CHECKLIST FOR FACILITY PLANNERS–cont'd

Electrical–cont'd

	Yes	No
4. An adequate number of electrical outlets are strategically placed.	___	___
5. Gymnasium and auditorium lights are controlled by dimmer units.	___	___
6. Locker-room lights are mounted above the space between lockers.	___	___
7. Natural light is controlled properly for purposes of visual aids and other avoidance of glare.	___	___
8. Electrical outlet plates are installed 3 feet above the floor unless special use dictates other locations.	___	___
9. Controls for light switches and projection equipment are suitably located and interrelated.	___	___
10. All lights are shielded. Special protection is provided in gymnasia, court areas, and shower rooms.	___	___
11. Lights are placed to shine between rows of lockers.	___	___

Walls

1. Movable and folding partitions are power-operated and controlled by keyed switches.	___	___
2. Wall plates are located where needed and are firmly attached.	___	___
3. Hooks and rings for nets are placed (and recessed in walls) according to court locations and net heights.	___	___
4. Materials that clean easily and are impervious to moisture are used where moisture is prevalent.	___	___
5. Shower heads are placed at different heights—4 feet (elementary) to 7 feet (university)—for each school level.	___	___
6. Protective matting is placed permanently on the walls in the wrestling room, at the ends of basketball courts, and in other areas where such protection is needed.	___	___
7. An adequate number of drinking fountains is provided. They are properly placed (recessed in wall).	___	___
8. One wall (at least) of the dance studio has full-length mirrors.	___	___
9. All corners in locker rooms are rounded.	___	___

Ceilings

1. Overhead-supported apparatus is secured to beams engineered to withstand stress.	___	___
2. The ceiling height is adequate for the activities to be housed.	___	___
3. Acoustical materials impervious to moisture are used in moisture-prevalent areas.	___	___
4. Skylights, being impractical, are seldom used because of problems in water-proofing roofs and the controlling of sun rays (gyms).	___	___
5. All ceilings except those in storage areas are acoustically treated with sound-absorbent materials.	___	___

Floors

1. Floor plates are placed where needed and are flush-mounted.	___	___
2. Floor design and materials conform to recommended standards and specifications.	___	___
3. Lines and markings are painted on floors before sealing is completed (when synthetic tape is not used).	___	___
4. A coved base (around lockers and where wall and floor meet) of the same water-resistant material used on floors is found in all dressing and shower rooms.	___	___

Continued.

CHECKLIST FOR FACILITY PLANNERS–cont'd

Floors—cont'd

5. Abrasive, nonskid, slip-resistant flooring that is impervious to moisture is provided on all areas where water is used—laundry, swimming pool, shower, dressing, and drying rooms. ____ ____
6. Floor drains are properly located and the slope of the floor is adequate for rapid drainage. ____ ____

Gymnasia and special rooms

1. Gymnasia are planned so as to provide for safety zones (between courts, end lines, and walls) and for best utilization of space. ____ ____
2. One gymnasium wall is free of obstructions and is finished with a smooth, hard surface for ball-rebounding activities. ____ ____
3. The elementary school gymnasium has one wall free of obstructions; a minimum ceiling height of 18 feet; a minimum of 4,000 square feet of teaching area; and a recessed area for housing a piano. ____ ____
4. Secondary school gymnasia have a minimum ceiling height of 22 feet; a scoreboard; electrical outlets placed to fit with bleacher installation; wall attachments for apparatus and nets; and a power-operated, sound-insulated, and movable partition with a small pass-through door at one end. ____ ____
5. A small spectator alcove adjoins the wrestling room and contains a drinking fountain (recessed in the wall). ____ ____
6. Cabinets, storage closets, supply windows, and service areas have locks. ____ ____
7. Provisions have been made for the cleaning, storing, and issuing of physical education and athletic uniforms. ____ ____
8. Shower heads are placed at varying heights in the shower rooms on each school level. ____ ____
9. Equipment is provided for the use of the physically handicapped. ____ ____
10. Special provision has been made for audio and visual aids, including intercommunication systems, radio, and television. ____ ____
11. Team dressing rooms have provisions for:
    a. Hosing down room ____ ____
    b. Floors pitched to drain easily ____ ____
    c. Hot- and cold-water hose bibbs ____ ____
    d. Windows located above locker heights ____ ____
    e. Chalk, tack, and bulletin boards, and movie projection ____ ____
    f. Lockers for each team member ____ ____
    g. Drying facility for uniforms ____ ____
12. The indoor rifle range includes:
    a. Targets located 54 inches apart and 50 feet from the firing line ____ ____
    b. 3 feet to 8 feet of space behind targets ____ ____
    c. 12 feet of space behind firing line ____ ____
    d. Ceilings 8 feet high ____ ____
    e. Width adjusted to number of firing lines needed (1 line for each 3 students) ____ ____
    f. A pulley device for target placement and return ____ ____
    g. Storage and repair space ____ ____
13. Dance facilities include:
    a. 100 square feet per student ____ ____
    b. A minimum length of 60 linear feet for modern dance ____ ____
    c. Full-height viewing mirrors on one wall (at least) of 30 feet; also a 20-foot mirror on an additional wall if possible ____ ____
    d. Acoustical drapery to cover mirrors when not used and for protection if other activities are permitted ____ ____

CHECKLIST FOR FACILITY PLANNERS–cont'd

Gymnasia and special rooms–cont'd

	Yes	*No*
e. Dispersed microphone jacks and speaker installation for music and instruction	___	___
f. Built-in cabinets for record players, microphones, and amplifiers, with space for equipment carts	___	___
g. Electrical outlets and microphone connections around perimeter of room	___	___
h. An exercise bar (34 inches to 42 inches above floor) on one wall	___	___
i. Drapes, surface colors, floors (maple preferred), and other room appointments to enhance the room's attractiveness	___	___
j. Location near dressing rooms and outside entrances	___	___

14. Training rooms include:
    a. Rooms large enough to administer adequately proper health services
    b. Sanitary storage cabinets for medical supplies
    c. Installation of drains for whirlpool, tubs, etc.
    d. Installation of electrical outlets with proper capacities and voltage
    e. High stools for use of equipment such as whirlpool, ice tubs, etc.
    f. Water closet, hand lavatory, and shower
    g. Extra hand lavatory in the trainer's room proper
    h. Adjoining dressing rooms
    i. Installation and use of hydrotherapy and diathermy equipment in separate areas
    j. Space for the trainer, the physician, and the various services of this function
    k. Corrective-exercise laboratories located conveniently and adapted to the needs of the handicapped

15. Coaches' rooms should provide:
    a. A sufficient number of dressing lockers for coaching staff and officials
    b. A security closet or cabinet for athletic equipment such as timing devices
    c. A sufficient number of showers and toilet facilities
    d. Drains and faucets for hosing down the rooms where this method of cleaning is desirable and possible
    e. A small chalkboard and tackboard
    f. A small movie screen and projection table for use of coaches to review films

Handicapped and disabled

Have you included those considerations that would make the facility accessible to, and usable by, the disabled? These considerations include:

1. The knowledge that the disabled will be participants in almost all activities, not merely spectators, if the facility is properly planned.
2. Ground-level entrance(s) or stair-free entrance(s) using inclined walk(s) or inclined ramp(s).
3. Uninterrupted walk surface; no abrupt changes in levels leading to the facility.
4. Approach walks and connecting walks no less than 4 feet in width.
5. Walks with a gradient no greater than 5%.
6. A ramp, when used, with rise no greater than 1 foot in 12 feet.
7. Flat or level surface inside and outside of all exterior doors, extending 5 feet from the door in the direction that the door swings, and extending 1 foot to each side of the door.
8. Flush thresholds at all doors.
9. Appropriate door widths, heights, and mechanical features.
10. At least 6 feet between vestibule doors in series, i.e., inside and outside doors.
11. Access and proximity to parking areas.

Continued.

CHECKLIST FOR FACILITY PLANNERS–cont'd

Handicapped and disabled–cont'd

	Yes	No
12. No obstructions by curbs at crosswalks, parking areas, etc.	___	___
13. Proper precautions (handrails, etc.) at basement-window areaways, open stairways, porches, ledges, and platforms.	___	___
14. Handrails on all steps and ramps.	___	___
15. Precautions against the placement of manholes in principal or major sidewalks.		
16. Corridors that are at least 60 inches wide and without abrupt pillars or protrusions.	___	___
17. Floors which are nonskid and have no abrupt changes or interruptions in level.	___	___
18. Proper design of steps.	___	___
19. Access to rest rooms, water coolers, telephones, food-service areas, lounges, dressing rooms, play areas, and all auxiliary services and areas.	___	___
20. Elevators in multiple-story buildings.	___	___
21. Appropriate placement of controls to permit and to prohibit use as desired.	___	___
22. Sound signals for the blind, and visual signals for the deaf as counterparts to regular sound and sight signals.	___	___
23. Proper placement, concealment, or insulation of radiators, heat pipes, hot-water pipes, drain pipes, etc.	___	___

Swimming pools

1. Has a clear-cut statement been prepared on the nature and scope of the design program and the special requirements for space, equipment, and facilities dictated by the activities to be conducted?	___	___
2. Has the swimming pool been planned to meet the total requirements of the program to be conducted as well as any special needs of the clientele to be served?	___	___
3. Have all plans and specifications been checked and approved by the local board of health?	___	___
4. Is the pool the proper depth to accommodate the various age groups and types of activities it is intended to serve?	___	___
5. Does the design of the pool incorporate the most current knowledge and best experience available regarding swimming pools?	___	___
6. If a local architect or engineer who is inexperienced in pool construction is employed, has an experienced pool consultant, architect, or engineer been called in to advise on design and equipment?	___	___
7. Is there adequate deep water for diving (minimum of 9 feet for 1-meter boards, 12 feet for 3-meter boards, and 15 feet for 10-meter towers)?	___	___
8. Have the requirements for competitive swimming been met (7-foot lanes; 12-inch black or brown lines on the bottom; pool 1 inch longer than official measurement; depth and distance markings)?	___	___
9. Is there adequate deck space around the pool? Has more space been provided than that indicated by the minimum recommended deck/pool ratio?	___	___
10. Does the swimming instructor's office face the pool? And is there a window through which the instructor may view all the pool area? Is there a toilet-shower-dressing area next to the office for instructors?	___	___
11. Are recessed steps or removable ladders located on the walls so as not to interfere with competitive swimming turns?	___	___
12. Does a properly constructed overflow gutter extend around the pool perimeter?	___	___
13. Where skimmers are used, have they been properly located so that they are not on walls where competitive swimming is to be conducted?	___	___

CHECKLIST FOR FACILITY PLANNERS–cont'd

Swimming pools–cont'd

Yes   No

14. Have separate storage spaces been allocated for maintenance and instructional equipment?   — —
15. Has the area for spectators been properly separated from the pool area?   — —
16. Have all diving standards and lifeguard chairs been properly anchored?   — —
17. Does the pool layout provide the most efficient control of swimmers from showers and locker rooms to the pool? Are toilet facilities provided for wet swimmers separate from the dry area?   — —
18. Is the recirculation pump located below the water level?   — —
19. Is there easy vertical access to the filter room for both people and material (stairway if required)?   — —
20. Has the proper pitch to drains been allowed in the pool, on the pool deck, in the overflow gutter, and on the floor of shower and dressing rooms?   — —
21. Has adequate space been allowed between diving boards and between the diving boards and sidewalls?   — —
22. Is there adequate provision for lifesaving equipment? Pool-cleaning equipment?   — —
23. Are inlets and outlets adequate in number and located so as to ensure effective circulation of water in the pool?   — —
24. Has consideration been given to underwater lights, underwater observation windows, and underwater speakers?   — —
25. Is there a coping around the edge of the pool?   — —
26. Has a pool heater been considered in northern climates in order to raise the temperature of the water?   — —
27. Have underwater lights in end racing walls been located deep enough and directly below surface lane anchors, and are they on a separate circuit?   — —
28. Has the plan been considered from the standpoint of handicapped persons (e.g., is there a gate adjacent to the turnstiles)?   — —
29. Is seating for swimmers provided on the deck?   — —
30. Has the recirculation-filtration system been designed to meet the anticipated future bathing load?   — —
31. Has the gas chlorinator (if used) been placed in a separate room accessible from and vented to the outside?   — —
32. Has the gutter waste water been valved to return to the filters, and also for direct waste?   — —

Indoor pools

1. Is there proper mechanical ventilation?   — —
2. Is there adequate acoustical treatment of walls and ceilings?   — —
3. Is there adequate overhead clearance for diving (15 feet above low springboards, 15 feet for 3-meter boards, and 10 feet for 10-meter platforms)?   — —
4. Is there adequate lighting (50 footcandles minimum)?   — —
5. Has reflection of light from the outside been kept to the minimum by proper location of windows or skylights (windows on side walls are not desirable)?   — —
6. Are all wall bases coved to facilitate cleaning?   — —
7. Is there provision for proper temperature control in the pool room for both water and air?   — —
8. Can the humidity of the pool room be controlled?   — —
9. Is the wall and ceiling insulation adequate to prevent "sweating"?   — —
10. Are all metal fittings of noncorrosive material?   — —
11. Is there a tunnel around the outside of the pool, or a trench on the deck which permits ready access to pipes?   — —

Continued.

CHECKLIST FOR FACILITY PLANNERS—cont'd

Outdoor pools

		Yes	*No*
1.	Is the site for the pool in the best possible location (away from railroad tracks, heavy industry, trees, and open fields which are dusty)?	——	——
2.	Have sand and grass been kept the proper distance away from the pool to prevent them from being transmitted to the pool?	——	——
3.	Has a fence been placed around the pool to assure safety when not in use?	——	——
4.	Has proper subsurface drainage been provided?	——	——
5.	Is there adequate deck space for sunbathing?	——	——
6.	Are the outdoor lights placed far enough from the pool to prevent insects from dropping into the pool?	——	——
7.	Is the deck of nonslip material?	——	——
8.	Is there an area set aside for eating, separated from the pool deck?	——	——
9.	Is the bathhouse properly located, with the entrance to the pool leading to the shallow end?	——	——
10.	If the pool shell contains a concrete finish, has the length of the pool been increased by 3 inches over the "official" size in order to permit eventual tiling of the basin without making the pool "too short"?	——	——
11.	Are there other recreational facilities nearby for the convenience and enjoyment of swimmers?	——	——
12.	Do diving boards or platforms face north or east?	——	——
13.	Are lifeguard stands provided and properly located?	——	——
14.	Has adequate parking space been provided and properly located?	——	——
15.	Is the pool oriented correctly in relation to the sun?	——	——
16.	Have windshields been provided in situations where heavy winds prevail?	——	——

Questions and exercises

1. Prepare a sketch of what you consider to be an ideal physical education plant. In your plans consider both outdoor and indoor facilities.
2. Plan a health suite that you consider to be ideal.
3. What are ten basic considerations in planning facilities?
4. Discuss the following statement: The trend in schoolhouse construction is away from the so-called frills.
5. Develop a list of standards for outdoor play areas and locker, shower, and drying room facilities in the following areas: (a) lighting, (b) heating and ventilation, (c) plant sanitation, (d) furniture.
6. What are some of the essential factors to keep in mind when planning the gymnasium?
7. What should be provided in the school in the way of special activity areas?
8. What are some of the essential factors to keep in mind when planning the swimming pool?
9. What considerations should be made in school facilities for recreation?
10. Draw up a list of references for obtaining authoritative information on various aspects of facility construction and maintenance.

Reading assignment in *Administrative Dimensions of Health and Physical Education Programs, Including Athletics:* Chapter 12, Selections 63 to 69.

Selected references

American Association for Health, Physical Education, and Recreation: Planning areas and facilities for health, physical education, and recreation, Washington, D. C., 1965, The Association.

Architectural Research Group: Shelter for physical education, College Station, Texas, 1961, Publications Department, Texas Engineering Experiment Station, A & M College of Texas.

Athletic Institute and American Association for Health, Physical Education, and Recreation: Equipment and supplies for athletics, physical education, and recreation, Chicago, 1960, The Institute.

California State Department of Education: Brief statement of principles involving the construction of school health unit, State Health Committee Bulletin, Sacramento, The Department.

California State Joint Committee on School Health: Guide and check list for healthful and safe school environment, Sacramento, The Committee.

DeWeese, A. O., and Moore, V. M.: The organization of a school health service comprising from 500 to 1000 pupils from kindergarten through high school, Journal of School Health **34:**415, 1964.

Dickey, D. D.: Athletic lockers for schools and colleges, Minneapolis, Minnesota, Post Office Box 6630, 1967.

Educational Facilities Laboratories, Inc.: Air structures for school sports, New York, 1964, The Laboratories.

Gabrielsen, M. A.: Swimming pool planning and utilization, a speech to the Conference on Planning, Constructing, Utilizing Physical Education, Recreation, and Athletic Facilities at Columbus, Ohio, December 10, 1969.

Gabrielsen, M. A., and Miles, C. M.: Sports and recreation facilities for school and community, Englewood Cliffs, N. J., 1958, Prentice-Hall, Inc.

Grieve, A.: Legal considerations of equipment and facilities, The Athletic Journal **47:**38, 1967.

Joint Committee on Health Problems in Education of National Education Association and American Medical Association: Healthful school environment, Washington, D. C., 1969, The Association.

Leu, D. J.: Planning educational facilities, New York, 1965, The Center for Applied Research, Inc. (The Library of Education).

New York State Department of Education: Planning the indoor physical education facilities, Albany, 1962, The State Department of Education.

Scott, H. A., and Westkaemper, R. B.: From program to facilities in physical education, New York, 1958, Harper & Row, Publishers.

The State Education Department, The University of the State of New York: Planning the outdoor physical education facilities for central schools, Albany, 1964, The Department.

Wetzel, C. H.: Planning gym seating for long-range needs, Scholastic Coach **30:**48, 1961.

Annuals and periodicals

Professional architectural and educational magazines devote considerable space to the planning, designing, constructing, equipping, and managing of school facilities. The school facilities articles appearing in the annuals and periodicals listed below are usually concerned with specific school plants of recent construction and are illustrated with drawings and photographs. Some of these periodicals issue special editions that are devoted entirely to school facilities.

Architectural

Architectural Forum, Time, Inc., 9 Rockefeller Plaza, New York, N. Y. 10020

Architectural Record, F. W. Dodge Corp., 119 W. 40th St., New York, N. Y. 10018

Progressive Architecture, Reinhold Publishing Corp, 430 Park Ave., New York, N. Y. 10022

Educational

American School and University, Buttenheim Publishing Corp., 470 Park Ave. South, New York, N. Y. 10016 (annual).

American School Board Journal, Bruce Publishing Co., Milwaukee, Wis.

Nation's Schools, Modern Hospital Publishing Co., Inc., 1050 Merchandise Mart, Chicago, Ill. 60654

Overview, Buttenheim Publishing Corp., 470 Park Ave. South, New York, N. Y. 10016

School Management, School Management, Inc., 22 W. Putnam Ave., Greenwich, Conn.

School Planning, School Planning, Inc., 75 E. Wacker Dr., Chicago, Ill. 60601

Budgeting and financial accounting provide the necessary administrative machinery and operations to request funds, make them available for special facilities, programs, projects, and individuals, and then exercise control to see that they are used in an efficient manner. Administration is responsible for this function. It is an important duty and one that requires special qualities of integrity, foresight, wisdom, and firmness.

Fiscal management reflects the administrative program. It shows where the emphasis is, what is considered important in long-term planning, and the activities that need developing. The administration must therefore closely coordinate program with budgeting and financial accounting. The two go hand in hand.

IMPORTANCE OF FISCAL MANAGEMENT

The services that a school system provides, whether personal help, facilities, instructional materials, or other items, usually involve the disbursement of money. This money must be secured from proper sources, be expended in the light of educational purposes, and be accounted for item by item. The budget, the master financial plan for the entire school or college system or any subdivision, is constructed with this purpose in mind.

There must be well-thought-through policies for the raising and spending of school or college money. Educators should know the procedures for handling such funds with integrity, the basic purposes for which the educational program exists, the school

laws, and the codes and regulations concerning fiscal management. Education is big business and is rapidly occupying a major role in the fiscal planning of national, state, and local units of government. Only as the funds are used wisely and in the best interests of the students and all people concerned can the large outlay of monies be justified.

PLACE OF FINANCIAL MANAGEMENT IN HEALTH AND PHYSICAL EDUCATION PROGRAMS

Of all the subject matter areas in elementary, secondary, or college and university educational systems, health and physical education require one of the largest outlays of funds in order that the educational programs may be conducted effectively. The cost of personnel, health services, facilities, and supplies and equipment are only a few of the items that amount to large sums of money. As much as 25% of many school and college plants are devoted to these programs. There are probably 200,000 physical educators and coaches getting paid at least $1 billion annually in salaries. More than 60 million children and young people are the focus of attention in health and physical education.

Gymnasia, swimming pools, health suites, playgrounds, and other facilities are being constructed at the cost of astronomical sums to taxpayers.

With such a great outlay of funds for health and physical education programs, there must be sound financial management to see that the monies are utilized in the best way possible. This is one of the most important responsibilities that educators, and particularly administrators, have.

Purposes of financial management

Some of the principal purposes for which financial management exists in health and physical education programs are as follows:

1. To prevent misuse and waste of funds that have been allocated to these special fields.
2. To help coordinate and relate the objectives of health and physical education programs with the money appropriated for achieving such outcomes.
3. To ensure that monies allocated to health and physical education will be based upon research, study, and a careful analysis of the pertinent conditions that influence such a process.
4. To involve the entire staff in formulating policies and procedures and in preparing budgetary items that will help ensure that the right program directions are taken.
5. To utilize funds in a manner that will develop the best programs of health and physical education possible.
6. To exercise control over the process of fiscal management in order to guarantee that the entire financial process has integrity and purpose.
7. To make the greatest use of personnel, facilities, supplies, equipment, and other factors involved in accomplishing educational objectives.

Responsibility

The responsibility for fiscal management, although falling largely upon the shoulders of the administration, involves every person who is a member of the school staff, as well as the pupils themselves.

Formulation and preparation of the budget, for example, is a cooperative enterprise in many respects. It is based on information and reports that have been forwarded by faculty and staff through the various departments and subdivisions of the organization. These reports must contain information on programs, projects, obligations that exist, funds that have been spent, and monies that have been received from various sources. Staff members help in this process. Administrators must have an overall picture of the entire enterprise at their fingertips. They must be cognizant of the work being done throughout the establishment, functions that should be carried out, needs of every facet of the organization, and other items that must be considered in the preparation of the budget. The larger the organization, the larger should be the budget organization under the administrator. The efficiency of the enterprise depends upon expert judgment in fiscal matters. Students themselves play a part in many school and college systems. For example, through general organizations, budgets are prepared and outlays of funds relating to many activities, such as plays and athletics, are either approved, amended, or rejected. Fiscal management involves many people, but the job of leadership and direction falls upon the administration.

COST ANALYSIS

Cost analysis of materials consumed or used in a program is a derivative of cost accounting. The need for cost analysis is to aid the administrator to evaluate present operations as well as to project future planning. Cost analysis is limited to the types of accounting systems being used as well as designating the unit to be compared. For example, some schools operate on grades one to eight, kindergarten to grade twelve, or some other educational pattern. Naturally, there would be a great difference in expenditures per pupil in the various patterns or organization.

Various units are used in cost analysis for the general education fund. The number of pupils in attendance, the census, average daily attendance, and average daily membership are some of those that are used. There are advantages and disadvantages to each of the various units.

Knezevich and Fowlkes* found in their study that the most common raw per capita unit used in cost analysis is per pupil in average daily attendance. In other words, educational costs are figured on a per pupil basis and the total number of pupils involved is computed by determining what the average daily pupil attendance is in a school or educational system. This figure is arrived at by adding the aggregated days of attendance of all pupils and then dividing by the number of days school was in session. The number of pupils in average daily attendance is then divided into the total of the educational costs in order to obtain the cost per pupil in average daily attendance. It should be recognized, however, there is no universally accepted definition of average daily attendance. Whereas some states would permit all pupils to be counted in attendance when teachers are attending a state teachers meeting, others would not.

Knezevich and Fowlkes also pointed out that as a raw measure of educational burden, the average daily membership is a better measure than the average daily attendance. Teachers' salaries must be paid whether pupils are in 90% or 100% attendance, and desks and school books must be available whether pupils are in attendance or not. As raw per capita units go, the average daily membership is a better unit to measure the educational burden than the more commonly used average daily attendance unit. Tradition, however, has favored the average daily attendance

unit over that of average daily membership.*

Cost analysis as it relates to equipment and supplies for health and physical education may be simply handled by allowing a certain number of dollars per pupil enrolled in the district or on the various levels in the school system. The New York State Education Department, for example, publishes an analysis of the monies spent on different budget categories on a pupil basis, depending on the type and size of the school.† This is very helpful and offers the business administrator a guide to the problem of budget allocation.

Good business administration should allow a space on the budget sheet for personnel in all departments to list any needs over the specified allocations and a place to state reasons for the listing. One of the drawbacks of using cost analysis sheets is that it is physically impossible for the data to be current.

Some experts in fiscal management feel that a per capita expenditure allocation for health and physical education represents a good foundation program. However, they recommend, in addition, (1) an extra percentage allocation for program enrichment, (2) an extra percentage allocation for variation in enrollment, and (3) a reference to a commodity index (current prices of equipment and supplies) that may indicate need for changes in the per capita expenditure because of current increase or decrease in the value of the items being purchased.

Cost analysis in practice in physical education programs

In order to provide the reader with an understanding of the amount of money

---

*Knezevich, S. J., and Fowlkes, J. G.: Business management of local school systems, New York, 1960, Harper & Row, Publishers, p. 157.

*Knezevich, S. J., and Fowlkes, J. G., op. cit., p. 15.

†Bureau of Statistical Services: Expenditures per pupil in average daily attendance, Division of Educational Management Services, State Education Department, The University of the State of New York, Albany, N. Y.

allocated to physical education programs throughout the United States and how it is determined, a survey of selected school systems was accomplished. The following paragraphs are cited examples of money allocation in several cities.

California. A large city system in California reports that physical education supplies are included in each school's allocation for instructional supplies, with the amount being based upon the number of pupils enrolled—elementary schools, $3.25 per pupil; junior high schools, $2.44 per pupil; and senior high schools, $2.15 per pupil.

Physical education equipment was in-

AVERAGE P.E. BUDGETS
(NOT INCLUDING INTERSCHOLASTIC ATHLETIC PROGRAM)

Level	Cost/student	Avg'e cost/District
ELEMENTARY	$ .67	$ 6,000.00
JR. HIGH	2.34	6,670.00
HIGH SCHOOL (By District Enrollment) under 1000	13.70	6,610.00
1000 – 5000	10.20	11,120.00
over 5000	2.40	22,200.00

COST - HIGH SCHOOL INTERSCHOLASTIC ATHLETIC PROGRAM

District Enrollment	Cost/student	Avg'e cost/District
under 1000	No. of participants not known	$ 8,585.00
1000 - 5000		20,900.00
over 5000		95,625.00

DEFICIT SPENDING - HIGH SCHOOL INTERSCHOLASTIC ATHLETIC PROGRAM

District Enrollment	% of Districts reporting cost of program exceeds gate receipts	Am't of deficit reported by individual schools Min.	Max.
under 1000	62%	$ 21.00	$ 22,296.00
1000 - 5000	43%	1500.00	20,500.00
over 5000	37%	15,652.00	164,445.00

Cost analysis in physical education. Reports on sixty-eight school districts in forty states. (From *A study of the feasibility of the use of limited shelters for physical education: partial shelter for physical education*, College Station, Texas, 1961, Texas Engineering Experiment Station, Texas A & M University.)

cluded in the budget for the year at a figure of $32,000. The maintenance of physical education equipment was provided for, as needed, by the board of education. The board of education also provided the towels and laundry service. In regard to the athletic program, the board of education provided extra pay for coaches and intramural directors, all the necessary athletic uniforms, the cleaning and repair of these uniforms and equipment, officials, and accident insurance for all boys and girls participating in the extramural and interschool athletic programs.

In another large school district in California, there was an allocation of $1.35 per pupil (boys) in junior and senior high schools for physical education programs. Girls were allocated the amount of $1.05 per pupil at the same educational level for the same period. The amount varied from year to year based upon need and prior experience. If the total amount allocated was not used during the school year, an amount not to exceed 20% of the total year's allocation could be carried over. The school district provided the expenses of transportation and instruction for the athletic program. Supplies needed in connection with the athletic program were provided through student body funds derived from student fees, sales at student stores, and admissions to athletic activities.

Florida. As reported to the author, Florida as a general policy does not favor earmarked funds for any single program in the schools. The procedure recommended is that county school districts receive what is called a teacher-unit allocation from the state for each twenty-seven students in average daily attendance. Each unit carries with it a certain amount of money for expendable supplies. The local school district holds a percentage of this money for general district-wide use and reallocates the remaining amount to individual schools based on formulas such as pupil enrollment. Each individual school is encouraged to involve its faculty in determining the priority of needs for the coming year. Therefore, health and physical education could have a high priority one year and a low one another year. As a general rule, health and physical education appear to have the same consideration as other phases of the curriculum. In a few instances, physical education needs are met through such fund-raising activities as dances and PTA drives.

Illinois. A high school in Illinois reported that no set figure or set formula was used to arrive at the allocation for health or physical education programs. The board of education subsidized the program of physical education beyond the gate receipts. At the time of the survey there was an equipment budget of $1,000 and a supplies budget of $1,300. The board of education reviews the anticipated budget each year for approval. The Director of Health and Physical Education submits a list of anticipated expenditures for such items as equipment, supplies, transportation, and officials. Gate receipts are also estimated. The difference between the two figures is the amount the board must approve or adjust before approval.

Indiana. One medium-sized school system in Indiana reported that each school (elementary, junior high, senior high, and so on) is allocated so much money for each student enrolled, and then the principal assigns the amount for each phase of the school program.

A county school corporation in Indiana budgets 10 cents per pupil for elementary schools in two accounts—one for instructional supplies and one for repair and replacement. Junior high and senior high schools are budgeted 35 cents per pupil in both accounts. In addition to the above-mentioned accounts, each junior and senior high school principal is budgeted 35 cents per pupil per school as additional money that he can use where he feels the greatest need exists.

A large city school system in Indiana does not have a formula for determining the amount of money allocated for physical education. Budget requests are prepared by the high school department heads for grades nine to twelve and by the supervisor of health and physical education for grades one to eight. The amount requested is based on inventory, program needs of individual schools, and requirements for supplying new schools and additions to present plants.

Another Indiana school system finances the entire interscholastic athletic program from gate receipts. Extra pay for coaches and maintenance of athletic facilities is financed through the general fund. In respect to the physical education program, each department is given an allocation of funds based on the number of students served.

New Jersey. One large school system in New Jersey reported an allocation of 50 cents per student for physical education supplies, and a smaller school system reported an allocation of $3,000 to $6,000 for supplies and coaches' salaries for athletics. Most school districts in New Jersey, it was reported, do not seem to have difficulty in getting reasonable physical education supplies based on needs. For athletics, most schools in New Jersey are subsidized in whole or part by board of education funds.

New York. Twenty-five New York State schools were surveyed to determine the amount of money allocated to their physical education programs. The amounts allocated were then changed into a per pupil allotment so as to provide a means of comparison. The items for which said money was allocated included athletic and gymnasium supplies and equipment, various athletic fees, officials, transportation, police, reconditioning of equipment, supplies and equipment needed in physical education classes, and intramurals and extramurals for both men and women. In those schools in which the administrative pattern grouped grades seven to twelve, the highest allocation per pupil was $33.86 and the lowest was $10.07. In those schools in which budgets were figured on a kindergarten to grade twelve school administrative pattern, the highest per capita allocation was $13.22 and the lowest was $5.30. In those schools in which the administrative pattern included grades nine to twelve, the highest per capita allocation was $35.24 and the lowest was $13.68.

Each school surveyed was asked how the amount that was allocated per student was determined. The general practice was that the Director of Health and Physical Education submitted and substantiated the following:

1. Needs—for the coming school year
2. Increased expenditures—a sound estimate of projected increases in regard to pupil program participation based on increased enrollments, pupil interest, program changes, and the anticipated cost of equipment and supplies to be used
3. Inventory—present equipment and supplies on hand and the condition of these items
4. Previous year's budget—amounts allocated in previous year or years

These four items represent the basis on which most allocations of funds to programs of health and physical education were determined.

Directors of health and physical education programs surveyed felt that where they were granted increases in per capita allocations it was the result of such factors as increase in the number of participants, a careful evaluation of the number of participants and the time they spent using the equipment and supplies, the cost per hour (for example, it was determined in one community that it cost less than 50 cents per hour per child to participate in football), and an excellent working rapport with the board of education.

The survey also disclosed that most schools have a contingency fund to meet emergency needs, that many schools used the money that was saved when the proposed budget allocation was in excess of the actual bid price on certain supplies and equipment, that some schools used part of the money received from gate receipts, and that some other schools used part of the money from the sale of general organization tickets.

Oklahoma. A city school system in Oklahoma reported that budget allocations for health and physical education programs for boys and girls vary according to pupil enrollment. The superintendent of schools and the board of education decide the amount that will be allocated to each of the special programs. Athletics are self-supporting and the board of education does not allocate money directly to them.

Texas. An independent school district in Texas pointed out that they do not have a formula for physical education or health education. The board of education and school administration decide the total budget.

BUDGETING

Budgeting is the formulation of a financial plan in terms of work to be accomplished and services to be performed. All

---

SCHOOL DISTRICT — TAX BUDGET.

Assessed Valuation $59,681,265.00
Rate per $1,000.00 .... 32.34
Amount of Budget to be Raised by Taxation   1,930,067.00

GENERAL CONTROL:

2/2	Board of Education—Legal, Auditing	$ 1,225.00
2/3	Board of Education—Supplies, Travel, etc.	5,700.00
2/7	Central Office—Salaries	66,680.00
2/8	Central Office—Supplies, Travel, etc.	4,600.00
2/10	Attendance & Census Service—Salaries	450.00
2/11	Attendance & Census Service—Supplies	165.00
	Total General Control	$ 78,820.00

INSTRUCTIONAL SERVICE:

3/3	Salaries of Principals	$ 87,225.00
3/4	Salaries of Clerical & Other Help	36,405.00
3/6	Other Expenses of Supervision—Supplies, Travel, etc.	8,850.00
3/9	Salaries of Teachers	1,277,015.00
3/10	Textbooks	18,800.00
3/11	Supplies Used in Instruction	38,250.00
3/13	Tuition to Other Districts	12,600.00
3/14	Other Expenses of Instruction	10,100.00
	Total, Instructional Service (Day Schools)	$ 1,489,245.00

OPERATION OF SCHOOL PLANT:

4/1	Wages—Building Service Employees	$ 110,575.00
4/2	Fuel Oil	20,900.00
4/3	Water	3,875.00
4/4	Light & Power	21,800.00
4/5	Custodial Supplies	5,600.00
4/7	Services Other Than Personal (Telephone, Laundry, Piano Tuning)	7,100.00
	Total, Operation of School Plant	$ 169,850.00

MAINTENANCE OF SCHOOL PLANT:

5/1	Upkeep of Grounds	$ 8,175.00
5/2	Repair of Buildings	57,160.00
5/3	Repair & Replacement of Heating, Lighting & Plumbing Equipment	20,400.00
5/4	Repair & Replacement of Instructional Equipment	14,182.00
5/5	Repair & Replacement of Furniture	9,920.00
5/6	Repair & Replacement—Other Equipment	5,457.00
5/11	Other Expenses of Maintenance	1,985.00
	Total, Maintenance of School Plant	$ 117,279

FIXED CHARGES:

6/1	Pensions—State Teachers' Ret. System	$ 226,000.00
6/2	Pensions—Other Employees	35,525.00
6/3	Insurance	37,410.00
6/4	Taxes	3,200.00
6/5	Membership—State School Boards Assn.	400.00
6/6	Employers Contrib. to F.I.C.A. (Soc. Sec.)	37,500.00
	Total, Fixed Charges	$ 340,035.00

DEBT SERVICE:

7/1	Payment of Bonds	$ 175,000.00
7/4	Payment of Interest on Bonds	56,555.00
7/7	Refunds	
7/8	Other Expenses of Debt Service	225.00
	Total, Debt Service	$ 231,780.00

CAPITAL OUTLAY:

8/2	Improvement of Grounds	$ 800.00
8/3	Architect & Engineer Fees	2,500.00
8/4	New Buildings & Bldg. Equipment	—
8/9	Alteration of Bldgs. (Not Repairs)	1,920.00
8/11	Instructional Equip. & Furniture	19,157.00
8/12	Other Equipment	1,971.00
8/15	New Library Books	5,700.00
8/14	Gift Fund	—
	Total, Capital Outlay	$ 32,048.00

AUXILIARY AGENCIES AND OTHER SUNDRY ACTIVITIES:

9/1	Library Salaries	$ 20,800.00
9/2	Library—Repair & Repl. of Books	3,500.00
9/3	Library—Other Expenses	1,350.00
9/4	Health Service—Med. Inspection	5,100.00
9/5	Health Service—Nurses' Salaries	32,800.00
9/6	Health Service—Dental Hyg. Salary	500.00
9/7	Health Service—Other Expenses	1,400.00
9/8	Transportation Services	19,000.00
		22,500.00
9/10	Cafeteria	8,400.00
9/12	Recreation & Sports	4,135.00
9/13	Other Expenses	50.00
9/14	Psychological Services	11,175.00
	Total, Auxiliary Agencies	$ 130,710.00
	Grand Total of Budget	$ 2,596,067.00
	Amount of State Aid (Estimated)	550,000.00
	Miscellaneous Receipts (Estimated)	53,000.00
		$ 1,930,067.00
	Reduction of Contingent Fund	63,000.00
	Amount to be Raised by Taxes	$ 1,930,067.00
	Assessed Valuation	$59,681,265.00
	Tax Rate per $1,000.00 (Estimated)	$ 32.34

Certified to be a true and correct copy
Sgd:
Sgd: .... District Clerk

Sample budget summary for a school system.

of the expenditures should be closely related to the objectives that the organization is trying to achieve. In this aspect the administration plays a very important part in the budgeting process.

Budgets should be planned and prepared with a thought to the future. They are an important part of the administration's 3-, 5-, or 7-year plan and the program of accomplishment that has been outlined for a fiscal period. Projects of any size should be integrated progressively over many years. Thus the outlay of monies to realize such aims requires long-term planning.

According to the strict interpretation of the word, a budget is merely a record of receipts and expenditures. As used here, however, it reflects the long-term planning of the organization, pointing up the needs with their estimated costs, and then ensuring that a realistic program is planned that will fit into the estimated income.

The budget forecasts revenues and expenses for a period of 1 year, known as the fiscal year, which is not always synonymous with the school or college year.

Purposes of budgets

The purposes of budgets are as follows:

1. They express the plan and program for the departments of health and physical education. They determine such things as (a) size of classes, (b) supplies, equipment, and facilities, (c) methods used, (d) results and educational values sought, and (e) personnel available.

2. They reflect the school's or college's educational philosophy and policies and those of the professional fields of health and physical education. They provide an overview of these specialized areas.

3. They determine what phases of the program are to be emphasized. They aid in an analysis of all aspects of health and physical education programs.

4. They interpret to the principal, superintendent of schools, board of educa-

tion (or trustees), dean, and the public in general the needs of health and physical education.

5. They assist, together with the budgets of other educational subdivisions, in determining the tax levy for the school district.

6. They make it possible, upon approval by the recognized officials, to authorize expenditures for the program of health and physical education.

7. They make it possible to administer the health and physical education program economically by improving accounting procedures.

Types of budgets

There are short-term and long-term budgets. The short-term is usually the annual budget that runs for a 12-month period. The long-term budget represents long-term fiscal planning, possibly for a 10-year period. Most health and physical education personnel will be concerned with short-term or annual budgets whereby they plan their financial needs for a period covering the school year.

Responsibility for budgets

The responsibility for the preparation of the overall school or college budget may vary from one locality to another. In most systems the superintendent of schools is responsible. In colleges it is the responsibility of the president and the dean. Where these situations exist, it is often possible for principals, department heads, teachers, and professors to participate in preparation of the budget by submitting various requests for budget items. In other situations the budget may be first prepared in nearly all its details and then submitted to the subdivisions for consideration.

In some large school systems the superintendent of schools frequently delegates much of the budget responsibility to a business manager, a clerk, or an assistant or associate superintendent.

The final official school authority in re-

THE ROLE OF THE ADMINISTRATOR IN BUDGETING*

A. Preliminary considerations in preparing the budget
    1. Program additions or deletions
    2. Staff changes
    3. Inventory of equipment on hand

B. Budget preparation: additional considerations
    1. Athletic gate receipts and expenditures — Athletic Association fund
    2. Board of education budget — allocations for physical education, including athletics
    3. Coaches requests and requests of teachers and department heads
    4. Comparison of requests with inventories
    5. Itemizing and coding requests
    6. Budget conferences with administration
    7. Justification of requests

C. Athletic association funds: considerations
    1. Estimated income
        a. Gate receipts
        b. Student activities tickets
        c. Tournament receipts
    2. Estimated expenditures
        a. Awards
        b. Tournament fees
        c. Films
        d. Miscellaneous
        e. Surplus

D. General budget: considerations
    1. Breakdown
        a. By sport or activity
        b. Transportation
        c. Salaries of personnel
        d. Insurance
        e. Reconditioning of equipment
        f. Supervision
        g. General and miscellaneous
        h. Equipment
        i. Officials
    2. Codes
        a. Advertising
        b. Travel
        c. Conferences
        d. Others

E. Postbudget procedures
    1. Selection of equipment and supplies
    2. Preparation of list of dealers to bid
    3. Request for price quotations
    4. Requisitions
    5. Care of equipment
    6. Notification of teachers and coaches of amounts approved

F. Ordering procedures
    1. Study the quality of various products
    2. Accept no substitutes for items ordered
    3. Submit request for price quotations
    4. Select low quotes or justify higher quotes
    5. Submit purchase orders
    6. Check and count all shipments
    7. Record items received on inventory cards
    8. Provide for equipment and supply accountability

*Adapted from recommendations of Director's Workshop, New York University, 1968.

THE ROLE OF THE ADMINISTRATOR IN BUDGETING—cont'd

G. Relationships with administration
   1. Consultation — program plans with building principal and/or superintendent
   2. Make budget recommendations to administration
   3. Advise business manager of procedures followed
   4. Discuss items approved and deleted with business manager
   5. Advise teachers and coaches of amounts available and adjust requests

H. Suggestions for prospective directors of physical education programs
   1. Develop a philosophy and approach to budgeting
   2. Consult with staff for their suggestions
   3. Select quality merchandise
   4. Provide proper care and maintenance of equipment and supplies
   5. Provide for all programs on an equitable basis
   6. Budget adequately but not elaborately
   7. Provide a sound well-rounded program of physical education
   8. Emphasize equality for girls and boys
   9. Provide for basic instructional, adapted, intramural and extramural, and interscholastic parts of the program
   10. Conduct a year-round public relations program
   11. Try to overcome these possible shortcomings:
      a. Board of education not oriented to needs of physical education
      b. Program not achieving established goals
      c. Staff not adequately informed and involved in administrative process

---

spect to school budgets is the board of education. This body can approve, reject, or amend. But even beyond the board of education rests the authority of the people, who in most communities have the right to approve or reject the budget.

In colleges the budget may be handled in the dean's office, or the director or chairman of the physical education department may have the responsibility. In some cases the director of athletics is responsible for the athletic budget.

Within school departments of health and physical education the chairman, supervisor, or director is the person responsible for the budget. However, he or she will usually consult with members of the department and receive their suggestions.

Criteria for a good budget

A budget for health and physical education should meet the following criteria:

1. The budget will clearly present the financial needs of the entire program in relation to the objectives sought.

2. Key persons in the organization have been consulted.

3. The budget will provide a realistic estimate of income to balance the expenditures that are anticipated.

4. The possibility of emergencies is recognized through flexibility in the financial plan.

5. The budget will be prepared well in advance of the fiscal year so as to leave ample time for analysis, thought, criticism, and review.

6. Budget requests are realistic, not padded.

7. The budget meets the essential requirements of students, faculty, and administrators.

Budget preparation and planning

Four general steps for procedure in budget planning that health and physical education personnel might consider are as follows:

1. Actual preparation of the budget by the chairman of the department with his or her staff, listing the various estimated receipts, expenditures, and any other information that needs to be included.

2. Presentation of the budget to the principal, superintendent, dean, board of education, or other person or group that represents the proper authority and has the responsibility for reviewing it.

3. After formal approval of the budget, its use as a guide for the financial management and administration of the department or organization.

4. Critical evaluation of the budget periodically to determine its effectiveness in meeting educational needs, with notations being made for the next year's budget.

The preparation of the budget, representing the first step, is a long-term endeavor that cannot be accomplished in a day or two. The budget is something that can be well prepared only after a careful review of program effectiveness and appraisal over an extended period of time. However, the actual finalization of the budget usually is accomplished in the early spring after a detailed inventory of program needs has been taken. The director of health and/or physical education, after close consultation with staff members and the principal, dean, superintendent of schools, or other responsible administrative officer, should formulate the budget.

In preparing the budget many records and reports will be of value. The inventory of equipment and supplies on hand will be useful, and copies of inventories and budgets from previous years will provide good references. Comparison of budgetary items with those in schools and colleges of similar size may be of help. Accounting records will be valuable.

The preparation of the budget should be accomplished in such a way that it is flexible and will allow for readjustments to be made, if necessary. It is difficult to accurately and specifically list each detail in the way that it will be needed and executed.

The budget should represent a schedule that can be justified. This means that each budgetary item must satisfy the most meaningful educational needs and interests of all concerned. Furthermore, each item that constitutes an expenditure should be reflected in budget specifications.

Richard G. Mitchell, writing on "administrative planning," lists these five important considerations in budget preparation:

1. What was planned last year? This constitutes the tying together of the proposed budget with the one approved last year to check on long-term planning goals.
2. What was accomplished last year? This step relates last year's accomplishments to the achievement of the department's long-term objectives.
3. What can realistically be accomplished this year? In light of past years, future trends, and the master plan, what can be accomplished this year?
4. What needs to be done? This constitutes the minimum essentials that must be accomplished this year. These items have priority.
5. How is it to be done? Such items as staff, equipment, supplies, and other requirements for accomplishment and meeting of needs would be outlined.*

Budget organization

Budgets can be organized in many ways. One pattern that consists of four sections or divisions and that might prove useful for a health or physical education administrator is described here:

1. An introductory message enables the administration to present the financial proposals in terms that a board of education or person outside the specialized fields might readily understand. This section offers to persons who have specialized in these areas an opportunity to discuss some

---

*Mitchell, R. G.: Administrative planning—its effective use, Recreation **44**:426, 1961.

aspects of the program in lay terms and some of the directions that need to be taken in order to provide for the health and physical fitness of the students.

2. The second section presents an over-all view of the budget, with expenditures and anticipated revenues arranged in a clear and systematic fashion so that any person can compare the two.

3. A third section, with an estimate of receipts and expenditures in much more detail, should enable a principal, superintendent of schools and/or board of education, or other interested person or group to understand the budget specifically and to follow up any item of cost.

4. A fourth section might include supporting schedules to provide additional evidence for the requests outlined in the budget. Many times a budget will have a better chance of approval if there is sufficient documentation to support some items. For example, extra pay for coaching may be thought to be desirable. Salary schedules for coaches in other school systems could be included to support such a proposition.

Another type of budget organization might be one that consists of the following three parts: (1) an introductory statement of the objectives, policies, and program of the health and physical education department; (2) a résumé of the objectives, policies, and program interpreted in terms of proposed expenditures; and (3) a financial plan for meeting the educational needs during the fiscal period.

Not all budgets are broken down into these four or three divisions. All budgets do, however, give an itemized account of receipts and expenditures.

In a physical education budget common inclusions are items concerning instruction, such as extra compensation for coaches; matters of capital outlay, such as a new swimming pool or handball court; the replacement of expendable equipment, such as basketballs and baseball bats; and pro-

vision for maintenance and repair, such as refurbishing football uniforms or doing some grading on the playground. It is difficult to estimate many of these items without making a careful inventory and analysis of the condition of the facilities and equipment.

Sources of income

The sources of income for most school and college health and physical education programs include the general school or college fund, gate receipts, health, general organization, and activity fees, and some other revenues.

General school or college fund. At the elementary and secondary levels the health program would be supported, usually entirely, through general school funds, and the physical education program would be financed in the same way, to a large extent. At the college and university level the general fund of the institution would also represent a major source of income.

Gate receipts. Gate receipts play an important part in some schools in the financing of at least part of the physical education program. Although there is usually less stress on gate receipts at lower educational levels, colleges and universities sometimes finance their entire athletic, intramural, and physical education programs through such a medium. At a few high schools throughout the country, gate receipts have been abolished because of the feeling that if athletics represent an important part of the education program, they should be paid for in the same way that science and mathematics programs, for example, are financed.

Health, general organization, and activity fees. Some high schools either require or make available to students separate health, general organization, or activity fees and tickets or some other inducement that enables them to attend the athletic, dramatic, and musical events that are offered. In colleges and universities a similar plan is generally used, thus providing students

Table 16-1. General organization athletic account — financial report (September-December)

Expenses		
Football		
Officials (four home games)	$ 240.00	
Equipment and supplies	1,182.01	
Transportation	87.50	
Supervision (police, ticket sellers and takers)	476.00	
Reconditioning and cleaning equipment	656.60	
Medical supplies	62.70	
Scouting	30.00	
Film	15.68	
Guarantees	260.00	
Football dinner	115.50	
Miscellaneous (printing tickets, meetings)	86.00	
Total football expense		$3,211.99
Cross country		
State and county entry fees	$ 5.00	
Transportation	32.00	
Total cross country expense		$ 37.00
Basketball		
Supervision (three games)	$ 18.00	
Custodian (three games)	13.00	
Police (one game)	6.00	
Total basketball expense		$ 37.00
Cheerleaders		
Transportation	$ 26.10	
Sixteen sweaters	160.00	
Cleaning sweaters	48.00	
Total cheerleader expense		$ 234.10
Total expenses		$3,520.09
Receipts		
Football		
Newburgh game	$ 655.85	
Norwalk game	909.80	
Yonkers game	564.75	
Bridgeport game	550.00	
Guarantee (New Haven)	60.00	
Total receipts		$2,740.40

with reduced rates to the various out-of-class activities offered by the institution. A health fee also is quite common at higher education levels. Table 16-1 shows a general organization financial statement.

Other sources of income. Some other sources of income, not so common to all educational levels, are (1) *special foundation, governmental, or individual grants or gifts* intended to promote physical fitness, athletics, or some phase of health and physical education programs; (2) the sale of *radio and television rights* at the college level, especially for those institutions that have nationally ranking teams and where the athletic contests have great public appeal; (3) *concessions* at athletic contests and other activity events; and (4) *special fund-raising events* such as a faculty-varsity basketball game or a gymnastic circus.

Linn* has listed some steps that might profitably be followed for estimating receipts in the general school budget and that are also application to the preparation of budgets for health and physical education:

1. Gathering and analyzing historical data
2. Collecting current data
3. Preparing income estimates
4. Organizing and classifying receipts into proper categories
5. Preparing revenue estimates from accumulated data
6. Making comparisons with estimates for preceding years and preparing final draft of receipts

Expenditures

In health and physical education budgets, typical examples of expenditures are items of *capital outlay*, such as a dental chair or swimming pool; *expendable equipment*, such as tongue depressors or basketballs; and a *maintenance and repair provision*, such as towel and laundry service and the repair of pure-tone audiometers or refurbishing of football uniforms. See Table 16-2 for a sample list of expenditures for athletics.

Some expenditures are very easy to estimate but others are more difficult, requiring the keeping of accurate inventories, examination of past records, and careful

*Linn, H. H.: School business administration, New York, 1956, The Ronald Press Co.

Table 16-2. A sample list of expenditures for athletics

	Baseball	Basketball	Football	Cross country	Girls' sports	Golf	Hockey	Soccer	Swimming	Tennis	Track	Total
Equipment and supplies	$369.55	$116.70	$278.68	$45.80	$41.60	$36.10	$251.65	$70.40	$80.05	$27.20	$231.77	$1,549.50
Transportation	208.50	248.70	39.60	83.20	84.98	48.40	495.00	63.70	108.80	8.80	120.90	1,510.48
Officials	122.00	391.35	50.00					52.00				615.35
Cleaning	65.70	30.95	129.40				95.60	57.20			141.10	519.95
Supervision		66.00										66.00
Custodian		37.00										37.00
Additional coaching			350.00					100.00				450.00
Entry fees						7.00			17.21	4.00	22.50	50.75
Rental, boys' club pool									250.00			250.00
Totals	$765.75	$890.70	$847.68	$129.00	$126.58	$91.50	$842.25	$343.20	$456.10	$40.00	$516.27	$5,049.03

analysis of the condition of the equipment. Some items and services will need to be figured by averaging costs over a period of years, such as cleaning and mending athletic equipment. Other examples of items that require careful consideration in order to list expenditures accurately are awards, new equipment needed, guarantees to visiting teams, and medical services for emergencies.

Linn* suggests some sound procedures to follow in estimating expenditures:

1. Prepare a budgetary calendar that will include what is to be accomplished and when.
2. Gather and analyze historical data.
3. Collect current information and data pertinent to expenditures.
4. Prepare estimates from accumulated data.
5. Organize and classify various items of expenditure, stating the purposes for which money will be expended.
6. Clarify expenditure estimates to show how they represent meaningful educational needs.
7. Compare estimates with expenditures for previous years.
8. Reevaluate estimates and prepare final draft.

Budget presentation and adoption

Budgets in health and physical education, after being prepared, should usually be submitted to the superintendent through the principal's office. The principal represents the person in charge of his particular building and, therefore, subdivision budgets should be presented to him for his approval. Good administration would mean, furthermore, that the budgetary items would have been reviewed with him during their preparation so that approval is usually a routine matter.

In the case of college and university, the

proper channels should be followed. This might mean clearance through a dean or other administrative officer. Each person, of course, who is responsible for budget preparation and presentation should be very familiar with the proper working channels.

For successful presentation and adoption, the budget should be prepared in final form only after careful consideration so that little change will be needed. Requests for funds should be justifiable, and ample preliminary discussion of the budget with persons and groups most directly concerned should be held so that needless difficulty will be avoided.

Budget administration

After the presentation and approval of the budget, the next step is to see that it is administered properly. This means that it should be followed as closely as possible with periodic checks on expenditures to see that they fall within the budget appropriations that have been provided. The budget should function as a good guide for economical and efficient administration.

Budget appraisal

Periodic appraisal calls for an audit of the accounts and an evaluation of the school program resulting from the administration of the current budget. Such appraisal should be done in all honesty and with a view to eliminating weaknesses in current budgets and strengthening future ones. It should also be remembered that the budget will be only as good as the administration makes it and that the budget will improve only as the administration improves.

FINANCIAL ACCOUNTING

The great amount of money involved in health and physical education programs means that strict accountability must be observed. This means the maintenance of accurate records, proper distribution of ma-

---

*Linn, H. H., op. cit.

terials, and adequate appraisal and evaluation of procedures. Financial accounting should provide:

1. A record of receipts and expenditures for all departmental transactions
2. A permanent record of all financial transactions for future reference
3. A pattern for expenditures that is closely related to the approved budget
4. A tangible documentation of compliance with mandates and requests either imposed by law or by administrative action
5. Some procedure for evaluating, to see that funds are dealt with honestly, and proper management in respect to control, analysis of costs, and reporting

Most of the state departments of education publish manuals on school accounting. Each chairman of health and physical education should have a copy of his or her own state's school accounting procedure and should read and follow it carefully.

Reasons for financial accounting

Some reasons why financial accounting is needed in health and physical education include those listed below:

1. To provide a method of authorizing expenditures for items that have been included and approved in the budget. This means proper accounting records are being used.

2. To provide authorized procedures for making purchases of equipment, supplies, and other materials and to let contracts for various services.

3. To provide authorized procedures for paying the proper amounts (a) for purchases of equipment, supplies, and other materials, which have been checked upon receipt, (b) for labor that actually has taken place, and (c) for other services that have been rendered.

4. To provide a record of each payment

Table 16-3. Sample sports program, general organization, and board of education report of expenditures and receipts

Sports	Board of education	General organization	Total
Total expenditures			
Baseball	$ 765.75		$ 765.75
Basketball	890.70	$ 106.34	997.04
Football	847.68	3,943.09	4,340.77
Cross country	129.00	37.00	166.00
Girls' sports and cheerleaders	126.58	249.10	375.68
Golf	91.50		91.50
Hockey	842.25	48.95	891.20
Soccer	343.20		343.20
Swimming	456.10	41.10	497.20
Tennis	40.00	4.00	44.00
Track	516.27	15.03	531.30
Total	$5,049.03	$3,994.61	$9,043.64
Total general organization receipts			
Football		$2,740.40	
Basketball		381.30	
Total			$3,121.70

that has been made, including the date, to whom, for what purpose, and other pertinent material.

5. To provide authorized procedures for handling various receipts and sources of income.

6. To provide the detailed information that is essential for proper auditing of accounts, such as confirmation that money has been spent for accurately specified items.

7. To provide material and information for the preparation of future budgets.

8. To provide a tangible base for the development of future policies relating to financial planning.

Administrative principles and policies for financial accounting

The Athletic Institute* has prepared some excellent material on accountability, in which it brings out such important principles and policies as the following:

1. The administrative head has the final responsibility for accountability for all equipment and supplies in his or her organization.

2. Departments should establish and enforce policies covering loss, damage, theft, misappropriation, or destruction of equipment and supplies or other materials.

3. A system of accurate record keeping should be established and be uniform throughout the department.

4. Accountability should demonstrate the close relationship that exists between equipment and supplies and the program objectives.

5. A system of policies should be developed that will guarantee the proper use and protection of all equipment and supplies within the department.

6. The person to whom equipment and supplies are issued should be held accountable for these materials.

*The Athletic Institute: Equipment and supplies for athletics, physical education and recreation. Chicago, 1960, The Institute, chap. 5.

7. Accurate inventories are essential to proper financial accounting.

8. A system of marking equipment and supplies as proof of ownership should be instituted.

9. A meaningful procedure should be established for the proper distribution of all equipment and supplies.

10. The discarding of equipment and supplies should take place only in accordance with established procedures and by authorized persons.

Accounting for receipts and expenditures

A centralized accounting system is very advantageous, with all funds being deposited with the school treasurer or business manager. Purchase orders and other procedures are usually then countersigned or certified by the school treasurer, thus better guaranteeing integrity in the use of funds. A system of bookkeeping wherein books are housed in the central office by the finance officer helps to ensure better control of finances by the school and allows for all subdivisions or departments in an educational system to be financially controlled in the same manner. Such a procedure also provides for better and more centralized record keeping. The central accounting system fund accounts, in which are located the physical education and health funds, should be audited annually by qualified persons not associated with the school funds. Finally, an annual financial report should be made and publicized to indicate receipts, expenditures, and other pertinent data associated with the enterprise.

All receipts and expenditures should be recorded in the ledger in the proper manner, providing such important information as the fund in which it has been deposited, or from which it was withdrawn, and the money received from such sources as athletics and dues to school organizations should be shown with sufficient cross references and detailed information. Supporting vouchers should also be at hand. Tickets to athletic and other events should be numbered consecutively and checked to get an accurate record of ticket sales. Students should not be permitted to handle funds except under the supervision of some member of the administrative staff or faculty. All accounts should be properly audited at appropriate intervals.

Purchase orders on regular authorized forms issued by the school should be used, so that accurate records may be kept. To order verbally is a questionable policy. By preparing written purchase orders, on regular forms and according to good accountability procedure, legality of contract is better ensured, together with prompt delivery and payment. For more information see Chapter 17 on the purchase and care of supplies and equipment.

CHECKLIST FOR BUDGETING AND FINANCIAL ACCOUNTING

Yes   *No*

1. Has a complete inventory been taken and itemized on proper forms as a guide in estimating equipment needs?
2. Does the equipment inventory include a detailed account of the number of items on hand, size and quantity, type, condition, etc.?
3. Is the inventory complete, current, and up-to-date?
4. Are budgetary estimates as accurate and realistic as possible without padding?
5. Are provisions made in the budget for increases expected in enrollments, increased pupil participation, and changes in the cost of equipment and supplies?
6. Have supply house and the school business administrator been consulted on the cost of new equipment?
7. Has the Director of Health and Physical Education consulted with his staff on various budget items?
8. Has the Director of Health and Physical Education consulted with the school business administrator in respect to the total budget for his department?
9. Are new equipment and supply needs for health and physical education determined and budgeted at least one year in advance?
10. Was the budget prepared according to the standards desired by the chief school administrator?
11. Are statistics and information for previous years indicated as a means of comparison?
12. Is there a summary of receipts and expenditures listed concisely on one page so that the total budget can be quickly seen?
13. If receipts from athletics or other funds are to be added to the budget, is this shown?
14. Are there alternate program plans with budgetary changes in the event the budget is not approved?
15. Has a statement of objectives of the program been included that reflects the overall educational philosophy and program of the total school and community?
16. Has the budget been prepared so that the major aspects may be viewed readily by those persons desiring a quick review and also in more detail for those persons desiring a further delineation of the budgetary items?
17. Is the period of time for which the budget has been prepared clearly indicated?
18. Is the health and physical education budget based on an educational plan developed to attain the goals and purposes agreed upon by the

Continued.

CHECKLIST FOR BUDGETING AND FINANCIAL ACCOUNTING–cont'd

	Yes	No
director and his staff within the framework of the total school's philosophy?	___	___
19. Is the health and physical education plan a comprehensive one reflecting health science instruction, health services, and a healthful environment, physical education class, adapted, intramural and extramural, and interscholastic program?	___	___
20. Does the plan include a statement of the objectives of the health and physical education programs and are these reflected in the budget?	___	___
21. Are both long-range and short-range plans for achieving the purposes of the program provided?	___	___
22. Have provisions been made in the budget for emergencies?	___	___
23. Are accurate records kept on such activities involving expenditures of money as transportation, insurance, officials, laundry and dry cleaning, awards, guarantees, repairs, new equipment, medical expenses, and publicity?	___	___
24. Are accurate records kept on the receipt of monies from such sources as gate receipts and advertising revenue?	___	___
25. Once the budget has been approved, is there a specific plan provided for authorizing expenditures?	___	___
26. Are specific forms used for recording purchase transactions?	___	___
27. Are purchases on all major items based on competitive bidding?	___	___
28. Are requisitions used in obtaining supplies and equipment?	___	___
29. Are requisitions numbered and do they include such information as the name of the person originating the requisition, when the item to be purchased will be needed, where to ship the item, the description and/or code number, quantity, unit price, and amount?	___	___
30. With the exception of petty cash accounts, is a central purchasing system in effect?	___	___
31. Is the policy of quantity purchasing followed wherever possible and desirable in the interests of economy?	___	___
32. If quantity purchasing is used, is advanced thought and planning given to storage and maintenance facilities and procedures?	___	___
33. Are performance tests made of items purchased? Are state, regional, or national testing bureaus or laboratories utilized where feasible?	___	___
34. Are receipts of equipment and supplies checked carefully?	___	___
35. Is an audit made of all expenditures?	___	___
36. Are specific procedures in effect to safeguard money, property, and employees?	___	___
37. Is there a check to determine that established standards, policies, and procedures have been followed?	___	___
38. Are procedures in operation to check condition and use of equipment and supplies?	___	___
39. Is a financial report made periodically?	___	___
40. Are there proper procedures for the care and maintenance and accountability of all equipment and supplies?	___	___
41. Are accurate records kept on all equipment and supplies including condition, site, and age?	___	___
42. Have established procedures been developed and are they followed in regard to the issuance, use, and return of equipment?	___	___
43. Have provisions been made for making regular notations of future needs?	___	___

Questions and exercises

1. Prepare a budget for a high school or college department of physical education.
2. What are five reasons for fiscal management in health and physical education?
3. Collect budgets from five school systems or colleges and critically evaluate them.
4. Where does the responsibility fall for budget preparation?
5. Outline the procedure you would follow in the preparation of a budget if you were chairman of the department of health and physical education for a city educational system.
6. What are the criteria for a good budget?
7. What are the most common sources of receipts and expenditures in a health and/or physical education department?
8. What records would you keep in order to ensure good financial accounting?
9. Formulate ten policies to ensure good financial accounting.

Reading assignment in *Administrative Dimensions of Health and Physical Education Programs, Including Athletics:* Chapter 13, Selections 70 to 76.

Selected references

Athletic Institute: Equipment and supplies for athletics, physical education, and recreation, Chicago, 1960, The Institute.

Casey, L. M.: School business administration, New York, 1964, The Center for Applied Research in Education, Inc. (The Library of Education).

Cosgrove, J. N., editor: Budgeting—experts say it's wise planning, not pinching pennies, The National Underwriter **50:**42, 1967.

Gehric, E. A.: Budget procedure for extracurricular organizations, Business Education World **32:**17, 1951.

Knezevich, S. J., and Fowlkes, J. G.: Business management of local school systems, New York, 1960, Harper & Row, Publishers.

Linder, I. H., and Gunn, H. M.: Secondary school administration, Columbus, Ohio, 1963, Charles E. Merrill Books, Inc.

Ranney, D. C.: The determinants of fiscal support for large city educational systems, Administrators Notebook, vol. 15, December, 1966.

Roe, W. H.: School business management, New York, 1961, McGraw-Hill Book Co.

Thomas, J. A.: Education decision-making and the school budget, Administrators Notebook, vol. 12, December, 1963.

Wilsey, C. E.: Budget for equipment replacement, School Board Journal, p. 10, May, 1967.

CHAPTER *17* THE PURCHASE AND CARE OF SUPPLIES AND
EQUIPMENT INCLUDING
AUDIOVISUAL MATERIALS

Health and physical education programs utilize many supplies and equipment that cost thousands of dollars. *Supplies* are those materials that are expendable and that need to be replaced at frequent intervals, such as shuttlecocks and adhesive tape. *Equipment* is the term used for those items that are not considered expendable but are utilized over a period of years, such as parallel bars and audiometers.

Since so much money is expended upon supplies and equipment and since such materials are vital to school and college health and safety, to good playing conditions, and to values derived from the programs, it is important that this administrative phase of the specialized fields of health and physical education be considered carefully.

Many different sources for purchasing equipment exist, many grades and qualities of materials are available, and many methods of storing and maintaining such merchandise are prevalent. Some of these sources, grades, and methods are good and some are questionable. In order to obtain the greatest values for the amount of money spent, basic principles of selecting, purchasing, and maintaining need to be known and understood. This chapter includes a brief discussion of these matters and also a discussion of audiovisual materials. In Appendix A the reader will find a listing of organizations and companies where various health and physical education supplies and equipment may be purchased. Appendix B contains an extensive

chart on the subject of the care, repair, and storage of physical education supplies and equipment. All types of health, physical education, and athletic equipment and supplies are included.

SUPPLY AND EQUIPMENT NEEDS VARY

Supplies and equipment needed in a school or college system will vary according to certain influencing factors. These include, first, the programs themselves and the activities that are to be offered. The geographic location of the school will help to determine the activities scheduled, as will such other elements as the interests of students and their physiologic, psychologic, and sociologic needs. A second factor would be the other facilities and the health rooms and playing space available. Some schools and a few colleges do not have a health suite and have only limited physical education facilities. Under such conditions the supplies and equipment needed will differ from those required in settings where spacious accommodations exist. Other factors that will need to be taken into consideration are the nature of the clientele (in regard to age, sex, and number of students), the money available, the length of playing seasons, and provisions for the health and safety of participants. Those persons responsible for purchasing supplies and equipment should carefully study their own particular situations and estimate their own needs in an objective and realistic manner.

Gymnastic equipment courtesy Nissen Corporation, Cedar Rapids, Iowa.

Gymnastic equipment courtesy Nissen Corporation, Cedar Rapids, Iowa.

Gymnastic equipment courtesy Nissen Corporation, Cedar Rapids, Iowa.

As pointed out previously, the types of equipment and supplies will vary with the program. In the health education area such articles as microscopes, mannequins, test materials, laboratory equipment, and audiovisual equipment will be needed. In the health service area there will be a need for such items as equipment for screening vision and hearing, first-aid supplies, scales, examining table, dental equipment and supplies, beds, towels, and sheets. In the physical education area, of course, all types of balls, apparatus, uniforms, timers, and racks will be needed if individual, team, formal, aquatic, dance, and other activities are to be offered. Different types of materials will be required for the interschool and intercollegiate athletic programs, the intramural and extramural programs, the adapted programs, and the class programs. Many decisions in the purchasing of equipment and supplies will depend upon the objectives being sought by the administration.

In general, however, the administration is interested in:

1. Trying to standardize supplies and equipment as much as possible
2. Supervising the entire process of selection, purchase, storage, and maintenance
3. Maintaining a list of sources of materials
4. Preparing specifications for various items that are to be purchased
5. Securing bids for large purchases and those required by law
6. Deciding upon or recommending organizations where materials are to be purchased
7. Testing products to see that specifications are satisfactorily met
8. Checking supplies and equipment to determine if all that were ordered have been delivered
9. Expediting the delivery of purchases so that materials are available as needed

10. Continually seeking new products that meet needs of program
11. Providing overall supervision of purchase, care, and use of supplies and equipment

SELECTION OF SUPPLIES AND EQUIPMENT

A discussion of some of the principles that should be observed in the selection of supplies and equipment for school and college health and physical education programs, including athletics, follows.

Selection should be based upon local needs

Supplies and equipment should be selected because they are needed in a particular school or college situation and by a particular group of students. Items should be selected that represent materials needed to carry out the program as outlined in the course of study and that represent essentials to fulfilling program objectives.

Selection should be based upon quality

In the long run, the item of good quality is the cheapest and the safest. Bargains too often represent inferior materials that wear out much earlier. Only the best grade of football equipment should be purchased. I did a study of football deaths that occurred during a 25-year period and found that many of these deaths had resulted from use of inferior helmets and other poor equipment. What is true of football is also true of other activities.

Selection should be made by competent personnel

The persons carrying out the assignment of selecting the supplies and equipment needed in health and physical education programs should be competent to assume such a responsibility. To perform such a job efficiently means examining many types and makes of products, conducting experiments to determine such qualities as economy and durability, listing and weighing the advantages and disadvantages of different items, and knowing how each item is going to be used. The person selecting supplies and equipment should be interested in this responsibility, have the time to do the job, and possess those qualities needed to perform the function in an efficient manner. Some schools and colleges have purchasing agents who are specially trained in these matters. In small organizations the chairman, director, or coach frequently performs this responsibility. One other point is important: regardless of who the responsible person may be, the staff member who utilizes these supplies and equipment in his or her particular facet of the total program should have a great deal to say about the specific items chosen. He or she is the one who understands the functional use of the merchandise.

Selection should be continuous

A product that ranks as the "best" available this year may not necessarily be the "best" next year. Manufacturers are constantly conducting research in order to come out with something better. There is keen competition among them. The administration, therefore, cannot be complacent and apathetic, thinking that because a certain product has served them so well in the past, it is the best buy for the future. Instead, there must be a continual search for the best product available.

Selection should take into consideration service and replacement needs

Items of supplies and equipment may be difficult to obtain in volume. Upon receipt of merchandise, sizes of uniforms may be wrong and colors may be mixed up. Additional materials may be needed on short notice. Such facts mean that in the selection process consideration should be given to selecting items that will be available in volume, if needed, and that con-

KEY TO FIGURES

1. **CHEST.** Be sure the tape is snug under the arms and over the shoulder blades.

2. **WAIST.** Place the tape above the hips around waist like a belt to determine waist measurements.

3. **HIPS.** Measure hips around the widest part.

4. **INSEAM.** Measure inseam from close up the crotch to top of the heel of the shoe when full-length pants are ordered. For shorter pants, like baseball and football pants, check on the measurement recommendations of the manufacturer of the clothing you select.

5. **OUTSEAM.** Measure from the waistline to top of heel of shoe for full-length pants. For baseball, football, and shorter pants check the measurement recommendations of the particular manufacturer involved.

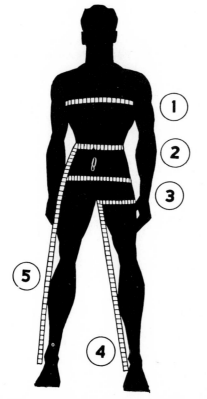

6. **SLEEVE.** Take measurments from center of back over elbow to wrist. Keep elbow bent, straight out from shoulder.

HEAD. (Not shown in diagram). The tape should run across forehead about 1½ inches above eyebrows and back around the large part of the head.

How to measure for athletic equipment. Correct measurement is essential for proper sizing of athletic equipment to ensure the comfort of the wearer, durability of equipment, proper protection, and appearance on the field. This illustration may be used as a measuring guide to ensure the proper fit of uniforms, jerseys, protective equipment, and warmup suits. This is a basic measuring guide for most types of athletic equipment. For a perfect fit it is also recommended that you state height, weight, and any special irregularities of build. See also p. 489. (From How to budget, select, and order athletic equipment, Chicago, 1962, The Athletic Institute.)

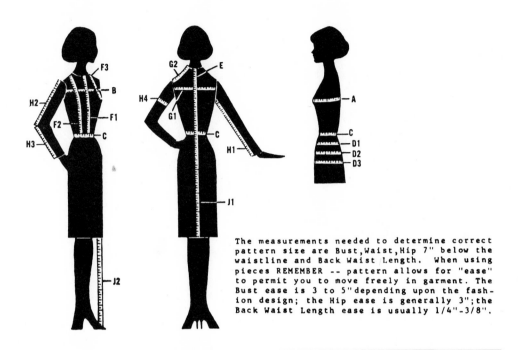

The measurements needed to determine correct pattern size are Bust, Waist, Hip 7" below the waistline and Back Waist Length. When using pieces REMEMBER -- pattern allows for "ease" to permit you to move freely in garment. The Bust ease is 3 to 5" depending upon the fashion design; the Hip ease is generally 3"; the Back Waist Length ease is usually 1/4"-3/8".

NAME .... DATE ....

A. **BUST**... **in.** — Measure around fullest part — a little higher in back

B. **CHEST** .... **in.** — Measure straight across front from seam to seam

C. **WAIST** .... **in.** — Put string or elastic around waist to locate natural waistline.

D. **HIP   1**................................... **in.** — Measure 3" below natural waistline

      2 .... **in.** — Measure 7" below natural waistline

      3 .... **in.** — Measure 9" below natural waistline

E. **BACK WAIST LENGTH** .... **in.** — Nape of neck to waistline

F. **FRONT WAIST LENGTH   1** .... **in.** — Neck to waistline at Center Front

                    2 .... **in.** — Mid-shoulder to waist over bust

                    3 .... **in.** — Base of neck at shoulder seamline to tip of bust

G. **SHOULDERS   1** .... **in.** — Seam to seam across back 4" below neckline

             2 .... **in.** — One shoulder from base of neck to seamline

H. **SLEEVE   1** .... **in.** — Underarm to wrist

          2 .... **in.** — Shoulder to elbow

          3 .... **in.** — Elbow to wrist

          4 .... **in.** — Around upper arm

J. **LENGTH   1** .... **in.** — Waist to hemline at Center Back

        2 .... **in.** — From floor to hemline

printed in u. s. a.

How to take a girl's measurements. (Courtesy McCall's Patterns.)

Gymnastic equipment courtesy Nissen Corporation, Cedar Rapids, Iowa.

Gymnastic equipment courtesy Nissen Corporation, Cedar Rapids, Iowa.

sideration should be given to dealing with a business firm that will service and replace materials and take care of emergencies without delay and controversy.

PURCHASING SUPPLIES AND EQUIPMENT

A discussion of several important considerations in making purchases of supplies and equipment follows.

Purchases should meet the requirements established by the educational system and have administrative approval

Each educational system has its own policy providing for the purchase of supplies and equipment. It is essential that the prescribed pattern be followed and that proper administrative approval be obtained. Requisition forms that contain such information as description of items, amounts, and costs; purchase orders that place the buying procedure on a written or contract basis; and voucher forms that show receipt of materials should all be utilized as prescribed by school or college regulations. The health and physical education administrator and staff should be familiar with and follow local purchasing policies.

Below are listed a series of steps that one school system uses in purchasing equipment:

1. Initiation—A request is made by the teacher for equipment to fulfill, augment, supplement, or improve the curriculum.
2. Review of request—The building principal and central administration approve or disapprove request after careful consideration of need.
3. Review of budget allocation—A budget code number is assigned after availability of funds in that category has been determined.
4. Preparation of specifications—Specifications are prepared in detail, giving exact quality requirements, and made available to prospective contractors or vendors.
5. Receipt of bids—Contractors or vendors submit price quotations.
6. Comparison of bids to specifications—Careful evaluation is made to determine exact fulfillment of quality requirements.
7. Recommendations to the board of education—The business administrator prepares comparisons for the board of education, with specific recommendations for their approval.
8. Purchase order to supplier—After board of education approval, a purchase is made that fulfills the requirements at a competitive price.

Purchasing should be done in advance of need

The main and bulk purchases of supplies and equipment for programs of health and physical education should be completed well in advance of the time that the materials will be utilized. Late orders, rushed through at the last moment, may mean mistakes or substitutions on the part of the manufacturer. When purchase orders are placed early, manufacturers have more time to do their jobs and can carry out their responsibilities more efficiently. Goods that do not meet specifications can be returned and replaced, and many other advantages result. Items that are needed in the fall should be ordered not later than the preceding spring, and items desired for spring use should be ordered not later than the preceding fall.

Supplies and equipment should be standardized as far as possible and practical

Ease of ordering is accomplished and larger quantities of materials can be purchased at a saving when standardized items of supplies and equipment are used. Standardization means that certain colors,

ORIGINAL
(To Superintendent's Office)

BOARD OF EDUCATION
———— , **NEW YORK**

REQUISITION FORM

DATE_____

The following supplies, equipment, or services are required for the use of

_____
Teacher or Department

_____
Signed

Quantity	Description—give complete information	Purpose	Cost	
			Unit	Total

PURCHASE REQUISITION

Comment:

    Purchase requisitions are generally initiated by a school or department to cover requirements which are needed during the school year and which are to be purchased from a supplier. Requisition should be made out in duplicate:

    1. Original sent to business office for processing

    2. Duplicate retained in initiating school or department

APPROVED

_____
Superintendent of Schools

BOARD OF EDUCATION
——————— , New York

DEPARTMENT OF PURCHASE AND SUPPLIES

Req. No. ....

For ....

School   Department

TO......................................   Date ....

....   Return to be made by ....

....

THIS IS NOT AN ORDER

Gentlemen:

    Kindly fill in **the quotations** requested below. If unable to quote, please note and return blank.
Be sure to quote unit price and total amount. **This form must be returned.**   ——————————— **Purchasing Agent**

Notice: Resolution of the Board of Education of the city of   prohibits the purchase of materials, supplies,
    and/or services, produced by child labor, and the provisions thereof are made a part hereof.
    The Board of Education is exempt from paying manufacturers' excise, floor, or sales tax. Tax exemption
    certificate will be issued when requested.

Approximate number wanted	Articles and description	Vendor's description (Give manufacturer's name and number, when not as per our description)	Unit price	Total

QUOTATION FORM

Comment:

    This form is made out in the purchasing office and sent to
a vendor to obtain prices on items specified. If sent to the
vendor in duplicate, it permits the vendor to fill out the form,
indicating what he proposes to furnish and the price, and also
gives him a copy for his files. On receipt of the various
quotations covering the transaction, a summary may be made for
use of the purchasing official.

IMPORTANT - Please Specify Delivery Date   Extend total cash of each item

The following terms will be expected unless
  otherwise specified: Vendor ....
    Cash discount 2% - 30 days
    Quotations will be f. o. b. point of delivery,   Signature ....
      with all charges paid.
    Prompt delivery

ⓘ **ORIGINAL**
Copy to
vendor

PURCHASE ORDER
BOARD OF EDUCATION

№ 100

To:

Date of order ....
Quotation Bid No. ....
Requisition No..........................
DELIVERY INSTRUCTIONS
WHEN WANTED
Send to
At
Via   Terms

Please enter our order for the following goods:
All claims must be mailed in duplicate to Clerk's office at the above address

Quantity and unit	Description	Unit price	Total amount	✓	Delivery checked by	Code

PURCHASE ORDER

Comment:

    It is a generally accepted practice to make four copies of
the purchase order form. In this case, the disposition might
be as follows:

    1. Original copy to vendor

    2. One copy for purchasing department files

    3. One copy to finance or auditing division

    4. One copy to requisitioner which may become the receipt
        copy and returned to business office when goods called
        for have been received

If shipment cannot be made as requested, notify us at once.
CONDITIONS — READ CAREFULLY

1 Please acknowledge receipt of this order by return mail.
2 Make invoice in duplicate; send one with goods and mail the other to the purchasing agent.
3 Each shipment should be covered by a separate invoice.
4 The right is reserved to cancel this order if it is not filled within the contract time.
5 The conditions of this order are not to be modified by any verbal understanding.
6 Charges for boxing and cartage will not be allowed unless previously agreed upon.
7 If the price is stated in the order, material must not be billed at a higher price.
8 Acceptance of this order includes acceptance of all terms, prices, delivery instructions, specifications, and conditions stated.

There is a balance to credit of proper appropriation or fund to meet the expenditure covered by this purchase.

....
                        Clerk

....
          School Purchasing Agent

styles, and types of material are ordered consistently. This procedure can be followed after careful research to determine what is the best, most reliable, and most serviceable product for the money. However, standardization of supplies and equipment should never mean that further study and research to find the best materials in the light of program objectives is terminated.

Specifications should be clearly set forth when making purchases

The trademark, item number, catalogue number, type of material, and other important specifications should be clearly stated when purchasing material so as to avoid any misunderstanding as to what it wanted and is being ordered. This procedure en-sures that quality merchandise will be received when it is ordered. It also makes it possible to compare bids of competing business firms in a more meaningful manner.

Cost should be kept at the lowest figure possible without loss of quality

Quality of materials is a major consideration. However, among various manufacturers and business concerns, prices vary for products of equal quality. Since supplies and equipment are usually purchased in considerable volume, a few cents on each unit of purchase could represent a saving of many hundreds of dollars to taxpayers. Therefore, if quality can be maintained, materials should be purchased at the lowest cost figure.

Gymnastic equipment courtesy Nissen Corporation, Cedar Rapids, Iowa.

MONTH	TYPE OF ATHLETIC EQUIPMENT			
	FOOTBALL	**BASEBALL**	**BASKETBALL**	**TRACK**
JANUARY	ORDER NEW EQUIPMENT	ORDER NEW EQUIPMENT	PRACTICE FREE THROWS DURING STUDY HALL	ORDER NEW EQUIPMENT
FEBRUARY	ORDER NEW EQUIPMENT	TIME IS RUNNING OUT		TIME IS RUNNING OUT
MARCH	ORDER NEW EQUIPMENT	DELIVERY	TAKE INVENTORY	MAKE PLANS FOR VACATION
APRIL	TIME IS RUNNING OUT	MARK EQUIPMENT	ORDER NEW EQUIPMENT	GO FISHING
MAY	MOW PRINCIPAL'S LAWN		ORDER NEW EQUIPMENT	
JUNE	GO TO SCHOOL BOARD PICNIC	TAKE INVENTORY	ORDER NEW EQUIPMENT	TAKE INVENTORY
JULY	DELIVERY		ORDER NEW EQUIPMENT	
AUGUST	MARK EQUIPMENT	ATTEND COUNTY FAIR	TIME IS RUNNING OUT	
SEPTEMBER			DELIVERY	DELIVERY
OCTOBER		ORDER NEW EQUIPMENT	MARK EQUIPMENT	MARK EQUIPMENT
NOVEMBER	TAKE INVENTORY	ORDER NEW EQUIPMENT		ORDER NEW EQUIPMENT
DECEMBER	ORDER NEW EQUIPMENT	ORDER NEW EQUIPMENT		ORDER NEW EQUIPMENT

ORDER NEW EQUIPMENT   TIME IS RUNNING OUT   YOU MAY BE TOO LATE

Athletic equipment buyers' almanac. (From How to budget, select, and order athletic equipment, Chicago, 1962, The Athletic Institute.)

Purchases should be made from reputable business firms

In some cases the decision concerning the firm from which supplies and equipment are to be purchased may be determined by the local board of education or college authorities. In the event of such a procedure, this principle is academic. However, where the business firm from which purchases will be made is determined by health and physical education personnel, it is wise to deal with established, reputable businesses that are known to have reasonable prices, reliable materials, and good service. In the long run this is the best and safest procedure to follow.

Local firms should be considered

The administration's main concern is to obtain good value for money expended. If local firms can offer equal values, render equal or better service for the same money, and are reliable, then preference should probably be given to local dealers. If such conditions cannot be met, however, a question can be raised as to the wisdom of such a procedure. In some cases it is advantageous to use local dealers, since they are more readily accessible and can provide quicker and better service than firms located farther away.

Bids should be obtained

A good administrative procedure that helps to eliminate any accusation of favoritism and that assists also in obtaining the best price available is use of competitive bidding. This procedure requires that special forms be distributed to many dealers who handle the supplies and equipment

Gymnastic room with equipment. (University of California at Irvine.)

desired. In such cases, the specifics in regard to the kind, amount, and quality of articles desired should be clearly stated. After bids have been obtained the choice can be made. Low bids do not have to be accepted. However, where they are not honored, proper justification should be set forth.

Gifts or favors should not be accepted from dealers

Some dealers and salesmen are happy to present an administrator or staff member with a new rifle, set of golf clubs, tennis racquet, or other gift if, in so doing, they believe it is possible to get a school or college on their account. It is poor policy to accept such gifts or favors. This places a person under obligation to an individual or firm and can only result in difficulties and harm to the program. An administrator or staff member should never profit personally from any materials that are purchased for use in his or her programs.

A complete inventory analysis is essential before purchasing

Before purchases are made such information should be available as the amount of supplies and equipment on hand and the condition of these items. This knowledge prevents overbuying and large stockpiles of materials that may be outdated when they become needed.

CHECKING, ISSUING, AND MAINTAINING SUPPLIES AND EQUIPMENT

Some guidelines for checking, issuing, and maintaining supplies and equipment are discussed in the following paragraphs.

All supplies and equipment should be carefully checked upon receipt

Equipment and supplies that have been ordered should not be paid for until they have been checked as to amount, type,

quality, size, and other specifications that were listed on the purchase order. If any discrepancies are noted, they should be corrected before payment is made. This represents a very important procedure and responsibility and should be carefully followed. It represents good business practice in a matter requiring good business sense.

Supplies and equipment requiring organization identification should be labeled

Equipment and supplies are often moved from location to location within the school plant and also are issued to students and to staff members on a temporary basis. It is a good procedure to stencil or stamp the school or college identification in some appropriate location in order to have a check on such material, to help trace missing articles, to discourage misappropriation of such items, and to know what is and what is not departmental property.

Procedures should be established for issuing and checking in supplies and equipment

There can be considerable loss of material if poor accounting procedures are followed. Procedures should be established so that items are issued in a prescribed manner, proper forms are completed, records are maintained, and there is a clear understanding at all times as to where the material is located. Articles should be listed on the records according to various specifications of amount, size, or color, together with the name of the person to whom the item is issued. The individual's record should be classified according to name, street address, telephone, locker number, or other information important for identification purposes. In all cases the person or persons to whom the supplies and equipment are issued should be held accountable.

Text continued on p. 505.

NOTICE TO BIDDERS

(For use in advertising)

The board of education of ___(legal name)___ School District

No. ____ of the Town(s) of _____ popularly known

as _____ , (in accordance with Section 103 of

Article 5-A of the General Municipal Law) hereby invites the sub-

mission of sealed bids on _____ for use in the

schools of the district. Bids will be received until _____ on the
$\overline{\text{(hour)}}$

_____ day of _____ , 19 ____, at _____
(date)   (month)   (place of bid

_____, at which time and place all bids will be publicly opened.
opening)

Specifications and bid form may be obtained at the same office. The

board of education reserves the right to reject all bids. Any bid

submitted will be binding for _____ days subsequent to the date of

bid opening.

Board of Education

_____ School District No. ____

of the Town(s) of _____

County(ies) of _____

_____
(Address)

By _____
(Purchasing Agent)

_____
(Date)

Note: The hour should indicate whether it is Eastern Standard or
Eastern Daylight Saving Time.

Sample notice to bidders form. (From School Business Management Handbook Number 5, The University of the State of New York, Albany, N. Y.)

INVENTORY							
Date	Manufacturer	Dealer	Cat. No.	Total on Hand	Number Purchased	Cost	Comment

Year	New	Good	Fair	Obs.	Total	Numbers or Sizes							

Inventory form.

EQUIPMENT RECORD CARD
TO BE RETURNED TODAY

Name_____ Teacher_____ Period_____

No.	Article	No.	Article	No.	Article
	Archery, Arm Guard		Handball		Sponge Ball
	Archery, Arrow		Hockey Ball		Tape Measure
	Archery, Bow		Hockey Sticks		Table Tennis Net
	Archery, Glove		Jacks - Ball		Tennis Ball
	Badminton Racket		Jump Rope		Tether Ball
	Badminton Shuttlecock		Marbles		Timer (Stop Watch)
	Basketball		Pick-up Sticks		Whistle
	Bean Bag		Ping Pong Ball		
	Checkerboard		Ping Pong Paddle		
	Checker Men		Playground Ball		
	Chest Protector		10" 16"		
	Chinese Checkers		Quoits		
	Clip Board		Softball		
	Darts		Softball Bat		
	Deck Tennis Rings		Shin Guards		
	Dominoes		Shuffleboard Cue		
	Eye-glasses Guard		Shuffleboard Disc		
	Goal Guards		Shuttlecock		
	Golf Ball		Shuttle Loop		
	Golf Club		Soccer Ball		

Equipment record form. (From Bucher, C. A., Koenig, C. R., and Barnhard, M.: Methods and materials in secondary school physical education, ed. 3, St. Louis, 1970, The C. V. Mosby Co.)

EQUIPMENT ISSUE

Date...

I .... have

accepted school property ....

.... (write in article and its number)

and agree to return it clean and in good condition or pay for said uniform.

Signed ....

H. R. #

Home Phone #   Home Address..

Equipment issue form. (From Bucher, C. A., Koenig, C. R., and Barnhard, M.: Methods and materials in secondary school physical education, ed. 3, St. Louis, 1970, The C. V. Mosby Co.

DEPARTMENT OF HEALTH AND PHYSICAL EDUCATION

Re: Lost Property Report

Student owner_____ H.R._____ R___ S___

Date of loss_____ Time_____ Period_____

List missing articles:

Description of known details:

Instructor's follow-up:

(Signed)___ _____

(Use reverse side if additional space is necessary.)

Lost property report. (From Bucher, C. A., Koenig, C. R., and Barnhard, M.: Methods and materials in secondary school physical education, ed. 3, St. Louis, 1970, The C. V. Mosby Co.)

EQUIPMENT CHECKOUT RECORD

Player_____ Home Room_____

Address_____ Phone_____

Class_____ Height_____ Weight_____ Age_____

Parents Waiver_____ Examination_____ Insurance_____

Football   Cross Country   Basketball   Swimming   Wrestling

Baseball   Track   Tennis   Golf

	Out	In	Game Equipment	Out	In
Blocking pads			White jersey		
Shoulder pads			Maroon jersey		
Hip pads			White pants		
Thigh pads			Maroon pants		
Knee pads			Warm-up pants		
Helmet			Warm-up jacket		
Shoes			Stockings		
Practice pants					
Practice jersey					

I hereby certify that I have received the above-listed athletic equipment and will return same not later than the day following the last game of the season for the sport checked.

Signature_____

Equipment checkout record. (From Bucher, C. A., Koenig, C. R., and Barnhard, M.: Methods and materials in secondary school physical education, ed. 3, St. Louis, 1970, The C. V. Mosby Co.)

BOYS' PHYSICAL EDUCATION DEPARTMENT

Equipment Inspection

Please write on this sheet the names of boys not wearing clean gym clothing. Also give the advisers' names. Thank you.

Inspection may involve any day with special emphasis on each MONDAY. The instructor should place his initials following the date of each recording.

Date	Instr. Init.	Boy's Name	Adviser	Dirty Clothes	Partial Equipment	Torn Clothing	*Borrowed Equipment

*Borrowed equipment with or without owner's consent should always be followed up with a discipline note.

Equipment inspection form. (Courtesy Boys' Physical Education Department, New Trier Township High School, Winnetka, Ill.; from Bucher, C. A., Koenig, C. R., and Barnhard, M.: Methods and materials in secondary school physical education, ed. 3, St. Louis, 1970, The C. V. Mosby Co.)

Laundry for washable supplies. (University of California at Irvine.)

Equipment should be in a state of constant repair

Equipment should always be maintained in a serviceable condition. Procedures for caring for equipment should be routinized so that repairs are provided as needed. All used equipment should be checked and then repaired, replaced, or serviced as is needed. Repair can be justified, however, only when the cost for such is within reason. Supplies should be replaced when they have been expended.

Equipment and supplies should be stored properly

Supplies and equipment should be handled efficiently so that space has been properly organized for storing, a procedure has been established for ease of location, and proper safeguards have been taken against fire and theft. Proper shovels, bins, hangers, and other accessories should be available. Temperature, humidity, and ventilation are also important considera-

---

ADMINISTRATOR'S CODE OF ETHICS FOR PERSONNEL INVOLVED IN PURCHASING*

1. To consider first the interests of the school district or college and the betterment of the educational program.
2. To be receptive to advice and suggestions of colleagues, both in the department and in the field of business administration, and others insofar as advice is compatible with legal and moral requirements.
3. To endeavor to obtain the greatest value for every dollar spent.
4. To strive to develop an expertise and knowledge of supplies and equipment that ensure recommendations for purchases of greatest value.
5. To insist on honesty in the sales representation of every product submitted for consideration for purchase.
6. To give all responsible bidders equal consideration in determining whether their product meets specifications and the educational needs of your program.
7. To discourage and to decline gifts that in any way might influence a purchase.
8. To provide a courteous reception for all persons who may call on legitimate business missions regarding supplies and equipment.
9. To counsel and help other educators involved in purchasing.
10. To cooperate with governmental or other organizations or persons and help in the development of sound business methods in the procurement of school and college equipment and supplies.

*Adapted from the New York State Association of School Business Officials: Code of ethics for school purchasing officials.

Rolling equipment cart, one of several designed for specific classes of the physical education program. These are stored in the equipment room and transported to activity areas by student helpers. (University of California at Irvine.)

Storage cart for folding chairs. This is an interesting and functional system for storing over 1,000 chairs. Lightweight carts roll into compartments under the stage. (University of California at Irvine.)

tions. Items going into the storeroom should be properly checked as to quality and quantity. An inventory should be constantly available as to all items on hand in the storeroom. Every precaution should be taken to provide for the adequate care of the material so that a wise investment has been made.

Appendix A contains much useful information applicable to the purchase and care of supplies and equipment for health and physical education programs.

AUDIOVISUAL MATERIALS

Audiovisual aids and materials have become such an important part of health and physical education programs that space is provided for a discussion of the use, types, and guidelines for such supplies and equipment.

A recent survey among 100 schools and colleges found that more than one-half of them used some form of visual or audio aid in their programs. All of the persons surveyed felt that audiovisual media served as a valuable supplement to instruction in the learning of motor skills. The survey also found that videotaping is on the increase as an instructional tool. The audiovisual media used with the most frequency by those persons surveyed included cartridge films, loopfilms, 16- and 8-mm. films, wall charts, slide films, film strips, and instructional television.

Reasons for increased use of audiovisual materials

There are several reasons why there is an increased use of audiovisual materials in health education and physical education programs. Some of these are:

1. *They enable the student to better understand concepts and the performance of a skill, events, and other experiences.* The old cliché, "One picture is worth a thousand words," has much truth. The use of a film, pictures, or other materials gives a clearer idea of the subject being taught, whether it is how a heart functions or how to perfect a golf swing.

2. *They help to provide a variety to teaching.* There is increased motivation, the attention span of children is prolonged, and the subject matter of a course is much more exciting when audiovisual aids are used in addition to other teaching techniques.

3. *They increase motivation on the part of the student.* To see a game played, a skill performed, or an experiment conducted in clear, understandable, illustrated form helps to motivate the student to engage in a game, perform a skill more effectively, or want to know more about the relation of exercise to health. This is particularly true in video replay, for example, where a student can actually see how he performs a skill and then can compare his performance to what should be done.

4. *They provide for an extension of what can normally be taught in a classroom, gymnasium, or playground.* Audiovisual aids enable the student to be taken to other countries, to experience sporting events that occur in other parts of the United States, and to witness events that are significant to health. All of these are important to health and physical education programs and the instructional program for students.

5. *They provide a historical reference for the fields of health and physical education.* Outstanding events in sports, physical education, and health that have occurred in past years can be brought to life before students' eyes. In this way the student obtains a better understanding of these fields and the important role they play in our society and other cultures of the world.

Selected types of audiovisual aids

A partial list of audiovisual materials that are commonly used today by health and physical education teachers follows.

Visual aids (audiovisual in some cases)

Reading materials—books, magazines, encyclopedias, and almanacs

Chalkboards—for recording plays, thoughts, and ideas

Wall charts—of self-explanatory terms

Flat pictures, cartoons, posters, photographs

Graphs—bar, circle, line, and other types

Maps and globes

Bulletin boards—for posting materials pertaining to program

Models and specimens—the human body, skeleton, animals, insects, and others

Opaque projector—used to display on a screen an enlarged picture that is too small in the original for all students to readily see and understand its message

Overhead projector—a compact, lightweight machine that can be operated with ease and used to project materials on a screen. The material projected is in the form of a transparency, made of film that can either be purchased or made

Stereoscopes—machines that project a picture in three dimensions and thus give a better understanding of space relationships

Silent films

Slides—three types, generally speaking: 35-mm. individual slide encased in a cardboard holder; the larger lantern slide usually 3¼ by 4 inches, and the lantern slide that may be prepared for immediate use by a Polaroid transparency film

Filmstrips

Loop films—available in cartridges that can be inserted into a projector and shown with comparative ease. There are three types: a free 8-mm. loop film that can be shown in an 8-mm. projector; an 8-mm. cartridge film encased in a plastic cartridge that requires a special projector; and the super-8-mm. film encased in a plastic cartridge that requires a still different type of projection.

Motion pictures—usually in 8-, 16-, and 35-mm. sizes

Television—educational and closed circuit television and the kinescope recorder. Video-tape recording that enables a student to actually see how he performs a particular skill, for example, has proved effective as an instructional medium.

Audio aids

Radio—educational and commercial programs

Records and transcriptions—of important events, speeches, musical productions, and music for dances

Tape recordings—special events are recorded and used to appraise student progress in conduct, skills, concepts, and appreciation and to cover current happenings pertinent to health and physical education

Administrative guidelines for the selection and use of audiovisual aids

1. *Audiovisual materials should be carefully selected and screened before using.* Such items as appropriateness for age and grade level of students, adequacy of subject matter, technical qualities, inclusion of current information, cost, and other factors are important to know when selecting audiovisual materials to be used.

2. *The presentation of materials should be carefully planned to provide continuity in the subject being taught.* Materials should be selected and used that amplify and illustrate some important part of the material being covered in a particular course. Furthermore, they should be used at a time that logically fits into the presentation of certain material and concepts.

3. *The materials should be carefully evaluated after they have been used.* Whether or not materials are used a second time should be determined on the basis of their worth the first time they were used. Therefore, a careful evaluation should take place after their use. Records of evaluation should be maintained.

4. *Slow-motion and stop-action projections are best when a pattern of coordination of movements in a skill is to be taught.* When teaching a skill the teacher usually likes to analyze the various parts of the whole and also to stop and discuss various aspects of the skill with the students.

5. *Proper maintenance and preparation of equipment should be done.* Projectors, record players, television equipment, and other materials need to be kept in good operating condition and operated by qualified personnel in order to have an effective audiovisual program.

CHECKLIST FOR SPORTS AND OTHER PHYSICAL EDUCATION EQUIPMENT AND SUPPLIES

Anthropometric apparatus

Anthropometric tape
Chest depth caliper
Dynamometer
Manuometer
Scale
Shoulder breadth
  caliper
Stadiometer
Wet spirometer

Aquatics

Clocks
Diving boards
  Boards
  1-meter
  3-meter
Diving tramp
Ear plugs
Fins
Guns
Kickboards
Lane markers
Life buoys
  15-inch diameter
  18-inch diameter
Lifeguard chair
Noseclips
Pool cleaning
  equipment
Pool ladders
  2 foot   4 foot
  3 foot   5 foot
Regulators
  (breathing tank)
Robe
Snorkles
Swim caps
Swim suits
  Men's
Tanks (air)
Underwater masks
  Women's
Warmups
  Jacket
  Pants
Water basketball
  (backboard and
    goal)

Aquatics—cont'd
Water polo balls
Water polo goals
Water polo nets
Water slides
Weight belt
Wet suit
  Boots
  Gloves

Archery
Arrow points
Arrows
  Field
  Hunting
  Target
Backstop net
Bow case
Bow sight
Bow strings
Bows
Feathers
Finger tabs
Fletching tool
Forearm guards
Gloves
Nocks
Quivers
Sets
Target face
Target standards
Targets

Audiovisual aids
Administrative aids
Coaching aids
Dance records
Film
Loudspeakers

Badminton
Net
Racquet press
Racquets
Sets
Shuttlecocks
Standards

Baseball
Backstop
Ball bag
Balls
Bases

Baseball—cont'd
Bats
  Baseball
  Fungo
  Little League
  Pony and Babe
    Ruth League
Bat bag
Batting cage
Batting tee
Belts
Caps
Catcher's mask
Chest protector
Gloves
  Catcher's mitt
  Fielder's
  First baseman's
Home plate
Leg guards
Pants
Pitcher's plate
Pitching machine
Protective helmets
Rosin
Rule book
Score book
Shirts
Shoes
Sliding pads
Socks
Umpire's body
  protector
Umpire's indicator
Umpire's leg guards
Umpire's mask
Uniforms (complete)
Warmup jackets

Basketball
Backboards
Ball return
Balls
Goals
Nets
Pants
Rebound ring
Shirts
Shoes
Target socks
Warmups

Bowling
Ball bag
Balls
Shirts
Shoes

Boxing
Bag bladder
Bag gloves
Bag platforms
Corner pillows
Ear protectors
Gloves
Hand wrappings
Head protectors
Platform rings
Ring canvas
Ring ropes
Robes
Rope wrappings
Shoes
Skip ropes
Speed bag
Striking bag swivel
Teeth protector
Training bags
Trunks

Cheerleading
Briefs
Majorette boots
Skirts
Sweaters

Crew
Oars
Sculls
Shells

Exercise equipment
Abdominal board
Body weights
Dumbbells
Exerciser sets
Isogyms
Isometric kits
Leg press machine
Multipurpose weight
  bench
Pulley weights
Squat stands
Weight sets
Weight shoes

Continued.

CHECKLIST FOR SPORTS AND OTHER PHYSICAL EDUCATION EQUIPMENT AND SUPPLIES—cont'd

Fencing
Chest protector
  Woman's protector
Electrical equipment
  Foils
  Epees
Gloves
Jackets
Masks
Rubber tips
Scoring device
Shoes
Trousers
Weapons
  Epees
  Foils
  Sabers

Field hockey
Balls
Goal
Net
Shin guards
Shoes
Sticks

Football
Ankle wraps
Balls
Belts
Bladders
Blocking sleds
  2-man
  5-man
  7-man
Capes
Cervical neck pad
Chin straps
Cleats
Downs marker
Dummies
Face guards
Flags (corner)
Helmet racks
Helmets
Hip pads
Jerseys
Kicking tee
Knee pads
Mouth guards
Pants
Rib pads

Football—cont'd
Scrimmage vests
Shoes
Shoulder pad rack
Shoulder pads
Socks
Thigh guards

Golf
Bags (club)
Balls
Cage (practice)
Club cart
Clubs
  Irons
  Putters
  Woods
Gloves
Head covers
Rubber driving mat
Shoes
Tees

Gymnastics
Balance beam
  Low beam
Buck (vaulting)
Chalk
Chalk holder
Hand guards
Horizontal bar
Parallel bars
  Low bars
Rings
Ropes (climbing)
Safety belts
Side horse
Springing and jumping
  apparatus
  Beat board
  Reuther board
  Spring board
  Trampolet
Tambourine
Trampoline
Trapeze
Uneven bars
  Conversion kit
Uniform
  Pants
  Shirts
  Shoes

Gymnastics—cont'd
Uniform—cont'd
  Warmups
    Pants
    Shirts
Vaulting box

Handball
Balls
Gloves

Ice hockey
Goal
Net
Skates
Uniform
  Jerseys
  Pants
  Socks

Instructor's equipment
Cap
Jacket
Pants
Shirts
Shoes
Women's tunic

Judo and karate
Punching board
Uniforms
  Judo
  Karate

Lacrosse
Balls
Body protectors
Goal
Net
Shoes
Sticks

Paddle tennis
Balls
Net
Paddles

Physical Education equipment
Basket holder
Baskets
Bicycle trainer
Bleachers
  4-row
  Seats 50

Physical education equipment—cont'd
  Seats 400
  Seats 750
Goal posts
  Football
  Soccer and field
    hockey com-
    bination
  Soccer and football
    combination
Heat lamp
Laundry equipment
  hamper
Line markers
Lockers
  Box type
  Double tier
  Single tier
Mat hangers
Mat trucks
Peg boards
Scoreboards
Stall bars
Steam cabinet
Wall ladder
Whirlpool bath

Physical education supplies
Athletic supporters
Awards
Ball carriers
Balls
  Cage
  Medicine
  Playground
Cups (protective)
Foot baths
Game standards
  (combination)
Indian clubs
Jump ropes
Locks
Mat envelope covers
Mats
Pinnies
Shower sandals
Soap
Spike wrench kit
Stop clocks
Table inflators

CHECKLIST FOR SPORTS AND OTHER PHYSICAL EDUCATION EQUIPMENT AND SUPPLIES—cont'd

Physical education supplies — cont'd
- Towels
- Tug-of-war ropes
- Uniform hangers
- Uniforms (physical education)
  - Boy's
  - Girl's
- Whistles

Playground equipment
- Benches
- Bicycle racks
- Castle towers
- Cooking grill
- Flag poles
- Flying rings
- Horizontal bar
- Horizontal ladders
- Merry-go-round
- Picnic table
- Seesaws
  - 3 Seesaws
  - 4 Seesaws
  - 6 Seesaws
- Slides
- Swing seats
  - Nursery seat
  - Rubber seat
  - Belt seat
  - Wood seat
- Swings
  - 2 Swings
  - 4 Swings
  - 6 Swings
  - 8 Swings
- Trapeze bar

Soccer
- Balls

Soccer—cont'd
- Goals
- Net
- Shin guards
- Uniforms
  - Pants
  - Shirts
  - Shoes
  - Socks

Softball
- Balls
- Bases
- Bat bag
- Bats
- Books
  - Rule book
  - Score book
- Caps
- Gloves
  - Catcher's
  - Fielder's
  - First baseman's
- Hose
- Jackets
- Jerseys
- Masks
- Protectors (body)
- Shoes
- Uniforms

Squash
- Balls
- Rackets

Tennis
- Balls
- Courts
- Nets
- Posts
- Racquet jacket

Tennis—cont'd
- Racquet press
- Racquets
- Rebound net
- Tennis ball machine
- Uniforms
  - Shirts
  - Shoes
  - Shorts

Track
- Batons
- Circles
  - Discus
  - Shot
- Competitors numbers
- Cross bar lifter
- Cross bars
- Discus
- Field marks
- Finish line yarn
- Hammer
- Heel cup
- High jump standards
- Hurdles
- Javelins
- Measuring tapes
  - 50-foot
  - 100-foot
  - 200-foot
- Pedometer
- Pits (jumping and vaulting)
- Pole vault box
- Pole vault poles
- Pole vault standards
- Shoe laces
- Shoes (indoor)
- Shoes (outdoor)
- Shot

Track — cont'd
- Shot—cont'd
  - Indoor
    - 8-pounds
    - 12-pounds
    - 16-pounds
  - Outdoor
    - 8-pound
    - 12-pound
    - 16-pound
- Spike wrench
- Spikes
- Starting blocks
- Starting pistol
- Stop watch
- Takeoff board
- Toe board
- Track surface
- Uniforms
  - Pants
  - Shirts
- Warmups
  - Pants
  - Shirts

Volleyball
- Balls
- Net
- Scorebook
- Sets
- Standards

Wrestling
- Head guards
- Knee guards
- Sweat suit
- Uniform
  - Shirts
  - Shoes
  - Tights
  - Trunks

Questions and exercises

1. What factors need to be taken into consideration in relation to the purchase and care of supplies and equipment?

2. List and discuss five principles that should be followed in respect to the selection of supplies and equipment. Apply these principles in the procedure involved in selecting a diving board for a swimming pool.

3. List and discuss five principles that should be followed in respect to purchasing supplies and equipment. Apply these principles to the procedure involved in purchasing a trampoline for the gymnasium.

4. Prepare a report on the various types of audiovisual aids that could be used effectively in the teaching of tennis.

5. Prepare an administrative plan that you, as a chairman of a health and physical education department, would recommend for the checking, issuing, and maintenance of physical education supplies and equipment. Be specific, pointing out the steps that should be followed and procedure implemented to ensure sound property accountability.

   Reading Assignment in *Administrative Dimensions of Health and Physical Education Programs, Including Athletics:* Chapter 13, Selections 73 to 76.

Selected references

American Association for Health, Physical Education, and Recreation: Equipment and supplies for athletics, physical education and recreation, Washington, D. C., The Association. (Published annually in the Journal of Health, Physical Education, and Recreation.)

American Athletic Equipment Co., Jefferson, Iowa.

Bourguardez, V., and Heilman, C.: Sports equipment: selection, care, and repair, New York, 1950, A. S. Barnes & Co.

Care and maintenance of lacrosse sticks, Towson, Md., 1965, Bacharach Rasin Co., Inc.

Care of athletic equipment, River Grove, Ill., Wilson Sporting Goods Co.

Casey, L. M.: School business administration, New York, 1964, The Center for Applied Research in Education, Inc. (The Library of Education).

De Kieffer, R. E.: Audiovisual instruction, New York, 1965, The Center for Applied Research in Education, Inc. (The Library of Education).

How to budget, select, and order athletic equipment. Available from Athletic Goods Manufacturers Association, Merchandise Mart, Chicago, Ill., also through MacGregor & Rawlings Sporting Goods.

Irwin, A.: Put your equipment on wheels, Scholastic Coach 35:10, 1966.

Meyer, K.: Purchase, care, and repair of athletic equipment, St. Louis, 1948, Educational Publishers, Inc.

Murray, F.: Perpetual inventory, Scholastic Coach 31:20, 1962.

Participants in National Facilities Conference: Planning areas and facilities for health, physical education, and recreation, Chicago, 1965. The Athletic Institute, Inc.

Selway, C. P.: Efficiency in the equipment and laundry rooms, Scholastic Coach 34:30, 1965.

CHAPTER 18 LEGAL LIABILITY AND INSURANCE MANAGEMENT

The growth of school and college health and physical education programs, including athletics, in this country has brought with it many problems in the field of administration. One of these problems is legal liability and insurance management. This is especially pertinent to these specialized areas because of the danger of accidents while engaging in the various activities that comprise the programs. Furthermore, the nature of these areas involves the use of special apparatus, excursions and trips, living in camps, utilizing first-aid practices, and other items that have implications for liability.

According to Bouvier's *Law Dictionary*, liability is "the responsibility, the state of one who is bound in law and justice to do something which may be enforced by action." Another definition states: "Liability is the condition of affairs which gives rise to an obligation to do a particular thing to be enforced by court action."

Leaders in the fields of health and physical education should know how far they can go with various aspects of their programs and what precautions are necessary in order not to be held legally liable in the event of an accident. The fact that approximately 67% of all school jurisdiction accidents involving boys and 59% involving girls occur in physical education and recreation programs has implications for these specialized fields. Furthermore, the fact that an estimated 3 million boys and girls participate in interscholastic athletic programs alone indicates a further administrative concern for physical education programs.

The administration, which in the final analysis is responsible for the program, should clearly understand the implications of their work in this respect. Fear of personal liability can thwart an otherwise good educational program.

When an accident resulting in personal injury occurs on school property, the question often arises as to whether damages can be recovered. The National Commission on Safety Education points out that all school employees run the risk of suit by injured pupils on the basis of alleged negligence that causes bodily injury to pupils. Such injuries occur on playgrounds, on athletic fields, in science laboratories, in shop classes, or in any place where students congregate.

The legal rights of the individuals involved in such cases are worthy of study. Although the law varies from state to state, it is possible to discuss liability in a general way that has implications for all sections of the country. First, it is important to understand the legal basis for health, physical education, and allied areas.

THE LEGAL BASIS FOR HEALTH EDUCATION, PHYSICAL EDUCATION, AND ALLIED AREAS*

All fifty states, the District of Columbia, and Puerto Rico have laws requiring or permitting the teaching of health, physical

---

*State school laws and regulations for health, safety, driver, outdoor, physical education, Washington, D. C., 1964, Office of Education, Department of Health, Education and Welfare.

education, safety education, driver education, and outdoor education. In addition to such laws, thirty-seven states, the District of Columbia, Puerto Rico, and the Canal Zone have a total of eighty-eight regulations regarding the teaching of these subjects.

Physical education, either as a separate subject or in combination with health education, is a matter of law and/or regulation in forty-eight states, the District of Columbia, Canal Zone, Puerto Rico, and the Virgin Islands.

Health education, as a separate subject or in combination with physical education, is a matter of law and/or regulation in forty-one states, the District of Columbia, Canal Zone, Puerto Rico, and the Virgin Islands.

Safety education, as a separate subject, is a matter of law and/or regulation in thirteen states.

Driver education is a matter of law and/or regulation in thirty-six states.

Outdoor education is a matter of law in six states.

Health, physical, safety, and outdoor education are a matter of law and regulations at the elementary school level in all fifty states, the District of Columbia, Canal Zone, Puerto Rico, and the Virgin Islands.

Physical education is a required daily experience for 4 years in three states at the secondary level, and health and physical education in varying amounts is a required daily experience in fifteen other states at the same educational level.

Thirty-two states require health and physical education for graduation from school: 4 years, twelve states; 3 years, two states; 2 years, two states; 1 or 2 years, two states; 1 year, three states, and as a requirement other than length of time listed, eleven states.

Two states do not have laws or regulations requiring teaching of physical education.

Included in Appendix C is a state-by-state analysis of school laws and regulations concerning the teaching of health, physical education, and allied areas.

LEGAL IMPLICATIONS FOR REQUIRING PHYSICAL EDUCATION

Shroyer* made a study of the legal implications of requiring pupils to enroll in physical education classes and found that the courts have handed down decisions from which the following conclusions may be drawn:

1. Students may be required to take physical education. However, there should be some flexibility to provide for those cases where an individual's constitutional rights might be violated if such activities are against his principles, for example, dancing.

2. Where reasonable parental demands for deviation from the physical education requirement are called for, every effort should be made to comply with the parent's wishes. However, unreasonable demands should not result in acquiescence.

3. Where rules and regulations may be questioned, the board of education should provide for a review of the rationale behind the rule or regulation and why the policy is needed.

4. A student may be denied the right to graduate and receive a diploma when a required course such as physical education is not taken.

LEGAL LIABILITY

Some years ago the courts recognized the hazards involved in the play activities that are a part of the educational program. An injury occurred to a boy while he was playing tag. The court recognized the possibility and risk of some injury in

---

*Shroyer, G. F.: Legal implications of requiring pupils to enroll in physical education, Journal of Health, Physical Education, and Recreation **35:** 51, 1964.

physical education programs and would not award damages. However, it pointed out that care must be taken by both the participant and the authorities in charge. It further implied that the benefits derived from participating in physical education activities such as tag offset the occasional injury that might occur.

The cited decision regarding the benefits derived from participating in physical education programs was handed down at a time when the attitude of the law was that no government agency, which would include the school, could be held liable for the acts of its employees unless it so consented. Since that time a changing attitude

in the courts has been in evidence. As more accidents occurred, the courts frequently decided in favor of the injured party when negligence could be shown. The immunity derived from the old common-law rule that a government agency cannot be sued without its consent is slowly changing in the eyes of the courts so that both federal government and state may be sued.

Those elements of a school curriculum that are compulsory, such as physical education, prompt courts to decide on the basis of what is in the best interests of the public. Instead of being merely a moral responsibility, safety has become a legal

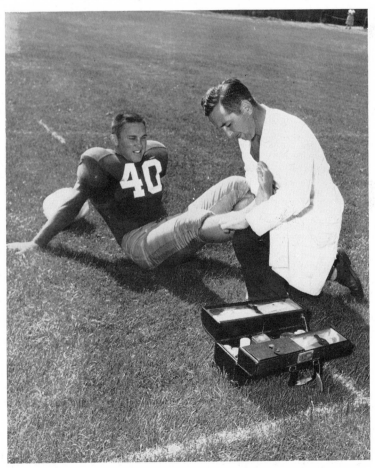

Many accidents occur on playgrounds and athletic fields. (Stanford University, Stanford, Calif.)

responsibility. Those who uphold the doctrine that a government agency should be immune from liability maintain that payments for injury to constituents is a misapplication of public funds. On the other hand, the liberal thinkers feel it is wrong for the cost of injuries to fall on one or a few persons and, instead, should be shared by all. To further their case these liberals cite the constitutional provision that compensation must be given for the taking or damaging of private property. They argue that it is inconsistent that the government cannot take or damage private property without just compensation on the one hand, yet on the other can injure or destroy the life of a person without liability for compensation. The liberal view is being used more and more by the courts.

The rule of immunity (since school districts are instrumentalities of the state, and the state is immune from suit unless it consents, the state's immunity extends to the districts) is the law, with a few exceptions, in almost all the states. Some exceptions are California, Washington, and New York. However, as has been pointed out above, the doctrine of immunity is starting to crumble. The case *Bingham v. Board of Education of Oregon City,* 223 P2d 432, handed down by the Supreme Court in Utah in October, 1950, involved a 3-year-old child who, while riding her tricycle on the school grounds, fell into some burning embers left on the grounds and suffered severe burns. The school maintained an incinerator adjacent to the playground area in which rubbish was burned. From time to time embers and ashes were removed and scattered around the adjoining area. The parents sued to recover damages and the court held the district was not liable. Judge Latimer, who wrote the court's opinion, said: "While the law writers, editors, and judges have criticized and disapproved the foregoing doctrine of government immunity as illogical and unjust, the weight of precedent of decided cases sup-

ports the general rule and we prefer not to disregard a principle so well established without statutory authority. We, therefore, adopt the rule of the majority and hold that school boards cannot be held liable for ordinary negligent acts."

The importance of this case lies in the fact that two judges dissented. The dissenting opinion pointed out: "I prefer to regard said principle for the purpose of overruling it. I would not wait for the dim distant future in never-never land when the legislature may act." It was also pointed out that the rule rests upon the "immortal and indefensible doctrine" that "the king (sovereign) can do no wrong" and that a state should not be allowed to use this as a shield.

There has been considerable court activity in regard to the principle of governmental immunity. In 1959 the Illinois Supreme Court (*Molitor v. Kaneland Community Unit,* District No. 302, 163 N.E. 2d 89) overruled the immunity doctrine. The supreme courts of Wisconsin, Arizona, and Minnesota followed suit, but in 1963 the Minnesota legislature restored the rule but provided that where school districts had liability insurance they were responsible for damages up to the extent of the coverage. The principle of governmental immunity has also recently been put to the test in courts in such states as Colorado, Iowa, Kansas, Oregon, Pennsylvania, and Utah. However, the courts in these states are hesitant to depart from the precedent that has been set and furthermore insist that it is the legislature of the state rather than the courts that should waive the rule.*

In thirty-nine of fifty states school districts have governmental immunity, which means that as long as they are engaging in a governmental function they cannot be sued, even though negligence has been

---

*Shapiro, F. S.: Your liability for student accidents, National Education Association Journal **54:** 46, 1965.

determined. In eleven states governmental immunity has been annulled either by legislation or judicial decision. In some states schools may legally purchase liability insurance (California requires and twenty-two other states expressly authorize school districts to carry liability insurance) protecting school districts that may become involved in lawsuits, although this does not necessarily mean that governmental immunity has been waived. Of course, in the absence of insurance and "save harmless" laws, which require that school districts assume the liability of the teacher, negligence, proved or not, any judgment rendered against a school district must be met out of personal funds. School districts in Connecticut, Massachusetts, New Jersey, and New York have "save harmless" laws. Wyoming permits school districts to idemnify employees.

School districts that still enjoy governmental immunity usually are either required or permitted to carry liability insurance that specifically covers the operation of school buses.

There is a strong feeling among educators and many in the legal profession that the doctrine of sovereign immunity should be abandoned. In fourteen states students injured as a result of negligence are assured recompense for damages directly or indirectly, either because governmental immunity has been abrogated or because school districts are legally required to indemnify school employees against financial loss. In eighteen other states, if liability insurance has been secured, there is a possibility that students may recover damages incurred.

Although school districts have been granted immunity in many states, teachers do not have such immunity. A decision of an Iowa court in 1938 provides some of the thinking in regard to the teacher's responsibility for his own actions (*Montanick v. McMillin*, 225 Iowa 442, 452-453, 458, 280 N.W. 608, 1938).

[The employee's liability] is not predicated upon any relationship growing out of his employment, but is based upon the fundamental and underlying law of torts, that he who does injury to the person or property of another is civilly liable in damages for the injuries inflicted. . . . The doctrine of *respondeat superior*, literally, "let the principal answer," is an extension of the fundamental principle of torts, and an added remedy to the injured party, under which a party injured by some act of misfeasance may hold both the servant and the master. The exemption of governmental bodies and their officers from liability under the doctrine of *respondeat superior* is a limitation of exception to the rule of *respondeat superior* and in no way affects the fundamental principle of torts that one who wrongfully inflicts injury upon another is liable to the injured person for damages. . . . An act of misfeasance is a positive wrong, and every employee, whether employed by a private person or a municipal corporation owes a duty not to injure another by a negligent act of commission. . . .

Tort

A tort is a legal wrong resulting in direct or indirect injury to another individual or to property. A tortious act is a wrongful act and damages can be collected through court action. Tort can be committed through an act of *omission* or *commission*. An act of omission results when the accident occurs during failure to perform a legal duty, such as when a teacher fails to obey a fire alarm after she has been informed of the procedure to be followed. An act of commission results when the accident occurs while an unlawful act is being performed, such as assault on a student.

The National Education Association points out that "A tort may arise out of the following acts: (a) an act which without lawful justification or excuse is intended by a person to cause harm and does cause the harm complained of; (b) an act in itself contrary to law or an omission of specific legal duty, which causes harm not intended by the person so acting or omitting; (c) an act or omission causing harm which the person so acting or omitting did not intend to cause, but which might and should, with due diligence, have been foreseen and prevented."* The teacher, leader, or other individual not only has a legal responsibility as described by law but also is responsible for preventing injury. This means that in addition to complying with certain legal regulations, such as proper facilities, there must be compliance with the principle that children should be taught without injury to them and that prudent care, such as a parent would give, must be exercised. The term *legal duty* does not mean only those duties imposed by law but also the duty that is owed to society to prevent injury to others. A duty imposed by law would be one such as complying with housing regulations and traffic regulations. A duty that teachers owe to society in general consists of teaching children without injury to them. For example, it was stated in one case (*Hoose v. Drumm*, 281 N.Y. 54): "Teachers have watched over the play of their pupils time out of mind. At recess periods, not less than in the classroom, a teacher owes it to his charges to exercise such care of them as a parent of ordinary prudence would observe in comparable circumstances."

It is important to understand the legal meaning of the word *accident* in relation to the topic under discussion. According to Black's *Law Dictionary*, accident is defined as follows: "An accident is an unforeseen event occurring without the will or design of the person whose mere act causes it. In its proper use the term excludes negligence. It is an event which occurs without fault, carelessness, or want of proper circumspection for the person affected, or which could not have been avoided by the use of that kind and degree of care necessary to the exigency and

in the circumstance in which he was placed." The case of *Lee v. Board of Education of City of New York* in 1941, for example, showed that prudent care was not exercised, and the defendant was liable for negligence. A boy was hit by a car while playing football in the street as a part of the physical education program. The street had not been completely closed off to traffic. The board of education and the teacher were found negligent.

Negligence

Questions of liability and negligence occupy a very prominent position in connection with the actions of teachers and leaders in school health and physical education programs.

The law in America pertaining to negligence is based upon common law, previous judicial rulings, or established legal procedure. This type of law differs from that which has been written into the statutes by lawmaking bodies and is called statutory law.

Negligence implies that someone has not fulfilled his legal duty or has failed to do something that according to common-sense reasoning should have been done. Negligence can be avoided if there are common knowledge of basic legal principles and proper vigilance. One of the first things that must be determined in event of accident is whether there has been negligence.

Rosenfield* defines negligence as follows: "Negligence consists in the failure to act as a reasonably prudent and careful person would under the circumstances involved." The National Education Association's report elaborates further: "Negligence is any conduct which falls below the standard established by law for the protection of others against unreasonable risk of harm. In general, such conduct may be of two types: (a) an act which a reason-

---

*National Education Research Division for the National Commission on Safety Education: Who is liable for pupil injuries? Washington, D. C., 1950, National Education Association, p. 5.

---

*Rosenfield, H. N.: Liability for school accident, New York, 1940, Harper & Row, Publishers.

able man would have realized involved an unreasonable risk of injury to others, and (b) failure to do an act which is necessary for the protection or assistance of another and which one is under a duty to do.*

According to Garber, a school employee may be negligent because of the following reasons:

1. He did not take appropriate care
2. Although he used due care, he acted in circumstances which created risks
3. His acts created an unreasonable risk of direct and immediate injury to others
4. He set in motion a force which was unreasonably hazardous to others
5. He created a situation in which third persons, such as pupils, or inanimate forces, such as shop machinery, may reasonably have been expected to injure others
6. He allowed pupils to use dangerous devices although they were incompetent to use them
7. He did not control a third person, such as an abnormal pupil, whom he knew to be likely to inflict intended injury on others because of some incapacity or abnormality
8. He did not give adequate warning
9. He did not look out for persons, such as pupils, who were in danger
10. He acted without sufficient skill
11. He did not make sufficient preparation to avoid an injury to pupils before beginning an activity where such preparation is reasonably necessary
12. He failed to inspect and repair mechanical devices to be used by pupils
13. He prevented someone, such as another teacher, from assisting a pupil who was endangered, although the pupil's peril was not caused by his negligence†

The National Education Association report includes the following additional comment:

The law prohibits careless action; whatever is done must be done well and with reasonable caution. Failure to employ care not to harm others is a misfeasance. For example, an Oregon school

bus driver who parked the bus across a driveway when he knew the pupils were coasting down the hill was held liable for injuries sustained by a pupil who coasted into the bus. (*Fahlstrom v. Denk,* 1933.)*

Negligence may be claimed when the plaintiff has suffered injury either to himself or to his property, when the defendant has not performed his legal duty and has been negligent, and when the plaintiff has constitutional rights and is not guilty of contributory negligence. The teacher or leader for children in such cases is regarded as *in loco parentis,* that is, acting in the place of the parent in relation to the child.

Since negligence implies failure to act as a reasonably prudent and careful person, necessary precautions should be taken, danger should be anticipated, and common sense should be used. For example, if a teacher permits a group of very young children to go up a high slide alone and without supervision, she is not acting as a prudent person would act. If the teacher of health education, after giving a demonstration, leaves a deadly drug on her desk and it later results in the death of a child, she is not acting as a careful person should act. In the case previously cited of *Lee v. Board of Education of City of New York,* when the physical education class was held in a street where cars were also allowed to pass, negligence existed.

A verdict by the jury in a California district court points up negligence in the sport of football. Press dispatches indicated that the high school athlete who suffered a disabling football injury was brought into court on a stretcher. The award was $325,000 (against the school district) in a suit in which the parent charged that the coach "was negligent in having the boy moved to the sidelines *too*

*National Education Research Division for the National Commission on Safety Education, op. cit., p. 6.

†Garber, L. O.: Law and the school business manager, Danville, Ill., 1957, Interstate Printers & Publishers, Inc., pp. 205-206.

*National Education Research Division for the National Commission on Safety Education, op. cit., p. 6.

soon after he was injured." The newspaper report seemed to infer that the negligence was involved not in the *method* of moving the boy from the field, but rather in the *time* at which he was moved.

An interesting case where the court ruled negligence occurred in New Jersey. In 1962 a student in the Chatham Junior High School was severely injured in an accident while participating in physical education. The testimony brought out that the physical education teacher was not present when the accident occurred but was treating another child for a rope burn. However, he had continually warned his class not to use the springboard at any time he was out of the room. (The student was trying to perform the exercise where he would dive from a springboard over an obstacle and finish with a forward roll.) The prosecution argued that the warning had not been stressed sufficiently and that the teacher's absence from the gymnasium, leaving student aides in charge, was an act of negligence. The court ruled negligence and in 1964 awarded the boy $1.2 million dollars for injuries. His parents were awarded $35,140. Upon an appeal, the award to the boy was reduced to $300,000, but the award to the parents remained the same. It is interesting to note that in this case the board of education felt there was no negligence on the part of the physical education teacher.

In respect to negligence, considerable weight is given in the law to the *foreseeability of danger*. One authority points out that "if a danger is obvious and a reasonably prudent person could have foreseen it and could have avoided the resulting harm by care and caution, the person who did not foresee or failed to prevent a foreseeable injury is liable for a tort on account of negligence."* If a teacher fails to take the needed precautions and care,

negligence is constituted. However, it must be established upon the basis of facts in the case. It cannot be based upon mere conjecture.

Teachers and leaders must realize that children will behave in certain ways, that certain juvenile acts will cause injuries unless properly supervised, that hazards must be anticipated, reported, and eliminated. The question that will be raised by most courts of law is: "Should the teacher or leader have had prudence enough to foresee the possible dangers or occurrence of an act?"

Two court actions point up legal reasoning on negligence as interpreted in one state. In the case of *Lane v. City of Buffalo* in 1931, the board of education was found not liable. In this case a child fell from a piece of apparatus in the schoolyard. It was found that the apparatus was in good condition and that proper supervision was present. In the case of *Cambareri v. Board of Albany*, the defendant was found liable. The City of Buffalo owned a park that was supervised by the park department. While skating on the lake in the park a boy playing "crack the whip" hit a 12-year-old boy who was also skating. Workers and a policeman had been assigned to supervise activity and had been instructed not to allow games that were rough or dangerous.

Although there are no absolute, factual standards for determining negligence, certain guides have been established that should be familiar to teachers and others engaged in the work under consideration in this book. Attorney Cymrot, in discussing negligence at a conference in New York City, suggested the following:

1. The teacher must be acting within the scope of his employment and in the discharge of his duties in order to obtain the benefits of the statute.
2. There must be a breach of a recognized duty owed to the child.
3. There must be a negligent breach of such duty.

---

*National Education Research Division for National Commission on Safety Education, op. cit., p. 6.

4. The accident and resulting injuries must be the natural and foreseeable consequence of the teacher's negligence arising from a negligent breach of duty.
5. The child must be a participant in an activity under the control of the teacher or, put in another way, the accident must have occurred under circumstances where the teacher owes a duty of care to the pupil.
6. A child's contributory negligence, however modified, will bar his recovery for damages.
7. The plaintiff must establish the negligence of the teacher and his own freedom from contributory negligence by a fair preponderance of evidence. The burden of proof on both issues is on the plaintiff.
8. Generally speaking, the board of education alone is responsible for accidents caused by the faulty maintenance of plants (schools) and equipment.*

Some states have a "save harmless" law. For example in New Jersey the law reads:

Chapter 311, P. L. 1938. Boards assume liability of teachers. It shall be the duty of each board of education in any school district to save harmless and protect all teachers and members of supervisory and administrative staff from financial loss arising out of any claim, demand, suit or judgment by reason of alleged negligence or other act resulting in accidental bodily injury to any person within or without the school building; provided, such teacher or member of the supervisory or administrative staff at the time of the accident or injury was acting in the discharge of his duties within the scope of his employment and/or under the direction of said board of education; and said board of education may arrange for and maintain appropriate insurance with any company created by or under the laws of this state, or in any insurance company authorized by law to transact business in this state, or such board may elect to act as self-insurers to maintain the aforesaid protection.

Defenses against negligence

Despite the fact that an individual is negligent, to collect damages one must show that the negligence resulted in or was closely connected with the injury. The

*Proceedings of the City Wide Conference with Principal's Representatives and Men and Women Chairmen of Health Education, City of New York Board of Education, Brooklyn, N. Y., 1953, Bureau of Health Education.

legal question in such a case is whether or not the negligence was the "proximate cause" (legal cause) of the injury. Furthermore, even though it be determined that negligence is the "proximate cause" of the injury, there are still certain defenses upon which a defendant may base his case.

Proximate cause. The negligence of the defendant may not have been the proximate cause of the plaintiff's injury.

Example: In the case of *Ohmon v. Board of Education of the City of New York,* 88 N.Y.S.2d 273 (1949), it was declared that when a 13-year-old pupil in public school was struck in the eye by a pencil thrown in classroom by another pupil to a third pupil, who stepped aside, the proximate cause of injury was an unforeseen act of the pupil who threw the pencil and that absence of the teacher (who was stacking supplies in a closet nearby the classroom) was not proximate cause of injury so as to impose liability for the injury on the board of education.

Act of God. An act of God is a situation that exists because of certain conditions that are beyond the control of human beings. For example, a flash of lightning, a gust of wind, a cloudburst, and other such factors may result in injury. However, this assumption applies only in cases where injury would not have occurred had prudent action been taken.

Assumption of risk. This legal defense is especially pertinent to games, sports, and other phases of the program in health education and physical education. It is assumed that an individual takes a certain risk when engaging in various games and sports where bodies are coming in contact with each other and where balls and apparatus are used. Participation in such activity indicates that the person assumes a normal risk.

Example: In the case of *Scala v. City of New York,* 102 N.Y.S.2d 709, where the plaintiff when playing softball on a public playground was aware of the risks caused by curbing and concrete benches near the playing fields, it was decided that the plaintiff must be held to have voluntarily and fully assumed the dangers and, having done so, must abide by the consequences.

Example: In an action by Albert Maltz (*Maltz v. Board of Education of New York City,* 114 N.Y.S.2d 856, 1952) against the Board of Education of the City of New York for injuries, the court held that a 19-year-old boy who was injured when he collided with a doorjamb in a brick wall 2 feet from the backboard and basket in a public school basketball court and who had played on that same court several times prior to the accident knew the basket and backboard were but 2 feet from the wall, had previously hit the wall or gone through the door without injury, was not a student at the school but a voluntary member of a team that engaged in basketball tournaments with other clubs, knew or should have known the danger, and thus assumed the risk of injury.

Contributory negligence. Another legal defense is contributory negligence. A person who does not act as would a normal individual of similar age and nature thereby contributes to the injury. In such cases negligence on the part of the defendant might be ruled out. Individuals are subject to contributory negligence if they expose themselves unnecessarily to dangers. The main consideration that seems to turn the tide in such cases is the age of the individual and the nature of the activity in which he engaged.

The National Education Association's report makes this statement in regard to contributory negligence:

Contributory negligence is defined in law as conduct on the part of the injured person which falls below the standard to which he should conform for his own protection and which is legally contributing cause, cooperating with the negligence of the defendant in bringing about the plaintiff's harm. Reasonable self-protection is to be expected of all sane adults. With some few exceptions, contributory negligence bars recovery against the defendant whose negligent conduct would otherwise make him liable to the plaintiff for the harm sustained by him. Both parties being in fault, neither can recover from the other for resulting harm. When there is mutual wrong and negligence on both sides, the law will not attempt to apportion the wrong between them.

Contributory negligence is usually a matter of defense, and the burden of proof is put upon the defendant to convince the jury of the plaintiff's fault and of its causal connection with the harm sustained. Minors are not held to the same degree of care as is demanded of adults.*

Contributory negligence has implications for a difference in the responsibility of elementary school teachers as contrasted with high school teachers. The elementary school teacher, because the children are immature, has to assume greater responsibility for the safety of the child. That is, accidents in which an elementary school child is injured are not held in the same light from the standpoint of negligence as those involving high school students who are more mature. The courts might say that a high school student was mature enough to avoid doing the thing causing him to be injured, whereas if the same thing occurred with an elementary school child, the courts could say the child was too immature and that the teacher should have prevented or protected the child from doing the act from which he was injured.

Sudden emergency. This legal defense is pertinent in cases where the exigencies of the situation require immediate action on the part of a teacher and, as a result, an accident occurs. For example, an instructor in a swimming pool is suddenly alerted to the fact that a child is drowning in the water. The teacher's immediate objective is to save the child. He runs to the assistance of the drowning person and in doing so knocks down another student who is watching from the side of the pool. The student who is knocked down hits his head on the tile floor and is injured. This would

---

*National Education Research Division for the National Commission on Safety Education, op. cit., p. 9.

be a case of sudden emergency and, if legal action is taken, the defense could be based on this premise.

Nuisance

Action can be instituted for nuisance when the circumstances surrounding the act are dangerous to life or health, result in offense to the senses, are in violation of the laws of decency, or cause an obstruction to the reasonable use of property.

An authentic source states in regard to a nuisance:

> There are some conditions which are naturally dangerous and the danger is a continuing one. An inherent danger of this sort is called at law a "nuisance"; the one responsible is liable for maintaining a nuisance. His liability may be predicated upon negligence in permitting the continuing danger to exist, but even without a showing of negligence the mere fact that a nuisance does exist is usually sufficient to justify a determination of liability. For example, a junk pile in the corner of the grounds of a country school was considered a nuisance for which the district was liable when a pupil stumbled over a piece of junk and fell while playing at recess (*Popow v. Central School District No. 1, Towns of Hillsdale et al., New York,* 1938). Dangerous playground equipment available for use by pupils of all ages and degrees of skill has also been determined to be a nuisance (*Bush v. City of Norwalk, Connecticut,* 1937).
>
> On the other hand, allegations that the district has maintained a nuisance have been denied in some cases; for example, when a small child fell into a natural ditch near the schoolyard not guarded by a fence, the ditch was held not to be a nuisance for which the district would be liable (*Whitfield v. East Baton Rouge Parish School Board, Louisiana,* 1949). The court said this ditch did not constitute a nuisance; nor did the principle of *res ipsa loquitur* apply. Under this principle the thing which causes the injury is under the management of the defendant and the accident is such that in the ordinary course of events, it would not have happened if the defendant had used proper care.[*]

Mr. Cymrot, attorney at law, in address-ing the Health Education Division of the New York City Schools had the following to say about an "attractive nuisance":

> Teachers need to be aware of decisions of the courts pertaining to "attractive nuisance," . . . an attractive contrivance which is maintained, alluring to children but inherently dangerous to them. This constitutes neglect. But it is not every contrivance or apparatus that a jury may treat as an "attractive nuisance." Before liability may be imposed, there must always be something in the evidence tending to show that the device was something of a new or uncommon nature with which children might be supposed to be unfamiliar or not know of its danger. Many courts have held, however, that for children above the age of 10 years the doctrine of "attractive nuisance" does not hold. Other children are expected to exercise such prudence as those of their age may be expected to possess.[*]

The following cases point up some court rulings in respect to "nuisance."

In the case of *Texas v. Reinhardt* in 1913, it was ruled that ball games with their noises and conduct were not a "nuisance" in the particular case in question and an injunction should not be issued stopping such activity.

In the case of *Iacono v. Fitzpatrick* in Rhode Island in 1938, a boy 17 years old, while playing touch football on a playground, received an injury that later resulted in his death. He was attempting to catch a pass and in so doing crashed into a piece of apparatus. The court held that the apparatus was in evidence and the deceased knew of its presence. It further stated the city had not created or maintained a nuisance.

In the case of *Schwarz v. City of Cincinnati, Ohio,* the city had permitted an organization to have fireworks in one of its public parks. Next day a 12-year-old boy was injured after lighting an unexploded

---

[*]National Education Research Division for the National Commission on Safety Education, op. cit., p. 6.

[*]Proceedings of the City Wide Conference with Principals' Representatives and Men and Women Chairmen of Health Education, City of New York Board of Education, Brooklyn, N. Y., March, 1953, Bureau of Health Education.

bomb that he found. The court ruled that the permit granted the association was "... not authority to create a nuisance ... not authority to leave an unexploded bomb in the park." The city, which was the defendant in the case, was not held liable.

Governmental versus proprietary functions

The government in a legal sense is engaged in two types of activity: (1) governmental in nature and (2) proprietary in nature.

The *governmental function* refers to those particular activities that are of a sovereign nature. This theory dates back to the time when kings ruled under the divine right theory, were absolute in their power, and "could do no wrong." As such the sovereign was granted immunity and could not be sued without his consent for failing to exercise governmental powers or for negligence. Furthermore, a subordinate agency of the sovereign could not be sued. The municipality, according to this interpretation, acts as an agent of the state in a governmental capacity. The logic behind this reasoning is that the municipality is helping the state to govern the people who live within its geographic limits.

Many activities are classified under the *governmental function* interpretation. Such functions as education, police protection, and public health fall in this category.

In regard to public education, the courts hold that this is a governmental function and, therefore, entitled to state's immunity from liability for its own negligence. However, as has previously been pointed out, the attitude of the courts has changed and has taken on a broader social outlook that allows in some cases for the reimbursement of the injured.

Proprietary function pertains to government functions that are similar to those of a business enterprise. Such functions are for the benefit of the constituents within the corporate limits of the governmental agency. An example of this would be the manufacture, distribution, and sale of some product to the public. A cafeteria conducted for profit in a school is a proprietary function. In functions that are proprietary in nature a governmental agency is held liable in the same manner as an individual or a private corporation would be held liable.

In the case *Watson v. School District of Bay City*, 324 Mich. 1, 36 N.W.2d 195, a decision was handed down by the supreme court of Michigan in February, 1949. In this case a 15-year-old child attended a high school night football game. In going to her car she was required to walk around a concrete wall. As she attempted to do this, she fell over the wall and onto a ramp. She suffered paralysis and died 8 months later. The parking area was very poorly lighted. The supreme court held that staging a high school football game was a governmental function and refused to impose liability upon the district.

From this discussion it can be seen that education, recreation, and health are governmental functions. While this distinction between governmental and proprietary functions precludes a recovery from the governmental agency if the function was governmental in nature, the federal government and some of the states by legislation have eliminated this distinction.

Fees

Most public recreation activities, facilities, and the like are offered free of charge to the public. However, there are certain activities that, because of the expenses involved, necessitate a fee in order that such activities may continue. For example, golf courses are expensive and charges are usually made so that they may be maintained. This is sometimes true also of such facilities as camps, bathing beaches, and swimming pools.

The fees charged have a bearing upon whether recreation is a governmental or a proprietary function. The courts in most states have upheld recreation as a governmental function, because of its contribution to public health and welfare and also because its devices are free to the public at large. When fees are charged, however, the whole picture takes on a different aspect.

The attitude of the courts has been that the amount of the fee and whether or not the activity was profit-making in nature are considerations in determining whether recreation is a governmental or a proprietary function. Incidental fees that are used in the conduct of the enterprise do not usually change the nature of the enterprise. However, if the enterprise is run for profit, the function changes from governmental to proprietary in nature.

Liability of the municipality

It has been previously pointed out that a municipality as a governmental agency performs both governmental and proprietary functions.

When the municipality is performing a governmental function, it is acting in the interests of the state, receives no profit or advantage, and is not liable for negligence on the part of its employees or for failure to perform these functions. However, this would not hold if there were a specific statute imposing liability for negligence. When the municipality is performing a proprietary function—some function for profit or advantage of the agency or people who comprise it—rather than the public in general, it is liable for negligence of those who are carrying out the function.

This discussion readily shows the importance of conducting recreation as a governmental function.

Liability of the school district

As a general rule the school district is not held liable for acts of negligence on the part of its officers or employees, provided a state statute does not exist to the contrary. The reasoning behind this is that the school district or district school board in maintaining public schools acts as an agent of the state. It performs a purely public or governmental duty imposed upon it by law for the benefit of the public and for the performance of which it receives no profit or advantage.

Some state laws, however, provide that the state may be sued in cases of negligence in the performance of certain duties, such as providing for a safe environment and competent leadership. Furthermore, the school district's immunity in many cases does not cover such acts as those that bring damage or injury through trespass of another's premises or where a nuisance exists on a school district's property, resulting in damage to other property.

Liability of school, park, and recreation board members

Generally speaking, members are not personally liable for any duties in their corporate capacities as board members that they perform negligently. Furthermore, they cannot be held personally liable for acts of employees of the district or organization over which they have jurisdiction on the theory of *respondeat superior* (let the master pay for the servant). Board members act in a corporate capacity and do not act for themselves. For example, in the state of Oregon the general rule as to the personal liability of members of district school boards is stated in 56C.J., page 348, section 223, as follows:

School officers, or members of the board of education, or directors, trustees, or the like, of a school district or other local school organization are not personally liable for the negligence of persons rightfully employed by them in behalf of the district, and not under the direct personal supervision or control of such officer or member in doing the negligent act, since such employee is a servant of the district and not of the officer or board members, and the doctrine of *respondeat superior* accordingly has no application; and members of a district board are not personally liable for the negligence or other wrong of the board as such. A school officer or member of a district board is, however, personally liable for his own negligence or other tort, or that of an agent or employee of the district when acting directly under his supervision or by his direction.

However, a board member can be held liable for a *ministerial* act even though he cannot be held for the exercise of discretion as a member of the board. If the board acts in bad faith and with unworthy motives, and this can be shown, it can also be held liable.

Liability of teachers and leaders

The individual is responsible for negligence of his own acts. With the exception of certain specific immunity, the teacher or leader in programs of health, physical education, and recreation is responsible for what he or she does. The Supreme Court of the United States has reaffirmed this principle and all should recognize the important implications it has. Immunity of the governmental agency such as a state, school district, or board does not release the teacher or leader from liability for his or her own negligent acts.

In New York a physical education teacher was held personally liable when he sat in the bleachers while two strong boys, untrained in boxing, were permitted by the instructor to fight through nearly two rounds. The plaintiff was hit in the temple and suffered a cerebral hemorrhage. The court said: "It is the duty of a teacher to exercise reasonable care to prevent injuries. Pupils should be warned before being permitted to engage in a dangerous and hazardous exercise. Skilled boxers at times are injured, and . . . these young men should have been taught the principles of defense if indeed it was a reasonable thing to permit a slugging match of the kind which the testimony shows this contest was. The testimony indicates that the teacher failed in his duties in this regard and that he was negligent, and the plaintiff is entitled to recover." (*LaValley*

v. Stanford, 272 App. Div. 183, 70 N.Y.S. 2d 460.)

In New York (*Keesee v. Board of Education of City of New York*, 5 N.Y.S.2d 300, 1962) a junior high school girl was injured while playing line soccer. She was kicked by another player. The board of education syllabus listed line soccer as a game for boys and stated that "after sufficient skill has been acquired two or more forwards may be selected from each team." The syllabus called for ten to twenty players on each team and required a space of 30 to 40 feet. The physical education teacher divided into two teams some forty to forty-five girls who had not had any experience in soccer. A witness who was an expert in such matters testified that in order to avoid accidents no more than two people should be on the ball at any time and criticized the board syllabus for permitting the use of more than two forwards. The expert also testified that pupils should have experience in kicking, dribbling, and passing before being permitted to play line soccer. The evidence showed that the teacher permitted six to eight inexperienced girls to be on the ball at one time. The court held that possible injury was at least reasonably foreseeable under such conditions and that the teacher had been negligent and that the teacher's negligence was the cause of the pupil being injured.[*]

Teachers and leaders are expected to conduct their various activities in a careful and prudent manner. If this is not done, they are exposing themselves to lawsuits for their own negligence. As respects administrators, the National Education Association's report has the following to say:

The fact that administrators (speaking mainly of principals and superintendents) are rarely made

---

[*]School Law Series: The pupil's day in court: review of 1963, Washington, D. C., 1964, Research Division, National Education Association, p. 43.

defendants in pupil-injury cases seems unjust to the teachers who are found negligent because of inadequate supervision, and unjust also to the school boards who are required to defend themselves in such suits. When the injury is caused by defective equipment, it is the building principal who should have actual or constructive notice of the defect; when the injury is caused by inadequate playground supervision, the inadequacy of the supervision frequently exists because of arrangements made by the building principal. For example, a teacher in charge of one playground was required to stay in the building to teach a make-up class; another teacher was required to supervise large grounds on which 150 pupils were playing; another teacher neglected the playground to answer the telephone. All of these inadequacies in playground supervision were morally chargeable to administrators; in none of these instances did the court action direct a charge of responsibility to the administrator. Whether the administrator in such cases would have been held liable, if charged with negligence, is problematical. The issue has not been decided, since the administrator's legal responsibility for pupil injuries has never been discussed by the courts to an extent that would make possible the elucidation of general principles; the administrator's moral responsibilities must be conceded.*

Accident-prone settings

Since many accidents occur on the playgrounds, during recess periods, in physical education classes, and at sports events, some very pertinent remarks are included here that have been stated in the National Education Association's report:

Playground and recess games

. . . [T]he unorganized games during recess and noon intermissions are more likely to result in pupil injuries than the organized games of physical education classes. Playground injuries may be pure accidents, such as when a pupil ran against the flagpole while playing (*Hough v. Orleans Elementary School District of Humboldt County, California,* 1943), or when a pupil was hit by a ball (*Graff v. Board of Education of New York City, New York,* 1940), or by a stone batted by another pupil (*Wilbur v. City of Binghamton, New York,* 1946). The courts have said in connec-

tion with this type of injury that every act of every pupil cannot be anticipated. However, the school district should make rules and regulations for pupils' conduct on playgrounds so as to minimize dangers. For example, it was held to be negligence to permit pupils to ride bicycles on the playground while other pupils were playing. (*Buzzard v. East Lake School District of Lake County, California,* 1939.)

Playgrounds should be supervised during unorganized play and such supervision should be adequate. One teacher cannot supervise a large playground with over a hundred pupils playing (*Charonnat v. San Francisco Unified School District, California,* 1943), and when the supervision is either lacking or inadequate districts which are not immune are liable for negligence in not providing adequate supervision (*Forgnone v. Salvadore Union Elementary School District, California,* 1940). Pupils are known to engage in fights and may be expected to be injured in fights; it is the responsibility of the school authorities to attempt to prevent such injuries. The misconduct of other pupils could be an intervening cause to break the chain of causation if the supervision is adequate; but when the supervision is not adequate, misconduct of other pupils is not an intervening superseding cause of the injury.

If a pupil wanders away from the group during playground games and is injured by a dangerous condition into which he places himself, the teacher in charge of the playground may be liable for negligence in pupil supervision (*Miller v. Board of Education, Union Free School District, New York,* 1943), although the district would not be liable in common-law state because of its immunity (*Whitfield v. East Baton Rouge Parish School Board, Louisiana,* 1949).

Supervision of unorganized play at recess or noon intermissions should be by competent personnel. A school janitor is not qualified to supervise play. (*Garber v. Central School District No. 1 of Town of Sharon, New York,* 1937.)

All injuries sustained by pupils on playground equipment are excluded in the Washington statute imposing liability for certain other kinds of accidents. Injuries may occur because playground equipment is in a defective condition. The New York courts have not been consistent in their rulings on this point. In one New York case the district was not liable for injury caused by a defect in a slide because there was no evidence that the defect had existed a sufficient length of time for the school authorities to have knowledge of it (*Handy v. Hadley-Luzerne Union Free School District No. 1, New York,* 1938), but another district in New York was held liable for a defect

---

*National Education Research Division for the National Commission on Safety Education, op. cit., p. 14.

in a slide (*Howell v. Union Free School District No. 1, New York*, 1937).

Nor have the New York courts been consistent in fixing liability when the injury was sustained on playground equipment which was not defective but was dangerous for the individual pupil who played on it. One pupil who fell off a monkey bar was unable to collect damages because the court held specific supervision of each game and each piece of playground equipment would be an unreasonable requirement. The pupil merely met with an accident which was not the fault of the playground supervisor. (*Miller v. Board of Education of Union Free School District No. 1, Town of Oyster Bay, New York*, 1936.) However, another district was declared liable for injuries sustained by a pupil who fell from a ramp during recess, the court holding that liability rested upon the maintenance of a dangerous piece of playground equipment. This ramp had been constructed for the use of older boys and even they were to use it only under supervision; the injured pupil was a small child. (*Sullivan v. City of Binghamton, New York*, 1946.)

Where children of all ages share a playground extra precautions should be taken to prevent accidents, since some children are more adept in using equipment than others and some playground equipment is dangerous to the unskilled.

Physical education and sports events

Pupil injuries in this area occur when playground or gymnasium equipment is defective, when pupils attempt an exercise or sport for which they have not been sufficiently trained, when there is inadequate supervision of the exercise, when other pupils conduct themselves in a negligent manner, and even when the pupils are mere spectators at sports events.

It has been held that physical education teachers, or the school district in States where the district is subject to liability, are responsible for injuries caused by defective equipment. For example, there was liability for the injury to a pupil who was injured in a tumbling race when the mat, not firmly fixed, slipped on the slippery floor. (*Cambareri v. Board of Education of Albany, New York*, 1940.)

Defects in equipment should be known to the physical education instructor. There may be what is called actual or constructive notice of the defect. Actual knowledge is understandable; constructive notice means that the defect has existed for a sufficient time so that the instructor should have known of its existence, whether he did or not. Teachers of physical education should make periodic examination of all equipment at rather frequent intervals; otherwise they may be charged with negligence in not having corrected defects in equipment which have existed for a sufficient time that ignorance of the defect is a presumption of negligence.

Physical education teachers may be liable also for injuries which occur to pupils who attempt to do an exercise which is beyond their skills. A running-jump somersault is one such instance (*Govel v. Board of Education of Albany, New York*, 1944); boxing is another (*LaValley v. Stanford, New York*, 1947); and a headstand exercise is another (*Gardner v. State of New York, New York*, 1939). All of these exercises were found to be inherently dangerous by the courts, and the evidence showed that previous instruction had been inadequate and the pupils had not been warned of the dangers. However, where the previous instruction and the supervision during the exercise are both adequate, there is no liability so long as it cannot be proved that the teacher is generally incompetent (*Kolar v. Union Free School District No. 9, Town of Lenox, New York*, 1939). These cases suggest that teachers should not permit pupils to attempt exercises for which they have not been fully prepared by warnings of the dangers and preliminary exercises to develop the required skills.

As in other types of pupil injuries, the physical education teacher is not liable if the injury occurred without his negligence. If caused by the negligence of another pupil, the teacher will likely be relieved of liability if the other pupil's misconduct was not foreseeable. Pure accidents occur in sports also and if there is no negligence there is no liability (*Mauer v. Board of Education of New York City, New York*, 1945).

Sports events to which nonparticipating pupils and even the public are invited raise other problems of liability for the district or the physical education teacher in charge. If the locality is in a common-law State where the district is immune, the charge of an admission fee does not nullify the district's immunity or make the activity a proprietary function as an exception to the immunity rule (*Watson v. School District of Bay City, Michigan*, 1949). If the accident occurs in a State where the district is liable for at least certain kinds of injuries, such as California, the invitation to attend a sports event includes an invitation to use the nearby grounds and equipment, imposing liability for injury from hidden glass or other dangers (*Brown v. City of Oakland, California*, 1942). If a spectator is accidentally hit by a ball, however, there is no liability; even when a pupil was injured by being hit by a bottle at a game there was no liability because the misconduct of the other spectator was not foreseeable (*Weldy v. Oakland High School District of Alameda County, California*, 1937).*

Common areas of negligence

Common areas of negligence in health and physical education activities listed by Begley† in a New York University publication are situations involving poor selection of activities, failure to take protective procedures, hazardous conditions of buildings or grounds, faulty equipment, inadequate supervision, and poor selection of play area. Cases involving each of these common areas of negligence are as follows.

Poor selection of activities. The activity must be suitable to the child or youth. In *Rook v. New York*, 4 N.Y.S.2d 116 (1930), the court ruled that tossing a child in a blanket constituted a dangerous activity.

Failure to take protective measures. The element of "foreseeability" enters here and proper protective measures must be taken to provide a safe place for children and youth to play. In *Roth v. New York*, 262 App. Div. 370, 29 N.Y.S.2d 442 (1941), inadequate provisions were made to prevent bathers from stepping into deep water. When a bather drowned, the court held the state was liable.

Hazardous conditions of buildings or grounds. Buildings and grounds must be safe. Construction of facilities and their continual repair must have as one objective the elimination of hazards. In the case of *Novak et al. v. Borough of Ford City*, 141 Atl. 496 (Pa., 1928), unsafe conditions were caused by an electric wire over the play area. In the case of *Honaman v. City of Philadelphia*, 185 Atl. 750 (Pa., 1936), unsafe conditions were caused by failure to erect a backstop.

---

*National Education Research Division for the National Commission on Safety Education, op. cit., pp. 18-20.

†Begley, R. F.: Legal liability in organized recreational playground areas, Safety Education Digest, 1955.

Faulty equipment. All play and other equipment must be in good condition at all times. In the case of *Van Dyke v. Utica*, 203 App. Div. 26, 196 N.Y. Supp. 277 (1922), concerning a slide that fell over on a child and killed him, the court ruled that the slide was in a defective condition.

Inadequate supervision. There must be qualified supervision in charge of all play activities. In the case of *Garber v. Central School District No. 1, Town of Sharon, N.Y.*, 251 App. Div. 214, 295 N.Y. Supp. 850, the court held that a school janitor was not qualified to supervise school children playing in a gymnasium during the lunch hour.

Poor selection of play area. The setting for games and sports should be selected with a view to the safety of the participants. In the case *Morse v. New York*, 262 App. Div. 324, 29 N.Y.S.2d 34 (1941), when sledding and skiing were permitted on the same hill without adequate barriers to prevent participants in each activity from colliding with each other, the court held that the state was liable for negligence.

Supervision

Children are entrusted by parents to recreation, health, and physical education programs, and it is expected that adequate supervision will be provided so as to reduce to a minimum the possibility of accidents.

Questions of liability in regard to supervision pertain to two points: (1) the extent of the supervision and (2) the quality of the supervision.

Regarding the first point, the question would be raised as to whether adequate supervision was provided. This is a difficult question to answer because it would vary from situation to situation. However, the answers to these questions: "Would additional supervision have eliminated the accident?" and "Is it reasonable to expect that additional supervision should have been provided?" will help to determine this.

In regard to the quality of the supervision, it is expected that competent personnel will handle specialized programs in health, physical education, and recreation. If the supervisors of such activities do not possess proper training in such work, the question of negligence can be raised.

Waivers and consent slips

Waivers and consent slips are not synonymous. A waiver is an agreement whereby one party waives a particular right. A consent slip is an authorization, usually signed by the parent, permitting a child to take part in some activity.

In respect to a waiver, a parent cannot waive the rights of a child who is under 21 years of age. When a parent signs such a slip, he is merely waiving his or her right to sue for damages. A parent can sue in two ways, from the standpoint of his rights as the parent and from the standpoint of the child's own rights that he has as an individual, irrespective of the parent. A parent cannot waive the right of the child to sue as an individual.

Consent slips offer protection from the standpoint of showing that the child has the parent's permission to engage in an activity.

SAFETY

It is important to take every precaution possible to prevent accidents by providing for the safety of students and other individuals who participate in programs of health education, physical education, and recreation. If such precautions are taken, the likelihood of a lawsuit will diminish and the question of negligence will be eliminated. A few of the precautions that the leader or teacher should make provision for are as follows:

1. Instructor should be properly trained and qualified to perform specialized work.

2. Instructor should be present at all organized activities in the program.

3. Classes should be organized properly according to size, activity, physical condi-

---

Gen. No. 1 100M-1-54-3181

WAIVER FORM
LONG BEACH PUBLIC SCHOOLS

Long Beach, California

Date_____

We,_____, are the parents or guardians

of_____, and in consideration of the special benefits of the extracurricular activity being afforded the student by the Long Beach Board of Education and the school districts whose school the aforementioned child attends, hereby permit_____

_____to participate in_____

_____

and we hereby release and discharge the said Long Beach Board of Education, the said school district, and each and all their agents and employees from any liability whatever to the undersigned resulting from or in any manner arising out of any injury or damage which may be sustained by the said_____, on account of his participation in

_____or in the transportation in connection therewith. We further agree that in case of any action being brought for, or on behalf of the aforementioned child on account of any injury received during his participation in the above mentioned events, or in the transportation connected therewith, that we will be personally responsible to the school district, the Board of Education, and any of its officials or agents concerned, and will repay to them and hold them harmless against any judgment recovered in any such action against them or either of them.

Signed this_____day of_____, 195____

Signature of Parent or Guardian	Address
Signature of Parent or Guardian	Address

NOTE: Parents or Guardians, read the reverse side of this form.

tion, and other factors that have a bearing on safety and health of the individual.

4. Health examinations should be given to all pupils.

5. A planned, written program for proper disposition of students who are injured or become sick should be followed.

6. Regular inspections should be made of such items as equipment, apparatus, ropes, or chains, placing extra pressure upon them and taking other precautions to make sure they are safe. They should also be checked for deterioration, looseness, fraying, splinters, and so on.

7. Overcrowding athletic and other events should be avoided, building codes and fire regulations should be adhered to,

and adequate lighting for all facilities should be provided.

8. Protective equipment such as mats should be utilized wherever possible. Any hazards such as projections or obstacles in an area where activity is taking place should be eliminated. Floors should not be slippery. Shower rooms should have surfaces conducive to secure footing.

9. Sneakers should be worn on gymnasium floors and adequate space provided for each activity.

10. Activities should be adapted to the age and maturity of the participants, proper and competent supervision should be provided, and spotters should be utilized in apparatus and other similar activities.

Every precaution should be taken to prevent accidents. Students learn to handle a canoe in water safety course. (University of Florida, Gainesville, Fla.)

11. Students should be instructed in the correct methods of using apparatus and performing in physical activities. Any misuse of equipment should be prohibited.

12. The buildings and other facilities used should be inspected regularly for safety hazards such as loose tiles, broken fences, cracked glass, and uneven pavement. Defects should be reported immediately to responsible persons and necessary precautions be taken.

13. In planning play and other instructional areas the following precautions should be taken:

a. There should be sufficient space for all games.

b. Games that utilize balls and other equipment that can cause damage should be conducted in areas where there is minimum danger of injuring someone.

c. Quiet games and activities that require working at benches, such as arts and crafts, should be in places that are well protected.

14. Truesdale lists certain questionable practices in which teachers, coaches, nurses, and trainers sometimes engage:

1. Supply "pills" for headaches or as laxatives or for menstrual discomfort.
2. Examine and diagnose by the stethoscope.
3. Prescribe anticold pills or capsules.
4. Strap joint injuries under supposition of sprain without expert assessment for possible fracture.
5. Permit return to play of a player with a head injury.
6. Play injured players not medically certified.
7. Permit return of students without medical certification to class, or particularly to activity, after illness.
8. Prescribe gargles or swabs for sore throats.
9. Use cutting tools (knives or razor blades) on calluses, corns, blisters, ingrown nails, etc.
10. Administer local anaesthesia to permit play after injury.
11. Employ physical forces such as heat or electric current to produce tissue change and decongestion and repair without medical order, or by unqualified persons.
12. Possibly further damage unconscious players

by dashing water in the face, by slapping the face or by unwarranted use of aromatic spirits of ammonia to "bring them to."*

Truesdale also points out that "it is the duty of adults engaged in education not only to know of and be skillful in the proper techniques for protecting persons against injury, or protecting injured persons against aggravation, but also to know the limits beyond which the untrained or the partially trained person may not go."

15. In the event of accident the following or a similar procedure should be followed:

a. The nearest teacher or leader should proceed to the scene of the accident immediately, notifying the person in charge and nurse, if available, by messenger. Also, a doctor should be called at once if one is necessary.

b. A hurried examination of the injured person will give some idea as to the nature and extent of the injury and the emergency of the situation.

c. If the teacher or leader is well versed in first aid, assistance should be given (a qualified first-aid certificate will usually absolve the teacher of negligence). Every teacher or leader who works in these specialized areas should and is expected to know first-aid procedures. In any event everything should be done to make the injured person comfortable and reassure the injured until the services of a physician can be secured.

d. If the injury is serious an ambulance should be called.

e. After the injured person has been provided for, the person in charge should fill out the accident forms and take the statements of witnesses and file for future reference. Reports of accidents should be prepared promptly and sent to proper persons. They should be accurate as to detail

---

*Truesdale, J. C.: So you're a good samaritan! Journal of the American Association for Health, Physical Education, and Recreation 25:25, 1954.

STANDARD STUDENT ACCIDENT REPORT FORM
Part A. Information on ALL Accidents

1. Name: _____ Home Address. _____
2. School _____ Sex M ☐; F ☐. Age: _____ Grade or classification· _____
3. Time accident occurred Hour _____ A.M., _____ P.M. Date· _____
4. Place of Accident   School Building ☐   School Grounds ☐   To or from School ☐   Home ☐   Elsewhere ☐

5. **NATURE OF INJURY**	Abrasion _____ Amputation _____ Asphyxiation _____ Bite _____ Bruise _____ Burn _____ Concussion _____ Cut _____ Dislocation _____ Other (specify) _____	Fracture _____ Laceration _____ Poisoning _____ Puncture _____ Scalds _____ Scratches _____ Shock (el.) _____ Sprain _____	**DESCRIPTION OF THE ACCIDENT** How did accident happen? What was student doing? Where was student? List specifically unsafe acts and unsafe conditions existing. Specify any tool, machine or equipment involved. _____
PART OF BODY INJURED	Abdomen _____ Ankle _____ Arm _____ Back _____ Chest _____ Ear _____ Elbow _____ Eye _____ Face _____ Finger _____ Other (specify) _____	Foot _____ Hand _____ Head _____ Knee _____ Leg _____ Mouth _____ Nose _____ Scalp _____ Tooth _____ Wrist _____	

6. Degree of Injury. Death ☐   Permanent Impairment ☐   Temporary Disability ☐   Nondisabling ☐
7. Total number of days lost from school: _____ (To be filled in when student returns to school)

Part B. Additional Information on School Jurisdiction Accidents

8. Teacher in charge when accident occurred (Enter name) _____
   Present at scene of accident: No _____ Yes· _____

9. **IMMEDIATE ACTION TAKEN**
   First-aid treatment _____ By (Name) _____
   Sent to school nurse _____ By (Name) : _____
   Sent home _____ By (Name) : _____
   Sent to physician _____ By (Name) : _____
   Physician's Name: _____
   Sent to hospital _____ By (Name) : _____
   Name of hospital: _____

10. Was a parent or other individual notified? No.___ Yes.___ When._____ How· _____
    Name of individual notified· _____
    By whom? (Enter name). _____
11. Witnesses· 1. Name: _____ Address: _____
    2. Name· _____ Address: _____

12. **LOCATION**

Specify Activity		**Specify Activity**		**Remarks**
Athletic field	_____	Locker	_____	What recommendations do you have for pre-
Auditorium	_____	Pool	_____	venting other accidents of this type? _____
Cafeteria	_____	Sch. grounds	_____	
Classroom	_____	shop	_____	
Corridor	_____	Showers	_____	
Dressing room	_____	Stairs	_____	
Gymnasium	_____	Toilets and		
Home Econ.	_____	washrooms	_____	
Laboratories	_____	Other (specify)	_____	

Signed: Principal: _____ Teacher: _____

(National Safety Council—Form School 1)   Printed in U.S.A. Rep. 200M—25302

Form recommended by National Safety Council.

and complete as to information. Among other things they should contain information about:

Name and address of injured person
Activity engaged in
Date, hour, and place
Person in charge
Witnesses
Cause and extent of injury
Medical attention given
Circumstances surrounding incident

f. There should be a complete followup of the accident, an analysis of the situation, and an eradication of any hazards that exist.

Herman Rosenthal, Assistant to the Law

GROVER CLEVELAND HIGH SCHOOL
HIMROD & GRANDVIEW AVE.
Ridgewood, New York
STATEMENT BY WITNESS
(Write in Ink)

Witness...Address...

Age................................Rank..........................Class......................................

Name of one injured.......................Injured's Official Class.............Age of Injured.............

Date of accident.........................Time.................Day of week...................

A. Circumstances of Accident

1. Locate the position from which you witnessed the accident, using such phrases as, in front of, as I entered, standing on the, in back of, etc.....................................

....

....

....

2. Locate the position where the accident occurred, using such phrases as, on the landing, exit 8 up, on the horizontal bar, etc..

....

....

3. Tell what you saw..

....

....

....

B. Additional remarks, if any..

....

....

C. Signature of Witness...

Statement by witness to accident. (Grover Cleveland High School, Ridgewood, N. Y.)

Secretary, City of New York, in addressing a health education conference in New York City, pointed up the following remarks in respect to reporting accidents:

Reports should be complete, full and in detail. He advised that where a case does go into litigation, there is a delay in the court calendar of 2 to 3 years before the case is tried. A complete and detailed report is always better than a teacher's or a child's memory. He pointed out that the completion of accident reports was the function and duty of the teacher and in no case should a child be expected to prepare the report. Reports in the handwriting of children, he said, should be limited only to the statements and signatures of the injured and of the witnesses to the accident. He emphasized that should an injured child at the time of the accident be unable to prepare a written statement or affix his signature to a report, the teacher should prepare the necessary statement and signature and indicate the reasons for so doing. He further focused attention on the fact that teachers should not attempt to color or distort facts in order to protect the school or the child, because such a practice does more harm than good. An extremely important point, he said, was the need to report where the teacher was at the time of the accident, the extent of the supervision, and the teacher control of the activity at the time of the accident. Also, he said that with few exceptions reports should be submitted within 24 hours of the time of the accident. He explained that in some cases this might not be possible, but in such cases no report need be delayed more than 48 hours.*

g. Thelma Reed, Chairman of Standard Student Accident Report Committee of the National Safety Council, listed the reasons why detailed injury reports are important for school authorities:

1. Aid in protecting the school personnel and district from unfortunate publicity and from liability suits growing out of student injury cases;
2. Aid in evaluating the relative importance of the various safety areas and the time each merits in the total school safety effort;
3. Suggest modifications in the structure, use, and maintenance of buildings, grounds, and equipment;
4. Suggest curriculum adjustments to meet immediate student needs;
5. Provide significant data for individual student guidance;
6. Give substance to the school administrators' appeal for community support of the school safety program;
7. Aid the school administration in guiding the school safety activities of individual patrons and patrons' groups.

Some suggestions to help reduce injuries on the gridiron

Approximately 700 American boys have been killed directly or indirectly playing football in the last quarter century. Studies show that football is by far the most dangerous part of the educational program. According to the National Safety Council, in a recent year football accounted for one out of every five accidents occurring under the school's jurisdiction to students in the sophomore year, one out of every four to junior-year students, and one out of every three to seniors. By contrast baseball accounted for one out of twenty-six to sophomore students, one out of twenty-nine to the juniors, and one of thirty-three to the seniors.

Football can be made a much safer game. Many times chances are taken, players are urged to participate when not in the best of physical condition, the safest type of uniforms and equipment are not used, and the necessary precautions are not taken. In some cases there is negligence on the part of school authorities. Some suggestions to help make football a safer game are as follows:

1. A qualified coaching staff and a qualified trainer should be hired.
2. The best equipment that money can buy should be purchased.
3. Qualified officials should be present for all games and scrimmages.
4. Safe facilities, such as good turf, adequate space, and elimination of all hazards should be required.

*Proceedings of the City Wide Conference with Principals' Representatives and Men and Women Chairmen of Health Education, City of New York Board of Education, Brooklyn, N. Y., 1953, Bureau of Health Education.

5. A doctor should be present at all games and at all scrimmages.

6. A thorough physical examination before the season starts and again at midseason is a *must*. It should include a detailed study of the health history of each player. If health history shows heart abnormalities or other defects that might be aggravated, the boy should not be permitted to play.

7. Provisions should be available for such essentials as an x-ray study, encephalogram, physical therapy, and bandaging.

8. Accident insurance to cover full cost of diagnosis and treatment of all injuries should be obtained.

9. No boy should be allowed to return to a game after a head injury until an x-ray film has been taken and a doctor has approved return to action. If injury is diagnosed as severe concussion, he should never be allowed to participate in gridiron activities again.

10. The temptation to send in the star who insists that he is not hurt and wants to return to play should be resisted. Decision to return to play should not be permitted unless approved by the doctor in writing.

11. Each school should play only schools of its own size and teams of its own stature.

12. More stress should be placed on training and conditioning: at least twenty practices spaced over a 3-week period before the first game for each player, longer warmups for reserves sitting on the bench and for all players at halftime of the game, and greater emphasis on fundamentals, such as blocking, tackling, and techniques of play.

13. If the rules could be changed as follows, injuries could be reduced:

a. Eliminate second-half kickoff.

b. Increase the penalty for piling on. Ban from the game the player who persists in ignoring this rule.

c. Allow for substitutions to the extent that exhausted players will not be in the game.

d. Provide 5 minutes longer between halves of the game, with specific stipulation that this time is to be used for warmup.

Safety code for the physical education teacher

The following safety code should be followed by the physical education teacher:

1. Have a proper teacher's certificate in full force and effect.
2. Operate and teach at all times, within the scope of his employment as delimited and defined by the rules and regulations of the employing board of education and within the statutory limitations imposed by the state.
3. Provide the safeguards designed to minimize the dangers inherent in a particular activity.
4. Provide the amount of supervision for each activity required to ensure the maximum safety of all the pupils.
5. Inspect equipment and facilities periodically to determine whether or not they are safe for use.
6. Notify the proper authorities forthwith concerning the existence of any dangerous condition as it continues to exist.
7. Provide sufficient instruction in the performance of any activity before exposing pupils to its hazards.
8. Be certain that the task is one approved by the employing board of education for the age and attainments of the pupils involved.
9. Not force a pupil to perform a physical feat which the pupil obviously feels he is incapable of performing.
10. Act promptly and use discretion in giving first aid to an injured pupil, but nothing more.
11. Exercise due care in practicing his profession.
12. Act as a reasonably prudent person would under the given circumstances.
13. Anticipate the dangers which should be apparent to a trained, intelligent person (a legal principle known as "foreseeability").*

---

*Munize, A. J.: The teacher, pupil injury, and legal liability, Journal of Health, Physical Education, and Recreation 33:28, 1962.

INSURANCE MANAGEMENT

There are three major types of insurance management that school districts utilize to protect themselves against loss. The first type is insurance for *property,* owned by the school district. The second type is insurance for *liability protection,* where there might be financial loss arising from personal injury or property damage for which the school district is liable. The third type is insurance for *crime protection* against a financial loss that might be incurred as a result of theft or other illegal act. This section on insurance management is primarily concerned with the second type of insurance, namely, liability protection.

A definite trend can be seen in school districts toward having some form of school accident insurance to protect students against injury. School administrators and boards of education in many communities feel this is one additional and important way of giving service to its school population. Along with this trend can be seen the impact upon casualty and life insurance companies that offer insurance policies for school children and staff. The premium costs of school accident policies vary from community to community and also in accordance with age of insured and type of plan offered. The area of interscholastic athletics has been responsible for the development of many state athletic protection plans as well as the issuance of special policies by commercial insurance companies. When it is realized that accidents are the chief cause of death among students between the ages of 5 and 18, it can readily be seen that some protection is needed.

Common features of insurance management plans

Some common features of insurance management plans across the United States are as follows:

1. Premiums are paid for by the school, by the parent, or jointly by the school and parent.

2. Schools obtain their money for payment of premiums from the board of education, general organization fund, or a pooling of funds for many schools taken from gate receipts in league games.

3. Schools place the responsibility upon the parents to pay for any injuries incurred.

4. The blanket type coverage is a very common policy for insurance companies to offer.

5. Insurance companies frequently offer insurance coverage for athletic injuries as part of a package plan that also includes an accident plan for all students.

6. Most schools have insurance plans for the protection of athletes.

7. Most schools seek insurance coverage that provides for benefits whether x-ray films are positive or negative.

8. Hospitalization, x-ray films, and medical fees and dental fees are increasingly becoming part of the insurance coverage in schools.

Some school boards have found it a good policy to pay the premium on insurance policies because the full coverage of students provides peace of mind for both parents and teachers. Furthermore, it has been noted by some educators that many liability suits have been avoided in this manner.

Other school officials investigate the various insurance plans available and then recommend a particular plan and the parents deal directly with the company. Such parent-paid plans are frequently divided into two options: (1) they provide coverage for the student on a door-to-door basis (to and from school, while at school, and in school-sponsored activities) and (2) they provide 24-hour accident coverage with premiums usually running to four times higher than the "school only" policy. The "school only" policy rates are based upon age with rates for children in the elementary grades less than those in the higher grades. These policies also usually run only for the school year.

Student accident insurance provides coverage for all accidents regardless of whether the insured is hospitalized or treated in a doctor's office. Such medical plans as Blue Cross and Blue Shield are limited in the payments they make. Student accident insurance policies, as a general rule, offer reasonable rates and are a good investment for all concerned. Parents should be encouraged, however, to examine their existing family policies before taking out such policies to avoid overlapping coverage.

A survey of nine school districts in Ohio a few years ago indicated some practices and problems concerned with answering the question: "What to look for in selecting an insurance policy for athletics?"* These facts were disclosed by this survey:

1. The chief school administrator was the person who usually selected the insurance company from whom the policy would be purchased.
2. Medical coverage on policies purchased ranged from $30 to $5,000 and dental coverage from nothing to $500.
3. The claims collected for one particular type of injury ranged from nothing to $792.30.
4. Companies did not follow through at all times in paying the amount for which the claim was made.
5. Most insurance companies writing athletic policies have scheduled benefit plans.
6. Catastrophe clauses were absent from all policies.
7. Athletes covered ranged from 80% to 100%.
8. In most cases part of each athlete's premium was paid for from a school athletic fund.

*Rockhold, J.: How to buy athletic insurance, The Ohio High School Athlete **23:**169 1964.

9. Football was covered in separate policies.

As a result of this survey the following recommendations were made:

1. Some person or group of persons should be delegated to explore insurance policies and, after developing a set of criteria, to purchase the best one possible.
2. Where feasible, cooperative plans with other schools on a county or other basis should be encouraged in order to obtain less expensive group rates.
3. Criteria for the selection of an insurance policy should, in addition to cost, relate to such important benefits as maximum medical, excluded benefits, maximum dental, hospital, death or dismemberment, surgical, and x-ray.
4. The greatest possible coverage for cost involved should be an important basis for the selection of policy.
5. In light of football programs especially, the catastrophe clause should be investigated as possible additional coverage.
6. Deductible clause policies should not be purchased.
7. Dental injury benefits are an important consideration.
8. Determine what claims the insurance company will and will not pay.
9. The school should insist on 100% enrollment in the athletic insurance program.
10. Schools should have a central location for keeping insurance records, and there should be an annual survey to ascertain all the pertinent facts about the cost and effectiveness of such coverage.

Procedure for insurance management

Every school should be covered by insurance. There are five types of accident insurance that can be used: "(1) commercial insurance policies written on an individual basis; (2) student medical benefit plans written on a group basis by commercial insurers; (3) state high school athletic association benefit plans; (4) medical benefit plans operated by specific city school systems; and (5) self-insurance."* Before adoption by any school each type of insurance should be carefully weighed so that best coverage is obtained for the type of program sponsored.

A suggested procedure to be followed as a guide for the administration of an insurance program follows:

(1) the entire school should be organized to study the insurance problems and needs, (2) a survey should be made to ascertain the need for insurance before it is purchased, (3) after the need has been established, specifications should be constructed indicating the kind and amount of insurance needed, (4) the specifications should be presented to several insurers to obtain estimates of coverage and costs, (5) the plans presented to the school by the several insurers should be studied, and the one best suited to that particular situation should be selected, (6) parents should be given full information about the insurance, (7) workable and harmonious relations should be established with the insurer selected (8) continuous evaluation of the insurance program should be carried out, and (9) records should be carefully kept of costs, accidents, claims payments, and other pertinent data.

School administrators should insist upon the following conditions and requirements when purchasing accident insurance: (1) the coverage should include all school activities and provide up to $500 [more today] for each injury to each pupil, (2) the medical services should include (a) cost of professional services of physician or surgeon, (b) cost of hospital care and service, (c) cost of a trained nurse, (d) cost of ambulance, surgical appliances, dressings, x-rays, etc., and (e) cost of repair and care of natural teeth, (3) the policy should be tailor-made to fit the needs of the school, (4) the coverage should be maximum for minimum cost, (5) all pupils as well as all teachers, should be included, (6) a deductible clause should be avoided unless it reduces the premium substantially and the policy still fulfills its purpose, (7) blanket rather than schedule type coverage should be selected, and (8) claims payment must be simple, certain, and fast.†

School athletic insurance*

According to Grimes, prior to 1930 there was very little accident insurance carried by school districts to protect their athletes, and there was little activity on the part of commercial insurance companies in this area. Only a very few schools were self-insured, and if they were it was primarily for football. Grimes further relates that the Wisconsin High School Athletic Association provided the first movement in school athletic insurance coverage when it established its plan in 1930 and made it available to member schools. Thereafter, many other states followed the example set by Wisconsin, and athletic associations established their own athletic insurance plans. The practice grew and by the 1940's, twenty-five states had such plans. By the 1950's commercial insurance companies, recognizing the possibilities in this area, started to penetrate the high school athletic field and provided special policies to cover athletes in various sports. The commercial insurance companies became so competitive that they made deep inroads into the nonprofit state athletic association plans. Also, according to Grimes, as a result of the commercial insurance company inroads, insurance plans became more comprehensive and coverage was extended to pupils for all school activities for all grades. Today, only eight high school athletic associations sponsor their own insurance plans. These plans stay in business largely because they have adopted many of the features of commercial insurance plans, such as nonallocated benefits, catastrophic coverage, group coverage, nonduplication of benefits, and varying premium rates.

Athletic protection funds usually have these characteristics: they are a nonprofit

*Joint Committee: Administrative problems in health education, physical education and recreation, Washington, D. C., 1953, American Association for Health, Physical Education, and Recreation, p. 105.

†Joint Committee, op. cit., p. 106.

*From Grimes, L. W.: Trends in school athletic insurance. In Secondary school athletic administration—a new look, Washington, D. C., 1969, The American Association for Health, Physical Education, and Recreation.

venture, they are not compulsory, a specific fee is charged each person registered with the plan, and there is provision for recovery for specific injuries. Generally the money is not paid out of tax funds but instead is paid either by the participants themselves or by the school or other agency.

In connection with such plans, it should be recognized that an individual, after receiving benefits, could in most states still bring action against the coach or other

CLAIM NO.	**REQUEST FOR ACCIDENT BENEFIT**	Dr.
	INTERSCHOLASTIC	X-Ray
To be filled in by School	SPORT	Total
		DO NOT WRITE IN ABOVE SPACE

1. School _____ 4. Grade _____
2. Name _____ 5. Age _____
3. Date and Time of Injury _____ 6. No. of years of competition _____

7. Game _____ 8. Type of play at time of injury 9. Boy activity at time of injury
   Practice _____ Offense ____ Run ____ Block ____
   Scrimmage _____ Defense ____ Pass ____ Tackle ____
   Skills _____ Rebound ____ Kick ____ Shooting ____
   Night Football Game _____ Etc. ____ Etc. ____

10. Explain exactly where and how the injury occurred _____

11. Name of the doctor who first attended or examined your injury _____
    Date and hour? _____ **STATE DATES** of treatment _____
12. After the injury I returned to the squad on _____ (date), was not in school for _____ days.
13. Does the parent have other insurance to cover this expense _____

I, Principal of _____ High School, have examined the above statements, and the statements of the Doctor or Dentist who attended this student. The statements are true to the best of my knowledge and I believe this claim to be just.

(Date) _____ (Principal) _____

(Signature of Claimant)
This boy was given a Physical Examination on
(DATE) _____ at the beginning of **THIS SPORTS SEASON,** which was recorded on the regulation Physical Examination Card which is on file in the school.

(Signature of Coach present at time of injury)

AFFIDAVIT OF ATTENDING PHYSICIAN

1. Date of first treatment _____ 2. Diagnosis _____

(Here state the nature, character and extent of injury to claimant)

3. **X-RAY READING REPORT MUST ACCOMPANY ALL CLAIMS FOR INDEMNITY FOR FRACTURE OR DISLOCATION.**

4. In your opinion was there any predisposing factor contributory to the injury? _____
5. Give name of any consulting or assistant physician _____
6. Describe your treatment and **State Dates** of examination or treatment _____

7. Prognosis and General Remarks _____

Facsimile of Physician's Fees

( ) Office Calls @ $3.00 ____ $ ____
( ) Home Calls @ $4.00 ____ $ ____
( ) Operation ____ $ ____
( ) X-ray ____ $ ____
_____ $ ____
Total ____ $ ____

X-RAY not taken by you — attach official copy of report and statement for charge.

SINCE THE PROTECTION PLAN IS A NON-PROFIT ORGANIZATION ESTABLISHED TO SERVE THE SCHOOLS, THE MAXIMUM SCHEDULED INDEMNITY IS NOT TO BE CLAIMED UNLESS ITEMIZED PROFESSIONAL SERVICES JUSTIFY THAT AMOUNT AS LISTED ON REVERSE SIDE.

8. The above named student is again able to PARTICIPATE in athletics and physical education on _____ date
9. Patient discharged from my care on _____ date

I, a Duly Licensed Physician, personally performed the above services.
Signature of Physician: _____ M. D.
Address _____

Form No. 3
25M—5-62

PHYSICIAN: RETURN FORM TO SCHOOL WITH STUDENT ON LAST VISIT
All Bills Must Be Presented Within 90 Days of Accident If Claims Are To Be Paid

Request for accident benefit form. (New York State High School Athletic Protection Plan, Inc.)

leader whose negligence contributed to the injury.

In respect to paying for liability and accident insurance out of public tax funds, the states vary as to their practices. Some states do not permit tax money to be used for liability or accident insurance to cover students in physical education activities. On the other hand, the state legislature of Oregon permits school districts to carry liability insurance. This section is stated as follows in the revised code, O.R.S.:

332.180 Liability insurance; medical and hospital benefits insurance. Any district school board may enter into contracts of insurance for liability coverage all activities engaged in by the district, for medical and hospital benefits for students engaging in athletic contests and for public liability and property damage covering motor vehicles operated by the district, and may pay the necessary premiums thereon. Failure to procure such insurance shall in no case be construed as negligence or lack of diligence on the part of the district school board or the members thereof.

Some athletic insurance plans in use in the schools today are entirely inadequate. These plans indicate a certain amount of money as the maximum that can be collected. For example, a boy may lose the sight of an eye. According to the athletic protection. fund, the loss of an eye will draw, say, $1,500. This amount does not come even remotely close to paying for such a serious injury. In this case a hypothetical example could be taken by saying that the parents sue the athletic protection fund and the teacher for $30,000. In some states if the case is lost, the athletic fund will pay the $1,500 and the teacher the other $28,500. It can be seen that some of these insurance plans do not give complete and adequate coverage.

In many states teachers need additional protection against being sued for accidental injury to students. Legislation is needed permitting school funds to be used as protection against student injuries. In this way a school would be legally permitted to and could be required to purchase liability insurance to cover all pupils.

Questions and exercises

1. Consult the legal files in your local governmental unit to determine any court cases on record that have implications for the fields of health education, physical education, and/ or recreation. Describe the circumstances surrounding each.
2. Arrange a mock trial in your class. Have a jury, prosecutor, defendant, witnesses, and other features characteristic of a regular court trial. Your instructor will state the case before the court.
3. Why is it important that leaders in health, physical education, and recreation have knowledge in respect to legal liability?
4. Define and illustrate each of the following: (a) liability, (b) tort, (c) negligence, (d) in loco parentis, (e) plaintiff, (f) nuisance, (g) misfeasance, (h) respondeat superior, and (i) proximate cause.
5. What are the defenses against negligence? Illustrate each.
6. What is the difference between governmental and proprietary functions? Illustrate each.
7. How does the charging of fees affect liability?
8. What is the extent of liability of (a) municipality, (b) school district, (c) board member, and (d) coach?
9. What are some safety procedures that should be followed by every physical education teacher?
10. Prepare a form to be used for the reporting of accidents.
11. What are the advantages of waivers and consent slips?

Reading assignment in *Administrative Dimensions of Health and Physical Education Programs, Including Athletics:* Chapter 14, Selections 77 to 82.

Selected references

American Association for Health, Physical Education, and Recreation, National Association of Secondary School Principals, and National Commission on Safety Education: The physical education instructor and safety, Washington, D. C., 1948, National Education Association.

American Association for Health, Physical Education, and Recreation: Secondary school athletic administration—a new look, Washington, D. C., 1969, The Association.

Bucher, C. A.: Football can be made safer, New

York World-Telegram and Sun, Saturday Feature Magazine, Sept. 1, 1956.

Casey, L. M.: School business administration, New York, 1964, The Center for Applied Research in Education, Inc. (The Library of Education).

Curtis, P.: Safety and fun synonymous, Chicago, 1955, National Safety Council.

Doscher, N., and Walke, N.: The status of liability for school physical education accidents and its relationship to the health program, The Research Quarterly 23:280, 1952.

Dyer, D. B., and Lichtig, J. G.: Liability in public recreation, Milwaukee, 1949, C. C. Nelson Publishing Co.

Elkow, D.: Safety for recreation areas and playgrounds, Safety Education Digest, 1955 (entire issue).

Foraker, T., and others: School insurance, School and Community, p. 28, October, 1967.

Garber, L. O.: Tort and contractual liability of school districts, Danville, Ill., 1963, The Interstate Printers & Publishers, Inc.

Garber, L. O.: Yearbook of school law, Danville, Ill., 1963, The Interstate Printers & Publishers, Inc.

Gauerke, W. E.: School law, New York, 1965, The Center for Applied Research in Education, Inc. (The Library of Education).

Grieve, A.: Legal aspects of spectator injuries, The Athletic Journal 47:74, 1967.

Guenther, D.: Problems involving legal liability in schools, Journal of the American Association for Health, Physical Education, and Recreation 20:511, 1949.

Hamilton, R. R.: School liability, Chicago, 1952, National Safety Council.

Kurtzman, J.: Legal liability and physical education, The Physical Educator 24:20, 1967.

Liebee, H. C.: Liability for accidents in physical education, athletics, recreation, Ann Arbor, Mich., 1952, Ann Arbor Publishers.

National Education Association, Research Division: School laws and teacher negligence: summary of who is responsible for pupil injuries, National Education Association Research Bulletin 40:75, 1962.

National Education Association: The pupil's day in court: review of 1968, Washington, D. C., 1969, The Association.

National Education Association: Tort liability and liability insurance, School Law Summaries, NEA Research Division, March, 1969.

Proceedings of the City Wide Conference with Principals' Representatives and Men and Women Chairmen of Health Education, City of New York Board of Education, Bureau of Health Education, 1953.

Research Division for the National Commission on Safety Education: Who is liable for pupil injuries? Washington, D. C., 1950, National Education Association.

Rosenfield, H. N.: Liability for school accidents, New York, 1940, Harper & Row, Publishers.

Shroyer, G. F.: Coach's legal liability for athletic injuries, Scholastic Coach 34:18, 1964.

State school laws and regulations for health, safety, driver, outdoor, and physical education, Washington, D. C., 1964, Department of Health, Education, and Welfare.

Truesdale, J. C.: So you're a good samaritan! Journal of the American Association for Health, Physical Education, and Recreation 25:25, 1954.

CHAPTER 19 CURRICULUM DEVELOPMENT

One of the most striking changes to be observed in education during the last few years is the national curriculum reform movement. There is a new mathematics, a new physics, a new English, and a new social studies. Many of the approximately 85,000 public elementary and 24,000 public secondary schools have felt the impact of change, with the movement being most pronounced in suburban schools. A recent study conducted by the Educational Testing Service of Princeton, New Jersey, covered 38,000 students from more than 7,500 academic high schools. It reported that curriculum innovations had a substantial effect in the teaching of school subjects.

In curriculum development, tradition and other pressures are difficult to overcome. Proposals for change encounter obstacles in trying to penetrate the school and college structures in many communities and campuses. Yet the explosion of knowledge, the growth of education in America, the complexity of society, and the impact of social change make it imperative that educators and the public alike examine what they have been doing in the past, evaluate what they are doing now, and plan for the future.

Each subject matter field must relate to and help each student approach self-realization and effective social behavior through an involvement of pertinent ideas, people, and activities. Individual differences must be provided for. Each school system's program must reflect the fact that learning is a continuous and individual process that proceeds at various rates and to various degrees in the attainment of each student's maximum potential.

The curriculum in health education or physical education represents the experiences that are provided children and young people so that the objectives of the profession may be met. The curriculum functions as the vehicle for achieving such objectives as organic development, skill development, mental development, and social development. It provides for experiences in terms of courses, subject matter, and activities that will best approach those goals. It creates the environment that will enable sound and meaningful education to take place. The experiences provided are means to an end—that end being the realization of the broad goals that we have established as a profession and that enrich human living. Each student is, through the experiences provided, helped to develop his abilities and to realize his full potential.

IMPORTANCE OF CURRICULUM DEVELOPMENT AND ROLE OF ADMINISTRATION

Curriculum development is important as a service to the student. It should be concerned with matching the experience and the student; it must meet the needs of boys and girls. Since no two students are exactly alike, there is great need for flexibility and for a wide range of experiences that meet the requirements of all pupils. Continuous curriculum development is a way of determining what needs to be learned and of providing the means for seeing that it is accomplished.

The administration plays a very important part in curriculum planning. The end result of all administrative effort is to provide better instructional services, better programs, better learning situations, and better experiences to achieve the objectives that have been established. Since new problems constantly arise and since unmet needs continue to exist or go unrecognized, there is an urgent need for continuous curriculum planning. It is the administrator who provides the required leadership. The educational philosophy that represents the foundation of curriculum development should reflect faculty thinking as determined by their study of pupil needs. If an administrator possesses what he considers to be a better philosophy, he should discuss this with the faculty, bringing forth facts, good reasoning, and logic to support his concept. If it is then accepted by the faculty, it can be utilized. Otherwise, it will not receive extensive practical application because it is not understood or accepted.

Curriculum construction requires the selection, guidance, and evaluation of experiences in the light of both long-term and more immediate goals. It provides for an orderly periodic evaluation of the total program, both the inclass and the out-of-class, with changes being made whenever necessary. It takes into consideration such factors as students, total community, existing facilities, personnel, time allotments, national trends, and state rules and regulations. It sets up a framework for orderly progression from the kindergarten through college. It offers a guide to health education and physical education teachers so that they are better able to achieve educational goals.

Curriculum development is very important and school administrators have the responsibility for making the necessary provisions to see that it is accomplished.

CATALYSTS THAT BRING ABOUT CURRICULUM CHANGE

Changes occur in health education and physical education curricula as they do in other areas of the school offering. There is usually a continuous list of myriad proposals for change. Each proposal should be considered on its own merits and put to the test of whether or not it has value.

What are the influencing factors in regard to change? A few associations, agencies, and individuals who produce change in health and physical education are discussed in the following paragraphs.

National associations and agencies

The President's Council on Physical Fitness and Sports is an outstanding example of one national governmental agency that brought about much change in programs of health, physical education, and recreation throughout the United States and the world. Through their speakers, publications, and communication media pronouncements, many changes have taken place in the schools and colleges of this nation. Physical fitness in some communities has become the overriding purpose of programs of health education and physical education, sometimes at the expense of the other objectives of these fields and a well-balanced program of activities.

Examples of other national associations and agencies that play a part in curriculum change are the National Education Association, the American Association for Health, Physical Education, and Recreation, the United States Office of Education, the Association for Supervision and Curriculum Development, and The American Medical Association.

State associations and agencies

As national organizations influence the curricula of our schools and colleges, so do state organizations. State boards of education or departments of public instruction, state bureaus, departments or divisions of health and physical education, state education associations, citizens committees, teachers associations, and associations for health, physical education, and recreation are a few examples of organizations that influence curricula. Through the publication of syllabi, sponsorship of legislation, enactment of rules and regulations, exercise of supervisory powers, allocation of funds, and initiation of projects, organizations promote certain ideas and programs that initiate changes in schools and colleges.

Research

Research brings about change. As new knowledge is uncovered, more information is known about the learning process, new techniques are developed, and other research is conducted. Change eventually ensues if the research is significant, but the change may be slow in coming. It usually takes a long period of time for the creation of knowledge to penetrate to the grass roots, where it becomes part of an action program.

In the fields of health education and physical education, research on motor learning, the relationship of health and physical fitness to academic achievement, movement education, cognitive learning, physiologic changes that occur in the body through exercise, smoking, ecology, and the relationship of mental health and physical activity represent a few examples of research that have or will have a bearing upon programs of health education and physical education throughout the country.

College and university faculties

The leaders in education from the campuses of this nation who serve as consultants, write textbooks, make speeches, and are active in professional associations, help to bring about changes in education in general and in the special fields of health education and physical education.

Social forces

Such social forces in the American culture as the civil rights movement, automation, mass communication, student activism, black studies, sports promotion, and collective bargaining through unions are a few of the movements sweeping the nation that have implications for curricula in schools and colleges. In addition, the social trends of the times involving attitudes toward sex, driving, alcohol, tobacco, and narcotics bring about curricula change. Times change, customs change, the habits of people change, and with such change the role of educational institutions and their responsibilities to their society frequently change.

THE HEALTH EDUCATOR AND PHYSICAL EDUCATOR AND CURRICULUM CHANGE

Since there are so many factors that continually influence curricula, it is important for the health educator and physical educator to assess the recommended changes so that informed and wise decisions may be made. Four questions that administrators and teachers might ask themselves in rationalizing the importance of suggested changes are as follows:

1. *What are the functions of the schools and colleges?* To what extent is the suggested change in conformance with the philosophy and purpose of education in the American society? How will it better help the students?

2. *Am I sufficiently well informed so that I can make an intelligent decision?* Teachers and administrators will need to be knowledgeable about the learning process, the patterns of human growth and development, current program needs, and such matters as the needs and interests of the people in the local community who are served by the educational institution. The responsibility rests with administrators and teachers to be well informed in the areas pertinent to the decisions that need to be made.

3. *How does the change relate to staff, plant, budget, and other important administrative items?* The change must be prac-

tical of implementation and the best use of staff, plant, and other items taken into consideration in making the decision.

4. *What do the experts say?* What is the thinking of professionals who have done research, studied the problem intensively, and tested the proposal on a wide scale? Expert opinion may be of help as an additional source of information for making a wise curriculum decision.

PROCEDURAL CONSIDERATIONS FOR CURRICULUM CHANGE

Curricular revision cannot occur without taking into consideration an investigation into such procedural matters as the following:

1. *Students.* The number of students, their characteristics and needs, and their socioeconomic backgrounds and interests need to be considered prior to initiating any pertinent curriculum change.

2. *Faculty.* The members of the staff play a key role in curricular revision. For example, the attitude of faculty toward change, present teaching loads, comprehension of goals of the school, attitudes toward inclass and out-of-class programs, competencies in areas of curriculum revision, and past training and experience are a few important considerations. Change in curriculum might well mean new members being added to the faculty or a different type of competency being represented on the staff.

3. *Physical plant.* Information in regard to the adequacy of the physical plant for present and future programs must be considered. Information should be available on capabilities and limitations of the present plant. There may be new demands placed upon facilities through a curricular revision that brings about changes in such matters as class size.

4. *Budget.* The financial plan is another important consideration in curriculum change. What will the new program cost? What are the sources of support? Before the faculty expends large amounts of time and effort in a study of curriculum change, there should be a reasonable assurance that proposed changes are economically feasible.

5. *Curriculum.* Since any new curricular proposal is likely to reflect present practices to some degree, it seems logical that the present curriculum needs careful scrutiny to determine what has happened over the years, the degree to which the faculty has brought about change, and the general direction in which the institution is moving.

6. *Administration.* It is important for the faculty to take a hard look at the administrative leadership of the school or college, including the principals, superintendents, deans, and presidents, as well as the boards of education and boards of trustees. The philosophy of the administration and its views toward change should be carefully weighed. Administrators will need to approve budgetary allocations and necessary expenditures as well as, in many cases, pass upon the proposed changes.

PEOPLE INVOLVED IN CURRICULUM DEVELOPMENT

Curriculum planning should be characterized by broad participation on the part of many people. The consideration of administrators, teachers, state groups, students, parents, and other individuals is important.

Administrators

Administrators—whether the college president in the field of higher education, the superintendent of schools or principal of an elementary, middle, junior high, or senior high school, or the chairman or director of the health and physical education department—are key personnel in curriculum planning. These individuals serve as the catalytic forces that set curriculum studies into motion; as the leadership that encourages and stimulates interest in providing better learning experiences for students; as the obstacle clearers who provide the time, place, and materials for doing an effective job; and as the implementors who help to see that the fruits of such studies are actually put into practice.

Teachers

Teachers, because they are the persons representing the grass-roots level of the curriculum enterprise, are the ones who actually know what is feasible and what will or will not work. They mingle daily with the pupils and they play a key role in curriculum planning. In smaller school systems each member of the health education and physical education staff should take part in curriculum planning. In larger school systems volunteers or representatives from the various schools might make up the study group.

The teacher's role in active curriculum development can involve contributing his or her experiences and knowledge and presenting data to support recommendations of desired changes. An effective way to utilize faculty groups is the committee system. Committees can be established for the study of such considerations as school philosophy, specific instructional areas, pertinent case studies, immediate and specific objectives for each grade level, needs of children, student readiness for various activities, experiences to satisfy the needs

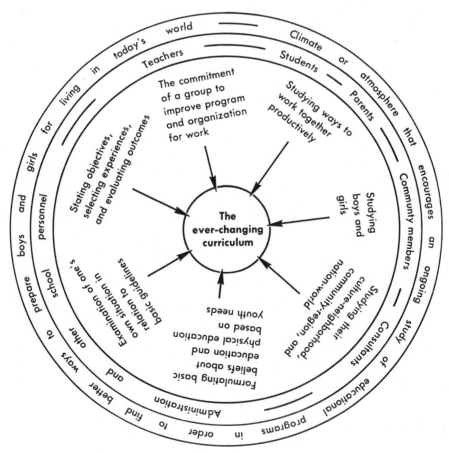

The curriculum merry-go-round. (From Cassidy, R.: Curriculum development in physical education, New York, 1954, Harper & Row, Publishers.)

The curriculum must take into consideration the needs of each student. A camp junior counselor helps a special education (handicapped) student with a bow and arrow. Archery is one of many activities offered the special education students during a week-long summer camp near Ellensburg, Wash., as part of the Broadfront Program.

High school physical education instructor Sherry Ortman checks the stopwatch as a student finishes a jog around the track, as part of the Broadfront Program.

Broadfront Project physical education specialist Clyde Buehler times a sixth-grade student in a 50-yard dash, one of the physical fitness test items administered in the fall and spring.

Junior high school physical education instructor Sue Kennedy readies a student for a leg-lift test, using a dynamometer. The leg-lift is one of the physical fitness tests administered in the fall and spring, as part of the Broadfront Program.

Two students work with the "Exer-Genie" exerciser as part of their developmental physical education program, a part of the Broadfront Program. The developmental program is aimed at improving students with low fitness ability.

of children, means of implementing curriculum changes, and the program of evaluation.

Each teacher in the school should be regarded as a curriculum planner in regard to his or her own instructional offering and, in addition, as a contributor to the total departmental and all-school educational program.

State groups

Throughout most states are located many people and agencies that can help in health and physical education curriculum planning. These include the state department of public instruction or education, the state department of health, colleges and universities, and voluntary health agencies. These

groups may provide curriculum guides, courses of study, advice, teaching aids, other materials, and help that will prove invaluable in curriculum planning.

Students

Students can play a part in curriculum development. As a result of an indication of their thinking in regard to such items as their interests, significant learning experiences, obstacles to desirable learning, and learning experiences recommended in the out-of-class program, guides may be provided that will help in curriculum development. The suggestions and ideas of students can be taken and evaluated by adults, in the light of their own thinking; it may be that the adults will find much merit and substance in the thinking of students.

Parents and community leaders

Discussions with parents and other interested citizens can sometimes help in curriculum development. Since the home plays such an important part in a child's learning and since parents are in essence one-half of the teaching team, there is an opportunity present, in group planning, to communicate to the public what the school is trying to achieve and how it can best be accomplished. Mothers and fathers and other community-minded people can also make significant contributions in evaluating students' behavior in terms of desired outcomes, as established and delineated by the schools.

Other individuals from specialized areas

Curriculum development should utilize the services of individuals who are interested and who can make a worthwhile contribution. For example, such persons as doctors, nurses, and recreation leaders should not be overlooked. It is desirable to look at the curriculum from all sides and all angles, to look at it right side up and upside down, to look at it from the student's as well as the teacher's point of view, and from the parent's as well as the administrator's. Desirable results will flow from a continuous appraisal of the curriculum, made by many persons whose efforts, resources, qualifications, and interests are utilized in a meaningful manner.

STEPS IN CURRICULUM DEVELOPMENT

Krug,* in discussing curriculum development from the general educator's point of view, classifies the following steps involved in curriculum planning: determining the purposes of education, translating the pur-

poses into an all-school program, translating the purposes into specific subject matter areas, providing curriculum guides and instructional aids and materials, and carrying on the teaching-learning process. These appear below in adapted form.

Determining the purposes of education

This step involves studying the various factors that contribute to and result in the formulation of objectives, such as the nature of society, the learning process, and the needs of children and youth. After consideration has been given to such important factors by a faculty or presentations have been made by curriculum specialists, educational objectives can be more clearly formulated.

Translating the purposes into an all-school program

Having determined the objectives of education as a whole and knowing the characteristics of children of different grade levels, those persons developing a curriculum can focus attention on outlining and analyzing broad categories of learning experiences and assigning relative emphases to the various phases of the educational process. The specialized fields of health and physical education should be viewed as part of the total educational program. Consequently, their specific objectives should relate to the overall educational objectives.

Translating the purposes into specific subject matter areas

The next step is to focus attention on subject matter and the activities of the teaching-learning process. Relating this to one phase of the physical education program, for example, it is obvious that the physiologic needs of children would necessitate provision of ample opportunities for a wide range of physical movements involving the large muscles. Growth and development characteristics of children,

---

*Krug, E. A.: Curriculum planning, New York, 1950, Harper & Row, Publishers.

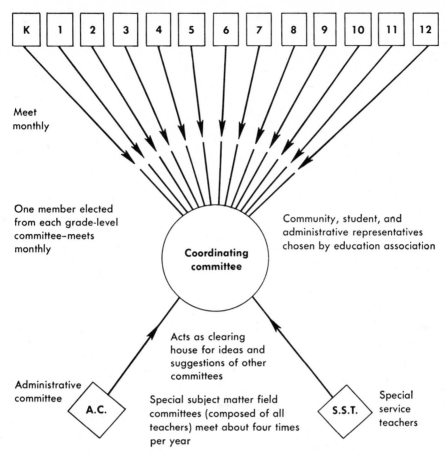

Grade-level committees. Purpose of program is to ascertain the needs of children and to devise means of meeting those needs. (From Oliver, A. I.: Curriculum improvement—a guide to problems, principles, and procedures, New York, 1965, Dodd, Mead & Co.)

physical capacities and abilities, and other considerations also would need to be studied.

Providing curriculum guides and instructional aids and materials

Curriculum guides and instructional aids such as textbooks, visual aids, and other materials are an important consideration in curriculum development. An opportunity is presented here to utilize educationally sound materials that will assist the teacher in exploiting the educational environmental situation most effectively so that desirable learnings will take place and objectives will be accomplished.

Carrying on the teaching-learning process

This step represents the culmination of the curriculum development process—what actually takes place in the classroom, gymnasium, playfield, or swimming pool. The effectiveness with which learning takes place, the aids and materials utilized, the good methods used, and the desirable outcomes accomplished determine the success or the failure of curriculum development.

Cassidy, discussing steps in curriculum development from the point of view of physical education, lists the following as the most effective in curriculum building in the process of cooperative program planning:

1. The commitment of a group of individuals to the importance of the task and organization of the group to work cooperatively in the study and formulation of program experiences which include both methods and materials.
2. Formulation of a philosophy of education and of physical education or a set of guiding principles or basic beliefs which will serve to give direction in program making and in evaluation.
3. In order to complete step 2, the group must study foundation facts concerning the needs of youth—this includes the demands of the culture and the developmental tasks required of youth by that culture.
4. Clarification of the objectives of education and of physical education.
5. Study of one's own students, the school and community situation, relationships, values, attitudes, program, and facilities in the light of stated principles.
6. Statement of objectives based on student needs, consistent with the basic point of view of the group and the situation in which the program must operate.
7. Selection of units of activity or experiences to accomplish these objectives.
8. Development of the materials of instruction—the resource and the teaching units.
9. Development of tools for evaluating the progress toward the stated objectives.
10. Provision for ongoing machinery to assure the continuance of such study.*

A CONCEPTUAL APPROACH TO PHYSICAL EDUCATION

The goal of education is to help boys and girls to become mature adults, possess ability to make wise decisions, and be capable of intelligent self-direction.

Physical education, as a part of education, should provide each boy and girl with carefully planned experiences that result in knowledge about the value of physical activity, essential motor skills, strength, stamina, and other essential physical characteristics and about the social qualities that make for effective citizenship.

---

*Cassidy, R.: Curriculum development in physical education, New York, 1954, Harper & Row, Publishers, pp. 12-14.

Over the years physical educators in many of our schools have attempted to achieve these goals in a dedicated and conscientious manner. However, most physical educators will agree there is still much room for improvement. Those persons who advocate change cite educational systems where there is lack of progression, sequential treatment of subject matter, and an orderly developmental pattern for teaching motor skills. Furthermore, they say, physical education curricula vary from school to school and state to state without any degree of uniformity. As a result of these conditions, they lament, students are not becoming as physically educated as they could be, and, also, physical education is not gaining the respectability in the educational process it justly deserves.

A new development that has won the acclaim of educators in recent years is the concept approach to curriculum planning. This innovation may have possibilities for helping physical education to achieve a more important and respected place in the schools of this nation.

Each subject matter field has objectives toward which they teach and that represent the worth of the field for the students. Physical education has traditionally advocated the four objectives of organic development, neuromuscular development, mental development, and social development. These goals have proved valuable as targets toward which both the teacher and student strive. At the same time, they are rather general in nature and may not provide the best basis for the most effective structural organization of physical education.

The student should be aware of the general objectives of physical education but, in addition, as a result of his school experiences, should be sensitive to, understand, and know the framework that constitutes the field of physical education. He should be aware of the unity, the wholeness, and the interrelatedness of the many activities in which he engages from kindergarten through college. He should even think at times as a physical educator might think, particularly from the standpoint of recognizing the importance and value of such course experiences to human beings. He should understand what constitutes the master plan of education and the structure of physical education as it fits into this master plan.

In creating this structure of physical education, one might draw an analogy between our field and the construction of a house. Just as there are key pillars and beams that give the house form and support, so the key unifying elements within physical education that give it a strong foundational framework and hold it together as a valuable educational experience for every boy and girl should be identified. These unifying threads would tie together the various parts of the discipline into a meaningful and cohesive learning package.

These unifying threads would be the *concepts* and, as such, would represent the basic structure of physical education in the school program. They would be the *key ideas, principles, skills, values,* or *attitudes* that represent points upon which we as physical educators should focus our efforts throughout the school life of the child. They would be part of both the teacher's and student's thinking and would range from very simple ideas to high-level abstractions. They would start with simple, elementary, fundamental experiences and in a sequential, progressive, and developmental pattern gain depth and comprehensiveness over the years as schooling progresses and the student matures. They would as unifying threads define the domain of physical education.

Concepts in physical education would not be memorized by the students. Rather, they would be ideas—analytic generalizations that would emerge and be understood by the student as a result of his school experiences in physical education. They would also provide him with a reservoir of information, skills, and understandings that would help him to meet new problems and situations.

The concepts, of course, would need to be carefully selected according to acceptable criteria and be scientifically sound. Furthermore, after the concepts had been identified, there would be need for extensive testing of their validity by many experts, including teachers in the field and specialists in curriculum development.

To implement the concepts within the physical education structure, there would be a need to delineate the identified concepts into meaningful units and topics that would be progressive in nature and reinforce the concepts that had been identified. The subdivisions of concepts in the structure would represent basic elements needed to develop a meaningful course of study and bring about desirable behavior. Furthermore, they would emanate and flow from the key concepts and would help to give greater meaning and understanding to them. As the conceptual, unifying threads were developed at each ascending grade and educational level, the student would be provided with new challenges, where the information, skills, and understanding he has acquired could be applied. The result would be that finally the student would reach a point where he could on his own arrive at valid answers and make wise decisions in the area of physical education.

As a result of the concept approach, students would have a greater mastery of the field of physical education, increased understanding and power in dealing with problems related to their physical self that are new and unfamiliar, and motivation to want to become physically educated in the true sense of the term. The approach would provide a stable system of knowledge and provide guideposts for thinking intelligently about physical education.

The concept approach would have par-

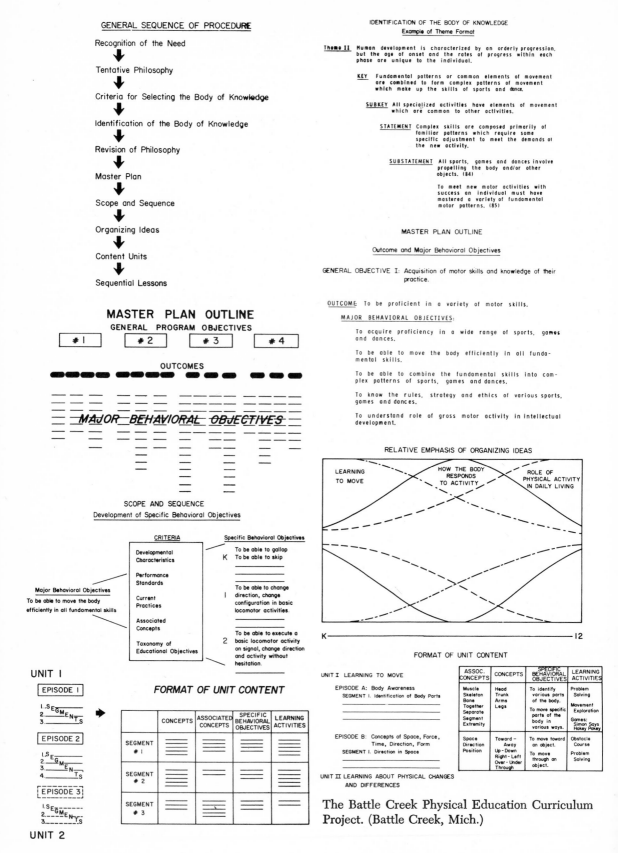

The Battle Creek Physical Education Curriculum Project. (Battle Creek, Mich.)

ticular value to physical education because of such things as the great breadth of skills, knowledge, and values that make up this field of endeavor. It would provide a logical and systematic means for identifying among the many elements those that give form and structure to the type of physical education program professionals want taught in schools. The identified concepts would have permanence, and as the explosion of knowledge takes place in the years ahead through the efforts of our scholarly researchers, this new information can become part of the structure, wherever applicable. Finally, the concept approach would be readily adaptable to individual differences that exist among students as well as sufficiently flexible to provide for the many geographic types of facilities and other factors that differentiate one community or school from another.

Some physical educators might say that the subject matter, skills, and other elements of physical education are the same under the concept approach as under the traditional approach. It may be that the facts will be the same in some cases but the approach will be different. For example, in the new mathematics, as developed by one professional group in grade nine, there is still concentration upon algebra, but the emphasis is not on the solving of algebraic equations but, instead, on the behavior of numbers—a verbalization of concepts.

Under the traditional approach, the organization of courses involved topics and activities, but without sufficient regard to the relationship of the topic and activity to what had gone on previously for the student and what lies ahead. This new method would still discuss topics and conduct activities, but topics and activities would be related to key concepts that the topic and activity are designed to elaborate upon, contribute more understanding, and make the area of learning more meaningful in the life of the student.

Physical education needs a curriculum study with careful consideration being given to the concept approach. At a time when the curriculum reform movement is sweeping the nation and when there already is a new mathematics, a new physics, a new English, and a new social studies, physical education can no longer be apathetic about what it teaches and how it teaches. The concept approach is one that should be very carefully weighed for the *new physical education*.

CURRICULUM DEVELOPMENT IN PRACTICE

A noteworthy example of practical curriculum planning is the work of leaders in the Columbus, Ohio, public schools,* who developed a curriculum guide for a school health science course. The procedures for curriculum development were formulated by a committee consisting of a supervisor of health education, six health teachers, two advisory committee members, a school physician, and a director of public information. This committee consulted with curriculum authorities in health education and read literature on curriculum research. The plan involved the following eight-point process:

1. *Study of the existing program.* A review of course offerings, teaching guides, textbooks, and other curriculum materials was made.
2. *Collection and review of pertinent literature.* Thirty cities, counties, states, and professional health associations were canvassed and thirty health textbooks reviewed.
3. *Aims and objectives of guide determined.* The basic philosophy of health education as viewed by the committee was formulated.

---

*Cauffman, J. G.: How to develop a curriculum guide for a school health science course, Journal of Health, Physical Education, and Recreation 33:19, 1962.

4. *Needs and interests identified.* The needs and interests of the students who would represent the consumer of the teaching were studied.

5. *Judgments obtained from selected individuals.* The thinking of administrators, health teachers, nurses, counselors, parents, and health authorities was sought on problem areas of health education.

6. *Available resources screened.* Resources within the school system, within the community, and out-of-town resources were surveyed relating to selected health problem areas and what was available to help in solving problems.

7. *The organization of resource units.* After problem areas had been identified and resources screened, resource units were developed for teaching.

8. *Experimental use of guide.* The guide was used experimentally for 2 years in the Columbus schools. Evaluations were done and changes made where it was thought they were needed.

An example of one community of more than 50,000 people that made a curriculum study is White Plains, New York. The methods and materials utilized by this community have been described elsewhere* and may be of help to other communities or school districts.

The study was initiated by the director of health and physical education for the public schools after a discussion with several faculty members. The board of education allocated $750 for the study, and these funds enabled the staff to secure, as a consultant, a university professor who was well versed in the field of physical education.

---

*Bucher, C. A., Koenig, C., and Barnhard, M.: Methods and materials for secondary school physical education, St. Louis, 1970, The C. V. Mosby Co.

The consultant and the director prepared the outline for the study group that consisted of the physical education staff. The board of education allowed the experience to be credited toward inservice education credit that was recognized on the salary increment scale. The workshop experience required that staff members meet one evening each week as a group. All administrative arrangements were handled by the director and leader. During the actual deliberations, however, the director remained in the background, allowing the staff to act on its own.

The physical education staff was divided into committees according to school level —elementary, junior high school, and senior high school. Each committee prepared its recommendations, worked with the study leader, and presented its findings to the staff as a whole. The entire faculty discussed and made suggestions to each committee. In the light of these deliberations each group then reworked its recommendations into final form.

The curriculum guide that was developed . as a result of these deliberations contains the following:

1. A general statement of philosophy in regard to the curriculum guide
2. A statement of objectives for each educational level
3. A grouping of activities to meet objectives
4. The time requirement for each grade
5. The percentage of total time used for each grade activity at each grade level
6. A statement on evaluation—its purposes and its use as a basis for grading
7. A cumulative record card

The White Plains curriculum guide placed the physical education program in a more favorable light among the students, administrators, and teachers and in the community. Most important, it helped to ensure that the right experiences were provided each school child as part of his or her education.

EVALUATION OF THE CURRICULUM

Once a curriculum has been developed, evaluation is essential. The major purpose of such an evaluation is to determine the extent to which the experiences provided are reflected in desirable learnings on the part of the students. Unless the educational outcomes are desirable and are acceptable to educators, the curriculum cannot be considered successful. Saylor and Alexander have pointed out essential characteristics of an evaluation program:

1. The integral relationship of curriculum planning and evaluation should be clearly understood by all persons who participate in planning the school program.
2. Changes in the procedure of curriculum planning and in over-all curriculum plans should be based on evaluative evidence.
3. The planning of learning experiences for all learning groups should include provisions for evaluation by the groups and their teachers of the experiences.
4. A systematic set of procedures for securing evaluative evidence should be in operation.
5. These procedures should be based on values agreed upon by all who participate in curriculum planning.
6. Evidence should be secured regarding (a) the progress of pupils during the period concerned toward specific curriculum goals; (b) the progress of pupils after completing phases of the curriculum; (c) the opinions of parents and teachers bearing on curriculum planning.*

Curriculum evaluation to date has used four means of determining whether or not a new program has worth.† One method is through observations of students who have been exposed to the new program and the progress they have made. A second method is systematic questioning of teachers and students involved in the program. A third procedure involves testing of students periodically to determine their progress. A fourth method is the comparative testing of students under the "new" and under the "old" programs to determine progress under each.

Suggested outline

A score card or outline by which the curriculum of any school system may be checked has been developed by the Bureau of Curriculum Research of Teachers College, Columbia University. The suggested outline for evaluation follows:

A. Recognition of Basic Educational Objectives
   1. General aims or objectives
   2. Statement of objectives or aims
   3. Validity (soundness, worth) of the stated and implied objectives
   4. Degree in which objectives have been consistently carried out in the selection and organization of subject matter and methods suggested
B. What to Teach—Organization of Subject Matter
   1. Nature of subject matter
   2. Major emphasis
   3. Form of development of subjects
   4. Use made of scientific studies in selection and organization of subject matter
C. Recognition of, and Adaptation to, Pupil Needs
   1. Effective utilization of pupils' experiences
   2. Course of study so organized as to provide for individual differences in children's interests and abilities
   3. Gradation of material on basis of pupils needs for immediate use
   4. Regard for relative value of topics within a subject
   5. Suggested use of varied forms of activities
   6. Use made of scientific studies in provision for pupil needs
D. Adaptation to Teacher Needs—Suggestions as to Methods and Materials
   1. Respect for the judgment and initiative of the teacher
   2. Suggestions for correlations between subjects

---

*Saylor, J. G., and Alexander, W. M.: Curriculum planning for better teaching and learning, New York, 1954, Holt, Rinehart & Winston, Inc., p. 607.

†Goodlad, J. I.: School curriculum in the United States, New York, 1964, The Fund for the Advancement of Education, p. 59.

3. Definite suggestions for work dealing with materials and topics of local interest
4. Illustrative and type lessons given
5. Suggested standards for checking results of teaching
6. Reference to proper use of maps
7. Use of scientific studies in determining methods and materials
8. References, basic and supplemental, for children

E. Course of Study Itself—Mechanical Make-up
1. Clearness and conciseness
2. Proper methods of emphasizing important phases of work
3. Attractiveness, useableness
4. Convenience
5. Ease of revision
6. Economy of space and expense*

PRINCIPLES TO CONSIDER IN CURRICULUM DEVELOPMENT

In summary, it can be pointed out that although curriculum development will vary from school to school and from community to community, some general principles are applicable to all situations:

1. Learning experiences should be selected and developed that will be most helpful in achieving educational outcomes.

2. Curriculum development is a continuous effort rather than one that is accomplished at periodic intervals.

3. The leadership in curriculum development rests primarily with the administration and supervisory staffs.

4. The administration should utilize (wherever possible and practicable) the services of teachers, laymen, students, state consultants, and other persons who can contribute to the development of the best curriculum possible. The work should not, however, place an unreasonable demand on any person's time and effort.

5. Curriculum development is dependent upon a thorough knowledge of the needs and characteristics, developmental

levels, capacities, and maturity levels of the students, as well as an understanding of the environments in which those students live.

6. Curriculum development should permit teachers to exploit sound principles of learning in the selection and development of learning experiences.

7. Curriculum development should take into account out-of-school learning experiences and integrate them with school experiences.

8. The main value of curriculum development is determined by the degree of improved instruction that results.

EDUCATIONAL INNOVATIONS AFFECTING CURRICULUM DEVELOPMENT

There are many new developments that affect the curriculum, both from the standpoint of administrative innovations that affect school organization and scheduling and what is taught and from the standpoint of new teaching techniques that influence how the subject matter is taught and the degree to which learning takes place.

Teaching machines, language laboratories, educational television, tape recorders, super-8 films, and opaque projectors are affecting school programs. Too few teachers and administrators are familiar with the "new" media that have come not from educators themselves but from individuals with vision and creativeness outside the schools. Educators need to get away from the routine administrative detail and traditional ways of teaching, at least to the point where they are familiar with and know the advantage of new ways of doing things. Although nothing has been developed as a substitute for sound teacher-student relationships, much has been introduced that can make this relationship more meaningful and productive. With the great expansion in school enrollments, teacher shortages, and international em-

*Reeder, W. G.: The fundamentals of public school administration, New York, 1958, The Macmillan Co., pp. 497-499.

phasis, innovations need to be evaluated for their possible use in the classroom.

Constant evaluation is, of course, necessary. The innovation must stand the test of making it possible to have higher quality education, including more individualized instruction, better learning, and freedom for the teacher to do more important work.

A few of the innovations include flexible school structures, newer audiovisual aids, programmed learning, ungraded classes, team teaching, teacher aids, hidden talent projects, paperbacks and other variations in text materials, automated data processing, language laboratories, and new approaches to grouping. Discussed in this chapter are selected administrative innovations and also some new teaching innovations with which each health educator and physical educator should be familiar.

Administrative innovations affecting curriculum development

Administrative innovations affecting curriculum planning include flexible scheduling, nongraded schools, middle school, and year-round school.

Flexible scheduling. Flexible scheduling, sometimes called modular scheduling because of the time units involved—most frequently about 20 minutes each—is a term used to describe a school schedule in which classes do not meet for the same length of time each day. Flexible scheduling uses blocks of time to build periods of different length. For example, one module might be 20 minutes in length, a double module would be 40 minutes, a triple module would be 60 minutes, and a quadruple module would be 80 minutes. Time is left between each module for purposes of organization of classes.

One advantage of flexible scheduling over the traditional pattern of fixed scheduling, or the same allotment of time per day to a subject, is that flexible scheduling enables subjects to have varying times for instruction. For example, teachers say that usually more time is necessary in a science laboratory than for instruction in a foreign language newly introduced to students. It has been pointed out that a foreign language can be most effectively taught in shorter time periods at more frequent intervals. Flexible scheduling also provides more instructional time, more opportunity for small group instruction, and less time in study halls where learning time is not always put to the best use. With flexible scheduling it is possible to have subject matter and courses presented under optimum conditions, on an individual basis, and in smaller or larger groups, as best meets the needs of the subject and teacher. Flexible scheduling also helps the teacher by permitting more time for instruction.

It can no longer be assumed that all subject matter and all courses should be taught in the same unit of time to the same number of students. New research shows that some subjects are taught best in shorter periods of time, given more frequently, and with a smaller group of students.

The use of the computer has made flexible scheduling a reality. The principal can tell a 707 computer how many teachers he has, what courses they can teach, how many students there are, and what courses each student wants to take. Within 60 minutes the answers are provided in the form of a complete master schedule and individual schedules for each student enrolled.

Operation G.A.S.P. (Generalized Academic Simulation Programs) is one example of flexible scheduling. It was developed at the Massachusetts Institute of Technology under a grant from the Ford Foundation's Education Facilities Laboratories. As a result of G.A.S.P., time and money have been saved, flexibility in schools has been provided, and preplanning space utilization before construction blueprints are made is much more accurate and meaningful.

Form No. 1

LESSON JOB ORDER

Date needed _____

From _____
    Teacher   Subject

Total number of modules in group	Number of modules needed	Number of groups	Class size request	Module request	Room request	Additional teacher	Method of instruction (large group, small group, individual study group, etc.)

Bulletin notice: _____

_____

Approved _____
        Team leader   Date

Lesson job order for flexible scheduling. (Courtesy Gardner Swenson, Principal, Brookhurst Junior High School, Anaheim Union High School District, Anaheim, Calif.)

One example of a school district where flexible scheduling is carried out is the Anaheim Union High School District in Anaheim, California (see accompanying illustrations). It has utilized the Brookhurst Plan, encompassing both team teaching and flexible scheduling. Some of the characteristics of this plan are that the faculty is organized into teams in each subject matter area, teachers submit daily job orders that include number of students desired in a group, length of time needed, facilities required, and method of instruction to be used. A master schedule is developed from the job orders, and students schedule a 14-modular day using the master schedule as a guide. The student's schedule becomes operational 3 days after the construction of the master schedule, a procedure that is completed each day throughout the year. The method of instruction is determined according to the following criteria: (1) When facts and data are presented, large group instruction is utilized. (2) When it is desired to use information presented in large group discussion as a means of developing insight and effectively using the information, small group discussion is scheduled. (3) When the goal is to help students develop study habits, use research techniques effectively, and develop self-direction, independent study is utilized.

Nongraded school. The practice of grouping students into grades according to chronologic age has been a part of American education for more than 100 years. However, this procedure has been challenged along the way. Dr. Francis W. Parker, as early as 1870, and John Dewey, in the 1930's, raised questions about this method of grouping boys and girls. Today, it is not only being questioned but the nongraded school has also become a reality in

The keysort card used in flexible scheduling at Anaheim, Calif. This is the student schedule. There are four parts to the keysort card: the original, which after being processed, becomes the student's copy; the attendance ticket section, made up of two sheets with four sections to each sheet, which goes to the teacher; and the last copy, which is used by the attendance officer. The card is coded so that specific notches may be made, indicating what has been printed on the card. Based upon achievement and ability, teacher's recommendation, as well as counselor's recommendations, the student's card is notched to indicate his class section in the required courses. The grooves on the top of the card indicate the fourteen modules of the school day. They are used in the scheduling process by the office in eliminating conflicts of time. (Courtesy Gardner Swenson, Principal, Brookhurst Junior High School, Anaheim Union High School District, Anaheim, Calif.)

many school districts from coast to coast. It is being used most extensively at the elementary level, but it finds use at the secondary level as well.

The dissatisfaction with the grouping of children according to chronologic age came about because it was thought to prevent the academic progress of many youngsters. The graded school was not in harmony with modern research and theory on human behavior and child development. Students vary in readiness to learn, ability, social and mental development, home environments, rate of achievement, and other similar factors. Studies show sharp differences in academic achievement among children entering the first grade and also in any one grade. They also show sharp differences in both physical and social development.

In the nongraded school children are grouped on the basis of age, abilities, and other pertinent factors essential to success in school, and then the child is permitted to advance at his own speed. Continuous pupil progress becomes the policy with grade names and nonpromotion policies eliminated. The chonrologic age system of grouping and promotion is abandoned and a new plan established that calls for four areas each with a 3-year span, including primary, intermediate, junior high school, and senior high school. Within each area the student may move freely and progress as rapidly as he can master the subject matter and requirements. Various phases in each 3-year span are established through which the student may move and progress. In one high school in Florida, for example, there are five phases in each subject area: (1) remedial program, (2) basic skills, (3) intermediate program for students seeking an average education, (4) depth study for students desiring depth in education, and (5) independent study and research. Students are placed in the proper phase for each subject according to the results achieved on standard achieve-

ment tests and teacher evaluations. There are opportunities for regular appraisals and frequent reclassification.

For the nongraded school to be a success there must be a cooperative and sympathetic faculty, good guidance and counseling program, and parental support. Team teaching and both large and small group instruction are also part of the nongraded program.

There are many problems associated with the nongraded schools and also many advantages. Before accepting the nongraded concept wholeheartedly, a school needs to determine how much a plan affects the child, the teachers, and the curriculum.

Physical educators and health educators must carefully weigh the value of the nongraded school as it relates to their fields of specialization. They must decide its value as it relates to skill, organic, social, and mental development. They need to ask such questions as: How should a student be scheduled in advanced skills—with his own age group or with older groups? How should a student be classified in the nongraded school where each of the objectives—social, emotional, and mental development—is a determining factor?

Middle school. The question as to what is the most desirable pattern of grade organization is the topic of many discussions among school administrators, teachers, and the lay public. One survey of 366 unified school systems with pupil enrollment of 12,000 or more, conducted by the Educational Research Service, showed that 71% of these school systems were organized on the 6-3-3 plan, 10% on the 8-4 organization, and 6% on a 6-2-4 pattern. Other patterns include 7-5, 6-6, 5-3-4, and 7-2-3.

The pattern of organization being considered by many school systems today is the middle school concept. Most simply, a middle school is for boys and girls between the elementary and high school years—grades six, seven, eight, and sometimes five. New York City, for example, the nation's largest school system, has middle schools grouped by grades five to eight or six to eight. The secondary schools have become 4-year comprehensive high schools. Other places that are embarked on the middle school pattern are Bridgewater, Massachusetts; Bedford Public Schools in Mount Kisco, New York; Sarasota County, Florida; Saginaw, Michigan; Easton, Connecticut; and Independence, Ohio.

Some of the reasons for the middle school concept are as follows:

1. There is an opportunity for more departmentalization than found in the elementary schools but less than found in the high schools, especially in such fields as science, mathematics, art, and music.

2. There is an opportunity for greater stimulation of students and better facilities and equipment, such as laboratories and shops.

3. There is an opportunity for special teachers and special programs essential for children passing through the early adolescent period.

4. Students today have subjects that were taught much later in the school program years ago. For example, in terms of the required curriculum, the fourth grader today is in advance of the sixth grader years ago. Therefore, the middle school concept is applicable to the present educational era.

5. There is a better opportunity for student grouping and meeting individual differences.

6. There is a better opportunity for guidance services to be extended into the lower grades.

7. There is better opportunity for a more personalized approach than is possible under other types of organization.

8. The ninth grade youngsters are more mature and can fit into the high school program, permitting them to take advanced courses.

9. There is better opportunity for a gradual change from self-sustained classroom to complete departmentalization.

Some of the reasons against the middle school are as follows:

1. There is lack of evidence to support its value because of its relative newness.

2. There are social adjustment problems in placing ninth graders with twelfth graders.

3. Youngsters in the middle school will be pushed too hard academically and socially.

4. Administrative techniques and procedures would need to be altered.

An example of the middle school in operation is the Saginaw Township Community Schools in Saginaw, Michigan. In Saginaw the administrative plan includes the neighborhood school (grades one to four), the middle schools (grades five to eight), and the community high school (grades nine to twelve).

Students at the middle school have a self-contained classroom environment in the fifth grade, where there is an educational climate that provides the needed security with one base and one teacher but at the same time provides for a more open school plan in which there is not complete isolation between fifth-grade classrooms. Also, fifth graders begin to learn how to operate in a more flexible pattern utilized in the succeeding grades.

The sixth grade provides for a marked transition that involves a departure from the self-contained classroom, with the teachers working in informal teams, although the student spends most of his time with one teacher in one classroom. Students assume more responsibility for their own and each other's welfare and become acquainted with several teachers and different groups of children.

In the seventh and eighth grades, students spend two periods of each school day in their homerooms but the rest of the time is spent in specialized classrooms receiving instruction from specialists in

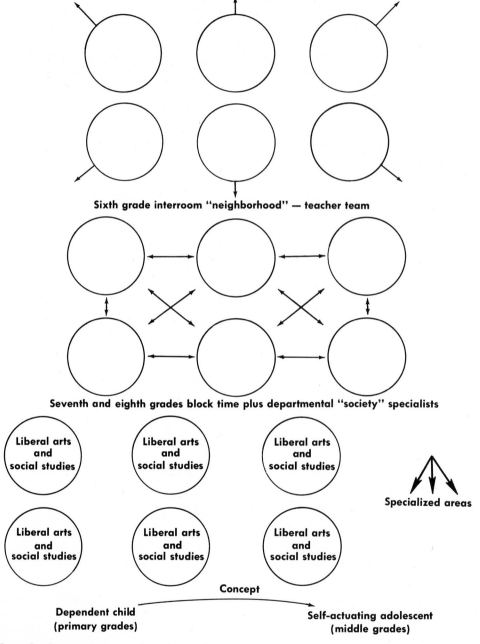

Middle school concepts—graphic representation. (Courtesy Saginaw Township Community Schools, Saginaw, Mich.)

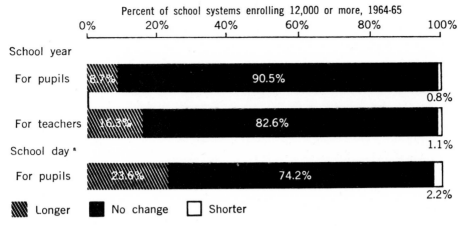

Percent of school systems enrolling 12,000 or more, 1964-65

School year

For pupils — 8.7% / 90.5% / 0.8%

For teachers — 16.3% / 82.6% / 1.1%

School day *

For pupils — 23.6% / 74.2% / 2.2%

▨ Longer   ■ No change   ☐ Shorter

* Information not available on changes in length of teachers' day.

Lengthening the school year and school day. Change during 1962 to 1967. (From NEA Research Bulletin **43**:105, 1965.)

such areas as physical education, music, arts, mathematics, and science. Students are encouraged to do more independent study in seventh and eighth grades. (See accompanying graphic representation.)

Health and physical educators will want to evaluate the middle school concept in respect to their special fields. It has many implications for the utilization of specialists, the presentation of skills and subject matter, and the organization of intramural and extramural athletic activities.

Year-round school. The need for a year-round school program is being increasingly heard whenever educational topics are discussed. Such developments as the child's becoming an economic liability in our modern industrial society, the great technologic advance that has resulted in a raising of the minimal requirements for vocational adequacy, the knowledge explosion, and the taking over of many functions of the home by other agencies and institutions have resulted in many people asking the question—why not have the children in school for a longer period of time?

The year-round school also makes sense to some educators because the school plant is idle during the summer months, although

costs for administration, insurance, and capital outlay remain constant. Also, many school-age children do not have constructive programs for the summer months, and teachers would be available in many cases.

Some of the plans suggested for extending the school year include the staggered quarter plan, in which the calendar year is divided into four quarters with pupils attending three of four quarters and having a vacation the fourth quarter. Teachers could be hired for either three or four quarters.

A second suggestion is the 48-week school year, which would be divided into four 12-week periods, with the remaining 4 weeks being used for vacation purposes. Teachers would be employed on a 12-month basis.

A third suggestion would be the voluntary summer program that students could attend if they so desired for purposes of remedial work, avocational, recreational, and enrichment type courses.

The fourth suggestion is the summer program for professional personnel plan. Under this arrangement teachers would be employed on a 12-month basis and would work 48 weeks and have a 4-week vacation. The students would go to school from

36 to 40 weeks. Teachers would spend the other weeks working on curriculum and instructional planning.

Health educators and physical educators should study the year-round school patterns and draw implications for their special fields. If school were conducted on a year-round basis, many of the objectives health and physical educators seek could be accomplished in a much better way. There would be more time for skill teaching. There could be greater relief from academic pressures, and healthful habits could be better encouraged and implemented.

New developments affecting methods and techniques of teaching

In recent years new approaches to the presentation of subject matter and other educational experiences have gained widespread recognition. These new innovations have implications—for the teacher, by utilizing special talents and saving time, and for the student, by promoting learning and recognizing individual differences and abilities. A few of the innovations that have special implications for health education and physical education are briefly cited here since they are of concern to all teachers, administrators, and leaders in these special fields.

Creativity. Creativity is a process whereby the student or individual formulates and produces new ideas, patterns of thinking, products, or something entirely new. Since creativity is designed to help each person reach his fullest development, it should be encouraged on the part of students and teachers. The teacher is a very important factor in encouraging creativity among students. By being interested in seeking new and better ways of creativeness among her students, she recognizes its value and nurtures it constantly.

Environment also plays an important part in creativity. The school must be characterized by a congenial and friendly atmosphere. Freedom must be afforded the student since creativity does not occur during a particular period or time of day. Also, the physical environment should be conducive to creativity by being cheerful, colorful, and challenging.

Courses in health education and physical education should encourage boys and girls to explore, investigate, express themselves, and experiment. Each student should be recognized for his uniqueness. Movement education, gymnastics, dance, and many other activities in physical education, as well as such experiences as problem-solving in health education, offer opportunities for creativity.

Teachers of health education and physical education should try to think up new and different approaches to subject matter presentation. By being creative in the teaching process itself, the instructor may stimulate new interests among the students in the subject matter being taught and the experiences being provided.

Movement education. Movement education is primarily concerned with the teaching of physical education through a sound understanding and application of the basic and scientific fundamentals of movement. Movement education had its origin in England, where Rudolf Laban gave it considerable thought, emphasis, and impetus. It can be the basis for teaching all forms of physical activity.

Movement education is based upon the concept that movement involves time, space, force, and flow. All sports and activities in the physical education program require basic movements for accomplishment. The student attempts to determine what he can achieve through problem-solving situations. Students try to discover why they move in a particular way, how they move differently than other persons, where they may move, and with what and with whom they may move. They become aware of body movements and how they affect not only the activities in physical education but also daily living.

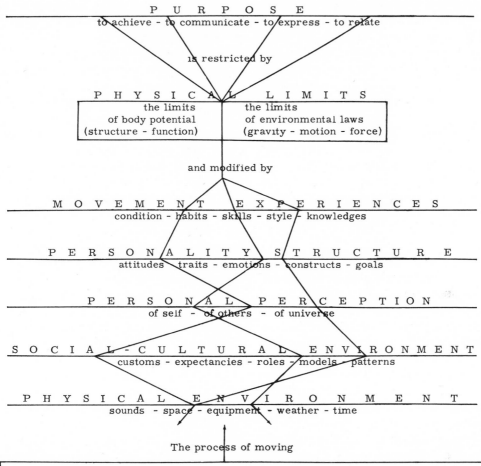

Human movement is initiated by

P U R P O S E
to achieve - to communicate - to express - to relate

is restricted by

P H Y S I C A L L I M I T S

the limits of body potential (structure - function)	the limits of environmental laws (gravity - motion - force)

and modified by

M O V E M E N T E X P E R I E N C E S
condition - habits - skills - style - knowledges

P E R S O N A L I T Y S T R U C T U R E
attitudes - traits - emotions - constructs - goals

P E R S O N A L P E R C E P T I O N
of self - of others - of universe

S O C I A L - C U L T U R A L E N V I R O N M E N T
customs - expectancies - roles - models - patterns

P H Y S I C A L E N V I R O N M E N T
sounds - space - equipment - weather - time

The process of moving

Occurs through space, in time, with quality (level-tempo-force). Can be described in terms of its components-dimensions, basic movements, fundamental skills; its design-patterns and style. Can be used to control equilibrium and to give and receive impetus. May or may not be efficient in terms of mechanics and purpose. Is perceived variantly with occurrence, the mover, and observers.

and
IS A MODIFIER OF ITS OWN DETERMINANTS

Movement education—an approach to the study of observable movement. (From Abernathy, R., and Waltz, M.: Toward a discipline: first steps first, Quest, monograph II, p. 3, April, 1964.)

Movement education may be utilized in physical education in different ways. In some cases it represents a different and separate course, whereas in other situations it may represent the basic philosophy underlying the entire program.

Team teaching. Team teaching usually refers to an arrangement in which two or more teachers cooperatively work together in planning, instructing, and evaluating one or more class groups so as to utilize the special competencies and qualifications of the team members. In some team teaching projects, the team is made up of two or more experienced and inexperienced teachers, a student teacher, a master teacher, teacher aids, consultants, and secretary.

The purpose of team teaching is to involve the talents of many teachers and specialties. As a team they formulate the program of study and plan a schedule that consists of lecture sessions for large groups of students, small study group classes for practice, review, and discussion, and independent study time or individual projects to meet the individual needs and interests of students. A student might find himself following a schedule that consisted of 40% of his time in large group instruction, 40% in smaller group discussions, and 20% in individual study or research.

Team teaching in essence means that planning is done by a team, the material is presented by a team, and the educational experiences are evaluated by a team. Some obvious advantages of team teaching are that it utilizes a teacher's talents to best advantage, individual differences are better realized, duplication of effort is avoided, and pupil self-responsibility is developed.

Educational television. Teaching with the aid of television has been introduced into health and physical education programs with considerable success. Areas of first aid and instruction in many health problems and various forms of physical activities have been successfully brought to large groups viewing televised lectures or demonstrations by specialists. Furthermore, such a technique has also permitted questions and answers on the part of students, with the entire audience benefiting from such an exchange.

One of the most impressive studies in educational television was performed by the Board of Education, Washington County, Hagerstown, Maryland, where this medium was used on a closed-circuit basis for 8 years. The results showed that pupil achievement was enhanced, the teacher's professional growth was accelerated, the curriculum was enriched and

upgraded more readily, more pupils were reached, and the team teaching concept with the studio teacher and the classroom teacher was enhanced.

Programmed instruction. Programmed instruction was introduced by B. F. Skinner, a psychologist at Harvard. It is a process that arranges materials to be learned in a series of small steps designed to help the student educate himself by progressing from what he actually knows to areas of learning that are new and more complex. The student is usually checked as he progresses to determine his mastery of the material to be learned. If he is successful, he proceeds to the next material, but if he is not correct, he has to go back and review the material that he missed. The learning program represents an orderly, sequential route to the mastery of the subject.

Programs are found in two major forms —the teaching machine and the programmed textbook. However, both forms operate on the basic principles outlined in the previous paragraph. Both techniques have proved of value in supplementing classwork and in meeting individual differences.

The fields of health education and physical education are fertile territory for programmed instruction. New materials are starting to appear on the market for programmed teaching. Much more will be available in the months and years ahead. Obvious advantages to such teaching are that students will be able to learn much more on their own outside of class, the student who is absent because of illness will have a medium for making up what has been missed, and large classes may be broken down, with some of the students doing programmed instruction.

RESEARCH IN HEALTH EDUCATION AND PHYSICAL EDUCATION

There is an urgent need to advance the frontiers of knowledge in the fields of health education and physical education.

There have been too many unsupported claims for the value of physical education and health in education. There is a need to determine their worth through valid research findings—basic research that will advance knowledge and also applied research that will determine the best ways of applying this knowledge to these fields of endeavor.

There are many questions left unanswered. A few problems that need considerable investigation include the following: Why do school accidents happen? Why are health practices not followed? How much can retarded children learn? What is the value of programmed learning materials? What are the attitudes toward physical education? What should be the place of international studies in education? What are the biomechanics of human movement? What do we know about exercise physiology? What is the scientific basis for human movement? What is the relationship of personality development to motor performance? What is the relationship of scholastic achievement to physical fitness? What are the best ways to develop creativity? What social changes take place through outdoor education and camping? What is the therapeutic value of recreational activity? What are the qualities of leadership needed for working with mentally disturbed patients?

Research can help physical education and health to develop a better understanding as to the accepted body of knowledge, skills, attitudes, and practices that should be imparted through educational means and how they can best be transmitted. In so doing the status of these professions will be enhanced.

Graduate schools in particular should sponsor and encourage research. They should extend a student's range of knowledge and understanding of his field of special interest, as well as provide opportunities to engage in creative research.

There is a need for effective channels for the communication of research findings to the practitioners in the field. The *Research Quarterly* of the American Association for Health, Physical Education, and Recreation is one good outlet but offers an opportunity for only comparatively few research studies. One estimate points out that the field of medicine has more than 400 journals published monthly, as well as some published weekly, such as the *Journal of the American Medical Association.*

There is a need for the professions of health, physical education, and recreation to more clearly delineate the answers to such questions as the following:

1. What areas need research in health, physical education, and recreation?
2. What questions does research raise about present programs in health, physical education, and recreation?
3. How can research findings be disseminated and used most effectively in our professional programs?
4. What constitutes a desirable program of research for health, physical education, and recreation?
5. What are some of the problems concerning financing, misconceptions, and poor techniques in research in the professional fields of health and physical education?

STATE AND FEDERAL LEGISLATION—FINANCIAL AID TO EDUCATION PROGRAMS

State and federal legislation, philanthropic foundations, and other agencies are becoming increasingly interested in education and are providing financial help to schools and colleges.

Education and the pursuit of learning are becoming a major point of emphasis in the American culture. At the turn of the century the population was approximately 76 million and only about 6% of the nation's 17 year olds graduated from high school, and only approximately 4% of the college-age boys and girls went to college. Today, better than 70% of the 17 year olds are graduating from high school and about 30% of the college-age population is on campus. The bill for education is more than $50 billion a year and going up. There are approximately 125,000 schools, 100,000 administrators, and 2 million teachers in America's largest industry.

With the explosion in knowledge playing such a prominent role in American life, there are many concerns for the types of programs to be offered and individuals to be served. Consequently, dollars are being poured into facilities, personnel, programs, and other essentials.

The health educator and physical educator need to be conscious of these grants-in-aid monies that are being given to educational pursuits. Many of the sources of funds can be tapped for programs in the special fields of health education and physical education. Furthermore, it may be possible for specialists in these fields to influence legislation at the state and/or national level so that the bills passed include allocations for these special fields in the wording of the legislation.

Some of the specific ways in which the professions of health education and physical education may use this money might be to correct weak spots in the lack of facilities, sponsor research, hire additional personnel, offset low salaries, and purchase equipment.

A sampling of suggested projects, activities, and programs that might receive funds for research and grants-in-aid at the federal level in programs of health, physical education, recreation, and safety are as follows:

1. Employment of specialists to help in developing and implementing programs in adapted physical education
2. Inservice education programs for teachers
3. The development of curriculum guides
4. The purchase of special types of equipment, supplies, and facilities
5. The employment of specialists to

work with underprivileged children who have special health problems
6. The employment of consultants who are specialists on various health and physical education problems
7. The development of health guides
8. The conduct of research for more effective teaching and better meeting the needs of children
9. The conduct of workshops
10. Immunization programs
11. The development of programs for physically underdeveloped children

Questions and exercises

1. Outline the steps you think should be followed in curriculum planning by a chairman of a health and physical education department.
2. What is the relationship between curriculum planning and objectives?
3. Examine the health and/or physical education curriculum of three high schools. What are their strong and their weak points?
4. What are three references that the teacher can use for curriculum planning?
5. How can community resources be used effectively in curriculum planning?
6. Prepare what you consider to be an outstanding curriculum for health and/or physical education at the elementary, junior high school, or senior high school level. Analyze the steps you followed in constructing this curriculum.
   Reading assignment in *Administrative Dimensions of Health and Physical Education Programs, Including Athletics:* Chapter 15, Selections 83 to 86.

Selected references

Allen, D. W.: Elements of scheduling a flexible curriculum, Journal of Secondary Education **38:** 84, 1963.

Association for Supervision and Curriculum Development: Assessing and using curriculum content, Washington, D. C., 1965, The Association.

Blair, M., and Woodward, R.: Team teaching in action, Boston, 1964, Houghton Mifflin Co.

Bucher, C. A.: Foundations of physical education, ed. 5, St. Louis, 1968, The C. V. Mosby Co.

Bucher, C. A., and Reade, E.: Physical education and health in the elementary school, New York, 1971, The Macmillan Co.

Bucher, C. A., Koenig, C., and Barnhard, M.: Methods and materials for secondary school physical education, ed. 3, St. Louis, 1970, The C. V. Mosby Co.

Bush, R. N.: New design for high school education: assuming a flexible schedule, Bulletin of the National Association of Secondary-School Principals **46:**30, 1962.

Cassidy, R.: Curriculum development in physical education, New York, 1954, Harper & Row Publishers.

Daniels, A. S.: The potential of physical education as an area of research and scholarly effort, Journal of Health, Physical Education, and Recreation **36:**32, 1965.

Eichhorn, D. H.: The middle school, New York, 1966, The Center for Applied Research in Education, Inc. (The Library of Education).

Evaul, T. W.: The automated tutor, Journal of Health, Physical Education, and Recreation **35:** 27, 1964.

Good, C. V., and Seates, D. E.: Methods of research: educational, psychological, sociological, New York, 1964, Appleton-Century-Crofts.

Goodlad, J. I.: School curriculum reform in the United States, New York, 1964, The Fund for the Advancement of Education.

Goodlad, J. I., and Anderson R. H.: The nongraded elementary school, rev. ed., New York, 1963, Harcourt, Brace & World, Inc.

Koopman, G. R.: Curriculum development, New York, 1966, The Center for Applied Research in Education, Inc. (The Library of Education).

Lloyd, F. V.: Curricular responsibilities of today's school board, Administrator's Notebook, vol. 14, October, 1965.

Meyers, K.: Administering the curriculum, The Clearing House **39:**145, 1964.

Nixon, J. E., and Jewett, A. E.: Physical education curriculum, New York, 1964, The Ronald Press Co.

Nunnelley, W. A.: Physical education goes on television, Journal of Health, Physical Education, and Recreation **36:**66, 1964.

Oliver, A. I.: Curriculum improvement—a guide to problems, principles, and procedures, New York, 1965, Dodd, Mead & Co.

Report of the Second National Conference on Curriculum Projects: Assessing and using curriculum content, Washington, D. C., 1964, Association for Supervision and Curriculum Development.

School Health Education Study: Health education: a conceptual approach, New York, 1965, sponsored by the Samuel Bronfman Foundation of New York City.

Sliepcevich, E.: A conceptual approach to curriculum development in health education, Journal of Health, Physical Education, and Recreation **36:**12, 1965.

The University of the State of New York, The State Education Department, Bureau of Secondary Development: Physical education in the secondary schools, Albany, 1964, State Department of Education.

Wisconsin Department of Public Instruction: A guide to curriculum building in physical education—elementary schools, Curriculum Bulletin No. 28, Madison, 1963, The Department.

There are many reasons why each health and physical education program must be vitally concerned with public relations today. The increased costs of programs in these specialized areas, including allocations of funds for facilities, personnel, and other essential items, has raised many questions in the minds of the public. The changes taking place in education and in our programs have confused many persons and thus raised the need for clarification. Criticism of the schools and of such programs as athletics, physical education, sex education, sensitivity training, and others has resulted in increased public involvement in our programs.

Sometimes when the terms *public* or *professional relations* are used, the reader, administrator, physical educator, or other person frequently associates the term with radio, television, and other communications media. However, one should not forget that the most effective avenues of public and professional relations include: (1) relations with students, (2) relations with parents of students, (3) personal contacts with the public at large, (4) the leadership role exerted by physical educators and health educators in their communities, (5) contacts established with various groups in the community, and (6) communications media such as correspondence, records, and telephone conversations.

PUBLIC RELATIONS DEFINED

Public relations is a much-defined term. Some of the common definitions for this term as given by experts in this specialized field are as follows: Philip Lesly speaks of it as comprising the activities and attitudes that are used to influence, judge, and control the opinion of any individual, group, or groups of persons in the interest of some other individuals. Professor Harwood L. Childs defines it as a name for those activities and relations with others that are public and that have significance socially. J. Handly Wright and Byron H. Christian, experts in public relations, refer to it as a program that has the characteristics of careful planning and proper conduct, which in turn will result in public understanding and confidence. Edward L. Bernays, who has written widely on the subject of public relations, lists three items in his definition: first, information that is for public consumption, second, an attempt to modify the attitudes and actions of the public through persuasion, and third, the objective of attempting to integrate the attitudes and actions of the public and of the organization or people who are conducting the public relations program. Benjamin Fine, a specialist in educational public relations, defines public relations as the entire body of relationships that go to make up our impressions of an individual, an organization, or an idea.

These selected definitions of public relations help to clarify its importance for any organization, institution, or group of individuals trying to develop an enterprise, profession, or business. Public relations takes into consideration such important factors as consumer's interests, human relationships, public understanding, and good will. In business, it attempts to show the important place that specialized enterprises

One purpose of school public relations is "to inform the public about the work of the schools." (Wisconsin State College, La Crosse, Wis.)

have in society and how they exist and operate in the public interest. In education, it is concerned with public opinion, the needs of the school or college, and acquainting constituents with what is being done in the public interest. It also concerns itself with acquainting the public with the educational problems that must be considered in order to render a greater service.

The American Association of School Administrators points out these purposes of school public relations: "(a) to inform the public about the work of the schools, (b) to establish confidence in the schools, (c) to rally support for proper maintenance of the educational program, (d) to develop awareness of the importance of education in a democracy, (e) to improve the partnership concept by uniting parents and teachers in meeting the educational needs of children, (f) to integrate the home, the school, and the community in improving educational opportunities for all children, (g) to evaluate the offerings of the schools in meeting the needs of the children in the community, and (h) to correct misunderstandings as to the aims and objectives of the schools."[*]

Public relations means that the opinions of the populace must be taken into consideration. Public opinion is very powerful, and individuals, organizations, and institutions succeed or fail in terms of its influence. Therefore, in order to have good public relations the interests of human beings and what is good for people in general must be considered.

---

[*]American Association of School Administrators: Public relations for America's schools, Twenty-eighth Yearbook, Washington, D. C., 1952, The Association, p. 14.

The practice of public relations is pertinent to all areas of human activity: religion, education, business, politics, military, government, labor, and other affairs in which individuals engage. A good public relations program is not hit-and-miss. It is planned with considerable care, and great amounts of time and effort are necessary to produce results. Furthermore, it is not something in which only the "top brass," management, executives, or administrative officers should be interested. In order for any organization to have a good program, all members must be public relations–conscious.

The extent to which interest has grown in the field of public relations is indicated by the number of individuals specializing in this area. The *Public Relations Directory and Yearbook* lists personnel who specialize in this work. A recent edition of this publication listed more than 800 individuals who are doing work in this area on an independent basis, approximately 4,500 who were directors of public relations with business firms, approximately 1,900 who were associated with trade and professional groups, and nearly 700 who were with social organizations. In a recent Manhattan telephone directory there were over 500 names listed under the heading of "Public Relations." In contrast, in 1935, there were only ten names.

The importance of public relations is being increasingly recognized for the part it can play in educational, business, or social advancement. All need public support and understanding in order to survive. Public relations helps in obtaining these essentials.

PLANNING THE PUBLIC RELATIONS PROGRAM

Public relations programs are much more effective when they are planned by many interested and informed individuals and groups. Such individuals and groups as school boards, teachers, administrators, and citizens' committees can provide valuable assistance in certain areas of the public relations program. These people, serving in an advisory capacity to health and physical education departments, can help immeasurably in fulfilling the following specific steps that should be followed in planning a public relations program, which have been identified by McCloskey:

1. Establish a sound public-communications policy.
2. Determine what educational services and developments benefit pupils.
3. Obtain facts about what citizens do and do not know and believe about educational values and needs.
4. Decide what facts and ideas will best enable citizens to understand the benefits children obtain from good schools and what improvements will increase these benefits.
5. Make full use of effective teacher-pupil planning techniques to generate understanding and appreciation.
6. Relate cost and tax facts more closely to opportunity for boys and girls to achieve.
7. Decide who is going to perform specific communication tasks at particular times.*

McCloskey further suggests that after putting the public relations plan into operation, it is important to test and evaluate its results and then improve the educational program accordingly.

PUBLIC RELATIONS MEDIA

There are many media that can be utilized in a public relations program. Some have more significance in certain localities than others. Some are more readily accessible than others. Health and physical education persons should survey their communities to determine media that can be utilized and will be most effective in their public relations program.

It should be pointed out, however, that the *program* and the *staff* represent the best media for an effective public relations pro-

---

*McCloskey, G.: Planning the public relations program, National Education Association Journal **49**:17, 1960.

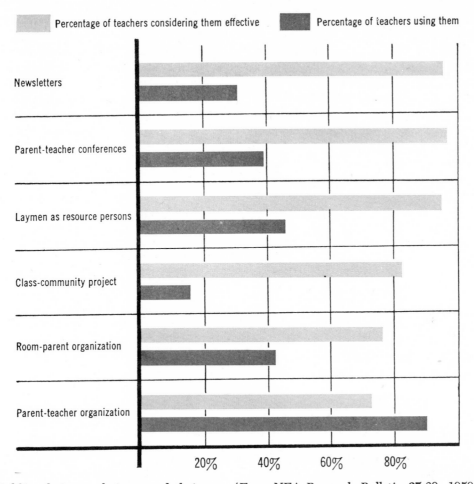

Percentage of teachers considering them effective   Percentage of teachers using them

Public relations techniques and their use. (From NEA Research Bulletin **37**:39, 1959.)

gram. Through the activities and experiences provided and the leadership given, much good will may be built for any school, or college, department or profession. This should never be forgotten.

Another important consideration is that the most effective public relations is carried on through the person-to-person medium. This might be teacher to student, student to parent, or teacher to citizen. In all cases the child is a very important consideration, being really the most important means of communication between the school and the home. What is accomplished in school or college, the effectiveness of a teacher's work, and the material learned become subjects of conversation around the dinner table and other places in the home. The attitudes developed in students often become those of the parents as well.

Newspapers

The newspaper is one of the most common and useful media for disseminating information. It reaches a large audience and can be very helpful in interpreting health and physical education to the public at large. Some questions that might be asked to determine what makes a good news story are: Is the news of interest to the public? Are the facts correct? Is it direct in style, written in the third person in a layman's vocabulary, and well organized? Does it include news on individuals who are closely related to the schools or colleges? Does the article have a plan of action, and does it play a significant part in interpreting the school or college program?

When a story is submitted to a newspaper there are certain standard rules that apply in the preparation of copy:

1. Prepare all copy in typewritten form as neatly as possible, double spaced, and on one side of the paper only.

2. The name, address, and telephone number of your organization should be on page one, in the upper left-hand corner. Also at the top of page one, but below the address, should be the headline and release date for the story.

3. Paragraphs should be short, and if the story necessitates more than one page, write the word "More" at the end of each page. At the top of each additional page, list the name of the story in the upper left-hand corner. The symbols # # # should be placed at the end of the article to indicate the end.

One expert on newspapers has pointed out that the most common reasons for rejecting material includes limited reader interest, poor writing, inaccuracies, and insufficient information.

Pictures and graphic materials

Pictures represent a very effective medium for public relations. Two words should be kept in mind by the persons who take and select the pictures for publication. These words are "action" and "people." Pictures that reflect "action" are much more interesting and appealing than "still" pictures. Furthermore, pictures that have people in them are much more effective than ones that do not possess this essential ingredient. It should also be recognized that usually a few people are better than many persons. Finally, such considerations as good background, accuracy in details, clearness, and educational significance should not be forgotten.

Educational problems, such as budgets, statistical information in regard to growth of school population, information about participation in various school or college activities, and many other items can be made more interesting, intelligible, and appealing if presented through colorful and artistic charts, graphs, and diagrams.

Magazines

There are thousands of popular magazines, professional journals, trade publications, and other periodicals being published today.

Such national magazines as *Look, Life, McCall's,* and *Reader's Digest* are excellent for publicity purposes. It is, however, very difficult to get stories in such publications because of their rigid requirements and the fact that they like to cover the stories with their own staff. Many times it is better to suggest ideas to them rather than to submit a manuscript. There are other methods that may be used. One can attempt to interest the editors in some particular work being done and have them send a staff writer to cover the story. It might be possible to get a free-lance writer interested in the organization and have him develop a story. Someone on the department staff who possesses writing skill can be assigned to write a piece for magazine consumption and then submit it to various periodicals for consideration.

Public speaking

Public speaking can be a very effective medium for public relations. Through public addresses to civic and social groups in the community, public affairs, gatherings, professional meetings, and any organization or group that desires to know more about the work that is being performed, a good opportunity is afforded for interpreting one's profession to the public. However, it is very important to do a commendable job or the result can be poor rather than good public relations.

In order to make an effective speech one should observe many fundamentals. A few that may be listed are mastery of the subject, sincere interest and enthusiasm, interest in putting thoughts across to the public rather than in putting the speaker across, directness, straightforwardness, preparation, brevity, and clear and distinct enunciation.

If the organization is of sufficient size, a speakers' bureau may be an asset. This may be utilized if there are several qualified speakers within an organization. Various civic, school, college, church, and other leaders within a community can be informed of the services that the organization has to offer along this line. Then, when the requests come in, speakers can be assigned on the basis of qualifications and availability. The entire department or organization should set up facilities and make information and material available for the preparation of such speeches. If desired by the members of the organization, inservice training courses could even be worked out in conjunction with the English department or some experienced person in developing this particular phase of the public relations program.

Discussion groups

Discussion groups, forums, and similar meetings are frequently held in various communities. At such gatherings, representatives from the community, which usually include educators, industrialists, businessmen, physicians, lawyers, clergymen, union leaders, and others, discuss topics of general interest. This is an excellent setting to clarify issues, clear up misunderstandings, enlighten civic leaders on particular fields of endeavor, and discuss the pros and cons of community projects. Health and physical education persons should play a larger role in such meetings than has been the case in the past. Much good could be done for these specialized fields through this medium.

Radio and television

Radio and television are powerful media of communication because of their universal appeal. These public relations media are well worth the money spent for the purpose, if this is the only way they are available. First, however, the possibilities of obtaining free time should be thoroughly examined. The idea of public service will influence some radio and television station managers to grant free time to an organization. This may be in the nature of an item included in a newscast program, a spot announcement, or a public service program that utilizes a quarter, half, or even a full hour.

There are some radio and television stations that are reserved for educational purposes. This possibility should be examined carefully. Many schools and colleges have stations of their own that may be utilized.

Sometimes one must take advantage of these media on short notice; therefore, it is important for an organization to be prepared with written plans that can be put into operation immediately. This might make the difference between being accepted or rejected for such an assignment. The organization must also be prepared to assume the work involved in rehearsals, preparation of scenery, or other items that are essential in presenting such a program.

Radio and television offer some of the best means of reaching a very large number of people at one time. As such, organizations concerned with specialized work of health and physical education should continually utilize their imaginations to translate the story of their professions into material that can be utilized effectively by these media.

Films

Films can present dramatically and informatively such stories as an organization's services to the public and highlights in the training of its leaders. They constitute a most effective medium for presenting a story in a short period of time. A series of visual impressions will remain long in the minds of the audience.

Since such a great majority of the American people enjoy movies today, it is important to consider them in any public relations program. Movies are not only a form of entertainment but also an effective medium of information and education. Films stimulate attention, create interest, and provide a way of getting across information not inherent in printed matter.

Movies, slides, slidefilm, and other phases of these visual aids have been utilized by a number of departments of health and physical education to present their programs to the public and to interest individuals in their work. Voluntary associations, professional associations, and official agencies in these fields have also used them to advantage.

Posters, exhibits, brochures, demonstrations, miscellaneous media

Posters, exhibits, and brochures should be recognized as playing an important part in any public relations program concerned with health and physical education. Well-illustrated, brief, and attractive brochures can visually and informatively depict activities, facilities, projects, and services that a department or organization has as part of its total program.

Drawings, paintings, charts, graphs, pictures, and other aids, when placed upon posters and given proper distribution, will illustrate activities, show progress, and present information visually. These media will attract and interest public thinking.

Exhibits, when properly prepared, interestingly presented, and properly located, such as in a store window or some other prominent spot, can do much to demonstrate work being done by an organization.

Demonstrations that present the total program of an organization or profession in an entertaining and informative manner have a place in any public relations program.

Other miscellaneous media, such as correspondence in the forms of letters and messages to parents, student publications, and reports, offer opportunities to develop good relations and favorable understanding in respect to schools and colleges and the work they are doing. Every opportunity must be utilized in order to build good public relations.

THE MANY PUBLICS

In order for any public relations program to be successful, accurate facts must be presented. To establish what facts are to be given to the public, the particular public at which the program is directed must be known. Contrary to general belief there is no *one* public. There are an infinite number of publics varying according to interests, problems, and other factors that make individuals different.

A public is a group of people who are drawn together by common interests, who are located in a specific geographic area, or who are characterized by some other common feature. There are over 220 million people in the United States composing hundreds of different publics—farmers, organized laborers, unorganized workers, students, professional people, and veterans. The various publics may be national, regional, and local in scope. They can be classified according to race or nationality, age, religion, occupation, politics, sex, income, profession, economic level, or business, fraternal, and educational backgrounds. As one can readily see, there are many publics. Each organization or group that has a special interest is a public. The public relations–minded person must always think in terms of the publics with which he desires to promote understanding and how they can best be reached.

In order to have a meaningful and purposeful public relations program, it is essential to obtain some facts about these various publics. It is necessary to know their understanding of the professions, their needs and interests, their health practices and hobbies, and other essential information.

Public opinion decides whether a profession is important or not, whether it meets an essential need, whether it is making a contribution to enriched living. It determines the success or failure of a department, school, institution, or profession. Public opinion is dynamic and continually changing. Public opinion results from the interaction of people. Public opinion is king in this game of life and it behooves any group of individuals or organization that wants to survive to know as much about it as possible.

To get information on what the public thinks, why it thinks as it does, and how it reaches its conclusions, various techniques may be used. Surveys, questionnaires, opinion polls, interviews, expert opinion, discussions, and other techniques have proved valuable. Anyone interested in public relations should be acquainted with these various techniques.

Public opinion is formed to a great degree as a result of influences in early life, such as the effect of parents, home, and environment; on the basis of people's own experiences in everyday living, what they see, hear, and experience in other ways; and finally by media of communication such as newspapers, radio, and television. It is important not only to be aware of these facts but also to remember that one

Demonstrations as part of a public relations program. Gamma Phi gym circus. (Illinois State University, Normal, Ill.)

is dealing with many different publics, each requiring a special source of research and study in order to know the most effective way to plan, organize, and administer the public relations program.

PUBLIC RELATIONS IN PRACTICE

A survey was recently conducted among eleven school systems to determine the nature and scope of their professional and public relations programs. Several questions were asked of health and physical education personnel through the personal interview technique. The information gained from these interviews is highlighted in the following paragraphs.

In respect to policies

1. The director of health and physical education was directly responsible for all public relations releases to the press.

2. All printed matter needed the approval of the director of health and physical education and the superintendent of schools before being released.

3. The coaches of interscholastic athletics were responsible for preparing all releases in regard to their programs.

4. Each staff member in the health and physical education program was urged to recognize that his or her activities were part of the professional and public relations programs of his or her school.

In respect to communication

In respect to communications media, the following were utilized:
Total physical education program
Newspaper
Posters
Films
Public speaking
School publications
Newsletter
Letters to parents
Demonstrations and exhibits
Personal contact
Pictures
Radio
Television

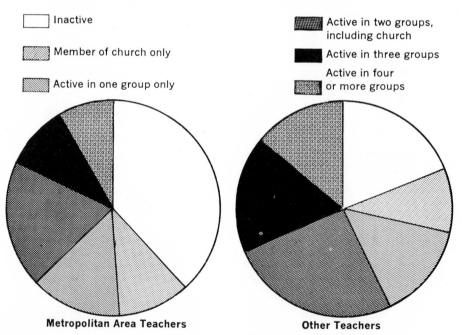

Metropolitan area teachers are less inclined to be joiners than are teachers in smaller districts. (From NEA Research Bulletin **40:**73, 1962.)

Window displays
Brochures
Sports days
Bulletin boards

The five media found to be most effective in their professional and public relations programs were (1) the total physical education program and the total health education program, (2) personal contact, (3) newspapers, (4) public speaking, and (5) demonstrations and exhibits.

All of the directors of health and physical education indicated that athletics received more publicity than any other phase of the physical education program. When asked why they thought this was so, some typical comments were: "The public demands it," "It is required because of public interest," and "The newspapers will only accept and print releases on athletics."

In respect to the message that was desired to be communicated to the public

When the directors were asked, "What message are you trying to convey to the public?" the following are typical answers that were given:

1. The value of the total physical education and health program
2. The importance of the program to the student
3. Recognition and achievement of all students in all areas of health and physical education, not just athletics
4. Efforts and energies being expended to give each child a worthwhile experience in health and physical education
5. The role of the health and physical education program in enhancing the health and welfare of the student
6. The aims and objectives of the total health and physical education programs

Guiding principles

In summary, the professional and public relations programs in the eleven school districts were conducted in light of the following principles:

1. Each physical education and health department recognized the importance of an active public relations program.
2. Definite policies guided the program.
3. Responsibility for public relations was shared by all members of the department, with the central authority residing with the director.
4. Many different communications media were used to interpret the program to the numerous publics.
5. The total health and physical education program was recognized as being the most effective medium of professional and public relations.
6. Efforts were made to interpret accurate facts about physical education and health to the public.
7. Considerable planning was needed for the effective utilization of public relations media.

Limitations of program of professional and public relations

Some obvious limitations of the professional and public relations programs surveyed were as follows:

1. Information had not been gained through research as to how various publics thought and felt about health and physical education—what they did and did not know concerning these special fields.
2. There was a lack of budgetary allocations to carry on a professional and public relations program.
3. No specific plans had been established to evaluate the professional and public relations programs in the various schools.
4. Communications media overemphasized the role of athletics in the total physical education program.
5. Information had not been gained through research as to what services most benefited pupils and what facts best enabled the public to understand the benefits children derive from such programs.

6. There was a lack of effective pupil-teacher planning techniques.

PRINCIPLES OF PUBLIC RELATIONS

A few of the principles that should be observed in developing a public relations program are listed:

1. Public relations should be considered internally before they are developed externally. The support of everyone within the organization, from the top administrator down to the last worker, should be procured. Furthermore, such items as purpose of program, person or persons responsible, funds available, media to be utilized, and tools to carry on the program should be primary considerations.

2. A public relations program should be outlined and put in writing, and every member of the organization should become familiar with it. The better it is known and understood, the better chance it has of succeeding.

3. The persons directly in charge of the public relations program must have complete knowledge of the professional services that are being rendered; the attitudes of those who are members of the profession and of the organization represented; and the nature, background, and reactions of the consumers and of all the "publics" that are directly or indirectly related to the job being performed.

4. After all the information has been gathered, a program should be developed that meets the needs as shown by the research that has been done.

5. There should be adequate funds available to do the job. Furthermore, the person or persons in charge of the public relations program should be given freedom in spending this money in whatever ways they feel will be most helpful and productive for the organization.

6. The formation of a public relations staff will be determined by the needs of the organization, the amount of money avail-able, the attitude of the administration, and the size of the organization. If additional staff is available, special talents should be sought so as to provide effectively for a well-rounded program.

7. Individuals assigned public relations work should modestly stay in the background instead of seeking the limelight, keep abreast of the factors that affect the program, develop a wide acquaintance, and make contacts that will be helpful.

8. In developing a public relations program, such items as the following should be checked: Is there a handbook or a newsletter to keep members of the organization informed? Is there a system for dispensing information to local radio and press outlets? Is there a booklet, flyer, or printed matter that tells the story of the organization? Do members of the organization participate regularly in community affairs? Is there provision for a speakers' bureau where civic clubs and other organizations may procure speakers on various topics? Does the organization hold open house for parents and interested persons? Does the organization have a film or other visual material that can be shown to interested groups and that explains and interprets the work?

9. A good public relations program will utilize all available resources and machinery to disseminate information to the public in order to ensure adequate coverage.

PUBLIC RELATIONS AND EDUCATION

Education is recognized as essential in present-day society. In order that knowledge and experience may be transmitted from generation to generation, education is necessary. This is the essential that gives continuity to any culture.

A major obstacle today to education is in the area of public relations. Unless the public understands the work being performed by the schools, educators cannot expect their support. Today a great segment of the American public does not

The Physical Education Department
of the
Rapid City Public Schools
PRESENTS THE
FOURTH ANNUAL

FITNESS IS FUN

Public relations. (Rapid City Public Schools, Rapid City, S. D.)

understand and appreciate the work that is being performed in the schools and colleges.

The need for a broad public relations program is evidenced by many facts in American life. The American people spend more for tobacco each year than they do for education and twice as much for liquor. Schools and colleges are overflowing and there is a need for $10 to $20 billion for new buildings alone. Schools and colleges must absorb thousands of pupils a year, yet the necessary provisions have not been made. There is need for greater financial support, increased teachers' salaries, more buildings, and better teacher training. The necessary improvements cannot be obtained without public understanding and public support.

The National Education Association conducted a survey several years ago that included the factor of teachers' salaries. Of the persons surveyed, 33% felt that teachers' salaries were satisfactory, 2% thought they were high, and 20% did not have sufficient information on which to base an opinion.

A Gallup poll showed that 87% of the people are satisfied with the schools their children attend.

Elmer Roper conducted a poll that showed that 71.6% of the people in this country are either very satisfied or fairly well satisfied with the public school system. Less than one-half of the people indicated that teachers were underpaid and yet the poll showed that teachers received the highest percentage when the public was asked to "rank the order of importance to the community of public school teachers, clergymen, public officials, merchants, and lawyers."

The public in general is not informed in respect to education. What is true of education in general is even more true of health and physical education, which are important phases of the educational program. This has important implications for a well-

organized and long-term public relations program.

Bernays, in addressing the American Association of School Administrators, listed some pertinent remarks that he felt were essential to public understanding and action on the part of the American people.

He pointed out that three forces are responsible for social change: namely, public opinion, voluntary groups, and the law, which is dependent upon public opinion. In the light of this principle, voluntary groups are needed to aid in informing the public about education. These voluntary groups should consist of leading civic leaders as well as professional educators. Lay and professional groups must coordinate their programs closely and gear their campaigns to everyone, from kindergarten to college, throughout the entire country. One of the most important considerations is that a unified front be presented to the public. All should agree on the issues and present them in the same light. If the various professional associations that are now organized and exist on national, district, state, and local levels and the various lay organizations could speak with one voice and with unison and similarity of purpose, much could be accomplished.

Bernays also recommended that a central board of strategy establish policy and goals and iron out problems so that a unified approach would be followed. Through such a board, research could be conducted to ascertain and reach a common agreement at the various levels as to what the needs of education are. It could also determine the reasons for the apathy, indifference, and misunderstanding on the part of the public. It could wage a unified battle against enemies of public education.

Another step in the overall public relations program would be a clear-cut operational program. Such a program would provide for a continuous campaign, personnel, money, utilization of mass communications media, close cooperation between school, college, and parents and between the school, college, and community in general, and a more active role for teachers in community activities.

The American Association of School Administrators lists various principles that it considers essential to school public relations:

a. School public relations must be honest in intent and execution.
b. School public relations must be intrinsic (school program should be recognized as worthwhile in itself).
c. School public relations must be continuous.
d. School public relations must be positive in approach.
e. School public relations should be comprehensive.
f. School public relations should be sensitive to its publics.
g. The ideas communicated must be simple.*

Through such a public relations program, all the people would have a better understanding of education in this country.

PUBLIC RELATIONS IN SCHOOL HEALTH AND PHYSICAL EDUCATION PROGRAMS

A definition of public relations heard some time ago stated: "Public relations is getting the *right facts* to the *right people* at the *right time* and in the *right way."*

Some of the facts that we need to get across to the public are these:

1. Physical education, health education, and recreation are closely allied but not the same. Each is separate and distinct; each needs its own specialists and deserves its own place in the educational program.

2. The professional fields of physical education, health education, and recreation are more than muscle and perspiration. Skills are not performed in a vacuum. Something happens to behavior, ethics, and mental development.

3. Athletics are an integral part of phys-

ical education, but physical education is not just athletics.

4. A well-rounded health program is an essential and integral part of modern education.

Some of the right people we must reach are the following:

1. Superintendents of public instruction, school administrators, presidents and deans of colleges and universities, mayors, and others. They are the ones who make the decisions, determine the main points of emphasis, and decide how funds will be allocated. They can help us to grow into that dynamic force for good that we are capable of becoming.

2. Other members of the faculty. The teachers of English, mathematics, industrial arts, and other disciplines are very important cogs in the educational system. We should not isolate ourselves from them. They can help us and we can help them. We are all in this business together, working toward common goals. "United we stand and divided we fall."

3. Consumers of our products and services. Let's reach those for whom we exist. And let's get to more than just the star player—let's contact the dub as well as the skilled, the girl as well as the boy, the oldster as well as the youngster. Let's reach everyone, from the cradle to the grave.

The right time is now. Now is the time when:

1. There is a "bull market" in education —enrollments are booming, budgets skyrocketing, facilities expanding. And there is tremendous interest in education, America's largest industry.

2. There is interest in the *whole* individual. The theory of dualism of mind and body has been exploded. We are interested in the physical as well as the mental, emotional, and social aspects of human beings.

3. Research is pointing up the importance of our fields of endeavor. This research shows the importance of exercise, the value of hobbies, the need for health

---

*American Association of School Administrators, op. cit., pp. 16-33.

instruction and recreation, and the contribution that sports can make in helping conquer physical and mental problems.

4. The President of the United States is interested in fitness. He places a high priority on our fields of endeavor.

5. The automation era is at hand, with its increased hours of leisure. Education also consists of knowing what to do when you have nothing to do.

6. The interest in such areas as drugs, ecology, sports, sex education, and smoking is at an all-time high.

The right facts, the right people, and the right time will lose effectiveness unless we *act in the right way:*

1. Since close national-community relationships are important, keep the lines of communication constantly open from the national organizations down to the grass roots programs. There should be a constant flow of ideas that can be translated into action.

2. Develop the best possible programs of health and physical education. Have satisfied children and youth go out from your programs.

3. Utilize every opportunity available to sell someone else on the worth of your professional field of endeavor. If you are sold, yourself, it will not be difficult to sell someone else.

4. Exploit every medium of communication to get your message across.

5. Think in positive terms—think *success,* and our chances of achieving big things will be better assured.

Questions and exercises

1. Outline what you consider to be an effective public relations plan for a school program of health or physical education.
2. Prepare a news release on some event or phase of the department program. Follow through with it for publication or broadcast.
3. Analyze the strengths and weaknesses of the present public relations program of the American Association for Health, Physical Education, and Recreation. Send a letter to headquarters on your findings.
4. After careful firsthand study, list the main features of the public relations program of some successful business concern. Show how some of the same techniques, media, and ideas may be applied to your professional field of endeavor.
5. What is meant by the fact that we are dealing in public relations with not just one but many "publics"?
6. Why is a knowledge of public relations important to teachers and administrators alike?
7. Discuss the potentialities of five public relations media in promoting physical education, health education, and recreation.
8. Prepare a speech that is to be given before a lay audience on the importance of physical education and health education to community welfare. Give the speech before class.
9. Prepare a bibliography of films that could be utilized effectively to interpret your profession to the public.
10. What qualifications would you need to become a full-time public relations person in your field?
11. List and discuss some principles that should be observed in public relations.
12. To what extent have the schools done a good public relations job?

Reading assignment in *Administrative Dimensions of Health and Physical Education Programs, Including Athletics:* Chapter 16, Selections 87 to 90.

Selected references

American Association for Health, Physical Education, and Recreation: Physical education—an interpretation, Washington, D. C., The Association.

American Association for Health, Physical Education, and Recreation, and National School Public Relations Association: Putting PR into HPER, Washington, D. C., 1953, The Association.

American Association of School Administrators: Public relations for America's schools, Twenty-eighth Yearbook, Washington, D. C., 1952, The Association.

Baughman, M. D.: The school's role in community life, School and Community 51:9, 1969.

Bernays, E. L.: Public relations, Norman, 1952, University of Oklahoma Press.

Bucher, C. A.: Sportswriters—physical educator's nemesis, The Physical Educator 10:51, 1953.

Chester, E. B.: School district in trouble, American School Board Journal 150:17, 1965.

Ciernick, S.: Getting more mileage from school publications, National Education Association Journal 49:24, 1960.

Dapper, G.: Public relations for educators, New York, 1964, The Macmillan Co.

Douglas, H. R.: Trends and issues in secondary education, New York, 1962, The Center for Applied Research, Inc. (The Library of Education).

Flesch, R.: The art of readable writing, New York, 1949, Harper & Row, Publishers.

Harral, S.: Tested public relations for schools, Norman, 1952, University of Oklahoma Press.

Humphrey, J. W.: Educators at your service, The Clearing House 38:556, 1964.

Jones, J. J.: School public relations, New York, 1966, The Center for Applied Research, Inc. (The Library of Education).

McCloskey, G.: Planning the public relations program, National Education Association Journal 59:17, 1970.

National Recreation Association: The ABC's of public relations for recreation, New York, 1946, National Recreation Association.

National School Public Relations Association: It starts in the classroom, Washington, D. C., 1951, National Education Association.

National School Public Relations Association: Print it right, Washington, D. C., 1953, National Education Association.

Scherer, D. J.: How to keep your district in the public eye, School Management 10:22, 1966.

Suttoff, J.: Local cosmopolitan orientation and participation in school affairs, Administrator's Notebook, vol. 9, No. 3, November, 1960.

Torpey, J.: Interpreting physical education for the public, The Physical Educator 24:131, 1967.

CHAPTER 21 OFFICE MANAGEMENT

The health and/or physical education office is one of the key centers for these professional fields. Too often health and physical educators give considerable attention to the development of their programs, the construction of facilities, and detailed measurement and evaluation programs but give little thought to the conduct of the office. As a result the program, facilities, public relations, and other factors often suffer. Office management is important because the office has many functions. It is the place for first impressions, center of communications, focus of administrative duties, and point of contact for administration and staff.

IMPORTANCE OF OFFICE MANAGEMENT

Colleagues, pupils, visitors, and other persons frequently have their initial contacts with departments of health and physical education in the central office. Their reception, the courtesies they are shown, the efficiency with which the office work is carried out, and other operational details leave a lasting impression upon their minds. Friends are often made or lost at this strategic point.

Center for communications

Office work, broadly conceived, is the handling and management of information. The office is usually the place where schedules are arranged and distributed, telephone calls made and received, reports typed and mimeographed, bulletins prepared and issued, conferences arranged and held, appointments made and confirmed, and greetings voiced and exchanged. The office represents the setting for a hub of activity around which revolves the efficient functioning of the work of health and physical education personnel. Unless these communications are carried out with dispatch, accurately and courteously, the entire administrative process breaks down.

Focus of administrative duties

The chief administrative personnel, secretarial assistants, and clerical help comprise the office staff. The filing system, key records, and reports are usually housed in the office. When inventories need to be examined, letters pulled from the files, or the chairman of the department consulted on important matters, the office is frequently the point of contact. Administrative responsibilities are carried out in the office, making this space a central point or focus for the entire organization.

Point of contact for administration and staff

Staff members visit the office regularly. Mailboxes are located there, and telephone calls may be taken in the office. Conferences and appointments with pupils and visitors often bring the teacher to the office. Constant communication takes place between administration and staff in this setting. High staff morale, efficiency, a friendly climate, and a feeling of working toward common goals can be imbued to a large degree through the atmosphere that exists in the office.

OFFICE SPACE

The central office for the health and/or physical education department, in accordance with its clearinghouse activities, should be located in a readily accessible position in the school or college plant. This office should be as near the entrance of the building as possible and at the same time have ready accessibility to health service offices, gymnasia, locker rooms, athletic fields, and other facilities of the department.

Most central offices for health and physical education should consist of at least three divisions: general reception area, clerical space, and private office. Other desirable features to be considered are a toilet, a storage room, and a conference room for staff and other meetings.

General reception area

The general reception office is that part of the office layout used by visitors as a waiting room or information center, for teachers and pupils who desire to get their mail, have appointments, or wish information, and for office services in general. It should be attractive, with some pictures on the wall, comfortable chairs, bulletin boards, and other items essential to carrying out the necessary administrative routines and creating a warm, friendly climate. A counter or fence should separate the general waiting room from the rest of the office facilities. This helps to ensure greater privacy and more efficient conduct of office responsibilities.

Clerical space

The clerical space should be separated from the general waiting and reception room. It should be equipped with such necessary materials as typewriters, files, tables,

and telephones. It is often desirable to have a private alcove or office for one or more of the secretaries, depending upon the size of the department and office. Privacy is often needed for the typing of letters, the preparation of reports, or the convenience of visitors and other personnel. There should be ample lighting, freedom of movement, and sufficient space for the various administrative duties to be carried out with a minimum of confusion and of difficulty.

Private offices

The chairman of the department and possibly other personnel, depending upon the size of the department, should have private offices. The offices should be such that the persons in charge of administration can concentrate on their work without interruptions, have private conferences with students, faculty members, or visitors, and in general carry out their duties in the most efficient way possible. The offices should be decorated and equipped in an appropriate manner. There should be desks of sufficient working size that are neat in appearance, with calendars, schedule pads for appointments and conferences, and other essential materials. Filing cases, storage cabinets, and other equipment should be provided as needed. Faculty should also be provided with offices as much as possible.

OFFICE PERSONNEL

The number of office personnel will depend upon the size of the department. The staff could consist of secretaries, stenographers, transcribing machine operators, a receptionist, switchboard operator, and typists in a large department in a school or college. However, the usual office will probably consist of one secretary. In some small schools, student help may be all the personnel available.

The *secretary* should be a "good right arm" to the chairman and to the department as a whole. To be most helpful, she

The secretary should be a "good right arm" to the administrator. (Office in senior high school, Mamaroneck, N. Y.)

will be a typist, a stenographer, and a public relations representative, will operate a dictaphone and mimeograph machine, and will see that the office runs smoothly. She will help the chairman and other staff members to remember facts, appointments, and other important information. She should know where materials are filed and be able to obtain them on a moment's notice, relieve the "boss" of minor details, and see that reports are sent out on time and that accurate records are kept.

A *stenographer* is a typist who can also take shorthand. A stenographer, however, differs from a secretary. She usually takes dictation and types letters and other material but does not have the personal relationship and confidential duties that a secretary has. Large departments frequently have stenographic "pools" wherein girls are on call to do work for any faculty member having work to be done.

A *transcribing operator* takes correspondence and other material that has been dictated and listens to a dictaphone or other playback mechanism upon which such information has been recorded. Using earphones, she sits at a typewriter and listens and types in accordance with the instructions that have been given.

A *receptionist's* position will vary with the department. In some departments a receptionist is a "greeter" who presents an attractive appearance and is polite, courteous, and helpful to callers. Some departments also assign her certain typing, filing, and telephone duties, in addition to the reception of callers.

Large departments frequently have *switchboard operators* who cover the phones for many faculty members and other personnel. Frequently staff members are not in, and messages are then relayed by the switchboard operator through the prescribed channels.

Office personnel should be selected very carefully. Experience, character, personality, looks, and ability should play important roles in the selection process. The secretary should have, as a minimum of education, a high school diploma. The achievements of a girl who has been through the commercial course and who has a good background in typewriting, bookkeeping, English, and secretarial practice will help to ensure her value to the department.

The chairman of the department and other faculty members should treat a secretary and other office personnel with respect and make them feel that they are very important parts of the work being accomplished. The staff should be patient and see that clerical help know the details of their jobs, recognize the importance of each, and appreciate the responsibilities that rest with their positions.

In smaller high schools, elementary schools, and colleges, the administrator may have to rely partially or entirely upon *students* to get some of the clerical work accomplished. Probably, senior students who have particular inclinations along this line will be most successful. Inservice education should take place for these students to see that acceptable precedures are followed in filing, typing, mimeographing, maintaining records, and performing other office duties.

EQUIPMENT AND SUPPLIES

Whether or not an office is efficient in its clerical and other responsibilities will depend upon the equipment and supplies available. It must be recognized that the materials needed will vary with the size of the school or college. In smaller schools and colleges such equipment as adding machines might readily be available in the central office but not in departmental offices. Following are some of the items that should be considered:

Adding machine	Maps of school district
Bookcases	Paper cutter
Bulletin boards	Paste
Buzzers	Pencil sharpeners
Calendars	Pencils and pens
Chairs	Reproducing machines
Clips	Rulers
Cloak racks	Safe
Clock	Scissors
Desk baskets	Scrapbooks
Desk lights	Stamps
Desk pads	Stapling machine
Desks	Stationery and paper
Dictionaries	Tables
Ditto machine	Telephone
First-aid cabinet	Typewriters
Letter trays	Umbrella rack
Magazine racks	Wardrobe cabinets
	Wastebaskets

In some large offices where many, many details are handled, data processing equipment should be available.

OFFICE WORK AND AUTOMATION

The rapid progress made in recent years begs the question as to whether or not new automated equipment should be installed in the office. The way this question is answered will depend upon such factors as the extent of the program the office serves, the amount of clerical work that needs to be done, and the size of the allocated budget.

Automation as used here refers to the processing of data by some mechanical device or system other than typewriters, adding machines, calculators, and photocopiers. Automation can be used in respect to handling such items as accounts payable, cumulative records, health records, inventories, personnel records, schedules, work requests, and transcripts.

Automation can be utilized by an organization either by installing their own machines or by working through some business organization that processes educational data for a fee. Also, the procedure of joining with several other school or college systems for such a service will work very well in some situations. Depending upon the size of the operation, it may be that a job can be done better, the hiring of additional personnel can be eliminated, and the cost will be less without automation.

REFERENCE MATERIALS

An area that high school and college offices should not overlook is the area of reference materials. The elementary, high school, and college offices will find it valuable to develop professional libraries that contain some of the outstanding professional books, periodicals, and standard references for their professional fields. In addition, there should be such references as books and periodicals; bulletins of the state department of education, state department of health, state and national professional organizations; facility references; and catalogues of athletic equipment and supplies.

Although there may be such material in the school library, it may be of value in many locations to have such references in the central office. In this way faculty members utilize them to a greater extent and thus keep up to date with their professional fields.

ADMINISTRATIVE ROUTINE

The administrative routine or manner in which the day-to-day business of the department is carried out by the office represents the basic reason why such a facility exists. Therefore, this matter should receive very careful consideration.

Hours

The office should be open during regular school hours. This usually means from 8 or 9 A.M. to 4 or 5 P.M. During this time there should always be someone present to answer the telephone, greet visitors, and answer students' questions. There may be some exceptions to these hours in a small school, but even in these cases there should be regular office hours that have been publicized as widely as possible.

Teachers should also have regular office hours at which they will be accessible to students, colleagues, and other persons who would like to see them. These office hours should be posted, office personnel informed, and the schedule carefully observed so that requests for information and assistance can be properly handled.

Assignments

All assignments, whether for office personnel or faculty, should be made very clear, be in writing, and be properly publicized. Office personnel may be required to ring electric bells to signal a change in periods, set clocks, take messages, mimeo-

graph daily or weekly bulletins, distribute minor supplies, check the calendar of school events, provide messenger service to teachers and pupils, or assist in the health examination. These details should be clearly understood and carried out at the proper time. Specific responsibilities should be fixed and a schedule of duties prepared so as to prevent any misunderstanding.

Correspondence

Correspondence represents a most effective public relations medium. Letters can be written in a cold, impersonal manner or they can carry warmth and help to interpret what a program expects and is trying to do for a student or other person. Letters should be prepared carefully, using only correct English, and in a neat manner that meets the highest standards of secretarial practice. If a health or physical education teacher has to do his own letters, these same standards should be met. Letters should convey the feeling that the department is anxious to help and to be of assistance wherever possible. Letters should be answered promptly, not placed in a drawer and left for weeks or months. Carbon copies of letters should be made and filed for future reference.

Files and filing

The office should contain steel filing cases for vertical filing. The filing system used will depend upon the number of personnel involved and the person doing the filing, but in any case it should be simple and practical. Files will usually consist of correspondence and informational material. For ease of finding material some form of alphabetical filing should usually be utilized, although numerical filing may at times be practical. The alphabetical files can be done on a name or subject basis, such as "Brown, Charles A.," or "Health Examinations," using a Manila folder for all the material to be filed under the name or subject. Cross references should be included to facilitate finding material. Guide cards can be used to show which divisions of the file pertain to each letter of the alphabet, thus making the search for material much more rapid.

A visible filing system for any records and reports that are used currently and constantly will prove helpful. These are usually prepared on cards, and the visible filing case contains flat drawers that at a moment's notice will show the names or index numbers when pulled outward.

Office files should be kept very accurately. The person doing the filing should be careful to see that the letter or other material gets into the proper folder and that folder into its correct location. Filing should also be kept up to date. A periodic review of the files should be made in order to weed out material that is no longer pertinent to the department. Files that for any reason are removed from the cabinet should be returned. If they are to be kept out for any length of time, an "out" sign should be substituted, showing where they are.

Telephone

The use of the office telephone is a major consideration for good departmental public relations. A few simple rules that should be observed are indicated below.

Promptness. The telephone should be answered as promptly as possible. It should not be allowed to ring for some length of time before the receiver is taken off the hook. Answering promptly reflects efficient office practice and consideration for the person calling.

Professional purposes. The telephone is installed in an office for professional purposes. Secretaries or other office personnel should not be permitted to talk for long periods of time about personal matters that have no relationship to departmental affairs. The telephone should be kept clear for business that is of importance to the achievement of professional objectives.

Courtesy, friendliness, and helpfulness. The person answering the phone should be pleasant in manner and courteous in approach and should desire to be of assistance to whoever is calling. This should be the procedure not only when one is feeling his or her best but at all times. Such a telephone manner represents a professional responsibility that should be carried out with regularity.

Messages. At times faculty or staff members who are being called will not be available. A pencil and telephone pad should be kept at hand for recording calls in such cases, and a definite procedure should be established for relaying these messages to the proper person.

Appointments

Appointments should not be made unless it is believed that they can be kept. Furthermore, all appointments should be kept as nearly at the time scheduled as possible. Many times the person making an appointment has arranged his day with the understanding that he will have his conference at a certain time. If this time is not adhered to it means the schedule has to be altered, and complications frequently arise as a result of such a procedure. The secretary should keep an accurate list of appointments. If no secretary is available, the staff member should keep his own schedule of appointments and check it regularly to see that it is met.

RECORDS AND REPORTS

At times, records and reports are not prepared and maintained accurately because the directions given by the chairman of the department or the teachers are not clear and definite. When complicated reports are to be prepared, oral instructions, by themselves, will usually not be sufficient. Instead, directions should be written, typed, and distributed. The preparation of a sample will also help to ensure better results.

Text continued on p. 600.

B = Boys
G = Girls

School	Accident	Adapted program	Application for participation in interscholastic sports	Attendance	Cumulative class record	Equipment	Extracurricular activities	Game reports	Health	Interscholastic sports	Intramurals	Inventory	Medical form for inter-scholastic sports	Medical form for physical education	Parental permission sports	Physical fitness
School 1	B-G			B-G	B-G				B-G	B-G	B-G					B-G
School 2					B-G						B	B-G			B-G	B-G
School 3	B-G	B-G		B-G				B	B-G	B					B-G	B-G
School 4	B-G			B-G		B-G						B-G	B	B-G	B	B-G
School 5		B-G			B-G					B			B		B	B-G
School 6	B-G			B-G	B-G			B			B-G		B		B-G	B-G
School 7	B-G		B	B-G						B		B-G				B-G
School 8	B-G			B-G			B-G				G	B-G			B-G	B-G
School 9				B-G	B-G											
School 10	B-G	B-G	B	B-G					B-G	B	B-G			B-G	B-G	B-G
School 11	B-G			B-G							B-G	B-G	B-G		B	
School 12		B-G		B-G							B-G	B-G				B-G
School 13	B-G	B-G		B-G		B-G				B-G	B-G	B-G			B-G	B-G
School 14				B-G		B-G	B-G			B-G						
School 15	B-G			B-G				B		B-G					B-G	B-G
School 16	B-G								B-G					B		
School 17			B	B	B	B			B						B	
School 18												B-G			B-G	B-G
School 19				B-G					B-G					B-G	B-G	B-G
School 20	B-G			B-G									B		B-G	B-G
School 21	B-G		B-G	B-G	B-G	B-G	B-G		B-G	B-G	B-G		B			B-G

Physical education records used in twenty-one schools.

Name

Year

	HT.	WT.	OFF.	HT.	WT.	OFF.	HT.	WT.	OFF.	HT.	WT.	OFF.	HT.	WT.	OFF.	HT.	WT.	OFF.
Hockey																		
Soccer																		
Volleyball																		
Basketball																		
Softball																		
Lacrosse																		
Archery																		
Tennis																		
Badminton																		
Gym club																		
Synchronized swimming																		
Leader's club																		
Junior varsity cheerleader																		
Varsity cheerleader																		
Subtotal																		
Total																		

Comments

(HT.) = Honor team; (WT.) = Winning team; (OFF.) = Officiating.

Girl's physical education extracurricular activity card.

SCHOOL HEALTH EXAMINATION

Please return this report as soon as the examination has been completed. All reports must be in within 30 days after school opens. A physical examination made any time between June 1 and October 1 is acceptable.

Name .... Exam Date ....

Address ....

School .... Grade .... Wt. .... Ht. ....

reveals the following defects (leave blank if normal)

Nutrition ....

Skin ...   Scalp   Hands   Feet ....

Eyes ....

Ears ....

Nose.. ....

Teeth ....

Tonsils and Adenoids..

Lymphatics ....

Heart ....

Lungs ....

Abdomen...

Genito-urinary ....

Hernia ....

Orthopedic ....

Other..

General Physical and Emotional Status ....

REMARKS: *(Defects and recommendations for care in school to be noted on reverse side.)*

DATES OF IMMUNIZATION: **(Not previously recorded):**

		Initial	Booster
Smallpox	_____		
Diphtheria	_____		
Pertussis	_____		
Tetanus toxoid	_____		
Polio	_____		
Previous illness & operation	_____		

X-RAY OF CHEST—Report and date: _____

....**M.D.**

(Please print or write legibly)

Phys. Education   **Address**..
yes ☐ no ☐

Report for school health examination.

NOTICE REGARDING ANNUAL VISION TEST

Pupil's name_____ School_____

Address_____ Nurse _____

To Parent or Guardian:

The results of the annual vision test suggest that your child may have some eye difficulty. We recommend that the child have a complete eye examination in order to determine whether an eye defect exists and, if so, the need for correction or care.

Please ask the examiner to complete this form. We ask that you return the completed form to the school.

* * * * *

To Examiner:

Your diagnosis and recommendations will be appreciated and will assist us in planning this child's school program.

School observations:

Visual acuity   R_____ L_____   Test used _____

Other observations _____

_____

_____

_____   _____
       Supervising Principal   School Nurse or Physician

* * * * *

Examiner's diagnosis and recommendations:

1.   Diagnosis   R _____ L_____

2.   Visual acuity   (a) Without   R _____ (b) With   R _____
                          correction L _____   correction L _____

3.   Are glasses to be worn?   _____Yes   _____No

4.   If yes, indicate extent of use. _____

5.   Should activities be limited because of eye conditions? _____ Yes _____No

6.   If yes, please specify. _____

7.   Recommendations and remarks. _____

_____
Examiner's signature

_____
Title

_____   _____
   Date   Address

Health report for vision test.

AUDIOGRAM

Name_____   Parent notified _____

Grade_____   Doctor's slip in _____

Teacher _____   Remarks_____

_____

_____

Frequency — cyles per second

	125	250	500	1000	2000	4000	8000	

Hearing loss in decibels

-10 ... -10
0 ... 0
10 ... 10
20 ... 20
30 ... 30
40 ... 40
50 ... 50
60 ... 60
70 ... 70
80 ... 80
90 ... 90
100 ... 100

Average normal hearing

X = Left ear

O = Right ear

Health report form for testing of hearing.

OFFICE OF THE SCHOOL NURSE

Dear Parent:

A recent health appraisal of your child _____

indicates a condition of _____

_____

which we feel warrants more complete diagnostic study and/or treatment

if such is indicated. It is urged that this condition be given immediate

professional attention. If for any reason you are unable to do so, please

advise the school nurse-teacher, who may be able to assist you.

Kindly ask your professional advisor to complete the lower portion

of this notice and return it to me.

_____
School Nurse-Teacher

Telephone No. _____

= =

TO THE EXAMINER

The following information will help us to better understand the health

needs of this child:

Findings: _____

Recommendations given parents: _____ _____

_____

Are any modifications of the school program indicated? If so, what?

_____

Do you wish to see this child again? If so, when? _____

Date _____

_____
Signature of Examiner

Address _____

Health report to parents.

Administrators are often responsible for poorly kept records, inaccurate reports, and late submissions. There should be clear directions, announcements at regular intervals, reminders as to when reports are due, and a prompt checking of reports to see if they are all in and whether there are omissions or other inaccuracies.

A survey was conducted of twenty-one school systems to determine the types of records that were kept in departmental files for health and physical education

SUPPLIES AND EQUIPMENT INVENTORY
(Special Teachers)

Name of teacher _____   School _____

Location of materials* _____   Date _____

Quantity	Description of articles	Condition		
		Good	Fair	Poor

* If the instructor who is preparing this report does not have a homeroom or if equipment used by the instructor is located in cabinets or storage space in more than one room, a notation as to the exact location of articles listed above should be made. If more than one room is used to store supplies, a separate report should be filed to note the contents of each storage location.

(SUBMIT IN DUPLICATE)

Inventory form for supplies and equipment.

personnel. The result of this survey showed that some of the schools were very conscientious in regard to record keeping; others were not. In general, most of the department heads and teachers admitted they should put more time and effort into this phase of health and physical education administration.

In the school systems surveyed, the boys' departments usually kept more records and forms than the girls' departments. See p. 594. This can be explained partially by the fact that athletic programs for boys have many more records associated with it.

The survey showed that in some schools records were kept in the department of health and physical education, while in other schools these same records were kept in another department. For example, in some schools attendance records were kept by the health and physical education department, while in other schools an attendance officer had complete control. In some schools the health and physical education department kept records on health, while in other schools these records were kept by the school nurse. The same was true in regard to budgetary and inventory records.

Pupil's Name .... Gr. ....

Permission is hereby given to .... to
Pupil's Name
participate in the After-School Play Program for the

.... season. I understand (he) (she) will
Fall, Winter, Spring

participate in .... on .... of each
Activity   *Days*

week from about .... to ....
Hour   *Hour*

Date ....
Parent or Guardian

Enrollment in this program is voluntary. However, once enrolled regular attendance is expected unless prevented for reasons of health or family plans. The pupil is expected to notify the activity supervisor of the reason for each absence.

Details of each season's program are given each pupil to take home in September of each year. Another copy will gladly be sent on request.

5M-7/63-BP

Parental permission form.

Name_____   _____ H. R._____
      Last   First

Lock No._____

Combination_____

Locker No._____

Floor Spot_____

Equipment record.

Some heads of health and physical education departments kept these records, while the business administrator and principals kept them in other schools.

The forms on pp. 595 to 601 show some of the most common types of records kept in the twenty-one school systems surveyed.

Examples of reports and records that are maintained by the health and/or physical education departments include the following:

Health
  Health consultation request
  Medical examination record
  Health history
  Growth records
  Excuse forms
  Exercise card
  Height and weight card
  Body mechanics inspection form
  Films and visual aids list
  Health habits record form
  Accident records

Physical education activity, skill, and squad records and reports
  Basket card
  Physical education record
  Field event report card

Physical education test and achievement forms
  Physical fitness record
  Report to parents
  Résumé of personality traits
  Citizenship guide sheet
  Athletic report

Physical education attendance and excuse records and reports
  Squad card attendance record
  Appointment slip
  Absence report
  Change of program

Physical education equipment forms
  Padlock record
  Equipment record
  Equipment inventory and condition report
  Lost property report

CHECKLIST OF SOME IMPORTANT CONSIDERATIONS FOR OFFICE MANAGEMENT

Space and working conditions   *Yes*   *No*

1. Does the reception room provide ample space for waiting guests?   ——   ——
2. Is the clerical space separated from the reception room so that office   ——   ——
   work is not interrupted by the arrival of guests?
3. Are there private offices for the Director of Health and Physical Edu-   ——   ——
   cation and as many of the staff as possible?
4. Is there an up-to-date health suite that provides an office and other   ——   ——
   essential facilities for the school nurse?
5. Is there adequate space and equipment for filing?   ——   ——
6. Are file drawers arranged so that papers can be inserted and removed   ——   ——
   easily and with space for future expansion?
7. Is the office arranged so that as many workers as possible get the best   ——   ——
   natural light with glare from sunlight or reflected sunlight avoided?
8. Has the office space been painted in accordance with the best in color   ——   ——
   dynamics?
9. Have provisions been made so that unnecessary noise is eliminated,   ——   ——
   distractions are kept to a minimum, and cleanliness prevails?
10. Is there good ventilation, appropriate artificial lighting, and satisfac-   ——   ——
    tory heating conditions?

CHECKLIST OF SOME IMPORTANT CONSIDERATIONS FOR OFFICE MANAGEMENT–cont'd

Personnel   *Yes*   *No*

11. Is a receptionist available to greet guests and answer queries?   _____   _____
12. Is there a recorded analysis of the duties of each secretarial position?   _____   _____
13. Are channels available for ascertaining causes of dissatisfaction among   _____   _____
    secretarial help?
14. Do secretaries dress neatly and conservatively?   _____   _____
15. Do secretaries maintain a desk that has an orderly appearance and   _____   _____
    clear their desks of working papers each day?
16. Do secretaries concern themselves with the efficiency of the office?   _____   _____
17. Are secretaries loyal to the department and staff members?   _____   _____
18. Do staff members have regular office hours?   _____   _____
19. Are appointments kept promptly?   _____   _____

Procedures

20. Is up-to-date reading material furnished for waiting guests?   _____   _____
21. Does the office help continually pay attention to maintaining offices   _____   _____
    that are neat, with papers, books, and other materials arranged in
    an orderly manner?
22. Are the secretaries knowledgeable about departmental activities so   _____   _____
    that they can answer intelligently queries about staff members and
    activities?
23. Do secretaries wait upon guests promptly and courteously?   _____   _____
24. Are letters typed neatly, well placed on the sheet, properly spaced,   _____   _____
    free from erasures and smudge and typographical errors?
25. Is correspondence handled promptly?   _____   _____
26. Is the filing system easily learned and is the filing done promptly so   _____   _____
    that the work does not pile up?
27. Is the office routine efficient of human time and energy with the   _____   _____
    elimination of duplicate operations or forms?
28. Are the most effective and efficient office methods utilized?   _____   _____
29. Is the clerical output satisfactory, with work starting promptly in the   _____   _____
    morning and after lunch, breaks taken according to schedule, and
    work stoppage taking place as scheduled?
30. Has a streamlined procedure been developed so that telephones are   _____   _____
    answered promptly, guests are courteously treated, and personal argu-
    ment and gossiping eliminated?
31. Are all essential records properly maintained and kept up to date?   _____   _____
32. Have procedures for typing and duplicating course outlines, committee   _____   _____
    reports, examinations, bulletins, fliers, letters, announcements, etc.,
    been developed to eliminate uncertainty or confusion on the part of
    staff members?
33. Are regular office hours for staff posted and known so that office staff   _____   _____
    can make appointments as needed?
34. Are secretaries acquainted with such details as securing films and   _____   _____
    other visual aids, obtaining reference material, helping in registration,
    duplicating material, and obtaining additional forms and records?
35. Is the office covered continuously during working hours?   _____   _____

Questions and exercises

1. Why is good office management essential for good public relations? What are some important reasons why office management is important to a department of physical and/or health education?
2. What three main divisions should office space include? Discuss the physical layout of each of these three divisions.
3. What office personnel should be available in a small high school, in a large high school, and in a college or university?
4. List the equipment and supplies that should be readily available in the average physical education office.
5. What importance can be attributed to a professional list of references in an office? Prepare a list of outstanding references for both the fields of health and physical education.
6. Prepare rules for effective administrative routine in respect to (a) hours, (b) assignments, (c) records and reports, (d) correspondence, (e) files and filing, (f) telephone, and (g) appointments.

Reading assignment in *Administrative Dimensions of Health and Physical Education Programs, Including Athletics:* Selections 16 and 71

Selected references

Courtesy in correspondence, The Royal Bank of Canada Monthly Letter **46:**1, 1965.

Doris, L., and Miller, B.: Complete secretary's handbook, Englewood Cliffs, N. J., 1951, Prentice-Hall, Inc.

Fawcett, W.: Policy and practice in school administration, New York, 1964, The Macmillan Co.

Leffingwell, W. H., and Robinson, E. M.: Textbook of office management, New York, 1950, McGraw-Hill Book Co.

Pittman, J.: Office may become a leader of management, The Office **67:**110, 1968.

Shiff, R. A.: Satellite administrative service centers, Administrative Management **30:**26, 1969.

Siegel, G. B.: Management development and the instability of skills: a strategy, Public Personnel Review **30:**15, 1969.

CHAPTER 22 MEASUREMENT OF PUPIL ACHIEVEMENT*

Measurement programs are gaining increasing prominence in school and college health and physical education programs. In order to show the benefits derived from participation in these programs and in order to conduct them in the most efficient way possible, measurement is an essential consideration.

The term *measurement* is used here to refer to the use of techniques to determine the degree to which a trait, ability, or characteristic exists in an individual.

During the last 35 years many measurement techniques have been developed in the fields of health and physical education. Some of these have been carefully constructed in a scientific manner, but many fall below acceptable standards. The administration should focus its attention on the materials that give valid and reliable results. Furthermore, all interested persons should be encouraged to construct new techniques in areas where shortages exist.

There are measurement techniques other than tests. Some of these are rating scales, checklists, photographic devices, controlled observation, and various measuring instruments.

The Joint Committee on Health Problems in Education of the National Education Association and the American Medical Association† states that the most common instruments or procedures used by health teachers are (1) observations, (2) surveys, (3) questionnaires and checklists, (4) interviews, (5) diaries and other autobiographic records kept by students, (6) health and growth records, (7) other records of health conditions or improvements, (8) samples of students' work, (9) case studies, and (10) health knowledge tests.

PURPOSES OF MEASUREMENT

Many purposes exist to support the utilization of measurement techniques in the administration of school health and physical education programs. A few of these will be discussed.

Measurement helps to determine the progress being made and the degree to which objectives are being met. It aids in discovering the needs of the participants. It identifies strengths and weaknesses of students and teachers, aids in curriculum planning, and shows where emphasis should be placed. It also gives direction and helps to supply information for guidance purposes.

Measurement helps in determining where emphasis should be placed in teaching and the procedures that are effective and ineffective. It also has use in aiding pupils to determine their own progress in respect to health and physical education practices, as a basis for giving grades, and as a means of interpreting programs to administrators and the public in general.

The information provided by measurement techniques can also be utilized in other ways. In the area of measurement, findings can be used for such purposes as grouping individuals according to similar mental, physical, and other traits that will

---

*See also Chapter 11 on Administering School and College Physical Fitness Programs for information on physical fitness tests.

†Joint Committee on Health Problems in Education of National Education Association and American Medical Association: Health education, Washington, D. C., 1961, National Education Association, p. 343.

Table 22-1. Extent of use of pupil evaluation techniques*

Techniques used†	Percent of 38 city school systems	Percent of 44 county school systems
Tests	100.0	100.0
Cumulative records	92.0	77.0
Interviews	89.5	71.0
Case studies	84.2	57.0
Case conferences	81.6	55.0
Group discussion	68.4	68.0
Anecdotal records	63.2	32.0
Observation	60.5	73.0
Files of sample materials	57.9	48.0
Questionnaires	53.3	30.0
Rating scales	44.7	11.0
Checklists	36.8	21.0
Inventories	31.6	18.0
Logs or diaries	13.2	16.0
Sociograms	10.5	2.0

*From Bonney, M. E., and Hampleman, R. S.: Personal-social evaluation techniques, New York, 1962, The Center for Applied Research in Education, Inc. (The Library of Education), pp. 4-5.
†Other techniques mentioned only once by either city, county, or both are the following: followup studies, autobiographies, clinics, case work, stenographic reports, films, recordings, psychiatric consultation, parental interviews, graphs of pupils' progress, interaction content records, and photographs.

Testing in physical education. (Henderson County Schools, Hendersonville, N. C.)

ensure better instruction. Measurement yields information that can be used as an indication of a person's achievement in various skills and activities. It provides information that can be used to predict future performance and development. It affords data on attitudes that determine whether or not the participant has proper motiva-tion, and it focuses attention on future action that should be taken in the program.

THE COMPUTER AND MEASUREMENT

The computer has many implications for the management of data concerned with pupil achievement in health and physical education programs. It enables the teacher and the administration to reduce the amount of time they devote to the analysis of data. The computer permits the analysis of test scores for thousands of students with comparative ease. It enables the physical educator to identify differentiating characteristics of students, such as scores that are high or low. The computer enables a battery of test items on such characteristics as speed, strength, or power to be analyzed item by item. It is an aid in scheduling in light of the results of measurement, for example, for purposes of grouping students with similar deficiencies into the same class. The computer makes it possible to prepare a profile of each student on the various health and physical education tests that are administered. Test scores of one class of students can be compared with other classes within the same school or with other schools where national norms are available.

These represent only a few examples of how the computer can be of value in the administration of a pupil measurement program. The uses of this device for the imaginative and creative administrator and teacher are limitless. The nation and world are rapidly being run on an electronic basis. Physical education and health education, if they desire to make their measurement programs most effective and meaningful, should examine the possibilities of the computer for their programs.

CRITERIA FOR TEST CONSTRUCTION AND SELECTION

Criteria refer to those particular standards that may be used to evaluate measurement and evaluation materials in the field of education. Such criteria as validity, reliability, objectivity, norms, and administrative economy provide the scientific basis for the selection and construction of tests. Administrators should be particularly concerned that the tests they utilize meet these criteria. If they do, properly interpreted results should aid considerably in developing adequate school health and physical education programs.

A definition of each criterion for test construction and selection and questions that could be asked by the administrator to determine whether or not the tests he desires to use meet the criteria listed are stated here*:

A. Validity
   Accuracy in measuring what it claims to measure.

*Larson, L. A.: Lecture notes, Course No. 280.62 in Advanced Methods and Materials in Physical Education, Health, and Recreation, New York University, 1946-1947.

1. Does it cover the area for which it is designed?
2. Is it applicable to proper ages and grades?
3. Is the criterion with which material was correlated acceptable?
4. Is the size of the correlation coefficient acceptable?
5. Does the technique give information concerning objectives?
6. Is the sampling adequate, representative, and random?
7. Is evidence cited as to whether it is a classification, achievement, diagnostic, or prognostic technique?
8. Has the technique been tried in the recommended area of application?

B. Reliability
   The consistency of measurement and evaluation on the same individual or group under the same conditions and by the same examiner.
   1. Is the size of the coefficient correlation acceptable?
   2. What are the means of the two tests?
   3. What are the conditions under which reliability has been determined?
   4. Is the method used for the determination of reliability valid (test-retest, split-halves, parallel forms)?
   5. Is the sample adequate, representative, and random?
   6. Has the reliability of the technique been determined by using the same group or individuals for which the technique is recommended?

C. Objectivity
   The degree to which a technique may be administered to the same individuals or group by a different examiner and obtain the same results.
   1. Is there a simple and complete manual of instructions?

2. Is the method used for determination of objectivity valid (test-retest, parallel forms)?
3. Is the sample adequate, representative, and random?
4. Has the objectivity of the technique been determined by using the same group for which the technique is recommended?
5. Are the means cited?
6. What is the difference in the mean scores?
7. Are the conditions under which objectivity has been determined satisfactory?
8. Are the procedures easily understood by the examiner and by the subject?
9. Are alternate forms of tests provided in instances where they are necessary?

D. Norms
   Levels of group performance or a statistical average most frequent for a group.
   1. What is the basis for construction of the norm (age, grade, ability)?
   2. Is the sample adequate, representative, and random?
   3. Are norms local or national?
   4. Are norms tentative, arbitrary, or experimental?
   5. Are all significant extraneous factors eliminated?
   6. Is the statistical refinement sufficient?
   7. Is the appropriate statistical tool used?

E. Administrative economy
   Procedures that deal with the conduct of the program.
   1. How much time is required to administer the technique?
   2. What is the approximate cost of the equipment used in the administration of the technique?
   3. Is the technique easy to administer?

4. How much training is necessary for the examiners?
5. Are the objectives of the test compatible with the objectives of the program?
6. Is the measurement or evaluational technique designed for school or research purposes?
7. How many examiners are needed?
8. Is the technique within the scope of a health or physical educator's training?

FRAMEWORK FOR MEASUREMENT PROCEDURES

To give the reader a clearer knowledge of some of the types of information that can be measured concerning some of the objectives of health and physical education, a partial framework is listed on the following pages. It is presented for the purpose of giving an indication of the vast scope of measurement and how it can influence these specialized programs. Objectives and terms used in framework are defined for purposes of clarification.

Objectives

1. *Organic development objectives* refer to the activity phase of the program that builds physical power in an individual through the development of the various organic systems of the body.
2. *Skill development objective* deals with the phase of the program that develops coordination, rhythm, and poise, through which some particular act may be performed with proficiency.
3. *Mental development objective* deals with the phase of the program that develops a comprehensive knowledge of principles, historical background, rules, techniques, values, and strategies.
4. *Human relations development objective* refers to the phase of the pro-

gram that aids an individual in making personal and group adjustments and in developing desirable standards of conduct essential to good citizenship.

Definitions

1. *Classification information* refers to those elements that can be used as a basis for segregating individuals into homogeneous groups for which they are reasonably well suited mentally, physically, emotionally, and socially.
2. *Achievement information* refers to those elements that can be measured to determine the scope and magnitude of an individual's achievement in organic development, skills, knowledge, and adaptability.
3. *Diagnostic information* refers to those elements that can be used to determine the causal factors of development and performance.
4. *Prognostic information* refers to those elements that can be used as valid forecasters of development and performance.
5. *Basic element* is an aspect of organic, neuromuscular, or mental growth that is a foundation for, and makes possible the development of, a skill.
6. *Fundamental skill* refers to a basic skill that is common to, and essential for participation in, most forms of activity.
7. *Activity skill* refers to a skill that is pertinent to successful participation in a particular activity.

Types of information concerning the objectives

1. *Organic development objective*
   a. Classification information
   (1) Age, weight, height
   (2) Strength
   (3) Posture
   (4) Sensory capacity
   (5) Physical fitness
   (6) Anthropometric measurements
   (7) Mental capacity
   (8) Power
   (9) Energy
   (10) Cardiac efficiency
   b. Achievement information
   (1) Strength
   (2) Endurance
   (3) Speed
   (4) Sensory capacity
   (5) Physical fitness
   (6) Power
   (7) Energy
   (8) Posture
   (9) Cardiac efficiency
   (10) Nutrition
   c. Diagnostic information
   (1) Age, weight, height
   (2) Strength
   (3) Endurance
   (4) Nutrition
   (5) Speed
   (6) Sensory capacity
   (7) Physical fitness
   (8) Power
   (9) Energy
   (10) Cardiac efficiency
   (11) Posture
   d. Prognostic information
   (1) Age, weight, height
   (2) Posture
   (3) Speed
   (4) Endurance
   (5) Sensory capacity
   (6) Physical fitness
   (7) Power
   (8) Energy
   (9) Cardiac efficiency
2. *Skill development objective*
   a. Classification information
   (1) Basic elements (concerned mainly with physical activity—would need development for other types)
   (a) Age, weight, height
   (b) Endurance
   (c) Strength
   (d) Native motor ability

YORKTOWN HEIGHTS ELEMENTARY SCHOOLS

PHYSICAL EDUCATION Progress Record	Grade Weight Height	3				4				5				6			
		Dec. 196	Grade Average	June 196	Grade Average	Dec. 196	Grade Average	June 196	Grade Average	Dec. 196	Grade Average	June 196	Grade Average	Dec. 196	Grade Average	June 196	Grade Average
Name																	
CHIN-UPS (Arm strength)																	
JUMPING ROPE - number of jumps completed in 30 seconds (Endurance, leg strength, coordination)																	
STANDING BROAD JUMP (Body movement forward) (feet)																	
JUMPING FOR HEIGHT (Jump - Reach - Body movement upward) (inches)																	
CLIMBING 20-FOOT ROPE (General strength & coordination) (feet)																	
TRAVEL HORIZONTAL LADDER (Arm strength & coordination) (feet)																	
SIT-UPS* (Abdominal strength)																	
50-YARD DASH (Speed) (seconds)																	
SOFTBALL THROW 30 FEET, 10 THROWS (Accuracy)																	

* Maximum sit-ups:
3rd - 20
4th - 30
5th - 50
6th - 50

FOUR YEAR FITNESS REPORT CARD

Fitness report card reflects growth and progress. Parents in Yorktown Heights, N. Y., know just how their children did in every phase of the semiannual physical fitness test because they receive fitness report cards twice each year and can check progress and growth. (From Klappholz, L., editor: Successful practices in teaching physical fitness, New London, Conn., 1964, Croft Educational Services. Reprinted by permission.)

(e) Motor educability	(a) Running
(f) Reaction time	(b) Throwing
(g) Motor interest	(c) Kicking
(h) Sensory capacity	(d) Jumping
(2) Fundamental skills (mainly concerned with physical activity—other aspects would need to be developed)	(e) Dodging
	(f) Leaping
	(g) Vaulting
	(h) Climbing

(i) Skipping
(j) Accuracy
(k) Objective body control
(l) Agility
(m) Timing
(n) Balance
(o) Spring
(p) Hand-eye, foot-eye, arm-eye coordinations
(3) Activity skills (would need to be broken down into the various components affecting the development of each skill)

b. Achievement information
(1) Basic elements (similar to basic elements under classification information)
(2) Fundamental skills (similar to fundamental skills under classification information)
(3) Activity skills (would need to be broken down into the various components affecting the development of each skill)

c. Diagnostic information
(1) Basic elements
(a) Nutrition
(b) Health habits such as sleep, rest, and mental state
(c) Cardiac efficiency
(d) Sensory capacity
(e) Motor interest
(f) Reaction time
(g) Motor educability
(h) Native motor ability
(i) Strength
(j) Endurance
(k) Age, weight, height
(2) Fundamental skills (similar to fundamental skills under classification information)
(3) Activity skills (would need to be broken down into the various components affecting the development of each skill)

d. Prognostic information
(1) Basic elements (similar to basic

elements under diagnostic information)
(2) Fundamental skills (similar to fundamental skills under classification information)
(3) Activity skills (would need to be broken down into the various components affecting the development of each skill)

3. *Mental development objective*
a. Classification information
(1) Mental capacity
(2) Health education, physical education, and recreation background
(3) Academic background
(4) Moral background
(5) Home environment

b. Achievement information—such knowledge, attitudes, and practices as:
(1) Rules of games
(2) First-aid procedures
(3) General health, health habits, proper living, health knowledge
(a) Personal
(b) Community
(c) Mental
(d) Social
(e) Emotional
(4) Rules of safety
(5) Proper forms in games, athletic events, swimming, dancing, and other physical activities
(6) Etiquette in certain game situations
(7) Team play
(8) Strategy in games and events
(9) Regulations governing meets, tournaments, and other athletic events
(10) Duties of officials
(11) Physical activities
(12) Values of health and physical education
(13) Techniques
(14) Historical background of games and activities

(15) Principles of hygiene and sanitation

(16) Effect of exercise on body

(17) Best kind of exercise to take under certain circumstances

c. Diagnostic information

    (1) Mental capacity

    (2) Health and physical education background

    (3) Academic background

    (4) Interest

    (5) Home environment

    (6) Physical fitness

    (7) Achievement records

    (8) Health records

d. Prognostic information

    (1) Mental capacity

    (2) Interest

    (3) Physical fitness

    (4) Achievement records

    (5) Health records

4. *Human relations development objective*

a. Classification information

    (1) Character

    (2) Personality

    (3) Mental health

    (4) Social attitudes

    (5) Conduct

    (6) Habits

    (7) Citizenship

    (8) Emotions

    (9) Drives

    (10) Appreciations

    (11) Interests

    (12) Capacity for leadership

    (13) Ability to transfer training

    (14) Group living

    (15) Sportsmanship

    (16) Service to community

b. Achievement information

    (1) Character and personality

        (a) Honesty

        (b) Loyalty

        (c) Fair play

        (d) Good sportsmanship

        (e) Courage

        (f) Unselfishness

    (2) Leadership

        (a) Initiative

        (b) Cooperation

        (c) Quickness of decision

        (d) Fairness and judgment

        (e) Vision and imagination

        (f) Executive ability

        (g) Ability to get along with others

        (h) Personal magnetism

(3) Transfer of training

    (a) From game situations to other situations in life

    (b) Motor transfer—capacity to solve motor situations and to make a new coordinated movement accurately

(4) Habits and practices

    (a) Health (eating, sleeping, bathing, and so on)

    (b) Exercise and recreation

(5) Attitudes and appreciations

    (a) Value of health

    (b) Value of physical recreation

    (c) Good sportsmanship

    (d) Team play

    (e) Value of acquiring certain skills

    (f) Appreciation of recreation and exercise

    (g) Appreciation of health and practicing health habits

    (h) Attitude toward cheating

    (i) Attitude toward winning

    (j) Attitude toward intraschool versus interschool competition

    (k) Appreciation of playing with the "dub"

    (l) Appreciation of training for competition

    (m) Appreciation of ways of spending leisure time

    (n) Appreciation of awards and rewards

(6) Social attitudes

    (a) Toward individuals of different race, color, and creed

(b) Toward good citizenship
(7) Emotions
(8) Service to community
c. Diagnostic information
(1) Health and physical education background
(2) Mental capacity
(3) Character
(4) Family background
(5) Companions
(6) Personality
(7) Emotional control
(8) Drives
(9) Interests
(10) Group living
(11) Sportsmanship
(12) Physical fitness
d. Prognostic information
(1) Sportsmanship
(2) Character
(3) Personality
(4) Mental capacity
(5) Group living
(6) Leadership
(7) Emotional control
(8) Habits
(9) Attitudes and appreciations
(10) Physical fitness
(11) Interests
(12) Personal ambitions
(13) Home environment
(14) Parental influence

TECHNIQUES AND INSTRUMENTS FOR OBTAINING DESIRED INFORMATION ABOUT STUDENTS

There are many techniques and instruments that can be utilized to obtain the various types of classification, achievement, diagnostic, and prognostic information about students. A few examples are listed for each category.

Classification information

An example of an instrument that would yield classification information is McCloy's Classification Index I.* This classification index takes into consideration such items as age, height, weight, and athletic skill, with a simple formula developed for the calculation of the index.

Another example of an instrument that could prove helpful for classification purposes is the Wetzel Grid.† This is valuable in either school health or physical education programs since it takes into consideration such elements as physique, developmental level, and nutritional progress with respect to weight, age, and height.

Achievement information

An example of an instrument that reflects achievement information would be the Indiana Physical Fitness Text.‡ This instrument involves such test items as straddle chins, squat-thrusts, push-ups, and vertical jumps. Norms have been developed for boys and girls.

There are many achievement tests available that can be utilized by school and college programs of health and physical education. Some excellent tests are listed in a later section of this chapter.

Diagnostic information

Examples of diagnostic techniques for a school or college health program would be the health examination, audiometer, and vision tests. These techniques or instruments yield information on an individual's health, including heart, lungs, teeth, hearing, vision, and posture.

An example of a diagnostic instrument

*McCloy, C. H., and Young, N. D.: Tests and measurements in health and physical education, ed. 3, New York, 1954, Appleton-Century-Crofts, pp. 59-60.

†Wetzel, N. C.: Grid for evaluating physical fitness, Cleveland, 1948, National Education Association Service, Inc.

‡State of Indiana Department of Public Instruction: High school physical education course of study, Bulletin 222, Indianapolis, 1958, The Department.

in physical education would be the Dyer Backboard Test* for tennis. This test evaluates general tennis ability. It does not analyze the various strokes and elements of the game. It merely consists of volleying a tennis ball as rapidly as possible against a backboard.

Prognostic information

An example of a prognostic instrument would be a sociometric test, which reflects a person's ability to get along with others. Another instrument would be a test of mental capacity to forecast academic achievement. Also, it could be a health record to forecast certain aspects of mental health essential to success in various endeavors. It could be a test of general motor ability to forecast achievement in specific skills. Several types of measurement instruments yield information that would forecast future performance in many of life's activities.

TECHNIQUES AND INSTRUMENTS FOR OBTAINING INFORMATION ABOUT OBJECTIVES

In addition to gaining classification, achievement, diagnostic, and prognostic information about students, it also is necessary to identify particular instruments, materials, resources, and methods for evaluating pupil status in respect to organic, neuromuscular, mental, and social development.

Organic development objective

A medical examination is a valuable technique for obtaining information about the organic development of the pupil. Such an examination should be given at least once a year by a competent physician.

Physical fitness tests will be helpful in determining student status in regard to this objective. Several excellent tests are listed in Chapter 11.

Other tests that should be reviewed as possible instruments for determining the organic development status of pupils are as follows*:

Circulatory-respiratory tests
Cureton All-Out Treadmill Test
Henry Tests of Vasomotor Weakness
MacCurdy-Larson Organic Efficiency Test
Schneider Cardiovascular Test
Turner Test of Circulatory Reaction to Prolonged Standing
Tuttle Pulse-Ratio Test

Anthopometric, posture, and body mechanics measurements
Cureton Technique for Scaling Postural Photographs and Silhouettes
Cureton Tissue Symmetry Test
Cureton-Grover Fat Test
Cureton-Gunby Conformateur Test of Antero-Posterior Posture
Cureton-Holmes Tests for Functional Fitness of the Feet
Cureton-Nordstrom Skeletal Build Index
Cureton-Wickens Center of Gravity Tests

Muscular strength, power, and endurance tests
Anderson Strength Index for High School Girls
Carpenter Strength Test for Women
Cureton Muscular Endurance Tests
Larson Dynamic Strength Test for Men
MacCurdy Test of Physical Capacity
McCloy Athletic Strength Index
Rogers Physical Capacity Test and Physical Fitness Index
Wendler Strength Index

---

*Dyer, J. T.: The backboard test of tennis ability, Supplement to the Research Quarterly 6:63, 1935; Revision of backboard test of tennis ability, Research Quarterly 9:25, 1938.

*These tests may be found in copies of Research Quarterly, American Association of Health, Physical Education, and Recreation, or in one of the measurement and evaluation texts listed in the selected references at the end of this chapter.

Flexibility tests
Cureton Flexibility Tests
Leighton Flexometer Tests

Neuromuscular development objective

Physical skills represent a major part of the physical education program; therefore, appropriate valid tests of physical skills should be utilized. Such qualities as *motor educability, motor capacity, physical capacity, motor ability, and motor efficiency* are terms frequently utilized in connection with neuromuscular development.

Tests have been developed for skills in sports such as archery, badminton, soccer, basketball, bowling, football, golf, handball, field hockey, and ice hockey. Descriptions of these tests are given in some of the source books listed at the end of this chapter. These suggested tests should be studied carefully to determine their suitability or adaptability to a particular school situation. Some of the instruments that should be explored in measuring this objective in students are as follows:

Motor fitness tests
Bookwalter Motor Fitness Tests
Cureton-Illinois Motor Fitness Tests
O'Connor-Cureton Motor Fitness Tests for High School Girls

General motor skills tests
Brace Test of Motor Ability
Carpenter Test of Motor Educability for Primary Grade Children
Cozens Test of General Athletic Ability
Humiston Test of Motor Ability for Women
Iowa Revision of the Brace Motor Ability Test
Johnson Test of Motor Educability
Larson Test of Motor Ability for Men
Metheny Revision of the Johnson Test
Powell-Howe Motor Ability Tests for High School Girls
Scott Test of Motor Ability for Women

Sports skills tests
Borleske Touch Football Test for Men
Cureton Swimming Endurance Tests
Cureton Swimming Tests
Dyer Backboard Test of Tennis Ability
Johnson Basketball Test for Men
Lehsten Basketball Test for Men
Rodgers-Heath Soccer Skills Tests for Elementary Schools
Russell-Lange Volleyball Test for Girls
Schmithals-French Field Hockey Tests for Women
Young-Moser Basketball Test for Women

One of the most significant new developments in the area of skill measurement is being encouraged under the sponsorship of the American Association for Health, Physical Education, and Recreation. During the past few years their Research Council has been working to devise tests and norms for effective evaluation of boys and girls, grades five through twelve, in physical education programs across the United States. This total project includes skill tests for such activities as:

Archery	Football	Softball
Badminton	Golf	Swimming
Baseball	Gymnastics	Tennis
Basketball	Lacrosse	Track and field
Field hockey	Soccer	Volleyball

Administrators should obtain the sports skills test manuals that have been developed. They will be most helpful not only for testing purposes but for instructional suggestions as well. Sample class composite record forms, data, and profile forms are also available from the Association.

Mental development objective

In the field of health education there are several tests for measuring health knowledge and attitudes. Solleder[*] has compiled a list of several of these instruments

---

[*]Solleder, M. K.: Evaluation instruments in health education, Washington, D. C., 1965, American Association for Health, Physical Education, and Recreation.

for each educational level. Such tests could be used to evaluate the effectiveness of teaching procedures, weaknesses in the instructional program, and health knowledge of students and for the purpose of grouping students in health classes. They could also be used to determine the impact of health instruction on health knowledge and the attitudes and practices of students, as well as to grade students.

In order to illustrate the types of tests available in health education, one test is listed for each educational level as taken from Solleder's compilation of health evaluating instruments:

Elementary school—Dzenowagis, J. G.: Self-Quiz of Safety Knowledge. This test has been developed to measure safety preparedness of pupils at the fifth- and sixth-grade levels. Available from the National Safety Council, School and College Department, 425 N. Michigan Ave., Chicago, Ill.

Junior high school—Kilander, H. F.: Nutrition Information Test. This test is designed for students in junior high school through college. Norms are available from Dr. H. F. Kilander, Wagner College, Staten Island, N. Y.

Senior high school—Thompson, C. W.: Thompson Smoking and Tobacco Knowledge Test. This test includes the most important physiologic, psychologic, and socioeconomic facts relating to smoking and tobacco. For more information on this test see Thompson, C. W.: Thompson Smoking and Tobacco Knowledge Test, Research Quarterly 35:60, 1964.

Junior college—Junior College Health Knowledge Test. This multiple-choice test covers eleven areas of health instruction. For more information write to Supervisor of Health Education, P. O. Box 3307, Terminal Annex, Los Angeles, Calif. 90054.

College or university—Dearborn, T. H.: College Health Knowledge Test. For more information write to Stanford University Press, Stanford, Calif.

In the field of physical education, several standardized tests are available for written tests in various sports. Also, some tests may be found in rule books and source books. Some knowledge and understanding tests in physical education that should be explored are the French Tests for Professional Courses in Knowledge and Sports, Hewitt Comprehensive Tennis Knowledge

---

COMPARISON OF ESSAY AND OBJECTIVE TESTS

Characteristic	Essay test	Objective test
Preparation of test item	Items are relatively easy to construct	Items are relatively difficult to construct
Sampling of the subject matter	Sampling is often limited	Sampling is usually extensive
Measurement of knowledges and understandings	Items can measure both; measurement of understanding is recommended	Items can measure both; measurement of knowledges is emphasized
Preparation by pupil	Emphasis is primarily on larger units of material	Emphasis is primarily on factual details
Nature of response by pupil	Pupil organizes original response	Except for supply test items, pupil selects response
Guessing of correct response by pupil	Successful guessing is minor problem	Successful guessing is major problem
Scoring of pupil responses	Scoring is difficult, time-consuming, and somewhat unreliable	Scoring is simple, rapid, and highly reliable

From Ahmann, J. S.: Testing student achievements and aptitudes, New York, 1962, The Center for Applied Research in Education, Inc. (The Library of Education), p. 35.

Tests, Scott Badminton Knowledge Test, Scott Swimming Knowledge Test, and Scott Tennis Knowledge Test.

Teachers may devise their own tests appropriate to the subject and age level being taught. When teachers develop their own tests, however, they should keep in mind the following principles of test construction:

1. The items selected should stress the most important aspects of the material.
2. The length of the test should be determined in relation to the time available for testing.
3. The test should be appropriately worded and geared for the age level to be tested.
4. Questions or test items should be worded so as to avoid ambiguity.
5. Statements should be simple and direct, not tricky or involved.

Social development objective

There have been several tests developed in the school and college health program to indicate pupil attitudes and behavior. Solleder* has listed several of these in her publication. A sampling of these behavior and attitude instruments are as follows:

Elementary school—Yellen, S.: Health Behavior Inventory, 1963. Designed for grades three to six and covers such items as health habits, nutrition, safety, rest, and disease prevention. For more information on this test write to California Test Bureau, Monterey, Calif.

Junior high school—Colebank, A. D.: Health Behavior Inventory, 1963. Designed for grades seven to nine and covers various health information items through a 100-item test. For more information write to California Test Bureau, Monterey, Calif.

Senior high school—Johns, E. B., and Juhnke, W. L.: Health Practice Inventory, 1952. Covers thirteen health areas. Manual of directions and norms also available for senior high students. For more information write to Stanford University Press, Stanford, Calif.

College or university—Leonard, M. L., and

Horton, C. W.: An Inventory of Certain Practices in Health, 1949. Instrument can be used to study health behavior of college students. For more information write to California State Department of Education, Sacramento, Calif.

General tests of social adjustment have also been developed, such as the Bell Adjustment Inventory, Science Research Associates Inventory, Minnesota Multiphasic Personality Inventory, and Bernreuter Personality Inventory. The guidance department in almost any school or college would be a good source of information for many tests of social adjustment.

Attitudes may be measured in different ways. Three techniques utilized in this area are teacher evaluation (observation of students with an anecdotal record being kept by the teacher), opinion polls, and rating scales. The physical education teacher should ask for the assistance of other teachers, particularly of the guidance personnel, in this type of testing.

Sociometrics is being used extensively for measurement of social relationships as determined by use of a sociogram. The sociogram points out the natural leaders in the groups and the outsiders trying to become members. When used more than once with the same group, a comparison of the results indicates social growth or change. A sociogram may be taken, for example, by asking all members of a team to list two people whom they would like to have as their friends, with their choices limited to a given group or team. Results may be pictured with arrows pointing to the names listed.

MINIMUM AND DESIRABLE STANDARDS

Larson and Yocom* have developed a list of minimum and desirable standards

---

*Solleder, M. K., op. cit.

*Larson, L. A., and Yocom, R. D.: Measurement and evaluation in physical, health, and recreation education, St. Louis, 1951, The C. V. Mosby Co., p. 450.

RÉSUMÉ OF PERSONALITY TRAITS

Date_____

_____   _____ _____   _____
     Student   Home Room   Teacher   Subject

Please check directly above the word or group of words which you think best
describes the pupil. Give specific examples, if possible, in parentheses
on same line with check or below under COMMENTS if you prefer.

1. INDUSTRY_____|_____|_____|_____|_____
         Needs   Needs   Prepares   Completes   Seeks
         constant   occasional assigned   supplementary additional
         prodding   prodding   work   work   tasks

2. STUDY HABITS_____|_____|_____|_____
            Poor   Fair   Good   Excellent

3. RESPONSIBILITY_____|_____|_____|_____|_____
            Unreliable Somewhat   Usually   Thoroughly Assumes
                        dependable dependable dependable responsi-
                                                            bility

4. COOPERATION_____|_____|_____|_____
           Poor   Fair   Good   Excellent

5. HONESTY_____|_____|_____
        Questionable at times Generally reliable Completely reliable

6. MATURITY_____|_____|_____
         Immature   Of average maturity   Exceptionally mature

7. EMOTIONAL STABILITY_____|_____|_____
              Usually well balanced Well balanced Exceptionally
                                                     stable

8. MANNERS_____|_____|_____
       Discourteous and   Usually courteous   Always courteous
       inconsiderate   and considerate

9. INFLUENCE_____|_____|_____|_____
       Occasionally Passive   Average   Generally   Strong
       detrimental   beneficial

10. FURTHER COMMENTS: Outstanding personality traits, chief interests, social
                      adjustments, unusual achievements, etc.

Résumé of personality traits. (From Bucher, C. A., Koenig, C. R., and Barnhard, M.: Methods and materials in secondary school physical education, ed. 3, St. Louis, 1970, The C. V. Mosby Co.)

Table 22-2. Minimum and desirable standards for a measurement program in health and physical education

Measurement of program outcomes (product)	Minimum standards	Desirable standards
Organic	Medical examination or a cardiovascular test Physical (motor) fitness test	Medical examination (including a cardiovascular test) Muscular strength Body build Growth, nutrition, development Posture and body mechanics
Skills	General motor ability	Tests for each sport
Knowledge	Teacher-made tests	Standardized tests and teacher-made tests
Adjustment	Controlled observation	Standardized tests

for a measurement program in health, physical education, and recreation based on the premise that these specialized fields, as pertains to measurement, contribute to the attainment of objectives of organic development, skill or motor development, knowledge or mental development, and adjustment or human relations development. These standards are reproduced in Table 22-2.

Phillips* listed what she considered to be a *minimal program of measurement.* She pointed out that these are stated in general terms and that to prescribe standards for any particular situation, it would be necessary to have information on the quality and/or quantity of such factors as personnel, facilities, equipment, program teacher-pupil ratio. She listed the following six points:

1. A *health examination,* conducted by a medical doctor. The absolute minimum would be for the examination to be given to all incoming freshmen (or sophomores in the 3-year high school). It would be greatly improved if the physical education teacher could administer a posture screening test at the same time.

2. *Tests of neuromuscular skills.* These tests should be given during the final periods of instruction for each motor activity learned. This

provides the teacher and pupil with objective evidence of the pupil's status in the skill and may be used additionally for classification purposes for further instruction and/or for the developing of intramural teams in those cases where the activity is of the intramural type.

3. *Knowledge tests.* These tests should be given at least once a semester and should sample the information and knowledge learned during that time.

4. *Attitude tests.* While no specific recommendation will be made for giving attitude tests in this minimum program, it will be very strongly suggested that the teacher should be constantly alert in observing the behavior of his students. One of the most important of our physical education objectives is the development of good attitudes. The thoughtful teacher will understand that a real effort must be made if this objective is to be realized. Hence, the teacher must carry on a constant program of evaluation in his daily associations with his students and use his observations as a basis for discussion with the individual students.

5. An annual *motor fitness or physical fitness test.* This would provide the teacher and pupil with a yearly check on the progress of the pupil in this vital area of his development.

6. *Self-evaluation.* One of the most important recommendations for this program is one that may not have too much supporting evidence in the formal literature on physical education measurement and evaluation. This is to the effect that the teacher should be carrying on a constant program of self-evaluation, relative to his own professional, personal, and social growth and development, as well as to the quality and effective-

*Letter dated Nov. 15, 1955, from Marjorie Phillips, Indiana University.

ness of the program he is providing for his students.

If the program of self-evaluation is ineffective, then it would be reasonable to expect that the program of pupil evaluation will be equally ineffective.

KEEPING RECORDS AND USING TEST RESULTS

There are many clerical duties associated with the measurement program. For most effective use records should be kept up-to-date and new test results constantly analyzed in terms of student progress and program planning. In some school districts teacher aides and community volunteers have been used to do the clerical work. Also, in today's automation era some schools and colleges have found it advantageous to use IBM cards to record test results. It may also be helpful to maintain a record file of measurement instruments used, adding comments concerning possible success or problems involved in their administration. This would prevent repetition of testing with unsuitable instruments.

The purpose of testing is to help the student and improve the educational program. As pointed out earlier in this chapter, tests can yield classification, achievement, diagnostic, and prognostic information. Therefore, after the testing has been accomplished, the results should be used appropriately.

NEED FOR A STANDARDIZATION OF MEASUREMENT MATERIALS

There are at least three reasons why the need is great for a standardization of measurement materials for the fields of health and physical education.

In the first place, many of the techniques being used today have been developed by individuals who have failed to use or interpret correctly scientific methods of construction. As a result, there are materials being used in our schools and colleges that have either failed to be scientifically evaluated or else have fallen below acceptable standards. In light of these conditions, it is necessary to ensure that only materials that meet acceptable criteria will be used. Standardization would make such a practice possible.

In the second place, it is impossible to make comparisons between individuals of different localities because of the different

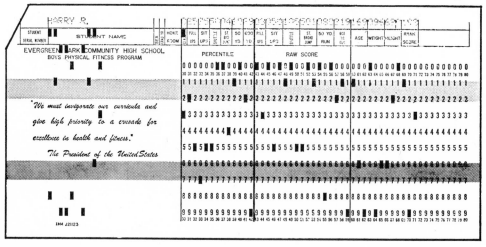

IBM card for recording test results. (From Bucher, C. A., Koenig, C. R., and Barnhard, M.: Methods and materials for secondary school physical education, ed. 3, St. Louis, 1970, The C. V. Mosby Co.)

techniques being used in each section. When a student transfers from one geographic locality to another, the instructor is at a loss to analyze his status, because of the lack of standards for all sections of the country. As a result, the instructor must start from the beginning in determining an individual's physical condition, traits, or characteristics. Standardization would make it possible for records to be interpreted intelligently, regardless of who administers the technique or the locality in which it is administered.

In the third place, it is difficult to measure progress on a national basis without the use of standards. It is imperative that measurement materials be standardized so that the professions can know whether they are meeting the objectives that have been set, can evaluate the various types of programs and instruction, and can know what they are achieving through these programs. Standardization would make it possible to better determine individual and program weaknesses, quality of instruction, and progress achieved. Furthermore, standardization would serve as a means of motivation and comparison.

GRADING

The giving of grades in school programs of health and physical education represents

Physical education progress report, Barrington, Ill., Junior High School. (From Bucher, C. A., Koenig, C. R., and Barnhard, M.: Methods and materials for secondary school physical education, ed. 3, St. Louis, 1970, The C. V. Mosby Co.)

an administrative necessity. The purposes for grading include the following:

1. It serves as a means of indicating student achievement in the areas for which the course or experience is offered.
2. It serves as a means of informing such persons as parents, employers, colleges and universities, honorary societies, and other groups of the quality of a pupil's work.
3. It serves as a motivational device for some students.
4. It serves as a guide to program planning and for the grouping of students (grades identify areas of strength and weakness in the curriculum and in the students) and as a basis for counseling students (abrupt changes in a student's grades might be indicative of problems).

Since grading is an established custom

PHYSICAL EDUCATION REPORT CARD

NASHVILLE CITY SCHOOLS

Pupil_____School_____

Homeroom_____Classroom _____Year 19_____ 19_____

GRADE LEVEL	FALL					SPRING					YEAR'S AVERAGE
	1	2	3	Ex	Av	4	5	6	Ex	Av	

Items checked (✔) below need improvement

	1	2	3	4	5	6
Develops co-ordination						
Shows knowledge of rules						
Develops physically						
Strength						
Endurance						
Weight						
Participates						
Dress						
Playing						
Shower						
Attendance (Days absent from class)						
Conduct						

CODE

(Teacher may add plus or minus if she wishes)

A=90 - 100—Consistently does ex-   C=75 - 81—Does fair work
    cellent work   D=70 - 74—Low, but passing
B =82 - 89—Does good work   F =Below 70—Failing

Comments enclosed   Date_____ Date_____ Date_____
                  Date_____ Date_____ Date_____

Teacher_____

Physical education report card, Nashville city schools. (From Bucher, C. A., Koenig, C. R., and Barnhard, M.: Methods and materials for secondary school physical education, ed. 3, St. Louis, 1970, The C. V. Mosby Co.)

in the educational system of this country, physical education must conform and grant grades or utilize some other method of denoting the progress that has been achieved.

Grades have been issued in physical education in several ways, ranging from granting letter or numeral grades to ranking in a class. These grades have also been based on many factors, many of which have questionable value. Some present practices base grades on such factors as attendance, punctuality, effort, costume, achievement, general attitude, initiative, hygiene, skill, knowledge of rules, cooperation, posture, strength, and endurance. Nationally, there seems to be no set formula or procedure. Each individual instructor establishes the basis on which grades should be granted.

The following recommendations represent some of the more advanced thinking among educators in general. At the elementary level especially, the feeling is increasing that it is not wise to issue a single

ATTITUDES AND PRACTICES	Items checked (✓) below need improvement					
	1	2	3	4	5	6
SOCIAL						
Uses self-control						
Is courteous in speech and action ..						
Co-operates						
Cares for property (incl. textbooks)						
Is considerate toward others						
Respects and obeys school rules						
WORK						
Makes good use of abilities						
Follows directions promptly						
Completes each task						
Works independently						
Uses initiative						
HEALTH						
Maintains personal cleanliness						
Maintains correct posture						
Obeys safety precautions						

PARENT'S SIGNATURE

1. _____

2. _____

3. _____

4. _____

5. _____

6. _____

For legend see opposite page.

grade or numerical rating. It is felt that a descriptive paragraph telling in more detail what progress is being made by the pupil is much better. Discussing such items as a student's strengths and weaknesses and where he needs to improve is much more meaningful and purposeful. This type of report and talks with parents will better achieve the purpose of showing to what degree educational objectives are being attained and what needs to be accomplished in the future. This method also has implications for grading above the elementary level.

When grades are given, they should be based on the achievement of objectives— the degree to which the student has achieved the desired outcomes. These objectives should be clear in the instructor's and students' minds at the outset of the course so that the desired direction will be known. The individuals getting the best grades would be those students most nearly achieving the objectives that have been listed as desirable goals for the course. In physical education the physical, motor, mental, and human relations objectives would all be kept in mind.

A further recommendation is that, as far as possible, the degree to which desired objectives are achieved should be determined objectively rather than subjectively. This means that wherever possible scientific evaluation and measurement techniques should be utilized. Since there is a dearth of such techniques, some subjective judgments will have to be made.

Grades should be understood by the student. He or she should know how they are arrived at and how the factors that go into the grades are weighed. The grades should also be easily understood by parents, particularly as to how they relate to the objectives of the course the student is taking. As far as possible, the grades should be expressed in the same manner as grades in other subject matter areas throughout the school. This not only facilitates record keeping and transfer of credits but also places health and physical education on the same level as other subjects.

The State Department of Public Instruction at Bismarck, North Dakota, has established some standards for grading in that state. Some excerpts* from their grading policy read as follows:

The hit or miss method of purely subjective grading in physical education so widely used cannot be too strongly condemned. The grade in physical education should be an accurate reflection of how well the pupil has achieved the objectives. It is suggested that the following points be considered in grading:

(a) The system for reporting grades should conform to the system generally used by the school as a whole.

(b) Basis for the grade:

50%, Achievement of physical skill and activity.

30%, Specific health and social qualities.

20%, Knowledge of rules and techniques.

An 'A' student is *superior* in that he:

(a) Is keenly enthusiastic. Persists industriously at his tasks.

(b) Acts intelligently on his own initiative.

(c) Shows positive leadership.

(d) Carries out responsibilities faithfully and honestly.

(e) Displays superior general ability and form.

(f) Is well liked by most of his fellow students, tactful to those in authority and to those he leads.

(g) Is a gracious winner and a good leader and encourages the same in others.

A 'B' student is *excellent* in that he:

(a) Is usually enthusiastic and generally industrious.

(b) Cooperates well with leaders.

(c) Follows directions intelligently without much help.

(d) Generally carries out his share of group activity.

(e) Has good general ability and form.

(f) Has few enemies and gets along well with others.

(g) Seldom displays poor sportsmanship.

*Department of Public Instruction: Health education in secondary schools, Bismarck, N. D., 1950, State Department of Public Instruction, pp. 48-49.

A 'C' student is *average* in that he:
  (a) Is passive as a rule. Willing to do as told.
  (b) Is not outstanding in understanding. A little slow at times.
  (c) Usually cooperates. Never assumes leadership.
  (d) Will work with assistance.
  (e) Has some friends and some enemies but none outstanding.
  (f) Has fair ability. Learns slowly at times.
  (g) Displays poor sportsmanship occasionally.

A 'D' student is *below average* in that he:
  (a) Is disinterested and reticent. Tends to avoid work.
  (b) Does not understand directions. Makes frequent errors.
  (c) Must be led and watched.
  (d) Will avoid responsibility frequently.
  (e) Has poor ability and little form. A slow learner.
  (f) Tends to be reclusive or unsociable.

  (g) Is poor in skill. Either has no skill or won't use it.

A student will probably not be completely described by any one of the descriptive groups listed, but as a rule traits above and below the group most descriptive of the individual will level each other into the middle group.

The thinking in regard to grading in physical education is well summarized by the American Association for Health, Physical Education, and Recreation*:

1. Specific goals and objectives should be established with students.

*American Association for Health, Physical Education, and Recreation: Administrative problems in health education, physical education, and recreation, Washington, D. C., 1953, The Association, p. 74.

PASSING OR FAILING IN PHYSICAL EDUCATION*

In response to numerous inquiries from school officials, the following is intended to clarify the statement that boards of education may not refuse graduation or promotion because of failure in physical education.

Physical education is required for all pupils by Education Law and Regulations of the Commissioner of Education. It is expected that each pupil will participate in such classes and that he will exert sufficient effort to enable him to achieve his optimal progress toward all program objectives. If a pupil refuses to attend physical education classes and otherwise does not fulfill course requirements approved by the board of education, and prompt and appropriate notification is given to all concerned, a failing mark may be given and graduation withheld until such time as the deficiency has been removed.

On the other hand, a pupil who fulfills all the requirements and has exhibited acceptable evidence of satisfactory progress in terms of his abilities but who has been unable to meet minimal standards of physical performance may not be given a failing mark in physical education.

Pupils who act in ways deemed undesirable as good school citizens while participating in physical education classes, such as disobeying the teacher, refusing to exert reasonable effort or deliberately violating stated policies and procedures, should be treated as disciplinary cases.

Physical education is an integral part of the school curriculum. It is recognized that achievement of the program's major goals including physical fitness, skills, knowledge, social qualities and attitudes will help provide valuable assets for each pupil. Therefore, every effort should be made to insure that physical education is a meaningful and profitable experience for each boy and girl, particularly for those who possess lower levels of physical ability. One of the most valuable outcomes of a physical education program is the inculcation of a strong appreciation of, desire for and interest in participation in physical activities which will endure throughout life. Would failing in physical education help to reach this goal?

Reviewed and Approved by Division of Law,
State Education Department,
January, 1969

*From New York State Education Department: Curriculum guide: physical education in the secondary school, 1964, p. 21.

Student ....

....   **19**............ - **19**......
Grade

RICHWOODS COMMUNITY HIGH SCHOOL

Progress Report in Physical Education

Teacher ....   Counselor

1st pd.	2nd pd.	3rd pd.	Sem. exam	Sem. avg.	4th pd.	5th pd.	6th pd.	Sem. exam	Sem. avg.	Units crdt.

EXPLANATION OF MARKING SYSTEM

Achievement—Grading for actual work done by the student

A—94-100—Excellent   D—70-77—Below Average
B—86- 93—Above Avg.   F—Below 70—Failure
C—78- 85—Average   E—Conditional
                              Inc.—Incomplete

ACTIVITIES INCLUDED IN GRADING PERIODS

ACTIVITIES	1	2	3	4	5	6
Flicker Ball						
Flag Football						
Soccer						
*Field Hockey						
*Speed Ball						
*Campcraft						
Basketball (beginning) (advanced)						
Volleyball (beginning) (advanced)						
Tumbling (beginning) (advanced)						
Apparatus (beginning) (advanced)						
Wrestling (beginning) (advanced)						
Handball						
Badminton						
Recreational Games						
*Fundamental Rhythms—Modern Dance						
Track and Field						
Softball						
Archery						
Golf						
Co. P.E. Social Dance						
Co. P.E. Square Dance						
Co. P.E. Volleyball & Rec. Games						
Driver Training (Classroom)						
Health Education (Classroom)						
*Indicates Girls' Activity Only						

GRADING PROCEDURE

The six week grade is evaluated in the following areas:
1. Performance of Skills
2. Knowledge of Skills and Physical Fitness
3. Social Attitudes including cooperation, sportsmanship, and leadership
4. Hygiene conditions (uniforms, showers), and attendance.

PHYSICAL FITNESS TESTS
(Based on National Norms)

	Trial 1 (Fall)		Trial 2 (Spring)	
	Score	% ile	Score	% ile
Pull-Ups (Boys) (shoulder strength)				
Modified Pull-Ups (Girls) (shoulder strength)				
Sit-Ups (abdominal strength)				
Shuttle Run (agility)				
Standing Broad Jump (leg power)				
50-Yard Dash (speed)				
Softball Throw (arm power)				
600-Yard Run-Walk (endurance)				

The National Norms and Scores are based on Age, Weight, and Height.

PARENT'S SIGNATURE

Your signature means only that you have seen this report.

1st Period...

2nd Period...

3rd Period..

4th Period..

5th Period..

Each absence, however short, interferes with the student's progress.

Progress report in physical education, Richwoods Community High School, Peoria Heights, Ill. (From Bucher, C. A., Koenig, C. R., and Barnhard, M.: Methods and materials for secondary school physical education, ed. 3, St. Louis, 1970, The C. V. Mosby Co.)

2. Marks should relate to the attainment of these goals and objectives.
3. Students should be informed of how marks will be determined.
4. Marks shall be based upon several factors rather than a single item alone.
5. Evaluation techniques should be valid, reliable, objective, and standardized whenever possible.
6. The place of improvement shall be determined in advance.
7. Personalities shall be removed as a factor in the final mark.
8. The mark should not only inform but it should also suggest ways of improvement.

Table 22-3 outlines a proposed plan by Dr. Lynn McCraw for grading as a means

Table 22-3. Proposed plan for grading*

Components	Weightings	Instruments
Attitude in terms of Attendance Punctuality Suiting out Participation	5% to 25%	Attendance and other records Teacher observation
Skills in terms of Form in execution of skill Standard of performance Application in game situation	20% to 35%	Objective tests Teacher observation Student evaluation
Physical fitness with emphasis on Muscular strength and endurance Cardiovascular-respiratory endurance Agility Flexibility	20% to 35%	Objective tests Teacher observation
Knowledge and appreciation of Skills Strategy Rules History and terms	5% to 25%	Written tests Teacher observation
Behavior in terms of Social conduct Health and safety practices	5% to 25%	Teacher observation Student evaluation

*From McCraw, L. W.: Principles and practices for assigning grades in physical education, Journal of Health, Physical Education, and Recreation **35:**2, 1964.

of assessing the various objectives in an objective manner.

Questions and exercises

1. Define the term *measurement.* Why is it important to the successful administration of any program of health, physical education, or recreation?
2. List as many measurement techniques as possible that are utilized in the schools. Take three of these and describe their use in detail.
3. What is the relationship of measurement to objectives?
4. Why is it important to have classification, achievement, diagnostic, and prognostic information about each individual participating in the program of health, physical education, and/or recreation?
5. What are some general guides in respect to the measurement program that should be known by every administrator and teacher?
6. List and describe the various criteria essential to the construction and selection of scientific tests.
7. How would the standardization of measurement materials contribute to better programs of health, physical education, and recreation?
8. What are the minimum and desirable standards for a measurement program?
9. Develop what you consider to be a satisfactory and practical measurement program for a health, physical education, and/or recreation program.

Reading assignment in *Administrative Dimensions of Health and Physical Education Programs, Including Athletics:* Chapter 17, Selections 91 to 93.

Selected references

Ahmann, J. S.: Testing student achievements and aptitudes, New York, 1952, The Center for Applied Research in Education, Inc. (The Library of Education).

American Association for Health, Physical Education, and Recreation: Research methods applied to health, physical education, and recreation, Washington, D. C., 1949, The Association.

American Association of Health, Physical Education, and Recreation: Sports skills test manuals (archery, basketball, football, softball), 1966, 1967, The Association.

American Association for Health, Physical Education, and Recreation: Grading in physical education, Journal of Health, Physical Education, and Recreation 38:34, 1967.

Bonney, M. E., and Hampleman, R. S.: Personal-social evaluation techniques, New York, 1962, The Center for Applied Research in Education, Inc. (The Library of Education).

Boyd, C. A., and Waglow, I. F.: The individual achievement profile, The Physical Educator 21:3, 1964.

Clarke, H. H.: Application of measurement to health and physical education, ed. 4, Englewood Cliffs, N. J., 1967, Prentice-Hall, Inc.

Fabricius, H., and others: Grading in physical education, Journal of Health, Physical Education, and Recreation 38:5, 1967.

Herman, W. L.: Teaching attitude as related to academic grades and athletic ability of prospective physical education teachers, The Journal of Educational Research 61:40, 1967.

Jensen, C.: Evaluate your testing program, The Physical Educator 21:149, 1964.

Jorndt, L. C.: Point systems—motivational devices, The Physical Educator 23:1, 1966.

Larson, L. A., and Yocom, R. D.: Measurement and evaluation in physical, health, and recreation education, St. Louis, 1951, The C. V. Mosby Co.

Latchaw, M., and Brown, C.: The evaluation process in health education, physical education, and recreation, Englewood Cliffs, N. J., 1962, Prentice-Hall, Inc.

Lawrence, T.: Appraisal of emotional health at the secondary school level, The Research Quarterly 37:2, 1966.

Liba, M. R., and Loy, J. W.: Some comments on grading, The Physical Educator 22:4, 1965.

Link, F. R.: To grade or not to grade, The PTA Magazine 62:10, 1967.

Mathews, D. K.: Measurement in physical education, ed. 2, Philadelphia, 1963, W. B. Saunders Co.

Meyers, C. R., and Blesh, T. E.: Measurement in physical education, New York, 1962, The Ronald Press Co.

National Education Association: Reports to parents, National Education Association Research Bulletin 45:2, 1967.

National Research Council, American Association for Health, Physical Education, and Recreation: Measurement and evaluation materials in health, physical education, and recreation, Washington, D. C., 1950, The Association.

Oxendine, J. B.: Social development—the forgotten objective? Journal of Health, Physical Education, and Recreation 37:5, 1966.

Piscopo, J.: Quality instruction: first priority, The Physical Educator 21:4, 1964.

Smithells, P. A., and Cameron, P. E.: Principles of evaluation in physical education, New York, 1962, Harper & Row, Publishers.

Solleder, M. K.: Evaluation instruments in health education, Washington, D. C., 1965, American Association for Health, Physical Education, and Recreation.

Trump, C.: Meaningful grading, Scholastic Coach 35:44, 1966.

CHAPTER 23 TEACHER AND PROGRAM EVALUATION

Evaluation as used in this chapter refers to the process of administration. The purpose of evaluation is to improve programs of health and physical education for the students. This includes attention to such items as determining the strengths and weaknesses of the leadership, program, facilities, and activities. A framework of evaluation procedures is discussed below to give the reader a clearer understanding of the types of information that may be evaluated.

FRAMEWORK FOR EVALUATION PROCEDURES

There are many items that can be evaluated in terms of the process of administration. These include an evaluation of various aspects of each category: in administration, this might include policies, finance, publicity, community relationship, and records; in leadership, performance, results, training, and qualifications; in facilities, the various factors that pertain to effective construction, use, and maintenance; in equipment, supply, use, cost, number, and maintenance; in activities, time, facilities, participation, and conduct; and in participation, utilization of facilities, and amount of time permitted.

MEANS FOR EVALUATION

Various means of evaluating educational programs have been devised. These range from very elaborate and detailed checklists, rating scales, and score cards to a list of questions that the administration should ask to determine the relative merit of certain administrative practices and programs.

For example, score cards such as the LaPorte Score Cards have been developed to rate health and physical education programs; Score Card 1 relates to the evaluation of health and physical education programs in the elementary school, and Score Card 2 is used for junior and senior high schools and 4-year high schools. These score cards cover such items as program of activities, class program, and intramural and interschool athletics. Each area can be rated according to a possible score that would represent an excellent program. The score cards have been successfully applied in several thousands of schools. Norms have been developed for purposes of comparison. Also some states, such as Ohio and Indiana, have developed program score cards that are pertinent to their respective states.

Many aspects of evaluation are discussed in this text in chapters that relate to such specific items as facilities, equipment and supplies, class program, health services, and a healthful environment. Therefore, this chapter is designed to cover the broad field of evaluation and to pay particular attention to teacher evaluation, which is of considerable concern to administration today. Recent advances in education have necessitated development of sound methods of rating teachers and their abilities.

TEACHER EVALUATION

In recent years, administrators, parents, teachers, and community have been concerned with developing ways and means of establishing methods to measure teacher effectiveness for the purpose of making sound decisions for retention, salary adjustments, and promotion, as well as to help teachers to improve.

The administration has an important role to play in the evaluation of teachers. Leadership needs to be provided in this area to establish a planned program of evaluation. Teachers need to be helped to improve their own effectiveness. Records should be kept to determine progress.

Some guidelines for the evaluation of teachers are as follows:

1. *Appraisal should involve the teachers themselves.* Evaluation is a cooperative venture and teachers should be involved in the development of the criteria for evaluation and need to understand the process.

2. *Evaluation should be centered on performance.* The job that is to be accomplished should be the point of focus with other extraneous factors omitted.

3. *Evaluation should be concerned with helping the teacher to grow on the job.* The purpose of evaluation is to help the teacher evaluate himself and maintain his strengths and reduce his weaknesses.

4. *Evaluation should look to the future.* It should be concerned with developing a better health program, a better physical education program, and a better school system.

5. *Evaluation of teachers should be well organized and administered*, with the step-by-step approach clearly outlined.

Fawcett* suggests the following outline, which includes some of the broad areas in which a teacher might be evaluated, as a means of initiating an evaluation program.

Interpersonal relations
  Teacher-teacher
  Teacher-students
  Teacher-parents
  Teacher-community
  Teacher-administrators

---

*Fawcett, C. W.: School personnel administration, New York, 1964. The Macmillan Co., pp. 58-59.

Classroom management
  Setting of classroom goals and individual learning goals for each student.
  Assignment and acceptance of individual responsibility by each student in the class.
  Confirmation of desired behavior of students and redirection of undesirable behavior.
  Exercise of authority to secure necessary decisions in the classroom.
  Research behavior of the teacher to keep goals and activities of the classroom consistent with the culture.
  Record-keeping behavior of the teacher essential to the conduct of the classroom.
  Coordination of the instruction in the classroom not only with other instructional activities of the school but with out-of-school learning experiences of the students.
  Inclusion of each student in the learning activities of the class.
  Communication in the classroom not only to make the teacher understand, but to make it possible for each person to share in classroom activities.
  Judgment in the allocation of time and resources to different activities in the classroom.

Teacher-learning
  1. Analysis of students:
       Skills
       Attitudes
       Knowledge
  2. Presentation of subject matter through:
       Lectures
       Group discussions
       Student research
       Programmed learning
  3. Utilization of instructional material and resources:
       Libraries
       Books
       Machines
       Television
       Radio
       Films
       Supplementary materials, organizations, and people of the community
  4. Creation of an efficient learning environment through organization of the physical surroundings in the classroom

Some methods of evaluating teachers are:

1. *Observation of teachers in the classroom or in the gymnasium.* The National Education Association Research Division, in studying this method, reported that the

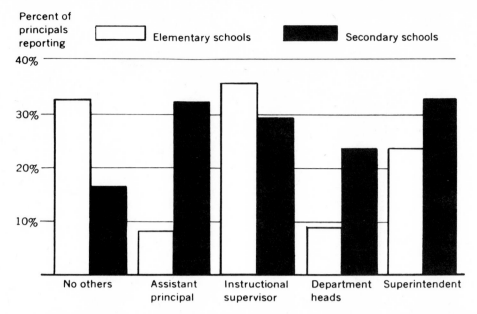

Who shares responsibility for evaluating probationary teachers with the school principal (limited to systems with written evaluations)? (From NEA Research Bulletin **42**:85, 1964.)

median length of time for the most recent observation was 22 minutes, about 25% of the teachers were notified 1 day in advance that the observation would take place, and about 50% of the teachers reported that a conference followed up the observation with the teacher's performance being discussed and evaluated. Nearly one-half of the teachers reported that the observation was helpful to them.

2. *Student progress.* With this method standardized tests are used to determine what progress the student has made as a result of exposure to the teacher.

3. *Ratings.* Ratings vary and may consist of an overall estimate of a teacher's effectiveness or consist of separate evaluations of specific teacher behaviors and traits. Self-ratings may also be used. Ratings may be conducted by the teacher's peers, by students, or by administrative personnel and may include judgments based on observation of student progress. In order to be effective, rating scales must be based on such criteria as objectivity, reliability, sensitivity, validity, and utility.

At college and university levels the evaluation of teacher performance is sometimes more difficult than at precollege levels because of the unwillingness of the faculty to permit members of the administration, or other persons, to observe them. Various methods have been devised in institutions of higher learning to rate faculty members, including statements from department heads, ratings by colleagues, ratings by students, and ratings by deans and other administrative personnel.

A question that frequently arises in the development of any system of teacher evaluation is: what constitutes effectiveness as it relates to a teacher in a particular school or college situation? Several studies have been conducted with some interesting findings. For example, there is only a slight correlation between intelligence and the rated success of an instructor. Therefore, the degree of intelligence a teacher has, within reasonable limits, seems to have little value as a criterion. The relation of knowledge of subject matter to effectiveness appears to relate most in particular

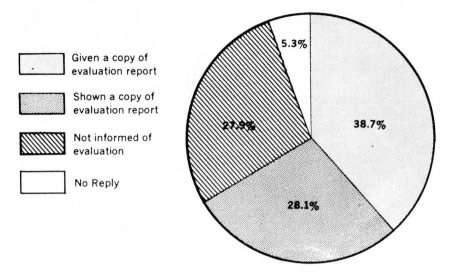

How teachers are informed of their evaluations. (From NEA Research Bulletin **42:**86, 1964.)

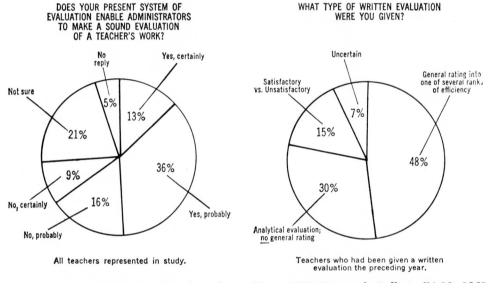

What teachers say about evaluation of teachers. (From NEA Research Bulletin **54:**38, 1965.)

teaching situations. A teacher's demonstration of good scholarship while in college appears to have little positive relationship to good teaching. There is some evidence to show that teachers who have demonstrated high levels of professional knowledge on National Teachers Examinations are more effective teachers. However, the evidence here is rather sparse. The relationship of experience to effectiveness also

seems to have questionable value. Experience during the first 5 years of teaching seems to enhance teacher effectiveness but then levels off. There is little, if any, relationship between effectiveness and cultural background, socioeconomic status, sex, and marital status. Finally there is little evidence to show that any specified aptitude for teaching exists. The studies indicate that more research needs to be done in

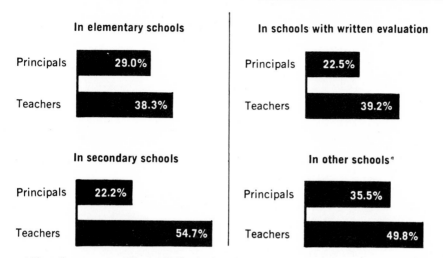

In elementary schools

Principals 29.0%

Teachers 38.3%

In schools with written evaluation

Principals 22.5%

Teachers 39.2%

In secondary schools

Principals 22.2%

Teachers 54.7%

In other schools[a]

Principals 35.5%

Teachers 49.8%

[a] Where there was no written evaluation in the school systems, or teachers did not receive a written evaluation in 1961-62, or were employed in a different school system in 1961-62, or who did not know whether there was written evaluation.

Principals and teachers express doubt or a negative opinion on the system of teacher evaluation. (From NEA Research Bulletin 42:111, 1964.)

order to establish what constitutes teacher effectiveness on the job.

EVALUATING SCHOOL AND COLLEGE HEALTH PROGRAM ADMINISTRATION

Evaluation of the school or college health program represents a major undertaking. Checklists and other forms have been developed to rate the health instruction, health services, and healthful school or college environment aspects of the total program. Such instruments that have been developed to evaluate various aspects of school and college health programs are as follows:

1. Criteria for evaluating the elementary health program, Sacramento, Calif., 1962, California State Department of Education.
2. Evaluation criteria, health education, Washington, D. C., NSSSD, American Council on Education.
3. Illinois Curriculum Program: Health education program, inventory B; What should we do to strengthen our schools' health education program? Inventory C, Springfield, 1952, Department of Public Instruction.
4. LaPorte, W. A.: Health and physical education scorecard no. 1 and no. 2, College

Book Store, 3413 S. Hoover Blvd., Los Angeles, Calif.
5. Los Angeles City Schools: Health tests (for various grade levels), Los Angeles, 1962, Division of Educational Services, Los Angeles City Schools, School Publication 673.
6. Michigan School Health Association: Appraisal form for studying school health programs, 1962, The Association
7. Oregon State College: A school health program evaluation scale, Corvalis, 1955, Oregon State College.
8. Texas Education Agency: A checklist appraising the school health program, Bulletin 519, Austin, 1955, State Education Department.

To give the reader a clearer understanding of what a checklist for health education is like, a very abbreviated one developed in the state of Colorado is included (p. 635).

Other means of evaluating school and college health programs that have been utilized in addition to checklists and score cards in various parts of the nation are *questionnaires* that have been developed and sent to parents, students, and other individuals; *surveys* of interested groups of people; *expert evaluations* by authorities, such as sanitarians or curriculum special-

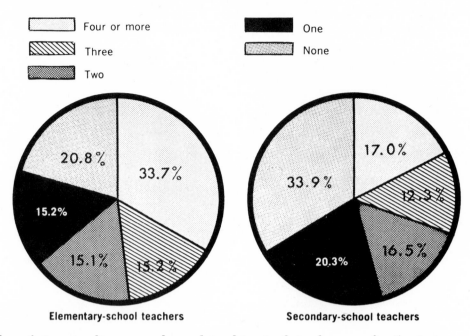

Number of times teachers were observed teaching in their classroom for 5 minutes or more, as reported by teachers from beginning of 1962-1963 term to February 1, 1963. (From NEA Research Bulletin 43:14, 1965.)

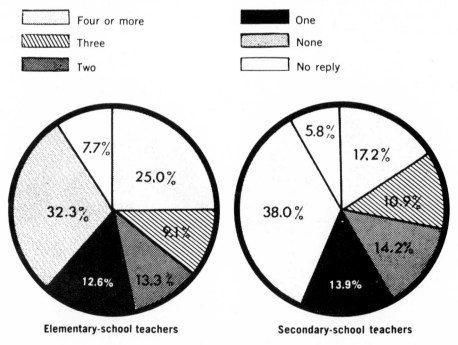

Number of individual conferences of 10 minutes or more that teachers had with principals or other school system official, as reported by teachers from beginning of 1962-1963 term to February 1, 1963. (From NEA Research Bulletin 43:17, 1965.)

CHECKLIST FOR HEALTH EDUCATION*   *Yes*   *No*

1. *Sanitary, safe, and wholesome environment*
   a. Are the state-approved medical certificates required for all personnel?   ___ ___
   b. Is there a written plan for first-aid care of illness and accidents?   ___ ___
   c. Do the buildings and grounds meet state or local sanitary standards?   ___ ___
   d. Are cases of communicable disease detected and excluded promptly according to state policy?   ___ ___
   e. Are the state policies for busses being followed?   ___ ___
   f. Are the state policies for lunchrooms being followed?   ___ ___
2. *Graded health and safety education*
   a. Is there a written plan of health instruction throughout all the grades?   ___ ___
   b. Is physical education a regular part of the program for all pupils?   ___ ___
   c. Are pupils prepared to understand the health services offered in the school and community?   ___ ___
   d. Are first-aid courses offered in the high school?   ___ ___
3. *Detection of health problems that may diminish effectiveness of the educational program*
   a. Is vision of all pupils periodically checked?   ___ ___
   b. Is hearing of all pupils regularly checked?   ___ ___
   c. Are you using the new state bulletin on testing vision and hearing?   ___ ___
   d. Is attention paid to periodic growth measurements?   ___ ___
   e. Are children screened regularly for dental health?   ___ ___
   f. Are medical evaluations of all pupils made periodically?   ___ ___
   g. Are cumulative health records maintained on all pupils?   ___ ___
4. *Guidance on these health problems of individual pupils, including counsel with parents and others*
   a. Is professional follow-up given to known health problems?   ___ ___
   b. Are the community health facilities known and used?   ___ ___
   c. Are these community facilities adequate for pupil needs?   ___ ___
5. *Special facilities for physically, mentally, and emotionally exceptional children*   ___ ___
   who are educable
   a. Are these pupils accurately classified for their learning potential?   ___ ___
   b. Are special programs available for all exceptional children?   ___ ___

*From the Colorado Education Association's Journal, October, 1956.

---

ists; *analysis of health records; tests and inventories;* and *interviews and conferences.*

Evaluation is a continuous process to determine if the program is accomplishing the purposes for which it exists.

Johns* points out an evaluation experience with selected schools and colleges in the Los Angeles area where there was a concerted effort to determine the answers to such questions as: How good is the school health program? How well is it being carried out? How well does it compare to

what should be done? Evaluations were carried out through self-appraisal as well as by outside consultants and resource persons. Three approaches to evaluation were utilized: (1) appraisals of the health education program, (2) appraisals of behavior changes in pupils as a result of exposure to the program, and (3) appraisals of the process of evaluation. Such procedures were followed as formulating, classifying, defining, and suggesting situations in which the achievement of objectives could be evaluated, tryout of different evaluation methods, developing and evaluating appraisal methods, and interpreting

---

*Johns, E.: An example of a modern evaluation plan, Journal of School Health **32**:5, 1962.

results in light of a more effective health program. A handicapping condition in the study was the lack of available valid appraisal instruments for the total health program. The findings of this study were used to justify the significance of health education in the curriculum. Such an experiment has implications, it seems, for other schools and colleges throughout the United States.

Following is a list of pertinent questions compiled by Smolensky and Bonvechio to evaluate the total school health program:

School health and safety education

1. Which curriculum areas should be emphasized at the various grade levels?
2. What are the most significant present, future, and contemplated health and safety needs of the school-age population?
3. Where and how does health and safety instruction best fit into the crowded school curriculum?
4. What should be the scope and sequence of the health and safety units in the curriculum?
5. What experiences are most conducive to developing health-educated pupils and communities?
6. How can health instruction be best integrated through experiences in the school environment?
7. How can health services be made educational in nature and scope?
8. What instructional techniques and materials are needed?
9. How can in-service staff education be practically accomplished?

School health services

1. How can health appraisal of pupil and school personnel best be accomplished?
2. What is the most effective way to counsel pupils, parents, teachers, and others in interpreting the findings of health appraisal?
3. What can be done to encourage the correction of remediable health defects in children?
4. What is the most effective way to identify, health educate, and generally educate handicapped children?
5. How can the school best control and prevent the spread of disease?
6. What kinds of services, policies, and procedures best meet the needs for emergency services for school children?

7. How can school health service be made educational in nature?
8. What are the responsibilities of the home, school, family physicians, and public health organization for health services?
9. What is the most effective way to ensure communication and coordination between all persons and groups interested in improving child health?
10. Are the duties of the school health team well defined?

Healthful school living (environment)

1. Are all educational programs of the school contributing to the health and safety of the pupils and school employees?
2. Do school administrative policies and procedures contribute to the physical and emotional health of pupils, teachers, and school employees?
3. Is the school's physical and emotional environment conducive to effective learning?
4. Is the school lunch program contributing to nutritional education and good nutrition?
5. How can school sanitation be best maintained, improved, and promoted?
6. Are regular and continuous sanitary inspections made by qualified personnel?

Administration

1. Does the school administrator help to formulate, clarify, and evaluate the goals of the school health program?
2. Does the school administrator coordinate the efforts of all school personnel who work in the school health program?
3. Does he (school administrator) assign the most qualified personnel to the various tasks in the school health program?
4. Does the school make the best possible use of local health resources?
5. Does he (school administrator) adapt the school health program to local needs and interests?
6. Does he (school administrator) motivate others in the school health program through leadership?
7. Does the school have an effective school health council?
8. Does the school district have an effective school health committee?*

---

*Smolensky, J., and Bonvechio, L. R.: Principles of school health, Boston, 1966, D. C. Heath & Co., pp. 101-102 As adapted from Davis, R L: Quality in school health administration, National Elementary Principal 39:8, 1960.

EVALUATING SCHOOL AND COLLEGE PHYSICAL EDUCATION PROGRAM ADMINISTRATION

Evaluation of student achievement in physical education represents only part of the evaluation responsibility. Evaluation of program administration is also important. Such phases of the program as classes, intramurals, interscholastics, intercollegiates, and adapted physical education activities should be evaluated in terms of activities, leadership, equipment, facilities, participation, records, research, and budgetary allotment.

The following are sample questions such as might be formulated for use in evaluation of program administration. They might either be answered with ratings of poor, fair, good, or excellent or be scored on a numerical basis of 1 to 10.

Class program

1. Does the teaching program devote equitable time to team sports, individual sports, rhythms and dance, and gymnastic activities?
2. Are the equipment and facilities adequate to allow maximum student participation?
3. Are reasonable budgetary allotments made for the class teaching program?
4. Are accurate evaluation procedures carried out and worth-while records kept?
5. Are minimal participation requirements met by all students?
6. Are students meeting proper physical education requirements in regard to dressing and showering?
7. Are proper safety measures taken in all activities?
8. Are opportunities for developing student leadership being afforded in the class program?

Adapted program

1. Do adequate screening procedures determine all possible participants in this program?
2. Are adequate facilities, equipment, time, and space made available to the program?
3. Are proper supervision and instruction afforded each individual participant?
4. Is medical approval obtained for each individual's regimen of activity?
5. Do participants engage in some of the regular class work, as well as remedial classes, when advisable?
6. Are careful records and progress notes kept on each student?
7. Is the financial allotment to the program adequate?
8. Does student achievement indicate the value of the program?

Healthful school living. (Mamaroneck High School, Mamaroneck, N. Y.)

Intramural and extramural programs

1. Are intramural and extramural sports offered to all students in as many activities as possible?
2. Has participation in these programs increased during the past year?
3. Is maximum coaching supervision available to players?
4. Is adequate financial assistance given to this phase of the program?
5. Are accurate records maintained concerning the participants, their honors, awards, and electives?
6. Does the reward or points system emphasize the joys of participation rather than stress the value of the reward?
7. Is equipment well cared for and properly stored to gain the most use from it?
8. Are competitive experiences wholesome and worth while for all participants?

Interscholastic program

1. Is financial support for this program provided by the physical education budget?
2. Is there equitable financial support for all sports in the interscholastic or intercollegiate program?
3. Are interscholastic and intercollegiate sports available to all students, boys and girls alike?
4. Are adequate health standards being met in respect to amount of practices, number of games, fitness of participants, and type of competition?
5. Is competition provided by schools and colleges of a similar size?
6. Is the program justifiable as an important educational tool?
7. Are academic standards for participants maintained?
8. Are good public relations with the community furthered through this program?

Administration

1. Is the teaching staff well qualified and capable of carrying out the program?
2. Is the program run efficiently with little loss of teaching time or space, and is maximum use made of facilities?
3. Are professional standards maintained as to class size and teacher assignment?
4. Is the departmental organization on a democratic basis, with all members sharing in the decisions?
5. Do members of the staff have a professional outlook, attend professional meetings, and keep up with the latest developments in the field?

6. In what areas have scientific tests and research been made for contribution to the profession?*

These sample questions represent only a few that can be used in the evaluation process. The key to successful evaluation of this type lies in the followup steps taken for improvement.

CHECKLIST AND RATING SCALE FOR THE EVALUATION OF THE PHYSICAL EDUCATION PROGRAM

An analysis of evaluation standards required by several state departments of education and those recommended by leading authorities in the field resulted in the formulation of the accompanying checklist and rating scale for evaluating various components of the physical education program. Space prevents a complete and extensive instrument; however, many of the most desirable professional standards are listed. Some of the evaluative criteria may not be directly applicable to a particular program. It is therefore recommended that the criteria be adapted where needed so as to better meet specific local needs.

In regard to scoring, it is recommended that each specific area of the rating form be scored so that a better picture can be gained of a department's strengths and weaknesses in respect to each aspect of the program. The first major section of the checklist and rating scale, "General administrative considerations" requires the checking of appropriate statements where applicable to a particular program of physical education. Each of the statements will be checked if the program meets the professional standards listed. If a statement cannot be checked, consideration should be given to upgrading this aspect of the

---

*Bucher, C. A., Koenig, C., and Barnhard, M.: Methods and materials for secondary school physical education, ed. 2, St. Louis, 1970, The C. V. Mosby Co.

STATE *of* NEBRASKA
DEPARTMENT OF HEALTH
DIVISION, HEALTH EDUCATION
STATE CAPITOL, LINCOLN

School's Name
....

Address
....

Signature of Representative

A GUIDE FOR EVALUATING PHYSICAL EDUCATION PROGRAMS

(Adapted from the evaluating criteria of the American Association for Health, Physical Education, and Recreation)

It should be understood that these are minimum standards. It is hoped that many schools will surpass the minimum and will continue to improve each semester.

To qualify for the citation, elementary schools should comply with **FIVE** of the first six standards; secondary schools should comply with **NINE** for the banner. The committee welcomes comments accompanying this application explaining your school's program on the back of this page.

YES   NO

1. Teacher-pupil ratio in a physical education class should not exceed 40 pupils.   ....

   a. Average size physical education class:

   Elementary (K-6)......................... High School (7-12).........................

2. There is balance in the physical education program with emphasis given to individual body building activities as well as to team sports and it is under a professionally qualified physical educator who follows an approved guide.   ....

   a. Person who is general supervisor of physical education classes or teachers:

   Elementary................................ Secondary....................................

   b. Basic guide followed:...

   c. Check areas of activity in your program:

Elementary	Secondary	Secondary
☐ 1. Low organized games & relays	☐ 1. Touch or flag football	☐ 11. Calisthenics
☐ 2. Track and field	☐ 2. Track and field	☐ 12. Soccer or speed ball
☐ 3. Self-testing	☐ 3. Testing	☐ 13. Field hockey
☐ 4. Rhythm	☐ 4. Rhythm	☐ 14. Bowling
☐ 5. Basketball	☐ 5. Basketball	☐ 15. Deck tennis
☐ 6. Flag or touch football	☐ 6. Softball	☐ 16. Handball
☐ 7. Softball	☐ 7. Tumbling & Apparatus gymnastics	☐ 17. Fencing
☐ 8. Tumbling	☐ 8. Wrestling	☐ 18. Tennis
☐ 9. Wrestling	☐ 9. Swimming	☐ 19. Shuffleboard
☐ 10. Calisthenics	☐ 10. Golf or tennis	☐ 20. Table tennis

3. Co-educational activities are included in the instructional program and are co-operatively planned and conducted by the men and women instructors.   ....

   a. List some co-educational activities carried out:

4. Modified or adapted activities are provided for students with special needs as based on information from medical data.   ....

   a. Briefly describe some plan you use for taking care of students with special needs:

5. A fitness test is given at least annually (twice per year is desired) and covers such components of fitness as muscular strength, endurance, speed, and agility.   ....

   a. Name of test used..................... b. Dates administered...................................

6. Efforts are made to publicize the physical education activities through demonstrations and public appearances and through local publications or news media.   ....

   a. List several specific instances:

7. Appropriate credit is given for class instruction in physical education and is required for graduation from junior and senior high school.   ....

   a. Amount credit given........................... b. Amount credit accepted for graduation...........................

8. Activities such as band, marching, cheerleaders, driver education, and interscholastic athletics are not substituted for physical education.   ....

9. Physical education class participation is required for a minimum of 8 semesters in grades 7-12 and two days each week.   ....

   a. How many semesters of physical education are required 7-12?.............................

   b. How many days per week required for each child?.............................

10. An intramural program is open to boys and girls and provides competitive participation opportunities.   ....

    a. List two or three activities in which intramural competition is provided:

11. Appropriate uniforms and showering are required of all participants in secondary schools.   ....

These awards are made available by the Woodmen of the World Life Insurance Society, Omaha, Nebraska

A guide for evaluating physical education programs. (Nebraska Department of Health, Division of Health Education, Lincoln, Neb.)

program. The checklist and rating scale that follow, starting with the section on "Considerations in administering physical education programs," provide for a graded scoring system so that the highest rating in each instance would be 5. If rating is less than 5, the school or college system in question may wish to consider upgrading this particular administrative phase of the total physical education program.

CHECKLIST AND RATING SCALE FOR THE EVALUATION OF THE PHYSICAL EDUCATION PROGRAM

General administrative considerations

Philosophy—Physical education and the total school or college program:

——1. Physical education is a part of the total educational program.

——2. Objectives of physical education are a part of and contribute to the achievement of general education objectives.

——3. Physical education is viewed as education of and through the physical.

——4. The students represent the primary point of focus in the physical education program.

——5. Physical education is different from, but allied to, the areas of health, recreation safety, and outdoor education.

——6. The physical education program respects the worth and dignity of each individual.

Objectives—The physical education program strives to meet the following five general objectives:

——1. Physical

——2. Social

——3. Emotional

——4. Intellectual

——5. Personal

Curriculum

——1. The program has a complete, effective, and up-to-date curriculum guide.

——2. The curriculum guide and its related aspects are periodically evaluated and improvements are made on the basis of that evaluation.

——3. The curriculum calls for instruction in all areas as listed under facilities (see Facilities).

General administrative responsibilities

——1. Regular departmental meetings are held and all staff members attend.

——2. Uniform written policies and procedures are in effect for the entire department and are made available to appropriate school personnel.

——3. Other areas of the curriculum, such as driver education, interschool or intercollegiate athletics, band, etc., are not substituted for physical education.

——4. All physical education instructors are involved in program planning and evaluation in a meaningful way.

——5. Organizational structure permits the most efficient scheduling of instructional staff members.

——6. Assignments for class and extraclass activities result in an equitable and reasonable teaching load for all teachers.

——7. The development of a sound accident policy has been carried out, including safety procedures, first aid, hospitalization, reporting, etc.

——8. There is a qualified and designated person to inspect, maintain, and repair equipment.

——9. Individual conferences are held with all students.

——10. Economic, cultural, and social background are considered when screening students.

CHECKLIST AND RATING SCALE FOR THE EVALUATION OF THE PHYSICAL EDUCATION PROGRAM—cont'd

General administrative considerations–cont'd

——11. Lesson plans of a modified or complete nature are required where necessary for those on the instructional staff.

——12. A professional library is available and is continually being updated, including references and resource material.

——13. Periodic reports on the status of equipment and facilities are required.

——14. All committees are required to turn in written reports periodically.

——15. Complete records exist on grades, tests, and performances of each student.

——16. Test results and other evaluative materials are used to improve the program.

Considerations in the administration of physical education programs

Excuses from physical education classes
5 = In writing, by physician only.
3 = In writing, by parents or by decision of school personnel.
1 = By verbal request of student.

Recording attendance
5 = Well-designed and accurate means of determining absences, latenesses, excuses, etc.
3 = Accurate, but time consuming.
1 = Poorly done and lacks authoritativeness.

Provisions for excused students from regular class period
5 = Remedial or adaptive classes as recommended by physician.
3 = Aided and assisted by instructor within limits of physical disability.
1 = Excused from physical education to attend study hall, etc.

Required program
5 = Physical education is required at all grade levels for all pupils and includes adaptive classes.
4 = Physical education is required at all grade levels only for those who can qualify for the regular program.
3 = Physical education is required for all those who do not participate in extramural activities.
2 = Physical education is required only for those who are very low in physical fitness.
1 = Physical education is purely elective in nature.

Required classes per week
5 = Five times per week, not including out-of-class activities, for precollege level and two times per week for college level.
4 = Five times per week supplemented with intramurals or extramurals. (Two times per week supplemented with intramurals or extramurals at college level.)
3 = Four times per week in any combination. (One time per week in any combination at college level.)
2 = Three times per week in any combination. (One time per week in any combination at college level.)
1 = Less than three times per week in any combination. (Less than one time per week in any combination at college level.)

Length of each class
5 = 60 minutes or more.
4 = 50 to 59 minutes.
3 = 40 to 49 minutes.
2 = 30 to 39 minutes.
1 = Less than 30 minutes.

Continued.

CHECKLIST AND RATING SCALE FOR THE EVALUATION OF THE PHYSICAL EDUCATION PROGRAM—cont'd

Considerations in the administration of physical education programs–cont'd

Time provided for showers and dressing
5 = 10 to 12 minutes, including shower.
3 = 13 to 15 minutes, 7 to 9 minutes.
1 = Less than 7 minutes or more than 15 minutes.

Class grouping
5 = By needs and abilities of students.
4 = By physical maturity.
3 = By grades.
2 = By interests (students elect activities).
1 = Haphazardly (for example, whatever period is left after scheduling academic program).

Determining class size
5 = Consideration of personnel, facilities, and activity.
4 = Consideration of two of the above (for example, facilities and activity).
3 = Consideration of one of the above (for example, facility available).
2 = By dividing number of students by number of classes.
1 = Controlled by academic program.

Pupil-teacher ratio in each class
5 = 30 pupils or less.
4 = 31 to 35 pupils.
3 = 36 to 40 pupils.
2 = 41 to 50 pupils.
1 = 51 pupils or more.

Total program financed
5 = Completely through regular school or college budget.
4 = Taxes plus pooling receipts of *all* school or college activities.
3 = Taxes plus gate receipts.
2 = Taxes plus contributions from organizations or individuals and/or gate receipts.
1 = Other.

Extramural program
5 = Administered and controlled by regular school or college authorities.
3 = Administered and controlled by schools and colleges with nonschool or noncollege personnel assisting.
1 = Outside personnel contracted to conduct program.

Public relations
5 = Department makes every effort to keep community informed of the total physical education program.
3 = Full coverage is given to intramural and extramural activities.
2 = Only interscholastic activity news releases are given out for public consumption.
1 = No effort is made by the department to make the community aware of its program.

Athletic standards
5 = Every effort is made to follow league and state eligibility requirements, including setting up individual school standards—also, provide medical examinations, insurance, and supervision when needed.
4 = State and league eligibility requirements conscientiously adhered to, as well as providing medical examinations, insurance, and supervision.
3 = Follow state and league eligibility requirements with modified medical coverage.
2 = State and league eligibility requirements known, occasionally bypassed for the benefit of the student.
1 = Complete disregard of rules and regulations.

CHECKLIST AND RATING SCALE FOR THE EVALUATION OF THE PHYSICAL EDUCATION PROGRAM—cont'd

Considerations in the administration of physical education programs–cont'd

Supervision of intramural and extramural activities
- 5 = Instructional personnel knowledgeable about given activity plus a background in physical education, including athletic training and first aid.
- 4 = Instructional personnel knowledgeable about given activity with a background in general education and special training in athletic injuries and first aid.
- 3 = Instructional personnel knowledgeable about activity and is a classroom teacher without additional preparation.
- 2 = Instructional personnel knowledgeable about activity but in no other way associated with the school program.
- 1 = Volunteer from the faculty to coach and/or supervise.

Adjusting teaching schedules to enable effective planning, organizing, and supervising of intramural and extramural programs
- 5 = Personnel are given released time to adequately prepare for intramural and extramural programs.
- 3 = Some free time is usually provided to enable some preparation during the school day.
- 1 = No free time is given personnel during the regular school day to prepare for intramural and extramural activities.

Coeducational instruction and supervision
- 5 = Both men and women physical educators pool their time and talents to offer a coeducational program.
- 3 = A limited program for coeducational activities may be offered upon occasion.
- 1 = No effort is made to offer a coeducational program.

Providing proper equipment
- 5 = Effort is made to buy the best equipment suitable to the program, and equipment that is wearing out is quickly replaced or rebuilt, taking into consideration high standards and quality.
- 3 = Usually first quality equipment is purchased. Occasionally, that of a secondary quality is bought so as to stay within the means of the budget.
- 1 = All efforts are made to buy the best "deal" regardless of quality and long wear but more suited to immediate needs.

The physical education program is supervised by a specially trained professional
- 5 = The program has a director whose education exceeds the Master's degree, whose major area of study is physical education, and who has a minimum of 5 years' experience.
- 3 = The director has a major degree in physical education but lacks experience academically (beyond a Bachelor's degree) and professionally (at least 5 years in the field).
- 1 = There is no director or single person responsible for coordinating the total physical educational program.

Components of the physical education program

Program designed to:
- 5 = Provide experiences that are related to the normal growth and development of the students, including needs, interests, and abilities.
- 4 = Offer a variety of activities both of an individual and a dual sport nature so as to appeal to the individual student.
- 3 = Provide a curriculum of activities that vary but are dependent upon interests and abilities of instructors.
- 2 = Give the athlete a chance to improve his interscholastic or intercollegiate ability with a general program for the regular student body.
- 1 = Offer as much physical activity as possible but with a lack of direction.

Continued.

CHECKLIST AND RATING SCALE FOR THE EVALUATION OF THE PHYSICAL EDUCATION PROGRAM—cont'd

Components of the physical education program–cont'd

Specific activities are offered to:
   5 = Improve the physical fitness and recreational potential of every individual in the program.
   3 = Meet the minimum physical fitness levels *or* to teach recreational games.
   1 = Entertain and to gain the approval of the students participating to make physical education more popular.
Activities include:
   5 = A variety of activities including *all* of the following: individual and dual sports, rhythms and dances, gymnastics, stunts and self-testing activities, team games, and aquatics.
   3 = Basically, a program emphasizing team sports with a few individual activities and dual sports to supplement the program.
   1 = Several activities of each nature but lacking any set design.
Aquatics
   5 = A full program of aquatics from beginning swimming to life saving as part of the required program.
   4 = Part of the required program for beginners and intermediates regardless of grade level.
   3 = A required part of the program but only for certain grade levels.
   1 = No program offered or available.
Intramural program
   5 = Full year-round program.
   3 = Part time year-round program.
   1 = No program offered.
Interscholastic and intercollegiate activities
   5 = Activities are offered which meet the needs of the individual students who have achieved the necessary competencies.
   3 = An emphasis on team sports with a few major individual and dual sports offered.
   2 = Basically a team sports program.
   1 = No interscholastic or intercollegiate program.
A special program of a recreational nature including:
   5 = Camping skills, nature hikes, fishing, hunting, etc.—all of which are required.
   3 = Several or all of the above but on an elective basis.
   1 = No such program available.
A special program of combative activities offered
   5 = Judo, wrestling, etc., are part of the required program.
   3 = Only a very few combative activities are part of the required program.
   2 = Combative activities are not part of the required program but may be elected.
   1 = No combative activities offered.
All aspects of the program of physical education should be concerned with the following (all items should be checked if high professional standards prevail):
   ——1. Designing a program that helps to meet the school's or college's educational objectives.
   ——2. Achieving specific objectives relative to physical education.
   ——3. Biologic and sociologic factors when planning the program for the individual.
   ——4. Physical fitness tests, health appraisal, and health records when classifying for physical education.
   ——5. The use of visual aids, including slides, films, posters, demonstrations by leaders in the field, etc.
   ——6. Requiring proper physical education uniforms.

CHECKLIST AND RATING SCALE FOR THE EVALUATION OF THE PHYSICAL EDUCATION PROGRAM—cont'd

Components of the physical education program–cont'd

———7. Providing logical progression and continuity.

———8. Opportunities for student leadership.

———9. Instruction on rules of safety.

———10. A series of warmup drills *directly* related to the activities to be taught.

———11. Providing a series of lectures and discussions to enable the student to understand the human organism, the physiology of exercise, body mechanics, and other related areas.

———12. Showers *required* of all students who are physically able.

———13. Not substituting recess and lunch time for the required physical education program.

———14. Scheduling boys' and girls' classes to achieve maximum efficiency of all facilities.

———15. Offering intramurals for the faculty as well as the students.

———16. An intelligent and *minimal* award system for intramurals and interscholastic athletics.

———17. Sports conducted with concern for sportsmanship, fair play, individual values, etc.

Staff

Members of the instructional staff, having the same status and tenure as other teachers, include the following:

5 = All instructors of physical education classes, intramurals, and interscholastic athletics.

3 = All instructors of the regular class program and intramurals.

1 = Only those involved with the regular class program.

Background preparation includes courses in general liberal education, biologic sciences, social sciences, physical sciences, psychology, and professional courses

5 = Required of all those in the instructional classes, including intramurals and interscholastic athletics.

3 = Required only from those in the regular class program and intramurals.

1 = Required only from those in the regular class program.

All members of the staff (all items should be checked if high professional standards prevail)

———1. Are active participants in educational and professional organizations.

———2. Are working toward improving the professional status (refresher courses, etc.).

———3. Are active participants in inservice training programs.

———4. Are active members of departmental committees, such as committee on evaluation.

———5. Help to plan programs with other content areas of the school when appropriate, such as health, recreation, science, guidance, etc.

———6. Are involved in planning, budgeting and ordering of equipment and supplies.

———7. Maintain a high degree of total fitness for the obvious values inherent in total fitness so as to provide the image to their students of which they profess.

———8. Receive at least one free planning period per day.

———9. Have a teaching load maximum of 5 or 6 clock hours per day (college 15 hours per week).

———10. Have a teaching load with a maximum of 250 pupils per day.

———11. Have a minimum of 20 semester hours in the field of physical education.

Supervision in the locker room

5 = By professionally trained instructor.

3 = By experienced adult.

1 = By student leaders.

Continued.

CHECKLIST AND RATING SCALE FOR THE EVALUATION OF THE PHYSICAL EDUCATION PROGRAM—cont'd

Facilities and equipment (check when applicable—items that can be checked will help to determine if high professional standards prevail)

General facilities meet the following standards:

——1. Facilities are designed for and used by the community as well as the school or college.

——2. Facilities are free from obstruction, free from safety hazards, and meet high standards of health and safety.

——3. Facilities have the necessary safe entrances and exits.

——4. There are a sufficient number and variety of teaching facilities (indoor and outdoor) to permit the realization of all the objectives of the program.

——5. New facilities are planned cooperatively by the physical education department, the school administration, the community, and the architect.

——6. Permanent fixtures (backstops, stall bars, etc.) are placed to afford maximum use and safety.

Indoor facilities include:

——1. Well-designed gymnasia that meet official regulations for specific areas and proper floor markings (for example, basketball court, volleyball area, etc.).

——2. Sound, safe, and practical flooring (no splinters, etc.).

——3. Adequate seating capacity for spectators.

——4. Well-placed drinking fountains and cuspidors.

——5. Adequate and regulation lighting.

——6. Adequate heating and temperature control.

——7. Adequate acoustical features.

——8. A public address system.

——9. Launderette for towel service and the cleaning of certain athletic wear.

——10. Adequate storage space on same level as gymnasia.

——11. An equipment room with:

    ——a. Proper ventilation, temperature, and humidity control.

    ——b. Enough area for storage and efficient dispensing of equipment and supplies.

    ——c. An area for repairing, rebuilding, and checking of equipment and supplies.

    ——d. Room or area for drying athletic gear.

——12. Main gymnasium measuring a minimum of 50 by 80 feet of open space.

——13. Secondary gymnasia for weight-lifting, dancing, etc., measuring at least 15 by 25 feet.

——14. Minimum clearance of 22 feet for ceilings in all gymnasia.

——15. Fixtures recessed and/or protected (such as water fountains, scoreboards, clocks).

——16. Adequate ventilation in all gymnasia.

——17. Areas for:

——a. Badminton.	——f. Swimming pool.
——b. Basketball.	——g. Table games (cards, checkers).
——c. Dancing.	——h. Volleyball.
——d. Gymnastics.	——i. Weight-lifting.
——e. Ping pong.	——j. Wrestling.

Major equipment for indoor activities include:

——1. Necessary nets and standards.	——7. Long horse.
——2. High bar.	——8. Trampoline.
——3. Low bar.	——9. Mats.
——4. Balance beam.	——10. Vaulting box.
——5. Parallel bars.	——11. Still rings.
——6. Side horse.	——12. Flying rings.

CHECKLIST AND RATING SCALE FOR THE EVALUATION OF THE PHYSICAL EDUCATION PROGRAM—cont'd

Facilities and equipment–cont'd

——13. Spring boards.
——14. Climbing ropes.
——15. Chalk boards.
——16. Bulletin boards (strategically placed).
——17. Official electric scoring device.
——18. Peg boards.
——19. Stall bars.
——20. Backboards and rims for basketball.
——21. Record library.
——22. Phonograph.
——23. Film library.

Training room includes:
——1. Equipment necessary for the prevention and cure of injuries (whirlpool, diathermy, etc.).
——2. Supplies necessary for sound and safe operation, such as first aid equipment and supplies.

Faculty offices
——1. Separate for men and women.
——2. Includes private locker room facilities.
——3. Appropriately equipped with chairs, desks, shelves, etc.
——4. Window view into locker room and gymnasium or pool.

Locker, shower, and drying rooms include:
——1. Moisture- and shock-proof electric fixtures.
——2. Separate locker rooms for boys and girls.
——3. Individual storage lockers.
——4. One large dressing locker for each student during peak load.
——5. Proper ventilation.
——6. Proper heating.
——7. Proper lighting.
——8. Locker room adjacent to lavatory.
——9. Minimum of 12 square feet per pupil during peak load.
——10. One shower head for every four pupils during peak load.
——11. Gang showers for boys.
——12. Gang showers for girls.
——13. Cubicle stall showers for girls.
——14. One hair dryer to every four girls during peak load.
——15. Urinals, sinks, and toilets in boys' locker room.
——16. Sinks and toilets in girls' locker room.
——17. Drying room between shower and lockers.
——18. Water temperature automatically controlled.
——19. Floor, ceiling, walls, and other permanent fixtures constructed of a type of material that withstands extreme moisture conditions and is sanitary, safe, and easy to maintain.
——20. Proper facilities for visiting teams.
——21. Soap dispensers provided.
——22. Towel service provided.
——23. Proper size permanent benches, mirrors, and open aisle space.

Outdoor facilities include:
——1. Proper equipment intelligently and safely installed (goal posts, back stops, nets, etc.).
——2. Adequate storage space for outdoor facilities.
——3. Being immediately adjacent to school building with safe access to locker rooms.
——4. Grass area on fields.

Continued.

CHECKLIST AND RATING SCALE FOR THE EVALUATION OF THE PHYSICAL EDUCATION PROGRAM—cont'd

Facilities and equipment–cont'd

———5. Safe fencing around all areas.
———6. A minimum of 2½ acres for every 250 pupils.
———7. Areas for the following activities:

———a. Archery.
———b. Badminton.
———c. Basketball.
———d. Baseball.
———e. Croquet.
———f. Cross country.
———g. Cycling.
———h. Field hockey.
———i. Football.
———j. Golf.
———k. Handball.
———l. Horseshoes.

———m. Ice skating.
———n. Lacrosse.
———o. Marching.
———p. Open fields for relays, games, etc.
———q. Shuffleboard.
———r. Skiing.
———s. Soccer.
———t. Softball.
———u. Tennis.
———v. Track and field.
———w. Tetherball.
———x. Volleyball.

———8. Provision for all-year-round activities.
———9. Proper surfacing, grading, and drainage.

Measurement and evaluative techniques

The following should be incorporated into a measurement and evaluation of the program, its staff, its students, etc.

Measurement of student status and progress

———1. Standardized tests (knowledge and skill).
———2. Locally designed tests (knowledge and skill).
———3. Medical examination.
———4. Orthopedic screening test.
———5. Motor ability tests.
———6. Observation.
———7. Records on social, mental, and emotional development.
———8. Grading:

———a. Grading is consistent with other subjects in the school program, including credit toward graduation.
———b. Grades are based upon individual ability relative to skills, fitness, knowledge, and health attitudes.
———c. Grading is added by established criteria for measuring student progress.
———d. The final grade indicates the extent to which each pupil has achieved the objectives of the course.

Staff evaluation

———1. Controlled student analysis.
———2. Self-evaluation.
———3. Departmental review.
———4. Academic preparation.
———5. Professional experience.
———6. Inservice participation.
———7. Critical contributions to the school, college, and profession.

Questions and exercises

1. Survey five teachers to determine what they think constitutes the most objective method of evaluation of their performance on the job.
2. Should teachers of health education and of physical education be evaluated in the same way? Why? Why not?
3. What contributions can evaluation make to helping the teacher grow professionally?
4. You are responsible for evaluating a school health program and/or a school physical education program. Select the instrument for evaluation, conduct the evaluation, and report to the class on your findings.
5. What areas of school health and physical education programs, according to your observation and evaluation, need the most professional upgrading?

   Reading assignment on *Administrative Dimensions of Health and Physical Education Programs, Including Athletics:* Chapter 18, Selections 94 to 97.

Selected references

Billet, R. E.: Evaluation: the golden fleece, New York State Education **55**:42, 1968.

Brian, G.: Evaluating teacher effectiveness, National Education Association Journal **54**:2, 1965.

Bucher, C. A., Koenig, C., and Barnhard, M.: Methods and materials for secondary school physical education, ed. 3, St. Louis, 1970, The C. V. Mosby Co.

Caldwell, S. F.: Evaluation in the elementary physical education program, The Physical Educator **22**:153, 1965.

California State Department of Education: Criteria for evaluating the elementary health program, Sacramento, 1962, The Department.

Fawcett, C. W.: School personnel administration, New York, 1964, The Macmillan Co.

Goldman, S.: The school principal, New York, 1966, The Center for Applied Research in Education, Inc. (The Library of Education).

Howsam, R. B.: Facts and folklore of teacher evaluation, The Education Digest **29**:7, 1964.

Johns, E.: An example of a modern evaluation plan, Journal of School Health **32**:5, 1962.

La Porte, W. A.: Health and physical education scorecard no. 1 and no. 2, College Book Store, 3413 S. Hoover Blvd., Los Angeles, Calif. 90056.

Malone, W. C.: A checklist for evaluating coaches, Coach & Athlete **29**:3, 1966.

Michigan School Health Association: Appraisal form for studying school health programs, 1962, The Association.

National Education Association: Methods of evaluating teachers, National Education Association Research Bulletin **43**:1, 1965.

National Education Association: What teachers and administrators think about evaluation, National Education Association Research Bulletin **42**:4, 1964.

Roundy, E. S.: Are our physical education programs meeting todays needs? Journal of Secondary Education **41**:221, 1966.

Simpson, R. H., and Seidman, J. M.: Student evaluation of teaching and learning, Washington, 1962, American Association of Colleges for Teacher Education.

Vander Werf, L. S.: How to evaluate teachers and teaching, New York, 1960, Holt, Rinehart & Winston, Inc.

PART
five

ADMINISTRATION OF RECREATION, CLUB, OUTDOOR EDUCATION, AND CAMPING PROGRAMS

Louisville, Ky., City Division of Recreation.

CHAPTER 24 COMMUNITY AND SCHOOL RECREATION, CLUB, AND ACTIVITY PROGRAMS

Recreation may be defined as that field of endeavor concerned with those socially acceptable and worthwhile activities in which a person voluntarily participates during leisure hours and through which he may better develop physically, mentally, emotionally, and socially.

The key concepts of any form of recreation that is advocated here are five in number. First, the activity must be conducted in hours other than work. It is a *leisure-time activity*. The activity must not be associated with productive labor that is aimed at profit or that is a regular part of one's daily routine as a means of making a living. Second, recreation is an *enjoyable activity*. It is something from which one gains satisfaction, serenity, and happiness. Third, recreation is *constructive* in nature —it is *wholesome*. A person could go out and become inebriated every night and say it is recreation. However, this is not the kind of recreation that is recommended. Recreation should do something to contribute to the individual's physical, mental, emotional, or social welfare. Fourth, recreation is *nonsurvival in nature*. Therefore, such things as sleep cannot be labeled as forms of recreation in the sense that it is discussed in this chapter. Finally, recreation is *voluntary*. The person engages in the activity because he has chosen to participate. There has been no compulsion. He has made the choice freely. These five criteria or concepts must be satisfied if it is the type of recreation that this text is advocating for the benefit of people everywhere.

TYPES OF RECREATION

Some of the better-known kinds of recreation are community, industrial, hospital, school, family, and commercial. The kinds of recreation that will be considered primarily in this chapter are those concerned with community and school recreation.

Community recreation

Community recreation is that in which villages, towns, and cities sponsor a recreation program for their inhabitants. It is controlled, financed, and administered by the community.

Industrial recreation

Industrial recreation is the type wherein an industrial concern, such as Eastman Kodak, Lockheed Aircraft, or other business establishment, sponsors a recreation program for its own employees.

Hospital recreation

Hospital recreation refers to a program that is set up in a veterans, municipal, or other hospital for the benefit of the patients. It includes recreation for the ill and disabled. The therapeutic values of recreation are increasingly being recognized.

School recreation

School recreation refers to the program provided by a board of education for the students that attend a particular school system. Boards of education also provide recreation programs for the adult population of a community.

The human relations objective represents a major contribution of recreation to enriched living. "Canoemanship"—one of the activities of recreation course. (University of Connecticut, Storrs, Conn.)

Family recreation

Family recreation means the activities that are engaged in by a family unit during their leisure hours and that have resulted from their own initiative.

Commercial recreation

Commercial recreation is that form of recreation such as is found at amusement parks and that is conducted for profit.

GOALS OF RECREATION

Community recreation is a field of endeavor that deserves increasing recognition for the work that it is doing in enriching individual lives. The goals reflect this contribution. Many goals have been listed for the field of recreation. Some of those that have received attention are the following: physical, mental, emotional, and social health; happiness; satisfaction; balanced growth; creativeness; competition; learning; citizenship; socialization; and the development of one's talents.

Following are six goals for American recreation that have been stated by The Commission on Goals for American Recreation.* They represent one of the best professional statements on recreational goals.

1. *Personal fulfillment.* The democratic ideal is based on the concept that the individual is the most important consideration in our society. To achieve his most important place in our culture, each person needs to fulfill the basic need for adequacy or self-fulfillment. Each person

---

*The Commission on Goals for American Recreation: Goals for American recreation, Washington, D. C., 1964, American Association for Health, Physical Education, and Recreation.

There is insufficient stress on family recreation today.

wants to belong and to feel important. Each person should strive to become all that he is capable of becoming. Therefore, recreation should help each person to achieve full integration of his total personality; contribute to his mental, physical, social, and emotional development; and help to fill in the gaps that work and on-the-job activity do not provide. The many activities offered through a well-organized recreation program can contribute to the self-fulfillment of each person who participates.

2. *Democratic human relations.* The democratic society functions best through associated effort directed and channeled toward the accomplishments of those goals that are in the best interests of the majority. The recreation profession recognizes that its goals exist on the level of the individual as well as on the level of the democratic society of which it is a part. Recreation, therefore, constantly keeps in mind such important tenets as (a) each individual has worth and each personality must be respected, (b) the citizen in a democracy cooperates for the common good, (c) the citizen abides by the laws—rules that have been established to guard

each individual's rights, and (d) the citizen living in a democracy guides his behavior by acceptable moral and ethical values.

3. *Leisure skills and interests.* Recreation is concerned with meeting the interests of those people who voluntarily participate in its programs, developing skills that will provide the incentive, motivation, and medium for spending free time in a constructive and worthwhile manner. As such, recreation must be concerned with a breadth and variety of interests, ranging from physical activities, social activities, and artistic activities to community service programs and learning activities.

4. *Health and fitness.* Recreation is cognizant of the nature of many individuals who live a sedentary existence with the implications this has for poor health and fitness. It also recognizes the importance of a vigorous and active life and seeks to meet the challenge of a society in which mental illness, stress, and inactivity prevail in many quarters.

5. *Creative expression and esthetic appreciation.* There is increased realization today of the need for each individual to give vent to his own personal expression, to creativity, and to the appreciation of the

most beautiful and cultured activities in the various cultures of the world. Recreation seeks to contribute to each individual's desire for creative expression and esthetic appreciation by providing the environment, leadership, materials, and motivation for such experiences, recognizing that creativity can flourish only in a climate that has been properly prepared for its development and growth.

6. *Environment for living in a leisure society.* Recreation recognizes that the environment plays an important role in the determination of the quality and extent of the recreative experience. Therefore, recreation is particularly interested in preserving our natural resources; in the construction of parks, playgrounds, hobby centers, and other recreation centers; in seeing that recreation programs are taken into consideration in city planning; and in awakening the populace to the need for an appreciation of esthetic and cultural values.

I have formulated four objectives for the recreation profession:

1. *The health development objective.* The health development objective is important in the field of recreation. Health to

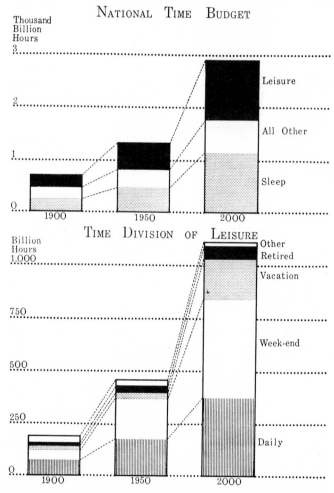

National time budget and time division of leisure—1900, 1950, and 2000. (From The American Academy of Political and Social Science: Leisure in America: blessing or curse? Philadelphia, 1964, The Academy.)

a great degree is related to activity during leisure hours as well as during hours of work. The manner in which a person spends his free time determines in great measure whether his physical, mental, emotional, and spiritual health is of high quality. Through recreation, adaptive physical activity is available that is conducive to organic, mental, emotional, and spiritual health. A range of activities exists that offers opportunities for every individual to promote his organic health. Activities are available in which the individual may relax, escape from the tensions of work, forget about problems, and thereby improve mental health. Activities are planned and conducted that provide individual enjoyment and pleasure and in this way contrib-

ute to emotional health. Activities requiring the participation of many individuals are included and are conducive to better social relations and higher standards of moral and spiritual values, thus promoting spiritual health. Public recreation programs are designed to provide activities that counteract the deteriorating effects of strenuous or routine work or study and thus complement the overall routine that an individual follows. They overcome many of the shortages that exist when the man leaves the office, the child leaves school, or the housewife completes her work. In this way they contribute to the integration and development of the whole individual.

2. *The human relations objective.* The human relations objective represents a ma-

Campcraft class. Mt. Olympus, their ultimate goal, is in the background. (Olympic College, Bremerton, Wash.)

jor contribution of recreation to enriched living. Recreational programs develop many individual qualities that make for better adjustment. Such attributes as courage, justice, patience, tolerance, fairness, and honesty are only a few that are possible of development while individuals are playing and recreating together in the many activities that comprise the total recreation program. Attitudes that promote good human relations are also developed. Wholesome attitudes of social cooperation, loyalty to the group, recognition of the rights of others, and the idea that one receives from a group in direct proportion to what one gives it are a few that make for better relations and enable worthy goals and projects to be accomplished. The growth of family recreation is a trend that also helps to make for a more unified home life. This is very important, since the family group represents the foundation on which good human relations are built. Furthermore, to develop good social traits it is necessary to bring people together in a situation in which there is a feeling of belonging and in which each individual is recognized. There are innumerable opportunities for such interaction in the many recreational programs that exist throughout the country.

3. *The civic development objective.* The civic development objective is a noteworthy goal for recreation. Recreation contributes in many ways to the development of any community. It contributes to community solidarity by uniting people in common projects regardless of race, creed, economic status, or other discriminatory factors. It helps to build the morale of the members of the community. It is a contributing factor in alleviating crime in that it provides settings and activities in which youth and other individuals may engage in constructive, worthwhile activities, rather than in destructive antisocial activities. It helps make the community a safer place in which to live through providing adequate playgrounds and other recreational

centers that keep children and youth off the streets. It helps make the community more prosperous by contributing to the health of the individual, by cutting down on the dollar appropriation for crime, and by increasing the total work output of an individual. It helps the growth and development of the individual so that he becomes a more valuable citizen in the community and has more to contribute in its behalf.

4. *The self-development objective.* The self-development objective refers to the potentialities that participation in a program of recreational activities has for developing the individual to his fullest capacity. Recreation does this through a variety of means. It contributes to the balanced growth of an individual. It allows for growth in ways other than in mere production of material things for utilitarian purposes. In other words, it satisfies the human desire for such things as creative music, art, literature, and drama. It allows an individual to create things not for their material value but for the joy, satisfaction, and happiness that go with creating something through one's own efforts. It allows for the development of latent and dormant skills and abilities of the individual until they are aroused by leisure hours with proper settings and leadership. These skills help to make a better-integrated individual.

Recreation provides an avenue for the individual to experience joy and happiness through some activity in which he has the desire to engage. In this chaotic world where there are so many sorrows, heartbreaks, and frowns, it is essential for people to revitalize themselves through the medium of activities. These provide smiles and hearty laughs and release from the tension associated with day-to-day routine. They afford a place for many individuals to excel. Such an urge is many times not satisfied in one's regular job or profession. An opportunity is provided in recreation to satisfy this desire. It offers an educational experience. The participant learns new skills, new knowledges, new techniques, and develops new abilities. He is filing away new and different experiences that will be helpful in facing the situations he will encounter from day to day.

GUIDING PRINCIPLES FOR PLANNING RECREATION PROGRAMS

Recreation programs should not be developed on a "hit-or-miss" basis. Instead, outstanding leaders in recreation have studied very thoroughly and carefully the types of programs that best serve the needs of people and have developed principles that can be used as guides for leaders who are engaged in program planning.

Brightbill* set forth his program principles, which, in adapted form, are as follows:

1. Individual interests, characteristics, needs, and capabilities should be taken into consideration in the planning of recreation programs.

2. The recreational interests and skills of individuals may be determined to some degree as a result of the cultural, economic, religious, and social phenomena that characterize them.

3. Recreation should be planned cooperatively, with the recreator taking into consideration interested individuals, departments, agencies, and organizations.

4. Program planning requires consideration of national standards modified to local conditions.

5. Program planning should take into consideration individual differences in skills and the progressive planning of skill experiences.

6. Creativity and self-expression are considerations in program planning.

7. Opportunities should be made available for individuals to be of service to others so that the personal satisfaction that

comes from such service can be realized by such persons.

8. Recreation programs should provide for a wide spectrum of activities.

9. Leadership, financial means, and facilities are essential considerations in program planning.

10. Physical and human resources of the community should be mobilized for the recreation program.

11. The recreation program should seek to provide equality of opportunity for participation for all persons in the community.

12. Flexibility should be possible within a recreation program to provide for such exigencies as changed interests on the part of human beings and other conditions that affect program planning.

13. The health and safety of participants should always be a consideration in planning recreation programs.

14. The recreation program should seek to help each person exemplify acceptable standards of human behavior.

15. The participant in the recreation program should never be exploited for such means as raising money, personal glory, or other similar motives.

16. Recreation should be the object of continual evaluation to determine the measure to which the worthwhile goals are being achieved in light of the investment being made.

Brightbill's goals reflect recreation programs in general, with particular consideration for community recreation. The following principles developed for school recreation by a national conference of experts in this area* are much the same as those established by Brightbill:

1. The recreation program should be characterized by many different activities that are related to the needs and interests of the people they serve.

---

*Langton, C. V., Duncan, R. O., and Brightbill, C. K.: Principles of health physical education, and recreation, New York, 1962, The Ronald Press Co., pp. 251-261.

*National Conference on School Recreation: School recreation, Washington, D. C., 1960, American Association for Health, Physical Education, and Recreation.

2. The welfare of the individual and group should be continually kept in mind when planning the recreation program.

3. The program should be planned so that each individual can realize some of the goals that have been established for recreation.

4. Opportunities should be provided for individuals to participate in the planning of the program. Also, the program should be adapted to local conditions.

5. The recreation program should take into consideration community mores and folkways.

RECREATION ACTIVITIES

The range of recreation activities is infinite in scope. Any activity that meets the criteria listed earlier in the chapter can be a recreational activity. This means that drama, music, art, crafts, games, sports, camping, literature, fairs, nature study, dance, and community work are possible avenues for millions of people to obtain the benefits that recreation can offer.

A list of a few of the possible activities for recreation purposes follows:

Dramatics
  Clubs
  Festivals
  Plays

Arts and crafts
  Ceramics
  Graphic arts
  Leathercraft
  Metalcraft
  Photography
  Plastics
  Sewing
  Stenciling and block
    printing

Outdoor activities
  Campfires
  Camping
  Canoeing
  Conservation
  Fishing
  Orienteering
  Outdoor cooking
  Woodcraft

Music
  Barber shop quartets
  Choral groups
  Community sings
  Instrumental
  Orchestral

Dancing
  Folk
  Modern
  Social
  Square

Sports and games
  Archery
  Badminton
  Bowling
  Fencing
  Golf
  Hopscotch

Miscellaneous
  Cards
  Flowers
  Forums
  Hobby clubs

RECREATION AGENCIES

There are three major types of recreation agencies in the United States: (1) public recreation agencies, (2) private or voluntary agencies, and (3) commercial agencies. Some examples of each type are listed:

1. Public recreation agencies
   a. Municipal public agencies—the park department, recreation department, youth commission, education department, and other city or community departments that operate recreation programs
   b. State public agencies—state park departments, state conservation departments, and state education departments
   c. Federal public agencies—national parks, Forestry Service, Children's Bureau, Fish and Wild Life Service, and Tennessee Valley Authority
2. Private or voluntary agencies
   a. Youth-serving organizations—Boys' Clubs of America, Young Men's Christian Associations, Young Women's Christian Associations, Campfire Girls, Boy Scouts, and church centers
   b. Organizations serving an entire population—museums, libraries, athletic clubs, outdoor clubs, and granges
   c. Private voluntary agencies organized around special interests of certain groups—music specialties, photographic specialties, and sports specialties
3. Commercial agencies (operated for profit)—theaters, bowling alleys, art galleries, night clubs, and concert halls

National Recreation and Park Association

A major development in the field of recreation was the unification of five of the national organizations serving laymen and professional recreation. The American Institute of Park Executives, the American Recreation Society, the American Zoological Association, the National Council of State Parks, and the National Recreation Association were merged into a unified national organization known as the *National Recreation and Park Association*. Lawrence S. Rockefeller was elected as the first president of this association. The merger was designed to bring together a single organization supported by private citizens and professional groups and dedicated to helping all Americans to devote their free time to constructive and satisfying activities.

WAYS IN WHICH RECREATION PROGRAMS ARE ADMINISTERED

Recreation programs are not all administered in the same manner in this country. Government agencies, schools, business, and voluntary agencies play a role in many communities. Jenny* has listed five major types of administration of recreation programs in the United States that apply to community recreation.

The recreation board

A recreation board can be set up in any community where enabling legislation exists and permits such action. The board usually consists of five to nine members. The group is frequently composed of representatives of the city government, the school district, the recreation or park department, and the community at large. Terms of office usually run for varying periods of time depending upon the community, and the members usually serve without compensation. Members of the board are either elected or appointed to their positions.

The school board

In many communities the board of education, under a broad interpretation of its powers or under the provisions of state ex-

*Jenny, J. J.: Introduction to recreation education, Philadelphia, 1955, W. B. Saunders Co., pp. 31-35.

tension education laws or enabling acts, conducts recreation programs. In some communities this responsibility is interpreted as providing a program only for its children and youth, whereas other programs are provided for persons of all ages.

The park board

In such cities as Detroit and Seattle, the department of parks administers the recreation program. Since the community parks are used so extensively for recreation purposes, and to avoid duplication of facilities, budgeting, and planning, some citizens feel that the park board is the logical form of administration for community recreation programs. Those opposed to this arrangement, however, point out that recreation does not get priority under such an administrative setup.

The recreation board and the school board

In some communities the recreation board and school board cooperatively work together in administering the recreation program. The school board, for example, may provide the facilities and sometimes the funds, while the recreation board provides the personnel, equipment, and supplies. Regardless of how the responsibilities are shared, a close working relationship is developed between the two groups in providing a recreation program for the inhabitants of the particular geographic locality they serve.

The recreation association, nonprofit agency, and corporation

In villages and other communities where the park, recreation, or school board has not assumed the administration of the recreation program, sometimes recreation associations, clubs, and other organizations provide a program. The Boys' Clubs of America, Young Men's Christian Associations, and Recreation Promotion and Service Corporations are examples of this type of administrative organization. These or-

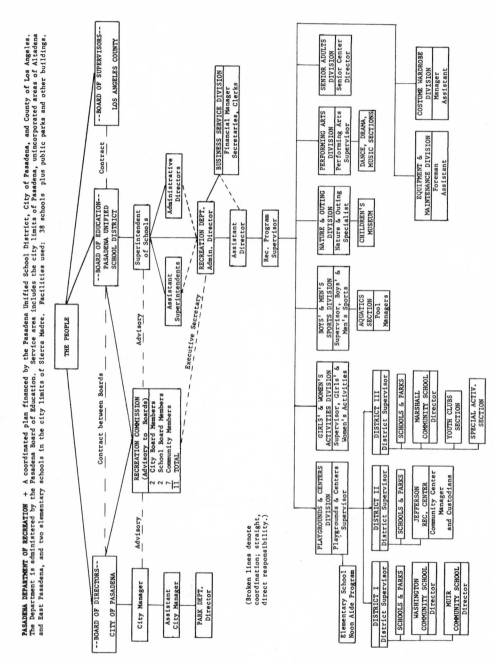

PASADENA DEPARTMENT OF RECREATION + A coordinated plan financed by the Pasadena Unified School District, City of Pasadena, and County of Los Angeles. The Department is administered by the Pasadena Board of Education. Service area includes the city limits of Pasadena, unincorporated areas of Altadena and East Pasadena, and two elementary schools in the city limits of Sierra Madre. Facilities used: 38 schools plus public parks and other buildings.

New organization chart of the Pasadena Department of Recreation, Pasadena, Calif.

ganizations have made outstanding contributions in many communities.

THE SCHOOL AND RECREATION

The recommendations of the Second National Conference on School Recreation[*] included setting forth a series of principles and statements regarding school-centered recreation and municipal-school recreation. These principles and statements are presented in adapted form:

Role of school

1. Schools should accept, as a major responsibility, education for leisure.

2. Schools and colleges should provide their students with opportunities for participation in wholesome, creative activities.

3. The facilities and resources of a school should be made available for recreation purposes when needed.

4. Where community recreation programs are missing or inadequate, the school should take the initiative and provide recreation programs for young and old alike.

5. The school should cooperate with community organizations and agencies interested in or sponsoring recreation programs.

6. The school should appoint a person to act as a community school director; he would be responsible for the recreation-education program in the school.

7. Recreation and education are not identical, but each has its own uniqueness and distinctive features.

8. The community-school director should provide inservice recreation education for his staff.

9. The federal level of government has a responsibility to stimulate recreation programs.

10. Recreation depends upon public understanding and support for its existence.

11. Recreation should be concerned with exploiting the interests of people.

12. The recreation program should consist of many varied activities.

13. Recreation should be concerned with contributing to the mental health of the individual.

Municipal-school recreation

1. The school should accept the responsibility to educate for the worthy use of leisure, contribute to recreation in the instructional program, mobilize community resources, and cooperatively plan facilities for recreation. The college and university should promote research in recreation and provide professional preparation programs in this specialized area.

2. There should be joint planning of municipal school recreation based on stated principles and brought about by state departments of education and local boards of education.

3. School facilities should be available for recreational use.

Some recreation leaders have raised the question as to whether or not recreation should be school centered. Hjelte and Shivers[*] list some arguments pro and con in respect to this issue.

School-centered recreation

The reasons that Hjelte and Shivers list *for* a school-centered program are as follows: The school possesses the facilities essential to a good recreation program, and duplicating these facilities results in waste and inefficiency. Schools are located within a community in much the same way as recreational centers are located—to meet the needs of the people within a particular geographic area. The school comes in con-

[*]Report of the Second National Conference on School Recreation: Twentieth century recreation, re-engagement of school and community, Nov. 7-9, 1962, Washington, D. C., 1963, American Association for Health, Physical Education, and Recreation.

[*]Hjelte, G., and Shivers, J. S.: Public administration of parks and recreational services, New York, 1963, The Macmillan Co.

tact with all the children and, therefore, the consumer of recreation can best be helped through this agency. The objectives of schools and the objectives of recreation are similar. The schools are a source of leadership for recreation programs.

Hjelte and Shivers' arguments *against* a school-centered recreation program are as follows: Education should restrict itself to intellectual training and not be concerned with experiences that are only indirectly related to intellectual training. Public schools have too many responsibilities without adding any more. Teachers are poorly paid and facilities are inadequate in many localities, and so a heavier burden should not be placed upon these resources. Recreation is hampered by the formality of the school environment and becomes regimented. Consequently, recreation is able to realize its potentialities to a greater extent through the establishment of a special agency. School facilities, equipment, and supplies are damaged through a recreation program and alterations are necessary, which raises the question as to whether other facilities might not be provided more economically. Finally, in attempting to join the forces of education and recreation, difficulties are encountered in securing financial aid for both. Greater public support can be gained if recreation is not grafted onto the educational program.

Regardless of the arguments for or against school-centered recreation, the schools should play a vital part in the field of recreation. At the present time they are contributing staff and facilities. The program of studies in the schools, however, has a long way to go before it realizes its potentialities for developing resources for leisure.

TEN GUIDELINES FOR THE ADMINISTRATION OF SCHOOL RECREATION *

1. The acceptance and commitment of the administration regarding the role of recreation in education.
2. The establishment of a representative ad hoc committee by the Board of Education to survey recreational needs and interests in the school district. Appropriate funds should be provided for the routine services for such a committee, including secretarial and consultant services.
3. The appointment of a qualified professional staff member, preferably the school district director of health, physical education, and recreation, to serve as coordinator of the study and liaison to the ad hoc committee.
4. The conduct of the study by the committee to determine the status of organized recreation in the school district. This should include: a review of the understanding and philosophy of people in the school district regarding recreation; existing recreational services available.
5. Arranging for technical, professional, consultant services in recreation through recognized agencies for the purpose of appraising the findings of the survey in terms of quality recreation for the school district.
6. Develop, in cooperation with the professional consultant, a proposed plan of recreation for the school district. Such a plan should include a statement of philosophy, principles, policies, procedures, and a financial plan.
7. A review of the ad hoc committee plan by the Board of Education and administration.
8. The acceptance or modification of the plan by the Board of Education.
9. The ratification of the plan and the adjustment of general school district administrative policies to appropriately provide for recreation.
10. The administrative implementation of recreation as officially adopted by the Board of Education, with emphasis on clear communication.

*New York State Department of Education, Albany, N. Y.

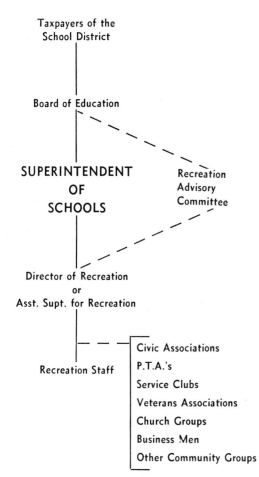

Taxpayers of the School District

Board of Education

SUPERINTENDENT OF SCHOOLS

Recreation Advisory Committee

Director of Recreation
or
Asst. Supt. for Recreation

Recreation Staff

Civic Associations
P.T.A.'s
Service Clubs
Veterans Associations
Church Groups
Business Men
Other Community Groups

Recommended organization chart for school-operated recreation programs. (From School recreation, Report of the National Conference on School Recreation, copyrighted 1960.)

Contributions the regular school program can make

All subjects in the educational program have a contribution to make in developing resources for leisure. The school, with wide and varied educational offerings in such fields as science, art, music, physical education, and industrial arts, has infinite opportunities to develop many resources for leisure. During this age of mass production, application of atomic energy to industry, and increasing amounts of leisure, the schools are being challenged to accept this responsibility.

Schools should help young people to adjust to the way of life that they will encounter after leaving school, aid them in solving the problems they will meet, and help them to become responsible citizens. Education most certainly must concern itself with leisure-time education. Leisure hours represent a challenge facing the nation's schools.

Contributions the out-of-class program can make

The school's job does not end when the 3 o'clock bell rings. Its influence extends into the child's life throughout the school day and is also reflected in those activities in which he engages after regular school hours. How the child spends his free time after school and on Saturdays, Sundays, and holidays will influence his health and also his success in life. During his school years he may want to find out more about photography, choral singing, dramatics, or sports. The extracurricular program provides the opportunity to pursue these interests further. Probably one of the greatest values that out-of-school activities have for children is realized in later years. The interests they develop will carry over to adult life and supply them with many happy and profitable hours.

The school can help to enrich leisure

One of the best statements of how the school can help to enrich leisure of students was stated in an editorial by Joy Elmer Morgan, which is as true today as when it was written. He points out that the school can help to enrich leisure:

1. By introducing young people to a wide range of life interests.
2. By teaching the use of books and libraries and developing wholesome reading appetites closely related to each of the great objectives of education and life.
3. By developing appreciation of fine music and skill in singing, playing, and dancing.

4. By having children participate in games and sports which may be easily continued in after years.

5. By providing experience in pleasant social life through school activities.

6. By cultivating in children a love of the out-of-doors—appreciation of flowers, animals, landscape, sky, and stars.

7. By giving children an opportunity to develop hobbies in various creative fields—gardening, mechanics, applied arts, fine arts, architecture, city planning.

8. By making the school and its playfields the center and servant of a wholesome and satisfying neighborhood life.

9. By calling attention to various recreational agencies and the values which they serve—theaters, concerts, libraries, radio, periodicals and newspapers, museums, parks, playgrounds, travel.*

THE RECREATION LEADER

The recreation leader should have most of the qualifications of the health education and physical education specialists and in addition some that are pertinent especially to his field of work.

Qualifications

Various personal attributes are important for the recreation leader who is working with people so much of the time. These include such characteristics as integrity, friendly personality, enthusiasm, initative, organizing ability, and others that will aid in the achievement of recreation objectives.

Recreation leaders should possess a broad cultural background, with an understanding of the needs and problems facing society. This implies a fundamental knowledge of history, sociology, and anthropology. In addition, they should have the skills and competencies necessary for coping with such needs and problems. This would include the communicative arts, knowledge of psychology, and other allied areas.

It is especially important that the recrea-

---

*Morgan, J. E.: Editorial, Journal of the National Education Association **19**:1, 1930.

tion leader understand and appreciate human beings. He or she must have respect for the human personality; a broad social viewpoint; the desire to inculcate a high standard of moral and spiritual values; a recognition of the needs, interests, and desires of individuals; an appreciation of the part that recreation can play in meeting these needs and interests; and a desire to serve humanity.

There is special need for an understanding and appreciation of community structure and the place of recreation at the "grass roots" level of this structure. The ability to utilize scientific survey techniques and other methods of social research is also an essential qualification.

There should be ability in the performance of skills in many of the areas with which recreation is concerned. These skills should not be limited to games and sports but in addition should branch out into such areas as arts and crafts, dramatics, camping and outdoor education, music, social recreation, and other important aspects of the total offering.

The philosophy of recreation, with the importance of constructive leisure-time activities to human beings, should be understood. In addition, there is the necessity for the special knowledge, attitudes, and skills concerned with methods and materials, safety, first aid, principles of group work, health, juvenile delinquency, and crime prevention.

Recreation positions and areas of recreation service

The following represent various types of recreation positions for which the aspiring student can prepare and the areas of recreation service:

Recreation positions
  Superintendent of recreation
  Assistant superintendent
  Recreation director
  Consultant
  Field representative
  Executive director

Hospital recreation supervisor
Campus recreation coordinator
Extension specialist
Service club director
Girls' worker—boys' worker
District recreation supervisor
Recreation leader
Supervisor of special activities
Recreation therapist
Recreation educator

Areas of recreation service
Community recreation departments
Park departments
Schools
Service clubs for the armed forces
Churches and religious organizations
Hospitals
Institutions—public and private
Voluntary youth-serving agencies
Rural
Colleges and universities
Industry
State and federal agencies

SCHOOL CLUB AND ACTIVITY PROGRAMS

There are many out-of-class experiences that have educational value for students. Agricultural, cheerleading, music, camping, and journalism clubs and student government represent only a few of these experiences. In some cases these activities are run by the students themselves, whereas in other cases the faculty plays a significant role. The purpose of these programs, however, should be focused on helping the student to obtain a fuller and more total educational experience. Some of the objectives of such clubs are social, service, cultural, recreational, and exploratory in nature. They can provide students with opportunities for self-expression, leadership, constructive use of leisure time, creativity, responsibility, and practice skills.

The school club and activity programs should be planned as unified and integrated programs that dovetail with the curriculum. They should be organized and controlled in a manner that best serves the student's interests, develop special aptitudes and abilities, afford constructive use of leisure time, promote social assets, and provide intellectual and career information. The administration must also recognize that school activities cannot run themselves. They need continuous stimulation and guidance as well as financial support to be successful. The administration should be involved in the process by which the aims of a group are determined, its plans carried out, and the results evaluated to determine if the goals are being met. Problems can develop if the budget is not planned carefully, if qualified personnel are not available to give guidance to the activity, and if inadequate organization and control exist.

School club and activity programs can be a very important part of a well-balanced school program. They can provide opportunities for students to further their education in ways that the formal classroom situation does not permit. If properly administered, they can contribute to cutting down on dropouts, delinquency, and nonconstructive use of leisure hours.

The accompanying checklist highlights some of the important considerations for school club and activity programs.

CHECKLIST FOR SCHOOL CLUB AND ACTIVITY PROGRAMS

	Yes	No
1. Are club activity programs a normal outgrowth of the regular school program?	——	——
2. Are there clearly stated objectives for the club or activity program?	——	——
3. Does the club program supplement the formal curriculum by increasing knowledge and skills?	——	——

Continued.

CHECKLIST FOR SCHOOL CLUB AND ACTIVITY PROGRAMS—cont'd

	Yes	No
4. Are clubs organized in terms of educational value rather than administrative convenience?	——	——
5. Does the administration set adequate policies to guide the program?	——	——
6. Have the aims and objectives of the club or activity program been determined?	——	——
7. Can any student join a club?	——	——
8. Is a student limited to the number of clubs he may join?	——	——
9. Does each club have a simple constitution and bylaws that can guide students in the conduct of the organization?	——	——
10. Do the clubs prepare the student for democratic living?	——	——
11. Do the activities help to develop school spirit?	——	——
12. Does the school schedule club activities so that they do not conflict with regularly scheduled school activities?	——	——
13. Does the school administrator ensure the program of adequate space and funds to carry on a worthwhile program?	——	——
14. Can a student discover and develop special aptitudes and abilities through the club and activity program?	——	——
15. Does the club and activity program offer opportunities for vocational exploration?	——	——
16. Is the individual student able to develop socially acceptable attitudes and ideals through the club program?	——	——
17. Does the club experience provide situations that will contribute to the formation of improved behavior patterns in the student?	——	——
18. Do all club members actively participate in program planning?	——	——
19. Are the projects and activities of the club initiated primarily by the students?	——	——
20. Do the activities performed pertain to the club purposes?	——	——
21. Are students allowed to select clubs and activities according to interests?	——	——
22. Are students issued a calendar of events?	——	——
23. Does the school library make available books and periodicals needed by club and activity groups?	——	——
24. Does the club faculty adviser enlist the confidence of boys and girls?	——	——
25. Is the club faculty adviser willing to give time and thought to making the club or activity program a success?	——	——
26. Is the club faculty adviser able to find his chief satisfaction in pupil growth and not in appreciation of his efforts?	——	——
27. Does the administration of the school evaluate the club periodically?	——	——
28. Does the club allow time for the evaluation of activities?	——	——

Questions and exercises

1. Survey a community recreation program. In the light of this survey list the contributions the program makes to the community, its organization aspects, relation to schools, activities included in its program, and degree to which it is achieving professional objectives.

2. What are the objectives of recreation? Develop a group of guiding principles for the achievement of each of these objectives.

3. To what degree is recreation understood by the American public in general?

4. Discuss what you consider to be the outstanding accomplishments of the recreation profession during the last 50 years.

5. How can the recreation profession turn its shortcomings into accomplishments during the next 50 years?
6. Develop a plan whereby physical education, health education, and recreation can work together most productively in the community.
7. To what extent is your school achieving recreational objectives through its educational offering?
8. Read and critically review one article in *Recreation* magazine.
9. How can television be utilized most advantageously by the recreation profession?
10. Describe what you consider will be a community recreation program in the year 2000.

Reading assignment on *Administrative Dimensions of Health and Physical Education Programs, Including Athletics:* Chapter 19, Selections 98 to 100.

Selected references

American Association for Health, Physical Education, and Recreation: Leisure and the schools, Washington, D. C., 1961.

American Association for Health, Physical Education, and Recreation: Your community-school-community fitness inventory, Washington, D. C., 1959, The Association.

Bentz, C.: Operating a school swimming pool for the benefit of the total community, School Activities **39**:12, 1968.

Brimm, R. P.: The junior high school, New York, 1963, The Center for Applied Research in Education, Inc. (The Library of Education).

Bryant, A.: Activities program beginnings in a new junior college, School Activities **38**:5, 1966.

Bucher, C. A., editor: Methods and materials in physical education and recreation, St. Louis, 1954, The C. V. Mosby Co.

Bullock, N.: Aviation clubs in secondary schools, School Activities **39**:5, 1968.

Bunte, G. V.: Skin diving club, Student Life **27**:20, 1960.

California Association for Health, Physical Education, and Recreation and California State Department of Education: The roles of public education in education, Burlingame, 1960, The Association.

Carlson, R., Deppe, T. R., and Maclean, J. R.: Recreation in American life, Belmont, Calif., 1963, Wadsworth Publishing Co., Inc.

Danford, H. G.: Creative leadership in recreation, Boston, 1964, Allyn & Bacon, Inc.

Douglas, H. R.: Trends and issues in secondary education, New York, 1962, The Center for Applied Research in Education, Inc. (The Library of Education).

Frederick, R. W.: Student activities in American education, New York, 1965, The Center for Applied Research in Education, Inc. (The Library of Education).

Heller, M. P.: School activities need an open door policy, Clearing House **40**:42, 1965.

Hjelte, G., and Shivers, J. S.: Public administration of park and recreational services, New York, 1963, The Macmillan Co.

Kraus, R.: Recreation and leisure in modern society, New York, 1971, Appleton-Century-Crofts.

Kraus, R.: Recreation today—program planning and leadership, New York, 1966, Appleton-Century-Crofts.

Kraus, R. G.: Recreation for rich and poor: a contrast, Teachers College Record **67**:568, 1966.

McKenzie, R. F.: Those extra curricular activities, Texas Outlook **52**:35, 1968.

Meyer, H. D., and Brightbill, C. K.: Community recreation—a guide to its organization, ed. 3, Englewood Cliffs, N. J., 1964, Prentice-Hall, Inc.

Nash, J. B.: Philosophy of recreation and leisure, St. Louis, 1953, The C. V. Mosby Co.

National Conference on School Recreation: School recreation, Washington, D. C., 1960, American Association for Health, Physical Education, and Recreation.

Nelson, R. L.: School recreation, The Physical Educator **20**:111, 1963.

Report of the Second National Conference on School Recreation: Twentieth century recreation, re-engagement of school and community, Washington, D. C., 1963, American Association for Health, Physical Education, and Recreation.

Rodney, L. S.: Administration of public recreation, New York, 1964, The Ronald Press Co.

Shivers, J. S.: Leadership in recreational service, New York, 1963, The Macmillan Co.

The Commission on Goals for American Recreation: Goals for American recreation, Washington, D. C., 1964, American Association for Health, Physical Education, and Recreation.

The International City Managers' Association: Municipal recreation administration, ed. 4, Chicago, 1960, The International City Managers' Association.

Willgoose, C. E.: Recreation—obligation of the schools, Instructor **75**:39, 1966.

Yukic, T. S.: Fundamentals of recreation, New York, 1963, Harper & Row, Publishers.

The pupils of Bowling Green Elementary School in Sacramento, California, experience outdoor learning on their own school grounds where they have a nature center and arboretum. Students at Alberton in western Montana, under a Title III project, developed a 7-day camp for sixth and seventh graders where conservation was stressed by studying such things as timber management, forest fire control, air and water pollution, and the management of animals, plant, and soil. Boys and girls in the public schools of Le Mars, Iowa, go to Camp Quest and participate in an academic curriculum based on the discovery method of learning to stimulate interest in the life and earth sciences. More than 50,000 children have benefited from studying nature's resources at Camp Tyler, Texas, which is operated as part of the school system.

The president* of the Minnesota Outdoor Education Association discussed in the *Journal of the National Education Association* how a kindergarten teacher takes her class outside to study the clouds in the sky, a third-grade class utilizes a compass to measure distances and determine directions preliminary to beginning a map for social studies, a sixth-grade class goes to a park and discovers fossils, and an eighth-grade class finds a spider web and relates it to what they were doing on conservation. Outdoor education is not just nature study but instead represents a vital part of the educational program at all education levels and in all subjects including art, social studies, mathematics, physical education, and industrial arts.

The out-of-doors is nature's laboratory. It is a setting that offers excellent opportunities to learn many knowledges and skills and to develop wholesome attitudes. Experiments and research have shown that boys and girls who use nature's classroom will learn more readily those things that directly relate to the out-of-doors and be more interested in doing so.

Outdoor education and school camping are not synonymous. Outdoor education includes school camping. The camp provides a laboratory by which many facets of the out-of-doors can be studied at first hand. And the camp experience helps to develop qualities important to preparing young people for the lives they will live.

One hundred leaders in education, conservation, and recreation participated in a National Conference on Outdoor Education. This conference reaffirmed the importance of outdoor education and came to the following conclusions*:

1. There is an urgent need during the times in which we live for education in the out-of-doors.

2. There is a need to stress outdoor education in schools and colleges as well as in conservation, recreation, and other agency programs.

3. Those agencies and organizations involved in outdoor education should

---

*Brinley, A.: Classrooms as big as all outdoors, NEA Journal 53:45, 1964.

*Professional Report from the National Conference on Outdoor Education, Journal of Health, Physical Education, and Recreation 33:29, 1962.

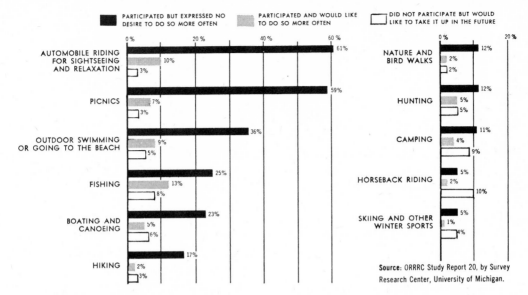

Expression of preference of participants and nonparticipants in outdoor activities. (From *Action for Outdoor Recreation for America: A digest of the report of the Outdoor Recreation Resources Review Commission, with suggestions for citizen action, 1964.*)

work cooperatively together to provide as many young people and adults as possible with experiences in this area.

4. The American Association for Health, Physical Education, and Recreation should make provision for outstanding leadership in this field of endeavor.

BEGINNINGS

In May, 1948, representatives of such well-known organizations and agencies as the American Association for Health, Physical Education, and Recreation; United States Office of Education; National Secondary School Principals Association; American Association of School Administrators; and the American Council on Education made recommendations that camping and outdoor education should be a part of every child's educational experience, that cooperative arrangements should be worked out with conservation departments and other agencies directly related to natural resources, and that experimental

camping programs, as a phase of the educational program, should be established in Michigan and any other states that were interested in trying out this educational trend. Since 1948, camping and outdoor education have grown tremendously in this country.

Outdoor education and camping are rapidly being recognized as having an educational value that should be experienced by every boy and girl. Although there are comparatively few camps throughout the United States that are associated with school systems, the trend is more and more in the direction of required camping and outdoor education as part of the educational offering.

Many teacher education institutions preparing teachers of science, elementary education, health education, recreation, and physical education recognize the value of camping and its importance in education. Prospective teachers in some training programs are required to spend one or more sessions at a camp. The experience orients the student in camp living and in the organization and administration of a camp and emphasizes the value of outdoor education. It is also felt by some professional preparing institutions that the student should have a broad understanding of camping in education. This should include a study of the role of camping and outdoor education in the total educational process, the aims and objectives of camping and outdoor education, procedures essential in the conduct of a camp, qualifications and duties of the camp counselor in his relation to the director and to the campers, safety precautions and procedures, the program of activities for all types of weather conditions, and facilities.

SETTINGS FOR OUTDOOR EDUCATION

A publication of the American Association for Health, Physical Education, and Recreation lists some of the significant settings for outdoor education activities*:

1. *School sites and adjacent areas.* The trees, shrubs, streams, ponds, and outdoors in general offer many opportunities to develop outdoor laboratories that can be utilized for experiences related to such areas as science, social studies, arts and crafts, and physical education.

2. *Parks, forests, and farms.* Most communities have parks, farms, or other available outdoor areas nearby that can be utilized for outdoor education.

3. *School farms.* School farms are being developed in some communities and are providing agricultural experiences and a variety of learning situations that revolve around rural living. Such farms offer opportunities for studying birds, animals, conservation, gardening, milk production, home management, care of farm machinery, and community life.

4. *School forests.* School forests or nearby municipal, county, state, or national forests provide excellent outdoor education settings. School experiences relating to art, music, conservation, forestry, zoology, shop, archery, shelter construction, fire protection, camp crafts, and hiking can be provided.

5. *School and community gardens.* The opportunity to till the soil, see plants grow, and other similar activities can be provided for in school and community gardens.

6. *Museums and zoos.* An opportunity to study animals, collections of historic materials, works of art, and other important aspects of our culture is provided by museums and zoos.

7. *School camps.* The utilization of camps, either as a day camp or for an extended period of time, offers opportunities for group living, work experience, development of outdoor skills, and many other experiences important to the well-rounded education of every boy and girl.

VALUES OF OUTDOOR EDUCATION AND SCHOOL CAMPING

The values of outdoor education and school camping are very much in evidence as a result of the many experiments that have been conducted throughout the United States. For purposes of discussion, it might be said that the values of such experiences are threefold: (1) they meet the social needs of the child, (2) they meet the intellectual needs of the child, and (3) they meet the health needs of the child.

A camping experience is an essential part of every child's school experience because it helps to develop the child socially. In a camp setting children learn to live democratically. They mix with children of other creeds or national origin, color, economic status, and ability. They aid in planning the program that will be followed during their camp stay; they assume part

*American Association for Health, Physical Education, and Recreation: Leisure and the schools, Washington, D. C., 1961, The Association, p. 108.

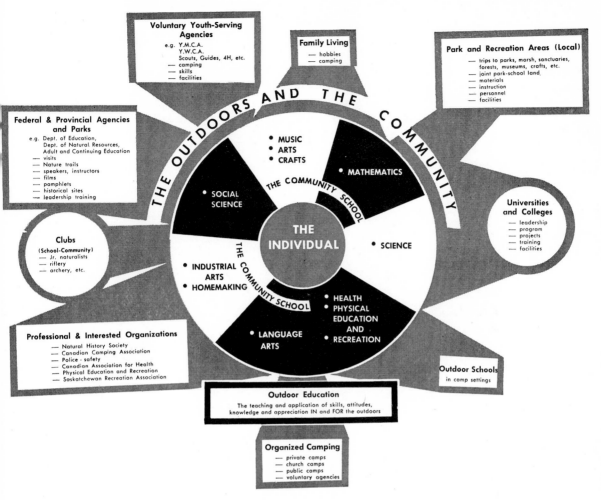

The world of outdoor education. (From MacKenzie, J.: Saskatchewan Community 14:4, 1963-1964.)

of the responsibility for the upkeep of the camp, such as making their own beds, helping in the kitchen, sweeping their cabins, and fixing the tennis courts; and they experience cooperative living. The children get away from home and from their parents. They lose their feeling of dependency upon others and learn to do things for themselves. The child learns to rely on his own resources. The camp also provides an enjoyable experience for the child. A child is naturally active and seeks adventure. This experience provides the opportunity to release some of this spirit

of adventure and to satisfy the "wander-lust" urge.

A camping experience is an essential part of every child's school experience because it helps to develop the child intellectually. While living in a camp, the child learns about soil, forests, water, and animal and bird life. He learns about the value of the nation's natural resources and how they should be conserved. He learns of ecology, the science concerned with the interrelationship between living organisms and their environment and between organisms themselves. He learns by doing rather than through the medium of text-books. Instead of looking at the picture of a bird in a book, he actually sees the bird chirping on the branch of a tree. Instead of reading about soil erosion in a textbook, he sees how it actually occurs. Instead of being told about the four basic groups of food, he has the opportunity to live on a diet that meets the right standards. Instead of reading about the value of demo-cratic living, he actually experiences it. The child experiences many new things that he cannot possibly do at home or within the four walls of a school building. Camping is also of special value to children who do not learn easily from books. In many cases the knowledge accumulated through actual experience is much more enlightening and beneficial.

Camping is an essential part of every

Camping and outdoor education are rapidly being recognized as having an educational value that should be experienced by every boy and girl.

child's school experience because it helps to meet the health needs of the child. Camps are located away from the turmoil, confusion, noise, and rush of urban life. Children experience having their meals at a regular time, obtaining sufficient sleep, and participating in wholesome activity in the out-of-doors. They wear clothing that does not restrict movement, that shields from the sun, and that they are not afraid to get dirty. The food is good. They are doing things that are natural for them to do. It is an outlet for their dynamic personalities. It is much more healthful, both physically and mentally, than living in a "push-button" existence with its lack of recreation, relaxation, and opportunity for enjoyable experiences. It is like living in another world, and children come away refreshed from such an experience.

THE SCHOOL CAMP PROGRAM

The program in most camps consists of such sports activities as swimming, boating, fishing, horseback riding, tennis, badminton, hiking, horseshoes, basketball, and softball; such social activities as campfires, frankfurter and marshmallow roasts, dancing mixers, and cookouts; and opportunities to develop skills and an appreciation in arts and crafts, photography, Indian lore, drama, music, and nature study.

The educational aspects can include a variety of experiences. Some of these are campfires, outdoor cooking, woodcraft, camp sites, canoeing, conservation, astronomy, birds, animals, indoor and outdoor gardening, fishing, hiking, hunting, and orienteering.

A publication of the American Association for Health, Physical Education, and Recreation* points out some experiences

---

*Joint Committee: Administrative problems in health education, physical education, and recreation, Washington, D. C., 1953, American Association for Health, Physical Education, and Recreation, p. 47.

that might take place and yield educational results:

While the camp program is well integrated with the aims and purposes of general education, there are many implications for essential learnings usually associated with health, physical education, and recreation. A student at a school camp, as a member of a program group made up of boys and girls, might have some of the following experiences: (a) a trip with a cookout; (b) a work project such as planting trees, building shelter for game, repairing boats, and others; (c) responsibility for the common living activities for the day, such as preparation of food, cleaning of the camp, cutting wood for the fire, and the like; (d) participation in activities of interest, such as crafts, dramatics, and music; (e) helping to plan the evening activities for the camp; (f) helping evaluate the day's program; (g) meeting with the camp council; (h) participating in a special campfire program; and (i) countless other kinds of experiences appropriate to the age of the group and the location of the camp.

Julian W. Smith, one of the nation's leaders in the fields of camping and outdoor education, has listed a sample elementary school program (Table 25-1).

SCHOOL CAMPS IN OPERATION

These are some outstanding examples of school systems that are using camping as an effective and worthwhile educational experience.

The sixth-grade children in the city of San Diego and San Diego County, California, have the opportunity to experience one week of camp life at Camp Cuyamaca. This is a former Civilian Conservation Corps Camp and is located in the nearby mountains. Year-round camping is included as part of the education of the boys and girls going to these schools. The staff is made up largely of school personnel, and the financial outlay is assured by the city council and county board of supervisors. From sixty to seventy children at a time experience all sorts of camp activities including arts and crafts, nature study, hikes, and care of living quarters. Teachers accompany the children on camp-

Table 25-1. A sample elementary school camp program*

Day	Teamsters	Cruisers	Lumberjacks
Monday	Planning Hike around lake Cookout Paul Bunyan stories	Planning Hike to abandoned farm Crafts	Planning Camp cruise Tapping trees Square dance
Tuesday	Blacksmiths shop Scavenger hunt Sock hop	Logging Make ice cream Cookout	Treasure hunt Plant trees Fishing
Wednesday	Boiling sap Crafts Square dance	Hike around the lake Fishing Square dance	Fire building Compass hike Crafts
Thursday	Breakfast cookout Compass hike Council fire	Compass hike Plan for council fire Council fire	Cookout Boating Council fire
Friday	Evaluation Clean up and pack Go home	Evaluation Clean up and pack Go home	Evaluation Clean up and pack Go home

*From Smith, J. W.: Outdoor education, Washington, D. C., 1956, American Association for Health, Physical Education, and Recreation, p. 26.

Camp Quest. (Central Junior High School, Le Mars Community School District, Le Mars, Iowa.)

Camp Quest. (Central Junior High School, Le Mars Community School District, Le Mars, Iowa.)

ing trips. One main emphasis in the camp is to have children experience living together with other children in a democratic, healthful, and stimulating environment.

Another notable school camping experience takes place in the public school system of Battle Creek, Michigan, at Saint Mary's Lake Camp. As provided in the arrangements established in this educational setup, children have the opportunity of 2 weeks' camping experience, which may occur at any time during the year. The camp staff is made up of faculty members of the Battle Creek schools. A novel feature of this camp is the banking experience that each child has. All boys and girls deposit their money in the camp bank, and a banking system is established analogous to that used by commercial banks. The campers also run their own post office. The only cost to each child for this valuable experience is the price of the food.

Long Beach, California, also offers a valuable camping experience to the children and faculties of its schools. Their camp, Camp Hi-Hill, is located about 50

Table 25-2. School camping is an extension of the classroom*

Basic scientific understandings and appreciations	*Spiritual values*
How soil is formed	Experiencing the beauty of nature
How plants grow	Appreciation of living things developed from personal contact
The rain-water cycle	Better appreciation of the personal worth of others, from living together
How forest animals live	Development of finer group unity
Dependence of man upon plants and animals	Appreciation of the beauty and worth of the out-of-doors
Causes of soil erosion and prevention	
Operation of a weather station	

Basic scientific understandings and appreciations (continued):

How soil is formed
How plants grow
The rain-water cycle
How forest animals live
Dependence of man upon plants and animals
Causes of soil erosion and prevention
Operation of a weather station
Use of map and compass
Significance of fire damage
Study of stars
Meaning of contour, grade, and slope

Study of seasonal changes

Bird, animal, and insect life
Uses of flood control dams
How snow is used for protection and water supply for vegetation
Migration, fire hazards
Barometric pressure
Weather observations
How animals use the food they stored
Watersheds

Worthy skills in recreation

Hiking to discover, study, explore, and collect native craft materials
Outdoor cooking techniques
Outdoor survival skills
Outdoor sports such as: skiing, boating, canoeing, fly-chasing, bait-casting, swimming, skating, and mountain climbing
Crafts
Nature workshop
Square dancing
Building outdoor shelters
Appreciating wholesome outdoor recreation

Spiritual values

Experiencing the beauty of nature
Appreciation of living things developed from personal contact
Better appreciation of the personal worth of others, from living together
Development of finer group unity
Appreciation of the beauty and worth of the out-of-doors

Wholesome work experiences

Conservation projects
Planting and terracing to arrest erosion
Repairing trails
Building small check dams
Planting and maintaining a forest nursery
Setting tables
Washing dishes
Cleaning cabins
Caring for animals and pets
Learning safe use and care of simple hand tools

Democratic social living

Cooperative planning by groups
Evaluation by students
Discussing camp safety standards
Living in cabin groups
Participating in campfire activities
Solving problems arising from living together
Understanding duties of the forest ranger
Acting as host, hostess, and hopper at dining table
Improving relationships of pupils and teacher
Enriching and fostering democratic living

Healthful living

Maintaining personal health, cleanliness
Maintaining regular hours of sleeping
Keeping cabin neat and clean
Participating in wholesome exercise
Developing better table manners and eating habits
Planning menus
Practicing first aid

---

*Adapted from State Board of Education, Concord, N. H.: School camping and outdoor education; and from Division of Instruction, Long Beach, Calif., Public Schools: Guide for the Camp Hi-Hill Program, Long Beach, Calif., June, 1952.

---

miles from Long Beach in the San Gabriel Mountains. This camp is primarily for sixth graders and faculty members, and the emphasis is on giving these children an opportunity to cope with various problems that arise when a group of individuals start living together in a democratic manner. This camp is also conducted on a year-round basis with winter activities playing just as important a role as summer activities. Table 25-2 shows how the camp experience at Long Beach is an extension of classroom learning activities.

Some states have passed legislation making tax money available to the schools for the support of camping provided for the public school children. This trend in state-level provision for camping in the public schools means that more and more opportunities are going to be made available for children to have this worthwhile experience. For example, in the state of Michigan a bill was passed providing that boards of education, with the exception of those in primary school districts, could operate camps independently or jointly with other boards of education or governing bodies for purposes of recreation and instruction. Provision was made for the charging of fees, if necessary, to cover expenses incurred in maintaining the camp. However, these camps are to be run on a nonprofit basis. Provisions were also made for boards of education to employ personnel to operate these camps, to maintain essential facilities,

and to locate camps on property other than that owned by the board of education, provided that the consent of the owner of said property had been secured. Finally, a provision was made stipulating that the cost of operating a school camp should not be included in the determination of per capita costs of the regular school program.

In the state of New York legislation has provided that boards of education may operate camps on land secured by the school district for camp purposes. The legislature of the state of New York passed the Desmond School Camp Bill, which made it possible for school districts to appropriate funds for instructional programs deemed advisable for school children. Camping is one experience that is being recognized more and more as being an essential for all children of school age.

When historians look back at the twen-

Education in the out-of-doors that is meaningful.

tienth century there is a good possibility they will credit the school camping movement as the greatest educational innovation of the era and acclaim Michigan as one of the pioneer states in proving that nature's classroom helps to prepare the child much more effectively for living in today's world. The history of school camping in this state goes back some 25 years. In the early 1930's Tappan Junior High School in Ann Arbor utilized a camp setting for its junior high school students, and the Cadillac board of education developed a summer camp for its elementary school children. A little later, schools in Battle Creek, Decatur, and Otsego utilized camps in their educational programs. In 1945 the state government passed legislation making it possible for school districts to acquire and operate camps as part of their educational program. In 1946 their Departments of Public Instruction and Conservation, together with the W. K. Kellogg Foundation, joined forces to develop the program further. The late Lee M. Thurston, State Superintendent of Public Instruction, and P. J. Hoffmaster, State Director of Conservation, set as the goal for the state of Michigan: "A week of school camping for every boy and girl in the state."

The rapid development of camping in Michigan has resulted to a great degree because of the educationally significant way in which the program is operated. The groups going to camp usually include fifth- or sixth-graders on the elementary level, or home rooms and special subject matter areas on the secondary level. The camps are run by the teachers and students. Preplanning takes place in the classroom where such essentials as clothing needed, projects to be developed, and job assignments are arranged. The usual procedure is to have two teachers for the average classroom-size group, plus extra help for food preparation and camp maintenance. The parents assume the cost of food, with special provisions being made for those children whose families are unable to pay the expenses. Any child who wants to go to camp is given the opportunity. Schools assume the instructional cost. The school district or government agency bears the cost of the camp and its facilities.*

Over 100 educational systems include camping in their school programs at the present time in the state of Michigan. This state is pioneering in an educational movement that has many potentialities for furthering the social, mental, physical, and emotional growth of children. The fact that fewer than 10% of the children of camp age in America ever get any type of camp experience presents a challenge for other states to follow Michigan's lead.

The years ahead will undoubtedly find camping becoming more and more a part of the school program. Administrators, teachers, and educators in general should examine the potentialities that camping and outdoor education have for their own school systems.

---

*Smith, J. W.: The Michigan story of camping and outdoor education, The Journal of Educational Sociology **23**:508, 1950.

Questions and exercises

1. Prepare a speech to be given to a parent-teacher's association on the importance of camping in education. Point up the values of camping to the children in the community.
2. What is the responsibility of professional preparing institutions in the field of camping and outdoor education?
3. Make a study of the program of camping and outdoor education in the state of Michigan and give a report to the class.
4. Cite specific examples to show how camping and outdoor education can develop a child socially and intellectually.
5. Prepare a report for a board of education to justify taking all the sixth-grade children of a school to camp on school time.
6. What should constitute some of the experiences provided in a camp setting?
7. Make a study of school camping in the fifty states and report to class on the progress that has been made during the last 5 years.

8. How can school camping contribute to the wise use of natural resources?
9. What is meant by enabling legislation? What type of enabling legislation is needed in your state to promote school camping? List a series of logical steps that should be followed to achieve such legislation.
10. Write an essay of 250 words on the subject: School camping is an extension of the classroom.

Reading assignment in *Administrative Dimensions of Health and Physical Education Programs, Including Athletics:* Chapters 19 and 20, Selections 100 to 103.

Selected references

American Association for Health, Physical Education, and Recreation: Leisure and the schools, Washington, D. C., 1961, The Association.

Brinley, A.: Classrooms as big as all outdoors, NEA Journal 53:45, 1964.

For these children: everything that camp should give, Michigan Education Journal (editorial), 43:26, 1965.

Freeberg, W. H.: Programs in outdoor education, Minneapolis, 1963, Burgess Publishing Co.

Fewer, R. D.: Administrative responsibilities for outdoor education, Illinois Journal of Education 55:7, 1964.

Gabrielson, M. A., and Holtzer, C.: Camping and outdoor education, New York, 1965, The Center for Applied Research in Education, Inc. (The Library of Education).

Hammerman, D. R., and Hammerman, W. M.: Teaching in the outdoors, Minneapolis, 1964, Burgess Publishing Co.

Hammerman, D. R.: Research implications for outdoor education, Journal of Health, Physical Education, and Recreation 35:89, 1964.

Illinois State Superintendent of Public Instruction: Know about outdoor education. Illinois Journal of Education, December, 1964. (Available from Superintendent, Room 302, State Office Building, Springfield.)

Isenberg, R. M.: Education comes alive outdoors, NEA Journal 54:24, 1967.

Report of the Committee on Camping in Education: The place of camping in education, Journal of the American Association for Health, Physical Education, and Recreation 21:15, 1950.

Shanklin, J. F.: Outdoor recreation land, Journal of Health, Physical Education, and Recreation 36:19, 1965.

Shivers, J. S.: Camping — administration counseling, programming, New York, 1971, Appleton-Century-Crofts.

Smith, J. W.: Outdoor education for American youth, Washington, D. C., 1957, American Association for Health, Physical Education, and Recreation.

Appendices

A SOURCES OF EQUIPMENT AND SUPPLIES FOR ATHLETIC, PHYSICAL EDUCATION, RECREATION, OUTDOOR EDUCATION, AND SCHOOL HEALTH PROGRAMS*

AAHPER's seventh annual directory of equipment and supplies is in two parts. The first lists companies and suppliers under sixteen categories. Many of the companies distribute goods in more than one category and are so listed. Only the company name appears under the category heading. Addresses are shown in the second part of the directory, which is an alphabetical listing of suppliers.

Each entry contains the full company name and address, plus a brief description of its services as prepared by the company. The companies listed in this directory have been accepted for advertising in the Journal and for exhibiting at AAHPER national conventions. All have met certain standards of advertising and exhibiting. Those listed in boldface type have advertised and exhibited with AAHPER over a long-term period.

ATHLETIC AND SPORTS EQUIPMENT

AA-Belco All-Automotive Phys-Ed &
   Athletic Laundry Equip. Co.
ADIRONDACK INDUSTRIES, INC.
AMERICAN ATHLETIC EQUIPMENT CO.
American Gym Corporation
**ATLAS ATHLETIC EQUIPMENT
   COMPANY**
R. E. Austin & Son
BALL-BOY CO.
Benson Optical Company
Bike Athletic Prod. Div., Kendall Co.
Bolco Athletic Co.

*From Journal of Health, Physical Education, and Recreation **40**:61-68, 1969.

Brunswick Corp./Bowling Division
Buc-Ol Mfg. Co.
The J. E. Burke Company
CASTELLO FENCING EQUIP. CO. INC.
Chicago Roller Skate Co.
CONVERSE RUBBER COMPANY
COSOM CORPORATION
CRAN BARRY INC.
DAYTON RACQUET CO. INC.
Dekan Timing Devices
DeVac, Inc., Sportation Division
Andy Douglass, Inc.
DUDLEY SPORTS CO. INC.
Exercycle Corporation
Flex-I-Flag Company
The Harry Gill Company
J. E. Gregory Co.
Gulbenkian Swim Inc.
GYM MASTER CO.
Hadar Athletic Mfg. Co.
Hanhart Stop Watch Factory, Ltd.
HARGAL ALL-SPORTS CARRYALL
Harvard Table Tennis Corporation
HILLERICH & BARDSBY CO.
Jayfro Corp.
Adolph Kiefer & Co.—Div. of McNeil Corp.
Kwik-Kold, Inc.
LIND CLIMBER COMPANY
McGregor Company, Consumer Division,
   Brunswick Corp.
MARCY GYMNASIUM EQUIPMENT CO.
Mason City Tent & Awning Co.
McArthur Towels Inc.
Medart Division, Jackes-Evans Mfg. Co.
Mid-Valley Sports Center
3M Company, Recreation & Athletic Products
Mitchell Division/Royal Industries
Monsanto Company—AstroTurf®
   Recreational Surfaces
National Sports Division—Medalist Industries
NISSEN CORPORATION
OCEAN POOL SUPPLY CO. INC.

Oregon Worsted Co.
Pennsylvania Athletic Products
PHYSICAL EDUCATION SUPPLY ASSOCIATES, INC.
PORT-A-PIT INC.
Premier Products
J. A. PRESTON CORPORATION
Program Aids Inc.
Protection Equipment Sales Division—
  Vogt Mfg. Corp.
Quinton Instruments
Randolph Mfg. Co., Inc.
Rawlings Sporting Goods Company
Saunders Archery Company
Scott & Company-GM Baseball
SEAMLESS
Sells Aerial Tennis Co.
SERON MFG. CO.
Shield Mfg., Inc.
Sorensen-Christian Industries, Inc.
A. G. Spalding & Bros., Inc.
STERLING RECREATION PRODUCTS
Strand Case Co. (Div. of SNR Golf, Inc.)
Top Star Inc.
Universal Athletic Sales Co.
UNIVERSAL BLEACHER CO.
Videonetics, Div. Newell Industries
W. J. VOIT RUBBER CORP.
WILSON SPORTING GOODS CO.
Wittek Golf Range Supply Co., Inc.
Wolverine Sports Supply

ATHLETIC AND SPORTS CLOTHING

M—Men's
W—Women's
B—Both

ALDRICH & ALDRICH INC.— B
Algy Dance Costumes—W
Bike Athletic Prod. Div., Kendall Co.—M
TOM BRODERICK COMPANY, INC.— B
CAPEZIO DANCEWEAR— B
CASTELLO FENCING EQUIP. CO. INC.
CHAMPION PRODUCTS INC.— B
CONVERSE RUBBER COMPANY— B
CRAN BARRY INC.— W
Dolfin Sportswear Company—B
Gulbenkian Swim Inc.—B
GYM MASTER CO.— B
Hanes Sports Division—Hanes Corp.—M
The Hanold Company and its Sylvia
  Putzinger Div.—B
Jean Lee Originals—W
Adolph Kiefer & Co.—Div. of McNeil
  Corp.—B
Loshin's Costume Center, Inc.—W
McArthur Towels Inc.—B

E. R. MOORE CO.— W
National Sports Division—Medalist Industries
New Balance Athletic Shoe Co.—B
NISSEN CORPORATION
OCEAN POOL SUPPLY CO. INC.
PHYSICAL EDUCATION SUPPLY ASSOCIATES, INC.
Randolph Mfg. Co., Inc.
Rawlings Sporting Goods Company—M
Wheelan and Wheelan, Inc.—W
White Stag-Speedo—B
WILSON SPORTING GOODS CO.
Wilton Mfg. Co. Inc.—B

RESEARCH EQUIPMENT

Warren E. Collins, Inc.
Dekan Timing Devices
E & M Instrument Co., Inc.
Exercycle Corporation
Lafayette Instrument Co.
NISSEN CORPORATION
J. A. PRESTON CORPORATION
Quinton Instruments
Reedco, Inc.
Technology/Versatronics, Inc.

SCOREBOARDS AND TIMERS

R. E. Austin & Son
CRAN BARRY INC.
Dekan Timing Devices
Gulbenkian Swim Inc.
Hanhart Stop Watch Factory, Ltd.
Adolph Kiefer & Co., Div. of McNeil Corp.
NISSEN CORPORATION
Program Aids Inc.
Sorensen-Christian Industries, Inc.
Wolverine Sports Supply

AUDIOVISUAL MATERIALS

ALLYN AND BACON, INC.
American Cancer Society, Inc.
THE ATHLETIC INSTITUTE
R. E. Austin & Son
BALL-BOY CO.
Bowmar Records, Inc.
Stanley Bowmar Co., Inc.
George F. Cram Company, Inc.
Denoyer-Geppert Company
Walt Disney Educational Materials Company
Ealing Corporation
EDUCATIONAL ACTIVITIES, INC.
EDUCATIONAL RECORDINGS OF AMERICA, INC.
Educators Progress Service, Inc.
Film Distributors International

G. N. Productions
Harcourt, Brace & World, Inc.
HARPER & ROW, PUBLISHERS
D. C. Heath and Company/A Div. of
    Raytheon Education Co.
HOCTOR EDUCATIONAL RECORDS
HOLT, RINEHART AND WINSTON
KIMBO EDUCATIONAL RECORDS
Lafayette Instrument Co.
Marjorie S. Larsen
J. B. Lippincott Company
Loshin's Costume Center, Inc.
Medical Plastics Laboratory, Inc.
FREDA MILLER RECORDS FOR DANCE
3M Company, Visual Products Division
National Dairy Council
The National Foundation—March of Dimes
National Golf Foundation
NISSEN CORPORATION
Physical Education Aids
**PHYSICAL EDUCATION SUPPLY
    ASSOCIATES, INC.**
Popular Science and Audio Visuals, Inc.
Program Aids Inc.
Rhythms Productions Records
School Aid Co., Inc.
Society For Visual Education, Inc.
Syracuse University Film Marketing Division
TAMPAX INCORPORATED
United States Air Force
Videonetics, Div. Newell Industries

FACILITIES

THE ATHLETIC INSTITUTE (planning)
California Products Corporation (surfacing)
DeBourgh Mfg. Co. (lockers)
J. E. Gregory Co.
Adolph Kiefer & Co., Div. of McNeil Corp.
Medart Division Jackes-Evans Mfg. Co.
    (lockers, bleachers)
3M Company—Recreation and Athletic
    Products (Surfacing)
Monsanto Company—AstroTurf® (surfacing)
NISSEN CORPORATION (bleachers)
STERLING RECREATION PRODUCTS
Superior Wire & Iron Products, Inc. (lockers)
Universal Athletic Sales Co.
Universal Bleacher Co.
    (bleachers, port-a-pool)

EDUCATIONAL MATERIALS

AAHPER-USLTA Joint Committee on Tennis
ALLYN AND BACON, INC.
American Cancer Society, Inc.
American Institute of Baking
American Junior Bowling Congress

THE ATHLETIC INSTITUTE
**ATLAS ATHLETIC EQUIPMENT
    COMPANY**
BALL-BOY CO.
Stanley Bowmar Co., Inc.
WM. C. BROWN COMPANY PUBLISHERS
BURGESS PUBLISHING CO.
George F. Cram Company, Inc.
Denoyer-Geppert Company
Walt Disney Educational Materials Company
Ealing Corporation
**EDUCATIONAL RECORDINGS OF
    AMERICA, INC.**
Educators Progress Service, Inc.
Encyclopaedia Britannica, Inc.
Film Distributors International
Harcourt, Brace & World, Inc.
HARPER & ROW, PUBLISHERS
D. C. Heath and Company/A Div. of
    Raytheon Education Co.
HOCTOR EDUCATIONAL RECORDS
HOLT, RINEHART AND WINSTON
Instructional Materials Laboratories, Inc.
KIMBERLY-CLARK CORPORATION
KIMBO EDUCATIONAL RECORDS
LEA & FEBIGER
Licensed Beverage Industries, Inc.
J. B. Lippincott Company
McGraw-Hill Book Co., Webster Division
Medical Plastics Laboratory, Inc.
**CHARLES E. MERRILL PUBLISHING
    COMPANY**
FREDA MILLER RECORDS FOR DANCE
3M Company, Visual Products Division
National Dairy Council
The National Foundation—March of Dimes
National Golf Foundation
National Rifle Association of America
Personal Products Company
The Physical Education Association of
    Great Britain and Northern Ireland
Program Aids Inc.
Reedco, Inc.
Rhythms Productions Records
W. B. SAUNDERS COMPANY
Scott Paper Company
Signal Press
Society For Visual Education, Inc.
Standard Brands Incorporated
Stepping Tones Records
Syracuse University Film Marketing Division
TAMPAX INCORPORATED
Videonetics, Div. Newell Industries

EMBLEMS, AWARDS, TROPHIES

CHAMPION PRODUCTS INC.

CRAN BARRY INC.
Gulbenkian Swim Inc.
**PHYSICAL EDUCATION SUPPLY
ASSOCIATES, INC.**
Program Aids Inc.
Wolverine Sports Supply

PUBLISHERS

Academic Press, Inc.
ALLYN AND BACON, INC.
The W. H. Anderson Company
THE ATHLETIC INSTITUTE
WM. C. BROWN COMPANY PUBLISHERS
BURGESS PUBLISHING CO.
Denoyer-Geppert Company
Ealing Corporation
Educators Progress Service, Inc.
Encyclopaedia Britannica, Inc.
Goodyear Publishing Company, Inc.
Harcourt, Brace & World, Inc.
HARPER & ROW, PUBLISHERS
D. C. Heath and Company
HOCTOR EDUCATIONAL RECORDS
KIMBO EDUCATIONAL RECORDS
LEA & FEBIGER
LIND CLIMBER COMPANY
J. B. Lippincott Company
LYONS & CARNAHAN
THE MACMILLAN COMPANY
McGRAW-HILL BOOK COMPANY
McGraw-Hill Book Co., Webster Division
**CHARLES E. MERRILL PUBLISHING
COMPANY**
FREDA MILLER RECORDS FOR DANCE
THE C. V. MOSBY COMPANY
The National Foundation—March of Dimes
National Sporting Goods Association
O'Brien & O'Brien
The Physical Education Association of
Great Britain and Northern Ireland
Physical Education Aids
**PHYSICAL EDUCATION SUPPLY
ASSOCIATES, INC.**
Program Aids Inc.
Rhythms Productions Records
The Ronald Press Company
W. B. SAUNDERS COMPANY
School Aid Co., Inc.
Charles C Thomas, Publisher
**WADSWORTH PUBLISHING COMPANY,
INC.**

TRAINING ROOM EQUIPMENT AND SUPPLIES

AA-Belco All-Automatic Phys-Ed &
Athletic Laundry Equipment Co.

American Gym Corporation
Bike Athletic Prod Div., Kendall Co.
CRAN BARRY INC.
Exercycle Corporation
Kwik-Kold, Inc.
MARCY GYMNASIUM EQUIPMENT CO.
Master Lock Company
Medical Plastic Laboratory, Inc.
Mitchell Division/Royal Industries
Premier Products
J. A. PRESTON CORPORATION
Program Aids Inc.
Sani-Mist Inc.
SCHOOL HEALTH SUPPLY CO.
SERON MFG. CO.
STERLING RECREATION PRODUCTS
Top Star Inc.
Wolverine Sports Supply

RECREATION AND OUTDOOR EDUCATION EQUIPMENT AND FACILITIES

R. E. Austin & Son
BALL-BOY CO.
Brunswick Corp./Bowling Division
Buc-Ol Mfg. Co.
The J. E. Burke Company
COSOM CORPORATION
Daisy/Heddon, Division Victor
Comptometer Corp.
DeVac, Inc., Sportation Division
Flex-I-Flag Company
J. E. Gregory Co.
Gulbenkian Swim Inc.
Hadar Athletic Mfg. Co.
THE DELMER F. HARRIS CO.
Jayfro Corp.
Adolph Kiefer & Co., Div. of McNeil Corp.
MARCY GYMNASIUM EQUIPMENT CO.
Mason City Tent & Awning Co.
Master Lock Company
Medart Division, Jackes-Evans Mfg. Co.
Mid-Valley Sports Center
3M Company—Recreation and Athletic
Products
Mitchell Division/Royal Industries
Monsanto Company—AstroTurf®
Recreational Surfaces
National Sports Division—Medalist Industries
NISSEN CORPORATION
Pennsylvania Athletic Products
Playground Corporation of America
PORT-A-PIT INC.
Premier Products
J. A. PRESTON CORPORATION
Program Aids Inc.

Saunders Archery Company
SEAMLESS
Shield Mfg., Inc.
Sorensen-Christian Industries, Inc.
STERLING RECREATION PRODUCTS
Superior Wire & Iron Products, Inc.
T. F. Twardzik & Co., Inc.
Universal Athletic Sales Co.
UNIVERSAL BLEACHER CO.
Videonetics, Div. Newell Industries
Wittek Golf Range Supply Co., Inc.
Wolverine Sports Supply

GAMES

COSOM CORPORATION
DAYTON RACQUET CO., INC.
Hanhart Stop Watch Factory Ltd.
Harvard Table Tennis Corporation
Marjorie S. Larsen
Mason City Tent & Awning Co.
PORT-A PIT INC.
J. A. PRESTON CORPORATION
Sells Aerial Tennis Co.
STERLING RECREATION PRODUCTS
R. E. Titus Gym Scooter Co.
T. F. Twardzik & Co., Inc.
Wolverine Sports Supply

CAREER INFORMATION

American Cancer Society, Inc.
Educators Progress Service, Inc.
O'Brien & O'Brien
The Physical Education Association of
    Great Britain and Northern Ireland
United States Air Force
U.S. Army Recruiting Command
U.S. Marine Corps
U.S. Navy
YWCA of the USA

FACILITIES AND EQUIPMENT MAINTENANCE

AA-Belco All-Automatic Phys-Ed &
    Athletic Laundry Equip. Co.
Hillyard Chemical Company
Master Lock Company
McArthur Towels, Inc.
Medart Division Jackes-Evans Mfg. Co.
PELLERIN MILNOR CORPORATION
Sani-Mist Inc.
STERLING RECREATION PRODUCTS

DANCE SUPPLIES

ALDRICH & ALDRICH INC.
Algy Dance Costumes

BALL-BOY CO.
Bowmar Records, Inc.
TOM BRODERICK COMPANY, INC.
CAPEZIO DANCEWEAR
CRAN BARRY INC.
**EDUCATIONAL RECORDINGS OF
    AMERICA INC.**
J. E. Gregory Co.
HOCTOR EDUCATIONAL RECORDS
KIMBO EDUCATIONAL RECORDS
Kling's Theatrical Shoe Co.
Leo's Advanced Theatrical Co.
Loshin's Costume Center, Inc.
FREDA MILLER RECORDS FOR DANCE
**PHYSICAL EDUCATION SUPPLY
    ASSOCIATES, INC.**
Rhythms Productions Records
SELVA
Stepping Tones Records
Wheelan and Wheelan, Inc.
Wolff-Fording & Co., Inc.

MISCELLANEOUS

American Junior Bowling Congress
    (bowling programs)
Benson Optical Company
    (athletic eyewear)
COCA-COLA USA (concessions)
CRAN BARRY INC.
    (cheerleading fashions & supplies)
DeBourgh Mfg. Co. (lockers)
Jean Lee Originals
    (cheerleader & majorette fashions)
Mason Candies, Inc. (fund raising)
Master Lock Company (locks)
Monsanto Company—AstroTurf®
    Recreational Surfaces (synthetic turf)
National Sporting Goods Association
    (national trade association for the
    sporting goods industry)
PELLERIN MILNOR CORPORATION
    (laundry machinery)
Reedco, Inc. (tests and measurements)
Superior Wire & Iron Products, Inc.
    (athletic lockers & benches)

A

AA-Belco All-Automatic Phys-Ed &
    Athletic Equipment Co.
P. O. Box 652
Charlotte, North Carolina 28201
Specialized all-automatic physical education and
athletic laundry equipment for doing all gym
uniforms, towels, and game and practice uniforms.

AAHPER-USLTA Joint Committee on Tennis

Norris Gymnasium
University of Minnesota
Minneapolis, Minnesota 55455
Educational materials and teaching aids pertaining to tennis instruction.

Academic Press, Inc.
111 Fifth Avenue
New York, New York 10003
Texts and reference works in physical education and health.

ADIRONDACK INDUSTRIES, INC.
McKinley Avenue
Dolgeville, New York 13329
Manufacturer of "Big Stick Bats."

ALDRICH & ALDRICH INC.
1859 Milwaukee Avenue
Chicago, Illinois 60647
Apparel for physical education, pool, and dance.

Algy Dance Costumes
148 West 24 Street
New York, New York 10011
Sequined uniforms for majorettes, cheerleaders, and twirlers.

ALLYN & BACON, INC.
470 Atlantic Avenue
Boston, Massachusetts 02210
Publishers of preschool through high school and college textbooks.

AMERICAN ATHLETIC EQUIPMENT CO.
Box 111
Jefferson, Iowa 50129
The manufacturer of gymnasium and gymnastic equipment.

American Cancer Society, Inc.
219 East 42nd Street
New York, New York 10017
Health-educational teaching aids, films, film cartridges, filmstrips and printed materials.

American Gym Corporation
North Greengate Road
Greensburg, Pennsylvania 15601
American Gym Corp. manufacturers of the Super Gym Weight Training Machine 8, 9, 10, 11, 13, 14, and 15 Stations.

American Institute of Baking
400 East Ontario Street
Chicago, Illinois 60611
Graded educational literature for teaching nutrition in the health education curriculum.

American Junior Bowling Congress
1572 East Capitol Drive
Milwaukee, Wisconsin 53211
Bowling program for boys and girls.

The W. H. Anderson Company
646 Main Street
Cincinnati, Ohio 46201

THE ATHLETIC INSTITUTE
805 Merchandise Mart
Chicago, Illinois 60654
Audiovisual and published instructional aids on athletics, physical education, and recreation.

ATLAS ATHLETIC EQUIPMENT COMPANY
2339 Hampton Avenue
St. Louis, Missouri 63139
Gymnasium apparatus and gymnasium mats.

R. E. Austin & Son
705 Bedford Avenue
Bellmore, New York 11710
Quality field and gym athletic equipment.

B

BALL-BOY CO.
27 Milburn Street
Bronxville, New York 10708
New designs—equipment and teaching aids for sports, athletics, dance.

Benson Optical Company
1812 Park Avenue
Minneapolis, Minnesota 55440
All-American athletic eyewear, all-nylon frame and safety lenses—comfortable, lightweight, safe.

Bike Athletic Prod. Div., Kendall Co.
309 W. Jackson Boulevard
Chicago, Illinois 60606
Athletic supporters, supports, mouthguards, trainer's tape, trainer's supplies, first aid supplies, and socks for the prevention and care of injuries.

Bolco Athletic Company
1751 N. Eastern Avenue
Los Angeles, California 90032
Baseball bases, home plates, pitchers plates, base anchors, helmets.

Bowmar Records, Inc.
622 Rodier Drive
Glendale, California 91201
Music for physical fitness and records of singing, games, and folk dances.

Stanley Bowmar Co., Inc.
4 Broadway
Valhalla, New York 10595
We sell multi-media materials, including records, tapes, filmstrips, and transparencies, for all grade levels.

TOM BRODERICK COMPANY, INC.
2400 Broadway

Parsons, Kansas 67357
Gymwear, poolwear, dancewear, team uniforms.

WM. C. BROWN COMPANY PUBLISHERS
135 South Locust Street
Dubuque, Iowa 52001
Publisher of college textbooks and supplementary
materials.

Brunswick Corporation, Bowling Division
69 West Washington
Chicago, Illinois 60602
The finest and most complete line of bowling supplies and equipment including bowling balls, bags,
and shoes.

Buc Ol Manufacturing Co.
1017 South Locust Street
Oxford, Ohio 45056
Mac-Col, the safe, all rubber practice golf ball that
eliminates the need for nets indoors and large
space outdoors.

BURGESS PUBLISHING CO.
426 South 6th Street
Minneapolis, Minnesota 55415
Educational texts and manuals for elementary,
high school, and college use.

The J. E. Burke Company
P. O. Box 549
Fond du Lac, Wisconsin 54935
Playground, sports, and recreation equipment.

C

California Products Corporation
169 Waverly Street
Cambridge, Massachusetts 02139
Plexipave tennis courts and Reslite® running
tracks.

CAPEZIO DANCEWEAR
1855 Broadway
New York, New York 10023
Dance, theatre, and recreation footwear; leotards,
tights, and accessories.

CASTELLO FENCING EQUIP. CO. INC.
30 East 10th Street
New York, New York 10003
Fencing, judo, karate uniforms and equipment.

CHAMPION PRODUCTS INC.
115 College Avenue
Rochester, New York 14607
Athletic knitwear and campus sportswear.

Chicago Roller Skate Co.
4498 West Lake Street
Chicago, Illinois 60624
Boot and clamp-on roller skates, repairs and accessories suitable for physical education programs.

COCA-COLA USA
P. O. Drawer 1734
Atlanta, Georgia 30301
Manufacturers of a complete line of soft drinks—
Coca-Cola, Sprite, TAB, Fresca, and Fanta Flavors.

Warren E. Collins, Inc.
220 Wood Road
Braintree, Massachusetts 02184
Ergometers and treadmills for determining work
output in mild, moderate, and excessive exercise.

CONVERSE RUBBER COMPANY
392 Pearl Street
Malden, Massachusetts 02148
Manufacturers of tennis, basketball, football, wrestling, and yachting shoes; football and band par-
kas, warm-up jackets.

COSOM CORPORATION
6030 Wayzata Boulevard
Minneapolis, Minnesota 55416
Safe-T-Play sporting goods—"The First Step in
Sports."

George F. Cram Company, Inc.
301 S. LaSalle Street
Indianapolis, Indiana 46206
Anatomical, health, and personality charts and
models.

CRAN BARRY INC.
31 Green Street, Box 354
Marblehead, Massachusetts 01945
Complete suppliers of sports equipment and apparel for women.

D

Daisy/Heddon, Division Victor
    Comptometer Corporation
South Highway 71
Rogers, Arkansas 72756
School training programs.

DAYTON RACQUET CO. INC.
302 South Albright Street
Arcanum, Ohio 45304
Steel racquets—tennis, badminton, paddle tennis,
and racquet ball.

DeBourgh Mfg. Co.
9300 James Avenue South
Minneapolis, Minnesota 55431
Fully ventilated athletic and physical education
lockers and locker room benches.

Dekan Timing Devices
Box 712
Glen Ellyn, Illinois 60137
Automatic performance analyzer, timing automat-
ically and the 1/100th second range with mul-
tiple start and stop methods.

Denoyer-Geppert Company
5235 Ravenswood Avenue
Chicago, Illinois 60640
Designed and producer of unbreakable anatomical models, skeletons, charts, transparencies, and related visual aids for health sciences.

DeVac, Inc., Sportation Division
10122 Highway 55
Minneapolis, Minnesota 55427
Golf machines for direct teaching of proper swing via muscle memory, non-shanking golf clubs.

Walt Disney Educational Materials
    Company
800 Sonora Avenue
Glendale, California 91201
Upjohn/Disney Health Series: Four Films. This is Your Health Films: Eight Films.

Dolfin Sportswear Company
South Sterley and Catherine Streets
Shillington, Pennsylvania 19607
Swim suits used for competition, swimming classes, and practice in general, all around pool, and beach use.

Andy Douglass, Inc.
2758 Orchid Street
New Orleans, Louisiana 70119
Completely safe weight-lifting machine that eliminates all problems, including safety, economy, time, and space.

DUDLEY SPORTS CO., INC.
19 West 34th Street
New York, New York 10001
Softballs, baseballs, baseball and tennis machines.

E F

E & M Instrument Co., Inc.
7651 Airport Boulevard
Houston, Texas 77017
Multi-channel, ink-writing recorders and accessories and biotelemetry systems.

Ealing Corporation
2225 Massachusetts Avenue
Cambridge, Massachusetts 02140
Super 8mm, silent, single-concept film loops and related projection equipment.

EDUCATIONAL ACTIVITIES, INC.
P. O. Box 392
Freeport, New York 11520
Records, tapes, cassettes, filmstrips, and books.

**EDUCATIONAL RECORDINGS OF
    AMERICA, INC.**
P. O. Box 231
Monroe, Connecticut 06468

Everything in educational records—folk, square, social dance, physical fitness.

Educators Progress Service, Inc.
214 Center Street
Randolph, Wisconsin 53956
Guides to free materials for schools.

Encyclopaedia Britannica, Inc.
Chicago, Illinois
Encyclopaedia Britannica, Great Books of the Western World, Britannica Junior, and other related materials.

Exercycle Corporation
630 Third Avenue
New York, New York, 10017
Distributor of Exercycle,® the world's leading motorized exerciser, the PEP,™ Personal Exerciser Planner, Torg™ exercise equipment.

Film Distributors International
2223 South Olive Street
Los Angeles, California 90007
16mm films—"Narcotics: Pit of Despair" and "Drug Abuse: The Chemical Tomb."

Flex-I-Flag Company
2238 N.E. Buchanan
Minneapolis, Minnesota 55418
Inexpensive field flags to be used as boundary markers for physical education activities.

G H

G. N. Productions
1019 North Cole Avenue
Los Angeles, California 90038
Educational films and film production services.

The Harry Gill Company
201 Courtesy Road
Urbana, Illinois 61801
Track and field equipment.

Goodyear Publishing Company, Inc.
15115 Sunset Boulevard
Pacific Palisades, California 90272
Goodyear Physical Activities Series edited by J. Tillman Hall.

J. E. Gregory Co.
922 West First
Spokane, Washington 99204
Physical education equipment and supplies.

Gulbenkian Swim Inc.
87 Greenwich Avenue
Greenwich, Connecticut 06830
Nylon swim wear, nylon physical education suits for swim classes, kickboards, racing lanes, swim equipment.

GYM MASTER CO.
3200 South Zuni Street
Englewood, Colorado 80110
Gymnasium, gymnastic apparatus, weight lifting equipment, gymnastic clothing.

Hadar Athletic Mfg. Co.
1108 North 13th Street
Humboldt, Iowa 50548
Physical education, track and field, and football equipment.

Hanes Sports Division, Hanes Corp.
Box 3073
Winston-Salem, North Carolina 27102
Manufacturers of athletic and sports clothing.

Hanhart Stop Watch Factory, Ltd.
3 Chestnut Street
Suffern, New York 10901
Hanhart stop watches for timing all sporting events.

Hanold Company and its
    Sylvia Putziger Division
Standish, Maine 04084
Sports clothing and gym wear including the Putziger Blazer.

Harcourt, Brace & World, Inc.
757 Third Avenue
New York, New York, 10017
Textbooks and other instructional materials for grades K-12.

HARGAL ALL-SPORTS CARRYALL
Box 1094
Wilmington, California 90744
The Versatile Cart—the kids cannot tear apart.

HARPER & ROW, PUBLISHERS
49 East 33rd Street
New York, New York 10016
Texts and references—health, physical education, recreation.

THE DELMER F. HARRIS CO.
Box 288
Concordia, Kansas 66901
"Swedish Gym" apparatus and other Playmate playground equipment.

Harvard Table Tennis Corporation
265 Third Street
Cambridge, Massachusetts 02142
Table tennis equipment.

D. C. Heath and Company/A Division of
    Raytheon Education Company
125 Spring Street
Lexington, Massachusetts 02118
Heath produces films and filmstrips in science, history, and health education for elementary and secondary schools.

HILLERICH & BRADSBY CO.
P. O. Box 506
Louisville, Kentucky 40201
Louisville Slugger bats, golf clubs, and hockey sticks.

Hillyard Chemical Company
302 North 4th Street
St. Joseph, Missouri 64502
All supplies that will make your floors look beautiful yet practical for sports.

HOCTOR EDUCATIONAL RECORDS
115 Manhattan Avenue
Waldwick, New Jersey 07463
Records and manuals for all phases of dance and physical education—Bogen phonographs also.

HOLT, RINEHART AND WINSTON
383 Madison Avenue
New York, New York 10017
Vince Lombardi's The Science and Art of Football —a series of 12 teaching-training films.

I J

Instructional Materials Laboratories, Inc.
18 East 41st Street
New York, New York 10017
Industry-sponsored school programs in areas of first aid and driver safety.

Jayfro Corp.
P. O. Box 50
Montville, Connecticut 06353
Manufacturers of a top quality line of athletic, gym, and recreation equipment.

Jean Lee Originals
P. O. Box 207
Goshen, Indiana 46526
United States' largest manufacturer and distributor of cheerleader and majorette fashions.

K

Adolph Kiefer & Co., Div. of McNeil Corp.
2741 Wingate
Akron, Ohio 44314
Swimming pool equipment including racing lanes, swimwear, and deck equipment.

KIMBERLY-CLARK CORPORATION
Life Cycle Center
Neenah, Wisconsin 54956
Family life educational booklets and teaching aids.

KIMBO EDUCATIONAL RECORDS
P. O. Box 55
Deal, New Jersey 07723
Educational albums, filmstrips, teacher's manuals for physical education, dance, gymnastics, rhythms, and sports at all grade levels.

Kling's Theatrical Shoe Co.
218 South Wabash Avenue
Chicago, Illinois 60604
Manufacturers and retailers of dance wear.

Kwik-Kold, Inc.
First Federal Building
Moberly, Missouri 65270
Training room supplies including instant cold packs, Desenex skin protection.

L

Lafayette Instrument Co.
Box 1279
Lafayette, Indiana 47902
Manufacturers of laboratory testing devices.

Marjorie S. Larsen
1754 Middlefield
Stockton, California 95204
Speed-a-Way guide book. Film, audiovisual charts and tests.

LEA & FEBIGER
600 Washington Square
Philadelphia, Pennsylvania 19106
Distinctive texts in health, physical education, and recreation, described in new 1969 catalog.

Leo's Advance Theatrical Co.
125 North Wabash Avenue
Chicago, Illinois 60602
Shoes, body garments, records, makeup, tights, material, costumes for children and adults in dance and physical education.

Licensed Beverage Industries, Inc.
155 East 44th Street
New York, New York 10017
Free educational reprints for teacher use dealing with the area of alcohol education as a field of instruction in schools and colleges.

LIND CLIMBER COMPANY
807 Reba Place
Evanston, Illinois 60202
Gymnastic equipment for elementary schools and schools for exceptional children, textbook of apparatus activities.

J. B. Lippincott Company
East Washington Square
Philadelphia, Pennsylvania 19105
Books in medicine, dentistry, pharmacy, nursing, and allied professions.

Loshin's Costume Center, Inc.
215 East 8th Street
Cincinnati, Ohio 45202
Leotards, trunks, tights, dance and recreation footwear, dance and recreation records and manuals.

Lyons & Carnahan
Educational Division/Meredith Corporation
407 East 25th Street
Chicago, Illinois 60616
Publishers of elementary and secondary education materials.

M

THE MACMILLAN COMPANY
866 Third Avenue
New York, New York 10022
Book publishers in all areas of health, physical education, and recreation.

MacGregor Company Consumer Division
Brunswick Corporation
I-75 and Jimson Road
Cincinnati, Ohio 45215
Manufacturers of golf equipment and athletic goods.

MARCY GYMNASIUM EQUIPMENT CO.
1736 Standard Avenue
Glendale, California 91201
Manufacturers of the circuit-trainer™ and complete gym installations.

Mason Candies, Inc.
P. O. Box 500
Mineola, New York 11501
Fill your treasury with Mason Candies' no-risk, no-investment protected fund raising plan.

Mason City Tent & Awning Co.
403 South Federal Avenue
Mason City, Iowa 50401
Rip Flag is the quality belt and flag set made to give maximum help to the physical education instructor or coach.

Master Lock Company
2600 North 32nd Street
Milwaukee, Wisconsin 53245
Padlocks and built-in locks for lockers.

McArthur Towels Inc.
Box H
Baraboo, Wisconsin 53913
School gym towels, laundry equipment, related products.

McGRAW-HILL BOOK COMPANY
330 West 42nd Street
New York, New York 10036
Publishers of outstanding education textbooks.

McGraw-Hill Book Co., Webster Division
Manchester Road
Manchester, Missouri 63011
Physical Education for Life, a physical training text with film loops on various sports.

Medart Division, Jackes-Evans Mfg. **Co.**
11737 Administration Drive
St. Louis, Missouri 63141
Telescopic gymseats, basketball backstops, lockers, locks.

Medical Plastics Laboratory, Inc.
P. O. Box 38
Gatesville, Texas 76528
Authentic plastic anatomical reproductions.

**CHARLES E. MERRILL PUBLISHING
    COMPANY**
1300 Alum Creek Drive
Columbus, Ohio 43216
Elementary physical education materials and text-books for prospective elementary and secondary health educators.

Mid-Valley Sports Center
5350 North Blackstone
Fresno, California 93726
The E. Mason "Shorty" Tennis racket—a tennis racket five inches shorter than the regular racket.

FREDA MILLER RECORDS FOR DANCE
Dept. E, Box 383
Northport, New York 11768
Modern dance and rhythms from basic movements to advanced for dance, physical education, and the elementary classroom teacher.

3M Company, Recreation & Athletic Products
3M Center, Adv. Display, 220-6E
St. Paul, Minnesota, 55101
"Tartan" brand surfacing for recreation and athletic playing surfaces.

3M Company, Visual Products Division
3M Center
St. Paul, Minnesota 55101
Complete line of equipment and accessories for overhead projection.

Mitchell Division/Royal Industries
1500 East Chestnut Street
Santa Ana, California 92701
Protective playground cushion and matting products.

Monsanto Company
    Astro Turf® Recreational Surfaces
800 North Lindbergh Boulevard
St. Louis, Missouri 63166
AstroTurf® athletic fields, playgrounds, field houses, golf tees, and greens.

E. R. MOORE CO.
7230 North Caldwell Avenue
Niles (Chicago), Illinois 60648
Gymwear for girls and young women in physical education classes.

THE C. V. MOSBY COMPANY
11830 Westline Industrial Drive
St. Louis, Missouri 63141
Publishers of outstanding college text and reference books in the field of health and physical education.

N O

National Dairy Council
111 North Canal Street
Chicago, Illinois 60606
Publishers of booklets, posters, films, and filmstrips on nutrition education for use in professional, educational, and consumer groups.

The National Foundation—March of Dimes
800 Second Avenue
New York, New York 10017
Free supplementary materials on genetics, birth defects, and prenatal care.

National Golf Foundation
Room 804 Merchandise Mart
Chicago, Illinois 60654
Golf films and publications.

National Rifle Association of America
1600 Rhode Island Avenue, N.W.
Washington, D. C. 20036
National organization promoting marksmanship, firearms safety, hunting safety, and conservation.

National Sporting Goods Association
717 North Michigan Avenue
Chicago, Illinois 60611
National trade association representing sporting goods retailers as well as manufacturers of all types of sporting goods equipment.

National Sports Division Medalist Industries
19 East McWilliams
Fond du Lac, Wisconsin 54935
Complete line of wrestling and gymnasium mats and accessories.

New Balance Athletic Shoe Co.
176 Belmont Street
Watertown, Massachusetts 02172
Athletic-track shoes.

NISSEN CORPORATION
930 27th Avenue S.W.
Cedar Rapids, Iowa 52406
Manufacturing heavy-duty gymnasium equipment for schools and colleges.

O'Brien & O'Brien
Educational Consultants
P. O. Box 271
Buffalo, New York 14221
Guide to Educational Opportunities: Listing of faculty and staff vacancies in universities, colleges, and junior colleges.

OCEAN POOL SUPPLY CO., INC.
17 Stepar Place
Huntington Station, New York 11746
The first and finest in swimwear, equipment, and accessories.

Oregon Worsted Co.
P. O. Box 02098
Portland, Oregon 97202
Manufacture and sale of Flying Fleece balls.

P

PELLERIN MILNOR CORPORATION
P. O. Box 398
Kenner, Louisiana 70062
Manufacturers of heavy duty laundry machinery for school and college use.

Pennsylvania Athletic Products
P. O. Box 951
Akron, Ohio 44309
Athletic products for institutional use.

Personal Products Company
Milltown, New Jersey 08850
Complete program of feminine hygiene instructional materials including motion picture, teacher's guides, and student booklets.

The Physical Education Association of
  Great Britain and Northern Ireland
Ling House, 10 Nottingham Place
London, W. 1, England
The professional association of physical educators in Britain and publishers and distributors of a wide variety of books.

Physical Education Aids
P. O. Box 5117
San Mateo, California 94402
Textbooks, wall charts, teaching units for gymnastic and tumbling activities.

**PHYSICAL EDUCATION SUPPLY
  ASSOCIATES, INC.**
P. O. Box 292
Trumbull, Connecticut 06611
For the new movement, hoops, balanced jump ropes, magic stretch ropes, wevau balls, wevau ball primer, "Who Can," corrective gymnastics.

Playground Corporation of America
29-16 40th Avenue
Long Island City, New York 11101
Planned physical play environments for children 2-12.

Popular Science Audio Visuals, Inc.
355 Lexington Avenue
New York, New York 10017
Producer-distributor of audiovisual materials.

PORT-A-PIT, INC.
P. O. Box C
Temple City, California 91780
Safety skill development equipment for gymnastics and physical education.

Premier Products
River Vale, New Jersey 07675
Gymnasium, physical education equipment and mats.

J. A. PRESTON CORPORATION
71 Fifth Avenue
New York, New York 10003
Adapted physical education and related research equipment.

Program Aids Inc.
161 MacQuesten Parkway
Mount Vernon, New York 10550
Manufacturers of innovative physical education equipment.

Protection Equipment Sales Division
  Vogt Mfg. Corp.
100 Fernwood Avenue
Rochester, New York 14621
Makers of Polvonite wrestling mats and Voplex gym mats.

Q R

Quinton Instruments
3051 44th Avenue West
Seattle, Washington 98199
Treadmills, bicycle ergometers, exercise cardio-tachometers, respiratory gas analysis, telemetry equipment.

Randolph Mfg. Co., Inc.
32 South Main Street
Randolph, Massachusetts 02368
Athletic footwear and water sports equipment.

Rawlings Sporting Goods Company
2300 Delmar Boulevard
St. Louis, Missouri 63166
Complete line of athletic goods.

Reedco, Inc.
5 Easterly Avenue
Auburn, New York 13021
Equipment for the testing and teaching of body mechanics and posture.

Rhythms Productions Records
Box 34485
Los Angeles, California 90034
Producers of educational records, audiovisual materials, and folk dance costume picture prints.

The Ronald Press Company
79 Madison Avenue

New York, New York 10016
Books on physical education, sports, gymnastics, and conditioning.

S

Sani-Mist Inc.
3018 Market Street
Philadelphia, Pennsylvania 19104
Foot spray dispenser for the prevention of athletes foot.

Saunders Archery Company
P. O. Box 476
Columbus, Nebraska 68601
Saunders accessories complete your profit picture.

W. B. SAUNDERS COMPANY
West Washington Square
Philadelphia, Pennsylvania 19105
Textbooks, handbooks, and reference books in health and physical education.

School Aid Co., Inc.
911 Colfax Drive
Danville, Illinois 61832
The leader in athletic books.

SCHOOL HEALTH SUPPLY CO.
300 Lombard Road
Addison, Illinois 60101
First aid and athletic training room supplies and equipment.

Scott & Company-GM Baseball
P. O. Box 583
Reseda, California 91335
The GM baseball—finest baseball made.

Scott Paper Company
1133 Avenue of the Americas
New York, New York 10036
World of a Girl—Free educational materials for teaching menstrual hygiene—color, sound film, color illustrated booklets, available in quantity, teaching guides.

SEAMLESS
253 Hallock Avenue
New Haven, Connecticut 06503
Manufacturer of athletic and leisure sports equipment and supplier of tapes and gauzes for trainers.

Sells Aerial Tennis Co.
Box 3042
Kansas City, Kansas 66103
A low-cost indoor, outdoor game, junior high school through adult ages.

SELVA
1607 Broadway
New York, New York 10019
Dance shoes and accessories.

SERON MFG. CO.
15 West Jefferson Street
Joliet, Illinois 60431
Glass-Gard eyeglass holder and other physical education protective products.

The Seven-Up Company
121 South Meramec Avenue
St. Louis, Missouri 63105
7UP, the Uncola and Like, just for girls.

Shield Mfg. Inc.
9 St. Paul Street
Buffalo, New York 14209
Manufacturer of protective mouth guards for all contact sports.

Signal Press
1730 Chicago Avenue
Evanston, Illinois 60201
Materials for teaching the effects of alcohol, narcotics, and tobacco.

Society For Visual Education, Inc.
1345 Diversey Parkway
Chicago, Illinois 60614
Filmstrips, slides, study prints, 8mm loops, and records.

Sorensen-Christian Industries, Inc.
P. O. Box 1
Angier, North Carolina 27501
Metal and electronic products for athletics and recreation.

A. G. Spalding & Bros., Inc.
270 New Jersey Drive
Ft. Washington, Pennsylvania 19034
Manufacturers of quality athletic and field equipment for all major sports.

Standard Brands Incorporated
625 Madison Avenue
New York, New York 10022
Planters Peanuts will offer information and booklets with reference to physical fitness programs for children under 11, and other educational material.

Stepping Tones Records
P. O. Box 64334
Los Angeles, California 90064
Technique for tap, ballet, jazz, training aids—for all grades.

STERLING RECREATION PRODUCTS
7 Oak Place
Montclair, New Jersey 07042
Manufacturers and distributors of full line equipment for all the carry over sports and individual development.

Strand Case Co., Div. of SNR Golf, Inc.
631 East Center Street

Milwaukee, Wisconsin 53212
Team luggage, flag football, athletic, and sports equipment.

Superior Wire & Iron Products, Inc.
16400 South Lathrop Avenue
Harvey, Illinois 60426
Ventilated athletic lockers and locker benches, portable basketball standards.

Syracuse University Film Marketing Division
1455 East Colvin Street
Film Rental Library
Syracuse, New York 13210
Offering seven gymnastics 16mm films for sale—both boys and girls—also super 8 loops.

T

TAMPAX INCORPORATED
161 East 42nd Street
New York, New York, 10017
Free educational materials on menstrual health including student booklets, teaching aids, anatomical charts, and consultant services.

Technology/Versatronics, Inc.
506 South High Street
Yellow Springs, Ohio 45387
Oxygen consumption computer.

Charles C Thomas, Publisher
301-327 East Lawrence Avenue
Springfield, Illinois 62703
Books in the field of health, physical education, and recreation.

R. E. Titus Gym Scooter Co.
1719 Hackney
Winfield, Kansas 67156
Gym scooters and scooter accessories.

Top Star Inc.
P. O. Box 728
Arlington, Texas 76010
Liquid nutrition, ballmate and tiremate sealants, Padphil 4:19 scientific passer development machine.

T. F. Twardzik & Co., Inc.
600 East Center Street
Shenandoah, Pennsylvania 17976
Leases dispensers for table tennis balls and sale of table tennis equipment.

U

United States Air Force
Randolph Air Force Base, Texas 78148
Materials about education and training opportunities in the U.S. Air Force.

**UNITED STATES ARMY
RECRUITING COMMAND**
Hampton, Virginia 23369
Career and educational opportunities literature.

United States Marine Corps
Commandant of the Marine Corps
(Code DPO)
Headquarters
Washington, D. C. 20380
Career Information.

United States Navy
Bureau of Naval Personnel (Pers-B6e)
Washington, D. C. 20370
Education and occupations available in the U.S. Navy.

Universal Athletic Sales Co.
4707 East Hedges Avenue
Fresno, California 93703
The Universal "Gladiator" gym machine with over 14 exercise positions.

UNIVERSAL BLEACHER CO.
Box 638
Champaign, Illinois 61820
Roll-a-way bleachers, basketball backstops, outdoor bleachers, port-a-pool water safety classrooms.

V W Y

Videonetics, Div. Newell Industries
1216 Kifer Road
Sunnyvale, California 94086
Instant replay stop-action recorder.

W. J. VOIT RUBBER CORP.
Subsidiary of American Machine &
Foundry Company of New York
3801 South Harbor Boulevard
Santa Ana, California 92704
Athletic balls and equipment, exercisers, golf clubs and balls, and scuba diving equipment.

**WADSWORTH PUBLISHING COMPANY,
INC.**
Belmont, California 94002
Provides textbooks for professionals in recreation and physical education and publishes a series of sports skills instruction books.

Wheelan and Wheelan, Inc.
129 North 12th Street
Philadelphia, Pennsylvania 19107
Manufacturer of girls and women's physical education clothing.

WILSON SPORTING GOODS CO.
2233 West Street
River Grove, Illinois 60171
A complete line of athletic and recreation equipment.

White Stag-Speedo
5203 S.E. Johnson Creek Boulevard
Portland, Oregon 97206
Nylon tank suits for competition and physical education classes, coaches, and lifeguards.

Wilton Mfg. Co., Inc.
Ware, Massachusetts 01082
Athletic clothing and campus wear.

Wittek Golf Range Supply Co., Inc.
3650 Avondale
Chicago, Illinois 60618
World's largest manufacturer and distributor of driving range and miniature equipment.

Wolff-Fording & Co., Inc.

88 Kingston Street
Boston, Massachusetts 02111
Manufacturers of leotards, dance costumes, gym slippers, shoes, and theatrical supplies.

Wolverine Sports Supply
745 State Circle
Ann Arbor, Michigan 48104
Complete line of athletic and playground equipment.

YWCA of the USA
600 Lexington Avenue
New York, New York 10022
Career information for work with private social agency.

B CARE, REPAIR, AND STORAGE OF UNIFORMS AND EQUIPMENT

Following are instructions for the care of uniforms (see also accompanying chart for laundering and cleaning procedures):

1. Clean garments immediately after each wearing. If this is not possible, hang on rust-proof hangers in a well-ventilated room.
2. If garment is saturated with mud and cleaning is to be done immediately, remove excess mud by rinsing under shower.
3. Avoid excessive heat in washing and drying since this will cause shrinkage. Lukewarm water is recommended.
4. Wash white garments separately—do not mix with colored ones.
5. Use a bleaching agent only on white cotton garments.
6. To prevent stains from becoming set, wet-clean or dry-clean garments before they dry.
7. Protect clothing from moisture and dry as soon as possible to prevent mildew.
8. Usually dry-clean brushed or woven wool fabrics.
9. Restore knit goods that may have shrunk to original size by dampening and drying in a stretched condition.
10. When wet garments must be packed, separate jerseys from pants and fold neatly in trunks. Place a layer of plain paper, or a towel, between each jersey. Use same method for pants, but remove knee pads and thigh guards from pants before packing. As soon as possible, unpack and clean or hang to dry.
11. Recommended procedures regarding cleaning of practice equipment is every second or third day under dry conditions. If practice is held during muddy, wet weather, a daily washing should be performed.
12. Send equipment at completion of the season to a reliable cleaner or reconditioner with complete and exact cleaning instructions.
13. Check accessories, such as metal snaps, zippers, slides, and buttons, for rust, breakage, or loss before being stored.
14. Fold repaired garments and pack in storage bins located in cool, dry, well-ventilated area.
15. Store colored textiles in separate containers with napthalene flakes or moth balls.

Following is a chart that indicates the recommended procedures for the care, repair, and storage of various pieces of physical education equipment.

BASEBALL

UNIFORMS		Code
HOF	Wool and Nylon	2
A	Wool and Nylon	2
B	Nylon, Acrilan, Cotton and Orlon	2
F	Cotton, Orlon, Nylon and Rayon	2
H	Nylon, Acrilan, Rayon and Cotton	2
X	Rayon, Cotton, Orlon and Dacron	2
P	Cotton	2
K	Cotton and Nylon Knit	1

JACKETS	Code
Melton Cloth	5

UNDERSHIRTS	Code
Wool	2
Cotton	2
Wool and Cotton	2

T-SHIRTS	Code
Cotton	2

SOFTBALL

SHIRTS	Code
Cotton and Rayon	2
Cotton	2
Fineline Twill	1

PANTS	Code
Cotton	2

ATHLETIC STOCKINGS

	Code
Worsted	1
Worsted and Cotton	1
Cotton and Rayon	1
Cotton	1
Durene and Coylon	1
Durene and Rayon	1
Durene	1
Stretch Nylon	1

WRESTLING

CLOTHING		Code
#24	Stretch Nylon-Spandex	1
#25	Durene Cotton-Nylon-Spandex	1
#28	Stretch Nylon and Cotton Durene	1
#29	Cotton and Nylon	1
#35	Durene Cotton and Nylon	1
#44	Durene Cotton and Nylon	1

TRACK

SHIRTS	Code
Nylon and Durene Cotton	1
Durene Cotton and Rayon	1

PANTS	Code
Cotton	1
Satin	2
Nyl-Weave	2

MEN'S WARM-UP SHIRTS AND PANTS	Code

GIRLS' SHIRTS AND PANTS	Code
Orlon Acrylic	1
Nylon	1
Stretch Nylon and Durene Cotton	1
Durene Cotton and Nylon	1
Durene Cotton and Rayon	1
Cotton and Rayon	1
Nylon and Durene Cotton	1

BASKETBALL

SHIRTS		Code
#19	Stretch Nylon and Durene Cotton	1
#17	Nylon and Durene Cotton	1
#18	Durene Cotton and Nylon	1
#16	Durene Cotton and Rayon	1
#14	Durene Cotton and Rayon	1
#10	Cotton and Rayon	1

PANTS	Code
Nylon Contact Cloth	1
Nyl-Twill	2
Royal Label Twill	1
Royal Label Satin	2
Nyl-Weave	2
Hi-Glo Acetate Satin	2

WARM-UP JACKETS, SHIRTS AND PANTS	Code
Brushed Wool	5
Nylon Fleece	1
Orlon Fleece	1
Nyl-Twill	2
Royal Label Twill	1
Nyl-Weave	2
Hi-Glo Acetate Satin	2
Durene Cotton and Nylon	2
Durene Cotton and Rayon	1
Stretch Nylon and Durene Cotton	1

ICE HOCKEY

JERSEYS	Code
Durene Cotton and Nylon	1
Cotton and Nylon	1
Cotton and Rayon	1

PANT	Code
Royal Label Twill, Rayon and Cotton	1
Nylon	1
Cotton	1

FOOTBALL

JERSEYS		Code
#12	Nylon and Stretch Nylon	1
#28	Stretch Nylon and Durene	1
#30	Nylon and Durene	1
#33	Stretch Polypropylene and Nylon	1
#35	Durene and Nylon	1
#38	Cotton and Nylon	1
#45	Cotton and Rayon	1
#52	Durene	1

PANTS (half and half)		Code
(Front)	(Back)	
Nylon Contact Cloth	Stretch Nylon-Spandex	2
Nyl-Knit	Stretch-Nylon-Spandex	2
Nyl-Twill	Stretch Nylon-Spandex	2
Nylon Contact Cloth	Durene Cotton-Nylon-Spandex	2
Nyl-Twill	Durene Cotton-Nylon-Spandex	2
Scrimmage Cloth	Cotton and Nylon	1

KNIT SHELLS	Code
Stretch Nylon	1
Nyl-Knit	3
Stretch Nylon-Durene	1
Durene and Nylon	1
Cotton and Nylon	1

COACHES PANT	Code
C. A. Cloth	1

PARKAS AND SIDELINE CAPES	Code
Vinyl Twill	4

SOCCER

JERSEYS	Code
Durene Cotton and Nylon	1
Cotton and Nylon	1

PANT	Code
Cotton	2

LAUNDERING SPANDEX MATERIALS
Rawlings SPANDEX should be laundered in warm (100° Fahrenheit), not hot water, using a mild no-bleach detergent. Drip dry at room temperature or use a no-heat dryer. Under no circumstances should SPANDEX materials be dry cleaned.

LAUNDERING AND CLEANING PROCEDURE

1 Machine wash for 15 minutes with water at 100° Fahrenheit. Use a mild no-bleach detergent. Drip dry at room temperature or use a no-heat dryer.

2 Machine wash for 15 minutes with water at 100° Fahrenheit. Use a mild no-bleach detergent. Drip dry at room temperature.

3 Machine wash for 15 minutes with water at 120° Fahrenheit. Use a mild no-bleach detergent. Drip dry at room temperature.

4 Hand wash using a soft-bristled brush and mild detergent with water at tap-water temperature. Brush should be applied in the direction of the weave of the material. **Do not use cleaning solutions.**

5 Dry clean and steam press.

Chart of laundering and cleaning procedures. (From Rawlings Athletic Equipment Digest, ed. 4, St. Louis, 1966, Rawlings Sporting Goods Co.)

Equipment	Care	Repair	Storage
Archery			
Arrows	1. Carry arrows by pile end so that feathers will not be damaged. 2. Use steel wool for cleaning wooden arrows and then apply a coat of wax. 3. Rub metal piles with oil to prevent rusting. 4. On a wet day collect arrows on ground first and wipe with a tassel. 5. Smooth out arrow feathers that are out of shape. 6. Remove arrows by grasping them in close to target face and pulling straight out while your other hand holds target face against bale.	1. Repair minor splits and cracks by putting cement on both broken edges and then bind tightly with strong thread. 2. Arrows that are broken at pile end can be cut off and new piles applied. 3. Straighten arrow by carefully taking shaft and bending it in opposite direction. 4. Remove a broken pyroxylin nock by using a lighted match; then sand wood to a smooth finish and apply a new nock with a very thin coat of quick-drying cellulose cement. Nock should be perpendicular to cock feather. 5. Cement a loose feather in place and tie with thread until cement is dry. Correctly align feather when tied. 6. Return arrows to manufacturer for refletching, recresting, repolishing, and straightening.	1. Store arrows in racks rather than in boxes. 2. Protect feathers from from moths with a good moth preventive.
Bows Wood	1. Rub Simoniz or Johnson's Wax on bows at end of season to protect finish. 2. Oil leather grip periodically.	1. Send bows to manufacturer for any major repairs.	1. Unbrace bows, hang vertically on wooden pegs, and store in a cool, humid place.
Metal	1. Oil steel occasionally to prevent rusting.		

Special thanks are given to Miss Sharon Irwin of Frostburg State College, Frostburg, Maryland, for her help in the gathering and organizing of this material.

Equipment	Care	Repair	Storage
Archery—cont'd			
Bowstrings	1. Beeswax bowstrings at least once weekly.	1. Replaced badly frayed strings. If only one or two strands are broken, cut them off and wax string. 2. Mark nocking points and replace worn servings. Use carpet thread or dental floss for this.	
Fingertabs and armguards	1. Clean with saddle soap. 2. Oil leather occasionally to keep it from drying out and cracking.	1. Repair broken stitches immediately.	1. Store in cool, humid place.
Targets	1. Cover targets with a waterproof covering if left outside overnight. 2. Reinforce target faces with cardboard or heavy paper backings. 3. Varnish target stand occasionally to protect it from moisture.	No specific recommendations.	1. Keep targets flat and stack or lay singly on a platform several inches from floor. 2. Spread powdered sulfur among the butts to keep animals away.
Athletic shoes			
Canvas shoes	1. Wash with lukewarm water and mild detergent. 2. Keep soles of basketball shoes free of dust and dirt so that maximum gripping action can be maintained.	No specific recommendations.	No specific recommendations.
Leather shoes	1. Allow damp or wet shoes to dry at room temperature after being cleaned of dirt and mud. 2. Place a dry rag in toe of each shoe to aid drying process. 3. Apply leather conditioner, neat's-foot or viscol oil, to shoe—uppers and leather outsoles. 4. Polish shoes regularly.	1. Repair rips and tears immediately to prevent further deterioration. 2. Replace worn-out cleats and spikes to prevent injury and to provide longer wear.	1. Insert shoe trees in shoes to maintain proper form.

Continued.

Equipment	Care	Repair	Storage
Badminton			
Net	1. Check nets regularly for holes, tears, and other damage.	1. Repair immediately with string or very strong thread.	1. Fold nets before they are stored. 2. Lay them flat on a smooth surface protected from dirt and rodents.
Rackets			
Metal	1. Occasionally wipe and strip with oil and then wipe off frame to prevent rusting. Copper-plated strings will not rust.	1. Rackets that break may be welded, but are not too satisfactory.	
Wood	1. Apply a thin coat of gut preserver to strings to improve durability. 2. Apply a good brand of wax to wood frame occasionally and polish.	1. Have frame restrung with gut at sports dealers. 2. Broken frame may sometimes be repaired with fiber glass, depending on extent of breakage.	1. Keep in press and in a waterproof case.
Shuttlecock	1. Straighten out feathers of shuttle frequently. 2. Kept shuttles humidified, so that they do not become brittle.	1. Replace a broken feather with a good one by inserting it through stitching and cementing it carefully with a minimum amount of cement so as not to destroy balance.	1. Store shuttlecock in an upright position with base down so that there is no pressure on feathers.
Baseball			
Balls	1. Do not use leather-covered balls on damp ground for longest use. 2. Keep rubber-covered balls inside when not in use since heat and direct sunlight for long periods of time will reduce their durability. 3. Wipe rubber-covered balls with a damp rag.	1. Resew broken threads.	1. Store in dry area and out of direct light. 2. Do not store balls under other objects.

Equipment	Care	Repair	Storage
Baseball—cont'd			
Bases	1. Remove canvas-covered bases after every game to prevent water damage. 2. Brush and reshape bases. 3. Wipe rubber bases with a damp rag.	1. Repair rips in bases as soon as possible.	1. Store bases flat.
Bats	1. Treat bats with linseed oil prior to storage.	1. Repair grips or replace with leather or cork.	1. Store in dry room at normal temperature.
Gloves	1. Dry gloves if they are wet. 2. When leather becomes rough or cracks, treat it with neat's-foot oil. 3. Do not wear a glove made for left hand on right hand since this will destroy pocket and cause padding to move. 4. Occasionally clean gloves with saddle soap, using a moist cloth to rub soap over glove. Wipe off lather with clean cloth.	1. Repair a rip or tear occurring in seam. Cover large rips with a leather patch.	1. Store gloves in a cool, dry place. 2. Do not store under other equipment.
Basketball			
Leather	1. Inflate only to specified pressure; never over-inflate. 2. Moisten inflating needle and insert with rotary motion up to shoulder of needle. 3. Use saddle soap to clean balls.	1. Send a damaged ball to manufacturer.	1. Store balls partially inflated, but with enough air to hold their shape. 2. Store in a cool, dry place.
Rubber	1. Inflate same as leather balls. 2. Wipe ball with damp rag to remove dirt. 3. If ball has mud, oil, or grease on it, use soap and warm water.	1. Return to manufacturer a basketball that is badly punctured. 2. A latex repair might prove sufficient for a small puncture.	1. Reduce pressure to prevent constant strain. 2. Store in a cool, dry place. 3. Do not expose to direct sunlight for a period of time.

Continued.

Equipment	Care	Repair	Storage
Bowling			
Ball	1. Clean ball often with soap and water 2. Use a special bowling ball liquid cleaner if ball has accumulated wax from alley.	No specific recommendations.	1. Keep ball in a bowling bag.
Pins	1. Remove pins that are cracked or broken. 2. Clean both plastic and wood pins as often as necessary.	No specific recommendations.	1. Store in a dry place.
Shoes	1. Wear bowling shoes only while bowling. 2. Give same care as street shoes.	No specific recommendations.	No specific recommendations.
Fencing			
Jackets	1. Wash and fluff jackets regularly.	1. Repair tears or rips immediately.	1. Store in area with maximum ventilation.
Masks	1. Remove lipstick before putting a mask on. 2. Check mask for gaps or rust spots. 3. Wash padding and bibs frequently. 4. Masks that are tinned or chrome plated do not require any treatment other than wiping with soap and water. 5. Clean leather trimming with saddle soap. 6. Wipe leatherette trimming off with warm water and soap. 7. Clean canvas trimming with soap and water.	1. Repaint masks if paint is wearing off.	1. Store masks so that no outside pressure will be exerted on them. 2. Allow for maximum ventilation.
Weapons	1. Secure pommels to prevent guards and blades from rubbing. 2. Put a slight set on blade before using it so that it will always bend in same direction.	1. Remove small nicks in blade with fine emery cloth. 2. Replace broken blades by unscrewing pommel and slipping old blade out.	1. Store foils in a hanging position so that blades are not damaged.

Equipment	Care	Repair	Storage

Fencing—cont'd

Weapons—
cont'd

3. To bend or straighten blade, rub it between shoe sole and floor. Friction heats blade and makes it more pliable. Hands should not be used.
4. Wipe off blade periodically during very humid weather or in damp climates.
5. Oil blade occasionally to prevent it from rusting.

3. A new blade might require filing before fitting properly.

Field hockey

Balls

1. Reenamel leather-covered balls when protective covering is worn.
2. If match is played on a wet surface use a number of balls.

1. Before paint is applied, scrape off all old paint. Use denatured alcohol or a paint thinner and medium-coarse steel wool for this purpose.
2. A board in which nails have been driven will serve as a ball rack for wet balls.
3. If a leather-covered ball has ripped at seams, it might be repaired at a shoe repair shop.

1. Store away from dampness.

Goalie pads and shin guards

1. Allow wet guards to dry at normal room temperature before putting them away.
2. Remove dirt and mud with a stiff brush.
3. Oil leather straps occasionally to prevent drying out and cracking.

1. Leather straps, elastic understraps, and buckles that have come loose can be repaired at a shoe repair shop.

1. Attach matching guards by buckling and store in pairs on a flat surface.
2. Store goalie pads in a dry, well-ventilated area.

Stick

1. Keep head of stick clean. Scrape off mud or dirt with a knife or steel wool; then wipe blade with a slightly dampened cloth.

1. Sandpaper and wax a stick that has frayed at edges.
2. If stick splinters, shave down, working toward open end of splinter.

1. Store sticks away from dampness and heat.
2. Store sticks flat without pressure of other sticks on them.

Continued.

Equipment	Care	Repair	Storage
Field hockey—cont'd			
Stick—cont'd	2. Wipe off blades of new sticks with linseed oil to preserve wood. 3. Repeat this procedure occasionally during season. 4. At end of season remove excess dirt with steel wool, rub blade with beeswax, and paint it with shellac or varnish. 5. Avoid sitting or leaning on stick when testing its resiliency. 6. Wipe stick immediately after use in rain or on wet ground.	Then sand and protect with a piece of adhesive tape. Use only one layer of tape since heavy taping will cause an unbalance of stick. 3. Replace if rubber grip rots and dries.	
Football			
Ball	Same as for basketball	Same as for basketball.	Same as for basketball.
Football pads	1. Allow thorough drying after each use. 2. Wash pads that have fiber parts sewn on by hand with a soft bristle brush with soap and water, then rinse entire pad in clear water. Dry fabric at normal temperature in well-ventilated room. 3. Brush-coat fiber parts with clear lacquer. 4. Clean Armorlite parts with soap or detergent and water, rinsing thoroughly. 5. Remove pads from pockets before washing girdle pads. 6. Clean pads with no exposed fiber parts by wrapping any exposed metal with cloth or tape (to prevent damage to washer); then wash in automatic washer with detergent.	1. Send to a qualified renovator for major repairs.	1. Store in a dry, well-ventilated room. 2. Do not stack pads on each other since this will distort their form. 3. Do not hang by elastic straps since this will weaken strap. 4. Store hip pads by hanging from buckle.

Equipment	Care	Repair	Storage
Football—cont'd			
Football pads— cont'd	Dry under room temperature in well-ventilated room.		
Helmet	1. Several times during season clean padding in each helmet with saddle soap. 2. Work up a heavy lather on brush or cloth; then scrub leather surface to loosen dirt. Wipe off surface with clean cloth; then apply light coating of castor oil to leather lining to keep it from becoming harsh. 3. Make sure chin strap is always in position shaped to chin contour when not in use.	1. When refinishing a helmet, use steel wool or fine sand paper to thoroughly remove surface dirt or loose paint. 2. Replace worn straps and snaps. 3. Use a thin coat of clear lacquer on outside of helmet to restore glossy appearance.	1. Store helmets in a cool, dry area. 2. Store on helmet hangers, on helmet racks, or in their original boxes.
Golf			
Bag	1. Clean with detergent and water.	1. Replace broken straps or mend them with leather and rivets.	1. Store at normal room temperature.
Balls	1. Wash balls frequently. 2. Paint practice balls.		
Clubs Irons	1. If grips of any clubs have become loose, or if a change in thickness is desired, remove string at top and bottom of leather and then unwind. 2. Little care is required to maintain irons other than drying and oiling occasionally to prevent rusting. 3. File club nicks smooth when they appear on surface. 4. Clean iron heads occasionally with fine grade steel wool and detergent.	1. Replace damaged or worn grips at pro shop. 2. If head of wooden-shafted iron becomes loose, taken it to a club maker.	1. Store at normal room temperature.

Continued.

Equipment	Care	Repair	Storage
Golf—cont'd Irons—cont'd	5. When playing, clean grooves in head with tee after each use. 6. Clean shaft with a moistened cloth and detergent. Dry immediately.		
Woods	1. If club has been used in rain or wet grass, wipe with an oily rag. 2. Occasionally wash with mild soap and water and clean grooves on faces with a soft brush or a wooden tee. 3. Wax (paste wax) wooden clubheads to prevent warping and cracking. 4. Apply a light oil to steel shaft. 5. Head covers protect head from scarring. 6. Check sole plates frequently to see that they remain tight. 7. Use a file to smooth out nicks to prevent damage to balls 8. Rub leather grips lightly with neat's-foot oil several times a year.		1. When storing, put a few drops of linseed oil on a cloth and wipe club thoroughly. 2. Use another cloth with a mixture of a few drops of oil and shellac and give wooden heads of clubs a vigorous rubbing. This will coat surface and help repel moisture. 3. Store at normal room temperature.
Gymnastic equipment Balance beam	1. Sand wood balance beam. 2. When original lacquer sealer is worn, apply another coat 3. Be careful not to build up a high gloss heavy finish since this will make it slippery.	No specific recommendations.	No specific recommendations.

Equipment	Care	Repair	Storage
Gymnastic equipment—cont'd			
Horizontal bar	1. Sand steel horizontal cross bars with emery cloth to keep them bright and to keep rust and chalk from accumulating. 2. Check mechanical connections regularly.	1. Refinish metal bases of all these pieces with spray enamels.	No specific recommendations.
Horse	1. Pommels need no finish and excess chalk can be sanded off. 2. A periodic application of saddle soap to clean horse body is recommended to keep leather soft.	1. When leather becomes badly worn, have it replaced by manufacturer.	No specific recommendations.
Mats	1. Wash vinyl-covered mats with ordinary soap and water. 2. Clean canvas mats every week with a vacuum cleaner. 3. Repair small rips and tears immediately. 4. Send badly worn mats back to factory where they will be recovered using old filler.	1. In repairing rubber mats, roughen rubber surface and cut a patch with the sides rounded. Roughen one surface of patch with sandpaper and apply coat of cement with a brush to both mat surface and rough side of patch. Allow about 5 to 10 minutes for cement to dry and then apply second and third coats, allowing each time to dry thoroughly. Roll cemented side of patch onto prepared cemented place on mat. Also cement a patch on opposite side of mat cover, using same technique. Allow 40 hours for the cement to cure fully at room temperature.	1. Hang mats on mat hangers when not in use or stacked upon each other. 2. Keep them in a rolled position.
Parallel bars	1. Leave rails unfinished and smooth. Use 6/0 or 8/0 sandpaper to maintain texture and remove excess chalk.	No specific recommendations.	No specific recommendations.

Continued.

Equipment	Care	Repair	Storage
Gymnastic equipment—cont'd Parallel bars —cont'd	2. Do not use waxes and preservatives on wood. 3. Clean paint finish on most apparatus with a mild solvent. 4. To keep adjustment staffs moving freely, use a spray can of silicone product sparingly.		
Rings	1. Wipe leather covering with a moist cloth and allow time to dry. 2. Check all mechanical connections regularly.	No specific recommendations.	No specific recommendations.
Ropes	1. Check constantly for frayed areas. Also, check connections for support. 2. Replace worn ropes.	No specific recommendations.	No specific recommendations.
Trampoline	1. Wash trampoline beds with cold water and mild soap and put back on trampoline under spring tension while they are still wet. Never use warm water or harsh detergent on nylon trampoline beds.	No specific recommendations.	1. Fold and store out of way.
Lacrosse Balls	1. Rinse balls in a warm, soapy solution and dry.	No specific recommendations.	1. Store in an area with low humidity and normal room temperature.
Gloves	1. When gloves become wet, allow drying to take place at normal room temperature. Mineral or vegetable oil will remove harshness caused by drying. 2. Clean with saddle soap only. Apply saddle soap with a moist cloth by rubbing cloth over soap to work up a cream on cloth. Rub soiled leather with cloth until a lather	1. Repair broken stitches.	1. Store at normal room temperature.

Equipment	Care	Repair	Storage
Lacrosse—cont'd Gloves—cont'd	has been worked up and dirt is loosened. Wipe off dirty lather with a clean cloth and rub leather briskly with a clean cloth.		
Goalie pads	Refer to instructions for field hockey goalie pads.	Refer to instructions for field hockey goalie pads.	Refer to instructions for field hockey goalie pads.
Helmet	Refer to instructions for football helmet.	Refer to instructions for football helmet.	Refer to instructions for football helmet.
Nets	1. Moisture-proof leather portions of net with coat of Lexol. 2. Tarred nets are best for damp areas.	No specific recommendations.	No specific recommendations.
Stick	1. Loosen lead string after play. 2. Wipe crosse with a dry rag after playing. 3. Oil wood with linseed oil after rain and about once a month. This should be just enough to moisten the rub. 4. Use petroleum jelly or leather conditioner on thongs and gut. 5. Occasionally apply varnish or furniture wax to protect wood from moisture. 6. Place tongue depressors vertically in gut wall when it becomes wet after play in inclement weather.	1. Sandpaper any wood surface that has splintered. Tape small breaks with a very light tape, used sparingly so as not to disturb balance of crosse. 2. Mend broken gut by making a split in broken end as well as in one end of piece being used for repair; then thread one end through other. 3. Tape angles that have split. This may not prove satisfactory if crosse is put to hard use.	1. When crosses are stored at end of season, insert small sticks in guard, parallel to short strings. A thin coat of shellac applied to guard will stiffen it and hold it in place. After shellac dries, remove sticks. 2. In order to avoid pressure on bridge or guard, hang crosses on a peg or nail, with weight of crosse resting against peg. Crosses can also be placed on a shelf in horizontal position, wood down, with space between crosses. 3. Store crosses in a place protected from rodents at normal room temperature.
Skiing Boots	1. Remove excess snow or surface moisture at end of the day with a soft cloth. If moisture has seeped inside of boot, a temporary stuffing of	No specific recommendations.	1. Insert ski boot trees to maintain proper form.

Continued.

Equipment	Care	Repair	Storage
Skiing—cont'd Boots—cont'd	newspaper will help to absorb it quickly. 2. Never dry boots next to direct heat. 3. When boots are dry, check their surface for cuts and scrapes, massage immediately, preferably with the fingers with wax. Polish all over as often as necessary to maintain protective finish of leather.		
Poles	1. Check cane poles for splits and loose laminations.	1. Use only water-resistant glue in regluing.	1. Cover metal with a thin coat of oil before storing. 2. Oil all leather parts carefully.
Skis	1. Thoroughly scrape skis with sandpaper, a knife, or steel wool and wax base with a liquid wax containing pine tar. Following this they should be surfaced waxed. 2. Use "wax wax" for powdered snow and "tar wax" for wet snow. Use paraffin as a final application. 3. Wax can be applied in several ways—by hand, with an iron, with a cork, or in liquid form with a brush. Brush method is most durable. Apply the wax in lengthwise strokes from tail to tip. 4. Two or three coats of ski lacquer are recommended for skis that do not have plastic bottoms. 5. Wax tops of skis with a good floor wax to prevent snow collecting on them.	No specific recommendations.	1. Place skis back to back and fastened together with ski ties near tips and near tails. A 2 × 4 inch block of wood sandwiched between them at level of binding will preserve their camber and their shape.

Equipment	Care	Repair	Storage
Skiing—cont'd Skis—cont'd	6. Never bring skis directly from a warm place into contact with snow since running surface will freeze.		
Soccer Ball	Refer to basketball.	Refer to basketball.	Refer to basketball.
Net	Refer to lacrosse.	Refer to lacrosse.	Refer to lacrosse.
Softball	Refer to baseball.	Refer to baseball.	Refer to baseball.
Squash Ball	No specific recommendations.	No specific recommendations.	1. Store balls in a cool, dry place.
Racket	Refer to instructions for badminton rackets. 1. After play wash squash racket in a mild soap and water solution to remove dirt and perspiration.	Refer to instructions for badminton rackets.	Refer to instructions for badminton rackets.
Tennis Ball	1. Brush off dirt and dust before putting away. 2. Allow sufficient time for drying if balls are wet before putting away. 3. Replace balls that become damp during play.	No specific recommendations.	1. Store balls in can with a cap on it. 2. Store at normal room temperature.
Net	1. Take twine nets indoors when weather is damp or wet. 2. Slacken rope cables at end of day. 3. During dry seasons and at end of a season, wash nets with a hose to remove dust and dirt. 4. Dip cord nets into commercial creosote once during season and before storing. 5. Wipe steel cable occasionally with an oily rag, and remove rust with emery cloth dipped in kerosene.	1. Repair holes or tears using a fisherman's knot.	1. Be sure that nets are thoroughly dry before storing them at end of season. 2. Store nets in a cool, dry place away from rodents.

Continued.

Equipment	Care	Repair	Storage
Tennis—cont'd			
Net—cont'd			
	6. Occasionally wipe metal nets with an oily rag.		
Racket			
Metal	Same as for badminton.	No specific recommendations.	No specific recommendations.
Wood	Same as for badminton.	Same as for badminton.	Same as for badminton.
Track and field			
Discus	1. Clean and polish metal rim of discus. 2. Varnish wood portion to prevent water absorption.	No specific recommendations.	No specific recommendations.
Javelin	1. Check binding and steel points for looseness. A loose wrapping will interfere with throwing, and a loose point may cause the javelin to snap.		1. Store javelins in a dry place and hang them from a nail or hook.
Shot	1. Clean shot with kerosene and emery cloth.		1. Oil and store in a dry place.
Vault pole	1. Replace worn or torn tape. Do not add more tape than is needed for a satisfactory grip since tape adds weight. 2. Catch poles after jump to avoid splintering (bamboo) or denting (aluminum).		1. Store poles in a rack in a horizontal position.
Volleyball			
Ball	Same as for basketball.	Same as for basketball.	Same as for basketball.
Net	Same as for badminton.	Same as for badminton.	Same as for badminton.

C SCHOOL LAWS AND REGULATIONS ON THE TEACHING OF HEALTH, SAFETY, DRIVER, OUTDOOR, AND PHYSICAL EDUCATION

State	All subjects in this table							Health education (separate subject)			Health and physical education (combined subject)		
	Laws				Regulations			Authorization			Authorization		
	Total	Mandatory		Permissive (P and PI)	Total	Auth. state board	Auth. state dept.	Law	Reg.	Grade or level	Law	Reg.	Grade or level
		Specific law (M)	Course of study (MC)										
1	2	3	4	5	6	7	8	9	10	11	12	13	14
Total laws and regulations: States and D. C.	216	138	23	55	81	49	32	11	22	—	20	17	—
Outlying areas	1	1	0	0	7	3	4	1	3	—	0	1	—
Aggregate U. S.	217	139	23	55	88	52	36	12	25	—	20	18	—
Alabama	2	2	0	0	2	2	0	—	(SB[1])	1-9	—	—	—
Alaska	2	2	0	0	1	1	0	([2])	—	—	—	—	—
Arizona	2	1	0	1	1	0	1	—	—	—	—	(SD[3])	E
Arkansas	4	4	0	0	1	1	0	—	—	—	(M[3])	—	E-S
California	10	7	1	2	1	1	0	(MC[4])	—	E	—	—	—
Colorado	2	1	0	1	0	0	0	—	—	—	—	—	—
Connecticut	5	4	1	0	0	0	0	—	—	—	(MC[5])	—	E-S
Delaware	4	2	1	1	2	0	2	—	SB	E-S	—	—	—

*From State school laws and regulations for health, safety, driver, outdoor, and physical education, Washington D. C., 1964, De
†E, Elementary; M, mandatory, required by specific law; MC, required by law through specific mention among subjects to be inclu
secondary; SB, state board of education; SD, state department of education; 0, zero in colums 2 through 8; and —, zero in colu

Physical education (separate subject)			Safety education (separate subject)			Driver education			Outdoor education			Special health and/or safety topics			
Authorization			Authorization			Authorization			Authorization				Authorization		
Law	Reg.	Grade or level	Law	Reg.	Grade or level	Law	Reg.	Grade or level	Law	Reg.	Grade or level	Topic	Law	Reg.	Grade or level
15	16	17	18	19	20	21	22	23	24	25	26	27	28	29	30
17	28	—	8	5	—	33	7	—	6	0	—	—	121	2	
0	3	—	0	0	—	0	0	—	0	0	—		0	0	
17	31	—	8	5	—	33	7	—	6	0	—	Fire drills	121	2	
M	SB	E-S	—	(¹)	—	—	—	—	—	—	—	Fire drills	M	—	E-S
—	SB	S	—	—	—	—	—	—	—	—	—	Alcohol and narcotics	(M²)	—	E-S
												Fire drills	M	—	E-S
—	—	—	—	(³)	—	—	—	—	—	—	—	Alcohol and narcotics	M	—	E-S
												Use of firearms and safe hunting	P	—	E-S
—	SB	S	(³)	—	—	—	—	—	—	—	—	Alcohol and narcotics	M	—	3-8
												Fire drills	M	—	E-S
												Fire prevention	M	—	E
(M⁴)	—	E-S	(M⁴)	—	E-S	(M⁴)	—	S	(P⁴)	—	E-S	Alcohol and narcotics including manners and morals	M	—	E-S
	SB	S	—	—	—	—	—	—	—	—	—	Fire drills	M	—	E-S
												School safety patrol	P	—	E-S
												Fire prevention	M	—	E-S
—	—	—	—	—	—	P	—	S	—	—	—	First-aid instruction	M	—	S
												Physiology and hygiene, including alcohol and narcotics	M	—	E-S
—	—	—	—	—	—	M	—	S	—	—	—	Alcohol and narcotics	M	—	E-S
												Fire drills	M	—	E-S
												Highway safety	M	—	E-S
M	SB	E-S	—	—	—	PI	—	S	—	—	—	Physiology and hygiene, including alcohol, stimulants, and narcotics	MC	—	E-S
												Fire drills	M	—	E-S

partment of Health, Education, and Welfare.
ded in course of study; P, permissive law; PI, permissive by implication—law implies recognition of school's responsibility; S,
mns 9 through 29.

Continued.

State	All subjects in this table							Health education (separate subject)			Health and physical education (combined subject)		
		Laws				Regulations		Authorization			Authorization		
			Mandatory										
	Total	Specific law (M)	Course of study (MC)	Permissive (P and PI)	Total	Auth. state board	Auth. state dept.	Law	Reg.	Grade or level	Law	Reg.	Grade or level
_1_	_2_	_3_	_4_	_5_	_6_	_7_	_8_	_9_	_10_	_11_	_12_	_13_	_14_
Florida	3	1	1	1	3	3	0	—	SB	E-S	—	—	—
Georgia	3	3	0	0	1	1	0	—	SB	S	(M³)	—	E-S
Hawaii	1	0	0	1	3	0	3	—	(SD⁶)	E-S	—	—	—
Idaho	3	2	0	1	2	2	0	—	SB	S	—	—	—
Illinois	7	3	0	4	1	0	1	—	—	—	M	—	E-S
Indiana	7	6	0	1	3	3	0	—	SB	S	—	—	—
Iowa	3	3	0	0	0	0	0	—	—	—	M	—	E-S
Kansas	1	0	1	0	2	0	2	MC	—	E	—	SD	S
Kentucky	2	1	0	1	3	3	0	—	(SB³)	E	—	(SB³)	S
Louisiana	2	1	1	0	1	1	0	(MC⁹)	—	E	—	—	—

Physical education (separate subject)			Safety education (separate subject)			Driver education			Outdoor education						
Authorization			Authorization			Authorization			Authorization						
Law	Reg.	Grade or level	Law	Reg.	Grade or level	Law	Reg.	Grade or level	Law	Reg.	Grade or level	Topic	Law	Reg.	Grade or level
15	16	17	18	19	20	21	22	23	24	25	26	27	28	29	30
—	SB	E-S	—	SB	E-S	P	—	S	—	—	—	Alcohol and narcotics	MC	—	E-S
												Fire drills	M	—	E-S
—	—	—	(3)	—	—	—	—	—	—	—	—	Alcohol on human health and behavior, social and economic conditions	M	—	E-S
												Temperance day designated	M	—	E-S
—	SD	E-S	—	(6)	—	PI	—	S	—	—	—	Fire drills	—	SD	E-S
—	SB	S	—	—	—	P	—	S	—	—	—	Physiology and hygiene, including alcohol, stimulants, and narcotics	M	—	E-S
												Alcohol, narcotics, and tobacco	M	—	E-S
—	SD	E-S	P	—	E-S	(P7)	—	S	P	—	E-S	Physiology and hygiene, including alcohol and narcotics	M	—	E-S
												Highway safety	(M7)	—	E-S
												School safety patrol	P	—	E-S
M	—	E-S	M	—	8	(P8)	—	S	—	—	—	Alcoholic drinks, tobacco, sedatives, and narcotics	M	—	4-8
—	SB	S	—	(8)	—	—	SB	S	—	—	—	Fire drills	M	—	E-S
												Moral instruction	M	—	E-S
												Hygiene and sanitary science	M	—	5
—	—	—	—	—	—	—	—	—	—	—	—	Physiology and hygiene, including stimulants, narcotics, and poisonous substances	M	—	E-S
												Fire drills	M	—	E-S
—	—	—	—	—	—	—	—	—	—	—	—	Fire drills	—	SD	E
—	SB	E	—	(3)	—	—	—	—	—	—	—	Alcohol and narcotics	M	—	4-10
												Moral instruction	P	—	E-S
—	SB	E-S	—	—	—	—	—	—	—	—	—	Alcohol and narcotics	(M9)	—	E-S

Continued.

State	All subjects in this table							Health education (separate subject)			Health and physical education (combined subject)		
	Laws			Regulations				Authoriza-tion			Authoriza-tion		
	Total	Mandatory		Permis-sive (P and PI)	Total	Auth. state board	Auth. state dept.	Law	Reg.	Grade or level	Law	Reg.	Grade or level
		Specific law (M)	Course of study (MC)										
1	2	3	4	5	6	7	8	9	10	11	12	13	14
Maine	4	3	0	1	2	2	0	—	SB	E-S	(M[3])	—	E-S
Maryland	5	3	1	1	0	0	0	—	—	—	—	—	—
Massachusetts	4	1	1	2	0	0	0	—	—	—	(MC[11])	—	E-S
Michigan	4	3	0	1	0	0	0	—	—	—	M	—	E-S
Minnesota	7	4	0	3	2	0	2	—	SD	E-S	M	—	E-S
Mississippi	4	2	1	1	0	0	0	—	—	—	(M[12])	—	E-S
Missouri	2	2	0	0	1	1	0	—	—	—	—	—	—

Physical education (separate subject)			Safety education (separate subject)			Driver education			Outdoor education			Special health and/or safety topics			
Authorization			Authorization			Authorization			Authorization				Authorization		
Law	Reg.	Grade or level	Law	Reg.	Grade or level	Law	Reg.	Grade or level	Law	Reg.	Grade or level	Topic	Law	Reg.	Grade or level
15	16	17	18	19	20	21	22	23	24	25	26	27	28	29	30
—	SB	1-11	(3)	—	—	P	—	S	—	—	—	Physiology and hygiene, including alcohol, stimulants, and narcotics	M	—	E-S
												Temperance day designated	M	—	E-S
(M10)	—	E-S	—	—	—	P	—	S	—	—	—	Physiology and hygiene, including alcohol and narcotics	M	—	E-S
												Hygiene and sanitation	MC	—	E
												Fire drills	M	—	E-S
—	—	—	(11)	—	—	(P11)	—	S	—	—	—	Fire drills	M	—	E-S
												School safety patrols	P	—	E-S
—	—	—	—	—	—	P	—	S	—	—	—	Physiology and hygiene, including alcohol and narcotics	M	—	E-S
												Fire drills	M	—	E-S
—	SD	E-S	—	—	—	PI	—	S	P	—	E-S	Alcohol on human system and character and upon society	M	—	E-S
												Morals, physiology and hygiene, narcotics, and stimulants	M	—	E-S
												School safety patrol	P	—	E-S
												Fire drills	M	—	E-S
—	—	—	—	—	—	P	—	9-12	—	—	—	Physiology and hygiene, including alcohol and narcotics, home and community sanitation; highway safety	(MC12)	—	E-S
												Fire drills	M	—	E-S
M	SB	E-S	—	—	—	—	—	—	—	—	—	Physiology and hygiene, including tobacco, alcohol, narcotics, and stimulants	M	—	E-S

Continued.

State	All subjects in this table							Health education (separate subject)			Health and physical education (combined subject)		
	Laws				Regulations			Authorization			Authorization		
		Mandatory											
	Total	Specific law (M)	Course of study (MC)	Permissive (P and PI)	Total	Auth. state board	Auth. state dept.	Law	Reg.	Grade or level	Law	Reg.	Grade or level
1	2	3	4	5	6	7	8	9	10	11	12	13	14
Montana	5	4	1	0	1	1	0	—	—	—	(M[13])	SB	E-S
Nebraska	3	2	0	1	0	0	0	(M[9])	—	E-S	—	—	—
Nevada	6	5	0	1	1	2	0	M	SB	E	—	—	—
New Hampshire	5	2	0	3	0	0	0	—	—	—	—	—	—
New Jersey	5	3	0	2	0	0	0	—	—	—	(M[3])	—	E-S
New Mexico	5	4	0	1	4	4	0	—	SB	E	(M[15]) (SB[15])	—	E-S 1-8
New York	7	5	0	2	3	0	3	M	SD	1-8 E-S	—	—	—

Physical education (separate subject)			Safety education (separate subject)			Driver education			Outdoor education			Special health and/or safety topics			
Authorization		Grade or level	Authorization		Grade or level	Authorization		Grade or level	Authorization		Grade or level	Topic	Authorization		Grade or level
Law	Reg.		Law	Reg.		Law	Reg.		Law	Reg.			Law	Reg.	
15	16	17	18	19	20	21	22	23	24	25	26	27	28	29	30
												Narcotics, drugs, use and abuse	M	—	E-S
—	—	—	—	—	—	—	—	—	—	—	—	Physiology and hygiene, including alcohol, stimulants, and narcotics	MC	—	E-S
												Fire prevention	M	—	E
												Fire drills	M	—	E-S
—	—	—	—	—	—	PI	—	S	—	—	—	Fire prevention	M	—	E-S
(M[10])	—	S	—	—	—	P	—	S	—	—	—	Physiology and hygiene, including stimulants and narcotics	M	—	E-S
	SB	E-S										Fire drills	M	—	E-S
												Fish and game laws	M	—	E-S
(M[14])	—	E-S	—	—	—	PI	—	E-S	—	—	—	Physiology and hygiene, including alcohol and narcotics	M	—	E-S
		E										Use of firearms and safe hunting	P	—	E-S
—	—	—	([3])	—	—	PI	—	S	—	—	—	Alcohol and narcotics	M	—	E-S
												Fire drills	M	—	E-S
												School safety patrol	P	—	E-S
—	SB	E-S	—	—	—	P	—	9-12	—	—	—	Physiology and hygiene, including alcohol and narcotics	M	—	E-S
							SB	S				Fire prevention	M	—	E-S
												Fire drills	M	—	E-S
												Physiology and hygiene, including alcohol, narcotics, and drugs	(M[7])	—	3-9 / 9-12
												Fire prevention	M	—	E-S
												Fire drills	M	—	E-S
M	SD	E-S	—	(SD[7])	E-S	—	—	—	P	—	E-S	Highway safety, traffic regulations, safety patrols	P	—	E-S
												Use of firearms and safe hunting	MC	—	E-S

Continued.

State	All subjects in this table							Health education (separate subject)			Health and physical education (combined subject)		
	Laws				Regulations			Authorization			Authorization		
		Mandatory											
	Total	Specific law (M)	Course of study (MC)	Permissive (P and PI)	Total	Auth. state board	Auth. state dept.	Law	Reg.	Grade or level	Law	Reg.	Grade or level
1	2	3	4	5	6	7	8	9	10	11	12	13	14
North Carolina	4	2	1	1	4	0	4	(M[11])	SD	E-S 1-8	—	SD	S
North Dakota	6	4	1	1	1	0	1	—	—	—	—	—	—
Ohio	2	0	1	1	4	4	0	—	SB	E	(MC[17])	SB	E-S
Oklahoma	3	0	1	2	3	0	2	—	(SD[18])	E	(MC[18])	SD	E-S S
Oregon	3	2	0	1	1	1	0	—	—	—	—	SB	E-S
Pennsylvania	4	2	1	1	3	0	3	—	(SD[19])	E	(MC[19])	SD	E-S
Rhode Island	6	5	0	1	0	0	0	M	—	E-S	M	—	E-S
South Carolina	8	7	1	0	3	3	0	(M[20])	SB	E-S	—	—	—
South Dakota	1	0	1	0	5	5	0	—	(SB[21])	7-8	—	SB	9

Physical education (separate subject)			Safety education (separate subject)			Driver education			Outdoor education			Special health and/or safety topics			
Authorization			Authorization			Authorization			Authorization				Authorization		
Law	Reg.	Grade or level	Law	Reg.	Grade or level	Law	Reg.	Grade or level	Law	Reg.	Grade or level	Topic	Law	Reg.	Grade or level
15	16	17	18	19	20	21	22	23	24	25	26	27	28	29	30
(M[11])	SD	E-S 1-8	([11])	—	—	(P[11])	SD	S	—	—	—	Alcohol and narcotics	MC	—	E-S
												Fire prevention, fire drills, fire prevention day	M	—	E-S
M	—	E-S	—	([16])	—	PI	(SD[16])	S	—	—	—	Physiology and hygiene, including alcohol, narcotics, and tuberculosis	MC	—	E-S
												Temperance day designated	M	—	E-S
												Fire drills	M	—	E-S
												Moral instruction	M	—	E-S
—	SB	E-S	([17])	(SB[17])	E	PI	—	S	—	—	—	—	—	—	—
(P[18])	—	E-S	([18])	—	—	([18])	—	E-S	—	—	—	—	—	—	—
—	—	—	—	—	—	P	—	S	—	—	—	Alcohol, narcotics, and moral instruction	M	—	E-S
												Fire dangers and drills	M	—	E-S
—	SD	E	([19])	—	—	P	—	E-S	—	—	—	Physiology and hygiene, including alcohol, narcotics, and tuberculosis	M	—	E-S
												Fire drills	M	—	E-S
—	—	—	—	—	—	P	—	S	—	—	—	Physiology and hygiene, including alcohol, stimulants, and narcotics	M	—	E-S
												Fire prevention	M	—	E-S
												Fire drills	M	—	E-S
M	SB	E-S E-S	([20]) ([20])	([20])	E	—	(SB[20])	S	—	—	—	Physiology and hygiene, including alcohol, narcotics, and moral instruction	MC	—	E-S
												Alcohol and narcotics	M	—	E-S
												Traffic laws	M	—	E-S
												Fire prevention	M	—	E
												Fire drills	M	—	E-S
—	SB	7-8 and 9-12 optional	—	SB	S	—	SB	S	—	—	—	Alcoholic drinks and narcotics, including moral temperance	MC	—	E-S

Continued.

State	All subjects in this table							Health education (separate subject)			Health and physical education (combined subject)		
		Laws				Regulations		Authorization			Authorization		
		Mandatory											
	Total	Specific law (M)	Course of study (MC)	Permissive (P and PI)	Total	Auth. state board	Auth. state dept.	Law	Reg.	Grade or level	Law	Reg.	Grade or level
1	2	3	4	5	6	7	8	9	10	11	12	13	14
Tennessee	5	4	1	0	2	2	0	—	(SB[22])	E-S	(MC[22])	—	E
Texas	3	1	1	1	2	2	0	(M[23])	—	E-S	—	(SB[23])	E-S
Utah	6	4	0	2	2	2	0	—	SB	S	—	—	—
Vermont	6	2	2	2	0	0	0	—	—	—	(MC[5])	—	S
Virginia	7	4	1	2	1	1	0	—	SB	1-7	M	(SB[24])	E-S
Washington	5	3	1	1	1	0	1	—	—	—	—	SD	9-10

Physical education (separate subject)			Safety education (separate subject)			Driver education			Outdoor education			Special health and/or safety topics			
Authorization			Authorization			Authorization			Authorization				Authorization		
Law	Reg.	Grade or level	Law	Reg.	Grade or level	Law	Reg.	Grade or level	Law	Reg.	Grade or level	Topic	Law	Reg.	Grade or level
15	16	17	18	19	20	21	22	23	24	25	26	27	28	29	30
M	(SB[22])	E-S	M	—	S	—	([22])	—	—	—	—	Temperance day designated	M	—	E-S
												Fire drills	M	—	E-S
M	SB	E-S 7-8	—	([23])	—	(PI[3])	—	E-S 9-12	—	—	—	—	—	—	—
—	SB	S	—	—	—	P	—	9-12	—	—	—	Physiology and hygiene, including stimulants and narcotics	M	—	E-S
												Sanitation and prevention of diseases	M	—	8-12
												Alcohol, narcotics, and tobacco; school safety patrol	M	—	E-S
—	—	—	—	—	—	—	—	—	—	—	—	Physiology and hygiene	MC	—	E
												Physiology and hygiene, including alcohol and narcotics	M	—	E-S
												Alcohol education	M	—	E-S
												Firearms, game laws, and hunting	P	—	E-S
												Fire drills	M	—	E-S
												School safety patrol	P	—	E-S
—	—	—	(M[24])	—	E-S	(P[24])	—	S	P	—	E-S	Physiology and hygiene, including alcohol and narcotics	M	—	E-S
												Physiology and hygiene	MC	—	E
												Fire drills	M	—	E-S
M	—	E-S	—	—	—	—	—	—	—	—	—	Physiology and hygiene, including alcohol, stimulants, and narcotics	MC	—	E-S
												Temperance and citizenship day, including alcohol and narcotics	M	—	E-S
												School safety patrol	P	—	E-S
												Fire drills	M	—	E-S

Continued.

State	All subjects in this table							Health education (separate subject)			Health and physical education (combined subject)		
	Laws				Regulations			Authorization			Authorization		
		Mandatory											
	Total	Specific law (M)	Course of study (MC)	Permissive (P and PI)	Total	Auth. state board	Auth. state dept.	Law	Reg.	Grade or level	Law	Reg.	Grade or level
1	2	3	4	5	6	7	8	9	10	11	12	13	14
West Virginia	3	2	0	1	5	0	5	([25])	SD	E	—	(SD[25])	E
Wisconsin	9	6	0	3	0	0	0	—	—	—	—	—	—
Wyoming	4	3	0	1	1	1	0	PI	—	E-S	—	SB	E
District of Columbia	2	1	0	1	2	0	2	—	—	—	—	SD	E-S
Canal Zone	0	0	0	0	2	0	2	—	SD	E-S	—	—	—
Guam	0	0	0	0	0	0	0	—	—	—	—	—	—
Puerto Rico	1	1	0	0	2	0	2	(M[27])	SD	E	—	—	—
Virgin Islands	0	0	0	0	3	3	0	—	(SB[28])	E	—	SB	S

[1]Combined subjects of health, science, and safety.
[2]Law on alcohol and narcotics refers to health education by implication in elementary schools.
[3]Combined subjects of health, physical education, and safety.
[4]Combined subjects of training in healthful living, morals, and manners; outdoor science and conservation education; safety and accident prevention. Driver education required to be offered in secondary schools.
[5]Combined subjects of health and physical education, alcohol and narcotics.
[6]Combined subjects of social studies, science, health, and safety—elementary grades only; health (separate subject) in secondary grades.
[7]Highway safety—on elementary level strong emphasis in traffic safety; on secondary level strong emphasis on driver education.
[8]Combined subjects of health and safety. Driver education—established division of school traffic safety in state department of education to initiate, promote, and supervise the development and expansion of driver education.
[9]Combined subjects of health, alcohol, and narcotics.
[10]Combined subjects of physical education and training.
[11]Law on driver education refers to safety education. Combined subjects of health and physical education, physiology and hygiene, physical education and good behavior, alcohol, stimulants, and narcotics.
[12]Combined subjects of hygiene, health training through physical exercise, games, recreation, and athletics; special health and/or safety topics.
[13]Combined subjects of health, physical education, and recreation.
[14]Combined subjects of military drills and physical exercises. Physical exercises must be included in the program.
[15]Combined subjects of physiology and hygiene, morals, health, and physical exercises. (Regulation—combined subjects with recreation.)
[16]Combined subjects of driver education and safety education.

Physical education (separate subject)			Safety education (separate subject)			Driver education			Outdoor education			Special health and/or safety topics			
Authorization			Authorization			Authorization			Authorization				Authorization		
Law	Reg.	Grade or level	Law	Reg.	Grade or level	Law	Reg.	Grade or level	Law	Reg.	Grade or level	Topic	Law	Reg.	Grade or level
15	16	17	18	19	20	21	22	23	24	25	26	27	28	29	30
—	SD	S	—	(SD[25])	E	P	SD	S	—	—	—	Scientific temperance, including alcohol and narcotics			
												Fire prevention	M	—	E-S
M	—	E-S	(M[26])	—	E-S	PI	—	S	P	—	E-S	Physiology and hygiene, including stimulants and narcotics	M	—	E-S
												Fire drills	M	—	E-S
												Fire prevention	M	—	E-S
												Dairy products—vitamin content	M	—	E-S
												School safety patrol	P	—	E-S
—	—	—	M	—	E-S	—	—	—	—	—	—	Alcohol and narcotics	M	—	E-S
												Fire drills	M	—	E-S
—	SD	S	—	—	—	PI	—	S	—	—	—	Physiology and hygiene, including alcohol and narcotics	M	—	E-S
—	SD	S	—	—	—	—	—	—	—	—	—	—	—	—	—
—	—	—	—	—	—	—	—	—	—	—	—	—	—	—	—
—	SD	E-S	—	—	—	—	—	—	—	—	—	—	—	—	—
—	SB	E	—	([28])	—	—	—	—	—	—	—	—	—	—	—

[17]Combined subjects of health and physical education, alcohol, and narcotics, first aid, safety, and fire prevention. Combined subjects of first aid, safety, and fire prevention.

[18]Combined subjects of health and safety. Combined subjects of health and physical education, fitness and safety, alcohol, narcotics, and driver education (high school only). Combined subjects of military training, athletic training, and physical examinations.

[19]Combined subjects of health, physical education, and safety. Health education—combined subject with science or separate subject.

[20]Combined subjects of health and safety. Combined subjects of driver education and safety, cigarettes.

[21]Health education—may be combined with science or physical education.

[22]On secondary level, health education course includes physical education and driver education. Combined subjects of health and physical education, hygiene and sanitation, alcohol, narcotics, and cigarettes.

[23]Combined subjects of health, physiology, alcohol and narcotics; health, physical education, and safety; driver education and traffic safety.

[24]Combined subjects of safety, accident prevention, highway and motor vehicle safety (high school only). Driver education as part of health and physical education curriculum.

[25]Law on special health topics refers to health education by implication. Combined subjects of health and physical education, first aid, and safety.

[26]Combined subjects of safety, accident prevention, and highway safety; physiology and hygiene, including stimulants and narcotics—½ school term, grades 6, 7, or 8.

[27]Division of school hygiene "to carry out a complete program of health and physical development of pupils."

[28]Units on health and safety are included in general science and biology courses in grades 7 to 10, and home economics courses, grades 8 to 12.

D FIELD AND COURT DIAGRAMS

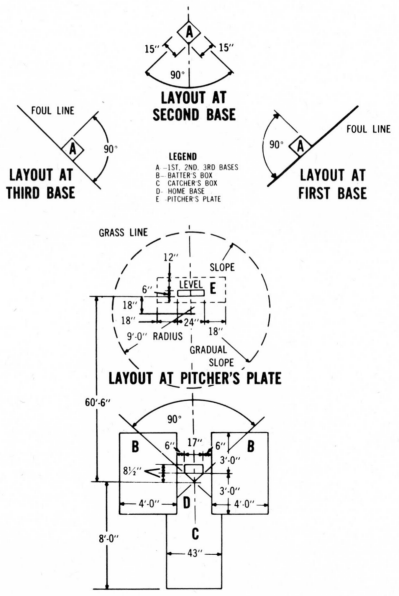

Reprinted courtesy McGregor-Consumer Division, Brunswick Company, Cincinnati, Ohio.

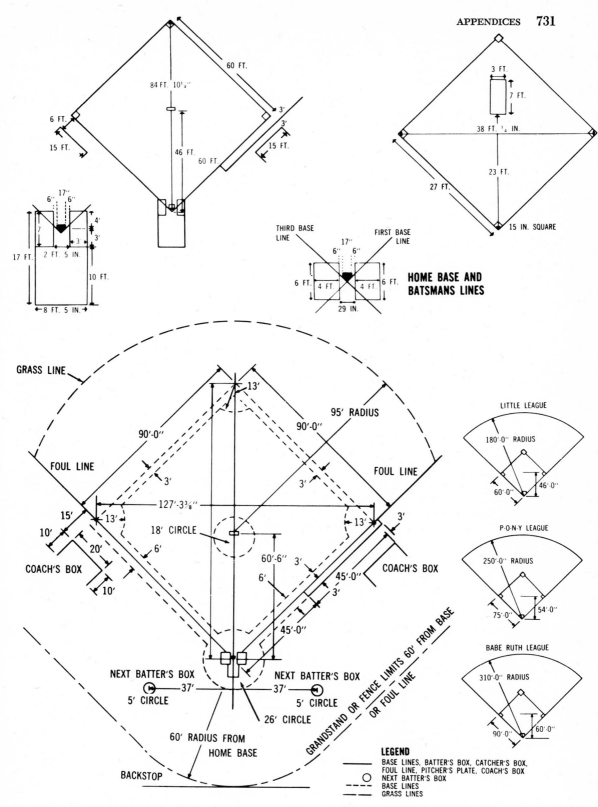

HOME BASE AND BATSMANS LINES

LITTLE LEAGUE

P-O-N-Y LEAGUE

BABE RUTH LEAGUE

GRASS LINE

FOUL LINE

COACH'S BOX

COACH'S BOX

NEXT BATTER'S BOX

NEXT BATTER'S BOX

BACKSTOP

GRANDSTAND OR FENCE LIMITS 60' FROM BASE OR FOUL LINE

60' RADIUS FROM HOME BASE

LEGEND
BASE LINES, BATTER'S BOX, CATCHER'S BOX, FOUL LINE, PITCHER'S PLATE, COACH'S BOX
○ NEXT BATTER'S BOX
--- BASE LINES
— — GRASS LINES

THIRD BASE LINE   FIRST BASE LINE

Reprinted courtesy McGregor-Consumer Division, Brunswick Company, Cincinnati, Ohio.

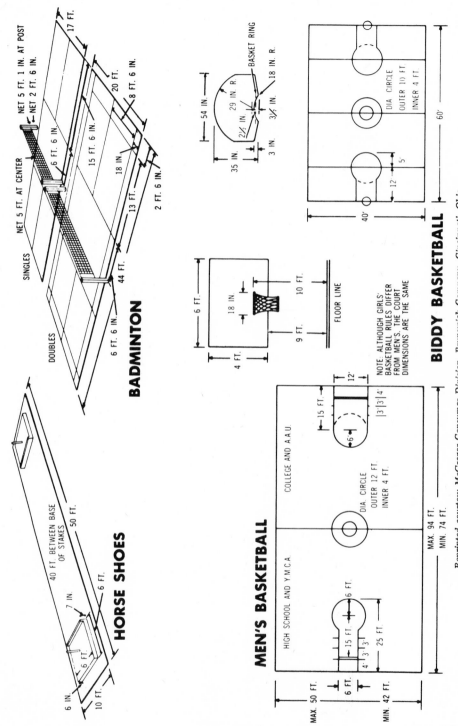

BADMINTON

HORSE SHOES

MEN'S BASKETBALL

BIDDY BASKETBALL

Reprinted courtesy McGregor-Consumer Division, Brunswick Company, Cincinnati, Ohio.

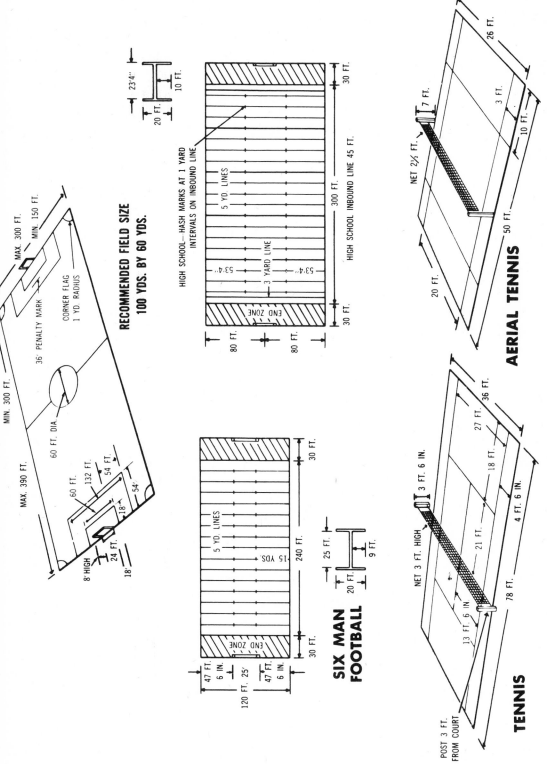

RECOMMENDED FIELD SIZE
100 YDS. BY 60 YDS.

MAX. 300 FT.

MIN. 150 FT.

CORNER FLAG
1 YD. RADIUS

36' PENALTY MARK

MIN. 300 FT.

MAX. 390 FT.

60 FT. DIA.

60 FT.

132 FT.

54 FT.

54'

18'

8' HIGH

24 FT.

18'

HIGH SCHOOL—HASH MARKS AT 1 YARD
INTERVALS ON INBOUND LINE

5 YD. LINES

3 YARD LINE

53'4"

53'4"

HIGH SCHOOL INBOUND LINE 45 FT.

300 FT.

30 FT.

30 FT.

END ZONE

80 FT.

80 FT.

23'4"

10 FT.

20 FT.

SIX MAN
FOOTBALL

5 YD. LINES

15 YDS.

END ZONE

30 FT.

240 FT.

30 FT.

47 FT.
6 IN.

FT. 25'

47 FT.
6 IN.

120 FT.

25 FT.

20 FT.

9 FT.

AERIAL TENNIS

26 FT.

7 FT.

NET 2½ FT.

3 FT.

10 FT.

50 FT.

20 FT.

TENNIS

36 FT.

3 FT. 6 IN.

NET 3 FT. HIGH

27 FT.

18 FT.

21 FT.

4 FT. 6 IN.

1 IN.

3 FT. 6 IN

78 FT.

13 FT. 6 IN

POST 3 FT.
FROM COURT

Reprinted courtesy McGregor-Consumer Division, Brunswick Company, Cincinnati, Ohio.

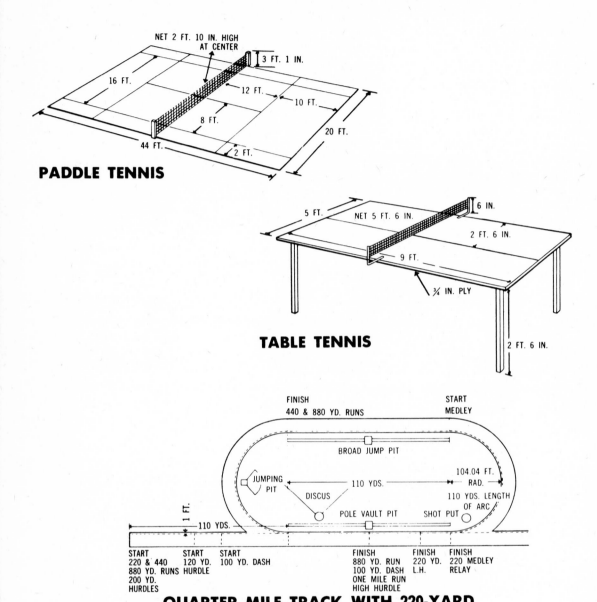

PADDLE TENNIS

TABLE TENNIS

QUARTER MILE TRACK WITH 220-YARD STRAIGHTAWAY

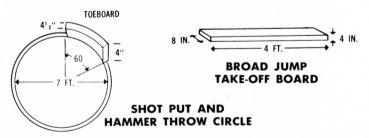

BROAD JUMP TAKE-OFF BOARD

SHOT PUT AND HAMMER THROW CIRCLE

Reprinted courtesy McGregor-Consumer Division, Brunswick Company, Cincinnati, Ohio.

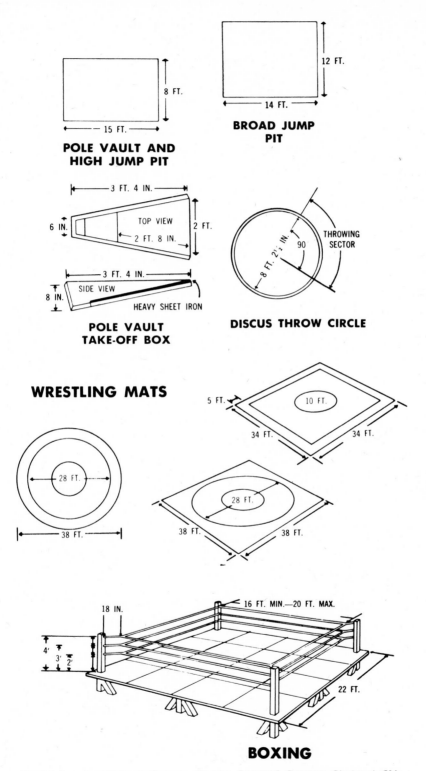

**POLE VAULT AND
HIGH JUMP PIT**

**BROAD JUMP
PIT**

**POLE VAULT
TAKE-OFF BOX**

DISCUS THROW CIRCLE

WRESTLING MATS

BOXING

Reprinted courtesy McGregor-Consumer Division, Brunswick Company, Cincinnati, Ohio.

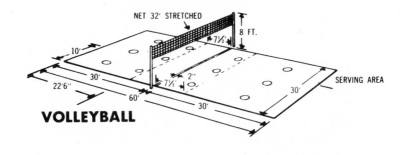

VOLLEYBALL

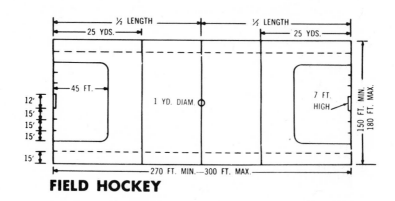

FIELD HOCKEY

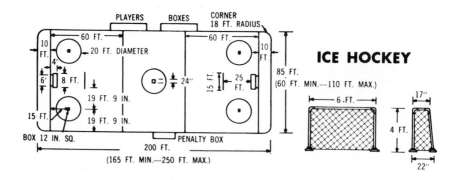

ICE HOCKEY

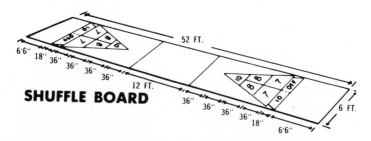

SHUFFLE BOARD

Reprinted courtesy McGregor-Consumer Division, Brunswick Company, Cincinnati, Ohio.

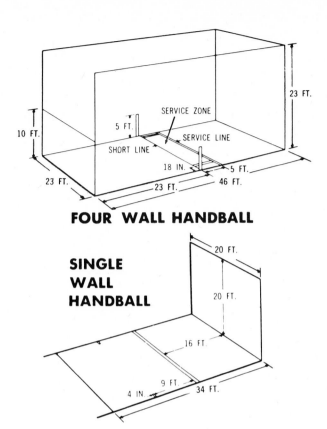

FOUR WALL HANDBALL

SINGLE WALL HANDBALL

Reprinted courtesy McGregor-Consumer Division, Brunswick Company, Cincinnati, Ohio.

Index

A

Abernathy, R., 567
Accidents
  accident-prone settings, 527–529
  football deaths and injuries, 535–536
  insurance against, 538–539
  precautions against, 530–532
  reporting of, 532–535
Accounting, 478–482
  principles and policies, 480
  provisions of, 478–479
  reasons for, 479–480
  receipts and expenditures, 480–481
Achievement information instrument, 613
Achievement information yielded by tests, 613
Acoustics, 389
Action for Outdoor Recreation for America, 671
Activities
  for adapted physical education, 200–201
  in intramurals and extramurals, 209–211
  in physical education, 154–158
    classification of, 155–157
    coeducational, 158
    selection of, 154–155
  for recreation, 660
Activity fees, 475–476
Adapted physical education program, 179–205, 637
  activities for, 200–201
  administrative principles, 203–204
  defined, 179
  evaluation, 637
  objectives of, 183–184
  planning of, 184–185
  records for, 183
  scheduling of, 197–200
  schools and colleges and, 201–203
  teacher and, 201
  types of conditions and contribution of, 185–197
Adapted program, 66
Adee, Don, 69
Administration
  of budgets, 478
  and challenge of modern education, 19–22
  curriculum development, 543–544

Administration — cont'd
  definition of, 3
  democratic, 16–19
  fitness and, 279–302
  health education and, 45–47
  health science instruction, 312–313
  importance of, 6–8
  interschool athletics and, 234–278
  intramurals and extramurals and, 224–232
  nature of, 3–29
  personnel for health programs, 90–115
  personnel for physical education programs, 90–115
  philosophy of, 4–6
  physical education and, 45–47
  physical fitness and, 279–302
  policy formation and, 14–16
  recreation programs and, 661–663
  of school recreation, 664
  teacher evaluation and, 629–633
  theory, 8–14
    and administrative organization, 13–14
    and administrative skills, 12
    and administrative tasks, 12
    and decision making, 12–13
    and leadership, 11–12
    preparation of administrators in, 9–11
    traditional and modern administration, 8–9
Administrative changes in school organization, 48–49
  school districts, 48
  school organization patterns, 49
  state and federal control, 48–49
Administrative emphasis and a healthful environment, 396
Administrative guidelines for audiovisual aids, 508
Administrative guides for emergency care, 379–383
Administrative innovations affecting curriculum development, 559–566
  flexible scheduling, 559–561
  middle school, 562–565
  nongraded school, 561–562
  year-round school, 565–566
Administrative mind, 93–94

Administrative patterns of school organization, 49
Administrative personnel, 53–56
Administrative policies for intramurals and extra-murals, 224–232
Administrative policies in physical education class program, 140–148
  class attendance, 142–148
  class handling, 147–148
  credit for physical education, 142
  elective program, 141–142
  excuses from class, 143–146
  required program, 141
  self-defense courses, 148
  sex separation, 146–147
  substitutions for physical education, 142
Administrative practices and the mental and emotional health of the students, 392–397
  attendance, 394
  discipline, 396–397
  emphasis, 396
  homework, 394
  personnel policies, 394–396
  play and recreation, 393–394
  school day organization, 392
  student achievement, 392–393
Administrative principles for the adapted physical education program, 203–204
Administrative principles for financial accounting, 480
Administrative relationships and objectives, 30–47
Administrative routine in the office, 592–593
  appointments, 593
  assignments, 592
  correspondence, 592
  files and filing, 592–593
  hours, 592
  telephone, 593
Administrative setting, 48–78
Administrative staff offices, 431
Administrative theory; see Administration, theory of
Administrator
  budgeting and role in, 472–473
  business, 79–89
  conflict with health and physical educators, 110–112
  in curriculum development, 546–547
  duties of, 98–100
  leadership of, 97–98
  qualifications of, 92–97
  responsibilities of, 109–110
  worries of, 112
Administrator's code of ethics for personnel involved in purchasing, 505
Adult health education, 332
Agencies for recreation, 660
Ahmann, J. S., 616
Airshelters, 422

Alabama College, 398, 443
Alexander, W. M., 557
American Academy of Pediatrics, 258–259
American Academy of Political and Social Science, 656
American Association for Health, Physical Education, and Recreation, 100–101, 128–129, 138, 140, 203–204, 220–221, 226, 257, 265–268, 282–283, 297–298, 434, 539, 625, 654, 659, 663, 672, 675
American Association of School Administrators, 10, 79, 573, 585
American Medical Association, 317–318, 326–327, 337, 345, 346, 348, 352, 361–362, 367, 370, 375–376, 378, 380–381, 391
Appointments, 593
Appraisal of budgets, 478
Architect in facility planning, 415–418
  critique with, 418
  design, 417–418
  educational specifications, 417
  meeting with, 417–418
  qualifications, 416
Areas of negligence, 518–521, 529
Areas of recreation service, 667
Association of School Business Officials, 79
Athlete and health services, 344–346
Athletes, examination of, 357
Athletic
  associations, 269–272
  contracts, 246–247
  council, 236
  director, 236–237
  eligibility, 256
  expenditures (table), 477
  game management, 252
  injuries, 246
  insurance, 539–541
  medical examinations, 244–245
  records, 254
  schedules and practices, 252–254
  scholarships, 256
Athletic Institute, 207, 210, 213–214, 217–219, 221–223, 226, 228, 229–230, 433, 435–437, 451, 480, 488, 496
Athletics; see also Interschool athletics; Intramurals and extramurals and a healthful environment, 391
Attendance in physical education, 142–143
Attendance of schools, 394
Audiovisual materials, 507–508
  guidelines for selection and use of, 508
  reasons for use of, 507
  types, 507–508
Automation and office work, 591
Auxiliary rooms, 438
Awards, 215–216, 253–254

B

Battle Creek Physical Education Curriculum Project, 554
Battle Creek Physical Education Project, 130
Beginnings of outdoor education and camping, 671–672
Begley, R., 529
Berelson, B., 97–98
Bethesda Public Schools, 85
Board of education, 51–53
  members, qualifications of, 53
Bonney, M. E., 606
Bonvechio, L. R., 636
Bookwalter, K. W., 40, 407–410
Brigham Young University, 408, 438–439
Brightbill, C. K., 659
Brinley, A., 670
Broadfront program, 130, 548–549
Brookhurst Junior High School, 560–561
Budget making and financial accounting, 464–483
  checklist for, 481–482
  cost analysis, 465–470
  defined, 464
  financial accounting, 478–482
  importance, 464
  place in health and physical education programs, 464–465
Budgets
  administration of, 100
  and budgeting, 470–478
    administration, 478
    administrator role in, 472–473
    appraisal of, 478
    criteria, 473
    defined, 470–471
    expenditures, 477–478
    organization, 474–475
    preparation and planning, 473–474
    purposes of, 471
    responsibility for, 471–473
    sources of income, 475–477
    types, 471
Business administrator, 79–89
  auxiliary services, 84–88
  facilities and equipment and, 85–86
  function of, 82
  guidelines for educators, 88
  and health departments, 82–84
  insurance, 86
  medical examinations and, 87–88
  objectives of, 82
  and physical education departments, 82–84
  problems of, 88
  responsibilities of, 80–82
  team transportation, 84–85

C

Cafeteria, 448
California and allocation of money, 467–468
California Interscholastic Federation, 261–262
California State College, 240
California State Department of Education, 156, 184–185
Camp Quest, 676
Camps, 453–454; *see also* Outdoor education and camping
Carra, L. D., 169
Cassidy, R., 547, 552
Cauffman, J. G., 555
Certificate for teaching health education, 102
Certificate for teaching physical education, 103
Challenge of modern education, 19–22
Chandler Street Junior High School, 58, 62
Checklist and rating scale for physical education program, 638–648
Checklists for
  facility planners, 454–462
  office management, 602–603
  school club and activity programs, 667–668
  supplies and equipment, 509–511
Cheyenne Public Schools, 419
Chicago Public Schools, 151
Cincinnati Reds, 408
City of New York Board of Education, 521, 523, 535
Civic development, objective of recreation, 658
Class management in physical education, 148–154
  costume, 150–151
  dressing and showering, 150
  organization, 148–150
  records, 154
  roll taking, 151–154
Class membership in health science, 336
Class scheduling in physical education, 133–140
Class size in physical education, 137–138
Classification
  information instrument, 613
  information yielded by tests, 613
  of physical education activities, 155–157
Classroom teacher handling of physical education classes, 147–148
Classrooms for health instruction, 444–445
Coach, 238–240
Coeducational activities, 158
College
  adapted program and, 201–203
  business managers, 79–80
  health programs, 56–63
  health science instruction program in, 331–332
  health service program, 345–350
  intramurals and extramurals, 222–224
  physical education class program, 167–172
  physical fitness and, 287–293

College — cont'd
  and university faculties and curriculum change, 545
  varsity athletics, 262–264
Colorado Springs Public Schools, 125
Commercial organizations for health education, 338
Commercial recreation defined, 654
Communicable disease control, 376–379
  attendance at schools, 379
  epidemics, 379
  healthful environment, 378
  immunization, 378–379
  isolation and readmittance of students, 378
  responsibility for, 376–378
Communication of public relations to public, 581
Community leaders and parents in curriculum development, 550
Community organization for health, 73–77
Community organization for physical education, 77–78
Community recreation, 653–669
  activities, 660
  administration, 661–663
  agencies, 660
  defined, 653
  goals, 654–656
  leader, 666–667
  National Recreation and Park Association, 660–661
  objectives
    civic development, 658
    health development, 656–657
    human relations, 657–658
    self-development, 658–659
  principles for planning, 659–660
  recreation, kinds of, 653–654
  school-centered recreation, 663–666
  school club and activity programs and checklist for, 667–668
Competition, 211–215
Competitive bidding, 497–498
Components of physical fitness, 280–281
Computer and measurement of pupil achievement, 606–607
Concept approach to health science instruction, 320–322
Concept approach to physical education, 552–555
Concord, New Hampshire, State Board of Education, 677
Content areas in health science instruction program, 315–320
Contribution of physical education to atypical conditions, 185–197
Contributory negligence, 522
Cooperative program in educational administration, 8
Corliss, L. M., 317–318, 347, 350

Correction of remediable defects, 369–371
Correspondence, 592
Cost analysis, 465–470
  defined, 465–466
  money allocations, 466–470
Costumes in physical education, 150–151
Counseling for health; see Health counseling
Court decisions on legal liability, 514–517
Court decisions on physical education class requirement, 514
Crawford, E., 268
Creativity, 566
Credit for physical education, 142
Criteria for evaluating physical education activity classes, 173–176
Crowd control, 240–243
Culturally disadvantaged students, 192–194
Cureton, T. K., 281
Curriculum
  development, 543–571
    catalysts of change in, 544–545
    conceptual approach, 552–555
    evaluation, 557–558
    health and physical educator and curriculum change, 545–546
    importance of, 543–544
    new developments affecting, 558–568
      administrative innovations, 559–566
      teaching methods and techniques, 566–568
    people involved, 546–550
    in practice, 555–557
    principles, 558
    procedural considerations, 546
    research, 568–569
    state and federal legislation, 569–570
    steps in, 550–552
  reform, 26
Custodian of building in health science instruction program, 315

D

Daniels, A. S., 184, 203
Dartmouth College, 439, 440, 441
Davenport, Iowa, Public Schools, 32
Davies, E. A., 184
Decision making, 12–13
Defenses against negligence, 521–523
  act of God, 521
  contributory negligence, 522
  proximate cause, 521
  risk assumption, 521–522
  sudden emergency, 522–523
DeGroot, D. S., 258
Democratic administration, 16–19
Dental examinations and services, 357–360
Dental hygienist, 83–84
  in health science instruction program, 315

Dentist in health science instruction program, 315

Denver Public Schools, 187–188, 347, 350, 353, 359, 361, 369

Department of Health, Education, and Welfare, 513

Design of the facility, 417–418

Developing physical fitness, 281–283

Developments in health and physical education facilities, 420–428

DeWeese, A. O., 445

Dexter, G., 184

Deyton, J. W., 183

Diagnostic information yielded by tests, 613–614

Diagnostic techniques, 613–614

Diagrams, field and court; *see* Appendix D

Director of health and physical education, 82–83

Director of health, physical education, and recreation, 55–56

Discipline, 396–397

Division for Girls' and Women's Sports, 265–269

Division of Instruction, Long Beach, California, 677

Dressing and showering, 150

Drugs in health science instruction, 322–325

Duncan, R. O., 94, 659

Dupee, R. K., Jr., 263

Duties of administrator, 12, 98–100

Dyer, J. T., 614

E

East Stroudsburg State Teachers College, 137

Education
    business management function in, 82
    changing nature of, 22–27
    of exceptional students, 371–376
    outdoor; *see* Outdoor education and camping
        and public relations, 582–585
    structure of, 21
    versus treatment as part of health service program, 351

Educational Facilities Laboratories, 424

Educational innovations affecting curriculum development, 558–568
    administrative innovations, 559–566
    teaching methods and techniques, 566–568

Educational Policies Commission, 31, 277

Educational specifications for facility planning, 417

Educational television, 568

Educators' errors in facility management, 415

Eiland, H. J., 172

Elective physical education, 140–142

Elementary school
    health science instruction in, 325–328
    interscholastic athletics, 258–259
    intramurals and extramurals, 220–222
    physical education class
        activities, 156

Elementary school — cont'd
    physical education class — cont'd
        class handling, 147–148
        program for, 159–161
        sex separation in, 146–147
    play areas, 449–450
    teaching stations, 429

Eligibility in intramurals and extramurals, 220

Ellensburg Public Schools, 285

Emergency care, 379–383

Emergency, sudden, 522–523

Emma Woerner Junior High School, 33

Emotionally disturbed students, 191–192

Environment for students; *see* Healthful environment for students

Environmental sanitation, 383

Epidemics, 379

Equipment
    and clothing, 389–390
    and supplies; *see* Supplies and equipment
    and uniform care, repair, and storage; *see* Appendix B

Evaluation
    of the curriculum, 557–558
        outline, 557–558
    framework of procedures, 629
    of health programs, 633–636
    means, 629
    of physical education programs, 637–638
        checklist and rating scale, 638–648
    of school and college health science instruction program, 339–341
    of teachers, 629–633

Exceptional students
    adaption of program for, 372–376
    care and education of, 371–376
    identification of, 371–372
    personnel for, 376

Excuses from physical education class, 143–146

Expenditures
    for athletics, 477
    in health and physical education, 477–478
    and receipts, accounting for, 480–481

Extramurals; *see* Intramurals and extramurals

F

Facilities,   85–86,   389–390,   415–428,   431–438, 443–462; *see also* Physical plant
    checklist for planners, 454–462
    construction trends, 418–420
    equipment and supplies, 85–86
    health science instruction, 443–448
    indoor, 389, 431–438
        administrative and staff offices, 431
        auxiliary rooms, 438
        cafeteria, 448
        classrooms, 444–445

Facilities — cont'd
  indoor — cont'd
    gymnasia, 433–437
    health science instruction, 443–448
    health services, 445
    locker, shower, and drying rooms, 390, 431–433
    special activity areas, 437–438
    swimming pools, 438–443
  new features, 420–428
  outdoor, 389, 448–454
    camps, 453–454
    game areas, 452
    outdoor swimming pools, 452–453
    play areas, 448–452
  planning, 415; *see also* Planning considerations for physical plant
  working with architect, 415–418
Factors in curriculum change, 544–545
  faculties, 545
  national associations and agencies, 544
  research, 545
  social forces, 545
  state associations and agencies, 544–545
Family recreation, defined, 654
Fawcett, C. W., 630
Features of insurance management plans, 537–538
Fees, 524–525
Felshin, J., 264
Files and filing, 592–593
Finances in intramurals and extramurals, 229–230
Financial accounting; *see* Accounting
Financial aid to education programs, 569–570
Financial management, 464–465
  defined, 464
  importance of, 464
  place in health and physical education programs, 464–465
  purposes, 465
  responsibility for, 465
Fiscal management; *see* Financial management
Fitness programs; *see* Physical fitness
Flexible scheduling, administrative innovation, 559–561
Flint Community College, 73
Florida and allocation of money, 468
Football deaths and injuries, reduction of, 535–536
Forman School, 422
Formulas for determining teaching stations needed, 428–429
Forsythe, C. E., 252
Fowlkes, J. G., 466
Framework for measurement procedures, 608–613
  information concerning the objectives, 609–613

G

Gabrielsen, M. A., 438

Game
  area dimensions, 451
  areas, 452
  management, 252
Garber, L. O., 519
Gate receipts, 255, 475
General education
  contribution of health education to, 31–33
  contribution of physical education, 31–33
  purposes of, 30–31
Geodesic field house, 425
Girls'
  health record, 356
  interschool athletics, 264–269
  intramurals and extramurals, 224
Glastonbury High School, 152
Goals of recreation, 654–656
Goodlad, J. I., 557
Gould, A. G., 136
Governmental versus proprietary functions, 524
Graceland Fieldhouse, 196, 422–424
Grades, 392–393
Grading, 621–627
Griffiths, D., 3
Grimes, L. W., 539
Grouping in physical education classes, 139–140
Grover Cleveland High School, 534
Guidance counselor in health science instruction program, 315
Gulick, L., 98
Gymnasia, 433–437

H

Hampleman, R. S., 606
Health administration, 63
Health appraisal, 351–367
  athletic examinations, 357
  dental examinations, 357–360
  health records, 364–367
  medical examinations, 354–357
  screening for vision and hearing defects, 360–363
  teachers' observations, 363–364
Health attitudes, 36–37
Health coordinator, 63
Health council, 63, 75
Health counseling, 367–369
  conference method, 368–369
  counselors, 368
  purposes of, 367–368
Health department, 73–75
Health department and business administrator, 82–89
  dental hygienist, 83–84
  director of health and physical education, 82–83
  facilities and supplies, 85–86

Health department and business administrator — cont'd
   health educator, 83
   insurance, 86–87
   medical examinations, 87–88
   team transportation, 84–85
Health development, objective of recreation,
   656–657
Health education
   administration of, 27–28
   administration personnel, 90–115
   checklist for, 635
   contribution to general education, 31–33
   definition, 30
   expenditures in, 477–478
   financial management and, 464–465
   measurement of pupil achievement; see Pupil
      achievement
   objectives of, 34–38
   office management, 588–604
   physical education, relationship to, 33–34
   physical fitness and, 289–294
   public relations and, 585–586
   recommendations of President's Council for, 294
   research, 568–569
   teaching certificate of, 102
Health educator
   curriculum change and, 545–546
   general school administrators and, 108–115
   guidelines, 88–89
   qualifications of, 100–101
   responsibilities of, 110
Health features of the physical environment; see
   Physical environment
Health insurance, 86–87
Health, knowledge of, 35–36
Health practices, 37
Health program, 56–77
   aspects of, 59–62
   coordinator of, 63
   council of, 63
   public health and relation to, 75–77
   terminology, 58–59
   two-year college, 71–73
Health programs, evaluation of, 633–636
Health records, 364–367
Health reports, 596–599
Health room, 381–383
Health and safety education, evaluation of, 636
Health science instruction, 59–61, 305–343, 443–
   448
   administration of program, 312–313
   for adults and at college level, 331–332
   content areas, 315–325
      critical, 322–325
      curriculum selection, 315–316
      student needs and interests, 316–320

Health science instruction — cont'd
   coordinator in, 313–314
   definition and importance, 305–308
   evaluation of, 339–341
   facilities, 443–448
      cafeteria, 448
      classrooms, 444–445
      health service facilities, 445
      health service suite, 445–448
      standards for, 443–444
   health concepts, 320–322
   methods of teaching, 332–334
   organization of classes, 336–337
   for preschool and elementary school, 325–328
   resources, 337–339
   School Health Education study, 308–312
   school health team, 313–315
   at secondary level, 328–331
   teaching
      concentrated, 334
      correlated, 334–335
      incidental, 336
      integrated, 335–336
Health service facilities, 445
Health service suite, 445–448
Health services, 61–62, 344–385
   appraisal; see Health appraisal
   athlete and, 344–346
   care and education of exceptional students, 371–
      376
   communicable disease control, 376–379
   correction of remediable defects, 369–371
   defined, 344
   education versus treatment, 351
   emergency care, 379–383
   environmental sanitation, 383
   health counseling, 367–369
   for personnel, 383–384
   place in schools and colleges, 345–350
   responsibility for, 350–351
Health studies, 37–38
Healthful environment for physical education,
   389–391
   athletics, 391
   clothing and equipment, 389–390
   indoor facilities, 389
   outdoor facilities, 389
   shower and locker facilities, 390
   swimming pools, 390–391
Healthful environment for students, 386–403
   defined, 386
   physical environment, 386–391
   psychologic environment, 391–401
Healthful living, 62
Healthful school living, 101
   evaluation of, 636
Hearing and screening of defects, 362–363

Heathcote School, 414
Heating and ventilation, 388
Henderson County Schools, 129, 134, 136, 279, 606
Highland Park High School, 356
Hill, F. W., 81
Hilleboe, G. L., 185
Hjelte, G., 663
Homework, 394
Hospital recreation, defined, 653
Houston's Astrodome, 421
Hoyman, H. S., 306, 321
Human relationships, 398–399
Hunsicker, P. N., 292, 298–299

I

Illinois League of High School Girls' Athletic Asso-
    ciations, 264
Illinois State University, 105, 579
Illuminating Engineering Society, 387
Immunity from liability, 515–517
Immunization, 378–379
Income sources, 475–477
    activity fees, 475–476
    gate receipts, 475
    general funds, 475
Indiana and allocation of money, 468–469
Indiana Department of Public Instruction, 613
Indiana State Department of Health, 358
Indoor facilities, 431–438
Industrial recreation, defined, 653
Injuries and interschool athletics, 246
Instructional program, 65–66
Insurance, 86–87
Insurance for interschool athletics, 246
Insurance management, 537–541
    features of, 537–538
    procedure for, 538–539
    school athletic insurance, 539–541
    types of, 537
Intelligence ratings, 393
Intercollegiate athletics, 262–264
Interscholastic program, evaluation of, 638
Interschool athletics, 65, 67–68, 207–208, 234–278
    administrative considerations in, 240–255
    administrative problems in, 255–258
    associations for, 269–272
    athletic director, 236–237
    awards, 253–254
    coach, 238–240
    college and university, 262–264
    contracts for, 246–247
    crowd control and, 240–243
    defined, 234
    elementary and junior high school, 258–261
    extra pay in, 272–276
    game management, 252
    girls', 264–269

Interschool athletics — cont'd
    high school, 261–262
    insurance for, 246
    medical examinations for, 244–245
    officials and, 247–248
    programs in, 65, 67–68
    protests and forfeitures in, 248–252
    relation to intramurals and extramurals, 207–208
    relation to physical education, 235–236
    safety and, 245–246
    schedules and practices, 252–254
    transportation, 255
Intramurals and extramurals, 65–67, 206–233, 638
    activities in, 209–211
    administrative policies for, 224–232
    athletics, 65–67
    awards, points, records, eligibility for, 215–220
    college, 222–224
    defined, 206
    elementary school, 220–222
    evaluation, 638
    finances, 229–230
    girls', 224
    health examinations for, 229
    junior high school, 222
    objectives of, 206–207
    play, sports, and invitation days, 208–209
    publicity and promotion, 230
    relation to interschool athletics, 207–208
    senior high school, 207–208, 222–224
    time for, 230–231
    units and types of competition, 211–215
Inventory analysis, 498
Inventory form, 500
Invitation days, 208–209
Irwin, L. W., 325
Issuing, checking, and maintaining supplies, 498–
    507

J

Jenny, J. J., 661
Johns, E., 635
Joint Committee on Health Education Terminol-
    ogy, 30, 58–59
Joseph P. Kennedy, Jr., Foundation, 189
*Journal of the American Association for Health,
    Physical Education, and Recreation,* 261
*Journal of the California Association for Health,
    Physical Education, and Recreation,* 137
Journal of School Health, 325–326, 328, 330
Junior college physical education program,
    171–172
Junior high school
    health science instruction, 328–330
    interscholastic athletics, 258–261
    intramurals and extramurals, 222
    play and recreation area, 450

K

Keller, I. A., 234
Kelliher, M. S., 236–237
Kephart, N. C., 32
Knezevich, S. J., 466
Krug, E. A., 550

L

Labeling supplies, 498
Langan, J. J., 320
Langton, C. V., 659
LaPorte, W. R., 138–139, 156, 186
Larson, L. A., 281, 607, 617
Leader of recreation program, 666–667
Leaders' Clubs, 119–121
Legal liability, 513–542
    accident-prone settings, 527–529
    court decisions, 514–517
    definition, 513
    fees, 524–525
    governmental versus proprietary functions, 524
    immunity from liability, 515–517
    insurance management, 537–541
    of municipality, 525
    negligence, 518–523, 529
        common areas of, 518–521, 529
        defenses against, 521–523
    nuisance, action for, 523–524
    safety, 530–536
    of school district, 525
    school laws and regulations, 513–514
        state-by-state analysis; see Appendix C
    school, park, and recreation board members, 525–526
    supervision, 529–530
    of teachers and leaders, 526–527
    tort, 517–518
    waivers and consent slips, 530
Leu, D. J., 416
Liability; see Legal liability
Lighting, 387–388
Limitations of public relations, 581–582
Linn, H. H., 79, 477–478
Locker, shower, and drying rooms, 431–433
Long Beach California Public Schools, 202, 357
Louisville, Kentucky, City Division of Recreation, 652

M

MacConnell, J. D., 414
MacKenzie, J., 673
Mamaroneck Senior High School, 590, 637
Massachusetts Department of Education and Department of Public Health, 363–364
Materials and resources for health education, 337–338
    commercial organizations, 338

Materials and resources for health education — cont'd
    official agencies, 338
    professional agencies, 337–338
Matthews, D. O., 210, 229
Mauro, D. R., 273
Mayshark, C., 307, 325
McCall's Patterns, 489
McCloskey, G., 574
McCloy, C. H., 281, 613
McCraw, L. W., 627
McPherson High School, 68, 429
Measurement material standardization, 620–621
Measurement of pupil achievement; see Pupil achievement
Media in public relations, 574–578, 580–581
    discussion groups, 577
    films, 577–578
    magazines, 576
    miscellaneous, 578
    newspapers, 575–576
    pictures, 576
    public speaking, 576–577
    radio and television, 577
Medical examinations, 87–88, 354–357
Menninger, Wm., 393
Mental development tests, 615–617
Mental and emotional health of students and administrative practices, 392–397
Mentally retarded students, 189–190
Michigan State College, 220
Michigan State Department of Education, 311, 320, 335
Middle school, 9
Middle school, administrative innovation, 562–565
Mikeal, R. L., 324
Miller, A. T., Jr., 281
Miller, J. L., 334
Mitchell, R. G., 474
Money allocations, survey of, 466–470
Moore, V. M., 445
Morehouse, L. E., 281
Morgan, J. E., 666
Movement education, 129, 566–567
Municipality liability, 525
Municipal-school recreation, 663
Munize, A. J., 536

N

National Association of Intercollegiate Athletics, 271
National Collegiate Atheltic Association, 271
National Commission on Safety Education, 519–520, 522–523, 527, 529
National Conference of City and County Directors of the AAHPER, 241–243
National Conference on Outdoor Education, 670

National Conference of Physical Education for Children of Elementary School Age, 159–162

National Conference of Professors of Educational Administration, 8

National Conference on School Recreation, 665

National Congress of Parents and Teachers, 272

National Council of Schoolhouse Construction, 386

National Council of Secondary School Athletic Directors, 270–271

National Education Association, 317–318, 326–327, 348, 391, 518, 526, 605

National Facilities Conference, 428–429, 430, 444–445

National Federation of State High School Athletic Associations, 271

National Intramural Sports Council, 226

National Junior College Athletic Association, 271–272

National Recreation and Park Association, 660–661

National Safety Council, 533

National School Boards Association, 53

National and state associations and agencies and curriculum change, 544–545

Nation's Schools, 112

Nature and scope of public relations programs, 580–582

  limitations, 581–582

  media, 580–581

  message, 581

  policies, 580

  principles, 581–582

NEA Research Bulletin, 275, 395, 565, 575, 580, 631–634

Nebraska Department of Education, 314

Nebraska Department of Health, 314, 639

Nebraska Western College, ii

Negligence, 518–523, 529

  common areas of, 518–521, 529

  defenses against, 521–523

Neuromuscular development tests, 615

New Jersey and allocation of money, 469

New Trier Township High School, 181, 223

New York and allocation of money, 469–470

New York Committee on Educational Leadership, 53

New York Health Education Program, 319

New York State Association of School Business Officials, 505

New York State Department of Education, 198, 259, 452, 625, 664

New York State Heart Assembly, Inc., 198

New York State High School Athletic Protection Plan, Inc., 540

New York State Physical Fitness Conference, 138

New York State Public High School Athletic Association, 247

New York University, 472–473

Nissen Corporation, 485–486, 490, 495

Nolte, A. E., 322

Nongraded school, administrative innovation, 561–562

North Central Association of Colleges and Secondary Schools, 257, 263

Nuisance, action for, 523–524

Nurse in health science instruction, 314–315

Nutritionist in health science instruction program, 315

O

Objectives

  of adapted program in physical education, 183–184

  of business management, 82

  of health education programs, 34–38

    administration, role of, 45–46

  of health and physical education, measurement of, 608–613

  of intramurals and extramurals, 206–207

  of physical education, 38–45

    administration, role of, 45–46

    human relations, 43–45

    mental development, 42–43

    motor development, 39–42

    physical development, 38–39

  for recreation profession, 656–659

    civic development, 658

    health development, 656–657

    human relations, 657–658

    self-development, 658–659

Office management, 588–604

  administrative, importance of, 588

  administrative routine, 592–593

  automation and, 591

  checklist, 602–603

  communications center, 588

  equipment and supplies, 591

  importance, 588–589

  personnel, 589–591

  point of contact, 588–589

  records and reports, 593–602

  reference materials, 591–592

  space, 589

Office space, 589

  clerical space, 589

  general reception area, 589

  private offices, 589

Official agencies for health education, 338

Officials, 247–248

Ohio State Department of Education, 340

Oklahoma and allocation of money, 470

Oliver, A. I., 551

Oliver, James N., 32

Olympic College, 657

Organic development tests, 614–615

Organization
  administration, 13–14
  budgets, 474–475
  community health, 73–77
  health science classes, 336–337
  physical education, 68–71, 77–78
  physical education classes, 148–150
  school day, 392
Osborn, B. M., 339
Outdoor education and camping, 670–680
  early beginnings, 671–672
  importance and need for, 670–671
  school camp program, 675
  school camps in operation, 675–679
  settings for, 672
  values of, 672–675
Outdoor facilities, 448–454
Outdoor swimming pools, 452–453
Outline for checking curriculum, 557–558
Oxendine, J. B., 169

P

Park board, 661
Parker, R., 183
Park-school facilities, 428
Pasadena Department of Recreation, 662
Pay, extra, for extra services, 272–276
Peiffer, Tom, 143–144
Perceptual-motor foundations, 129–130
Personnel administration, 53–56, 90–115
  assistant superintendent, 54
  beginning teachers, problems with, 108
  clerk of the board, 54–55
  director, 55–56
  duties of, 98–100
  health educators, qualifications, 100–101
  leadership of, 97–98
  physical educators' qualifications, 101–107
  principal, 55
  principles of, 90–92
  qualifications of, 92–97
  superintendent of schools, 53–54
  supervisor, 55
Personnel in curriculum development, 546–550
Personnel errors in facility management, 415
Personnel for exceptional students, 376
Personnel involved in purchasing, 505
Personnel office, 589–591
Personnel policies and a healthful environment, 394–396
Phillips, M., 619
Philosophy of administration, 4–6
Physical education
  activities, 154–158
  activity class evaluation, 173–176
  adapted program, 179–205
    evaluation of, 637

Physical education – cont'd
  administration of, 27–28
  basic instructional program, 127–178
    administrative policies, 140–148
    class management, 148–154
    evaluation of activity classes, 173–176
    guidelines, 131–133
    interrelationships of, 172–173
    scheduling classes, 133–140
    student health, 173
    teaching developments in, 127–130
  checklist and rating sale, 638–648
  community organization of, 77–78
  conceptual approach to, 552–555
  contribution to general education, 31–33
  cost analysis and, 466–470
  definition, 30
  evaluation of programs, 637–638
  expenditures in, 477–478
  facilities, 420–428
  financial management and, 464–465
  health education, relationship to, 33–34
  healthful environment for, 389–391
  insurance program, 86–87
  interschool athletics, 67–68, 234–278
  intramural and extramurals, 66–67, 206–233
  legal liability, 513–542
  measurement of pupil achievement; *see* Pupil achievement
  new teaching developments, 127–130
  objectives of, 38–45
  office management, 588–604
  personnel administration, 90–115
  physical fitness and, 289–295
  public relations and, 585–586
  recommendations of President's Council for, 294–295
  research, 568–569
  student leadership, 116–126
  teacher safety code, 536
  teaching certificate, 103
Physical education department
  and business administrator, 82–89
  director of health and physical education, 82–83
  facilities and supplies, 85–86
  insurance, 86–87
  medical examinations, 87–88
Physical education program, 63–71
  adapted program of, 66
  instruction in, 65–66
  interschool athletics, 67–68
  intramurals and extramurals, 66–67
  organization of, 65, 68–71
  terminology in, 64–65
  two-year college, 71–73
Physical educator
  and curriculum change, 545–546

Physical educator — cont'd
    general school administrators and, 108–115
    guidelines for, 88–89
    health science instruction program, 315
    qualifications of, 100–107
    responsibilities of, 110
Physical environment, 386–391
    acoustics, 389
    building, 386–387
    furniture, 388
    heating and ventilation, 388
    lighting, 387–388
    plant sanitation, 388–389
    site, 386
Physical fitness, 279–302
    background of, 283–286
    components of, 280–281
    defined, 279
    development of, 281–283
    materials for, 300–301
    recommendations of President's Conference on
        Youth Fitness, 286
    recommendations of President's Council for,
        293–295
    role of schools and colleges in, 287–293
    testing for, 295–300
Physical plant, 407–463
    architect, 415–418
    facility construction trends, 418–420
    health science instruction facilities, 443–448
    indoor facilities, 431–438
    new features in facilities, 420–428
    outdoor facilities, 448–454
    personnel errors in facility management, 415
    planning considerations, 407–415
    planning team, 415
    swimming pools, 438–443
    teaching stations, 428–430
Physically gifted students, 195–197
Physically handicapped students, 185–189
Piscope, J., 173
Pittsfield Public Schools, ii
Planning
    the adapted physical education program,
        184–185
    a budget, 473–474
    considerations for physical plant, 407–415
Plant sanitation, 388–389
Play
    areas, 448–452
        elementary school, 449–450
        junior high school, 450
        senior high school, 451–452
    and recreation and mental health of students,
        393–394
Playdays, 208–209
Playground and recess games, 527–528

Point systems, 216
Policies of public relations, 580
Policy formation, 14–16
Poorly coordinated students, 194–195
Practical curriculum planning, 555–557
Precautions against accidents, 530–532
Preschool health science instruction, 325
President's Conference on Fitness of American
    Youth, 286
President's Council on Physical Fitness, 286–287,
    293–295
President's Council on Physical Fitness and Sports,
    137, 171
Preston, G. H., 391
Princeton University, 409
Principal, 55
Principles
    for adapted program, 203–204
    in curriculum development, 558
    for facility planning, 407–415
    for planning recreation programs, 659–660
    and policies for financial accounting, 480
    of public relations, 582
Problems of beginning teachers, 108
Procedural considerations for curriculum change,
    546
Procedure for insurance management, 538–539
Procedures in curriculum development, 550–552
Professional agencies and associations for health
    education, 337–338
Professional preparation of the coach, 239–240
Professional and public relations, 572–587
    definitions and purposes, 572–574
    education and, 582–585
    health and physical education and, 585–586
    media, 574–578
    nature and scope, 580–582
    principles, 582
    program planning, 574
    publics and public opinion, 578–580
Professional services for individual behavior
    problems, 399
Prognostic information yielded by tests, 614
Prognostic instrument, 614
Program of measurement, standards for, 617–620
Program planning for public relations, 574
Programmed instruction, 568
Programs for physical education, 158–172
    colleges and universities, 167–171
    grades nine through twelve, 166–167
    grades seven and eight, 159, 162–166
    junior college, 171–172
    kindergarten through grade six, 159–161
Proselyting, 257
Protests and forfeitures, 248–252
Proximate cause, 521
Psychologic environment, 391–401

Psychologic environment — cont'd
  administrative practices, 392–397
  defined, 391–392
  human relationships, 398–399
  professional services, 399
  teacher, 397–398
Public health, 73–75
  council of, 75
  department, 73–75
  relationship of school to health programs, 75–77
  voluntary agencies of, 75
Public relations; *see* Professional and public relations
Public school organization, chart of, 44
Publicity and promotion in intramurals and extramurals, 230
Publics and public opinion, 578–580
Pupil achievement, measurement of, 605–628
  computer, 606–607
  criteria, 607–608
  definition, 605
  framework, 608–613
  grading, 621–627
  minimum and desirable standards, 617–620
  purposes, 605–606
  recording and testing, 620
  standardization of materials, 620–621
  techniques and instruments, 613–617
    mental development, 615–617
    neuromuscular development, 615
    organic development, 614–615
    social development, 617
Purchasing supplies and equipment, 491–498

Q

Qualifications
  of administrator, 92–97
  of architect in facility planning, 416
  of health and physical educators, 100–107
  of student leader in physical education, 118–119
Qualities for successful teaching, 107–108

R

Rapid City Public Schools, 583
Reasons for financial accounting, 479–480
Reasons for use of audiovisual materials, 507
Records
  of handicapped children, 183
  in intramurals and extramurals, 216–220
  in physical education classes, 154
Recreation, kinds defined, 653–654; *see also* Community recreation
Recruitment of athletes, 256–257
Reeder, W. G., 558
Reference materials in the office, 591–592
Reiff, G., 292

Relationship of interschool athletics to physical education program, 235–236
Reporting of accidents, 532–535
Reports and records in the office, 593–602
Required physical education program, 140–141
Research and curriculum change, 545
Research and health education and physical education, 568–569
Research Quarterly, 614
Resources for physical fitness, 300–301
Responsibilities
  of business administrators, 80–82
  of general administrators, 109–110
  of health educators, 110
  of physical educators, 110
Responsibility
  for budgets, 471–473
  for financial management, 465
  for school health services, 350–351
Rich Township High School, 117
Richwoods Community High School, 240, 390, 626
Risk assumption, 521–522
Rockhold, J., 538
Roll taking, 151–154
Rosenfield, H. N., 518

S

Safety, 245–246, 530–536
  code for physical education teacher, 536
  football injuries, 535–536
  interschool athletics and, 245–246
  precautions, 530–532
  reporting accidents, 532–535
Saginaw Township Community Schools, 564
San Mateo College, 406, 434, 450
Saylor, J. G., 557
Scheduling
  the adapted program, 197–200
  physical education classes, 133–140
    class size, 137–138
    elementary and secondary levels and, 136–137
    grouping, 139–140
    teaching loads, 138–139
    time allotment, 135–136
  time for intramurals and extramurals, 230–231
Schneider, E. C., 295
Scholarships, 256
School administrative changes, 48–49
  districts, 48
  organization patterns, 49
  state and federal control, 48–49
School athletic insurance, 539–541
School attendance, 394
School board and administration of recreation programs, 661
School camp program, 675

School camps in operation, 675–679
School-centered recreation programs, 663–666
School club and activity programs, and checklist for, 667–668
School or college administrator in health science instruction program, 314
School and college health program, 56–77, 633–636
    evaluation of, 633–636
School and college physical education program, 63–71
School or college physician in health science instruction program, 314
School and college structure, 49–56
    administrative personnel, 53–56
    board of education, 51–53
    health programs, 56–63
    lay groups, 56
    physical education programs, 63–71
School district liability, 525
School districts, 48
School and emergency care, 379–383
School Health Education Study, 37, 308–312
School health and physical education facilities, 407–463
School health program, 56–63
School health services, 100, 636
    evaluation of, 636
School health team, 313–315
School laws and regulations for teaching health and physical education, 513–514; see also Appendix C
School, park, and recreation board members' liability, 525–526
School recreation, defined, 653
Schools and the adapted program, 201–203
Schools, growth of, 20
Schools and health service program, 345–351
Schools and physical fitness, 287–293
Scouting in athletics, 257–258
Screening for vision and hearing defects, 360–363
Secondary school physical education class, 136–137
    program for, 159, 162–166, 168–169
Secondary schools teaching stations, 429
Selection of physical education activities, 154–155
Selection of supplies and equipment, 487–491
Self-defense courses, 148
Senior high school
    health science instruction in, 328–331
    interscholastic athletics, 261–262
    intramurals and extramurals, 222–224
    recreation areas, 451–452
Settings for outdoor education, 672
Sex education in health science instruction, 322–325
Sex separation in elementary school physical education classes, 146–147

Shapiro, F. S., 516
Shivers, J. S., 663
Shroyer, G. F., 514
Sliepcevich, E. M., 322
Smiley, D. F., 136
Smith, J. W., 676, 679
Smith, M. C., 324
Smolensky, J., 636
Social development tests, 617
Social forces and curriculum change, 545
Solleder, M. K., 615, 617
Solley, P. M., 274
Special activity areas, 437–438
Speno-Brydges Bill, 37–38
Sports days, 208–209
Sports events and physical education as accident-prone settings, 528–529
Sports participation and disqualifying conditions, 352
Spring Branch Independent School District, 432
Standards
    interschool athletics, 234–278
    intramurals and extramurals, 206–233
Stanford University, 235, 515
State Department of Public Instruction, Bismarck, North Dakota, 624
State and federal legislation, financial aid to education, 569–570
State groups and curriculum planning, 549
Steiner, G. A., 97–98
Steinhaus, A. H., 281
Stevens, H. J., 79
Stogdill, R. M., 11, 97
Stone, E. B., 183
Structure of education, 21
Student achievement, 392–393
    grades, 392–393
    individual differences, 392
    tests and examinations, 393
Student health in physical education, 173
Student leaders in physical education
    advantages and disadvantages for, 116–118
    evaluation of, 124
    qualifications of, 118–119
    selection of, 119–120
    training of, 120–121
    utilization of, 121–124
Student leadership in physical education, 116–126
    mental and emotional health, 392–397
    mental health and the teacher, 397–398
Students in adapted physical education
    culturally disadvantaged, 192–194
    curriculum development and, 549–550
    emotionally disturbed, 191–192
    mentally retarded, 189–190
    physically gifted, 195–197
    physically handicapped, 185–189

Students in adapted physical education — cont'd
  poorly coordinated, 194–195
Substitutions for physical education, 142
Superintendent of schools, 53–54
Supervision and liability, 529–530
Supplies and equipment
  including audiovisual materials, 484–512
    checking, issuing, and maintenance, 498–507
    checklist for, 509–511
    definitions, 484
    purchasing, 491–498
    selection of, 487–491
    varying needs for, 484–487
  for an office, 591
  sources of; see Appendix A, 683–697
Sutton, W., 339
Swimming pools, 390–391, 438–443, 452–453

T

Taylor, J. M., 324
Teachers
  in adapted program, 201
  age distribution of, 24
  in curriculum development, 547–549
  evaluation of, 629–633
  in health science instruction program, 313, 325–332
  liability of, 526–527
  observations in health services program, 363–364
  student mental health and, 397–398
Teaching developments in physical education, 127–130
  Battle Creek Physical Education Project, 130
  Broadfront Program, 130
  movement education, 129
  perceptual-motor programs, 129–130
Teaching-learning process, carrying on, 551–552
Teaching loads in physical education, 138–139
Teaching methods for health, 332–334
Teaching methods and techniques, 566–568
  creativity, 566
  educational television, 658
  movement education, 566–567
  programmed instruction, 568
  team teaching, 567–568
Teaching profession
  measurement as a member, 106–107
  problems of beginning teachers, 108
  qualities for success, 107–108
Teaching stations, 428–430
  elementary schools, 429
  secondary schools, 429
Team teaching, 567–568
Team transportation, 84–85
Techniques and instruments for obtaining information about objectives, 614–617

Techniques and instruments for obtaining information about objectives — cont'd
  mental, 615–617
  neuromuscular, 615
  organic, 614–615
  social, 617
Techniques and instruments for obtaining information about students, 613–614
  achievement information, 613
  classification information, 613
  diagnostic information, 613–614
  prognostic information, 614
Telephone coverage, 593
Test construction and selection, criteria for, 607–608
Testing and recording in the measurement program, 620
Tests and examinations, 393
Tests for physical fitness, 295–300
Texas A & M University, 135, 426, 567
Theory of administration, 8–14
Thurston, J. P., 275–276
Time allotment for physical education, 164–165
Time arrangement for health science classes, 336–337
Timing and frequency of routine health services, 347
Tort, 517–518
Tournaments
  and championships, 255–256
  consolation, 213–214
  double-elimination, 213–214
  ladder, 213, 215
  pyramid, 214–215
  round robin, 212–213
  single-elimination, 212
  spider web, 214–215
Training of the student leader in physical education, 120–121
Transportation of athletes, 254–255
Trinity College, 235, 239, 345
Truesdale, J. C., 532
Two-year college, 71–73
Types of audiovisual aids, 507–508
Types of insurance management, 537

U

United States Office of Education, 373–374
United Teaching Profession, 106–107
Units of competition, 211–215
University of Alaska, 411–413
University of California, 38, 41, 387, 428, 431, 497, 505–506
University of Connecticut, 206, 654
University of Florida, 531
University of Maine, 437
University of Michigan, 132, 248, 292

University of the State of New York, 164–166, 184–186, 288–289, 299–300, 466, 499
Urwick, L., 98
Utilization of the student leader in physical education, 121–124

V

Valley Winds Elementary School, 49
Values of outdoor education and school camping, 672–675
Vision and screening of defects, 360–362
Visual aids; *see* Audiovisual materials
Voluntary health agencies, 75

W

Waivers and consent slips, 530
Wallace Rider Farrington High School, 453
Waltz, M., 567
Washington Irving Elementary School, 396
Washington State College, 126, 155, 171, 280
Waterloo, Iowa, Junior High School, 268
Wetzel, N. C., 613
Wisconsin State College, 159, 573
Working effectively with health and physical educators, 108–115

Y

Year-round school, administrative innovation, 565–566
Yocom, R., 281, 617
Young, N. D., 281, 613